D1605088

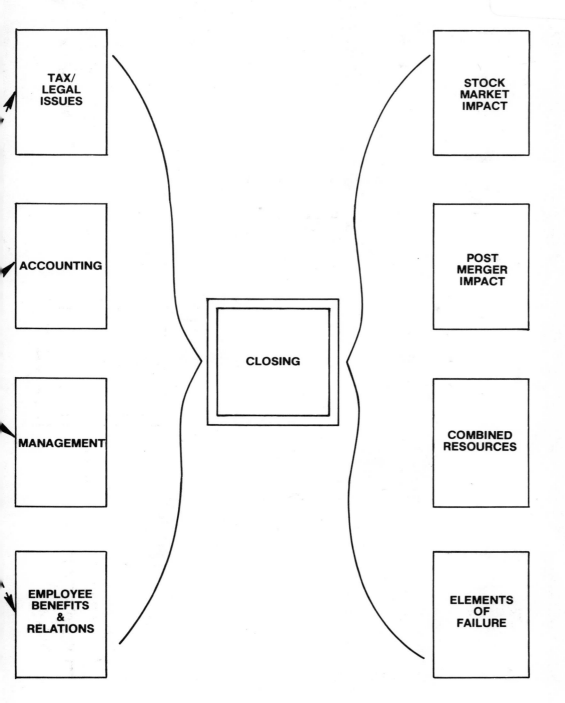

Alma College

Library

SIGILLUM ALMAE COLLEGII · IN NOMINE DEI, AMEN. · INCORPORATED A.D. 1886

HANDBOOK OF
MERGERS, ACQUISITIONS
AND BUYOUTS

HANDBOOK OF MERGERS, ACQUISITIONS AND BUYOUTS

Edited By

STEVEN JAMES LEE

and

ROBERT DOUGLAS COLMAN

PRENTICE-HALL, INC.
ENGLEWOOD CLIFFS, NEW JERSEY

Prentice-Hall International, Inc., *London*
Prentice-Hall of Australia, Pty. Ltd., *Sydney*
Prentice-Hall of Canada, Ltd., *Toronto*
Prentice-Hall of India Private Ltd., *New Delhi*
Prentice-Hall of Japan, Inc., *Tokyo*
Prentice-Hall of Southeast Asia Pte. Ltd., *Singapore*
Whitehall Books, Ltd., *Wellington, New Zealand*

© 1981 *by*

Prentice-Hall, Inc.
Englewood Cliffs, N.J.

*All rights reserved. No part of this book may be
reproduced in any form or by any means, without permission in writing from the publisher.*

"This publication is designed to provide accurate and authoritative
information in regard to the subject matter covered. It is sold with the
understanding that the publisher is not engaged in rendering legal,
accounting, or other professional service. If legal advice or other expert
assistance is required, the services of a competent professional person
should be sought."
—*From the Declaration of Principles jointly adopted by a
Committee of the American Bar Association and a Committee
of Publishers and Associations.*

Library of Congress Cataloging in Publication Data
Main entry under title:

Handbook of mergers, acquisitions, and buyouts.

Includes bibliographical references and index.
1. Consolidation and merger of corporations—
United States—Addresses, essays, lectures. I. Lee,
Steven James. II. Colman, Robert Douglas.
HD2746.5.H36   658.1′6   80-21347
ISBN 0-13-380360-0

Printed in the United States of America

820459

LIBRARY
ALMA COLLEGE
ALMA, MICHIGAN

DEDICATION

To my daughter, Megan—I hope that she will never shrink from the responsibility of standing and acting alone.

S.J.L.

To Jane and Eric—This is where some of the time went.

R.D.C.

Contributors

PAUL D. ARDLEIGH
Bankers Trust Company

PAUL F. BALSER
Thomson McKinnon Securities, Inc.

DANIEL G. BERGSTEIN
Greenbaum, Wolff & Ernst

RICHARD J. BERMAN
Bankers Trust Company

HAROLD BIERMAN, JR.
Cornell University

THEODORE BIRNBAUM
Birnbaum Associates

ARTHUR M. BORDEN
Sage Gray Todd & Sims

MICHAEL D. BOXBERGER
Heidrick and Struggles, Inc.

RONALD G. CARR
Morrison & Foerster

DONALD C. CARTER
The Carter Organization

ROBERT DOUGLAS COLMAN
Bankers Trust Company

CONNIE A. COX
Cox, Lloyd Associates, Ltd.

SAMUEL M. FEDER
Wender, Murase & White

BERTRAM FRANKENBERGER, JR.
Deloitte Haskins & Sells

ROBERT L. FROME
Olshan, Grundman & Frome

ELEANOR J. FURLAUD
Towne, Dolgin & Furlaud

ALAN M. GETZOFF
Olshan, Grundman & Frome

MILTON L. GLASS
The Gillette Company

DONALD GLICKMAN
First National Bank of Chicago

WILLARD T. GRIMM
W. T. Grimm & Co.

ROBERT JAY HABER
Bondy & Schloss

RALPH A. HARRIS
Drexel Burnham Lambert Incorporated

ROBERT H. HAYES
Hayes/Hill, Incorporated

DAVID I. KARABELL
O'Sullivan, Wolff, Karabell & Graev

STEVEN JAMES LEE
Nordic American Banking Corporation

I. ROBERT LEVINE
Ernst & Whinney

ROBERT A. McTAMANEY
Carter, Ledyard and Milburn

RICHARD MILLER
Ernst & Whinney

JAMES M. NEEDHAM
Arthur Young & Company

WILLIAM C. PELSTER
Skadden, Arps, Slate, Meagher & Flom

DEAN D. PORTER
Thomson McKinnon Securities, Inc.

ALFRED RAPPAPORT
Northwestern University

Contributors

ROBERT D. RAVEN
Morrison & Foerster

ALBERT F. REISMAN
Otterbourg, Steindler, Houston and Rosen, PC

ROBERT G. ROBISON
Wender, Murase & White

GERALD ROKOFF
Kramer, Levin, Nessen, Kamin & Soll

LEONARD SCHNEIDMAN
Spengler Carlson Gubar & Brodsky

TOMISLAVA SIMIC
W. T. Grimm & Co.

LAURENCE E. SIMMONS
Simmons & Company International

W. PETER SLUSSER
Blyth Eastman Paine Webber

DR. ROBERT C. SORENSEN
Sorensen Marketing/Management Corporation

JAMES STEVRALIA
Squadron, Ellenoff, Plesent & Lehrer

ROBERT S. TAFT
Miller, Montgomery, Sogi, Brady & Taft

ROBERT W. TAFT
Hill & Knowlton, Inc.

MARTIN R. WADE, III
Bankers Trust Company

NEIL A. WASSNER
Main Hardman & Cranstoun

MARTIN J. WHITMAN
M. J. Whitman & Co., Inc.

JOHN C. WILCOX
Georgeson & Co., Inc.

JAMES B. YOUNG
Arrowhead Puritas Waters Division
Coca-Cola of Los Angeles

CONTENTS

OVERVIEW

PEOPLE IMPACT IN BUYER AND SELLER COMPANIES

MARKET AND FINANCIAL ANALYSIS

ACQUISITION METHODS

ACCOUNTING ASPECTS

POST TRANSACTION IMPACT

FINANCING THE ACQUISITION OR BUYOUT

TAX CONSIDERATIONS

ANTITRUST SECURITIES AND STATE LAW GUIDELINES

TENDER OFFERS

BUYOUTS

DISSOLUTION AND DIVESTITURE

SPECIAL TOPICS

HANDBOOK OF
MERGERS, ACQUISITIONS
AND BUYOUTS

OVERVIEW

THE EDITORS

STEVEN JAMES LEE is a Vice President of the Nordic American Banking Corporation with responsibilities for financing, negotiating, and structuring U.S.-based acquisitions for Nordic-controlled companies, actively doing business in the United States. He was formerly a Vice President of Bankers Trust Company in the Corporate Financial Services Department. His responsibilities included financial consulting in mergers and acquisitions, corporate valuations and appraisals, financial planning, ESOP's and leveraged buyouts Mr. Lee holds a Doctor of Jurisprudence from Fordham University School of Law, a Master of Business Administration from the Wharton School of Finance and Commerce of the University of Pennsylvania, and a Bachelor of Arts from Lehigh University. He is a member of the New York State Bar Association and the United States Court for the Southern and Eastern Districts of New York.

In recent years Mr. Lee has written, or been featured in, articles appearing in numerous financial publications including *The Wall Street Journal, The New York Times, Nation's Business, Financial Executive, Newsweek* and *American Banker.* He is also the author of *Buyer's Handbook for Cooperatives and Condominiums* (Van Nostrand, 1978), *Buyers Handbook for Single Family Homes* (Van Nostrand, 1978), *Woman's Handbook of Independent Financial Management* (Van Nostrand, 1979), and *Conservative Real Estate Investment: Hedging Against the 1980's* (Boardroom Books, 1981).

ROBERT DOUGLAS COLMAN has had broad and varied corporate experience during the past eleven years, having worked for Bankers Trust Company, Western Electric Company, and Sperry Corp. For the past three years at Bankers Trust he has been engaged in corporate finance, and in the structuring of mergers and acquisitions, management and leveraged buyouts, valuations and Employee Stock Ownership Plans. Prior to this time he was a practicing attorney in New York.

Mr. Colman is a graduate of Union College, Schenectady, New York. He has a M.B.A. in Finance from the New York University Graduate School of Business, and a J.D. from the Fordham University School of Law. He is a member of the New York Bar.

1

Organization and Structure of This Handbook

STEVEN JAMES LEE

ROBERT DOUGLAS COLMAN

THERE ARE AT LEAST TWO SCHOOLS OF THOUGHT regarding the field of mergers, acquisitions, and buyouts. Adherents of the first school believe that transactions are accomplished by a handshake over cocktails between the principals of the two concerns. Everything that follows is mere detail: the tax "angles" can be worked out by tax counsel; the financing will be raised by the bankers or investment bankers; the optimal accounting treatment will be attended to by the accountants; and a variety of miscellaneous considerations such as public relations, employee benefits, state law and antitrust aspects will be ironed out by an assortment of specialists and experts.

It is indisputable that transactions have been accomplished, and will continue to be accomplished, along the lines discussed in the preceding paragraph. However, these are the exceptions, and it is the editors' belief that transactions accomplished in such a fashion have the least likelihood of long-run success.

The second school of thought, which this handbook exemplifies, acknowledges the depth and complexity of the field of mergers, acquisitions, and buyouts, and develops a systematic approach to the field. It is based on the belief that a broad but thorough technical knowledge forms the basis of, and generates the opportunities for, successful transactions.

We believe that this handbook is the most comprehensive and *usable* one-volume work ever produced on the subject of mergers, acquisitions and buyouts. Although the literature in the field is extensive, we have found the other standard works to be lacking in one or more respects. They are either too large and technical, too general and without practical case-study illustrations, non-current and lacking the significant developments of the past three years, or slanted toward a particular professional audience (such as law or accounting) to the detriment of certain major topics and issues.

The 14 topical areas in the handbook cover the essential information needed by the "non-professional practitioner" for an understanding of the field. By this we mean that we have not produced a "handbook" in the traditional sense (that is, like a step-by-step guide for the construction of an automobile). Rather, this work can be used by the practitioner or executive to understand the issues and thinking of the other professionals on the acquisition team. It can be used by the accountant to understand the impact of the merger upon public relations with shareholders and the investment community, and by the lawyer to appreciate the concerns of the banker.

The period from the initial conception of the handbook through printing and production was an effort of almost three years' duration for the editors and the contributors. Each of the 49 experts who has made a contribution was selected because he or she is a recognized specialist on the material contained in that chapter. Every attempt was made to provide the essentials of each subject in a minimum of space. We strove to maintain a balance between a work that is usable and readable and a handbook that is comprehensive. We have endeavored to direct the individual contributions away from an overemphasis on seldom-encountered details. In general, each topic will cover completely only the elements which a relatively sophisticated person should understand to have a good grasp of that topic as it commonly impacts on mergers, acquisitions, and buyouts. The reader of this handbook will be able to deal with atypical or very specialized problems through further research in the literature of the legal, accounting and financial professions.

There are a considerable number of case-study examples throughout this work. They have been drawn, whenever possible, from the actual experiences of our contributing experts. Sometimes the proprietary nature of these examples has required that they be referred to as ''ABC Company'' or ''XYZ Inc.'' The editors believe that material drawn from actual situations will be the most valuable and practical for the reader. Our contributors have faced the difficult task of imparting to the reader the approach and basic problem-solving methodologies used in specific transactions. Where appropriate, balance sheets, income and cash flow statements have been included as exhibits to further elucidate the text.

The subject of mergers, acquisitions, and buyouts does not have a ''starting point'' as does, say, Euclidean geometry, which builds upon several neatly defined theorems. The subject at hand is much more amorphous, and can be likened to a circle whose center is everywhere and circumference is nowhere. In order to impose structure upon the issues and perspectives involved, this handbook proceeds roughly along chronological lines. That is, it begins with the seller's decision to sell and the buyer's decision to buy, and proceeds through the myriad issues involved between inception and closing. A schematic diagram of the process would look like this:

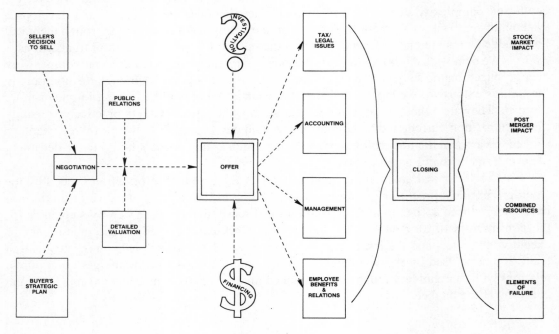

Figure 1-1

The seller's decision to sell involves a determination of the value that it will find acceptable as well as important tax planning considerations. A buyer has frequently developed a detailed strategic plan with specific acquisition criteria. Once the buyer identifies a specific property, he will ascribe a certain valuation to that property. His initial offer will be based upon an understanding of the intrinsic value of the property to be purchased. The question of value and purchase price is a recurring theme throughout the work. Two entire chapters (one by Ralph A. Harris and another by Martin J. Whitman) are devoted exclusively to it, while other chapters throughout the handbook also discuss the value issue.

The negotiation process, which begins with the offer, is approached from several points of view. The chapter by Richard J. Berman and Martin R. Wade shows the progression from the initial formulation of a strategic plan through valuation and consummating in an offer. The *Acquisition Contract Through Closing* by David I. Karabell develops an actual merger in intricate detail, from initial offer through closing. It offers down-to-earth advice on how to document a closing after the parties have struck the final business deal. These two chapters complement each other; one is written from a financial point of view and the other from a legal framework.

Robert W. Taft, in his chapter on *The Public Relations Aspects of Mergers and Acquisition* examines an often-neglected subject which is of tremendous significance. This chapter points out the pitfalls, to buyer and seller alike, of neglecting the promotional and external factors of a transaction.

The question of public relations points to a factor which adds to the uniqueness of this handbook. This first factor is an emphasis on the ''soft'' elements of mergers, acquisitions, and buyouts. Aside from public relations impact upon creditors, shareholders and suppliers, soft elements include human resources, business atmosphere and employee benefits. These often-neglected considerations, as opposed to the ''hard'' elements (tax, legal, accounting, financial) are perhaps as significant to the long-range success of a transaction.

There are numerous chapters which treat the ''soft'' side of mergers, acquisitions, and buyouts. Aside from the *Public Relations Aspects,* these include *Picking the Right Man to Run Things* (L.E. Simmons and Michael Boxburger), *What Happens to My People After I Sell* (Robert H. Hayes), *Marketing Information and The Determination of Value* (Robert C. Sorenson), *Marshalling the Combined Resources* (Connie A. Cox), *Employee Benefits as Related to Acquisitions and Mergers* (Robert S. Taft), *Most Asked Questions* (Theodore Birnbaum), and *The Causative Elements of Failure* (James B. Young).

Although we are attempting to approach our subject in chronological fashion, it should be clear that the numerous elements are interwoven and must be approached simultaneously. Inherent in the question of purchase price is the ability of the buyer to obtain the financing, and the manner and form of financing. *Strategic Analysis for More Profitable Acquisitions* (Alfred Rappaport), *Stock Market Impact* (Harold Bierman, Jr.), *Examining the Credit Resources of the Buyer* (Donald Glickman), *Leveraged Business Acquisitions* (Albert F. Reisman), as well as the chapters previously mentioned by Ralph A. Harris and Martin J. Whitman address the question of financing.

Special types of financing are utilized in buyout transactions, which are a species of acquisition. In buyouts and leveraged buyouts the purchaser is a new and nominally capitalized entity rather than an ongoing business with substantial resources. It is a type of transfer of ownership which has come into vogue in the past three years, particularly with the Houdaille and Congoleum transactions. The steady growth, high asset value company has become the target for a new group of investors. *Leveraged Buy-Out Financing* (Paul F. Balser and Dean D. Porter), *Structuring the Buyout* (Robert L. Frome) and *Overview of Leveraged Buyouts* (Robert D. Colman) analyze buyouts and leveraged buyouts. To date, there is very little which has been written on this important subject.

Another special topic related to the area of buyouts is the *Use of Employee Stock Ownership Plans (ESOP's)* by Paul D. Ardleigh. This technique allows employees to purchase their company while financing the purchase with pretax earnings. The increased cash flow can often accommodate a more highly leveraged structure than traditional approaches would accommodate.

There are a myriad of legal, tax and accounting problems that can arise in a particular acquisition. The two chapters on antitrust treat this difficult subject in a manner which adds to the overall usability of the handbook. The *Procedural Framework of Antitrust Considerations* (Robert D. Raven and Ronald G. Carr) treats the procedural aspects while *Basic Guidelines in Federal and State Law* (William C. Pelster) focuses on the question of what is or is not an antitrust violation. Taking these together, the reader should be able to identify a potential antitrust problem and anticipate the procedural steps, including notice and waiting period requirements. An understanding of these chapters is obviously no substitute for the use of professionals in an actual situation. Failure to comply with the rules set forth carries the potential of severe legal sanctions. However, these chapters can be used rewardingly by "the non-professional practitioner" to identify and structure problem areas at the first instance.

Lawyers and accountants are indispensable in accomplishing a merger, acquisition, or buyout, and the majority of the contributing authors belong to one of these groups. We believe the reader will find these chapters extremely readable and lacking in excessive professional jargon. *Certain State Laws Affecting Acquisitions* (Robert Jay Haber) provides an overview of the varying incorporation statutes and "Blue Sky" laws. It also treats some novel problems that arise in product liability situations. *Securities Law and Federal Registration Requirements* (Samuel M. Feder and Robert G. Robison) is a concise overview of the federal securities laws and their impact upon mergers. The pitfalls are explored in a way which cuts through red tape and concentrates on the key facts.

Taxes and tax planning have a tremendous impact on purchase price and in the financing of the transaction. *Non-Taxable Methods* (Neil A. Wassner), *The Dreyfus Formula* (Leonard Schneidman), *Taxable Sales and Liquidations* (James Stevralia), and *Tax Treatment of Shareholders* (Gerald Rokoff) attest to the importance of taxes. *Employee Benefits* (Robert S. Taft) treats the peculiar tax impact upon employees and executives.

Tender offers, both friendly and hostile, are treated in the chapters *Tender Anatomy* (John C. Wilcox), *Resistance to Takeover Attempts* (Donald C. Carter), and *Going Private* (Arthur Borden). Both tender offers and going private transactions have produced a good deal of controversy in the past five years. These are sensitive areas from the point of view of compliance with federal securities laws, shareholder satisfaction, and the general public market. The most current information in these volatile and rapidly changing areas is explored by the authors.

As with the area of tender offers, the question of accountability and proper accounting methods have come under close public scrutiny. *Painting a Clear Picture of the Acquisition* (Bertram Frankenburger, Jr.), *Accounting For Business Combinations* (I. Robert Levine and Richard P. Miller) and *When to Consolidate* (James M. Needham) provide an integrated examination of the accounting dimension.

The topics covered in the accounting, financing, tax, antitrust, securities, state law chapters have an unavoidable amount of technical material because it is the nature of their subject matter. This is the "hard" side of mergers, acquisitions and buyouts. We believe that the manner of presentation allows for use by the student as well as the relatively sophisticated manager. When desirable, the authors have included footnotes and bibliographies as a guide for further research.

There are a number of chapters which do not fit neatly into a chronological outline of the acquisition process. *A Conclusive Investigation Into the Causative Elements of Failure In Acquisitions and Mergers* (James B. Young) is a unique look at the failure of businesses to produce a planned, coordinated methodology in acquisitions and mergers. The author explains why almost half of acquisitions and mergers fail, and brings out clearly the key elements which mean success. There are many case studies and suggestions which will aid the layman as well as the professional in avoiding initial errors. Common pitfalls are also examined in *Marshalling of Combined Resources* (Connie A. Cox). There is also the fine statistical work and background information of Willard T. Grimm and Tomislava Simic covering the last decade.

Another special topic of particular relevance today involves acquisitions by foreign buyers. This whole subject has been highlighted during the past year by the acquisition of Marine Midland Bank by the Hong Kong Shanghai Banking Corporation. *Special Problems of Dealing with Foreign Buyers* (Daniel G. Bergstein and Eleanor J. Furlaud) addresses this subject, as does a portion of the chapter by Robert W. Taft on *Public Relations Aspects of Mergers and Acquisitions.*

Two subjects closely related to mergers and acquisitions are divestiture and dissolution. A divestiture is often the result of an ill-fated acquisition several years before, as is explained by Milton L. Glass in *The Troubled or Non-Essential Subsidiary.* Liquidation or dissolution as an alternative to or in combination with a merger is treated in *Liquidating the Company to Realize Value* (W. Peter Slusser). Such ''giants'' as the Shell/Belridge and UV liquidations are lucidly analyzed.

An important consideration of the editors has been the psychological similarities and differences between the attitudes of the buyer and seller. Thus there is a specially designed chapter on the *Most Asked Questions of the Buyer and Seller* (Theodore Birnbaum). It is a keen study of the mental process which commonly occurs during transaction negotiations.

Contrary to some opinions, the editors believe that today's environment provides numerous opportunities for successful mergers, acquisitions and buyouts. There are still large pools of equity capital available to consummate transactions. Some of these sources are domestic, while others are in foreign hands. The number of venture capital groups that have turned their attention to investment opportunities in going concerns is on the rise. Stocks of some relatively stable companies have become ridiculously cheap by all the standard statistical measures. It would not be possible to buy most going businesses or start a new business at anything like the value of the attractive stock prices currently given to many listed firms.

The remarkable interest rate structure which evolved in 1979-1980 may also open some new opportunities which might not otherwise be available. The cost of capital has become a much more significant element in corporate overhead. Plans for penetration into new markets, expansion of basic product lines, and modernization of facilities may have to be curtailed because of the historically high cost of funding such activities. However, one solution to this problem for many large corporations would be the sale of secondary businesses. Even if such businesses are substantial in size and quite profitable, it might still be beneficial to sell them and deploy the capital in the basic company business to assure a continued competitive posture.

There is little doubt that it has become more difficult to arrange financing for mergers, acquisitions and buyouts. In recent years several new techniques have allowed the marketplace to adapt to changes in the cost of money. A new emphasis has been placed on tax deferral and tax-saving techniques in the leveraged buyout. The use of tax losses, tax carryback provisions and specialty employee benefits like the ESOP have become much more common. There has also been a larger recognition and utilization of federal and state low-cost funds or guarantees by qualifying companies. More such innovations are likely to be developed and used in the coming years.

Another area of change has been the approach used by aggressive buyers. In the past, it was common for the purchaser to overwhelm the enterprise which had been targeted for takeover. The financial community nicknamed such raids the "Saturday Night Special" because a bidder gave very little regard to the attitude of management or shareholders in the acquired company. Now, a new network of state and federal regulation provides the target company with legal barriers which make such unsolicited takeovers much more difficult. This handbook has excellent chapters on resistance to takeover attempts and antitrust guidelines.

A classic example of the effects of this new and cautious approach to takeovers is offered by the attempt of American Express to acquire McGraw-Hill. At first, American Express had a hostile approach which was vigorously resisted by the management of McGraw-Hill. American Express realized that continuing its aggressive posture would only provide the management of McGraw-Hill with the basis for a protracted legal dispute. American Express completely reversed its public attitude and assumed a reserved posture with a willingness to purchase common stock at $40 a share in cash. This left the management and the board of directors of McGraw-Hill in an awkward position. They had to decide if they were obstructing the shareholders' opportunity of obtaining a very good price for their stock. The directors of McGraw-Hill felt they could justify rejecting the offer and so American Express quietly walked away.

Many authorities have expressed concern about the conflict of interest questions in evaluation of merger or acquisition proposals by the board and management and also about target tender techniques in general. The Securities and Exchange Commission has gone on record to suggest that "legislative action is warranted to correct" law and policy questions relating to tender offers. Present proposals would make formal tender offer provisions generally applicable to all acquisitions of 10 percent of a company's securities. The formal provisions which have been suggested include a requirement that any bank with a present or prior commercial relationship with the acquiror disclose its identity; a preemption of state takeover laws; the creation of statutory private rights of action for shareholders; and a grant of authority to the SEC to regulate banks and financial advisors to the company making the offer. These proposals would make very significant inroads in the law governing takeovers.

This handbook addresses these larger issues, while offering much step-by-step information for both the buyer and seller. The editors believe that the *Handbook of Mergers, Acquisitions and Buyouts* is an integrated balance of technical and practical advice. We believe that the reader will find clear and concise guidance for almost all aspects of this complex subject matter.

WILLARD T. GRIMM

Chairman of W.T. Grimm & Co.

After graduation from The School of Commerce at Northwestern University in 1924, Mr. Grimm was employed for 13 years in the Chicago office of First Boston Corporation. Kidder-Peabody & Company then hired him to open a Chicago office for that firm, which Mr. Grimm managed for 14 years.

He withdrew from the partnership in July, 1951, to form W.T. Grimm & Co., which originally specialized in private placement loans. In the later 1950's, the firm entered the merger and acquisition business, serving as intermediary for buyers and sellers.

Over the past 20 years, the Research Department of W.T. Grimm & Co. has built up the most complete merger data bank in the country.

Mr. Grimm has always been active in various civic and community organizations and was a recipient of a Northwestern University Alumni Merit Award.

TOMISLAVA SIMIC

Director of Research, W.T. Grimm & Co.

Tomislava Simic, a graduate of Northwestern University, with a major math degree, has been with W.T. Grimm & Co. four years and earned the title Director of Research. She is responsible for the firm's merger data bank and edits the Annual and Mid-year Merger Summaries. In addition, she prepares special merger studies utilizing data assembled over the previous two decades.

= 2 =

Background Information

WILLARD T. GRIMM

TOMISLAVA SIMIC

MERGER AND ACQUISITION ANNOUNCEMENTS

Net merger and acquisition announcements in 1979 rose 1 percent to 2,128 from the 2,106 reported for 1978. Following the record-breaking level of activity for 1969, mergers had declined every year except for the 4 percent increase in 1972 (Figure 2-1).

NET MERGER & ACQUISITION ANNOUNCEMENTS
1969 — 1979

Year	Number	Year to Year Percentage Change
1969	6,107	+37%
1970	5,152	−16%
1971	4,608	−11%
1972	4,801	+ 4%
1973	4,040	−16%
1974	2,861	−29%
1975	2,297	−20%
1976	2,276	− 1%
1977	2,224	− 2%
1978	2,106	− 5%
1979	2,128	+ 1%

Figure 2-1   *Source: W. T. Grimm & Co.*

The slight increase in 1979 may signal a rise in total acquisition activity during the 1980s.

In the bar graph shown in Figure 2-2, the number of acquisition announcements is divided into four categories: (1) divestitures, (2) acquistions of privately owned companies, (3) acquisitions of publicly traded companies, and (4) acquisitions of foreign companies by U.S. buyers. Observe the concentration of activity among private sellers and the decline in divestitures.

RECORD DOLLAR VOLUME

The 1979 total dollar volume paid for all mergers and acquisitions providing a purchase price reached a record $43.5 billion, surpassing the previous peak of $43 billion in 1968 and the $34.2 billion recorded for 1978. In 1969, when acquisition activity was at its highest level, the dollar volume totaled $23.7 billion. (Figure 2-3 on page 11).

One may properly question the effect of inflation on the dollar prices paid for companies. Valuing the dollar at 100 cents at the end of 1969, it had a purchasing value of but 50.5 cents at the end of 1979.

The continual trend toward sizable acquisitions greatly contributed to the rise in dollar volume during the past few years. The 1979 surge in interest rates and the impending economic slowdown did not deter the hectic pace of these giant takeovers. Completed or still pending transactions having a purchase price of $100 million or more totaled 83 in 1979, compared with 80 in 1978 and 41 in 1977. Comparable figures for 1976 and 1975 were 39 and 14, respectively.

In addition to the 83 completed or still pending deals of 1979, there were 48 other $100 million or larger transactions which were terminated. There were 20 such terminations in 1978. A discussion of canceled acquisitions appears later in this chapter. Figure 2-4 lists the 20 largest pending or completed acquisitions since 1968. Note that 12 of the top 20 were announced during 1979.

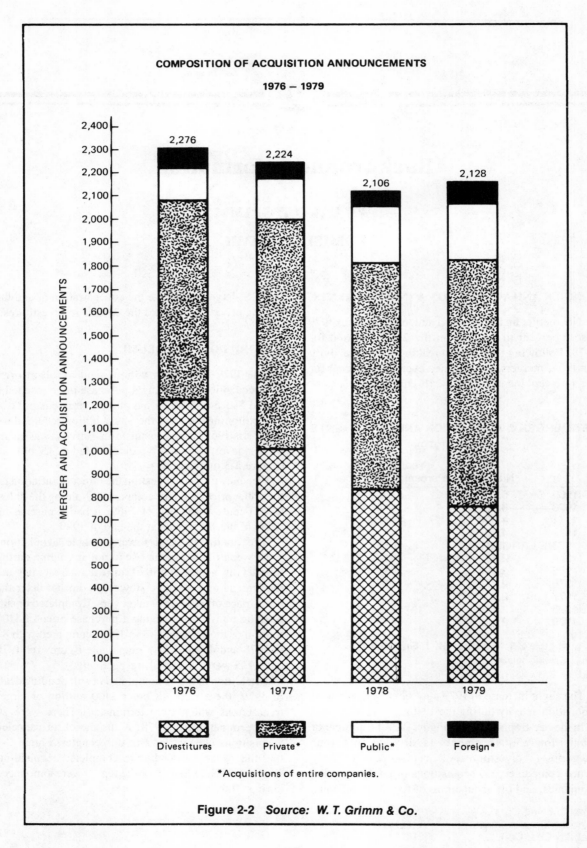

COMPOSITION OF ACQUISITION ANNOUNCEMENTS

1976 — 1979

Divestitures   Private*   Public*   Foreign*

*Acquisitions of entire companies.

Figure 2-2   Source: W. T. Grimm & Co.

10

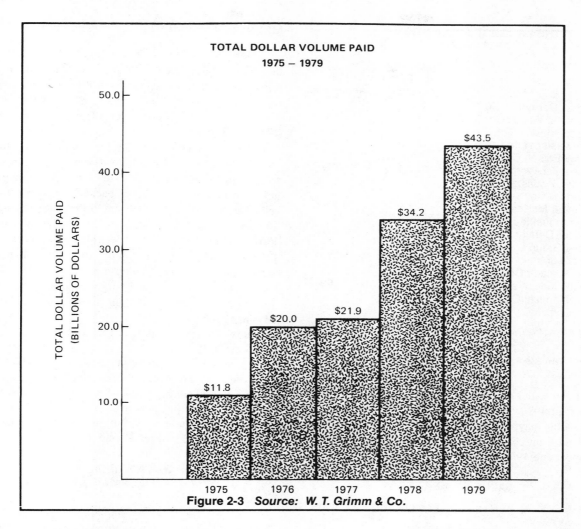

TOTAL DOLLAR VOLUME PAID
1975 — 1979

TOTAL DOLLAR VOLUME PAID (BILLIONS OF DOLLARS)

1975	$11.8
1976	$20.0
1977	$21.9
1978	$34.2
1979	$43.5

Figure 2-3 *Source: W. T. Grimm & Co.*

Figure 2-4
THE LARGEST ACQUISITIONS
1968 — 1979

Buyer/ Seller	Approximate Price Paid (Millions)	Year Announced
Shell Oil Co.		
Belridge Oil Co.	$3,653.0	1979
General Electric Co.		
Utah International, Inc.	1,906.5	1975
Mobil Oil Corp.		
Marcor, Inc.	1,687.2	1974 & 1976

Mobil acquired 54% in 1974 and purchased the remaining interest in 1976.

Buyer/ Seller	Approximate Price Paid (Millions)	Year Announced
Schering Corp.		
Plough, Inc.	1,428.6	1970
RCA Corp.		
C.I.T. Financial Corp.	1,350.0	1979
Newmont Mining Corp., Williams Cos., et al		
Kennecott Copper Corp.		
(Peabody Coal Co.)	1,200.0	1976

Figure 2-4
THE LARGEST ACQUISITIONS
1968 — 1979

Buyer/ Seller	Approximate Price Paid (Millions)	Year Announced
Exxon Corp.		
Reliance Electric co.	1,160.0	1979
Chessie Systems, Inc.		
Seaboard Coast Line Industries, Inc.	1,037.5	1978
Xerox Corp.		
Scientific Data Systems, Inc.	999.9	1969
United Technologies Corp.		
Carrier Corp.	821.7	1978 & 1979

United acquired 49% in 1978 and purchased the remaining interest in 1979.

Buyer/ Seller	Approximate Price Paid (Millions)	Year Announced
International Paper Co.		
Bodcaw Co.	805.0	1979
Mobil Corp.		
International Paper Co. (oil & gas operations of General Crude Co.)	800.0	1979

11

THE LARGEST ACQUISITIONS
1968 — 1979

Buyer/ Seller	Approximate Price Paid (Millions)	Year Announced
J. Ray McDermott & Co. Babcock & Wilcox Co.	758.5	1977
Tenneco, Inc. Southwestern Life Corp.	757.3	1979
McGraw-Edison Co. Studebaker-Worthington, Inc.	727.8	1979
Kohlberg, Kravis, Roberts & Co. Foremost-McKesson, Inc.	648.0	1979*
Cooper Industries, Inc. Gardner-Denver Co.	629.3	1979
Imperial Group Ltd.—Britain Howard Johnson Co.	618.5	1979
Boise Cascade Corp. Ebasco Industries, Inc.	598.4	1969
Allied Chemical Corp. Eltra Corp.	587.7	1979

This transaction was canceled in 1980.

Figure 2-4   Source: W. T. Grimm & Co.

Even with some of the largest acquisitions taking place in 1979, an analysis of the 1,047 transactions providing payment terms shows that 64 percent involved a purchase price of $15 million or less. The comparable 1969 figure was 86 percent.

VALUE OF MERGERS

Price Paid Value	Percent of Transactions 1978	1979	*1969*
$1 million or less	9%	6%	*24%*
$1.1 — 2.0 million	8%	8%	*15%*
$2.1 — 3.0 million	9%	8%	*14%*
$3.1 — 4.0 million	7%	7%	* 7%*
$4.1 — 5.0 million	6%	7%	* 6%*
$5.1 — 7.0 million	9%	10%	* 5%*
$7.1 — 15.0 million	19%	18%	*15%*
Over $15 million	33%	36%	*14%* ******

Figure 2-5   Source: W. T. Grimm & Co.

While most people think of mergers in terms of high-multiple million dollar transactions, Figure 2-5 will surprise them as to the high percentage of acquisitions each year valued at less than $15 million. In this area are the many deals resulting in the sale of companies by the founders to provide liquidity for estate tax purposes or the need of rapid growth companies to merge with larger companies to finance their expansion.

MEDIUM OF PAYMENT

Among the 1,233 merger announcements disclosing the medium of payment, 654 or 53 percent were *cash* transactions, up from 46 percent in 1978. Acquisitions involving the use of *equity-type securities* numbered 323 or 26 percent, down from 30 percent in 1978 (Figure 2-6 on page 13).

Cash has been the dominant form of payment since 1974, when the Dow Jones Industrial Average plunged to a low of 577.60. Corporate acquirers were no longer able to offer a favorable *stock* package to prospective sellers as they often did in the late 1960s. The exchange of *stock* had been the primary means of payment from 1967 to 1973, but had been declining since 1968. In 1969, *stock* acquisitions accounted for 57 percent of all transactions, while *cash* comprised 32%.

A *combination* of cash/stock and/or debt was utilized in 247 deals or 20% in 1979, compared with 23% in 1978.

There were only 9 transactions consisting of *debt* payments in 1979.

The subsequent figure compares the various forms of payment with respect to the value of the transaction. Despite the recent high cost of money, cash was the dominant form of payment in each category. However, note the substantial use of combination offers in deals valued over $100 million (Figure 2-7).

PAYMENT MEDIUM
COMPARISON BY VALUE OF DEALS
1979

Price Paid Value	Percent of Transactions Cash	Stock	Combination	Debt
Under $25 million	49%	33%	17%	1%
$25.1 — 50.0 million	67%	15%	17%	1%
$50.1 — 100.0 million	62%	15%	22%	1%
Over $100 million	50%	13%	36%	1%

Figure 2-7   Source: W. T. Grimm & Co.

This increase in combination deals reflects the recent trend in tender offers, particularly those paying less than 50 percent in cash (taxable) and the balance in stock (tax-free). This formula of purchase combines some advantages to both buyer and seller.

ANALYSIS OF MERGER ACTIVITY BY INDUSTRY

The W.T. Grimm & Co. Research Department classifies merger-acquisition announcements into 40 industry categories. The ten most active seller industries are presented in Figure 2-8 along with their number of transactions and respective rankings from prior years.

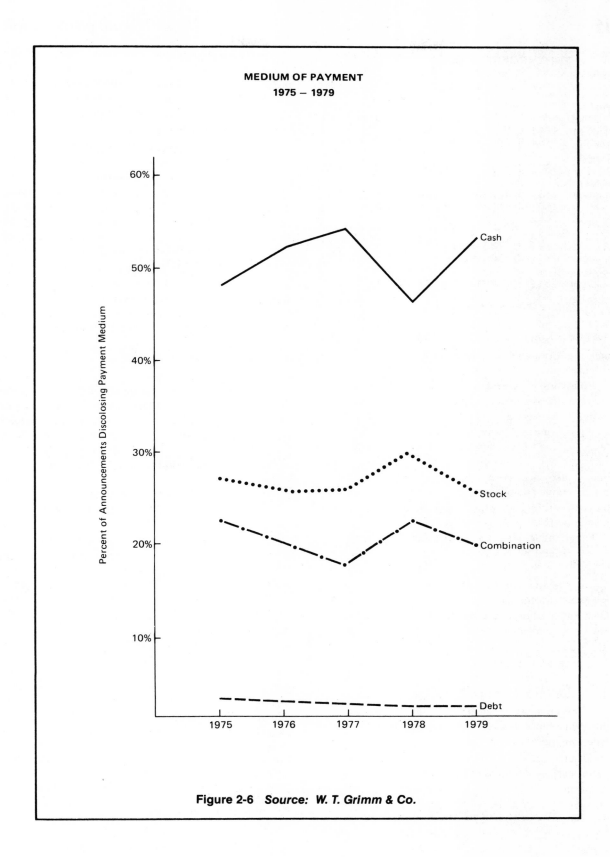

Figure 2-6 *Source: W. T. Grimm & Co.*

TOP TEN INDUSTRY CLASSIFICATIONS

Industry Classification of Seller	1975	1976	1977	1978	1979
Finance, Banks & Insurance	425 (1)	313 (1)	291 (1)	253 (1)	326 (1)
General Services	174 (2)	221 (2)	266 (2)	240 (2)	222 (2)
Wholesale & Retail	155 (3)	202 (3)	190 (3)	192 (3)	213 (3)
Food Processing & Agriculture	138 (4)	106 (6)	134 (4)	112 (4)	126 (4)
Machinery, Equipment & Farm Equipment	113 (5)	112 (5)	116 (5)	95 (5)	91 (5)
Electronics	50 (14)	60 (12)	65 (8)	66 (8)	82 (6)
Chemicals, Paints & Coatings	70 (11)	79 (8)	70 (7)	60 (10)	78 (7)
Public Utilities	76 (8)	72 (9)	84 (6)	68 (7)	67 (8)
Computer Services	34 (20)	39 (19)	41 (17)	52 (13)	62 (9)
Drugs, Cosmetics & Medical Equipment	51 (13)	62 (11)	60 (9)	60 (10)	62 (9)

Figure 2-8   Source: W. T. Grimm & Co.

Notice the increasing activity within the Electronics and the Computer Services industry classifications (Figure 2-8).

Following a six-year decline in the number of transactions, the Finance, Banks & Insurance industry category witnessed a 29 percent increase in merger activity. Contributing to the increase is the ''takeover fever'' among life insurance companies. These concerns are not only acquired by other insurance firms, but are also attractive candidates for industrial buyers. Life insurance companies are recognized for their stability in earnings growth, cash-generating ability, and insulation from business cycles.

Other industries attracting corporate acquirers include General Services and Wholesale & Retail, particularly the distribution sector. Service and distribution companies are less cyclical and not very capital intensive. Moreover, according to a U.S. Commerce Department study, service and distribution concerns have been growing faster in recent years than manufacturing firms.

Figure 2-9 lists the top ten seller industries of 1969. In comparison to the top ten of 1979, there is no difference among the first five entries.

More than half of the 1979 record total dollar volume was concentrated in the industry classifications listed in Figure 2-10.

ACQUISITION LEADERS

The top ten buyers in 1979 accounted for a total of 62 acquisitions. This compares with 278 transactions for the ten most aggressive acquirers of 1969. Figures 2-11 and 2-12 present the comparable listings. For the

1969 entries, we have provided some interesting data on their stock market performance. The range of stock prices from 1960 through 1977 is supplied for each company together with the 1979 year-end prices. Much of the acquisition boom in the 1960s was fueled by soaring conglomerate stock prices.

TOP TEN INDUSTRIES 1969

Industry Classification of Seller	Number of Transactions
General Services	1,009
Finance, Banks & Insurance	812
Wholesale & Retail	596
Machinery, Equipment & Farm Equipment	371
Food Processing & Agriculture	294
Entertainment & Leisure Time Products	281
Real Estate	212
Electronics	196
Apparel	185
Printing & Publishing	172

Figure 2-9   Source: W. T. Grimm & Co.

TOP TEN INDUSTRY CLASSIFICATIONS BY DOLLAR VOLUME 1979

Industry Classification of Seller	Total Dollar Volume Paid (Millions)
Finance, Banks & Insurance	$ 8,192.0
Petroleum	6,947.1
Mining, Timber & Minerals	3,062.4
General Services	2,839.3
Food Processing & Agriculture	1,965.0
Wholesale & Retail	1,916.8
Electrical Equipment	1,372.6
Electronics	1,281.5
Public Utilities	1,120.7
Drugs, Cosmetics & Medical Equipment	1,082.7
	$29,780.1

Figure 2-10   Source: W. T. Grimm & Co.

TOP TEN BUYERS 1979

Buyer Name	Number of Acquisitions
W.R. Grace & Co.	8
Parker-Hannifin Corp.	7
Allied Bancshares Corp.	6
Anacomp, Inc.	6
Gannett Co., Inc.	6
Harte-Hanks Communications, Inc.	6
Ingredient Technology Corp.	6
Peabody International Corp.	6
Rollins Burdick Hunter Co.	6
Campbell Soup Co.	5

Figure 2-11   Source: W. T. Grimm & Co.

TOP TEN BUYERS
1969

Buyer Name	Stock Prices 1960-1977 High	Low	1979 Dec. 31st
U.S. Industries, Inc.	35-5/8	2	8-5/8
Republic Corp.	255-1/4	4-1/16	27-7/8
Whittaker Corp.	45-7/8	3/4	19-1/8
American Medicorp, Inc.	Acquired in 1978.		
Beatrice Foods Co.	30-1/4	5-1/4	20-1/2
Alco Standard Corp.	40-1/2	3/8	32-1/4
Intermark Investing, Inc.	43-3/8	1/2	12
Beck industries, Inc.	Assets sold in 1971.		
National Student Marketing Corp.	35-3/4	1/16	5-1/2
*National selling its insurance subsidiary.			
International Telephone & Telegraph Corp.	67-3/8	12	25-1/2

Figure 2-12   Source: W. T. Grimm & Co.

Looking at both periods, we find that today's acquisition activity is not restricted to opportunistic conglomerates. All but three of the corporate purchasers in 1969 are diversified concerns. Among the top buyers of 1979, W.R. Grace & Co. is the only conglomerate. Noting the present variety of corporate acquirers, the purchase of companies has become an effective component of their overall plan to accomplish growth goals. Managements have realized the advantages of supplementing internal expansion with external growth. Parker-Hannifin Corp., a newcomer to the 1979 list, describes its strategy for profitable growth in these words: "acquire profitable companies in growth markets within our basic business lines ...... lessen cyclical vulnerability through acquisition and internal growth."

INTERNATIONAL TRANSACTIONS

Foreign corporations purchased 236 American companies in 1979, up 19 percent from the 199 acquisitions reported a year ago.

As indicated in Figure 2-13, the presence of foreign purchasers has played a significant role in the merger scene. Foreign corporations have developed acquisition strategies which increasingly include the takeover of prominent American companies. Paying higher prices than U.S. buyers, foreign concerns in recent years have acquired such well-known companies as Miles Laboratories, Inc., Colonial Stores, Inc., Peter Paul Inc., Alcon Laboratories, Inc., Lawry's Foods, Inc., and Jovan, Inc. (Figure 2-14).

In contrast to their own political and economic environment, foreign corporations are attracted to the rela-

FOREIGN ACQUISITIONS OF U.S. COMPANIES
1976 — 1979

	1976	1977	1978	1979
Number of Transactions	178	162	199	236
*Total Dollar Volume Paid (Billions)	$2.360	$3.147	$6.308	$5.862
*Average Price/Earnings Ratio Paid	12.7X	15.9X	14.0X	20.9X
*Average Premium Paid Over Market	41.6%	49.7%	50.5%	56.9%
*Based on those transactions supplying data.				

Figure 2-13   Source: W. T. Grimm & Co.

tive stability of the United States. More important, acquisitions of U.S. companies enable foreign concerns to enter the world's largest market. Hence, foreign buyers are willing to pay higher premiums. Furthermore, the decline in the U.S. dollar, the depressed U.S. stock market conditions, and the less demanding accounting rules are added incentives for foreign acquirers to offer higher prices.

FOREIGN BUYERS
SIZABLE TRANSACTIONS
1979

Foreign Buyer/ American Seller	Price Paid (Millions)
Imperial Group Ltd.—Britain Howard Johnson Co.	$618.5
Toyo Kogyo Ltd.—Japan Ford Motor Co. (Ford Industries Co.)	400.0
Allianz Versicherungs AG—West Germany Fidelity Union Life Insurance Co.	369.8
Nationale-Nederlanden N.V.—Netherlands Life Insurance Co. of Georgia	360.0
Genstar Ltd.—Canada Flintkote Co. (remaining 78.5%)	305.8
Schweizerische Aluminum AG—Switzerland Maremont Corp.	168.8
Allianz Versicherungs AG—West Germany Mutual Life Insurance Co. (North American Life & Casualty Co.)	138.3
Triumph Adler—West Germany Pertec Computer Corp.	118.8
Lloyds & Scottish Ltd.—Britain Talcott National Corp. (James Talcott Factors, Inc.)	118.0
Beecham Group Ltd.—Britain Jovan, Inc.	85.0

Figure 2-14   Source: W. T. Grimm & Co.

Industries having the highest number of foreign purchasers are listed in Figure 2-15, along with comparable year-earlier totals.

INDUSTRIES ATTRACTING FOREIGN BUYERS
1979

| | Number of Acquisitions | | Percent |
Seller Industry Category	1979	1978	Change
Finance, Banks & Insurance	24	17	+ 41%
Wholesale & Retail	23	18	+ 28%
General Services	20	18	+ 11%
Food Processing & Agriculture	18	16	+ 13%
Machinery, Equipment & Farm Equipment	15	7	+114%
Drugs, Cosmetics & Medical Equipment	14	6	+133%
Chemicals, Paints & Coatings	12	12	---
Primary Metal Processing	12	6	+100%

Figure 2-15 *Source: W. T. Grimm & Co.*

Figure 2-16 lists those countries which acquired the most American firms. Note the recent aggressiveness of France and the Netherlands.

LEADING FOREIGN PURCHASERS
1979

| | Number of Acquisitions | | Percent |
Foreign Purchaser	1979	1978	Change
Britain	60	62	− 3%
Canada	50	49	+ 2%
West Germany	37	27	+ 37%
France	18	6	+200%
Switzerland	16	11	+ 45%
Netherlands	11	4	+175%
Japan	11	9	+ 22%

Figure 2-16 *Source: W. T. Grimm & Co.*

The purchase of foreign companies by American corporations rose 21 percent to 119 transactions from the 98 counted in 1978. Comparable 1977 and 1976 aggregates were 112 and 126, respectively. This renewed acquisitiveness toward foreign concerns coincides with the relative strength of many foreign subsidiaries belonging to U.S. multinationals.

Over 46 percent of the transactions involving foreign sellers were concentrated in 5 industry categories: General Services with 18 deals; Food Processing & Agriculture with 13; Drugs, Cosmetics & Medical Equipment with 10; Chemicals, Paints & Coatings with 7; and Finance, Banks & Insurance with 7. However, 4 of the 5 largest acquisitions occurred in the petroleum industry. See Figure 2-17.

FOREIGN SELLERS
SIZABLE TRANSACTIONS
1979

American Buyer/ Foreign Seller	Price Paid (Millions)
Superior Oil Co. Canadian Superior Oil Ltd. (remaining 47%)	$576.4
Gulf Oil Corp. Amalgamated Bonanza Petroleum Ltd.—Canada	141.0
Southland Royalty Co. Peninsular & Oriental Steam Navigation Co.—Britain (P&O Oil Corp.)	131.0
General Foods Corp. Hag AG—West Germany	110.0
Houston Oil & Minerals Corp. Colombo-Brazileros S.A./ Colbras—Columbia	55.0

Figure 2-17 *Source: W. T. Grimm & Co.*

Of the 119 foreign sellers, 90 had headquarters in the countries listed in Figure 2-18.

LEADING FOREIGN SELLERS
1979

| | Number of Acquisitions | | Percent |
Foreign Seller	1979	1978	Change
Britain	35	29	+ 21%
France	17	3	+467%
Canada	15	23	− 35%
West Germany	10	7	+ 43%
Spain	7	1	+600%
Australia	6	8	− 25%

Figure 2-18 *Source: W. T. Grimm & Co.*

DIVESTITURES

Divestment activity further subsided during 1979. Sales of divisions, subsidiaries or product lines constituted 752 transactions, 35 percent of net merger and acquisition announcements. Divestitures accounted for 39 percent or 820 transactions in 1978, while 1,002 or 45 percent were reported for 1977. In comparison, 1969 witnessed 801 divisional sales which represented only 13 percent of all acquisitions.

During the 1970s, divestments averaged over 40 percent of total acquisition activity, with 54 percent and 53 percent occurring in 1975 and 1976, respectively. Resulting from the conglomerate acquisitions of the late 1960s, corporations were disposing of those divisions which had marginal profits or did not "fit" into future development plans.

In addition to the sale of marginal-profit and unrelated corporate units, divestments also provided the required funds to improve cash flow. A case in point is Itel Corp. which appears in our list of aggressive sellers (Figure 2-19). Anticipating a pretax loss of about $43 million for 1979, Itel pursues an intense divestment program.

LEADERS IN DIVESTMENT ACTIVITY
1979

Seller	Number of Divestitures
Chrysler Corp.	7
Interpace Corp.	7
Beatrice Foods Co.	6
Itel Corp.	6
Lone Star Industries, Inc.	6
Allied Chemical Corp.	5
Bankers Trust Co.	5
Genesco, Inc.	5
NL Industries, Inc.	5

Figure 2-19 *Source: W. T. Grimm & Co.*

TENDER OFFERS

Tender offer announcements numbered 140 in 1979, a 14 percent increase over the 123 such offers in 1978. However, cancellations also rose from 20 a year ago to 32 in 1979. The remaining 108 completed or pending transactions represents only a 5 percent gain from the 103 comparable deals of 1978.

Of the 140 tender offer announcements, 106 involved publicly held targets, up from the 90 public tenders counted in 1978 (Figure 2-20).

PUBLIC TENDER OFFERS
1975—1979

	1975	1976	1977	1978	1979
Total Announced	58	70	69	90	106
Contested by Target Firms	20	18	11	27	26
Contested and then Canceled	6	12	6	14	17
Cancellations for Other Reasons	9	9	5	4	10
Total Unsuccessful Tenders	15	21	11	18	27
Completed or Pending Tenders	43	49	58	72	79

Figure 2-20 *Source: W. T. Grimm & Co.*

As shown above, the tender offer has become a common acquisition strategy over the last few years. Of late, target companies have included sizable and well-established concerns. This, in turn, has enhanced the possibility of any firm becoming a takeover candidate. Such an environment has prompted many corporations to adopt various defense tactics, including super-majority vote requirements, protective takeover statutes, purchase of a business related to the suitor, and legal proceedings against the suitor.

In some instances, target companies are obliged to search for more compatible suitors, or "white knights," which, most likely, are companies willing to pay higher prices. Among the 17 target companies of 1979 which were able to ward off the original bidder, 9 were acquired by other concerns at higher prices.

A premiums-paid distribution for the 79 completed or pending public tender offers is illustrated in a bar graph (Figure 2-21 on page 18).

The 1979 median value of 49.6 percent is higher than the 41.3 percent computed in 1978, but is significantly lower than the 60.0% calculated for the first six months of 1979. The recent "tight-money" policy initiated by the Federal Reserve Board may well have lessened the acquirer's ability to pay a high premium. Bidders will have to think twice before paying "fat takeover premiums" which could create an undersirable Goodwill item on their balance sheets. (Figure 2-22).

VALUE OF TENDER OFFERS
1978 — 1979

	Number of Offers	
Size of Offer	1978	1979
$ 0.1 — 5.0 million	22	7
$ 5.1 — 10.0 million	8	10
$10.1 — 25.0 million	20	23
$25.1 — 50.0 million	11	18
$50.1 — 75.0 million	11	11
Over $75 million	28	30

Figure 2-22 *Source: W. T. Grimm & Co.*

ACQUISITIONS OF PUBLICLY
HELD COMPANIES*

Owing to the increased cancellation rate, completed or pending acquisitions of publicly traded companies dropped 5 percent to 248 transactions from 260 in 1978. Cancellations totaled 95 in 1979, compared with 65 in 1978. Takeovers of public firms had been rising since 1974 (Figure 2-23 on page 18).

*Any purchase of a controlling interest or more in a publicly traded company.

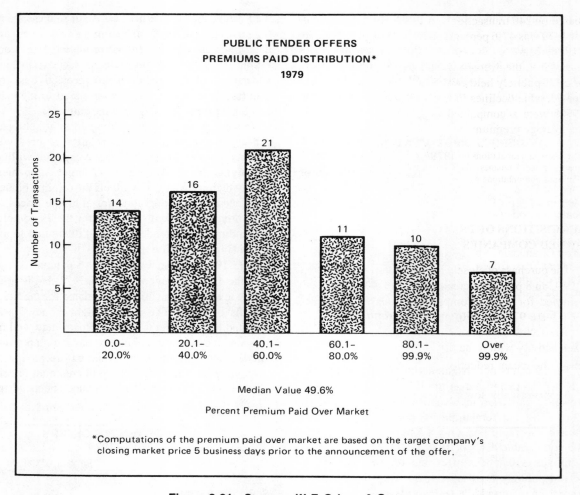

Figure 2-21   *Source: W. T. Grimm & Co.*

ACQUISITIONS OF PUBLICLY HELD COMPANIES
1974 — 1979

Year	Announced	Cancelled	Completed or Pending
1979	343	95	248
1978	325	65	260
1977	267	74	193
1976	232	69	163
1975	174	44	130
1974	133	65	68

Figure 2-23   *Source: W. T. Grimm & Co.*

PUBLIC TAKEOVERS
VALUE OF ACQUISITIONS
1978 — 1979

Value of Purchase Price	Percent of Transactions Disclosing Price	
	1978	1979
$10 million or less	19%	20%
$10.1 — 15.0 million	5%	9%
$15.1 — 25.0 million	16%	14%
$25.1 — 50.0 million	16%	17%
$50.1 — 100.0 million	20%	16%
Over $100 million	24%	24%

Figure 2-24   *Source: W. T. Grimm & Co.*

Despite the high cost of financing, *cash* was widely used as a form of payment. *Cash* transactions accounted for 67 percent of all public takeovers, while *stock* and *combination* payments amounted to 14 percent to 19 percent, respectively. Comparable 1978 and 1979 percentages were *cash,* 57 percent; *stock* 23 percent; and *combination,* 19 percent.

PERCENT PREMIUM PAID
OVER MARKET PRICE*

Calculated on 229 acquisitions of publicly traded companies, the 1979 average premium paid over market was 49.9 percent, compared with 46.2 percent (based on 240 transactions) in 1978. The median value for 1979 was 47.6 percent, up from the 1978 median of 41.5 percent.

In 1969, the average premium paid over the market price of publicly held companies was 25 percent. The considerable declines in market conditions during the 1970s were accompanied by substantial increases in the average premium.

*Premium paid tabulations for 1979 are based on the seller's closing market price 5 business days prior to the initial announcement. Previous computations were based on 2 business days.

ACQUISITIONS OF PRIVATELY OWNED COMPANIES

The purchase of closely held corporations numbered 1,049, an 8 percent increase from the 969 transactions recorded for 1978. Comparable totals for 1977 and 1976 were 971 and 856, respectively.

The following factors have influenced the heightened activity within the private sector:

— the recent reduction in the federal capital gains tax

— historically low P/E ratios for publicly traded stocks

— low level of investor interest in new stock offerings

— rising costs of public offerings.

We expect a further increase in acquisitions of privately owned companies. High interest rates along with inflationary pressures will force many undercapitalized firms to consider selling out or merging.

The preferred method of payment in private transactions, unlike public takeovers, was *stock*. The exchange of *stock* took place in 41 percent of the deals, while *cash* payments accounted for 39 percent.

A breakdown of privately held acquisitions by the value of the purchase price is displayed in Figure 2-25.

CLOSELY HELD SELLERS VALUE OF ACQUISITIONS 1979

Value of Purchase Price	Percent of Transactions Disclosing Price
$5 million or less	51%
$ 5.1 — 10.0 million	23%
$10.1 — 15.0 million	8%
$15.1 — 25.0 million	7%
$25.1 — 50.0 million	6%
$50.1 — 100.0 million	3%
Over $100 million	2%

Figure 2-25   Source: W. T. Grimm & Co.

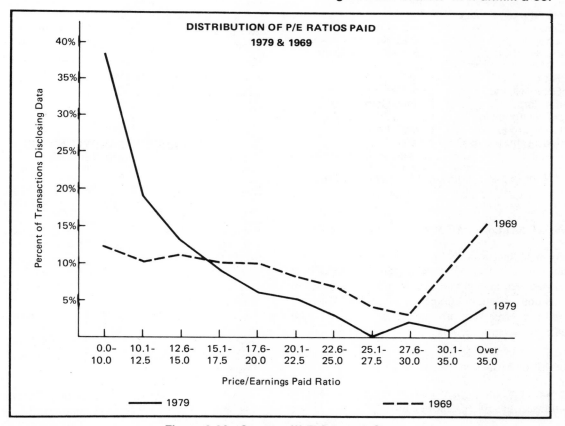

Figure 2-26   Source: W. T. Grimm & Co.

PRICE/EARNINGS RATIOS PAID

An aggregate of 333 transactions supplied the requisite data with which to compute the price/earnings ratios paid. These deals represented only 16 percent of net announcements. Thus, the subsequent multiples should not be construed as characteristic of all mergers and acquisitions. Based on the 333 transactions, the average P/E paid held steady at 14.3, the same as in 1978. However, at midyear 1979, the average multiple was 15.2. The decline in the last half is another indication that acquirers are moderating their offers. The 1979 median P/E paid was 11.6, compared with 11.5 in 1978.

The average multiple in 1969 was 21.0. A distribution of P/E ratios paid during 1969 is compared with those of 1979 in Figure 2-26 on page 19.

Examples of acquisitions commanding high multiples are listed in Figure 2-27.

ACQUISITIONS: P/E-PAID MULTIPLES HIGHER THAN 15.0 TIMES

Buyer Name	Seller Name
Siemens AG	Aerotron, Inc.
SmithKline Corp.	Allergan Pharmaceuticals, Inc.
Santa Fe International Corp.	C.F. Braun Co.
Holec N.V.	BTU Engineering Corp.
Trans World Corp.	Century 21 Real Estate Corp.
NCR Corp.	Comten, Inc.
McGraw-Hill, Inc.	Data Resources, Inc.
Harris Corp.	Farinon Corp.
Imperial Group Ltd.	Howard Johnson Co.
Unilever Group Ltd.	Lawry's Foods, Inc.
United Technologies Corp.	Mostek Corp.
Mattel, Inc.	Western Publishing Co.

Figure 2-27   Source: W. T. Grimm & Co.

ANNUAL SALES OF ACQUIRED COMPANIES

An aggregate of 1,376 transactions involved the sale of an entire company. Of these acquisitions, 644 sellers disclosed their annual sales. In 1978, there were 1,286 acquisitions of entire companies and sales of the acquired concerns were provided in 673 cases (Figure 2-28).

CANCELLATIONS

Over 9 percent of gross merger announcements, or 219 transactions, were canceled in 1979, versus 171 or

8 percent in 1978. Comparable percentages for 1977 and 1976 were 8 percent and 7 percent, respectively.

DISTRIBUTION OF SELLERS BY SALES
1978 — 1979

	Percentage of Sellers	
Annual Sales Volume	1978	1979
$5 million and Less	26%	28%
$ 5.1 — 10.0 million	16%	16%
$10.1 — 15.0 million	7%	7%
$15.1 — 25.0 million	10%	10%
$25.1 — 35.0 million	8%	6%
$35.1 — 45.0 million	5%	4%
$45.1 — 50.0 million	2%	2%
$50.1 — 75.0 million	7%	7%
$75.1 — 100.0 million	4%	4%
Over $100 million	15%	16%

Figure 2-28   Source: W. T. Grimm & Co.

Among the last ten years, 1975 had the highest cancellation rate, 10.4 percent of the gross total.

In 1969, canceled acquisitions numbered 620 or 9 percent. The majority of these terminations resulted from the deterioration of the market price of the buyer's shares or merger package, thereby substantially lowering the value of the offer.

Of those cancellations identifying cause of termination in 1979, inability to agree on terms was most frequently cited, followed by the intrusion of competing bidders, and economic conditions, namely high interest rates which lessened the availability of adequate financing (Figure 2-29).

TEN LARGEST CANCELLATIONS
1979

Buyer/ Seller	Approximated Value (Millions)	Reason for Cancellation
Borg-Warner Corp. Firestone Tire & Rubber Co.	$1,326.9	Firestone asked for a higher price.
Brascan Ltd.—Canada F.W. Woolworth Co.	1,020.0	Brascan abandoned offer; suffered a number of U.S. legal setbacks.
American Express Co. McGraw-Hill, Inc.	974.2	American withdrew its "hotly contested" offer.
Tenneco, Inc. & Southland Royalty Co. (joint buyers) International Paper Co. (oil & gas operations of General Crude Co.)	705.0	Operations acquired by Mobil Corp.

Buyer/ Seller	Approximated Value (Millions)	Reason for Cancellation
Weyerhaeuser & Co. Bodcaw Co.	695.0	International Paper Co. acquired Bodcaw at higher price.
Gulf Oil Corp. International Paper Co. (oil & gas operations of General Crude Co.)	650.0	Operations acquired by Mobil Corp.
Midland Bank Ltd.—Britain Walter E. Heller International Corp.	493.9	Not given.
Mobil Corp. Bodcaw Co.	475.0	Bodcaw acquired by International Paper Co.
Reliance Group, Inc. UV Industries, Inc.	449.2	Outbid by NVF Co.
Denison Mines Ltd.—Canada Reserve Oil & Gas Co.	443.5	Reserve received higher offer from Getty Oil Co.

Figure 2-29 *Source: W. T. Grimm & Co.*

PERSPECTIVE ON THE 1970's

Mergers and acquisitions during the past few years, as distinguished from the late 1960's, differ in many respects, ranging from the structure of deals to the reasoning behind them. Philosophically, the acquisition process in the 1970's progressed from a management fad to a significant method of achieving corporate goals. While hyperactivity within the merger market was more or less induced by artificial elements in the 1960's, the business consolidations during the past few years have been determined by corporate needs and changing economic conditions. The haphazardness of a decade ago matured into a cautious and selective approach to the acquisition process. Today's merger and acquisition strategies have become highly organized schemes consisting of comprehensive searches, detailed industry reports and a thorough evaluation of acquisition candidates.

The interaction of three conditions actuated the unprecedented acquisition growth during the 1960's: the science of management; lax accounting procedures; and investment institutions. Computer-oriented innovations within the science of management promoted the philosophy that an effective manager could manage anything. This, in turn, encouraged the "conglomerate" acquisition—the purchase of unrelated businesses. Certain acquisition accounting methods in the late 1960's, notably "pooling of interest," enabled conglomerate acquirers to immediately boost their earnings per share. Pooling allowed acquirers to combine their sales and earnings with those of sellers as if the constituent companies had always been one.

These rapid increases in per share earnings gave conglomerate builders the appearance of instant success—so much so that investors, particularly mutual funds, turned their attention to these diversified concerns. Conglomerate stock prices soared. Rising stock prices and earnings multiples further stimulated the merger movement. Due to the pumped-up stock prices, stock was widely used as a medium of payment. By 1968, stock transactions accounted for 62 percent of all deals compared with 26 percent in 1964. But "the Chinese paper game" came to an abrupt end with the drop in the market during 1970. At the same time, the accounting profession imposed stricter limits on the "pooling" treatment of mergers, and the general disregard for internal growth in earnings became apparent. Illusory profits disappeared, stock prices dropped, and any remaining possibility of "easy" acquisitions evaporated.

After a short period of retrenchment, the acquisitions and mergers market in the 1970's emerged with different players and game rules. First, the volume of merger activity hardly approached the record levels of the previous decade. Second, motivations were different. The single most important merger development was adoption of the "planned growth-through-acquisition" strategy. Corporate managements recognized the value of planning. Merger and acquisition strategies became effective components of overall plans to accomplish growth goals. Managements realized that supplementing internal expansion with external growth offered certain advantages—most importantly, cost.

In today's economic environment, plants, new markets and technological skills may be obtained at a lower cost through acquisitions than by construction, research and/or development. And, the acquisition of such items takes less time than starting from scratch. There is also the matter of uncertainty. An acquisition may involve less risk since the acquired concern has already shown its earning potential. Because there is a lower degree of risk, financing may be easier to obtain. Loans to develop or market new products are particularly risky.

While acquisition goals differ widely, the philosophies of today's acquisition-oriented managers all entail a theme of "synergistic combinations," which result in sounder business consolidations than those of a decade ago. Today, acquisition candidates are judged on the basis of potential performance and capabilities to provide a solid "business fit" and a fixed return on investment. In contrast to the 1960's, sellers' P/E ratios are now usually higher than acquirers' P/E multiples. Buyers will accept temporary dilution of their own shares to make advantageous acquisitions. Also, unlike the 1960's, companies acquired today are often financially healthy, well-managed and enjoy strong market positions. Owing to the takeover of these established and profitable companies, sizable mergers have increased dramatically, pushing the 1979 dollar volume paid to its record $43.5 billion.

Certain motivations are always present with respect to mergers. They include opportunities for real economies, increased profits, and achieving growth objectives. External influences have a negative or positive effect on these motivations. The merger and acquisition process will continue to adapt to these influences so that corporate goals can be accomplished.

SPECIAL CONSIDERATIONS OF THE SELLER AND BUYER

PRIOR TO CONSUMMATION OF THE TRANSACTION, the buyer and seller find themselves in an adversary position. Although both parties may seek successful solutions, the methods and psychology of the buyer and seller are quite different. Responses to the same situation, or even the identical question, will evoke actions and answers which reflect opposite mental attitudes. The buyer has the assignment of minimizing the purchase price to be paid while still inducing the seller to complete the transaction. The seller, on the other hand, is out to maximize the purchase price he will receive without going beyond the limits of the buyer's ability or willingness to pay. Interestingly enough, at the point of consummation of the deal, both parties frequently feel they have received the better of the bargain.

The conflicting perspectives of the buyer and seller are often evidenced by the public relations aspects of the transaction. In his chapter, Robert W. Taft takes a serious look at the public relations activities which can benefit all parties to the transaction. There is a discussion of appropriate pre-merger activities, an outline of communications with the public during the negotiation process, and an examination of public relations for the new corporate entity. Unique to this discussion is an appendix of typical press releases which have been effectively used in some of the more noteworthy merger and acquisition situations in the recent past.

In the next chapter, Daniel G. Bergstein discusses the uniqueness of foreign corporate structures and how to deal effectively with them as potential buyers. There is practical advice on how to research buyers and their backgrounds, anticipate legal and financial issues, deal with language and collateral problems and where to seek professional help. Case studies of actual experiences in completing a transaction between an American seller and a foreign buyer help illustrate Mr. Bergstein's points.

In examining corporate growth, Messrs. Berman and Wade focus on determining the goals of an acquisition program and translating the goals into planned actions. These experts view a proper planning process as the key ingredient to elimination of the incompatible or unprofitable acquisition. They go on to propose that the buyer establish basic guidelines as to acquisitions, fix form and magnitude of the payment which can be supported, determine an optimum ownership strategy, assess the importance of geography, and truthfully estimate the risk posed by any weakness in present management. Other information in this chapter will guide the potential buyer in making the approach to a seller in a well-thought-out manner.

The final chapter in this topical area, co-authored by Laurence E. Simmons and Michael D. Boxberger, considers the guidelines for who should run the new entity. This subject is a major problem area which deserves separate treatment in understanding the ultimate position of the buyer and the seller. The lines of authority should be clearly drawn to accommodate efficiency in the combination business.

ROBERT W. TAFT

Senior Vice President
Hill and Knowlton, Inc.

ROBERT W. TAFT is a senior vice president of Hill and Knowlton, Inc., New York public relations counseling firm. Mr. Taft is an accredited member of the Public Relations Society of America and a director of its Investor Relations Section. He served on the PRSA committee which drafted the Financial Public Relations Code of Ethics in 1972. In addition, he is a member of the National Investor Relations Institute and a former president of the New York Chapter.

Mr. Taft is an adjunct professor of New York University and chairs an annual seminar on investor relations. He received his undergraduate education at Amherst College, and graduated from Yale Law School with a J.D. in 1962. He is a member of the Cleveland, Ohio, and American bar associations.

Mr. Taft, born and raised in Cleveland, Ohio, resides in Manhattan.

3

Public Relations Aspects of
Mergers and Acquisitions

ROBERT W. TAFT

INTRODUCTION

The role of public relations in merger and acquisition activities is important, but too often overlooked.* Effective public relations activities well in advance of a merger can benefit the seller by contributing to the best possible price, attracting suitable potential purchasers, and organizing and presenting useful information in an efficient way. Such activities can benefit the buyer by enhancing the reputation and recognition of the purchase and minimizing post-acquisition assimilation problems.

In this chapter I will discuss the role of public relations in pre-merger activities of both buyer and seller. Since a merger is generally a ''material'' event for one or both parties to the transaction, I will also outline the rules (which are quite specific and strict) about public communications activities immediately preceding and during the merger process. To complete the chapter, I have added brief comments on post-merger activities to clarify and redirect the communications functions of the merged entity.

Included in the appendix are a number of typical press releases used at various stages in actual merger and acquisition situations. These releases are illustrative of what can and cannot be said, but are not intended to be exhaustive of the possibilities. Continuing evolution of the rules (such as the recent adoption of the Hart-Scott-Rodino Act) and the apparently limitless resourcefulness of investment bankers who structure these transactions, insure that additional ways of reporting developments will continue to be created.

PUBLIC RELATIONS FOR THE SMALL SELLER

The small company seeking to attract potential buyers faces enormous communications obstacles. The objective is simple: to make the company's strengths well known and to attract inquiry from appropriate buyers. A secondary objective is to create a visibility and reputation for the company which can support the efforts of an investment banker or finder in convincing a potential buyer that the company is attractive.

In most cases, traditional avenues of publicity are foreclosed to a small company. This is particularly so if a company is unlisted or, worse, privately held. While going public and listing may make certain types of publicity easier to obtain, no company should consider either act simply to create publicity opportunities.

The most common mistakes that small companies make are starting communications activities too late and doing too little. In most cases these companies make a third mistake by expecting too much of their first try at communications.

Any public relations effort should commence a year, and preferably two years, before a sale is contemplated. Since the press and even the investment community are likely to be indifferent at the start, the company must approach the problem by exploiting its strengths.

Small companies tend to shape communications programs that say what the management wants to hear. Such programs are generally a waste of money because they fail to address the interests or needs of the real

*Portions of this chapter are drawn from *The SEC, The Securities Markets and Your Financial Communications,* Fifth Edition, 1979, published by Hill and Knowlton, Inc.

25

audience. In this case a company looking for a buyer should "think like a buyer." What is a buyer looking for?

Most buyers are looking for similar information about a company. For example, they want the best available information on a company's future growth potential (as opposed to its historical growth record). They want to know as much as possible about a company's existing products, product development record, and the prospects for new products about to come into production. They want to know as much as possible about a company's customers (What is the nature of the relationship? How dependent is the company on one or a few customers? How effective is the company in competing for new customers?). They want to know about relationships with suppliers and sources of materials.

In a word, a potential buyer wants to know as much as possible about what he is actually buying, both tangible assets and intangible prospects.

Companies, both large and small, tend to present themselves in company releases and publications with restraint and in guarded terms. Most frequently, they hold back important information for "competitive reasons." It is difficult to refute this argument because it is so vague. But the secretive instincts of corporate managers must be overcome and dealt with—commonly from the very top of the organization—if a company is to develop usable information about itself. This need not involve "giving away the store." But it probably will involve a much higher degree of disclosure than a small company has ever before experienced.

A good starting point for developing a package of information about the company is to study the annual reports and SEC filings of publicly traded companies in similar businesses. Most industries share a common pattern of disclosure. A selling company seeking attention should conform as closely as possible to the disclosure patterns of the publicly traded members of his industry group.

Even large companies need time to develop their disclosure documents. A small company should begin with a relatively simple document, perhaps a short history of the company. Then, layer by layer, it can add to this document such information as:

— lists of the company's plant locations and the products produced at each;
— information on the uses and markets for each product group;
— biographical information about key members of management.

Rather quickly, the company will come to sensitive subjects like the following:

— future plans, including sources of future capital;
— candid discussion of the company's competitive position;
— the relative contribution of various products to sales and earnings;
— some assessment of that latest concern, the impact of inflation on the business.

Eventually the master document will have to include specific financial information (on a three-to-five-year basis because this is what any reasonable buyer would be interested in) and enough additional material so that the buyer can understand such fundamentals as:

— the company's accounting methods;
— how the company reserves for bad debts and what its experience has been;
— the impact of extraordinary items on results in recent years;
— the cost of goods sold in relation to inventory;
— profit margins.

These and other pieces of information are painful for most companies to disclose. But no company can undertake any type of communications program, much less the tricky business of finding a buyer, unless it is prepared to share information about itself with the public. The debate over what and how to disclose information will continue as long as the company operates. But initial agreement that management will support and cooperate with some minimum level of public disclosure is essential.

Focus on Management

A company seeking a buyer must make itself visible to potential buyers. Companies work with various intermediaries discussed elsewhere in this book. But almost without exception, a program that increases company visibility makes the intermediary's work easier and makes a seller's negotiating position with a potential buyer stronger.

One of the best sources of visibility for a small company is not the company's activities, but the character of the company's management. It is a truism in the financial community that investors at all levels of sophistication are concerned with the quality of a company's management. Any company program should seek to present this management story.

The management story should be shaped so that it conveys information of value to a reader. For example, a good way to illustrate management ability is to discuss how management solved a particular problem in a new or more effective way. An article concerning management's problem-solving ability can be submitted with a byline to many trade or general business publications. It may be possible to interest a writer in developing such a story on his own.

The following section provides a simple illustration of how one company prepared a brief "pitch" letter to attract interest from several different publications.

Press Relations

There are numerous opportunities for companies of all sizes to obtain considerable visibility in the press. The process takes time and some effort but almost always pays off. The biggest problem for inexperienced companies is dealing with reporters. This is generally true because most businessmen forget that the reporter has a job to do too. The reporter is looking for news. Most corporate stories, at least the first time they are discussed, really aren't newsworthy to anyone other than the company itself.

The solution is simply to think like the reporter. Try to identify the items of interest at your company, even though they may not be central to the business. Give the reporter an interesting lead and he will flesh out his story with one or more of the items that you feel are important.

Another problem is identifying the right publications to contact. One of the easiest is the daily newspaper. Local business writers are always looking for new story leads, particularly stories about local companies.

Reporters are easy to approach. Most answer their own phones. While it is common to simply call a reporter you know well, it is better to approach an unfamiliar reporter in writing. There are several advantages to this:

— it forces you to develop a story line on paper as a reporter would;
— it saves the reporter time;
— it provides basic information in accurate form which will probably be used in the story.

These letters are called "pitch" letters in the trade. Here is a sample pitch letter developed by a very small company which will be seeking a buyer in about 18 months:

"Mr. Alan Jones
Editor
Middletown Gazette
Middletown, Connecticut

Dear Mr. Jones:

"The Brown Company of Middletown has a new lease on life thanks to the innovative leadership of Leon Gold. We think the turnaround story of this 120-year-old textile supplies manufacturing concern will interest your readers.

"Gold, a Harvard MBA and former securities analyst, bought Brown in 1976. After years of analyzing other people's companies, he wanted to run his own.

"The Brown Company's fortunes were declining, but Gold's strategy has transformed a potential loser into the textile materials industry's fastest moving marketer ($2.7 million estimated 1979 sales). The once sleepy world of textile supplies is now charged with a new competitive spirit.

"Gold saw potential in the textile supply industry back in 1976. Its steady growth and recession-resistance helped him attract a stable of blue-chip, low-profile investors to the private concern. These included: (list prominent individuals).

"Before Gold's buyout, the company—a subsidiary of the East Coast's largest textile supplies wholesaler—had lost its sense of direction. Gold's ambition was to rebuild Brown into the highly regarded textile materials manufacturer that it had been for over 100 years. To that end, he cut the low-margin fat from the product line and instituted the company's first financial controls.

"Marketing strategy, Gold knew, would be one of the key points in the turnaround. But he didn't know the industry. He beefed up management depth late in 1977 by hiring Bob Smith out of the president's seat at a (competitor's) division. Smith's reputation and experience were critical in building distributor support and developing new products.

"Gold also lured the Sales Promotion Director of (competitor) to give his strategy a consumer orientation. Together, they started the industry's first in-depth market research, and the results inspired the following innovations:

• Customers complained about damaged materials so Brown's products are now plastic-packaged and deliveries are up 50 percent.
• The entire textile line has been renamed, redesigned and supported by a new ad campaign with heavy promotion. Customers have reacted and products are back-ordered for the first time.
• They acquired a renowned line of imported textiles and other materials which has become the door-opener for Brown's expanded sales force. Twelve-month sales figures for the new line have doubled.
• The company's reestablished prominence helped attract *Better Homes & Gardens* to

sponsor Brown's craft kit, and the leading authority in the field has been signed for promotion. This new program will require no major capital expense for Brown, but should throw off a lot of cash.

"Although there are no market share figures available, Brown's increased sales volume indicates a growing position in a number of product areas. The gamble is paying off for Gold as the turnaround continues. This should be the company's first profitable year out of the last five.

"Gold is articulate, knowledgeable and eager to talk. If you are interested in speaking with him, I'd be glad to arrange it.

"I will call you soon to see if you need additional information and to get your reaction.

"Sincerely,"

Such a letter can be sent by any company executive or consultant.

The letter's tone is enthusiastic. Rather than asking for a story, it suggests that there is information of interest to the reporter's audience. The letter implies that there are several story opportunities. Most important, the letter makes it clear that the company is eager to cooperate.

Essentially the same letter can be used with appropriate trade publications and, depending on the company's business, with some general interest magazines.

All or portions of that disclosure document I discussed earlier should be made available to the reporter if he does show interest in doing a story about the company. The document will help him get his facts straight and may even interest him in doing something else on the company.

While publication of such articles is valuable, the use of article reprints will considerably enhance the benefit to the company. In addition to sending reprints to customers and suppliers, the company can use them selectively in the financial community to increase its visibility.

Other Publicity Opportunities for the Small Seller

Public Service: Initially, this may seem remote from the issue of mergers and acquisitions. But it has been demonstrated repeatedly that the company benefits when management's skills as a business leader are recognized by an appointment to undertake a public service function. This assumes, of course, that management does a conscientious and capable job. Clearly, the public service position provides a base for additional visibility to the man and, by association, to the

company. This exposure will bring management visibility among a broad segment of the public, including potential buyers. A variation on this approach is to initiate a new public activity. Of course, a risk of undertaking a program using this strategy is that a prospective buyer may become concerned that the business is being neglected.

Speeches: Speeches on virtually any subject will increase management's visibility. A business topic appeals to business audiences. Similarly, testimony before governmental agencies can serve to advance management visibility. Any talk should be reinforced with widely distributed speech reprints.

Financial Reports: Above all, the company should consider preparing financial reports, complete with president's message and text, for distribution to possible interested audiences such as banks and local investment bankers. Distribution can also be made to local media in any city where the company has operations. Many companies also distribute to political leaders and executives at other in-the-community companies to open avenues for common discussion.

A basic annual report can be a treacherous undertaking for a company that has no experience in writing about itself. Common mistakes are to overproduce and, especially, overwrite such documents.

My favorite example of a particularly dreadful "first" annual report began with these words:

"Knighthood was still in flower in the year 1066 when William the Conqueror led the Norman conquest of the British Isles.

"Exactly nine hundred years later—far past the Age of Chivalry, through the Renaissance and the Industrial Revolution and a couple of world wars, into the midst of the Space Age—another 'Norman Conquest' of sorts was to begin.

"History books will perhaps ignore this one. Its men-at-arms appeared in business suits. The field to be won was the fast-growing business and industrial complex of the American South.

"Norman Jones, Inc.* entered the lists like Ivanhoe, with a borrowed suit of armor, steel nerves, and a sharp lance—with everything to gain and the determination to unhorse all comers."

* Not the real name.

There may be a place for this kind of writing but it is surely not in a company's annual report. It took a reader several more pages to find out what business the company was in. The report disclosed virtually nothing about the company's financial condition but unintentionally said a good deal about the management.

An "annual report" can be designed as a non-registered sales tool for the company. Although a small company will not necessarily want to include as much as a company filing with the SEC, some financial information should be provided in the annual report. Financial information about the company is, after all, what any interested buyer wants to know first.

Advertising and Product Exposure: Opinions about a company, based on little more than its advertising, both corporate and product, can be readily formed by potential buyers. The reputation of a company's products can precede it in the financial community. Frequently, careful placement of product ads in financial publications can dramatically increase a company's visibility among potential buyers.

Summary: Above all, whatever activities a small company undertakes, work should begin well in advance of any serious sales effort. The company will benefit from successful activities like those described above whether or not they result directly in attracting a buyer's attention. The company's employee relations, and relations with customers and the community, will certainly improve.

Research on the Buyer

Before leaving the small seller it is worth suggesting a different role for public relations. A seller normally wants to know as much about a prospective buyer as the buyer wants to know about the seller. A person with some training in public relations can provide invaluable assistance in researching the buyer. For example, newspaper accounts, conversations with various types of media people, customers, security analysts and others can develop information to answer such questions as:

— How good are the buyer's labor relations?
— How do the buyer's managers feel about their employer?
— How independent have other acquired companies remained after the buyer took over?
— Does the buyer have financial or product problems that could drag you both down?

The seller should not overlook the opportunity for independent investigation of this type of information by parties who do not have any financial stake in seeing the acquisition completed.

PUBLIC RELATIONS FOR THE LARGER SELLER

The problems are somewhat different for the large seller. In this case, most publicity tools are available. The issues which public relations must deal with are more subtle, particularly the issue of positioning the company (or, more commonly, that part of the company which is for sale) to attract buyers without undercutting existing operations.

There are several different strategies which have been developed in recent years to deal with this problem:

Public Announcement: Many companies simply announce that certain divisions are for sale. Here is an example of a statement in the annual report that a company operation is for sale:

"After a careful study of the market potential for Bard, coupled with the added investment to develop this market, we have decided to terminate further work on the new membrane for kidney dialysis. We think the product has potential to a company already in the field of kidney dialysis and are attempting to sell our operation to such a company. If we do not sell it, we will close down the operation during the first half of 1980. Either way, there will be no material impact on Bard's 1980 results."

This course of action clearly requires substantial preparation among employees and customers to avoid work stoppages and loss of business. Nevertheless, this course of action may be forced by tax considerations which make it desirable to set up reserves against the sale of a business in a tax year other than the year of sale. Here is an example of a company announcement triggered by the decision to account for a specific division as a discontinued operation:

"(Dateline)—NL Industries, Inc. today announced that it is holding preliminary discussions with several prospective purchasers of its magnesium operation in Utah.

"The company is maintaining the current rate of full production, and will continue its ongoing program of technical and production improvements to meet the requirements of its customers.

"NL's 1979 financial statements will reflect a decision to write the magnesium operation down to its estimated net realizable value and to provide for its present and anticipated operating results as a discontinued operation. This decision was reached even though the operation generates a positive cash flow and the long-range economic and technical viability of the Great Salt Lake facility has been proven in more than 30 months of continuous operation. The NL board of directors recommended that the company continue to emphasize its investments in petroleum services rather than magnesium.

"The write-down of the magnesium investment together with three other major factors—the net gain from the sale of 19 other metal and chemical units, the overall net income from operation of discontinued units, and the benefit from a change in the company's accounting for investment tax credit—is not expected to have any significant impact on net income.''

Another compelling reason to make such an announcement is where it becomes useful to separate an unprofitable operation from other activities in terms of financial reporting. The less attractive operation may be obscuring otherwise good results. Other examples of direct announcements of intention to sell a problem division are included in the appendix.

Statement of Corporate Strategy: Increasingly, large companies are outlining their financial objectives in annual reports and meetings with security analysts. The company normally also indicates its intention to sell off operations which do not meet certain criteria. Where this is done, interested buyers can quickly identify likely problem areas that may be shortly on the block.

Annual Report Positioning: It has become clear by examining the annual reports of companies that are contemplating the divestiture of certain operations, that they frequently change the emphasis in descriptions of operations which are for sale. It is normal to reduce the space devoted to an operation which has the potential to be sold. It is also normal to reduce or eliminate the information on the operation's contribution to sales and earnings.

Corporations are rarely publicly critical of operations which they are attempting to sell. The public relations problem is to find the appropriate level of description to make casual readers understand that the operation is sound, but to eliminate surprise when the operation is sold. A secondary problem in cases where several facilities or subsidiaries are to be sold is to avoid the impression of piecemeal sale and the possibility of being left with unsold pieces of a larger operation.

A good example of how to deal with such a discussion appears in the 1978 annual report of NL Industries, Inc.:

> "NL continues to monitor the long-term market outlook and profit potential of the recycled lead industry. While growth for the business appears moderately optimistic, new and proposed government regulations on lead in the environment and in the workplace are highly restrictive to producers and users. In view of these regulations, each of NL's plants is being reviewed to ensure that additional capital requirements can

be justified relative to NL's alternative investment opportunities. Based upon this analysis, NL has already sold two West Coast facilities and closed one of its older smelters.''

Secrecy: The discussion to this point has assumed that a larger company is selling a portion of its business. In cases where the entire company is to be sold, the watchword is secrecy. Generally, the public relations people at the company are not advised until shortly before the announcement. The first announcement is normally made by the acquiring company or jointly. To insure secrecy in such cases, an outside public relations firm is frequently used.

PUBLIC RELATIONS FOR POTENTIAL BUYERS

There are essentially two public relations issues for any potential buyer:

1. To attract appropriate sellers;
2. To minimize resistance from potential sellers to efforts to make acquisitions.

Companies are increasingly more open and direct in their public posture on acquisitions. There is little risk in letting the world know that the company is seeking to grow through acquisition. From the financial community's point of view there are clear advantages. Wall Street dislikes surprises. One form of surprise is an unexpected merger. Where the financial community considers the merger unworkable or otherwise inappropriate, the transaction can have serious long-term consequences for the stock. On the other hand, companies can benefit from clearly articulated merger policies that are discussed with and understood by the Street.

Statement of Acquisition Policy

There is an increasing trend for companies to articulate their acquisition policies. Sometimes this is done in meetings with analysts. Increasingly, too, these statements are appearing in corporate annual reports. Here are three recent examples:

Example #1: Peabody International Corporation Annual Report 1979—Page 22

Acquisition Philosophy

> "Peabody has an ongoing, well-defined program for seeking acquisitions that meet five primary criteria:
>
> > 1. They must make conceptual sense —that is, complement our existing operations and fit within Oil Field, Quality Assurance or Environment.

2. They must have profit margins at least as good as Peabody's and should enhance both our per-share earnings and balance sheet.

3. They must be well-managed companies with good track records in proven businesses.

4. We want to join with companies whose managers wish to retain their full management responsibility. We recognize that unique skills are developed in the course of running any business, and we have an unusually strong record of retaining the managements of acquired companies, either within those companies or assuming expanded responsibilities within Peabody.

5. The acquisitions must be friendly. We have never taken over an unwilling management group. In every acquisition we have merged under mutual agreement of both managements.''

Example #2: Black & Decker Annual Report 1978— Page 14

New Business

''Black & Decker has programs to encourage inventors of products that are consistent with the Company's marketing and manufacturing strengths. Likewise, the Company does consider appropriate acquisitions, but only in support of existing business plans and corporate objectives.

''Black & Decker is fortunate to be in a business that has provided a record of high growth and offers a favorable outlook for the future. While the Company continues to explore new products and markets in related businesses, it has retained its focus on labor-saving products.''

Example #3: Becton Dickinson Annual Report 1978— Pages 10-11

Acquisitions are Profiled

''Part of the company's growth will come from acquisitions, and its executives look at several possibilities a week. Traditionally, much of the innovation in the health field has come from single entrepreneurs or scientists, many of whom aren't working directly in the field. 'Becton Dickinson's acquisition strategy,' says Photios T. Paulson, vice president for planning and development, 'is to position ourselves in the market so that the entrepreneurs and researchers come to us, either for funding or a buyout.'

''The company's criteria for acquisitions also relate closely to its overall strategy. An acquisition must either enhance one of Becton Dickinson's basic businesses—as its acquisition last summer of Energetics Science, Inc.

strengthened the safety monitoring business—or the acquired company must have a strong position in a new embryonic or growth-stage business—as Telemed Corp., a pending acquisition, has in the business of computer analysis of electrocardiograms.

''Acquisition candidates are put through the same SBU profile analysis that Becton Dickinson's own businesses are. 'In some cases,' says John Gabel, 'that rigorous screening has deflated some ideas and led to the rejection of an acquisition that didn't fit the company's businesses or didn't have a commanding market potential.' In another case, however, an apparently ugly duckling turned into a swan. 'And I've got one,' says Frank Iris candidly, 'that I wouldn't have made if we had looked at it in a profile.'''

Solutions to the buyer's second problem, to minimize resistance from potential sellers, take many forms. One approach is to state publicly, as Peabody did, that the company will not attempt to take over a company that is unwilling to be acquired. Such statements facilitate the sharing of information during negotiations. Occasionally, of course, a company may change its mind about such a policy. A recent example illustrates the kind of response which an unsuspecting target can make (although the companies did later combine).

''(Dateline)—C.T. Bowring & Co. Limited, London, England, announced today that it is commencing actions against Marsh & McLennan Companies, Inc. in the Federal District Court for the Southern District of New York and in the High Court in England to restrain the use or publication of confidential information concerning Bowring supplied to Marsh & McLennan. The information was supplied in connection with negotiations between the two companies relating to a possible pooling arrangement and in the course of subsequent discussions between them.

''Marsh & McLennan had unilaterally announced on December 17, 1979, that it was considering making an offer to acquire all of the issued share capital and convertible loan stock of Bowring. Bowring's complaints in the court actions allege that any such offer would constitute an illegal use or publication of such confidential information, in violation of confidentiality undertakings and fiduciary relationships between the parties.

''Bowring and Marsh & McLennan commenced discussions in June 1978 with a view to implementing proposals for the coordination of the operations and the combination of the results of their insurance interests, on a mutually agreeable basis not involving an exchange of stock or control. Such discussions led to the initialing of a draft agreement by the end of 1978. However, it subsequently became apparent that Marsh & McLennan was no longer willing to pursue the proposals envisaged by the agreement. As a result, although this remains the preferred route so far as Bowring is concerned, alternative forms of structuring an association were then examined but without success.

"In the course of these negotiations a very substantial amount of highly confidential and detailed information relating to its insurance operations was supplied by each party to the other. Such information was exchanged on the basis of understandings that the information was to be used solely for the purpose of such negotiations and not for any other purpose. In fact, express representations were made by Marsh & McLennan to Bowring on several occasions that no unilateral offer to the shareholders of Bowring would be made by Marsh. Bowring provided information to Marsh relying on these understandings.

"Since Marsh & McLennan has now publicly indicated the possibility of an offer to shareholders on a unilateral basis, the Board of Directors of Bowring has concluded that it has no recourse but to seek to restrain through court action the improper use and publication of confidential information which such an offer would inevitably involve."

"Mr. Peter Bowring, Chairman of Bowring, commented as follows:

"'The Board of Bowring has unanimously determined that the acquisition of control of Bowring by Marsh & McLennan would not be in the best interests of the Group, its staff, and the shareholders. However, Bowring continues to be actively interested in pursuing a solution which combines and coordinates their own and Marsh & McLennan's insurance operations, but with each Group preserving its integrity and independence. We stand ready to reopen discussions with Marsh on a pooling basis and, subject of course to obtaining the necessary governmental and other consents, to implement the draft agreement already initialed.'"

Another strategy to reassure nervous sellers is to include, as a part of the company's continuing public relations objectives and activities, a flow of information which underscores the positive benefits that continue to result from earlier acquisitions.

Companies in two or more distinctly different businesses devote considerable time and energy to telling the world about the continuing success of acquired companies.

A classic study of the integration of very different companies can be seen in the gradual accommodation of Montgomery Ward and Container Corporation into a company called Marcor, and the subsequent assimilation, in 1976, of Marcor by Mobil. The handling of all three companies in a single annual report has differed from year to year in an attempt to integrate certain central management concepts, yet preserve some elements of individuality for each company.

MAKING THE ACQUISITION WORK

There are three areas that most handbooks of this type do not discuss adequately: employee relations, community relations, and customer relations. They play a central role in making the acquisition work, and they all require prior planning.

Employee Relations

Experience has shown that most mergers and acquisitions produce confusion in the employee population and generate a tremendous need for information. If information is not forthcoming, rumors fly. Judgments and opinions of the new management, based on scant information, are formed in the minds of the employees.

A staged approach to communications must be planned. For example, key management personnel should be told before an announcement is made to line workers or other management. Do not assume that people, especially employees, will understand if they get their news secondhand. An employee is likely to feel deceived if he hears of the acquisition on the radio as he drives home one evening. His immediate reaction might be to look for another job.

The announcement should be as complete as possible. A slide presentation is an effective way of highlighting your firm's financial strength, overall capabilities, and policies. Following the slide presentation, the president might give a short address reassuring the employees of their job security. An information kit, similar to the one prepared for the press, can be distributed to the employees.

As other relevant news items develop, newsletters or memos can be sent to the workers, and meetings with managerial personnel can take place. As part of your mechanism for employee communications, management should consider an internal newsletter as well as memoranda issued as needed to keep the employees informed.

If labor in the acquisition company is unionized, you should also keep the unions well informed of corporate developments through distribution of the background information kits or slide presentations to union leaders.

Community Relations: Acquiring Company New to Community

If you establish a good line of communications with your employees, they will help gain a favorable reception for your firm in the community where it operates. It is important that a company coming into a community through acquisition establish itself as a responsible corporate citizen. A good community relations program can smooth the way for constructive taxation policies, laws, and regulations.

When dealing with plant communities, the new management should explain the impact of the acquisition on the local employment situation and emphasize plans for any increase in production capacity or innovations in research, energy use, or environmental protection.

Because the corporation's reception in the community is based on the experiences of the first few days, it is imperative that a community relations program be planned during negotiating stages of an acquisition and that contacts within the community be established quickly.

The key community audiences include municipal, county, and state governments; special revenue districts which might see the acquisition as a new tax source; official planning boards and zoning authorities; community opinion leaders, including the clergy; environmental, consumer and other special interest groups; school officials and teachers; and, of course, your employees in their role as community residents.

The first step in a community communications program is to evaluate the business and social structure of the community. This might be done through meetings with small groups of community opinion leaders, including elected officials on both the local and national levels.

Assess the environment of the local community. There may be problems that you, as outsiders, are not aware of. There are political, economic, and social issues that you must contend with. Some community members might be opposed in principle to certain types of industries growing in the community. Others might be concerned with questions of pollution control or occupational safety. By understanding the motivations

and actions of state and federal regulatory agencies, and the attitudes of community leaders, you can better anticipate potential problems and deal with them on a pro-active basis.

After you have developed an understanding of the community structure and made initial contact, work to build stronger contacts and to portray the company to each group as a constructive member of the community. For example, the existing manager of the acquired company should introduce the president of the firm to the community. Other methods of community communications include interviews with the local media and speeches at local forums such as the Chamber of Commerce or Rotary Club.

Customer Relations

Do not overlook the existing trade relationships of the acquisition target.

Customers, suppliers, and distributors should be made familiar with the acquiring company and its management. Distributors and customers must be reassured on supply and pricing. Good relationships must be maintained with suppliers.

Begin with a letter from the president explaining the acquisition. A presentation might also be given for these audiences by your company's management. And also consider an information kit for customers, suppliers and distributors.

SPECIAL PROBLEMS FOR FOREIGN ACQUIRORS

It appears likely that in coming years foreign investment and acquisition of American companies will continue and perhaps grow. Such foreign investment is considered by many to be a growing political issue in the United States. At this writing there appears to be growing interest in some quarters for various forms of legislation to restrict or regulate such investment.*

Foreign investors facing the complexity and diversity of American society for the first time must develop a careful understanding of, and communication with, American audiences. Many foreign companies appear to undertake effective communications programs at home, but fail to conduct effective communications programs in the U.S. Foreign companies often appear to underestimate the impact of their presence in the United States.

A foreign company should assess its image in the U.S. (if any) in advance of any acquisition it is considering. The company's name or logo may be a household word at home, but it could be virtually unknown

*The Foreign Investor In the American Marketplace: A Hill and Knowlton Study; Published 1979 by Hill and Knowlton, Inc.

in the U.S. An objective assessment of the company's image in the U.S. would reveal the possible misconceptions it needs to correct as soon as possible.

As part of a media communications program, a background information kit detailing the foreign company should be developed for U.S. readers. The information kit should contain a summary of the company's activities, an annual report, organization and management structure charts, and biographies and photographs of the chairman and key members of senior management. The kit should be distributed in the U.S. to appropriate business/financial and trade press editors.

News releases subject to legal review concerning the company's operations, and releases of a more general nature, can also be distributed to the U.S. business press and to the national press.

Because the media can reflect the xenophobia of the community, misconceptions of corporate intentions, insensitivity to community opinion on the part of a firm, or an inconsistent company message, it is essential that all public statements be carefully planned. A primary corporate spokesperson should be named to insure that the company articulates a consistent point of view on sensitive issues.

Many foreign investors have problems in complying with U.S. labor laws, particularly the Equal Employment Opportunity Act. Several cases have been filed against foreign investors over the right to impose different management styles. One case involves the C. Itoh Company in which that company had a dual compensation system, one for its American and one for its Japanese employees. The firm also conducted management meetings in Japanese, thereby excluding the American managers' participation. American managers of C. Itoh sued the company charging they were being discriminated against because they were American nationals.

Another case is a class action suit against Sumitomo, another Japanese company. The American employees alleged that the Japanese company violated civil rights laws by allowing only those employees who knew the Japanese marketplace, as well as Japanese business practices, culture and language, into top positions. If the U.S. government succeeds in its suit, it will be able, at least to a limited extent, to impose management practices on foreign companies.

It is obvious that a definite connection exists between management styles and employee relations. Foreign investors taking this into account are reorienting their personnel policies for the U.S. market. Foreign companies operating in the United States can foster an improved employment policy by better defin-

ing the differences in job positions, by providing uniform benefits and by communicating with the employees.

One foreign company that has effective employee communications in the U.S. is Matsushita Electric, which acquired the American T.V. manufacturing operations of Motorola in 1974. *The Wall Street Journal* reported that at the beginning of the merger, the American workers were upset at the idea of working for a foreign company. However, four years later, these workers cited better working conditions, improved quality control, decision-making by consensus and more open communications between management and line workers. The American workers applauded the ten-minute meetings held twice a day between foremen and workers to discuss production, quality control and other problems.

LIMITATIONS ON DISCUSSING THE MERGER

It is quite natural for the parties to a merger to want to draw public attention to the benefits that will accrue to all parties from the successful completion of the transaction. However, in many, if not most cases today, this is illegal. Until the early 1970's, the SEC took the position that when two companies merged on terms requiring an exchange of shares, no sale of shares took place. But in late 1972, the SEC reversed itself and concluded that, as of January 1, 1973, mergers involving stock would in fact be "sales," therefore requiring the registration of shares and subject to all the limitations on "market conditioning" and "selling" associated with any registration.

Therefore, today, most public statements about mergers prior to shareholder approval and completion are extremely circumscribed. SEC Rule 145(b) (1) limits initial communications about the proposed merger to no more than the following:

— "the name of the issuer of the securities to be offered, or the person whose assets are to be sold in exchange for the securities to be offered, and the names of other parties to (the transaction);

— "a brief description of the business of parties to such transaction;

— "the date, time and place of the meeting of security holders to vote on or consent to any such transaction;

— "a brief description of the transaction to be acted upon and the basis upon which such transaction will be made;

— "any legend or similar statement required by State or Federal law or administrative authority."

Companies should realize that issuance of such a

release normally will put the company in the registration period if it is not already in it. Any communications should be reviewed with legal counsel.

While it is beyond the scope of this chapter to discuss in detail the difficulties of communications activities during the so-called "blackout" registration period, the following brief discussion may be helpful to those unfamiliar with the subject. However, it should be noted that this area is subject to widely different interpretation by the lawyers involved. Some prefer an extremely strict construction of the rules, meaning that the company can say virtually nothing during registration. Other lawyers, generally reflecting the recently expressed intentions of the SEC itself, tend toward a more liberal (and, in my opinion, common-sense) construction of the rules.

Companies are permitted to issue a news release *at the time they file* a registration statement. Rule 134 provides that such a release must be preceded or accompanied by a written prospectus, or state from whom a prospectus may be obtained. A Rule 134 release must be limited to the following additional information:

— the name of the security issuer;
— the full title of the security being offered;
— a brief statement about the general nature of the issuer's business;
— the price of the security or the method of determining the probable price range as specified by the issuer or managing underwriter;
— in the case of a debt security with a fixed interest provision, the yield, or probable yield range, as specified by the issuer or managing underwriter;
— the name and address of the sender of the communication and the fact, if so, that he is participating or intends to participate in the distribution of the security;
— the names of the managing underwriters;
— the approximate date on which it is expected that the proposed sale will begin;
— whether the security is a "legal investment" for certain regulated purchasers such as banks, insurance companies, etc.;
— whether, in the opinion of counsel, the security is exempt from specified taxes, or the extent to which the issuer has agreed to pay any tax with respect to the security;
— whether the security is being offered through rights issued to security holders and, if so, the class of securities whose holders will be entitled to subscribe; the subscription ratio; the actual or proposed record date; the date upon which the rights were issued or are expected to be issued; the actual or anticipated date upon which they will expire; and the approximate subscription price—or any of the foregoing;
— any statements or legend required by any state law or administrative authority.

Since releases under Rules 145 and 134 contain only basic information, they are not considered "selling" documents and need not be filed with the SEC.

In addition, most states have "Blue Sky" laws governing securities offerings and related matters. A release to be issued under Rules 145 and 134 should be reviewed with counsel to determine whether it conforms to the requirements of state law.

Proxy Solicitation

Because of the strict limitations on management's discussion of the possible benefits of a merger, most companies use experienced proxy solicitors to insure that all shareholders are reached and that shareholders have adequate access to knowledgeable people who can answer basic questions about the transaction. In most cases, management itself will undertake an organized solicitation of the larger shareholders.

Another increasingly common tool which managements use to gain shareholder approval of mergers is basic advertising. Since it is generally too expensive (and ineffective) to reproduce the entire joint proxy statement as an advertisement, these ads take the form of calling attention to the upcoming vote. Here is a portion of a recent full-page ad to shareholders of UV Industries urging that they vote on a complex merger/liquidation proposal:

Full-Page Ad—The Wall Street Journal—Excerpt

"AN IMPORTANT MESSAGE FOR SHAREHOLDERS OF UV INDUSTRIES, INC.

"Your vote 'FOR' the following proposals is needed at the Stockholders' Meeting scheduled to be held on March 26:

1. "To adopt the Plan of Liquidation and Dissolution providing for the liquidation of the Company and the distribution of its cash and assets to all the stockholders.
2. "To sell Federal Pacific Electric Company, a wholly owned subsidiary of UV, for $345,000,000 in cash.
3. "To approve an alternative proposal to sell substantially all of the assets of the Company and distribute the proceeds in cash or in kind to all of the stockholders, in the event the Plan of Liquidation (Proposal #1) is not approved.

"Let me tell you why YOUR vote is so important.

"We believe that Sharon Steel intends to vote against the Plan of Liquidation in an attempt to prevent it from being adopted.

"If the Plan of Liquidation is not adopted, the gain from the sale of Federal would then be taxable, which would cost UV approximately $42,000,000 in federal income taxes, or nearly $3 for each share of UV Common Stock.

"The closing sales price of the Company's Common Stock on December 15, 1978, the last business day prior to the December 18, 1978, announcement that the Company had agreed to sell Federal and was considering liquidation, was $19-3/8 per share. If the Plan of Liquidation is approved, the initial liquidating distribution alone will be $18 per share. This initial distribution will be followed by an additional distribution or distributions. While the aggregate distributions to stockholders if the alternative proposal (item #3 above) is adopted will be less than the aggregate distributions pursuant to the Plan of Liquidation (item #1 above), the initial distribution under the alternative proposal will also be $18 per share.

"Adoption of the Plan of Liquidation requires the affirmative vote of two-thirds of all outstanding stock. Adoption of the alternative proposal requires the affirmative vote of a majority of the outstanding stock.

SINCE THE OUTCOME IS IN NO WAY CERTAIN, YOUR VOTE IS ABSOLUTELY ESSENTIAL. PLEASE ACT PROMPTLY.

Thank you,

Marvin Horwitz
March 16, 1979   Chairman of the Board

"If your shares are held in the name of your broker, dealer, bank or other nominee, contact the party responsible for your account and direct him to immediately have a proxy executed by them on your behalf. If you have any questions or any difficulty in voting your shares, please call us collect at (phone number) or (proxy solicitor and phone number) which is assisting your company."

In addition, there is a growing trend to include a transmittal letter to shareholders bound to, and covering, the joint proxy statement. The language is reviewed by the SEC. Nevertheless, these transmittal letters do appear to be growing more promotional in character. Such a letter should be explored as a possible platform when a merger is unusual or faces possible opposition or dispute.

The following excerpts from a two-page covering letter attached by The Penn Central Corporation to its nearly 250-page joint proxy statement illustrates what is currently being done:

"Dear Fellow Shareholders:

"A Special Meeting of the Shareholders has been called for December 18, 1979 to vote on the acquisition by PCC of Marathon Manufacturing Company. Marathon will become a subsidiary of PCC.

"Marathon is the world's largest manufacturer of mobile self-elevating (jackup) drilling rigs, which are used for offshore drilling of oil and gas wells. (For your information we have enclosed a photograph of a typical Marathon jackup rig.) Marathon also manufactures heavy equipment for moving and loading earth and other materials in the coal mining, timber, port and railroad industries. In addition, Marathon produces several other diversified products, including fabricated steel products, white mineral oil and aircraft starting batteries.

"The Joint Proxy Statement is unavoidably lengthy and detailed in order to give certain financial and business information concerning PCC and Marathon as required by securities laws and accounting regulations. However, for your convenience, we have included a summary at the beginning of the Statement. It may be helpful to you to read the summary before reading the more expanded descriptions in the remainder of the Statement.

"I want to assure you that the acquisition of Marathon has been thoroughly investigated and analyzed. This has been done not only by PCC management but, in addition, we have utilized outside firms of experts to assist us in specific areas of our review, including analyses of Marathon's financial affairs, industries and facilities.

"We have also engaged the investment banking firms of Morgan Stanley & Co. Incorporated and Lehman Brothers Kuhn Loeb Incorporated to evaluate the acquisition of Marathon. As can be seen in Annexes II and III to the Joint Proxy Statement, both firms determined that the terms of the proposed transaction are fair to the shareholders of PCC from a financial point of view.

"In structuring the terms of the acquisition of Marathon, we have considered a number of alternatives including various types of securities. After taking into account the relevant factors, we believe the proposed structure of the acquisition is the most desirable for PCC shareholders. It combines the use of cash from certain bank loans with the issuance of a new series of convertible preference stock which is subject to the prior rights of the now outstanding Series A and B Preference Stock. The new series of special preference stock was made possible by a charter amendment that was overwhelmingly approved by the PCC shareholders at the June 1979 annual meeting. The Marathon acquisition presents PCC with a favorable opportunity to use that new preference stock for the benefit of all its shareholders.

"We are convinced that Marathon is a particularly attractive investment for PCC.

"Marathon is a major corporation and its acquisition will result in a significant expansion of PCC's revenues, earnings and asset base. Marathon also is strong financially and currently has a relatively low amount of outstanding debt.

"Marathon's energy-related businesses will complement PCC's existing activities in the increasingly important energy field. Marathon is the market leader in its principal business, the manufacturing of jackup rigs, for which we believe there will continue to be strong demand. Thus, PCC will have an additional avenue for participating in the anticipated expansion of the energy industry.

"PCC management anticipates that no federal income taxes will be paid on the post-acquisition earnings of Marathon for the next several years due to the inclusion of such earnings in PCC's consolidated federal income tax returns where they are expected to be offset by an accelerated use of PCC's unexpired 'loss carryforward' from loss operations in prior years. Consequently, in our view, the Marathon acquisition should be considered on a pre-federal income tax basis, as well as on an after imputed tax basis, because PCC is not currently paying federal income taxes. For those who wish to see the particular figures, the table on page 13 in the Joint Proxy Statement shows projected 1979 earnings per common share with and without the acquisition of Marathon, both before and after deduction of imputed, but non-payable, federal income taxes.

"In summary, Marathon represents a major step in our continuing program to re-establish PCC as one of America's preeminent corporations and is an attractive investment opportunity that will provide important benefits to PCC and its shareholders. Although the future cannot be predicted with certainty, we believe that Marathon's principal businesses have favorable growth prospects which, when combined with Marathon's proven management team, will provide PCC with an attractive stream of earnings and cash flow that will produce a desirable return on PCC's investment in Marathon.

"PCC's Board of Directors (by a 12-to-1 vote) and PCC management strongly recommend approval of this acquisition as being in the long-term best interests of PCC and its shareholders. We therefore urge you to vote FOR the acquisition on the enclosed proxy card and to sign and return it promptly.

Sincerely yours,

"YOUR VOTE IS IMPORTANT. PLEASE SIGN, DATE, AND RETURN PROMPTLY THE ENCLOSED PROXY CARD EVEN IF YOU PLAN TO BE PRESENT AT THE SPECIAL MEETING."

Since this kind of material is frequently replayed in press coverage of the merger and through broker word of mouth, it increases management's chances of telling its side of the story.

Proxy Fights and Tender Offers

Both proxy fights and tender offers have their own communications requirements. The rules in these areas are under continuing revision by the SEC and I have excluded a discussion of them from this chapter. At the present time the communications requirements applying to proxy fights and tender offers provide numerous traps for the unwary communicator. For example, a recent change in the SEC's rules requires a company announcing its intention to make a tender offer to actually move ahead with that offer within five days or withdraw it. This is in direct conflict with most state takeover rules which require pre-notification to state securities departments of ten or more days. The matter is currently in the courts.

These areas of merger and acquisition work require highly specialized public relations skills. Just as there are a handful of lawyers who specialize in takeovers, there are, similarly, a handful of public relations specialists in the field.

TIMING THE FIRST ANNOUNCEMENT

There is no "right" time to make the first announcement of merger discussions or completion of a merger. The announcement's timing depends on several factors, including:

— the degree of certainty that a final agreement is likely to be reached (since repeated announcements of merger discussions which are subsequently terminated suggest either stock puffery or inept or indecisive negotiating ability on the part of those involved);

— the number of people who are aware of discussions;

— the existence of unusual market activity which could suggest that rumors about the merger talks have leaked out;

— the size or importance to the parties of the merger, should it occur.

Premature Release

Because rules in this area are vague, a good deal of judgment is required. However, it is clear that an unnecessary, premature or misleading disclosure can create as many problems as improper disclosure. Before considering the right things to do, I'd like to spend a few minutes on an example of poor disclosure.

The following press release (company name disguised) created serious business problems for the issuing company. Lawyers for the company drafted the release because there appeared to be unusual market activity in the stock. The company was, in fact, in continuing discussions for the sale of one of its plants. The company had previously indicated its intention to find a buyer. The release read as follows:

"(Dateline)—John Smith, Chairman and Chief Executive Officer of Acme Company, announced today that the Company is continuing its previously announced efforts to explore all possibilities concerning its business and the deployment of its assets. As part of this evaluation, the Company is in the process of holding initial exploratory discussions with third parties concerning the possible merger of Acme and the possible sale of certain of Acme's assets. Mr. Smith emphasized that no agreements or understandings had been reached and that discussions were on a very preliminary basis. Smith indicated that this announcement was being made in response to the current market activity in Acme's common stock. Even if the current discussions are terminated, similar discussions may take place in the future, Smith noted."

In this case, the release incorrectly conveyed the impression that the company was seeking to be acquired *in toto,* and that it would go out of business. Lawyers for the company refused to permit management to make any additional explanation of what the release meant. Stories appeared across the country reporting that the company was going to be sold.

Worst of all, competitors copied the release and the negative press coverage and put packets of this material in the hands of "Acme's" customers. The customers, believing that the company was shortly going to go out of business, immediately began shifting their business to competitors. Employee morale at Acme sank to a new low and company products deteriorated in quality. Acme did not recognize the problems for more than

a month, and was still devoting substantial management time to answering questions raised by the release a year later. The moral is clear: it is better not to speak until it is absolutely necessary; when it is necessary to speak, speak clearly.

Handling Confidential Information

The *NYSE Company Manual* states:

"Judgment must be exercised as to the timing of a public release on those corporate developments where ... disclosure would endanger the company's goals or provide information helpful to a competitor. In these cases, it is helpful to weigh the fairness to both present and potential stockholders who at any given moment may be considering buying or selling the company's stock."

The *Amex Company Guide* adds:

"The ... circumstances where disclosure can be withheld are limited and constitute an infrequent exception to the normal requirement of immediate public disclosure. Thus, in cases of doubt, the presumption must always be in favor of disclosure."

In connection with merger discussions "where the risk of untimely and inadvertent disclosure of corporate plans is most likely to occur," the NYSE does make this specific exception:

"Where it is possible to confine formal or informal discussions to a small group of the top management of the company or companies involved, and their individual confidential advisors where adequate security can be maintained, premature public announcement may properly be avoided."

The NYSE, under this rule, considers an executive of a public relations counseling firm an "individual confidential advisor" if, in a particular situation, a company determines that such consultation is necessary. The executive would participate as an individual only, but it is understood he might consult with one other—but no more than one —specified executive of the counseling firm at the request of the top management of the company.

The NYSE also suggests that each company periodically review its internal procedure for handling confidential information. The Amex recommends that companies remind employees regularly of their policies on confidentiality, and adds:

"If counsel, accountants, or financial or public relations advisors or other outsiders are consulted, steps should be taken to ensure that they maintain similar precautions within their respective organizations to maintain confidentiality.''

According to the SEC, ''the policy of prompt disclosure of material business events is embodied in the … directives of the major exchanges.'' It appears that the SEC intends to leave regulation of the timing of disclosures to the stock exchanges and the NASD.

The SEC has not insisted on immediate disclosure. In a 1970 release it said only that a company ''has an obligation to make full and prompt'' disclosure. The Commission has not said that failure to make prompt disclosure is, in itself, a violation of Rule 10b-5.

Risks of Delay

Until recently, a corporation generally had no duty under Rule 10b-5 to make *immediate* disclosure of material information in the absence of trading. This policy is now subject to serious limitations.

In a 1973 case, *Financial Industries Fund v. McDonnell Douglas Corporation,* a U.S. Court of Appeals decided that ''an undue delay (in disclosure) not in good faith, can be deceptive, misleading, or a device to defraud under Rule 10b-5.'' Similar cases since 1973 seem to indicate that prompt disclosure is mandatory unless valid business reasons exist for nondisclosure, or unless information to be disclosed is not yet verified.

Stock Watch

The exchanges and the NASD maintain ''stock watch'' departments which continuously monitor trading for unusual activity. In such instances, companies may be contacted by the exchanges or the NASD to inquire about the possibility of undisclosed corporate developments that might account for the activity. When such information exists, the exchanges and the NASD normally will require companies to make immediate public disclosure. They may halt trading in the company's stock until the news is disseminated.

Unusual Market Activity

Both major exchanges and the NASD recommend that when unusual market activity takes place in listed companies' securities, they should attempt to determine whether information on impending developments has leaked or whether there are rumors circulating.

The NYSE suggests that companies notify its Corporate Services Department, the Amex its Securities Division and the NASD its Market Surveillance Department, for assistance in determining what course of action to take. Such notification enables the exchanges and the NASD to decide whether the company should issue a clarifying statement. *(Amex Company Guide,* p.110; *NYSE Company Manual,* A-23)

Rumors

''A corporation,'' the *NYSE Company Manual* states, should

''…act promptly to dispel unfounded rumors which result in unusual market activity or price variations… If rumors or unusual market activity indicate that information on impending developments has leaked out, a frank and explicit announcement is clearly required. If rumors are in fact false or inaccurate, they should be promptly denied or clarified.''

The *Amex Company Guide* includes a similar requirement.

Corrections

It is well established that a company violates Rule 10b-5 when it issues a false and misleading press release dealing with material information. However, a once accurate press release may become false and misleading through the passage of time. In several cases, it has been held that a company must correct and revise such inaccurate releases or else risk Rule 10b-5 liability.

Stand-by Release

It is useful to draft and hold in reserve a short stand-by release on the merger discussions in the event unexpected market activity makes comment necessary.

Insider Trading

It is also desirable for counsel to review with the involved parties the SEC's disclosure rules and the current state of laws concerning insider trading.

The antifraud provisions of Rule 10b-5 prohibit a person from purchasing or selling stock when in possession of undisclosed material information. ''Insiders,'' under Rule 10b-5, are those who come into possession of undisclosed material information in the course of their business activities and those (''tippees'') who receive such information from an insider or third party. Thus, employees, consultants, retained counsel, accountants, underwriters, broker-dealers, analysts, investment advisors and those who are informed directly or indirectly by any of these people are all insiders within the purview of Rule 10b-5.

The SEC has stated that it

''considers the elements (necessary to establish liability for insider trading) to be that the information in question be (1) material and nonpublic; (2) that the tippee, whether he receives the information directly or indirectly, know or have reason to know that it was non-public and had been obtained improperly by selective revelation or otherwise; and (3) that the information be a factor in his decision to effect the transaction (in the security of the company involved)."

Liability under Rule 10b-5 could, in fact, result where persons innocently come into possession of and use information which they have reason to know is intended to be confidential and then, on the basis of such information, effect a transaction in the securities involved.

Stock Exchange Guidelines for Insider Trading

The stock exchange rules set forth useful guidelines for corporate insiders on questions of securities trading.

The NYSE states:

"Where a development of major importance is expected to reach the appropriate time for announcement within the next few months, transactions by officers and directors should probably be avoided. Corporate officials should wait until after the release of ... important developments (has) appeared in the press before making a purchase or sale."

The Amex recommends that "as a basic policy ...

insiders should wait for at least 24 hours after the general publication of the release in a national medium. Where publication is not so widespread, a minimum waiting period of 48 hours is recommended. Where publication does not occur, or if it should otherwise appear appropriate, it may be desirable to obtain an opinion of counsel before insiders trade."

The NYSE further recommends that corporate officials acquire their holdings of company stock: (1) according to a periodic investment program; (2) following the release and dissemination of company financial results, such as in an annual or quarterly report, proxy statement or prospectus; or (3) during times of stability in company operations and the market for its securities.

DISTRIBUTION

There are no special rules for the distribution of press releases announcing merger or acquisition developments. They are, almost without exception, considered "material" and as such, should receive the same wide distribution that a company's earnings, dividends, and other major releases receive.

For reference, we have included below the rules governing distribution of material releases by the major stock exchanges.

The NYSE's "Procedure for Immediate Disclosure" requires that "news which ought to be the subject of immediate publicity must be released by the fastest available means." The Exchange adds that this is ordinarily accomplished by "a release to the public press by telephone, telegraph or hand delivery, or some combination thereof." A release to the press solely by mail is not considered satisfactory by the NYSE.

The *NYSE Company Manual* states that material information "should be given to the wire services and the press for IMMEDIATE RELEASE," rather than be held for release at a later time. However, the NYSE states that "the spirit of the IMMEDIATE RELEASE policy is not considered to be violated on weekends where a 'Hold for Sunday or Monday A.M.'s' is used to obtain a broad public release of the news."

The NYSE and Amex prescribe that, at a minimum, news requiring immediate disclosure be released to the two major financial wire services (Dow Jones & Company, Inc. and Reuters Economic Services), Associated Press and United Press International, and to one or more of the general circulation newspapers in New York City which contain financial news. In addition, the Amex requries companies to distribute to Moody's Investors Service, Inc. and Standard & Poor's Corporation (*NYSE Company Manual*, A-24; *Amex Company Guide*, §403).

Both exchanges encourage the additional distribution of such news releases to newspapers and broadcast media in cities where the company is headquartered or has major plants or facilities, and to trade publications. Circulation of announcements requiring immediate disclosure can be further expedited by use of services that distribute press releases over private teletype networks such as PR Newswire.

NYSE-listed companies should send a copy of all press releases subject to immediate disclosure to: Corporate Services Department, New York Stock Exchange, 20 Broad Street, New York, New York 10005.

For Amex-listed companies, ten copies of all financial releases should be sent to: Securities Division, American Stock Exchange, 86 Trinity Place, New York, New York 10006.

Companies quoted on the NASDAQ (National Association of Securities Dealers Automated Quotations) system should forward copies of all press releases and stockholder information to the attention of: Issue Information, NASD, 1735 K Street, N.W., Washington, D.C. 20006.

"Telephone Alert" Procedure

Frequently, NYSE-, Amex- and NASDAQ-listed companies may have disclosures of a material nature to make either shortly before or during trading hours. The

NYSE expects companies in such cases to notify its Corporate Services Department at least five minutes in advance of release, and the Amex expects companies to notify its Securities Division no later than the time of release of the information to news media. The NASD requests that NASDAQ issuers contact its Market Surveillance Department prior to making a material news announcement.

This "Telephone Alert" is designed to place the exchanges in a position to determine whether trading in the affected securities—or quotations, in the case of NASDAQ—should be halted temporarily to allow for publication, dissemination and public evaluation of the information released.

As the *Amex Company Guide* states:

"Such a step frequently helps avoid rumors and marketing instability, as well as the unfairness to investors that may arise when material information has reached part but not yet all of the investing community. Thus, in appropriate circumstances, the Exchange can often provide a valuable service to investors and listed companies by arranging for such a halt."

POST-MERGER COMMUNICATIONS

Communications problems following completion of the merger or acquisition are beyond the scope of this chapter. However, a brief summary of some considerations will illustrate that mergers involve a great deal more than just getting the participants to the altar. The marriage must be made to work over the long term. Communications problems are at the heart of most rocky mergers. A little forward planning can avoid at least the more fundamental problems during the months and years following a merger.

Here, as elsewhere in the merger process, the character and past activities of the parties will play a major role in shaping the problems and solutions which communications can effectively deal with.

Corporate communications programs come in all shapes and sizes and it is rare that the communications activities of two companies are completely compatible at the start. Therefore, it is generally safe to assume that a transitional period of several months will be necessary to identify and solve problems. During this period, however, every effort should be made to sustain essential communications activities such as annual and quarterly reports.

Getting Down to Work

Initially, the subject of communications deserves attention at the highest level. Early post-merger meetings between the companies should decide in broad terms when and how the communications functions at each company should relate to each other. Most important, the question of who is in charge of the communications function should be resolved quickly and communicated widely.

Integrating the Staffs

It is common that mergers cause considerable redundancy in communications staffs. Among other things, one or the other company may have a substantially larger communications function engaged in a range of activities which the other company does not undertake. Cuts in staff are almost inevitable.

Experience suggests that cutting early is probably preferable to delaying basic communications decisions. There will be loss and slippage, sometimes serious, in the department's knowledge and skill. But the merged company is likely to chart a new communications tack in a matter of months. Public relations results are almost always better at a merged company when "tradition" is laid to rest early in favor of a department climate receptive to new approaches and ideas.

Activities for the Acquired Company's Communications Department

There are several transitional projects that the communications department of the acquired company can undertake during the early months of the merger. Ideally, these should be joint projects in which the acquiror's staff learns more about the business of the new acquisition. However, in practice, the acquired company staff is normally permitted to display its abilities on projects like the following:

— completion of all mandatory filing requirements;
— development of a special section for the annual report (necessarily a joint effort in terms of concept and planning);
— development of a presentation for the Board to explain the business of the acquired company;
— a pre-packaged presentation with slides or other visuals and a script which can be used in all plant locations to explain the acquiree's business to the acquiror's management and employees; note that acquiror may wish to develop a similar project for acquiree audiences;
— analyst presentation (normally developed as a ten - to twelve-minute segment of the acquiror's presentation);
— special report to shareholders with visuals for use at next annual meeting;
— development of a special mailing to shareholders about the new acquisition;

— factbook or factbook supplement about new acquisition compatible with acquiror's factbook. This is desirable in any event since it becomes a substitute document for back annual reports of acquired company which will be in short supply in a period of months.

Performance on projects like the above will allow the individual with senior communications responsibility to make judgments of staff member competence.

The Communications Audit

At some point relatively early in the new relationship, it is desirable and almost mandatory to conduct a thorough audit of the existing communications activities of both the acquiror and the acquiree. While this can be done by either of the two parties to the merger, it is more commonly done by qualified outsiders such as an experienced public relations firm. The outside perspective contributes objectivity and can make impartial judgments of the relative effectiveness of existing activities. It is not uncommon to find that major portions of the communications efforts of both parties to a merger are ineffective, wasted, or irrelevant to the needs of the newly merged entity.

The audit should include discussions with senior managements as well since development of a new program must begin with the establishment of clear communications objectives that are consistent with corporate objectives.

The final audit report should be made to top management (particularly where there are major disagreements as to future direction uncovered during the interview process) and should form a communications plan for the company in the next 12 to 18 months or longer.

Delivery of this plan should precede final staff and department structure decisions. At this point the company is ready to proceed with some confidence that its communications activities have value and serve the broader corporate purpose.

COST/BENEFIT ANALYSIS

Public relations is peculiarly resistant to cost/benefit analysis. Few if any experts in the field attempt to quantify the results of their work. Efforts at counting published lines of copy, or linking articles with movements in the price of company stock have generally failed.

To a large extent, judgment of the effectiveness of a communications effort must be subjective. Have there been any results? If not, are the reasons for no action valid and are efforts continuing to achieve a breakthrough? Are the results of value or has the public relations person simply followed the line of least resistance, substituting quantity for substance?

Perhaps most important, has management supported the effort or simply created additional obstacles to success?

The Public Relations Society of America gathers information, on a continuing basis, on what corporations of various size pay for public relations services. This information can be misleading since expenditures vary widely in all categories. But it is a rare company with sales of $100 million or more that does not spend at least $100,000 annually on all forms of public relations activities. Agency fees vary from flat retainer arrangements of as little as $500 per month to monthly minimums of $4,000 or more. Generally, when working with an agency it is preferable to contract for services on an hourly basis rather than for a flat fee. This insures that there will be some relationship between fees and services performed. It is also generally preferable to have at least one in-house person assigned full or part-time public relations responsibility, whether or not an agency is retained, to provide continuity, develop basic information and provide liaison with management.

SUMMARY

In today's business environment, mergers and acquisitions are a fact of life. In this chapter I have attempted to suggest that they should not be taken for granted. On the other hand, most public relations people do not, and probably should not, think of a merger project as a special activity or a separate project. Rather, they will approach it as one element of a company's overall ongoing communications objectives. This seems to me a sound approach on the whole.

Much of what I have discussed here is "good public relations" whether or not there is a merger pending. Although many aspects of mergers and acquisitions require the services of highly specialized experts, for example, in finance and negotiations, the public relations aspects of mergers generally are within the skills range of most public relations practicers.

Except where confidentiality is essential or a proxy fight or tender offer is involved, managements should use the public relations people already available to them. The advantages are significant: your people know the company and are known widely throughout the company and the community. Their sense of employee attitudes and their access to "the grapevine" will be indispensable. Outside consultants can provide guidance and help with elements of planning and behind-the-scenes drafting, but, if management has confidence in them, the available public relations staff should execute the visible portions of the project, particularly in company facilities and plant communities.

APPENDIX—SAMPLE MERGER AND ACQUISITION RELEASES

Included in this section are examples of typical press releases issued by companies involved in actual merger or acquisition situations. These releases cover most aspects of a merger or acquisition situation, from the initial incidence of rumors and increased market activity to announcements of completion and handling terminations. These examples are not intended to exhaust all of the possibilities; they represent examples of what other companies have done in such situations.

These releases were, for the most part, collected during January and February of 1980. Names of the issuing companies have been retained in all cases. Some releases have been edited to exclude material not pertaining to mergers or acquisitions.

I have also included several examples of company "rationales" for the suitability of various types of mergers. Those releases are dispersed through the material but identified "with rationale" in the Index.

Index

I. HANDLING RUMORS

1. Response to Market Action—Negative

(Dateline)—Cedar Point, Inc., stated that, while as previously announced it is continuing discussions concerning the possible acquisition of all of Cedar Point, it knows of no reason for the recent market activity in its common stock.

2. Response to Rumors and Market Action—Negative

(Dateline)—Claude Ramsey, chairman and president of Akzona Inc., said today that he knew of no reason for the heavy trading activity in the company's stock this week. He said, "We hear there are rumors that Akzo N.V., owner of about 66 percent of Akzona's stock, is purchasing additional shares. Akzo is neither buying nor selling the stock. Certainly the state of our business currently would not warrant the unusually high volume and run-up in price. Based on the mildness of the weather so far, we cannot anticipate the outstanding earnings International Salt Company has enjoyed in recent years. Unless there is a sudden and prolonged change in the weather, we expect first quarter earnings to be substantially lower than in the first quarter of last year."

3. Response to Inquiries About Market Action

(Dateline)—In response to an inquiry from the American Stock Exchange, Huck Manufacturing Co. (ASE) advised that it is engaged in very preliminary discussions for possible negotiations for its sale.

From time to time, in the past, the company has received inquiries from various companies and has entered into such discussions.

The company has emphasized that no offer is pending, nor is there any assurance that the current limited discussions will lead to a definitive agreement.

The company further advised that while the present discussions have not reached a stage which, in the company's opinion, would normally necessitate public disclosure, such announcement is being made because of the company's concern over the recent activity in its stock.

II. ANNOUNCEMENTS OF INTENT

4. Announcement of Acquired Interest— By Target

(Dateline)—Interpace Corporation (NYSE) disclosed today that it has been advised that Wheelabrator-Frye, Inc., has acquired approximately 242,000 shares of Interpace's common stock. Interpace said that this amount represents more than 5 percent of its total common stock outstanding and that Wheelabrator-Frye intends shortly to file a Form 13-d with the Securities and Exchange Commission as required.

5. Announcement of Intent—Denial

(Dateline)—Chemed Corporation announced today that it had acquired in the open market approximately 7 percent of the outstanding common stock of Quaker Chemical Corporation, a Conshokocken, Pennsylvania-based specialty chemical company whose principal products include rolling lubricants, corrosion preventives, metal finishing compounds, machinery, grinding and forming compounds, textile production products, paper production products and hydraulic fluids.

Edward L. Hutton, president and chief executive officer of Chemed, stated that Chemed has been acquiring Quaker common stock as an investment. Mr. Hutton noted that Chemed views Quaker's prospects for continued growth in sales and earnings as quite favorable.

Chemed presently intends to continue to acquire Quaker common shares either in open market purchases or through privately negotiated transactions until Chemed's holdings approach 10 percent of all outstanding Quaker shares. To enable Chemed to account for its investment in Quaker on an equity basis, Chemed may eventually determine to continue its ac-

quisition of Quaker common stock until Chemed holdings aggregate 20 percent -25 percent of all such outstanding shares. Chemed does not presently intend to make a tender opposed by the board of directors of Quaker.

Chemed Corporation, headquartered in Cincinnati, is a specialty chemical company with leading positions in water and waste treatment chemicals, industrial and institutional cleaning compounds and germicidal and maintenance products. Chemed is an 87 percent-owned subsidiary of W.R. Grace & Co.

6. Letter of Intent Submitted

(Dateline)—Minnesota Fabrics Inc. announced today that it has submitted a letter of intent proposing to purchase a Canadian private fabric retailer. By the terms of the proposal, the purchase price will be paid in cash based upon the net worth of the business together with additional payments based upon future earnings. The letter of intent proposes that a definitive purchase agreement will be entered into by the parties. During the calendar year 1979, retail sales of the Canadian retailer were approximately $15 million.

7. Confirmation of Negotiations

(Dateline)—Scott Paper Co. today confirmed that it and Crown Zellerbach Canada Ltd. are jointly negotiating the sale of Elk River Timber Co. Ltd., a Vancouver Island logging operation owning some 100,000 acres of timberland and other property near Campbell River, British Columbia.

Scott holds a two-thirds interest in Elk and Crown Zellerbach Canada holds a one-third interest.

The transaction is expected to have a favorable effect on Scott's 1980 earnings.

8. Confirmation of Negotiations— With Rationale

(Dateline)—Phelps Dodge Corporation announced today that it is discussing with several potential buyers the sale of Phelps Dodge's 40 percent equity interest in Consolidated Aluminum Corporation ("Conalco"), a large domestic producer of aluminum metal and aluminum products. Phelps Dodge has received written advice from two potential buyers, each expressing interest in purchasing Phelps Dodge's Conalco shares for $125 million. Discussions intended to lead to a purchase agreement on these terms will continue with these and possibly other companies.

The transaction as proposed is subject to the obtaining of consents and approvals from various parties and to the right of first refusal of Swiss Aluminum Ltd. ("Alusuisse"), which holds the remaining 60 percent equity interest in Conalco, under a shareholders' agreement between Alusuisse and Phelps Dodge. Under that agreement, Phelps Dodge has now offered Alusuisse its Conalco shares on the same terms as discussed with the potential buyers; Alusuisse has 30 days to decide whether to accept.

George B. Munroe, Phelps Dodge Chairman, commenting on the discussions, stated: "We have entered into talks looking toward the sale of our interest in Conalco with some regret. The aluminum industry should do well over the next several years, and we expect Conalco will share in those good times. However, to realize its full potential, Conalco will probably have to undertake substantial investments, and Alusuisse has indicated it wants to begin to move ahead with an investment program. While we might participate in the needed investments if we remain a Conalco shareholder, we would prefer to keep our capital resources available for our own operations. Our discussions are therefore aimed at finding a new partner for Alusuisse—one that is fully in step with its investment approach."

Conalco owns and operates two aluminum smelters, in Tennessee and Louisiana, and 11 fabricating plants, all in the United States, and also owns 66 percent of Ormet Corporation, the assets of which include an alumina plant in Louisiana and an aluminum smelter in Ohio. In 1979, Conalco earned $4 million, after taxes, on sales of about $825 million. Phelps Dodge's investment in Conalco at Dec. 31, 1979, on the equity basis was $76.5 million.

9. Announcement of "Discussions" Naming Parties

(Dateline)—Telecom Corporation and Spector Industries, Inc. announced that they have held discussions recently concerning a possible merger involving the two companies. The boards of directors of the two companies will meet later today concerning the transaction, and it is anticipated that a joint announcement will be issued later today as to whether or not an agreement in principle concerning the merger has been reached.

10. Announcement of Cash Offer and Discussions Naming Amount and Parties

(Dateline)—Harry K. Wells, chairman of the board of McCormick & Company, Inc., announced that yesterday he received a letter from Dr. Y. Dunant, chairman of Sandoz Ltd., proposing discussions, requesting a meeting and making an offer for a cash merger in which holders of McCormick common stock, both voting and non-voting, would receive $37 per share. Mr. Wells said that he had advised Dr. Dunant that Dr. Dunant could meet with McCormick on March 12, 1980, and that, thereafter, the McCormick board would consider the matter at a regularly scheduled meeting in March. Mr. Wells emphasized that

"McCormick has many times expressed its historical and present policy of independence and management views the prospects for McCormick's business and for its shareholders under that continuing policy to be excellent. There should be no inference or expectation that there will be any transaction."

11. Decision to Seek Buyer for Certain Operations

(Dateline)—Ward Foods, Inc., (NYSE), a diversified food company, today said that a tentative decision has been reached to consider the sale and/or disposition of its three baked goods locations which are incurring substantial cash losses.

Two locations under consideration are in Detroit, Mich., and the other is in White River Junction, Vermont.

The company will continue its more viable bakery operations in Chicago, Ill., and East Orange, N.J., which have potential for sustained growth.

A pre-tax provision in the range of $10-12 million for estimated losses, including expenses during the phase-out period associated with these dispositions, will be charged against 1979 earnings. The actual cash costs will be materially less.

Through the third quarter (42 weeks ended Oct. 20, 1979), the company reported net income of $5,265,000 or $1.31 per share on sales volume of $244,398,000. Except for this provision, full-year 1979 results would have shown a substantial net profit for the third consecutive year. The company expects its final results for 1979, including this provision, to be available within the next few weeks.

III. PRELIMINARY STEPS TO AGREEMENT

12. First Announcement Prior to Terms

(Dateline)—Leesona Corporation/NYSE/ announced that its management was engaged in serious negotiations with another company regarding a possible acquisition of Leesona. The price being discussed is $40.00 per share in cash. Certain conditions remain to be resolved before an agreement can be reached; however, a definitive announcement is expected to be made tomorrow morning.

13. First Announcement by Target—"Unsolicited" Offer

(Dateline)—Guardsman Chemicals, Inc., has received from Grow Group, Inc., an unsolicited merger proposal dated January 29, 1980, pursuant to which Guardsman would be merged into Grow or a subsidiary of Grow.

Under the proposal, up to 200,000 shares of Guardsman (approximately 20 percent of

Guardsman's present outstanding shares) would be exchanged for $15 cash. All remaining Guardsman shares other than the approximately 20 percent of the outstanding shares presently owned by Grow which would be canceled, would be exchanged, on a one-for-one basis, for a new issue of 10 percent cumulative convertible preferred voting stock of Grow.

Keith C. Vander Hyde, president and chief executive officer of Guardsman, stated that the proposal by Grow will be studied by the Board of Directors of Guardsman at a special meeting to be called promptly.

14. "Preliminary Memorandum of Understanding" with Rationale

(Dateline)—Early California Industries Inc. (NASDAQ) announced that its Early California Foods Division had entered into a preliminary memorandum of understanding for the purchase of the Spanish green olive and pepper businesses of Riviana Foods, a subsidiary of Colgate-Palmolive Co.

According to Billy J. McFarland, president of Early California Foods, the company will be purchasing all of Riviana's Spanish green olive and pepper inventories located in the United States and will continue to sell Riviana's Towie and So-Li-cious brands to retail and institutional customers through the existing network of brokers.

Early California will also acquire Riviana's wholly-owned subsidiary, Riviana Espana, located in Seville, Spain. Riviana Espana is a processor and packager of Spanish green olives for export principally to the United States and also to Europe, Australia and other international markets.

Riviana's $10 million domestic sales of Spanish green olives and peppers will substantially augment Early California Foods' ripe and green olive sales of about $32 million. Early California Foods is the second largest U.S. processor of California ripe olives. With regard to this substantial expansion of the company's green olive business, McFarland stated: "We believe that the addition of this Spanish source of supply will significantly strengthen Early California Foods' ability to service the $275 million U.S. olive market.

"Since our primary thrust has been in the $125 million ripe olive market, the potential for our participation in the $150 million market for green olives is greatly enhanced by this acquisition. We welcome the opportunity to become an international processor of olives and to work closely with the important Spanish olive industry."

Consummation of the acquisition is contingent upon the execution of definitive contracts, approval by the respective boards of directors and other conditions contained in the preliminary memorandum of understanding.

Early California Industries, in addition to its olive business, is also one of the largest rice millers in the United States, and its Sierra Wine Corporation is the nation's largest bulk winery. Its other food products include salad dressings and specialty food items. The Company is also engaged in newspaper publishing and commercial printing, fire retardant manufacturing and agribusiness consulting.

15. Preliminary Agreement— Joint Announcement

(Dateline)—Frederick A. Godley, chairman, and C. Lawson Reed, president of Xomox Corporation, and Charles F. Knight, chairman and chief executive officer of Emerson Electric Co., jointly announced the execution today of an agreement under which Xomox will be merged with Emerson.

Under the terms of the agreement, each Xomox shareholder will receive .838 shares of Emerson stock for each share of Xomox held, or if greater, that portion of a share of Emerson calculated by dividing $28.50 by the average closing price of Emerson stock during the 10 days preceding the Xomox shareholder meeting called to vote on the transaction. A Xomox shareholder may also elect to receive $28.50 in cash instead of Emerson stock. Since it is intended that the transaction be tax-free to Xomox shareholders electing to receive Emerson shares, the foregoing is subject to the requirements of the Internal Revenue Code which limit the total amount of cash which can be used as consideration in such a transaction.

The transaction, for those accepting Emerson stock, will be tax-free and is subject to completion of the usual requirements, including the execution of a definitive agreement, approval of both Boards of Directors, approval of Xomox shareholders and the obtaining of a favorable tax ruling. Officers and shareholders representing in excess of 43 percent of Xomox shares have executed agreements committing themselves to vote their shares in favor of the merger.

The Boards of Directors will meet as soon as practical to act on the proposed transaction.

16. Agreement in Principle—Joint Announcement

(Dateline)—Richard D. Wood, chairman of the board of Eli Lilly and Company and Bagley Wright, chairman of the board, and W. Hunter Simpson, president and chief executive officer of Physio-Control Corporation, Seattle, jointly announced today that the two corporations have approved an agreement in principle for the acquisition of Physio-Control by Lilly.

Physio-Control designs, manufactures and sells specialized electronic instrumentation for use in the cardiovascular and dialysis fields of medicine. It also makes and sells other products used for monitoring human physiology. Lilly manufactures and sells a broad line of human health, agricultural, and cosmetics products.

The transaction would involve the issuance of .7 share of common stock of Lilly for each share of common stock of Physio-Control and would be structured as a tax-free reorganization for federal income tax purposes. Approximately 2.6 million shares of Lilly common stock would be issued in connection with the acquisition. At Dec. 31, 1979, Lilly had 72,907,214 shares outstanding.

The transaction is subject to the negotiation and execution of a definitive agreement and approval by the boards of directors of both companies and by the shareholders of Physio-Control. The issuance of the Lilly shares is subject to the registration requirements of the Securities and Exchange Commission.

17. Agreement in Principle—Joint Announcement

(Dateline)—Victor Posner, chairman of the board, president and chief executive officer of NVF Company, Miami Beach, Fla. (NYSE), and Harold L. Schwartz, Jr., chairman of APL Corporation, Great Neck, N.Y. (NYSE), announced today that the managements of the two companies had reached an agreement in principle for the merger of APL into NVF. Under the proposal, shareholders of APL would receive, for each share of APL Common Stock, $6.00 in cash and $10.75 face amount of a new 25-year 10 percent NVF subordinated debenture (substantially similar in terms to NVF's outstanding 10 percent Subordinated Debenture due 2003). The proposal is subject to the execution of a definitive contract, all requisite directors', shareholders' and other consents and approvals and the effectiveness of a registration statement to be filed with the Securities and Exchange Commission covering the debentures to be issued by NVF in the transaction.

APL has approximately 3,179,015 shares of common stock outstanding, of which NVF owns approximately 23.9 percent.

18. Agreement in Principle—Joint Announcement with Rationale

(Dateline)—The Signal Companies, Inc. (NYSE) and Ampex Corporation today jointly announced that the two companies have entered into an agreement in principle for the merger of Ampex into Signal through an exchange of common stock.

The terms of the agreement in principle call for the exchange of 0.79 Signal common share of stock for each common share of Ampex Corporation. Ampex has approximately 11 million common shares outstanding and an additional 1.7 million shares reserved for issuance upon exercise of employee stock options and conversion of convertible debentures.

The merger is subject to termination by either party if, at any time up to 10 days before it becomes effective, the average of the closing prices of the Signal common stock on the New York Stock Exchange for any consecutive five-day period shall have exceeded $51 per share or been less than $40 per share.

Completion of the merger is also subject to approval by the board of directors and shareholders of each company, a favorable tax ruling and approval by various regulatory agencies. The merger should close in mid-1980.

Agreement was jointly announced by Forrest N. Shumway, Signal chairman and chief executive officer, and Arthur Hausman, Ampex president and chief executive officer.

Shumway stated that Ampex is a premier high-technology company, well respected in its markets. "Ampex meets our investment criteria in that it is non-cyclic and a leading company in a growth industry. It manufactures high-quality products," said Shumway.

"Ampex is a well-managed company with a great future. We contemplate no changes in its operating philosophy or in its existing management," added Shumway.

Ampex Corporation is headquartered in Redwood City, Calif. It principally designs, manufactures and markets worldwide professional audio and video systems, computer memories and data handling products, magnetic tapes and accessories. At the end of its fiscal year ended April 28, 1979, it reported sales of $380 million. It employs 12,000.

The Signal Companies, a worldwide multi-industry company, reported sales of more than $4 billion. It employs 53,000. Its units include The Garrett Corporation, Mack Trucks, Inc., UOP, Inc., Signal Landmark Properties, Inc., and Dunham-Bush, Inc. Signal's investments include Golden West Broadcasters and Natomas Company.

19. Agreement in Principle—Two Versions:

(A) Announcement By Both Parties

(Dateline)—An agreement in principle for the sale of Random House, Inc., to the Newhouse Publications for between $65 and $70 million was announced today by Edgar H. Griffiths, chairman and chief executive officer of RCA, and S.I. and Donald Newhouse of Newhouse Publications.

The sale is subject to a definitive agreement and to approval by the board of directors of RCA.

Upon final approval, Random House will become a wholly owned subsidiary of Newhouse Publications and will continue to operate as a separate entity with its present personnel and management, according to the Messrs. Newhouse.

Mr. Griffiths said the sale of Random House "is in line with RCA's announced decision to focus on four basic areas of business—Hertz, NBC, financial and consumer products and services, and electronics and communications. Random House is a well-managed company, a leader in the publishing field, but it does not relate to our conception of the RCA of the future."

The Messrs. Newhouse said "We are delighted to be associated with Random House—a company of great cultural and business achievements. We look forward to a very exciting future together."

RCA acquired Random House in 1966. The publishing company was incorporated in 1925 and is engaged in a broad range of publishing activities. Among its divisions and subsidiaries are such famous imprints as Random House, Alfred A. Knopf, Inc., Pantheon Books, The Modern Library, Vintage and Ballantine.

(B) Announcement By One Party

An agreement in principle for Random House, Inc., one of America's most prominent book publishing companies, to be bought by Newhouse Publications from the RCA Corporation was announced today.

Random House, Inc., is a group of publishing houses that includes the Random House, Alfred A. Knopf, Pantheon, Vintage and Ballantine imprints. The company was founded in 1925 by the late Bennett Cerf and Donald Klopper, now chairman emeritus. Since 1966, Random House has been headed by Robert L. Bernstein, who currently serves as chairman and president. RCA announced its intention to sell the publishing house late last year.

The Newhouse organization is a privately held company that publishes 29 newspapers in metropolitan areas throughout the United States; Parade magazine, a Sunday newspaper supplement; and magazines through its affiliate, the Conde Nast Publications, Inc. It also has interests in broadcasting and cable television.

Commenting on the sale, Mr. Bernstein said, "In a period when authors have been expressing concern about the growing trend toward ownership of publishing houses by large public corporations, Random House has been fortunate to have enjoyed 14 years of undiminished editorial independence under the ownership of RCA. We now look forward to the continuation of this basic strength of our publishing company under strong, private ownership."

Mr. Bernstein continued, "Edgar Griffiths, RCA's chairman and chief executive officer, made it plain to me that he would sell us only to a company which our management felt would allow us to function with complete editorial freedom. He has kept that promise. The Newhouse publications represent the full spectrum of American opinion, and each operation is run by autonomous management with total editorial independence. I'm confident that all of Random House's authors, editors and employees will thrive in the kind of environment the Newhouses will provide."

20. Agreement in Principle—Two Acquisitions

(Dateline)—Kenai Corp. (AMEX) announced today that it had reached two agreements in principle to acquire corporations located in Oklahoma and Texas. The companies are engaged in contract drilling and the manufacturing of oilfield equipment. The aggregate price will be approximately $9,000,000.

The larger proposed acquisition, Pearson Drilling Co., Inc. located in Enid, Okla., owns and operates six drilling rigs with depth capacities ranging from 8,000 to 15,000 feet. Michael R. Green, Kenai's chief operating officer, said this acquisition, if consummated, will increase the number of the company's drilling rigs to 37 and open a new region for Kenai's drilling operations. The present 31 rigs are located in Texas and New Mexico, the Rocky Mountain area and California.

The other agreement is to acquire a manufacturer and supplier of specialty oilfield equipment.

The acquisitions are subject to the execution of definitive purchase contracts to contain several representations, warranties and covenants. No assurance can be given that such contracts will be successfully concluded.

21. Agreement to Purchase

(Dateline)—Hawker Siddeley Group Limited of London, England, announced that Hawker Siddeley has entered into an agreement to acquire all the outstanding shares of FASCO Industries, Inc., a privately owned U.S. corporation incorporated in New York, for a consideration of $100-million in cash. The acquisition is subject to certain conditions, including, among others, expiration of the required waiting period under the Hart-Scott-Rodino Antitrust Improvements Act of the United States and confirmation that there will be no reference under the Fair Trading Act of 1973 in the United Kingdom.

FASCO is principally a manufacturer of fractional horsepower electric motors for use in a wide variety of consumer and commercial products. It also manufactures and markets electric motor-driven products for domestic and commercial premises, and pressure and temperature controls.

FASCO, headquartered in Boca Raton, Fla., has three production facilities in Missouri and two in North Carolina, employing in total around 3,150 people.

The acquisition of FASCO will broaden Hawker Siddeley's product lines in the United States and, it is believed, will also enhance FASCO's opportunities to participate in export markets.

The Hawker Siddeley Group is comprised of more than 140 operating companies supplying a wide range of electrical and mechanical engineering products manufactured on six continents.

Its annual sales to international markets are in excess of $2-billion, and it employs about 55,000 people.

Hawker Siddeley has been advised by S.G. Warburg and Co., Ltd. and Warburg, Paribas, Becker Inc. The First Boston Corporation conducted the sale of FASCO on behalf of FASCO shareholders.

22. Agreement to Purchase—With Rationale

(Dateline)—Saxon Industries, Inc. (NYSE) today announced that it has signed an agreement to purchase for approximately $5 million Westvaco Corporation's paper cold-cup manufacturing plant located at Williamsburg, Pa.

Saxon is a leading manufacturer, converter and distributor within the paper and paper products industry.

Stanley Lurie, president and chief executive officer of Saxon Industries, stated: "Saxon Industries is actively engaged in strengthening its existing business base. The Williamsburg paper cup plant will add the important category of cold drink cups to our manufactured paper disposables product line. We also plan to increase the plant's production capabilities to include the manufacturing of paper plates, bowls and trays."

Mr. Lurie also pointed out that "this facility is ideally situated to complement Saxon's other plants for food service disposable products which are located in Santa Clara, Calif.; Fort Wayne, Ind.; and St. Albans, Vt. We now will have a network of plants strategically located to meet our customers' demands on a nationwide basis much more efficiently and well positioned to increase our potential for further market penetration," he said.

Saxon Industries stated that the financing for the purchase of the Williamsburg plant will be accomplished through industrial revenue bonds.

23. Modification of Previously Announced Preliminary Agreement—Joint Announcement

(Dateline)—Xomox Corporation and Emerson Electric Co. jointly announced today a modification in the terms of their previously reported agreement for the merger of Xomox and Emerson and that discussions toward a definitive agreement are continuing.

Under the modified terms, each Xomox shareholder will receive .838 shares of Emerson common stock in exchange for each Xomox share held; provided, that the average closing price of Emerson stock, as determined during a pricing period consisting of the 10 trading days preceding the Xomox shareholders' meeting called to vote on the transaction, remains between $34.00 and $36.00 per share. If the average price rises to above $36.00, but to not more that $40.00 per share, the ratio will be determined by dividing $30.16 by the average price of Emerson stock determined during the pricing period. If the average price of Emerson stock falls below $34.00 per share, but to not less than $30.00 per share, the ratio will be determined by dividing $28.50 by the average price of Emerson stock as determined during the pricing period. If, however, during the pricing period, the average price exceeded $40.00 per share or was less than $30.00 per share, the pricing terms will be subject to renegotiation by the parties. The option under which a Xomox shareholder previously could have elected to receive $28.50 in cash has been eliminated, and no cash will be paid for Xomox stock other than in lieu of fractional shares and in connection with possible dissenters' rights. The transaction will be structured to be tax-free.

Approvals by the respective boards of directors are subject to satisfactory resolution of the normal business review and to final negotiation of the definitive agreement. In addition, the transaction is subject to the usual requirements, including a favorable vote of the Xomox shareholders as well as satisfactory evidence as to the tax-free nature of the transaction.

24. Board Approval of Agreement in Principle—Joint Announcement

(Dateline)—Spector Industries, Inc., and Telecom Corporation jointly announced that their respective boards of directors have today agreed in principle to a merger of Spector with Red Ball Motor Freight, Inc., a wholly owned subsidiary of Telecom. Under the proposed terms of the transaction, the shareholders of Spector would receive, on a tax-free basis, one share of Telecom common stock for each share of Spector common stock outstanding.

The proposed transaction is subject to negotiation of

a definitive merger agreement, approval by the shareholders of Telecom and Spector, approval of the Interstate Commerce Commission and other appropriate regulatory bodies, and other conditions.

Telecom is a Houston-based holding company. In addition to Red Ball Motor Freight, Inc., which represents the bulk of Telecom's revenues, Telecom is engaged through other subsidiaries in manufacturing, wholesale distribution of heating and air conditioning equipment and financial services. Spector Industries, based in Chicago, is also predominantly a motor common carrier.

25. Filing of Preliminary Proxy Statement and Registration Statement—Joint Announcement

(Dateline)—Eli Lilly and Company and Physio-Control Corporation jointly announced that they have filed with the Securities and Exchange Commission a preliminary proxy statement and registration statement relating to the previously announced proposed acquisition by Lilly of Physio-Control. In addition, the required notification and report forms were filed on Feb. 15 with the Federal Trade Commission and the Department of Justice.

The transactions [are] subject to the execution of a definitive agreement and approval by the board of directors of both companies and by the stockholders of Physio-Control. A special meeting of Physio-Control stockholders to consider the acquisition is tentatively planned for the latter part of April.

26. Definitive Agreement—Joint Announcement

(Dateline)—Millipore Corporation of Bedford, Massachusetts and Waters Associates, Inc. of Milford, Massachusetts, jointly announced today the execution of a definitive agreement providing for the combination of the two companies. The agreement, which has been approved by the directors of both companies, provides for the shareholders of Waters to receive one share of Millipore common stock for each share of Waters common stock held by them in a tax-free exchange.

The agreement will be submitted to the shareholders of both companies for approval at meetings to be held the first week in May and, in this connection, an appropriate filing with the SEC is anticipated within the next two to three weeks. Certain officers, directors and other shareholders of Waters owning at least 34 percent of the outstanding stock of Waters have agreed with Millipore to support the proposed combination and to vote their shares accordingly.

Millipore is a leader in microstate technology, the analysis and processing of fluids for the removal, separation and identification of chemical, biological and inert substances. Waters is a leader in high-performance liquid chromatography instrumentation for chemical analysis and purification.

27. Definitive Agreement—Subject to Conditions

(Dateline)—H.J.Heinz Company announced today that it had executed a definitive agreement with Gagliardi Brothers, Inc., a frozen meat company, that provides for the acquisition of Gagliardi by Heinz. The consummation of this transaction is subject to certain conditions set forth in the definitive agreement.

Located in West Chester, PA., Gagliardi markets a range of portion-controlled beef, veal and pork products under the Table Treats brand name for the retail and the foodservice trades. Among the best known is "steak-umm R," a flaked and formed sliced beef steak that can be cooked in a minute.

In announcing the signing, Anthony J.F. O'Reilly, Heinz president and chief executive officer, said that Gagliardi will operate as a subsidiary of Ore-Ida Foods, Inc. upon consummation of the transaction later this year. He did not disclose the purchase price.

"We are particularly pleased," Mr. O'Reilly said, "that Gagliardi products are high-quality pure meat and contain neither salt nor preservatives, because such products are harmonious with Heinz quality standards."

Ore-Ida Foods, Inc. is located in Boise, Idaho and was acquired by Heinz in 1975.

Gagliardi's work force numbers 365.

28. Definitive Agreement and Outline of Merger Process

(Dateline)—John Brown and Company Limited, London, and Leesona Corporation (NYSE), Warwick, R.I., jointly announced today that they have entered into a definitive agreement providing for the acquisition of Leesona by John Brown at a price of $40 per share in cash pursuant to a cash tender offer and merger. The total consideration is expected to approximate $80 million.

Under the terms of the agreement, which was approved by the respective boards of directors of Leesona and John Brown, a wholly owned subsidiary of John Brown will make a cash tender offer for any and all outstanding shares of Leesona at $40 per share. The offer will commence as soon as practicable but not later than Jan. 31, 1980. The purchase of shares under the tender offer is subject to various conditions including, among others, the tender of a majority of Leesona's shares outstanding (including for this purpose 228,571 shares covered by a warrant) and the approval of John Brown's shareholders.

It is anticipated that John Brown's shareholders will

meet no later than Feb. 22, 1980, to approve the offer. Any Leesona shares not acquired by the John Brown subsidiary in the tender offer will be acquired at $40 per share in a subsequent merger transaction. The proposed merger is subject to various conditions including, among others, the approval of Leesona's stockholders, if required by applicable law.

John Brown stated that the tender offer will be made only pursuant to definitive offering documents to be filed with the Securities and Exchange Commission. Henry Schroder Corporation will act as dealer manager in connection with the offer.

Leesona stated that its board of directors has unanimously approved the making of the tender offer and has recommended acceptance of the offer by Leesona's stockholders.

"The business of the two companies would complement each other effectively," Robert G. Page, president of Leesona, said. "Each would benefit by the combination." The arrangement contemplates that Leesona will continue its present business under its present management, with Mr. Page continuing as president and chief executive officer. He stated the combination should not result in loss of employment at any Leesona plant.

The business of John Brown is comprised of three principal divisions (described).

Leesona is a leading manufacturer of machines for the plastics and textile industries, with manufacturing facilities in the United States, England, and Italy (described).

Leesona recently estimated earnings of $7.8 million for 1979 on sales of $167 million.

29. Seller Announces Agreement to Sell Facility

(Dateline)—Industrial America Corporation here today announced that it has reached an agreement in principle for sale of its Vancouver, Wash. foundry to privately held Rich Manufacturing Co. of Portland, Ore., for an undisclosed amount of cash. The sale is scheduled to be effective January 31, 1980.

Industrial America President Robert R. Bowen said that the foundry is the only such operation within the company and that its sale will not only rationalize the company's activities in the forest products industry, but will expedite expansion in areas where it is more active. Rich Manufacturing operates exclusively in the ferrous foundry industry.

Bowen added that annual sales of the Vancouver plant have amounted to less than 7 percent of Industrial America's total sales.

Industrial America is an operating company with manufacturing and industrial distribution interest which employs more than 700 persons at seven U.S. and Canadian manufacturing plants and eight sales offices and warehouses. Its Moore International Division manufactures and installs custom-designed systems for the treating and handling of forest products, and subsidiary East Carolina Supply Co. warehouses and distributes a wide variety of industrial supplies and truck parts from the Carolinas to Florida.

IV. INTERMEDIATE STEPS TO AGREEMENT

30. Progress Report on Completion of Merger

(Dateline)—Board Chairman William H. Seay advised Southwestern Life Corporation shareowners by letter today that work is proceeding toward submitting for their consideration the Tenneco, Inc. proposal to acquire Southwestern.

The text of the letter follows:

You have probably received word of Tenneco, Inc.'s agreement to acquire Southwestern Life Corporation in which each of our shareowners would receive .75 of a share of Tenneco, Inc. common stock and .20 of a share of a new issue of Tenneco, Inc. non-voting preference stock in exchange for each share of Southwestern stock. As a result of this announcement, we have received a number of inquiries from shareowners concerning the transaction and the anticipated time schedule.

Consummation of the acquisition is subject to the approval of owners of a majority of the shares of Southwestern, the existence of certain business and economic conditions customary in this type of transaction and clearance by several state and federal regulatory agencies.

A meeting of Southwestern shareowners to consider the proposal tentatively is planned for the first half of this year. Notice of the meeting will be mailed to shareowners of record on the record date along with a prospectus/proxy statement meeting the requirements of the federal securities laws. This mailing will include detailed information about Southwestern, Tenneco and the proposal with instructions as to voting procedures.

The Tenneco preference stock will be noncallable for five years after issuance. It will have the benefit of a sinking fund beginning 10 years after issuance requiring redemption of 6-1/4 percent of the issue per year with any balance to be redeemed 25 years after issuance. The dividend rate will be determined by the companies' respective investment bankers at the time of mailing the prospectus/proxy statement so that the preference stock's market value will be approximately equal to its liquidation value of $100 per share, provided that the dividend rate will not be less than $8.50 nor more than $11 per share.

If the acquisition is consummated, the shareowners of Southwestern will, as soon as practicable thereafter, receive through the mails instructions concerning the surrender for cancellation of Southwestern share certificates in exchange for certificates of Tenneco common and preference stock. The receipt of Tenneco shares by our shareowners will be taxable for federal income tax purposes.

No assurances can be given at this time as to the precise dates for mailing the prospectus/proxy statement, holding the shareowners meeting or the distribution of Tenneco shares in the event the acquisition is consummated. The agreement between Southwestern and Tenneco, Inc., however, provides that it shall terminate if the transactions contemplated therein have not been consummated by August 31, 1980, or such later date as Tenneco, Inc. and Southwestern may agree upon.

Though we cannot be specific in many details, we hope this information will answer at least some questions you may have had.''

31. Hart-Scott-Rodino Request for Additional Information

(Dateline)—Pay Less Drug Stores Northwest, Inc. (NYSE) (Pay Less Northwest) stated today that it received on Jan. 23 a request, pursuant to the Hart-Scott-Rodino Antitrust Improvements Act of 1976, from the Federal Trade Commission for certain additional information in connection with its proposed acquisition of Pay Less Drug Stores (OTC), a California company (Pay Less California). Pay Less Northwest's subsidiary will thus be unable to purchase and pay for shares of Pay Less California pursuant to its tender offer until 10 calendar days after Pay Less Northwest substantially complies with such request. Pay Less Northwest presently contemplates that it will substantially comply with the request by Feb. 1, 1980.

Pay Less Northwest previously announced that its subsidiary had commenced a tender offer for all outstanding shares of Pay Less California at $22.50 net in cash per share. The offer is conditioned, among other things, upon the tender of at least 917,000 shares prior to the expiration of the offer, scheduled for Thursday, Feb. 14, 1980 at 5:00 P.M. New York City time.

32. Hart-Scott-Rodino Request for Additional Information—Explanation of Process

(Dateline)—Hudson Bay Mining and Smelting Co., Limited announced that the FTC has requested additional information from it relating to the tender offer by Hudson Bay's wholly owned subsidiary for any and all outstanding shares of the capital stock of Rosario Resources Corporation at $65 a share. Hudson Bay filed a premerger notification and report on January 10, 1980 with the Department of Justice and the FTC as required by the Hart-Scott-Rodino Antitrust Improvements Act of 1976. The request by the FTC extends the waiting period, during which no shares can be purchased and paid for pursuant to the tender offer, until 10 days after Hudson Bay delivers the additional information requested. Hudson Bay said that it will comply with the FTC's request as promptly as practicable.

Hudson Bay noted that because Rosario owns 19.5 percent of the outstanding shares of common stock of Heola Mining Company and because Hudson Bay purposes to acquire more than 50 percent of the capital stock of Rosario, it is deemed to be making a secondary acquisition of the Heola shares. The waiting period for this secondary acquisition is 30 days and will expire on Feb. 9, 1980, unless prior to that time, the FTC or the Department of Justice requests additional information or material. Hudson Bay has requested that the FTC terminate the waiting period in respect of the secondary acquisition upon the termination of the waiting period in respect of the primary acquisition of the Rosario shares pursuant to the offer. It has not received a response from the FTC on its request.

33. Acquisition of Partial Interest—Subject to Approvals

(Dateline)—Robert C. Pew, chairman and president of Steelcase, Inc., of Grand Rapids, Mich., today announced the acquisition of a 50 percent interest in a leading West German office products company, Pohlschroder GmbH, KG. Financial details were not disclosed.

Pohlschroder, headquartered in Dortmund, West Germany, and founded in 1855, employs 1,250 people and manufactures high quality metal office furniture, filing shelves and cabinets, library shelving and security products such as safes for banks. The acquisition was made jointly by Steelcase and Forges de Strasbourg, a French public company, and is subject to authorization by the French government's exchange control authorities.

A division of Forges de Strasbourg, Strafor, S.A., with factories in Sarrebourg and Strasbourg, France, will manufacture and distribute Steelcase chairs in Europe. In 1979, Steelcase/Strafor also began manufacturing the Steelcase Series 9000 Systems Furniture for the European market.

Henri Lachmann, general manager of Strafor, cited the acquisition of Pohlschroder as an action which "creates for the first time, a clear European leader in the office furniture business." He went on to name four reasons for the acquisition:

1) The combination creates one group with the size and financial strength to capitalize on the changes taking place in today's office environment, i.e., the emergence of systems furniture as opposed to traditional file, desk and chair business; 2) Pohlschroder has one of the finest distribution organizations in the German market, Europe's largest; 3) The Pohlschroder and Steelcase/Strafor lines are not duplicated so both companies will benefit from a future exchange of products and the elimination of duplication in design and engineering effort; 4) The three-company combination will benefit from the proven sales approaches of Steelcase and Strafor.

Steelcase's senior vice president of marketing, Fred A. Bell, also explained that the rapid change from traditional office furniture to more complex office furniture systems has caused buyers to seek out those companies that offer more than just furniture. Buyers today, whether in Europe or the United States, are looking for solutions to office environmental problems and for ways to improve productivity. Steelcase, with its highly accepted products, energetic sales approach, state-of-the-art technical and research facilities and its continuing study of the office on a national scale, will be able to contribute significantly to the continued success of Pohlschroder and Strafor.

V. FINAL STEPS TOWARD COMPLETION

34. Decision to Proceed After Review

(Dateline)—Penn Pacific Corporation announced today that it has completed the review of the corporate records, contracts and title documents, etc. of the Delhi Contract Units and based upon that review, has decided to go forward with the acquisition of the Delhi Contract Units.

Daniel Lezak, president of Penn Pacific Corporation, stated that there are 6,278,371 Delhi Contract Units that are presently issued and outstanding. The purchase of the Units requires 627,837 shares of Penn Pacific Corporation $3.20 par value preferred stock or one share of preferred stock for each 10 Contract Units.

Lezak further stated that the preferred stock was convertible into Penn Pacific Corporation common stock on the basis of two shares of preferred stock for one share of common stock. The preferred stock will be non-voting, without dividends, and will be callable at par ($3.20) after three years from the date of issue.

The preferred shares shall be redeemable from a sinking fund on a pro rata basis. Such sinking fund will be formed from 50 percent of the proceeds of royalties, overrides or settlements accruing to the various properties owned by the Contract Units.

Lezak added that since these Contract Units were under the jurisdiction of the Federal District Court of Dallas, that Penn Pacific Corporation would wait for a formal filing with the Court until such time as its Form 10-K and audited financial statements have been completed so that both the Court and the approximately 6,000 holders of the Contract Units could have current financial information on Penn Pacific Corporation which they could utilize in their acceptance procedure.

It is anticipated that the Form 10-K for Penn Pacific Corporation will be available for distribution by mid-February 1980, therefore, the Hearing in which this Form 10-K would be approved would not occur until the first week in March.

35. Registration for Merger Becomes Effective

(Dateline)—The Holiday Inns, Inc. S-14 registration statement filed with the Securities and Exchange Commission in connection with the pending merger between Holiday Inns, Inc. and Harrah's was declared effective today according to an announcement by the two companies.

The shareholders of both companies are scheduled to vote on the merger February 28, 1980. The joint proxy materials will be mailed to shareholders within a few days. Holiday Inns shareholders will meet in Memphis and Harrah's shareholders at Lake Tahoe, Nevada.

Terms of the merger agreement provide that each share of Harrah's common stock will be exchanged for $17.75 in cash and $17.75 principal amount of 9-5/8 percent convertible subordinated debentures of Holiday Inns, Inc. convertible into Holiday Inns, Inc. common stock at $20 per share. The estate of William Harrah, which owns 70 percent of the outstanding shares of Harrah's has agreed to take $45 million of its cash portion of the transaction in a two-year installment promissory note.

The transaction has been approved by Nevada gaming authorities and is also subject to favorable tax rulings as well as other customary conditions.

36. Shareholder Approval by Acquired Company

(Dateline)—John B. Mencke, president and chief executive officer of Empire National Bank, announced that merger of Empire into The Bank of New York had been approved at a special meeting of shareholders of Empire held today. Of a total of

1,276,399 shares of common stock outstanding, 1,154,676, or 90 percent, were voted in favor of the proposed merger and 9,657, or less than 1 percent, were voted against the proposed merger. Mr. Mencke pointed out that consummation of the merger was still subject to the satisfaction of certain conditions set forth in the merger agreement and to the approval of various regulatory agencies. He further stated that the necessary applications to these regulatory agencies are expected to be filed as soon as practicable. Under terms of the proposed merger the shareholders of Empire would receive $22 per share in cash upon consummation of the merger.

37. Shareholder Approval by Acquiring Company

(Dateline)—John Brown and Company Limited, London, England, announced that its shareholders had approved the tender offer by an indirect wholly owned subsidiary of John Brown for outstanding shares of common stock of Leesona Corporation at $40 per share net to the seller in cash, which has commenced on Jan. 30, 1980. The purchase of and payment for shares pursuant to the tender offer remains subject to various other conditions, including the tender of a majority of the total number of Leesona Shares outstanding on Jan. 25, 1980 (including, for this purpose, 228,571 shares covered by a warrant). The tender offer expires at 5:00 P.M., New York City time, on Thursday, Feb. 28, 1980, unless extended.

As previously announced, an agreement between John Brown and Leesona provides that any Leesona shares not acquired by the John Brown subsidiary in the tender offer will be acquired at $40 per share in cash in a subsequent merger transaction. The proposed merger has also been approved by John Brown's shareholders but is subject to various other conditions, including the approval of Leesona's stockholders, if required by applicable law.

38. Shareholder Approval—With Rationale

(Dateline)—Sanders Associates (NYSE) shareholders approved a merger with California Computer Products, Inc. (Calcomp) at their 28th annual meeting, Saturday, Feb. 16, 1980. Calcomp shareholders had approved the merger at a special meeting Friday, in Anaheim, Calif.

The merger agreement provides for the exchange of .34 shares of Sanders common stock for each share of Calcomp common stock.

Sanders acquired 1,260,000 shares of Calcomp common stock in a cash tender offer in May 1979 and purchased 500,000 shares of Calcomp preferred stock in November of last year, bringing Sanders voting power in Calcomp to approximately 54 percent.

Sanders president, Jack L. Bowers, told shareholders "The merger links Sanders, a supplier of defense systems and graphic display products, with Calcomp, a supplier of computer graphic systems and products."

Bowers said, "The acquisition provides Sanders with additional graphics product lines, principally digital plotters and interactive graphic systems, servicing such markets as computer-aided design. In addition, Calcomp's extensive sales and field engineering organizations provide Sanders with direct access to end-user markets for Sanders own graphic display technology."

More than 99 percent of the 4,290,602 shares voted at Sanders annual meeting were cast in favor of the merger. At the Calcomp meeting, 1,418,276 shares, or 62 percent of eligible shares, excluding Sanders shares, favored merging with Sanders, and 96,999 shares voted against.

VI. ANNOUNCEMENTS OF COMPLETION

39. Completion of Acquisition

(Dateline)—Kaman Bearing and Supply Corporation, a wholly owned subsidiary of Kaman Corporation, announced today the acquisition of United Industrial Supply, Inc., Garden Grove, Calif.

Servicing the large aerospace and extractive industries in the Los Angeles basin as a distributor of industrial hydraulic hose fittings and accessories, United Industrial Supply will operate as a division of Kaman Bearing and Supply Corp. California. United Industrial will also serve as a hose specialist resource for all the Kaman Bearing locations in California, according to J.M. McCririe, president of Kaman Bearing and Supply California. Red Harle and Bill Houck, the founders of United Industrial Supply, will remain in management.

Operating in 21 states and British Columbia with 104 locations, Kaman Bearing and Supply distributes over 50,000 industrial products, including bearings, chains, sprockets, V-Belts, pulleys, conveyor idlers, hydraulic components and systems, lubricants and seals.

Headquartered here, Kaman Corporation is designed for diversification in five market groups: bearing and supply, music and aerospace, aviation services, and sciences.

40. Completion of Acquisition—With Rationale

(Dateline)—Siecor Optical Cables Inc. of Horseheads, N.Y., said today it has acquired the assets of privately held Superior Cable Corporation of Hickory,

N.C., a producer of copper cable and other products for the telecommunications industry. Cost was not disclosed.

Siecor said it will operate Superior Cable as a wholly owned subsidiary.

Siecor Optical Cables is owned jointly by Corning Glass Works of Corning, N.Y., and Siemens Corporation of Iselin, N.J. Siecor provides a line of optical waveguide cables and related hardware to the communications industry.

Siecor Chairman Leroy Wilson said the merger will provide for the rapid development of a manufacturing base for optical waveguide cable. In addition, he said, "it will establish for Siecor and Superior a strong position in the telephone cable field—both optical and conventional cable."

A.L. Viles, president and chief operating officer of Superior, will continue in that position. The company's annual sales approximate $115 million.

41. Completion of Acquisition—With Rationale

(Dateline)—Rockwell International Corporation announced today that it had completed the purchase of all outstanding stock in Wescom, Inc., a privately held telecommunications supplier headquartered in Downers Grove, Illinois.

Donald R. Beall, president and chief operating officer of Rockwell International, said Wescom "Adds another order of strength" to Rockwell's commercial telecommunications business.

The acquisition, he said, combines "The proven technical capabilities associated with two highly regarded names in the telecommunications field—Collins and Wescom."

"Wescom's product lines in voice frequency, pulse code modulation, and voice switching equipment, including a newly developed digital PABX, complement our Collins telecommunications product lines," Beall said.

Wescom has approximately 2,000 employees and four principal plants in the United States and Canada.

Rockwell and the Wescom stockholders had announced the signing of a definitive agreement on Dec. 27, 1979.

As a wholly owned subsidiary, Wescom will become a part of the company's electronics operations, reporting to electronics president D.J. Yockey.

Yockey made the following related organization announcements:

Kerry R. Fox, vice president and general manager of the Collins Transmission systems division at Rockwell, becomes president of Wescom, reporting to Yockey. He succeeds Win Shiras, a management consultant who had been interim president.

J.C. Culp becomes vice president and general manager of the Collins Transmission systems division, succeeding Fox. Culp had been worldwide director of marketing for microwave and a regional director in the company's international business.

Rockwell International is a major, multi-industry company applying advanced technology to a wide range of products in its automotive, aerospace, electronics and general industries businesses.

42. Completion of Small Acquisition—No Terms Announced

(Dateline)—International Harvester has purchased all outstanding stock of Iowa Industrial Hydraulics, Inc., a small Pocahontas, Iowa, manufacturer of hydraulic cylinders for excavation and mining equipment.

Financial terms of the transaction were not announced.

The Iowa firm had 1979 sales of $10.5 million, and 125 employees. International Harvester had 1979 sales of $8.4 billion in trucks, farm equipment, construction equipment and turbomachinery.

Iowa Industrial Hydraulics will operate as an IH subsidiary and continue to produce its present line of hydraulic cylinders for cranes and mining equipment to broaden IH's offering in the hydraulics market, according to IH. International Harvester's Precision Products Division currently produces hydraulic cylinders for use in agricultural and construction equipment.

No major expansions are planned at Pocahontas, according to IH, although some modifications will be made to the 124,000 square foot plant, and a warehouse will be added this year.

The Pocahontas City Council has passed enabling legislation to permit issuance of up to $10 million in Industrial Revenue Bonds by the city to finance expansion and improvement of Iowa Industrial Hydraulics in the future if business conditions warrant.

43. Consummation of Merger

(Dateline)—The previously announced merger of Midwestern Fidelity Corporation into a wholly owned subsidiary of Guardian Royal Exchange Assurance Limited (U.K.) has been consummated, it was reported today. The announcement was made by Victor Yerrill, president of Albany-Atlas Group, the U.S. operating arm of Guardian Royal Exchange Assurance. Pursuant to the merger, Midwestern shareholders, other than Guardian and its affiliates, are entitled to receive $27 in cash in exchange for each share held by them or to seek relief as dissenting shareholders under Ohio law. The subsidiary of Guardian had previously acquired 94.5 percent of the Midwestern common stock pursuant to a tender offer and an agreement with certain Midwestern shareholders.

Guardian is one of the largest insurance companies in the United Kingdom.

44. Consummation of Merger— Joint Announcement

(Dateline)—National Education Corporation (AMEX, PSE) and Intext, Inc. (OTC) announced today that the previously announced merger of Intext with a subsidiary of National Education Corporation has been consummated.

As a result of the merger, Intext is now a wholly owned subsidiary of National Education Corporation.

All operations of the combined companies are in the field of education with combined annual revenues of approximately $90 million. The nationwide operations include technical and vocational training and textbook publishing. Educational materials and services extend from kindergarten, through post-secondary and on-the-job training.

National Education, headquartered in Newport Beach, Calif., has reorganized its operations into four groups in anticipation of the Intext merger. They are the publishing and services group, the technical schools group, the business schools group and the home study group.

45. Completion of Sale of Subsidiary— No Terms Announced

(Dateline)—Western Union Corporation announced today that it has sold National Sharedata Corporation to a group composed of present and former National Sharedata Management personnel.

Terms of the transaction were not immediately disclosed, but a spokesman said that the sale did not result in any loss to Western Union.

National Sharedata, headquartered in Dallas, is in the business of providing computer facilities management and related data processing services, on a contract basis, primarily to commercial banks. It was acquired by Western Union Corporation in 1973 and had been operated as a wholly owned subsidiary since that time.

46. Completion of Sale of Unprofitable Subsidiary

(Dateline)—Allied Chemical has announced it has sold the Sugar Bowl Gas Corporation and Sugar Bowl Industrial Gas Corporation to Tatham Corporation for $25 million in notes plus the assumption by Tatham Corporation of long-term lease obligations approximating $9 million. Thomas P. Tatham, a Houston-based independent oil and gas operator, is chairman, president and principal stockholder of Tatham Corporation.

The Sugar Bowl companies, which were wholly owned subsidiaries of Allied Chemical, own and operate an intrastate pipeline system in Louisiana which transports and sells natural gas. The system has incurred substantial losses for several years under certain long-term, fixed-price contracts which expire by the end of 1981.

Under the sales agreement, Tatham Corporation has assumed all obligations under the gas contracts effective from Jan. 1, 1980. However, Allied Chemical continues as guarantor of the pipeline system's performance under those long-term contracts.

Under the terms of the financing arrangements, Tatham Corporation has secured a $125 million irrevocable letter of credit agreement against which the pipeline system may draw to meet pipeline losses through the end of 1981.

Under the bank's agreement, the bank may arrange for additional credits if the pipeline system provides additional collateral. If additional credit is not established prior to the full drawdown under the initial letter of credit, Allied Chemical is committed to provide up to $80 million through 1981 of subordinated loans if needed to cover further operating losses. Funds provided by Allied will be repayable with interest over a five-year period beginning 1982. Under certain conditions relating to Allied Chemical's commitment and the making of future loans under the commitment, Allied Chemical would be entitled to a minority equity interest in the pipeline system.

In the third quarter of 1979, Allied Chemical identified the pipeline as one of several businesses earmarked for divestiture and disclosed that negotiations were under way with a potential purchaser. A sales agreement was reached with Tatham Corporation in December, 1979.

Tatham Corporation intends to employ all of the approximately 50 Allied Chemical employees who currently manage and operate the pipeline.

47. Purchase of Majority Interest in Small Foreign Company

(Dateline)—The acquisition of Claude S.A., a leading French lighting manufacturer, was announced today by General Telephone & Electronics Corp.

GTE has purchased the majority interest in Claude held by a subsidiary of International Telephone and Telegraph Corporation. The ITT unit held 99.7 percent of Claude's stock, with the remainder being publicly owned.

Claude, with annual sales of approximately $85 million, has its principal plants in Lyon, Reims and St. Etienne. The company markets incandescent, high intensity discharge and fluorescent lamps and special products in the French, European and International markets.

"We intend to maintain Claude, which has one of the best known and respected brand names in France, as an independent and separate company manufacturing and marketing lamps for the European market," said Kemp V. Dwenger, senior vice president, GTE Sylvania Lighting Products - International. GTE Sylvania Lighting - Europe, with headquarters in Geneva, has manufacturing operations in West Germany, Belgium and England and marketing subsidiaries in all western European countries, including France.

GTE is one of the four largest producers of lighting products in the world and has the largest share of the world market for photolighting products. The corporation's overall sales and revenues in 1978 were $8.7 billion. One of the largest enterprises in the world, GTE operates 152 manufacturing plants and also has telephone operating companies which serve more than 17 million telephones.

"It is our intention to make available to Claude the extensive capabilities of GTE to strengthen its product and manufacturing capabilities and to help it expand its position in the European lighting market," Mr. Dwenger said.

Claude, founded in 1930, employs about 1,600 persons, its headquarters is in Boulogne, near Paris.

Claude's largest facility is a 220,000 square-foot plant in Lyon which manufactures incandescent lamps. It produces high intensity discharge lamps and special products at a 98,000 square-foot plant in Reims and fixtures at smaller plants in St. Etienne and Ivry, near Paris. Signs, both illuminating and non-illuminating for advertising, direction and other purposes, are made at Nantes and at facilities in Rouen and in Belgium at Brussels.

Sales offices and warehouses are maintained at strategic locations throughout the country.

VII. HANDLING TERMINATIONS

48. Termination of Merger Discussions

(Dateline)—National Silver Industries, Inc. (AMEX) announced today that it had terminated the previously reported exploratory discussions concerning the sale of its business.

Milton Bernstein, chairman of the board, stated that National Silver continues its full, normal operations in all divisions and areas.

49. Termination of Merger Agreement

(Dateline)—Harvey E. Pittluck, president of PBA, Inc., today announced that the previously reported agreement pursuant to which PBA, Inc. was to acquire 50 percent of the capital stock of Carolina Cartage Company, Inc. had been terminated by the mutual consent of the parties.

Carolina Cartage Company, Inc. is a certified motor carrier which operates principally in the southeastern United States.

As initially stated, the acquisition was not expected to have any material impact on the short-term earnings of PBA, Inc.

Note to editors—Profit By Air has offices or agents in most major cities throughout the world including Atlanta, Boston, Chicago, Cleveland, Dallas, Louisville, Los Angeles, Memphis, Miami, Minneapolis, Newark, New York, Philadelphia, Portland, San Francisco, San Juan, Seattle and Washington, D.C.

50. Withdrawal of Merger Proposal— Announcement by Target

(Dateline)—Guardsman Chemicals, Inc., has received word from Grow Group, Inc., that the merger proposal initiated by Grow on Jan. 29, 1980, has been withdrawn.

Guardsman had earlier challenged the legality of the Grow proposal in a federal court suit filed in Grand Rapids, Mich., claiming that the combination of the two companies would be flatly illegal under the federal antitrust laws because of the possible anticompetitive effects that such combination would have in certain concentrated markets common to both companies.

Keith C. Vander Hyde, president and chief executive officer of Guardsman, commented that Guardsman will prosecute this suit so long as Grow continues to own a substantial block of Guardsman shares.

51. Rejection of Merger Proposal by Board

(Dateline)—Levitz Furniture Corporation today announced that its board of directors, at a special meeting held here today, voted to reject the offer to merge Levitz Furniture Corporation into a new company which would have been owned by the Levitz and the Pritzker families.

On Dec. 4, 1979, Levitz Furniture Corporation announced that it had received a formal proposal for the merger under which the public shareholders of Levitz would receive $27 per share for their stock. The Levitz board, on Dec. 4, appointed a committee of outside directors to engage an investment banking firm to evaluate the offer. After consideration of the investment banker's report, the board rejected the offer as inadequate.

52. No Comment After Termination

(Dateline)—Columbia Pictures Industries announced today that in light of the announcement late Friday, by Kirk Kerkorian and Tracinda Investment Corporation that they had stopped consideration of their two-year option tender offer for Columbia stock, the company would have no further statement with respect to the withdrawn proposal. Columbia said it had not taken a position with respect to the offer and had, in fact, planned to consider the matter at the next regular meeting of its board of directors on January 29. In view of the Kerkorian decision, which had not been discussed with or communicated to Columbia prior to its release, the company said a Board decision would not be necessary.

53. Agreement to Halt Stock Purchases Pending Court Ruling

(Dateline)—The Reece Corporation [NYSE] announced today that the company's counsel had reached an agreement with counsel for Walco National Corporation whereby Walco will not acquire any additional Reece common stock, pending a hearing on Feb. 29, 1980. At that time Reece's application for a temporary restraining order and preliminary injunction to restrain Walco from purchasing any more Reece stock will be heard.

54. Court Order to Stop a Pending Merger (Competing Bidders)

(Dateline)—Pay Less Drug Stores Northwest Inc. (NYSE) ("Pay Less Northwest") announced today that a federal court had granted its request for a temporary restraining order enjoining Jewel Companies, Inc. (NYSE) ("Jewel") and certain others from acquiring or seeking to acquire, directly or indirectly, any additional shares of the common stock of Pay Less Drug Stores (OTC), a California company ("Pay Less California"), pending the hearing and determination of Pay Less Northwest's Motion for a preliminary injunction. It is expected that a hearing on such motion, as well as upon a request by Jewel for preliminary injunctive relief against Pay Less Northwest, will be held during the first week of February.

Jewel recently obtained from the Securities and Exchange Commission an exemption from certain provisions of the Federal Securities Laws which would otherwise have prevented it from making open market purchases of Pay Less California stock during the pendency of the previously announced proposed merger of a Jewel subsidiary with Pay Less California. Pay Less Northwest has contended in court that such purchases by Jewel would violate the Federal Securities Laws, particularly those regulating tender offers. The restraining order entered last Friday, January 18, by Judge Charles Renfrew of the U.S. District Court for the Northern District of California, stated that "there is a substantial question whether such purchases would constitute a violation of the Federal Securities Laws and the fiduciary duties of Jewel as dominant shareholders" of Pay Less California.

On January 17 Northwest's wholly owned subsidiary commenced a tender offer for all outstanding common shares of Pay Less California. The offer is conditioned, among other things, upon the tender of at least 917,000 shares prior to the expiration of the offer, scheduled for Thursday, February 14, 1980 at 5 P.M. New York City time. Northwest's subsidiary presently owns 269,000 shares of Pay Less California (approximately 12.2 percent of the outstanding shares); Jewel has stated that it holds 297,000 shares of Pay Less California (approximately 13.5 percent of the outstanding shares) and has an option to acquire an additional 421,486 shares (approximately 79.2 percent of the outstanding shares), which is exercisable if the previously announced proposed Jewel merger is not consummated.

Pursuant to the terms of the proposed Jewel merger, each share of Pay Less California would be converted in a non-taxable exchange into .652 of a share of Jewel common stock, which, based on Friday's closing price, had a market value of approximately $18.91. Pursuant to Pay Less Northwest's tender offer, shareholders of Pay Less California are being offered $22.50 net per share in cash (which would be a taxable transaction).

DANIEL G. BERGSTEIN

DANIEL G. BERGSTEIN is a member of the Bars of the States of New York and Florida and a member of the New York City law firm of Greenbaum, Wolff & Ernst. Mr. Bergstein specializes in corporate and securities law, including acquisitions and mergers. He was admitted to practice in 1968 and served as law clerk to the Honorable Edward Jordan Dimock of the Federal District Court for the Southern District of New York, after receiving his Juris Doctor degree from the Brooklyn Law School.

ELEANOR J. FURLAUD

ELEANOR J. FURLAUD is a member of the New York City law firm of Towne, Dolgin & Furlaud, and specializes in corporate securities law. She received her Juris Doctor degree from Columbia Law School and is a member of the Bar of the State of New York.

4

Guidelines to Foreign Direct
Investment in the United States

DANIEL G. BERGSTEIN

ELEANOR J. FURLAUD

INTRODUCTION

This chapter addresses the major legal considerations for a foreign corporation commencing certain types of operations in the United States.

The specific legal problems which will be encountered by the foreign corporation are innumerable, and there is no doubt that the foreign corporation's U.S. counsel will play the greatest role in addressing the most significant technical legal aspects of the proposed transaction.

For example, there are highly complicated and technical statutes and rules with respect to the sale or exchange of equity and debt securities in the United States. They are generally governed at the national level by the Securities Act of 1933 and the Securities Exchange Act of 1934. The situation is further complicated by the fact that each of the 50 states has adopted its own statutes and regulations governing the sale or exchange of securities.

There are myriad other statutes which must be complied with and which may apply to specific industries. Areas such as banking, insurance, air commerce, communications and the maritime industries are restricted, often on both Federal and state levels. Accordingly, the authors have addressed themselves to the most straightforward forms of transaction that might be entered into by first-time entrants in the United States market in an effort to give the reader some feeling both for the manner in which most transactions of this type are conducted and for the basic elements and considerations that will come into play.

MARKET EXPANSION

The United States has traditionally welcomed, and indeed encouraged, foreign investment in its economy. In 1791, Alexander Hamilton spoke warmly of encouraging the introduction of foreign capital into the fledgling United States economy:[1]

"It is not impossible that there may be persons disposed to look with a jealous eye on the intro-

---

[1] From time to time, Americans have expressed strong negative feelings towards the influx of foreign capital. For example, in 1832, there were struggles over the first and second Banks of the United States, thought to be forerunners of foreign capital advances into American life. Equally, there were American reactionary feelings towards alien capital, particularly concerning American farmlands but also concerning industrial investment. These feelings resulted in Congressional action in the form of the Alien Land Act of 1887. During the period of World War I and directly thereafter, legislation restricting alien participation in radio, aircraft, shipping and petroleum production proliferated. Since World War II, the United States has backed off from some of the hostile reaction articulated during that time, and even moved towards encouraging foreign investment in the United States. *See,* Sturm, *Taxation of Foreign Investors in the United States*, 55 TAXES 542 (1977) (hereinafter cited as Sturm), and Vagts, *The Corporate Alien: Definitional Questions in Federal Restraints on Foreign Enterprise*, 74 HARV. L. REV. 1489, 1493-94 (1961).

duction of foreign capital, as if it were an instrument to deprive our own citizens of the profits of our own industry; but, perhaps, there never could be a more unreasonable jealousy. Instead of being viewed as a rival, it ought to be considered as a most valuable auxiliary, conducing to put in motion a greater quantity of productive labor, and a greater portion of useful enterprise, than could exist without it.''[2]

For some time, the economic atmosphere in the United States has been very attractive to foreign companies. Foreign companies are increasingly realizing that efficient penetration into U.S. markets involves doing business in the U.S. rather than just with it.[3] Uncertainty about the long-term political and economic prospects in Latin American and European home countries, combined with a weakened dollar, large amounts of dollars in Europe and the Middle and Far East, a decline in prices of shares in U.S. securities markets and the comparable declines in the market value of shares of privately held domestic corporations have created an acceleration in the trend of foreign corporations acquiring controlling interests in existing domestic enterprises or independently establishing production and marketing facilities in the United States.[4] Many overseas companies must take over or start up U.S.-based businesses in order to compete effectively in American markets.[5]

While foreign corporations have generally preferred portfolio investments rather than major direct investments in American corporations in order to take advantage of the greater depth and stability of U.S. capital markets, direct investments have advantages for foreign investors similar to those for U.S. companies investing abroad.[6] Direct investment, defined as ''[giving] the investor operating control of the business firm involved, as opposed to indirect or portfolio in-

vestment, which does not provide operational control,''[7] allows the establishment of production facilities and branch offices to reach markets unreachable otherwise,[8] whether as a result of trade barriers in the form of import/export controls, tariff restrictions or excessive transportation costs.[9]

The large increase in foreign direct investment and national concern that government-controlled foreign investments would be used as a tool of political-economic warfare have started a flood of recent legislation, the main thrust of which has been to require reporting and disclosure of foreign investment in order to improve the United States government's monitoring of foreign investment activity.[10]

For example, pursuant to the Foreign Investment Study Act of 1974, the Treasury and Commerce Department collected extensive data on the nature and extent of foreign investment. It was concluded on the basis of this data that the available information on foreign investment was insufficient to suggest new regulatory schemes. Therefore, it was recommended that the U.S. government conduct improved data collecting activities on a continuing basis. Congress thereafter enacted the International Investment Survey Act of 1976[11] to provide clear and unambiguous authority for the President to collect information on international investment. Disclosure was also required by the Agricultural Foreign Investment Disclosure Act of 1978,[12] passed as a result of anxiety caused by an increase in farmland values leading to a decline in family farming. This Act requires that any ''foreign person who acquires or transfers any interest, other than a security interest, in agricultural land'' must report to the Department of Agriculture.

Further, the growth in the number and size of foreign banking institutions led to the enactment of the International Banking Act of 1978.[13] The Foreign

---

[2]ANNALS OF CONG. 994 (1791).

[3]Sturm, *supra* note 1, at 542.

[4]*Id*.

[5]Young, *The Acquisition of United States Businesses by Foreign Investors*, 30 BUS. LAWYER 111, 111 (1979).

[6]Under the Foreign Investment Study Act of 1974, P.L. 93-479, 88 Stat. 1450 (codified at 15 U.S.C.A. §78b note (1976)), foreign ''direct investment'' was defined as 10% or more foreign ownership of voting shares, and foreign ''portfolio investment'' was defined as investment in ''voting stocks involving less than 10% ownership...in non-voting stocks and in debt instruments with maturity of more than one year.''

[7]FLANIGAN, U.S. POLICY ON FOREIGN INVESTMENT IN THE UNITED STATES 7 (Chamber of Commerce of the United States 1974).

[8]*See* 6 Inter-Economics, June 1974, at 84.

[9]Often, foreign investment is characterized as ''upstream.'' In other words, foreign investors come to gain technological or marketing skills and to benefit from the skilled United States labor force, as well as to gain access to financial markets, and create markets for parent company goods. *See* Note, *U.S. Regulation of Foreign Direct Investment: Current Developments and the Congressional Response*, 15 VA. J. INT'L L. 611 (1975).

[10]For a complete description of recent federal disclosure regulations, *see* AMERICAN BAR ASSOCIATION, A GUIDE TO FOREIGN INVESTMENT UNDER UNITED STATES LAW 10-21 (1979) (hereinafter cited as A GUIDE TO FOREIGN INVESTMENT).

[11]P.L. 94-472, 90 Stat. 2059 (1976) (amended P.L. 95-381 [92 Stat. 726 (1978)) (codified at 22 U.S.C. §§3101-3108 (1976 and Supp. II 1978)).

[12]P.L. 95-460, 92 Stat. 1263 (1978) (codified at 7 U.S.C. §3501-3508 (Supp. II 1978)).

[13]P.L. 95-369, 92 Stat. 607 (1978) (codified at 12 U.S.C. §§3101-3108 (Supp. II 1978)).

Sovereign Immunities Act,[14] was enacted to clarify the jurisdiction of U.S. courts over foreign governments and their property.

Finally, the Domestic and Foreign Investment Improved Disclosure Act of 1977 amended the reporting requirements of §13(d) of the Securities Exchange Act of 1934 to add citizenship and residency requirements to the facts that must be disclosed by beneficial owners of 5 percent or more of equity securities of United States issuers. Under 13(d) and (g) of the Securities Exchange Act of 1934, a foreign investor who directly or indirectly acquires beneficial ownership of 5 percent or more of a class of equity securities of a registered issuer must file reports with the Securities and Exchange Commission.[15]

As discussed, the effect of the recent legislation has been to enable the United States government to amass more accurate information on foreign investments. It is unlikely that the United States government will impose significant controls on foreigners interested in investing in the United States economy, or, indeed, that such controls could be imposed without violating the numerous Treaties of Friendship, Commerce and Navigation (the "FCN Treaties") to which the United States is a party.

The United States has entered into over 40 FCN Treaties which deal with such matters as tariffs and the entrance of goods and ships into the territories of the parties to the treaties. Eleven of the most recent treaties, including those with France, Germany, Japan and The Netherlands, contain express assurances of the foreign investors' right either to form corporations or acquire controlling interests in United States companies. For example, in the treaty with the Republic of Germany, German nationals and companies were granted the right to "organize companies under the general company laws...and to acquire majority interests in companies of such other Party...."[16] The most recent FCN Treaties[17] commit both parties to "national treatment" of the treaty alien investor. This is important to delineate the U.S. policy towards foreign investment in the U.S. Although all FCN Treaties may

be qualified by the "protocols" that accompany the treaties,[18] and all are terminable after ten years on one year's notice, the FCN Treaties have served to form a U.S. policy which would probably prohibit the Congress of the United States from enacting general restrictions against direct investments. It should be noted that most of the FCN Treaties do not go as far as the "national treatment" language of the eleven most recent FCN Treaties. About half the FCN Treaties allow only "most favored nation" treatment with respect to the organization of corporations, the acquisition of shares and the holding of executive positions in domestic U.S. corporations.

A further limitation on the ability of the United States government to impose limitations on foreign direct investment is the fact that the U.S. is a party to a multilateral agreement on investment, The Code of Liberalization of Capital Movements, as a consequence of the United States' membership in the Organization for Economic Cooperation and Development ("OECD"). All major U.S. investment and trading partners are members of the OECD. While the Code is not in the form of a treaty, it apparently has the force of one under international law.[19] The Code expressly allows creation or extension of a wholly owned enterprise, subsidiary or branch, acquisition of full ownership of an existing enterprise and participation in a new or existing enterprise.

The authors address three methods of expansion by foreign corporate investors into the United States markets: (i) direct qualification by the foreign corporation in one of the states, (ii) creation of a domestic subsidiary corporation, and (iii) foreign parent or U.S. subsidiary acquisition of an existing United States domestic corporation.[20] Each method has advantages and disadvantages which the authors will address in turn. In general, to transact any form of business in the United States, whether by qualification, formation of a subsidiary, or by the acquisition of an existing business, the foreign investor must submit to the laws of any state wherein it transacts business. The extent to which the state's rules will affect it depends upon its

---

[14]P.L. 94-583, 90 Stat. 2891 (1976) (codified at 28 U.S.C. §§1330, 1602-1611 (1976)).

[15]*See* Graphic Sciences, Inc. v. International Mogul Mines, 397 F. Supp. 112 (D.D.C. 1974); SEC v. General Refractories Co., 400 F. Supp. 1248 (D.D.C. 1975).

[16]Treaty of FCN, October 29, 1954, United States-Federal Republic of Germany, art. VII, para. 1 (1956), 7.2 U.S.T. 1839, T.I.A.S. No. 3593.

[17]Treaties with the following countries: France, Germany, Japan, The Netherlands, Israel, Thailand, Togo, Oman, Korea and Nicaragua.

[18]A GUIDE TO FOREIGN INVESTMENT, *supra* note 10, at ___29.

[19]See *The Rising Tide of Reverse Flow: Would a Legislative Breakwater Violate U.S. Treaty Commitments?*, 72 MICH. L. REV. 551, 578 (1974) for a good discussion of the above issue. The Code has not been consented to by the United States Senate. Such action is probably not necessary because executive action by the United States Executive Branch binds the U.S. through a vote in the council, which appears to be the authorized method of acceptance by the convention that established the OECD. The Code is not, by its terms, binding on any of the 50 states.

[20]Phillips, "Legal Restraints on Foreign Direct Investment in the United States," 7 Commerce Department, *Report to the Congress on Foreign Direct Investment in the United States*, Appendix K (1976) (hereinafter cited as Phillips). This article does not address other potential but less frequently used methods of entering the U.S. markets such as joint ventures or mergers.

legal status in the state and the nature of its operations there. Although the United States has no federal corporation law, most of the 50 states have adopted some form of the Model Business Corporation Act, which was prepared in 1946 and revised in 1969 by the Committee on Corporation Laws of the American Bar Association's Section of Corporation, Banking and Business Law. Thus, most states have enacted fairly uniform rules governing the formation and internal management of corporations. Each state must be examined carefully, however, to determine the governing rules.

Most state statutes do not make a distinction between an out-of-state corporation formed in a foreign country and an out-of-state corporation formed in another of the 50 states. Thus, because "foreign" United States corporations are afforded constitutional rights such as equal protection of the laws and freedom from unreasonable restraint on interstate commerce, [21] alien corporations should be equally protected.

QUALIFICATION

A corporation formed in a foreign country may qualify to do business directly in the United States, as the states rarely distinguish between alien corporations and U.S. corporations formed in one of the other 50 states in determining whether such corporation may transact business in the state. [22] A corporation must apply for the privilege of entering any state where it intends to "do business" and submit to the state's taxing authority. What constitutes "doing business" varies from state to state, but it generally is considered that opening a branch office and staffing it with even one employee is sufficient to require the state's approval.

The typical qualification process usually requires the submission of an application containing certain information about the corporation seeking to be qualified, the corporation's charter, by-laws, a resolution of the board of directors authorizing submission of the application and the appointment of an agent for service of process. Most states require a registered place of business or a registered agent, usually an individual, or both, for service of process within the state. [23]

Many states have provisions to the effect that (i) a qualified out-of-state corporation may enjoy the same but no greater rights and privileges as a domiciliary in the state, and is subject to the same duties, obligations, rights and privileges, or (ii) that no out-of-state corporation may be qualified to transact business that the domiciliary corporation is not permitted to transact. [24]

It is important that the foreign investor examine each state in which it wishes to transact business because several states have unusual qualification provisions. For example, Kansas Statute Annotated §17-7301 requires a statement of the assets and liabilities of the corporation. Hawaii Revised Statute §174-1 requires that a foreign corporation state the total value of the property owned and used by it in its businesses and the total value of property to be acquired by it in the twelve months following the statement and the total dollar amount of business transacted by it during its preceding fiscal year. Vermont Business Corporation Act §2119 states that the Secretary of State may require a foreign corporation to file for the benefit of creditors a "good and sufficient bond...in such sum and condition as the secretary of state may direct."

The penalties for failing to qualify to do business in the state where a branch office is located generally consists in the foreign corporation not being allowed to commence legal actions in the state. Although most states permit the non-complying foreign corporation to defend itself in legal actions and allow a retroactive cure of the failure to qualify, in Idaho, for example, failure to qualify results in permanent disqualification from bringing actions in any court of the state. Many states impose additional penalties on the corporations which transact business but which have failed to qualify, ranging from requiring payment of back taxes before maintaining an action within the state, [25] to rendering the employees of such corporations guilty of a misdemeanor punishable by imprisonment. [26] Finally, some states render void all agreements entered into by non-complying corporations. [27]

Where foreign investors have minimal direct contact with the United States, such as merely purchasing securities publicly traded in United States markets or depositing funds in United States banks, the tax impli-

[21]See Wheeling Steel Corporation v. Glander, 337 U.S. 562 (1949); International Textbook Co. v. Pigg, 217 U.S. 91, 110-111 (1910).
[22]Only the Washington statute distinguishes between the two. *See* WASH. REV. CODE ANN. §23A.36.010 (West supp. 1980).
[23]For a good description of the historical and present-day significance of the agent for service of process, see Phillips, *supra* note 20.
[24]*See, e.g.,* ILL. ANN. STAT. ch. 32, §157.103 (Smith-Hurd 1954); N.J. STAT. ANN §14A:13-2 (West 1969); N.Y. BUS. CORP. LAW. §1301 (McKinney 1963 and Supp. 1979); WASH. REV. CODE ANN. §23A.32.010 (West Supp. 1980). Only nine jurisdictions (Alabama, California, Connecticut, Delaware, Nevada, New Hampshire, Puerto Rico, Ohio and the Virgin Islands) have statutes or constitutions that lack all of these provisions. *Id.*
[25]N.Y. BUS. CORP. LAW §1312 (McKinney 1963).
[26]*See, e.g.,* OKLA. STAT. ANN. tit. 18, §1.201 (West 1953).
[27]*See* ALA. CODE §10-2-254 (1977).

cations of any income derived from such activities is clear. Any capital gains realized from the sale of such securities by foreign corporations and the interest paid the foreign investor by the bank where such funds are deposited is not income subject to taxation.[28]

On the other hand, dividends and interest (other than from bank deposits) paid to foreign corporations or nonresident alien individuals not engaged in trade or business are subject to a withholding tax imposed either at the rate of 30 percent or at a lower rate if provided for by treaty.[29]

A foreign corporation which actively conducts a trade or business in the United States, however, faces tax consequences a good deal more complex than the mere passive investment of funds. A threshold question is whether the foreign corporation is engaged in a trade or business within the United States for Federal income tax purposes. The level of activity required to subject the foreign investor to Federal income tax liability is different from that required to subject the foreign investor to state qualification statutes. For example, the opening of a branch office in a state would probably require the foreign corporation to file an application to qualify to transact business, even if the branch did not actively generate income. Such a branch would not, however, necessarily give rise to Federal income tax exposure.[30] Passive income derived from such a branch would nevertheless be subject to state taxes and a flat 30 percent tax rate, or lower if there is an applicable double tax treaty.[31] On the other hand, a foreign corporation may be found to be engaged in a U.S. trade or business even if it does not maintain an office or branch here. A foreign corporation which is so engaged is commonly referred to as a "resident" foreign corporation, although this term is not presently found in the language of the Code itself.[32]

TRADE OR BUSINESS INCOME

In general, if during any part of the taxable year a foreign corporation is engaged in a trade or business within the United States, any income derived that is "effectively connected with the trade or business," or which is deemed to be effectively connected under the "limited force of attraction" rules, is taxed at the applicable progressive rates.[33] Business expenses properly allocable to taxable trade or business income may be deducted from gross income.[34]

What constitutes "trade or business" within the meaning of the Code is not made clear by the statute or the regulations promulgated thereunder. Courts which have construed the question indicate that the U.S. commercial involvement must be "considerable, continuous and regular"[35] before it qualifies for "trade or business" status. For example, United States courts have stated that: "the ownership and leasing of real property, the collection of rentals therefrom and the performance of certain minimal acts customarily incident to the ownership of real property do not constitute engaging in trade or business...."[36] If the foreign investor is not engaged in trade or business and has income which is "fixed or determinable, annual or periodical," such income is subject to a tax of 30 percent.[37] Such "fixed" income specifically includes dividends, rents, interest and other passive income. Contingent and some fixed royalty payments[38] and interest, except interest on bank deposits, are also subject to a 30 percent tax under the Code. No deductions may be taken from the income on which the 30 percent tax rate is imposed. Income defined as "fixed or determinable, annual or periodical" income is "effectively connected" only when it is directly attributable to the foreign corporation's U.S. activities,[39] in which event it will be taxed at progressive rates.

---

[28]This is because interest paid to a foreign corporation or nonresident alien individual is not deemed to be from "sources within the United States" under §861(a)(1)(A) (if not deemed to be effectively connected with the conduct of a trade or business within the United States) and is, therefore, not included in the foreign corporation's gross income under §§882(b) and 881. *See* Garelik, *What Constitutes Doing Business Within the United States by a Non-Resident and Alien Individual or a Foreign Corporation,* 18 TAX L. REV. 423 (1963). Note, however, that a nonresident alien *individual* who is present within the United States for 183 days or more during the taxable year must pay a 30 percent tax (or lower if there is an applicable double tax treaty) on any capital gains derived during that year from United States sources. *See* I.R.C. §871(a)(2).

[29]*See* I.R.C. §§871(a)(1), 881.

[30]*See* Treas. Reg. §1.864-3(b), Examples (1) and (2).

[31]I.R.C. §881(a)(1).

[32]Sturm, *supra* note 1, at 545.

[33]*See* I.R.C. §864(c)(3). Such income is so taxed even if received or accrued during a part of the taxable year after the conduct of the U.S. business has ceased.

[34]*See* Treas. Reg. §1.873-1.

[35]Jan Casimir Lewenhaupt v. Commissioner, 20 T.C. 151 (1953), *aff'd*, 221 F.2d 227; 55-1 U.S. Tax Cas. ¶9339 (9th Cir. 1955).

[36]Herbert v. Commissioner, 20 T.C. 26, 33 (1958); Linen Thread Co. v. Commissioner, 14 T.C. 725, 736 (1950), *aff'd* 46-1 U.S. Tax Cas. ¶9125.

[37]*See* I.R.C. §881(a).

[38]I.R.C. §§881(a)(4), 871(e). Royalties are often exempted from taxation by treaties. *See, e.g.,* Income Tax Treaty, Apr. 29, 1948, United States-Netherlands, art. IX, 62 Stat. 1757, T.I.A.S. No. 1855. *See also* Sturm, *supra* note 1, at 546 n. 41.

[39]*See* Treas. Reg. §1.864-4(c).

Recurring income items or business operating income will, therefore, be subject to some form of taxation. However, disposition of investment assets which are not used in or related to a U.S. business can be accomplished without subjecting such dispositions to United States taxes. Income derived from the sale in the United States of such property, whether real or personal, is not "fixed" income,[40] and foreign corporations which sell or transfer capital assets not connected with any U.S. business are not liable for Federal taxation.[41] In order to receive the benefits of this treatment, the foreign corporation must ensure that the asset to be disposed of is not connected with any trade or business in which the foreign corporation is engaged. If the asset is attributable to a trade or business, the net gains are taxable at the capital gains rate normally attributable to domestic corporations because the income is "effectively connected."[42]

Foreign corporations must also be aware of the individual state and local taxes. Most states impose a tax on income even though it is sometimes called a franchise, privilege, or license tax.[43] States vary widely in the methods used to determine the amount of income of a corporation doing business there allocable between its jurisdiction and other states or foreign countries where the corporation also does business. Approximately half the states have adopted the Uniform Revision of Income for Tax Purposes Act.[44] Certain states tax income earned by corporate affiliates in other states or foreign countries, in the proportion allocated to the business conducted in the taxing state, even if the corporate affiliate itself does no business there. It should be noted that state taxes are a deductible item for Federal income tax purposes.[45]

Whether or not income is "effectively connected" with a U.S. business requires analysis within the framework of certain tests set out in the Internal Revenue Code. Income from commercial activities is separated into two components, consisting essentially of passive investment income and effectively connected business income.[46] If an investment is found to constitute an integral part of the business undertaking under either the "business activities" or the "asset use" tests outlined in the regulations, it will be exposed to Federal income tax liability just as will income derived from the business itself.[47] If the investment is a capital asset, the tax on sale would be at the capital gains rates otherwise applicable unless the rules set forth in *Corn Products v. Commissioner*[48] are applied, which would result in tax at the higher ordinary rates.

Code §864(c)(3) sets forth the additional "limited force of attraction" rule which extends the meaning of the term "effectively connected" so that the presence of any U.S. trade or business in the United States in effect causes all commercial profits earned from U.S. sources to be taxed at applicable progressive rates even though unrelated to that trade or business. Therefore, non-"trade or business" income may become taxable "effectively connected" income.[49]

Foreign investors may avoid problems of attribution of unrelated income to trade or business by establishing a separate corporate entity. Even where there is common control, the trade or business status of one corporation is not attributed either to its parent or to an affiliated corporation[50] unless there are common business dealings between the two companies.

ORGANIZING A SUBSIDIARY CORPORATION

The use of the corporate intermediary offers the foreign investor several advantages. Incorporation insulates the foreign investor from full liability and is an advantage in conducting an active business involving regular contact with suppliers, labor unions and customers.[51] Foreign investors should be aware, however, that income earned in the United States by a corporation is subject to double taxation: once at the corporate level at the applicable rates and again at the withholding rates when distributed as dividends to foreign shareholders.[52] Further, a U.S. corporation is taxed at corporate rates on its world-wide income of whatever character. Under the Code, dividend distributions and interest payments to its foreign shareholders and lenders are subject to the 30 percent withholding tax. The tax may be lowered or eliminated

---

[40]Treas. Reg. §1.1441-2(a)(3).

[41]*See* Sturm, *supra* note 1, at 547; Garelik, *supra* note 28, at 427.

[42]I.R.C. §864(c)(2).

[43]aA GUIDE TO FOREIGN INVESTMENT, *supra* note 10, at 59-60.

[44]*Id.* at 60.

[45]I.R.C. §164.

[46]Sturm, *supra* note 1, at 555.

[47]I.R.C. §864(c)(2); Treas. Reg. §1.864-4(c)(3); Sturm, *supra* note 1, at 555.

[48]350 U.S. 46 (1955).

[49]*See* Sturm, *supra* note 1, at 555.

[50]*See* Treas. Reg. §1.864-3(b), Example (2); Sturm, *supra* note 1, at 555. Note, however, that the Commissioner may allocate income, deductions, or credits between two or more organizations where he determines that such allocation is necessary to prevent evasion of taxes. *See* I.R.C. §482.

[51]*See* Sturm, *supra* note 1, at 558.

[52]*Id.*

by a treaty with the recipient's home country, and no tax is imposed where during the previous three years the paying corporation derived more than 80 percent of the gross income from abroad. Care should be taken, however, that a sufficient equity to debt ratio is maintained in order to prevent the Internal Revenue Service from reclassifying interest payments to creditor-shareholders as dividends.[53]

The advantages of incorporating are great, and in most cases, the foreign investor will decide to conduct its United States-related activities through a newly organized subsidiary corporation. Because the United States does not have a national corporations law, the foreign investor must choose one of the 50 states in which to incorporate.

Although many states have enacted some form of the Model Business Corporation Act,[54] there is a wide variety among the states with regard to treatment of such considerations as location requirements of corporate offices or shareholder meetings, number of directors, whether action is permissible by written consent, whether directors may meet by conference telephone calls and so on. The authors have attached as Annex A a chart setting forth, state by state, various items of interest to foreign investors intending to incorporate in the United States. The foreign investor should incorporate in the state where it intends to transact the bulk of its business, unless the restrictions of that state are too onerous. The foreign investor may always incorporate in a state which is highly flexible, such as Delaware or Arizona, and qualify to transact business in the state where it intends to transact business. A corporation must qualify to do business in every state where it transacts business. Whether a corporation is "doing business" in a state requires analysis of that state's particular rules.[55]

In general, the states do not restrict the rights of investors from outside the United States to hold shares in business corporations. Some states, however, restrict foreign holding of shares in certain specialized corporations. These corporations are generally those conducting businesses in certain highly regulated industries and are restricted on the Federal level as well. Other states have restrictions of their own. For example, in Texas, an international trading corporation involved in the sale of farm, ranch, mine, etc. products must have as a majority of its directors, officers and shareholders persons who are U.S. citizens.[56] Also, Hawaii limits fish marketing to residents.[57]

There are myriad other considerations which a foreign investor must consider when choosing a state in which to incorporate. Some are merely inconveniences; some are severe restrictions. For example, several states require shareholders' meetings to be held within the state or within the United States, as does Maryland.[58] In Iowa[59] and Indiana,[60] similar restrictions apply. The Indiana statute has been interpreted to mean that shareholders must meet in the state.[61] A state requirement that shareholders meet within the state could prove to be of great inconvenience to foreign investors resident abroad. Most states, however, provide that the shareholders may act without actually meeting if all shareholders sign a unanimous written consent to the taking of an action. Further restrictions to which foreign investors should pay attention include the requirements of some states that at least some of the incorporators be U.S. citizens or that the incorporator's meeting be held in the United States. These latter factors are not of great concern because investors will be consulting with their attorneys who may act as incorporators.

Generally, there are no citizenship or residency requirements for officers of general business corporations. Only three states require directors to be citizens or residents of the state in which the corporation is formed.[62] Generally, directors' meetings need not be held within the state.

In sum, if the subsidiary corporation's business will be conducted in one state only, by and large it will be preferable to organize the subsidiary in that state, assuming that such state's corporation laws are sufficiently flexible.

---

[53]*See* text accompanying note 69 *infra*.

[54]*See generally* Phillips, *supra* note 20.

[55]*See* text accompanying notes 22-23 *supra*.

[56]*See* TEX. REV. CIV. STAT. ANN art. 1527 (Vernon 1980).

[57]*See* HAWAII REV. STAT. §422-4 (1976). *See also* 46 U.S.C. §251 (1976).

[58]MD. CORP. AND ASS'NS CODE ANN. §2-502 (1975).

[59]IOWA CODE ANN. §491.14 (West Supp. 1980). The place of business is where shareholders' meetings should be held unless the board of directors designates somewhere else in the county.

[60]IND. CODE ANN. §23-1-2-9(a) (Burns 1972) (in state at principal place of business).

[61]*See generally* Phillips, *supra* note 20.

[62]HAWAII REV. STAT §416-4 (Supp. 1979); N.H. REV. STAT. ANN. §296:3 (1978); S.D. COMP. LAWS ANN. §47-5-1 (1969). However, Florida Law, FLA. STAT. ANN. §607.111(2) (West 1977 and Supp. 1980), states that directors need not be Florida residents unless the articles of incorporation or bylaws so require. Further, Nevada Law, NEV. REV. STAT. §78-115 (1979), requires that one director be a citizen of the United States.

ANTITRUST

A threshold question that every foreign investor must consider in determining whether to acquire an ongoing U.S. business is whether the acquisition will violate antitrust laws. United States antitrust laws may serve to block a contemplated U.S. acquisition. Broadly, United States antitrust laws prohibit the acquisition of the stock or assets of any corporation which in any line of commerce in any section of the country may substantially lessen competition or tend to create a monopoly.[63] Also, U.S. law prohibits any unreasonable "restraint of trade" or attempt to monopolize trade.[64] Other laws enable U.S. administrative agencies to take action against unfair methods of competition and unfair or deceptive acts or practices.[65]

Finally, there is a significant condition that must be met before acquired or acquiring corporations which engage in commerce may consummate an acquisition of a certain size.[66] The Clayton Act requires the filing of a prior notification of a proposed acquisition with both the Department of Justice and the Federal Trade Commission (the "FTC"). The notification requires the disclosure by both acquiring and acquired corporations of a substantial amount of data including revenue data with respect to each of the respective product categories.

Upon the expiration of the specified waiting period after the filing, the acquisition may be consummated. However, the expiration of the waiting period does not preclude either the Justice Department or the FTC from seeking at a future date any and all remedies afforded by the antitrust laws.

CAPITALIZING THE SUBSIDIARY

State law does not require that in the capitalization of the subsidiary corporation there be any particular ratio between debt and equity. The determination of the ratio between such debt and equity investment is left to the shareholders and board of directors of the subsidiary corporation. However, a provision of the Internal Revenue Code provides certain penalties which make it unattractive for the debt-to-equity ratio to be disproportionately large on the debt side when the debt is created by having the shareholders extend loans to, and thereby become the creditors of, their corporation.[67] This type of capitalization will result in the corporation being "thinly capitalized." By and large, thin capitalization must be considered as a poten-

tial problem to be dealt with whenever the debt-to-equity ratio of the investment of the foreign parent in the subsidiary is greater than one to one. If the debt-to-equity ratio exceeds one to one, the Internal Revenue Service may take the position that there is not a reasonable relationship between the equity and debt investment of the foreign parent, and that the debt, in fact, represents an equity investment. The Internal Revenue Service will also take corporate earnings, the term of the debt, the likelihood that the debt will be repaid, and the normal practice of the parties into account, even if there is a low debt-to-equity ratio. If a subsidiary corporation is held to be "thinly capitalized" the repayment of principal and interest by the subsidiary to the foreign parent may be treated as dividends and all interest payments on account of such debt will not be allowed as an ordinary interest deduction to the subsidiary.

The Internal Revenue Service has recently proposed regulations which would be effective with respect to debts to shareholders and others created after December 31, 1980, and which would provide fairly comprehensive and rather strict rules for determining whether a particular obligation is to be treated as a capital contribution (Proposed Treasury Regulations Sections 1.385-1 through 1.385-12, published Federal Register, March 20, 1980). Although the proposed regulations do not purport to cover debts incurred before December 31, 1980, they will undoubtedly be viewed as guidelines in reviewing such transactions. It is important to note that parent company guarantees of loans made to the subsidiary by third parties may raise a thin capitalization problem if it is not reasonable to expect that the loan can be enforced against the subsidiary in accordance with its terms. In such case, the guaranteed loan may be treated as a capital contribution by the foreign parent. However, such guarantees are often necessary in the establishment of new ventures in the U.S.

FOREIGN PARENT CORPORATION GUARANTEE

It is fair to conclude that in most cases the organization of a domestic United States corporation will be an advisable vehicle for the foreign corporation to make its investment in the United States. This course of action will assure maximum insulation of the foreign parent from any liabilities arising out of its United States operations, as well as avoiding undesirable tax effects previously discussed. It is well settled in state corporate law that a wholly owned subsidiary will afford corporate insulation to the foreign parent

---

[63]Clayton Act, 15 U.S.C. §18 (1976).
[64]Sherman Act, 15 U.S.C. §§1, 2 (1976).
[65]Federal Trade Commission Act, 15 U.S.C. §45 (1976).
[66]There are several size tests, including the "size of person" test and the "size of the acquisition" test.
[67]*See* I.R.C. §385; 3 STD. FED. TAX REP. (CCH) ¶2579.

shareholder, providing that certain formalities have been observed. Such formalities include the maintenance of separate books of account, the establishment of separate bank accounts, the holding of regular meetings of shareholders and of the board of directors, and in general, the treatment by the parent of its subsidiary as a wholly independent entity.

As a practical matter, however, the ability of the U.S. subsidiary to engage in any meaningful business activities in the United States may require the foreign parent initially to guarantee all or a portion of the U.S. subsidiary's obligations. As foreign investment in the United States has increased over the last several years, United States creditors (particulary lending institutions) have become far more sophisticated with respect to such guarantees. The guarantees have become exceedingly complex since they are not restricted to a simple guarantee of payment or collection. The guarantee also deals with such issues as who may accept service of any process in the United States that might be brought by the creditor against the foreign parent for the enforcement of the obligations, and the venue or place where any action to enforce the guarantee against the foreign parent may be instituted. Obviously, the United States creditor will seek to assure that the guarantee, by its terms, provides that any action involving the guarantee will be instituted in the United States and, more specifically, in the city in which the creditor is situated. Typically, the creditor who is receiving a guarantee will require that an opinion of counsel of the foreign parent be delivered attesting to the enforceability of such guarantee against the foreign parent. Normally, foreign counsel for the parent will be required to opine with respect to the enforceability of the guarantee in the jurisdiction of incorporation of the parent, and local United States counsel will be required to opine with respect to the enforceability of the guarantee against the foreign parent in the United States. Annex C is a typical form of guarantee used by one of the leading lending institutions in the United States.

COMMENCEMENT OF OPERATIONS

Once a foreign corporation has determined to commence business operations in the United States, it may either begin a new business operation from inception, or acquire an existing United States company and use that company as the base upon which to build.

Among the factors to be considered in starting up a new business organization in the United States are the difficulty involved in acquiring physical premises for the conduct of business, the purchase and acquisition of capital assets, the hiring of management at the executive, middle and lower levels, the establishment of relations with unions and compliance with existing state and federal statutes. Some business operations will most naturally lend themselves to commencement of new business operations if their activities are unique to the United States market. For example, recently a foreign manufacurer of vehicles established a new sales and distribution organization in the United States. In this case, it was not possible for the foreign corporation to acquire an existing operation in the United States since no similar operation existed. Accordingly, it was necessary for the new U.S. corporation to go through each of the steps recited above. Much of the effort of the new United States subsidiary was directed toward establishment of internal organizational mechanics and procedures and diverted management's energies from the sales and marketing aspects of the business to the organizational aspects. For these reasons its is often preferable to acquire existing U.S. operations rather than creating them anew.

With respect to the acquisition of existing U.S. businesses, whether in corporate form or otherwise, the four principal methods are:

(i) A negotiated sales transaction of either stock or assets;

(ii) A tender offer for the shares of a publicly held corporation, where the acquiring company offers to purchase shares directly from the public stockholders;

(iii) Open market purchases of shares of a publicly held corporation with the ultimate aim of obtaining control; and

(iv) A negotiated merger between the acquiring and acquired company.

The subject matter with respect to tender offers, open market purchases and negotiated mergers is extensive and in the eyes of some practitioners, infinite. Accordingly, due to the limited scope of this article, the authors believe it most useful to limit the balance of this discussion to the most typical method of acquisition, which is the negotiated sale transaction between the purchaser and seller and to analyze briefly the basic sale agreement. In this connection, we will look at a transaction involving the acquisition by the foreign parent, through a wholly owned United States subsidiary, of the controlling portion of the issued and outstanding stock of the U.S. corporation from its shareholders. The other method of effecting substantially the same results is to cause a newly formed U.S. subsidiary to acquire all, or substantially all, of the assets of the target company. In an assets transaction, insofar as the outside world is concerned, the business operations of the acquired company remain essentially the same; however, the business is conducted by and through the newly formed U.S. subsidiary.

Annex B is a typical stock acquisition agreement, the basic form of which has been used in several transactions. Although this form of agreement is by no means universal, every stock acquisition agreement will contain the major elements of the provisions which are set forth therein. Obviously, each transaction will have its own tax, legal and business considerations and, therefore, will be specifically tailored to meet the objectives of the parties involved.

A purchase agreement involving the sale of assets rather than the sale of stock will reflect the fact that generally there is a smaller risk of undisclosed carryover liability of the seller to the buyer. In a stock purchase transaction, however, the acquired company will retain all of its liabilities whether or not disclosed to the purchaser. Therefore, if the liabilities of the acquired company are greater than as disclosed to the purchaser, the purchase price will be effectively increased to that extent. Accordingly, a stock purchase agreement will tend to have more extensive indemnity provisions, and may in addition provide for the "holdback" or escrow of a certain portion of the purchase price until such time as undisclosed liabilities are reasonably expected to have surfaced. In an asset transaction the possibility that undisclosed liabilities of the seller will follow the purchased assets is less likely, and accordingly the sale agreement may be less extensive with respect to providing protection for the purchaser against such undisclosed liability. The other major respect in which assets and stock purchase agreements will differ will be with respect to the mechanics of transferring the assets. In a stock transaction the purchaser inherits all of the rights, titles, ownership, duties and obligations of the acquired company, generally without having to effect extensive documentation other than the transfer of shares. In an assets acquisition the transfer of the assets must be effected on an asset by asset basis and, therefore, will require more complex transfer mechanics.

In order to better understand the typical form of purchase agreement the authors believe it would be useful to analyze the form of agreement which was used in a recent acquisition made by a foreign corporation of a United States corporation. The foreign corporation already had a United States subsidiary corporation which in turn was the parent of several second tier operating subsidiaries. The corporation to be acquired ("New Corp.") would be a subsidiary of the foreign parent's first tier U.S. subsidiary. All of the U.S. subsidiaries had filed consolidated tax returns for some time. The foreign parent further expected that its then existing U.S. subsidiaries would generate taxable income for the foreseeable future and that New Corp. would generate operating losses for at least two to three years after its acquisition. Accordingly, it was advisable to bring New Corp. within the consolidated group for tax purposes. Although on a business basis it would

have been sufficient to acquire a 51 percent interest in New Corp., the reader will note that the purchaser acquired 80 percent of the issued and outstanding stock of New Corp. in order to meet the Internal Revenue Code requirements for filing of consolidated tax returns.[68]

One of the foreign parent's objectives in acquiring the business of New Corp. was to have in place existing management immediately after acquisition. Since the selling stockholders of New Corp. also constituted its senior management, a *sine qua non* of the transaction was the retention of the selling stockholders as senior management. This was effected by the execution of long-term employment agreements between New Corp. and the selling stockholders at the closing of the sale. In order to give the remaining management further incentive to perform to the best of their abilities for the new major stockholder, the purchase price for the stock included a provision for bonus payments to be made to senior management if they caused New Corp. to perform above certain levels of profitability. This method of building incentives into the purchase price of the stock rather than into the employment agreements provided certain tax advantages to the sellers. If similar bonus arrangements for services performed appeared in the employment agreements, such bonuses would be taxed to the selling stockholders at ordinary income tax rates. On the other hand, by incorporating the bonus payments as part of the purchase price, it was anticipated that such payments would be subject to the much lower long-term capital gains tax rate.

In connection with the transactions, there were fairly complicated employment agreements for each of the selling stockholders, as well as a shareholders' agreement between the selling stockholders and the first tier U.S. subsidiary of the foreign parent. From the point of view of the purchaser, the employment agreements set forth in specific detail the limitations upon management to act unilaterally without the consultation or approval of the board of directors, which was controlled by the foreign parent. For example, the foreign parent wished to assure that major corporate actions would not occur without the permission of the board. The shareholders' agreement, on the other hand, was the document employed by the selling stockholders to restrict the foreign parent's ability to cause the corporation to take certain actions inimical to their interests as stockholders during the first several years of the relationship.

PURCHASE AGREEMENT STRUCTURE

The purchase agreement, whether it be a stock or an asset agreement, will generally have a structure

---

[68]I.R.C. §§1501, 1504.

similar to the following:

A. Seller's Representations and Warranties

These representations and warranties will set forth the factual premises upon which the purchaser has made his investment decision to purchase either the stock or the assets in question. It is exceedingly important to set forth in the greatest detail possible the specific grounds upon which the buyer has made his investment decision. The truthfulness and accuracy of the seller's representations will provide a basis upon which the purchaser may withdraw from the transaction prior to consummation on the grounds that the buyer's investigation has indicated a breach thereof. The completeness of the seller's representations and warranties may also determine whether or not the buyer will have a later claim against the seller when the business or the assets which were anticipated to be acquired were not as believed to be by the buyer. It is, therefore, extremely important that the attorney for the buyer understands not only the nature of the transaction and the specifics such as the purchase price and the method of payment, but also the basis upon which the buyer made his decision to purchase.

Although the representations and warranties to be made by our seller in the purchase agreement were specifically tailored to the transaction in question, they were representative of those which will generally appear in every type of purchase agreement, whether the transaction is in stock or assets. These representations included the following:[69]

(i) That the seller is duly organized and in good standing in the jurisdictions where it conducts business.

(ii) Absence of provisions in the seller's charter, by-laws, indentures or agreements which would prohibit or otherwise restrict the transaction.[70]

(iii) Identification of the seller's financial statements upon which the purchaser has relied and the seller's statement concerning their truth and accuracy; that there are no liabilities except as disclosed to the purchaser; that since the date of such financial statements there have been no material adverse changes in the business of the acquired company; and that the financial statements do not contain special or non-recurring items except as stated therein.

(iv) That all seller's tax returns have been duly filed and that all taxes have been paid or reserved against.

(v) That the seller has good title to its properties free and clear of liens, claims or encumbrances, except as specifically disclosed. In asset transactions there is likely to be a specific schedule of fixed assets and personal property which is then embodied in a bill of sale.

(vi) A list of patents, trademarks and license agreements, together with the seller's assurances that there are no infringement claims.

(vii) A list of material contracts and a statement that they are in full force and effect.

(viii) Disclosure with respect to employment, consulting, purchase, supply, distribution, franchise, agency, pension, retirement, profit sharing, bonus, stock option, deferred compensation, collective bargaining and lease agreements to the extent demanded by the purchaser.

Strategically, the purchaser will want its counsel to prepare the first draft of the purchase agreement. The purchaser's counsel will then have great latitude in incorporating in the section dealing with seller's representations and warranties, representations which are very broad and the purpose of which is designed to elicit information concerning the seller's business. This technique is often referred to as the "smoke out": that is, the seller, by being presented with very broad, all-encompassing and generalized representations and warranties, will be required to inform the purchaser of modifications which must be made so that the seller will not be in default of those representations and warranties on signing of the agreement. The technique results in the purchaser having "smoked out," through the use of the purchase agreement, information concerning the seller's business that it might not have discovered in the context of a general businessman's review or investigation of the seller's business operations.

B. Purchaser's Representations and Warranties

The purchaser's representations and warranties are typically very limited and restricted to the following areas:

(i) That it is a corporation duly organized and in good standing and with power to enter into the contemplated transaction;

(ii) That it has the right and authority and has obtained all necessary consents and performed all corporate functions necessary to proceed with the transaction; and

---

[69]*See* Annex B, Section 1(a) through (q) inclusive.
[70]Annex B, Section 1(a).

(iii)   That the transaction is not prohibited by the buyer's articles of incorporation or by any other corporate document or agreement with third parties to which the buyer is a party under which the buyer is obligated.[71]

If the purchase price will be represented by some form of deferred payment as opposed to an all-cash transaction, the purchaser may be required to represent as to its financial condition in a manner as extensive as that which is normally required of the seller.[72]

C. Seller's Affirmative and Negative Covenants

The covenants of the seller are divided into two classes, namely, covenants to be observed by the seller prior to the closing,[73] and covenants to be observed by the seller after the closing.[74] Each class of covenant may also be divided into both affirmative covenants which require the seller to perform some act or acts,[75] and negative covenants which will require the seller to refrain from performing a particular act or acts.[76]

The negative covenants which most typically appear in purchase agreements will prohibit the seller from performing certain acts prior to the closing without the consent of the buyer. This is intended to assure that the seller will not take any major action which will result in changing the basic structure of the seller or its method of doing business or operations. Prior to closing, the purchaser will usually try to prohibit the seller from (i) incurring any unusual liabilities; (ii) modifying the compensation of employees; (iii) authorizing or making any unusual capital expenditures; (iv) issuing any capital stock or rights to acquire any capital stock; (v) paying any dividends or making any other distributions to shareholders; (vi) amending its articles of incorporation or by-laws; (vii) agreeing to merge, consolidate or otherwise alter its corporate structure: (viii) mortgaging any of its properties; (ix) waiving any of its rights or claims; and (x) in general, entering into any transaction between the contract execution and the closing which would not be in the ordinary course of business.[77]

The affirmative covenants which sellers are typically required to observe between the contract signing and closing include (i) a general agreement to carry on the business in substantially the same manner as in the past and not to introduce any methods or practices or enter into any agreements which are not in keeping with prior practice; (ii) using their best efforts to maintain the business organization intact and to preserve customer and business relationships; (iii) maintaining their properties in good working order; (iv) keeping their books and records in a manner consistent with prior practice; (v) observing all laws, rules and regulations which they are required to observe; and finally (vi) permitting the purchaser access to all of the corporate books, information and data which will enable the purchaser to verify the representations and warranties made by the seller in the purchase agreement.[78]

The affirmative and negative covenants typically made by sellers and which are of a post-closing nature are generally far less extensive since the relationship between the buyer and the seller will have already been consummated. However, there are general provisions for post-closing covenants which will appear in many agreements. The affirmative post-closing covenants most typically seen will be with respect to cooperating in the future with the buyer for the purpose of executing any further documents or taking any further actions which may be necessary to effectuate or finalize the details of the transfer of the stock or assets. The seller generally agrees that it will provide the purchaser with whatever additional documentation the purchaser reasonably requests.[79] Another post-closing negative covenant is a non-competition clause whereby the seller and/or the shareholders agree not to compete with the purchaser.

D. Transfer and Payment

Here, the provisions are basically straightforward although on occasion they may be somewhat complex because of the need to comply with legal requirements regarding such transfers. The transfer and payment section will set forth the consideration to be paid by the purchaser to the seller and the manner in which such payment is to be effected. In some cases (such as the one reflected in Annex B), the seller will negotiate a base purchase price[80] which is to be paid by the purchaser at the closing and will in addition negotiate a

---

[71]Annex B, Section 3.
[72]Annex B, Section 1(c).
[73]Annex B, Section 2.
[74]Annex B, Sections 14, 22, 25.
[75]Annex B, Section 2(b).
[76]Annex B, Section 2(a).
[77]Annex B, Section 2(a).
[78]Annex B, Section 2(b).
[79]Annex B, Section 14.
[80]Annex B, Section 4(b).

further price to be paid by the purchaser based upon the performance of the business acquired. This is referred to most typically as an "earn-out price."[81] That is, that to the extent that the purchaser realizes sales and/or profits in excess of a base figure recited in the agreement, the purchaser agrees that the seller will, in effect, "earn out" an additional sum of money which will be added to the purchase price. The earn-out formula most typically appears where, as in our case, the sellers are the individuals who form all or part of the management team of the acquired company. In such case, the earn-out price will give such management additional incentive to use its best efforts to maximize the sales and earnings of the acquired company for the benefit of the purchaser since they will share in such results to the extent provided by the earn-out price.

E. Conditions to Closing Which Must Be Met by Seller

The purchase agreement sets forth in very specific detail the conditions which must exist to trigger the purchaser's obligation to complete the transaction.[82] The omnibus condition to closing is that all of the representations and warranties of the seller be true as of the time of the closing to the same extent (except as otherwise contemplated by the agreement) as they were at the time given, and that the seller, or the company to be acquired, has performed all of the covenants that it was required to perform. In most cases, such condition will be tempered by the concept of materiality so that an inconsequential breach of a representation and warranty or failure to observe a covenant will not enable the purchaser to withdraw from the transaction.[83]

In the United States there is great emphasis placed upon obtaining an opinion from the seller's counsel attesting to certain facts or conditions which are within the knowledge of such counsel. Since most purchase agreements will recite that a condition to the purchaser's obligation to close will be the delivery of an opinion of the seller's counsel with respect to specific matters, a great deal of time in the negotiating process of the purchase agreement is spent on the determination of the ultimate form of the seller's opinion of counsel.[84] In most cases, if the opinion is fairly complex its text is substantially set forth in the pur-

chase agreement. Usually; the opinion of counsel is addressed by the seller's counsel to the purchaser and is intended by its recitation to induce the purchaser to rely thereon. Although not normally stated expressly, the intent of the parties is to create liability on the part of seller's counsel to the buyer in the event that the recitations in such opinion prove to be incorrect and to the material detriment of the purchaser. Accordingly, the seller's counsel will seek to limit the matters as to which he will opine to matters which are subject to factual verification by such counsel.

Seller's opinion of counsel will most typically affirm (i) the due incorporation and good standing of seller or the acquired company; (ii) that seller has the power and authority to enter into the sale; (iii) in the case of a stock purchase transaction, that the shares to be transferred are validly issued, fully paid and non-assessable; (iv) that to the knowledge of such counsel the acquired company and the seller will not be in default as a result of the consummation of the transaction; (v) that the purchase agreement is a valid and binding obligation upon the seller and the acquired company; (vi) that the shares (or in the case of an asset transaction, the assets) are owned by the seller and are free and clear of any liens, claims or encumbrances; and (vii) that if the transactions are consummated in the manner contemplated by the agreement, the purchaser will acquire good and valid title to the shares or the assets, as the case may be.[85]

Often a purchaser will insist that a closing condition be the delivery of a "cold comfort letter" by the purchaser's accountants.[86] The cold comfort letter is a communication addressed by the purchaser's accountants to the purchaser indicating that on the basis of the investigation conducted by such accountants of the acquired company's business, books, records and financial statements, nothing has come to their attention which would lead them to conclude that there was a material adverse change in its business, financial condition or prospects from that reflected in the financial statements upon which the purchaser is relying.

Other closicg conditions typically will deal with (i) the mechanical transfer of the property, whether it be stock or assets;[87] (ii) the absence of any material litigation adversely affecting the transaction or the business of the subject company,[88] and (iii) the execution and

---

[81] Annex B, Section 4(c).
[82] Annex B, Section 5.
[83] Annex B, Section 5(a).
[84] Annex B, Section 5(b).
[85] Annex B, Section 5(b).
[86] Annex B, Section 5(c).
[87] Annex B, Section 5(e).
[88] Annex B, Section 5(i).

delivery of ancillary documents.[89] As a result of the Hart-Scott-Rodino Antitrust Improvements Act, it is now necessary to include in many purchase agreements a requirement that the 30-day waiting period shall have passed without any action having been taken by the Federal Trade Commission.[90]

F. Conditions to Be Met by Purchaser

Every stock or asset purchase agreement will contain provisions which set forth the conditions which must exist in order to trigger the seller's obligation to close. In a cash transaction these conditions to closing are simple and generally not significant.[91] However, where the transaction contemplates some deferred payments by the purchaser, the closing conditions to be met by the purchaser may be somewhat more extensive. An opinion of the purchaser's counsel as extensive in nature as the opinion of counsel of the seller may be required.[92] Such conditions often require the purchaser to have executed the very same ancillary documents as required of the seller. In the case of the instant transaction, it is evident that the foreign parent guarantee was an ancillary document important to the sellers.[93]

OTHER IMPORTANT PROVISIONS OF A PURCHASE AGREEMENT

There are other provisions of a purchase agreement which will appear in most transactions.

A. Survival of Representations and Warranties

The purchaser will want to provide specifically that the representations and warranties of the seller will survive the closing.[94] This will provide the legal basis for a claim against the seller in the event that at some time subsequent to the closing it is discovered that the representations and warranties, or the fulfillment of the covenants of the seller, were not proper or correct and/or observed. The seller will attempt to limit the period of time during which the purchaser may make a claim against the seller based upon such breach. In most states, in the absence of any such contractual limitation, the purchaser will be able to bring a claim against the seller for a period of time determined by the applicable statute of limitations. Where there is a deferred payment of the purchase price, the agreement should provide that to the extent there is any such limitation on survival of representations and warranties they will extend out to the date that the last deferred payment is made. Agreements with deferred payment provisions will also generally contain a right of offset by the purchaser against any deferred payments which may become due.[95]

B. The Indemnification Provisions of a Purchase Agreement

Indemnification provisions normally operate in both directions, i.e., for the benefit of purchaser and seller, and contain the general mechanics to be observed in the event that a claim for indemnification is made.[96] Sometimes, the extent of indemnification is limited by the seller to the consideration which it received from the purchaser. In many cases this kind of limitation will make sense. However, where the breach of a representation and warranty by the seller would expose the buyer to liability significantly in excess of the amount of the purchase price because of various statutorily imposed liabiliites, the limitation on indemnity should be viewed more closely by the purchaser. This is especially true in the area of potential liability to third parties based upon statutes such as the Federal securities laws, environmental protection laws, etc.

C. Compliance with Bulk Sales Laws

In the case of an assets transaction only, the purchaser may insulate itself against the claims of the seller's creditors by complying with the bulk sales law of the applicable state. The bulk sales laws generally provide that if the purchaser of assets has given due notice to the seller's creditors that the purchaser will purchase all or substantially all of the assets of the seller, then the creditors will have no right to pursue those assets in the hands of the purchaser.[97] The theory behind the bulk sales laws is that by giving the seller's creditors advance notice that the consideration representing the purchase price will be paid to the seller on a date certain in the future, the creditors will have sufficient time to pursue their legal remedies against such consideration, rather than against the assets to be transferred. Accordingly, compliance with the bulk sales laws is most often effected by first obtaining from the seller a list of all of its creditors, including names,

---

[89]Annex B, Sections 5 (j)-(n).

[90]15 U.S.C. §18a (1976).

[91]Annex B, Section 6.

[92]Annex B, Section 6(b).

[93]Annex B, Section 6(g).

[94]Annex B, Section 13.

[95]Annex B, Section 7.

[96]Annex B, Sections 25 and 26.

[97]*See, e.g.,* U.C.C. §§6-101 to 111 (McKinney 1964 and supp. 1979).

addresses and amounts due. The purchaser then has the obligation of communicating in writing to each of such creditors and informing them of the proposed sale. As the reader can imagine, these notifications are often very disruptive of the business of the seller and may result in some dislocations in the continuity of the business. Accordingly, in many instances the purchaser will waive compliance with the bulk sales law to avoid such public notices. In lieu of compliance with the bulk sales law, the asset purchase agreement will often contain a prospective covenant by the seller to pay all of its debts as they become due. In order to secure that obligation, purchasers very often will make provision for retaining some portion of the purchase price and paying the creditors of the seller directly with the proceeds.

D. Where There Is More Than One Seller

In this case, the purchaser will wish to deal with one party only. Accordingly, purchase agreements which have multiple sellers will make provision for a seller's representative, who will have the power and authority to bind all of the sellers without requiring the purchaser to verify individually that all of such representative's actions are authorized.[98]

E. The Balance of the Purchase Agreement

This will contain what are referred to as "boilerplate clauses." These clauses will deal with the payment of expenses of each party,[99] the absence or presence of brokers who are interested in the transaction,[100] the recitation that the agreement contains the entire agreement between the parties with respect to the transaction,[101] that the transaction may not be modified except in writing,[102] the names and addresses to be used in the event that there are any notifications under the agreement,[103] the jurisdiction whose laws will be applied to any interpretation of the agreement,[104] the issuance of news releases,[105] confidential treatment of the information exchanged in connection with the agreement by each party,[106] and provision for the jurisdiction and venue where actions may be instituted under the agreement.[107]

---

[98]Annex B, Section 10.
[99]Annex B, Section 11.
[100]Annex B, Section 12.
[101]Annex B, Section 15.
[102]Annex B, Section 16.
[103]Annex B, Section 18.
[104]Annex B, Section 19.
[105]Annex B, Section 22.
[106]Annex B, Section 23.
[107]Annex B, Section 24.

ANNEX A

The following charts set forth information on the existence of various corporate characteristics and requirements in each of the fifty states. They are intended to give the reader a general overview of the corporate entity as interpreted by the several jurisdictions. Because state laws in this area are subject to frequent change, the authors caution that the foreign investor should consult counsel as to current requirements before making a decision to transact business in a particular state.

state	perpetual existence unless articles of incorporation specify otherwise	requires an office, which may be principal place of business	books and records may be kept anywhere	list of shareholders must be kept at an instate location	minimum capital requirement of a) $1,000	b) $500 or less	shareholders may act without holding a meeting if the action receives: a) unanimous written consent	b) % required for approval at a meeting	shareholders' meetings shall be held a) at instate office unless bylaws provide for other arrangement	b) at corporation's principal office unless	c) other
Ala.	X	X	□²	X	X		X				X
Alas.	X	X	X²	X²			X		X		
Ariz.	X	X	X	X			X		X		
Ark.	X	X	X	X		X	X		X		
Cal.	no ref.	no ref.	□²					X³			X
Colo.	X	X	X	X			X		X		
Conn.	X	X	X	X	X			X⁴	X		
Del.	X	X	X	□²				X³	X		
D.C.	X	X	X	X	X			X³	X		
Fla.	X	X	X	X				X³			X⁹
Ga.	X	X	X	X	X		X⁵		X		
Haw.	X	X	□²	□²			X		X		
Ida.	X	X	X	X			no ref.		X		
Ill.	X	X	X	X	X		X		X		
Ind.	X	X	X	X	X		X		X		
Iowa	X	X	X	X			X		X		
Kan.	X	no ref.	no ref.	no ref.			X⁶		X		
Ky.	X	X	X	X			X		X		
La.	X	X	X	no ref.			X⁴		X		
Me.	X	X	X	X			X		X		
Md.	X	X	X	no ref.			X				X⁹
Mass.	X	X		X			X				X⁹
Mich.	X	X	X					X⁴	X		
Minn.	X	X		X	X		X		X		
Miss.	□¹	X	X	X	X		X		X		
Mo.	X	X	X	X			X		X		
Mont.	X	X	X	X			X		X		
Neb.	X	X	X	X			X		X		
Nev.	X	X	no ref.	X²				X⁷			X⁹
N.H.	X	□²	□²		X		X				X⁹
N.J.	X	X	X	X			X		X		
N.M.	X	X	X	X			X		X		
N.Y.	X	X	X	X			X		X		
N.C.	X	X	X	X			X		X		
N.D.	X	X	X	X	X		X		X		
Ohio	X					X	X⁶		X		
Okla.	X	X	□²			X	X		X		
Ore.	X	X	X	X			X		X		
Pa.	X	X	X	X				X⁸	X		
R.I.	X	X	X	X			X¹⁰		X		
S.C.	X	X	X	X			X				X⁹
S.D.	X	X	X	X			X		X		
Tenn.	X	X	X				X			X	
Tex.	X	X	X	X	X		X		X		
Utah	X	X	X	X	X		X		X		
Vt.	X	X	X	X			X		X		
Va.	X	X	X	X			X				X⁹
Wash.	X	X	X	X			X			X	
W. Va.	X	X	X	X			X			X	
Wis.	X	X	X	X			X		X		
Wyo.	X	X	no ref.	no ref.			X		X		

1. In Mississippi a 99 year maximum.

2. In Alabama, minutes must be in state; in Alaska, copies must be available in state; in California, books and records of a domestic corporation must be kept in state; in Delaware, the list of stockholders must be available 10 days before meetings; in Hawaii, books and records must be available to directors, one of whom must live in Hawaii; in Nevada, articles and by-laws must be kept in state; in New Hampshire, books and records must be kept in state; in Oklahoma, originals or copies must be kept in registered office.

3. All must receive notice. By-laws can change the percentage required.

4. If articles of incorporation allow, then by percentage specified (more than 50%).

5. Restrictions on merger votes.

6. Unless articles of incorporation otherwise provide.

7. Excepts election of directors.

8. Minimum of 2/3 or whatever by-laws specify, whichever is higher.

9. In Florida, anywhere; in Nevada, South Carolina and Virginia, anywhere the by-laws specify; in Massachusetts and New Hampshire, somewhere in state unless otherwise provided; in Maryland, as provided by the by-laws, in the United States.

state	min. dir: a) 3 or number of shareholders if less than three	b) 3	c) 1	residency requirement for directors other than as provided in bylaws	meetings: a) in or out of state	b) in or out of state, unless articles of inc. or bylaws otherwise provide	act without meeting: a) unanimous written consent	b) % required for approval at a meeting	telephone: a) are permitted	b) unless prohibited by bylaws or articles.
Ala.		X			X		X[1]			
Alas.	X				X				X	
Ariz.			X		X		X[2]		X	
Ark.	X				X			X[3]		
Cal.	X					X			X	
Colo.		X			X		X[2]			X
Conn.	X				X		X[2]			X
Del.			X			X	X[2, 4]			X
D.C.		X				X	X[2]			
Fla.			X		X		X[5]			X
Ga.	X					X	X[2, 5]			
Haw.	X			X[6]	no ref.		X[2]			X
Ida.		X			X		X[2, 5]			X
Ill.	X				X		X[5]			
Ind.			X			X	X[2, 5]			
Iowa			X		X		X			X
Kan.			X			X	X[4]			X
Ky.			X		X		X			X
La.	X				X		X[2]			X
Me.	X					X	X[2, 5]			X
Md.	X					X	X			X
Mass.	X				X		X[5]			X
Mich.			X		X		X[2]			X
Minn.	X				X		X[2]		X	
Miss.		X			X		X			
Mo.	X					X	X[2, 5]			X
Mont.		X			X		X			
Neb.	□[7]				X		X[2]			
Nev.	X					X	X[4]			
N.H.	□[7]			X[8]	X		X[4]			X
N.J.			X			X	X[2, 5]			X
N.M.			X		X		X[5]			X
N.Y.	X					X	X[4]			X[9]
N.C.	X				X		X[10]			X
N.D.		X			X		no ref.			
Ohio	X					X	X[4]			X
Okla.		X				X	X			
Ore.			X		X		X			
Pa.	X				X		X[2]			
R.I.	X				X		X[2]			X[9]
S.C.	X					X	X			
S.D.			X	X[6]	X		X			
Tenn.	X				X		X[5]			X
Tex.			X		X		X[4]			X
Utah		X			X		X[2]			
Vt.	X				X		X			X[9]
Va.	X				X		X[5]			X
Wash.			X		X		X[2]			X
W. Va.			X		X		X[5]			
Wis.			X			X	X			
Wyo.	X				X		X			X

1. In Alabama, consent must come before action is taken.
2. These states allow for written consent of either board or committee meetings.
3. In Arkansas, all must consent that the meeting be waived.
4. Unless restricted by the articles or by-laws.
5. Unless the articles or by-laws otherwise provide.
6. One director must be a resident.
7. No requirement; as fixed by by-laws.
8. One director must be U.S. citizen.
9. Articles or by-laws must provide.
10. Oral consent may be acceptable.

state	powers of indemnification		shareholders' preemptive rights, if any:			penalties for doing business without authority			
	a) broad	b) limited	a) broad	b) limited	c) none, unless provided	a) cannot bring suit, must pay all back fees and penalties, contracts still valid	b) other monetary penalties	c) agent and/or director faces penalties	d) other
Ala.	X		X					X	X¹
Alas.	X			X		X	X		
Ariz.	X				X	X			X²
Ark.	X		X					X	X²
Cal.	X				X				X⁴
Colo.	X		X			X	X	X	
Conn.	X			X		X	X		
Del.	X				X		X	X	
D.C.		X	X			X	X		
Fla.	X				X	X	X		
Ga.	X			X		X			X³
Haw.	X			X			X	X	
Ida.	X		X			X			
Ill.	X		X			X	X		
Ind.	X				X			X	X⁸
Iowa	X			X		X			
Kan.	X				X	X			
Ky.	X			X		X	X		
La.	X				X	X			
Me.	X		X			X	X		
Md.	X			X		X	X	X	
Mass.	X				X	X			
Mich.	X				X	X	X		
Minn.	X		X			X	X		
Miss.		X			X	X			
Mo.	X		X						X⁵
Mont.		X			X	X			
Neb.	X			X		X			
Nev.	X		X					X	X⁶
N.H.		X	no ref.			X			X⁷
N.J.	X				X	X	X		
N.M.		X	X			X	X		
N.Y.	X		X			X			
N.C.		X	X			X	X		
N.D.		X	X			X			
Ohio	X		X			X	X		
Okla.	X				X	X	X	X	
Ore.	X			X		X			
Pa.	X		X			X			
R.I.	X			X		X			
S.C.		X		X		X	X		
S.D.		X	X			X			
Tenn.	X			X		X	X		
Tex.		X		X		X	X		
Utah	X		X			X			
Vt.		X			X	X			
Va.	X			X		X		X	
Wash.	X		X			X			
W. Va.	X		X			X			
Wis.	X			X		X	X		
Wyo.	X		X			X	X		

1. In Alabama contracts made by unauthorized corporation are void.
2. Atty general can sue to enjoin the corporation from doing business.
3. In Arkansas contracts are unenforceable. In Georgia other party can void contract.
4. In California fine is $20/day; $250 penalty before suing, all back fees.
5. Cannot bring suit; $1,000 fine.
6. Cannot sue or defend suit.
7. Refusal to comply is felony.
8. $10,000 fine, cannot sue.

ANNEX B

STOCK PURCHASE AGREEMENT

AGREEMENT, dated _____ , by and among Corporation A, a Delaware corporation (the "Purchaser"), Corporation B, a New York corporation ("B"), Corporation C ("C"), and each of the selling stockholders listed on Exhibit 1 hereto (the "Selling Stockholders").

WHEREAS, the Selling Stockholders collectively will own all the issued and outstanding shares of the common stock of B after giving effect to the redemptions contemplated herein; and

WHEREAS, subject to the express conditions herein set forth and on the other terms herein contained, the Purchaser desires to purchase, and the Selling Stockholders desire to sell, an aggregate of X shares of common stock of B (the "Shares"), which will represent 80 percent of the issued and outstanding shares of the common stock of B after giving effect to the redemptions contemplated herein.

NOW, THEREFORE, in consideration of the mutual covenants herein contained and for other good and valuable consideration, the receipt and sufficiency of which are hereby acknowledged, the parties hereto do hereby agree as follows:

1. *Representations and Warranties of Selling Stockholders and B.*

Except for the representations, warranties and agreements set forth in subsection (n) of this Section 1 which are made by each of the Selling Stockholders and C only for himself, each of the Selling Stockholders, C and B, jointly and severally, represents, warrants and agrees as follows:

(a) B has no subsidiaries other than Corporation D, a Canadian corporation ("D"), Corporation E, a New York corporation ("E"), and Corporation F, a New York corporation ("F"). Such subsidiaries are sometimes collectively hereinafter referred to as the "Subsidiaries." B is a corporation duly organized, validly existing and in good standing under the laws of the State of New York. The ownership or leasing of its properties and the conduct of its business do not require B to qualify to do business as a foreign corporation in any other jurisdiction. Each Subsidiary is a corporation duly organized, validly existing and in good standing under the laws of its jurisdiction of incorporation. Each Subsidiary is duly qualified to do business as a foreign corporation in each other jurisdiction in which the ownership or leasing of its properties or the conduct of its business requires it to so qualify. B has full power and authority (corporate and other) to own its properties and conduct the business in which it is now engaged. B has full right, power and authority to execute and deliver the Agreement and to carry out the transactions contemplated hereby; no consent or other approval of any governmental authority is necessary or required for the execution or performance of this Agreement by B or for its consummation of the transactions contemplated hereby. The Selling Stockholders have furnished the Purchaser with a copy of B's Articles of Incorporation as heretofore amended, certified by the Secretary of State of the State of New York, a copy of its By-Laws, certified by its Secretary, and a copy of a certificate of the Secretary of State of the State of New York, listing all corporate documents on file and evidencing its due organization, valid existence and good standing under the laws of the State of New York. The Selling Stockholders have also furnished the Purchaser with a true and correct copy of the Certificate of Incorporation and By-Laws of each Subsidiary certified by its Secretary.

(b) B is authorized to issue X number of shares of Common Stock without par value. X number of shares of Common Stock have been duly and validly issued, are outstanding and are fully paid and nonassessable. Except for X number of shares of Common Stock owned by Corporation G (the "G Shares"), all of the outstanding shares of Common Stock are owned by the Selling Stockholders and C in the manner set forth in Exhibit 1 hereto, the number of shares owned by each Selling Stockholder being set forth opposite his name in Exhibit 1. B has no authorized, issued or outstanding shares of capital stock other than those specified above, nor any securities convertible into capital stock. No person holds any option to purchase or otherwise to acquire from B any shares of capital stock of B or any securities convertible into such capital stock. Except for 3% of the outstanding capital stock of E owned by H and 10% of the outstanding capital stock of F owned by I, and except as set forth in paragraph (r) of this Section 1 with respect to D, B owns all the issued and outstanding Shares of capital stock of each Subsidiary, no Subsidiary has any authorized, issued or outstanding securities convertible into its capital stock, and no person holds any option to purchase or otherwise acquire from any Subsidiary any shares of capital stock of such Subsidiary or any securities convertible into such capital stock.

(c) Reference is made to a consolidated balance sheet of B and Subsidiaries at _____ (the "Balance Sheet"), and the consolidated statements of income and retained earnings of B and Subsidiaries for the year ended _____, including in each case the related notes, all certified by Company J, certified public accountants, copies of which are attached hereto as Exhibit 2. All of the information supplied to J by B, C and the Selling Stockholders in connection with the aforesaid financial statements is true and correct to the best knowledge and information of the Selling Stockholders and C, and the Selling Stockholders and C have no reason not to believe that such financial statements have been prepared in accordance with generally accepted accounting principles applied on a consistent basis throughout the period covered thereby and present fairly the financial condition of B and Subsidiaries at _____ and the results of their operations for the year then ended. In the foregoing financial statements, (i) all fixed assets are stated at cost less depreciation; (ii) all accounts payable arose in the ordinary course of business; (iii) adequate reserves are set up in accordance with generally accepted accounting principles for depreciation, amortization, contingent liabilities and all taxes; (iv) all material expense accruals have been made; and (v) all of the accounts receivable represented therein arose out of transactions in the ordinary course of business and are collectible in an amount equal to the book value thereof. Neither B nor any Subsidiary has any material indebtedness or liability, contingent or otherwise, not disclosed or adequately reserved for in accordance with generally accepted accounting principles on the Balance Sheet, except current obligations and liabilities incurred in the ordinary course of business since _____. There is no indebtedness owed to B or any Subsidiary by any officer, director or stockholder of B or any Subsidiary, except as set forth on Schedule A hereto.

(d) Except as set forth on Schedule B hereto, since _____, (i) B has not entered into any transactions or incurred any liabilities other than in the ordinary course of its business as theretofore conducted, or issued or sold or purchased any shares of its capital stock, or paid any dividends or made any other distributions on its capital stock to its stockholders, or incurred any indebtedness for borrowed money or any other indebtedness with a maturity of more than one year; (ii) there has not been any material adverse change in the business, financial position, net worth, results of operations or prospects of B; (iii) B has not sustained any material loss or damage to its properties,

whether or not insured; and (iv) none of the Subsidiaries has incurred any material liabilities.

(e) Neither B nor any Subsidiary owns any real property. The leases listed and described in Schedule C hereto, copies of which have been furnished to the Purchaser, constitute all the leases of real property under which B or any Subsidiary is presently bound or to which B or any Subsidiary presently is a party. Each lease so listed is valid, subsisting and enforceable in accordance with its terms, and neither B nor any Subsidiary is in default or in arrears in the performance or satisfaction of any agreement or condition on its part to be performed or satisfied thereunder, nor has B or any Subsidiary received any notice of default thereunder. Neither B nor any Subsidiary owns or uses any buildings, plants, offices, improvements or real estate in connection with its business, except for the real property subject to the leases listed on Schedule C hereto.

(f) B and the Subsidiaries own all of the furniture, fixtures, and other fixed assets and all of the inventories and supplies and all other personal property of every kind, character and description now held by them or used by them in their respective businesses, including, without limitation, all such properties and assets reflected in the Balance Sheet or acquired by B or any Subsidiary since _____, other than such properties and assets as have been disposed of since that date in the ordinary course of business, in each case free and clear of all liens, encumbrances, equities, claims and obligations (including obligations under leases) to other persons of any kind or character, except as may be reflected on the Balance Sheet. All furniture, fixtures, and other fixed assets, including but not limited to leasehold improvements, which are reflected on the Balance Sheet, are well maintained and in good repair and operating condition.

(g) There is set forth in Schedule D hereto a true and complete list of all employment contracts, collective bargaining or other labor agreements, all pension, retirement, stock option, stock purchase, savings, profit-sharing, deferred compensation, retainer, consultant, bonus, group insurance or other incentive or welfare contracts, plans or arrangements, and all trust agreements relating thereto, to which B or any Subsidiary is a party or by which B or any Subsidiary is bound. With respect to each item listed in Schedule D, neither B nor any Subsidiary nor any other person or entity which is a party thereto or bound thereby is in default thereunder, and neither B nor any Subsidiary has given or received a notice of any such default. Copies of each item listed on Schedule D have been furnished to the Purchaser.

(h) There is set forth in Schedule E hereto a true

and complete list of each material agreement or contract to which B or any Subsidiary is a party or by which B or any Subsidiary is bound which involves liability or obligations of B or any Subsidiary in excess of $5,000. With respect to each item listed in Schedule E, neither B nor any Subsidiary nor any other person or entity which is a party thereto or bound thereby is in default thereunder, and neither B nor any Subsidiary has given or received a notice of any such default. Copies of each item listed on Schedule E requested by the Purchaser have been furnished to the Purchaser.

(i) There is set forth in Schedule F hereto a brief description of all litigation or legal proceedings in which B or any Subsidiary (or any of Messrs. W, X, Y or Z, but only if such litigation or legal proceeding would affect his employment with B or his ability to perform his obligations hereunder) is now involved (including, without limitation, any voluntary or involuntary proceedings under any bankruptcy, reorganization or similar statute). Except as set forth in Schedule F hereto, neither B nor any Subsidiary nor any director, officer or stockholder of B or any Subsidiary is in default with respect to any judgment, order, writ, injunction, decree or assessment issued by any governmental agency or department relating to any aspect of the business or affairs or properties of B or any Subsidiary. Except as set forth in Schedule F hereto, neither B nor any Subsidiary nor any director, officer or stockholder of B or any Subsidiary is in violation of, or is charged or, to the best of their knowledge, threatened with any violation of, or under investigation with respect to any violation of, any provision of any federal, state, provincial or local law or administrative rule or regulation relating to any aspect of the business or affairs or properties or assets of B or any Subsidiary which could have a material adverse effect upon the business or affairs or properties or assets of B or any Subsidiary. There are no statutes, rules or regulations which are unique to the operations of currency brokers such as B.

(j) Except as set forth in Schedule G hereto, neither B nor any Subsidiary owns or has any proprietary interest in (or is in any way entitled to) any trademarks, trade names, patents, copyrights, registrations or applications with respect thereto, and licenses or rights under the same. There are no outstanding claims asserted against B or any Subsidiary alleging infringement of any trademark, trade name, patent, copyright or license of anyone else, and the Selling Stockholders do not know of any adversely held trademark, trade name, patent, copyright or license on which such a claim could reasonably be based.

(k) There is set forth in Schedule H hereto a true and complete list of all insurance policies in force and effect in respect of the business, properties and assets of B and the Subsidiaries. Neither B nor any Subsidiary is in default under any such policy and a copy of each such policy requested by the Purchaser has been furnished to the Purchaser.

(l) Neither B nor any Subsidiary is in default in the performance, observance or fulfillment of any of the terms, provisions or conditions of any charter, by-law, contract, indenture, agreement or other instrument or any commitment or obligation to which it is a party or by which it is bound or of any order, writ, injunction, decree or demand of any court or of any federal, state, provincial, municipal or other governmental department, commission, board, bureau, agency or instrumentality, domestic or foreign; and the execution and delivery of this Agreement and the consummation of the transactions contemplated hereby will not result in any conflict with or breach of or default under, or require the consent of any person which is a party to, any agreement, indenture, deed of trust or other instrument, or any order, judgment or decree of any governmental agency or any court, to which B or any Subsidiary is a party or by which B or any Subsidiary is bound.

(m) B and the Subsidiaries have timely filed all federal, state and local tax returns which are required to have been filed for the period ended and all prior periods, and have paid, or made adequate provision on the Balance Sheet for the payment of, all taxes (including, without limitation, income, franchise, excise, sales and property taxes) and any interest or penalities thereon, which have become due for such periods. The Selling Stockholders have delivered to the Purchaser true copies of all such tax returns, which include consolidated federal income tax returns for B, E and F for the year ended _____ and all prior years. All such federal, state and local tax returns have been accurately and completely made and, to the best knowledge of the Selling Stockholders and C, reflect all tax liabilities of B and the Subsidiaries for the respective periods to which they apply. None of such tax returns have been audited by the Internal Revenue Service or any federal, state or local taxing authority. There are no outstanding unsettled or unpaid claims, assessments or deficiencies for any federal, state or local taxes of B or any Subsidiary. Without limiting the generality of the foregoing or of any other provision of this Agreement, the Selling Stockholders, jointly and severally, agree to indemnify and hold the Purchaser and any member of any consolidated group of which Purchaser is a member harmless from any tax deficiency or any increase in taxes of B or any Subsidiary, or of the Purchaser of any consolidated group of which the Purchaser is a member at any time, and any penalties or interest relating thereto, whether or not any Selling Stockholder or B had knowledge thereof, in excess of an aggregate of $_____ attributable to any audit by the Internal Revenue Service or any federal, state or local taxing authority of the federal, state or local tax returns of B or the Subsidiaries (including consolidated returns), or attributable to the failure of B or any Subsidiary to file properly any tax return required to be filed by it, for any period or periods ending on or prior to the Closing Date, even if as a result of a decrease in any carry forward deductions or credits such increase in tax or deficiency is payable for a tax period subsequent to the Closing Date. There are no agreements affecting B or any Subsidiary for the extension of time for the assessment or payment of any federal, state or local tax.

(n) Each of the Selling Stockholders and C has good and valid title to the Shares to be sold by him to the Purchaser hereunder as set forth on Exhibit 1 hereto and to the shares of B's common stock to be redeemed by B from him as also set forth on such Exhibit 1, free and clear of any claims, liens, equities or encumbrances; each Selling Stockholder and C has full right, power, authority and capacity to execute and deliver this Agreement and to carry out the transactions contemplated hereby; no consent or other approval of any governmental authority is necessary or required for the execution or performance of this Agreement by any Selling Stockholder or C, or for the sale by any Selling Stockholder of the Shares to be sold by him to the Purchaser hereunder or for the sale by any Selling Stockholder or C of the Shares of B's to be sold by him to the Purchaser hereunder or for the sale by any Selling Stockholder or C of the shares of B's common stock to be redeemed by B hereunder; and the execution and delivery of this Agreement and the consummation of the transactions contemplated hereby will not result in any conflict with or breach of or default under, or require the consent of any person which is a party to, any agreement, indenture, deed of trust, will or other instrument, or any order, judgment or decree of any governmental agency or any court, to which any Selling Stockholder or C is a party or by which any Selling Stockholder or C is bound. Upon consummation of the transactions in the manner contemplated herein, the Purchaser will acquire good and valid title to the Shares and B will acquire good and valid title to the G Shares and to the shares of B's common stock to be redeemed

from the Selling Stockholders and C hereunder, free and clear of any claims, liens, equities or encumbrances other than as created by the Collateral Security Agreement (as hereinafter defined) with respect to the Shares deposited thereunder.

(o) No representation, warranty, statement or disclosure of B and the Selling Stockholders contained in this Agreement or in the schedules and exhibits attached hereto, and no certificate, document or other instrument prepared by B, the Selling Stockholders or their agents and furnished or to be furnished to the Purchaser by B or the Selling Stockholders pursuant hereto or in connection with the transactions contemplated hereby, contains or will contain any untrue statement of a material fact, or omits or will omit to state a material fact necessary to make the statements contained therein not misleading.

(p) The Selling Stockholders have furnished the Purchaser with true and complete copies of an agreement dated as of _____ and an agreement dated as of _____, both between G ("G"), B and the Selling Stockholders (the "G Agreements") and an agreement dated _____, between X, W and B (the "Senior Stockholders' Agreement").

(q) The representations and warranties of B and the Selling Stockholders herein contained shall be true on and as of the date thereof and, except as otherwise specifically contemplated herein, at all times to and including the Closing Date with the same effect as if made on and as of any such time.

2. *Covenants of B and the Selling Shareholders.* B and each of the Selling Stockholders, jointly and severally, covenant and agree with the Purchaser as follows:

(a) From and after the date of this Agreement until the Closing Date, except as otherwise specifically contemplated herein or agreed to in writing by the Purchaser, neither B nor any Subsidiary shall:

(i) incur or agree to incur any liability or obligation (absolute or contingent) except current liabilities incurred in the ordinary course of business, or prepay, satisfy, or agree to prepay or satisfy any liability or obligation (absolute or contingent) prior to maturity;

(ii) grant or promise to grant to any of its employees (whether hourly paid or salaried employees) any increase in their rates of compensation or any pension, retirement or other employment benefits;

(iii) authorize or make any capital expenditure (other than for ordinary repairs, renewals and replacements);

(iv) issue or sell any shares of its capital stock, acquire directly or indirectly any such shares, or grant any option, warrant or any other right to purchase or to convert any obligation into shares of its capital stock;

(v) declare or pay any dividend on, or make any other distribution in respect of, any shares of its capital stock;

(vi) amend its Articles of Incorporation or By-Laws:

(vii) enter into any contract to merge or consolidate with any other corporation, to acquire all or substantially all of the assets of any other corporation, to sell all or substantially all of its assets to any other corporation, or to cause any Subsidiary to be organized;

(viii) create, incur or suffer to exist any mortgage, lien, charge or encumbrance on, or pledge of, any of its assets, real or personal, tangible or intangible;

(ix) waive any of its rights or claims having value other than in the ordinary course of business; or

(x) enter into any transaction other than in the ordinary course of business.

(b) From and after the date of this Agreement until the Closing Date, except as otherwise specifically contemplated herein or agreed to in writing by the Purchaser, each of B and the Subsidiaries will:

(i) carry on its business in substantially the same manner as heretofore and will not make any purchase or sale, or introduce any method of management or operation in respect of its business or properties, except in a manner consistent with its prior practice;

(ii) use its best efforts to maintain and preserve its business organization intact, to retain its present employees, and to maintain its relationships with its customers and others;

(iii) maintain its properties in customary repair, working order and condition, and maintain in full force and effect insurance comparable in amount and scope of coverage to that now maintained by it;

(iv) maintain its books, accounts and records in the usual manner on a basis consistent with prior years, and comply in all material respects with all laws, ordinances and regulations of governmental authorities applicable to it and to the conduct of its business; and

(v) permit the Purchaser and its authorized representatives (including, without limitation, any attorneys and accountants designated by the Purchaser) to have full access at reasonable times to all its properties, records and documents and furnish to the Purchaser and such representatives such financial and other information with respect to its business and properties as they may from time to time reasonably request.

3. *Representations and Warranties of Purchaser.* The Purchaser represents, warrants and agrees as follows:

(a) The Purchaser is a corporation duly organized, validly existing and in good standing under the laws of the State of Delaware with full corporate power and authority to own its properties and conduct the business in which it is now engaged.

(b) The Purchaser has full right, power and authority to execute and deliver this Agreement and to carry out the transactions contemplated hereby; no consent or other approval of any governmental authority is necessary or required for the execution or performance of this agreement by the Purchaser or for the purchase by the Purchaser of the Shares hereunder; the execution and delivery of this Agreement and the consummation of the transactions contemplated hereby will not result in any conflict with or breach of or default under any agreement, indenture, deed of trust or other instrument, or any order, judgment or decree of any governmental agency or any court, to which the Purchaser is a party or by which the Purchaser is bound.

(c) The Purchaser has delivered to the Selling Stockholders a consolidated balance sheet of Purchaser and its subsidiaries at _____ and the consolidated statements of income and retained earnings of the Purchaser and its subsidiaries for the year ended _____, including in each case the related notes, all certified by J, certified public accountants. All of such financial statements are true and correct, have been prepared in accordance with generally accepted accounting principles applied on a consistent basis throughout the periods covered thereby and present fairly the financial condition of the Purchaser and its subsidiaries at _____ and the results of their operations for the year then ended. The Purchaser covenants and agrees that it will deliver to the Selling Stockholders the audited financial statements of the Purchaser and its Subsidiaries for the fiscal year ended _____ and for each year thereafter until the Earn-Out Price (as hereinafter defined) has been paid in full as soon as such financial statements have been prepared by the Purchaser's certified public accountants.

(d) Since _____, there has been no materially adverse change in the financial position, net worth or results of operations of the Purchaser.

4. *Purchase of Shares.* Subject to the terms and conditions herein set forth and on the basis of the representations, warranties and agreements herein contained:

(a) On the Closing Date, the Selling Stockholders shall sell, assign, transfer and deliver the Shares to the Purchaser, and the Purchaser shall purchase and receive the Shares, at the Base Purchase Price and the Earn-Out Price hereafter set forth. The Purchaser shall pay the Base Purchase Price for the Shares pursuant to subsection (b) of this Section 4, against delivery by the Selling Stockholders to the Purchaser of a certificate or certificates representing the Shares in transferable form and with signatures guaranteed by a bank or trust company satisfactory to the Purchaser.

(b) In consideration of the aforesaid sale, assignment, transfer and delivery, the Purchaser shall, on the Closing Date, pay to the Selling Stockholders the sum of X (the "Base Purchase Price"), which shall be allocated among the Selling Stockholders in accordance with each Selling Stockholder's proportionate share thereof as set forth in Exhibit 1 hereto. The Base Purchase Price shall be paid by delivery to the Selling Stockholders of a certified or official bank check or checks payable in New York Clearing House funds in the aggregate amount of X, plus the delivery to Messrs. N, O, P & Q of a certified or official bank check payable in New York Clearing House Funds in the amount of X (the "Escrow Funds"). The Escrow Funds shall be held by Messrs. N, O, P & Q in escrow as security for the representations and warranties of B and the Selling Stockholders made herein being true on the date hereof and on the Closing Date, all in accordance with an escrow agreement in the form of Exhibit 3 hereto to be entered into on the Closing Date by the Selling Stockholders, the Purchaser, the Agent (as hereinafter defined) and Messrs. N, O, P & Q (the "Escrow Agreement").

(c) The Selling Stockholders and B acknowledge that upon the consummation of the transactions in the manner contemplated herein, the fiscal year of B shall be changed to one ending on December 31 of each year commencing December 31, 19___, and that until full payment of the Earn-Out Price or amounts in lieu thereof B shall be maintained as a separate operating corporation, but this shall not affect B's right to consolidate with Purchaser for tax purposes. As additional contingent purchase price (the "Earn-Out Price") for the Shares, the Purchaser shall also pay the Selling Stockholders to the extent earned:

(i) an amount equal to 30% of the first X of consolidated pre-tax profits of B and 35% of such pre-tax profits in excess of X for B's fiscal year ending December 31, ___, and

(ii) an amount equal to 30% of the first X of consolidated pre-tax profits of B and 35% of such pre-tax profits in excess of X for B's fiscal year ending December 31, ___, and

(iii) an amount equal to 27% of the first X of consolidated pre-tax profits of B and 31.5% of such pre-tax profits in excess of X for B's fiscal year ending December 31, ___.

(d) For the purpose of determining the Earn-Out Price and for the purpose of determining payments in lieu of the Earn-Out Price pursuant to paragraph (f) of this Section 4, the consolidated pre-tax profits of B shall be determined by the then regularly employed independent certified public accountants of B in accordance with generally accepted accounting principles consistently applied and, unless consented to in writing by the Selling Stockholders, in accordance with the following provisions:

(A) B's current depreciation practices, policies and schedules shall be applied;

(B) there shall be no good will amortization resulting from this or any future transaction;

(C) there shall be no change in the treatment of pension and retirement plan costs;

(D) all brokerage transactions between B and the Purchaser or any of its affiliates shall be on arm's length terms agreed to by the Agent (as hereinafter defined) and by an authorized representative of Purchaser;

(E) no charge shall be made to B for general overhead expenses or home office charges of the Purchaser or any of its affiliates; however, charges for specific services performed for B upon the prior agreement of the Agent and an authorized representative of the Purchaser shall be charged to B in the amount agreed; such agreement may be oral but shall be confirmed in writing;

(F) capital gains and losses shall be excluded;

(G) interest on loans from Purchaser or any of its affiliates shall be allowed in amounts not exceeding the interest rate currently paid by Purchaser;

(e) The Earn-Out Price shall be paid by the Purchaser to the Selling Stockholders promptly after each installment thereof has been finally determined by B's then regularly employed independent certified public accountants, but in no event later than April 15, of ___, and ___, respectively. Each installment of the Earn-Out Price, if any, shall be allocated among the Selling Stockholders in accordance with each Selling Stockholder's proportionate share thereof as set forth in Exhibit 1 hereto, and shall be paid by a delivery to the Selling Stockholders of a certified or official bank check or checks payable in New York Clearing House funds.

(f) As collateral security for the payment by the Purchaser of the Earn-Out Price when and as it becomes due and payable, the Purchaser shall deliver to Messrs. N, O, P & Q on the Closing Date certificates representing X shares of Common Stock of B, registered in the Purchaser's name but in form transferable with signatures guaranteed by a bank or trust company satisfactory to the Selling Stockholders. Such certificates shall be held by Messrs. R in accordance with a collateral security agreement in the form of Exhibit 5 hereto to be entered into on the Closing Date by the Purchaser, the Selling Stockholders, the Agent and Messrs. R (the "Collateral Security Agreement").

(g) The sale, assignment, transfer and delivery of the Shares by the Selling Stockholders to the Purchaser and the payment of the Base Purchase Price therefor (the "Closing") shall take place at the offices of R, _____ , New York, New York, or at such other place as the Selling Stockholders and the Purchaser shall agree, at 10:00 a.m., or at such other time as the Selling Stockholders and the Purchaser shall agree, on _____ or such other date not later than _____ as the Selling Stockholders and the Purchaser shall mutually agree (the "Closing Date").

5. *Conditions to Obligation of Purchaser.* The obligation of the Purchaser to purchase the Shares pursuant to Section 4 of this Agreement is subject to the satisfaction on or prior to the Closing Date of the following conditions, but compliance with any of such conditions may be waived by the Purchaser in its discretion:

(a) All representations and warranties of B and the Selling Stockholders contained in this Agreement shall be true and correct on and as of the Closing Date with the same effect as if made on and as of the Closing Date, and B and each of the Selling Stockholders shall have performed all of the covenants and satisfied all of the conditions to be performed or satisfied by them on or prior to the Closing Date.

(b) Messrs. N, O, P & Q, New York, New York, counsel to B and the Selling Stockholders, shall have furnished to the Purchaser their written opinion, addressed to the Purchaser, dated the Closing Date, in form and substance satisfactory to the Purchaser's counsel, to the effect that:

(i) B has been duly incorporated and is validly existing as a corporation in good standing under the laws of the State of New York with full power and authority (corporate and other) to own its properties and conduct the business in which it is now engaged;

(ii) Each subsidiary has been duly incorporated and is validly existing as a corporation in good standing under the laws of its jurisdiction with full power and authority (corporate and other) to own its properties and conduct the business in which it is now engaged;

(iii) Each of B and the Subsidiaries has been duly qualified and is in good standing as a foreign corporation in each other jurisdiction in which B, to the knowledge of such counsel (after having made diligent inquiry), owns or leases properties or conducts business so as to require such qualification;

(iv) The Shares have been duly and validly authorized and issued and are fully paid and nonassessable;

(v) Neither B nor any Subsidiary is, to the knowledge of such counsel, in default in the performance, observance or fulfillment of any of the terms, provisions or conditions of any charter, by-law, contract, indenture, agreement or other instrument or any commitment or obligation to which it is a party or by which it is bound or of any order, writ, injunction, decree or demand of any court or of any federal, state, provincial, municipal or other governmental department, commission, board, bureau, agency or instrumentality, domestic or foreign;

(vi) B and each Selling Stockholder has full right, power, authority and capacity to execute and deliver this Agreement and all other agreements which are exhibits hereto and to which he or it is a signatory and to carry out the transactions contemplated hereby; no consent or other approval of any governmental authority is necessary or required for the execution or performance of this Agreement by B or any Selling Stockholder or for the consummation of the transactions contemplated hereby; this Agreement has been duly and validly executed by B and each Selling Stockholder and constitutes a valid and binding agreement of B and each Selling Stockholder in accordance with its terms subject to any federal or state bankruptcy, insolvency or similar statute affecting the rights of creditors generally; and the execution and delivery of this Agreement has not, and the consummation of the transactions contemplated hereby has not and will not, result in any breach of or default under any agreement, indenture, deed of trust, will or other instrument, or any order, judgment or decree of any governmental agency or any court, known to such counsel, to which B or any Selling Stockholder is a party or by which B or any Selling Stockholder is bound; and

(vii) Upon the consummation of the transactions in the manner contemplated herein, B has acquired good and valid title to the G Shares and to the X shares of B's common stock redeemed from the Selling Stockholders and C, free and clear of any claims, liens, equities or encumbrances.

(viii) Upon the consummation of the transactions in

the manner contemplated herein, the Purchaser will have acquired good and valid title to the Shares, free and clear of any claims, liens, equities or encumbrances other than as created by the Collateral Security Agreement. Such opinion shall also cover such other matters with respect to B, this Agreement and the transactions contemplated hereby as the Purchaser may reasonably specify. Such counsel may rely on opinions of other counsel satisfactory to the Purchaser in jurisdictions where such counsel is not qualified to practice. As to questions of fact material to such opinion, such counsel may rely upon certificates of officers of B and/or of the Selling Stockholders and of public officials.

(c) The Purchaser shall have received a letter of J., addressed to the Purchaser, dated the Closing Date, stating in effect that, on the basis of a limited review of the latest available interim consolidated financial statements of B, consultations with officers of B responsible for financial and accounting matters and other appropriate procedures, they have no reason to believe that during the period from _____ to a date not more than four days prior to the Closing Date there was any change in the capital stock of B (except as specifically contemplated herein) or net losses in excess of X and during the period from _____ to _____ there was no material adverse change in the financial position of B, or any material adverse change in the results of operations of B as compared with the period ended _____. Operating losses, including net losses from trade differences, of less than X incurred during the period from _____ to _____ shall not be deemed to be a material adverse change for the purposes of this paragraph.

(e) All of the Shares shall have been tendered for delivery to the Purchaser against payment therefor pursuant to this Agreement.

(f) The Selling Stockholders shall have furnished or caused to be furnished to the Purchaser certificates satisfactory to the Purchaser to the effect that the representations and warranties of the Selling Stockholders and B contained in this Agreement are true and correct on and as of the Closing Date and that all of the covenants to be performed and the conditions to be satisfied by the Selling Stockholders and B on or prior to the Closing Date have been performed or satisfied by them.

(g) All proceedings and related matters in connection with the organization of B and the authorization, issue, sale and delivery to the Purchaser of the Shares shall be satisfactory to R, counsel to the Purchaser, and R shall have been furnished with such papers and information relating to such matters as they may reasonably request.

(h) The Selling Stockholders shall have delivered with respect to each of B and the Subsidiaries a telegram from the Secretary of State of its jurisdiction of incorporation dated not more than two (2) days prior to the Closing Date to the effect that it is duly organized, validly existing and in good standing.

(i) No private or governmental suit or action shall have been instituted or threatened either to restrain the transaction contemplated by this Agreement or which would have a materially adverse effect upon B or its business, operations or prospects.

(j) B shall have entered into an employment agreement with each of X, W, Z and Y, each substantially in the form of Exhibit 4 hereto.

(k) All officers and directors of B shall have tendered their resignations as of the Closing Date.

(l) The Escrow Agreement and the Collateral Security Agreement shall each have been duly executed and delivered.

(m) A stockholders agreement among B, the Purchaser, X, W, Y and Z substantially in the form of Exhibit 6 hereto (the "Stockholders Agreement") shall have been duly executed and delivered.

(n) The Certificate of Incorporation of B shall have been amended in accordance with paragraph (j) of Section 4 hereof and B shall have issued X shares of its non-voting cumulative redeemable preferred stock to the Purchaser for X per share.

(o) B shall have redeemed the G Shares and an additional X shares of its common stock from the Selling Stockholders and C.

(p) The G Agreements and the Senior Stockholders' Agreements shall have been terminated in writing by the parties thereto and G shall have executed and delivered a general release in favor of B.

(q) The Subsidiaries shall have no outstanding material liabilities, including any liabilities to B.

6. *Conditions to Obligations of Selling Stockholders.* The obligation of the Selling Stockholders to sell the Shares pursuant to Section 4 of this Agreement is subject to the satisfaction on or prior to the Closing Date of the following conditions, but compliance with any of such conditions may be waived by the Selling Stockholders in their discretion:

(a) All representations and warranties of the Purchaser contained in this Agreement shall be true and correct on and as of the Closing Date with the same effect as if made on and as of the Closing Date, and the Purchaser shall have performed all of the covenants and satisfied all of the conditions to be performed or satisfied by it on or prior to the Closing Date.

(b) R, New York, New York, counsel to the

Purchaser, shall have furnished to the Selling Stockholders their written opinion, dated the Closing Date, in form and substance satisfactory to the Selling Stockholders' counsel, to the effect that:

(i) the Purchaser is a corporation duly organized, validly existing and in good standing under the laws of the State of Delaware with full corporate power and authority to own its properties and conduct the business in which it is now engaged;

(ii) the execution and delivery of this Agreement and the consummation of the transactions contemplated hereby have not and will not result in any conflict with or breach of or default under any agreement, indenture, deed of trust or other instrument known to such counsel or any order, judgment or decree of any governmental agency or any court known to such counsel, to which the Purchaser is a party or by which the Purchaser is bound; and

(iii) the Purchaser has full right, power and authority to execute and deliver this Agreement and all other agreements which are exhibits hereto and to which the Purchaser is a signatory and to carry out the transactions contemplated hereby; no consent or other approval of any governmental authority is necessary or required for the execution or performance of this Agreement by the Purchaser or for the consummation of the transactions contemplated hereby; this Agreement has been duly and validly authorized, executed and delivered by the Purchaser and constitutes a valid and binding obligation of the Purchaser in accordance with its terms, subject to any federal or state bankruptcy, insolvency or similar statute affecting the rights of creditors generally. Such opinion shall also cover such other matters with respect to the Purchaser, this Agreement and the transactions contemplated hereby as the Selling Stockholders may reasonably specify. Such counsel may rely on opinions of other counsel satisfactory to the Selling Stockholders in jurisdictions where such counsel is not qualified to practice. As to questions of fact material to such opinion, such counsel may rely upon certificates of officers of the Purchaser and of public officials.

(c) The Purchaser shall have furnished or caused to be furnished to the Selling Stockholders certificates satisfactory to the Selling Stockholders to the effect that the representations and warranties of the Purchaser contained in this Agreement are true and correct on and as of the Closing Date and that all of the covenants to be performed and the conditions to be satisfied by the Purchaser on or prior to the Closing Date have been performed or satisfied by it.

(d) All proceedings and related matters in connection with the organization of the Purchaser shall be satisfactory to N,O,P, & Q, counsel to the Selling Stockholders, and N,O,P, & Q shall have been furnished with such papers and information relating to such matters as they may reasonably request.

(e) No private or governmental suit or action shall have been instituted or threatened to restrain the transactions contemplated by this Agreement.

(f) B shall have entered into an employment agreement with each of X, W, Z and Y, each substantially in the form of Exhibit 4 hereto.

(g) Purchaser shall have delivered a limited guaranty of such employment agreements substantially in the form of Exhibit 7 hereto, executed by Corporation S and Corporation T and an opinion of British counsel in form and substance reasonably satisfactory to counsel for the Selling Stockholders, to the effect that such guarantors are validly existing and that such guaranty has been duly authorized and executed by such guarantors and is valid and binding on them.

(h) The Escrow Agreement and the Security Agreement shall each have been duly executed and delivered.

(i) The Stockholders' Agreement shall have been duly executed and delivered.

(j) The Certificate of Incorporation of B shall have been amended in accordance with paragraph (j) of Section 4 hereof and B shall have issued X shares of its non-voting X cumulative redeemable preferred stock to the Purchaser for X per share.

7. *Offset Against Earn-Out Price.*

(a) Any other provision of this Agreement to the contrary notwithstanding, any liability, loss, damage or expense of any kind or nature sustained by B or the Purchaser arising out of or resulting from the breach or falsity of any representation, warranty or covenant contained in this Agreement made by B or the Selling Stockholders on and as of the date of this Agreement or the Closing Date may, at Purchaser's option, be offset against the Earn-Out Price or any payment in lieu thereof.

(b) In the event that any such liability, loss, damage or expense of any kind or nature is claimed by Purchaser to have been sustained by B or the Purchaser as set forth in subsection (a) of this Section 7, notice thereof (including the claimed amount thereof) shall be given by Purchaser in writing to the Selling Stockholders. If within thirty (30) days of such notice the Selling Stockholders and the Purchaser cannot agree as to the amount of such claim by the Purchaser, either the Selling Stockholders or the Purchaser may cause the dispute to be submitted to arbitration before a board of three arbitrators in accordance with the rules then obtaining of the American Arbitration Association, and such arbitration shall be conducted in accordance with such rules. Each arbitration pursuant hereto shall be conducted in the City of New York. The amount payable for the services of the arbitrators, and all of the costs relating thereto (excluding fees and expenses of counsel to any party) shall be paid by any one or more of the parties to the arbitration in such proportions as the arbitrators may determine. The determination of the arbitrators shall be final and binding upon the parties and a judgment upon the determination of the arbitrators may be entered in any court having jurisdiction thereof.

(c) If the Purchaser claims that it or B has sustained any liability, loss, damage or expense as set forth in subsection (a) of this Section 7 or that it or B has received notice of any claim of any such liability, loss, damage or expense, and if Purchaser serves a notice thereof on the Selling Stockholders, and if the amount of such claim has not been finally determined (either by agreement or by arbitration) at the time when payment of any portion of the Earn-Out Price, or any payment in lieu thereof, becomes due and payable, then such portion of the Earn-Out Price, or the payment in lieu thereof, up to an amount equal to the amount of such loss, liability, damage or expense as claimed by Purchaser in such notice shall be paid in escrow to Messrs. N, O, P & Q until the amount of such claim has been finally determined (either by agreement or by arbitration). When the amount of such claim has been finally determined (either by agreement or by arbitration), Messrs. N, O, P & Q shall pay such finally determined amount, if any, plus any interest actually earned thereon to the Purchaser and shall pay the remainder of the amount held in escrow under this subsection plus any interest actually earned thereon to the Selling Stockholders.

(d) The rights and remedies contained in this Section 7 shall be in addition to other rights and remedies contained in this Agreement or permitted by law.

8. *Payment of Indebtedness of Certain Selling Stockholders to B*. The indebtedness to B set forth on Schedule B hereto shall be paid by the respective debtors thereof on or before December 31, ___. If such indebtedness has not been paid in full by such date, the Purchaser may defer paying to such debtor that portion of the Earn-Out Price, or any payment in lieu thereof, payable and allocable to such debtor equal in amount to the then unpaid amount of such indebtedness owed by such debtor to B.

9. *Binding Effect*. In the event of the incapacity or death of any individual who is a party to this Agreement, this Agreement shall be binding upon and inure

to the benefit of his or her guardian, executor or administrator, as the case may be, and said guardian, executor or administrator may exercise all of the rights and powers, and shall perform all of the obligations, of such individual hereunder as fully as if said guardian, executor or administrator were an original party hereto.

10. *Selling Stockholders' Agent*. (a) Each of the Selling Stockholders hereby irrevocably designates and appoints X (herein, in such capacity, called the "Agent") as his agent and attorney-in-fact for all purposes of this Agreement, with full right, power and authority to modify, amend or otherwise change this Agreement, or any of its terms or provisions, to give and receive consents, notices, certificates and receipts hereunder, and to perform any other act arising under or pertaining to this Agreement which such Selling Stockholder himself could do.

(b) Any claim by the Purchaser against the Selling Stockholders, or any of them, in respect of this Agreement may be asserted against, and settled with, the Agent.

(c) Any and all sums at any time owed hereunder by the Purchaser to any of the Selling Stockholders may, at the Purchaser's option, be paid to the Agent; and any such payment to the Agent shall be deemed to be the equivalent of a payment made directly to such Selling Stockholders, as their interests may appear, and the Purchaser and anyone acting on its behalf shall be under no obligation whatever to look to the application by the Agent of any such payments, and shall be released and discharged from any further obligation whatever to such Selling Stockholders or any of them in respect of any such payment, and shall be under no liability whatever to any such Selling Stockholder by reason of any disposition which the Agent may make of any such payment.

(d) In the event of the death or incapacity of X, then W, (or in the event of the death or incapacity of both X and W, then Messrs. N, O, P and Q) each hereby irrevocably agrees to be substituted to serve in his place as the Agent, with the same rights, powers and authority as hereinabove specified.

(e) The provisions of this Section 10 shall also apply to the Escrow Agreement and all powers conferred on the Agent herein with respect to this Agreement are hereby conferred on the Agent with respect to the Escrow Agreement. Without limiting the generality of the foregoing, the Agent is hereby authorized and empowered to execute the Escrow Agreement on behalf of each Selling Stockholder.

(f) Each Selling Stockholder represents and warrants that he is not entitled to immunity from judicial proceedings and agrees that, should the Purchaser or B bring any judicial proceedings in any jurisdiction to enforce any obligation or liability of such Selling Stockholder under this Agreement no immunity from such proceedings will be claimed by or on behalf of such Selling Stockholder or with respect to his property. Each Selling Stockholder agrees that any suit, action or proceedings (including arbitration) arising out of or relating to this Agreement may be instituted in any state or Federal court (or in the case of arbitration in accordance with the rules of the American Arbitration Association) in the County, City and State of New York, irrevocably waives to the fullest extent permitted by law any objection which he may have now or hereafter to the laying of the venue of any such suit, action or proceedings and any claim that any such suit, action or proceedings has been brought to an inconvenient forum, and irrevocably (i) acknowledges the competence of any such court (ii) to the fullest extent permitted by law, submits to the jurisdiction of any such court in any such suit, action or proceedings and (iii) agrees to be bound by and meet its obligations under any judgment rendered thereby.

(g) Each Selling Stockholder hereby designates and appoints Messrs N, O, P and Q, at its offices in the County, City and State of New York, as its authorized agent to accept and acknowledge on its behalf service of any and all process which may be served in any suit, action or proceedings of the nature referred to in paragraph (e) of this Section 10 in any state or Federal court in the County, City and State of New York and agrees that (i) service of process upon said Messrs. N, O, P and Q at its offices at New York, New York, and, if permitted by law, written notice of said service to such Selling Stockholder, mailed to such Selling Stockholder at its address set forth in Section 18 hereof, shall, to the fullest extent permitted by law, be deemed in every respect effective service of process upon such Selling Stockholder in any such suit, action or proceedings in the County, City and State of New York and shall be taken and held to be valid personal service upon such Selling Stockholder, whether or not such Selling Stockholder shall then be present, residing or doing business, or at any time shall have been present, resided or done business, within the County, City and State of New York and (ii) any such service of process shall be of the same force and validity as if service were made upon it according to the law governing the validity and requirements of such service in the State of New York. Each Selling Stockholder irrevocably waives all claim of error by reason of any such service.

(h) Each Selling Stockholder represents and warrants that said Messrs. N, O, P and Q have agreed in writing to accept such appointment. Said designation and appointment shall be irrevocable until the appointment by the Selling Stockholders of another agent satisfactory to the Purchaser and B and the acceptance by such successor agent of such appointment.

(i) Nothing in this Section 10 shall affect the right of the Purchaser or B to serve process in any other manner permitted by law or limit the right of the Purchaser or B to bring proceedings against any Selling Stockholder in the courts of any other jurisdiction or jurisdictions.

11. *Expenses.* Each party shall pay its own expenses incident to the preparation and carrying out of this Agreement, including all fees and expenses of its counsel and accountants for all activities of such counsel and accountants undertaken pursuant to this Agreement whether or not the transactions contemplated hereby are consummated. The Selling Stockholders shall pay the expenses of the Agent, and all expenses and taxes (including transfer taxes) incident to the sale and delivery of the Shares to the Purchaser.

12. *Brokers.* (a) The Purchaser agrees to indemnify and hold harmless each of the Selling Stockholders against any claims asserted against any of the Selling Stockholders for brokerage or finder's commissions or compensation in respect of the transactions contemplated by this Agreement by any firm or person purporting to act as broker or finder for the Purchaser.

(b) Each of the Selling Stockholders jointly and severally agrees to indemnify and hold harmless the Purchaser against any claims asserted against the Purchaser for brokerage or finder's commissions or compensation in respect of the transactions contemplated by this Agreement by any firm or person purporting to act in the capacity of broker or finder for any of the Selling Stockholders.

13. *Survival of Representations and Warranties.* No information furnished to, or investigation made by, the Purchaser or any of its employees, attorneys, accountants or other representatives in connection with the subject matter of this Agreement shall affect any representation, warranty or agreement of any of the Selling Stockholders herein contained, which shall survive the sale, assignment, transfer and delivery of the Shares hereunder.

14. *Further Assurances.* Each of the parties hereto agrees to execute all such further instruments and documents and to take all such further action as the other parties may reasonably require in order to effectuate the terms and purposes of this Agreement.

15. *Entire Agreement*. This Agreement, together with schedules and exhibits hereto, sometimes referred to herein collectively as "the Agreement", and the documents referred to herein and therein, and other writings signed by the parties hereto of even date herewith, supersede all prior agreements and understandings and constitute the entire agreement between the Selling Stockholders and the Purchaser with respect to the subject matter hereof and the transactions contemplated hereby and neither the Selling Stockholders nor the Purchaser has relied upon any representation or warranty by or on behalf of the other party except as so specifically set forth.

16. *Modification of Agreement*. This Agreement may not be changed or modified except by an agreement in writing signed by the party to be charged thereby or by any person authorized to act on its behalf.

17. *Waivers*. The waiver by either party hereto of any breach of any provision of this Agreement shall not constitute or operate as a waiver of any other breach of such provision or of any other provision hereof, nor shall any failure to enforce any provision hereof operate as a waiver of such provision or of any other provision hereof.

18. *Notices*. Any notice or other communications permitted or required under this Agreement shall be sufficiently given if sent by registered mail, postage prepaid, or by telegram, addressed as follows:

To Purchaser:
c/o Corporation U

Attention:
with copy to:
R

Attention:
To any Selling Stockholder: to the address set forth in Exhibit 1 hereto
with copy to:
NOPQ

Attention:
To B:
B

Attention:
and Corporation U

Attention:

with copies to:
N, O, P and Q

Attention: _____
and
R

Attention:

or to such other person or persons and/or at such other address or addresses as shall be furnished in writing by any party hereto to the other. Any such notice or communications required or permitted herein shall be deemed to have been given as of the date so mailed or telegraphed, as evidenced by the postmark on the envelope or the official notation of time and date on a telegram. Any notice delivered otherwise than as provided above shall be deemed given only at the time actually received by the person to whom it is addressed.

19. *Governing Law*. This Agreement is made pursuant to and shall be construed in accordance with the laws of the State of New York, irrespective of any forum in which an action may be brought to enforce or secure an interpretation of this Agreement and irrespective of the principal place of business, residence or domicile of the parties hereto.

20. *Section Headings*. The section and subsection headings contained herein are for reference purposes only and shall not in any way affect the meaning and interpretation of this Agreement.

21. *Counterparts*. For the convenience of the parties, this Agreement may be executed in one or more counterparts, each of which shall be deemed an original but all of which together shall constitute one and the same document.

22. *News Releases*. Any news releases, public announcements or publicity proposed to be released by any party hereto concerning this Agreement, shall be subject to review by and the written approval of the other parties hereto prior to release.

23. *Confidential Treatment*. If this Agreement is terminated or if the Closing does not occur, the Purchaser will deliver to the Selling Stockholders all originals and copies of documents, work papers and other material obtained from the Selling Stockholders relating to B and the transactions contemplated hereby, whether so obtained before or after the execution hereof, and will promptly destroy all documents based on material obtained from the Selling Stockholders and will use its best efforts to have all information so obtained kept confidential.

24. *Jurisdiction and Service of Process Upon the Purchaser*. (a) The Purchaser represents and warrants that it is not entitled to immunity from judicial proceedings and agrees that, should any Selling Stockholder or B bring any judicial proceedings in any jurisdiction to enforce any obligation or liability of the Purchaser under this Agreement no immunity from such proceed-

ings will be claimed by or on behalf of the Purchaser or with respect to its property. The Purchaser agrees that any suit, action or proceedings (including arbitration) arising out of or relating to this Agreement may be instituted in any state or Federal court (or in the case of arbitration in accordance with the rules of the American Arbitration Association) in the County, City and State of New York, irrevocably waives to the fullest extent permitted by law any objection which it may have now or hereafter to the laying of the venue of any such suit, action or proceedings and any claim that any such suit, action or proceedings has been brought to an inconvenient forum, and irrevocably (i) acknowledges the competence of any such court (ii) to the fullest extent permitted by law, submits to the jurisdiction of any such court in any such suit, action or proceedings and (iii) agrees to be bound by and meet its obligations under any judgment rendered thereby.

(b) The Purchaser hereby designates and appoints Messrs. R, at its offices in the County, City and State of New York, as its authorized agent to accept and acknowledge on its behalf service of any and all process which may be served in any suit, action or proceedings of the nature referred to in paragraph (a) of this Section 24 in any state or Federal court in the County, City and State of New York and agrees that (i) service of process upon said Messrs. R at its offices at _____, New York, New York, and, if permitted by law, written notice of said service to the Purchaser, mailed to the Purchaser at its address set forth in Section 18 hereof, shall, to the fullest extent permitted by law, be deemed in every respect effective service of process upon the Purchaser in any such suit, action or proceedings in the County, City and State of New York and shall be taken and held to be valid personal service upon the Purchaser, whether or not the Purchaser shall then be doing, or at any time shall have done, business within the County, City and State of New York and (ii) any such service of process shall be of the same force and validity as if service were made upon it according to the law governing the validity and requirements of such service in the State of New York. The Purchaser irrevocably waives all claim of error by reason of any such service.

(c) The Purchaser represents and warrants that said Messrs. R have agreed in writing to accept such appointment. Said designation and appointment shall be irrevocable until the earlier of (x) 60 days after the Earn-Out Price or any payments in lieu thereof shall have been paid in full and (y) the appointment by the Purchaser of another agent reasonably satisfactory to the Selling Stockholders and B, and the acceptance by such successor agent of such appointment.

(d) Nothing in this Section 24 shall affect the right of any Selling Stockholder or B to serve process in any other manner permitted by law or limit the right of any Selling Stockholder or B to bring proceedings against the Purchaser in the courts of any other jurisdiction or jurisdictions.

25. *Indemnification by the Selling Stockholders.*

(a) The Selling Stockholders agree to indemnify and hold the Purchaser and B harmless from and against any and all claims, demands, causes of actions, suits, proceedings, judgments, decrees and liabilities, losses, damages and costs, including but not limited to all legal fees and expenses of any kind whatsoever, incurred by the Purchaser or B in defense thereof, which may be asserted against the Purchaser or B, caused by, arising out of or resulting from a breach of any of the representations, warranties, undertakings, covenants or agreements of the Selling Stockholders set forth in this Agreement or in any schedule, exhibit, instrument or document delivered to the Purchaser pursuant hereto. The Selling Stockholders shall not be liable for any damages under this Section 18 unless the Purchaser or B, as the case may be, shall have given the Selling Stockholders written notice of any alleged breach within sixty (60) days after the Purchaser or B, as the case may be, actually learns of the occurrence of any such breach and shall have afforded the Selling Stockholders a period of thirty (30) days after the receipt of such notice to remedy such alleged breach.

(b) If any action or proceeding is brought against the Purchaser or B under circumstances which indicate that the Selling Stockholders may be required to indemnify the Purchaser or B, as the case may be, pursuant to subsection (a) above, the Selling Stockholders shall be entitled to participate therein, and to assume the defense thereof with counsel reasonably satisfactory to the Purchaser or B, as the case may be, and after notice from the Selling Stockholders to the Purchaser or B, as the case may be, of the Selling Stockholders' election to so assume such defense (and in the event of such assumption), the Selling Stockholders shall not be liable to the Purchaser or B, as the case may be, under subsection (a) above for any legal or other expenses subsequently incurred by the Purchaser or B, as the case may be, in connection with the defense of such action or proceeding, but shall continue to be liable to the Purchaser and B as otherwise provided in subsection (a) above.

26. *Indemnification by the Purchaser.*

(a) The Purchaser agrees to indemnify and hold the Selling Stockholders harmless from and against any and all claims, demands, causes of action, suits, proceedings, judgments, decrees and liabilities, losses, damages and costs, including but not limited to any legal fees and expenses of any kind whatsoever, incurred by the Selling Stockholders in defense thereof, which may be asserted against the Selling Stockholders, caused by, arising out of or resulting from a breach of any of the representations, warranties, undertakings, covenants or agreements of the Purchaser set forth in this Agreement or in any instrument or document delivered to the Selling Stockholders pursuant hereto. The Purchaser shall not be liable for any damages under this Section 26 unless the Selling Stockholder shall have given to the Purchaser written notice of any alleged breach within sixty (60) days after the Selling Stockholders actually learn of the occurrence of any such breach and shall have afforded to the Purchaser a period of thirty (30) days after the receipt of such notice to remedy such alleged breach.

(b) If any action or proceeding is brought against the Selling Stockholders under circumstances which indicate that the Purchaser may be required to indemnify the Selling Stockholders pursuant to subsection (a) above, the Purchaser shall be entitled to participate therein and to assume the defense thereof with counsel reasonably satisfactory to the Selling Stockholders, and after notice from the Purchaser to the Selling Stockholders of its election to so assume such defense (and in the event of such assumption), the Purchaser shall not be liable to the Selling Stockholders under subsection (a) above for any legal or other expenses subsequently incurred by the Selling Stockholders in connection with the defense of such action or proceeding, but shall continue to be liable to the Selling Stockholders as otherwise provided in subsection (a) above.

IN WITNESS WHEREOF, the parties have executed this Agreement as of the date first above written.

[SIGNATURES]

ANNEX C

THE FOREIGN CORPORATION ADDRESS IN A FOREIGN NATION

December —, 19—

The United States Corporation
New York Address
New York, New York
U.S.A.

GUARANTY AGREEMENT

Dear Sirs:

The Foreign Corporation, a foreign corporation (the "Guarantor"), hereby agrees with the United States Corp., a Delaware corporation ("the Lender"), as follows:

1. The foreign corp.'s subsidiary (the "Borrower") and the Lender have entered into an agreement dated the date hereof (the "Loan Agreement") providing for the borrowing by the Borrower from the Lender of $0,000,000. Such borrowing is to be evidenced by a promissory note of the Borrower substantially in the form of Exhibit A to the Loan Agreement as such form may be modified by the Borrower with the consent of the Lender (the "Note"). The Note will be subject to acceleration and prepayment as provided in the Loan Agreement. In connection with the Borrowing, the Borrower is delivering to the Lender a letter of credit issued by the New York Branch (the "New York Branch") of the foreign corp.'s Foreign Bank ("Foreign Bank"), substantially in the form of Exhibit C to the Loan Agreement as such form may be modified with the consent of the Lender (the "Letter of Credit"). Payment by the New York Branch when due under the Letter of Credit is guaranteed by Foreign Bank in the Guaranty Agreement of even date herewith between Foreign Bank and the Lender (the "bank-Guaranty"). The Guarantor acknowledges receipt of a copy of the form of each of the foregoing documents, acknowledges due execution and delivery of the Loan Agreement and the Note, and waives any notice of borrowing under the Loan Agreement, any notice of claim, payment or any other action at any time under the Loan Agreement, the Note, the Letter of Credit or the bank Guaranty and the acceptance of this Guaranty Agreement or the bank Guaranty.

2. The Guarantor represents and warrants that:

2.1. The Guarantor is a corporation duly organized, validly existing and in good standing under the laws of foreign nation and has all necessary power and authority (corporate and other) to execute, deliver and perform this Agreement.

2.2 This Guaranty has been duly authorized, executed and delivered by the Guarantor and constitutes a legal, valid and binding agreement of the Guarantor in accordance with its terms, except as may be limited by bankruptcy, insolvency or other similar laws generally affecting the rights of creditors.

2.3 The execution, delivery and performance of this Guaranty Agreement do not and will not contravene any law, rule, regulation, judgment, order or injunction applicable to the Guarantor or the *statuten* of the Guarantor, and does not and will not contravene or constitute a default under any indenture, agreement or instrument binding upon the Guarantor.

2.4 No authorization, consent, approval or license of, or declaration, filing or registration with any governmental body, authority or agency is required in connection with the execution, delivery or performance by the Guarantor of its obligations hereunder other than the authorization represented by Foreign Exchange License No. _____ issued by Foreign National Bank, which authorization (a true and complete copy of which has been delivered to the Lender) has been duly obtained, has not been amended, supplemented or rescinded and is in full force and effect on the date hereof.

2.5 There are no actions, suits or proceedings pending or, to the knowledge of the Guarantor, threatened, against or affecting the Guarantor in any court or before any governmental department, agency or instrumentality, an adverse decision in which (i) might materially affect the ability of the Guarantor to perform its obligations hereunder or under this Guaranty Agreement, or (ii) would materially adversely affect the business or condition, financial or otherwise, of the Guarantor.

2.6 In connection with the transactions contemplated by the Loan Agreement, the Guarantor has delivered or caused to be delivered to the Lender: (i) the Consolidated Balance Sheet and

Balance Sheet dated January, 19__ and 19__ of the Guarantor included in the offering memorandum referred to in Section __ of the Loan Agreement, and the related Consolidated Profit and Loss Account, and Source and Application of Funds for the years then ended (including in each case the notes thereto), which financial statements have been examined and certified by Foreign firm, Accountants and (ii) the unaudited consolidated balance sheet dated June __, 19__ and the related unaudited consolidated profit and loss account and source and application of funds for the six-month period then ended. Such financial statements present fairly the financial position of Guarantor as of the respective dates of such balance sheets and its results of operations and sources and applications of funds for the respective periods then ended in conformity with generally accepted accounting principles in foreign nation applied on a consistent basis, and include in the case of unaudited interim statements all adjustments necessary to a fair statement of the information contained therein subject only to year-end adjustments which will not be material. Since June __, 19__, there has not been any change in the business, assets, financial position or results of operations of Guarantor and its subsidiaries, considered as a whole, from that set forth in the offering memorandum (including exhibits thereto) referred to in Section __ of the Loan Agreement, except for changes in the ordinary course of business which have not, either individually or in the aggregate, been materially adverse.

3. The Guarantor covenants and agrees that:

3.1 It will maintain its corporate existence, rights and franchises in full force and effect.

3.2 The Guarantor will not consolidate or merge with or into any other corporation or sell, transfer, lease, or otherwise dispose of all or substantially all of its properties and assets (in a single transaction or a series of related transactions), unless (i) the survivor corporation of any such consolidation or merger, or the corporation to whom such sale, transfer, lease or other disposition shall have been made, immediately prior and after giving effect thereto shall be a corporation enjoying company status substantially similar to that enjoyed by the Guarantor and organized under the laws of the foreign nation) or any other jurisdiction approved in writing by the Lender or any holder of the Note) and shall immediately upon such consolidation, merger, sale, transfer, lease or other disposition, expressly assume in a writing satisfactory to the Lender or any holder of the Note all

of the obligations and agreements of the Guarantor under this Agreement and (ii) after giving effect to such consolidation, merger, sale, transfer, lease or other disposition, there shall not exist any Event of Default under the Loan Agreement or condition or event which, with notice or lapse of time or both would constitute such an Event of Default. In case of any consolidation, merger, sale, transfer, lease or other disposition, the successor corporation resulting therefrom or, as the case may be, the corporation to which such sale, transfer, lease or other disposition shall have been made, shall, for all purposes of this Agreement be deemed to be the Guarantor.

3.3 It will at all times own, directly or indirectly through a Subsidiary, all of the capital stock of the Borrower, free and clear of any lien, pledge, claim, option, security interest or other encumbrance. For the purposes of this Section 3.3, the term "Subsidiary" shall mean a wholly owned subsidiary (incorporated in the foreign nation or the United States of America or any State thereof) of the Guarantor or any other Subsidiary.

3.4 It will not at any time permit or suffer to exist any mortgage, pledge, security interest or encumbrance of any kind on all or substantially all of the properties and assets of the Guarantor without making effective provision, and the Guarantor will make or cause to be made effective provision, whereby all of the Guarantor's obligations under this Agreement will be secured equally and ratably with (or prior to) all debt then outstanding incurred, assumed or guaranteed by, and any debt thereafter incurred, assumed or guaranteed by the Guarantor which is secured, directly or indirectly, by any mortgage, pledge, security interest, or other encumbrance.

3.5 It will deliver to the Lender or any subsequent holder of the Note, (a) promptly as the same become available, all annual, semi-annual and quarterly reports and other reports, documents and notices furnished by the Guarantor to the holders of any of its securities or publicly available reports, documents and notices filed by the Guarantor with any stock exchange or any governmental board, agency or authority; and (b) with reasonable promptness, such further information with respect to the Guarantor as the Lender may from time to time reasonably request.

3.6 For the purpose of permitting the Lender to

evaluate the financial condition of the Guarantor and its compliance with the terms of this Agreement, the Guarantor will permit the Lender or its duly authorized representatives to visit and discuss its affairs, finances and accounts with the officers of the Guarantor, at such reasonable times and as often as may be reasonably requested.

3.7 It will take all action necessary to be taken by it to maintain the Foreign Exchange License of the Foreign National Bank referred to in Section 2.4 hereof in full force and effect.

3.8 If at any time the Guarantor obtains knowledge of (i) any Event of Default (as defined in the Loan Agreement) or condition or event which, with notice or lapse of time or both, would constitute such an Event of Default or (ii) any event or conditon specified in Section __ (a), (d) or (e) of the Loan Agreement, there shall be delivered forthwith to the Lender a certificate of an officer on behalf of the Guarantor specifying the nature and period of existence thereof.

3.9 All amounts guaranteed under this Guaranty Agreement will rank equally and ratably, without priority by reason of date of issue, currency or payment or otherwise, with all other unsecured and unsubordinated indebtedness for borrowed money for which the Guarantor is directly, potentially, contingently or otherwise liable.

4. For value received, the Guarantor, as primary obligor and not as surety merely, herby absolutely and unconditionally guarantees the due and punctual payment in United States dollars of all amounts due from the Borrower under the Note and the Loan Agreement and the due and punctual payment of the principal of, and premium, if any, and interest on the Note, including all fees, expenses and indemnities, at the time and place and otherwise in accordance with the terms thereof, irrespective of the validity, binding effect or enforceability of, or any change in or amendment to, the Note, the Loan Agreement, the Letter of Credit, the bank Guaranty or any other instrument, any attempt or the absence of any attempt to collect from the Borrower, the New York Branch or Foreign Bank or any other action or the absence thereof to enforce the Loan Agreement, the Note, the Letter of Credit, the bank Guaranty or any other instrument, any action or failure to act prior thereto or concurrently therewith by the Lender or any other person or party in respect of the Loan Agreement, the Note, the Letter of Credit or the Guaranty or any other instrument, or whether the Note or the Loan Agreement shall have been duly executed by the Borrower or the Letter of Credit shall have been duly executed by the New York Branch or the bank Guaranty shall have been duly executed by Foreign Bank, or any other circumstance which might otherwise constitute a legal or equitable discharge or defense of a guarantor. The Guarantor hereby agrees that upon default by the Borrower in the payment when due of any amounts due under the Loan Agreement or under the Note, whether at maturity or by acceleration or otherwise, the Guarantor will, without notice or demand, forthwith pay the same, at the time and place and in the funds, currency and money specified in the Note, without any withholding for, or in respect of, taxes or charges or deductions of any kind in connection therewith. The Guarantor hereby expressly waives diligence, presentment, demand, protest or notice of any kind whatsoever, as well as any requirement that the Lender or any holder of the Note assert or exhaust any right, give any notice or take any other action in respect of the Borrower, the New York Branch, Foreign Bank or any other person or party and hereby consents to any and all extensions of time of payment of and renewals of the Note. This Guaranty is a guaranty of payment and not of collection merely and will not be discharged except by complete performance of all obligations of the Borrower contained in the Note and in the Loan Agreement.

5. All payments by the Guarantor in respect of the principal of, premium (if any) or interest on the Note or any other amounts due hereunder shall be made free and clear of any set-off or counterclaim and without deduction for all present and future taxes, duties, fees, deductions, withholdings, restrictions or conditions of whatsoever nature, if any, now or hereafter imposed by the foreign nation or by any political subdivision or taxing or other authority thereof or therein, and if the Guarantor is compelled by applicable law to deduct any such taxes or make any such deductions it will pay to the Lender or any holder of the Note such additional amounts as may be necessary in order that the Lender or any holder of the Note shall realize without deduction the full amount of the principal of, premium (if any) and interest due on the Notes or (as the case may be) any other amount provided for herein, and in the event that the Guarantor shall be required to make any such deduction or withholding, and to increase the amount of any payment to _____ or any such holder hereunder as aforesaid, the Guarantor shall furnish the Lender certified copies of all applicable tax receipts evidencing the payment of any such additional amounts, in order to enable the Lender or any such holder to substantiate a claim for credit against any such taxes paid by the Guarantor for its account.

6.

6.1 The Guarantor represents and warrants that it is not entitled to immunity from judicial proceedings and agrees that, should any holder of the Note bring any judicial proceedings in any jurisdiction to enforce any obligation or liability of the Guarantor under this Agreement, no immunity from such proceedings will be claimed by or on behalf of the Guarantor or with respect to its property. The Guarantor agrees that any suit, action or proceedings arising out of or relating to this Agreement may be instituted in any state or Federal court in the State of New York, United States of America or in any court having jurisdiction in foreign nation, irrevocably waives to the fullest extent permitted by law any objection which it may have now or hereafter to the laying of the venue of any such suit, action or proceedings and any claim that any such suit, action or proceedings has been brought in an inconvenient forum, and irrevocably (i) acknowledges the competence of any such court, (ii) to the fullest extent permitted by law, submits to the jurisdiction of any such court in any such suit, action or proceedings and (iii) agrees to be bound by and meet its obligations under any judgment rendered thereby.

6.2 The Guarantor hereby designates and appoints The Law Firm, _____ , at its offices in The Borough of Manhattan in the City and State of New York, United States of America, as its authorized agent to accept and acknowledge on its behalf service of any and all process which may be served in any suit, action or proceedings of the nature referred to in Section 6.1 in any state or Federal court in the State of New York and agrees that (a) service of process upon said Law Firm at its street address, New York, New York, as the Borrower's agent for service of process made at its said office in The City of New York and, to the extent lawful, written notice of said service to the Guarantor, mailed to the Guarantor at its foreign address _____ , attention of _____ Managing Director, shall, to the fullest extent permitted by law, be deemed in every respect effective service of process upon the Guarantor in any such suit, action or proceedings in the State of New York and shall be taken and held to be valid personal service upon the Guarantor, whether or not the Guarantor shall then be doing, or at any time shall have done, business within the State of New York (provided that no mailing to the Guarantor at said address shall be required if such mailing would be unlawful or impossible) and (b) any such service of process shall be of the same force and validity as if service were made upon it according to the law governing the validity and requirements of such service in the State of New York. The Guarantor irrevocably waives all claim of error by reason of any such service.

6.3 The Guarantor represents and warrants that said Law Firm has agreed in writing to accept such appointment and that a true copy of such acceptance has been furnished to the Lender. Said designation and appointment shall be irrevocable until the principal of and interest and premium, if any, on the Note and all other sums owing by the Guarantor in accordance with the provisions of this Agreement have been paid in full. If such agent shall cease so to act or advises any holder of the Note or the Guarantor that it is unable to carry out the terms of its appointment (or if the Lender shall in good faith advise the Guarantor that the agent has ceased so to act or is unable to carry out the terms of its appointment), the Guarantor covenants and agrees that it shall forthwith appoint another such agent satisfactory to the Lender or any holder of the Note.

6.4 Nothing in this Section 6 shall affect the right of the Lender or any holder of the Note to serve process in any other manner permitted by law or limit the right of the Lender to bring proceedings against the Guarantor in the courts of any other jurisdiction or jurisdications.

7. The obligations of the Guarantor hereunder to make payment in United States Dollars of the principal of, premium (if any) and interest on the Note and all other amounts which may be payable hereunder shall not be discharged or satisfied by any tender, or any recovery pursuant to any judgment, which is expressed in or converted into any currency other than United States Dollars, except to the extent to which such tender or recovery shall result in the effective receipt in The City of New York by the Lender of the full amount of United States Dollars expressed to be payable hereunder. The obligation of the Guarantor to make payments in United States Dollars shall be enforceable as an alternative or additional cause of action for the purpose of recovery in United States Dollars of the amount (if any) by which such effective receipt shall fall short of the full amount of United States Dollars expressed to be payable hereunder, and shall not be affected by judgment being obtained for any other sums due hereunder.

8. All communications and notices provided for in this Agreement shall be in writing securely wrapped, mailed first class mail or delivered, if to the Guarantor, to it at its foreign address or, if to the Lender, to it at its address, New York, New York, Attention: Loan De-

partment (or such other address as the party receiving any such notice may have designated by a notice in writing to the party giving such notice).

9. All notices, communications, reports, opinions and other documents given under this Agreement, unless submitted in the English language, shall be accompanied by one English translation for each copy of the foregoing so submitted; provided that the English version of all such notices, communications, evidences, reports, opinions and other documents shall govern in the event of any conflict with the non-English version thereof.

10. To the extent permitted by applicable law, the Guarantor hereby expressly excludes, waives and negates, insofar as it is concerned, the provisions of all moratorium legislation and regulations of the foreign nation now and hereafter in force.

11. Notwithstanding any investigation at any time by or on behalf of the Lender or any holder of the Note, all covenants, agreements, representations and warranties made by the Guarantor in this Guaranty Agreement and in the certificates or other documents delivered pursuant hereto (a) shall survive the borrowing contemplated under the Loan Agreement, and shall continue in full force and effect until all amounts payable hereunder and under the Note are paid in full and (b) shall be binding upon the Guarantor and its respective successors and assigns and shall be enforceable by and inure to the benefit of the Lender and its successors and assigns (including each subsequent holder of the Note, whether or not an express assignment to such holder of rights under this Agreement shall have been made).

12. Any corporation deemed to be the Borrower pursuant to the last sentence of Section 5.6(a) of the Loan Agreement shall, for all purposes of this Agreement (including without limitation Sections 3.3 and 4), be deemed to be the Borrower. Each reference herein to the bank Guaranty shall be deemed to include reference to the bank Letter of Credit referred to therein.

13. This Agreement may be executed in one or more counterparts, each of which when executed and delivered shall be an original and all of which shall together constitute one and the same instrument.

14. No course of dealing between the Borrower and the Lender or any holder of the Note or failure or delay by the Lender or such holder in exercising any right, power or privilege under this Agreement and no oral waiver, discharge or modification of rights under the provisions hereof or thereof shall operate as a waiver, discharge or modification of any rights of the Lender or such holder, except to the extent expressly waived discharged or modified in writing by the Lender or such holder; nor shall any single or partial exercise thereof or the exercise of any other right, power or privilege preclude any other or further exercise thereof or the exercise of any other right, power or privilege.

15. This Guaranty Agreement is to be delivered in, and shall be construed in accordance with and governed by the laws of, the State of New York of the United States of America.

The Foreign Corporation

By _____

Title _____

RICHARD J. BERMAN

RICHARD J. BERMAN joined Bankers Trust Company in 1975 and is Vice President and Director of Mergers and Acquisitions. Prior to that, he was Director of Mergers and Acquisitions for Norton Simon, Inc. for five years.

Mr. Berman holds a BS and MBA in Finance, both from New York University, a J.D. from Boston College Law School and a Special Certificate from The Hague Academy of International Law.

MARTIN R. WADE, III

MARTIN R. WADE has worked in mergers and acquisitions for Bankers Trust Company since December 1976. He is a Vice President and is responsible for international mergers and acquisitions for Bankers Trust.

Mr. Wade holds a BS in Finance from West Virginia University and a MBA from University of Wyoming.

5

The Planned Approach to Acquisitions

RICHARD J. BERMAN

MARTIN R. WADE, III

I. THE PLANNING STAGE

How many times recently have we read or heard about companies that are entering into massive divestiture programs subsequent to many years of feverish acquisition activity? Most of these companies' problems could have been eliminated by proper planning.

Merger and acquisition planning should include, at the minimum, determining the goals of the acquisition program, selecting an acquisition strategy and rationale, determining acquisition criteria and matching them against available financial resources. It must then be determined that after careful examination of alternative methods of corporate growth, such as new product development, licensing arrangements, and joint ventures, acquiring another company is the most effective path to realize corporate growth objectives.

An acquisition program should ameliorate strengths and/or eliminate weaknesses. Before embarking upon a program the company should undertake a broadly based study of its basic strengths and weaknesses.

Perhaps a company will find itself obtaining a majority of its sales from a mature industry which is exhibiting a slow rate of growth. The solution could be to cut back on capital expenditures and use the significant cash flow being generated for an acquisition program. Another goal for an acquisition program could be to provide strong executives with additional challenges within the company. Another strength could be a particularly strong international distribution network that is in great need of additional products. This marketing network could be leveraged if a complementary product line could be appended.

Another goal in the planning process is to eliminate weaknesses. For instance, ironically enough, the company may find itself with a very weak balance sheet, overloaded with debt because of a previously ill-conceived acquisition. This problem could be eliminated by acquiring a company that has a very strong balance sheet. Furthermore, a large stodgy company might find that it has not provided for management succession. A tactic then would be to acquire a smaller growth company whose expert and ambitious management would be able to take on additional responsibilities and reposition the company.

Without question, some companies aim in their acquisition program to make themselves less attractive as an acquisition candidate by others. One of the most common methods is to make an acquisition which absorbs excess cash and increases debt. In addition, while the theory is yet untested, some companies believe that by acquiring an FCC-regulated broadcast license, they are immune from an unfriendly takeover.

All that can be said at this time is that a TV or radio broadcast license possibly will protect a company from a foreign acquiror. However, there is also a possibility that a U.S. company could utilize some legal technique which would render this defensive measure ineffective. Any such defensive tactic should be reviewed with great skepticism.

In the planning stage of the acquisition process a company must spend time in serious self-examination to determine its own strengths and weaknesses. Mergers, acquisitions and divestitures in and of themselves are neither good nor bad. It is only when they serve a significant purpose that they make any sense as a corporate goal.

After determining the goals of the acquisition program, it is time to select the acquisition strategy and criteria which will help to achieve these objectives. Some basic guidelines must be set down even before determining the acquisition criteria.

The order in approaching strategic questions is not important. Nevertheless, they should address the following issues: Would the company be willing to enter into a non-negotiated or unfriendly transaction if the circumstances warrant it? Many issues will draw as their impetus the decision to pursue or not to pursue unfriendly transactions. If the company is unsuccessful in an unfriendly takeover attempt, will its management expertise and acquisition program be publicly questioned? Will it end up paying greater premiums for companies with which it initiated a non-negotiated transaction? Can the company afford to overlook what would be otherwise attractive acquisitions merely because senior management was initially opposed to this type of transaction?

The form of payment which the acquiror is willing to make for acquisitions will play a very great part in the acquisition program. The ramifications of using cash or stock must be examined against the possible benefits of using other forms of payment, such as notes, earn-outs, stock options, bonus clauses, and non-compete contracts. Thus it is obvious that the buyer's flexibility in structuring the transaction will enhance his negotiating position in the competitive acquisition arena.

Other issues to be addressed in formulating the acquisition strategy will include the following: Should privately held companies be considered as acquisition candidates? If so, the financial and operating implications of majority versus minority ownership should be carefully studied. Will legal problems arise as the result of vertical or horizontal integration? Is geographic diversification desirable? If so, international acquisition should be considered. The ability to integrate the acquisitions into the existing control systems must be examined. The implications of getting involved in turnaround situations should be thoroughly analyzed. Last, what is to be done with the company after the acquisition is the most important question.

A well-conceived plan will insure that, first, time is not wasted on transactions that should not or cannot be completed, and second, a company, once acquired can be comfortably integrated into the existing organization. Objectives can be tested and refined by developing a detailed acquisition criteria and updating it periodically.

Just as the acquisition strategy will help accomplish corporate goals, the acquisition criteria should support the acquisition strategy. The criteria should not be so restrictive as to severely limit the number of acquisition candidates that would be evaluated or so broad as to cause the buyer to examine a plethora of candidates that are beyond the scope of the available resources. At

a minimum, the criteria should include the following:

- Industries of Interest
- Financial Characteristics
- Minimum Size
- Market Position (i.e. #1)
- Profitability

When establishing criteria for an acceptable industry, one should determine the following:

- Growth prospects
- Competition
- Cyclicality
- Ease of entry
- Regulatory environment
- Labor or capital intensiveness

In the area of profitability and alternative investment opportunities, one should look at the following:

- Stability/Risk
- Quality
- Growth rate
- Payback
- Capital expenditures
- Return on investment

The acquiror must also be cognizant of the impact of an acquisition on his balance sheet, specifically on debt capacity. In an inflationary high interest rate environment, corporations will be obliged to increase debt/equity ratios and risk in order to increase return on investment and compensate for lower margins.

Total debt can be examined in terms of changes in current debt ratings and maximum tolerable debt ratios. Some acquisitions can be partially financed by divesting non-consonant or unimportant subsidiaries.

The maximum purchase price should be expressed in terms of:

- A range of price/earning ratios
- Amount of goodwill
- Earnings dilution or leverage

Some statement in the criteria should be made about the age and depth of management of a candidate, including whether and under what circumstances there would be a preference for management to continue.

The last stage in planning the acquisition program is to allocate management resources. A very senior executive should have the responsibility for the day-to-day supervision of the acquisition program, but it is also important to establish an Acquisition Committee, which according to the By-Laws of the corporation should be empowered to approve or disapprove any acquisitions before submission to the Board of Directors. Because of the difficult credit environment, it is beneficial to open up credit lines with commercial banks to facilitate the rapid consummation of any acquisition opportunity.

II. ACQUISITION CANDIDATE RESEARCH

Anyone actively involved as an intermediary in mergers and acquisitions can name several companies that have extensive and detailed acquisition criteria, nonetheless, their acquisition program is unsuccessful. One cause of failure is that companies have not placed as much effort into planning and managing an acquisition search as they did into developing and distributing detailed acquisition criteria.

The sources for acquisition leads can be divided into two broad categories; leads generated *inside* the company and those generated *outside* the company.

One very obvious good source of potential acquisition candidates that is often overlooked comes from one's own employees, suppliers, and customers. Normally the wide ranging contacts of the members of the board of directors can yield a number of acquisition possibilities. Depending on the type of acquisition that is being sought, senior corporate, group or divisional executives, through constant contact with sources in the trade will know of several companies that could be susceptible to an approach. Of course, the utilization of internal sources for acquisition leads must be counter balanced against having management time drawn away from day to day business requirements.

Many companies with active corporate development programs draw upon the various computer data bases to help define the universe of potential acquisition candidates. These data banks can also be used to sift through companies that fit many of the acquisition criteria. The selection of the most effective data base depends on the general type of company that will most likely be the target of the search. For example, if we expect our candidate will most likely be a publicly traded company that is listed on the New York or American Stock Exchanges, then Standard and Poor's Compustat data base will be most effective. The Compustat data includes extensive financial data on most listed companies, but does not include many private firms. Dun and Bradstreet has a service used by many banks and corporations for credit analysis of prospective customers. The Dun and Bradstreet data base is much larger because it includes both private and public companies. As with Compustat, the Dun and Bradstreet information is available on magnetic tape and is readily manipulated. Also, with both data bases a software package will be required which will program the computer to screen and select companies according to certain criteria such as sales, net worth and type of business. Once a data base has been selected and software developed a company can run as many screens as necessary using different variables to define the universe of potential acquisition candidates.

Another source of leads is probably best characterized as external to the company. This large and diverse group of intermediaries is made up of commercial and investment banks, finders or brokers, accountants, management consultants and attorneys.

If one looks at the most successful saleman in a company, often it is the person who follows up the most leads and makes the most calls. A similar correlation exists with a successful corporate development program. One needs as many good leads as possible. To develop candidates it is helpful to attract leading intermediaries and gain access to their contacts and inventory of sellers. It may be advantageous at this stage to retain a major institution on an exclusive basis, one with a record of achievement.

There are many methods to generate attention in a company's acquisition program. Besides making its activities known to the general public through news releases and annual reports, the company should let commercial and investment bankers know of its acquisition program through establishing personal contact. Also, it should inform its accountant, attorney, and Board of Directors of its plans.

One way to insure a flow of submissions is to develop a reputation for being fair with all who attempt to work with the company. The buyers establish a system whereby all proposals from intermediaries are formally handled and respond quickly and politely to whoever submitted the idea. Adequate records should be maintained, not only because it makes good administrative sense, but for protection. Many companies time-stamp all submissions. This excellent idea will cut down the number of law suits considerably. Until a working relationship has been established with an intermediary, all submissions should be on a blind or no-name basis. This will allow verification as to whether the candidate has been submitted from another source. If there is interest in a particular submission, always establish from the outset the amount and responsibility of the fee. Once an agreement on the matter of the fee has been established, it should be reduced to writing and all parties concerned should sign it. This will prevent many disputes which usually arise much later. Lastly, all submissions should be handled with complete confidentiality. This will enhance the buyer's credibility and increase the amount of quality submissions that it ordinarily would be receiving. The best deals normally are submitted to a buyer who has a reputation for impeccable character and knowledge of how to settle the issue of fees quickly and fairly.

Not all those who seek to fulfill the role of finder have the same capabilities. The acquisition strategy may require concentration in a specific industry. In industries such as insurance, communications, or natural resources, certain firms have developed extensive expertise and can quickly provide ample leads and contacts in those industries.

If one is seriously contemplating an unfriendly takeover, or at least not ruling it out, it would be wise to develop a working relationship with a firm that has had extensive experience in handling such transactions. If an actual project requiring specific expertise is required, the buyer may want to consider retaining an organization that has had such experience to efficiently assist with this phase of the program.

Each lead or contact submitted should be matched against the company's acquisition criteria. A ranking system should then be devised for each of the leads. Naturally, there are many methods to rank individual acquisition candidates. The point is that as soon as some sort of ranking system is applied, all efforts will be focused on a small group of targets which present the most attractive opportunities.

III. APPROACH AND CONTACT

The atmosphere which is set in the first meeting with a potential acquisition candidate may well prevail throughout the rest of the negotiations, and will be extremely difficult to alter. At the first meeting therefore, it is crucial to create a favorable impression of the buying firm on the senior management or principal of the acquisition candidate. The buyer's management should be prepared to talk at some length about the company's acquisition plans, future directions, and how it believes that the target company would meld with these objectives.

Obviously, to accomplish a discussion such as this convincingly, management will have had to develop detailed information on the candidate company, its principal officers, markets and competition. No effort should be spared in developing this type of information and this holds true whether one makes the approach directly or through an intermediary.

Unless the buyer is very experienced and has a successful record of completing acquisitions, it is more advantageous not to make the initial approach directly to the chief executive officer or principal of the candidate but to utilize an intermediary to introduce the concept of an affiliation with the company. The intermediary acts as a catalyst in the transaction —evaluating candidates, providing negotiating skills, basic legal, accounting and tax expertise, and even

offering the buyer anonymity until it is discovered that the target is probably for sale. Even the most prolific acquirors have close working relationships with one or two well respected intermediaries such as major commercial banks or investment bankers.

In essence, the role of the intermediary can vary enormously according to the needs of the acquiror. However, the major institutions which act in this capacity are generally prepared to assist in most of the following areas:

1. Defining Objectives
2. Establishing Criteria
3. Obtaining the Necessary Outside Legal, Accounting and Tax Assistance
4. Identifying Acquisition Candidates, Including Computer Screens
5. Evaluating Candidates
6. Structure Transactions
7. Assist in Negotiations
8. Help to Close the Transaction
9. Render a Fairness Opinion
10. Act as Dealer Manager

There are two avenues to be aware of when deciding on the proper approach. One frequently overlooked avenue is interlocking directors, attorneys or accountants. Obviously, this connection will not occur in the majority of cases. In the case where the submission is presented by a finder, then consideration should be given to the rapport the finder has with the potential acquiree. If he has a close relationship, e.g., written authorization of fee agreement from the seller, this is probably the best channel of approach.

One case which demonstrates the advantages of using an intermediary is the acquisition of a public company based in Texas by a major NYSE acquiror. The Texas company had spurned direct approaches by perhaps a dozen companies in the past but granted a meeting to the representative of a major New York financial institution. The 74 year old Chairman and largest shareholder confided at the first meeting that he was horrified that his Board would force him to sell because of his advanced age and lack of succession. The sympathetic intermediary stressed the character, compatible management style and autonomy available only through his client. He also mentioned that the Chairman, who had no other interests than his company, could obtain a life-time contract.

The Chairman then agreed to meet the prospective acquiror. Two months later, the transaction was consummated with the purchase price involving less negotiation than the terms of the apparently crucial life-time contract. Using considerable discretion as to tactics, the intermediary had gained the key shareholders' confidence, established the selling price for the business and provided the idea of the life-time contract. This was something that none of the prospective suitors had achieved by direct approach.

At the first meeting between the buyer and seller, the buyer should also take the initiative and ask questions regarding the prospective seller's business. Inquiries should address the company's present position, prospects, competition, and importantly, the personal goals and objectives of the senior management or principals.

A well-phrased direct question can frequently determine whether a company would consider selling and what are their price expectations. In the case of potential sellers who appear to be disenchanted by being forced to come to a decision before their concerns, some of which are emotional, can be relieved, it is possible to test the water by examining the reaction to a number of critical points in the discussion. If the seller agrees to exchange financials, or agrees to an additional meeting—perhaps even at the buyer's headquarters, then you have some indication that perhaps he may be interested.

Some of these courtships can lead to wasted time and effort. It is nearly impossible to assure a correct reading of the reactions of every potential seller with whom the buyer comes into contact. Very often the situation comes down to the buyer having to take some action to move the transaction off dead center. Submitting an acquisition proposal to the target is often one way to keep the transaction moving.

IV. STRUCTURING THE PROPOSED TRANSACTION

The first step in coming up with a proposal is to value the company. The accuracy of the valuation will, of course, depend on the degree of access that is available to the company's detailed financial information. Many fine texts have been written which discuss the techniques of valuing companies, and most major commercial and investment banks, as well as public accounting firms, can provide a creditable valuation. All valuation studies should include, at the minimum, an analysis of projected growth rates of the company's liabilities and assets (including hidden values not indicated on the balance sheet), and rates of return as well as leverage or dilution on earning at various price levels. This valuation should serve only as the basis for the aggregate dollar amount which the buyer is prepared to pay for the company and is not necessarily valid for other purposes.

The information gleaned from previous meetings with the seller-candidate can now be used to further refine a proposal. Particularly, one should concentrate on the seller's interest in the financial and non-financial aspects of the transaction. Are they retiring or staying with the business? What is their tax situation? If future projections are overly optimistic, should their bluff be called with a contingent payout?

Having valued the company and ascertained the status of the seller, the buyer should weigh these considerations against the strategic acquisition plan and formulate a proposal in terms of cash, stock or a combination of cash and securities, earn-out and employment contracts. Assuming the seller does not have a firm asking price, the initial proposal might as well be structured in the most flexible and advantageous terms. It should be kept in mind that this proposal is only intended to provide a basis for negotiations and will undergo, in all probability, numerous changes.

V. NEGOTIATIONS

Once a proposal has been drafted, this preliminary offer should be discussed with the senior management or principals of the seller. The initial proposal is likely to meet with one of three possible outcomes: an outright rejection, an acceptance with some modifications you feel are insignificant or a counteroffer. Assuming that a rejection has not been received, the buyer has been able to gain more information. At this time, the approximate asking price for the company should be revealed as well as more about the other expectations of the seller. The buyer should be able to take that information and, assuming that overall it is within the parameters of the acquisition strategy, work out a proposal that is acceptable.

As the next step, an agreement-in-principle, hopefully, should be reached on the acquisition of the company. The contents of the agreement-in-principle will vary, but certainly, it will include the aggregate asking price and the terms and conditions of the sale. Many buyers at this point attempt to put together a letter of intent which both parties can sign. In most cases, however, the letter of intent will be conditional, not binding. The buyers now knows the amount which must be financed in order to consummate the acquisition.

VI. FINANCING

No acquisition that has reached this point should fail because of a lack of financing. If the buyer has utilized a planned approach, he has already established some contact with the appropriate institutions and made them aware of his potential requirements. Even though this can be said, companies frequently are forced to terminate acquisitions because suitable financial arrangments could not be arranged. After wooing and winning the favor of a target company, many buyers fail to consummate the transaction because of lack of funds. Instead, they are forced to the sidelines as a well heeled suitor captures the now vulnerable and abandoned seller.

For smaller acquisitions, the acquiror may pay the entire purchase price from cash on hand. On larger transactions, the principal source of funds will be commercial banks. Commercial banks normally provide bridge financing as well as permanent working capital financing. Bridge financing can later be replaced by more permanent long-term financing, which in theory should be arranged during an advantageous rate environment. Many large companies also can utilize the commercial paper market, but probably only if they have been in the market previous to the acquisition and all the appropriate ratings and agency arrangements have been completed. In most cases, long-term financing will occur only after some short-term source of funds has been utilized.

The two basic sources of funds are the public and private markets, principally through insurance companies and pension funds. Raising money through the public markets requires the appropriate SEC filings as well as an underwriter, not only to manage but actually issue securities. Both debt and equity can be raised through a private arrangement, either directly with insurance companies or pension funds, but more typically by utilizing either a commercial or an investment bank as an agent. An element which is not commonly used in acquisition financing, but which is one which should not be overlooked, is the possibility of a lease financing for at least part of the financing requirements. Lease transactions can be put together by leasing companies, commercial banks or investment banks. Once there is an acceptable financing plan the parties now can move to the final stage of the acquisition.

VII. CLOSING

There are a number of formalities which must be accomplished in order to close the acquisition. Fortu-nately, they can be pursued concurrently with obtaining the financing package.

Acquisition agreements are relatively standard. The emphasis should be on thoroughness, not on complexity. About half of the agreement is expressed by the representations and warranties; some of the most important are:

(1) the financial statements are audited and pre-pared on a consistent basis;
(2) since the date of the last statement there has been no material change in the balance sheet (i.e. sale of assets, distribution of cash) or oper-ations of the company (i.e. acquisitions, loss of major customer, supplier, decline in earnings);
(3) seller will use best efforts to close the transac-tion as soon as possible;
(4) seller is expected to carry on the business and assist in the transition period.

The exhibits to an acquisition agreement are almost as important to the contract as the representations and warranties are. They provide the battle plan for the new management team, if one is required, and thus facili-tate the transition. Included in the exhibits are the contracts, customers, pensions, patents and exceptions to the representations and warranties.

Where public companies are concerned, it may be necessary to receive a fairness opinion on the transac-tion. One should select a firm which has had experi-ence in providing such opinions, and one which is not involved as a finder or as a financial adviser to you in the transaction. This opinion from a disinterested third party will provide the extra margin of safety should a lawsuit arise from the transaction. There can be reg-ulatory filings which must be made prior to closing. Where public companies are involved, these filings are governed by federal securities laws; however, there may also be state securities laws which must be adhered to. Depending on the size of the transaction, there is a possibility of various FTC filings which might be required under the Hart-Rodino-Scott Act.

All during this period the buyer has been working very closely with the seller, the seller's attorney and legal counsel in putting together a purchase agreement. Once all the conditions of the purchase agreement have been satisfied and both parties have signed the agree-ment, the transaction has been closed.

MICHAEL D. BOXBERGER

MICHAEL D. BOXBERGER is a Vice President of the international executive search firm of Heidrick and Struggles, Inc. He holds a BS in Biological Sciences from the University of Denver and an MBA from the University of Texas. He joined Heidrick and Struggles as an associate in 1977 and was named Vice President and Manager of the firm's Houston office in early 1980. Prior to joining Heidrick and Struggles, Mr. Boxberger was Senior Vice President of the Corporate Banking Group of Capital National Bank in Houston and an Account Executive in the International Department of the Northern Trust Company in Chicago.

Heidrick and Struggles is one of the oldest and largest consulting firms specializing in executive search. Founded in 1953, the firm has 19 offices in North America, Europe and Asia.

LAURENCE E. SIMMONS

LAURENCE E. SIMMONS is Executive Vice President of Simmons & Company International. He holds a B.S. degree in Economics from the University of Utah and an M.B.A. from Harvard Business School. He also studied international monetary theory at the London School of Economics. He was a co-founder of Simmons & Company in 1974. Prior to that time, he was a Corporate Finance Officer for the First National Bank of Chicago and had worked for Citicorp Leasing International.

Simmons & Company is an investment banking firm, located in Houston, Texas, specializing in the oil service industry. Since its founding in 1974, the firm has completed in excess of $800 million of corporate finance projects in the oil service industry, about two-thirds of which has been merger related.

6

Selecting the Executive to Run Things

MICHAEL D. BOXBERGER

LAURENCE E. SIMMONS

Selecting and motivating the right executive to run an acquired or merged business is possibly the single most important factor in a happy marriage. In many cases the financial analysis tells the buyer where the acquired company has been; the management determines to a significant degree where it will go.

If the acquired company already has a management team that meets the quality and financial objectives of the buyer, there is obviously little reason to change. If changes are required for any number of reasons, however, the selection of the executive to run things will become a very important task.

Selecting the key individual to head up the new venture in a merger or acquisition is not totally different from the same process undertaken to fill a vacancy in any organization. The basic questions that make up the selection process are essentially the same as those a board of directors might ask in a more customary succession process. The added pitfalls and pressures inherent in a merger compound the challenges to both parties.

The analysis of who should run the new operation should be one of the earliest factors the buyer considers in preparing for the merger or acquisition. More emphasis should be placed on this aspect than is given it in many cases. The analysis should also involve not only the top spot in the new structure, but also the key management positions that will report to the very top.

What then are some of the considerations that should be taken into account during the pre-acquisition phase? Surely, early in the negotiations, the prospective buyer should begin to explore several different aspects of the management personnel portion of the contemplated purchase. Such considerations would include, but certainly not be limited to, the following:

1. Where and how does the management situation of the selling company fit into the proposed new structure?
2. What steps should be taken to analyze both the prospective acquisition and the buyer in terms of the key managers who will direct the new organization?
3. What are the professional and personal parameters of the individual who should head the operation?
4. If no suitable internal candidate can be located, will the buyer handle the search for the top executive internally or should he seek outside assistance from an executive search firm?

The buyer is apt to find very different qualities and levels of sophistication in the acquired management. Insofar as the personnel analysis for the buyer is concerned, however, certain information must be discovered about the key people in the seller's organization.

Obviously, this involves only the pivotal members of the acquiree's management team, not the entire management staff. Depending somewhat on the size of the organization being acquired, there are probably from one to five prime individuals who impel the organization, make key decisions and make things happen. No doubt, there may be many more who are more or less vital to that organization's past track record and who may be under consideration for top positions in the new structure. In evaluating them for the very top post, however, only a pivotal few should be considered in this phase of the analysis.

What about the seller himself? Or what about the chief executive of the selling organization? What appear to be their intentions?

The buyer should ascertain in direct conversation with the seller at the earliest possible point in the discussions what his intentions are for himself as well as for his circle of key associates. Does he, himself, intend to stay on as manager, and what plans does he have for those top people now reporting to him?

One of the first steps that should be taken in the personnel phase of the acquisition is the evaluation not only of the management staff to be acquired, but also of the buyer's own management team. The buyer should assign someone within his organization at the level of vice president or higher to interview and check references of each of the key people in both organizations who are being considered for the top post and those who will report to him. An alternative would be to retain an outside consultant to handle this assignment on a time-and-expense basis.

Another point in the early stages of the analysis is to compare the "management styles"of the two organizations. Has the seller's been a highly structured and disciplined organization, or has it operated in a more free-wheeling, seat-of-the-pants entrepreneurial style? What about the buyer's management style? Will the two mesh easily or will possible conflicts arise?

The buyer's analysis should also include a comparison of the salary, incentive, option, retirement and benefits packages of buyer and seller. Consider whether or not all or any part of the seller's package must be integrated with the buyer's, and also what ramifications might result from adjustments to the seller's management's package.

The findings of this thorough analysis should be discussed with the seller for his comments and appraisal before the agreement is finalized. An acquisition or merger is always traumatic for the acquired company and its personnel, and such pre-agreement discussions may help to alleviate some potential problems that might greatly hinder the operation once it is on-going.

An interesting dichotomy sometimes appears in many discussions in evaluating top personnel for the new structure. The acquired company will often feel that industry background is of critical importance for the new top executive and his team. The buyer, on the other hand, may feel that a capable functional specialist will be fully qualified in that function no matter what the industry or service involved in the acquisition might be. Obviously, both feelings stem from the fact that the seller's personnel all have the industry background, while the buyer's personnel have the functional experience but may be lacking the specific industry experience and familiarity.

Both attitudes have some merit. The important factor for the buyer to keep in mind is the danger of adopting one viewpoint to the exclusion of the other. The buyer may be counting heavily upon the acquired company's particular industry skills to carry the new organization through the difficult initial phases of the new operation. Where such industry background is missing in the buyer's own personnel, such experience is a valid consideration until his own management staff is better versed in and more familiar with the problems of the new industry.

SELECTION OF THE TOP EXECUTIVE

If the seller or the seller's chief executive is not to be designated as the man to run the new operation, and if no suitable candidate surfaces from analyses of the two staffs, the buyer is forced to go to the outside to find the key man to fill the top post in the new organization. Even if possible internal candidates are identified as prospects, the buyer may still wish to go to the outside to see if even better-qualified individuals might be found to strengthen the management team of the new organization.

The first step in the search process should be to establish a detailed set of specifications for the position and the person expected to fill it. The position description should include both professional and personal parameters. The specifications for the position should set forth the title, responsibilities, reporting relationships (both those reporting to him as well as to whom he will report), compensation (including salary, any incentives, perquisites and benefits), education, minimum experience (including functional, industry and international, if necessary), and personal attributes.

The personal attributes portion of the description may be more critical in a merger or acquisition than it would be in filling a top vacancy in an existing organization. Corporations more and more are seeking individuals who are functionally tops, who are broader in perspective and who command good "people skills." The ability to work with and to motivate people is most acute in a merger situation, where the top executive is attempting to mold a new management team, to motivate them and to retain the best possible talent. The buyer's key personnel, who will be involved in the final selection of the top executive, should concur on the personal "chemistry" the successful candidate must possess to succeed in the new organization. The professional parameters are more clearly defined and more quantifiable, but the personal traits or ''chemistry'' are essential elements of the search parameters.

Earlier it was noted that the personnel analysis should include identifying the management ''style'' of both organizations. This should be a consideration in establishing personal attributes the top candidate must possess to succeed in the new structure. Not only must the new organization's management be able to function with their new chief, but the buyer's top officers should also feel that they can work well with the candidate under consideration.

Those setting specifications for the position should identify at the outset what factors in the position description are actually required as opposed to those which are merely desirable. The selection of any conditions that have not been thoroughly reviewed and agreed upon may overly complicate the selection process. It may also unduly restrict the number of potential candidates who are fully qualified, yet who may be omitted from consideration for failing to measure up to less essential parameters.

The buyer should be flexible to some degree with specifications for the position. We know from experience with surveying senior echelon executives that the scope of responsibility and challenge are their primary reasons for accepting a promotion or an offer from another organization. In fact, these two factors have consistently risen in importance over the past few years, while compensation has declined in significance. Yet such elements as an unusual ''perk'' or a slightly different title may be necessary to lure a truly attractive candidate into the new post.

Another factor that must be considered in establishing specifications for the position are legal requirements that must be complied with in executive selection. Among the major federal laws that apply to employment are the Equal Pay Act of 1963, Title VII of the Civil Rights Act of 1964, Executive Order No. 11246 issued in 1965, the Age Discrimination in Employment Act of 1967 and the Vocational Rehabilitation Act of 1973. In addition to federal laws, state and local governments have also enacted legislation governing employment that must be complied with.

Once specifications of the position have been established and agreed upon, the buyer must identify the person or persons who will actually carry out the search. A full-time employee who possesses the necessary experience and qualifications is generally best suited for such an assignment because of his familiarity with the organizations and industries involved in the

merger or acquisition. If such an individual is not present within the organization, then the buyer must select an executive search firm qualified to assist in the identification and selection of the top executive.

For such a top level search as that involving the selection of the man to run the new organization, the only employee qualified for such a responsibility may be the buyer's chief executive or other senior officer.

DOING THE SEARCH YOURSELF

Once the position description and specifications have been agreed upon and the individual chosen to conduct the search, the first step in the in-house search process should be to establish a reasonable timetable. It might be helpful to work backward from a desired completion time for having the new executive in place and functioning in his new position. Though the amount of time required to complete the search will vary for nearly every organization and every industry, it will seldom be less than 12 weeks from the time the search is actually initiated. In periods of high demand for superior executive talent such as we have seen recently, this period could extend substantially beyond three months, and organizations generally find that such a search extends beyond their initial expectations.

Assuming the buyer established 12 weeks as the timetable for selecting the new executive, the following might be considered as a starting point for allocating time to each element of the search:

Weeks 1-3:	Research and initial contacts with prospects.
Weeks 4 and 5:	Meet and evaluate candidates.
Week 6:	Select final candidates; schedule visits.
Weeks 7-9:	Host interviews with candidates.
Weeks 10 and 11:	Have selected finalists return; check references.
Week 12:	Extend and negotiate acceptance of final offer.

The person conducting the search should plan on spending at least half his time researching and identifying potential candidates and then the remaining half for interviews. Because of the levels of candidates as well as interviewers within the company, the interview phase will probably take at least one month due to travel schedules and other business commitments.

In the initial research stage of the search process, the searcher should attempt to reduce the total field of potential candidates by ascertaining where such individuals might be found. Where would such a person be today? The searcher should start by identifying target companies where such a person might be employed and by establishing where candidates might be found in terms of industry, functional area, responsibilities and income.

The person conducting the search should then set about trying to find sources who would be helpful in locating such an individual. These sources could include those previously contacted in other searches, or employees within the firm. Sources outside the firm would include acquaintances within the same function or industry, trade associations, bankers, lawyers, accountants, suppliers and possibly even customers.

There are a number of means of identifying possible candidates. Many industries and functions have associations which publish lists of members and member companies. There are also a number of corporate reference books, including *Dun & Bradstreet's Reference Book of Corporate Management* and *Standard & Poor's Register*.

Contacting sources either by phone or in person plus checking some of the trade and industry associations and corporate reference books will help the searcher build an initial list of prospects. While advertisements may be suitable for building a list of prospects for lower-level positions, advertising is seldom used for identifying individuals capable of coming into a new merger or acquisition as the top executive. Generally, at this level, nearly all executives are identified either through personal contact or by executive search consultants.

Once the searcher has compiled his list of prospects and sources, and before the first contact is made, he should set up some means of record-keeping. This procedure will help in keeping track of who has been contacted and the results of that contact. Bear in mind that the searcher may be in contact with hundreds of people either as prospects or sources, and some means must be established for monitoring the results of those contacts.

Also, before the first contact, the searcher should review the pluses and minuses of the merger situation, the industry, the position, and the reporting relationships. This helps to provide an accurate portrayal of the position and the company. He should prepare a packet of information that could be sent to interested prospects. Such a packet might include the annual reports of the two parties to the merger, plus 10-K's, literature on the products and/or services involved, and reprints of any articles that have appeared recently on the companies' recent accomplishments and their outlook for the future.

Once the searcher begins contacting possible candidates, he should record those in whom he will have a continuing interest and eliminate from further consideration any in whom he has no interest and those who express no interest in the position. In the contact the searcher should ask for a resume from those in whom he has some continuing interest. The resume will help conserve the searcher's time and the company's expense in a more detailed follow-up telephone conversation.

As contacts with prospects proceed, the searcher will gain a better understanding of the pool of talent available for the position as well as the suitability of the position's specifications. In some cases, the searcher may find through his contacts that the target compensation level is unacceptable to those with the experience and qualifications capable of assuming the post. The buyer is then faced with deciding whether to raise the level of compensation or to lower some of the qualifications that have been established. In some cases, raising the compensation level may not be in line with corporate policies and norms. Such instances may call for adding perquisities that offset a potential candidate's reluctance on a straight cash compensation basis.

After the initial phone contacts with prospects have established a common mutual interest and after the resumes are in hand, the searcher should study each resume before making the follow-up phone contact. That follow-up phone interview should establish whether or not it is desirable to proceed with a personal interview with the prospect.

As the search process nears the interview phase, the searcher should plan carefully for conducting the interviews. Most candidates will, no doubt, be brought in to the buyer's location at his expense. Some may be visited in their own communities during the screening interview phase. Still others may be able to arrange their travel schedules to be in the company's area while on other business matters. In any event, the searcher needs to plan and schedule the screening interviews to conserve his time as well as to control expenses of the search.

In certain instances, more than one meeting may be required with some individuals. Since the searcher will have no more than a few hours to spend with each prospect, he should carefully plan interviews to gather as much information as possible, while still complying with legal restrictions placed upon the questions.

The number of prospects to be interviewed may be only a handful or it could reach 20 or more. To help narrow the field to the three to five most attractive prospects, the searcher should note which candidates most closely match essential and desirable specifications discussed when the specifications were first established.

Once the three to five final candidates have been identified, the searcher should confirm their educations and check with at least one reference to verify essential elements of each candidate's background.

Far too often, searchers fail to check references or else do it in such a haphazard manner that it is of little value to the selection process. The well-conducted reference check can help confirm the prospect's probable success in the environment of the new merger or acquisition. Therefore, the referencing should not only verify the candidate's background experience and achievements, but also should verify his strengths and weaknesses. The weaknesses may be especially critical in the merger or acquisition situation.

Those contacted as references should be limited to those qualified and most helpful in terms of their association with the candidate and the closeness of their relationship. For best results, this referencing is done face-to-face, but telephoning is acceptable if done properly.

Legal restrictions apply to rereferencing as well to referencing. The searcher must comply with federal, state and local regulations regarding the individual's right to privacy.

Once the field of candidates has been narrowed and their backgrounds referenced, they should be invited to the buyer's headquarters to meet with all who will be involved in the final selection process. The searcher should provide each interviewer with a summary of the candidates' education, career background, current situation, and the searcher's evaluation of each individual.

The searcher should also brief the interviewers as to their responsibilities. The searcher should then check back with each party a few days prior to the slated interview to be certain that all involved are still available. Any necessary changes, of course, should be communicated as quickly as possible to all involved.

Before conducting the interviews, the searcher should send each candidate a confirming letter specifying the time, date and place. He should extend every courtesy to the candidates by providing them with travel tickets and a confirmation of hotel accommodations when necessary.

Ideally, these interviews should be held promptly, before the candidates's interest drops and so that company representatives may make better comparisons. Each executive involved should be ready to arrive at a reasonable decision while making a positive image for the organization.

Often prime candidates have been lost because of poor impressions from an interview. Those conducting the interviews should hold to the agreed-upon schedule and extend to the candidate every courtesy that they would to a personal guest. Once the interviews have been completed, the searcher should see to it that all of the interviewee's questions have been answered and confirm his interest in the position.

The searcher should then get feedback from each interviewer as soon as possible. When the initial interviews are completed, the buyer may wish to invite one or two back again for subsequent interviews. Before extending such an invitation, the searcher should inquire of the finalists as to their desired compensation and their availability date, both of which may have a significant bearing on the buyer's ultimate choice.

Following the last series of interviews, the searcher should again seek reactions from the interviewers and then make the final offer. If the prime candidate does not agree for one reason or another to accept the offer, the second candidate should be approached. Once agreement is reached, the final details should be confirmed in writing to the successful candidate. Other finalists should then be notified of the final decision as quickly as possible, and letters should go out to all others contacted as sources or prospects during the course of the search.

THE EXECUTIVE SEARCH CONSULTANT

If no one in the buyer's organization possesses the qualifications and ability to conduct such a search, the buyer may retain an executive search firm to identify and assist in the selection of the top executive for the new organization.

There may be other reasons for not conducting an in-house search. The buyer's own personnel may not only lack the necessary qualifications but also may not be suitable due to the level and type of positition being filled, which may be the case with a merger or acquisition.

The beginnings of the executive search industry can be traced to the talent-short era shortly after World War II. Executive search consultants today serve the majority of major American businesses and organizations of all sizes and types. They also work on behalf of not-for-profit organizations, governments and educational institutions.

If the buyer decides to retain an executive search firm, he should not hesitate to ask consultants to identify other clients in the same industry or clients active in mergers and acquisitions for which the consultant has assisted in executive search. The buyer should develop a list of questions and then contact previous clients who have been identified by the consultant.

Some of the questions that might be asked of the consultant's clients include:

1. What were the consultant's main strengths and weaknesses?
2. How well did the consultant identify with the client's problems?
3. How much time did the consultant spend with candidates, and did he help them gain an accurate understanding of the organization and the position?
4. How helpful was the consultant in checking references and verifying backgrounds?
5. How many candidates were presented for the client's final decision?
6. How does the client compare this consultant with others which his firm has retained?

If the buyer decides to utilize a search firm, he should request a written proposal, including details of the consultant's fee and invoicing method. Most search consultants charge 30 to 35 percent of the successful candidate's total estimated cash compensation for the first year, including the base salary and guaranteed or probable bonus. There are other arrangements used by consultants, including a fixed fee, a retainer fee for a specific time period, and a time charge sometimes limited to an agreed-upon maximum. Consultants generally invoice the client each month based upon the agreed upon fee arrangement, plus out-of-pocket expenses.

The buyer's selection of a consultant should be based upon his past performance on behalf of client organizations. Some search firms have built up an enviable record over the years and do their best to maintain that reputation. Some may be willing to work longer than the anticipated three months without additional fees to reach a satisfactory solution, and some are willing to resume the search if the successful candidate does not remain with his new employer for at least a year of service.

The buyer should be prepared to work closely with the consultant. Executive search consultants stress the need for partnership between the client and consultant on any successful search activity. The buyer should provide the consultant with all information he feels will be helpful on the search throughout its course. Any candidates who come to the attention of the buyer in the course of the search should be brought to the attention of the consultant for consideration in the search activity.

Both the buyer and the consultant should remain in close contact as the search progresses to ensure that the activity is progressing as planned and to correct any problems that develop along the way. The buyer should also keep the consultant posted on any changes or developments within the organization that might have an impact upon the position to be filled and potential candidates' final decision.

The consultant will devote his time during the first half of the search to research, telephoning and traveling to identify, evaluate and present candidates to the client. Once he has established the list of candidates, the search process becomes primarily the buyer's responsibility. How quickly the buyer acts upon meeting with candidates and making decisions regarding the finalists will affect whether or not the candidates retain their interest in the position and their willingness to accept if an offer is extended.

PRACTICAL POINTERS

Whether the buyer elects to conduct the search in-house or to retain an executive search consultant to find the man to head the new merger or acquisition, it is best to bear in mind the shortage of available talent. The problems inherent in finding superior performers have generated the growth of the executive search industry. Finding the superior performer who possesses the necessary experience and skills to lead a new merger or acquisition will not be a brief or simple process.

Added to that is the dimension of "chemistry." Finding the qualified individual with the necessary people skills to steer the new organization through the rough early stages of a merger or acquisition requires an exceptionally skilled manager and leader.

PEOPLE IMPACT IN BUYER AND SELLER COMPANIES

MANAGEMENT IS THE KEY ELEMENT which differentiates companies competing in the same marketplace. Human resources are often more important than any other single element of a business. The buyer and the seller need to assess management and factor it in as a positive or negative element of the sale. Indeed, lenders attach such importance to the expertise and reputation of the people who will ultimately be responsible for profitability, that they will dramatically change the terms and cost of borrowing depending on the quality of management. A respected management team with a good track record frequently can be the basis for success in obtaining financing and in ultimately completing a transaction.

This topical area examines the question of human resources from both the viewpoint of the buyer and the seller. The buyer should be aware that strong management is a true asset worth paying for in the purchase price. Weak management, on the other hand, will have to be supported with more resources and that can substantially affect profitability. The seller has an emotional tie of loyalty to workers who have helped shape a successful business. Their ultimate reward can be a factor for which other concessions are made during the transaction negotiations.

The subject of employee benefits as related to mergers, acquisitions and buyouts is covered by Robert S. Taft. He points out that in putting two corporations together the parties often lose sight of the fact that each company's employee compensation structure may differ substantially. Compensation packages must eventually affect the acquisition price. This is particularly true when there are large, unfunded past service costs, medical costs or fringe benefit retirement programs. Mr. Taft discusses pension plans, profit sharing plans, long-term deferred compensation, supplemental pensions, and stock option plans. There is also relevant material on key man insurance, employee moving expenses and interest-free loans.

Robert H. Hayes probes the age old problem of an owner who worries about loyal employees when selling his company. The question of retaining acquired employees, the importance of autonomy, retention, employee contracts and organization plans are also covered. Mr. Hayes believes that there is a need for understanding during and after negotiations about the interests of key management. Being oblivious to the human side of a merger, acquisition or buyout will likely produce misunderstanding and resentments. Often, this is the cause of costly mistakes and even failure of the enterprise.

ROBERT S. TAFT

ROBERT S. TAFT is a partner in the New York law firm of Miller, Montgomery, Sogi, Brady & Taft, and is a member of the New York and Florida Bars. He has a B.A. degree from Dartmouth College, an LL.B. from Columbia University, and an LL.M. from New York Law School. He is the author of numerous articles in the *Journal of Taxation, New York State Bar Journal, Antitrust Bulletin, The Tax Executive, Notre Dame Lawyer, The Family Law Quarterly, St. John's Law Review, The Tax Magazine,* and is the co-author of *Pension Plans, Deferred Compensation and Executive Benefits; Drafting Matrimonial Agreements and Property Settlements; Tax Free Organizations and Other Corporate Acquisitions; Practitioner's Guide to the Tax Reform Act of 1969;* and *New York State Personal Taxations.*

Mr. Taft has been a Professor of Law at New York Law School since 1973. He has served as Trustee of the Practicing Law Institute and as a Director of Odyssey House, and is an active member of the New York and American Bar Associations in the areas of pensions and employee benefits.

7

Employee Benefits as Related to Acquisitions and Mergers

ROBERT S. TAFT

In approaching an acquisition or merger, the parties must remember that employees are very important assets. In order to preserve the work force, one must preserve or improve employee benefits. In putting two corporations together, the negotiators often lose sight of the fact that each corporation's employee compensation structure may differ substantially. Integration of such structures could be difficult and could impede or destroy the success of the merger or acquisition.

Employee benefits must be thought of as an interrelated "bundle of rights." Each corporation may have put the "bundle" together differently. The "bundle" includes: salaries and current bonuses; qualified plans—pension and profit sharing; deferred payment plans—short-term; stock bonus plans—current; stock bonus plans—deferred; stock purchase plans— qualified; restricted stock plans—nonqualified; thrift or savings plans; affiliate stock purchase plans; shadow stock plans, management stock plans; key man insurance; split dollar insurance; group life insurance; medical insurance; miscellaneous fringes—vacation fund, company facilities, travel expenses, entertainment allowance, legal representation, home entertainment allowance, educational foundation and awards; and, of great interest in recent years, the Employee Stock Ownership Plan.

As can be seen by this list, the problem of putting together two corporate benefit programs can be enormous. It can even overshadow the other technical aspects of the merger or acquisition. Let us examine, for the moment, the standard merger of the two corporations as related to employee compensation. In the first analysis, we must determine benefit goals. One must consider discarding or terminating present programs of one or both corporations. Similarly there is the question of adopting new programs, continuing or amending present programs, extending transferee's programs to the employees of the transferor or extending transferor's programs to employees of the transferee. Overriding these policy decision are the cost factors and the tax implications for both the employers and the employees.

The compensation package will affect the acquisition price, especially if the corporation to be acquired has benefit programs with large unfunded past service costs. If there are funds established for employee benefits, such as a pension plan trust, one must determine if the fund assets are undervalued or overvalued. Are there unused contribution carryovers? How are these items to be reflected as adjustments in the purchase price?

Often, in the acquisition of a closely held company, the former owners are given consulting agreements. These types of agreements place these employees or consultants on a different benefit status from other general employees. They may not be eligible for all of the benefit programs available in the merged corporation. This must be fully analyzed before the old owners become consultants with limited benefits, as opposed to regular employees with full benefits.

If regular employment contracts are to be issued, how will they affect the payroll scale of the acquiring corporation? This is the problem of combining payrolls. A similar problem may exist with union contracts. Such contracts would have to be renegotiated before consummation of the merger or acquisition if,

117

by their terms, they could not be integrated with each other.

FLEXIBLE BENEFIT PACKAGE

The leading approach to compensation integration is the "flexible benefit package." This system is based upon calculating flexible credits expressed in dollars for each employee and then allowing the individual employees to allocate such credits among the alternative compensation components. A compensation committee determines each year the dollar value of each employee's benefits. The employee is then advised how many credits (based upon such dollar value) he or she has. The employee may then allocate such credits among the various benefit programs in a fashion most advantageous to him or her. Thus, if the employee is of a relatively young age, he or she may pass up the pension plan in favor of a bonus program or an extended vacation benefit. An older employee may use his credits for a retirement plan, life insurance and medical benefits. The choice is the employee's. The election is made annually on a "benefits election" form which sets forth all of the various benefits available to the employee, the flexible credits for a given year for the employee, the cost of each type of benefit option if selected by the employee, and the payroll deduction cost if the item is one that is reflected by a payroll deduction. Certain benefits will carry tax implications, and the benefits election form clearly sets forth each tax aspect so that the employee will understand it.

For the moment, let us focus on the medical coverage benefit. This benefit is now almost standard among corporate compensation programs. However, the extent of medical coverage varies from plan to plan.

Under the flexible benefit approach, the corporation offers, at its cost, a basic medical program for all employees. Superimposed on this program would be additional add-on programs providing more comprehensive coverage with varying deductible amounts. These add-ons would cost specified benefit credits. The employee would thus have his or her basic coverage with the ability to increase it to include such items as medical coverage, et cetera.

Another key element of employee fringe benefits is the retirement program. A flexible credit retirement program would have a basic program for all employees at the corporation's expense, and then a matching contribution program superimposed on the basic program. A matching contribution could be in any given ratio and the employee would make the election as to how he or she wishes his or her fund to be built up. The employee would allocate credits and the corporation would fund those credits with dollars and then match (in a specified ratio) these dollars. If, in a given year, the employee has more of a need for current income than a deferred income, he or she would allocate the credits for a bonus plan for said year rather than for the retirement plan. The Internal Revenue Service has ruled that since the election of optional benefits does not result in a reduction of compensation, the flexible benefit program is not a "cafeteria plan." Thus, participating employees will not realize immediate income merely by reason of their election of optional benefits through the allocation of flexible credits under the program.

As can be seen, the flexible benefit approach allows for a very easy integration of employee compensation programs when the merger or acquisition takes place. The balance of this segment of the chapter will outline the various elements of the flexible benefit package. Such a survey will enable the reader to understand the scope of the problem and the importance of considering the compensation problem as part of the merger or acquisition.

BENEFITS IN A FLEXIBLE TITLE BENEFIT PACKAGE

The primary form of providing for an employee is the "salary". Salaries are paid currently and taxed currently at ordinary income rates. The Salary is frequently used as a base for measuring other forms of compensation.

"Take-home pay" is that which most people use for everyday living; however, with the graduated tax rate, high salaries have netted the employees relatively too little to be satisfactory as total compensation. Since 1972, the tax rate on earned income is limited to 50 percent.

Current bonuses are taxed in the same manner as salaries. The obvious advantage of the current bonus is receiving a lump sum payment but the tax treatment makes this a limited form of compensation.

Both salaries and current bonuses must be realistic in the light of today's cost of living. Employees who share similar responsibilities should not receive dissimilar salaries unless there are circumstances which justify a difference. Variations, if any, are frequently found in this type of situation in the other forms of compensation.

QUALIFIED PLANS

The next type of compensation to consider comes under the heading of a "qualified plan". A "qualified plan'' (pension or profit-sharing) is one which meets the requirements of Sections 401(a) and 501(a) of the Internal Revenue Code of 1954, as amended. It has either definitely determinable benefits or contributions. Such a plan offers many tax advantages both to the employer and to the employee. Contributions by the employer are currently deductible, while tax to the employee is deferred until receipt of benefits or the making available of benefits, and the plan's fund build-up is tax-free. In addition, lump sum payouts under certain circumstances convert ordinary income tax treatment thereon to capital gain tax treatment, or are given a special income averaging treatment. Death benefits may pass to a beneficiary estate tax-free; and the first $5000 of the death benefit from a deceased employee's account (attributable to employer contributions) can go to the beneficiary free of income tax.

A qualified plan must be funded under specific rules. It must not favor the more highly paid employees, officers, or stockholders. It must be established by the employer for the exclusive benefit of its employees or their beneficiaries; its sole purpose must be to offer employees either (a) a share of the profits of the business, or (b) an income after retirement. The plan must be (1) permanent, (2) in writing, (3) communicated to employees, and (4) meet certain other requirements specified in Code Section 401 as to coverage, etc.

A profit sharing plan, as opposed to a pension plan, is a plan designed to provide participation in profits by the covered employee. The contributions by the employer to a profit sharing plan may be a predetermined percentage of annual profits, or may be left to the discretion of the employer on an annual basis. Since the employer's contributions to a profit sharing plan may and ordinarily will fluctuate substantially from year to year, the benefits ultimately to be paid to the covered employee will necessarily be indeterminate. Hence, the essential difference between a pension plan and a profit sharing plan is that in a pension plan the benefits ultimately to be paid are fairly well fixed at the inception of the plan, whereas in a profit sharing plan the benefits are not determinable at any time prior to distribution.

Contributions to a pension or profit sharing plan are deductible if they are actually paid within a prescribed time. As a general rule, the payment must be made within the year in which the deduction is claimed. For employers on the cash method, the rule is inflexible. For those on the accrual method, a grace period of up to 2 1/2 months may be allowed. An obligation to make a payment into a pension or profit-sharing plan cannot accrue unless a plan is in existence and depends on how far the corporation has gone in taking the necessary affirmative action. For example, if the plan is not a trusteed plan and it is evidenced only be annuity contracts with an insurance company, the IRS has ruled that it will not be in effect until the annuity contracts are executed and issued. In a trusteed plan where the trustee is to hold a group annuity contract, the plan will be considered to be in effect, if before the end of the year the corporation has taken all the necessary steps to establish the plan, has applied for the contracts, has had the application accepted, has prepared the contracts in sufficient detail to outline the term of the plan, has made an irrevocable part payment of the premium, and has communicated the plan to the employees.

Payment to a pension or profit sharing plan may be made in the form of cash or other property, but a payment by promissory note is not acceptable.

A pension or profit sharing trust may make limited investments in the securities of the employer corporation. The trust may make the investment directly from its available funds, provided that the exclusive benefit of the employees is the sole purpose for the purchase. The employer corporation also may make (within specified limits) its contribution in the form of its own securities or those of a subsidiary or parent corporation. In that event, the corporation will have no taxable gain, even if it had acquired its own securities at a lower cost than the value of the securities at the time of the contribution. If the original pension or profit sharing plan directs such an investment in the securities of the employer, potential fiduciary problems can be avoided.

Amounts placed in pension or profit sharing plans are considered together with salaries in determining the reasonableness of compensation. Besides that limitation, the Internal Revenue Code imposes a statutory limit to the amounts that an employer can deduct for contributions to a profit sharing plan. The primary limitation on the employer's deduction is 15 percent of the compensation otherwise paid or accrued during the taxable year to all employees covered under the plan. Compensation otherwise paid or accrued means every item for which the employer takes a compensation deduction. If the employer contributes less than the maximum in any one or more years, he may catch up in future years through carrying over to such years the ability to contribute amounts up to the maximum in each year the plan is in operation. There is a limitation on this carryover, in that the total deduction, including the regular allowance for the year, cannot exceed 25 percent of eligible compensation. Similarly, if contributions in excess of the 15 percent primary limit to a profit-sharing plan are made, the excess may be carried over to the earliest future year, but only to the extent that the current contributions for that year are less than the 15 percent primary limit.

For pension plans, the Employees Retirement Income Security Act (ERISA) has established minimum funding standards. Each covered plan must maintain an account called the "funding standard account," and each year this account is to be charged with liabilities which must be paid to satisfy minimum funding standards. If contributions are less than the minimum, the funding standard account will show an accumulated funding deficiency, which will result in the imposition of an excise tax of 5 percent of the amount of the accumulated funding deficiency.

One advantage of a profit sharing or pension plan is that although the corporation obtains an immediate tax deduction for its contributions, the employee beneficiary ordinarily does not currently include any part of the contribution in his taxable income. This is true even though a part or all of the contribution may be irrevocably vested in the employee or his designated beneficiary.

There is no requirement that all eligible employees participate in a plan. But where a plan discriminates in favor of a certain class of employees, contributions are not deductible and the covered employee may be subject to immediate tax consequences.

Where a pension or profit sharing trust purchases life insurance on an employee participant which is payable directly to the employee's beneficiaries, or is payable to the trust, which then pays it to the employee's beneficiaries, the Treasury Department has concluded that the life insurance protection thus obtained by the employee is a current benefit which must be currently taxed rather than treated as deferred compensation. The amount currently taxed to the employee, however, is only that portion of the total premium which represents the net one year term cost of the difference between the face amount of the policy and the surrender value at year end.

An employee is not taxed on his share of the qualified plan until it actually is distributed or until it is made available to him. A plan that contemplates some leeway by allowing early withdrawals must draw a careful line between those that will be sanctioned and those that can result in premature taxability.

Perhaps the most significant advantage of a pension or profit sharing plan to the executive is that the executive is given the opportunity to draw the share contributed by the employer plus all the increments on both that share and on the share he may have contributed himself at a long term capital gain rate or as specially

averaged ordinary income. This special treatment applied only if the entire amount that is payable is actually distributed within one taxable year and if the distribution is made on account of the employee's death, his attainment of age 59½, his separation from service of the employer or after his becoming disabled. Any other distributions will constitute ordinary income to the extent that they exceed contributions of the employee himself.

Obviously, the qualified plan is an exceedingly good method of building a retirement fund and as an estate planning tool. But, because of the anti-discrimination requirements for qualified plans, they have a somewhat limited application to executives. For them, we look to the next item of the compensation package.

LONG-TERM DEFERRED PAY PLAN

When the concept of the long-term deferred pay plan was first developed, it was facilitated by the use of a contract entered into between employer and employee whereby, as a rule, the employer agreed to pay the employee a fixed amount of money during a specific period of time; in return, the employee agreed that during this time period, (which would generally begin at the employee's retirement, when his taxable income dropped off, reducing his tax bracket,) the employee would act as consultant to the employer and fulfill certain other conditions (non-compete, etc.)

Then in 1960, the Internal Revenue Service issued what is now the theology in deferred compensation - Revenue Ruling 60-31. The Service stated that an employer and an employee could agree, prior to the time the compensation is earned, to defer all or a portion of such compensation to a later date. The tax on such income would similarly be deferred until the income was paid out. No conditions such as consideration were necessary.

This opened the door to the wide use of deferred compensation in tax planning. Then, in recent years, as inflation eroded the value of the dollar, employees began to feel that the dollar deferred today came back in the future worth less than a currently received dollar upon which tax was paid.

Thus was born the "investment account" This is a bookkeeping entry—a reserve on the employee's books equal to the amount of the deferred compensation. The employer then invests and reinvests its own funds equivalent to all or part of the investment account in marketable securities listed on the New York or American Stock Exchange of a caliber and diversity normally purchased by institutional trustees for trust accounts. Said investments are held by the employer and any amount realized therefrom (as a result of dividends, appreciation in security value, etc.) serves to increase the amount of the investment account and the ultimate amount to be paid to the employee. Any loss realized from such investment program serves to decrease the amount of the investment account and the ultimate amount to be paid to the employee. Similarly, the investment account is reduced by direct expenses and taxes incurred by the employer as a result of making such investments.

The investments and all the income therefrom are the property of the employer and are invested and reinvested by the employer in its sole discretion and the employee has no rights whatsoever to the investments. His rights are solely limited to receiving from the employer the annual payments of deferred compensation set forth in the agreement. The employee is given no right to direct the employer with respect to any investment or reinvestment. The deferred compensation is to be paid out to the employer over a fixed period of years beginning with the first day of the month subsequent to the day his full-time employment with the employer terminates or as soon thereafter as is practicable. In this manner, the employee benefits from the investing of deferred moneys during the deferred period.

When the funds are finally paid out, they are taxed as ordinary income, but by spreading the years of pay out, the tax rates can hopefully be kept low. This affords great flexibility in balancing taxes with compensation. It is also useful as an estate planning device.

SUPPLEMENTAL PENSION

Another type of compensation that has some popularity is the supplemental pension. This is a non-qualified plan which may be either non-contractual or contractual. As to the former, a policy may be adopted, without a contractual obligation of any sort, of paying certain employees stated amounts each year subsequent to their retirement. This is not funded in advance, nor is a formal contract entered into. The particular employee relies upon the employer's general policy to that effect. When he retires, the Board of Directors votes the amount to be paid to him each year.

The tax results under this arrangement are relatively simple. The employer gets a deduction only if, as and when it makes a payment to the employee. The payment becomes taxable income to the employee when he receives it.

The disadvantages of non-contractual pensions are (1) if an employer makes this arrangement for a number of employees, it is undertaking a substantial liability for the future; (2) it may be deferring a deduction from a current high tax year to a future lower tax year; and (3) from the employee's point of view, he has no assurance that he will ever receive anything; that even after payments begin, they will be continued; or that his employer will be financially able to meet its liabilities after he retires.

The contractual non-qualified pension is the basic deferred compensation agreement as discussed previously, except that as geared to a pension benefit, the employee's interest is forfeitable until he retires or dies or becomes permanently disabled, whichever may occur first.

SHORT-TERM DEFERRED PAY-PLAN

The next item in the compensation package is the short-term deferred pay plan. This is similar to the regular deferred pay plan but it is geared to specific needs of particular employees. Most people have special times during their lives when they need relatively large sums of additional funds, such as their children's college years, the year in which a house is purchased or when a wedding is held. Therefore, compensation planners have developed a program to provide payments at these times. By prudent planning with the employee, his financial needs can be met and great loyalty to the employer can be attained.

Another type of compensation program is the stock bonus plan. Here payment is made to the employees in the form of a bonus in the employer's stock. There is no cash outlay by the employer, but there is a dilution of its stock. The tax result is a current income tax attribution to the employee, which is not a happy result as the employee may find himself in a short-cash position.

Perhaps a better approach would be the deferred stock bonus plan. If the stock is paid out in installments, the tax will be spread accordingly. Dividends can be paid to the employee even though the stock has not been distributed to him at the time that the dividends were declared.

Next, we come to the qualified stock purchase plan. Being "qualified", this plan cannot discriminate in favor of Key employees or shareholders and this has a relatively limited use. Under such a plan, there is no tax when the employees receive or exercise their options. The gain on the sale of the stock is capital gain if certain conditions (holding period and price) are met.

There is also the non-qualified stock purchase plan

under which the Key employee purchases stock of the employer below market price on the installment basis. There is usually a special class of stock for this purpose. This is a good incentive to build the value of the corporation. The bargain purchase of corporate stock results in current taxation on the bargain element of the stock but the tax effect can be somewhat mitigated by the terms applied to the special class of stock used for this plan.

Another type of stock plan is the qualified restricted stock option plan. Stock options have historically been the recipients of special tax treatment, and thus have been a favorite "fringe benefit" with which to compensate Key employees. A qualified option under Section 422 of the Internal Revenue Code of 1954, as amended, is one where the option price is at least equal to the market price of the stock at the time of grant. If a good faith effort is made to set the option price at or above the fair market value, and it is determined that the effort failed, the stock option is not disqualified as it had been in the past. However the employee must report ordinary income when the option is exercised in the amount of 150 percent of the spread between the option price and the fair market value of the stock at the time of grant, or if less, 100 percent of the spread when the option is exercised.

A plan under which the option is granted must be approved by the corporation's shareholders within twelve months before or after adoption and must indicate total shares issuable under the options and the class of employees to receive the options. Grants must be made within ten years after adoption by the corporation or approval by the shareholders, whichever is earlier, and the option itself must be exercised within five years of grant, during the employee's lifetime, and only by the employee or by a transferree under laws of descent and distribution. The option may not be exercised while a prior qualified or restricted option held by the employee is outstanding. The employee's stock ownership immediately subsequent to the grant, must not exceed 5 percent of the voting power or value of the stock of the corporation (or its subsidiary or parent as the case may be) unless the equity capital of such corporation or corporations is less than two million dollars.

Then, in order to obtain capital gain treatment for the spread between option price and sale price of the stock acquired under a qualified stock option, the employee must hold the stock for at least three years. A sale prior thereto will split the tax treatment resulting in ordinary income on the spread between option price and value of stock at exercise, and capital gain on the spread between value of stock at exercise and sale price.

The qualified stock option plan is both an excellent incentive program and a useful estate planner's tool.

The non-qualified stock option plan results in ordinary income tax measured at the time the option is exercised, if there is no readily ascertainable value when the option is granted. If there is a readily ascertainable value at grant, tax is incurred when the option is granted. There may be capital gain on sale of the stock if the holding period requirement is met. There is limited use of the non-qualified stock option plan because of these tax consequences.

A special hybrid of the employee stock option plan is the Employee Stock Ownership Plan (ESOP), which may be a qualified or nonqualified employee benefit plan. It consists of a trust which has as its primary objective the acquisition of stock issued by the employer. The stock acquired by an ESOP is allocated annually to the accounts of participating employees in proportion to their annual compensation.

There is also the Thrift or Savings Plan. This is like offering the employee an employer operating savings account with additional advantages. Voluntary employee contributions are matched (but not necessarily to 100 percent) by the employer. The employer operates the Fund, usually utilizing payroll deductions for the employer's contributions. The Funds are often invested in the employee's stock so that the growth of the employee's account will be related to the employer's growth. If the plan is non-discriminatory, tax consequences will be deferred. This is a very effective program for non-Key employees and is often incorporated with a qualified pension plan.

There is also the "Affiliate stock purchase plan" which is a prime method of compensating Key employees. This occurred in the Ford-Dearborn Motors situation where executives are permitted to invest in one of the employer's newly created subsidiaries or affiliates (which may have been created just for this purpose). Stock in the new company is acquired at a relatively low cost at the time of organization and then the value thereof is built up by the employers feeding the new company business. When the executive retires from the employer, he sells his now highly valuable stock in the new company to the employer under capital gain circumstances.

Another program is the shadow stock plan. This is an ordinary income situation in which the employer establishes a plan whereunder a number of "units of participation" are set aside for employees. These units are each equivalent in value to the value of a share of stock of the employer. The units are bookkeeping entries, not actual stock. The employer then allocates part or all of such units among its Key employees, setting up on its books a separate account for each such employee. As the years pass, stock dividends increase the number of units of participation; cash dividends are recorded in the employee's account as equivalency dollars and are accumulated until there are enough equivalency dollars to theoretically purchase a share of equivalency stock at its existing value. At such time, the cash dividend account is debited and the employee is credited with another unit of participation in his account. When the employee retires or terminates his service after a "vesting period," he is paid in cash the difference between the market value of the employee's stock when the units of participation were allocated to him and the market value of said stock at the date of retirement or vested termination.

The income is taxed as ordinary income, but income averaging would mitigate against severe tax consequences, or the payments could be spread out over a number of years to reduce the overall tax rate. Since the employee's return is geared to the market performance of the employer's stock, this is a fine incentive program. It is also useful for estate planning.

The next type of program is the Management stock plan whereunder an employer issues to its Key employees a special class of stock for low cost purchase. The stock then appreciates, as does the employer's other stock, with the growth of the employer. The employer enters into a "buy-sell" agreement with the employees who receive the management stock whereby it will repurchase such stock from the employees at retirement or termination of service after a specified number of years. The repurchase formula can include measuring elements of company performance as compared to the employee's department's performance, increase in book value of stock, increase in market value of stock, a multiple of earnings, or, perhaps a combination thereof. The Key employee will realize capital gain on the sale of his management stock to his employer. This type of plan is also very useful in estate planning.

INSURANCE AND MEDICAL PLANS

The next type of compensation plan swings over to the insurance field. Here, we have "Key man" insurance, which is used primarily in connection with closely held corporations in order to protect the corporation should a "Key man" die. Then there is split dollar insurance which provides family protection at minimal tax cost to the employee. This is a very valuable estate planning tool and can also be used to fund deferred compensation agreements.

Life insurance is an absolute necessity for an employee fringe benefit program. The same is true for a medical insurance program; Blue Cross, Blue Shield,

Major Medical, or their equivalents. Employers frequently provide such coverage for their employees and permit the employees to pay for coverage for their families.

A corporation can provide tax-free insurance to its employees for (1) medical expenses which are acutally incurred by the employee or his dependents; (2) qualified sick pay; and (3) permanent injury to the employee or his dependents. Neither the premium payments nor the proceeds are taxable to the employee. The amounts so paid are treated as though they are received through accident and health insurance plans, which generally are exempt from tax.

The corporate employer may deduct the cost of insuring employees against illness and accidents as an ordinary and necessary business expense. However, in a closely held corporation, the costs of supplying insurance to stockholder officers again may be subject to the rule of reasonable compensation or be deemed a constructive dividend to the insured.

Unlike pension and profit sharing plans, health and accident insurance plans need not be non-discriminatory. They can be limited to top management.

As an alternative, a corporation may arrange to pay its employees' actual medical, hospital or surgical expenses. It can do so either through an insured plan or through direct payment. The corporation is entitled to deduct these sums, while, if the plan is non-discriminatory, no part of the payments will be taxable to the employee. If the plan is discriminatory, there may be some taxable income element to the employee. The plan need not be formal nor need it be in writing. Like health and accident insurance, coverage may be limited to a small group of employees or even to one employee. The plan must be in existence and communicated to the employee beneficiaries before the circumstances calling it into play arise. A resolution of the board of directors creating the plan and authorizing payments is a sound precautionary measure to prove the pre-existence of the plan.

The cost of individual hospital and medical insurance procured by employees may be reimbursed by the employer. If the employer makes the reimbursement check payable to the employee's insurance company or to the employee and the insurance company jointly, the payment may not be taxable income to the employee.

Up to $5,200 a year in sick pay may be excluded from the income of retirees under age 65 who are permanently and totally disabled. The exclusion is reduced by the amount by which the adjusted gross income of the retiree exceeds $15,000.

Death benefit payments up to $5,000 can be made to the beneficiaries of a decedent employee if the payments are made by the employer because of the employee's death. This tax-free privilege does not apply if the employee would have had a non-forfeitable right to receive the money during his life. In addition, the transferor's intentions must be that of detached and disinterested generosity. Payments that are made in corporate self-interest will not be excludable from the gross income of the taxpayer. Usually the existence of a plan or practice, even though disbursement is discretionary with the employer, strongly indicates that the payments are not benefits.

The employer may compensate his employees by carrying group term life insurance for their benefit. Premiums are deductible by employers and not included in the gross income of employees. The non-taxable amount of such term insurance is limited to $50,000. However, where the group term life insurance is provided for by contract under an employee annuity or pension or profit-sharing plan, the $50,000 limitation is not applicable. In addition, the limitation is not applicable where the policy is on an individual who has terminated his employment and has reached retirement age or is disabled.

In order to be able to give insurance benefits to selective employees, some employers prefer the split dollar arrangement, which has the advantage of allowing discrimination in favor of individual executives without granting the same benefits throughout the company. Split dollar insurance generally involves the purchase of a permanent form of insurance by the employer on the employee's life. The employer pays the annual premiums to the extent of the yearly increases in the cash surrender value of this policy, and the employee pays only the balance of the premium.

The amount of insurance proceeds payable to the employee's beneficiaries decreases with each annual payment by the employer, who is entitled to the increasing amount of the cash surrender value. Nevertheless, the employee receives valuable insurance protection for a long time at a relatively small outlay for premiums in the early years. After a short period, the earnings on the employer's investment are sufficient to cover the insurance costs, and the employees will not be required to make any further payment. The employee must include in his income each year the cost of one year's term insurance on the declining amount of protection enjoyed less any part of the premium he pays.

The rates on which executives will be taxed on a split dollar arrangement still are low enough to constitute an advantage to them over the rates they will have to pay after tax without the benefit of a company loan.

Moreover, there is the advantage of having the use of company funds to pay the major part of the premiums. On the other hand, the employer will not be entitled to a deduction for compensation paid.

MISCELLANEOUS BENEFITS AND PERQUES

Finally, there is the bundle of miscellaneous fringe benefits which must not be overlooked in the compensation package.

If an employer makes an interest-free loan to an employee, the net economic effect is the same as if it had paid him an additional compensation equal to the interest rate on the loan. If the employee itemizes his deductions on his tax return, the theoretical interest deduction would match the theoretical income. Thus, interest-free loans to employees are not considered a taxable benefit.

In tight money periods, when an employee might have to pay a finance company a higher rate than his corporate employer would pay, the interest-free loan could prove to be a substantial economic benefit. Moreover, for an employee who does not itemize his deductions, it can prove to be a tax benefit at any time. Interest-free loans to stockholders who are not employees may not necessarily obtain such favorable treatment. The interest-free loan could be treated as a divident to the stockholder.

Employee moving expenses may be deductible by the employee if the move and expense meet certain requirements. Employer reimbursement, whether direct or indirect, must be included in the employee's gross income. Any move must be made pursuant to the change of a principal place of work which must be 35 miles farther from the old residence than was his old principal place of work. Moreover, the taxpayer must be a full-time employee in the general location of his new place of work for at least 39 weeks of the 12-month period immediately following his arrival in order to take advantage of this deduction.

An employer may provide his employee with free meals or lodging or both if certain tests are met. The value of the meals will not be taxable if they are furnished for the convenience of the employer and they are furnished on the business premises of the employer. The value of lodging will not be taxable if in addition to the above two conditions, the employee is required to accept such lodging on the business premises as a condition of his employment.

President Carter attempted to cut down on executive prerequisites, and consequently Congress eliminated certain entertainment facilities such as yachts, hunting lodges and club dues. However, certain other prerequisites still remain. Among these are:

A. Business Meals: Expenditures for food and beverages under circumstances which are conducive to a business discussion (considering the surroundings in which furnished), the taxpayer's trade, business or income producing activity, the relationship to such trade, business or activity of the persons to whom the food and beverages are furnished, and to any other relevant facts. There is no requirement that business actually be discussed. Thus, if the described circumstances are established and if the amounts are deductible as ordinary and necessary business expenses or as expenses for the production of income, the expenses for food and beverages will be deductible without reference to the "directly related to or associated with" requirements of §274 of the Internal Revenue Code detailed below.

B. Food and Beverages for Employees: The cost of food and beverages furnished on the business premises primarily to employees of the taxpayer will not be taxed to the employees, and are deductible to the employer. Also expenses for food and beverages furnished to non-employee business guests will be deductible to the employer and not taxable to the guests, if furnished in a dining room which is primarily for the taxpayer's business premises. This rule applies both to the typical company cafeteria and to meals furnished to employees because their presence on the job at all times is essential.

C. Entertainment Expense "Compensation": Expenses for goods, services and facilities are deductible to the employer to the extent that the expenses are treated by the employer as compensation paid to the employee on the employer's income tax return and as wages for the purposes of withholding.

D. Reimbursed Expenses: Expenses paid or incurred by an individual in connection with the performance by him of services for an employer for which the individual is reimbursed by the employer under a reimbursement or other allowance arrangement are deductible by the employer, and not taxed to the employee.

E. Recreational Expenses: Expenses for recreational, social or similar activities primarily for the benefit of employees of the taxpayer are deductible by the employer and not taxable to the employee. For example, expenses of operating a bowling alley or swimming pool, tennis facility or handball court will be deductible if the facilities are available to all employees. These recreational expenses apply only with respect to activities which are primarily for employees who are officers, shareholders or other owners who own at least a 10 percent interest in the business, or are highly compensated employees.

F. Business Meetings: Expenses incurred by an employer which are directly related to business meetings of its employees, stockholders, agents or directors are deductible by the employer and not taxed to the employees.

G. Business League Meetings: Expenses directly related to and necessary for attendence at business meetings or conventions or of organizations such as business leagues, real estate boards, chambers of commerce, and boards of trade are deductible by the employer and not taxed to the employees.

H. Items Available to Public: Goods and services which are made available by the employer to the general public are deductible. Thus expenses for entertainment of the general public by means of television, radios, newspapers and the like are deductible. Moreover, the maintenance of private parks, golf courses and similar facilities also is deductible to the extent these facilities are available for public use.

An employee who is reimbursed by his employer for travel and entertainment expenses incurred in the course of his employment, must report the reimbursement as part of his income unless he accounts to his employer or does not claim the expenses as deductions on his return. Under §274 of the Internal Revenue Code, no deduction is allowed for income tax purposes (with the exception of the above-mentioned items), for any expense respecting an activity which is of a type generally considered to constitute entertainment, amusement or recreation except to the extent that the businessman or business organization establishes that the expense was either directly related to the active conduct of his trade or business or was associated with the actual conduct of the taxpayer's business and that the entertainment occurred directly before or after a substantial and bona fide business discussion.

Entertaining guests at nightclubs, country clubs, theatres, football games and prize fights, and on hunting, fishing, vacation and similar trips are examples of activities that constitute "entertainment amusement and recreation." In addition, "entertainment" includes any business expense incurred in the furnishing of food and beverages, a hotel suite, a vacation cottage, or an automobile either to a customer or to any member of a customer's family.

To demonstrate that such entertainment is "directly related" to the active conduct of a trade or business, the taxpayer must further show that (1) he had more than a general expectation of deriving some income and other specific trade or business at some indefinite future time; (2) he actively engaged in business discussions or negotiations during the entertainment period; and (3) the principal character or aspect of the combined business and entertainment was the transaction of business.

All ordinary or necessary business related travel expenses are deductible, provided they are incurred away from home and are not lavish and extravagant under the particular circumstances. Travel expenses include transportation fares, meals and lodging and incidental expenses such as telephone charges and the like. In order to be allowable, the expenses must be reasonable and necessary for the operation of the taxpayer's business and must be primarily related to it. To be primarily related to the business, the amount of time spent on the taxpayer's business as compared with the amount of time spent on personal affairs often is determinative.

Expenditures paid or incurred away from home by an individual for travel outside the United States are deductible only to the extent that they are made in the pursuit of trade business or income production activity. If the travel was primarily for business and some non-business activities also occurred, an allocation must be made between the two activities in order to determine the amount that is deductible. The allocation rule, however, applies only where the travel away from home is longer than one week or where the non-business portion of the trip represents 25 percent or more of the total time of the travel.

No deduction is allowed for expense paid or incurred by an individual in attending more than two foreign conventions a year. If an individual attends more than two foreign conventions a year he must select which of the two foreign conventions are to be taken into account for the purposes of determining the allowable deductions.

With all expenditures for travel, entertainment or gifts, the taxpayer must substantiate: (1) the amount of the expense; (2) the time and place of the travel, entertainment, or date and description of the gift; (3) the business purpose of the expense; and (4) the business relationship of the recipient to a taxpayer. These should be demonstrated by adequate records or sufficient evidence corroborating the taxpayer's own statement.

Often, an employer will establish an educational foundation to provide scholarships for children of its employees. This can be an important incentive for employees and should not be overlooked.

The above materials are an indication of the complexity of the employee compensation area. No attempt has been made to go into great detail with respect to any of the elements discussed. Any corporate package in this area must be tailored to the particular needs of the corporation, its employees and its shareholders. This requires meticulous and detailed work in setting up the total flexible benefit package. The end results are satisified employees and a structure that will not hinder or defeat a merger or acquisition.

It should be noted that the surviving corporation in a statutory merger or the acquiring corporation in an asset acquisition reorganization, can generally assume the liability to make payments to employees under the above-mentioned compensation programs. Moreover, such successor corporation may receive a deduction when it makes the payments.

By way of contrast, if the assets are purchased for cash, payment made by the successor corporation under an assumed benefits program, such as a deferred compensation plan, may be treated as a capital expenditure.

An ancillary area to employee compensation is that of the compensation received by the seller of a corporation. The seller may receive an immediate payment of the sales price, subject to capital gains tax and tax preference application. Or, the seller may take payment on the installment method of payout and pay the capital gains tax on each installment as received. Or, the acquisition might be a "tax-free" reorganization whereby the seller receives stock of the acquiring or surviving corporation. In such event, no tax will be paid until the said stock is sold. If the seller dies owning said stock, under present law, his estate will be able to take advantage of a stepped-up basis in such stock. This means that if the stock has increased in value over the decedent's basis (which will have been a transferred basis from his basis in his original corporation, which he sold in exchange for such stock), this increase is reflected in his estate valuation for estate tax purposes and then becomes part of the estate's basis for such stock for income tax purposes. Obviously, the health and age of the seller are a consideration in planning how he is to be compensated for the sale of his corporation.

Since capital gains rates are exceedingly low at present, and since inflation is running rampant, many sellers will want their money up front and will pay their taxes now. This is a sensible approach in today's economy. On the other hand, the installment method should be considered, under certain circumstances.

Section 453 of the Internal Revenue Code of 1954, as amended, permits a taxpayer to report a gain, but not a loss, from a casual sale or other casual disposition of personal property (other than inventory in the hands of the vendor) where the selling price exceeds $1,000.00, in personal property, electing the installment method. Unlike dealers in personal property, taxpayers seeking to use §453 with respect to casual personal property sales must restrict payments in the year of sale (exclusive of evidences of indebtedness of the purchaser and liabilities assumed by the purchaser) to not more than 30 percent of the selling price.

It is not necessary, for a valid installment election, that the seller receive any payments in the year of sale. A casual personal property disposition should qualify for the installment method in a transaction in which a small payment is made in the year of sale, or in any other year prior to the year of the second and final "balloon" payment. Moreover, the payments, regardless of the number stipulated, need not be regular, periodic, or in identical amounts. If a payment is made in the year of sale, there can be rights of prepayment in years following the year of sale.

The fact of an installment sale election does not change the tax consequences as between ordinary income and capital gains. The nature of the personalty sold will determine this.

The sales transaction itself, to qualify for the installment method, must be possessed of economic substance. If a seller structures a deferred payment sale through a related party as a conduit to a subsequent cash sale, the deferred payment sale will be ignored for purposes of the installment election.

Since personal property dispositions subject to the installment sale rules include sales of stock or securities by one not a dealer, the sale of the stock of a closely held company by the owner thereof would most certainly be eligible for §453 treatment. A redemption of stock of a shareholder by the redeeming corporation will also constitute a sale or other disposition for purposes of §453, so that gain, assuming all other requirements are met, will be subject to reporting under the installment method. The selling price is the total consideration received by the seller, including liabilities assumed by the purchaser as well as the amount of any mortgage to which the property is sold subject, whether or not assumed by the purchaser. In computing the selling price, the obligations of the purchaser are included at their face amount regardless of their actual fair market value. All other property (including an obligation of a third party) is included in the computation of selling price at its fair market value. If the selling price is not precisely ascertainable at the time of sale, the installment method may not be available. Thus, contingent consideration based upon future

performance may well eliminate the availability of §453. On the other hand, where the selling price has been reduced in a year after the year of sale, both the Courts and the Internal Revenue Service have treated the transaction as a renegotiation of the selling price. If it appears likely from the facts involved in such instance that the renegotiation was contemplated under the original contracts, the downward adjustment of the selling price could kill the installment sale treatment.

In general, evidence of indebtedness of the purchaser is not included in computing payments in the year of sale. Stock warrants issued by a corporation in connection with the acquisition of property are not evidences of indebtedness of the purchaser and therefore must be treated as a payment in the year of sale to the extent of their fair market value. However, a convertible debenture is an evidence of indebtedness and the conversion feature is neither valued separately nor considered an additional payment in the year of sale. If the seller, in the year of sale, disposes of the evidences of indebtedness of the purchaser, due and payable in subsequent years, to a third party, the amount received from such a disposition is not considered a payment in the year of sale, though the disposition itself may cause recognition of gain or loss. However, a payment of the purchaser in the year of sale in liquidation or an evidence of indebtedness of the purchaser given at the time of sale, will be considered as a payment in determining whether the 30 percent test has been met. Also if a payment or an evidence of indebtedness of the purchaser is due in the year of sale, but is not made to the seller because the seller disposes of the purchaser's obligation prior to the time for payment, the amount of such payment must nevertheless be treated as a payment in the year of sale. On the other hand, a satisfaction of evidence of indebtedness by the purchaser at less than face amount in the year of sale may be regarded as a disposition rather than an installment payment.

An advance payment, if regarded as an option payment or a contingent deposit, will generally be added to payments in the year of sale in determining if the 30 percent limitation has been met. Similarly, if the purchase price or more than 30 percent thereof is escrowed during negotiations, the installment sale treatment may not be available.

Where a taxpayer disposes of a going business, the transaction is regarded as a disposition of its separate assets. And where the business is sold under an installment arrangement, the sale of the business is regarded as a disposition of the individual assets, so that §453 would be available to virtually all assets, except inventory, so long as the 30 percent test is met. The sale of a single asset, even though having multiple uses, would be regarded as a single disposition for purposes of determining qualification under §453.

The regulations under §453 provide that any portion of any payment subject to §483(b), which is the imputed interest section of the Code, is not included as part of the selling price or the total contract price. If the contract provides for interest at the rate of at least 4 percent simple interest per annum, payable on each installment of principal at the time such an installment is payable, there is no unstated interest and §483 does not apply. If the contract does not provide for interest in an amount equal to or greater than the specified rate, total unstated interest is determined by discounting each payment due at an interest rate of 5 percent per annum compounded semi-annually, reduced by the present values of the interest, if any, provided under the contract. Section 483 does not apply to any payment due under a sale or exchange where the sales price can be determined, at the time of sale, not to exceed $3,000.

Ordinarily, an installment obligation held by a decedent at death is not subject to the disposition provisions of §453 at the time the obligation passes to the beneficiary from the decedent's estate. However, if an installment obligation is generated by an estate or trust upon the sale of an asset, any disposition of the obligation to a beneficiary is regarded as a disposition by the estate or trust under §453(d). Since the disposition is other than by sale or exchange, the gain or loss recognized will be the difference between the fair market value of the obligation at distribution and its basis.

If the estate receives an installment payment or an obligation acquired from the decedent, it will report income in the amount and character as would have been reported by the decedent had he lived and received the payment. If the estate disposes of the obligation by sale or exchange, including distributions in satisfaction of a pecuniary bequest or in discharge of a debt of the decedent, the estate will recognize income to the extent of the difference between the consideration received and the basis of the obligation. The income reportable by the estate upon such a sale or exchange retains the same character as that which would have been reported by the decedent had the obligation been disposed of by him.

The beneficiary who receives an installment obligation upon distribution from an estate (except in satis-faction of a pecuniary bequest) will continue to report income upon receipt of the installment obligation in the amount and character as would have been reportable by the decedent had he lived and collected the installment payments. Upon the death of the beneficiary, prior to completion of the installment payments, the obligation in turn passes to his estate and, if not collected during the period of administration, to his beneficiaries. The same rules would apply throughout.

It may thus be seen that §453 provides a method whereby the owner of a closely held corporation can spread the tax implications on the sale of his company for many years, including passing such spread of tax implications through his estate and his estate's beneficiaries.

Often, a seller of a corporation will be offered an employment opportunity in the continuing entity as part of the survivor's management. No seller should anticipate a long-continuing relationship with the new management. However, during the duration of such a relationship, a written employment contract is essential. Such agreement should carefully spell out all of the terms and conditions of employment (even to the "Bigelow" on the floor) and should be related to the available employee compensation programs discussed earlier. If a "non-compete" clause is to be part of such agreement, so that at the termination of the seller's employment, he cannot compete, said clause must be limited in time, and geographically, to be valid. A separate element of compensation should be allocated for this provision, to be paid during the non-compete period, with a death payment to the seller's estate should he die prior to the end of the period.

The primary concern relating to such an employment agreement is that the compensation be reasonable. This is especially important if the seller has participated in a "Tax-free" reorganization and has received stock in the surviving corporation as his sales price. If the compensation structure under the employment agreement is deemed unreasonable, the Internal Revenue Service will claim that the unreasonable part is a constructive dividend, not subject to the 50 percent earned income limitation.

Needless to say, in constructing a sales price where the seller will continue employment with the acquiring or surviving corporation, the sales price can be arranged on a "flexible benefit" structure to best accommodate the seller, his family, and the purchaser.

ROBERT H. HAYES

ROBERT H. HAYES knows the human side of acquisition firsthand from some 20 years as a management consultant and from the 1979 merger of his own firm, Robert H. Hayes and Associates, Inc., Chicago and Dallas, with William E. Hill & Company, New York. He founded Hayes in 1963 and is now President and chief executive officer of Hayes/Hill Incorporated. Mr. Hayes has spoken extensively on acquisitions, and has written on the subject previously for *Management Review,* a publication of the American Management Association.

8

"What Happens to My People After I Sell?"

The Human Side of Acquisitions

ROBERT H. HAYES

After spending several decades building his company into a profitable, successful concern, the middle-aged president of a medium-sized manufacturing business sold his company, with the understanding that he would stay on as CEO until his retirement some eight years hence. At the time the sale took place, both the seller and buyer said it was the best thing to happen to them.

But as soon as the deal was struck, things began to sour. The seller describes what happened:

> Immediately following the acquisition, we were descended upon by a hoard of corporate staff personnel from the home office. Each was a 'specialist' in a particular functional area, and their stated purpose was to acclimate us to 'our new parent's operations method.' What they actually succeeded in doing was driving our people crazy.
>
> We couldn't make a move without being told that our methods were outdated and that we'd have to adjust to the company's way of doing things. When I complained to Corporate about the situation, I was told that if I squawked too loud, my position would be in jeopardy. The net result was that company morale was destroyed and my key people began leaving. It wasn't long before I followed them.

This gentleman experienced a not uncommon series of events, and his story ended as many others do. Another seller in a similar situation reports:

> I knew the acquisition had been a mistake when they started insisting that we 'modernize' our operation through mechanization. The first thing they did was enlarge our plant and install new equipment. The labor savings they were counting on never materialized ... and our costs rose substantially. When they made us raise our prices, our sales volume began dropping. The last straw was when they insisted we cut corners on quality to reduce costs. Whenever I tried to dissuade them, they'd imply that I wasn't being progressive in my thinking. Throughout this entire period I felt like a helpless bystander.

It is this feeling of helplessness that is perhaps most compelling in such stories of acquisitions gone awry. Over and over, sellers tell of the enormous frustration and sadness they experience when—after years of being successfully in charge—they suddenly find they no longer run their own show.

But why should they be surprised? After all, they sold their companies willingly, didn't they? The answer is that in most cases where acquisition leads to such disillusionment, the sale was probably not conducted with the care and forethought necessary to ensure a "good fit" after the acquisition. A great deal has been written in management literature on how to find companies which are good acquisition prospects and how to evaluate these firms once they are located. But very little is written on how to manage the acquisition process itself and how to manage the personnel problems which can result.

Generally, both parties are oblivious to the human side of an acquisition until misunderstandings and resentments start to develop. Often these troubles grow quickly and become impossible to manage. They then end in a costly and demoralizing personnel loss which could have been avoided if more care had been taken all along for the human side of the acquisition.

The purpose of this chapter is to examine what can be done to assure that the human side of acquisition is handled well. While the bulk of this discussion focuses on the seller's concerns—"What Happens to My People After Selling?"—perhaps the best place to begin is with the acquirer. When all is said and done, it is the buyer who will be in control after the sale, and so everyone involved in the acquisition process should start being very clear what the buyer's intentions will be.

THE BUYER'S VIEW—IS RETENTION GOOD?

Management retention is not necessarily a good thing in itself; rather it depends on the buyer's broader strategic goals. Whether or not management stays on after a sale depends on what the buyer wants to accomplish. Two actual cases illustrate this well.

The first is a buyer which fits the high management retention mode precisely. The second is a highly profitable company which has many of the characteristics common to low retention companies. They are called Company "A" and Company "B" to protect their individual identities.

Company "A" which fits the high retention mode, is a large organization in the 2 to 3 billion dollar range. It was built by acquisitions and it confines its acquisitions to large, highly successful companies doing no less than 100 to 200 million in sales volume. Its acquisition requirements are quite high; it is looking for cash flows and returns on investment, which makes it turn down about four of every five acquisitions at which they look seriously.

As a result, Company "A" is always buying successful, fairly large, free-standing companies that have excellent management. And perhaps as important as excellent management, these companies have management depth, so selection for replacements can usually be made from inside the acquired company's own organization.

Company "A" has a very small staff group. In fact, other than clerical employees and people working on new acquisitions, this $3-billion company probably doesn't have more than 20 people at the corporate level. Company "A" controls its subsidiaries through detailed annual strategic plans and measurement against plans. As previously mentioned, this parent has a very high management retention rate in its subsidiaries.

Company "A" has no corporate personnel function; it sees personnel as a subsidiary function. The only corporate personnel function it recognizes is dealing with the top managements of the acquired companies, and Company "A" sees this function as being too important to delegate to a staff activity. Top personnel questions are handled by the chief executive officer.

How does this company evaluate management organization and depth in its pre-acquisition evaluation work? The chief executive officer and the head of the acquisition group do it themselves. Although they use consultants liberally for information collection and the like, they see this human evaluation as one of their key jobs in deciding whether they want to make the acquisition.

To illustrate the relationship between the CEO and a subsidiary president in this organization take the hypothetical situation of a subsidiary president in Company "A" who is making unorthodox and highly questionable organization changes, and say the corporation's chief executive officer hears about it from people within the subsidiary. What do you suppose he will do about it? The answer is, nothing. He considers the affairs of a subsidiary to be the subsidiary's business. As long as the subsidiary submits adequate plans—which means earning an adequate return—and meets its objectives, he negotiates with the subsidiary in a manner similar to the way two chiefs of state would negotiate at a summit meeting.

This strategy fits the desirable post-acquisition management retention mode. Management retention is not a big problem for Company "A". In fact, Company "A"'s management retention rate is in the 90 percent range.

Now take Company "B", a highly successful $1 billion company which displays many of the characteristics common to low management retention companies. It acquired a similar sized conglomerate active in electronics, metal fabrication, automotive aftermarket and several other fields. The acquired conglomerate was on the West Coast and had a headquarters staff of about 350 people. It was an extremely unfriendly take-over which ended in the courts. Company "B"'s basic strategy was to integrate this acquisition. Company "B" management wished to sell off the losers and dismantle the corporate staff, since they already had what they considered to be an adequate staff of their own. To accomplish this, it was essential that Company "B" achieve direct management control of the individual divisions which made up the acquisition.

The first thing Company "B" management did was move the subsidiary headquarters to New York. The second thing they did was to reduce the subsidiary staff from 350 people to 10 people, and then they sold off about a third of the acquired company's divisions. They are now earning a very handsome return on the acquisition. When they took it over, it was what might be termed "marginally" profitable.

Company "A" has a retention rate in the 90 percent range. Company "B" has a retention rate which is less than 30 percent. Is Company "A" doing a better human relations job than Company "B"? Not necessarily. It depends on the extent to which you want to integrate an acquisition. It depends on your strategy.

People management in acquisitions must follow directly from the overall acquisition strategy. Once the strategy is understood, the people actions flow rather easily. That is not to say that they are easy to implement, but they are generally easy to conceptualize.

It should also be remembered that mergers provide an excellent vehicle for culling ineffective or surplus managers. This opportunity should not be overlooked if integration is desirable.

Anthony Jay in his book *Management and Machiavelli* makes another very sound point about people in merger situations. Though he is talking about senior people, the point could be extended to management people in general. He says, "In an acquisition you should do one of two things. Either welcome the management warmly, encourage them, make them happy and make them yours, or terminate them and get them out of there as quickly as possible. Don't downgrade them, don't ignore them and don't leave them in the organization where they can cause trouble."

THE SELLER'S VIEW—
HOW IMPORTANT IS AUTONOMY?

"It turned out bad for me, the company, the employees—even the town. The company was kind of a leader in the community. Now it's just another business that has had to lay off a lot of people.

"I've never regretted anything in my life any more than I do this. I feel as though they defaced my baby."

These comments from unhappy sellers indicate a terrible feeling of loss and of no longer being in control. They reflect the heart of the human side of acquisition. Managerial autonomy and control are clearly the most important factors influencing what will happen to acquired top management after a sale.

Hayes/Hill Incorporated recently conducted a study of what happened to top executives after they sold their companies. Among those sellers who had planned to remain with their companies but who decided to leave when things went badly, extensive control or interference by the parent company in the operation of their business was reported to be the prime reason for leaving by over two-thirds of executives who left their companies following acquisition. The situation among executives who remained is almost the reverse, with over 75 percent reporting a satisfactory degree of autonomy. These relationships are depicted in Figure 8-1.

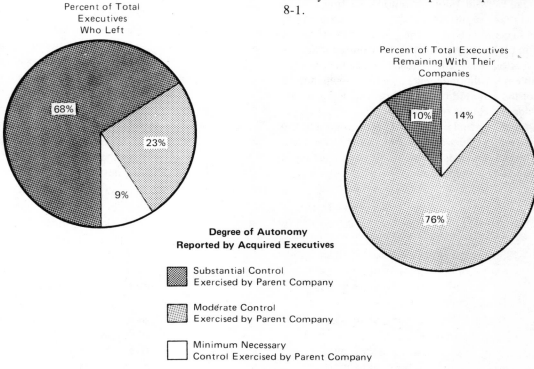

Percent of Total Executives Who Left

Percent of Total Executives Remaining With Their Companies

Degree of Autonomy Reported by Acquired Executives

- Substantial Control Exercised by Parent Company
- Moderate Control Exercised by Parent Company
- Minimum Necessary Control Exercised by Parent Company

A more precise definition of "autonomy" is appropriate at this point. Autonomy refers to the amount of day-to-day operating freedom an acquired division president is given to manage his business in pursuit of specific and agreed-upon goals and objectives. It does not imply that the division is ignored by corporate management or that the division president is free to operate without performance standards and objectives.

Quite the contrary, close involvement between division top management and the parent company is expected in establishing explicit goals and strategies, and relatively tight financial and budgetary control is naturally maintained to insure that these standards are achieved. It does mean, however, that the subsidiary president is free to make the day-to-day operating decisions involved in achieving these goals without close control by parent company management.

The impact of autonomy on acquired management retention is substantiated by the contrast in attitude and approach between companies with good and bad retention records. The differences are often subtle, but nevertheless real, and are basically a matter of emphasis.

Companies in the Hayes/Hill study which retained 50 percent or more of their acquired executives consistently reported a heavy emphasis on division independence and made every effort to maintain an autonomous environment for acquired subsidiary executives.

Companies with poorer retention records do not appear to attach significant importance to autonomy as a factor. In certain instances they do not appear to have a specific philosophy pertaining to acquired management retention, while others tend to place the onus for the problem on the independent and unsophisticated nature of the acquired owner and deal with the results rather than the causes of poor retention.

The following table comparing retention rates and expressed philosophies clearly depicts this contrast. As company retention rates fall below 50 percent, changes in philosophies become evident.

Company	Retention Rate	Representative Statements Depicting Philosophy Regarding Acquired Management Retention Problem
A	83%	"It is the expressed philosophy of our company to give as much autonomy as possible to acquired companies."
B	75%	"We give our divisions every opportunity to run their own businesses and solve their own problems. We have no operating or policy manuals, etc. Our divisions are on their own."
C	74%	"The single most important aspect in an acquisition is the management Our best results have always been where we've not tried to change a company's method of operation. We make every effort to give them as much autonomy as we can."
D	69%	"It really gets down to corporate philosophy and organization. You have to have autonomy in the divisions, and we make sure it's there.
E	68%	"Our divisions have a fair degree of autonomy. We never force them to do anything against their judgment."
F	67%	"We give our division management a pretty free hand. They get a minimum of interference from the home office."
G	58%	"An entrepreneur has to have leeway, and the parent company has to have confidence in him. Here he is treated with the same respect as the corporate president and he's never bothered by dictates or policy matters from Corporate."
H	50%	"Our company is very decentralized. We maintain the attitude that management is essential to the success of the acquisition. We never interfere except to review major capital expenditures."
I	48%	"We try to be as people-oriented as we can and really let them know their importance to the company."
J	47%	"The answer is to go out of your way not to buy small companies in new industries unless you've got the manpower ready as a backup. Too many entrepreneurs just can't accept that a big company doesn't revolve around one man."
K	47%	"We try to guide and assist the owner in getting acclimated to our methods. We try not to interfere in his decision making, but we do maintain tight control and insist on compliance with our operating procedures."

Company	Retention Rate	Representative Statements Depicting Philosophy Regarding Acquired Management Retention Problem
L	33%	"We try not to be unneccessarily rigid, but we do not leave acquired managers substantially independent. Some acquired managements just can't handle sophisticated systems of control.
M	33%	"Some autonomy is OK, but the important thing is how well your acquisition plan is followed."
N	29%	"The key is to make sure you have good people at the second level of management to move up when top management leaves. Entrepreneurs tend to become too provincial and can't accept new ways of doing things."
O	25%	"No particular approach."
P	20%	"Too many people lead you on about staying when they really don't intend to. Most men who sell out don't want to stay, and even if they do, they never last long in a big organization."

From the standpoint of the individual acquired company owner, the question of what does or does not constitute a satisfactory degree of autonomy is a subjective one. Nevertheless, acquired executives are surprisingly consistent in their descriptions of past problems and conflicts which resulted from a lack of operating autonomy. These can be categorized into four problem areas:

- Unsolicited Parent Company Directives and Decisions
- Excessive Operating Control
- Excessive Reporting Requirements
- Corporate Staff Interference.

It is essential that both prospective buyers and sellers carefully examine the probable degree of management autonomy which will be in effect after an acquisition.

A look at what frequently goes wrong in the personal relationships resulting from acquisitions is instructive for managers interested in avoiding such problems. In the Hayes study of 200 acquisitions made by a core group of Fortune 500 companies, only 42 percent of top management remained as long as five years. And this low figure is just the tip of the iceberg, because only companies that pride themselves on rather good post-retention records would participate in such a voluntary study.

Of the top managers who left after their companies were acquired, 82 percent said if they had it to do over again they would not sell at all. Some admitted that if they were selling again, knowing what they do now, they would gladly sacrifice dollars to assure that they could maintain management autonomy after the sale, or that the business would be run along lines they approved. To get a better understanding of why their experiences turned out so badly, the Hayes study compared them to the top men who stayed on.

HOW TO GET WHAT YOU BARGAIN FOR

In almost all of the cases where top management was retained, the pre-acquisition negotiations took place on both social and business levels and usually included wives. The acquiror put more substantial top management involvement into the negotiations and took the negotiations a little slower and more professionally. *And* perhaps most important from the seller's point of view, the owners of the acquired companies were much more thorough and thoughtful in their approach to selling their companies than were the men who ended up leaving.

The study determined that acquired executives who stayed on with their companies took several significant steps to satisfy themselves that the prospective buyer was, in fact, the kind of company they were counting on.

One of the sellers who left shortly after acquisition admitted, "I was hypnotized by the money." Only 29 percent of those who left felt, on reflection, that they had done an adequate job of investigation before they sold.

The sellers who became dissatisfied were naive and actually rather stupid about negotiations. They did not ask the simplest questions, such as "What are your plans for our company?" They did not consult management from other companies the prospective buyer had acquired to determine what its track record might be. They did not review the factors which could become post-acquisition points of contention, such as annual compensation, the acquiror's objectives, reporting relationships and the degree of autonomy allowed to existing management. The following are some considerations a wise seller will take into account before selling.

Employment Contracts

Experience shows that neither party is above breaking contracts if a deal goes sour. However, if the buyer breaks an employment contract, he will end up paying severance pay, benefits or other compensation.

Therefore, negotiating employment contracts may give the seller a good idea of the prospective buyer's intentions. If the parent is not quite serious about retaining management, it is not likely to tie itself to financially binding contracts. Contracts can serve to protect the seller and his top management not only by assuring a pay-off if the post-acquisition period does not go well, but also by telling—before the sale—whether the buyer is really interested in retaining existing management.

Compensation and Benefits

Compensation usually emerges as an issue on the human side of acquisition when the buyer seeks to lower acquired management's total package. The following comments from the Hayes/Hill study indicate how this sometimes happens:

> "I was guaranteed a bonus based on earnings. When it came time to settle up, however, they told me it was out of the question because I'd be earning more than the president of the company."
> "They took away our profit sharing plan and put their own in. It meant a reduction in money for me and excluded all my key people."
> "First they took away my company car. Then they reduced my salary to bring it in line with other division presidents. I wouldn't have minded so much if they had told me before the acquisition, but this way was really underhanded."

The best way to preclude such unhappy scenarios is to insist upon thorough, well-managed negotiations in the first place. Such post-acquisition compensation disputes often reflect a deeper problem of incompatible management styles or corporate goals which would probably have surfaced in careful pre-acquisition negotiations.

When the subject of long-term compensation comes up, many executives find the myriad of parent company incentive programs confusing and sometimes even mysterious. But this field is much simpler than most managers think. There may be a dozen different names for incentive plans, but they really boil down to just a few basic concepts related to overall company strategy. From there, it's just variations on a theme. The seller should make it his business really to understand the implications of these programs before he sells his company.

As for benefits, sellers are often told "Your people's benefits will equal or be better than what you have now." This really cannot be believed any more—some benefits will be reduced and others will be increased, just in the nature of the ERISA requirements and good business practice. A seller concerned

that his people retain the benefits package they now enjoy should work this out in specific pre-acquisition discussions.

Organization Plans and Reporting Relationships

Many of the organization changes made after a company is sold would not have been acceptable to the seller and his management before the deal was closed. Thus, the seller has more control over his company's future if he tried to pin down such matters during the negotiation process.

A problem here is that a buyer that plans to purge the seller's management might not be wise to communicate its plans to reduce the acquired company's staff. One way the seller can investigate what probable organization plans would evolve after the sale is to talk with companies that the buyer has already acquired. Some questions to ask:

- How autonomous is existing management?
- Does management report to the Corporate CEO directly or through channels?
- Are organizational changes communicated clearly and quickly to the people involved?
- Does affiliation with the parent company serve to bog down, or to expedite, work flow?
- Does management find it has to devote more time than is warranted to corporate meetings and reporting requirements?

Though it is impossible to predict precisely what post-acquisition organizational changes will come about, asking these questions can help give the seller an idea of whether the buyer will provide a good home for his company and his employees.

Communications

Communicating what is going on, and how employees will be affected, is an important part of handling the people concerns in an acquisition. A good communications program should be developed before the deal is consummated. It is generally best if the news and details of the sale come directly from the seller's management, rather than from the buyer. People naturally feel insecure after their organization is bought, so if they continue to receive their major communications from their old management, it usually makes them feel better.

THE NEED FOR UNDERSTANDING

Over and over in acquisitions that go sour, bitterness arises because the buyer "doesn't understand" the acquired company. The sellers complain that the parent is not familiar with their products or their market.

One seller grumbles, "They had always been involved in high volume, low margin operations that lent themselves to mass production techniques. On the other hand, we were in a low volume, high margin industry that required skilled craftsman labor."

Another seller says, "The corporate president called me in and explained that in keeping with the overall corporate growth plan we should redirect our sales efforts away from our existing, smaller accounts and concentrate only on the 'big boys.' When I tried to point out what might happen as a result, I was informed in no uncertain terms that the matter was not negotiable."

Still another disillusioned seller tellls of having to fill out corporate tonnage reports for his fine furniture manufacturing company just because the parent manufactures products for which tonnage reports are appropriate. "It's almost laughable, except that they're serious. They've even told me it doesn't matter so much whether our reports are accurate, just so we get them in on time."

This kind of insensitivity to the acquired company's products, markets and management is a bad way for a buyer to begin its relationship with a new division or subsidiary. It is also the best possible argument for both the buyer and the seller doing a thorough investigation before a deal is struck.

No matter how well a seller feels his management style meshes with that of the buyer, no matter how many assurances the seller may have that he will remain in control, he should understand that the sale will be a change and may bring unexpected consequences.

Without a doubt, well-managed negotiations are the key to dealing successfully with questions of "What happens to my people after I sell?"

A seller must be aware that over the years of developing his company into the salable entity it has become, he has largely considered it his baby. He has taken a parental interest in his key management. He should be very careful before he gives it over to a new parent.

MARKET AND FINANCIAL ANALYSIS

THE UNDERLYING VALUE OF A BUSINESS is still the cornerstone to any deal which is struck between a buyer and a seller. In order to obtain an objective appraisal a buyer must consider financial elements such as cash flow, balance sheet analysis, income statement analysis, and other accounting calculations. However, in some situations the value of a company may not relate directly to either earnings or physical asset base. Predominant elements of value may stem from so-called intangible items such as ownership or control of licenses, contracts, patents, market domination, expertise or special processes. In such instances it is essential to perform an analysis of intangibles to arrive at a realistic value for the company.

In the chapter by Robert C. Sorensen, the author explores the marketing facts behind the financial figures. He shows how such information can aid the buyer in determining whether or not projected earnings are real and obtainable. The advice in this chapter is as practical as suggestions that potential buyers contact management who retired from key positions or officials of an organization that negotiated to buy out the company and then elected not to proceed.

Ralph A. Harris explores the methods used by professional appraisers to ascribe value to companies. He details for the reader how to value cash flow and earnings, how to make cash flow estimates, the calculation and interpretation of present value, terminal values and their impact, and risk analysis. There are also sections on comparative analysis and acquisition premiums. The editors believe this to be one of the most comprehensive and readable pieces that has been written on the subject of determining price.

Previously, we noted that there is a large array of intangible items which should fairly be given value in a transaction. Martin J. Whitman explains some of these factors which ascribe exceptional value. Included is a discussion on minimization of tax bills, undervalued securities, absence of encumbrances, discount from net asset value and non-economic considerations.

Last in this topical area is Alfred Rappaport who considers strategic analysis for more profitable acquisitions. He points out that the actual acquisition price paid by the buyer must be reviewed in light of the contribution the new company makes to the combined entity. Among the supply of acquisition candidates there will be only a limited number available at a price which enables the acquiror to earn an acceptable return on investment. Mr. Rappaport illustrates his points in a detailed case study of Alcar Corporation's interest in acquiring Rano Products.

DR. ROBERT C. SORENSEN

DR. ROBERT C. SORENSEN is President of Sorensen Marketing/Management Corporation, a New York City consulting firm specializing in acquisitions and market planning, marketing information and expert testimony in trademark and antitrust litigation, and new product introduction. In years past he has been a faculty member of the University of Nebraska College of Law, team leader and operations analyst at Operations Research Office of The Johns Hopkins University, Executive Director of The Center For Advanced Practice of The Interpublic Group of Companies, and an early publisher and executive editor of Psychology Today. He has written many articles in professional and law reviews as well as appeared before many professional, business and academic groups in the United States and Europe. Dr. Sorensen has an extensive market planning and market research practice in the United States and overseas.

9

Marketing Information and the Determination of Value

ROBERT C. SORENSEN, Ph. D.

Conventional wisdom instructs: "Show me the 'bottom line'. I am not interested in anything else." The true importance of actual or potential profit is compromised by the frequent preoccupation with how much profit is indicated rather than how that profit came to be. "Numbers crunching" will make any balance sheet communicate a desired earnings picture in anticipation of a proposed acquisition or merger. But this often signals a disregard for the marketing facts behind the financial figures, facts that have a strong bearing on whether or not the projected earnings are real.

The value of any company is subject to judgment by many criteria which are traditionally used: sales, return on investment, book value, market share, prestige or good will and operating revenues. Dollar values are furnished by dollar records of the corporate operation; they are fixed by appraisers whose word is customarily accepted in particular fields of expertise, and by market value which is what people will pay for the item at the moment, to name but a few criteria.

But certain assumptions inevitably lie behind these presumed values, and it is in these assumptions that critical potential gains and losses lurk for the buyer or seller. The basic, often unstated, assumptions are these:

1. Demand will continue for whatever products and services are the major source of the profits, with any diminution or termination accounted for by other sources or potential losses.

2. Any intervening variables which can seriously affect a company's profit picture but over which the company does not exert control (e.g., the economy, a speech by the Federal Reserve Bank head, a military incursion by the Soviet Union) will either not occur or are provided for by contingency actions or other counter intervening variables.

3. The difference between the cost of doing business and the revenues gained from the sale of resulting products and services will remain at its present or specified level.

4. Agreements and commitments with distributors, franchisees and others have been prudently implemented and are at least minimally cost-effective.

NEGOTIATIONS AND THE FIXING OF VALUE

This is not a treatise on negotiations, but it is critical to the mission of the buyer in any merger and acquisition effort that everything done be consistent with the sole objective of any buy-sell negotiations: *to maximize the value for your group* of what you gain on the basis of what you seek to obtain and *to minimize the value for your group* of what you lose on the basis of what you sought but failed to obtain. In accomplishing this mission, unless you have certain unique concerns with the subsequent competitive strength or stock value of the company you are negotiating to acquire, disregard the other group's perceived value. Forget what they seek to obtain for themselves, and the concessions they seek to obtain from you, and do what you can to *maximize the value to them* of their gains and your concessions to them.

Unless one party holds an unmitigated economic or government supported advantage (e.g., impending bankruptcy status or orders to divest), parties give and take on the basis of each side securing a sufficiently beneficial outcome to warrant continuing the negotiations and signing the agreement. Acquisition negotiations are effective because their main purpose is obviously the *exchange of value* whereby one side's debits become the basis for the other side's credits and *vice versa*. Otherwise, one risks uncompromising disputation or later expensive concessions with respect to points at issue that are of similar value to both parties and can best be traded off in the negotiation process.

To accomplish this mission, it is sometimes necessary to generate objectives for the other side, to introduce concessions that are not real concessions, and to enhance the seeming market value of what you are giving up beyond its real cost to you. In doing so, of course, it is urgent that you not seem to depreciate the value of your concessions by your willingness to make them.

THE ADVANTAGE OF MARKETING INFORMATION IN NEGOTIATIONS

Obviously, acquiring marketing information offers many special advantages in the negotiation process:

1. Special marketing knowledge may mean an extra incentive for wanting to acquire or sell a company that is unknown to your opposite number. That additional knowledge enables you to have more staying power or be willing to pay more (or less), for example.

2. Your knowing something your opposite number does not think you know may mean that he will assume he possesses an advantage that he does not really enjoy, thus causing him to assume that a concession or indication of cooperation on your part is the signal to close the agreement sooner than he would have otherwise been willing.

3. Your opponent may be shaken by what is evidently your superior knowledge, and so there will be less effort to conceal facts you nonetheless may not have known and a far greater desire to cooperate with and respect you.

4. On your part, of course, it will mean that knowing what you know will encourage a greater degree of prudence than you may otherwise have exercised.

THE SELLER'S KNOWLEDGE AND INSIGHTS

A mistaken assumption in any acquisition or merger negotiation is that the seller or those negotiating in the seller's behalf are aware of all critical marketing facts. This is not true for several reasons:

1. The seller, sometimes subconsciously but often deliberately, does not acquaint himself with information challenging the purported true value of the company as he sees it. The seller is asking "What is right with our value?", not what is wrong with it.

2. Knowledge of the root causes of some of the problems in question is frequently the responsibility of marketing and research staff personnel who are the first to go when payrolls are reduced in anticipation of the need to present a low payroll profile.

3. The seller will frequently have been insulated from certain threatening facts of life by lower echelon individuals who are not invited to participate in the negotiations. This "protection" occurs for many reasons incidental to the daily functioning of business which need not be itemized here.

Suffice to say, it is urgent that the would-be buyers raise basic questions concerning salient marketing facts not only to the negotiators but to a network of potential key sources of information in the company under consideration, requesting the opportunity to interview or depose such persons only after preferably seeking independent access to them without the presence of the seller. These individuals to be contacted independently of and prior to the negotiations include the following: (1) The purchasing agent; (2) The marketing director; (3) The market research director; (4) The director of sales; (5) The advertising and/or media research director; (6) Key distributors; and (7) Sales managers located in key sales areas throughout the country.

Individuals not directly connected with the company under consideration who should be contacted also include (1) People retired from the above named positions within the previous three years; (2) Learned individuals employed by the trade press or trade associations relevant to the product category; (3) Analysts or brokers who are known to specialize in the company or product categories in question; (4) Local marketing professors or graduate students who have made the company an object of interest; (5) An official of any other organization that has recently negotiated for the buy-out of the company.

In the nonpublic company, there can prevail an inverse correlation between the extent of the seller's personal involvement with the company for sale and his concern with accurate current market values. The founder of a company is frequently discouraged from participating in selling negotiations for obvious reasons. Yet he or she will often be present and strongly committed to the value of a company based on previous investment of dollars that have little value today, the intense amount of his personal time given to the company, and his personal relations. All these factors may have little current market value for their own sake. This is the one element of negotiations where the wisest counsel is to manifest strong *interest and sympathy* in what the founder has to say, indicate respect for all that the founder feels he has done, indeed agree that the worth of the founder's contribution has been invaluable—which indeed it has despite the nonaffordable compensation that may be sought for what no other person or persons could have accomplished.

SALIENT MARKETING CONSIDERATIONS

What follows here are not new marketing propositions that are routinely ignored in any ongoing company operation. What is given particular consideration herein are considerations that are often not visible during negotiations even though they are by no means invisible. They are easy to overlook, are usually not represented by experts present at the negotiations or experts made available to would-be purchasers, and they do not carry easily ascertainable dollar equivalents in balance sheets and projections.

Salient marketing considerations in addition to the obvious ones of sales, market share and competitive positions include the following:

1. *Knowledge of customers.* Understand the company's knowledge of the key characteristics of its existing and prospective customers, its techniques for getting, maintaining and updating this knowledge, and its methods for putting it to use.

2. *Ability to change.* Understand the company's ability to diagnose and factor into the making of its products and services what its existing and prospective customers want. Many companies are famous for the products they have invented and the product capabilities they have perfected in their laboratories, but they do not have the management ability to harness corporate resources and bring the new product to full development in the marketplace. Worse still is that inability to maintain the appeal of the current product: learning or inventing new uses for it, amending its image for efficacy, adding a new scent, color, flavor, or other innocuous but vital characteristics to maintain a product's freshness against new competition or the tiresomeness of its continuous use.

To be working at acceptable cost-effective levels, a company must know or be seeking to know the characteristics and needs of its target customers that match what the company products and services can offer them. The absence of such information is the greatest source of wasted sales efforts to nonexistent prospects and miscalculated selling efforts to potential customers who showed considerable promise.

There are varieties of marketing intelligence methods that can be used including a customer census, a conservation effort that seeks to determine the explanation of every lost sale, a content analysis of anything that customers have had to say in letters, personal conversations and the media. The response rate on the part of people asked to fill out essential information in a customer census ranges from low in the instance of the innocuous appeal to well over 50 percent when people are asked to fill out a warranty card, a request for information, or an expression of willingness to be represented in a lobbying or other self-serving effort.

3. *Product excellence.* In the absence of total credentials which are lacking in most products, a company's profit makers may be lacking certain characteristics enabling it to clear safety and underwriting requirements, comply with state and federal rules, or to include an ingredient or other characteristics that would qualify it for certification by the appropriate organization. So-called pending approvals, postponement of final government compliance date, delay in securing the acceptable flavor ingredient—all raise questions about whether or not a company's products are the source of past or anticipated profits that are claimed for them.

4. *A company's marketing obligations.* Some companies have business obligations that are not classified as debts or even as liabilities despite the fact that their fulfillment must take place over a period of time and the cost of their fulfillment may be problematical or dangerous. This is frequently the case with magazines that have subscription fulfillment obligations, franchised organizations such as television cable companies or public utilities that are obligated to serve residents of specific territories, companies with unamortized but less than usable assets, and certain types of organizations with government contracts. These obligations can be the murky underside of the new balance sheet and need to be identified and understood if their true loss potential is to be evaluated.

There are obligations and commitments about which one has to make point-blank inquiry, past commitments that may have been necessary and even invaluable for the predecessor ownership but which may need to be taken into consideration in terms of whether or not they can be terminated by a certain date. These marketing commitments are of certain specific varieties including purchase arrangements with certain parties that may constitute *quid pro quo* for matters long since compensated, favoritism in distribution, franchise or other relationships with individuals and companies that no longer pay for themselves.

The company to be acquired may be working under certain legal or voluntary constraints as a result of a government or court finding, an agreement with a competitor, or a felt need to avoid litigation which may result in a change in name, ingredients, distribution pattern or advertising claims that can radically affect the revenues previously thrown off by a product or service profit maker in years past.

5. *Physical or psychological product obsolescence.* No product is secure from the effects of competition and social change, fatigue growing out of tiresome use, and company inability to turn over its customers or to generate the product in new forms or colors, or to extend its product line. The subtleties are substantial, because cost, pattern of use and frequency of purchase may encourage new model changes, product innovation or new positioning of the same product in the marketplace. These questions must be answered in advance of determining the true value of a product over a period of time.

6. *Product name troubles.* A product that has been doing very well may suffer from potential troubles with its name, a particularly serious problem with respect to trademarks. Four basic problems can undermine a name, all of which threaten potential deprivation in sales and increases in costs.

(A) Another product (directly competing or otherwise) may have been named in such a manner that it is confused with the product in question, causing consumer misunderstanding and lost sales. This may be remedied in trademark litigation, but the road to resolution may be long and expensive and the problem should be understood when purchasing the company and not inherited by surprise.

(B) Even worse is the possibility that the name is becoming or has become generic for all practical purposes. When a product name is legally found to be generic (e.g., Bayer's aspirin), it loses its uniqueness for representing a single product, its owners lose their property rights in the name, and other companies are free to use the name as synonymous with product category rather than a brand name.

(C) Sometimes a product will be thought to originate from a service other than the actual manufacturing source. This can cause confusion incapable of profitable resolution.

(D) A name that is descriptive is often in danger of being generic. Advertising agencies or companies naming their new products frequently fail to realize that a serious error in product naming is to embody in the name the process whereby the product works. The more ubiquitous the product and its process, the more likely that product name will be commonly used to identify the process. How many times does one hear the request: "Please xerox this for me" in companies that have photocopy devices other than Xerox, despite the fact that the Xerox people are thought to perform yeoman efforts to protect its trademark and to educate people about its use.

7. *Advertising eclipse.* The dynamics of the advertising and mass media balance among brand name products are crucial to the profit potential of each product. Some product marketing and advertising strategies are cyclical in the amount they spend; some expend tremendous amounts of money once every several years and woe to the competitors during those few months. To know this is going to happen is to anticipate sales difficulties or augmented advertising budgets which may be totally lacking in the advertising sales budget of the company to be taken over.

More critical is the understanding of a product's brand name and goodwill which are functions of how long the product has been advertised, the amount of money expended on its advertising and promotion, all in comparison with competitve products.

8. *Product sales eclipse.* Even more fundamental is the decision of a competitor to introduce a new product that will minimize or nullify the reason for being of the product that may be the main or leading source of profits on the part of the company to be acquired.

In this context, a manufacturer's desire to "milk" the brand in the past may have contributed to external conditions which threaten to ruin the product over the next several years. Depriving a brand of its essential marketing and merchandising support may have been economical and more profitable than ever over a short time period, but the delayed impact often converts into a downhill sales slide that is seldom remediable.

9. *Sudden increasing costs of marketing:* Costs change, sometimes in an orderly evolving fashion or a predictable cyclical manner or in an unpredictable wild pattern that needs to be anticipated. Input-output economics must be applied to the raw materials of marketing that are essential for making or servicing the product—particularly creative and production costs of generating advertising, advertising print space and broadcast.

10. *Social and economic change:* Product demand depends above all on whether or not people have a felt need for the product, like it, and use it. Incidence of felt

need, brand preference, and tendency to use are very dependent on factors over which the manufacturer and even the advertiser totally lack control. These changes include the business cycle, energy costs and the threat or existence of war.

These ten marketing information warning points are not meant to suggest conspiracies or happenstance that prevail only at acquisition and merger time. But each is unique, is often concealed for reasons of prudence and is hard to evaluate in terms of its fiscal consequences. Yet each exerts an impact on sales and the cost of doing business that will potentially depress the net worth and therefore the value of a company under consideration for purchase. Accordingly, marketing facts such as these must be identified in the language of specific inquiry or what attorneys call interrogatories. Lurking behind the financial figures as they frequently are, the potential advantages or pitfalls need to be exposed for what they are.

But there are more important positive considerations to check out when considering a company that is for sale. These are the "invisible assets" that are frequently overlooked, meaning that the buyer who overlooks them fails to realize how much more he might be willing to concede or pay in order to acquire the company. And if such assets are unknown to the seller, he too is at a disadvantage in his negotiations. These include:

1. *Potential profits from economies in purchasing.* Unfortunately the job of purchasing agent is filled by a clerical type rather than a skilled executive who understands that the purchase of materials, equipment and services for input offer opportunities for product or service redesign and savings that can strongly influence the company's profit potential. If the effort were given to effective negotiations in the purchase function that is given to effective negotiations in the sales function, a company's profit potential would have greater assurance of achievement.

2. *New uses for existing facilities.* A company frequently has machinery and labor skills that can be adapted to the manufacture and sale of additional products other than those being sold. This can present a problem if the new products are for uses by groups that are not anticipated in the company's marketing and distribution system. Care should be taken not to make unwarranted assumptions about the value of new additional product outlets, but their potential yield should be searched out and carefully discovered. The writer has discovered on more than one occasion that special unique equipment secured by a specialist to perform a particular series of tasks can often perform other specialized missions as well, particularly in contingent

situations such as weapons mobilization or contracts with companies seeking entirely new supply sources.

3. *Extension of existing sales resources:* Although errors are frequently made in this regard, no assumption should go untested with respect to the fit that one company's sales organization will have with another. The fact that a corps of salespersons exist is not enough, any more than the fact, for example, that a group of salespersons visits the same group of customer stores as those of the company being acquired. But if careful attention is paid to merging the functions and individuals of two sales departments, assuring their single unified management may effect significant economies of scale. The similarity of products, however, is not the answer—even when they are silverware and watches, to give one example of two sales groups that turned out to be totally incompatible in sales routines, time of calls, and work obligations.

4. *New markets:* New markets may exist that have been untapped due to policy, personnel or apathy on the part of a company that once taken over can be mobilized to accomplish profitable results. I have not found skeletons, but rather free spirits buried alive in corporate closets who when freed accomplished important results: a malingering scientist who was not being used, a small budget increase that revolutionized the output of a product design department and tripled sales within one year, a gruff but perceptive researcher who, once listened to, provided new sales opportunities heretofore lost to a blind sales force that was led by a one-eyed egocentric. New uses for existing products are less expensive to translate into new sales opportunities than new products, and usually considerably less risky.

New sales opportunites for existing customers add substantial potential to projected profits that are often lost to an existing management. Financial institutions and retail outlets are major examples of organizations that have tremendous sales potential among their existing customers who frequently tend to fragment their buying among several outlets for reasons of variety, assumed confidentiality, or the simple desire to be exposed to more new people or more new ideas.

SOURCES OF DATA

Considerable data exists about almost every company of any size that is independent of its own sources. The basic categories of data are these:

1. *United States Census data*: Of particular concern is not specific company data which is unavailable in census data, but information about the industry as a whole and various products therein. Product specifica-

tions, dollar volume costs, total retail sales and sales predictions are often useful in determining the relative value of the sales and other marketing efforts of the company under consideration.

2. *Syndicated service data*: Many companies utilize a variety of research and reporting services that provide useful data in certain product categories and industries, i.e., total sales, market share (at least of the company commissioning the service), consumer choices, sales behavior, brand loyalty and attrition, and reasons for purchase and non-purchases. These services include detailed diaries placed with households and industry buyers, electronic ratings of radio and television set exposure, magazine audience definition and readership, records of product placements, store audits and consumer interviews.

3. *Past litigation*: The litigation a company has been in, particularly including the complaint and answer documents, the adversaries' briefs, and the court decisions will often be a rich mine of marketing and related data about a company, its marketing problems, and the structure and substance of its industry. Because almost all trial proceedings are a matter of public record, the transcripts of evidence introduced at these trials and in pretrial depositions can be an immensely rich and rewarding source of insight and information.

4. *The trade press*: When purchase of a company is even contemplated, instructions should be given a clipping service to search on a regular basis for information that has been printed with reference to the company in question. It is remarkable how much is printed in the trade press about company policies, personalities, sales, and special problems or events. In this regard, the speeches of present and past corporate officers associated with the firm are useful.

5. *Discovery*: Another method of obtaining information is to utilize the legal process of discovery in an intelligent albeit modified manner: address a series of questions requesting answers and relevant documents thereto well in advance of the negotiations. Negotiations should not proceed until these marketing information requests have been complied with, and the option to continue this discovery effort should not expire until the negotiations have been completed.

Under certain circumstances, it is recommended that a technique of modified cross-examination be utilized with key people whose information and opinions are vital to understanding a company's values. I say this because in matters of marketing where opinion, perception, and prediction prevail (so-called "softer" expressions as opposed to "hard" dollar figures), it is urgent to secure such information on as direct a basis as possible.

6. Above all, a *marketing situation analysis* should be done of the subject company, utilizing one's own research and marketing personnel or consulting a marketing expert who has spent a great deal of time in identifying the marketing facts behind the financial figures. The essential elements in any such marketing situation analysis are the major companies involved in the industry of the subject company and their relative ranking in total sales volume (market shares), product output, marketing policies, profit as a percentage of total sales or as a return on investment, diversity of products, and relative profits. In this regard strong attention must be paid to the trends of this data over the past five year and 24 month periods and its projections for the next 24 month and five year periods, the unique selling proposition of each product in the subject and competitive companies, amount and kinds of media advertising, and the industry census data mentioned earlier.

CONCLUSIONS

The price to settle upon for the acquisition or merger transaction should be the last item to be resolved in the negotiations. It is always preferable that the other person be encouraged to make the first offer, no matter what one's role as buyer or seller. Nonetheless, price should be in the negotiator's mind from the very beginning, and one should have his own private conversion chart with which to evaluate the dollar worth of each gain and each loss during negotiations.

But when one publicly fixes a price to each phase of the negotiations, the function of money breaks down with respect to each individual marketing consideration. Some elements are price sensitive and some are not; many are valued in accordance with one's own unique perceptions and experiences that may not be duplicated by those of the next person. It is easier to find compatibility with another individual in matters of price when a group of problems are considered together. People are frequently less exacting when they are pricing a group of items rather than one at a time. A company's gas reserves, the value of its distribution system, its pension fund liabilities, and the replacement cost of its truck fleet, to suggest a few examples, may be valued differently when they are perceived together than when they are viewed separately.

This has been a discussion of estimated values rather than hard values. Marketing information will present many obvious opportunities for fixing hard values that must not be overlooked. But the so-called soft marketing information under discussion herein presents serious vulnerabilities to hard financial figures unless it is carefully searched out, identified and assessed.

RALPH A. HARRIS

Since 1978, Ralph A. Harris has been a Vice President of Corporate Finance-Special at Drexel Burnham Lambert Incorporated where he works on acquisitions and divestitures by U.S. and foreign companies.

Mr. Harris started his career at Bankers Trust Co. where he headed a group responsible for capital budgeting analysis of the Company's overseas investments and domestic and international loan commitments. Subsequently he became an advisor on policy for Bankers Trust's U.S. corporate loan portfolio. For a time, Mr. Harris was a director in the Corporate Financial Services Division of Bankers Trust, advising its clients on financing strategies and private placements.

Mr. Harris was educated at Brown University and Harvard's Graduate School of Business Administration where he majored in Finance. He did post-graduate work in operations research and international finance at New York University.

10

Determining the Right Price to Pay

RALPH A. HARRIS

I. INTRODUCTION

A. Purpose of Valuation of Acquisition

In the cases of private companies, or those with closely held stock, the need for valuation as a part of the acquisition process is obvious. Both acquiror and seller must determine their respective views as to the value of the company before negotiations can proceed. In the cases of acquisitions of publicly held companies, while the companies are already valued by the market, potential acquirors will have to determine whether the premium over the market value, which is often required today in making acquisitions, is sound.

The analysis of the value of an acquisition may have several different purposes, and different methods may be employed to arrive at a valuation. There may be a need for:

— determing whether a price under consideration is reasonable and fair;

— determining whether the acquisition is at a price which will provide a benefit (economic or otherwise) to the acquiror.

Because of the speed with which acquisitions must be considered, methods of performing evaluations of prospective targets need to be practical, requiring relatively limited data and portable computational tools. The methods employed herein are based on use of data which is generally available and involve calculations no more sophisticated than can be performed on most of the pocket-sized electronic calculators available today to financial analysts.

1. *Fairness and Reasonableness of Price.* By definition, a fair or reasonable price is one at which a buyer and seller who are each able and willing, and each of whom are informed about the company to be sold, would conclude a transaction. Each party's point of view toward what that price should be will be different due to its own circumstances and outlook, but a convergence to a narrow range of values is desirable in bringing about a merger or acquisition transaction. Even if there is a common ground of assumptions about the business to be acquired, the desire on the part of each company to take advantage of the other will obstruct the process of arriving at a reasonable value in negotiations. In this case, an independent valuation which examines the value of the potential acquisition may facilitate the process of arriving at an agreement. In this valuation the economic worth of the company is considered from several points of view, not necessarily just those of the potential acquiror.

2. *Valuing the Benefits of the Acquisition.* To an individual prospective acquiror the acquisition will have a unique and special value which is a function of the combination of unique strategic elements in each company's business. The prospective acquiror wants to know what that value may be in order to determine the maximum price that may be paid. The prospective acquiror must anticipate that he may be involved in a number of types of bidding contests or negotiation tactics in which he will be motivated to keep raising his offer. He must know when the price is too high.

Types of Bidding & Negotiating Tactics

- *Bid/Asked:* Each party states a position with an expectation of settling in between.
- *Acceptance Price:* Seller has a price deemed to be acceptable and will take the first offer which is acceptable.
- *Auction:* May be "open" in which case each party makes a bid higher than the last until one party is left; or "closed" in which case each party makes one secret bid and the highest bid wins.

149

B. Methods of Evaluation

The methods of evaluation may fall into two broad classes:

Economic Analysis by forecasting and evaluation of the target's asset value, future income and/or cash flow potential and valuing these factors appropriately;

Comparative Analysis of the historical performance of the target to that of other similar companies and using the value of those companies to define the value of the target.

1. *Economic Analysis*. Economic Analysis, the first method discussed, approaches the valuation of an acquisition as a capital budgeting procedure. Since the factors included in determining the income, cash flow or asset values may be related quite specifically to the situation or plans of the potential acquiror, it is an approach normally used to examine the impact on the acquiror. A constraint on the level of sophistication of economic analysis in evaluating acquisitions is the difficulty in getting sufficient information about acquisition targets, even when public and independent. While sophisticated methods of economic analysis are useful in many applications, the shorthand methods for acquisition evaluation, which do not depend on extensive data collection or computer models, are important, especially as screening tools. There are some very sophisticated quantitative approaches which may be used to forecast and model the benefits of an acquisition, such as those dealt with in operations research literature. The approaches described herein are intended for use by financial analysts without special quantitative training and are useful for quick evaluation of an acquisition's potential.

In our discussion of economic analysis, we will show how simple cash flow forecasts for the prospective acquisition can be constructed and discounted to obtain their Present Values. We will describe shorthand methods for finding estimates of Terminal Values and for performing risk analysis.

2. *Comparative Analysis*. Since, in Comparative Analysis, it is usually assumed that the object of the evaluation is similar to other companies being analyzed, this type of analysis is most useful as (i) a consistency check to see that a valuation is fair and reasonable or (ii) a guide to what the value may be to third parties. These purposes usually occur as a part of the bidding and negotiation process. To provide comparative analysis, collection of data for a large number of companies is required. Usually, due to time and data availability constraints, the financial information will be at a high level of aggregation and, therefore, the accuracy of comparative analysis is usually limited.

Another drawback of this type of analysis is that only historical data can be used. The analyst uses an aggregate of the results for a group of companies to estimate the value of a prospective acquisition. Anticipated future events affecting the value of the whole group of companies selected for comparison will be incorporated in the valuation of the acquisition. However, future events affecting only the acquisition itself will not be reflected in valuation by comparative means.

In discussing comparative analysis, we will show the importance of properly selecting examples for comparison, how to screen for relationships between the value of the comparison companies and their performance, and, finally, the seeming importance of book value as a factor in valuation in today's market.

C. Business Benefits and Acquisition Premiums

1. *Business Benefits*. Behind almost every acquisition is the belief that the combination of acquiror and the acquired company will create more value than the sum of their two separate values. This "2 + 2 = 5" concept has been called "synergism." This increase in value can occur through various means):[1]

a. financial effects;
b. operating effects.

Among the financial effects may be real and illusory advantages of the acquisition:

- tax savings (real);
- stability of income (often illusory, risk/return tradeoff changes);
- earnings per share increase with higher P/E company acquiring lower P/E company (illusory).

The operating effects may include:

- elimination of duplicate functions;
- horizontal or vertical integration;
- technological or "know-how" cross-fertilization.

Because these benefits are available, acquirors are willing to pay premiums for the kind of control which permits the acquiror to (i) achieve these benefits and (ii) include these benefits in its reporting of financial performance.

2. *Acquisition Premiums and Their Effect on Evaluation*. Because forecasting the impact of changes in strategic variables that occur from the operating effects on an acquisition is difficult, many purchasers

---

[1]Harry H. Lynch, *Financial Performance of Conglomerates*, Harvard University (Boston 1971), pp. 4-13.

insist that a prospective acquisition be economically rewarding on the basis of its status as a "stand alone." In part, this may be an attempt to avoid the excesses resulting from the quest for synergism in the late 'sixties. However, in today's market, acquisition targets often fetch large premiums over market value and substantial price/earnings ratios in tender offers. (See Table 10-1). Acquirors who look at the value of a target only on a "stand alone" basis may be precluded from making any acquisitions unless this constraint is relaxed or, alternatively, the hopeful acquiror may lose opportunities for growth as it purchases situations with low growth potential.

Since one purpose of an evaluation of an acquisition is to estimate what other parties may feel it would be worth, we have to deal with two measures of value: first, the value of the company on a "stand alone" basis as its shares might sell in the market, and, second, its value to potential acquirors or the price at which the company may be purchased in an acquisition. The difference between the two is the acquisition premium. Since the acquisition premium may be a function of factors other than the performance and outlook for the prospective acquisition, we have approached the valuation process as though in two steps:

- determine the value of the acquisition as though a publicly traded company (if it is not);
- determine the acquisition premium required given the objectives of the purchaser and the requirements of the seller.

II. ECONOMIC ANALYSIS

The foundation of this analysis is the determination of the value of the benefits of acquiring the target company. This value is to be derived from the potential incremental income, cash flow or asset value arising from the acquisition. Unless liquidation is contemplated, this value is usually in the form of the capitalization of a stream of income or cash flow which stretches into the future after the acquisition. The analysis should take into account the risks of the investment.

A. Valuing Cash Flow or Earnings?

The question of whether measurement of incremental income of cash flow effects is more relevant is not one to which there are any universal answers. Some companies are extremely conscious of earnings-per-share-growth and others are almost obsessive about maximizing cash flow. As a practical matter for the public company, both would seem to be important: projects (including acquisitions) must be examined on the basis of cash flow potential but checked to see that their impact on the earnings forecast for the company as a whole is not unduly disruptive.[2]

B. Simple Cash Flow Defined

In order to analyze a potential acquisition, a model for the cash flow prospects of the target needs to be developed. While this may be a complex, highly interactive simulation of the target's operations, often a very simple model will result in useful information.

Table 10-1
Acquisitions of Selected
Consumer Product Companies

Date	Target Company	Acquiring Company	Tender P/E Ratio	Tender Premium Over Market Price Before Announcement
11/21/78	Tiffany	Avon	15.8X	108.5%
09/13/78	Green Giant	Pillsbury	13.6	63.7
08/26/78	Entenmann's	Warner-Lambert	19.9	66.6
08/25/78	Del Monte	R.J. Reynolds	11.4	84.8
06/03/78	Pet	I.C. Industries	12.8	51.7
05/05/78	Weight Watchers	Heinz	16.6	39.1
05/01/78	Seven-Up	Philip Morris	20.2	90.1
04/07/78	Scholl	Schering-Plough	16.7	122.2
03/03/78	Tropicana	Beatrice	16.7	62.5
02/22/78	Foodways	Heinz	11.9	51.2
02/18/78	Peter Paul	Cadbury Schweppes	12.6	66.7
11/24/77	Chef Pierre	Consolidated Foods	11.6	76.5
09/08/76	Taylor Wine	Coca Cola	16.3	61.0
02/05/76	Mrs. Smith's Pie	Kellogg	12.1	58.4
		Average	14.9X	68.7%
		DJII Average (1978)	8.3X	

[2]Alfred Rappaport and Eugene M. Lerner, *Harvard Business Review*, "Limit DCF in Capital Budgeting", September/October 1968, Volume 68508, p. 133.

The cash flow to be analyzed would be the net cash generated by the operations (not including financing costs) of the company to be acquired as its operations would be carried out under the policies of the purchaser. In the absence of better information a good approach is to use Operating Cash Flow[3] as outlined below:

	Net Income (adjusted)
plus:	Depreciation
less:	Planned Capital Expenditures
less:	Changes in Working Capital
Equals:	Operating Cash Flow

In a relatively stable situation, the most recent values for net income and depreciation may be used as a base. Adjustments to net income are needed to reflect consolidation of operations by the purchaser and to keep separate the investment and financing issues.

Typical of these adjustments would be:

— elimination of interest expense to obtain operating earnings base;

— reduction in expenses due to consolidation of operations such as (i) administrative costs which may be eliminated (e.g. for computer systems, accounting and systems staff, office rental, etc.); (ii) public reporting and regulatory compliance costs, including expenses for legal staff;

— reduction in expenses for perquisites for owner/managers, especially in the case where a private company is being acquired and the owners or managers are not to remain with the company;

— change in the tax liability resulting from (i) changes in pre-tax income due to the adjustments above and the amortization of goodwill and (ii) changes in the tax computation to reflect the acquiror's tax status.

Capital expenditure plans, having been estimated by the prospective purchaser as part of his strategic plan for the business, are entered into the forecast. If working capital requirements are closely tied to sales levels, examination of historical relationships between working capital and sales will be helpful in defining additional working capital requirements. Discussion with industry people may help determine if inventory, receivables and payable policies have changed so that historical relationships may be misleading.

C. "Bottom Up" Cash Flow Estimation

In a more dynamic situation a "bottom up" approach may be required. Sales and direct expenses product line by product line would be estimated. Advertising and research and development budgets may be reviewed. Forecasts should be made for a number of years into the future. This is so the dynamics of the target's business may be understood. Frequently, the forecasted cash flow will show the negative cash flow effects of funding the expansion of a business (i.e., investment in plant and equipment, working capital "human capital") and positive cash flow effects as the business reaches maturity. We will look at an example of a major consumer product manufacturer that has entered negotiations to acquire from its inventor a new consumer product, say a "bionic" floor wax, which promises to have significantly superior powers to other products in its market. The acquiror evaluation of the cash flows might look something like Table 10-2.

Each row in this forecast may be the result of a number of man-hours of analysis of markets, the company's operations, capital plans, labor rates, and many other variables. The forecast may be based on the compilation of plans about the smallest elements of the company's business plan.

Table 10-2
Estimated Cash Flows of Acquisition Target
($000)

	Year					
	1	2	3	4	5	6
Revenues	$1,000	$ 2,000	$ 4,000	$ 4,500	$ 5,000	$ 5,000
Direct Costs (60% of Sales)	(600)	(1,200)	(2,400)	(2,700)	(3,000)	(3,000)
G & A (10% of Sales)	(100)	(200)	(400)	(450)	(500)	(500)
R & D	(500)	(250)	—	—	—	—
Advertising & Promotion	—	(240)	(240)	(270)	(300)	(400)
Capital Expenditures	(500)	(500)	(100)	(100)	(100)	(100)
Working Capital (17% of Sales Increase)	(167)	(163)	(333)	(83)	(83)	—
Operating Cash Flow	(867)	(557)	527	897	1,017	1,000
Present Value @ 15%	(754)	(421)	347	513	506	2,818(1)
Cumulative Present Value	$(754)	$(1175)	$(828)	$(315)	$(191)	$3,009

(1) sum of present values for years 6+

---

[3]This value is a special case of the Free Cash Flow defined by Joel M. Stern. Except for the fact that we have made adjustments to reflect the impact of the acquisition, these concepts are similar. Joel M. Stern, *Analytical Methods in Financial Planning* (New York, 1975).

D. Present Value Approach

In order to relate the estimated future cash flows of the acquisition to its price (investment), the cash flows are discounted to obtain their Present Value (PV).

1. *Obtaining the Present Value.* The discounting of cash flows in the Present Value approach has the following features:

a. It values the estimated stream of cash that the acquisition is to produce, thereby indicating the value of the acquisition;

b. The discount rate, if the Present Value process is properly defined, provides for a comparison of the investment in the acquisition to other opportunities for the firm.

The form of the present value calculation is:

$$PV(1) = CF_0 + \frac{CF_1}{(1+r)^1} + \frac{CF_2}{(1+r)^2} + \ldots + \frac{CF_n}{(1+r)^n}$$

The values of cash flows (CF) may be negative (representing investments or losses) in any period.[4]

2. *Interpreting the Present Value Result.* If the analyst is comfortable with the thought that the discount rate accurately describes the acquiror's opportunities for alternative investments, the Present Value should be the maximum price the company would pay for the acquisition:

Maximum Price = PV acquisition cash flows

In the example in Table 10-2 we see the acquisition is estimated to have a value of $3.0 million (the highest price the acquiror should be willing to pay).

In theory, those projects (including potential acquisitions) which, subject to the constraint of the firms' available capital, sum to the largest Net Present Value should be undertaken. In practice this portfolio approach is difficult to implement and is rarely used in the case of acquisitions which are usually considered un-

usual types of investments. Frequently the discount rate used by the corporation in performing its capital budgeting is not felt to be high enough to reflect the uncertainty which an acquisition is felt to embody.

Because of these difficulties, a discount rate used in determining the Present Value is often used only to account for the time value of money rather than serving as an investment criterion. Such a discount rate may be easily approximated by using the company's marginal cost of borrowing[5]. To evaluate the Present Value of the acquisition, common practice is to find the Present Value of an acceptable (as determined in the corporate budgetary framework of the potential acquiror) alternative investment, often that of developing a business internally rather than purchasing a business. Two calculations are performed: one, the Present Value of a selected alternative to the acquisition and the second, the Present Value of the acquisition itself.

$$PV\ acquisition = CF_0 + \frac{CF_1}{(1+r)^1} + \frac{CF_2}{(1+r)^2} + \ldots + \frac{CF_n}{(1+r)^n}$$

$$PV\ alternative = CF'_0 + \frac{CF'_1}{(1+r)^1} + \frac{CF'_2}{(1+r)^2} + \ldots + \frac{CF'_n}{(1+r)_n}$$

where CF_0 does not include acquisition price.

The maximum acquisition price would be equal to the difference between the two Present Values.

Maximum Price = PV acquisition − PV alternative

An example of how this type of analysis may work can be seen by extending our earlier example of the new product acquisition. Posit the case where the hypothetical acquiror assumes an internal effort to develop the product (rather than make an acquisition) would cost $500,000 a year and would take two years to develop the product to the stage of that of the prospective acquisition. To construct the analysis of the alternative, the cash flows of Table 10-2 would be

Table 10-3
Estimated Cash Flows of New Product Program
($000)

	Year							
	1	2	3	4	5	6	7	8+
After Tax Operating Cash Flow	$(500)	$(500)	$(867)	$(557)	$527	$897	$1,017	$1,000
Present Value @15%	(435)	(378)	(656)	(366)	302	446	440	2,130(1)
Cumulative Present Value	(435)	(813)	(1,469)	(1,835)	(1,533)	(1,087)	(647)	1,483

(1) sum of present values for years 8+

---

[4]Note that the "net present value" terminology is for a special case of this approach where the cash returns are separated from the investment cash flows and the equation takes the form:

$$NPV = \frac{CF_1}{(1+r)^1} + \frac{CF_2}{(1+r)^2} + \ldots + \frac{CF_n}{(1+r)^n} - I$$

where CF_1, CF_2, etc. are the positive cash flows in each period and I is the amount of the investment. There is no difference, except definitional, between these approaches.

[5]A weighted average cost of capital, which reflects the costs of equity to the corporation, would be inappropriate since the business risk test is met by comparing the acquisition to a project with similar risk which has been deemed to be an acceptable alternative.

assumed to be deferred for two years and during each of the first two years a negative cash flow of $500,000 would occur. Thus, the cash flows and their Present Values as in Table 10-3.

The Present Value of the returns from the acquisition is about $3.0 million (Table 10-2). By comparison the value of an internally generated product, as shown in Table 10-3, is $1,483,000 or roughly $1.5 million less than the acquisition Present Value. An acquisition price of $1.5 million would give the acquisition the same Net Present Value (NPV) as an investment in the internally generated product and would, therefore, represent the value of this acquisition to the acquiror. One difficulty with this approach is that, implicitly, the internally generated product investment has a higher rate of return than 15 percent, which could be inappropriate for valuing the acquisition because the risks involved are different for these two investments.

3. *Computational Convenience in Using Present Values.* One of the benefits of using a Present Value analysis is that the Present Values themselves are computationally convenient, facilitating sensitivity analysis and permitting a complicated problem to be solved in parts.

Present Values are Additive.

If:

$$PV_1 = \sum_{i=0}^{n} \frac{CF_{i1}}{(1+r)^i}$$

$$PV_2 = \sum_{i=0}^{n} \frac{CF_{i2}}{(1+r)^i}$$

Then:

$$PV_1 + PV_2 = \sum_{i=0}^{n} \frac{CF_{i1} + CF_{i2}}{(1+r)^i}$$

A Present Value Multiplied by a Constant Value is the same as Multiplying Each Cash Flow by that Value

If:

$$PV = \sum_{i=0}^{n} \frac{CF_i}{(1+r)^i}$$

Then:

$$kPV = \sum_{i=0}^{n} \frac{kCF_i}{(1+r)^i}$$

In approaches developed in later sections, we will see how these attributes may be used. These attributes *do not* apply to Internal Rate of Return (IRR) calculations.

E. Terminal Values and Their Impact

Unless there are specific plans or reasons for terminating the target's business in the near term, the evaluator is faced with the prospects of making forecasts very far into the future or estimating the value of the business at the end of the period of the near-term forecasts. The latter approach, in which a Terminal Value (TV) is estimated, is generally used. The total valuation of the acquisition is often sensitive to the choice of the Terminal Value; therefore some care in estimating it must be exercised. Two simple approaches for arriving at that value are:

- use the book value (or some ratio of it);
- a discounted value of the cash flow beyond the end of the near-term forecast period.

1. *Book Value Based Terminal Values.* We will see, in the later sections on Comparative Analysis, that a Market Value to Book Value ratio is useful in deriving a value for a company. The Market Value to Book Value ratio in existence at the time of the acquisition may be assumed at the end of the near-term forecast period, although admittedly this is a crude assumption. The book value may be computed by adding the interim earnings (adjusted for the interest cost of a "normal" debt load for this type of business if borrowing is not expected at the subsidiary level) to the beginning book value and reducing the result by any cash that may be considered "excess" (relative to other companies in the same business). These adjustments are meant to view the operation as though it were independent. The adjusted book value would then be multiplied by the Market Value/Book Value ratio to obtain an estimated market value which is the Terminal Value. However, to this Terminal Value should be added an amount equal to the amount of "excess" cash deducted from the book value before multiplying it by this ratio (see Table 10-4).

Table 10-4
Estimated Income of Acquisition Target
($000s)

	Year				
	1	2	3	4	5
Revenues	$1,000	$2,000	$4,000	$4,500	$5,000
Direct Costs	(600)	(1,200)	(2,400)	(2,700)	(3,000)
G & A	(100)	(200)	(400)	(450)	(500)
Advertising & Promotion	—	(240)	(240)	(270)	(300)
R & D	(500)	(250)	—	—	—
Depreciation (1)	—	—	(100)	(100)	(100)
Imputed Interest (2)	—	(67)	(133)	(176)	(195)
Net Income	(100)	43	727	804	905
Book Value	(100)	57	784	1,588	$2,493
Market Value/Book Value Ratio					2.0X
Terminal Value					$4,986
Present Value @ 15%					$2,479

(1) Assume 10 year life
(2) At 10%; assume debt equal to 30 percent of investment in fixed assets and working capital

The Present Value of this Terminal Value may be added to the Present Value of the first five years' cash flow to obtain a total Present Value for the acquisition because the Present Values are additive as pointed out in the previous section:

PV acquisition = PV 1st 5 years'
Cash Flow + PV Terminal Value

In the example of Table 10-2 we have

PV acquisition = 191 + 2,479 = $2,670

2. Terminal Values from Discounting Perpetual Cash Flows. Another method for estimating Terminal Values is to forecast far enough into the future the cash flows discussed in the Sections IIB and IIC so that estimated cash flows beyond the forecast period have a regular behavior which, for the purpose of analysis, may be assumed to continue forever. As long as this regular behavior is not constituted of a growth rate greater than the discount rate, the present value of all future cash flows is finite and often can be arrived at by simple computation.

The following are calculations to find the Terminal Value for a number of simple Present Value (discount rate r) models of cash flow behavior.

1) Assume constant cash flow for each period of perpetuity;

$$TV = \sum_{i=1}^{\infty} \frac{CF}{(1+r)^i} = \boxed{\frac{CF}{r} - CF}$$

2) Assume cash flow increasing by a constant dollar amount in each period of perpetuity:

$$TV = \sum_{i=1}^{\infty} \frac{CF + ig}{(1+r)^i} = \boxed{\frac{CF}{r} + g\frac{(1+r)}{r^2} - CF}$$

3) Assume cash flow increasing at a constant rate (r) in each period to perpetuity, so long as that rate is less than the discount rate:

$$TV = \sum_{i=1}^{\infty} CF\left(\frac{1+k}{1+r}\right)^i = \boxed{CF\left(\frac{1+k}{r-k}\right)}$$

where:

TV = Terminal Value   k = Rate of increase
r = Discount rate   CF = 1st Period cash flow
g = Dollar amount of increase

If the Example in Table 10-2 is continued and assuming the cash flow at the end of the fifth year is about $1,000 then the various methods of computing terminal value would result in:

Table 10-5
Perpetual Cash Flows of the Acquisition Target
($000)

Year	Constant Cash Flow	Constant Dollar* Increase Per Period	Constant Rate** Increase Per Period
		* ($100/period)	** (10%/period)
6	1,000	$1,100	$1,100
7	1,000	1,200	1,210
8	1,000	1,300	1,331
9	1,000	1,400	1,464
10	1,000	1,500	1,611
11	1,000	1,600	1,772
—	—	—	—
—	—	—	—
Terminal Value(1)	$5,667	$10,778	$22,000
Present Value(2)	$2,818	$5,359	$10,938
Plus Present Value First Five Years' Cash Flow (see Table 10-2)	$ 191	191	$ 191
Present Value Acquisition	$3,009	$5,550	$11,129

(1) Present value of all cash flows occuring in year 6 and beyond, discounted to the beginning of year 6 as per equations above.

(2) Present Value of Terminal Value at beginning of year 1

Again, we may arrive at a total Present Value for the acquisition through adding the Present Value of the first five years' cash flows to the Present Value of subsequent years' cash flows.

We also see that, depending on our determination of how best to find the Terminal Value, the Present Value of our acquisition target may take on a great range of values (Table 10-6):

Table 10-6
Effect of Different Methods
of Estimating Terminal Values
($000)

	Present Value of:	
	Terminal Value	Acquisition
Book Value-Based	$2,479	$2,670
Perpetual Cash Flow Present Value		
• Constant Cash Flow	2,818	3,009
• Constant Dollar Increasing Cash Flow ($100/yr)	5,359	5,550
• Constant Rate Increase Cash Flow (10%/yr)	10,938	11,129

F. Risk Analysis

The methods above, while depending on forecasts of the results of the target, do not reflect directly the uncertainty involved in the forecasting process itself. Acquiring a new business is a decidedly risky proposition in which the purchaser never has as much information about the prospective acquisition as the seller does. Often expected benefits do not occur as planned—costs rise after the acquisition, or technologies come up short in the market place. Many types of risks defy any type of organized analysis. However, some risks are identifiable and take the form of large ranges for the possible outcomes of key variables. There are several ways of expanding a valuation to include analysis of the impact of these types of risk on the value of the acquisition.

1. *Simulation.* Where a number of variables are uncertain as to outcome, simulation may be the only practical way of analyzing the risk of a project. There are a number of computer-based simulation "languages" and packages which may be employed to simplify this task. Each variable with uncertainty associated with it has a probability distribution of possible outcomes which may be developed. A simulation is constituted of a number of "trials," in each of which possible values for each variable are selected and the forecasted value of the acquisition is calculated based on that selection of values. A large number of such "trials" are performed, each with a different selection of values and a different outcome for the value of the

acquisition. The sum of the results of these "trials" divided by the number of "trials" is the "expected value" of the acquisition.

$$\text{Expected Value} = \frac{PV_1 + PV_2 + PV_3 + \dots + PV_n}{n}$$

where n is the number of the "trial."

More important, inspection of the range of resulting Present Values will give a good picture of the risk associated with the acquisition.

Example: In evaluating the acquisition of a manufacturer of precision and non-precision metal parts, simulation was carried out treating the following as "uncertain variables":

• the size of the market for precision products
• company's share of market for precision products
• company's sales of non-precision products
• indirect costs for each product line
• corporate sales expenses.

Rough graphs of the probability distributions of these variables are shown in Figure 10-1.

The result of a simulation of 100 trials is shown in Figure 10-2 on page 158.

A graph of the values resulting from simulation and their corresponding probability of occurrence indicated there was a 50 percent chance that the Present Value of this acquisition would be between $5 and $15 million (line segment x − x') and that the probability that a payment of $13 million (the target's asking price) would result in a negative Net Present Value was over 70 percent. Consequently the purchaser offered a lower price ($10 million, at which the probability of a loss was less than 50 percent). The offer was refused. Note that the "expected value" (the mean) of the acquisition was $12 million, very close to the asking price. In many cases, as in this one, it is not the expected value of the acquisition that is so important but the risk of loss at a given price. In this case, the $3 million difference in purchase price was viewed by the potential acquiror as the difference between a risky investment and a reasonable opportunity for a gain. Simulation techniques are generally only feasible if computer resources are available.

2. *Sensitivity Analysis.* When a relatively few critical variables are important, sensitivity analysis may be informative. This analysis is performed by selecting a critical variable, substituting a number of different likely values for that variable, and computing the effect on the cash flow and present value of the target. For example, a recent acquisition prospect was the manager of a $100 million mutual fund. A performance fee

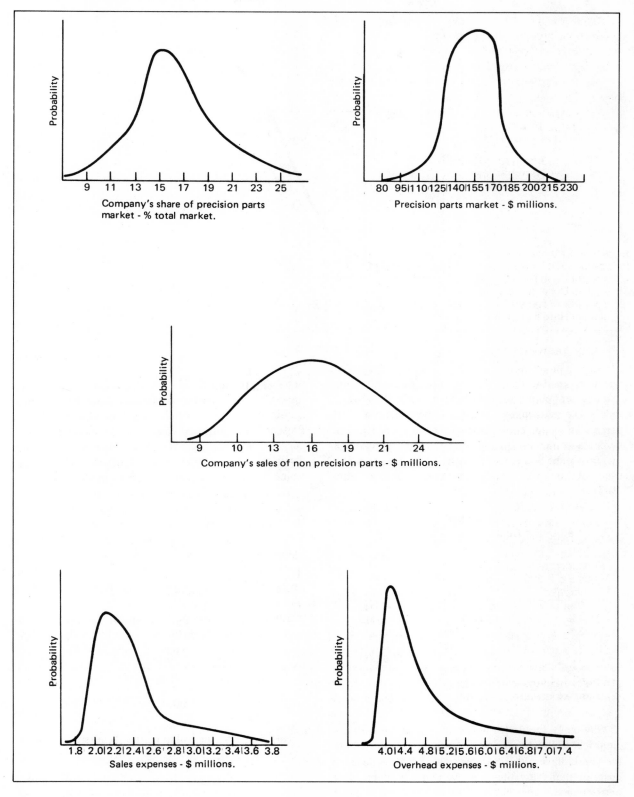

Figure 10-1

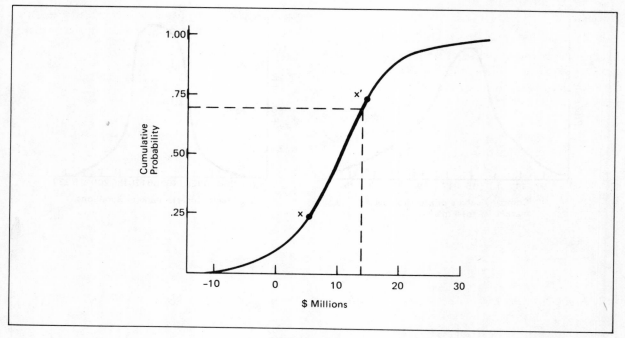

Figure 10-2

was to be paid to this company if the funds under its management outperformed the Standard & Poor's 500 index. The performance fee was to be equal to the 10 percent of dollar equivalent of the difference in the percentage increase in the fund over the percentage increase in the S & P 500. Sensitivity analysis could be used to show the impact of such a variable (Table 10-7).

Table 10-7
Estimated Cash Flows of Acquisition
Target Expenses

Fund Increase Minus S & P 500 Increase	Management Fee (1)	After Tax Cash Flow (2)
0%	$ 500,000	$100,000
1%	600,000	150,000
2%	700,000	200,000
3%	800,000	250,000
4%	900,000	300,000
5%	1,000,000	350,000

(1) Before expenses and taxes
(2) After expenses and taxes

Obviously the performance fee could have a very significant impact since, except for taxes, the whole fee would have a direct impact on cash flow because costs of managing the fund were not a function of performance. Since the impact of each additional 1 percent difference between the rate of increase of the fund's assets and the S & P 500 index can be determined ($50,000), the effect on the Present Value of the acquisition for this variable may be computed and the Present Value adjusted easily for any assumption regarding this variable. We may utilize the approach discussed in Section II.E.2 for finding the Present Value of a perpetual constant cash flow to find:

(i) The Present Value of the Cash Flow Assuming the Fund Performance Does Not Exceed S & P 500 Increase

$$PV = \frac{\$100,000}{(1+r)^1} + \frac{\$100,000}{(1+5)^2} + \ldots + \frac{\$100,000}{(1+r)^n}$$

$$= \frac{100,000}{r} - 100,000 = \$566,667, \text{ if } r = .15$$

(ii) Change in Present Value for Every 1 Percent the Fund Out Performs the S&P 500 Index

$$PV / 1\% \frac{50,000}{(1+r)^1} + \frac{50,000}{(1+r)^2} + \ldots + \frac{50,000}{(1+r)^n}$$

$$= \frac{50,000}{r} - 50,000 = \$283,333, \text{ if } r = .15$$

(iii) The Present Value of the Acquisition will be the sum of
• The first value
• The product of the second value and the percent (I) by which the fund outperforms the S&P 500.

That is:

$$PV \text{ acquisition} = \$566,667 + I(283,333)$$

In other words, each 1 percent difference between the rate of growth in the fund and the rate of growth of the S&P 500 Index would increase the value of the acquisition by $283,333 (Table 10-8).

Table 10-8
Present Value of Acquisition Target

Fund Increase S&P 500 Increase	PV Acquisition	Increase in PV Acquisition	
		$	%
0%	$ 566,667	0	0%
1	850,000	$283,333	50
2	1,133,333	283,333	33
3	1,416,666	283,333	25

3. *Break-even Analysis.* One of the most useful methods of evaluating risk is break-even analysis. The greatest limitation of this method is that it can be applied only by examining one variable at a time. Its popularity is based on the fact that the decision maker may avoid making explicit estimates or forecasts with respect to uncertain variables. In break-even analysis, the decision maker may stipulate the conditions under which the investment would be satisfactory. The problem is solved to find the value for the uncertain variable for which these conditions are satisfied. The decision maker hopes the value will be high enough or low enough to be easily considered within or outside the range of reasonable forecast for the uncertain variable.

With some ingenuity a break-even type of analysis may be used to analyze many different types of problems. Recently, an acquisition of a business was considered in which the chief attraction was the cash flow of the company. It was felt that by reducing advertising expenditures the business would generate substantial cash flow but that the business would probably decline to point of extinction within ten years. The question in the acquiror's mind was would the cash flow last long enough to justify the acquisition price. A simple "payback" calculation is a type of break-even calculation that would be commonly used but is deficient because it ignores the time value of money considerations. A discounted payback may give quite a different answer. In this case, the estimated cash flow was $2 million and the acquisition price about $9 million. A payback calculation would show a payback in 4.5 years; a discounted (at 15 percent) payback would show recovery of investment in a little more than 8 years (Table 10-9). In this case, the acquiror decided that this was too long a time to expect the business to remain healthy without advertising support and decided not to pursue the acquisition.

Table 10-9
Break-even Analysis: Payback of Investment of $9 Million
($000)

Years	Cash Flow	Cumulative Cash Flow	Present Value of Cash Flow	Cumulative Present Value
1	$2,000	$2,000	$1,739	$1,739
2	2,000	4,000	1,512	3,251
3	2,000	6,000	1,315	4,566
4	2,000	8,000	1,144	5,710
5	2,000	10,000	994	6,704
6	2,000	12,000	865	7,569
7	2,000	14,000	752	8,321
8	2,000	16,000	654	8,975
9	2,000	18,000	569	9,544
Payback Period:	4.5 Years			8+ Years

III. COMPARATIVE ANALYSIS

A. Approach

Comparative analysis is performed by identifying companies which are similar to the company to be valued and which are valued either (i) in the public market trading of their securities and/or (ii) by purchases of their securities in acquisitions transactions. It is reasonable that differences in value will occur among several companies in the same line of business. These differences can be attributed to the difference in the outlook for these companies. However, in performing a comparative analysis it is difficult to quantify the outlook for such companies. Therefore, the assumption is often made that relative historical performance among these companies will be a guide to future success. While this is obviously a weak assumption for any individual case, with a large enough group of companies errors due to this assumption should average out. The analyst must determine which indicators of performance (for the group of companies being employed as a basis for valuing the potential acquisition) are correlated to the values of the companies in the base. A model for the value of these companies and that of the acquisition can be built by defining the nature of this correlation. Then the acquisition may be valued by inserting into the model its performance values for those performance indicators chosen for the model.

For example, let us suppose that in analyzing a certain retailer, it was found that there was a high correlation between (i) the ratio of the price at which the stock of these companies traded in the market and

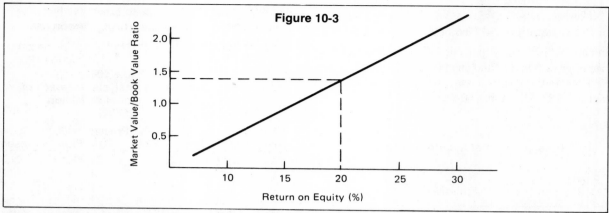

Figure 10-3

their book value per share and (ii) the return on equity. In other words, the market premium over the book value would be a function of return on equity of the company. The higher the return on equity the higher the market premium over the book value (Figure 10-3).

If a prospective acquisition in this line of business had a return on equity of, say, 20 percent, the market to book value ratio would be approximately 1.4; i.e. the premium of the market value over the book value would be 40 percent. If the prospective acquisition had a book value of $10 million, its market value would be estimated to be about $14 million. This is not to say that a reasonable price at which to acquire the company would be $14 million since premiums over market value are frequently paid in acquisitions. Another step is required to determine that premium (see Section IV).

The approach discussed above is a "two-step" procedure, in which the value of the company as it would sell in the public securities markets is estimated in the first step and the acquisition value estimated in the second step. An alternative but, we believe, less successful approach is to determine the acquisition value in one step. In this approach, the analyst would identify the relationship between acquisition prices paid and the performance indicators for a base of companies which have been acquired. The difficulty with this latter approach is that the factors affecting tender premiums are not necessarily related to the performance of the company but may depend more on the nature of the shareholdings in the company, the attitude of the shareholders toward a merger or acquisition, and other factors. Also, a larger number of cases for comparison may be possible if the analysis is split into two steps since not many companies may have similarities in both business and nature of acquisition method.

B. Selection of Comparative Companies

The key to successful comparative analysis is the selection of a universe of companies as a basis to indicate value. This is also the most difficult part of this type of analysis. Every company is in some ways unique. Selection may be made based on a number of different dimensions of the company's business:

— type of product produced;
— market segment to which product is sold;
— size;
— geographic area of operations;
— position in market place.

A valuation using comparative analysis can be heavily influenced by the type of feature which is felt to be important about a company. For example, in a recent study of acquisitions of consumer product companies with strong franchises, it was found that the average P/E paid for these companies was almost 15 times (see Table 10-1). On the other hand, the average P/E paid in the acquisition of various retail companies was about 11 times (see Table 10-10).

Table 10-10—Acquisitions of Selected Retail Chains

Target Company	Acquiring Company	Tender P/E Ratio	Tender Premium Over Market Price Before Announcement
Mervyn's	Dayton-Hudson	17.0X	8.5%
Howard Bros.	Gamble Skogmo	7.5	62.1
Volume Shoe	May Department Stores	12.5	42.1
Thalhimer Bros.	Carter-Hawley-Hale Stores	13.5	17.2
Marlene	Unishops	6.9	41.7
Winn's Stores	Heinrich Bauer Verlag	10.4	NA
Margo's La Mode	Alexander's	12.0	NA
	Group Average	11.4X	34.3%

If one were to consider Avon's acquisition of Tiffany as an acquisition of a retailer, it would appear as though Avon paid a high price (16X). However, that price is well within the range for companies with extremely strong consumer franchises as seen in Table 10-1.[6] Thus, the level of a fair acquisition price is a function of which group of companies is determined to best represent the essential elements or the company to be valued.

In cases where a company appears to be unique in product, markets addressed, and the other features listed above, the analyst may have to go to a higher level of abstraction in order to find companies with similar features. For example, WD-40, the product of which is a line of lubricants, would seem like an interesting but not exciting prospect. A closer look at WD-40, however, reveals that it is not so much a manufacturer of lubricants but a licensor of others to make a product using the WD-40 name. In making their products, these licensees use a formulation supplied by WD-40 and ingredients produced by the Company. WD-40 also has a very strong identity in its customers' minds. Thus this company has many of the characteristics of some of the great franchisers—Coca-Cola, McDonald's and others. Its valuation in the market, approximately 17 times earnings, would seem to reflect this.

Another difficulty may occur when the company to be valued is comprised of several different component businesses. Recently, an evaluation of a chemical company with five distinct lines of business was performed. For each line of business a different group of companies was used as a base of comparison for value and different valuation models for each group had to be developed. In addition, the company had a considerable amount of investments which had to be valued on a completely different basis.

Imagine performing a valuation of Norton Simon Inc. The selection on comparative companies would be done business by business (Table 10-11).

In types of business, Norton Simon's Avis car rental is closest to Hertz, National and Budget, which are parts of RCA, Household Finance and Transamerica, respectively. This example points out one of the difficulties of selecting comparable companies: in many cases, the closest comparisons will exist only as part of larger diversified corporations. There is no market value obtainable for these operations. Other companies that may be similar and publicly owned are in different segments of the business (truck rental in the case of

Table 10-11
Business Segments of Norton Simon Inc.

Norton Simon Business Segment (1)	Possible Comparative Companies
Foods	Beatrice Foods
•Hunt Tomato Products	Carnation
•Wesson Oil	General Foods
•Orville Redenbacher's	
Popcorn	General Mills
•Pfeiffer Salad Dressings	H.J. Heinz
•Hunt Snack Pack	Kraft
•Reddi Wip Dessert Topping	Nabisco
	Pillsbury
Vehicle Rental	Ryder
•Avis Car Rental	
Cosmetics & Fashion	Alberto-Culver
•Max Factor Cosmetics	Avon
•Halston Fragrances and	
Fashions	Eli Lilly
•McCall's Patterns	Neutrogena
	Revlon
Beverages	Annheuser-Busch
•Johnnie Walker Scotch	Brown-Forman
•Tanqueray Gin	Coca Cola
•Alexis Lichine Wines	Foremost-McKesson
•Canada Dry Mixers	Heublein Companies
and Drinks	National Distillers
•Barrelhead Root Beer	Pepsico
	Philip Morris
	Royal Crown
	Seagram
Packaging	American Can
•Glass Containers	American Hocking
•United Can	Ball Corp.
	Owens-Illinois

(1) Norton Simon Inc. 1979 Annual Report

Ryder) or have such small positions in the industry that they are unlikely to be good comparisons. Ryder may be used for comparison with Avis on the basis that, like Avis, it has a strong national franchise and a good image. The differences between the business of Ryder and Avis, however, are readily apparent.

Another difficulty which arises in analyzing a company is that its performance may not be measured against others in its industry since the major factors in the industry may be small parts of large corporations on which virtually no data is available. While recently the financial statements of publicly held corporations have begun showing more detail than before, there are still a great many limitations in gathering performance data on business segments. Since only revenue, profit, contributions and assets employed are generally reported, much useful information may never be reported even if

---

[6]Tiffany also had valuable real estate and inventory which were factors in its acquisition price.

the operation is reported as a separate "line of business." In the case of conglomerates, large operations sometimes with dominant positions in their market places, are lumped together for reporting purposes. A prime example would be ITT: its "Consumer Products and Services" group contains such leaders in their respective markets as Sheraton Hotels, Continental Bakeries and O.M. Scott lawn care products. If one were valuing a home garden and lawn care products company, recognition of O.M. Scott's dominant position would be necessary, but little data would be generally available on its operational performance.

To obtain reasonably reliable results, a number of companies similar to the company to be valued must be used to demonstrate a relationship between value and the characteristic(s) thought to determine that value. Since most companies to be included in a base for comparative analysis differ at least in some degree, the more companies included as a basis of comparison, the greater the diversity of the businesses included in the base. The boundaries of the base are usually not easily established. One example of the type of difficulty encountered is represented by GATX Corporation, historically a railroad car manufacturer and lessor. While this is still the principal business of GATX, the revenues and profits from this line of business represented less than one half of the Company's totals in fiscal 1978. It is questionable how worthwhile it would be to include GATX in the base for valuing a railroad car manufacturer and lessor since its performance is highly dependent on other lines of business as could be seen when several years ago the company suffered from its then heavy exposure in the shipping business.

Generally, an analyst who has dealt with the business under consideration will have a big advantage in performing comparative analysis. He has followed the companies in the industry and may have data on their operational performance, or that of business segments, that is not generally available. He will also know what companies provide the best comparisons and will know what elements in this business are the most important in predicting their success and their value in the market.

C. Data Collection and Consistency Requirements

In order to perform an evaluation based on comparable companies, the analyst must search for the reasons that the companies selected for comparison to the acquisition target take the values they do. Value may be analyzed in relationship to growth, earning power,

asset values, cash flow, advertising, research and development, rank in market segment, or any number of other variables which reflect the strength or performance of the companies. Some important variables may not be quantifiable. The search for relationships between values and these performance characteristics of the companies under study may be reduced in scope by the analyst who has an understanding of the business sufficient to know which variables are most important. It may also be limited, unfortunately, by data available to examine these variables. It is often difficult, for example, to obtain information on the average volume of sales per salesperson although it is recognized as being an important measure of a company's marketing performance.

What data is to be used should be on a consistent basis from company to company for those included in the base. Sales growth and profitability should be looked at over the same business cycle. Net income, when used in profitability calculations should be adjusted to eliminate the effect of one-time or extraordinary effects. If the companies in the base are not in the same industry, accounting conventions may vary drastically and sometimes great difficulties will be encountered in trying to get figures on a consistent basis. One difficulty which analysts have faced is how to deal with companies with very different amounts of excess cash. Earnings on the investment of these funds are not likely to be valued in the same way as the business itself. The opposite case, the unusually leveraged company, also results in difficulties in comparing its results to others.

D. Screening for Variables Important to Valuation

Having selected, and gathered data for, a base of comparable companies to use in valuing the prospective acquisition, the next task is to find what relationships exist between the value of the companies under study and their performance variables.

The fastest way to determine whether there is a correlation between valuation and a performance variable is to compare the rankings of the companies in the base by each type of variable. Data for a dozen selected department stores are displayed in Table 10-12. Notice that the rankings are performed in a special way with ties taking the same value and, when two values are tied, the next number is skipped. This form of ranking allows us to perform a simple statistical test to see whether the ranking of one variable is correlated to the ranking of another. The rank correlation coefficient, R, is computed:[7]

[7]The Spearman rank correlation coefficient, described in John E. Freund, *Mathematical Statistics* (Englewood Cliffs, 1971), p. 387 and the *International Dictionary of Applied Mathematics* (Princeton, 1960), p. 743.

$$R = 1 - \frac{6 \sum_{i=1}^{n} (Xi - X'_I)^2}{n(n^2 - 1)}$$

where Xi is the rank of one variable (e.g. the valuation variable) of company i and X'i is the rank of the other (e.g. performance) variable. The number of companies in the base is n.

For our twelve companies we will perform this computation for two sets of variables, one set which has a high correlation (Table 10-13) and one set with virtually no correlation (Table 10-15 on page 164). Since the difference in the rankings is squared in this computation, a number of small differences in ranking is likely to result in a higher correlation coefficient than a few large differences will.

The resulting rank correlation coefficient is:

$$R = 1 - \frac{6 \times 42}{12(12^2 - 1)} = .853$$

This looks like a pretty good correlation and we can check the significance of this coefficient by looking at Table 10-14 which shows the minimum coefficient required so that we can *reject* as improbable[8] the theory that the variables are *not correlated*.

We may conclude that there is less than a 1 percent chance that these two variables, Market/Book Value and 4 Year Growth in Sales are not correlated because the number of companies in our sample is 12 and, therefore, since R = .853 is greater than .658, the ranking is significant at the 1 percent level (Table 10-14).

Table 10-12
Selected Department Stores

| Department Stores | Valuation Variables | | | | Performance Variables | | | |
| | P/E | | Market/Book Value | | 4 Year Growth Sales(1) | | Net Income/Sales | |
	Ratio	Group Rank	Ratio	Group Rank	Ratio	Group Rank	Ratio	Group Rank
Alexanders Inc.	6.9X	3	0.42	12	7.1	9	0.9%	12
Allied Department Stores	5.3	10	0.71	8	6.9	10	4.0	3
Associated Dry Goods Corp.	6.0	7	0.47	11	5.4	12	2.3	11
Carter Hawley Hale Stores Inc.	6.8	5	0.81	5	14.9	3	2.9	7
Dayton-Hudson Corp.	8.0	2	1.14	1	16.5	2	5.1	1
Federated Department Stores	6.4	6	0.83	4	10.9	7	3.5	6
R.H. Macy & Co., Inc.	5.9	8	0.91	2	12.2	5	3.7	4
Marshall Field & Co.	8.1	1	0.66	9	8.6	8	2.4	10
May Department Stores Co.	5.6	9	0.78	7	11.0	6	3.5	4
Mercantile Stores Co.	5.3	10	0.81	5	13.1	4	4.4	2
Outlet Company	6.9	3	0.91	2	32.2	1	2.5	9
Carson Pirie Scott & Co.	5.0	12	0.62	10	5.6	11	2.9	7

(1) Four year compounded growth rate used because every annual report includes 5 years of historical data.

Table 10-13
Rankings of the Market Value/Book Value Ratios and the 4-Year Compound Growth Rate of Sales for 12 Department Stores

Company 1	Market/Book Rank	4 Year Growth in Sales Rank	Difference	Difference Squared
	Xi	X'i	Xi-X'i	(Xi-X'i)²
1	12	9	3	9
2	8	10	-2	4
3	11	12	-1	1
4	5	3	2	4
5	1	2	-1	1
6	4	7	-3	9
7	2	5	-3	9
8	9	8	1	1
9	7	6	1	1
10	5	4	1	1
11	2	1	1	1
12	10	11	-1	1
			Sum	42

Table 10-14
Minimum Correlation Coefficient (R)

| # of Companies Ranked | Probability Rankings Not Correlated Less Than | | |
	1%	2.5%	5%
5	.934	.878	.805
6	.882	.811	.729
7	.833	.755	.669
8	.789	.707	.621
9	.750	.666	.582
10	.715	.632	.549
11	.685	.602	.521
12	.658	.576	.497

Examining this table further, we see that if we have as many as 8 companies in our base we can be quite confident (1 percent level) of a correlation if the coefficient is greater than .8; but we need, to give us the same

---

[8] If R is the correlation coefficient, then $T = R\sqrt{R-2}/\sqrt{1-R^2}$ has the Student's t distribution t(n-2). If T is greater than the value in the Student's t distribution table for parameters α (the confidence level) and n-2, then the probability that the variables are uncorrelated is α; i.e. we reject the hypothesis that the variables are not correlated, if α is small.

Frank L. Wolf, *Elements of Probability and Statistics* (New York, 1962) pp. 291-294, Table A-8.

level of confidence, 11 companies if a coefficient of .7 is obtained. This explains the need to include as many comparable companies as possible.

Now see what happens when we try to compare the ranking of the Price/Earnings Ratio (P/E) to the 4 Year Growth Rate (Table 10-15).There can be no great confidence that these two variables are related since R = .392 is below the lowest value in our table (Table 10-14). With a little practice, ranking and computing rank correlation coefficient can be performed very quickly. As a rule of thumb, for a base of 6 to 12 companies, if the coefficients are less than .6 the relationship between variables may be ignored. If the coefficient is higher, the correlation between the variables may be the basis of a model for valuing the acquisition and the relationship between the variables should be examined further.

Table 10-15
Rankings of the Price/Earnings Ratios and
the 4 Year Compound
Growth Rate of Sales for 12 Department Stores

i	Price/Earnings Ratio Rank X_i	4 Year Growth Rate Rank X'_i	Difference $X_i - X'_i$	Difference Squared $(X_i - X'_i)^2$
1	3	9	−6	36
2	10	10	0	0
3	7	12	−5	25
4	5	3	2	4
5	2	2	0	0
6	6	7	−1	1
7	8	5	3	9
8	1	8	−7	49
9	9	6	3	9
10	10	4	6	36
11	3	1	2	4
12	12	11	1	1
				174

$$R = 1 - \frac{6 \times (174)}{12(12^2 - 1)} = .392$$

E. Relating the Performance of the Company to Its Value

The next step is to determine the nature of the relationship between the performance of the company and its value. At this point, graphing the values of a valuation variable (say, the Market/Book Value ratio) against the values of a performance variable (such as sales growth) for two such variables that have shown a high correlation is useful (see Figure 10-4). A straight line or a smooth curve drawn as close to as many of the graph points as possible will approximate the function of the relationship between the variables. By finding the value of the performance variable of the prospective acquisition (e.g. 15 percent sales growth) on the

horizontal axis (Point A), extending a line from that point straight up to our graph line (Point B), and moving horizontally from the point to the point on the vertical axis (Point C) which is at the same level, we find the estimated value of the valuation variable (.81 Market/Book Ratio) for our acquisition.

A more precise definition of the relationship may come from the use of regression analysis (simple bivariate regression analysis may be performed on many calculators commonly used by the financial analyst). Even if regression analysis is to be employed, it is a good idea to graph the variables to determine whether any transformations of the regression equations will be useful.

The regression analysis in this case produced the equation

Market/Book Ratio =

.552 + .017 × 4 Year Growth Rate (in %)

A company growing at a rate of 15 percent per year would have an expected market/book ratio of:

Market/Book Ratio = .552 + .017(15.0) = .81

At a book value of $50 million, the market value of our prospective acquisition would be estimated at about $40 million. The analysis performed here is unsophisticated in that the assumption is that just one variable is the determining factor in the valuation of a company. This is obviously not the case and many more elaborate models using multivariate regression analysis have been built. However, our approach may be excused for its simplicity because it is computationally easy, quite quick, and requires no computer analysis. There are a few reasons why a simple analysis such as this can be effective:

1. Companies are carefully selected for comparability, eliminating from consideration many variables of performance which are difficult to quantify;

2. The analysis is not done to predict the value of the company in the future, which presents greater difficulties, but is only a method of determining its value at the time of the acquisition.

F. Market/Book Value Ratio Is Often a Useful Approach

Recent experience indicates that the most likely valuation variable to show a strong relationship with a performance variable is the Market /Book Ratio. It would not be surprising if this did not reflect the climate of today's market in which acquisitions and liquidations are common. In the late 'sixties, when Price/Earnings multiples were more of a goal and a tool in corporate finance, different relationships would have existed. The analyst should be aware that rela-

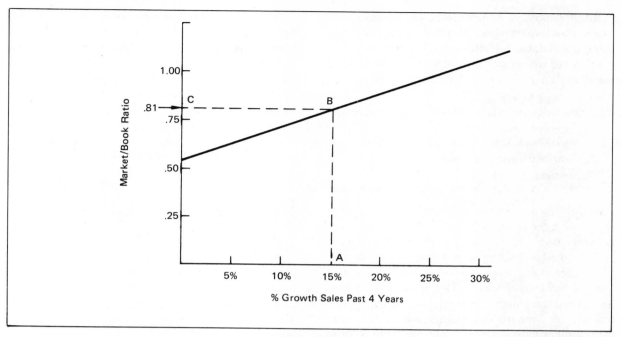

Figure 10-4

tionships which are useful today may not hold for future analysis.

In a recent study of retailing, correlations between valuation ratios and performance indicators were found as listed in Table 10-16. Of the eight cases where relationships for the Market/Book Ratio were sought, three showed correlation at a high level of confidence. Of the eight cases where relationships for Price/Earnings Ratio were sought, only one showed strong correlation.

Table 10-16
Correlation Coefficients Between Market Value Ratios
and Performance Variable for Various Retail Companies

Relationship	Correlation Coefficient	Probability That Relationship Does Not Exist
Department Stores		no more than
(base 12 companies)		
Market/Book to Net Income/Sales	.600	2.5%
Market/Book to 4 Year Sales Growth	.853	0.5
Price/Earnings to Net Income/Sales	−.392	*
Price/Earnings to 4 Year Sales Growth	.392	*
Mail Order Stores		
(base 7 companies)		
Market/Book to Net Income/Sales	.107	*
Market/Book to 4 Year Sales Growth	.893	0.5%
Price/Earnings to Net Income/Sales	−.125	40.0
Price Earnings to 4 Year Sales Growth	.857	1.0
Speciality Retailers		
(base 10 companies)		
Market/Book to Net Income/Sales	.794	0.5%
Market/Book to 4 Year Sales Growth	.521	10.0
Price/Earnings to Net Income/Sales	.406	15.0
Price/Earnings to 4 Year Sales Growth	.406	15.0
Supermarket Chains	($200-$300 million sales)	
(base 14 companies)	Market/Book to Net Income/Sales	.431	10.0%
Market/Book to 5 Years Sales Growth	.508	5.0
Price/Earnings to Net Income/Sales	−.313	15.0
Price/Earnings to 4 Year Sales Growth	.091	40.0

* Greater than 45 percent

The following definitions were developed for the Market/Book value relationship to 4 Year Growth performance variable for each group of companies for which there was significant correlation between these variables:

Department Store Chains:
    Market/Book Value = .55 + .017 (4 Year Growth)
Mail Order Companies:
    Market/Book Value = .52 + .034 (4 Year Growth)
Specialty Retailers: Not significant
Supermarket Chains:
    Market/Book Value + .16 + .029 (4 Year Growth)

The difference among the relationships for these segments of the retail business are shown graphically in Figure 10-5. From these relationships it would appear that mail order companies would have a valuation at a higher multiple of book value than supermarket chains at any level of growth. This may be due partly to the fact that less (equity) investment may be required to fund growth in the mail order business and partly due to the favorable outlook for the mail order business in an energy-conscious society. In viewing department stores this analysis suggests that growth may not be as important a valuation variable as it is for the other two types of retailers even though the Market/Book Ratio is highly correlated with this performance variable.

Table 10-17 offers an explanation: there is considerably less variability in the market/book value ratio for department store chains than for the other two categories of retailers.

Table 10-17
Market Value/Book Value Ratios for
Three Groups of Retail Companies

	Mean	Standard Deviation	Standard Deviation % of Mean
Department Store Chains	.76	.20	26%
Mail Order Companies	1.23	.59	48
Supermarket Chains	.55	.26	47

A question which has arisen in performing our studies is whether the book value used as a basis of the valuation should be adjusted for intangibles to arrive at a "Tangible Net Worth" type of value. A recent study of companies with large amounts of goodwill resulting from acquisitions seems to indicate that the amount of goodwill *per se* does not seem to affect the value of a company. The goodwill arises out of the accounting

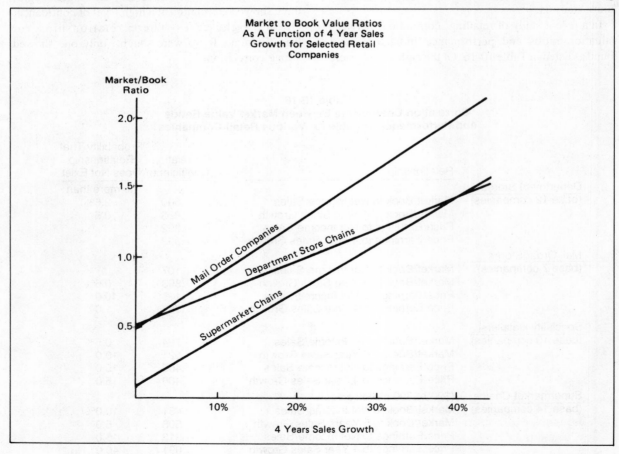

Market to Book Value Ratios
As A Function of 4 Year Sales
Growth for Selected Retail
Companies

Figure 10-5

conventions that do not recognize explicitly values of franchises, mailing lists, computer software, employee training, and other factors which may make an acquisition target unique and especially valuable. Purchasing companies, in paying the prices they do, must feel these values in the acquired companies exist even though they are not "tangible." It is consistent that stockholders, too, give credit for this value and therefore do not penalize a company for the goodwill component of its book value.

IV. ACQUISITION PREMIUMS

It may be expected that if a company's stock sells for one price in the market place as it is traded day-to-day in relatively small amounts, a sudden expression of interest in purchasing substantially all of the stock on the part of one party is likely to cause the stock to rise. The premium paid for acquisitions seems to be a function of acquiring companies' attitude of "all or nothing" in terms of control. This puts the acquiror in a position in which he must be sure of getting a large proportion of the shareholders to accept his offer to buy the stock of the prospective acquisition. The greater the hurdles the acquiror faces in achieving this goal, the larger the premium over the market price that will be required. The following is a representative list of the types of considerations which a premium is often intended to overcome:

— lack of desire on the part of present owners to sell their stock with unfamiliar reinvestment alternatives;
— threatened security for owner/manager (particularly in "unfriendly" takeovers);
— tax consequences if the acquisition is a taxable transaction;
— other potential suitors' bids;
— difficulties in rapidly acquiring a number of shares to exercise control and consolidate operations and tax reporting.

The relative importance of each of these factors can be judged only on a case-by-case basis. The distribution of stock holdings, attitude of primary stockholdings groups toward the acquiror and toward the form of the proposed transaction all must be known before an acquisition premium can be determined which will result in a reasonable level of success.

For convenience in analyzing acquisition premiums, we will classify all targets in two classes: private (or quasi-private) companies and companies with wide stock distribution.

A. Premiums for Purchasing Closely Held Companies

Measuring the acquisition premiums paid for strictly private companies, of course, is impossible since there is no market price to use as a reference. Some difficulty also exists if a very large proportion, say, 80 percent of the stock, is held by insiders since the trading of the remainder of the stock may be very thin and the stock price before any acquisition is imminent may be artificially high or low due to this illiquidity. For analysis of acquisition premiums, the best examples of quasi-private company acquisition targets are those in which the principal owners had 20 to 40 percent of the stock, where the rest is widely held, and where the owners are also in key management positions or otherwise critical to the company's success. Enough liquidity for the stock may exist so that a realistic market price may be established. On the other hand, an acquiror would be reluctant to try an unfriendly offer with such a large proportion of stock and the management of the company in one group's hands. Therefore, the acquiror will usually approach the holders of that controlling block and try to strike a deal that suits those holders. Since the same (or better) terms must be offered to the other shareholders (as required by the Securities and Exchange Commission), it may be reasonable to assume that the premium paid is a function of what is needed to satisfy the principal shareholding group. Because of tax considerations, it may be that an exchange of stock may result in a lower premium than a payment with cash or notes which may involve an immediate tax liability.

Some examples of acquisitions in which terms may have been set in recognition of the interests of a controlling group of shareholders are shown in Table 10-18.

B. Premiums for Purchasing with Widely Held Shares

The premiums paid for companies with widely distributed shares should be a function of the desire on the part of the purchaser to achieve control rapidly and the likelihood of competition arising in purchasing this control. The two extreme cases along this dimension of valuation would be (1) the case where a limited number of shares are sought for investment purposes and (2) the case of an aggressive bidding contest among parties.

In the first case, shares are often purchased in the open market, acquired in private transactions or in tender offers with low premiums. Recent examples of these types of purchases are shown in Table 10-19.

At the other extreme we have cases in which two potential purchasers vied for control (Table 10-20).

A sampling of cases where control was sought (and there were no large insider holdings) gave the results shown in Table 10-21.

Table 10-18
Selected Acquisitions of Companies with Large Shareholder Positions

Date	Target Company	Acquiring Company	Percentage of Shares Closely Held	Tender Premium Over Market Price Before Announcement	Method of Payment
12/28/78	Friendly Ice Cream	Hershey Foods	31%	61.4%	Cash
11/21/78	Tiffany	Avon	30	108.5	Stock
08/26/78	Entenmann's	Warner-Lambert	74	66.1	Cash
05/01/78	Seven-Up	Phillip Morris	51	90.1	Cash
04/07/78	Scholl	Schering Plough	46	122.2	Stock
03/03/78	Tropicana	Beatrice	51	62.5	Cash
02/22/78	Foodways National	H.J. Heinz	27	51.2	Cash
11/24/77	Chef Pierre	Consolidated Foods	37	76.5	Stock
09/08/75	Taylor Wine	Coca-Cola	27	61.0	Stock
02/05/76	Mrs. Smith's Pies	Kellogg	49	58.5	Stock
		Group Average		75.8%	

Table 10-19
Selected Acquisitions of Stock for Investment Purposes

Investor	Company in which Stock Purchased	% Shares Purchased	Tender Premium	Method
Henkel A.G.	Clorox	19%	—	Open Market
N.V.F.	Coachman	5	—	Open Market
Freidrick Flick	W.R. Grace	6 (1)	17.6%	Tender
Peter Eckes	Moxie	30	39.4	Tender
American Financial	Gulf United	19	39.5	Private Placement
Statesman Group	Wabash International	9	4.0	Open Market plus
Phyllis Quasha Family	Sparton	5	—	
	Group Average (2)		25.1%	

(1) Already owned significant amount of stock
(2) Of those paying premiums

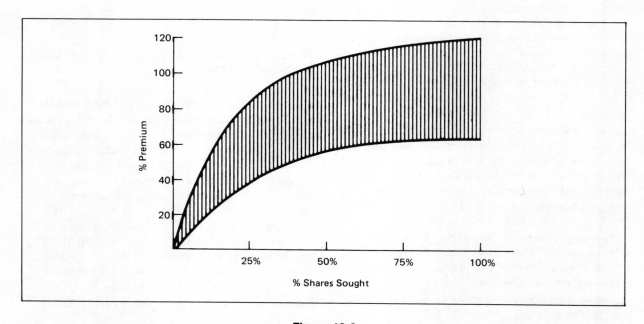

Figure 10-6

Table 10-20
Selected Contested Tender Offers

Date	Target Company	Acquiring Company	Other Bidder	Tender Premium
12/17/79	Warner & Swasey	Bendix (1)	Dominion Bridge(1)	127%
09/27/79	Mostek	United Technologies	Gould	100
06/05/79	Florida Mining & Minerals	Moore McCormick Resources	Kaiser Cement	123
04/17/79	Anken	Rhone Poulenc	Xidex	68
04/16/79	Interway	Gelco	Transamerica	116
02/09/79	Worthington Steel	Blount	Talloy	72
09/01/78	Servomation	City Investing	Liggett Group	91
06/30/78	Data 100	Northern Telecom	McDonnell Douglass	67
03/20/78	ASG Industries	Associated Imports	Fourco	132
04/25/79	Fairchild Camera	Schlumberger	Gould	75
			Group Average	97.1%

(1) At the date of this writing, this conclusion of this bidding contest has not been reached.

Table 10-21
Selected Acquisitions of Companies with Widely Distributed Shareholders

Date	Target Company	Acquiring Company	Tender Premium	% Share Sought in Tender
08/16/79	Microdata	McDonnell Douglas	48.8%	100%
05/11/79	California Computer Products	Sanders Associates	30.1	37
02/14/79	Gardner-Denver	Cooper Industries	77.2	45
02/09/79	Chicago River & Machine	Mite	47.0	100
01/19/79	Compten	NCB	54.3	45
11/21/78	P.R. Mallory & Co.	Dart Industries	30.8	100
11/13/78	Carrier Corp.	United Technologies	40.9	49
11/06/78	Risdon Manufacturing	Metal Box Limited	72.0	100
10/24/78	Simmons	Gulf & Western Industries	35.7	100
10/15/78	Tappan	A.B. Electrolux	87.0	100
		Group Average	52.4%	77.6%

From this data we see a rough relationship between the premium paid for acquisitions and the battle for control.

	Representative Premiums Paid
Little Interest in Control	0-25%
Control Important but not Contested	25-60%
Competition for Control	60-120%

Graphically, the relationship between premiums paid in acquiring shares and the proportion of shares sought may be represented as in Figure 10-6. The width of this band results from the numerous other variables which affect the tender premium determination.

SUMMARY

These approaches will be most successful when the evaluator has a familiarity with the business of the company subject to valuation as well as the techniques themselves. As is also apparent, access to data on stock prices, terms of tender offers and other acquisition methods, and historical performance of many public companies is essential for evaluating acquisition targets expeditiously in the often time-pressured environment of the field of mergers and acquisitions.

MARTIN J. WHITMAN

MARTIN J. WHITMAN, C.F.A., is Chief Executive Officer of M.J. Whitman & Co., Inc., members of the National Association of Securities Dealers, Inc., and he also holds the title of Professor (Adjunct) at Yale University and its Graduate School of Organization and Management. Mr. Whitman is a security analyst whose services are performed for a broad range of corporate and governmental clients. He also engages in brokerage activities with emphasis on the identification of, and the acquisition of, the securities of take-over candidates. Mr. Whitman conducts investment banking seminars at Yale.

Mr. Whitman, who has worked in various analytic capacities in the financial community since the early 1950's, has written and lectured extensively in various forums. He has authored, with Professor Martin Shubik of Yale University, the book, *The Aggressive Conservative Investor*, which was published in 1979 by Random House. Mr. Whitman is currently working on a new book reviewing a number of investment banking subjects including corporate contests for control, mergers and acquisitions, going public, going private, leveraged buyouts, bankruptcy and stockholder litigation.

11

Factors That Ascribe Exceptional Value

MARTIN J. WHITMAN

INTRODUCTION

There is one universal factor out of which exceptional value can be created—PRICE. The central fact that exceptional value can be created by acquiring securities, or businesses, when prices are ultra-low—or that exceptional value can be created by selling securities, or businesses, when prices are ultra-high—is all but ignored in scholarly and accounting literature about valuation. Rather, the underlying valuation assumption by most theoreticians is that the best determinant of value for a security or a business is found in the price at which that security trades in public markets; indeed, the most common schools of thought are that stock market price is such a good indicator of value that one need look no further than public markets to measure value where free, fair, and reliable public markets exist.

Whatever the merits of this value argument from the point of view of outside, passive, minority, non-control securities holders, the argument is wholly irrelevant for activists involved in mergers and acquisitions or any other activity where elements of control creep in as a real world consideration. Public stock market prices are frequently far too low or far too high in merger and acquisition contexts. Too low prices and too high prices are the royal road to ascribing exceptional values. The differences between evaluation approaches typically used by outside, passive stockholders and by control persons are described fully in *The Aggressive Conservative Investor*, by Martin J. Whitman and Martin Shubik, published in 1979 by Random House.

A too low or too high price, existing *in vacuo*, does not, of itself, create exceptional value for activists. Rather, the activist has to do something specific to obtain the benefits from the presence of a price disequilibrium—merge, acquire, recapitalize, reorganize, refinance, create tax shelter, go public, go private—i.e., engage in what I call asset conversion activity. The purpose of this Chapter is to examine concepts which should result in ascribing exceptional value because of the use of one, or more, asset conversion techniques.

In general, there are two types of factors which ascribe exceptional value-operational factors and finance factors. Of course, operational and financial factors are frequently related; in most transactions, the parties will look for both operational and financial benefits. However, for purposes of exposition, this chapter will examine the factors separately. Operational factors will be given short shrift, not because they may not be more important than financial factors over-all (they probably are), but because there appear to be few, if any, general rules concerning operational factors and such factors tend to be peculiar to particular businesses at specific times.

Operational factors which ascribe exceptional value are those that bring special benefits to acquirors including synergisms arising out of the ability to integrate businesses horizontally, vertically and circularly. Operational factors probably are the principal motivating factors behind most mergers and acquisitions. These activities (out of thousands) include Getty acquiring Reserve Oil and Gas to obtain control over petroleum reserves in the U.S. and Canada: Procter and Gamble acquiring Charmin Paper Mills as a means of gaining entry into the mass merchandising of certain consumer packaged goods; Brown-Forman Distillers acquiring the Canadian Mist trade name and inventories in order to expand its product base; Arvin Industries acquiring Calspan Corporation in order to obtain research and development capability; and American Motors and Renault making various arrangements so that, *inter alia*, American Motors dealers would be able to market small front wheel drive automobiles while Renault would obtain access to U.S. manufacuring and distribution facilities.

Strictly financial factors are those where little or nothing is changed in the operations of a business because of an asset conversion activity and where the objectives of the asset conversion are to create cheap equity for a control buyer, provide attractive finance for a company, provide a cash bailout for the seller or provide some combination of these three objectives. Examples of such financial activities which resulted in the creation of exceptional values include (out of thousands): Data 100 going public; the original venture capital financing of Federal Express and McDonald's; the leveraged buyouts of Big Bear Stores and Walls Industries; the hostile takeover by cash tender offer followed by mop-up merger of Veeder Root by Western Pacific Industies; and the going private of Kirby Lumber.

The remainder of this chapter consists of a general discussion of finance factors which ascribe exceptional value. These financial factors are of four types which tend to be related but which are discussed separately here:

1. Ability to Finance;
   a) Senior Funds
   b) Equity Funds
2. Tax Shelter;
3. Do-Ability of Deals;
4. Control Benefits or SOTT, i.e., Something Off The Top.

THE ABILITY TO FINANCE

The ability to finance—i.e., borrow or issue equity securities—is unquestionably the one non-operating factor that is crucial to creating exceptional value. And, the one crucial element that creates an ability to finance is *Credibility* with lenders and/or securities holders.

Creating credibility, especially with institutional lenders, usually involves objective substance about the business as well as lenders gaining trust and confidence in the people who are to be the borrowers or are to manage the company that will be the borrower.

In terms of objective substance, creditors will look to the financial strength of a business as measured by an absence of encumbrances, as well as a high quality asset base which could be security for borrowings. The creditor normally will also look for a stream of income out of which there can be reasonable expectations of sufficient cash flow to service debt.

In ascribing exceptional value for mergers and acquisitions, there is no primacy of earnings concept. In contrast, primacy of earnings is the dominant concept in security analysis for passive investors as is detailed in books such as *Security Analysis: Principles and Techniques* by Graham, Dodd & Cottle (McGraw-Hill

1962) and also in finance theory and accounting theory. Where asset conversion is involved, strong balance sheets and good earnings records are equally important in obtaining credibility with institutional lenders.

However, a strong balance sheet tends to be the key element which opens the door to obtaining exceptional value in the form of cheap stock or even virtually free stock. A strong balance sheet that can be used as a basis for borrowing allows one to "bootstrap." Bootstrapping creates values for all sorts of promoters whether in the context of going public or going private, including variations of going private such as leveraged buyouts and ESOT buyouts. The following is a simplified example of how promoters emphasizing financial position, i.e., a strong balance sheet, are able to create exceptional value for themselves by, in effect, taking advantage of the outside, passive investors' tendency to place undue emphasis on earnings and price earnings ratios, i.e., to the believers in a primacy of earnings concept.

Suppose that most publicly owned companies in the widget industry are selling at around 10 times earnings. Joe Promoter has his eye on Eastern Widget, a privately owned company that earns $2 million before taxes and $1 million after taxes. The company has a net worth of $5 million, no debt of any sort and a ratio of current assets to current liabilities of 3 to 1. Thus, it can be used as a source of other people's money. The owners of Eastern want to sell because they are getting older; to their way of thinking, they would be willing to sell their company for $8 million cash, equal to 8 times earnings and a 60 percent premium over book value. Joe Promoter has reason to believe the public will pay 8 times earnings for Eastern Widget, because it is a good company in an industry where the common stocks of other companies are selling at somewhat higher price-earnings ratios.

Joe wants to buy Eastern Widget for $8 million cash (using other people's money), turn the company into a public company and end up owning at least 30 percent of the common stock. If this public-company stock were to sell at around 8 times earnings, the market value of Joe's interest would be about $2 million - although he has invested virtually nothing other than his promotional efforts.

How does Joe accomplish this? He incorporates a new company, Midlantic Widgets. Midlantic is to be used to acquire Eastern. Midlantic initially has 250,000 common shares outstanding, all owned by Joe. Based on Eastern's strong balance sheet and record of profitability, as well as on Joe's plans to create a public company, Midlan-

FACTORS THAT ASCRIBE EXCEPTIONAL VALUE

tic raises $8 million (none of which is invested by Joe); it borrows $6 million from banks and insurance companies by selling 8 percent notes at par; and it sells to private individuals and venture capital firms, for $2 million cash, units consisting of debentures and common stock. The sale of these units results in Midlantic's issuing $2 million of 5 percent subordinated debentures and 137,500 common shares.

Using these $8 million of funds, Midlantic acquires Eastern. It can now report Eastern's earnings as its own. Midlantic's pro forma net income and earnings per share at this point will look like this:

Eastern's net income before taxes $2,000,000

Less interest on bank and insurance loans-
8% on $6,000,000   480,000
Interest on subordinated debentures -
5% on $2,000,000 $ 100,000
Amortization of purchase goodwill over
40 years   75,000*
Adjusted pretax net income $1,345,000
Less Income taxes at 50% without deduction
of good-will amortization   710,000
Net Income $ 635,000
Earnings per share on 387,500 common
shares $1.64
(of which Joe owns 250,000 and the private placement investors 137,500)

*The amortization of purchase goodwill is required by Accounting Principles Board Opinion 17 over periods not to exceed 40 years; 40 years times $75,000 equals $3 million, the amount over net worth that Joe paid for Eastern Widget.

Midlantic now has a public offering via an underwriting. It markets 375,000 newly issued Midlantic common shares at $8 per share, for proceeds of $3 million. These proceeds are then used to retire at par all of the 5 percent subordinated debentures and to pay down the $6 million of bank debt by $1 million. Midlantic's pro forma net income and earnings per share now look somewhat different:

Eastern's net income before taxes $2,000,000
Less interest on bank and insurance loans -
8% of $5,000,000   400,000
Amortization of purchase goodwill
over 40 years   75,000
Adjusted pretax net income $1,525,000
Less income taxes at 50% without
deduction of goodwill
amortization $ 800,000
Net income $ 725,000
Earnings per share on 762,500
shares $0.95

(375,000 shares owned by the public, which paid $8 per share: 250,000 shares owned by Joe Promoter, who now has no cash investment in Midlantic; and 137,500 shares owned by the private placement group, which now has no cash investment in Midlantic either)

Joe Promoter bought a company at 8 times earnings and then put other people's money into it. He turned around and sold an interest in the same enterprise (but a different company) to the public at about 8 times earnings. For his efforts, Joe ended up in control of a public company, with a 32.8 percent interest in its common stock, which has a market value of $2 million and for which he made virtually no cash payment.[1]

The same principles Joe Promoter used to create exceptional value for himself in a going public concept is also usable in other asset conversion contexts including reorganizations, recapitalizations and going privates, including leveraged buyouts.

There are various sources of senior finance if you have credibility, some of which entail lenders providing funds strictly on a senior basis and others of which entail the issuance of mezzanine securities to lenders who seek equity kickers from promoters in addition to their creditor, or preferred stock, positions. Some of these lender/investors always insist on senior positions, e.g., commercial banks, while others, e.g., venture capitalists or merchant bankers, not only take subordinate positions, but, also, lend credibility to a project so that additional financial support from senior lenders becomes available over and above the funds provided by, say, a merchant banker. The typical institutional providers of funds out of which exceptional values for corporate purposes can be created by promoters are commercial banks, life insurance companies, pension and related trusts, venture capitalists and merchant bankers, finance companies, and specialized investors such as small business investment companies and minority enterprise small business investment companies. Sometimes the creation of exceptional values is greatly facilitated because borrowings can be obtained which carry special benefits for lenders such as governmental guarantees and full or partial tax exemptions.

One of the most attractive methods for a corporation to obtain funds is by selling publicly new issues of common stocks and other equity-based securities such as convertible, subordinated debentures, convertible preferred stocks or warrants at prices far above any reasonable measure of the value of the business which

[1]Reprinted from the *Aggressive Conservative Investor*, pp. 145-147.

issued the security. Such overvaluations occur frequently for publicly traded equities. These overvaluations are the basis for creating exceptional value through either issuing such equity securities for cash or in merger and acquisition transactions.

Conventional financial theory notwithstanding, there is no reason why the stock market price for a common stock ought to have any necessary relationship to the control value of a business. Frequently, stock market prices will be far above the control value of a business and then exceptional value is created by issuing or selling stock. Such stock sales were the stuff out of which the new issue boom and conglomerate growths of the late 1960's were created. More recently, the ability to issue equity publicly on highly attractive bases has existed for start-up Atlantic City gambling casinos and many real estate tax shelter and oil and gas syndications, among others.

There are times when exceptional values are created because stock market prices are very low relative to business values. When this occurs, cheap stock is created by acquiring equity from the public in recapitalization exchange offers and going private transactions including leveraged buyouts. It is probable that the existence of ultra-low prices for common stocks arises more out of past prosperity for businesses whose growth is not reflected in changing stock market prices than it does out of bear markets in which stock prices become depressed.

TAX SHELTER

Income taxation is a complex field where tax shelters are created, *inter alia*, out of an ability of ongoing businesses to use tax loss carryforwards, or because participants in asset conversion transactions can obtain tax benefits out of tax-free exchanges, taxable exchanges which give rise to losses, installment transactions, contingent payout transactions, liquidations, spin-offs and blanket tax exemptions. The key to having exceptional value ascribed to tax benefits is to structure transactions so that the combined tax bills of the various participants in transactions—securities owners, acquiring companies and acquired companies—are minimized.

Minimization of tax bills in order to create exceptional values has three elements:

1. The tax bills should be at the lowest possible rates. No tax is preferable to capital gains tax which is usually preferable to tax on earned income which is usually preferable to tax on individuals at ordinary rates. Whether taxes should be paid by corporations or individual taxpayers depends on the very specific circumstances existing in each transaction.

2. Taxpayers are advantaged insofar as they can control the timing as to when a tax might become payable such as on the exercise of options and, correspondingly, taxpayers tend to be highly disadvantaged when they lose control of timing as to when a tax becomes payable such as upon constructive receipt of a dividend.

3. Probably the worst fate that can befall a taxpayer is to be involved in a profitable taxable event, e.g., a property sale, where the taxable event does not also give the taxpayer the cash with which to pay his tax, e.g., the consideration for the property sale was solely non-marketable, non-bankable debentures. In other words, cash, or the early promise of cash, is a *sine qua non* if exceptional value is to be created out of a profitable, but taxable, transaction.

DO-ABILITY OF DEALS

When one examines merger and acquisition or other asset conversion transactions, one always is examining within the context of obtaining control of a business or at least having elements of control. Generally, no matter how attractively priced a security may be for an outside, passive investor, that security will not ascribe exceptional value in the context of this chapter unless full or partial control is available, i.e., the deal has to be *do-able*. Baker Fentress, Kemper Corp. and Stanadyne Inc. are but a few of the many companies which are well-run, well-financed and which are selling at a substantial discount from the most conservative possible measures of their net asset values. Such securities probably ascribe exceptional values for passive, minority investors; they probably do not ascribe exceptional value in the context of this chapter, because control probably is not available; put simply, Baker Fentress, Kemper Corp. and Stanadyne probably are not do-able deals.

Deals become do-able in the context either of hostile takeovers or negotiated transactions conducted on a friendly or neutral basis. The vast majority of do-able deals become do-able because of non-hostile negotiations between parties who have something to gain by entering into transactions with each other.

In looking for exceptional values, it is much easier to uncover attractive situations than it is to uncover do-able deals. In a financial, non-operating context, attractive situations usually have four characteristics:

1. The business is well-financed, as measured by an absence of encumbrances whether on balance sheet, off balance sheet (such as pension plan liabilities), or not at all undisclosed (such as a need for massive capital expenditures).

2. The business is well-managed at least in the custodian sense, or in any event, the business has either been honestly managed—or new management can readily be obtained perhaps as an outgrowth of, say, a reorganization under Chapter 11 of the Bankruptcy Reform Act of 1978.
3. The business is understandable to the acquiror.
4. The price to be paid for the assets or securities to be acquired represents a substantial discount from any conservative valuation of net asset value.

CONTROL BENEFITS, OR SOTT

The factor that distinguishes control persons from outside, passive investors is that through security ownership, control persons, *a fortiori,* obtain certain benefits and assume certain responsibilities that the outside, passive investor does not. Frequently, these control benefits may be so large, relative to the control responsibilities assumed that they, of themselves, ascribe exceptional value.

These exceptional values encompass both economic and non-economic considerations. Economic considerations can run the gamut from salaries and perquisites to opportunities for nepotism and personal tax shelter. Non-economic considerations can include intangibles such as prestige and power.

A FINAL NOTE

In ascribing exceptional value for the benefit of control persons in asset conversion transactions involving public companies, there should be no conclusion that public stockholders suffer just because control persons benefit. Most often, this is just not so. Even where control persons benefit from asset conversions, so do public stockholders who, in going private and leveraged buyouts, may be offered substantial premiums over existing and historic market prices and who, in new public issues, frequently are offered opportunities to buy hot new issues which will sell at premium prices. Sometimes, public stockholders are treated unfairly when exceptional values are created for control persons. More frequently, the exceptional values for control persons are created because public stockholders are interested in, and apply, different analytic standards than do activists. Here, it is not that public stockholders are being cheated; it is that, by emphasizing such public stockholder concerns as earnings per share, industry identification, and near term stock market performance, to the exclusion of, say, financial position, the public stockholders are marching to the beat of a different drummer than is the activist trying to create exceptional values for himself.

ALFRED RAPPAPORT

Leonard Spacek Professor of Accounting and Information Systems
and Director of the Accounting Research Center
Graduate School of Management
Northwestern University

PROFESSOR RAPPAPORT, a member of the Northwestern faculty since 1967, received his undergraduate degree at Western Reserve University and M.S. and Ph.D. degrees at the University of Illinois. He is also a C.P.A. Before coming to Northwestern he taught at the University of Illinois and Tulane University and was employed by Price Waterhouse & Co. In 1979, he was appointed the Leonard Spacek Professor of Accounting and Information Systems and Director of the Accounting Research Center.

He is consulting editor for Prentice-Hall's series, "Contemporary Topics in Accounting"; was a member of the editorial board of *The Accounting Review;* served as director of the Center for Advanced Studies in Accounting and Information Systems at Northwestern from 1971 to 1975, was 1976-77 vice-president of the American Accounting Association; and was Coopers & Lybrand Research Fellow at Northwestern in 1977-78. Early in 1979 he was named to the Financial Accounting Standards Board Task Force on Funds Flow and Liquidity.

The author of books and many articles on a broad range of accounting, finance, and managerial topics, Rappaport is best known for his writings on the relationship between corporate financial reporting and management decision-making. He is a consultant to several corporations on strategic financial planning and merger-acquisition analysis. During the past few years he has been co-director of nationally-known seminars on mergers and acquisitions.

12

Strategic Analysis for More Profitable Acquisitions*

A seller's market demands more careful evaluation than ever before

ALFRED RAPPAPORT

Less than a decade after the frantic merger activity of the late 1960s, we are again in the midst of a major wave of corporate acquisitions. In contrast to the 1960s, when acquirors were mainly freewheeling conglomerates, the merger movement in the 1970s includes such long-established giants of U.S. industry as General Electric, Gulf Oil and Kennecott Copper. Because of the decline in the value of the dollar and the greater political stability of the United States, foreign companies also have come increasingly active buyers of U.S. companies during the past few years.

Most acquisitions are accomplished with cash today, rather than with packages of securities as was common in the 1960s. Finally, the current merger movement involves the frequent use of tender offers that often lead to contested bids and to the payment of substantial premiums above the premerger market value of the target company. In 1978 and 1979, cash tender offer premiums averaged more than 70 percent above premerger market values.

The popular explanation for the recent merger rage is that the market is "undervaluing" many solid companies, thus making it substantially cheaper to buy rather than to build. Couple this belief with the fact that many corporations are enjoying relatively strong cash positions and the widely held view that government regulation and increased uncertainty about the

economy make internal growth strategies relatively unattractive, and we see why mergers and acquisitions have become an increasingly important part of corporate growth strategy.

Despite all of the foregoing rationale, more than a few of the recent acquisitions will fail to create value for the acquiror's shareholders. After all, shareholder value depends not on premerger market valuation of the target company but on the actual acquisition price the acquiring company pays compared with the selling company's cash flow contribution to the combined company.

Only a limited supply of acquisition candidates is available at the price that enables the acquiror to earn an acceptable return on investment. A well-conceived financial evaluation program that minimizes the risk of buying an economically unattractive company or paying too much for an attractive one is particularly important in today's seller's market. The dramatic increase in premiums that must be paid by a company bidding successfully calls for more careful analysis by buyers than ever before.

Because of the competitive nature of the acquisition market, companies not only need to respond wisely but often must respond quickly as well. The growing independence of corporate boards and their demand for better information to support strategic decisions such

*Reprinted by permission of *Harvard Business Review*. "Strategic Analysis for More Profitable Acquisition" by Alfred Rappaport (July-August 1979). Copyright © 1979 by the President and Fellows of Harvard College; all rights reserved.

as acquisitions have raised the general standard for acquisition analysis. Finally, sound analysis convincingly communicated can yield substantial benefits in negotiating with the target company's management or, in the case of tender offers, its stockholders.

Malcolm S. Salter and Wolf A. Weinhold outlined seven principal ways in which companies can create value for their shareholders via acquisition.[1] In this article, I will show how management can estimate how much value a prospective acquisition will in fact create. In brief, I will present a comprehensive framework for acquisition analysis based on contemporary financial theory—an approach that has been profitably employed in practice. The analysis provides management and the board of the acquiring company with information both to make a decision on the candidate and to formulate an effective negotiating strategy for the acquisition.

STEPS IN THE ANALYSIS

The process of analyzing acquisitions falls broadly into three stages: planning, search and screen, and financial evaluation.

The acquisition planning process begins with a review of corporate objectives and product-market strategies for various strategic business units. The acquiring company should define its potential directions for corporate growth and diversification in terms of corporate strengths and weaknesses and an assessment of the company's social, economic, political, and technological environment. This analysis produces a set of acquisition objectives and criteria.

Specified criteria often include statements about industry parameters, such as projected market growth rate, degree of regulation, ease of entry, and capital versus labor intensity. Company critieria for quality of management, share of market, profitability, size and capital structure also commonly appear in acquisition critieria lists.

The search and screen process is a systematic approach to compiling a list of good acquisition prospects. The search focuses on how and where to look for candidates, and the screening process selects a few of the best candidates from literally thousands of possibilities according to objectives and criteria developed in the planning phase.

Finally comes the financial evaluation process, which is the focus of this article. A good analysis should enable management to answer such questions as:

— What is the maximum price that should be paid for the target company?

— What are the principal areas of risk?

— What are the earnings, cash flow, and balance sheet implications of the acquisition?

— What is the best way of financing the acquisition?

Corporate Self-Evaluation

The financial evaluation process involves both a self-evaluation by the acquiring company and the evaluation of the candidate for acquisition. While it is possible to conduct an evaluation of the target company without an in-depth self-evaluation first, in general this is the most advantageous approach.[2] The scope and detail of corporate self-evaluation will necessarily vary according to the needs of each company.

Two fundamental questions posed by a self-evaluation are: (1) How much is my company worth? (2) How would its value be affected by each of several scenarios? The first question involves generating a "most likely" estimate of the company's value based on management's detailed assessment of its objectives, strategies, and plans. The second question calls for an assessment of value based on the range of plausible scenarios that enable management to test the joint effect of hypothesized combinations of product-market strategies and environmental forces.

Corporate self-evaluation viewed as an economic assessment of the value created for shareholders by various strategic planning options promises potential benefits for all companies. In the context of the acquisition market, self-evaluation takes on special significance.

First, while a company might view itself as an acquiror, few companies are totally exempt from a possible takeover. During 1979 alone, 83 acquisitions exceeding $100 million were announced. The recent roster of acquired companies includes such names as Anaconda, Utah International, Babcock & Wilcox, Seven Up, Pet, Carborundum, and Del Monte. Self-evaluation provides management and the board with a continuing basis for responding to tender offers or acquisition inquiries responsibly and quickly. Second, the self-evaluation process might well call attention to strategic divestment opportunities. Finally, self-

---

[1]Malcolm S. Salter and Wolf A. Weinhold, "Diversification via Acquisition: Creating Value," HBR July-August 1978, p. 166.
[2]For a more detailed description on how to conduct a corporate self-evaluation, see my article, "Do You Know the Value of Your Company?" *Mergers and Acquisitions,* Spring 1979.

evaluation provides acquisition-minded companies a basis for assessing the comparative advantages of a cash versus an exchange-of-shares offer.

Acquiring companies commonly value the purchase price for an acquisition at the market value of the shares exchanged. This practice is not economically sound and could be misleading and costly to the acquiring company. A well-conceived analysis for an exchange-of-shares acquisition requires sound valuations of both buying and selling companies. If the acquiror's management believes the market is undervaluing its shares, then valuing the purchase price at market might well induce the company to overpay for the acquisition or to earn less than the minimum acceptable rate of return.

Conversely, if management believes the market is overvaluing its shares, then valuing the purchase price at market obscures the opportunity of offering the seller's shareholders additional shares while still achieving the minimum acceptable return.

Valuation of Acquisitions

Recently *Business Week* reported that as many as half of the major acquisition-minded companies are relying extensively on the discounted cash flow (DCF) technique to analyze acquisitions.[3] While mergers and acquisitions involve a considerably more complex set of managerial problems than the purchase of an ordinary asset such as a machine or a plant, the economic substance of these transactions is the same. In each case, there is a current outlay made in anticipation of a stream of future cash flows.

Thus the DCF criterion applies not only to internal growth investments, such as additions to existing capacity, but equally to external growth investments, such as acquisitions. An essential feature of the DCF technique is that it explicitly takes into account that a dollar of cash received today is worth more than a dollar received a year from now, because today's dollar can be invested to earn a return during the intervening time.

To establish the maximum acceptable acquisition price under the DCF approach, estimates are needed for (1) the incremental cash flows expected to be generated because of the acquisition and (2) the cost of capital—that is, the minimum acceptable rate of return required by the market for new investments by the company.

In projecting the cash flow stream of a prospective acquisition, what should be taken into account is the cash flow contribution the candidate is expected to make to the acquiring company. The results of this projection may well differ from a projection of the candidate's cash flow as an independent company. This is so because the acquiror may be able to achieve operating economics not available to the selling company alone. Furthermore acquisitions generally provide new post-acquisition investment opportunities whose initial outlays and subsequent benefits also need to be incorporated in the cash flow schedule. Cash flow is defined as:

(earnings before interest and taxes [EBIT]) × (1-income tax rate) + depreciation and other noncash charges − capital expenditures − cash required for increase in net working capital

In developing the cash flow schedule, two additional issues need to be considered: (1) What is the basis for setting the horizon date—that is, the date beyond which the cash flows associated with the acquisition are not specifically projected? (2) How is the residual value of the acquisition established at the horizon date?

A common practice is to forecast cash flows period by period until the level of uncertainty makes management too "uncomfortable" to go any farther. While practice varies with industry setting, management policy, and the special circumstances of the acquisition, five or ten years appears to be an arbitrarily set forecasting duration used in many situations. A better approach suggests that the forecast duration for cash flows should continue only as long as the expected rate of return on incremental investment required to support forecasted sales growth exceeds the cost-of-capital rate.

If for subsequent periods one assumes that the company's return on incremental investment equals the cost-of-capital rate, then the market would be indifferent whether management invests earnings in expansion projects or pays cash dividends that shareholders can in turn invest in identically risky opportunities yielding an identical rate of return. In other words, the value of the company is unaffected by growth when the company is investing in projects earning at the cost of

---

[3] "The Cash-Flow Takeover Formula," *Business Week,* December 18, 1978, p. 86.

capital or at the minimum acceptable risk-adjusted rate of return required by the market.

Thus, for purposes of simplification, we can assume a 100 percent payout of earnings after the horizon date or, equivalently, a zero growth rate without affecting the valuation of the company. (An implied assumption of this model is that the depreciation tax shield can be invested to maintain the company's productive capacity.) The residual value is then the present value of the resulting cash flow perpetuity beginning one year after the horizon date. Of course, if after the horizon date the return on investment is expected to decline below the cost-of-capital rate, this factor can be incorporated in the calculation.

When the acquisition candidate's risk is judged to be the same as the acquiror's overall risk, the appropriate rate for discounting the candidate's cash flow stream is the acquiror's cost of capital. The cost of capital or the minimum acceptable rate of return on new investments is based on the rate investors can expect to earn by investing in alternative, identically risky securities.

The cost of capital is calculated as the weighted average of the costs of debt and equity capital. For example, suppose a company's aftertax cost of debt is 5 percent and it estimates its cost of equity to be 15 percent. Further, it plans to raise future capital in the following proportions—20 percent by way of debt and 80 percent by equity. *Exhibit 1* shows how to compute the company's average cost.

EXHIBIT I
One company's average cost of capital

	Weight	Cost	Weighted cost
Debt	.20	.05	.01
Equity	.80	.15	.12
Average cost of capital			.13

It is important to emphasize that the acquiring company's use of its own cost of capital to discount the target's projected cash flows is appropriate only when it can be safely assumed that the acquisition will not affect the riskiness of the acquiror. The specific riskiness of each prospective candidate should be taken into account in setting the discount rate, with higher rates used for more risky investments.

If a single discount rate is used for all acquisitions, then those with the highest risk will seem most attractive. Because the weighted average risk of its component segments determines the company's cost of capital, these high-risk acquisitions will increase a company's cost of capital and thereby decrease the value of its stock.

CASE OF ALCAR CORPORATION

As an illustration of the recommended approach to acquisition analysis, consider the case of Alcar Corporation's interest in acquiring Rano Products. Alcar is a leading manufacturer and distributor in the industrial packaging and materials handling market. Sales in 1979 totaled $600 million. Alcar's acquisition strategy is geared toward buying companies with either similar marketing and distribution characteristics, similar production technologies, or a similar research and development orientation. Rano Products, a $50 million sales organization with an impressive new-product development record in industrial packaging, fits Alcar's general acquisition criteria particularly well. Premerger financial statements for Alcar and Rano are shown in *Exhibit II*.

EXHIBIT II
Premerger financial statements for Alcar and Rano (in millions of dollars)

Statement of income (year ended December 31)

	Alcar	Rano
Sales	$600.00	$50.00
Operating expenses	522.00	42.50
EBIT	78.00	7.50
Interest on debt	4.50	.40
Earnings before taxes	73.50	7.10
Income taxes	36.00	3.55
Net income	$37.50	$3.55
Number of common shares outstanding (in millions)	10.00	1.11
Earnings per share	$3.75	$3.20
Dividends per share	1.30	.64

Statement of financial position (at year-end)

	Alcar	Rano
Net working capital	$180.00	$7.50
Temporary investments	25.00	1.00
Other assets	2.00	1.60
Fixed assets	216.00	20.00
Less accumulated depreciation	(95.00)	(8.00)
	$328.00	$22.10
Interest-bearing debt	$56.00	$5.10
Shareholders' equity	272.00	17.00
	$328.00	$22.10

Acquisition for Cash

Acquimerge, the interactive time-sharing computer model for corporate planning and acquisition analysis used in the Alcar evaluation to follow generates a comprehensive analysis for acquisitions financed by cash, stock, or any combination of cash, debt, preferred stock, and common stock. In this article, the analysis will concern only the cash and exchange-of-shares cases. In the cash acquisition case, the analysis follows six essential steps:

— Develop estimates needed to project Rano's cash flow contribution for various growth and profitability scenarios.

— Estimate the minimum acceptable rate of return for acquisition of Rano.

— Compute the maximum acceptable cash price to be paid for Rano under various scenarios and minimum acceptable rates of return.

— Compute the rate of return that Alcar will earn for a range of price offers and for various growth and profitability scenarios.

— Analyze the feasibility of a cash purchase in light of Alcar's current liquidity and target debt-to-equity ratio.

— Evaluate the i pact of the acquisition on the earnings per share and capital structure of Alcar.

Step 1—cash flow projections: The cash flow formula presented earlier may be restated in equivalent form as—

$$CF_t = S_{t-1} (1+g_t) (p_t) (1-T_t) - (S_t-S_{t-1}) (f_t+w_t)$$

where

CF = cash flow,

S = sales,

g = annual growth rate in sales,

p = EBIT as a percentage of sales,

T = income tax rate,

f = capital investment required (i.e., total capital investment net of replacement of existing capacity estimated by depreciation) per dollar of sales increase,

w = cash required for net working capital per dollar of sales increase.

EXHIBIT III
Most likely estimates for Rano's operations under Alcar control

	Years		
	1-5	6-7	8-10
Sales growth rate (g)	.15	.12	.12
EBIT as a percentage of sales (p)	.18	.15	.12
Income tax rate (T)	.46	.46	.46
Capital investment per dollar of sales increase (f)	.20	.20	.20
Working capital per dollar of sales increase (w)	.15	.15	.15

Employing the cash flow formula for year 1:

$$CF_1 = 50(1+.15)(.18)(1-.46) - (57.5-50)(.20+.15) = 2.96$$

EXHIBIT IV
Projected ten-year cash flow statement for Rano (in millions of dollars)

	Years									
	1	2	3	4	5	6	7	8	9	10
Sales	$57.50	$66.12	$76.04	$87.45	$100.57	$112.64	$126.15	$141.29	$158.25	$177.23
Operating expenses	47.15	54.22	62.36	71.71	82.47	95.74	107.23	124.34	139.26	155.97
EBIT	$10.35	$11.90	$13.69	$15.74	$18.10	$16.90	$18.92	$16.95	$18.99	$21.27
Income taxes on EBIT	4.76	5.48	6.30	7.24	8.33	7.77	8.70	7.80	8.74	9.78
Operating earnings after taxes	$5.59	$6.43	$7.39	$8.50	$9.78	$9.12	$10.22	$9.16	$10.25	$11.48
Depreciation	1.60	1.85	2.13	2.46	2.84	3.28	3.74	4.25	4.83	5.49
Less capital expenditures	(3.10)	(3.57)	(4.12)	(4.74)	(5.47)	(5.69)	(6.44)	(7.28)	(8.22)	(9.29)
Less increase in working capital	(1.13)	(1.29)	(1.49)	(1.71)	(1.97)	(1.81)	(2.03)	(2.27)	(2.54)	(2.85)
Cash flow	$2.96	$3.41	$3.92	$4.51	$5.18	$4.90	$5.49	$3.86	$4.32	$4.84

Once estimates are provided for five variables g, p, T, f, and w, it is possible to project cash flow:

Exhibit III shows Alcar management's "most likely" estimates for Rano's operations, assuming Alcar control; *Exhibit IV* shows a complete projected ten-year cash flow statement for Rano.

Before developing additional scenarios for Rano, I should make some brief comments on how to estimate some of the cash flow variables. The income tax rate is the effective cash rate rather than a rate based on the accountant's income tax expense, which often includes a portion that is deferred. For some companies, a direct projection of capital investment requirements per dollar of sales increase will prove a difficult task.

To gain an estimate of the recent value of this coefficient, simply take the sum of all capital investments less depreciation over the past five or ten years and divide this total by the sales increase from the beginning to the end of the period. With this approach, the resulting coefficient not only represents the capital investment historically required per dollar of sales increase but also impounds any cost increases for replacement of existing capacity.

One should estimate changes in net working capital requirements with care. Actual year-to-year balance sheet changes in net working capital may not provide a good measure of the rise or decline in funds required. There are two main reasons for this:

(1) the year-end balance sheet figures may not reflect the average or normal needs of the business during the year, and (2) the inventory accounts may overstate the magnitude of the funds committed by the company.

To estimate the additional cash requirements, the increased inventory investment should be measured by the variable costs for any additional units of inventory required rather than the absolute dollar amount of increase in the inventory account.[4]

In addition to its most likely estimate for Rano, Alcar's management developed two additional (conservative and optimistic) scenarios for sales growth and EBIT-sales ratio. *Exhibit V* gives a summary of all three scenarios. Alcar's management may also wish to examine additional cases to test the effect of alternative assumptions about the income tax rate and capital investment and working capital requirements per dollar of sales increase.

Recall that cash flows should be forecast only for the period when the expected rate of return on incremental investment exceeds the minimum acceptable rate of return for the acquisition. It is possible to determine this in a simple yet analytical, nonarbitrary, fashion. To do so, we compute the minimum pretax return on incremental sales (P min) needed to earn the minimum acceptable rate of return on the acquisition (k) given the investment requirements for working capital (w) and fixed assets (f) for each additional dollar of sales and given a projected tax rate (T). The formula for P min is:

$$P_{min} = \frac{(f+w)\,k}{(I-T)\,(I+k)}$$

Alcar's management believes that when Rano's growth begins to slow down, its working capital requirements per dollar of additional sales will increase from .15 to about .20 and its effective tax rate will increase from .46 to .50. As will be shown in the next section, the minimum acceptable rate of return on the Rano acquisition is 13 percent. Thus:

$$P_{min} = \frac{(.20+.20)\,(.13)}{(I-.50)\,(I+.13)}$$
$$= .092.$$

Alcar's management has enough confidence to forecast pretax sales returns above 9.2% for only the next ten years, and thus the forecast duration for the Rano acquisition is limited to that period.

Step 2—estimate minimum acceptable rate of return for acquisition: In developing a company's average cost of capital, measuring the aftertax cost of debt is relatively straightforward. The cost of equity capital, however, is more difficult to estimate.

Rational, risk-averse investors expect to earn a rate of return that will compensate them for accepting greater investment risk. Thus, in assessing the company's cost of equity capital or the minimum expected return that will induce investors to buy the company's shares, it is reasonable to assume that they will demand the risk-free rate as reflected in the current yields available in government bonds, plus a premium for accepting equity risk.

Recently, the risk-free rate on government bonds has been in the neighborhood of 8.8 percent. By investing in a portfolio broadly representative of the overall equity market, it is possible to diversify away substantially all of the unsystematic risk—that is, risk specific to individual companies. Therefore, securities are

---

EXHIBIT V
Additional scenarios for sales growth and EBIT/sales

	Sales growth Years			EBIT/sales Years		
Scenario	1-5	6-7	8-10	1-5	6-7	8-10
1. Conservative	.14	.12	.10	.17	.14	.11
2. Most likely	.15	.12	.12	.18	.15	.12
3. Optimistic	.18	.15	.12	.20	.16	.12

---

[4]For an illustration of this calculation, see my article, "Measuring Company Growth Capacity During Inflation," HBR January-February 1979, p. 91.

likely to be priced at levels that reward investors only for the nondiversifiable market risk—that is, the systematic risk in movements in the overall market.

The risk premium for the overall market is the excess of the expected return on a representative market index such as the Standard & Poor's 500 stock index over the risk-free return. Empirical studies have estimated this market risk premium (representative market index minus risk-free rate) to average historically about 5 percent to 5.5 percent.[5] I will use a 5.2 percent premium in subsequent calculations.

Investing in an individual security generally involves more or less risk than investing in a broad market portfolio, thus one must adjust the market risk premium appropriately in estimating the cost of equity for an individual security. The risk premium for a security is the product of the market risk premium times the individual security's systematic risk, as measured by its beta coefficient.

The rate of return from dividends and capital appreciation on a market portfolio will, by definition, fluctuate identically with the market, and therefore its beta is equal to 1.0. A beta for an individual security is an index of its risk expressed as its volatility of return in relation to that of a market portfolio.[6] Securities with betas greater than 1.0, are more volatile than the market and thus would be expected to have a risk premium greater than the overall market risk premium or the average-risk stock with a beta of 1.0.

For example, if a stock moves 1.5 percent when the market moves 1 percent, the stock would have a beta of 1.5. Security with betas less than 1.0 are less volatile than the market and would thus command risk premiums less than the market risk premium. In summary, the cost of equity capital may be calculated by the following equation:

$$K_e = R_f + B_j (R_m - R_f)$$

where

K_e = cost of equity capital,

R_f = risk-free rate,

B_j = the beta coefficient,

R_m = representative market index.

The acquiring company, Alcar, with the beta of 1.0, estimated its cost of equity as 14 percent with the foregoing equation:

$$K_e = .088 + 1.0(.052)$$
$$= .140$$

Since interest on debt is tax deductible, the rate of return that must be earned on the debt portion of the company's capital structure to maintain the earnings available to common shareholders is the after-tax cost of debt. The after-tax cost of borrowed capital is Alcar's current before-tax interest rate (9.5 percent) times 1 minus its effective tax rate of 46 percent, which is equal to 5.1 percent. Alcar's target debt-to-equity ratio is .30, or equivalently, debt is targeted at 23 percent and equity at 77 percent of its overall capitalization as *Exhibit VI* shows Alcar's weighted average cost of capital. The appropriate rate for discounting Alcar cash flows to establish its estimated value is then 12 percent.

For new capital projects, including acquisitions, that are deemed to have about the same risk as the overall company, Alcar can use its 12 percent cost-of-capital rate as the appropriate discount rate. Because the company's cost of capital is determined by the weighted average risk of its component segments, the specific risk of each prospective acquisition should be estimated in order to arrive at the discount rate to apply to the candidate's cash flows.

EXHIBIT VI
Alcar's weighted average cost of capital

	Weight	Cost	Weighted Cost
Debt	.23	.051	.012
Equity	.77	.140	.108
Average cost of capital			.120

EXHIBIT VII
Risk-adjusted cost of capital for Rano acquisition

	Weight	Cost	Weighted Cost
Debt	.23	.054*	.012
Equity	.77	.153	.118
Average risk-adjusted cost of capital			.130

*Before-tax debt rate of 10% times 1 minus the estimated tax rate of 46%.

[5]For example, see Roger G. Ibbotson and Rex A. Sinquefield, *Stock, Bonds, Bills, and Inflation: The Past (1926-1976) and the Future (1977-2000)* (New York: Financial Analysts Research Foundation, 1977), p. 57. They forecast that returns on common stocks will exceed those on long-term government bonds by 5.4%.

[6]For a discussion of some of the problems in estimating beta as a measure of risk, see Eugene F. Brigham, *Financial Management: Theory and Practice* (Hinsdale, Ill.: The Dryden Press, 1977), p. 666.

EXHIBIT VIII
Maximum acceptable cash price for Rano—most likely scenario, with a discount rate of .130 (in millions of dollars)

Year	Cash flow	Present value	Cumulative Present value
1	$ 2.96	$ 2.62	$ 2.62
2	3.41	2.67	5.29
3	3.92	2.72	8.01
4	4.51	2.76	10.77
5	5.13	2.81	13.59
6	4.90	2.35	15.94
7	5.49	2.33	18.27
8	3.86	1.45	19.72
9	4.32	1.44	21.16
10	4.84	1.43	22.59
Residual value	11.48	26.02*	48.61
Plus temporary investments not required for current operations			1.00
Less debt assumed			5.10
Maximum acceptable cash price			$44.51
Maximum acceptable cash price per share			$40.10

*Year 10 operating earnings after taxes

$$\frac{\text{Year 10 operating earnings after taxes}}{\text{Discount rate}} \times \text{Year 10 discount factor} =$$

$$\frac{11.48}{.13} \times .2946 = 26.02$$

Rano, with a beta coefficient of 1.25, is more risky than Alcar, with a beta of 1.0. Employing the formula for cost of equity capital for Rano:

$$K_e = .088 + 1.25(.052)$$
$$= .153$$

On this basis, the risk-adjusted cost of capital for the Rano acquisition is as shown in *Exhibit VII* (page 183).

Step 3—compute maximum acceptable cash price: This step involves taking the cash flow projections developed in Step 1 and discounting them at the rate developed in Step 2. *Exhibit VIII* shows the computation of the maximum acceptable cash price for the most likely scenario. The maximum price of $44.51 million, or $40.10 per share, for Rano compares with a $25 current market price for Rano shares. Thus, for the most likely case, Alcar can pay up to $15 per share, or a 60 percent premium over current market, and still achieve its minimum acceptable 13 percent return on the acquisition.

Exhibit IX shows the maximum acceptable cash price for each of the three scenarios for a range of discount rates. To earn a 13 percent rate of return, Alcar can pay at maximum $38 million ($34.25 per share), assuming the conservative scenario, and up to $53 million ($47.80 per share), assuming the optimistic scenario. Note that as Alcar demands a greater return on its investment, the maximum price it can pay decreases. The reverse is, of course, true as well. For example, for the most likely scenario, the maximum price decreases from $44.51 million to $39.67 million as the return requirement goes from 13 percent to 14 percent.

Step 4—compute rate of return for various offering prices and scenarios: Alcar management believes that the absolute minimum successful bid for Rano would be $35 million, or $31.50 per share. Alcar's investment bankers estimated that it may take a bid of as high as $45 million, or $40.50 per share, to gain control of Rano shares. *Exhibit X* presents the rates of return that will be earned for four different offering prices, ranging from $35 million to $45 million for each of the three scenarios.

Under the optimistic scenario, Alcar could expect a return of 14.4 percent if it were to pay $45 million. For the most likely case, an offer of $45 million would yield a 12.9 percent return, or just under the minimum acceptable rate of 13 percent. This is as expected, since the maximum acceptable cash price as calculated in *Exhibit VIII* is $44.51 million, or just under the $45 million offer. If Alcar attaches a relatively high probability to the conservative scenario the risk associated with offers exceeding $38 million becomes apparent.

Step 5—analyze feasibility of cash purchase: While Alcar management views the relevant purchase price range for Rano as somewhere between $35 and $45 million, it must also establish whether an all-cash deal is feasible in light of Alcar's current liquidity and target debt-to-equity ratio. The maximum funds available for the purchase of Rano equal the post-merger debt capacity of the combined company less the combined premerger debt of the two companies plus the combined premerger temporary investments of the two companies. (Net working capital not required for everyday operations of the business is classified as "temporary investment.")

In an all-cash transaction governed by purchase accounting, the acquiror's shareholders' equity is unchanged. The post-merger debt capacity is then Alcar's shareholders' equity of $272 million times the targeted debt-to-equity ratio of .30, or $81.6 million. Alcar and

Rano have premerger debt balances of $56 million and $5.1 million, respectively, for a total of 61.1 million.

The unused debt capacity is thus $81.6 million minus $61.1 million, or $20.5 million. Add to this the combined temporary investments of Alcar and Rano of $26 million, and the maximum funds available for the cash purchase of Rano will be $46.5 million. A cash purchase is therefore feasible within the tentative price range of $35 to $45 million.

Step 6—evaluate impact of acquisition on Alcar's EPS and capital structure: Because reported earnings per share (EPS) continue to be of great interest to the financial community, a complete acquisition analysis should include a comparison of projected EPS both with and without the acquisiton. *Exhibit XI* contains this comparative projection. The EPS stream with the acquisition of Rano is systematically greater than the stream without acquisition. The EPS standard, and particularly a short-term EPS standard, is not, how-

ever, a reliable basis for assessing whether the acquisition will in fact create value for shareholders.[7]

Several problems arise when EPS is used as a standard for evaluating acquisitions. First, because of accounting measurement problems, the EPS figure can be determined by alternative, equally acceptable methods—for example, LIFO versus FIFO. Second, the EPS standard ignores the time value of money. Third, it does not take into account the risk of the EPS stream. Risk is conditioned not only by the nature of the investment projects a company undertakes but also by the relative porportions of debt and equity used to finance those investments.

A company can increase EPS by increasing leverage as long as the marginal return on investment is greater than the interest rate on the new debt. However, if the marginal return on investment is less than the risk-adjusted cost of capital or if the increased leverage leads to an increased cost of capital, then the value of the company could decline despite arising EPS.

EXHIBIT IX
Maximum acceptable cash price for three scenarios and a range of discount rates

Scenarios	Discount rates				
	.11	.12	.13	.14	.15
1. Conservative					
Total price ($ millions)	$48.84	$42.91	$38.02	$33.93	$30.47
Per share price	44.00	38.66	34.25	30.57	27.45
2. Most likely					
Total price ($ millions)	57.35	50.31	44.51	39.67	35.58
Per share price	51.67	45.33	40.10	35.74	32.05
3. Optimistic					
Total price ($ millions)	68.37	59.97	53.05	47.28	42.41
Per share price	61.59	54.03	47.80	42.59	38.21

EXHIBIT X
Rate of return for various offering prices and scenarios

	Offering price			
	Total ($ millions)	$35.00	$38.00	$40.00	$45.00
Scenarios	Per share	$31.53	$34.23	$36.04	$40.54
1. Conservative		.137	.130	.126	.116
2. Most likely		.152	.144	.139	.129
3. Optimistic		.169	.161	.156	.144

---

[7]See William W. Alberts and James M. McTaggart, ''The Short-Term Earnings Per Share Standard for Evaluating Prospective Acquisitions,'' *Mergers and Acquisitions,* Winter 1978, p. 4; and Joel M. Stern, ''Earnings Per Share Don't Count,'' *Financial Analysts Journal,* July-August 1974, p. 39.

EXHIBIT XI
Alcar's projected EPS, debt-to-equity ratio, and un-used debt capacity—without and with Rano acquisition

Year	EPS Without	With	Debt/equity Without	With	Unused debt capacity (in millions of dollars) Without	With
0	$ 3.75	$ 4.10	.21	.26	$25.60	$20.50
1	4.53	4.89	.19	.27	34.44	9.42
2	5.09	5.51	.17	.28	44.22	7.00
3	5.71	6.20	.19	.29	40.26	4.20
4	6.38	6.99	.21	.30	35.45	.98
5	7.14	7.87	.24	.31	29.67	−2.71
6	7.62	8.29	.26	.31	22.69	−7.77
7	8.49	9.27	.27	.32	14.49	−13.64
8	9.46	10.14	.29	.33	4.91	−22.34
9	10.55	11.33	.31	.34	−6.23	−32.36
10	11.76	12.66	.32	.35	−19.16	−43.88

Note: Assumed cash purchase price for Rano is $35 million.

Primarily because the acquisition of Rano requires that Alcar partially finance the purchase price with bank borrowing, the debt-to-equity ratios with the acquisition are greater than those without the acquisition (see *Exhibit XI*). Note that even without the Rano acquisition, Alcar is in danger of violating its target debt-to-equity ratio of .30 by the ninth year. The acquisition of Rano accelerates the problem to the fifth year. Whether Alcar purchases Rano or not, management must now be alert to the financing problem, which may force it to issue additional shares or reevaluate its present capital structure policy.

Acquisition for Stock

The first two steps in the acquisition-for-stock analysis, projecting Rano cash flows and setting the discount rate, have already been completed in connection with the acquisition-for-cash analysis developed in the previous section. The remaining steps of the acquisition-for-stock analysis are:

× Estimate the value of Alcar shares.
× Compute the maximum number of shares that Alcar can exchange to acquire Rano under various scenarios and minimum acceptable rates of return.
× Evaluate the impact of the acquisition on the earnings per share and capital structure of Alcar.

Step 1—estimate value of Alcar shares: Alcar conducted a comprehensive corporate self-evaluation that included an assessment of its estimated present value

based on a range of scenarios. In the interest of brevity, I will consider here only its most likely scenario.

Management made most likely projections for its operations, as shown in *Exhibit XII*. Again using the equation for the cost of equity capital, the minimum incremental EBIT as a percentage of incremental sales needed to earn at Alcar's 12 percent cost of capital is 10.9 percent. Since management can confidently forecast pretax return on sales returns above 10.9 percent for only the next ten years, the cash flow projections will be limited to that period.

Exhibit XIII presents the computation of the value of Alcar's equity. Its estimated value of $36.80 per share contrasts with its currently depressed market value of $22 per share. Because Alcar management believes its shares to be substantially undervalued by the market, in the absence of other compelling factors it will be reluctant to acquire Rano by means of an exchange of shares.

To illustrate, suppose that Alcar were to offer $35 million in cash for Rano. Assume the most likely case, that the maximum acceptable cash price is $44.51 million (*see Exhibit VIII*); thus the acquisition would create about $9.5 million in value from Alcar shareholders. Now assume that instead Alcar agrees to exchange $35 million in market value of its shares in order to acquire Rano. In contrast with the cash case, in the exchange-of-shares case Alcar shareholders can expect to be worse off by $12.1 million.

With Alcar shares selling at $22, the company must

exchange 1.59 million shares to meet the $35 million offer for Rano. There are currently 10 million Alcar shares outstanding. After the merger, the combined company will be owned 86.27 percent—i.e., (10.00)/(10.00 + 1.59)—by current Alcar shareholders and 13.73 percent by Rano shareholders. The $12.1

EXHIBIT XII
Most likely estimates for Alcar operations without acquisition

	Years		
	1-5	6-7	8-10
Sales growth rate	.125	.120	.120
EBIT as a percentage of sales	.130	.125	.125
Income tax rate	.460	.460	.460
Capital investment per dollar of sales increase	.250	.250	.250
Working capital per dollar of sales increase	.300	.300	.300

EXHIBIT XIII
Estimated present value of Alcar equity—most likely scenario, with a discount rate of .120 (in millions of dollars)

Year	Cash flow	Present value	Cumulative Present value
1	$ 6.13	$ 5.48	$ 5.48
2	6.90	5.50	10.98
3	7.76	5.53	16.51
4	8.74	5.55	22.06
5	9.83	5.58	27.63
6	10.38	5.26	32.89
7	11.63	5.26	38.15
8	13.02	5.26	43.41
9	14.58	5.26	48.67
10	16.33	5.26	53.93
Residual value	128.62	345.10*	399.03
Plus temporary investments not required for current operations			25.00
Less debt outstanding			56.00
Present value of Alcar equity			$368.03
Present value per share of Alca equity			$ 36.80

*Year 10 operating earnings after taxes

$$\frac{\text{Year 10 operating earnings after taxes}}{\text{Discount rate}} \times \text{Year 10 discount factor} =$$

$$\frac{128.62}{.12} \times .32197 = 345.10$$

million loss by Alcar shareholders can then be calculated as shown in *Exhibit XIV*.

Step 2—compute maximum number of shares Alcar can exchange: The maximum acceptable number of shares to exchange for each of the three scenarios and for a range of discount rates appears in *Exhibit XV*. To earn a 13 percent rate of return, Alcar can exchange no more than 1.033, 1.210, and 1.442 million shares, assuming the conservative, most likely, and optimistic scenarios, respectively. Consider, for a moment, the most likely case. At a market value per share of $22, the 1.21 million Alcar shares exchanged would have a total value of $26.62 million, which is less than Rano's current market value of $27.75 million—that is, 1.11 million shares at $25 per share. Because of the market's apparent undervaluation of Alcar's shares, an exchange ratio likely to be acceptable to Rano will clearly be unattractive to Alcar.

Step 3—evaluate impact of acquisition on Alcar's EPS and capital structure: The $35 million purchase price is just under ten times Rano's most recent year's earnings of $3.55 million. At its current market price per share of $22, Alcar is selling at about six times its most recent earnings. The acquiring company will always suffer immediate EPS dilution whenever the price-earnings ratio paid for the selling company is greater than its own. Alcar would suffer immediate dilution from $3.75 to $3.54 in the current year. A comparison of EPS for cash versus an exchange-of-shares transaction appears as part of *Exhibit XVI*. As expected, the EPS projections for a cash deal are consistently higher than those for an exchange of shares.

However, the acquisition of Rano for shares rather than cash would remove, at least for now, Alcar's projected financing problem. In contrast with a cash acquisition, an exchange of shares enables Alcar to have unused debt capacity at its disposal throughout the ten-year forecast period. Despite the relative attractiveness of this financing flexibility, Alcar management recognized that it could not expect a reasonable rate of return by offering an exchange of shares to Rano.

EXHIBIT XIV
Calculation of loss by Alcar shareholders (in millions of dollars)

Alcar receives 86.27% of Rano's present value of $44.51 million (see *Exhibit VIII*)	$38.4
Alcar gives up 13.73% of its present value of $368.03 million (see *Exhibit XIII*)	(50.5)
Dilution of Alcar shareholders' value	$12.1

EXHIBIT XV
Maximum acceptable shares to exchange for three scenarios and a range of discount rates (in millions)

	Discount rates				
Scenarios	.11	.12	.13	.14	.15
1. Conservative	1.327	1.166	1.033	0.922	0.828
2. Most likely	1.558	1.367	1.210	1.078	0.967
3. Optimistic	1.858	1.630	1.442	1.285	1.152

EXHIBIT XVI
Alcar's projected EPS, dept-to-equity ratio, and unused debt capacity—cash vs. exchange of shares

	EPS		Debt/equity		Unused debt capacity (in millions of dollars)	
Year	Cash	Stock	Cash	Stock	Cash	Stock
0	$ 4.10	$ 3.54	.26	.21	$20.50	$25.60
1	4.89	4.37	.27	.19	9.42	35.46
2	5.51	4.93	.28	.17	7.00	46.62
3	6.20	5.55	.29	.18	4.20	48.04
4	6.99	6.23	.30	.20	0.98	46.37
5	7.87	7.00	.31	21	−2.71	44.29
6	8.29	7.37	.31	.23	−7.77	40.90
7	9.27	8.22	.32	.24	−13.64	36.78
8	10.14	8.98	.33	.26	−22.34	29.90
9	11.33	10.01	.34	.27	−32.36	21.79
10	12.66	11.17	.35	.29	−43.88	12.29

Note: Assumed purchase price for Rano is $35 million.

CONCLUDING NOTE

The experience of companies that have implemented the approach to acquisition analysis described in this article indicates that it is not only an effective way of evaluating a prospective acquisition candidate but also serves as a catalyst for reevaluating a company's overall strategic plans. The results also enable management to justify acquisition recommendations to the board of directors in an economically sound, convincing fashion.

Many companies have used this approach for evaluation of potential candidates as well as for initial screening of potential candidates. In the latter case, initial input estimates are quickly generated to establish whether the range of maximum acceptable prices is greater than the current market price of the target companies. With the aid of the Acquimerge computer model, this can be accomplished quickly and at relatively low cost.

Whether companies are seeking acquisitions or are acquisition targets, it is increasingly clear that they must provide better information to enable top management and boards to make well-conceived, timely decisions. Use of the approach outlined here should improve the prospects of creating value for shareholders by acquisitions.

ACQUISITION METHODS

ONE OF THE KEY QUESTIONS IN ANY CORPORATE MERGER, ACQUISITION OR BUYOUT involves the tax ramifications for the parties concerned. In our approach to this topical area we have divided the material into two broad categories. The first views the acquired company as a continuation in modified form of the original investment of the shareholders and thus defers tax consequences until a final sale is consummated at a future date. The second method is to view the merger or acquisition as a sale resulting in a taxable event to selling shareholders. A shorthand terminology used by practitioners in the field is to call the former ''tax-free'' and the latter ''taxable'' transactions.

Neil A. Wassner details the tax-free rules in the Internal Revenue Code as they affect transaction structures. In this era of billion dollar mergers and acquisitions he points out how the stakes for following the proper rules have become enormous. Mistakes can mean the payment of hundreds of millions of dollars in taxes which might otherwise have been avoided. Mr. Wassner discusses the so-called type A through C forms of reorganization. These include the statutory merger or consolidation, stock-for-stock acquisitions and stock-for-asset acquisitions. There is also a discussion of contingent pay-out arrangements and treatment of the acquired company, the acquiring company, and their shareholders. This chapter is loaded with examples for each of its major subjects.

The discussion of taxable methods, by Leonard Schneidman, focuses on the Dreyfus formula which has gained considerable popularity in recent years. In such a transaction the acquired corporation sells its net assets for cash and puts the proceeds into an investment company which exchanges its assets for shares in a fund such as Dreyfus Tax Exempt Bond Fund. Turning to the topic of tax considerations in taxable transactions, the author then discusses stock sales, merger with a public company and the use of an ESOP as an alternative to the Dreyfus Formula. Further material on the subject of ESOPs is contained in the chapter by Paul D. Ardleigh.

NEIL A. WASSNER

NEIL A. WASSNER is the partner-in-charge of the merger and acquisition department of Main Hurdman & Cranstoun, a position which also includes directing his firm's consulting practice on employee stock ownership plans (ESOPs). He is a graduate of the Wharton School, University of Pennsylvania where he received a B.S. (Economics) and of the New York University School of Law where he received J.D. and L.L.M. (taxation) degrees. He is both a CPA and a member of the New York Bar.

Mr. Wassner has lectured on ESOPs and mergers throughout the United States before such groups as the American Management Association, the New York Attorney-CPA Society, the Long Island Commerce and Industry Association, the Atlanta Chamber of Commerce, and the Texas Tech Tax Institute. He has also written articles and has been quoted on these subjects by *Business Week, Newsweek, Fortune Magazine, Forbes Magazine, Administrative Management, Pension World, and North Eastern Industrial World.*

In December of 1975, he testified at the Joint Economic Committee hearings on ESOPs at the invitation of Senator Humphrey. He also submitted a position paper on ESOPs to the President Carter Campaign Organization, at the request of the issues coordinator. In September of 1977, he testified at a Brookings Institution hearing in Washington on other techniques for capital diffusion. In November of 1979 he testified before the Senate Banking Committee on aid to the Chrysler Corporation.

A significant amount of Mr. Wassner's work at the present time is in assisting overseas clients of his international accounting firm in acquiring corporations in the United States.

13

Non-Taxable Methods

NEIL A. WASSNER

INTRODUCTION

A key question in any corporate merger or acquisition is the tax consequences to the parties involved. Those parties are the two corporations involved in the merger as well as the shareholders and holders of other securities of the two corporations. In general, there are two possible approaches that the taxing authorities could take in a corporate merger situation. On one hand it would be possible for them to view the stock-for-stock merger or acquisition for example as a "sale" resulting in the holders of securities in the acquired company "selling" their stock for stock of the acquiring corporation. If viewed as a "sale" the transaction should be taxed to the shareholders just as if they had sold their shares for cash and the gain should be the difference between what the stock in the acquired corporation cost them and what the stock in the acquiring corporation is worth.

The second possible approach of the taxing authorities would be to view the transaction not as a sale but as a continuation of the old investment in another form. Under this approach there would be no taxable gain at the time of the exchange of stock since the original investment would be viewed as being unliquidated and the tax would therefore be deferred until such time as the investment is finally sold.

These two approaches, which are at the heart of the tax treatment of mergers and acquisitions, can perhaps best be seen by looking at two examples. In 1979, Southern Airlines Inc. and North Central Airlines Inc. merged to form a new corporation—Republic Airlines, Inc. Common shareholders of each of the merging corporations received common shares of the new corporation. Assume that a shareholder of Southern had owned 100 shares of Southern common stock that he had purchased many years ago for $1,000. On the

merger that formed Republic the exchange ratio was 2.1 shares of Republic for each share of Southern so he would receive 210 shares of Republic for his 100 shares of Southern. On the day of the merger, when Republic shares started trading, the shares sold for $6.88 per share so the total value of the 210 shares that he received would be worth $1,444, or a profit of $444 over the cost of his original investment in Southern.

Also in 1979, a Mr. X, sole shareholder of the X Corporation, a small local newspaper, "sold out" to a national newspaper chain whose shares are traded on the New York Stock Exchange. He received $1 million of stock in the national chain in exchange for his shares in his own corporation which had cost him $25,000 when he purchased the corporation in the 1940's. Thus he had a profit of $975,000 on the transaction. Mr. X retired to Florida and reads the stock pages daily!

How should the two transactions described above the taxed? Clearly, it would seem, the first transaction should not be viewed as a sale. The shareholders of Southern Airlines Inc. and the shareholders of North Central Airlines Inc. have not liquidated their investments but have merely "continued" their investments in a new form—that of the new Republic Airlines Inc. It would not appear to be appropriate to tax them at the time of the exchange unless they sell their shares in Republic at that time rather than remaining as shareholders.

But what of Mr. X, relaxing in Florida, living off his dividends in the national newspaper chain—is his situation the same? Has he "continued" his investment or has he, in effect, "cashed in his chips" by converting his investment into that of a liquid New York Stock Exchange company whose shares he can sell by merely picking up his phone and calling his broker? Is not the real effect of his transaction, as he no doubt tells his friends, that he "sold out" to the national chain rather than that he "merged" with the national chain?

Interestingly enough, if Mr. X had structured his transaction properly, he would be treated in the same way as the shareholders of Southern and of the North Central, that is as a "continuing" investor in the company that merged with or acquired his corporation. That is because the tax statute which deals with mergers and acquisitions—the so-called "reorganization" provisions of the Internal Revenue Code, depends heavily on the form rather than the substance of the transactions that it governs. The position taken in each of the examples is that the shareholder should not be taxed at the time of the transaction; hence, the mergers and acquisitions that are structured to take advantage of these tax provisions are usually called "tax-free acquisitions" or "tax-free reorganizations" or "tax-free exchanges."

While the term "tax-free" is commonly applied to these transactions to distinguish them from "taxable exchanges" discussed elsewhere in this volume, the term is really a misnomer. The relevant Internal Revenue Code provisions call for "tax-deferral" not "tax forgiveness" in the transactions covered by these sections. This is accomplished by providing for so-called "carryover basis" in merger or acquisition situations treated as "reorganizations." The workings of the carryover basis provisions can best be seen by returning to our examples.

We have seen that the shareholder of Southern Airlines who had paid $1,000 for his investment, has received 210 shares of stock in Republic Airlines each worth $6.88 per share. Since the transaction qualified as a "reorganization" he did not have to pay a tax on his gain of $444. However, suppose that several months after the exchange he wishes to sell 100 shares of Republic which are now selling for $5.88 per share. How does he determine his gain or loss on the transaction? This is calculated by dividing his "carried over" basis of $1,000 among the 210 shares of Republic that he received to get a basis of $4.76 per share of Republic shares. Thus a sale of 100 of these shares for $5.88 per share results in a gain of $1.12 per share even though the shares have declined in value from the date that he received them at the time of the merger. This gain is taxable to him, although the tax is likely to be at favorable capital gain rates (see the chapters on taxable acquisitions).

While the carryover basis rules tend to make "tax-free mergers" really "tax-deferred mergers" there is a circumstance under which the gain will not only be deferred but will go unrecognized forever. If Mr. X, the retired newspaper owner, were to die before he sold any of his shares in the New York Stock Exchange - listed stock of his acquiror, his heirs, under current law, would inherit his stock at the value on the date of his death. His basis would not carry over but would become irrelevant to his heirs in their calculation of their gain at the time that they sell the shares. Nor is Mr. X's estate taxed on the gain at the time of death although any estate tax that may be due is calculated at the value of the shares at the time of death.

By now, it should be apparent that the "reorganization" provisions of the Internal Revenue Code are by nature liberal provisions. They define, in a sense, exceptions to the general rules that a taxpayer should pay a tax at the time he has received income, and income includes gains on the sales of securities. Flowing from the fact that the provisions are basically favorable to the taxpayer are two corollaries. The first is that where a tax statute is essentially granting relief from the payment of tax it is almost certain that the requirements for falling within the relief provisions will be set out in some detail with the taxpayer having the responsiblity for following the form of the transaction as set out in order to be granted the relief. The second corollary that follows from this is that a taxpayer will want to be certain, *prior* to having entered the transaction, that he has properly followed the form dictated by the Code, by obtaining an advance ruling from the Internal Revenue Service.

The detailed requirements for qualifying as a "reorganization" or tax-free transaction are essentially set out in Section 368(a)(1) of the Internal Revenue Code. In addition, many court cases and Revenue Rulings have further defined these requirements and most of this chapter will deal with the statutory, administrative and court-imposed rules for a tax-free exchange. It should be apparent, particularly in this age of $1 billion mergers and acquisitions, that the stakes for following the rules are enormous, with hundreds of millions of dollars of taxes at stake in a transaction. For this reason, very few substantial mergers or acquisitions are attempted without obtaining a favorable ruling from the Internal Revenue Service.

The advance ruling procedure allows a taxpayer to go to the IRS before the transaction is completed and to determine whether the form that legal and business conditions have dictated will result in a finding that a "reorganization" has occurred. Of course, because of the huge potential taxes involved, if the transaction does not fit the IRS requirements, the legal and/or business considerations may have to give way to tax considerations or, if this is not possible, the transaction may be aborted. Most tax practitioners are aware of many acquisitions that would have made good business sense but floundered because the tax rules could not be met. No doubt many businessmen are also aware of situations where the deal was changed to meet tax considerations and the acquisition proved unsuccessful because of those changes!

Prior to taking a close look at the statutory language of the reorganization sections of the Internal Revenue Code, it is necessary to examine some of the requirements that are common to all transactions that wish to be classified as tax-free reorganizations. Some of these requirements are contained in the statute but others are gleaned from reading the court cases in this area. Regardless of whether the transaction is structured as a merger, a stock-for-stock exchange or a stock-for-asset exchange, it is necessary to clear the hurdles of the continuity of proprietary interest test, the continuity of business enterprise test, the business purpose test and the step-transaction doctrine.

The continuity of proprietary interest requirement arose early in the history of reorganization taxation and it should be easily understood from the examples that have been presented above. As we have seen, the essential tax philosophy in allowing a taxpayer to defer rather than pay his taxes is that his profit has not been realized in the reorganization. No sale has occurred, rather it is said that his investment has merely continued in another form. In an early court case a corporation's assets were acquired in a transaction in which it received some cash and some short-term notes. The question arose as to whether this transaction qualified as a reorganization since it met the statutory definition at that time. The court said no—since short-term notes did not represent a continuation of the interest in the new corporation. An ownership interest in assets was essentially converted into a creditor position by becoming a holder of short-term notes.

Over the years, many court cases have further clarified this requirement so that today it can be said that what is required is

1. that the transferor corporation or its shareholders retained a proprietary stake in the enterprise represented by an equity interest in the transferee corporation; and
2. that such retained interest represents a substantial part of the value of the property transferred.

As we will see in our consideration of stock-for-stock and stock-for-asset acquisitions, the statute defines quite precisely the type of security and the percentage that represents a ''substantial part of the value of the property transferred.'' However, in the case of statutory mergers, the statute is silent on these points and it is usual for the taxpayers to get a ruling when more complex types of securities than common

or preferred stock are used or when a significant portion of the acquisition price consists of cash or securities not representing a continuing proprietary interest.

In general, the Internal Revenue Service will favorably rule that a transaction has the requisite continuity of proprietary interest if at least 50 percent of the consideration paid represents equity-type securities. It is for this reason that many corporate mergers today are made for 51 percent stock and 49 percent cash or debt.

For example, in 1979, Carrier Corporation was merged into United Technologies Corporation with each common shareholder of Carrier receiving one share of a new United Technologies convertible preferred stock for each share of Carrier common stock. The new preferred stock has one-half vote, pays a dividend of $2.55 annually and is convertible into .375 shares of United Technologies common stock. It had a market value when issued of $28 per share.

In late 1978, United Technologies had purchased, via a tender offer, 49 percent of Carrier stock for cash of $28 per share. When the two transaction are viewed together, as required by the step-transaction doctrine discussed below, the merger was 51 percent for stock and 49 percent for cash.

Furthermore, the Internal Revenue Service and the courts agree that it is not necessary for voting rights to be present for the required proprietary interest to be found. Thus non-voting preferred stock is not an uncommon instrument in corporate mergers.

The continuity of business enterprise test, which is being restated in proposed regulations at the time of this writing, requires that the acquiring corporation either continue the transferor's business or use a significant portion of the transferor's business assets if it does not continue the business. This is discussed in greater detail in the following chapter.

The business purpose test and the step-transaction doctrine are not unique to the reorganization sections but are applied by the courts throughout the tax law. In essence, the business purpose test requires a finding that the transaction entered into was not done primarily for the purpose of tax avoidance but rather has a business purpose for the parties involved. It now seems clear that the business purpose looked to may be that of the corporation or the shareholder. Thus if the transaction has a business purpose for either of the parties it should pass muster. If the parties to the reorganization cease operating the combined business following a merger, it is likely that the transaction will be held to fail the business purpose test and the transaction might be treated, for tax purposes, as a liquidation.

The step-transaction doctrine often raises some of

the most complex questions in the merger and acquisition area. In almost any corporate transaction of some complexity certain significant corporate events occur prior to the transaction being examined and, of course, certain events occur after the transaction. They may be or may appear to be unrelated to the particular transaction. Yet in many cases the Internal Revenue Service or the taxpayer may argue that the prior or past occurrences should be viewed as a ''step'' in the entire transaction and thus change the nature of the particular deal.

If Buyer Inc. exchanges its shares for all the shares of Seller Inc. this would appear to be a tax-free acquisition. But suppose on the day after the acquisition Buyer Inc. buys back all of the shares issued to the shareholders of Seller Inc. for cash. Should the two steps be viewed as one changing the transaction to one where Buyer Inc. paid cash for all the shares of Seller Inc.? If so, the transaction clearly would fail to meet the continuity of proprietary interest test.

While it is often extremely difficult to determine when the step-transaction rule will be applied and when it will not, it is often helpful to apply the so-called ''but for'' test in this area. If the Internal Revenue Service can show that the second step would not have occurred ''but for'' the first step they will often try to argue, if it is in their interest to do so, that the two steps are not independent but should be viewed as one.

A's, B's AND C's OF CORPORATE ACQUISITIONS

Even beginners in the world of the taxation of corporate mergers and acquisitions are probably familiar with the terms ''A'', ''B'' or ''C'' acquisitions although they may not know their meaning or the derivation of the terms. The meanings can be found in Section 368(a)(1) of the Internal Revenue Code which defines reorganizations as follows:

Section 368(a)(1)(A)—The Type A reorganization: ''A statutory merger or consolidation.''

Section 368(a)(1)(B)—The Type B reorganization: ''The acquisition by one corporation, in exchange for all or part of its voting stock (or the voting stock of a parent corporation), of stock of another corporation, if the first corporation has control of the second immediately after the exchange.''

Section 368(a)(1)(C)—The Type C reorganization: ''The acquisition by one corporation, in exchange for all or part of its voting stock (or the voting stock of a parent corporation), of substantially all of the properties of another corporation.''

The Code then goes on to define Types D, E and F reorganizations. A Type D reorganization involves either a combination of affiliated corporations or a split-up of an existing corporation. Types E and F deal essentially with changes in a single corporation such as changes in its corporate structure or state of incorporation, for example.

Mergers and acquisitions then are primarily covered in the A, B and C sections and thus we will deal only with them in this chapter.

Statutory Merger or Consolidation (''A'' Reorganizations)

A Type ''A'' reorganization is defined in the Internal Revenue Code quite simply as ''a statutory merger or consolidation''—nothing more, nothing less and it is the simplicity of this definition, with the lack of specific technical requirements that makes the ''A'' and its derivatives the ''triangular A's'' the most flexible and thus the most often used of the merger and acquisition structures. A statutory merger or consolidation means that a combination is effected under the laws of the United States or any state, territory or the District of Columbia. The combination thus occurs ''by operation of law'' after the vote of the shareholders or whatever else is necessary to merge the companies under the laws of whatever state has jurisdiction in the matter.

In 1978, for example, Columbine Exploration Corp., a publicly held oil exploration company, agreed to merge with Brodie Exploration Corp., another publicly held corporation in the same business. According to documents filed with the SEC the transaction was to occur as follows:

Columbine will merge with and into Brodie under the laws of Colorado. Brodie will be the Surviving Corporation. At the effective date of the merger, the corporate existence of Columbine will cease and all of the business, properties and assets of Columbine will vest in Brodie, as the Surviving Corporation and Brodie, as the Surviving Corporation will assume all of the liabilities, obligations and debts of Columbine. The Articles of Incorporation and Bylaws of Brodie will continue to be effective following the merger ...

At the effective time of the merger, the 7,937,500 issued and outstanding shares of Columbine common stock ... will automatically be converted into 8,731,250 shares of the Surviving Corporation's common stock ... (and) the present holders of common stock of Brodie will continue to hold 8,733,333 shares of Brodie, the Surviving Corporation.

The SEC document then goes on to say that counsel for both Columbine and Brodie "have given opinions to the effect that if the merger is effectuated according to the Merger Agreement ... the transaction ... will constitute a "reorganization" within the meaning of Section 368(a)(1)(A) of the Internal Revenue Code ..." Further, the document states that ... "No ruling by the Internal Revenue Service as to the Federal Income Tax consequences of the merger has been requested or received by Brodie or Columbine, and there are no plans to request such a ruling."

Why was no ruling requested in a transaction that involved several millions of dollars of consideration? Because of the simplicity of the Type A transaction! The statute imposes no requirements other than a merger or consolidation under state law. The Brodie-Columbine deal above was a merger since one of the corporations survived. If the two corporations had merged into a newly-formed third corporation and the two older corporations had ceased to exist a consolidation would have occurred.

We have already seen that although the statute itself imposes little in the way of requirements for a valid "A" reorganization the continuity of proprietary interest doctrine may be a substantial hurdle in the structuring of a valid transaction of this type. Suppose, for example, that Columbine shareholders had received not only common stock of Brodie in this transaction but had received a combination of 50 percent cash and 50 percent common, or a package of securities consisting of 50 percent cash, 25 percent non-voting preferred stock and 25 percent common stock. While presumably both of these transactions would qualify as a valid "A" by continuing the requisite continuity of proprietary interest, they are sufficiently "borderline" to require a ruling in a significant transaction.

Flexibility is the major advantage of the type A transaction since it permits the use of liberal amounts of cash to be paid to dissenting shareholders who do not wish to go along with the merger and it permits the use of the "exotic" types of securities that have become popular in recent years such as non-voting preferred stock. (Of course, it is always possible that the Internal Revenue Service will find that your "exotically" designed non-voting, 10 percent, sinking fund, redeemable preferred stock is really a debt instrument in disguise and not find the requisite continuity of interest. Interestingly, the IRS will not give an advance ruling on the question of whether hybrid securities containing features of both equity and debt are sufficiently "proprietary." So one must not be too creative in this area!)

There are several disadvantages that a type A reorganization has and although they are essentially legal rather than tax in nature they should be briefly discussed here. First, since a merger combines all of both companies it is generally not possible to avoid the assumption of contingent or unknown liabilities in a merger because the surviving corporation automatically assumes all of the liabilities of the disappearing corporation.

Since a type "A" reorganization requires a valid transaction under state law, and since the laws of most states require appraisal rights for dissenters it may be necessary for a merging corporation to provide a significant amount of cash for those shareholders who do not wish to go along with the transaction. Essentially appraisal rights give the dissenter the opportunity to go to court to request cash equal to the value of his interest in the corporation. This subject will be examined more closely in other chapters of this book.

A pragmatic problem with type A reorganizations is that the laws of most states require shareholder approval by both corporations that are parties to the merger. Thus, for example, if giant A&P were to merge with a corner grocer it would be necessary for A&P shareholders to vote on it. This would require expensive SEC filings and other heavy costs associated with the calling of a shareholders meeting. While in a merger of two substantial companies a meeting would make sense it should not be necessary for A&P shareholders to approve a merger with a minute corporation. Prior to 1968 the tax flexibility of an "A" reorganization often had to give way to the impracticability and cost of holding shareholder meetings for small acquisitions. Then in 1968, the Internal Revenue Code was amended to provide for a new merger form—the "triangular A." This was followed in 1971 by the "reverse triangular A."

TRIANGULAR A

Early in 1979, The Creamette Company, a Minneapolis, Minn. corporation, was acquired by Borden,

Inc., the large food processing company. The transaction that effectuated this acquisition was the merger of Creamette into a wholly owned subsidiary of Borden known as Rovivrus (survivor spelled backwards for the analytical minded!) with the shareholders of Creamette receiving stock of Borden on the merger. After the merger Rovivrus changed its name to The Creamette Company (Figure 13-1).

The 1968 change in the Internal Revenue Code that allowed the development of the triangular merger was to permit the shareholders of Creamette to receive stock of Borden, the parent of Rovivrus, rather than the stock of Rovivrus on its merger into Rovivrus. Obviously, they would only want the stock of Borden, a publicly-traded corporation, on the merger but prior to 1968 it was not clear that shareholders could receive stock other than that of its direct merger partner on the combination.

The shareholders of Creamette met on January 31, 1979, in the city of Minneapolis to approve the merger. But did the stockholders of Borden have to approve the merger? No—they did not. Since Creamette was not merging with Borden but with Rovivrus only the shareholders of Rovivrus had to approve the merger. And who were they? Since all the stock of Rovivrus was owned by Borden, the Board of Directors of Borden, entitled under state law to vote the stock of subsidiaries, approved the merger. And this, of course, was the reason for the structure in the first place. By allowing the directors rather than the shareholders of Borden to vote on the merger the com-

pany saved a substantial amount of expenses that would have been incurred in holding a shareholders meeting. A further advantage of this structure is that Borden does not become liable for the liabilities of Creamette since they are not directly assumed by it in the merger. The liabilities become those of its subsidiary—New Creamette.

The requirements for a valid triangular A are that the merger would have been a valid "A" if it had been with the parent rather than the subsidiary, that no stock of the subsidiary be used in the transaction and that the subsidiary must acquire "substantially all" of the assets of the acquired corporation.

This final point, the *substantially all* test presents most of the problems in this type of reorganization. This requirement springs from a similar rule long required in the stock-for-asset or Type C reorganization and its discussion is deferred.

REVERSE TRIANGULAR MERGER

Vlasic Foods, Inc., a major company in the pickle business was acquired by Campbell Soup Company in 1978. The merger was structured as a reverse triangular merger with the shareholders of Vlasic becoming shareholders of Campbell. In actuality what really happened was that Capital Subsidiary, Inc., a newly formed wholly owned subsidiary of Campbell was merged into Vlasic with Vlasic becoming the surviving corporation and its shareholders receiving Campbell

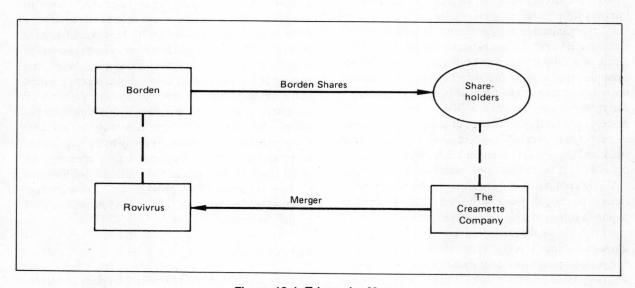

Figure 13-1. Triangular Merger

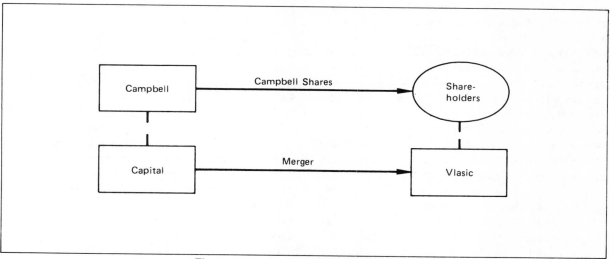

Figure 13-2. Reverse Triangular Merger

stock on the combination (Figure 13-2).

Of course, the similarity with the triangular merger should be quickly apparent—but so should the difference! Instead of the newly formed subsidiary being the survivor the reverse occurs. The acquired corporation survives as a wholly owned subsidiary of the acquiror. Hence, the term "reverse triangular" merger. The advantage of the reverse triangular over the "A" reorganization is again the elimination of the need for a stockholders meeting by the "true" acquiror, in our case Campbell. The advantage over the triangular merger is that the reverse triangular allows the legal attributes of the acquired company—leases, franchises, etc.—to survive the merger without having to be conveyed to another corporation. The acquired corporation is legally preserved in the reverse triangular.

Again the price one pays for the advantages of the reverse triangular merger is the loss of some flexibility, for several requirements are imposed not present in the straight "A reorganization. In addition to the "substantially all" requirement discussed above is the requirement that only voting stock of the parent company be issued in exchange for stock constituting control (80 percent) of the target company in the reverse triangular merger. Other types of consideration, such as cash, debt or non-voting stock may be used to acquire the remaining 20 percent. As a result, those using the reverse triangular form are more restricted in the type of consideration that can be used than those using the "A" or straight triangular route. This has not prevented the reverse triangular from becoming a popularly used format for corporate acquisitions involving public companies.

Stock-for-Stock Acquisitions ("B" Reorganizations)

In January of 1980, the X Corporation purchased approximately 8 percent of the stock of Y Corporation through market purchases on the New York Stock Exchange. In May of 1980, X and Y entered into merger negotiations and in July they agreed on terms. X would issue one share of a newly created voting preferred stock in exchange for each share of Y's common stock in an exchange offer that would be made to all of Y's shareholders. The offer was contingent upon acceptance by holders of 72 percent of the shares not already owned by X Corporation. In October, all the shares of Y Corporation were exchanged for shares of X Corporation pursuant to the exchange offer.

This transaction illustrates several of the key issues that arise in any discussion of stock-for-stock (Type B) acquisitions. The Internal Revenue Code requirement of a Type B reorganization is that the stock of the acquired corporation is obtained in exchange *solely* for either the acquiring corporation's or its parent's voting stock, provided that the acquiring corporation has *control* of the acquired corporation immediately after the acquisition.

Most of the problems that arise in stock-for-stock transactions involve difficulties in one of the two areas stressed above so it is therefore necessary to examine both of these requirements more carefully.

It is the word *solely* that presents most of the trouble in the stock-for-stock acquisition area and makes this type of acquisition the least flexible and therefore least used of the tax-free acquisition routes. Only voting stock may be given in the exchange—any other consideration paid, whether it be cash, non-voting securities or even stock warrants will cause the transaction to be taxable to all parties, even those receiving only voting stock. A Supreme Court case has stated that the word *solely* provides "no leeway" in the type of consideration that can be exchanged for the acquired company's stock. While the requirement is obviously very strict, a small exception has been recognized in the cases. It allows cash to pay for fractional shares where the exchange ratio of the stock-for-stock transaction leaves some shareholders with less than a full share of the acquiring company's stock.

The difficulties in this area can arise in several ways. Most troublesome is the question of expenses of the acquisition. The payment by the acquiring corporation of expenses that should clearly be those of the target company's shareholders, such as independent legal counsel or financial advisors, would constitute additional non-voting stock consideration and would destroy the tax-free nature of the transaction. Often, expenses of a transaction cannot clearly be allocated among the parties and since, theoretically $1 of cash consideration can thwart the transaction, the risks are enormous.

Another problem sometimes arises when the acquiring corporation enters into an employment agreement with the shareholder-managers of the target company. The IRS has argued, on occasion, that payments under the employment contract were really disguised payment of cash for the stock and has challenged the reorganization. Clearly, where bonuses are to be paid to shareholder-managers in proportion to their share ownership rather than to their salary and performance, a challenge from the IRS can be expected.

The "control" requirement in the stock-for-stock acquisition differs considerably with the common understanding of the term—enough votes to be able to elect a Board of Directors. Control in the "B" reorganization sense, and in many other areas of the Code, means ownership of stock possessing at least 80 percent of total combined voting power, plus as least 80 percent of the total number of shares of all other classes of stock. Assume a corporation had outstanding 100 shares of Class A common stock (voting); 100 shares of Class B common stock (voting); and 100 shares of nonvoting preferred stock. The ownership of 70 shares of Class A, 90 shares of Class B and 80 shares of preferred would meet the requirement since 160 shares of A and B represents 80 percent of the total "combined" voting power present in 200 shares.

In the example at the start of this section the transaction is conditioned on X Corporation obtaining 72 percent of Y Corporation on the offer so that, immediately after the exchange, X Corporation will own 80 percent of Y Corporation. But the example is meant to illustrate a common problem in the stock-for-stock cases—that of so-called "creeping control." If the purchase in January on the open market, for cash, is viewed as part of the same transaction as the stock-for-stock exchange in October, then the transaction will fail since the cash consideration paid in January would violate the *solely* for voting stock requirement. If, however, the transactions can be viewed as separate from the cash purchase, then the stock-for-stock exchange should be tax-free if X Corporation also meets the control test.

While we have seen in the discussion of the step transaction doctrine that it is not always clear when transactions will be considered to be part of a single plan, in the "B" reorganization area the IRS will generally view any transaction occurring within one year of the reorganization as part of the reorganization although the taxpayer may be able to prove the transactions were in fact unrelated. In our example, the one-year rule of thumb would destroy the "B" reorganization. Interestingly, sometimes it is the taxpayer who wishes the step transaction rule to be applied. Assume for example that X Corporation has acquired 8 percent of Y Corporation for voting stock, not cash, in January. Here application of the doctrine would make the January transaction tax-free as part of the subsequent reorganization while failure to apply the doctrine would make the January transaction taxable since the 8 percent purchase would not satisfy the "control" test.

Stock-for-Assets ("C" Reorganization)

Miniconglomerate Corp. had grown through acquisitions in the 1960's and, in 1980, was negotiating to be acquired itself, by the much larger Conglomerate Corp. Miniconglomerate was composed of 7 successful operating companies, one of which was in the same business as one of the businesses of Conglomerate. It was clear from discussions with the Justice Department that a merger of Miniconglomerate with Conglomerate would be attacked on antitrust grounds. Conglomerate was willing to proceed with the acquisition even if it could not acquire the one competing company but the shareholders of Miniconglomerate insisted on a tax-free transaction.

This example provides an opportunity to examine the stock-for-asset or Type "C" reorganization. This type of reorganization contemplates the acquisition by one corporation of *substantially all* of the properties of another corporation, in exchange *solely* for voting stock of the acquiring corporation or its parent, or in exchange for such voting stock and a limited amount of money or property.

The stock-for-asset acquisition usually results in the assets of the transferor corporation becoming a division of the acquiring corporation. This result is similar to the one attained when a statutory merger takes place but it is unlike a stock-for-stock acquisition where a parent-subsidiary relationship results. Since a newly formed subsidiary can issue its parent's stock in a "C" reorganization it is possible, however, to structure a "C" so as to create a parent-subsidiary relationship.

While in most stock-for-asset acquisitions the stock of the acquiring corporation is distributed to the shareholders of the acquired corporation in liquidation of the acquired corporation it is not necessary that this be done. Thus it is permissible for the corporation whose assets were acquired to remain in existence holding the stock of the acquiring corporation. This is rarely done, however, since, as we shall see, if the transaction qualifies as a valid "C" reorganization both the acquisition of the assets of the target company and the distribution of the acquiring corporation stock in liquidation of the transferor company will be tax-free to the transferor corporation and to its shareholders respectively.

The major complication in the stock-for-asset transaction is the question of what represents *substantially all* of the properties. In our example, let us assume that the division of Miniconglomerate that will not be sold to Conglomerate (because of the likely antitrust challenge) has assets worth $2 million and liabilities of $1 million for a net worth (at fair market value *not* cost) of $1 million. In total, Miniconglomerate has assets worth $10 million and liabilities of $6 million or a "net worth" of $4 million. Does the conveyance of all of the assets and liabilities of the other 6 divisions of Miniconglomerate to Conglomerate represent *substantially all* of the properties of Miniconglomerate? For purposes of issuing favorable rulings, the Internal Revenue Service holds that the *substantially all* requirement is met when there is a transfer of assets representing at least 90 percent of the fair market value of the net assets *and* at least 70 percent of the fair market value of the gross assets held by the target corporation immediately preceding the transfer. Thus, in our example, the proposed reorganization will fail; while $8 million of the $10 million (or 80 percent) of the gross assets will be transferred, only $3 million of the $4 million (or 75 percent) of the net assets will be conveyed. Since fair market value of the assets rather than historical cost is the key, it is not possible merely

from observing a company's balance sheet to determine whether the "C" will succeed. Further, the use of fair market value can lead to significant "second guessing" by the IRS, whose appraisers can challenge appraisals made by the taxpayer. Court decisions have held that intangibles, such as goodwill should be considered in applying the *substantially all* test and that the operating assets only should be used in applying the rule. Thus the court permitted the target company to retain *investment* assets making up 14 percent of total properties in an important case in this area.

Prior to 1954, only voting stock was permitted to be paid in a stock-for-asset acquisition. The 1954 Internal Revenue Code liberalized the Type C reorganization by permitting some cash or other property to be used in this type of acquisition so long as 80 percent or more of the fair market value of the property acquired is acquired for voting stock. In applying this 80 percent test it is necessary to include liabilities assumed as part of the purchase price, making the 1954 liberalization less flexible than might first appear. Thus, for example, if the target company has assets of $10 million and liabilities of $1 million, all of which are to be assumed in the acquisition, then the acquiror cannot pay more than $1 million in cash or property as part of the purchase price. Since fair market value is again used in applying the rule the taxpayer again runs the risk of second-guessing by the IRS. In our example above, if the assets thought to be worth $10 million are worth less, the reorganization would fail since the liabilities assumed and the cash paid will exceed 20 percent of the fair market value of the properties acquired.

The principal advantages of the stock-for-asset acquisition are that only the liabilities specifically assumed become the liabilities of the acquiror and that no dissenting shareholders of the transferor corporation become shareholders of the acquiring corporation. Further, as we have seen in the Miniconglomerate-Conglomerate example, unwanted assets, to some degree, can be withheld from the exchange. The principal disadvantages of the stock-for-asset transaction are that it is more burdensome for the attorneys to convey all of the assets to be acquired and hence may be more costly to accomplish and that the business and legal identity of the transferor corporation is not transferred to the acquiror. While the acquiror may transfer the assets of the transferor corporation to a newly formed subsidiary and change its name to the same name as the transferor company—to preserve business continuity and goodwill—the loss of legal identity can be more profound. Such assets as leases, franchises and licenses may not be transferable by their terms and therefore a stock-for-asset transaction may be precluded. A stock-for-stock or corporate merger may be mandatory under these conditions.

Contingent Pay-Out Arrangements

After months of negotiations the officers of Buyer, Inc. and Seller Corp. seemed to be getting nowhere in their merger discussions. Buyer, Inc. was convinced it was offering a fair price of 10 times Seller's 1979 earnings of $1 million, or $10 million, of Buyer, Inc. common stock in a stock-for-stock acquisition. This represented 1 million shares at Buyer's current price of $10 per share. Seller Corp. did not disagree that 10 was a reasonable multiple, but they did disagree on the earnings base period. Seller was convinced that its *future* earnings would greatly exceed $1 million per year and, after all, wasn't Buyer really buying the future rather than the past. While Buyer saw merit in Seller's case it was not prepared to pay in advance for earnings that might not materialize. Suppose, for example, that the newly wealthy, officer-shareholders of Seller quit their jobs after the acquisition. Could Seller reach its earnings goals without these key people? Late into the night a compromise began to develop. Buyer could pay Seller $10 million in stock now. Then, after three years, the average earnings of Seller would be calculated. If they exceeded $1 million, Buyer would pay Seller more stock, at the then current price of its stock, equal to 5 times the average earnings in excess of $1 million. The lower multiple was in recognition of the fact that, to some extent, Buyer would be helping Seller to achieve its goals.

Seller Corp. shareholders were happy with the opportunity to "earn" more shares after the acquisition. Buyer, Inc., while recognizing that it might have to pay more than originally anticipated, liked the idea that this type of transaction gave the officer-shareholders of Seller an incentive to remain with the company for three years and to work hard to achieve its goals. Buyer did feel, however, that prudence required that a limit be placed on the total number of additional shares that could be issued. Otherwise a combination of high earnings by the Seller subsidiary and a falling stock price of Buyer common stock could result in Seller's former shareholders controlling Buyer! After some more negotiations a ceiling of 800,000 additional shares was agreed to.

The above scenario has occurred numerous times in merger negotiations. The compromise solution— whether called "contingent pay-out" or "earnout" or "kicker" transaction—is both a logical way to resolve differences between forward-looking sellers and backward-looking buyers, and a way to provide incen-

tives for shareholder-management to work as hard for someone else as they did for themselves.

The tax question that arises in our transaction is two-fold; first, is the payment of 1 million shares in 1980 tax-free to the Seller shareholders and second, is the payment in 1983 of up to 800,000 additional shares, based upon earnings in the 1980-1982 period, tax-free to these shareholders? The Internal Revenue Service has not been unreasonable in this area. When these transactions began to proliferate in the "go-go" 1960's the IRS adopted a ruling policy, modified in 1977, that tried to reconcile the Service's desire for finality and definiteness in tax matters with the taxpayer's requirements to postpone a final accounting until the contingency period had run.

The result was an IRS statement that it would issue favorable rulings in this area if six requirements were met. The requirements can be examined in the context of our example. The first requirement is that all the shares that will be issued must be issued within 5 years of the date of the initial distribution. Our 3-year contingency period clearly meets this test. The second requirement is more subjective—that a valid "business reason" must exist for not issuing all of the stock immediately. Presumably, both resolving a difference in the valuation of Seller's worth and providing an incentive to Seller's shareholder-managers would meet this test. The third requirement is that the maximum number of shares which may be issued must be stated in the agreement of the parties, and the fourth requirement is that at least 50 percent of the maximum number of shares of each class of stock which could be issued must be issued initially. By providing a maximum total of 1.8 million shares and issuing 1 million shares initially, the Buyer, Inc.-Seller Corp. transaction has no trouble with these requirements.

The fifth requirement for a favorable advance ruling by the IRS is that the contingent right to additional stock must not be assignable, except by operation of law or, if assignable, the right must not be marketable or evidenced by a negotiable certificate of any kind. Since, in our transaction, Seller Inc. has few shareholders this is not a problem. In a public company the failure of a shareholder to be able to sell his contingent rights when, for example, he sells his stock in the acquiring company, is a problem. The final requirement that the IRS imposes is that the right to additional stock must be only with respect to stock of the acquiring corporation or a corporation in control of the corporation. This presents no problem in our example.

Some of the problems that can arise in the contingent payout area may be resolved by the use of an appropriate escrow agreement. For example, interest must generally be imputed on transactions involving a deferred delivery of shares. The IRS has been liberal in its interpretation of when stock is "issued" so that shares placed in escrow are considered "issued" for purposes of these IRS requirements. Thus no imputed interest need be calculated on escrowed shares.

Taxation of Parties to a Reorganization

Throughout this section we have examined numerous examples of corporate acquisition—some real and some imagined—to determine whether they qualify as "reorganizations" under the Internal Revenue Code. It now remains to examine the tax consequences to the various parties to the reorganization, assuming that the transaction does qualify for the favorable tax treatment of the reorganization provisions.

As we have seen there are usually three parties to a reorganization—the corporation whose stock or assets are acquired (the acquired or transferor corporation), the corporation which issues its stock to make an acquisition (the acquiring corporation) and the shareholders of the acquired or transferor corporation. The shareholders of the acquiring corporation are not parties since they do not exchange their interests in the transaction. Of course, in a statutory consolidation shareholders of both corporations will be viewed as shareholders of an acquired corporation.

Treatment of Transferor Corporation

A transferor corporation recognizes neither gain nor loss when it transfers property for stock or securities of another corporation, a "party to a reorganization", if the exchange is pursuant to a "plan of reorganization." While the terms "party to a reorganization" and "plan of reorganization" are terms of art, they contemplate all of the various types of acquisitions discussed in this chapter. Where stock or securities are the only consideration issued in an acquisition the result is clear. Suppose, however, that Corp. A issues $12 million of voting stock and $1 million of cash to acquire all the assets of Corp. B, a corporation with $1 million of liabilities, which are assumed by Corp. A. As we have seen from our discussion of stock-for-asset acquisitions, this transaction qualifies as a tax-free "C" reorganization since the voting stock represents 80 percent or more of the consideration paid.

While the transaction is a valid "C" it is still partially taxable to the transferor corporation. This is because only the gain that is represented by stock or securities received from the acquiring corporation is "forgiven" (really deferred) by the reorganization sections of the Code. Since Corp. B has received $1 million of cash on the reorganization it is taxable on gain of up to $1 million on the transaction. It must first

calculate its total gain on the transaction (called "gain realized") by valuing all the consideration it has received from Corp. A, cash and stock, and then subtracting its "basis" in the assets transferred to Corp. A in the exchange. Basis usually means a corporation's cost of its assets adjusted by certain factors, such as depreciation on fixed assets. In our example, if the "gain realized" exceeds $1 million, Corp. B still only "recognizes" $1 million of gain—the amount of the cash or other property (often called "boot"—a historically obscure term!) received in the exchange. A "gain realized" of under $1 million would result in a "gain recognized" of the same amount. No loss can be recognized by a transferor corporation in a reorganization.

Note that in our example the liabilities assumed do not constitute property giving rise to the recognition of gain. It should also be noted that if Corp. A had issued $1 million of non-voting stock instead of cash no gain would be recognized by Corp. B on the exchange, even though non-voting stock is "tainted" for purposes of determining whether the transaction qualifies as a valid "C" reorganization. Further, if Corp. B were to liquidate and distribute its stock in Corp. A and its cash to its shareholders, it would not have to recognize any gain on the transaction since, under those circumstances it would be viewed as a mere conduit in the reorganization with the consideration passing through it on the way to its shareholders. In most "C" reorganizations liquidation does in fact occur, leading to no gain being recognized by the transferor corporation.

At the beginning of this chapter, the subject of "carryover basis" was discussed and it was pointed out that the carryover basis rules are designed to ensure that unrecognized gain does not escape tax forever but is merely deferred until a later time. The workings of these rules can be observed by returning to our example. Corp. B has received $12 million of voting stock and $1 million cash for assets which we will now assume cost $5 million. Additionally, Corp. A assumed $1 million of Corp. B's liabilities. The "gain realized" on this transaction is $9 million; $13 million of stock and cash plus $1 million of assumed liabilities less $5 million "basis" in the assets transferred. However, as we have seen, the "gain recognized" is only $1 million—the amount of "boot" received. It now remains to determine the basis that Corp. B has in the stock of Corp. A. That is, assuming Corp. B does not liquidate but instead, at some later date, sells its stock in Corp. A, what basis should be used to determine the gain or loss on this subsequent transaction?

The Internal Revenue Code states that the basis that Corp. B has in the stock of Corp. A is equal to its basis in the assets it transferred ($5 million), increased by any gain recognized by Corp. B on the exchange ($1 million) and reduced by any liabilities assumed in the transaction ($1 million) and by any boot received ($1 million) or $4 million. Thus, if Corp. B were to sell the stock of Corp. A for $12 million it would have a gain of $8 million. The gain of $8 million that was unrecognized in the reorganization is taxed now—on the sale of the stock of Corp. A.

Treatment of Acquiring Corporation

The nonrecognition of gain or loss to an acquiring corporation that issues its stock in exchange for property of a second corporation is not covered by the reorganization provisions of the Internal Revenue Code but by another section of the Code which states that a corporation does not recognize gain or loss on the issuance of its own shares.

It is only the basis rules that are really of interest to the acquiror. Here the rules call for a carryover basis. The acquiror gets a basis in the property equal to the basis that the transferor corporation had in the property increased by any gain recognized by the transferor on the transaction. In our previous example, Corp. A will get a basis of $6 million in the property, equal to Corp. B's $5 million basis plus the $1 million gain recognized by Corp. B. If Corp. A were to later sell the property for its presumed value of $14 million (the $13 million of stock and cash paid plus the $1 million of liabilities assumed) its gain would be $8 million.

Treatment of Stockholders

The Internal Revenue Code provides that an exchanging stockholder in a reorganization recognizes neither gain nor loss if stock or securities in a corporation that is a "party to a reorganization" are exchanged "solely" for stock or securities in another corporation that is a "party to a reorganization", if the exchange is pursuant to a "plan of reorganization."

Once again, the Code provides that if there is boot in the transaction, the gain will be limited to the amount of boot that is received by the exchanging shareholder. One problem that frequently arises in this area, the question of whether the gain to be recognized is taxed at ordinary income or at capital gain rates, can be illustrated by the following example.

Smallco is a family-owned corporation equally owned by three sisters. Largeco proposes to form a subsidiary to enter into a "triangular merger" with Smallco, issuing $4 million of its stock and $1 million in cash to each of the three sisters for their stock having a basis of $2 million each. As we have seen from our previous discussions of "triangular mergers" and "continuity of interest," the transaction should qualify as a valid Type A reorganization. Further, it should be apparent that the $1 million in cash received by each sister is taxable boot resulting in a realized gain of $3 million and a recognized gain of $1 million to each sister. The remaining question is whether the $1 million gain should be taxed as a capital gain or as a dividend taxed at ordinary income rates.

Generally, capital gains treatment results from the "sale or exchange" of property that is a "capital asset"—a term which includes corporate stock. If the sisters had sold their shares for $5 million cash, the gain would unquestionably have been capital. However, by bringing the transaction within the purview of the reorganization provisions of the Code, we are faced with a rule that provides that if the exchange has the "effect of the distribution of a dividend" the taxpayer's gain must be so treated. Since a dividend, for this purpose, can only be payable out of "earnings and profits" of a corporation (a very complex tax term beyond the scope of this chapter but generally referring to a corporation's earnings since 1913—the year the Income Tax was enacted), it is possible that only a portion of the gain will be taxed as a dividend with the remainder taxed as a capital gain.

How then can an exchange have the "effect of a distribution of a dividend"? If we return to our three sisters, we may find a clue. Suppose that immediately prior to the acquisition of Smallco by Largeco, the sisters had the corporation declare a $3 million cash dividend and that Largeco had then acquired Smallco for only $12 million in stock. The sisters would be in no different position under either example. Yet in this latter example, the $1 million cash they each receive would clearly be a dividend. Why then, the IRS essentially is saying, should a capital gain result in the former example?

For a time, tax authorities were of the opinion that boot received in a tax-free exchange would "automatically" give rise to dividend treatment (the so-called "automatic dividend" rule), if "earnings and profits" were present. Recent cases however have changed this view so that each transaction is presently tested on its merits to determine whether the boot received has the "effect of a distribution of a dividend." Such factors as pro-rata or non-pro-rata distribution of boot, business purpose for boot distribution, and the percentage of acquiror to be owned by the former shareholders of the acquired corporation are observed in making the decision. Since this area is extremely "gray" it is strongly recommended that rulings be requested in cases of doubt.

Once it is established how much gain is to be recognized on the transaction, it is necessary to determine the basis that the shareholders receive in the stock of the acquiring corporation. Here the rule is that the basis of the stock received is equal to the basis of the property transferred increased by the amount of any gain recognized (whether capital gain or dividend) and decreased by the fair market value of any boot received.

Returning to our three sisters, each has a basis of $2 million in Smallco, each had a recognized gain of $1 million and each received $1 million of boot. Thus their basis in Largeco will be $2 million. If they sold Largeco stock for $4 million, its presumed value, they would recognize $2 million of further gain. Once again, the logic of the basis rules should be clear—$2 million of gain was deferred in the initial exchange and that gain is now picked-up when the stock received is sold.

LEONARD SCHNEIDMAN

LEONARD SCHNEIDMAN received his LLB from the Harvard Law School and an LLM in Taxation from New York University School of Law. Thereafter, he served as an attorney-advisor to Judge Graydon G. Withey of the United States Tax Court. Mr. Schneidman is a partner in the New York City law firm of Spengler Carlson Gubar & Brodsky, where he specializes in tax law and has been actively involved in the tax aspects of corporate acquisitions and dispositions. Mr. Schneidman has written and lectured on various tax topics and is a member of several committees of the tax sections of the American and New York State Bar Associations.

The Dreyfus Formula—"Now You 'C' It ..."

LEONARD SCHNEIDMAN

THE PROBLEM

A not uncommon situation confronted by many businesses, both large and small, involves the desire of a principal stockholder to retire at minimum tax cost from a business created by his efforts over many years and instead to obtain the benefits of ownership of a diversified investment portfolio, including, for example, tax exempt municipal bonds.

Assume, as a typical pattern, that Mr. A owns 75 percent of the stock of the corporation with the remaining 25 percent owned by his wife and children, both directly and in trust. Mr. A's basis in the stock of the corporation is $1,000,000 while the corporation's basis in its assets is $9,000,000. If Mr. A were to sell his stock for $10,000,000, he would realize a gain of $9,000,000, while, in contrast, the corporation's sale of its assets for the same amount would produce a gain of $1,000,000. Tax considerations, therefore, would dictate a sale of the corporation's assets. How can Mr. A. best achieve his personal objective of a diversified portfolio after such sale?

One solution might be that the corporation remain alive after the sale of its assets and invest the sales proceeds primarily in tax-exempt bonds. This solution, however, has a number of drawbacks, including possible personal holding company and/or accumulated earnings tax problems for the corporation; the lack of any market for the stock of the corporation; the dividend risk for any limited redemptions of the corporation's stock; and the taxable nature of any dividends declared by the corporation to Mr. A.

AN INGENIOUS SOLUTION

Although it may be true that there is "nothing new under the sun," old concepts may be used in ingenious new ways to produce a desired result. Such is surely the case with what is now known as the "Dreyfus Formula",[1] a combination of sale and reorganization transactions producing what might, in some sense, be characterized as a tax-free taxable disposition.

The Dreyfus Formula involves the following basic transactional format:

- The acquired corporation ("Target") sells its net assets for cash.
- Pursuant to a plan of reorganization, Target transfers all or substantially all of its assets (i.e. the cash proceeds) to an investment company (the "Fund") in exchange for Fund shares.
- Pursuant to the same plan, Target distributes the Fund shares to its own shareholders in complete liquidation of their stock interests in Target. Target is then dissolved pursuant to applicable state law.

Target is typically closely held, and its assets are usually sold to a third party unrelated either to itself or the Fund. However, Target may be publicly held, and its assets are sometimes sold to a new corporation whose shareholders include former key employees of Target. In most cases, the assets sold are those of an active business; but in some instances, Target may not have carried on active operations for a substantial period of time, having disposed of its operating assets in prior transactions and having replaced them with

---

The technique was named after the Dreyfus Tax Exempt Bond Fund which was involved in the pioneering 1978 transaction that was approved by the Internal Revenue Service. (See Appendix A).

various types of securities or other assets which yield passive income. The sale occurs just before the transaction with the Fund and is reported as a taxable transaction, with gain or loss and depreciation and investment credit recapture being recognized by Target as required.

The Fund is a diversified, open-end registered investment company which qualifies as a regulated investment company under Section 851 of the Internal Revenue Code[2] and generally pays tax exempt-interest dividends pursuant to Section 852(b)(5). Pursuant to a plan and agreement of reorganization entered into between the Fund and Target,[3] the Fund acquires Target's cash in exchange for Fund shares. It invests or otherwise utilizes such cash in conjunction with its normal business operations. Target's receipt of Fund shares in a qualifying reorganization is tax-free to Target and the receipt of these shares by Target's stockholders upon its liquidation is likewise tax-free.

In summary, the Dreyfus Formula eliminates the problems arising from keeping Target alive in order to avoid the taxable gain inherent in liquidating Target, e.g., in the case of Mr. A. $9,000,000; the Fund shares, directly held by Target stockholders are marketable; and the investment return to the Fund shareholders has the tax-free nature of direct ownership of municipal securities as opposed to possible personal holding company and other problems if Target is not liquidated.

The balance of this chapter will analyze the tax considerations involved in the sale and reorganization transactions, including the Internal Revenue Service's (the "Service") ruling policy with regard to the latter; the Securities laws aspects of these types of transactions; and, finally, a brief comparison of the Dreyfus Formula with other presently available techniques.

THE SALE TRANSACTION

Loss Sales. On the sale of assets, including the sale of a corporation's business, the purchase price must be allocated among the assets sold on an asset-by-asset basis.[4] Thus, the Target will recognize gain or loss on the sale of each asset. Computation of depreciation or investment tax credit recapture will likewise be computed on an asset by asset basis.[5]

If Target has high basis-low value assets, the disposition of its business in a taxable sale will produce little, if any, tax.[6] In fact, any loss generated on the sale of assets may be carried back for up to three years and could possibly produce tax refunds for Target.

Gain Sales. Where Target is not so fortunate to be able to sell its assets at book value or below, an interesting interplay between the reorganization and liquidation provisions of the Code is created. Section 337 provides in general terms that a corporation will not recognize gain or loss upon the sale of its assets effected pursuant to a plan of complete liquidation completed within 12 months.[6a] Can Target claim the benefits of Section 337 with regard to any gain realized on the sale of its assets or is such Section 337 treatment inconsistent with the subsequent Fund reorganization?[7] To date, the Service[8] and most (although not all courts)[9] have concluded that the provisions of Section 337 are not applicable to sales to outsiders in a liquidation occurring in the course of a reorganization.

THE REORGANIZATION TRANSACTION

Typically, the transaction between the Target and the Fund takes the form of an asset acquisition (i.e., Fund shares in exchange for Target's cash) meeting the requirements of Section 368(a)(1)(C).[10] All of the requirements for this form of reorganization, both statutory and non-statutory, must, therefore, be met.

Statutory Requirements. Among the statutory requirements are that the Fund acquire "substantially all" the assets of Target in exchange for its voting stock.[11]

(i) *"Substantially all."* The Service's present ruling policy is that "substantially all" means 90 percent

---

[2] Unless otherwise specified, all statutory references are to the Internal Revenue Code of 1954, as amended.

[3] The agreement for the sale of Target's assets is typically negotiated, and in some cases closed, prior to execution of the reorganization agreement.

[4] Revenue Ruling 55-79, 1955-1C.B, 370.

[5] Sections 47; 1245; 1250.

[6] Investment tax credit would be recaptured on the sale of the tangible personal property producing such credit regardless of the fact of a loss on such sale.

[6a] See generally, Rock, 18-5th T.M., *Corporate Liquidations Under Section 337*.

[7] The use of Section 337 as a backstop in case the Fund transaction fails to qualify as a reorganization is discussed hereinafter, at "Effect of Failure to Qualify as a Reorganization."

[8] Revenue Ruling 70-271, 1971-1 CB 166.

[9] See, e.g. *FEC Liq. Corp. v. U.S.*, 548 F.2d 924 (Ct. Cl. 1977) (Section 337 does not apply when transaction also constitutes a "C" reorganization); *General Housewares, Inc. v. U.U.S.*, 78-2USTC ¶9693 (D.C. Ala. 1977) (contra); see generally, Bittker & Eustice, Federal Income Taxation of Corporations and Shareholders, 4th ed. (1979) at §11.67; 14.32).

[10] Although in concept Target could merge into the Fund in a transaction meeting the requirements of Section 368(a)(1)(A), due to the possible contingent and/or undisclosed liabilities of Target, as a practical matter, a Fund will engage only in a 'C' reorganization.

[11] See, generally, Dailey, The Voting Stock Requirement of B and C Reorganizations, 26 Tax L. Rev. 725 (1971).

of the fair market value of Target's net assets and 70 percent of the fair market value of Target's gross assets.[12] It should be noted, however, that the case law is more liberal, particularly where the properties retained consist of non-operating assets and the transferor corporation is liquidated as part of the reorganization transaction.[13]

The prior sale of Target's assets should have no effect on determining whether Target transferred "substantially all" its assets to the Fund. The Service's ruling guidelines refer explicitly to substantially all of the "assets held by the corporation immediately prior to the transfer".[14] The guidelines provide exceptions for pre-reorganization payments to dissenters, and redemptions and irregular distributions which are part of the plan of reorganization. Neither the guidelines nor any other authority, however, appear to preclude a pre-reorganization sale of assets by the acquired corporation where the corporation receives in exchange assets (i.e., cash) of equivalent value.

Whether the "substantially all" requirements create a problem in any specific transaction will depend upon the particular facts, such as, for example, the ability of Target to sell all of its assets for cash prior to the reorganization, the amount of pre-reorganization payments to dissenters and any irregular "distributions" by Target prior to the reorganization.

(ii) *Investment company limitation*. Section 368(a)(2)(F), added to the Code by the Tax Reform Act of 1976, precludes tax-free reorganization treatment where immediately before the reorganization transaction, "2 or more parties to the transaction were investment companies."

The Fund, as a regulated investment company, is clearly an "investment company" for purposes of this provision.[15] Target, however, should not be an "investment company" under the statutory definition because, immediately before the reorganization takes place, its assets will consist solely of cash.[16] Since only one of the parties to the reorganization transaction (i.e. the Fund) is an "investment company", Section 368(a)(1)(F) should not affect the qualification of the transaction under Section 368 (a)(1)(c).

Where, as is sometimes the case, there is some delay between the sale transaction and the reorganization with the Fund, the Target must take great care with

regard to the assets it holds during that period. In order to avoid possible problems under Section 368 (a)(2)(F), Target should limit its investment of idle cash to United States Treasury Bills and bank savings accounts since the holding of these assets will not give rise to "investment company" status.[17]

Non-Statutory Requirements. In addition to the technical statutory requirements which must be satisfied under Section 368(a), a purported reorganization will not qualify for reorganization treatment unless it also meets certain non-statutory requirements which have been developed through regulations and case law. Despite certain overlaps, these requirements may be divided into three distinct categories— (i) business purpose; (ii) continuity of interest; and (iii) continuity of business enterprise.

(i) *Business purpose*. The business purposes for this type of transaction, for both the Target and the Fund,[18] are succinctly stated in Ltr. Rul. #7825045, which appears in Appendix A, as follows:

> "It is anticipated that the proposed transaction will provide the shareholders of Target with a more attractive corporate investment from the standpoint of current income, liquidity, diversification and stability. The Fund's investment of the cash received from Target will enable it to increase the value of its portfolio which will result in a lower per share expense ratio, thereby providing shareholders with a higher yield and making the Fund more attractive to the public as an investment vehicle."

These business purposes would appear to apply to essentially all Dreyfus Formula transactions and, hence, satisfaction of this non-statutory requirement should not ordinarily present any real problem.

(ii) *Continuity of interest*. The continuity of interest doctrine was developed by the courts to distinguish true reorganizations from transactions which, although they met the technical statutory definition of a reorganization, were properly taxable as sales.[19] In effect, the doctrine requires that after the transaction the acquired corporation or its stockholders retain a significant stock ownership interest in the acquiring corporation.

In the Dreyfus Formula, Target shareholders receive solely voting stock of the Fund, the corporation

---

[12] Revenue Procedure 77-37, §3.01, 1977-2 C.B. 568.

[13] See, for example, *James Armour, Inc.*, 43 T.C. 295 (1964); see generally, Bittker & Eustice, supra note 9, at §14.14.

[14] Revenue Procedure 77-37, supra, §3.01.

[15] Sections 368(a)(2)(F)(i) and (iii).

[16] In computing the percentage which determines whether a corporation is an "investment company" cash is ignored, Section 368(a)(2)(F)(iv). Therefore, a corporation whose assets consist entirely of cash cannot be an "investment company".

[17] Section 368(a)(2)(F)(iv).

[18] The regulations indicate that the business purpose test requires merely that the reorganization serve a business purpose or corporate purpose for one of the corporations involved. See Regulations, Sec. 1.368-2(g).

[19] For a general discussion of the continuity of interest doctrine, see Bittker & Eustice, supra note 9 at §14.11.

which acquires all or substantially all of Target's sole asset, the cash proceeds of the sale of Target's assets. This substitution of direct stock ownership interest would appear to satisfy the continuity of interest test as developed by the courts and applied by the Service for advance ruling purposes.[20] Nevertheless, as discussed below, the Treasury Department has raised the possibility that the Dreyfus Formula transaction, because of the prior sale of Target's assets, does not meet the requirement of continuity of interest.

(iii) *Continuity of business enterprise.* In addition to the business purpose and continuity of interest requirements, a reorganization must result in "a continuity of the business enterprise under the modified corporate form..."[21]

Cases and rulings appear to have established the following principles with regard to the application of the continuity of business enterprise requirement: (1) the former business of the acquired company need not be conducted by acquiring corporation after the reorganization (*American Bronze Corp.,* 64 TC 1111 (1975)); *Ernest F. Beecher,* 22TC 932 (1954), *aff'd,* 221 F.2d 252 (2d Cir. 1955); Revenue Ruling 63-29, (1963-1C.B.77); (2) The acquiring corporation must, however, engage in *some* business after the reorganization. *(American Bronze Corp. v. Commissioner,* supra (at p.1123)); (3) In cases where the acquired corporation's business is not continued, the courts may apply an additional criterion—use of the acquired corporation's assets—to establish the existence of continuity of business enterprise (*George R. Laure,* 70 TC 1087 (1978)); and (4) There is no limitation upon the type or character of assets which must be transferred, provided that the particular assets are transferred for reasons germane to the business activity conducted by the acquiring corporation (*Atlas Tool Co.,* 70 TC 86 (1978)).

The application of these principles to the Dreyfus Formula would appear to permit the transaction between Target and the Fund to satisfy the continuity of business enterprise requirement. As discussed hereafter, the Treasury Department, nevertheless, has strong reservations on this question.

Tax Effects of Reorganization Treatment. Among the tax consequences of the qualification of the Fund transaction as a reorganization are the following:

(a) no gain or loss will be recognized by Target upon the transfer to the Fund of cash solely in exchange for Fund shares;[22]

(b) no immediate gain or loss will be recognized by Target shareholders upon the receipt of the Fund shares pursuant to the plan of reorganization;[23]

(c) the basis of the Fund shares received will be equal to the basis of the exchanging shareholder in the shares of the Target's stock surrendered;[24] and

(d) the holding period of the Fund shares received in the hands of an exchanging shareholder will include his holding period in the Target's shares surrendered, provided the shares surrendered were capital assets in the hands of such Target shareholder.[25]

Effect of Failure to Qualify as a Reorganization. If the transaction with the Fund fails to qualify as a "C" reorganization, the Service would treat the receipt of Fund shares by Target shareholders as a taxable event, with the result that gain or loss would be recognized, measured by the difference between the value of the Fund shares received by each exchanging shareholder and the basis of such shareholder in the Target stock surrendered upon the liquidation. Such gain or loss would be capital or ordinary and long-term or short-term depending upon the particular circumstances of each exchanging Target shareholder.[26]

Since Target will be liquidated and its assets distributed to its shareholders, it should be possible, in case the "C" reorganization fails, to structure the transaction in such a manner as to qualify the cash sale of Target's assets for nonrecognition under Section 337.[27] Thus, the terms of the plan of reorganization should be drafted to comply with the requirements of Section 337, i.e., that all of Target's assets be distributed in liquidation within 12 months of the adoption of the plan.

---

[20] See Rev. Proc. 77-37, 1977-2 C.B. 568 (Section 3.02)
[21] Regulations, Section 1. 368-1(b)
[22] Section 361(a)
[23] Section 354(a)(1)
[24] Section 358(a)(1)
[25] Section 1223(1)
[26] Alternatively, Target might be treated as having distributed the cash to its shareholders in a liquidation with Target's shareholders being treated as having purchased the Fund shares for cash. This would result in the recognition of gain or loss by the Target shareholders measured by the difference between the cash deemed received by them and the adjusted bases for their Target stock.
[27] See Revenue Ruling 69-6, 1969-1 C.B. 104.

THE SERVICE SPEAKS—OR DOES IT?

During 1978, the Service issued at least two private rulings[28] according tax-free reorganization treatment as a "C" reorganization in connection with transactions essentially similar to Targets transfer of its assets (i.e., cash) to the Fund. These rulings, however, may be relied upon only by the taxpayers to whom they were issued and do not bind the Service with respect to other transactions, no matter how similar their facts and circumstances. In the summer of 1978 the issuance of rulings in this area was temporarily suspended pending reconsideration by both the Service and the Treasury Department. No further rulings have been issued since that time, and it is possible that the Service will ultimately decide that tax-free treatment should not be accorded under present law to transactions of this type.

Apparently, the Treasury Department is concerned with whether these transactions should be regarded for tax purposes as constituting taxable sales rather than tax-free reorganizations. More specifically, they questioned whether such transactions satisfy traditional notions of continuity of interest, in particular the "remote continuity" doctrine[29] since the Target's pre-sale assets do not come to rest with the Fund, but are instead transferred to an unrelated party. It should be noted, in assessing the strength of this assertion, that there does not appear to be any case or ruling in which reorganization treatment was denied under continuity of interest principles by reason of a prior sale of assets. To the contrary, the Tax Court has held on a number of occasions that continuity of interest was not destroyed by prior dispositions of the transferor's assets.[30]

The Treasury Department also raised related questions concerning the continuity of business enterprise doctrine. Despite the clear authority to the contrary,[31] the Treasury, relying upon cases which focus on continuation of the transferor's business in the context of "F" reorganizations[32] and liquidation—reincorporation transactions,[33] appears to be attempting to make such continuation of the enterprise a requirement of a "C" reorganization.

To date, neither the Service (other than in its two private rulings) nor the Treasury Department has made public its view with regard to the Dreyfus Formula transactions. In the absence of such clarification, and in light of the continuing ruling freeze, taxpayers who wish to engage in such transactions must do so at their own peril. A number of taxpayers, including public corporations[34], however, have consummated Dreyfus transactions on the strength of opinion of tax counsel.

THE SEC SPEAKS

The SEC, in view of the complexity and novelty of such transactions, their significance to shareholders and the conflicts of interest which may be involved, in Release No. 34-15572 (3/1/79), attached as Appendix C, published its views and practices in administering the existing disclosure requirements of the proxy rules in the context of certain multi-step sale of assets transactions, including the Dreyfus Formula.[35]

As stated in the Release, full and fair disclosure concerning the transaction should include discussion of:

(i) *Actual and potential conflicts of interest.* The principal areas of actual or potential conflicts of interest lie in the possibly different tax and estate needs of present management versus the public or minority shareholders and the fact that the purchaser often retains Target's management under long-term employment arrangements. Thus, for example, management may hold their shares at very low historical cost basis while later purchasers may have paid substantially higher amounts for their stock. A tax-free transaction, therefore, may be much more desirable to management than to other shareholders.

(ii) *Reasons for and effect of the transaction.* The reasons for the transaction should include both the reasons for the sale of assets itself and the reasons for the manner in which the sale is structured.

(iii) *Material features of the plan or transaction.* Material features of the transaction should include possible employment arrangements made by management with the purchaser; the terms of any financing arrangements (including the purchaser's financing arrangements with respect to the purchase); a brief description

---

[28] Ltr. Rul. #7825045; Ltr. Rul. #7829097 (see Appendix A).

[29] *Groman v. Commissioner,* 302 U.S. 82 (1937); *Helvering v. Bashford,* 302 U.S. 454 (1938).

[30] *See, e.g., American Bronze Corp. supra; Norman Scott Inc.,* 48 TC 598 (1967); *Ernest F. Becher,* supra.

[31] See discussion herein, at "Non-Statutory Requirements."

[32] "a mere change in identity, form or place of organization" Section 368(a)(1)(F).

[33] *See e.g., Pridemark, Inc. v. Commissioner,* 345 F.2d 35 (4th Cir. 1965); *Home Construction Corp. v. United States,* 439 F.2d 1165 (5th Cir. 1971); see also Revenue Ruling 75-561, 1975-2 C.B. 129.

[34] See for example, Proxy Statement, Camin Industries Corporation, dated August 27, 1979. The relevant tax discussion contained therein is attached hereto as Appendix B.

[35] Under certain conditions, such transactions may constitute "going private" or "Rule 13e-3" transactions, as defined in Securities Exchange Act Release No. 14185 (Nov. 17, 1977), 42 FR 60090 (Nov. 23, 1977).

of the facts which bear upon the fairness of the consideration received upon the asset sale; and the potential tax consequences.

(iv) *Rights of shareholders under state law.* Appraisal rights and other rights which may be available to Shareholders who object to the transactions must be discussed.

OTHER TECHNIQUES

In order to place the Dreyfus Formula in greater perspective, this final section briefly describes other possible "bailout" choices available to principal shareholders of, particularly, private corporations.

(i) *Stock sale.* As discussed previously, this route while incurring no corporate level tax and providing maximum liquidity, may produce very heavy capital gains taxes for the seller.

(ii) *Merger with a public company.* This approach, which avoids immediate tax liability at both the corporate and shareholder level, fails to create diversification and does not provide any means of tax-free present return.

(iii) *Sales of assets and use of personal holding or regulated investment company.*[36] These techniques, based upon keeping Target alive as the investment vehicle, present complex tax problems beyond the scope of this presentation.[37] In addition, operation as a closed-end regulated investment company will subject Target to SEC jurisdiction under its investment company regulations.

(iv) *Use of an ESOP.*[38] Sale of the stock of the principal shareholders to a qualified Employee Stock Ownership Plan permits, in effect, the purchase of the corporation with after-tax dollars, but like any sale of stock, may produce heavy capital gains taxes to the seller.

---

[36] See, *Business Week,* September 19, 1977, Inside Wall Street—"A new route around capital gains tax", p.104.
[37] See, Freeman, "Leveraged Buy-Outs: Cash Company and Investment Company Reorganizations," 6.*J. of Corp. Tax.* 332 (1980).
[38] See, Kaplan and Cowan, 354 T.M., *ESOPS and TRASOPS* (1979).

APPENDIX—EXHIBIT A

INTERNAL REVENUE SERVICE

Priv. Ltr. Rul. #7825045
Department of Treasury
Washington, DC 20224

COPY

Person to Contact:

T:C:R: 1:4

"This document may not be used or cited as precedent. Section 6110 (j) (3) of the Internal Revenue Code."

In re:

X =

Y =

A =

Dear Sir or Madam:

This is in reply to a letter dated November 17, 1977, in which rulings are requested as to the Federal income tax consequences of a proposed transaction. Additional information was received in a letter dated January 5, 1978. The facts submitted for consideration are substantially as set forth below.

X is a corporation engaged in business as a diversified open-end registered investment company. X intends to qualify as a regulated investment company as defined in section 851 of the Internal Revenue Code of 1954. The outstanding capital stock of X consists of _____ million voting shares of $.01 par value beneficial interest, which are widely held.

Y is a corporation engaged in the business of owning and operating _____ Y has outstanding 853 shares of $100 par value common stock and 36 shares of 5 percent cumulative non-voting preferred stock. The stock of _____ is closely held. A, the president of Y, owns approximately 11 percent of the outstanding common stock and approximately 14 percent of the preferred stock. A is the only shareholder actively involved in company affairs.

Prior to entering into the proposed transaction described below, Y plans to sell all of its assets to a newly formed corporation ("Newco") for a cash consideration of _____ million. In addition, all of the Y liabilities outstanding at the time of the sale will be assumed by Newco. Subsequent to the sale, the present business operations of Y will continue to be conducted by Newco.

A will own 79 percent of the outstanding Newco stock, with the remaining shares being owned by several key employees, none of whom hold shares in Y either directly or beneficially. The purchase price established for the Y assets is equal to the fair market value of those assets, based on an independent appraisal. Newco has recently obtained a _____ million commitment from a bank for the financing it will need to acquire Y. As part of these financing arrangements, A will pledge a portion of the X shares which he will receive in the transaction described below. So long as Newco is not in default under the agreements which specify the terms and conditions of the financing arrangements, A will retain dividend rights with respect to the pledged shares. In addition, barring default he will retain voting rights with respect to the pledged stock.

Subsequent to the sale of its assets to Newco, and pursuant to a proposed Agreement and Plan of Reorganization ("the Agreement"), Y will transfer to X all of the cash proceeds from the sale solely in exchange for X voting stock. The number of X shares to be received by Y will equal the amount of cash transferred, divided by the net asset value of X's shares computed as of the close of the New York Stock Exchange on the date of the exchange. As soon as practicable after the receipt of the X shares, but in any event within one year, all or substantially all of the X shares will be distributed on a pro rata basis to the Y shareholders in complete liquidation of their stock ownership interest in Y. It may be necessary for Y to sell a small portion of the X shares in order to provide funds for the payment of expenses or liabilities arising after the sale of Newco. Any excess cash not ultimately needed by Y will be distributed in liquidation pro rata to the former Y shareholders. Any X fractional shares to which the Y shareholders may be entitled will be issued in the form of a fractional share credit to the former Y shareholders' open account on the books of X. Under applicable state law, the Y shareholders will have dissenters' rights in connection with the proposed transaction. It is not anticipated that any Y shareholders will exercise their dissenters' rights. However, if any amounts do become payable to dissenters, such amounts will be paid by Y.

It is anticipated that the proposed transaction will provide the shareholders of Y with a more attractive corporate investment from the standpoint of current income, liquidity, diversification and stability. X's investment of the cash received from Y will enable it to increase the value of its portfolio which will result in a lower per share expense ratio, thereby providing shareholders with a higher yield and making X more attractive to the public as an investment vehicle.

With respect to the proposed transaction, the following representations have been made:

(a) X, Y and the shareholders of Y will each pay their own expenses, if any, incurred in connection with the proposed transaction.

(b) The management of Y is not aware of any plan or intention on the part of the Y shareholders to sell or otherwise dispose of the X shares to be received in the proposed transaction which will reduce the shareholders' ownership to a number of shares having, in the aggregate, a value of less than fifty percent of the total value of the Y stock outstanding before the transaction.

(c) At least ninety percent of the fair market value of the net assets and at least seventy percent of the fair market value of the gross assets of Y will be transferred to X in the proposed transaction. Expenses of Y and amounts paid to dissenters, if any, will be included as part of any determination of Y's net and gross assets for this purpose.

(d) There is no plan or intention on the part of X to discontinue its present business activities and it will invest or otherwise utilize the cash received from Y in connection with such business.

(e) There is no intercorporate indebtedness existing between X and Y which was acquired or issued or issued at a discount.

(f) Y is not an investment company within the meaning of section 368 (a) (2) (F) (iii), this being so whether the test of section 368 (a) (2) (F) (iii) is applied to the Y assets before or after the sale to Newco.

(g) X does not presently own, directly or indirectly, nor has it owned in the preceding 5 years, any stock of Y.

Based solely on the information submitted and on the representations set forth above, it is held as follows:

(1) The acquisition by X of substantially all of the assets of Y in exchange for X voting shares of beneficial interest, as described above, will be a reorganization within the meaning of section 368 (a) (1) (C) of the Internal Revenue Code of 1954. For purposes of this ruling, "substantially all" means at least ninety percent of the fair market value of the net assets and at least seventy percent of the fair market value of the gross assets of Y. X and Y will each be "a party to a reorganization" within the meaning of section 368 (b).

(2) No gain or loss will be recognized to Y on the transfer of substantially all of its assets to X in exchange for X voting shares of beneficial interest (section 361 (a)).

(3) No gain or loss will be recognized to the shareholders of Y upon the exchange of their shares of stock in Y for shares of X shares of beneficial interest (including fractional share interests to which they may be entitled) (section 354 (a)). However, should Y distribute to its shareholders any excess cash remaining after paying its expenses, the gain realized by the shareholders of Y in the exchange will be recognized under section 356 (a) (1) of the Code to the extent of the cash received and will be treated as a dividend under section 356 (a) (2) of the Code (Rev. Rul. 71-364, 1971-2 C.B. 182).

(4) The basis of the X shares of beneficial interest to be received by the Y shareholders (including fractional share interests to which they may be entitled) will be the same as the basis of the stock in Y surrendered in exchange therefor. Should any cash be distributed to the Y shareholders, the basis of the X shares of beneficial interest will be decreased by the amount of money received and increased by (i) the amount which was treated as a dividend and (ii) the amount of gain recognized (not including any portion of such gain treated as a dividend) (section 358 (a) (1)).

(5) The holding period of the X shares of beneficial interest to be received by the Y shareholders (including fractional share interests to which they may be entitled) will include the period during which they held the stock of Y exchanged therefor, provided the Y stock was held as a capital asset on the date of the exchange (section 1223 (1)).

(6) As provided by section 381 (c) (2) of the Code and section 1.381 (c) (2)-(1) of the Income Tax Regulations, X will succeed to and take into account the earnings and profits, or deficit in earnings and profits, of Y as of the date or dates of transfer. Any deficit in earnings and profits of either X or Y will be used only to offset earnings and profits accumulated after the date or dates of the transfer.

No opinion is expressed about the tax treatment of the transaction under other provisions of the Code and regulations or about the tax treatment of any conditions existing at the time of, or effects resulting from, the transaction that are not specifically covered by the above ruling.

Pursuant to a power of attorney on file in this office, a copy of this letter has been sent to your authorized representative.

Sincerely yours,

Chief, Reorganization Branch

Internal Revenue Service

Priv. Ltr. Rul. #7829097

Department of the Treasury
Washington, DC 20224

Dear XYZ:

This is in reply to a letter dated January 17, 1978, requesting rulings concerning the Federal income tax consequences of a proposed transaction. Additional information was received in letters dated February 22, March 3, 14, and 21, 31, and April 14, 1978. The information submitted is substantially as set forth below.

Acquired is a domestic corporation primarily engaged in the operation of a television station and it also owns certain oil wells. Acquired has 410 shares of voting common stock outstanding all of which is owned by A.

Corp. M is an open-end diversified investment company registered in the Investment Company Act of 1940 engaged in the business of investing in a diversified, professionally managed portfolio of municipal bonds, including industrial revenue bonds. Corp. M. is a Regulated Investment Company as such term is defined in Section 851 of the Internal Revenue Code of 1954, as amended. Corp. M. has approximately 67,812,017 shares of voting common stock outstanding.

Acquired has entered into a letter of intent with another unrelated corporation to sell all of Acquired's assets that are utilized in the direct operation of the television station owned by Acquired excluding therefrom all accounts receivable and cash on hand of Acquired. The purchase price for the assets pursuant to the letter of intent is approximately 6.3 million dollars cash.

Pursuant to a Plan of Reorganization, (Plan) and subsequent to the sale of its television station assets, Acquired will first collect its accounts receivable and shortly thereafter will sell all of its remaining non-cash assets including its uncollected receivables for their fair market value. Acquired will either sell its oil well assets for fair market value, or the oil well assets will be distributed upon dissolution in connection with the proposed transaction. Subsequent to the sale of its television station assets and its remaining non-cash assets excluding its oil well assets, Acquired will pay all of its liabilities and will file an estimated tax return. Acquired will then transfer all of its remaining assets to Corp. M in the proposed transaction excluding its oil well assets, if they have not been sold, and an amount of cash to pay the estimated expenses of the dissolution of Acquired. To the extent the cash retained by Acquired is not used to pay liquidation expenses, it will be transferred to Corp. M for additional Corp. M. shares.

Immediately following the exchange, Acquired will be dissolved; the Corp. M shares previously issued to Acquired in the proposed transaction, and the oil well assets, if not sold, will be distributed to the Accquired shareholder in dissolution.

In connection with the proposed transaction, the following representations have been made:

(1) Each party to the Plan will bear its own expenses except that the investment advisor to Corp. M will pay Corp. M's expenses.

(2) Management of Acquired has no knowledge of any concerted plan on the part of the shareholder of Acquired to dispose of more than 50 percent of the stock of Corp. M that he will receive.

(3) Acquired will be transferring in the proposed transaction assets representing at least 90 percent of the fair market value of its net assets and at least 70 percent of the fair market value of its gross assets held immediately prior to the transfer (including amounts used for expenses of the transaction on and amounts attributable to the oil well assets).

(4) The shareholders of Acquired and Corp. M will pay their own expenses attributable to the transaction, if any.

(5) Each party to the proposed transaction will receive approximately fair market value for their assets in the exchange.

(6) Acquired is not an investment company for purposes of section 368 (a) (2) (F) (iii) or (iv).

(7) There is no inter-corporate debt existing between Corp. M and Acquired that was acquired or issued at a discount.

(8) The proposed exchange of a portion of the stock of Acquired pursuant to the dissolution of Acquired for the oil well assets of Acquired will approximate a fair market value exchange. No portion of the oil well assets will be received by

the Acquired shareholder as salary or other compensation.

Based solely on the information submitted and the representations set forth above, it is held as follows:

(1) The acquisition by Corp. M of substantially all of the assets of Acquired in exchange solely for shares of voting stock of Corp. M, as described above, will be a reorganization within the meaning of section 368 (a) (1) (C) of the Internal Revenue Code of 1954. "Substantially all" means at least ninety percent of the fair market value of the net assets and at lease seventy percent of the fair market value of the gross assets of Acquired. Corp. M and Acquired will each be "a party to a reorganization" within the meaning of section 368 (b).

(2) No gain or loss will be recognized to Acquired upon the transfer of substantially all of its assets to Corp. M in exchange solely for voting shares of Corp. M (section 361 (a)).

(3) No gain or loss will be recognized to Corp. M upon the receipt of Acquired's assets, in exchange for Corp. M voting stock, as described above (section 1032)(a).

(4) The basis of the assets of Acquired to be acquired by Corp. M will be the same as the basis of those assets in the hands of Acquired immediately prior to the exchange (section 362(b)).

(5) The holding period of the Acquired assets in the hands of Newco will include the period during which those assets were held by Acquired (section 1223(2)).

(6) No gain or loss will be recognized to the shareholder of Acquired upon the receipt by them of Corp. M voting shares solely in exchange for Acquired stock (section 354 (a) (1)).

(7) The basis of the Corp. M stock to be received by the Acquired shareholder will be the same as the basis of the Acquired stock that the shareholder of Acquired surrendered in exchange therefor (section 358 (a) (1)).

(8) The holding period of the Corp. M stock to be received by the Acquired shareholder will include the period during which the Acquired stock surrendered in exchange therefor was held provided such stock was held as a capital asset on the date of the exchange (section 1223 (1)).

(9) A distribution of the oil well assets pursuant to the dissolution of Target to the shareholder of Acquired shall be treated under section 356 (a) (2) of the Code.

No opinion is expressed about the tax treatment of the transaction under other provisions of the Code and regulations or about the tax treatment of any conditions existing at the time of, or effects resulting from the transaction that are not specifically covered by the above rulings.

It is important that a copy of this letter be attached to the Federal income tax returns of the taxpayers involved for the taxable year the transaction covered by this ruling letter is consummated.

A copy of this letter is being sent to those representatives authorized to receive it.

Sincerely yours,

Chief, Reorganization Branch

APPENDIX—EXHIBIT B

TAX CONSEQUENCES

The Asset Sale Transaction will be reported by the Company as a taxable transaction, with gain or loss and depreciation and investment credit recapture being taken into account on an asset-by-asset basis. Except for dissenters, the Asset Sale Transaction will not result in any direct tax consequences to Company shareholders.

The Company has obtained an opinion from special tax counsel, Messrs. to the effect that the Fund Exchange will constitute a tax-free reorganization and that, consequently, the receipt of Fund Shares by shareholders pursuant to the Plan of Reorganization will not result in the recognition of gain or loss. Treatment of the Fund Exchange as a tax-free reorganization will, in general, be beneficial to those shareholders whose tax basis in their shares is less than the value of the Fund Shares received. Shareholders whose tax basis in their shares exceeds the value of the Fund Shares received will derive no immediate tax benefit from qualification of the Fund Exchange as a tax-free reorganization.

While the Internal Revenue Service (the "Service") has issued private rulings according tax-free treatment to similar transactions, its position in this area is now being reconsidered and advance rulings are not presently obtainable. Thus, the Company will not apply for a ruling from the Service with regard to the tax treatment of the Fund Exchange. It is therefore possible that, upon audit of individual shareholders' returns, the Service may assert that the receipt of Fund Shares pursuant to the Plan of Reorganization was a taxable event. Special tax counsel is of the opinion that a court would sustain tax-free treatment if that issue were litigated. However, no assurances can be given in this regard, and the cost of contesting any adverse determination by the Service would be the sole burden of the particular exchanging shareholder involved.

Provided the Fund Exchange qualifies as a tax-free reorganization, shareholders who subsequently redeem or otherwise dispose of Fund Shares in a taxable transaction will recognize gain or loss determined by reference to their tax basis in the shares held prior to the Fund Exchange, which gain or loss will be capital or ordinary, and long-term or short-term, depending upon the particular circumstances of the shareholder involved.

Dissenters to either the Asset Sale Transaction or the Fund Exchange will recognize gain or loss equal to the difference between the amount of cash received for their shares and their tax basis in such shares. Assuming consummation of the Asset Sale Transaction but not of the Fund Exchange, the Company will continue in existence, and shareholders who do not dissent to the Sale Transaction will recognize no gain or loss with respect to their shares unless and until such shares are sold or otherwise disposed of in a taxable transaction.

For a detailed discussion of the foregoing, see "Federal Income Tax Consequences."

FEDERAL INCOME TAX CONSEQUENCES

The Federal income tax aspects commented on with respect to the proposed transactions are necessarily general and may vary depending on a shareholder's individual circumstances. Any and/or all of the tax positions to be maintained by any shareholder, as discussed herein, may be challenged by the Internal Revenue Service (the "Service"). No assurance can be given that legislative or administrative changes or court decisions may not be forthcoming which would significantly modify the statements and conclusions expressed. EACH SHAREHOLDER IS, THEREFORE, URGED TO CONSULT HIS OWN TAX ADVISER WITH RESPECT TO THE FEDERAL AND STATE INCOME TAX CONSEQUENCES ARISING FROM THE PROPOSED TRANSACTIONS.

Sale Transaction

The sale of the Company's operating assets pursuant to the Purchase Agreement will be reported by the Company as a taxable transaction, with gain or loss and depreciation and investment credit being taken into account on an asset-by-asset basis. Tax deductions and credits previously taken by the Company for investment credit, accelerated depreciation and other items on the Purchased Assets would be recaptured to the extent of any gain on the sale. It is anticipated that because the amount subject to recapture would exceed the net profit, the sale would be a taxable transaction regardless of the structure of any subsequent corporate event, such as a liquidation to shareholders. Management of the Company presently estimates that the Company's Federal, state and local income tax liability as a result of the sale of assets will be approximately $____, which tax will remain the liability of the Company. The Purchaser has agreed to pay any sales, use, excise, transfer or other tax, except for income taxes, which may be levied or imposed with respect to the Asset Sale Transaction.

The sale of the Purchased Assets by the Company will, of itself, have no tax consequences to the shareholders, except for dissenting shareholders. (See "Dissenters" herein.)

PLAN OF REORGANIZATION

The Company has obtained an opinion from special tax counsel, Messrs., that the transfer of the Company's post-Sale Transaction assets to the Fund in exchange for the Fund Shares will qualify as a tax-free reorganization under Section 368(a)(1)(C) of the Internal Revenue Code, and that, among other consequences of such qualification: (a) no immediate gain or loss will be recognized by the Company's shareholders upon the receipt of the Fund Shares pursuant to the Plan of Reorganization; (b) the basis of the Fund Shares received will be equal to the basis of the exchanging shareholder in the shares of the Company's Common Stock surrendered; and (c) the holding period of the Fund Shares received in the hands of an exchanging shareholder will include his holding period in the shares surrendered, provided the shares surrendered were capital assets in the hands of such shareholder.

The opinion is based in part upon certain factual representations, including, among others: (i) that there is no plan or intention on the part of the Company's shareholders to sell or otherwise dispose of Fund Shares received pursuant to the Plan of Reorganization so as to reduce their combined ownership to a number of Fund Shares having, in the aggregate, a value of less than 50 percent of all the total value of the Company stock outstanding as of the closing date of the Fund Exchange; and (ii) that the sum of (a) the Company's expenses in connection with the Asset Sale Transaction and the Fund Exchange, and (b) any amounts payable to dissenting shareholders will not exceed 10 percent of the aggregate value of the Company's net assets immediately prior to the Fund Exchange.

No advance tax rulings are being sought from the Service in connection with the Fund Exchange or the subsequent distribution of Fund Shares to shareholders in exchange for their Common Stock. During 1978, the Service issued at least two private rulings according tax-free reorganization treatment in connection with transactions essentially similar to those contemplated here. Those rulings, however, may be relied upon only by the taxpayers to whom they were issued and do not bind the Service with respect to other transactions, no matter how similar their facts and circumstances. In the summer of 1978 the issuance of rulings in this area was temporarily suspended pending reconsideration by both the Service and the Treasury Department. No further rulings have been issued since that time, and it is possible that the Service will ultimately decide that tax-free treatment should not be accorded under present law to transactions of this type. In that event, the Service would likely seek upon audit to treat the receipt of Fund Shares by Company shareholders pursuant to the Plan of Reorganization as a taxable event. Such treatment would result in the recognition of gain or loss measured by the difference between the value of the Fund Shares received by each exchanging shareholder and the basis of such shareholder in the shares surrendered, which gain or loss would be capital or ordinary and long-term or short-term depending upon the particular circumstances of each exchanging shareholder.

If the Service were to challenge the tax-free treatment of the Fund Exchange upon audit and the issue were litigated, it is generally believed a court would reject the Service's position. However, no assurance can be given that, in the event of such a challenge, tax-free treatment could be ultimately sustained either administratively or through litigation. The cost of contesting any adverse determination by the Service would be the sole burden of the particular exchanging shareholder or shareholders involved. The Company will not set aside any reserves or be responsible for contesting any of these issues.

The Fund is a regulated investment company within the meaning of the Code and currently receives its income exclusively from tax-exempt interest on state and local obligations and capital gain from the sale of such securities. Such status allows the Fund to avoid taxation at the corporate level on any income distributed to stockholders. To achieve such status, the Fund must continue to be registered under the Investment Company Act of 1940 for each taxable year in question and to comply with certain investment restrictions which provide that it must derive at least 90 percent of its gross income from dividends, interest and gains from the disposition of stock or securities and it must diversify its investments. Although the Fund may make temporary investments in taxable securities, the Company has been advised that the Fund intends to invest all of its assets in tax exempt obligations and to distribute all of its net income to its stockholders.

Pursuant to a provision contained in the Tax Reform Act of 1976, a regulated investment company which invests at least 50 percent of the value of its total assets, determined at the close of each quarter of its taxable year, in certain state and local obligations (as defined in Section 103(a)(1) of the Code), the interest on which is tax-exempt, may distribute as a tax-exempt dividend to its stockholders the interest earned on such tax-exempt obligations if it designates such dividends as tax-exempt interest dividends and distributes annually at least 90 percent of such net tax-exempt interest to its stockholders.

Distributions by the Fund of net interest income received from certain temporary investments (such as certificates of deposit, commercial paper and obligations of the United States government, its agencies and instrumentalities) and net short-term capital gains realized by the Fund, if any, will be taxable to stockholders as ordinary income. Distributions to shareholders will not qualify for the $100 dividends received exclusion for individuals or the 85 percent dividends received deduction for corporations.

Any net long-term capital gains realized by the Fund, whether or not distributed, will be taxable to stockholders as long-term capital gains regardless of the length of time investors have held their Fund Shares. Long-term capital gains constitute an item of tax preference, potentially subject to either an "add-on" minimum tax under Section 56 of the Code or an "alternative" minimum tax under Section 55 of the Code, depending upon whether the taxpayer is a corporation or a person other than a corporation. A portion of the net long-term capital gains of the Fund may constitute an item of tax preference to stockholders, and each holder is advised to consult his own tax adviser in that regard.

For a more complete discussion of the tax consequences to holders of Fund Shares deriving from their ownership in the Fund, see the Fund Prospectus, annexed hereto as Exhibit A (pages 213-214).

A shareholder who receives Fund Shares would recognize gain or loss for Federal income tax purposes upon his redemption of the Fund Shares measured by the difference between the consideration received upon redemption and his basis in the Common Stock exchanged for the Fund Shares (assuming the Fund Exchange was a tax-free exchange). Subject to the application of Section 302, if the Fund Shares constitute a capital asset in the hands of the redeeming stockholder,

the gain or loss would constitute capital gain or loss, which would be long-term if the combined holding period for the Fund Shares and the shares is greater than 12 months as of the time of redemption.

APPENDIX—EXHIBIT C

[8010—01—M]
Title 17—Commodity and Securities Exchanges

CHAPTER II—SECURITIES AND EXCHANGE COMMISSION

[Release No. 34-15572]

PART 241—INTERPRETATIVE RELEASES RELATING TO THE SECURITIES EXCHANGE ACT OF 1934 AND GENERAL RULES AND REGULATIONS THEREUNDER

Disclosure in Proxy Statements Containing Certain Sale of Assets Transactions

AGENCY: Securities and Exchange Commission.

ACTION: Publication of staff interpretations.

SUMMARY: The Division of Corporation Finance is publishing its views and practices in administering the existing disclosure requirements of the proxy rules in the context of certain sale of assets transactions. Several proxy statements involving novel, multi-step sale of assets transactions have recently been filed with the Commission. In view of concerns that have been expressed by interested shareholders regarding the adequacy of disclosure, difficulties encountered in the administrative review process and enforcement actions which have been taken as a result of failure to comply with the existing disclosure requirements under the Securities Exchange Act of 1934, the Commission has determined that it is appropriate for the Division of Corporation Finance to provide information to the public about current practices and guidance to issuers in fulfilling their disclosure obligations. It should be noted, however, that these interpretations are not Commission rules, nor do they bear the Commission's approval. The release is being published at this time in order to promote the disclosure under the Commission's proxy rules

of meaningful information to affected shareholders. In appropriate contexts, however, the views expressed in the release may be applicable to disclosures in other filings.

DATE: February 15, 1979.

FOR FURTHER INFORMATION CONTACT:
Jennifer Sullivan, Division of Corporation Finance, 202-755-1750.

SUPPLEMENTARY INFORMATION: Recently, a number of proxy statements concerning novel, multi-step sale of assets transactions ("Sale of Assets Transactions") have been filed with the Commission. Typically, the transaction involves a cash sale of substantially all of the assets of a public company ("Public Seller" or "Seller") to another company, often a private company not otherwise engaged in a trade or business (the "Purchaser").[1] The Purchaser expects to continue the business of the Public Seller under the Seller's name and hires substantially all of the Public Seller's managers under long-term employment arrangements to manage the business. A significant percentage of the purchase price may be borrowed by the Purchaser and if so, the assets purchased are usually directly or indirectly pledged to secure repayment of the loan. Although the Purchaser assumes substantially all of the Public Seller's liabilities, the Public Seller may nevertheless be liable if those liabilities are not discharged by the Private Purchaser in the ordinary course.

In some cases, the sale of assets, if approved, may be followed by an issuer tender offer by the Public Seller to repurchase its shares for cash out of the proceeds received from the sale.[2] The Public Seller proposes, as part of the transaction, to amend its certificate of incorporation to change its business to that of an investment company. The proceeds from the sale remaining after the issuer tender offer is completed are to be invested in tax-exempt securities or preferred and other dividend paying stocks, depending on the Public Seller's status for Federal income tax purposes. Another variation involves a second sale of the Public

---

[1] Under certain circumstances, the transaction may well be a going private or "Rule 13e-3 transaction" as defined in Securities Exchange Act Release No. 14185 (Nov. 17, 1977), 42 FR 60090 (Nov. 23, 1977), which proposed for comment certain requirements and disclosures for going private transactions. See In the Matter of Woods Corporation, Securities Exchange Act Release No. 15337 (Nov. 16, 1978). The Commission expects in the near future to take action with respect to its pending rule proposals concerning going private transactions. Any rules adopted may require specific disclosures in addition to the existing proxy disclosure requirements discussed herein.
[2] See Securities Exchange Act Release No. 14234 (Dec. 8, 1977), 42 FR 63069 (Dec. 14, 1977), which proposed for comment new Rule 13e-4 and related Schedule 13E-4 that would, if adopted, impose substantive and disclosure requirements with respect to issuer tender and exchange offers.

Seller's assets (which after the sale of assets consist solely of cash) to a tax exempt bond fund. The Public Seller is dissolved and its shareholders receive shares of the tax exempt fund.

These transactions are often structured to benefit substantial shareholders in high tax brackets whose shares have a low tax basis. A review of proxy statements describing these transactions indicates that in many instances, the managers of the Public Sellers or their affiliates have had significant equity interests with a low tax basis. These persons are often able to convert their equity interests on a tax-free basis into an interest in an investment company paying regular income. In addition, if the Public Seller is able to qualify as a regulated investment company for Federal income tax purposes[3] and meets certain other conditions under the Internal Revenue Code,[4] it may make tax free distributions of the interest earned on investments in tax exempt securities. Because the Public Seller's managers are often in high tax brackets, they would significantly benefit from receiving tax-free distributions. At least some of the managers also benefit from the transaction because they receive long-term management arrangements with the Purchaser, some of which may allow the managers to benefit from any increased profitability of the business sold. In some instances, they may also receive other fees. These employment opportunities, fee arrangements and tax benefits are not generally available to the Seller's public shareholders, and thus create a conflict of interest on the part of the managers negotiating the transaction, including the price, such that under certain circumstances, the highest price for the Seller's assets may not be obtained.

If the Public Seller becomes a closed end investment company, to the extent that shareholders elect to tender their shares there will be a reduction in the number of shares outstanding and a consequent impact on a non-tendering shareholder's ability to later sell his investment company shares in the market.[5]

With respect to certain of these transactions, the Commission has received letters from concerned shareholders some of which have indicated that they believe that they were not provided with adequate information with which to make an informed voting decision. In addition, Commission inquiry in this area and certain of its enforcement actions have generated concerns and have focused public attention on such transactions.[6] In order to promote the disclosure of meaningful information to affected shareholders, the Commission has authorized the publication of a release setting forth Division views and practices in administering the existing disclosure requirements of the proxy rules in the context of these transactions. It should be noted, however, that these interpretations are not Commission rules and have not been officially approved by the Commission.

DISCUSSION

The following discusses the application of certain items of required information in the context of Sale of Assets Transactions. The specific items discussed are not exclusive and do not represent an exhaustive summary of information required in proxy statements concerning such transactions. In view of the complexity and novelty of such transactions, their significance to shareholders and the conflicts of interest which may be involved, meticulous care should be taken to assure that shareholders are provided with full and fair disclosure concerning the transaction.

A. ACTUAL AND POTENTIAL CONFLICTS OF INTEREST

The Division is concerned that disclosure has not in the past adequately highlighted the actual and potential conflicts of interest presented to management or its affiliates in transactions such as these, which are structured in part to accommodate their tax or estate needs and in which the Purchaser also retains the management under long-term employment arrangements.[7] Accordingly, the Division recommends that in appropriate cases a Special Factors section be included in the forepart of the proxy statement. The Special Factors discussed might include, where appropriate, items such as the following:

(1) Disclosure that the principal shareholders or management may have actual or potential conflicts of interest, and descriptions of such conflicts;

(2) Disclosure of the sale price per share compared to the net tangible book value per share;

(3) Disclosure that the Public Seller may remain secondarily liable with respect to liabilities assumed;

(4) Disclosure that certain officers and directors have entered into long-term employment contracts with the Purchaser, and if applicable, that they will receive increased salaries and/or the opportunity to share in future profits of the business; and

(5) Disclosure of such other factors with respect to the transaction which management believes require particular attention by shareholders in making their voting decisions.

---

[3] See Section 851 of the Internal Revenue Code of 1954, as amended.

[4] Id, at Section 852.

[5] In addition, the Seller's stock may be ineligible for trading on a national securities exchange and, in some instances, the Seller may be able to terminate its reporting obligations under the Securities Exchange Act. Securities Exchange Act Section 12(g)(4), 15 U.S.C. 78l (g)(4); Rule 12g-4, 17 CFR 240.12g-4; Rule 15d-6, 17 CFR 240.15d-6. These effects might, under certain circumstances, render the transaction a proposed Rule 13e-3 transaction. See note 1, supra. However, in connection with a Sale of Assets Transaction, the Public Seller would generally be required to register under the Investment Company Act of 1940, and would be subject to reporting, proxy solicitation and insider trading provisions under that Act. Investment Company Act of 1940 Sections 20 and 30 15 U.S.C. 80a-20, 80a-29. The Seller's registration may be terminated by the Commission on application or on its own motion if the number of persons who beneficially own the Seller's securities (other than short-term paper) is reduced to one hundred or less and it does not at that time make or propose to make a public offering of its securities. Id., at Sections 3(c)(1) and 8(f), 15 U.S.C. 80a-3(c)(1), 80a-8(f). However, most Seller's have indicated that they expect, and would desire for tax reasons, to continue to have more than one hundred shareholders and to continue to be registered under that Act. See Section 851 of the Internal Revenue Code of 1954, as amended.

[6] See, e.g., In the Matter of Woods Corporation, Securities Exchange Act Release No. 15337, supra; In the Matter of Spartek Corporation; Securities Exchange Act Release No. 15567 (February 14, 1979).

[7] In some instances employment and other arrangements between the Public Seller's managers and the Purchaser may be substantially equivalent to ownership interests, making the Purchaser an affiliate of the Public Seller. In such instances, the transaction might well be a going private transaction, as defined in the Commission's proposed rules. See note 1, supra.

B. REASONS FOR AND EFFECT OF
THE TRANSACTION

From a review of proxy statements involving Sale of Assets Transactions, and from information derived from investigations and enforcement actions related to these transactions, it appears that disclosures concerning the reasons for and the effect of the transaction have not always been adequate. Item 14 of Schedule 14A expressly requires that, in connection with a proposed sale of all or any substantial part of the assets of an issuer, the issuer disclose both the reasons for and the effect of the transaction.[8] These terms of Item 14a embody distinct disclosure requirements and are designed to elicit different information. Disclosure of the "effect" of the transaction should focus on the consequences to shareholders and to the issuer if the proposed transaction is approved, including legal effects, tax consequences and effects on market liquidity. By contrast, the disclosure of the "reasons for" the transaction should focus on the reasons management is proposing the transaction.[9] Such reasons are relevant because under state law the Board of Directors generally must authorize submission of the plan to shareholders for their approval.[10] It would be important in this regard to address both the reasons for the sale of assets itself and the reasons for the manner in which the sale is structured. Additionally, it would be appropriate, under certain circumstances, in order to clarify the reasons for the form in which the transaction is ultimately proposed, to also include a brief description of any prior offers or alternatives to the proposed transaction that were considered within a reasonable period prior to the date an agreement in principle was reached, and the reasons for rejecting them.[11]

Disclosures contained in some proxy statements filed with the Commission concerning Sale of Assets Transactions have indicated that management considered their own particular financial circumstances and personal goals as well as the benefits they derive from the transaction, in determining the structure of the transaction during negotiations for the sale. These have included diversification of their investments and the tax benefits discussed above, as well as the opportunity to continue to manage the operating businesses under favorable employment arrangements. The Division wishes to remind issuers of their obligations to make full and fair disclosure of both the reasons for and the effect of the transaction in order to provide shareholders with sufficient information to understand the nature of the transaction and to evaluate it on an informed basis.[12]

C. MATERIAL FEATURES OF THE
PLAN OR TRANSACTION

Both Items 14 and 16 of Schedule 14A require a description of the "material features" of the plan or transaction.[13] In this regard, the Division wishes to emphasize, that because of the conflicts that may exist if management, which may have the interests described above, negotiates the selling price of the assets as well as their own employment arrangements and the form of the transaction, it is important that material aspects of the transaction be adequately disclosed so that shareholders may fully appreciate the nature of the transaction for which their approval is sought.[14]

1. EMPLOYMENT ARRANGEMENTS

The Division believes it is particularly important that shareholders be apprised of the material terms of any employment arrangements to be entered into by management in connection with the Sale of Assets Transaction. The Division suggests that a comparison of the manager's compensation under the new arrangements with his average compensation from the Public Seller during an appropriate prior period be included in order to clarify the operation of the new compensation formula. If the compensation under the new arrangements is, in part, dependent upon earnings, it would be helpful if disclosure also indicates what the manager would have earned under such arrangements, based on the Public Seller's earnings for its last fiscal year, and for a reasonable time in the future, based on stated assumptions with respect to earnings.[15] In addition, any agreement by the Purchaser to make significant capital investments in the business would usually be pertinent. This information also may provide shareholders with some insight into the reasons for the transaction as well as the fairness of the consideration to be received.[16]

---

[8] 17 CFR 204.14a-101. That item provides in relevant part: Outline briefly the material features of the plan. State the reasons therefor and the general effect thereof upon the rights of existing security holders.

[9] See "Securities and Exchange Commission v. Parklane Hosiery," 558 F. 2d 1083 (C.A. 2, 1977). See also In the Matter of Woods Corporation, supra.

[10] See, e.g., Del. Code Ann. Title 8 §271 which provides: Every corporation may at any meeting of its board of directors sell, lease, or exchange all or substantially all of its property and assets … *as its board of directors deems expedient and for the best interests of the corporation,* when and as authorized by a resolution adopted by a majority of the outstanding stock of the corporation … (Emphasis supplied.) See "Securities and Exchange Commission v. Parklane Hosiery," supra, 558 F. 2d at 1088. Cf. "Santa Fe Industries, Inc., v. Green," 430 U.S. 462, n. 14 (1977).

[11] Whether or not the Public Seller had been seeking a buyer or was instead approached by the Purchaser may also be relevant.

[12] As is evidenced by the legislative history and subsequent interpretations thereof, Section 14(a) of the Securities Exchange Act, under which Schedule 14A is promulgated, is intended to promote "the free exercise of the voting rights of stockholders" by ensuring that proxies would be solicited with "explanation to the stockholder of the real nature of the questions for which authority to cast his vote is sought." H.R. Rep. No. 1383, 73d Cong., 2d Sess. 13 (1934). See also, "J.L. Case Co. v. Borak," 377 U.S. 426, 431 (1964); "Mills v. Electric Auto-Lite Co.," 396 U.S. 375, 381 (1970). It may, for example, be useful to show the amount of tax that would be payable, if the transaction were structured to be taxable, by hypothetical taxpayers in various tax brackets holding shares with various assumed bases.

[13] The relevant text of Item 14 is set forth in note 9, supra. Item 16, 17 CFR 204.14a-101, requires, in addition to a number of specified items of information, that the issuer: Outline briefly any other material features of the contract or transaction.

[14] See the discussion under "General" about certain steps that have been taken by some issuers to minimize such conflicts.

[15] The stated assumptions may be hypothetical and need not involve actual projections of earnings. See Securities Act Release No. 5992 (Nov. 7, 1978) 43 FR 53246 (Nov. 15, 1978).

[16] A brief outline of the facts bearing on the fairness of the consideration is required by Item 16 of Schedule 14A. See note 16, infra, for the relevant text of that item.

2. TERMS OF FINANCING

Although the Purchaser assumes the Public Seller's liabilities, the Public Seller may nevertheless remain obligated if any assumed liabilities are not discharged by the Purchaser because of inadequate financial resources or otherwise. The Purchaser's ability to discharge such liabilities depends upon its financial condition and the results of the Purchaser's future operations. In addition, the Purchaser's ability to secure the necessary financing is very often a condition to consummation of the sale. Shareholders should be provided with sufficient information to assess the risk that the Seller will be secondarily liable on debts assumed and the possibility that the transaction may not in fact be consummated due to financing problems. In addition to customary information, financial and otherwise, about the Public Seller's business, such information should generally include a detailed description of the Purchaser's financing arrangements with respect to the purchase and relevant financial data, including pro forma financial statements of the Purchaser. Under certain circumstances, the identity of persons controlling the Purchaser may be significant, especially if they have guaranteed payment of the liability assumed.

3. FACTORS WITH RESPECT TO CONSIDERATION

Proxy statements concerning Sale of Assets Transactions should also include, as is specifically required by Item 16 of Schedule 14A,[17] a brief discussion of the facts which bear upon the fairness of the price offered. In this regard, all factors should be outlined, including where appropriate, a discussion of whether other alternatives were considered or the terms of any recent prior offers or negotiations with respect to any extraordinary corporate transaction, such as the sale of a substantial portion of the Public Seller's assets or stock, a merger, reorganization, tender offer, purchase of stock or other similar transaction.

Under certain circumstances, it would be appropriate to disclose information known to management about any assets the fair market value of which is materially greater than their book value and which are (i) not necessary to the Selling Company's operations as a going concern and which could subsequently be sold by the Private Purchaser or the lender or (ii) to the knowledge of management are material to the lender's decision to finance the purchase price. Such assets might include marketable securities, real estate or mineral rights. Further, since consummation of the transaction is often conditioned on the obtaining of necessary financing, this information might also be pertinent to the extent such assets are to be used as collateral in connection with the financing of the purchase. Material terms of financing which the Private Purchaser is able to obtain to purchase the assets may also have a bearing on the fairness of the consideration.

4. TAX CONSEQUENCES

Because of the complexity of the tax consequences generally and the risk in some transactions that the Public Seller may become a personal holding company,[18] or may not be eligible for the favorable tax treatment accorded regulated investment companies,[19] care should be taken to fully discuss potential tax consequences in a manner that is easily comprehensible to the average investor.

D. RIGHTS OF SHAREHOLDERS UNDER STATE LAW

As discussed above, Item 14 of Schedule 14A requires a description of the material features of the plan and a discussion of its general effect on the rights of existing shareholders.[20] If under applicable state law appraisal rights are not available to dissenting shareholders, it is important that the proxy statement briefly outline what rights may be available under state law to shareholders who object to the transaction.

E. GENERAL

Some proxy statements filed with the Commission have involved plans which included provisions to ensure that the interests of the public shareholders are given careful consideration. The Division is publishing information about these provisions because other issuers may wish to consider their use.

One such provision neutralizes the votes of the individuals who may have conflicts of interest by requiring that their shares be voted for or against the proposed transaction in the same proportion as the votes of all other security holders.

Another provision involves the engagement of a "Special Review Person," who is disinterested in the transaction and has no material affiliations with the Purchaser or Public Seller, to represent and negotiate on behalf of the Public Seller's public stockholders. The Special Review Person may be authorized to negotiate on all matters regarding the agreement of sale, including the structure of the transaction and the consideration to be paid as well as to opine as to whether or not the transaction as structured is fair to the public stockholders. The Special Review Person's conclusions and recommendations are included in the proxy statement.

In addition, some plans have required an independent appraisal of the assets to be sold and/or an opinion with respect to the fairness of the considerations. In this regard, it would be important to disclose all material facts with respect to the fee arrangement and any material relationships between the individual rendering the opinion or appraisal and the company or its affiliates and to briefly describe the factors on which the opinion or appraisal are based, the procedures followed in making the determination and whether the price was determined by the board before consultation with the investment banker.[21]

---

[17]That portion of the item states: To the extent practicable, outline briefly the facts bearing upon the question of fairness of the consideration.

[18]See Section 542 of the Internal Revenue Code of 1954, as amended.

[19]See Id., at Section 851 and note 6, supra.

[20]in addition, Item 2 of Schedule 14A, 17 CFR 240.14a-101, specifically requires that an issuer: Outline briefly the rights of appraisal or similar rights of dissenters with respect to any matter to be acted upon …

[21]The Commission has expressed its concern that shareholders be provided with full disclosure in this regard. In the Matter of Woods Corporation, Securities Exchange Act Release No. 15337, supra.

Consistent with the recommendations of the Advisory Committee on Corporate Disclosure, the Division intends to carefully review proxy statements concerning Sale of Assets Transactions, with a view towards requiring more uniform and adequate disclosures of the potential conflicts of interest and other information necessary to permit shareholders to fully understand and evaluate the nature of the proposed transactions.[22] Issuers are reminded of their obligations under the antifraud provisions of the securities laws which, under certain circumstances, may necessitate disclosures in addition to those items specifically required.

Part 241 [Amended]

Accordingly, 17 CFR Part 241 is amended by adding "Statement of the views of the Commission's Division of Corporation Finance with respect to disclosure in proxy statements containing certain sale of assets transactions."

By the Division of Corporation Finance, pursuant to delegated authority.

GEORGE A. FITZSIMMONS,
Secretary

FEBRUARY 15, 1979.
[FR Doc. 79-6012 Filed 2-28-79; 8:45 am]

ADDENDUM

THE SERVICE REALLY SPEAKS

On December 28, 1979, the Treasury Department promulgated proposed regulations with respect to the continuity of business enterprise requirement in corporate reorganizations. In addition, on the same date, the Internal Revenue Service issued three pronouncements, *Rev. Rul.* 79-433, 1979-2 C.B. 155, *Rev. Rul.* 79-434, 1979-2 C.B. 155 and Rev. Proc. 79-68, 1979-2 C.B. 600 relating to the continuity of business enterprise requirement in corporate reorganizations. For a discussion of the Service's pronouncements see Beller and Brown, "IRS Mounts Double-barreled Attack on 'Cash Reorganizations' with Mutual Funds," 53 *J. of Tax.* 76 (1980). The proposed regulations and the Service pronouncements are attached as Exhibit A.

(i) *Proposed Regulations*. Prop. Regulations, Sec. 1.368-1 (d) provides, in general, that the continuity of business enterprise requirement in corporation reorganizations will be satisfied if the transferee either (i) continues the transferor's historic business or (ii) uses a significant portion of the transferor's historic assets in a business. Prop. Regulations, Sec. 1.368-1(d)(3)(iii) indicates that a corporation's historic business is the business that it has conducted most recently but that the corporation's historic business is not one which the corporation enters into as part of an overall plan intended to qualify as a reorganization. The proposed regulations contain five examples designed to illustrate the circumstances in which the continuity of business enterprise requirement will and will not be satisfied. Prop. Regulations, Sec. 1.368-1(d)(1) provides that the rules set forth in the proposed regulations are to

have prospective application only and, therefore, are limited to transfers occurring more than 30 days following the date the final regulations are published as a Treasury Decision in the Federal Register.

These proposed regulations have generated a substantial amount of comment. See, New York State Bar Association Tax Section, *Report on Proposed Regulations on Continuity of Business Enterprise in Corporate Reorganizations* (1980). The principal objection to the proposed regulations relates to the excessive scope of the regulations and their effect on transactions the proposed regulations are, presumably, not intended to apply to. At the present time, it appears that the final form of the regulations will deny reorganization treatment to an acquisition of Target by an investment company where the principal asset of Target is cash. Where, however, the Target has sold its assets and has acquired a portfolio of securities prior to a merger, a more difficult legal question is presented. Example (3) of the proposed regulations indicates that as long as a merger with an investment company is part of an overall plan, the passage of time between the sale of assets and merger with an investment company will not satisfy the continuity of business enterprise requirement even though a portfolio of securities is acquired in the interim period.

(ii) *IRS Pronouncements*. The Service issued two revenue rulings and a revenue procedure as described below.

(I) *Rev. Rul. 79-434. Rev. Rul.* 79-434 involved a situation in which a corporation engaged in the manufacturing business sold all of its assets to an unrelated

---

[22]The Advisory Committee on Corporate Disclosure ("Advisory Committee"), in its report to the Securities and Exchange Commission, urged the Commission to direct its staff, particularly in matters involving possible conflicts of interests, to review proxy statements more closely in order to obtain better and more uniform disclosures with respect to proposals which may substantially affect the interest of shareholders. Report of the Advisory Committee on Corporate Disclosure to the Securities and Exchange Commission, Committee Print 95-29, House Committee on Interstate and Foreign Commerce, 95th Cong., 1st Sess., Nov. 3, 1977, at pp. 399, 416. With respect to anti-takeover or similar proposals which were of particular concern to the Advisory Committee.

corporation for cash. The ruling specifically states that the sale was made in anticipation of the corporation's being acquired by a regulated investment company. Pursuant to an agreement between the corporation and the regulated investment company, the corporation transferred all of its assets (consisting of cash and short-term treasury notes) to the regulated investment company in exchange for shares of the regulated investment company. Thereafter, the corporation was liquidated and the shares of the regulated investment company were distributed to the corporation's shareholders.

Rev. Rul. 79-434 held that a reorganization under Section 368(a)(1) must satisfy both the terms of the statute and their underlying assumptions. The ruling concluded that the transaction was a "mere purchase" of the investment company shares by the acquired corporation followed by a distribution of such shares pursuant to a taxable liquidation of the acquired corporation.

Although the legal theory of *Rev. Rul.* 79-434, that the substance of the transaction is a purchase of the investment company shares, may be inconsistent with existing case law, taxpayers should expect the Service to take that position with respect to transactions entered into prior to the issuance of final regulations on continuity of business enterprise. This would seem to be the only purpose of *Rev. Rul.* 79-434 in view of the existence of the proposed regulations, which, if adopted, would only apply prospectively. The author understands that at least one formal application has been made to the Service to apply *Rev. Rul.* 79-434 prospectively only. The Service refused to act favorably on such application.

Whether *Rev. Rul.* 79-434 is at odds with existing relevant case law will in all likelihood ultimately be determined in the courts. On the other hand, the validity of the proposed regulations, if adopted, as a practical matter is beyond challenge. If the proposed regulations are adopted, the courts will, however, be called upon to interpret their language and scope.

(II) *Rev. Rul. 79-433. Rev. Rul.* 79-433 suspends *Rev. Rul.* 63-29, 1963-1 C.B. 77 because it is contrary to the position taken in Prop. Regulations, Sec. 1.368-1(d). *Rev. Rul.* 63-29 involved a situation in which the acquiring corporation was engaged in the manufacture of children's toys. Prior to the time of the consummation of the transaction in question, the acquiring corporation sold a substantial part of its operating assets for cash to another third party. Thus, the acquiring corporation's assets were essentially limited to cash and notes. Thereafter, the acquiring corporation

acquired all of the assets of a corporation engaged in the distribution of steel products in exchange solely for its voting stock. The acquiring corporation used its cash to expand the operations of the steel distributing business acquired. The ruling held that the continuity of business enterprise requirement was satisfied even though the toy business formerly conducted by the acquiring corporation was discontinued. Accordingly, the transaction qualified as a "C" reorganization.

(III) *Revenue Procedure 79-68.* Rev. Proc. 79-68 adds to the list of areas in which the Service will not issue advance rulings in situations in which the transferee corporation does not continue the historic business of the transferor corporation, or where the transferee corporation does not use a significant portion of the assets of the transferor corporation's historic business in the transferee corporation's business, pending Prop. Regulations, Sec. 1.368-1(d) becoming final.

LOOKING INTO THE CRYSTAL BALL

(i) *Cash Transaction.* Where the assets of Target consist primarily of cash from the sale of Target's operating assets, the issuance of *Rev. Rul.* 79-434 makes clear that the Service will challenge the tax-free nature of the asset transaction with the Fund. If and when the courts determine the legal correctness of *Rev. Rul.* 79-434 and if the courts approve reorganization treatment, the use of a cash reorganization may once again become a planning tool, at least until such time as the proposed regulations are made final in substantially their present form.

(ii) *Portfolio Transaction.* Where the assets of Target consist primarily of portfolio securities, the prognosis is less clear. Such transactions are addressed in the proposed regulations, but, as previously pointed out, the proposed regulations only apply prospectively. There is no published Service position with respect to a portfolio transaction under existing law. In addition, the preamble to the proposed regulations clearly states that "no inferences are intended regarding the law prior to the effective date of the proposed regulation." In any event, taxpayers going ahead with this type of transaction prior to the issuance of final regulations must be aware of the possibility the Service may challenge the tax-free nature of the transaction.

Even after the effective date of any final regulations, in light of the nature of the public comment to the proposed regulations, one could reasonably contemplate a greater latitude for such portfolio transactions in the regulations as adopted.

EXHIBIT A

DEPARTMENT OF THE TREASURY

Internal Revenue Service

26 CFR Part 1

[LR-93-79]

**Continuity of Business Enterprise
Requirement for Corporate
Reorganizations**

**AGENCY: Internal Revenue Service, Treasury.
ACTION: Notice of Proposed rulemaking.**

SUMMARY: This document contains proposed regulations clarifying the continuity of business enterprise requirement for corporate reorganizations. The continuity of business enterprise requirement is fundamental to the notion that tax-free reorganizations merely readjust continuing interests in property. Recent developments involving the availability of tax-free reorganization treatments for certain mutual fund transactions require clarification, in general, of the continuity of business enterprise requirement.

DATE: Written comments and requests for a public hearing must be delivered or mailed by February 25, 1980. The amendments are proposed to be effective for transfers made after 30 days after date this regulation is published as a Treasury Decision in the Federal Register.

ADDRESS: Send comments and requests for a public hearing to Commissioner of Internal Revenue, Attention CC:LP:T [LR-93-79], Washington, D.C. 20224.

FOR FURTHER INFORMATION CONTACT: Richard L. Mull of the Legislation and Regulations Division, Office of Chief Counsel, Internal Revenue Service, 1111 Constitution Ave., N.W., Washington, D.C. 20224, Attention CC:LR:T (202-566-3458, not a toll-free number).

SUPPLEMENTARY INFORMATION:

Background

This document contains proposed amendments to the Income Tax Regulations [20 CFR Part 1] under section 368 of the Internal Revenue Code of 1954. These amendments clarify the requirement of continuity of business enterprise in corporate reorganizations. The proposed regulations are to be issued under the authority in Code section 7805 [68A Stat. 917, 26 U.S.C. 7805].

Recent developments involving the availability of tax-free reorganization treatment for certain mutual fund transactions require clarification, in general, of the continuity of business enterprise requirement. The mutual fund transactions typically involve a sale by a closely held corporation of all of its assets and a transfer of the sale proceeds to a mutual fund for stock.

Assumption Underlying Tax-Free Reorganization

A tax-free reorganization assumes that "The new enterprise, the new corporate structure, and the new property are substantially continuations of the old [ones] still unliquidated." Treas. Reg. § 1.1002-1(c). The continuity of business enterprise requirement is fundamental to the notion that tax-free reorganizations effect only a readjustment of continuing interests in property under modified corporate forms. *See*, § 1.368-1(b).

The proposed regulations set forth certain basic concepts underlying the continuity of business enterprise requirement. Continuity of business enterprise requires that the transferee either continue the transferor's historic business or use a significant portion of the transferor's historic business assets. The transferee is not required to continue the transferor's business. However, if that business is not continued, there must be significant use of the transferor's historic business assets in the transferee's business.

The facts of the examples in the proposed regulations are based, in large part, upon administrative rulings and judicial opinions. Example (1) shows that continuity of business enterprise requires only that the transferree continue one of the significant lines of the transferor's business. Example (2) shows that continuity of business enterprise may exist even if the transferee's use of the transferor's assets differs from the transferor's use of those assets.

Example (3) shows that stocks and bonds acquired following the sale of a corporation's historic business as part of an overall plan intended to result in a reorganization are not historic business assets. *Compare, Lester J. Workman*, T.C. Memo 1977-378.

The facts in example (4) are a variation of those in Rev. Rul. 63-29, 1953-1, C.B. 77, although the example reaches a different result. Example (5) shows that a disposition of the transferor's assets by the transferee does not differ in result from a disposition of those assets by the transferor.

If the proposed regulation is adopted, the Service will resolve on a case-by-case basis the portion of a transferor's total assets considered to be "significant" for purposes of issuing advance letter rulings.

Related Legislative History

The continuity of business enterprise requirement described in the proposed regulation is closely related to the separate requirement of continuity of interest. While continuity of business enterprise is determined at the corporate level and continuity of interest is determined at the shareholder level, both are fundamental to the underlying assumption that a tax-free reorganization effects only a readjustment of continuing interests under modified corporate forms.

The continuity of interest requirement ensures that the

shareholders of the transferor retain a continuing interest in the corporate assets or business through ownership of a proprietary interest in the transferee corporation. *See, Pinellas Ice and Cold Storage Co. v. Commissioner,* 287 U.S. 462 (1933), and *Southwest Natural Gas Co. v. Commissioner,* 189 F.2d 332 (2d Cir.), cert. denied, 342 U.S. 860 (1951). *United States v. Groman,* 302 U.S. 82 (1937), and the *United States v. Bashford,* 302 U.S. 454 (1938), held that the shareholder's continuing interest was too indirect where the transferor's historic business was ultimately conveyed to a subsidiary (even a wholly owned subsidiary) of the transferee corporation.

Although the specific result in *Bashford* involving the continuity of interest requirement has been modified by statute (see section 368(a)(2)(c)), it remains true that a corporation may not acquire assets in a tax-free reorganization with the intention of "transferring them to a stranger." See the Ways and Means Committee Report on the Internal Revenue Code of 1954, H. Rep. No. 1337, 83d Cong., 2d Sess. A134 (1954). It makes no difference which party to a reorganization transfers the assets to a stranger. The continuing relationship between assets and shareholders is broken in either case. Thus, the committee report language is also directly related to the policy underlying the continuity of business enterprise requirement.

Effective Date

The proposed regulation relating to the continuity of business enterprise requirement will apply prospectively only to allow the public to comment and request a hearing. It will be effective for transactions that occur 30 days or more after it is adopted as a Treasury decision. No inferences are intended regarding the law prior to the effective date of the proposed regulation.

Related Documents

Shortly after publication of the proposed regulation, the Internal Revenue Service will publish three documents in the Internal Revenue Bulletin. First, a Revenue Ruling will hold that a mere purchase is not a reorganization. Second, Rev. Rul. 63-29 will be suspended pending revision. Third, the Service's list of no ruling areas contained in Rev. Proc. 79-14, 1979-1 C.B. 496, will be amended to include transactions that violate the continuity of business enterprise requirement as set forth in the proposed regulation.

Comments and Request for a Public Hearing

Before adopting these proposed regulations, consideration will be given to any written comments that are submitted (preferably six copies) to the Commissioner of Internal Revenue. All comments will be available for public inspection and copying. A public hearing will be held upon written request to the Commissioner by any person who has submitted written comments. If a public hearing is held, notice of the time and place will be published in the Federal Register.

Drafting Information

The principal author of this regulation is Richard L. Mull of the Legislation and Regulations Division, Office of Chief Counsel, Internal Revenue Service. However, personnel from other offices of the Internal Revenue Service and Treasury Department participated in developing the regulation, both on matters of substance and style.

Adoption of amendments to the regulation,— Accordingly, 26 CFR Part 1 is amended as follows:

§1.358 [Removed]

Paragraph 1. Section 1.368 is deleted.
Par. 2 §1.368-1 is amended as follows:
1. "The continuity of business enterprise requirement is described in paragraph (d) of this section," is added immediately following the third sentence in paragraph (b).
2. A new paragraph (d) is added to read as set forth below:

§1.368-1 Purpose and scope of exception of reorganization exchanges

(d) *Continuity of business enterprise*—(1) *Effective date.* This paragraph (d) applies to transfers occurring after 30 days after date this regulation is published as a Treasury Decision in the Federal Register.
To determine the date of transfer, see §1.381 (b)-1(b).

(2) *General rule.* Continuity of business enterprise requires that the transferee either (i) continue the transferor's historic business or (ii) use a significant portion of the transferor's historic business assets in a business.

(3) *Business continuity.* (i) The continuity of business enterprise requirement is satisfied if the transferee continues the transferor's historic business. The fact the transferee is in the same line of business as the transferor tends to establish the requisite continuity, but is not alone sufficient.

(ii) If the transferor has more than one line of business, continuity of business enterprise requires only that the transferee continue a significant line of business.

(iii) In general, a corporation's historic business is the business it has conducted most recently. However, a corporation's historic business is not one the corporation enters into as part of an overall plan intended to result in a reorganization. All facts and circumstances are considered in determining the existence of a plan.

(4) *Asset continuity.* (i) The continuity of business enterprise requirement is satisfied if the transferee uses a significant portion of the transferor's historic business assets in a business.

(ii) A corporation's historic business assets are the assets used in its historic business. Business assets include intangible operating assets such as good will, patents, and trademarks, whether or not they have a tax basis.

(5) *Examples.* The following examples illustrate this paragraph (d).

Example (1). Corporation P conducts three lines of business: manufacture of synthetic resins, manufacture of chemicals for the textile industry, and distribution of chemicals. The three lines of business are approximately equal in value. On July 1, 1981, P sells the synthetic resin and chemical distribution businesses to a third party for cash and marketable securities. On December 31, 1981, P transfers all of its assets to corporation Q solely for Q voting stock. Q continues the chemical manufacturing business without interruption. The continuity of business enterprise requirement is met. Continuity of business enterprise requires only that Q continue one of P's three significant lines of business.

Example (2). Corporation R manufactures computers and corporation S manufactures components for computers. S sells all of its output to R. On January 1, 1981, R decides to buy imported components only. On March 1, 1981, S merges into R. R continues buying imported components but retains S's equipment as a backup source of supply. The use of the equipment as a backup source of supply constitutes use of a significant portion of the transferor's historic business assets, thus, establishing continuity of business enterprise. R is not required to continue S's business.

Example (3). Corporation T is a manufacturer of boys' and men's trousers. On January 1, 1977, as part of an overall plan intended to result in a reorganization, T sold all of its assets to a third party for cash and purchased a highly diversified portfolio of stocks and bonds. On July 1, 1980, T transfers all of its assets to U, a regulated investment company, solely in exchange for U voting stock. The continuity of business enterprise requirement is not met. P's investment activity is not its historic business, and the stocks and bonds are not T's historic business assets.

Example (4). Corporation V manufactures children's toys and corporation W distributes steel and allied products. On January 1, 1981, V sells all of its assets to a third party for $100,000 cash and $900,000 in notes. On March 1, 1981, V merges into W. Continuity of business enterprise is lacking. The use of the sales proceeds in W's business is not sufficient.

Example (5). Corporation X manufactures farm machinery and corporation Y operates a lumber mill. X merges into Y. Immediately after the merger, Y disposes of X's assets. Y does not continue X's farm machinery manufacturing business. Continuity of business enterprise is lacking.

Jerome Kurtz,

Commissioner of Internal Revenue.

[FR Doc. 79-39594 Filed 12-27-79, 8:45am]
BILLING CODE 4830-01-M

REV. PROC. 79-68

Rev. Proc. 79-14, 1979-1 C.B. 496, provides a list of those areas of the Internal Revenue Code under the jurisdiction of the Assistant Commissioner (Technical) in which the Internal Revenue Service will not issue advance rulings or determination letters. Section 3.01 of Rev. Proc. 79-14 is amplified to include the following:

Section 368—Definitions Relating to Corporate Reorganizations. Whether the continuity of business enterprise requirement of section 1.368-1(b) of the regulations is satisfied if the transferee corporation does not continue the historic business (the business conducted most recently) of the transferor corporation or, when such business is not continued, the transferee does not use a significant portion of the assets of the transferor's historic business in the transferee's business. Rulings on this matter will be issued after the regulations clarifying the continuity of business requirement are finalized. These regulations were published as a notice of proposed rule making in the Federal Register of December 28, 1979. See Rev. Rul. 79-433, page 14, this Bulletin.

Rev. Proc. 79-14 is amplified.

1.368-1: *Purpose and scope of reorganization exchanges. Section 7805; 301.7805-1.)*

Reorganizations; continuity of Business Rev. Rul. 63-29, which concluded that the continuity of business enterprise requirement section 1.368-1(b) of the regulations was satis-

fied where the transferee sold its assets, discontinued its business and used the sales proceeds to expand the transferor's business, is suspended and will be revised.

Rev. Rul. 79-433

FACTS

Rev. Rul. 63-29, 1963-1 C.B. 77, holds that the continuity of business enterprise requirement of section 1.368-1(b) of the Income Tax Regulations was satisfied where the transferee corporation sold its assets and discontinued its business, then acquired the assets of another corporation in exchange for its voting stock, and used the sales proceeds realized on the sale of its assets to expand the business formerly conducted by the acquired corporation.

HOLDING

Rev. Rul. 63-29 is suspended and will be revised after the finalization of the regulations clarifying the continuity of business enterprise requirement that were published in proposed form in the Federal Register dated December 28, 1979. The Service will not issue rulings, in some circumstances, as to whether the continuity of business enterprise requirement is satisfied pending finalization of these regulations. See Rev. Proc. 79-68, page 000, this Bulletin.

PROSPECTIVE APPLICATION

Pursuant to the authority contained in section 7805(b) of the Internal Revenue Code, this revenue ruling will not be applied to transactions consummated before December 28, 1979, or to transactions consummated on or after December 28, 1979, pursuant to the terms of a binding written contract entered into before that date if such terms were in effect on that date.

Rev. Rul. 63-29 is suspended.

26 CRF 1.368-1: Purpose and scope of exception of reorganization exchanges.

Reorganizations; cash and notes for stock. A corporation that was engaged in a manufacturing business sold all of its assets to an unrelated corporation and purchased short-term Treasury notes with a portion of the cash proceeds. The subsequent transfer by the corporation of its cash and Treasury notes to a regulated investment company in exchange for stock in the company is not a reorganization under section 368(a)(1) of the Code.

Rev. Rul. 79-434

ISSUE

Does the transfer by a corporation, previously engaged in a manufacturing business, of its assets (cash and short-term Treasury notes) for stock of a regulated investment company qualify as a reorganization under section 368(a)(1) of the Internal Revenue Code?

FACTS

Corporation X, a corporation engaged in manufacturing, sold all of its assets to unrelated corporation Z for $1,000x$ cash. This sale was made in anticipation of X's acquisition by corporation Y, an open-end diversified investment company that qualifies as a regulated investment company as that term is defined in section 851 of the Code. Pursuant to an agreement between X and Y, X transferred all of its assets (cash and short-term Treasury notes that X had purchased with the proceeds from the sale of its assets) to Y in return for 1,000 shares of *Y*. As provided in the agreement, *X* dissolved after the transfer and distributed the stock of *Y* to its shareholders, individuals *A* and *B*, in exchange for their *X* stock.

LAW AND ANALYSIS

A tax-free reorganization assumes that "the new enterprise, the new corporate structure, and the new property are substantially continuations of the old [ones] still unliquidated." Section 1.1002-1(c) of the Income Tax Regulations. To exclude transactions that are not within the intended scope of a reorganization, the specifications of a reorganization are precise. A reorganization must satisfy both the terms of the specifications and their underlying assumptions. Section 1.368-1(b). Thus, section 368 of the Code does not apply to a transaction that "upon its face is outside the plain intent of the statute." See, *Gregory v. Helvering*, 293 U.S. 465 at 470 (1935). For example, a transaction that in substance is a mere sale of assets is not a reorganization. See, section 1.368-1(b) and *Cortland Specialty Co. v. Commissioner,* 60 F.2d 937 (2d Cir.), *cert. denied,* 288 U.S. 599 (1932). Similarly, a transaction that in substance is a mere purchase by one corporation of stock in another corporation is not a reorganization.

HOLDING

The transfer of cash or short-term Treasury notes for stock does not qualify as a reorganization under section 368(a)(1) of the Code because in substance it represents a purchase by *X* of the shares of *Y* prior to *X*'s liquidation.

The fair market value of the *Y* stock distributed by *X* to its shareholders in complete liquidation will be treated as in full payment in exchange for their *X* stock under section 331 of the Code. Gain or loss is recognized to the shareholders of *X* under section 1001.

ACCOUNTING ASPECTS

CORPORATE EXECUTIVES ARE INCREASINGLY TURNING TO THEIR AC-COUNTANTS for advice at the pre-transaction stage. There is a growing awareness that the accounting aspects of mergers, acquisitions and buyouts are a basic element in shaping the ultimate form of the business combination. Many accounting firms are establishing new services to meet the increased demands of their clients. Some maintain information on active buyers and sellers, screen companies for interested parties, evaluate the pros and cons of proposed acquisitions, review forecasts and their assumptions. The CPA is considered an independent advisor and not an advocate of any particular position.

The basis of financial statements and their attendant accounting policy is basic to understanding what the seller has to offer and what the buyer will acquire. Bertram Frankenberger, Jr. discusses financial statements and the CPA's report in light of obtaining a clear picture of the acquisition. He details disclosures which can be crucial in negotiating or structuring a transaction. This chapter also covers the equity method of accounting, cost and market value methods of accounting, pooling versus purchase accounting, the reverse purchase and how to handle goodwill. Mr. Frankenberger, also delves into matters under discussion by the FASB on business combinations, attitudes of the SEC on disclosure, and the professional ethics of the accountant as an intermediary. There is also an excellent list of references for the reader desirous of obtaining the actual releases summarized in this chapter.

In the chapter by James Needham, the important characteristics associated with consolidated financial statements are detailed for the reader. There is a discussion of when to consolidate, the content of the consolidating income statement and balance sheet, and an actual example is provided.

"Accounting for Business Combinations" is a thorough overview by I. Robert Levine and Richard P. Miller. They start out with several clear and simplified definitions and a bit of historical background. Then follow six detailed sections on accounting for a purchase, financial statement effects, classification of business combinations, pooling criteria, accounting for pooling, and disclosure requirements. The final part of this excellent chapter will help the reader understand some current developments in this topical area. The appendix to this chapter includes the basic accounting rulings and guidelines on the subject.

BERTRAM FRANKENBERGER, JR.

BERTRAM FRANKENBERGER, Jr. became a partner in the international public accounting firm of Deloitte Haskins & Sells in 1970, when it merged with the New Haven firm of Weinstein & Timm, in which he had been a partner since 1961. He is the Executive Office partner in charge of the Mergers and Acquisitions Department.

While studying at the University of Connecticut, where he received a BS, cum laude, he was named to Who's Who in American Colleges and a Distinguished Military Graduate. Upon graduation, he joined the U.S. Air Force, served under the Auditor General, attaining the rank of first lieutenant, and subsequently resigned from the Air Force Reserves as a captain.

Upon discharge from active duty, Mr. Frankenberger joined Deloitte Haskins & Sells as a staff accountant for five years before resigning to become a partner in Weinstein & Timm, CPA's.

Active in professional societies, Mr. Frankenberger has been chairman of the committees on management of an accounting practice and state taxation of the Connecticut Society of CPA's and has served on the Society's practice review committee. He is also a member of the American Institute of CPA's and the Association for Corporate Growth. He has been a frequent lecturer and author and has received several awards for speeches on accounting, auditing and taxes. He is a member of the advisory board of directors of the American National Bank and is a consultant and former treasurer of the Human Relations Area Files, Inc., an international research consortium of universities and colleges.

Mr. Frankenberger serves on the boards of the Union of American Hebrew Congregations, Congregation Mishkan Israel and Camp Laurelwood, Inc. (a community children's camp), the latter two as a past president. He is a former chapter president and active member of the University of Connecticut Alumni Association. He also belongs to the Probus Club, the Princeton Club of New York and the Woodbridge Country Club.

Mr. Frankenberger and his wife, the former Marjorie Green, live in Woodbridge, Connecticut. They have two daughters, Wendy Beth and Linda Sue Reason, and two grandsons, Casey and Dustin Reason.

15

Painting a Clear Picture of the Acquisition (The Important Role of Accounting and Your Accountant)

BERTRAM FRANKENBERGER, JR.

INTRODUCTION

Today, executives are taking a harder look than ever before at mergers and acquisitions as part of their long-range growth strategy. They are asking such questions as: What is the real business purpose of the proposed merger? Would a particular acquisition really fit into the corporation's overall plan? Are the objectives and goals of both companies compatible and supportive of each other? Are the managements compatible? Do the resources and capabilities of the companies complement one another? And what are the financial, accounting and tax implications of the proposed merger?

To answer such questions, executives generally turn to their corporate planning staffs, investment bankers and brokers, legal counsel, consultants, and public accountants for professional advice. These groups and individuals typically work together as a team, bringing together their respective skills and providing management with the best possible information on whatever proposed mergers and acquisitions are under consideration.

The role and services of the Certified Public Accountant (CPA) can be quite important throughout the merger or acquisition process, as outlined below:

Introductory services

Maintaining information on active buyers & sellers

Assisting companies in developing acquisition criteria

Screening companies according to established criteria

Introducing interested parties

Working with intermediaries

Performing businessman's reviews

Comprehensive analysis of a company—financial, operations, management

To evaluate proposed acquisitions, loans and investments

Due diligence review

Fair value study—not valuation

Consulting management on

Transaction structure

Negotiations and strategy

Contract terms

SEC and other regulatory requirements

Post-merger planning—integrating accounting, financial, and reporting systems

Tender offers

Analyzing assumptions

Consolidations

Forecasts

EPS projections

Pro forma financial statements

Analyzing alternatives

Pooling vs. purchase

Debt vs. equity

Stock vs. assets

Lump sum vs. payout

Assessing tax implications

Non-taxable reorganizations

Installment sales

Estate planning

Making referrals for

Appraisals and valuations

Counsel

Debt/equity financing

Private placements

It's evident, then, that companies can very well

benefit from their accountants ... and from thinking through the financial, accounting, and tax issues involved. In its role, the CPA firm, which must be independent of the parties to the transaction, serves as an advisor—not an advocate—and provides an objective view to either the acquiror (buyer) or the acquiree (seller). These services are generally consultative, and may result in formal letters or reports.

Regardless of the transaction's size, the parties involved should consult with their respective CPA firms early on—to establish an understanding of the services needed, the timeframe in which they will be rendered, and their estimated costs. The parties would be well advised to put such understandings in writing.

It is now appropriate to discuss some of the financial and accounting matters that arise in the process of considering a merger or acquisition.

WHAT THE SELLER SHOULD THINK ABOUT

Most sellers other than those involved in corporate divestitures are entrepreneurial—the founders of their companies—and are about to consummate what may well prove to be the only sale of a company that they will ever make. Their companies, and the financial statements, have been, in effect, an extension of themselves.

The principal sellers in a potential sale (or even a public offering) must recognize that a third-party buyer is going to be studying their financial statements as well as their operations and management styles. A buyer will be focusing on the seller's net income, cash flow, and balance sheet.

Sellers should therefore eliminate any unnecessary, non-productive expenses, such as company yachts and vacation retreats. They should rearrange and consolidate any financing through small and complex loan arrangements secured by multiple assets and leases, and eliminate contingent liabilities where possible. If possible, related party transactions should be reduced to insignificance or eliminated and minority interests should be purchased. Also, they might trade any employee participations in income for a profit-sharing plan that can be terminated by the company.

Further, the seller should examine alternative methods of accounting under generally accepted accounting principles (GAAP) that could improve net income and retained equity. One example is the percentage-of-completion vs. the completed-contract method of recording revenues and receivables under long-term contracts. Similarly, the seller might consider appropriate changes in present depreciation lives and methods (e.g., straight-line vs. double declining balance) and amortization policies.

These changes could boost net income and thereby enhance the selling price, while simplifying the transaction design. And the cleaner and healthier balance sheet resulting from the changes could make fewer off-balance-sheet explanations necessary.

The SEC requires most buyers to provide the seller's audited financial statements for at least the past three years. However, under Securities Act Release 4950, exemptions are granted when there is compelling and satisfactory supporting evidence, and when the balance sheet and income statement satisfy certain conditions ... gross sales and operating revenues, net income, total assets, total stockholders' equity, and total purchase price compared to total assets of registrant must be less than 45 percent and meet one of the following tests:

- If none of these items exceed 10 percent, no certified statements will be required
- If any of these items exceeds 10 percent, but none exceed 25 percent, certification of the balance sheet and the income statement for at least six months will be required
- If any of these items exceeds 25 percent, but none exceed 45 percent, certification of the balance sheet and the income statement for at least twelve months will be required

The sellers of most small businesses are not accustomed to developing budgets and forecasts. Nonetheless, almost all buyers want to learn how sellers view the company's future prospects. A well planned, readily understandable forecast, based upon reasonable assumptions, can impress a prospective buyer to the extent that it may result in a much greater purchase price.

ACCOUNTING ALTERNATIVES, DISCLOSURES, AND METHODS OF REPORTING

To appreciate the merger process fully, it is necessary to be aware of ths different methods of accounting available to buyers and other investors. For example, will an initial acquisition of a minority interest in common stock be accounted for under the cost, equity, or market value methods?

On the road to eventual control or takeover of companies, many of today's corporate merger-moguls find themselves acquiring different levels of voting stock. Depending on the degree of their controlling influence over an investee company and the percentage of voting stock ownership, alternative methods may be used to account for such investments and the income therefrom. It also helps to be aware of the financial statement captions and the relevant disclosures made in the notes thereto, as well as the language developed by corporate executives and their CPA's to state clearly and concisely the minimum information required under present day reporting standards.

Sometimes corporate management may disagree with the accounting principles applicable to their industry or business, or with the required disclosures. In such instances, the auditors must include in their report a disclaimer or qualification of their opinion, depending on the significance of such variances from GAAP or the standards of reporting, indicating the financial impact of such nonconformance.

An interesting example of the treatment of disagreements over the disclosures required in a purchase transaction appears in Note 7 to the financial statements of the annual report of Illini Beef Packers, Inc. for the year ended March 31, 1979. This treatment allowed management to express its disagreements while complying with GAAP, avoiding any disclaimers or qualification by the auditors:

7. ACQUISITIONS

On July 23, 1977, the Company, through its wholly owned subsidiaries, Schweigert Meat of Illini, Inc. and Copeland Sausage of Illini, Inc. purchased from Green Giant Company substantially all the assets, subject to certain liabilities, of Schweigert Meat Company, (including its Copeland Division) for approximately $9,079,000. The operations of these subsidiaries are included in the consolidated financial statements since the date of acquisition. The assets acquired constituted essentially all of the property, plant and equipment, inventories, accounts receivable, and prepaid expenses of Schweigert Meat Co. See Note 8 for information regarding the disposal in September of 1978 of the Copeland Sausage of Illini, Inc. plant.

Supplemental pro-forma information for net sales, net income, and net income per common share for the combined results of operations of the Company and subsidiaries, as though the acquisitions described above had been made at April 3, 1977, would be $235,037,000, $284,000 and $.35, respectively, for the year ended April 1, 1978. Appropriate adjustments have been made to the pro-forma data to recognize the acquisitions by the purchase method. The total purchase price was allocated to the net tangible assets acquired based upon their estimated fair value and included no goodwill.

The above information, while required by generally accepted accounting principles, is considered by management as misleading and meaningless disclosure as it is not indicative of the results that would have occurred had the Company acquired these operations on April 3, 1977. The net losses of the acquired operations, included above in such pro-forma information, in the previous year includes significant amounts of corporate overhead charged to the operations by the previous owners. More significantly, however, the reductions made in personnel and other cost and expenses since the acquisition of these operations by the Company are not considered in such pro-forma information.

The generally accepted accounting principles and disclosures referred to herein are those applicable in the U.S. They are not necessarily the same as those that will be found in reviewing the financial statements of a company whose corporate existence is governed by another country.

Therefore, when dealing with financial information about foreign operations, it is appropriate to determine the basis for accounting in those areas of paramount importance. Inquiries should be made of the CPA as to the differences in accounting principles from those of the U.S., and the consequences of any change to U.S. principles.

An interesting example of the nature and disclosure of differences in accounting principles appears in Note 1 to the consolidated financial statements of the annual report of Mitsubishi Corporation for the year ended March 31, 1979:

1. BASIS OF FINANCIAL STATEMENTS AND SUMMARY OF SIGNIFICANT ACCOUNTING POLICIES

The accompanying financial statements have been prepared on the basis of accounting principles generally accepted in the United States of America, other than the principles used in accounting for free distributions of shares at par as described below and in Note 8. In certain respects, effect has been given in the financial statements to adjustments which have not been entered in the companies' general books of account which are maintained principally in accordance with accounting practices in the country of incorporation. The major adjustments include those relating to (1) certain special provisions deductible for Japanese income tax purposes, (2) deferred income taxes, (3) accrual of certain expenses, (4) foreign exchange adjustments, (5) valuation of marketable equity securities, and (6) application of the equity method of accounting for investments in subsidiaries not consolidated and associated companies.

In the financial statements and the CPA's report of a potential buyer, merger partner or seller, certain disclosures are required other than those relating to the historical accounting for assets, liabilities, and net income. These disclosures can be crucial in negotiating or structuring a transaction.

More specifically, the CPA's report should apprise the reader:

- Whether the financial statements have been audited—and which ones
- If audited, whether generally accepted auditing standards (GAAS) have been applied
- Whether the statements were prepared in accordance with GAAP on a consistent basis, or delineate any significant exceptions
- Whether the statements are fairly presented, or why the accountants qualified their opinion
- The date of their report

Many of the more pertinent disclosures are generally found in the notes to the financial statements. Of particular interest to merger participants are:

- The significant accounting principles followed in areas such as acquisitions, consolidations, depreciation, revenue recognition, and taxes
- Unrecorded liabilities and contingencies relating to underfunded or unaccrued pension obligations, litigation, operating leases, employee contracts, capital commitments, disputes, warranties, and so forth
- Major customers (to comply with Financial Accounting Standards Board (FASB) Statement No. 30)
- The number of outstanding stock options and warrants and their exercise prices and rights
- Related party transactions (AICPA Statement on Auditing Standards No. 6, dated July 1975)
- Provisions of loan agreements, including interest rates, collateral, penalties, and restrictions on working capital and dividends
- Status of unused income tax loss carryforwards and investment tax credits

Public companies must include in their published annual report, or in their Form 10K filed with the SEC, information on their lines of business, management's discussion and analysis of summary of earnings and operations (ASR No. 159), and market price of publicly traded voting stock.

Companies with total assets of more than $1 billion, or with $125 million in inventories, property, plant and equipment (before deducting depreciation, depletion, or amortization), must report the effects of changing prices on business enterprises, in accordance with FASB Statement No. 33; this provides insight into management's opinion of the present value of its inventories, property, plant and equipment.

Also, proxy statements can be a source of information on percentages held by controlling interests, top management and their compensation, and other transactions. The monthly (Form 8K) and quarterly (Form 10Q) reports filed with the SEC are helpful in identifying current developments, such as changes in auditors, long-term debt, capital stock, status of litigation, and business segments.

Of particular significance in mergers and acquisitions are cost, market value, and equity methods of accounting; pooling vs. purchase accounting; goodwill and accounting for minority interests, as discussed below.

THE EQUITY METHOD OF ACCOUNTING

The equity method applies to common stock investments and corporate joint ventures, but not to partnerships. Companies holding investments of more than 50 percent in voting common stock are deemed to control the investee, usually referred to as a subsidiary. Fully consolidated financial statements are generally applicable for reporting their combined results of operations. The equity method is not a valid substitute when consolidation is otherwise appropriate, nor is it a basis for exclusion of a subsidiary from its consolidated financial statements.

Accounting Principles Board (APB) Opinion No. 18, effective for years beginning after December 31, 1971, provides the necessary ground rules to be applied in determining the applicability of the equity method of accounting.

In order to use the equity method, a company must be able to exercise a significant influence over operating and financial policies, even though it holds less than 50 percent of the voting common stock. A holder of more than 20 percent of the outstanding voting common stock of an investee is presumed to exercise such influence over the investee in the absence of evidence to the contrary. Such influence might be evident through board control, technological dominance, or interchange of personnel.

For example, Foster Wheeler Corporation is a company whose annual sales exceed $1 billion and whose parent controls only 11 percent of its common stock; the parent accounts for this interest using the equity method. Prominent users of the equity method include Teledyne Inc. and Gulf & Western Industries, Inc.

Under the equity method of accounting, the company with the equity investment records on its books its prorata share of the income or loss of the investee (net of income tax effect). The investor carries the investment as a separate item on the balance sheet, and ordinarily reports the share of the investee's income (or loss) as a single amount on the income statement. Intercompany profits and losses are eliminated until realized by the investor or investee. Losses would reduce the cost of the investment, but not below zero. The investor recognizes permanent losses in value of such equity investments as they are determined. However, a decline in the market value of such investments below the book value is not in itself evidence of other than a temporary impairment in value.

The following are the more pertinent of the disclosures that are generally applicable to significant investments accounted for under the equity method, and found in the investor's notes to the financial statements:

- The name of the investee company and the percentage of its common voting stock held by the investor
- The accounting policies with respect to its common stock investments
- The difference, if any, between the amount at which an investment is carried and the underlying equity in net assets, and the accounting treatment of the difference
- The names and reasons why investee holdings of more than 20 percent are not accounted for using the equity method, and why it is deemed appropriate for investee holdings of less than 20 percent
- The quoted market value (by investment), when available
- For investments in unconsolidated subsidiaries and corporate joint ventures, or other investments of 50 percent or less, that are material in relation to the investor's financial position or results of operations, it may be necessary to present information as to assets, liabilities, and results of operations of the investees in summary form, or in separate statements, as appropriate
- Possible material effects on an investor's share of income (or loss) of conversion, exercise, or contingent issuances of outstanding convertible securities, options, and warrants

An example of corporate disclosure of the accounting principles applied to investment in subsidiaries and affiliates appears in Note 1 to the financial statements of the annual report of Procter & Gamble Company for the year ended June 30, 1979.

1. SUMMARY OF SIGNIFICANT ACCOUNTING POLICIES

Principles of Consolidation: The financial statements include the accounts of The Procter & Gamble Company and its majority-owned subsidiaries. Investments in 20 percent to 50 percent owned affiliates in which significant manage-

ment control is exercised are included at original cost adjusted for the change in equity since acquisition. Other investments in affiliates are carried at cost.

The accounting for taxes provided on the investor's share of the investee's income would depend on the intentions of the investor's management, as provided in APB Opinion No. 24. That is, if management plans to hold its equity interest for investment purposes only, with eventual disposition and potential gain in mind, taxes would be provided at corporate capital gains rates. On the other hand, if management intends to retain its interests for the long haul, with expectations of increasing its influence and/or percentage of control, taxes would be provided at corporate income tax rates, recognizing appropriate exemptions and credits.

No income taxes need be accrued by the parent company, if sufficient evidence shows that the subsidiary has invested or will invest the undistributed earnings indefinitely or that the earnings will be remitted in a tax-free liquidation.

COST AND MARKET VALUE METHODS OF ACCOUNTING

Companies with investments of 50 percent or less in common stock of other companies that do not exert significant influence over the operations and financial policies of their investees generally account for the investment under the cost method.

Such an investor reports as income those dividends received from the investee's accumulated net earnings subsequent to the date of the investment, and reduces the carrying value of the investment to the extent that dividends received were paid in excess of the investee's earnings. Similarly, an investor reduces the carrying value of the investment to the extent of the investee's continued operating losses, which indicate that there is a permanent impairment in the value of the investment requiring such recognition.

The market value method is generally applied to temporary investments in marketable securities carried by investors in their current assets, or by investment companies.

Because of trends toward current valuation of financial statements and the significant number of companies with large holdings of less than 20 percent in other companies' marketable securities, some mention of this accounting method is appropriate. At times such holdings are interpreted, through filings with the SEC on Form 13D, as temporary investments that were not made with a view toward merger or acquisition. Under the market value method, the investor recognizes as income (or loss) changes in market values of the investment and dividends received. Simultaneously, the investor recognizes fluctuations in market prices of the investee's securities as adjustments of the carrying value of the investment.

FASB Statement No. 12 requires the valuation of all marketable securities not accounted for under the equity method at the lower of their aggregate cost or market. Such securities that are classified as noncurrent assets require recognition of the accumulated differences between cost and market as a valuation allowance, shown separately in the equity section of the balance sheet.

COMPARISON OF COST AND EQUITY METHODS

The following illustration compares two investor companies, C and E, using the cost and equity methods, respectively, to account for their 20 percent investment in I, which paid dividends of $40,000 during the year on its net income of $100,000, assuming that Company E will realize its equity in undistributed earnings through dividends:

	Company C	Company E
Method of accounting	Cost	Equity
Income accounts:		
Income of I		$20,000
Dividends received (85% non-taxable)	$ 8,000	
Income taxes provided (50% rate assumed)	(600)	(1,500)
Income from investment in I	$ 7,400	$ 18,500
Balance sheet account:		
Investment—beginning of year	$150,000	$160,000
Income of I		20,000
Dividends received		(8,000)
Investment—end of year	$150,000	$172,000

This example should clarify any doubts as to why investor companies strive to use the equity method for financial reporting purposes.

POOLING VS. PURCHASE ACCOUNTING

A business combination (merger or acquisition) is accounted for as either a pooling or a purchase. The present-day accounting for pooling grew out of the hectic environment surrounding public acquisitions in the late 1960's. Then, pooling was basically defined through its historic interpretation; that is, the "attendant circumstances." As the rules became so stretched the APB was forced to act, and as of October 31, 1970, simultaneously adopted Opinions Nos. 16 and 17, entitled "Business Combinations" and "Intangible Assets," respectively. Two separate opinions were required because the APB could not get unanimity on a single opinion.

Worth noting is the specific date that APB Opinions Nos. 16 and 17 became effective, since one of the major requirements of the latter opinion is that after that date any goodwill resulting from a business combination in a purchase transaction must be amortized over a period not to exceed 40 years. A reading of the notes to the financial statements concerning accounting principles, or goodwill in particular, may help determine whether a given transaction took place before or after the effective date, the amount of goodwill and the amortization policy.

APB Opinion No. 16 provides 12 basic criteria that a given business combination must meet in order for the transaction to be eligible for pooling treatment. Those business combinations that do not meet all 12 criteria are treated as purchases. The definitions are for accounting purposes only and are not necessarily legal distinctions, nor are they the basis for tax treatment in mergers and acquisitions.

Pooling accounting is analogous to a married couple who, from their date of marriage, are equally at risk, recognizing their respective assets, income, and potential as through they were one and the same. Contrast this with a couple who, having married after entering into a prenuptial agreement, are not equally at risk from their date of marriage with respect to their preexisting assets — the ultimate disposition of their assets could be governed by the prenuptial agreement. Such an arrangement is comparable to a purchase transaction, in which the assets and liabilities are valued as of its effective date. The accounting for the combined entities in a purchase transaction, and their subsequent reporting, give no recognition in the income statement to the acquired company's activities before the effective date of the acquisition.

Case studies of merger agreements indicate just how crucial the applicable accounting method can be to the successful completion of any given transaction. For example, the proposed acquisition by Alexander & Alexander Services, Inc. of R.B. Jones Corporation was contingent on A&A's auditors providing an opinion that the merger would be treated as a pooling of interests for accounting purposes.

Further, evidence of the effects of APB Opinions Nos. 16 and 17 on corporate mergers and acquisitions can be found in the W.T. Grimm statistics. In 1970, 6 percent of the reported merger transactions, public and private, were contingent transactions (which would spoil a pooling), whereas in 1978 and the first six months of 1979 they accounted for less than 1 percent of the merger activity. Based on other 1979 Grimm statistics, it is believed that substantially less than 27 percent of today's transactions would qualify for accounting under the pooling method.

During inflationary periods, purchase accounting will generally result in greater assets and net equity, as well as increased future expenses, than under pooling, due to the revaluation of assets, such as property, plant, and equipment in addition to goodwill. Such accounting will also result in higher charges against income from depreciation or amortization of these assets. This could be an advantage for an American Stock Exchange company in meeting the listing requirement of a minimum of $4 million for stockholders' equity following a merger, and make a purchase transaction using stock mandatory for such a company.

From a financial management viewpoint, if a company wishes to maintain a particular historical trend of growth in its earnings or sales, a pooling transaction might be desirable. Under pooling treatment the operating results of both the buyer and seller must be restated in the financial statements prior to the merger. In this way, the two companies are considered as though they had been a single entity from the earliest date that the financial statements are presented.

Another major difference between purchase and pooling accounting relates to the negative consequences of goodwill amortization. In addition to being a charge against future earnings, goodwill amortization is not deductible for tax purposes, thereby reducing the bottom line by 100 percent. It is, however, an adjustment of net income in measuring cash flow.

It is therefore necessary to become familiar with the twelve basic criteria of APB Opinion No. 16 in order to plan corporate development, identify potential acquirors or acquisition candidates, negotiate transactions, and consider the cost of an acquisition. The method of accounting will influence subsequent balance sheets and income and funds statements, once the merger is effected.

The following are the twelve criteria that must be met in order for a business combination to be accounted for as a pooling. Each is followed by the appropriate paragraph reference in APB Opinion No. 16, and some remarks.

1. Each of the combining companies is autonomous and has not been a subsidiary or division of another corporation within two years before the plan of combination is initiated (Para. 46a). (An autonomous new company, that is not a successor to a part of a company, incorporated within the two preceding years and forced divestitures to comply with governmental authority are exceptions to this criteria.)

2. Each of the combining companies is independent of the other combining companies (Para. 46b). (Thus, to qualify, none of the combining companies can collectively hold more than 10 percent of the outstanding voting stock of any of the other parties to the combination.)

3. The combination is effected in a single transaction or is completed in accordance with a specific plan within one year after plan is initiated (Para. 47a). (Amendments can extend the term, as can governmental proceedings or litigation.)

4. A corporation offers and issues only common stock with rights identical to those of the majority of its outstanding voting common stock in exchange for substantially all of the voting common stock interest of another company at the date the plan of combination is consummated (Para. 47b). ("Substantially all" means 90 percent or more. Cash may be issued to dissenting shareholders and for fractional shares, but not in excess of 10 percent in the aggregate.)

5. None of the combining companies changes the equity interest of voting common stock in contemplation of effecting the combination, either within two years before the plan of combination is initiated or between the dates the combination is initiated and consummated; changes in contemplation of effecting the combination may include distributions to stockholders and additional issuances, exchanges, and retirements of securities (Para. 47c).

6. Each of the combining companies reacquires shares of voting common stock only for purposes other than business combinations, and no company reacquires more than a normal number of shares between the dates the plan of combination is initiated and consummated (Para. 47d). (AICPA Accounting Interpretation No. 20 of Opinion No. 16 (1971) states that "In the absence of persuasive evidence to the contrary, ... however, it should be presumed that all acquisitions of treasury stock during the two years preceding the date a plan of combination is initiated ... and between initiation and consummation were made in contemplation of effecting business combinations ..." Board minutes are not considered "persuasive evidence." Systematic purchases to fulfill well documented stock option or compensation plans or to resolve an existing contingent share agreement would not normally spoil a pooling.)

7. The ratio of the interest of an individual common stockholder to those of other common stockholders in a combining company remains the same as a result of the exchange of stock to effect the combination (Para. 47e).

8. The voting rights to which the common stock ownership interests in the resulting combined corporation are entitled are exercisable by the stockholders; the stockholders are neither deprived of nor restricted in exercising those rights for a period (Para. 47f). (A

voting trust applicable to shares issued in the combination would spoil a pooling.)

9. The combination is resolved at the date the plan is consummated and no provisions of the plan relating to the issue of securities or other consideration are pending (Para. 47g). (Thus, contingent payouts are not allowed. Employment agreements providing for reasonable compensation are permitted. Under certain conditions, shares may be put in escrow to resolve pending contingencies, such as litigation or Federal tax examinations.)

10. The combined corporation does not agree directly or indirectly to retire or reacquire all or part of the common stock issued to effect the combination (Para. 48a). (As a result of this provision, the third party contingent purchase arrangement was developed, which was promptly destroyed by the SEC's adoption of Accounting Series Release (ASR) No. 130 in September 1972, as modified by ASR No. 135 in January 1973, commonly referred to as the "at risk" provisions. These ASRs require a recipient of the combined companies' shares not to market said shares until at least 30 days after the combined entities' financial information has been published, if the combination is to be accounted for as a pooling.)

11. The combined corporation does not enter into other financial arrangements for the benefit of the former stockholders of a combining company, such as a guaranty of loans secured by stock issued in the combination, which in effect negates the exchange of equity securities (Para. 48b). (Examples anticipated by this requirement are guarantees of stockholder loans collateralized by stock issued in the combination and the payment of unreasonable compensation or pensions to officer-stockholders of the combining company. The latter action could also destroy a tax free reorganization, if such payments were deemed to be boot.)

12. The combined corporation does not intend or plan to dispose of a significant part of the assets of the combining companies within two years after the combination other than disposals in the ordinary course of business of the formerly separate companies and to eliminate duplicate facilities or excess capacity (Para. 48c).

The financial disclosures required by the AICPA for transactions treated as a pooling are quite different from those for a purchase. The accounting treatment appears in a note to the financial statements, often entitled "Accounting Principles Applicable to the Merger." If pooling is applicable, mention is made of this in the note along with the number of shares issued, without reference to their value, the date of the transaction, and the name of the company combined. Also included are: the pertinent operating results of the previously separate companies for the period combined in the current financial statements, reconciliations of prior period revenues and earnings from those previously reported, descriptions of material adjustments of the net assets resulting from changes to conform the accounting principles, and an explanation of any increases or decreases in retained earnings caused by any change in the fiscal year of one of the parties due to pooling.

Included in the Notes to Financial Statements of the annual report of Alexander & Alexander Services, Inc. and Subsidiaries for the year ended December 31, 1978 is the following disclosure of its accounting for acquisitions that qualified for pooling treatment:

2. POOLINGS OF INTERESTS

The Company acquired 13 insurance brokerage, agency and consulting concerns in 1978 and 11 in 1977 in exchange for 1,558,216 and 1,078,374 shares of its common stock, respectively. The operations of the pooled businesses acquired in 1977 were included in the consolidated financial statements reported in the 1977 annual report to stockholders. The consolidated financial statements for 1977 and prior years have been restated to include the operations of 11 of the pooled businesses acquired in 1978. Complete financial information for two pooled businesses acquired in 1978 in exchange for a total of 116,000 shares of common stock was not available for periods prior to acquisition and have not been included in the consolidated financial statements. Annual commissions and fees of such businesses for their most recent years were (unaudited) approximately $1,150,000. The restated amounts for 1977 include commissions, fees and other income of $18,498,000 and net income of $3,206,000 applicable to pooled businesses acquired in 1978; similar amounts included in the 1978 financial statements for periods prior to acquisition amounted to $11,877,000 and $2,147,000, respectively.

PURCHASE ACCOUNTING

In accounting for a business combination as a purchase, it is important to determine the cost of the acquisition and the fair market value of the net assets received in order to establish the accounting and any goodwill that will become effective as of the date of the acquisition.

The cost of the acquisition is measured by the fair value of the consideration given, or that of the assets received, "whichever is more clearly evident." For example, when cash is paid, it is clearly the basis for determining the fair value of net assets received. However, when liabilities are assumed or issued as consideration, the present value of such liabilities must be determined to establish the cost of the acquisition. The fair market value of shares issued or the underlying assets received may have to be appraised by independent appraisers or investment bankers in order to determine their "value" in such an exchange. In either event, the cost of the transaction would be the basis on which the buyer would record on its books the net assets received.

Included in the total cost of a purchase transaction are those costs directly incurred in making the acquisition, such as accounting fees, legal fees, proxy solicitations, finder's fees, appraiser's fees, and printing costs. Contrast this with a pooling transaction where such expenses are deducted from income from operations during the period in which the business combination occurred. Also, normal expenses incurred in running an acquisition department are expensed as incurred, and are charged to operations under both the pooling of interest and purchase methods.

A different problem arises in transactions entered into with contingent future payments or other consideration to be paid to the sellers. Shares issued that are contingent on market values or security prices would not subsequently change the recorded costs of the acquisition.

Frequently, negotiated agreements provide for payments contingent on future earnings. In these circumstances, the intitial cost of the recorded transaction is adjusted to recognize the contingent future payments when incurred or determined. Most often this results in increased, noncurrent assets or intangible assets, such as goodwill, and the adjustment of future depreciation or amortization, as appropriate, over their remaining life. Should such future contingent consideration pertain to employment agreements, and the amounts are reasonable in relation to total compensation, the additional compensation is deducted during the periods earned in determining net income, and not added to the initial cost of the transaction and assets acquired.

On December 26, 1979, the FASB issued a draft memorandum, entitled "Accounting for Preacquisition Contingencies of Purchased Enterprises," as an amendment of APB Opinion No. 16. The proposed statement would specify how an acquiring enterprise should account for contingencies of a seller enterprise that were in existence at the purchase date, and for subsequent adjustments that result from those contingencies. It further proposes that amounts that can be reasonably estimated for probable contingencies would be recorded as a part of the purchase price, and that subsequent adjustments (except in limited circumstances) would be included in determination of net income in the period in which the adjustments are determined.

The cost of the acquisition must then be allocated to the individual assets acquired, and a determination must be made of the present values of liabilities assumed. These may often be reasonably estimated, depending upon their materiality and the available information on a given asset or liability and its maket value.

Many assets such as property, plant, and equipment are best determined by independent appraisals, as are liabilities, such as pension liabilities accrued and/or vested which may be determined by independent actuaries. Such information, along with known costs and/or estimated costs or values, would be utilized in compiling the fair value cost as of the effective date of the acquisition.

When such purchase costs exceed the fair value of the net assets acquired (the assets acquired less the liabilities assumed), the excess is generally allocated to intangible assets, such as those described in paragraph 88e of APB Opinion No. 16, quoted below. The remaining excess is allocated to goodwill.

In what are commonly referred to as "bargain purchases," the fair value of the net assets received exceeds the costs of the acquisition. In this event, the proportionate amount of the excess is first credited against the noncurrent assets acquired, excluding long-term investments in marketable securities, in determining the value of these assets. Should the excess credit exceed the fair value of the noncurrent assets, then the excess is credited to a deferred account commonly referred to as "negative goodwill" and amortized over a period not to exceed 40 years. The income statements for the anticipated years of amortization benefit from this credit.

Paragraph 88 of APB Opinion No. 16 provides the following "general guides for assigning amounts to individual assets acquired and liabilities assumed except goodwill":

a. Marketable securities at current net realizable values.
b. Receivables at present values of amounts to be received determined at appropriate current interest rates, less allowances for uncollectibility and collection costs, if necessary.

c. Inventories:
  (1) Finished goods and merchandise at estimated selling prices less the sum of (a) costs of disposal and (b) a reasonable profit allowance for the selling effort of the acquiring corporation.
  (2) Work in process at estimated selling prices of finished goods less the sum of (a) costs to complete, (b) costs of disposal, and (c) a reasonable profit allowance for the completing and selling effort of the acquiring corporation based on profit for similar finished goods.
  (3) Raw materials at current replacement costs.

d. Plant and equipment: (a) to be used, at current replacement costs for similar capacity[1] unless the expected future use of the assets indicates a lower value to the acquiror, (2) to be sold or held for later sale rather than used, at current net realizable value, and (3) to be used temporarily, at current net realizable value recognizing future depreciation for the expected period of use.

e. Intangible assets which can be identified and named, including contracts, patents, franchises, customer and supplier lists, and favorable leases, at appraised values.[2]

f. Other assets, including land, natural resources, and non-marketable securities, at appraised values.

g. Accounts and notes payable, long-term debt, and other claims payable at present values of amounts to be paid determined at appropriate current interest rates.

h. Liabilities and accruals—for example, accruals for pension costs,[3] warranties, vacation pay, deferred compensation—at present values of amounts to be paid determined at appropriate current interest rates.

i. Other liabilities and commitments, including unfavorable leases, contracts, and commitments and plant closing expense incident to the acquisition, at present values of amounts to be paid determined at appropriate current interest rates.

A buyer would not record the goodwill existing on the books of the seller, or recognize deferred income taxes. In line with fair value concepts at the time of the

acquisition, the goodwill is revalued and the actual liability for income taxes (such as investment credit recapture) is redetermined as of that date.

In a purchase transaction, the principal differences in disclosure from those required in a pooling are that the notes to the financial statements provide the cost of the acquired company, the description of the plan for amortization of acquired goodwill (if any), and the method and period of amortization. The notes also state the period for which the results of operations of the seller are included in the income statement of the buyer, along with the description of any contingent payments or commitments and their proposed accounting treatment.

Usually, the only opportunity for a buyer to disclose the results of operations of a seller, on a pro forma comparative basis for the current period and the preceding period, is in the notes to the financial statements in the year of acquisition. Such results at a minimum include revenues, income before extraordinary items, net income, and earnings per share.

The following note from the annual report of Elco Industries, Inc. for the year ended June 30, 1979 is representative of the disclosures required in a purchase transaction. However, because many different combinations of consideration may be issued, other disclosures may be needed, depending upon the nature of the consideration.

ACQUISITION OF BUSINESS

On November 1, 1978, the Company acquired the operating assets and business of Acme Rivet and Machine Corp. and affiliated companies ("Acme"). Acme has operations in Bristol, Connecticut and Ridgefield, New Jersey and is a full-line manufacturer and supplier of tubular rivets and related rivet setting machines, selling primarily to original equipment manufacturers to markets including appliances, electrical components, leather goods, and transportation equipment. The purchase price of approximately $12,000,000 included approximately $11,000,000 in cash and 57,142 shares of the Company's common stock, $5 par value. The acquisition has been accounted for as a purchase. The excess of cost over assets acquired is being amortized over 39 years on the straight line

---

[1]Replacement cost may be determined directly if a used asset market exists for the assets acquired. Otherwise, the replacement cost should be approximated from replacement cost new less estimated accumulated depreciation.

[2]Fair values should be ascribed to specific assets; identifiable assets should not be included in goodwill.

[3]An accrual for pension cost should be the greater of (1) accrued pension cost computed in conformity with the accounting policies of the acquiring corporation for one or more of its pension plans or (2) the excess, if any, of the actuarially computed value of vested benefits over the amount of the pension fund.

method. The accompanying financial statements include the operations and assets of this business since acquisition. Unaudited pro-forma results of operations for the fiscal years ended June 30, 1979 and 1978, assuming the purchase had taken place on July 1, 1977 are as follows:

	1979	1978
Net sales	$94,331,000	$82,493,000
Net earnings	4,228,000	4,313,000
Net earnings per common share	3.42	3.51

THE REVERSE PURCHASE

Those business combinations commonly referred to as "back-door" listings, like some other transactions, are fertile grounds for possible reverse purchase treatment. APB Opinion No. 16 devotes paragraphs 70 and 71 to this subject. The seller is usually the surviving corporation, as the combination results in issuing a controlling interest in the seller's shares in exchange for assets or shares of the "buyer." Reference must be made to the negotiated agreements and the circumstances to determine which entity is, in fact, the buyer, generally defined as the recipient of the greater portion of the voting rights of the combined corporation.

The significant factor in the reverse purchase is the determination of which entity's net assets are to be valued. For instead of the underlying assets of the company acquired being valued by the surviving entity, the assets of the surviving entity, deemed to be the acquiree, are revalued as of the effective date of the acquisition. Also, in such transactions there may be significant differences between the book and tax accounting attributable to the valuation of the surviving entity's assets, without any change in the tax basis of the acquiree's assets.

The following is a summary of some of the principal differences in pooling and purchase accounting practices:

	Pooling	**Purchase**
Assets	Basis carried forward	Adjusted to purchase cost on the basis of fair market values
Liabilities	Basis carried forward	Adjusted to fair market values
Valuation reserves	Basis carried forward	Eliminated
Net worth	Total carried forward	Eliminated or replaced by fair market value of equity securities issued
Revenues and expenses:		
Amount	Basis carried forward	Adjusted to reflect revised basis of assets and liabilities
Period	Retroactive restatement	From date of acquisition
Disclosures	Details of transaction and effect of restatement on current and prior period's revenues, extraordinary items, net income, and stockholders' equity	Details of transaction, goodwill amortization, and pro forma earnings for current and prior years
Costs of acquisition	Charged to expense	Capitalized as cost of assets acquired

GOODWILL

The goodwill as determined in a purchase transaction must be amortized over a period not in excess of 40 years in accordance with APB Opinion No. 17. Of particular significance to buyers is the fact that the amortization of goodwill is not tax deductible. Therefore, in taxable transactions, buyers may go to great extremes to reallocate costs in excess of net assets received to other assets whose depreciation or amortization is deductible.

A current trend in financial reporting is to refer to goodwill under other terminology, such as the "Excess of Cost Over Net Assets of Businesses Purchased."

The Clorox Company's annual report for the year ended June 30, 1979, Note to Consolidated Financial

Statements, includes an example of accounting for goodwill acquired both prior and subsequent to October 31, 1970:

1. SUMMARY OF SIGNIFICANT ACCOUNTING POLICIES

Goodwill represents the excess of the purchase prices over the values ascribed to net assets at dates of acquisition of businesses purchased. Goodwill arising from transactions after October 31, 1970 is amortized ($261,000 in 1979 and $23,000 in 1978) over the period of expected benefit, not exceeding 40 years. Goodwill ($42,118,000) arising from transactions prior to such date is not being amortized, since in the opinion of management there has been no reduction in the value of these assets.

While the life of goodwill depends on the facts and circumstances of each case, such as life cycle of the business or maturity of product, the following are some examples of lives ascribed to purchase transactions with a description of the industry of the acquiree:

Year of Acquisition	Acquiror (Acquiree)	Amount of Goodwill (000's)	Industry of Acquiree
	10-Year Amortization		
1976	United Technologies Corporation (Otis Elevator Company)	$5,000	Manufacturer of elevators
1976	Coleman Company (Coast Catamaran Corporation and Rand Manufacturing Company)	2,332	Manufacturers of sailboats and water skis
	20-Year Amortization		
1978	Lionel Corporation (P&M Distributors Inc.)	855	Retail toy stores
1978	Amsted Industries (Henry Pratt Company)	14,888	Manufacturer of valves and fluid control devices
	25-Year Amortization		
1978	United Technologies Corporation (Ambac Industries)	92,000	Manufacturer of scientific, medical, and environmental instruments; diesel and fluid power, electrical, industrial, and electronic products
1977	Tannetics, Inc. (Vacation Industries, Inc.)	2,079	Manufacturer of recreational vehicles
	30-to 40-Year Amortization		
1978	Angelica Corporation (Linen Systems for Hospitals, Inc.)	1,100	Renting of linens, uniforms, and other textile supplies
1976	Itel Corporation (Autex, Inc., Computer Dimensions, Inc.)	8,900	Information systems and data processing services
	40-Year Amortization		
1979	Trans World Corporation (Century 21 Real Estate Corporation)	75,997	Realty franchiser
1979	Trans World Corporation (Spartan Food Systems, Inc.)	44,753	Fast food restaurants
1978	The Clorox Company (Moore's Food Products, S.A., Casamitjana Mensa and Duraflame Inc.)	9,373	Processor of frozen foods and manufacturer of bleach and fireplace logs
1978	Eaton Corporation (Cutler Hammer, Samuel Moore, and Kenway)	42,900	Manufacturers of electronics and electrical equipment, fiber reinforced pressure hose, nylon tubing, and radiation chemistry; computer software

Year of Acquisi- tion	Acquiror (Acquiree)	Amount of Goodwill (000's)	Industry of Acquiree
1978	Meredith Corporation (WPCH, Suburban Newspaper Publications, WPGH, etc.)	Unknown	Radio and TV stations and newspapers
1978	Northern Telecom Limited (Data 100)	Unknown	Manufacturer of terminal systems
1976	American Brands, Inc. (Acushnet Company)	1,112	Manufacturer of golf equipment and molded rubber products
1974	National Distributing Company, Inc. (Alfred Hart Company, The Milford Company of California)	1,714	Liquor distributors
1974	Ward Foods, Inc. (La Crosse Milling Company)	864	Milling of grain
1973	Cooper Industries (Southwest Airmotive Company)	3,200	Servicing and distribution of aircraft parts

The consistent usage of 40-year amortization is attributable to the fact that companies are reluctant to reduce their earnings per share by increasing this non-deductible charge against net income, particularly when the life is not otherwise objectively measurable.

It is essential to review goodwill on a continuous basis, and to adjust the amortization period as appropriate. Faddish products, such as hula hoops or water beds, might warrant very short lives. The life of goodwill might be influenced by changing governmental regulations, e.g., restrictions on the importation of a particular product, increased duty rates, and new technologies—all of which can affect sales and net earnings significantly.

From an accounting viewpoint, goodwill does not arise from internally developed intangibles, such as advertising campaigns and money expended for employee training.

FUTURE OF POOLING AND PURCHASE ACCOUNTING

Under consideration by the FASB since August 1976 is its Discussion Memorandum on ''Accounting for Business Combinations and Purchased Intangibles.'' Following the completion by the FASB of its ''conceptual framework'' project, it will reconsider this Memorandum and the future treatment of pooling and purchase accounting. Special attention will be given to such matters as whether to permit pooling, whether the buyers or sellers or both should be revalued at the time of the acquisition, goodwill and its amortization, problems arising in business combinations due to differences in foreign accounting principles, and the treatment of the cost of the transaction.

Further influencing the FASB's deliberations on this Memorandum will be the general acceptance of accounting for inflation and changing prices.

MINORITY INTERESTS

One of the significant aspects of minority interests in subsidiaries is the fact that in most instances such interests are insignificant. A ''significant'' minority interest has been interpreted by the AICPA in its Interpretation No. 24 of APB Opinion No. 16 as a holding of 20 percent or more of the voting common stock of a subsidiary by persons not affiliated with the parent company. Generally speaking, a minority interest is an equity in a subsidiary held by another entity not affiliated with the parent company; it is an obligation to shareholders other than those controlling the consolidated entity. However, regardless of their size, such outside interests must be dealt with in the negotiation process or provided for in the agreements, as basically this will represent a claim by outsiders in any potential transaction.

The acquisition of a minority interest in a subsidiary, whether by the parent, the subsidiary itself, or even another affiliate, requires that the transaction be accounted for under the purchase method. Paragraph 99 of APB Opinion No. 16 does provide certain relief under ''grandfather'' provisions for certain minority interests, as does FASB Statement No. 10, issued in October 1975.

Should the minority interests in a subsidiary be so large in relation to the equity of the parent company's shareholders in its consolidated net assets, a presentation of separate financial statements for the parent and the subsidiary is appropriate. And should a subsidiary incur losses applicable to the minority interest that exceed the minority interest in the equity capital of the subsidiary, then such excess and any further losses applicable to the minority interest would be charged against the majority interest, since there is no obligation for the minority shareholders to make good on such losses.

An unusual example of corporate disclosure concerning the accounting for a 25 percent minority interest, solely attributable to its insignificance, appears in Outboard Marine Corporation's annual report in Note 2 to the consolidated financial statements for the year ended September 30, 1979:

2. BASIS OF CONSOLIDATION

The accounts of all subsidiaries are included in the Consolidated Financial Statements. Intercompany accounts, transactions and earnings have been eliminated in consolidation. All subsidiary companies are wholly owned except Outboard Marine Australia Pty. Limited which is 75 percent owned; the minority interest in this subsidiary's earnings and stockholders' investment is included in other expense and other accounts payable in the Consolidated Financial Statements. The amounts included in other expense are $568,000 and $606,000 in 1979 and 1978, respectively. The amounts included in other accounts payable are $3,196,000 and $2,854,000 at September 30, 1979 and 1978, respectively.

BUSINESSMAN'S REVIEWS

The SEC's "full disclosure" demands, high interest levels coupled with banking restraints on acquisition loans, and increasing shareholder litigation have escalated pressure on officers and directors to exercise greater due diligence in carrying out their corporate responsibilities. And hardly any area of business decisions is so fraught with danger signals as that of mergers and acquisitions or corporate divestitures. As a result, corporate officers and directors are seeking the outside expertise of independent consultants, while strengthening their own internal management reviews.

A Businessman's Review (BMR), sometimes referred to as a preacquisition review or investigation, is a comprehensive analysis of a company's organization, business components, operations, finances, and other matters that a potential buyer or seller might want to know about in making a decision. The BMR is not an audit, but instead a broad scale investigation of a company's business affairs. Should certain auditing services be required, such as confirming accounts receivable balances or observing inventories, they can be provided by independent CPAs.

In order to establish the scope of a BMR, coordinate it, and determine the participants and their roles, management should appoint a team or committee. The committee's responsibility should include determining the scope of the work to be performed, the information to be obtained, the outside consultants' required services, and which firms should be engaged.

Depending on the size of a buyer, the committee may consist of executives representing operations, finance, legal, corporate development, marketing, personnel or other areas affected by the proposed transaction. Consultants to the committee normally include corporate counsel, appraisers, investment bankers, CPAs, and marketing or management consultants. It is crucial that management designate a quarterback to coordinate the activities of the committee. One of the principal responsibilities of the coordinator is to ensure that the duties assigned to the committee members, including outside consultants, are put in writing. In so doing, all persons involved will have a clear understanding of their respective duties and the expected time frame necessary to complete the review.

The breadth of an independent CPA's participation in the review depends on the size of the transaction, the geographic sphere of operations of the company under review, as well as the qualifications of the buyer's internal staff to participate in the review and their availability. However, there is a minimum at which the outside CPAs should function. For example, most corporate executives expect theirs CPAs to review the:

- Proposed agreement and related commitments
- Financial statements for the past three years and interim statements to date
- Financial forecasts and budgets
- Federal and state income tax returns for the past three years
- Internal accounting controls and procedures
- Auditor's working papers for the most recent examination

In addition, some corporate executives want their CPAs to perform specific auditing procedures with respect to certain balance sheet assets or liabilities, or operating units. Others may want their CPAs to perform special industry studies or visit certain facilities. Depending on the nature of the underlying business, special analyses or queries are sometimes appropriate in relation to sales distribution, source of materials, the influence of inflation on sales or gross profit, and the like. More often than not, special studies of the tax aspects of the transaction are warranted, particularly as to the adequacy of the accruals or reserves.

Of paramount importance is the timing of the BMR. If possible, a limited portion of the BMR might even be performed before executing a letter of intent. In any event, a buyer should commence the BMR before all of the final terms are agreed on and, if possible, before the contract is executed. With the information derived from the BMR, the negotiating team may be able to make provisions in the agreement for any problem areas uncovered, and for adjusting the cost of the acquisition.

The degree of confidentiality required by a seller can also influence the timing of the BMR. In fact, because of the demand on the part of most sellers for extreme confidentiality, they would generally prefer to explain the presence of a CPA firm, as opposed to explaining that of a senior executive of another company. The reliability of a seller's information and the likelihood that a transaction will close might also influence the timing of the BMR. In the latter case, a buyer may want to terminate negotiations before the BMR is completed.

Another factor affecting the timing of the BMR or its segments is the extent of pressure to complete the BMR within a predetermined period. The review team may wish to get as much of a head start as possible. A review can take as little as a few days or as long as several weeks or even months, depending on the cooperation of the seller, the extent of the information required, the complexity of the financial structure of the company under review, and the scope of the seller's operations. In any event, the BMR should be performed in stages, with the matters that the buyer considers to be of most significance tackled first. This will serve to reduce the expense of the BMR, and the stress on the negotiating parties, if the transaction is aborted early in light of the results.

To gain real insight into the seller's affairs, and to surface any previously unrecognized liabilities, it is important to take a close look at various contracts, agreements, and other business and financial documents. These might include:

Corporate: Articles of incorporation; minutes of meetings of stockholders and the Board of Directors and its committees; house counsel's files, including those pertaining to litigation and regulatory matters
Accounting: Internal auditor reports; management letters of independent auditors; purchasing/sales contracts; agreements with related parties
Finance: Lines of credit; loan agreements; guarantees
Imports/Exports: Certificates of customs quotas; letters of credit
Marketing: Agreements with manufacturer's representatives; licensing agreements; salesmen commission plans; advertising contracts; warranty policies

Personnel: Executive compensation plans; employment contracts; profit-sharing and stock option plans; pension plans; union agreements
Plant and Equipment: Leases; property tax records; appraisals
Regulatory: Filings with government agencies (SEC, FTC, ICC, HEW, and so forth); currency restrictions
Taxes: Federal and state income tax returns; ruling requests; revenue agent reports

It is essential that a BMR determine whether a seller's accounting policies are being applied properly and consistently—that is, to make sure that assets are not inflated or liabilities understated by any unusual accounting techniques. Also, an analysis of seller's earnings should include a review of sales and income, justification for any deferred costs, and provision for adjustments of unusual or nonrecurring transactions. An attempt should be made to reconstruct the income statement to recognize seller's status as a separate operating entity, adjusting for operations to be discontinued, changes in interest rates, and other matters resulting from the transfer of ownership.

The underlying assumptions on which projections are based deserve a hard look. The CPA should determine the reasonableness of revenue growth, interest rates, inflation factors, raw material costs, inventory turnover, labor costs, and general and administrative expenses, and consider the consistency of the forecast from year to year—not only as to the accounting principles involved but also as to comparability.

In addition, the CPA should compare the related historical operating results with past projections and budgets as well as capital expenditures and, when appropriate, apply a correlation factor to current projections. Moreover, it is important to factor into a seller's financial forecasts and cash flows the proposed operational changes, goodwill amortization, depreciation changes, tax consequences, and interest cost differentials that would occur should the acquisition be consummated.

In addition to satisfying a buyer concerning the seller's assets, liabilities, and income, a BMR can establish the reasonableness of the seller's tax accruals and deferred tax credits, particularly to ascertain whether they are understated. Similarly, an analysis of the seller's past tax elections can determine compliance with Internal Revenue Service requirements, in relation to Subchapter S corporations, pension plans, LIFO inventories, and DISCs.

A buyer is also interested in the book and tax basis of the assets being acquired and their appraised values in determining alternatives for structuring the acquisition. Knowledge of the consequences of future depreciation or amortization and their ultimate effects upon taxes and cash flow would be of further benefit. And the tax implications of the transaction itself should certainly be considered to answer such questions as:

- Are there variable alternatives to be considered?
- Can the seller's tax burden be eased, while improving the buyer's cash flow by using the installment method for a portion of the transaction?
- Would a tax-free exchange that could result in accounting for the transaction as a pooling benefit the buyer's future earnings?
- What additional taxes may result from the acquisition—recapture of investment tax credit, and any deferred taxes that may become due, such as depreciation recapture?

The CPA firm does not issue an opinion on the financial statements of a seller as a result of a BMR, since it does not perform many of the auditing procedures required to render such an opinion. The report does not contain an opinion relative to the merits of the contemplated transaction nor does the CPA appraise the seller's assets. In essence, the reports are negative in tone, highlighting the potential pitfalls of the transaction and rarely elaborating on any positive considerations.

The review team should review the report draft with the acquisition committee before the draft is finalized. It should also work closely with the committee members throughout the conduct of the BMR, keeping them informed of results on a periodic basis, so that there are no surprises down the road, at which time it may be too late to do anything about them.

A natural question that often arises relates to the nature of BMR results and the circumstances that might cause a buyer to reconsider a potential acquisition. There are a wide variety of reasons, of course, for aborting a transaction. The most common one is that the earnings or equity anticipated by the buyer just was not there. Other reasons include: unauditable records, unrealistic projections, adverse legislation, downtrend in profitability, disagreement on tax allocations, improper inventory values, and understated liabilities.

A BMR should not be limited to the acquisition reviews of potential sellers. For example, if the BMR includes a fair value study, the accountants will include in their reports the property appraisals received from appraisers, as well as any actuarial reports on pension funds. (CPA firms do not make appraisals of corporate assets.) Further, the accountants can incorporate this information in a fair value balance sheet, showing the allocation of the purchase price to the relevant assets and liabilities.

There are also many other uses of the BMR. Companies might use the BMR approach in evaluating joint ventures, minority investments, and other forms of equity participation. Sellers might consider a BMR for evaluating a potential buyer. This can be quite important for sellers who will receive a significant portion of the consideration in the future, e.g., through sale of stock, debt payments, management contracts, and rentals.

Also, banks and insurance companies can use BMRs in connection with their studies of loans and investment opportunities. Investment bankers can use BMRs to help meet their due diligence requirements.

The BMR is a powerful management tool for investigation, analysis, and evaluation. The uses of the BMR are as wide-ranging as the user's imagination in applying this tool to today's corporate development needs.

ACCOUNTANTS' ROLE AS INTERMEDIARIES

Many accountants and accounting firms, like lawyers, bankers, brokers, and other professional intermediaries, serve as introductory parties in mergers and acquisitions. What is of significance to the business community is the fact that CPAs are barred from receiving finder's fees under two different edicts. Rule 302 of the AICPA's Code of Professional Ethics, effective March 1, 1973, bars AICPA members from receiving fees contingent upon a specified result or finding being reached. This may initially have been applied to tax cases, but its relevancy to the merger process has been interpreted by CPA firms as prohibiting them from undertaking the introductory role on a contingent fee basis. CPAs who perform such services do so on a no-fee basis, as part of their practice development or retention efforts.

In July 1979, the SEC Practice Section Executive Committee of the AICPA, considering matters relative to independence of the Section's members, required that its members refrain from performing merger and acquisition services for a finder's fee. The AICPA's SEC Practice Section membership consists of those firms serving public companies reporting to the SEC.

The SEC, in its Accounting Series Release No. 264, issued June 14, 1979, by reference, condones the AICPA's SEC Practice Section position with regard to its members. Further, it states "that the factors set forth in this release would normally preclude nonmembers from performing these services for their clients."

CONCLUSION

To successfully accomplish any "deal" or business combination in today's business environment, executives must have a good understanding of all the financial and accounting aspects—from the viewpoint of both the buyer and the seller. Familiarity with APB Opinions Nos. 16, 17, and 18, and their applicability to any business combination, is as important as knowing about a company's facilities and markets, particularly if the financial structure is paramount to one of the parties. The information in this chapter should provide executives with basic insight into these areas, and make them more fully aware of just how valuable the assistance of internal accounting personnel, independent CPAs, and outside legal advisors is in terms of sorting out the complexities of the proposed transaction.

REFERENCES

American Institute of CPAs (AICPA) Accounting Principles Board (APB) Opinion No. 16, Business Combinations, August 1970

AICPA APB Opinion No. 17, Intangible Assets, August 1970

AICPA Interpretations of APB Nos. 16 and 17

AICPA APB Opinion No. 18, The Equity Method of Accounting for Investments in Common Stock, March 1971

AICPA APB Opinion No. 24, Accounting for Income Taxes—Investments in Common Stock Accounted for by the Equity Method (Other than Subsidiaries and Corporate Joint Ventures), April 1972

AICPA APB Statement No. 4, Basic Concepts and Accounting Principles Underlying Financial Statements of Business Enterprises, October 1970

Financial Accounting Standards Board (FASB) Interpretation No. 4, Applicability of FASB Statement No. 2 to Business Combinations Accounted for by the Purchase Method, February 1975

FASB Interpretation No. 9, Applying APB Opinions No. 16 and 17, When a Savings and Loan Association or a Similar Institution is Acquired in a Business Combination Accounted for by the Purchase Method, February 1976

FASB Statement No. 10, Extension of "Grandfather" Provisions for Business Combinations, October 1975

FASB, Accounting for Business Combinations and Purchased Intangibles (Discussion Memorandum), August 19, 1976

SEC Accounting Release No. 130, Pooling-of-Interests Accounting, September 29, 1972, 37 F.R. 20937

SEC Accounting Release No. 135, Revised Guidelines for the Application of ASR No. 130, January 5, 1973, 38 F.R. 1734

SEC Accounting Release No. 146, Effect of Treasury Stock Transactions on Accounting for Business Combinations, August 24, 1973, 38 F.R. 24635

SEC Accounting Release No. 146-A, Statement of Policy and Interpretations in Regard to ASR No. 146, April 11, 1974, 39 F.R. 14588

JAMES M. NEEDHAM

JAMES M. NEEDHAM is a partner in Arthur Young & Company, New York. He has had extensive experience in assisting both domestic and non-U.S. based clients in the full range of merger and acquisition activity, including the development and implementation of acquisition and divestiture programs; leveraged buyouts and venture capital financing. Prior to joining Arthur Young, Mr. Needham was director of corporate development for a *Fortune* 200 company and held a management position on both the audit and consulting staffs of another international accounting firm.

16

When to Consolidate

JAMES M. NEEDHAM

In financial reporting the term "consolidation" refers to the combining of assets, liabilities, revenues, and expenses of subsidiaries and in some cases, joint ventures with the corresponding items of the parent company. In consolidated statements the emphasis is on the reporting of a business entity as opposed to a legal entity (i.e., individual subsidiary corporations or joint ventures).

An important characteristic associated with consolidated financial statements is that the separate corporations being consolidated should not report profits or losses on transactions with each other. Although the individual corporations will report these transactions on their books, the process of consolidating these individual corporations requires that the effect of these intercompany transactions be eliminated. If these transactions were not eliminated double counting of assets, liabilities, revenues, and expenses would occur and a premature recognition of income would result. The effect of the elimination process is to report on the combined activities of separate corporate entities as if all their financial transactions were recorded in one set of books.

In the consolidation of subsidiaries with the parent company, an investment by another entity, other than the parent, in a subsidiary may exist. That investment is called a minority interest and is shown on the consolidated balance sheet as a liability and on the income statement as a deduction in arriving at net income.

The effect of the consolidated process is to provide management, shareholders and other users of the financial statements with a summary of the separate legal entities as if they were a single economic entity. The emphasis is on the total entity and not with the individual subsidiaries. The effect is to show the individual subsidiary as a branch or a division. Accordingly, in the consolidation process we are creating an accounting abstraction—the business entity, as opposed to the legal abstraction—the corporation.

WHEN TO CONSOLIDATE

The constituent parts to be included in consolidated statements all have one thing in common—they are controlled through one corporation, the parent. This control is generally defined as ownership of over 50 percent of the outstanding voting shares of another company. For companies filing with the Securities and Exchange Commission (SEC), the SEC will not permit the consolidation of less than majority owned subsidiaries. Accordingly, control for purposes of consolidation has been defined as more than 50 percent ownership.

In arriving at a consolidation policy, the objective is to provide the financial presentation that is most meaningful under the circumstances. Accordingly, certain majority owned subsidiaries, the inclusion of which in consolidated statements would appear to distort the meaningfulness of those statements, are not consolidated. For instance:

a. The inclusion of foreign subsidiaries where the assets of those subsidiaries may be at risk due to political or economic instability or repatriation restrictions.

b. Subsidiaries in which a significant minority control exists and which control might preclude the flexibility necessary in a single business unit.

c. Subsidiaries in which control is temporary; a planned or forced disposition would be an example.

d. Certain subsidiaries that are part of a regulated industry such as banking or insurance where the flexibility or utility of assets of those subsidiaries is not at the disposal of the parent but a matter of law.

247

e. Subsidiaries, the inclusion of which in consolidation would significantly distort the capital structure and financial ratios of the parent. For instance, a captive finance subsidiary, a highly leveraged real estate subsidiary, or leasing company, would be examples.

f. Subsidiaries who have a year-end that is different by more than three months from the parent—the SEC applies a ninety-three day rule.

In those cases where the majority owned subsidiaries are not included in the consolidated financial statements, separate statements or combined statements of these nonconsolidated subsidiaries are normally presented separately. To exclude a more than 50 percent owned subsidiary from consolidation the reason for exclusion must be justified. It must be established why consolidated financial statements will be more meaningful if a particular subsidiary is excluded.

The current accounting literature is quite general with respect to requirements for consolidation. There is a basic presumption presented in Accounting Research Bulletin No. 51, which indicates that "consolidated financial statements are more meaningful than separate statements and that they are usually necessary for a fair presentation when one of the companies in the group directly or indirectly has a controlling financial interest in the other companies."

However there are many examples in practice today where full consolidation is employed but which may not provide the most meaningful presentation, particularly for the more sophisticated user who wishes to perform an in-depth financial analysis of a company. The many "conglomerates" are examples of this, particularly those that cross broad business classification boundaries such as manufacturing, financial and service industries. At a somewhat lower level, the combination of companies that are capital intensive vs. labor intensive, for instance, can also be difficult to analyze when presented as a single unit.

THE CONSOLIDATING INCOME STATEMENT AND BALANCE SHEET

The consolidating income statement and balance sheet provide a picture of the individual legal entities, namely, the subsidiary. To the extent that these subsidiaries are identifiable with pertinent or significant business segments, the consolidating statements offer the investor a more meaningful look at the consolidated entity. While inter-corporate borrowing and cost allocations among subsidiaries may limit the consolidating statements' utility, the potential to inform the investor is apparent—particularly, at the gross profit level which is not reflected in current business segment reporting.

There are, however, practical considerations that have prevented this approach from gaining much acceptance in practice, at least in publicly distributed financial reports. The volume of data, layout considerations, etc. make this approach unattractive, particularly for an annual report to shareholders. The auditor's professional literature, particularly for public companies, would require an expansion of the audit scope relative to each of the presented components of the consolidated group, an unattractive situation for most companies.

On the other hand, the Securities and Exchange Commission requires that separate financial statements be presented on an unconsolidated basis for parent companies and certain "finance type" subsidiaries that are included in consolidated financial statements when such entities meet certain specified criteria. This approach results, usually, in certain pieces of the consolidated group being presented separately but provides data relative to the balance only by subtraction.

If we accept the theory of eliminating legal entities in the *consolidation process* we can apply the same theory to the *consolidating process* and introduce, where possible, consolidating statements using business segments as the underlying unit rather than the subsidiary. The introduction of segment reporting may facilitate the introduction of this concept but due to the limited information required, it doesn't really satisfy the need.

If I were going to make a business review of an acquisition candidate for a client, one of the steps I would undertake would be to identify the significant business segments of the candidate and attempt to measure the profitability and growth rate of each segment so as to obtain a better picture of how the total income is produced, which segments are responsible and which have produced the growth. This type of analysis becomes more important as the diversity of the total entity increases. The analysis necessitates much of the work that should be required in a consolidating statement by business segment.

TAX CONSIDERATIONS

The requirements and practices for consolidation for federal corporation tax return purposes are generally independent of those for financial reporting.

In general, the federal tax regulations permit consolidation of an affiliated group wherein a company is controlled by 80 percent or more of the voting power. Certain types of corporations are not permitted to be consolidated even though the 80 percent control test is met.

An Illustration of the Alternatives

The following example shows the three basic reporting alternatives and demonstrates the information available in each of the three instances (Table 16-1). The alternatives are:

1. Equity accounting; the "Parent" column wherein the parent company records only its pro rata share of the net assets and net income of its subsidiaries.
2. Consolidated statements contain this one column, the only one usually presented in basic financial statement presentations.
3. Consolidating statements have all the columns presented together which obviously presents the most informative approach.

The illustration presents condensed balance sheet and income statement information. It is assumed that the parent company carries on no operations itself but only holds its investment in the two subsidiaries. The "Finance" subsidiary is wholly owned and carries on financing activities. The "Manufacturing" subsidiary has a minority interest of about 40 percent and is a basic manufacturing operation.

The equity accounting approach presented in the Parent column obviously is the least informative. Of course, in practice financial statements of this type would be supplemented with statements, or at least condensed information, of the principle subsidiaries.

The Consolidated statements by themselves still do not provide the whole story. In this illustration, the Finance subsidiary comprises over 75 percent of consolidated assets, less than 30 percent of revenues and almost 90 percent of net income. While the financial information by business enterprise, which is now required by generally accepted accounting principles, would provide this basic data, it still would not be sufficient for the detailed financial analysis that would be permitted by full consolidating statements.

TABLE 16-1
XYZ CORP.
CONSOLIDATING FINANCIAL STATEMENTS
(000's OMITTED)

	Parent Company	Finance Subsidiary	Manufacturing Subsidiary	Elimination	Consolidated Statement
Assets					
Cash, accounts receivable and inventory	$ 1800	$ 40800	$104100	$ —	$ 146700
Finance assets	—	854200	—	—	854200
Fixed assets	—	4700	144200	—	148900
Investments in and advances to subsidiaries	137000	—	—	(137000)	—
Other assets	—	63100	42700	—	105800
	$138800	$962800	$29100	$(137700)	$1255600
Liabilities and Equity					
Accounts payable and accrued expenses	$ —	$152600	$62700	$ —	$ 215300
Debt	70800	807700	171800	(100000)	950300
Minority interest	—	—	—	22000	22000
Equity	68000	2500	56500	(59000)	68000
	$138800	$962800	$291000	$(137000)	$1255600
Income Statement					
Revenues	$ —	$163500	$406800	$ —	$ 570300
Expenses	—	134300	399600	—	533900
Operating profit	—	29200	7200	—	36400
Income taxes	—	14700	3700	—	18400
	—	14500	3500	—	18000
Equity in income of subsidiaries	$ 16600	—	—	$ (16600)	—
Minority interest	—	—	—	(1400)	$ (1400)
Net income	$ 16600	$ 14500	$ 3500	$ (18000)	$ 16600

I. ROBERT LEVINE

I. ROBERT LEVINE received his A.B. Degree from Dartmouth College in 1954 and his MBA from The Amos Tuck School of Business Administration in 1955. He joined the Audit Department of the New York office of Ernst & Whinney in 1958 and became a Partner in 1968. In 1976, Mr. Levine was appointed Regional Partner in Charge of Merger and Acquisition Services. Currently, he is in the International Operations Office of Ernst & Whinney with responsibilities for international mergers and acquisitions.

Mr. Levine's background involves serving a wide variety of clients including those in publishing, manufacturing, retailing, real estate and construction. In addition to numerous speeches on merger and acquisition topics, Mr. Levine's related activities include assisting companies in planning and searching for acquisitions, advising on negotiating strategies and conducting acquisition reviews.

RICHARD P. MILLER

RICHARD P. MILLER received his B.B.A. Degree from the University of Notre Dame. He joined the New York Office of Ernst & Whinney as an Audit Manager in 1978 when Ernst & Whinney and S.D. Leidesdorf & Co. combined their accounting practices.

Mr. Miller's background includes experience in industry in addition to extensive and varied experience in public accounting in Cleveland, Ohio, Syracuse, New York and New York City. Prior to concentrating in accounting research and report review he served audit clients in a broad range of industries. He is a member of the American Institute of Certified Public Accountants and the New York State Society of Certified Public Accountants.

17

Accounting for Business Combinations

Purchases and Poolings

I. ROBERT LEVINE

RICHARD P. MILLER

INTRODUCTION AND OVERVIEW

Assuming a particular acquisition makes business sense, one of the early questions that should be raised involves the contemplated accounting treatment for the transaction. The purchase-pooling decision should be carefully reviewed, because each results in quite different financial statement effects.

Generally accepted accounting principles for business combinations are presently found in two opinions of the Accounting Principles Board (APB), the predecessor of the Financial Accounting Standards Board. These opinions are:

APB Opinion No. 16 — Business Combinations
APB Opinion No. 17 — Intangible Assets

APB No. 16 contains criteria for classifying business combinations either as purchases or as poolings of interests, and provides guidelines for the application of each method. While each method is acceptable, they are not alternatives in accounting for the same business combination. APB No. 17 requires the amortization of any goodwill that might arise in a purchase. Appendix B excerpts certain relevant portions of APB No. 16 and APB No. 17.

Definitions

A pooling of interests is the uniting of the ownership interests of two or more companies generally by an exchange of voting common stock. A pooling may also be obtained under certain conditions by an exchange of voting common stock for net assets. No acquisition is recognized in a pooling because the combination is accomplished without disbursing resources of the constituents.

This chapter differentiates between the two or more parties to a pooling by referring to them as either the "issuing company" or the "combining company." The term "combined company" is used to refer to the companies after consummation of the pooling.

A purchase is essentially the acquisition of assets. The purchase method of accounting is applicable to business combinations effected by paying cash, distributing other assets, incurring liabilities, or issuing equity securities, including voting common stock.

Major Differences

The major conceptual difference underpinning today's accounting rules for purchase versus pooling treatment relates to the stockholders of the issuing and combining companies. In a purchase, the combining company's stockholders usually do not participate as a group in the risks and rewards of the combined enterprise. In a pooling they do. Frequently in a purchase, the stockholders receive cash or debt, and assets of the buyer, or of the combined company, are ultimately distributed to the selling shareholders. In a pooling, stockholders receive voting common stock and the combined company has no obligation to distribute assets to shareholders.

The APB criteria for a pooling are quite detailed. Failure to qualify under any one of the criteria means that the acquisition will be accounted for as a purchase. Thus, it is usually fairly easy to qualify an acquisition as a purchase, if desired. On the other hand, accomplishing a pooling may be quite difficult.

Certain of the differences between the two methods are summarized in Exhibit 1. The major differences, from an accounting standpoint, relate to 1) the basis for recording the combining company's or the seller's assets and liabilities, 2) the recording of goodwill and 3) the income statement treatment of the combining company's or the seller's results of operations.

EXHIBIT 1

Characteristics	Purchase Method	Pooling Method
1. Theory	Acquisition of assets or stock.	Uniting of ownership interests. "Pooling of risks" concept is important.
2. Consideration	Buyer can use cash, notes, preferred or common stock; warrants or convertible securities. Contingent payment is allowed.	Must be an exchange of voting common stock for voting common stock. No shares to be issued can be contingent on future events.
3. Percent Sought	May purchase all or any part of assets or stock. May increase prior minority interest in stock.	90% or more of combining company's stock must be exchanged for issuing company's stock (10% or less can be cash or notes, *including* any stock acquired prior to the pooling).
4. Recorded Amounts	Seller's assets and liabilities are adjusted to their fair value. Previously unrecorded assets and liabilities are also recorded.	Combining company's assets and liabilities retain same basis as before.
5. Goodwill	Amortized over not more than 40 years. Amortization is not tax deductible. If cost is *less* than net assets acquired, noncurrent assets are reduced; if they are reduced to zero, then "negative goodwill" is recorded and amortized over not more than 40 years.	No goodwill recorded.
6. Reported Earnings	Earnings of seller included in operations from date of acquisition. Footnote disclosure of pro forma current and prior year earnings required. Subsequent periods' depreciation and other expenses are computed using adjusted asset and liability values.	All prior years earnings must be restated to include pooled company and effect of additional shares issued. No adjustments to methods of computing earnings.

Purchase Accounting in Brief

In a business combination accounted for as a purchase, one company purchases the other by acquiring its stock or its net assets. Either way, a purchase follows historical cost accounting principles for the recording of asset acquisitions: purchased assets are recorded at cost. This often becomes complicated in a business combination because many assets are acquired and many liabilities are assumed, all for one purchase price.

In a purchase, the buyer allocates its total purchase price to the assets acquired, less the liabilities assumed. It is almost as if individual assets were purchased and individual liabilities assumed: all on the acquisition date.

The difference between the cost of the acquired company and the fair values assigned to its net assets is recorded as goodwill. Frequently, the buyer will recognize and assign fair values to assets and liabilities that are not on the seller's books. Such assets might include patents and formulae. A typical liability would be unfunded vested pension liability.

Goodwill is considered by many to be a *soft* asset. It is not amortizable for tax purposes, whereas substantially all *hard* assets eventually become tax deductions. Financial analysts frequently subtract goodwill from stockholders' equity and emphasize the resulting *tangible stockholders' equity*. Accordingly, there is usually a great deal of attention paid to allocating as much of the purchase price as possible to *hard* assets, including identifiable intangibles such as patents. This allocation is especially important when the tax basis of an acquired company's assets will be stepped up to their fair value as of the acquisition date.

The income of the acquired company, after adjustments resulting from the purchase, is reflected in the income statement from the date of acquisition.

Pooling Accounting in Brief

In a pooling of interests, groups of stockholders combine to form *in effect* a new entity to carry on the previous businesses and continue their earnings streams. The future sharing of risks and rewards by the constituent stockholder groups is important but the form of the transaction, stock for stock or stock for net assets, is not.

In a pooling, a new basis of accounting does not arise for either of the constituent companies; the assets, liabilities and retained earnings of the issuing and the combining companies are combined at their recorded amounts. Aggregate income is not changed since the total resources are not changed. There is no newly invested capital nor have assets been withdrawn from either entity.

Adjustments caused by the issuance of voting common stock are typically reflected in the combined additional capital account. Income of both companies is combined for the entire fiscal period in which the acquisition occurs, as well as for prior periods.

Purchase—Pooling Preference

The two methods, purchase and pooling, are not alternatives for the same business combination. But depending upon the circumstances of the acquisition, one method may be preferred over the other, and, sometimes the acquisition can be structured to accomplish the desired result. Also, in some acquisitions, with adequate planning, the desired tax treatment (i.e., a taxable transaction with the resulting change in tax basis, or a nontaxable one in which the acquired company's tax basis does not change) can be achieved without impacting the desired accounting treatment. For example, it is possible for companies to arrange a taxable pooling.

Among the situations in which purchase accounting may be preferred are:

When the fair market value of the net assets exceeds the cost of acquiring the stock of the company. The resulting "negative goodwill" will have a positive impact on future earnings.

When the seller has had recent losses or poor earnings. A pooling would require restating all prior period earnings to include the seller's poor earnings performance, while a purchase would not.

Among the situations in which pooling accounting may be preferred are:

When the purchase price significantly exceeds

the fair value of net assets, and a material amount of goodwill would otherwise be recorded.

When the restated historic earning trends are improved by the pooling.

The decision about whether a particular acquisition is better treated as a purchase or a pooling should be made as early as possible. If a pooling is important, this can have a significant impact on negotiation strategy. The existence of specific pooling rules allows a company to plan a business combination to achieve desired goals. It is essential that each of the pooling criteria be reviewed to guard against inadvertent classification as a purchase when a pooling is desired or vice versa.

A company that considers itself a possible target can also do some advance planning. It can take steps to prevent being acquired in a pooling because certain of the specified pooling conditions must predate the initiation of the plan of combination by as much as two years; thus actions taken months or years before a business combination is conceived can preclude a pooling. Obviously, such defensive action should make economic sense. In any event, such action would not prevent its acquisition in a purchase.

Because of the complexities of the rules, it is often beneficial for both buyers and sellers to consult their independent accountants early in the planning process to determine if the desired result can be achieved.

HISTORICAL DEVELOPMENT

The pooling of interest concept did not gain momentum until the late 1940's. In fact, the purchase versus pooling alternative was not even a factor in business combinations up to that time. Rather, the major decision involving accounting for business combinations concerned accounting for goodwill.

Goodwill should "remain always on the books at cost," stated Roy A. Kester's 1917 text, *Accounting Theory and Practice*. When profits are large, Kester argued, goodwill is a very real asset: it represents excess earning power. And when profits are small, he continued, they could not stand the write-off. His was the "permanent capitalization" school of thought.

The "immediate write-off" school gained popularity in the 1930's, reflecting the accountant's conservatism reacting to depression economics. Thus goodwill, because of its intangible nature and nonmeasurable useful life, began to be written off as of the acquisition date, at first to capital surplus (paid-in capital), later to earned surplus (retained earnings). In the depression years, the idea of goodwill representing excess earning power ad infinitum clearly seemed naive.

The choice between permanent capitalization and immediate write-off was based upon one's balance sheet emphasis. If one considered it most important to reflect all of a company's assets, then one would opt for permanent capitalization. If on the other hand, one emphasized conservatism, the immediate write-off decision would be made. Income statement considerations such as matching revenues and related expenses were secondary.

Nevertheless, accountants were troubled by having companies pay hard dollars for something called goodwill and then suggesting that it all be written off in the name of balance sheet conservatism. In 1944, Accounting Research Bulletin No. 24 was issued discouraging, but not prohibiting the immediate write-off of purchased goodwill, especially against capital surplus. Concurrently, support was growing for a middle way: recording goodwill as an asset but amortizing it against income over the years during which the income was expected to be earned. One of the period's most respected authors, W.A. Paton, suggested in his *Advanced Accounting* (1941) ''... it seems clearly advisable to amortize (goodwill) through the period in which the (estimated excess) earnings are expected.''

But a real problem emerged in determining the period over which goodwill should be amortized. On one hand, W.A. Paton and A.C. Littleton in *An Introduction To Corporate Accounting Standards* (1940) stated that ''there is ample evidence ... to show that extraordinary earning power cannot be expected to persist indefinitely.'' Yet, almost ten years later, A.W. Holmes and R.A. Meier in their 1949 *Intermediate Accounting* text, commented that ''Purchased goodwill that apparently has no limited life need not be amortized, since the excess profits that result are a perpetuity.''

In ARB No. 24 and again in ARB No. 43 (the latter issued in 1953), goodwill was dealt with under the topic of intangible assets. It generally fell into that category of intangibles ''having no limited term of existence and no indication of limited life at the time of acquisition.'' The bulletins suggested either retaining goodwill on the books until a loss of value became evident or amortizing its cost against income. Practically speaking, most managements chose the former option, and as a result, significant amounts of permanently capitalized goodwill began to accumulate in the financial statements of acquisitive companies.

The post-World War II rise in common stock prices was paralleled by investors shifting their emphasis from the balance sheet toward the income statement. Price/earning ratios became newly discovered valuation methods. The ballooning valuation of companies in relation to the book value of their tangible assets began to result in larger and larger amounts of goodwill being recorded in acquisitions. Pressures grew for an alternative accounting method for acquisitions, especially where a large amount of goodwill would otherwise result.

Other pressures also fostered the poolings method. Because the income of the combining companies was retroactively combined, instant increases in earnings per share could be created in certain situations. Understandably the movement toward poolings gained popularity.

It was not until 1950 that the AICPA issued its first pronouncement dealing solely with business combinations. ARB No. 40 suggested that the accounting treatment of an acquisition should depend upon the attendant circumstances rather than its legal form. The bulletin briefly described a number of factors that suggest a pooling of interests, no one of which was to be considered conclusive, but whose presence would be cumulative in effect.

Such factors included relative size, continuity of management or power to control management and similarity of business. It noted that a pooling should result in carrying forward ''the book values of the constituent companies'' and stated that their retained earnings ''may be carried forward.'' ARB No. 43 restated but did not significantly revise ARB No. 40.

ARB No. 48 was issued in 1957 to clarify and in some areas expand on the accounting treatment of business combinations. It suggested, for example, some quantitative guidelines to judge whether one of the constituent companies was clearly dominant, thereby suggesting a purchase rather than a pooling. It suggested that in a pooling of interests, the retained earnings of the constituent companies *should* be carried forward, rather than stating, as previously, that it *may* be carried forward.

Issued in 1965, Opinion No. 6 of the Accounting Principles Board weakened ARB No. 48 somewhat by stating that the criteria set forth in ARB No. 48 were ''illustrative guides and not necessarily literal requirements.'' APB No. 10 in 1966 attempted to limit the number of post-year-end poolings to those where the transaction was consummated at or shortly after year-end.

Until the adoption of APB No. 16 in 1970 the purchase method had been an optional choice in many business combinations. But APB No. 16 stated that

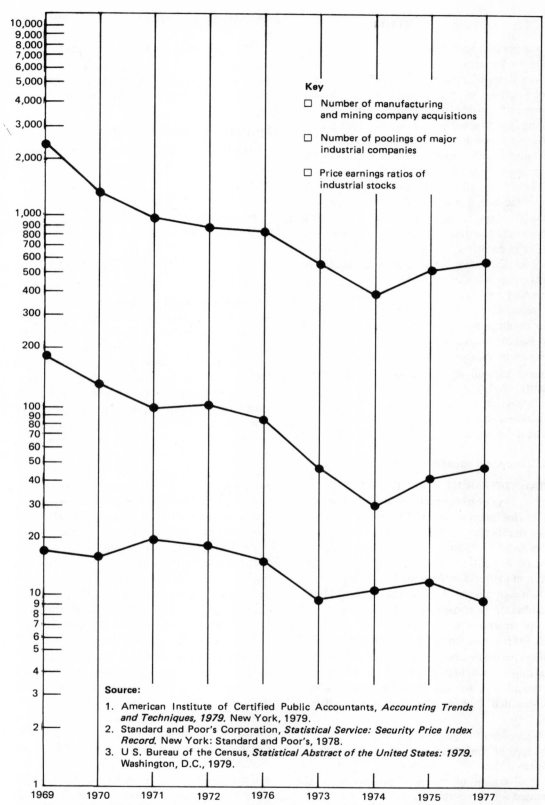

Figure 17-1. This illustrates the relationship of three merger-related statistics: total number of manufacturing and mining concerns acquired; total number of poolings among larger public companies; and the price earning ratios of public companies.

purchase and pooling accounting can not be considered alternatives for the same business combination. APB No. 16 also dropped certain prior conditions for a pooling of interests, such as management continuity and size similarity. Instead it substituted twelve criteria for a pooling, the absence of any one of which would require the use of purchase accounting.

Issued concurrently, APB No. 17 stated that the value of intangible assets eventually disappears, and that this should be reflected by periodic charges to income over the anticipated period of benefit, but not in excess of 40 years. It suggested periodic evaluation of the amortization period, although it added that one loss year, or even a few loss years together, did not necessarily justify a write-off of all or substantially all of the remaining unamortized cost.

In summary, pooling-purchase accounting and goodwill accounting have had diverse histories. The criteria for poolings have become more stringent over the years. But the treatment of goodwill has seen a bit of a roller coaster ride, as follows:

> Permanent capitalization (predominant treatment until early 1930's)
>
> Immediate write-off (to early 1940's)
>
> Capitalization and amortization (to 1950)
>
> Permanent capitalization (predominant treatment to 1970)
>
> Capitalization and amortization (to present)

FINANCIAL STATEMENT EFFECTS

While many considerations enter into the decision-making process, desired financial statement effects can significantly influence negotiations. As illustrated in Exhibits 2 and 3, the accounting treatment as a purchase or pooling usually results in a significantly different (1) reported financial position, and (2) earnings and earnings per share for the combined business. In addition, the consideration paid or exchanged and the tax treatment to the buyer can also affect differently (1) reported financial position, (2) earnings and earnings per share and (3) cash flow. All three of these will impact current and future financial reports. Pooling would also impact prior financials, which would be restated. Factors affecting these results include:

1. The amount of consideration
2. The type of consideration: cash, debt securities, preferred stock or common stock
3. The allocation of the purchase price (if accounted for as a purchase)
4. The tax treatment to the buyer: taxable (increase or decrease of tax basis) or non-taxable (no change in tax basis)

The following paragraphs and exhibits illustrate principles covered later in this chapter. In addition, Appendix A provides examples of disclosures of purchases and the related allocation of cost.

Purchase and Pooling Compared

Balance Sheet Effect: Exhibit 2 illustrates the balance sheet effect of four types of business combinations:

A. Purchase resulting in goodwill
B. Pooling
C. Purchase resulting in a pro rata reduction of noncurrent assets
D. Purchase resulting in negative goodwill

The amounts illustrated in Column A result from the purchase of all of the outstanding stock of Seller Corp. for $2,800 in cash. For tax purposes, the tax bases of the net assets are increased and are the same as the book amounts.

Column B illustrates the same situation except that 200 shares of voting common stock at $14 per share are exchanged for all of the outstanding voting common stock of Seller Corp. The pooling is tax-free and Seller Corp.'s cost basis continues as the tax basis.

Column C assumes $1,000 in cash is paid for all of the outstanding stock of Seller Corp. For tax purposes, there is no reorganization and Seller Corp.'s cost basis continues as the tax basis. Note that now because of the difference between book and tax basis, the amounts shown for inventories and 6 percent notes payable are different from the amounts in Column A. (Since the fair value increment for inventories is not deductible for tax purposes, the tax effect is recognized in allocating the cost to inventories; because the discount on the notes does not result in deductible interest, the tax effect is also reflected in the amounts allocated to the notes payable.) The amounts allocated to fixed assets and patents also reflect adjustments for the difference between book and tax basis. Because cost is less than the fair value of the net assets acquired, the noncurrent assets have been reduced pro rata using fair value as a base.

Column D assumes that only $100 in cash was paid for all of the outstanding stock of Seller Corp. As in Column C there is no reorganization for tax purposes (Seller Corp.'s cost basis continues as the tax basis) and the amounts shown for inventories and 6 percent notes payable are the same as the amounts in Column C. Because the excess of the fair value of the net assets acquired over cost is greater than amounts initially assigned to fixed assets and patents, they are reduced to zero and the remaining credit is classified as a deferred credit in the balance sheet between total liabilities and stockholder's equity. Negative goodwill is amortized into income over a period not in excess of 40 years.

Columns C and D reflect a *bargain purchase*, a purchase at less than the fair value of Seller Corp.'s net assets. When cost is less than the recorded carrying amounts of a seller's net assets, increased earnings can be expected in a buyer's income statement. That is because the reduced book basis assigned to certain of the seller's assets will result in lower depreciation and amortization expense in buyer's future consolidated income statements. Normally, if stock is acquired, the carrying amounts of assets for tax purposes will not be changed and thus cash flow is neither increased nor decreased. Thus, when a seller's tax basis is continued, tax deductions for depreciation and amortization will be the same after the acquisition as they were before. If seller's net assets are acquired, buyer's cash flow will typically be produced because tax basis is reduced.

EXHIBIT 2

SELLER CORP.—Balance Sheet Effects

	Cost Basis	Fair Value*	A Purchase	B Pooling	C Purchase Pro Rata Reduction	D Purchase Negative Goodwill
Current Assets:						
Inventories	$ 400	$ 450	$ 450	$ 400	$ 425	$ 425
Other	800	800	800	800	800	800
Noncurrent Assets:						
Excess of cost over net assets acquired			440			
Fixed assets (net)	1,100	2,000	2,000	1,100	845	
Patents		200	200		40	
TOTAL ASSETS	$2,300		$3,890	$2,300	$2,110	$1,225
Current Liabilities	$ 600	$ 600	$ 600	$ 600	$ 600	$ 600
Noncurrent Liabilities:						
6% notes payable—Note 1	300	260	260	300	280	280
Deferred income taxes—Note 2	150			150		
Deferred pension costs—Note 3			230		230	230
TOTAL LIABILITIES	1,050		1,090	1,050	1,110	1,110
Excess of Net Assets Acquired Over Cost						15
Stockholder's Equity	1,250		2,800	1,250	1,000	100
TOTAL	$2,300		$3,890	$2,300	$2,110	$1,225
Consideration						
Cash			$2,800		$1,000	$ 100
Stock (200 shares @$14 per share)				$2,800		

Note 1—Discount of $40 at current interest rates is assumed.

Note 2—Deferred taxes relate to depreciation—50% tax rate.

Note 3—The Company's pension plan has $460 in unfunded vested benefits. This amount is recorded net of tax because when paid, the Company will receive a 50% tax reduction but there will be no book expense because the liability is being recorded as part of the acquisition.

*Fair Values determined as follows:

1. Inventories—Finished goods and W.I.P. are valued at sales price, less cost to complete and/or dispose and a reasonable profit margin.
Raw materials are valued at *replacement* cost.
2. Fixed Assets—Generally recorded at replacement cost.
3. Patent is valued at "appraised" value. In a taxable purchase, the buyer will assign as much value as possible to intangible assets that can be deducted for income tax purposes, such as patents, employment contracts, etc.
4. Notes Payable—If the stated interest rates are substantially below (or above) current market, debt discount (premium) must be recorded. To substantiate a taxable deduction of any discount, the difference in rates should be supported by opinion of an investment banker.

EPS, Return on Equity and Cash Flow Effects:

Exhibit 3 illustrates the effects on earnings and cash flow of three business combinations:

Purchase for Cash
Purchase for Stock
Pooling

The facts are taken from Exhibit 2. The pre-merger income and per share data for Buyer Corp. and Seller Corp. are as follows:

	Buyer Corp.	Seller Corp.
Income:		
Income before taxes	$1,400	$ 600
Income taxes (50%)	700	300
Net income	$ 700	$ 300

	Buyer Corp.	Seller Corp.
Per share data:		
Shares outstanding	500	400
Earnings per share	$ 1.40	$ .75
P/E ratio prior to merger	10x	5x
Market value per share	$14.00	$ 3.75

Cash consideration of $2,800 was obtained by Buyer Corp.'s sale of a ten year, 10% note. The following information relates to the stock for stock exchanges:

Offer information:

Aggregate market value of stock	$7,000	$1,500
Book value	$8,000	$1,250
Exchange ratio for pooling		
	1 for 2	
Aggregate market value of offer:		
200 shares x $14.00 per share	$2,800	

EXHIBIT 3

Impact on EPS and Return on Equity

	Cash Purchase	Stock Issued Purchase	Pooling
Combined income before income taxes	$2,000	$ 2,000	$2,000
Acquisition adjustments:			
Inventory cost	(50)	(50)	
Patent ($200 ÷ 10 years)	(20)	(20)	
Depreciation on increased assets ($900 ÷ 10 years)	(90)	(90)	
Discount on notes ($40 ÷ 4 years)	(10)	(10)	
Reduced pension expense ($460 ÷ 15 years)	30	30	
Interest on debt ($2,800 at 10%)	(280)	-0-	
	1,580	1,860	2,000
Income taxes—50%	790	930	1,000
Goodwill amortization ($440 ÷ 10 years)	(44)	(44)	
PRO FORMA EARNINGS	$ 746	$ 886	$1,000
Number of shares outstanding	500	700	700
Earnings per share	$ 1.49	$ 1.27	$ 1.43
Combined equity	$8,000	$10,800	$9,250
Return on equity	9.3%	8.2%	10.8%

Impact on Cash Flow

	Cash Purchase	Stock Issued Purchase	Pooling
Tax reduction from stepped-up basis of assets:			
Inventory (1 year)	$ 50	$ 50	
Patent (10 years)	20	20	
Depreciation (10 years)	90	90	
Debt discount (4 years)	10	10	
	170	170	
Tax reduction—50%	85	85	$ -0-
Cash requirements of consideration paid:			
Interest on debt (10%)	(280)		
Debt principal (10 years)	(280)		
Dividends (5%)		(140)	(140)
Net cash drain to be provided by operations	$ (475)	$ (55)	$ (140)

Effects of a Purchase

In a purchase transaction, chances are that future earnings of the acquired company will be affected regardless of whether cash is paid, debt incurred or stock issued. Earnings of the acquired company included in future financial statements of the buyer will reflect the effects of using new carrying amounts for the assets acquired and liabilities assumed. They will also reflect the effects of amortization of any difference between the cost paid and the fair value of the net assets acquired, commonly known as goodwill or negative goodwill.

Further, earnings of the acquired company are included in the buyer's financial statements only from the date of acquisition. Prior years' earnings are not restated and thus a purchase can change the acquiring company's trend in earnings.

If the fair values of the net assets acquired are greater or less than the acquired company's carrying amounts, future earnings will be affected as these new amounts enter into the determination of income and expense. For example, if the current fair value of the acquired company's inventory is greater than its original cost, and it is sold in the next period, this higher amount will result in a higher cost of sales in the financial statements in the period following the business combination. Similarly, if the fair value of plant and equipment is greater than the carrying amounts before the merger, future financial statements will show larger depreciation charges.

If an amount greater than the fair value of all the acquired net assets is paid, that excess amount is considered goodwill, recorded as an asset and amortized over a period not to exceed forty years. Goodwill has an extra negative effect on earnings because it is not deductible for income tax purposes. This results in a higher tax provision in the income statement than would otherwise be expected based upon book income.

Conversely, if an amount less than book value is paid, income of future periods will be higher than that reported before the business combination. The excess of fair value of net assets acquired over cost is first allocated to noncurrent assets. This will result in lower charges to income, such as from depreciation. If noncurrent assets are reduced to zero, any remaining excess is recorded as a deferred credit, negative goodwill, and amortized to income over a period not to exceed 40 years. While goodwill is often determined to have an indefinite useful life and amortized over the maximum period allowed, the useful life of negative goodwill is less certain and, consequently, is usually amortized over a much shorter period; occasionally, periods as short as two or three years are used, but longer periods are more typical.

It should be noted that a purchase effected by an exchange of common stock will affect the earnings per share of the issuing company, but the impact may be less obvious than in a pooling because earnings of the acquired company are also affected by the fair values assigned in the purchase. This is because the additional earnings are only included for periods after the acquisition date.

Effects of a Pooling

The assets, liabilities, retained earnings and income of the combined enterprises are added together in the pooled financial statements. Prior years' financial statements are restated to give effect to the pooling as if the companies had always been together as one. Thus, both trends in earnings and earnings per share can be affected. Because common stock is issued in a pooling, the number of shares issued will impact the earnings per share of the combined enterprise.

Companies contemplating poolings pay close attention to the number of shares to be issued in relation to the earnings of the combining company. If too many shares are issued in exchange for the additional earnings of the combining company, then combined earnings per share will decrease from those reported by the issuing company before the acquisition.

The maximum number of shares that may be issued in a pooling without diluting the issuing company's earnings per share can be determined by dividing the estimated income of the combining company by the issuing company's earnings per share. For example, using the information in Exhibit 3, Buyer Corp. could issue up to 214 shares before combined earnings per share would be diluted.

$$\frac{\$300 \text{ (Seller Corp. Income)}}{\$1.40 \text{ (Buyer Corp. EPS)}} = 214 \text{ shares (Maximum Shares)}$$

A decrease in earnings per share is frequently unacceptable to management. If for example, Buyer Corp.'s stock price was only 8 x earnings, the combined EPS would have been diluted as follows:

Buyer Corp. EPS	$ 1.40
P/E ratio	× 8
Stock price	$11.20
$2,800 ÷ $11.20	= 250 shares to be issued
	+ 500 shares outstanding
	750
$1,000 net income (pooling method)	
÷ 750 shares	= $ 1.33 EPS

CLASSIFICATION OF BUSINESS COMBINATIONS

Business combinations must be classified as purchases or poolings of interests regardless of whether stock or assets are acquired or whether the combination results in (1) a new corporation which replaces all of the constituents, (2) one company remaining as the surviving corporation or (3) both companies remaining in a parent-subsidiary relationship.

When the net assets of one or more companies are acquired by the payment of cash, other assets, or the issuance of debt securities, the common stockholders of the acquired companies do not maintain an ownership interest in the combined firm, and the business combination is accounted for as a purchase.

If the combination involves an exchange of voting common stock for voting common stock or net assets for voting common stock, the common shareholders of the combining companies maintain their positions as owners of the combined company. APB No. 16 specifies 12 criteria for the classification of such business combinations. When all 12 criteria (conditions which must be present, or in some cases absent) are met, a business combination must be accounted for as a pooling of interests. If any one of the following criteria is not met, purchase accounting applies. Each of the twelve conditions is discussed later in the chapter.

Attributes of Companies

1. Each company is autonomous and not a division or subsidiary of another corporation.
2. The combining companies are independent of each other. (Neither owns more than 10 percent of the other.)

Method of Combining Interests

3. The combination will be effected in a single transaction or by a specific plan within one year after the plan is initiated.
4. The issuing company issues only voting common stock (e.g., not convertible preferred) for at least 90 percent of the combining company's outstanding voting common stock or substantially all of its net assets.
5. None of the combining companies has, within the past two years, changed the equity interest of its voting common stock in contemplation of combining. (Normal recurring dividends do not violate this rule.)
6. Treasury stock purchased by any of the combining companies within two years before the initiation of the combination (and between initiation and consummation) is for business purposes other than the combination and is in normal or nominal amounts in accordance with a systematic pattern of reacquisitions. (The SEC has even stricter requirements.)

7. The ratio of interest of one stockholder to the others in a company will remain the same after the exchange of stock in the combination.
8. Voting rights are fully exercisable by the stockholders without restriction.
9. No contingent shares are permitted except for settlement of events prior to the pooling.

Absence of Planned Transactions

After combining, the companies do not intend and have not agreed to do any of the following:

10. Retire or reacquire (or arrange to have a third party acquire) any of the common stock issued in the combination.
11. Enter into financial arrangements for the benefit of the former stockholders of a combining company.
12. Dispose of a significant part of the assets within two years after the combination (other than to eliminate duplicate facilities or excess capacity).

ACCOUNTING FOR A PURCHASE

APB Nos. 16 and 17 did not change generally accepted accounting principles for application of the purchase method of accounting but they did clarify accounting practice as the following sections indicate.

Determining Cost

Principles of historical cost accounting for the acquisition of an asset depend upon the nature of the transaction:

An asset acquired by exchanging cash or other assets is recorded at the amount of cash distributed or the fair value of other assets distributed.

An asset acquired by incurring liabilities is recorded at the present value of the amounts to be paid.

An asset acquired by issuing shares of stock is recorded at the fair value of the consideration received for the stock.

Often, however, the fair value of an asset acquired in an exchange is more reliably determinable than the fair value of non-cash assets given up. Or perhaps the fair value of an asset received for stock issued is not reliably determinable. In those situations, the general principle is modified as explained in APB No. 16 by a practical rule that when assets are acquired for other than cash, including shares of stock issued, "cost" may be determined either by the fair value of the consideration given or by the fair value of the property acquired, whichever is more clearly evident.

If equity securities are issued, the quoted market

price may be used to measure cost unless the quoted price is not a fair value. An example of this would be in the case of a lightly traded stock. Independent appraisals by investment or commercial bankers are frequently used to determine the fair value of securities issued in such cases, or where there is no quoted market price at all.

Indirect and Direct Costs of Acquisition

APB No. 16 intended that all internal costs associated with business combinations be expensed as incurred. Thus, the costs of maintaining an acquisitions department, including costs allocable to successful acquisitions, may not be treated as part of the cost of an acquired company. Rather, they are expensed in the period incurred.

Incremental external costs directly associated with an acquisition are capitalized as part of the cost of an acquired company. Such costs would include finder's fees and sums paid to outside consultants for accounting, legal, actuarial, engineering, investigation, and appraisal services. Practically speaking, many buyers request that their outside consultants identify the portion of their fees that are applicable to each acquisition.

Registration Costs

If the fair value of securities issued is used to measure the cost of an acquisition, that cost should be the same regardless of whether the shares issued were previously registered, are registered concurrent with the acquisition, or are to be registered in the future. Accordingly, cost is measured and allocated to the net assets acquired before accounting for any registration costs, which are treated as a reduction of the capital accounts.

If unregistered equity securities are issued in an acquisition and the buyer agrees to register those securities, the buyer should, if practicable, record the estimated costs of future registration as a liability and deduct those costs from the capital accounts. Thus, the same cost would be recorded as if previously registered shares had been issued.

Some acquisition agreements call for future "piggyback" registration (that is, the securities issued are to be included in the registration of a planned future offering). In such case, only the estimated incremental costs of registering the equity securities issued in the acquisition should be accrued.

Allocation of Cost to Assets Acquired and Liabilities Assumed

Book values previously reported in the financial statements of the seller are not relevant in the future financial statements of the buyer. Once the total cost is determined, a portion of that cost is assigned to each individual asset and liability on the basis of its fair value at the acquisition date. Any difference between the amount of the assigned costs of all tangible and identifiable intangible assets (which cannot include any goodwill previously recorded by the acquired company) less liabilities assumed and the total cost represents unspecified intangible value: goodwill if positive, negative goodwill if negative.

Valuation Guidelines

The valuation guidance given in APB No. 16 applies regardless of whether the purchase is of an entire company, a majority of its stock, or a segment of a company's business, and regardless of whether the consideration given is cash, other assets, debt, common or preferred stock, or a combination of these.

Independent appraisals are frequently needed to determine the fair values of certain of the assets acquired and liabilities assumed. Subsequent sales of assets or settlement of liabilities may also be a useful source of evidence of value. The effect of taxes is often a factor in determining assigned values.

The Opinion contains specific valuation guidelines for assigning amounts to individual assets and liabilities:

Assets acquired are valued generally at current net realizable values or current replacement costs, but care should be taken to consider the tax bases as discussed in the caption, "Tax Effects on Amounts Allocated."

• Accounts and notes receivable should be discounted to their present values using current interest rates appropriate for the acquiring company. Allowances for uncollectible accounts and collection costs should also be considered.

• Inventories should not be valued at the acquired company's cost. In a purchase, the acquiring company should earn a profit only on its efforts after the date of acquisition; accordingly, finished goods and work in process inventories should be valued at estimated selling prices less the sum of (a) costs to complete, (b) costs to sell, and (c) a reasonable profit allowance on the acquiring company's efforts to complete and sell the inventory. However, neither cost to sell or reasonable profit allowance are defined, and both are subject to varying estimates.

• Plant and equipment that will be used by the combined entity is valued at current replacement cost for similar capacity. Larger public companies report current replacement cost information for similar capacity under the FASB's Financial Accounting Standard

(FAS) No. 33, "Financial Reporting and Changing Prices" and guidance found in that statement for determining current cost may be useful in some acquisitions where independent appraisals are not needed.

• Plant and equipment, including items to be sold, and identifiable intangible assets such as contracts, patents, franchises, customer lists, and favorable leases may require independent appraisals of fair value. Intangibles frequently exist but are not carried as assets by the seller. Care should be taken to be sure all such existing intangibles are identified during the process of allocating cost.

Liabilities assumed are valued generally at the present values of amounts to be paid. Amounts should be discounted using an appropriate interest rate, which frequently is the buyer's borrowing rate for similar debt. More specific guidelines as to rates are set forth in APB No. 21 "Interest on Receivables and Payables."

• Liabilities for unfunded vested benefits should be recorded. Although APB No. 8 "Accounting for the Cost of Pension Plans," may have been appropriately followed by the acquired company, the liability for vested benefits may significantly exceed pension plan assets; this liability should be reflected during the process of assigning values to the liabilities assumed.

• Liabilities for warranties, vacation pay, etc. may not have been recorded because of their immateriality to the acquired company. But these liabilities may in fact be considered material to the acquiror in its process of allocating cost.

• Other liabilities and commitments such as unfavorable leases, contracts and commitments, and plant closing expense incident to the acquisition should also be identified if they exist and recorded at present values of amounts to be paid.

Tax Effects on Amounts Allocated

The fair values of specific assets acquired and liabilities assumed may differ from their income tax bases. Usually these differences in bases will arise when stock is acquired and the buyer does not elect to increase the tax basis of the acquired net assets (where elected, the increase in tax bases is normally effected by the liquidation of the acquired company).

The future tax effects of any differences between book and income tax bases are a factor in estimating fair value. Accordingly, values assigned to identifiable assets and liabilities should recognize that fair value may be less than market or appraisal value if all or a portion of the market or appraisal value is not deductible for income tax purposes by the buyer;

conversely, fair value may be greater if more than market or appraisal value is deductible for income tax purposes. The impact of these tax effects should be reflected in the amounts assigned to individual assets and liabilities. For example, if an excess of vested benefits over pension plan assets is to be accrued, the company will receive a tax deduction when these amounts are funded but there will be no book expense. Accordingly, the liability for pension costs would be recorded net of the related tax effect.

Any differences between the amounts recorded for book purposes and the tax basis are permanent differences, not timing differences. Accordingly, an acquiring corporation does not record separate deferred tax amounts at the date of acquisition.

Deferred income taxes previously recorded by a seller are not carried forward or recorded by the buyer. However, when a subsidiary is acquired and not liquidated, such amounts will continue to be carried on the subsidiary's books and eliminated in the preparation of consolidated financial statements.

Goodwill

When the total cost of an acquired company exceeds the sum of the amounts assigned to identifiable assets acquired less liabilities assumed, goodwill is recorded. In balance sheets, goodwill is often labeled "excess of purchase price over fair value of assets acquired."

Goodwill recorded in a purchase is amortized in accordance with the provisions of APB No. 17, "Intangible Assets." Based upon the concept that the value of all intangible assets eventually disappears, goodwill is amortized over the periods estimated to be benefited, but that period may not exceed 40 years. Amortization is generally computed using the straight-line method — equal annual amounts — unless another systematic method is more appropriate in the circumstances. Goodwill is often considered by management to have an indeterminate life expected to exceed 40 years; in such situations, it must be amortized over 40 years, not over either a longer or arbitrarily shorter period.

Negative Goodwill

In some business combinations the sum of the fair values of identifiable assets acquired, less liabilities assumed, exceeds the cost of the acquired company. If so, the fair values otherwise assignable to the noncurrent assets (except for long-term investments in marketable securities) are reduced proportionately by the amount of the excess. A resulting deferred credit may only be recorded after the noncurrent assets are reduced to zero value. This credit is usually known as negative goodwill and referred to in financial statements as "excess of net assets acquired over cost." Like goodwill, negative goodwill is amortized systematically to income over the period estimated to be benefited but not in excess of 40 years. Typically this period is 3-10 years.

Related Matters

Reverse Acquisitions: Identifying the acquiring corporation in a purchase is, in most cases, not difficult. The buyer is usually the entity that issues the consideration and is typically the larger company. But sometimes, when common stock is exchanged in a purchase transaction, the identity of the acquiring company is not obvious. In some combinations, the "acquired company" survives as the continuing corporate entity or its shareholders become the controlling group in the combined entity. The importance of identifying the buyer is that it is the seller's assets and liabilities that must be revalued as of the acquisition date.

APB No. 16 established a rebuttable presumption that the identity of the acquiring corporation is obtained by identifying the former common stockholder interests which either retain or receive the larger portion of the voting rights in the combined corporation. If a new corporation is formed to issue stock in a purchase, the stockholder group in control of the new entity will usually indicate the acquiring company. This presumption may be overcome if other evidence clearly indicates that another corporation is the buyer.

Frequently in a reverse acquisition the issuing company changes its name to the name of the company whose shareholders gave up their shares.

Equity Method: The acquisition by a corporation of voting control of another corporation's stock creates a parent-subsidiary relationship. Whether a purchase or a pooling, subsidiaries typically are consolidated. But occasionally they are not, as for example, when a manufacturing company owns a financial institution. In this situation, the subsidiary would be accounted for on the parent's books by the equity method of accounting. Under this method, the balance sheet carrying amount for the subsidiary would be the parent's cost of its investment plus its equity in the earnings of the subsidiary since acquisition, less dividends received. Individual assets and liabilities of the subsidiary are not reflected in the consolidated amounts. Similarly, in the income statement only the parent's equity in the subsidiary's earnings is reported; individual revenue and expense items are not consolidated.

Even though individual items are not included in the consolidated amounts, if the acquisition is a purchase, the fair value of the assets and liabilities must be determined when control is obtained. The resulting fair values are then depreciated (e.g., fixed assets) and amortized (e.g. goodwill) in determining the net income of the subsidiary for inclusion under the equity method.

Minority Interest: Accountants agree that when less than 100 percent control is acquired, the assets and liabilities of the controlled company should be reflected in the consolidated financial statements of the parent company unless the equity method of accounting is followed. But they disagree about the extent of recording the fair values of the net assets acquired when a minority interest exists.

To illustrate, if 75 percent of the voting stock of a company were acquired, some accountants would include the acquired net assets in the consolidated financial statements at the sum of 75 percent of the fair value of those net assets and 25 percent of historical cost; the reported minority interest would thus represent 25 percent of the historical cost of the acquired company's net assets. For example, assume $1,000,000 was paid for 75 percent of the common stock and that the fair value of the net assets acquired was $1,330,000 and the historical cost of those assets was $900,000. The acquired assets would be recorded in the consolidated balance sheet at $1,225,000 ($1,000,000 + [$900,000 x 25%]) and the minority interest would be recorded as $225,000. Thus the minority interest in the acquired company represents only the minority shareholders' interest in the separate entity. In the consolidated financial statements, the parent's cost and the allocation of that cost is not considered relevant to the minority shareholders.

Other accountants would reflect a minority interest equal to 25 percent of the entire fair value of the subsidiary's net assets. Those assets, using the above example, would be included in the consolidated balance sheet at $1,330,000 and $330,000 would be recorded as minority interest. Thus, the net assets would be recorded at cost, $1,000,000 and all assets and liabilities would be consolidated at their full fair value with the minority interest reflecting that value.

Acquisition of Minority Interest in Previously Purchased or Pooled Subsidiary: The acquisition of some or all of the stock held by minority shareholders is accounted for by the purchase method. Purchase accounting is applied even when a subsidiary had previously been pooled. For example, subsequent to a pooling in which 92 percent of the stock was exchanged, if the parent acquired the minority interest in a stock for stock exchange (or through the purchase of that stock by the subsidiary itself), that transaction would be treated as a purchase. In this situation, a full review would be necessary to determine the fair values of the net assets acquired and the amount of resulting goodwill, if any. But practically speaking, based on the immateriality of the amounts involved, companies often charge to goodwill the entire excess of cost over book value, rather than making allocations to the individual assets. Subsequent acquisitions of the stock of a subsidiary acquired in a purchase require that the fair values of the subsidiary's net assets be reviewed to determine whether they have changed materially enough to warrant reappraisals.

New Basis (Push-Down) Accounting: When stock is acquired in a purchase, the acquired company frequently continues on as a subsidiary of its new parent. Often, separate subsidiary company financial statements are prepared, particularly when there are minority shareholders or when the subsidiary has third party debt outstanding.

At present, some accountants prepare such subsidiary financial statements using the previous recorded historical cost carrying amounts of the subsidiary's assets and liabilities. Such statements reflect the view that only the company's stockholders have changed; that since the purchase transaction does not affect directly the continuing legal entity, the historical cost basis should not be changed.

Other accountants, however, would prepare financial statements allocating the parent company's cost to the subsidiary company's net assets. This method of reporting reflects the view that when there has been a substantial change in the ownership of a company, a new entity is in effect created and that its financial statements should reflect the new owner's basis in its net assets. That is, the new owner's basis should be "pushed down" to the company and used to establish a "new cost basis" in its financial statements.

In response to this diversity in practice, the AICPA submitted an "Issues Paper" on this subject to the FASB which later responded that it would not add this topic to its agenda as a separate project, but that it would consider this issue as part of the project on business combinations or in a possible project on consolidations.

Contingent Consideration: A business combination agreement may provide for the later issuance of additional shares of stock or the payment of cash or other consideration contingent on specified events or transactions occurring or not occurring in the future.

Consideration issuable at the expiration of a contingency period or issued and held in escrow pending the outcome of a contingency is disclosed in the buyer's financial statements but it is not recorded as a liability or shown as outstanding securities. When the contingency is resolved and consideration is issued or becomes issuable, the amount is recorded at the then current fair value of the consideration issued, either as additional cost or as an adjustment to stockholders' equity, as discussed below.

If the outcome of a contingency is determinable beyond reasonable doubt at the date of acquisition, the amount of such contingent consideration is used to determine the cost of an acquired company at that date.

Earnings Contingencies: The parties to a business combination may agree that if specified earnings are maintained or higher earnings are achieved in future periods additional consideration will be paid. When those earnings are achieved, the fair value of the additional consideration at the time it becomes issuable is recorded as additional cost of the acquired company and allocated to appropriate assets, usually goodwill, and amortized over the remaining life of those assets.

Some purchase agreements may provide for the issuance of additional consideration if specified earnings levels are maintained or achieved, but their intent is to provide compensation or a profit sharing arrangement. In these circumstances, the additional consideration should be accounted for as an expense of the appropriate period and not as a cost of the acquired company.

Market Price Contingencies: The recorded cost of an acquired company does not change because of contingencies based on security prices. The parties to a business combination may agree that should the market price of the securities issued not equal specified amounts on specified future dates, additional equity or debt securities, cash, or other assets will be issued to make the total consideration equal to the specified amount. Or they may agree that the securities previously issued will be repurchased at agreed amounts.

If additional consideration later becomes payable or shares are repurchased, the fair value of the additional consideration at that date is recorded as a reduction of stockholders' equity, if equity securities were originally issued. From a practical standpoint, when additional shares of stock are issued they are recorded at par or stated value because any excess of fair value over par or stated value would simply be added to and then deducted from the same account, additional paid-in-capital. If debt securities were issued, a discount is recorded and amortized from the date the additional consideration is issued.

Other Contingencies: In a purchase, the allocation of cost to identifiable assets and liabilities, including goodwill, if any, becomes complicated when there are assets and liabilities that are contingent on future events, such as income tax assessments or lawsuits pending at the date of a purchase or arising shortly thereafter. Accounting for subsequent settlements of these uncertainties is addressed in Financial Accounting Standards No. 38 "Accounting for Preacquisition Contingencies of Purchased Enterprises." This statement imposes a time limitation on the use of purchase price adjustments.

During the "allocation period" following a purchase, contingent assets and liabilities would be recorded if it is probable that future events would confirm their existence and the amounts could be reasonably estimated. Later adjustments of contingencies would be reflected in current income as they occur. The "allocation period" is limited to the time it takes the purchaser, after the purchase, to obtain the information needed (e.g., appraisals or actuarial determinations) to identify and allocate the purchase price to the acquired company's assets and liabilities. This period usually will be no more than a year and it could be much shorter.

Acquisition Date: APB No. 16 states that the date of acquisition is ordinarily the date assets are received and consideration paid. However, for convenience, the parties may designate an effective date between the dates a combination is initiated and consummated. A designated date may be used as the date of acquisition only if a written agreement provides that effective control of the seller is transferred to the buyer and there are no restrictions other than restrictions to protect the seller, such as not allowing significant changes in the operations before the closing and requiring dividends equal to those regularly paid before the designated date. Designating an effective date other than the date assets or securities are issued requires adjusting the cost of an acquired company and subsequent net income to compensate for recognizing income before any payment was made.

Typically, an acquisition does not close on the first or the last day of a month and a date is not designated in writing. But the acquisition is frequently recorded as of the beginning or end of that month, assuming the immateriality of the technical error. The cost and net income would require adjustment for any material dollar effect of the difference in dates.

Research and Development: Financial Accounting Standard (FAS) No. 2, "Accounting for Research and Development Costs," requires that the cost of tangible and intangible assets used in, or to be used in, research and development activities be charged to expense as incurred when those assets have no alternative future uses. Accordingly, most costs incurred in research and development activities are expensed immediately.

In a purchase the acquisition cost is allocated to all identifiable tangible and intangible assets acquired, including those intangibles resulting from the research

and development activities of the seller. These assets might include patents, blueprints, formulas, and specifications or designs for any new products or processes.

The acquired assets might also include materials and supplies, equipment and facilities and specific research projects to be used in future research and development activities. An FASB Interpretation (No. 4) of FAS No. 2 states that acquisition cost should be allocated to identifiable assets to be used in research and development activities, and if such assets have no alternative future use they must be charged to expense in the income statement of the combined company immediately after recording the acquisition. The Interpretation gives no guidance as to how the fair value of such assets should be determined, and some accountants view such assets as having no current net realizable value at the acquisition date.

Leases in Business Combinations: The fair value of a leasehold at an acquisition date may be different from the amount recorded by the seller and subject to revaluation under APB No. 16, if a purchase. But the classification of such a lease as a capital or operating lease probably would not be changed in either a purchase or a pooling. Leases, based on an FASB Interpretation (No. 21) of FAS No. 13, "Accounting for Leases," are classified only at the inception of the lease agreement or upon modification of the lease terms. Unless the terms of a lease agreement are modified as part of a business combination, the lease would not be reclassified at that time. For example, if the terms of a lease entered into by the seller ten years before a business combination were not changed, a lease classified as a capital lease would continue to be accounted for as a capital lease in the financial statements of the combined company even though it did not meet the criteria for a capital lease at the merger date.

LIFO Inventories: In taxable poolings, nontaxable purchases, and taxable purchases in which the book and tax allocations of the purchase price differ, the book amounts reported for LIFO inventories will differ from the LIFO tax basis. In a purchase this difference frequently results in the inventory being recorded net of the related tax effects. This often raises questions about compliance with the IRS requirement that book and tax amounts for LIFO inventories be in agreement. According to Rev. Proc. 72-29 a LIFO election will not be terminated by reason of application of APB No. 16 if certain disclosure requirements are met. Disclosure of income and LIFO inventory differences for book and federal income tax purposes is required to be made in the financial statements for all taxable years in which differences occur, regardless of the year of acquisition, and regardless of the materiality of such differences for financial statement purposes.

DISCUSSION OF POOLING CRITERIA

The pooling criteria set forth in APB No. 16 are elaborated upon in the Accounting Interpretations issued by the AICPA and the FASB. Altogether, the AICPA issued 39 interpretations of APB No. 16, of which 31 pertain to the criteria for classification of business combinations. To date, the FASB has issued two interpretations. While the AICPA interpretations are "unofficial," that is, not issued by an organization recognized by the accounting profession as authorized to establish generally accepted accounting principles, they have generally been followed.

The initiation of a pooling is defined in APB No. 16 as the earlier of (1) the date the major terms of a plan, including the ratio of exchange of stock, are publicly announced or formally made known to the stockholders of any one of the combining companies or (2) the date that stockholders of a combining company are notified in writing of an exchange offer. The initiation date is discussed in several accounting interpretations which make clear that for there to be an initiation, the exchange ratio must be set or a formula established by which the actual exchange ratio can be determined. Further, the terms of the exchange must be announced to those shareholders expected to tender their shares for shares of the issuing company. Notice to the shareholders of the issuing company or a public notice of intent to make a tender offer without also announcing set terms will not establish an initiation date. If an announced plan is formally terminated and subsequent negotiations result in another formal announcement of major terms, the new plan constitutes a new initiation even if the terms are the same as the terms of the old plan.

The following discussion of the pooling criteria includes applicable published accounting interpretations in addition to APB No. 16 comments.

Attributes of Combining Companies

The concept of pooling of interests requires the combining of independent ownership interests in their entirety to continue previously separate operations. Two essential attributes of combining companies are required for pooling of interests accounting.

AUTONOMY

> Criterion #1—Each of the combining companies is autonomous and has not been a subsidiary or division of another corporation within two years before the plan of combination is initiated.

Questions about the autonomy of a company frequently arise when a planned combination involves an entity controlled by one or a few individuals or by a personal holding company, established for federal income tax reasons, which also controls several other entities. In these situations, each entity is theoretically a "subsidiary" and the individual, group of individuals or the personal holding company, is the "parent." However, for purposes of applying this criterion of APB No. 16, the relationship between the businesses is more important than the fact that each business is theoretically a subsidiary. The intent of the criterion is to preclude fragmenting a business and pooling only a part of the business. Thus, if an owner had several related entities in the same line of business, the acquisition of only one or two and not all would require that purchase accounting be followed. Conversely, if the entities not being acquired are in unrelated lines of business the acquisition would qualify as a pooling, assuming all of the other pooling criteria were met.

A company that has been a subsidiary of another company within two years of initiation or consummation of a combination is not considered autonomous and, accordingly, is precluded from a pooling. However, a company divested to comply with an order of a governmental authority or judicial body is exempted from this criterion and is deemed autonomous and eligible to combine with another company in a pooling.

INDEPENDENCE

> Criterion #2—Each of the combining companies is independent of the other combining companies.

Combining companies are considered independent if, prior to the initiation of a plan of combination, neither company holds as an intercorporate investment more than 10 percent of the outstanding voting common stock of the other company. Independence of combining companies also means that at the date a plan of combination is initiated and at the date it is consummated, as well as all times between these dates, none of the combining companies holds more than 10 percent of the outstanding voting common stock of any other combining company. However, voting common stock acquired after the initiation date in exchange for the voting common stock issued to effect the combination is excluded from the 10 percent limitation.

APB No. 16 does not apply to transfers by a corporation of its net assets to a newly formed substitute corporate entity formed by an existing corporation or to a transfer of net assets or exchange of shares between companies under common control. Although the classification criteria of APB No. 16 do not apply to a combination of companies under common control, the accounting for these combinations is similar to accounting for poolings; the recorded amounts of assets and liabilities of the separate companies are combined to become the assets and liabilities of the combined corporation.

Manner of Combining Interests

Combining existing voting common stock interests and the subsequent mutual sharing in the combined risks and benefits is an essential ingredient of a pooling of interests. To assure that existing stockholder interests are appropriately combined, seven conditions relating to the exchange of common stock are required for pooling of interests accounting.

SINGLE TRANSACTION

Criterion #3—The combination is effected in a single transaction or is completed in accordance with a specific plan within one year after the plan is initiated.

The combination must be completed within one year after the initiation date if it is to qualify as a pooling. An exception is permitted, however, if the delay is beyond the control of the combining companies because proceedings by a governmental authority or litigation prevent completing the transaction. Altering the terms of exchange generally constitutes a new plan of combination and changes the initiation date to the date such revised terms are publicly announced.

SUBSTANTIALLY ALL SHARES EXCHANGED

Criterion #4—A corporation offers and issues only common stock with rights identical to those of the majority of its outstanding voting common stock in exchange for substantially all of the voting common stock interest of another company at the date the plan of combination is consummated. (Substantially all of the voting common stock means 90 percent or more.)

90 percent Test: The concept behind pooling of interest accounting requires a mutual sharing of risks

and rewards in the ongoing enterprise and, accordingly, substantially all of the voting common stock of the combining company must be exchanged for the voting common stock of the issuing company. In many exchange offers, cash is used to acquire shares from stockholders not satisfied with the issuing company's offer, and to acquire fractional shares. To eliminate problems over the definition of "substantially all," APB No. 16 requires that at least 90 percent of the outstanding voting common stock of the combining company be exchanged at the date the combination is consummated.

An issuing company generally may acquire other equity or debt securities of a combining company in any way it chooses. For example, it may redeem callable or redeemable securities for cash and retire them; it may assume debt securities, or exchange substantially identical securities or voting common stock for them; or it may leave the securities outstanding. However, if voting common stock or convertible securities are to be exchanged for convertible debt or convertible preferred stocks of the combining company, the number of voting common shares issued, or to be issued on conversion of the new securities, must equal the number of shares that would have been issued had the other securities been converted into the voting common stock of the combining company before consummation and exchanged for voting common stock of the issuing company.

Intercorporate Holdings: A pooling might be precluded when a combining company holds as an investment less than 10 percent of the issuing company's voting common stock. This could occur because an investment in the stock of the issuing corporation is treated as an investment by the issuing corporation in the stock of the combining company. To make the comparison with the 90 percent test the shares are converted to stock "as if" held by the issuing company using the announced exchange ratio. This calculation could result in the "issuing company" in effect holding more than a 10 percent intercorporate investment.

Intercorporate holdings also reduce the number of shares of voting common stock exchanged but they do not reduce the total number of outstanding shares of the combining company. This reduced number of shares deemed exchanged might result in less than 90 percent of the total outstanding voting common stock being received.

Disproportionate Payment: Payment for fractional shares must be reasonable in amount and proportional to each shareholder's fractional share interest. For example, if the issuing corporation exchanges its shares with a market value of $1,000,000 for 100,000 shares of the combining company ($10 per share) the amount paid for all the fractional shares must not be excessive in relation to that amount. If $1,000 was paid for each remaining fractional half share, such amount would be excessive and preclude a pooling. In addition, no individual shareholder may receive more for the same fractional interests than the holders of other fractional shares.

Acquisition of Net Assets: A business combination will also satisfy the voting common stock for voting common stock criterion if all the operating assets of a combining company are transferred in exchange for stock of the issuing company. Thus, a pooling of interests can be obtained even in those cases where the issuing company is reluctant, usually for legal reasons, to acquire the stock of the combining company. Special computations of equivalent shares may, however, be necessary if either company holds stock in the other company as an investment.

Restricted Stock: In a pooling, the issuing corporation may not issue voting common stock subject to restrictions, including restrictions imposed by it on the sale of its shares. However, a pooling is not precluded if such stock is temporarily restricted by governmental regulation because the shares are unregistered as long as the shares may be sold under the SEC's Rule 144, or the issuing company is in process of registering or has agreed to register those shares.

TWO YEAR CONTEMPLATION TEST

Criterion #5—None of the combining companies changes the equity interest of the voting common stock in contemplation of effecting the combination either within two years before the plan of combination is initiated or between the dates the combination is initiated and consummated; changes in contemplation of effecting the combination may include distributions to stockholders and additional issuances, exchanges, and retirements of securities.

Except for normal dividend distributions to stockholders, all changes in the equity interest of the outstanding voting common stock of either the issuing corporation or a combining company within two years before a plan of combination is initiated or between the dates a combination is initiated or consummated are presumed to have been in contemplation of the planned business combination and pooling accounting precluded. This presumption is rebuttable, but persuasive evidence to the contrary is needed.

Abnormal Dividends: Corporate assets may not be used as consideration in a pooling. Dividends paid to stockholders of either party to a proposed pooling that go beyond that company's normal dividend policy and do not have a demonstrated valid business purpose are viewed as a distribution of corporate assets.

If an issuing corporation's stockholders receive such a dividend the combination may be viewed as the issuance of corporate assets to one group of shareholders and common stock to the other group. On the other hand, if such a dividend is paid by the combining company, it has not exchanged all of its assets for stock of the issuing company. However, when a combining company has valid reasons for paying a special dividend, it might overcome the presumption that the dividend was paid in contemplation of a business combination. For example, a dividend paid to prevent incurring a tax liability for excessive accumulated earnings would usually not bar a pooling.

In most cases the issuing corporation will have monitored its dividend program if it knows that it will become involved in future business combinations.

Dilution of Possible Dissenters: A combining company expecting to become involved in a proposed pooling might want to assure that at least 90 percent of its voting common stock will be exchanged in any forthcoming offer. To do this, it might purposefully sell additional shares and thereby dilute the interests of possible dissenting shareholders to less than a 10 percent interest. Likewise, debt securities or preferred stocks might be exchanged for the voting common stock of holders thought likely to dissent. Unless a valid business purpose unrelated to the business combination could be demonstrated, these or similar transactions would preclude a pooling. However, an exchange of debt or other equity securities for voting common stock by a combining company could be reversed and "cured" and a pooling allowed if the issuing corporation exchanges its voting common stock for those debt or other equity securities in a ratio to restore the former shareholders to their original position. That is, they receive the same number of shares of the issuing corporation as if the earlier transaction had not occurred.

Partial Exchanges: An exchange of voting common stock for debt securities or preferred stock within two years of a business combination to allow some shareholders to retain only a portion of their original shares for a later exchange would preclude a pooling. Such an exchange however can be "cured" by the issuing corporation in the same manner as described immediately above.

TREASURY STOCK ACQUISITIONS

Criterion #6—Each of the combining companies reacquires shares of voting common stock only for purposes other than business combinations, and no company reacquires more than a normal number of shares between the dates the plan of combination is initiated and consummated.

Purchases by either party to a business combination of its own common stock can violate the pooling concept. Such purchases require the use of corporate assets and are presumed to be made in conjunction with the exchange of voting common stock. Treasury stock purchased to eliminate potential dissenting shareholders, to distribute assets to the common stockholders of the issuing corporation, or to redeem a portion of an individual shareholder's stock interests all violate the pooling concept.

If it were not for the treasury stock prohibitions, an issuing corporation might actually effect cash poolings by acquiring its own voting common stock for cash and then issuing voting common stock in a business combination. The same effect could also be obtained if the combining company acquired substantially all of its voting common stock for cash and then the remaining few shares were exchanged for stock of the issuing corporation.

In the absence of persuasive evidence to the contrary, it is presumed that all acquisitions of treasury stock during the two-year period preceding the date a plan of combination is initiated, and between initiation and consummation were made in contemplation of a pooling of interests. Lacking such evidence, the combination must be accounted for by the purchase method regardless of whether treasury stock or unissued shares or both are issued in the combination.

The pooling criteria of APB No. 16 permit certain limited acquisitions of treasury stock. These acquisitions must be for purposes other than business combinations. For example, it is permissible to acquire shares for stock option and compensation plans following a systematic pattern of reacquisitions established at least two years before the plan of combination is initiated. If less than two years, such reacquisitions must be coincident with the adoption of a new stock option or compensation plan. In addition, no more than a normal number of shares may be reacquired between the dates a plan of combination is initiated and consummated; the normal number of shares is established by the pattern of reacquisitions of stock before the plan is initiated.

Treasury stock may also be acquired without disturbing a concurrent pooling if such stock is for issuance in a specific business combination treated as a purchase, to resolve an existing contingent share agreement from a prior business combination or for issuance pursuant to contractual obligations, e.g., employee stock reacquistion agreements. However, such shares must be reissued for these specific purposes before consummation of the pooling or they must be specifically reserved for these purposes at consummation.

Treasury stock problems, sometimes referred to as "tainted" stock, may be "cured" by the sale of such stock prior to consummation of a proposed pooling. Further, a planned pooling would not be precluded if the number of tainted shares is not material in relation to the number of shares issued to effect the combination. Material is defined as less than 10 percent of the number of shares issued. Treasury shares not held for a specific purpose but acquired more than two years before the initiation of a business combination are not "tainted" shares and will have no effect on any pooling transaction; they may even be reissued in a pooling.

SEC Rules: The SEC, in Accounting Series Release (ASR) Nos. 146 and 146A, established stricter rules for treasury stock acquisitions than did APB No. 16. The ASR's established tests of purpose, systematic pattern and reasonable expectation if a combination is to be treated as a pooling.

Public companies, to protect future poolings, should acquire treasury stock only under a plan which meets each of the three above noted tests. ASR No. 146 requires that "The criteria of the reacquisition plan must be sufficiently explicit so that the pattern of reacquisitions may be objectively compared to the plan." Treasury stock acquisitions must satisfy these tests throughout the two years prior to the initiation of a pooling and between the dates of initiation and consummation. Treasury shares which do not meet the criteria of ASR No. 146 are considered tainted, but may be cured in the same manner as shares deemed tainted under the criteria of APB No. 16.

Purposes which usually satisfy the systematic pattern test include:

Recurring stock dividends
Stock option plans
Stock purchase plans
Stock compensation plans.
Plans to acquire shares to be exchanged for:
    Convertible debentures
    Convertible stock
    Warrants.

When determining the purposes of treasury stock acquisitions the ASR's state that it is important to focus on the intended subsequent distribution of the common shares rather than on assertions as to the reasons for acquiring treasury shares, even where the assertion is formalized by action of the board of directors. Thus, simply reserving treasury shares will not provide persuasive evidence that those shares were not reacquired in contemplation of pooling.

It is possible that treasury shares acquired shortly after the consummation of an intended pooling may be tainted and thus preclude pooling accounting. For example, the purchase of treasury shares from sources unrelated to the stockholders of the pooled company within 30 days of the intended pooling would be presumed to have invalidated the pooling. This presumption, however, can be overcome by evidence showing that the treasury shares were acquired for a specific purpose unrelated to the pooling of interest.

SHARES EXCHANGED IN ENTIRETY

Criterion #7—The ratio of the interest of an individual common stockholder to those of other common stockholders in a combining company remains the same as a result of the exchange to effect the combination.

A pooling of interests would be precluded even though more than 90 percent of the outstanding voting common stock of the combining company is exchanged if one or more shareholders exchange only a portion of their shares. The pooling concept requires a continued sharing of proportionate risks and rewards. This continued sharing is violated if an individual shareholder elects to participate to a lesser extent by exchanging only a portion of his shares. The 90 percent test is only to recognize that as a practical matter some shareholders of a combining company might refuse to exchange their shares even though most shareholders agree to the combination. In a pooling, each individual shareholder must exchange all of his shares or exchange none of his shares. The 90 percent test is not applied to individual shareholders; it is applied only to shareholders of a combining company as a group.

The determination of whether a shareholder exchanges all of his shares for voting common stock of the issuing corporation is usually made as of the consummation date. However, if an issuing corporation purchases common shares during the two year period prior to the initiation date directly from a shareholder who also exchanges common shares at consummation, that shareholder will be presumed to have exchanged only a portion of his shares and a pooling precluded, unless it can be shown that the original sale was not made in contemplation of the subsequent business combination.

Warrants: If a pooling is to be obtained, warrants may be used only to acquire warrants, debt or equity securities other than voting common stock of the combining company, and in some cases, up to 10 percent of the combining company's voting common stock. If warrants are exchanged for warrants of the combining company, the new warrants issued may not provide for the purchase of a greater number of shares than could be obtained if the combining company's warrants were exercised. For example, assume an issuing corporation exchanges 3 million common shares for 1 million shares of a combining company, and the combining company has 100,000 warrants outstanding that will allow the holder to purchase 200,000 common shares. At the 3-for-1 exchange ratio, 200,000 shares could be exchanged for 600,000 shares of the issuing company. Thus, each warrant may be exchanged for new warrants to purchase no more than 6 common shares of the issuing company.

EXERCISABLE VOTING RIGHTS

Criterion #8—The voting rights to which the common stock ownership interests in the resulting combined corporation are entitled are exercisable by the stockholders; the stockholders are neither deprived of nor restricted in exercising those rights for a period.

Shareholders of a combining company must be able to vote all shares issued to them. They also must be able to vote shares otherwise issuable to them but not distributed pending resolution of a contingency.

CONTINGENT SHARES IN A POOLING

Criterion #9—The combination is resolved at the date the plan is consummated and no provisions of the plan relating to the issue of securities or other consideration are pending.

A pooling transaction must be complete at the date the plan is consummated. Generally, there can be no agreement to issue additional shares or other consideration to the stockholders of the combining company and no shares can be issued to an escrow agent for return to the issuing corporation or release to the shareholders of the combining company upon the resolution of certain contingencies. The intent of this criterion is to prohibit a pooling if earnings or market price contingencies are present in a business combination agreement. APB No. 16 does, however, allow certain contingency agreements in a pooling to cover specific situations whose outcome cannot be determined at consummation or perhaps even for several years thereafter.

Any change made in the number of shares originally issued in a pooling for the final resolution of either a general or specific contingency is recorded as an adjustment to stockholders' equity. The related effect of the resolution of a contingency must be reflected in net income in the period the contingency is resolved. For example, an unfavorable resolution of a lawsuit could result in shares being returned to the issuing company. The return of those shares would be recorded as an adjustment to stockholders' equity and in accordance with the pooling concept the combined company would charge income for the settlement of the litigation.

General Contingencies: One contingency arrangement allowed in a pooling is the "general management representation" in which management of a combining company typically warrants that the assets exist, that recorded amounts are not less than realizable value and that all liabilities and their amounts have been recorded or disclosed. Such an agreement is acceptable in a pooling only if it provides immediately for a substantial sharing of risks and rewards and a complete sharing within a reasonable period of time. In this light, a contingency agreement is merely a device to provide time for the issuing corporation to determine that the representations are accurate so it does not issue shares for assets that do not exist or for losses that arose prior to consummation. The maximum time following consummation generally allowed for these determinations may not extend beyond the issuance of the first independent audit report on the combined company. That is, the audit should provide a check on management's general representations.

Specific Contingencies: A revision of the number of shares issued in a pooling is permitted for the settlement of a contingency known to exist at consummation at an amount different from that recorded by a combining company. An example would be pending anti-trust litigation or income tax returns under examination.

Employment Contracts: Granting employment contracts or entering into a deferred compensation plan with former stockholders of a combining company will not violate the pooling criterion if they are entered into for valid business purposes. The contracts should be reasonable in relation to existing contracts granted by the issuing corporation to its management.

Granting employment contracts to former stockholders of a combining company who were not or will not be active in management probably indicates a contingent pay-out arrangement, which would preclude a pooling. Likewise, "consultant" contracts for former stockholders often are in substance contingent pay-out arrangements that preclude a pooling.

Stock Options: Former stockholders of a combining company who become directors or employees of the combined corporation may participate in stock option plans adopted by the combined corporation for its employees and/or directors without affecting a pooling. However, a stock option plan that is in reality an arrangement to issue additional shares at a relatively low cost to these stockholders would violate the pooling criteria.

ABSENCE OF PLANNED TRANSACTIONS

Criterion #10—The combined corporation does not agree directly or indirectly to retire or reacquire all or part of the common stock issued to effect the combination.

Criterion #11—The combined corporation does not enter into other financial arrangements for the benefit of the former stockholder of a combining company, such as a guaranty of loans secured by stock issued in the combination which in effect negates the exchange of equity securities.

Criterion #12—The combined corporation does not intend or plan to dispose of a significant part of the assets of the combining companies within two years after the combination other than disposals in the ordinary course of business of the formerly separate companies and to eliminate duplicate facilities or excess capacity.

Certain transactions occurring after a business combination is consummated are inconsistent with the combining of existing common stockholders' interests. Including those transactions in the negotiations and terms of the combination, either explicitly or implicitly, counteracts the effect of combining stockholder interests.

Pooling With Bailout: The pooling criteria of APB No. 16 do not include a continuity of ownership interests requirement, a criterion for pooling under ARB No. 48. APB No. 16, however, does prohibit a combined corporation from agreeing to reacquire all or part of the stock issued to effect the combination. Stock issued must remain outstanding outside the combined corporation without arrangements on the part of any of the corporations involved to use their financial resources to buy out or "bailout" former stockholders or to induce others to do so. Further, a business combination can not be accounted for as a pooling if its consummation is contingent upon the purchase by third parties of any of the voting common stock to be issued. Former shareholders of a combining company are, however, free to dispose of their shares upon receipt without affecting the pooling. The corporation may even assist them in finding an unrelated buyer for their shares. Consummation of the business combination must occur first, however, without regard to such a sale and may not be contingent upon obtaining a firm commitment by a potential purchaser of the shares to be issued.

For public companies, the SEC requires a minimum holding period that must be complied with if a pooling is to be obtained. Under ASR No. 135, the former shareholders of a combining company may not sell their shares until such time as the first post-combination results, including interim results, covering at least 30 days of combined operations are published.

ACCOUNTING FOR A POOLING
Combining Financial Statements

To apply the pooling of interests method at the date a business combination is consummated, the recorded amounts of the assets and liabilities of the separate companies are combined to become the assets and liabilities of the combined corporation. The stockholders' equity accounts of the separate companies are also combined. If both corporate entities survive, this presents no problem as the pooling entries are made each time consolidated financial statements are prepared. But, only the issuing company survives, the historical balance sheet amounts from the nonsurviving company must be recorded on the survivor's books as of the consummation date.

The amount representing the outstanding shares of the combined corporation at par or stated value may exceed the total amount of capital stock of the separate combining companies. Any excess is deducted first from the combined additional paid-in capital account to the extent it is available, and thereafter from combined retained earnings.

Results of operations for the accounting period in which a pooling occurs are reported as though the companies had been combined as of the beginning of that period. Thus, the income statement will reflect the operations of the separate companies combined from the beginning of the period to the date the combination was consummated and those of the combined operations from that date to the end of the period. In a note to its financial statements, the combined entity is required to disclose the revenue, extraordinary items, and net income of each of the separate companies from the beginning of the period to the date the combination is consummated. For convenience, the information relating to the separate companies may be as of the end of the interim period nearest the date that the combination is consummated.

When financial statements and other financial information for prior years are presented they are to be restated and presented on a combined basis to furnish comparative information. All restated financial statements and financial summaries should indicate that the financial data of the previously separate companies has been combined. Generally, this is done by indicating

"restated" under the heading of the prior year column and including a reference to the footnote.

Consummation Date

A plan of combination is consummated on the date the voting common stock is exchanged. In a pooling, no other date may be used to record the effects of the business combination. This differs from a purchase in which the end of an accounting period between the initiation and consummation dates may be designated by the parties as the effective date.

Pooling After Year End

Because a pooling may only be recorded as of the date the combination is consummated, companies are prohibited from retroactively reflecting in their financial statements a pooling consummated after the close of their fiscal year but before financial statements are issued. However, companies are required to disclose in a footnote the substance of such a post-year end combination and its effects on reported financial position and results of operations.

Change in Accounting Methods

If the separate companies used differing methods of accounting for similar transactions or accounts, financial statement amounts may be adjusted to the same basis of accounting if the change would otherwise have been appropriate for the separate company. A change in accounting method to conform individual methods is applied retroactively and included as part of the pooling restatement when financial statements are presented for periods prior to the combination.

Expenses Related to Pooling of Interests

Costs incurred to effect a pooling and to integrate the continuing operations are recorded as expenses of the combined corporation in determining net income for the period in which the expenses are incurred. Expenses incurred before year end and applicable to a pooling consummated shortly after year-end should be recorded in the year the liability is fixed. However, when not material, such expenses frequently are recorded as of the consummation date. Typical expenses include registration fees, costs of furnishing information to stockholders, fees of finders and consultants, and costs incurred in combining the operations of the previously separate companies, including instituting efficiencies.

Differing Fiscal Years

Pooled companies generally adopt the same fiscal year. Subsidiaries included in consolidated financial statements of public companies must have fiscal year ends within 93 days of the parent's fiscal year end. If the previously separate companies prepared financial statements as of different fiscal year ends, and the 93 day requirement is not met, an adjustment is usually made to combined retained earnings to conform fiscal year ends, instead of recasting an entire fiscal year of one of the companies.

For example, assume an issuing company's fiscal year ends on September 30, 1980, the fiscal year of the combining company ends on March 31 and the consummation date is before September 30, 1980. The financial statement results of the two companies for their fiscal years ended March 31, 1980 and September 30, 1980 could be added together and reported as the combined results of operations for the year ended September 30, 1980 (prior years' income statements would be similarly combined). In this situation the earnings of the combining company from April 1, 1980 through September 30, 1980 would be added directly to the retained earnings of the combined corporation. After the combination, both companies would use the same fiscal year end of September 30.

Some companies might prefer to include the most recent income information and incur the cost, including additional audit costs, of recasting the financial information of the combining company. For instance, in the above example, financial data for the 12 months ended September 30, 1980 might be derived for the combining company.

Various other methods of restatement may also be appropriate depending upon the circumstances. APB No. 16 and Regulation S-X require certain disclosures about the amounts added to or deducted from retained earnings as a result of recasting the fiscal year of a combining company.

DISCLOSURES REQUIRED

Depending upon the accounting method used to account for a particular business combination, certain specific financial statement disclosures are required for the period in which the business combination is consummated.

Purchase Disclosures

Name and brief description of the companies combined.

Method of accounting for the business combination.

Period for which results of operations of the acquired company are included in the income statement of the acquiring corporation.

Cost of the acquired company and, if applicable, the number of shares of stock issued or issuable and the amount assigned to the issued and issuable shares.

Description of the plan for amortization of acquired goodwill, the amortization method and period.

Contingent payments, options, or commitments specified in the acquisition agreement and their proposed accounting treatment.

On a pro forma basis:

Results of operations for the current period as though the companies had combined at the beginning of the period, unless the acquisition was at or near the beginning of the period.

If comparative financial statements are presented, results of operations for the immediately preceding period as though the companies had combined at the beginning of that period.

The pro forma information should as a minimum show revenue, income before extraordinary items, net income, and earnings per share. To present pro forma information, income taxes, interest expense, preferred stock dividends, depreciation and amortization of assets, including goodwill should be adjusted to the accounting bases used in recording the combination. Pro forma presentations of results of operations of periods prior to the combination transaction should be limited to the immediately preceding period.

Information relating to several relatively minor acquisitions may be combined for disclosure.

Pooling Disclosures

Name and brief description of the companies combined.

Method of accounting for the business combination.

Description and number of shares of stock issued in the business combination.

Details of the results of operations of the previously separate companies for the period before the combination is consummated that are included in the current combined net income. This should include revenue; extraordinary items; net income; other changes in stockholders' equity; also amount of and manner of accounting for intercompany transactions.

Details of the nature of adjustments of net assets of the combining companies to adopt the same accounting practices and of the effects of the changes on net income previously reported by the separate companies and now presented in comparative financial statements.

Details of an increase or decrease in retained earnings from changing the fiscal year of a combining company. This should include at least revenue, expenses, extraordinary items, net income, and other changes in stockholders' equity for the period excluded from the reported results of operations.

Reconciliations of amounts of revenue and earnings previously reported by the corporation that issues the stock to effect the combination with the combined amounts currently presented in financial statements and summaries. A new corporation formed to effect a combination may instead disclose the earnings of the separate companies which comprise combined earnings for prior periods.

NEW YORK STOCK EXCHANGE REQUIREMENT

The New York Stock Exchange requires that in listing applications for shares to be issued in poolings, letters be received from the company and its independent accountants. The company's letter must contain certain information relating to its compliance with the pooling criteria. The accountants' letter must concur with the company's indicated treatment of the business combination as a pooling.

CURRENT DEVELOPMENTS

Over the years there has been criticism of the rationale for poolings and the treatment of goodwill. However, the 1970 rules still remain in effect. In 1976, the FASB issued a Discussion Memorandum on "Accounting for Business Combinations and Purchased Intangibles," but has not yet held a hearing to discuss the issues. This FASB project is inactive pending further progress on its conceptual framework project, especially the elements of financial statements segment. The Discussion Memorandum indicates that the FASB is planning a comprehensive reconsideration of accounting for business combinations and purchased intangibles and among the basic issues is whether or not there should be a recognition of new accounting basis and whether or not goodwill should be recognized as an asset in business combinations.

Thus, in the future the accounting for business combinations may be radically different, but for now, APB

Nos. 16 and 17 state the generally accepted accounting principles.

Bibliography

Accounting Principles Board, American Institute of Certified Public Accountants, "Business Combinations," Opinion No. 16, August 1970.

Accounting Principles Board, American Institute of Certified Public Accountants, "Intangible Assets," Opinion No. 17, August 1970.

American Institute of Certified Public Accountants, Accounting Interpretations of APB Opinion Nos. 16 and 17.

Committee on Accounting Procedure, American Institute of Accountants, "Accounting for Intangibles," Bulletin No. 24, December 1944.

Committee on Accounting Procedure, American Institute of Accountants, "Business Combinations," Bulletin No. 40, September 1950.

Committee on Accounting Procedure, American Institute of Certified Public Accountants, "Restatement and Revision of Accounting Research Bulletins," Bulletin No. 43, 1953.

Committee on Accounting Procedure, American Institute of Certified Public Accountants, "Business Combinations," Bulletin No. 48, January 1957.

Ernst & Whinney; *Accounting for Business Combinations.*

Holmes, Arthur W. and Meier, Robert A,; *Intermediate Accounting,* Richard D. Irwin Inc., Chicago, 1949.

Kester, Dr. Roy B.; *Accounting: Theory and Practice, Vol II.* The Ronald Press Company, New York, 1920.

May, George O.; *Financial Accounting: A Distillation of Experience.* The Macmillan Company, New York, 1951.

McCarthy, George D.; *Acquisitions and Mergers,* The Ronald Press Company, New York, 1963.

Paton, Dr. W.A.; *Advanced Accounting,* The Macmillan Company, New York, 1954.

Paton, Dr. W.A. and Littleton, A.C.; *An Introduction to Corporate Accounting Standards,* American Accounting Association, 1965.

APPENDIX A—EXAMPLES OF PURCHASES

EXCERPTS FROM PROXY STATEMENT
GEORGIA PACIFIC CORPORATION'S ACQUISITION
OF HUDSON PULP AND PAPER CORPORATION
(Proxy Statement Dated November 29, 1978)

The following unaudited pro forma combined statements of consolidated income, prepared by Georgia-Pacific, give effect to the proposed business combination on a purchase basis as described in Note (A). These statements should be read in conjunction with the related notes and the consolidated financial statements of the constituent companies and the related notes thereto and the related pro forma combined balance sheets, all of which are included elsewhere in this Joint Proxy Statement.

GEORGIA-PACIFIC CORPORATION AND SUBSIDIARIES
and
HUDSON PULP & PAPER CORP. AND SUBSIDIARY COMPANIES
PRO FORMA COMBINED STATEMENTS OF CONSOLIDATED INCOME
(Unaudited)

| | Year Ended December 31, 1977 | | | | Six Months Ended June 30, | | | | | | | |
| | | | | | 1977 | | | | 1978 | | | |
	Georgia-Pacific	Hudson	Adjust-ments	Pro Forma Combined	Georgia-Pacific	Hudson	Adjust-ments	Pro Forma Combined	Georgia-Pacific	Hudson	Adjust-ments	Pro Forma Combined
(Dollar amounts in millions, except per share amounts)												
Net sales	$3,675	$177	$—	$3,852	$1,719	$85	$—	$1,804	$2,022	$94	$—	$2,116
Costs and expenses												
Cost of sales	2,992	147	—	3,139	1,401	70	—	1,471	1,637	76	1	1,714
Selling, general and administrative	197	28	—	225	93	13	—	106	108	14	—	122
	3,189	175	—	3,364	1,494	83	—	1,577	1,745	90	1	1,836
Income from operations	486	2	—	488	225	2	—	227	277	4	(1)	280
Interest costs accrued, less interest capitalized	33	7	—	40	15	3	—	18	17	3	—	20
Income (loss) before income taxes	453	(5)	—	448	210	(1)	—	209	260	1	(1)	260
Provision (credit) for income taxes	191	(3)	—	188	86	—	—	86	111	—	—	111
Net income (loss)	$ 262	$ (2)	$—	$ 260	$ 124	$(1)	$—	$ 123	$ 149	$ 1	$(1)	$ 149
Net income applicable to common stock (Note B))				$ 249				$ 117				$ 143
Per share of common stock (Note (B))												
Primary				$2.41				$1.14				$1.39
Fully diluted				2.35				1.11				1.36
Shares of common stock (in thousands) (Note (B))												
Primary				103,000				102,990				102,840
Fully diluted				107,040				107,040				106,890
Ratio of earnings to fixed charges plus preferred dividends (Note (C))				5.78								6.00

Notes:

(A) The unaudited pro forma combined statements of consolidated income have been prepared on a purchase accounting basis and, accordingly, include such adjustments necessary to reflect on a pro forma basis the effects of recording the Hudson assets and liabilities as described in Notes (A) and (B) to the Pro Forma Combined Consolidated Balance Sheets. The separate consolidated statements of income of Georgia-Pacific for the year ended December 31, 1977 and for the six months ended June 30, 1977 and 1978 have been combined with those of Hudson for the year ended December 31, 1977 and for the six months ended June 25, 1977 and July 1, 1978. The following table describes the adjustments which are reflected in the pro forma combined income statements (in thousands):

Nature of Adjustment	Year Ended December 31, 1977	Six Months Ended June 30, 1977	Six Months Ended June 30, 1978
	Increase (decrease) cost of sales		
Excess of depletion based on fair value of timber over depletion based on book amount	$1,500	$800	$1,000
Excess of depreciation based on book amount of plant and equipment over depreciation based on fair value	(900)	(500)	(400)
Effect of the change in the excess of fair value of inventories over book amount	(600)	(400)	450
Rounding and miscellaneous	—	100	(50)
	$ —	$ —	$1,000

(B) Total pro forma combined net income per share of common stock is based upon the average number of shares of Georgia-Pacific outstanding during each period (as shown elsewhere in this Joint Proxy Statement), assuming issuance of the shares of Series A Stock (4,141,666 shares), necessary to give retroactive effect to the proposed merger (see "Proposed Merger" included elsewhere in this Joint Proxy Statement) on a purchase basis. Such shares of Series A Stock are not common stock equivalents with respect to primary earnings per share and they are anti-dilutive with respect to fully diluted earnings per share. During each of the years 1979 through 1988 net income applicable to common stock will include a charge of approximately $2 million per year for amortization of the excess of the involuntary liquidating value of the Series A Stock over the fair value of such Series A Stock. In addition, net income applicable to Common Stock will include charges for Series A preferred dividend requirements of $9.3 million for each of the years 1979

through 1988. Such charges will decrease by approximately $1 million per year beginning in 1989 until the mandatory sinking fund provisions have been satisfied. Such preferred dividend charges would be reduced by the amount of dividends applicable to any shares of Series A Stock converted into Georgia-Pacific Common Stock and any shares of Series A Stock acquired pursuant to scheduled purchase offers.

(C) The pro forma ratios of earnings to fixed charges plus preferred dividends have been computed as follows: (1) "Fixed charges plus preferred dividends" include interest cost accrued, one-third rent expense (which is deemed to be representative of an interest factor) and dividend requirements on Series A Stock (including amortization of the excess of the involuntary liquidation value over the fair value of such Series A Stock) adjusted to a pre-tax basis; (2) "Earnings" consist of (i) income before income taxes, (ii) interest expense and (iii) one-third rent expense.

GEORGIA-PACIFIC CORPORATION AND SUBSIDIARIES
and
HUDSON PULP & PAPER CORP. AND SUBSIDIARY COMPANIES
PRO FORMA COMBINED CONSOLIDATED BALANCE SHEETS
(Unaudited)

The following unaudited pro forma combined consolidated balance sheets, prepared by Georgia-Pacific, combine the condensed balance sheets of Georgia-Pacific at June 30, 1978 and Hudson at July 1, 1978. The combination will be accounted for as a purchase. The pro forma combined consolidated balance sheets give effect to the proposed transactions described in this Joint Proxy Statement and should be read in con-

junction with the consolidated financial statements of the constituent companies and the related notes thereto included elsewhere in this Joint Proxy Statement. Reference should also be made to the report of independent public accountants on Georgia-Pacific's 1977 financial statements, which report is qualified subject to the ultimate outcome of the plywood antitrust litigation referred to under "litigation of Georgia-Pacific".

ASSETS
June 30, 1978

	Georgia-Pacific	July 1, 1978 Hudson	Pro Forma Adjustments	Pro Forma Combined
			(in millions)	
Current assets	$ 960	$ 52	$ 1	$1,013
Natural resources, net	469	20	94	583
Property, plant and equipment, net	1,754	104	(32)	1,826
Other assets	25	1	—	26
	$3,208	$177	$ 63	$3,448

LIABILITIES

	June 30, 1978 Georgia-Pacific	July 1, 1978 Hudson	Pro Forma Adjustments	Pro Forma Combined
			(in millions)	
Current liabilities	$ 425	$ 19	$ 12	$ 456
Long-term debt	731	67	—	798
Convertible subordinated debentures	125	—	—	125
Deferred credits, including deferred income taxes	300	12	(10)	302
Employee stock purchase plan	1	—	—	1
Preferred shareholders' equity	—	1	139	140
Common shareholders' equity	1,626	78	(78)	1,626
	$3,208	$177	$ 63	$3,448

Notes:

(A) The $140 million purchase price of Hudson was calculated in July 1978 based on the fair value of the Series A Stock as represented by the estimated net proceeds which Georgia-Pacific could have reasonably expected to have received from a public offering of Series A Stock, after deducting appropriate amounts for underwriting discounts, commissions and expenses of such an offering. Such calculation was based on reviews of recent offerings of convertible preferred stock, trading markets for publicly-owned issues of convertible preferred stock as well as trading markets for preferred stocks without conversion privileges and the trading markets of various Georgia-Pacific securities. The calculation of fair value was made for financial reporting and accounting purposes and is not intended to represent a prediction of the market value of the Series A Stock when issued. The allocation of the purchase price to Hudson assets, in

accordance with generally accepted accounting principles, is based upon the respective assets and liabilities of Hudson recorded as of July 1, 1978, and such allocation is subject to changes in net book amounts between July 1, 1978 and the effective date of the merger, and to the determination of fair values of such assets, liabilities and Series A Stock on the effective date. However, it is not expected that any changes would have a material effect on the pro forma combined financial statements included herein.

(B) The following table describes the pro forma adjustments necessary to give effect to the proposed issuance of approximately 4,141,666 shares of Series A Stock in exchange for the 2,350,458 shares of Hudson Common Stock outstanding, based on the exchange ratio of 1.76207 shares of Series A Stock for each share of Hudson Common Stock, and to reflect an allocation of the purchase price as described in Note (A) above (amounts in millions):

Balance Sheet Caption	Pro Forma Adjustments Increase (Decrease)	Description of Basis for Adjustments
ASSETS		
Current assets		
Cash	$ (1)	Cash requirement to fund redemption of Hudson preferred stock at par as of the effective date of the merger
Inventories	2	Replacement cost less provision for reduction of Hudson's inventories necessary to conform to Georgia-Pacific policy
Total current assets	1	
Natural resources, net	94	Estimated current fair value of Hudson's timber and timberlands
Property, plant and equipment, net	(32)	Hudson's depreciated new replacement cost, after giving effect to Georgia-Pacific's planned capital expenditures at the Palatka, Florida, mill which Georgia-Pacific expects will achieve more efficient, lower cost operations
	$ 63	

Balance Sheet Caption	Pro Forma Adjustments Increase (Decrease)	Description of Basis for Adjustments
LIABILITIES		
Current liabilities		
Accrued pension liability	$ 5	Unfunded accrued vested pension benefits, net of applicable income tax effect, as determined by actuarial valuation of Hudson plans
Accrued income taxes	3	Additional tax provision, primarily applicable to undistributed earnings of Hudson's domestic international sales corporation
Accrued acquisition expenses	4	Provision, net of applicable income tax effect, for estimated fees and expenses directly related to acquisition, including legal fees, accounting services, investment banking services, printing, severance and /or relocation expenses
Total current liabilities	12	
Deferred credits, including deferred income taxes	(10)	Hudson's deferred income taxes arising prior to date of acquisition
Preferred shareholders' equity	139	Fair value of Series A Stock ($140), as described in Note (A), less redemption of Hudson preferred stock as of the effective date
Common shareholders' equity	(78)	Book amount of Hudson shareholders' equity
	$ 63	

EXCERPTS FROM ANNUAL REPORT
KENNECOTT COPPER CORPORATION ACQUISITION
OF THE CARBORUNDUM CORPORATION

Note 1. Summary of Accounting Policies:

Basis of Consolidation:

The financial statements are presented herein for both Kennecott Copper Corporation (Parent Company) and for Kennecott Copper Corporation and its subsidiaries (Consolidated). The Carborundum Company, which was acquired as of December 31, 1977, has been included in the consolidated balance sheet at December 31, 1977, but has not been included in the consolidated statement of income (see Note 2, Acquisition of The Carborundum Company).

Note 2. Acquisition of The Carborundum Company:

On November 29, 1977, Kennecott Industries, Inc., a wholly owned subsidiary of Kennecott, offered to purchase pursuant to an Offer to Purchase dated November 29, 1977 any and all shares of the Common Stock of The Carborundum Company for cash at $66 per share net. The Carborundum Company is a principal producer of abrasive products and an important manufacturer of advanced materials and pollution control and filtration products and systems. Through its tender offer, the Company and its consolidated subsidiaries acquired 97.3 percent of Carborundum's outstanding stock of which 75.3 percent was acquired before December 31, 1977. To finance the cost of acquiring the shares, $410,400,000 was borrowed from banks on a short-term basis and was outstanding at December 31, 1977. On January 3, 1978, cash payments of $565,000,000 were received from Peabody Holding Company representing payment of $365,000,000 of notes due on that date and the prepayment of the 9-1/2 percent, $200,000,000 notes due 1997 (see Note 3, Divestiture of Peabody Coal Company). The proceeds were used to liquidate the short-term loans of $410,400,000 on January 3, 1978 and to pay for shares of Carborundum acquired in early 1978. The receipt of the Peabody proceeds, repayment of short-term borrowings and payment for additional shares of Carborundum, all of which occurred in early January 1978, have been reflected in the balance sheet as of December 31, 1977. On January 12, 1978, The Carborundum Company became a wholly owned subsidiary, as a result of the merger of Carborundum into a Kennecott subsidiary. The acquisition of Carborundum has been accounted for as a purchase and the assets and liabilities of Carborundum, as of December 31, 1977, have been included in the consolidated balance sheet. The results of Carborundum will be included in the con-solidated statements of income beginning January 1, 1978. The purchase price of $571,500,000 exceeded the fair value of net assets acquired by approximately $40,335,000. This excess will be amortized on the straight-line method over a 40-year period.

Pro forma combined results of operations of Kennecott Copper Corporation and Subsidiaries and Carborundum for 1977, as though the acquisition had taken place on January 1, 1977 are as follows:

Combined sales	$1,638,082,000
Net income	$ 13,552,000
Net income per share	$0.41

APPENDIX B
EXCERPTS FROM APB OPINIONS

APB OPINION NO. 16

42. The Board finds merit in both the purchase and pooling of interests methods of accounting for business combinations and accepts neither method to the exclusion of the other. The arguments in favor of the purchase method of accounting are more persuasive if cash or other assets are distributed or liabilities are incurred to effect a combination, but arguments in favor of the pooling of interests method of accounting are more persuasive if voting common stock is issued to effect a combination of common stock interests. Therefore, the Board concludes that some business combinations should be accounted for by the purchase method and other combinations should be accounted for by the pooling of interests method.

43. The Board also concludes that the two methods are not alternatives in accounting for the same business combination. A single method should be applied to an entire combination; the practice now known as part-purchase, part-pooling is not acceptable. The acquisition after the effective date of this Opinion of some or all of the stock held by minority stockholders of a subsidiary—whether acquired by the parent, the subsidiary itself, or another affiliate—should be accounted for by the purchase method rather than by the pooling of interests method.

44. The Board believes that accounting for business combinations will be improved significantly by specifying the circumstances in which each method should be applied and the procedures which should be followed in applying each method. The distinctive conditions which require pooling of interests accounting are described in paragraphs 45 to 48, and combinations involving all of those conditions should be accounted for as described in paragraphs 50 to 65. All other business combinations should be treated as the acquisition of one company by another and accounted for by the purchase method as described in paragraphs 66 to 96.

Conditions for Pooling of Interests Method

45. The pooling of interests method of accounting is intended to present as a single interest two or more common stockholder interests which were previously independent and the combined rights and risks represented by those interests. That method shows that stockholder groups neither withdraw nor invest assets but in effect exchange voting common stock in a ratio that determines their respective interests in the combined corporation. Some business combinations have those features. A business combination which meets *all* of the conditions specified and explained in paragraphs 46 to 48 should be accounted for by the pooling of interests method. The conditions are classified by (1) attributes of the combining companies, (2) manner of combining interests, and (3) absence of planned transactions.

46. *Combining companies.* Certain attributes of combining companies indicate that independent ownership interests are combined in their entirety to continue previously separate operations. Combining virtually all of existing common stock interests avoids combining only selected assets, operations, or ownership interests, any of which is more akin to disposing of and acquiring interests than to sharing risks and rights. It also avoids combining interests that are already related by substantial intercorporate investments.

The two conditions in this paragraph define essential attributes of combining companies.

a. Each of the combining companies is autonomous and has not been a subsidiary or division of another corporation within two years before the plan of combination is initiated.

A plan of combination is initiated on the earlier of (1) the date that the major terms of a plan, including the ratio of exchange of stock, are announced publicly or otherwise formally made known to the stockholders of any one of the combining companies or (2) the date that stockholders of a combining company are notified in writing of an exchange offer. Therefore, a plan of combination is often initiated even though consummation is subject to the approval of stockholders and others.

A new company incorporated within the preceding two years meets this condition unless the company is successor to a part of a company or to a company that is otherwise not autonomous for this condition. A wholly owned subsidiary company which distributes voting common stock of its parent corporation to effect the combination is also considered an autonomous company provided the parent corporation would have met all conditions in paragraphs 46 to 48 had the parent corporation issued its stock directly to effect the combination.

Divestiture of assets to comply with an order of a governmental authority or judicial body results in an exception to the terms of this condition. Either a subsidiary divested under an order or a new company which acquires assets disposed of under an order is therefore autonomous for this condition.

b. Each of the combining companies is independent of the other combining companies.

This condition means that at the dates the plan of combination is initiated and consummated the combining companies hold as intercorporate investments no more than 10 percent in total of the outstanding voting common stock of any combining company. For the percentage computation, intercorporate investments exclude voting common stock that is acquired after the date the plan of combination is initiated in exchange for the voting common stock issued to effect the combination. Investments of 10 percent or less are explained in paragraph 47-b.

47. *Combining of interests.* The combining of existing voting common stock interests by the exchange of stock is the essence of a business combination accounted for by the pooling of interests method. The separate stockholder interests lose their identities and all share mutually in the combined risks and rights. Exchanges of common stock that alter relative voting rights, that result in preferential claims to distributions of profits or assets for some common stockholder groups, or that leave significant minority interests in combining companies are incompatible with the idea of mutual sharing. Similarly, acquisitions of common stock for assets or debt, reacquisitions of outstanding stock for the purpose of exchanging it in a business combination, and other transactions that reduce the common stock interests are contrary to the idea of combining existing stockholder interests. The seven conditions in this paragraph relate to the exchange to effect the combination.

a. The combination is effected in a single transaction or is completed in accordance with a specific plan within one year after the plan is initiated.

Altering the terms of exchange of stock constitutes initiation of a new plan of combination unless earlier exchanges of stock are adjusted to the new terms.

A business combination completed in more than one year from the date the plan is initiated meets this condition if the delay is beyond the control of the combining companies because proceedings of a governmental authority or litigation prevents completing the combination.

b. A corporation offers and issues only common stock with rights identical to those of the majority of its outstanding voting common stock in exchange for substantially all of the voting common stock interest of another company at the date the plan of combination is consummated.

The plan to issue voting common stock in exchange for voting common stock may include, within limits, provisions to distribute cash or other consideration for fractional shares, for shares held by dissenting stockholders, and the like but may not include a pro rata distribution of cash or other consideration.

Substantially all of the voting common stock means 90 percent or more for this condition. That is, after the date the plan of combination is initiated, one of the combining companies (issuing corporation) issues voting common stock in exchange for at least 90 percent of the voting common stock of another combining company that is outstanding at the date the combination is consummated. The number of shares exchanged therefore excludes those shares of the combining company (1) acquired before and held by the issuing corporation and its subsidiaries at the date the plan of combination is initiated, regardless of the form of consideration, (2) acquired by the issuing corporation and its subsidiaries after the date the plan of combination is initiated other than by issuing its own voting common stock, and (3) outstanding after the date the combination is consummated.

An investment in stock of the issuing corporation held by a combining company may prevent a combination from meeting this condition even though the investment of the combining company is not more than 10 percent of the outstanding stock of the issuing corporation (paragraph 46-b). An investment in stock of the issuing corporation by another combining company is the same in a mutual exchange as an investment by the issuing corporation in stock of the other combining company—the choice of issuing corporation is essentially a matter of convenience. An investment in stock of the issuing corporation must be expressed as an equivalent number of shares of the investor combining company because the measure of percent of shares exchanged is in terms of shares of stock of the investor company. An investment in 10 percent or less of the outstanding voting common stock of the issuing corporation affects the measure of percent of shares exchanged in the combination as follows:

The number of shares of voting common stock of the issuing corporation held by the investor combining company at the date the plan is initiated plus shares it acquired after that date are restated as an equivalent number of shares of voting common stock of the investor combining company based on the ratio of exchange of stock in the combination.

The equivalent number of shares is deducted from the number of shares of voting common stock of the investor combining company exchanged for voting common stock of the issuing corporation as part of the plan of combination.

The reduced number of shares is considered the number exchanged and is compared with 90 percent of the outstanding voting common stock of the investor combining company at the date the plan is consummated to determine whether the terms of condition 47-b are met.

Since the number of shares of voting common stock exchanged is reduced for an intercorporate investment in voting common stock of the issuing corporation, the terms of condition 47-b may not be met even though 90 percent or more of the outstanding common stock of a combining company is exchanged to effect a combination.

A combination of more than two companies is evaluated essentially the same as a combination of two companies. The percent of voting common stock exchanged is measured separately for each combining company, and condition 47-b is met if 90 percent or more of the voting common stock of each of the several combining companies is exchanged for voting common stock of the issuing corporation. The number of shares exchanged for stock of the issuing corporation includes only shares exchanged by stockholders other than the several combining companies themselves. Thus, intercorporate investments in combining companies are included in the number of shares of stock outstanding but are excluded from the number of shares of stock exchanged to effect the combination.

A new corporation formed to issue its stock to effect the combination of two or more companies meets condition 47-b if (1) the number of shares of each company exchanged to effect the combination is not less than 90 percent of its voting common stock outstanding at the date the combination is consummated and (2) condition 47-b would have been met had any one of the combining companies issued its stock to effect the combination on essentially the same basis.

Condition 47-b relates to issuing common stock for the common stock interests in another company. Hence, a corporation issuing stock to effect the combination may assume the debt securities of the other company or may exchange substantially identical securities or voting common stock for other outstanding equity and debt securities of the other combining company. An issuing corporation may also distribute cash to holders of debt and equity securities that either are callable or redeemable and may retire those securities.

However, the issuing corporation may exchange only voting common stock for outstanding equity and debt securities of the other combining company that have been issued in exchange for voting common stock of that company during a period beginning two years preceding the date the combination is initiated.

A transfer of the net assets of a combining company to effect a business combination satisfies condition 47-b provided all net assets of the company at the date the plan is consummated are transferred in exchange for stock of the issuing corporation. However, the combining company may retain temporarily cash, receivables, or marketable securities to settle liabilities, contingencies, or items in dispute if the plan provides that the assets remaining after settlement are to be transferred to the corporation issuing the stock to effect the combination. Only voting common stock may be issued to effect the combination unless both voting common stock and other stock of the other combining company are outstanding at the date the plan is consummated. The combination may then be effected by issuing all voting common stock or by issuing voting common and other stock in the same proportions as the outstanding voting common and other stock of the other combining company. An investment in 10 percent or less of the outstanding voting common stock of a combining company held by another combining company requires special computations to evaluate condition 47-b. The computations and comparisons are in terms of the voting common stock of the issuing corporation and involve:

Stock issued for common stock interest. The total number of shares of voting common stock issued for all of the assets is divided between those applicable to outstanding voting common stock and those applicable to other outstanding stock, if any, of the combining company which transfers assets (transferor company).

Reduction for intercorporate investments. The number of issued shares of voting common stock applicable to the voting common stock interests of the transferor combining company is reduced by the sum of (1) the number of shares of voting common stock of the issuing corporation held by the transferor combining company at the date the plan of combination is initiated plus shares it acquired after that date and (2) the number of shares of voting common stock of the transferor combining company held by the issuing corporation at the date the plan of combination is initiated plus shares it acquired after that date. The shares of the transferor combining company are restated as the equivalent number of shares of voting common stock of the issuing corporation for this purpose. Restatement is based on the ratio of the number of shares of voting common stock of the transferor combining company which are outstanding at the date the plan is consummated to the number of issued shares of voting common stock applicable to the voting common stock interests.

Comparison with 90 percent. The reduced number of shares of stock issued is compared with 90 percent of the issued number of shares of voting common stock applicable to voting common stock interests to determine if the transfer of assets meets the terms of condition 47-b.

c. None of the combining companies changes the equity interest of the voting common stock in contemplation of effecting the combination either within two years before the plan of combination is initiated or between the dates the combination is initiated and consummated; changes in contemplation of effecting the combination may include distributions to stockholders and additional issuances, exchanges, and retirements of securities.

Distributions to stockholders which are no greater than normal dividends are not changes for this condition. Normality of dividends is determined in relation to earnings during the period and to the previous dividend policy and record. Dividend distributions on stock of a combining company that are equivalent to normal dividends on the stock to be issued in exchange in the combination are considered normal for this condition.

d. Each of the combining companies reacquires shares of voting common stock only for purposes other than business combinations, and no company reacquires more than a normal number of shares between the dates the plan of combination is initiated and consummated.

Treasury stock acquired for purposes other than business combinations includes shares for stock option and compensation plans and other recurring distributions provided a systematic pattern of reacquisitions is established at least two years before the plan of combination is initiated. A systematic pattern of reacquisitions may be established for less than two years if it coincides with the adoption of a new stock option or compensation plan. The normal number of shares of voting common stock reacquired is determined by the pattern of reacquisitions of stock before the plan of combination is initiated.

Acquisitions by other combining companies of voting common stock of the issuing corporation after the date the plan of combination is initiated are essentially the same as if the issuing corporation reacquired its own common stock.

e. The ratio of the interest of an individual common stockholder to those of other common stockholders in a combining company remains the same as a result of the exchange of stock to effect the combination.

This condition means that each individual common stockholder who exchanges his stock receives a voting common stock interest exactly in proportion to his relative voting common stock interest before the combination is effected. Thus no common stockholder is denied or surrenders his potential share of a voting common stock interest in a combined corporation.

f. The voting rights to which the common stock ownership interests in the resulting combined corporation are entitled are exercisable by the stockholders; the stockholders are neither deprived of nor restricted in exercising those rights for a period.

This condition is not met, for example, if shares of common stock issued to effect the combination are transferred to a voting trust.

g. The combination is resolved at the date the plan is consummated and no provisions of the plan relating to the issue of securities or other consideration are pending.

This condition means that (1) the combined corporation does not agree to contingently issue additional shares of stock or distribute other consideration at a later date to the former stockholders of a combining company or (2) the combined corporation does not issue or distribute to an escrow agent common stock or other consideration which is to be either transferred to common stockholders or returned to the corporation at the time the contingency is resolved.

An agreement may provide, however, that the number of shares of common stock issued to effect the combination may be revised for the later settlement of a contingency at a different amount than that recorded by a combining company.

48. *Absence of planned transactions.* Some transactions after a combination is consummated are inconsistent with the combining of entire existing interests of common stockholders. Including those transactions in the negotiations and terms of the combination, either explicitly or by intent, counteracts the effect of combining stockholder interests. The three conditions in this paragraph relate to certain future transactions.

a. The combined corporation does not agree directly or indirectly to retire or reacquire all or part of the common stock issued to effect the combination.

b. The combined corporation does not enter into other financial arrangements for the benefit of the former stockholders of a combining company, such as a guaranty of loans secured by stock issued in the combination, which in effect negates the exchange of equity securities.

c. The combined corporation does not intend or plan to dispose of a significant part of the assets of the combining companies within two years after the combination other than disposals in the ordinary course of business of the formerly separate companies and to eliminate duplicate facilities or excess capacity.

Subsidiary Corporation

49. Dissolution of a combining company is not a condition for applying the pooling of interests method of accounting for a business combination. One or more combining companies may be subsidiaries of the issuing corporation after the combination is consummated if the other conditions are met.

Application of Pooling of Interests Method

50. A business combination which meets all of the conditions in paragraphs 45 to 48 should be accounted for by the pooling of interests method. Appropriate procedures are described in paragraphs 51 to 65.

Assets and Liabilities Combined

51. The recorded assets and liabilities of the separate companies generally become the recorded assets and liabilities of the combined corporation. The combined corporation therefore recognizes those assets and liabilities recorded in conformity with generally accepted accounting principles by the separate companies at the date the combination is consummated.

52. The combined corporation records the historical-cost based amounts of the assets and liabilities of the separate companies because the existing basis of accounting continues. However, the separate companies may have recorded assets and liabilities under differing methods of accounting and the amounts may be adjusted to the same basis of accounting if the change would otherwise have been appropriate for the separate company. A change in accounting method to conform the individual methods should be applied retroactively, and financial statements presented for prior periods should be restated.

Stockholders' Equity Combined

53. The stockholders' equities of the separate companies are also combined as a part of the pooling of interests method of accounting. The combined corporation records as capital the capital stock and capital in

excess of par or stated value of outstanding stock of the separate companies. Similarly, retained earnings or deficits of the separate companies are combined and recognized as retained earnings of the combined corporation (paragraph 56). The amount of outstanding shares of stock of the combined corporation at par or stated value may exceed the total amount of capital stock of the separate combining companies; the excess should be deducted first from the combined other contributed capital and then from the combined retained earnings. The combined retained earnings could be misleading if shortly before or as a part of the combination transaction one or more of the combining companies adjusted the elements of stockholders' equity to eliminate a deficit; therefore, the elements of equity before the adjustment should be combined.

54. A corporation which effects a combination accounted for by the pooling of interests method by distributing stock previously acquired as treasury stock (paragraph 47-d) should first account for those shares of stock as though retired. The issuance of the shares for the common stock interests of the combining company is then accounted for the same as the issuance of previously unissued shares.

55. Accounting for common stock of one of the combining companies which is held by another combining company at the date a combination is consummated depends on whether the stock is the same as that which is issued to effect the combination or is the same as the stock which is exchanged in the combination. An investment of a combining company in the common stock of the issuing corporation is in effect returned to the resulting combined corporation in the combination. The combined corporation should account for the investment as treasury stock. In contrast, an investment in the common stock of other combining companies (not the one issuing stock in the combination) is an investment in stock that is exchanged in the combination for the common stock issued. The stock in that type of intercorporate investment is in effect eliminated in the combination. The combined corporation should account for that investment as stock retired as part of the combination.

Reporting Combined Operations

56. A corporation which applies the pooling of interests method of accounting to a combination should report results of operations for the period in which the combination occurs as though the companies had been combined as of the beginning of the period. Results of operations for that period thus comprise those of the separate companies combined from the beginning of the period to the date the combination is consummated

and those of the combined operations from that date to the end of the period. Eliminating the effects of intercompany transactions from operations before the date of combination reports operations before and after the date of combination on substantially the same basis. The effects of intercompany transactions on current assets, current liabilities, revenue, and cost of sales for periods presented and on retained earnings at the beginning of the periods presented should be eliminated to the extent possible. The nature of and effects on earnings per share of nonrecurring intercompany transactions involving long-term assets and liabilities need not be eliminated but should be disclosed. A combined corporation should disclose in notes to financial statements the revenue, extraordinary items, and net income of each of the separate companies from the beginning of the period to the date the combination is consummated (paragraph 64-d). The information relating to the separate companies may be as of the end of the interim period nearest the date that the combination is consummated.

57. Similarly, balance sheets and other financial information of the separate companies as of the beginning of the period should be presented as though the companies had been combined at that date. Financial statements and financial information of the separate companies presented for prior years should also be restated on a combined basis to furnish comparative information. All restated financial statements and financial summaries should indicate clearly that financial data of the previously separate companies are combined.

Expenses Related to Combination

58. The pooling of interests method records neither the acquiring of assets nor the obtaining of capital. Therefore, costs incurred to effect a combination accounted for by that method and to integrate the continuing operations are expenses of the combined corporation rather than additions to assets or direct reductions of stockholders' equity. Accordingly, all expenses related to effecting a business combination accounted for by the pooling of interests method should be deducted in determining the net income of the resulting combined corporation for the period in which the expenses are incurred. Those expenses include, for example, registration fees, costs of furnishing information to stockholders, fees of finders and consultants, salaries and other expenses related to services of employees, and costs and losses of combining operations of the previously separate companies and instituting efficiencies.

Disposition of Assets After Combination

59. A combined corporation may dispose of those assets of the separate companies which are duplicate facilities or excess capacity in the combined operations. Losses or estimated losses on disposal of specifically identified duplicate or excess facilities should be deducted in determining the net income of the resulting combined corporation. However, a loss estimated and recorded while a facility remains in service should not include the portion of the cost that is properly allocable to anticipated future service of the facility.

60. Profit or loss on other dispositions of assets of the previously separate companies may require special disclosure unless the disposals are part of customary business activities of the combined corporation. Specific treatment of a profit or loss on those dispositions is warranted because the pooling of interests method of accounting would have been inappropriate (paragraph 48-c) if the combined corporation were committed or planned to dispose of a significant part of the assets of one of the combining companies. The Board concludes that a combined corporation should disclose separately a profit or loss resulting from the disposal of a significant part of the assets or a separable segment of the previously separate companies, provided

the profit or loss is material in relation to the net income of the combined corporation, and

the disposition is within two years after the combination is consummated.

The disclosed profit or loss, less applicable income tax effect, should be classified as an extraordinary item.

Date of Recording Combination

61. A business combination accounted for by the pooling of interests method should be recorded as of the date the combination is consummated. Therefore, even though a business combination is consummated before one or more of the combining companies first issues its financial statements as of an earlier date, the financial statements issued should be those of the combining company and not those of the resulting combined corporation. A combining company should, however, disclose as supplemental information, in notes to financial statements or otherwise, the substance of a combination consummated before financial statements are issued and the effects of the combination on reported financial position and results of operations (paragraph 65). Comparative financial statements presented in reports of the resulting combined corporation after a combination is consummated should combine earlier financial statements of the separate companies.

62. A corporation may be reasonably assured that a business combination which has been initiated but not consummated as of the date of financial statements will meet the conditions requiring the pooling of interests method of accounting. The corporation should record as an investment common stock of the other combining company acquired before the statement date. Common stock acquired by disbursing cash or other assets or by incurring liabilities should be recorded at cost. Stock acquired in exchange for common stock of the issuing corporation should, however, be recorded at the proportionate share of underlying net assets at the date acquired as recorded by the other company. Until the pooling of interests method of accounting for the combination is known to be appropriate, the investment and net income of the investor corporation should include the proportionate share of earnings or losses of the other company after the date of acquisition of the stock. The investor corporation should also disclose results of operations for all prior periods presented as well as the entire current period as they will be reported if the combination is later accounted for by the pooling of interests method. After the combination is consummated and the applicable method of accounting is known, financial statements issued previously should be restated as necessary to include the other combining company.

Disclosure of a Combination

63. A combined corporation should disclose in its financial statements that a combination which is accounted for by the pooling of interests method has occurred during the period. The basis of current presentation and restatements of prior periods may be disclosed in the financial statements by captions or by references to notes.

64. Notes to financial statements of a combined corporation should disclose the following for the period in which a business combination occurs and is accounted for by the pooling of interests method.

   a. Name and brief description of the companies combined, except a corporation whose name is carried forward to the combined corporation.
   b. Method of accounting for the combination—that is, by the pooling of interests method.
   c. Description and number of shares of stock issued in the business combination.
   d. Details of the results of operations of the previously separate companies for the period before the combination is consummated that are included in the current combined net income (paragraph 56). The details should include revenue, extraordinary items, net income, other changes in stockholders' equity, and amount of

and manner of accounting for intercompany transactions.

   e. Descriptions of the nature of adjustments of net assets of the combining companies to adopt the same accounting practices and of the effects of the changes on net income reported previously by the separate companies and now presented in comparative financial statements (paragraph 52).
   f. Details of an increase or decrease in retained earnings from changing the fiscal year of a combining company. The details should include at least revenue, expenses, extraordinary items, net income, and other changes in stockholders' equity for the period excluded from the reported results of operations.
   g. Reconciliations of amounts of revenue and earnings previously reported by the corporation that issues the stock to effect the combination with the combined amounts currently presented in financial statements and summaries. A new corporation formed to effect a combination may instead disclose the earnings of the separate companies which comprise combined earnings for prior periods.

The information disclosed in notes to financial statements should also be furnished on a pro forma basis in information on a proposed business combination which is given to stockholders of combining companies.

65. Notes to the financial statements should disclose details of the effects of a business combination consummated before the financial statements are issued but which is either incomplete as of the date of the financial statements or initiated after that date (paragraph 61). The details should include revenue, net income, earnings per share, and the effects of anticipated changes in accounting methods as if the combination had been consummated at the date of the financial statements (paragraph 52).

Application of Purchase Method

Principles of Historical-Cost Accounting

66. Accounting for a business combination by the purchase method follows principles normally applicable under historical-cost accounting to recording acquisitions of assets and issuances of stock and to accounting for assets and liabilities after acquisition.

67. *Acquiring assets.* The general principles to apply the historical-cost basis of accounting to an acquisition of an asset depend on the nature of the transaction:

   a. An asset acquired by exchanging cash or other assets is recorded at cost—that is, at the amount of cash disbursed or the fair value of other assets distributed.

b. An asset acquired by incurring liabilities is recorded at cost—that is, at the present value of the amounts to be paid.

c. An asset acquired by issuing shares of stock of the acquiring corporation is recorded at the fair value of the asset—that is, shares of stock issued are recorded at the fair value of the consideration received for the stock.

The general principles must be supplemented to apply them in certain transactions. For example, the fair value of an asset received for stock issued may not be reliably determinable, or the fair value of an asset acquired in an exchange may be more reliably determinable than the fair value of a noncash asset given up. Restraints on measurement have led to the practical rule that assets acquired for other than cash, including shares of stock issued, should be stated at "cost" when they are acquired and "cost may be determined either by the fair value of the consideration given or by the fair value of the property acquired, whichever is the more clearly evident." "Cost" in accounting often means the amount at which an entity records an asset at the date it is acquired whatever its manner of acquisition, and that "cost" forms the basis for historical-cost accounting.

68. *Allocating cost.* Acquiring assets in groups requires not only ascertaining the cost of the assets as a group but also allocating the cost to the individual assets which comprise the group. The cost of a group is determined by the principles described in paragraph 67. A portion of the total cost is then assigned to each individual asset acquired on the basis of its fair value. A difference between the sum of the assigned costs of the tangible and identifiable intangible assets acquired less liabilities assumed and the cost of the group is evidence of unspecified intangible values.

69. *Accounting after acquisition.* The nature of an asset and not the manner of its acquisition determines an acquirer's subsequent accounting for the cost of that asset. The basis for measuring the cost of an asset—whether amount of cash paid, fair value of an asset received or given up, amount of a liability incurred, or fair value of stock issued—has no effect on the subsequent accounting for that cost, which is retained as an asset, depreciated, amortized, or otherwise matched with revenue.

Acquiring Corporation

70. A corporation which distributes cash or other assets or incurs liabilities to obtain the assets or stock of another company is clearly the acquiror. The identities of the acquiror and the acquired company are usually evident in a business combination effected by the issue of stock. The acquiring corporation normally issues the stock and commonly is the larger company. The acquired company may, however, survive as the corporate entity, and the nature of the negotiations sometimes clearly indicates that a smaller corporation acquires a larger company. The Board concludes that presumptive evidence of the acquiring corporation in combinations effected by an exchange of stock is obtained by identifying the former common stockholder interests of a combining company which either retain or receive the larger portion of the voting rights in the combined corporation. That corporation should be treated as the acquiror unless other evidence clearly indicates that another corporation is the acquiror. For example, a substantial investment of one company in common stock of another before the combination may be evidence that the investor is the acquiring corporation.

71. If a new corporation is formed to issue stock to effect a business combination to be accounted for by the purchase method, one of the existing combining companies should be considered the acquiror on the basis of the evidence available.

Determining Cost of an Acquired Company

72. The same accounting principles apply to determining the cost of assets acquired individually, those acquired in a group, and those acquired in a business combination. A cash payment by a corporation measures the cost of acquired assets less liabilities assumed. Similarly, the fair values of other assets distributed, such as marketable securities or properties, and the fair value of liabilities incurred by an acquiring corporation measure the cost of an acquired company. The present value of a debt security represents the fair value of the liability, and a premium or discount should be recorded for a debt security issued with an interest rate fixed materially above or below the effective rate or current yield for an otherwise comparable security.

73. The distinctive attributes of preferred stocks make some issues similar to a debt security while others possess common stock characteristics, with many gradations between the extremes. Determining cost of an acquired company may be affected by those characteristics. For example, the fair value of a nonvoting, nonconvertible preferred stock which lacks characteristics of common stock may be determined by comparing the specified dividend and redemption terms with comparable securities and by assessing market factors. Thus although the principle of record-

ing the fair value of consideration received for stock issued applies to all equity securities, senior as well as common stock, the cost of a company acquired by issuing senior equity securities may be determined in practice on the same basis as for debt securities.

74. The fair value of securities traded in the market is normally more clearly evident than the fair value of an acquired company (paragraph 67). Thus, the quoted market price of an equity security issued to effect a business combination may usually be used to approximate the fair value of an acquired company after recognizing possible effects of price fluctuations, quantities traded, issue costs, and the like (paragraph 23). The market price for a reasonable period before and after the date the terms of the acquisition are agreed to and announced should be considered in determining the fair value of securities issued.

75. If the quoted market price is not the fair value of stock, either preferred or common, the consideration received should be estimated even though measuring directly the fair values of assets received is difficult. Both the consideration received, including goodwill, and the extent of the adjustment of the quoted market price of the stock issued should be weighed to determine the amount to be recorded. All aspects of the acquisition, including the negotiations, should be studied, and independent appraisals may be used as an aid in determining the fair value of securities issued. Consideration other than stock distributed to effect an acquisition may provide evidence of the total fair value received.

76. *Costs of acquisition.* The cost of a company acquired in a business combination accounted for by the purchase method includes the direct costs of acquisition. Costs of registering and issuing equity securities are a reduction of the otherwise determinable fair value of the securities. However, indirect and general expenses related to acquisitions are deducted as incurred in determining net income.

Contingent Consideration

77. A business combination agreement may provide for the issuance of additional shares of a security or the transfer of cash or other consideration contingent on specified events or transactions in the future. Some agreements provide that a portion of the consideration be placed in escrow to be distributed or to be returned to the transferor when specified events occur. Either debt or equity securities may be placed in escrow, and amounts equal to interest or dividends on the securities during the contingency period may be paid to the escrow agent or to the potential security holder.

78. The Board concludes that cash and other assets distributed and securities issued unconditionally and amounts of contingent consideration which are determinable at the date of acquisition should be included in determining the cost of an acquired company and recorded at that date. Consideration which is issued or issuable at the expiration of the contingency period or which is held in escrow pending the outcome of the contingency should be disclosed but not recorded as a liability or shown as outstanding securities unless the outcome of the contingency is determinable beyond reasonable doubt.

79. Contingent consideration should usually be recorded when the contingency is resolved and consideration is issued or becomes issuable. In general, the issue of additional securities or distribution of other consideration at resolution of contingencies based on earnings should result in an additional element of cost of an acquired company. In contrast, the issue of additional securities or distribution of other consideration at resolution of contingencies based on security prices should not change the recorded cost of an acquired company.

80. *Contingency based on earnings.* Additional consideration may be contingent on maintaining or achieving specified earnings levels in future periods. When the contingency is resolved and additional consideration is distributable, the acquiring corporation should record the current fair value of the consideration issued or issuable as additional cost of the acquired company. The additional costs of affected assets, usually goodwill, should be amortized over the remaining life of the asset.

81. *Contingency based on security prices.* Additional consideration may be contingent on the market price of a specified security issued to effect a business combination. Unless the price of the security at least equals the specified amount on a specified date or dates, the acquiring corporation is required to issue additional equity or debt securities or transfer cash or other assets sufficient to make the current value of the total consideration equal to the specified amount. The securities issued unconditionally at the date the combination is consummated should be recorded at that date at the specified amount.

82. The cost of an acquired company recorded at the date of acquisition represents the entire payment, including contingent consideration. Therefore, the issuance of additional securities or distribution of other consideration does not affect the cost of the acquired company, regardless of whether the amount specified is a security price to be maintained or a higher security price to be achieved. On a later date when the contingency is resolved and additional consideration is distributable, the acquiring corporation should record the current fair value of the additional consideration issued

or issuable. However, the amount previously recorded for securities issued at the date of acquisition should simultaneously be reduced to the lower current value of those securities. Reducing the value of debt securities previously issued to their later fair value results in recording a discount on debt securities. The discount should be amortized from the date the additional securities are issued.

83. Accounting for contingent consideration based on conditions other than those described should be inferred from the procedures outlined. For example, if the consideration contingently issuable depends on both future earnings and future security prices, additional cost of the acquired company should be recorded for the additional consideration contingent on earnings, and previously recorded consideration should be reduced to current value of the consideration contingent on security prices. Similarly, if the consideration contingently issuable depends on later settlement of a contingency, an increase in the cost of acquired assets, if any, should be amortized over the remaining life of the assets.

84. *Interest or dividends during contingency period.* Amounts paid to an escrow agent representing interest and dividends on securities held in escrow should be accounted for according to the accounting for the securities. That is, until the disposition of the securities in escrow is resolved, payments to the escrow agent should not be recorded as interest expense or dividend distributions. An amount equal to interest and dividends later distributed by the escrow agent to the former stockholders should be added to the cost of the acquired assets at the date distributed and amortized over the remaining life of the assets.

85. *Tax effect of imputed interest.* A tax reduction resulting from imputed interest on contingently issuable stock reduces the fair value recorded for contingent consideration based on earnings and increases additional capital recorded for contingent consideration based on security prices.

86. *Compensation in contingent agreements.* The substance of some agreements for contingent consideration is to provide compensation for services or use of property or profit sharing, and the additional consideration given should be accounted for as expenses of the appropriate periods.

Recording Assets Acquired and Liabilities Assumed

87. An acquiring corporation should allocate the cost of an acquired company to the assets acquired and liabilities assumed. Allocation should follow the principles described in paragraph 68.

First, all identifiable assets acquired, either individually or by type, and liabilities assumed in a business combination, whether or not shown in the financial statements of the acquired company, should be assigned a portion of the cost of the acquired company, normally equal to their fair values at date of acquisition.

Second, the excess of the cost of the acquired company over the sum of the amounts assigned to identifiable assets acquired less liabilities assumed should be recorded as goodwill. The sum of the market or appraisal values of identifiable assets acquired less liabilities assumed may sometimes exceed the cost of the acquired company. If so, the values otherwise assignable to noncurrent assets acquired (except long-term investments in marketable securities) should be reduced by a proportionate part of the excess to determine the assigned values. A deferred credit for an excess of assigned value of identifiable assets over cost of an acquired company (sometimes called "negative goodwill") should not be recorded unless those assets are reduced to zero value.

Independent appraisals may be used as an aid in determining the fair values of some assets and liabilities. Subsequent sales of assets may also provide evidence of values. The effect of taxes may be a factor in assigning amounts to identifiable assets and liabilities (paragraph 89).

88. General guides for assigning amounts to the individual assets acquired and liabilities assumed, except goodwill, are:

a. Marketable securities at current net realizable values.

b. Receivables at present values of amounts to be received determined at appropriate current interest rates, less allowances for uncollectibility and collection costs, if necessary.

c. Inventories:

(1) Finished goods and merchandise at estimated selling prices less the sum of (a) costs of disposal and (b) a reasonable profit allowance for the selling effort of the acquiring corporation.

(2) Work in process at estimated selling prices of finished goods less the sum of (a) costs to complete, (b) costs of disposal, and (c) a reasonable profit allowance for the completing and selling effort of the acquiring corporation based on profit for similar finished goods.

(3) Raw materials at current replacement costs.

d. Plant and equipment: (1) to be used, at current replacement costs for similar capacity unless the expected future use of the assets indicates a lower value to the acquirer, (2) to be sold or held for later sale rather than used, at current net realizable value, and (3) to be used temporarily, at current net realizable value recognizing future depreciation for the expected period of use.

e. Intangible assets which can be identified and named, including contracts, patents, franchises, customer and supplier lists, and favorable leases, at appraised values.

f. Other assets, including land, natural resources, and non-marketable securities, at appraised values.

g. Accounts and notes payable, long-term debt, and other claims payable at present values of amounts to be paid determined at appropriate current interest rates.

h. Liabilities and accruals — for example, accruals for pension cost, warranties, vacation pay, deferred compensation — at present values of amounts to be paid determined at appropriate current interest rates.

i. Other liabilities and commitments, including unfavorable leases, contracts, and commitments and plant closing expense incident to the acquisition, at present values of amounts to be paid determined at appropriate current interest rates.

An acquiring corporation should record periodically as a part of income the accrual of interest on assets and liabilities recorded at acquisition date at the discounted values of amounts to be received or paid. An acquiring corporation should not record as a separate asset the goodwill previously recorded by an acquired company and should not record deferred income taxes recorded by an acquired company before its acquisition. An acquiring corporation should reduce the acquired goodwill retroactively for the realized tax benefits of loss carry-forwards of an acquired company not previously recorded by the acquiring corporation.

89. The market or appraisal values of specific assets and liabilities determined in paragraph 88 may differ from the income tax bases of those items. Estimated future tax effects of differences between the tax bases and amounts otherwise appropriate to assign to an asset or a liability are one of the variables in estimating fair value. Amounts assigned to identifiable assets and liabilities should, for example, recognize that the fair value of an asset to an acquiror is less than its market or appraisal value if all or a portion of the market or appraisal value is not deductible for income taxes. The impact of tax effects on amounts assigned to individual assets and liabilities depends on numerous factors, including imminence or delay of realization of the asset value and the possible timing of tax consequences. Since differences between amounts assigned and tax bases are not timing differences (APB Opinion No. 11, *Accounting for Income Taxes,* paragraph 13),

the acquiring corporation should not record deferred tax accounts at the date of acquisition.

Amortization of Goodwill

90. Goodwill recorded in a business combination accounted for by the purchase method should be amortized in accordance with the provisions in paragraphs 27 to 31 of APB Opinion No. 17, *Intangible Assets.*

Excess of Acquired Net Assets Over Cost

91. The value assigned to net assets acquired should not exceed the cost of an acquired company because the general presumption in historical-cost based accounting is that net assets acquired should be recorded at not more than cost. The total market or appraisal values of identifiable assets acquired less liabilities assumed in a few business combinations may exceed the cost of the acquired company. An excess over cost should be allocated to reduce proportionately the values assigned to noncurrent assets (except long-term investments in marketable securities) in determining their fair values (paragraph 87). If the allocation reduces the noncurrent assets to zero value, the remainder of the excess over cost should be classified as a deferred credit and should be amortized systematically to income over the period estimated to be benefited but not in excess of forty years. The method and period of amortization should be disclosed.

92. No part of the excess of acquired net assets over cost should be added directly to stockholders' equity at the date of acquisition.

Acquisition Date

93. The Board believes that the date of acquisition of a company should ordinarily be the date assets are received and other assets are given or securities are issued. However, the parties may for convenience designate as the effective date the end of an accounting period between the dates a business combination is initiated and consummated. The designated date should ordinarily be the date of acquisition for accounting purposes if a written agreement provides that effective control of the acquired company is transferred to the acquiring corporation on that date without restrictions except those required to protect the stockholders or other owners of the acquired company — for example, restrictions on significant changes in the operations, permission to pay dividends equal to those regularly paid before the effective date, and the like. Designating an effective date other than the date assets or securities are transferred requires adjusting the cost of an acquired company and net income otherwise reported to compensate for recognizing income before consideration is transferred. The cost of an acquired

company and net income should therefore be reduced by imputed interest at an appropriate current rate on assets given, liabilities incurred, or preferred stock distributed as of the transfer date to acquire the company.

94. The cost of of an acquired company and the values assigned to assets acquired and liabilities assumed should be determined as of the date of acquisition. The statement of income of an acquiring corporation for the period in which a business combination occurs should include income of the acquired company after the date of acquisition by including the revenue and expenses of the acquired operations based on the cost to the acquiring corporation.

Disclosure in Financial Statements

95. Notes to the financial statements of an acquiring corporation should disclose the following for the period in which a business combination occurs and is accounted for by the purchase method.

    a. Name and a brief description of the acquired company.

    b. Method of accounting for the combination—that is, by the purchase method.

    c. Period for which results of operations of the acquired company are included in the income statement of the acquiring corporation.

    d. Cost of the acquired company and, if applicable, the number of shares of stock issued or issuable and the amount assigned to the issued and issuable shares.

    e. Description of the plan for amortization of acquired goodwill, the amortization method, and period (APB Opinion No. 17, paragraphs 27 to 31).

    f. Contingent payments, options, or commitments specified in the acquisition agreement and their proposed accounting treatment.

Information relating to several relatively minor acquisitions may be combined for disclosure.

96. Notes to the financial statements of the acquiring corporation for the period in which a business combination occurs and is accounted for by the purchase method should include as supplemental information the following results of operations on a pro forma basis:

    a. Results of operations for the current period as though the companies had combined at the beginning of the period, unless the acquisition was at or near the beginning of the period.

    b. Results of operations for the immediately preceding period as though the companies had combined at the beginning of that period if comparative financial statements are presented.

The supplemental pro forma information should as a minimum show revenue, income before extraordinary items, net income, and earnings per share. To present pro forma information, income taxes, interest expense, preferred stock dividends, depreciation and amortization of assets, including goodwill, should be adjusted to their accounting bases recognized in recording the combination. Pro forma presentation of results of operations of periods prior to the combination transaction should be limited to the immediately preceding period.

APB OPINION NO. 17

Acquisition of Intangible Assets

24. The Board concludes that a company should record as assets the costs of intangible assets acquired from other enterprises or individuals. Costs of developing, maintaining, or restoring intangible assets which are not specifically identifiable, have indeterminate lives, or are inherent in a continuing business and related to an enterprise as a whole—such as goodwill—should be deducted from income when incurred.

25. *Cost of intangible assets.* Intangible assets acquired singly should be recorded at cost at date of acquisition. Cost is measured by the amount of cash disbursed, the fair value of other assets distributed, the present value of the amounts to be paid for liabilities incurred, or the fair value of consideration received for stock issued as described in paragraph 67 of APB Opinion No. 16.

26. Intangible assets acquired as part of a group of assets or as part of an acquired company should also be recorded at cost at date of acquisition. Cost is measured differently for specifically identifiable intangible assets and those lacking specific identification. The cost of identifiable intangible assets is an assigned part of the total cost of the group of assets or enterprise acquired, normally based on the fair values of the individual assets. The cost of unidentifiable intangible assets is measured by the difference between the cost of the group of assets or enterprise acquired and the sum of the assigned costs of individual tangible and identifiable intangible assets acquired less liabilities assumed. Cost should be assigned to all specifically identifiable intangible assets; cost of identifiable assets should not be included in goodwill. Principles and procedures of determining cost of assets acquired, including intangible assets, are discussed in detail in paragraphs 66 to 89 of APB Opinion No. 16, *Business Combinations*.

Amortization of Intangible Assets

27. The Board believes that the value of intangible assets at any one date eventually disappears and that the recorded costs of intangible assets should be amortized by systematic charges to income over the periods estimated to be benefited. Factors which should be considered in estimating the useful lives of intangible assets include:

a. Legal, regulatory, or contractual provisions may limit the maximum useful life.

b. Provisions for renewal or extension may alter a specified limit on useful life.

c. Effects of obsolescence, demand, competition, and other economic factors may reduce a useful life.

d. A useful life may parallel the service life expectancies of individuals or groups of employees.

e. Expected actions of competitors and others may restrict present competitive advantages.

f. An apparently unlimited useful life may in fact be indefinite and benefits cannot be reasonably projected.

g. An intangible asset may be a composite of many individual factors with varying effective lives.

The period of amortization of intangible assets should be determined from the pertinent factors.

28. The cost of each type of intangible asset should be amortized on the basis of the estimated life of that specific asset and should not be written off in the period of acquisition. Analysis of all factors should result in a reasonable estimate of the useful life of most intangible assets. A reasonable estimate of the useful life may often be based on upper and lower limits even though a fixed existence is not determinable.

29. The period of amortization should not, however, exceed forty years. Analysis at the time of acquisition may indicate that the indeterminate lives of some intangible assets are likely to exceed forty years and the cost of those assets should be amortized over the maximum period of forty years, not an arbitrary shorter period.

30. *Method of amortization.* The Board concludes that the straight-line method of amortization—equal annual amounts—should be applied unless a company demonstrates that another systematic method is more appropriate. The financial statements should disclose the method and period of amortization. Amortization of acquired goodwill and of other acquired intangible assets not deductible in computing income taxes payable does not create a timing difference, and allocation of income taxes is inappropriate.

31. *Subsequent review of amortization.* A company should evaluate the periods of amortization continually to determine whether later events and circumstances warrant revised estimates of useful lives. If estimates are changed, the unamortized cost should be allocated to the increased or reduced number of remaining periods in the revised useful life but not to exceed forty years after acquisition. Estimation of value and future benefits of an intangible asset may indicate that the unamortized cost should be reduced significantly by a deduction in determining net income (APB Opinion No. 9, paragraph 21). However, a single loss year or even a few loss years together do not necessarily justify an extraordinary charge to income for all or a large part of the unamortized cost of intangible assets. The reason for an extraordinary deduction should be disclosed.

Disposal of Goodwill

32. Ordinarily goodwill and similar intangible assets cannot be disposed of apart from the enterprise as a whole. However, a large segment or separable group of assets of an acquired company or the entire acquired company may be sold or otherwise liquidated, and all or a portion of the unamortized cost of the goodwill recognized in the acquisition should be included in the cost of the assets sold.

POST TRANSACTION IMPACT

IN THE EYES OF THE INVESTMENT BANKERS, LAWYERS, NEGOTIATORS AND ACCOUNTANTS, the transaction is completed once all of the agreements are signed. In fact, the post merger or integration period is a difficult time which requires a great deal of attention. Two business entities must become one in order to realize the full potential of the combination. An unsuccessful integration will negate the results of the best structured transaction and can make the company so disaster prone that management will find it impossible to carry out its responsibilities.

The two chapters in this topical area are unique glimpses of the post transaction phase. Connie A. Cox discusses why the demands of post integration are so great and suggests that more post acquisition planning should be done early in the process. She addresses the elimination of redundancies, and debunks some myths of the integration process. She focuses the reader's attention on the critical four phases of the integration and outlines the steps to be completed during each phase.

Harold Bierman, Jr. discusses the two sets of stockholders in a merger or acquisition and evaluates the effects of the transaction on their well-being. He also covers the technical aspects of dealing with analysts in terms of earnings per share, the price earnings ratio, debt level, and diversification. There is also a list of references to aid the reader in following the calculations contained in the chapter.

CONNIE A. COX

CONNIE A. COX is founder and president of Cox, Lloyd Associates, Ltd., a management consulting firm specializing in strategic planning, competitive analysis and development of strategies for diversification, new business ventures and acquisitions. The firm also provides customized information gathering.

Prior to establishing her own firm, Ms. Cox was manager of Corporate Planning for General Foods Corporation. Previously, she was with Citicorp in New York as marketing manager, Master Charge Services.

Ms. Cox was also a consultant with McKinsey and Company, Inc. and an associate in Corporate Finance at Wertheim and Company.

A graduate of Northwestern University, Ms. Cox received her MBA from the Harvard Graduate School of Business Administration.

She has been published in *Boardroom Reports, Food Product Development* and *Management Practice*. Ms. Cox is listed in *Who's Who of American Women*. She is also a Director of Plant Industries, Inc., a company listed on the American Stock Exchange.

18

Marshalling the Combined Resources

CONNIE A. COX

Once the agreement is signed, the deal is done in the eyes of the investment bankers, the negotiators, the acquisition department, and the press. But the steps necessary to make the acquisition or merger a success are really just beginning. It is during the period known as the post merger integration that the potential of the combination of two companies should become a reality. Historically, however, the results have tended to be disastrous more frequently than successful during this period.

What makes this period so disaster prone? There are three primary reasons. First, few executives understand the importance of this part of the acquisition process. This is not surprising because integration is not a glamorous or popular subject. A search of published materials shows that less than ten articles were written in the last 15 years which cover the integration phase. This is compared to the hundreds written on identifying candidates, evaluating and analyzing, developing financial alternatives, and negotiating. In addition, no experts or specialists are selling their services for this phase, and, as a result, none are promoting its importance and difficulty. And yet, an unsuccessful integration can negate the results of the best negotiators, the best acquisition department, and the best investment bankers.

The second reason that integration is so disaster prone is that it is one of the most demanding tasks in business management. The intricacies and idiosyncrasies of two operating companies must be joined in some form of working relationship. This working relationship must provide for differences in

1. Size
2. Atmosphere
3. Industry
4. Financial strength
5. Management sophistication

but still produce the desired benefits of a combination.

The third reason is that without adequate knowledge of the task and little or no advice, certain operating philosophies have been adapted to minimize the problems. Unfortunately, these "myths of integration" lead to disaster.

In the following sections of this chapter, we will examine the scope of the task and these "myths of integration" to understand what will increase the ability to succeed during the integration process.

A DEMANDING ASSIGNMENT

Why are the demands of the post integration so great? It is because this task is not only extensive, but it is also complicated and difficult. No easy and automatic approaches can be used to speed and simplify the task. In addition, no experts or specialists appear to be available for counsel. This, in fact, is one rare occasion when a company is not beseiged by outsiders with ideas and suggestions. The company is truly on its own. We need to understand the scope of the task before we can identify what may help during this task.

The Task Extends ...

This is the only time in the history of most companies when the *many* details of an operating company must be dealt with simultaneously. These details are not just the frequently mentioned product lines, manufacturing and distribution facilities, accounting and information systems, and personnel. They also include the numerous forgotten, but critical, day-to-day necessities of business. Integration involves insurance policies for product liability, pollution liability and other business risks, labor contracts, suppliers' contracts, location of incorporation, and benefit packages and compensation programs for non-union personnel. And, I named just a few items.

With so many details to be covered simultaneously, mistakes are bound to occur and something is bound to be overlooked. Sometimes this produces major problems, and sometimes it produces minor problems. Sometimes, the detail which prevents a successful integration is never known; just its impact is seen. Take the case of the merger of Hornblower and Loeb Rhodes. The joke on Wall Street was that even in a romantic setting, with candlelight and soft music, their two computers refused to talk to each other. What went wrong? Maybe someone knows, but I wouldn't bet on it.

And the Complications Grow ...

If integration of two companies merely involved counting these details or just eliminating the redundancies, the task would not be so demanding. But, this is insufficient. The integration of two companies requires three steps for each and every detail before decisions are made. These critical steps are ...

1. Identifying and understanding each detail.
2. Evaluating the impact of the status quo on immediate and future profits versus alternative approaches.
3. Determining the strategic implications of each approach.

Completing one of these steps without the other two has led to many of the disasters of the past. Let's examine a few examples where only one step was overlooked.

Many companies have forgotten the importance of identifying and understanding each detail. Once a company is purchased, actions are immediately taken, in most acquisitions, to achieve the profit impact and strategic positioning which made the acquisition so attractive in the first place. Recently, a packaged foods company purchased a company producing non-food products appropriate for the future non-food section of the grocery store. The purchaser's rate of sales growth for food products was declining, and it sought increased volume to leverage the cost of its national sales force. And, with its contacts in groceries, it could substantially increase the sales of the acquired company. After purchasing the non-food company, it pursued these results immediately. The purchaser expanded production capacity, developed promotional programs and trained the sales force. But, the money and time were wasted. The non-food product was one of the few products in the grocery store not bought locally or regionally. Instead, these products were purchased only at the central headquarters of each grocery chain. Although the acquisition was directionally correct, those details of how the acquired company operated needed to be examined first, before substantial funds were invested incorrectly.

Ignoring the evaluation of profit impact has also led to several disasters. One example involves a frozen food company buying regional meat packers. Although the first acquisition was successful, the second turned into a disaster which almost broke the purchaser. Once the second meat packer was purchased, the purchaser immediately instituted its control system which eliminated *all* rebates to grocery chains; it was against company policy. But, the sales and profits of this meat packer were dependent on such rebates. Once they were stopped, the sales fell to zero, and the purchaser incurred substantial losses. Did those rebates really have to be eliminated overnight, or could a better solution have been found?

Another example shows the potential negative impact on the purchaser's business when a proper profit evaluation is not conducted. One company bought a small, rapidly growing company because it had a unique new product. In addition, the purchaser had been a primary supplier of raw materials to the acquired company prior to the acquisition. The acquisition offered substantial growth opportunities and exciting synergies. The new product was raced to the market. But when the purchaser introduced the new product, it realized that it was now competing directly with its own prime customers, and the purchaser's sales began to drop. The new product was withdrawn from the market and the acquisition was eventually shut down.

A further example involves a company which did not fully consider the strategic implications of one integration approach. Many years ago, as this large Midwestern company began to expand through acquisitions in its industry, it was determined that it was more efficient to integrate acquisitions with a master union contract. The contract was easier and less costly to administer in a rapidly expanding environment. For many years all went well. But after a number of acquisitions in similar industries, the company began to diversify into new industries. It later learned that these new companies could not afford, and did not need, the terms of the master contract. But, the purchaser was bound by the master contract. Each of the diversification acquisitions is now being sold. The new buyers are returning to contracts more relevant to those companies and their respective industries. And the companies are becoming profitable once again with different owners.

Post acquisition analysis is further complicated because no easy and automatic approaches can be used to speed and simplify the process. The details of the two companies are the critical ingredients of an integration and working with details requires time and effort to understand and evaluate them properly.

Integration requires more than just dealing with deals. It must be undertaken during a sensitive period for both the acquired and the purchaser. And because of the sensitivities, the difficulties of integration multiply.

Difficulties Abound

When the contract is signed, a sigh of relief is expressed, congratulations offered, and everyone involved feels happy. But this happiness is only temporary. It is usually followed by great confusion and disappointment. Many surprises may occur and most affected employees are tense and emotional.

The people at the acquired company are generally under great stress. What will be their future? Are the new owners reasonable? Will my job continue? Every word from the purchasing company is examined for clues. Each memo, telephone call, message or request is investigated for hidden meanings and indications of the future. And unfortunately, many actions of the purchaser are blown out of proportion.

Acquisitions with combinations of foreign and domestic companies increase the difficulties of this period. Geographical distances and language differences hamper communication. Unfamiliar cultural backgrounds, laws, and management approaches heighten the uncertainty.

Significantly, this is the first time both companies are permitted to see the realities of their new partner. Prior to the acquisition, the parties are on their best public behavior. This view is magnified in most situations by professionals involved in executing the transaction. After the closing, sophisticated, suave and polished deal men representing both the purchaser and the acquired firm are replaced by the nuts-and-bolts managers. An entirely new partnership must be formed in a new environment with new people.

The competitors of the acquired company frequently capitalize on the confusion and anxiety within the two companies. They rarely ignore this opportunistic period of vulnerability. When possible, they raid the company of its best managers. They also may aggressively move to take market share and prime suppliers.

And You Are Alone ...

After the acquisition the experts abandon the executives responsible for integration of operations. Rarely do the acquisition and development departments of the purchaser stay involved. A different executive is brought in at the closing to begin the integration. Generally, the executive left to implement the integration has little or no experience with mergers. This is a line manager, not a "deal" person. Executives with prior

successful integration experience have moved on to different positions while the executives who have failed to integrate companies are rarely given a second chance.

Frequently the new line manager has had no involvement with the specific company to be integrated. The acquired company and purchase contract are literally "hands off." In some instances, the knowledge of the purchased company gained during the negotiation stage is passed on, but frequently it is not. Even the details of the negotiation may not be communicated to the integration executive.

With no advisors to turn to and no procedures to automatically implement, many executives rely on the four myths of integration.

THE MYTHS OF INTEGRATION

These myths are operating philosophies that somehow have become incorrectly accepted as behavior which produces successful integration. The integration efforts of the past 20 years attest to their popularity and following. The four myths which have been the basis of so many integration efforts are ...

1. You must race to integrate.
2. Sameness is next to godliness.
3. The integration "stars" conquer.
4. Integration and "the deal" don't mix.

And yet, they lead so directly to disaster.

Race to Integrate ...

The operating philosophy that you must race to integrate appears to relate more to the need to produce results than to the requirements of integration. A substantial investment has been made and the directors and shareholders are watching. Most other large investments, such as new plant construction or new product introductions, can be made with little fanfare. And no one outside a company sees the exact dollars spent. But, with the reporting requirements of today, acquisitions are events with substantial disclosure. With these disclosures come the watchful eyes and critics. Management is under substantial pressure to produce results and move quickly to integrate. It must justify the acquisition.

Another pressure behind the race to integrate is the desire to obtain the synergies and tap the opportunities which made the acquisition attractive in the first place. Preparation prior to the closing can facilitate the task. However, the synergies and opportunities to be tapped must still be evaluated against those realities of the acquired company which only become evident after the closing. Some opportunities will be reclassified as unattainable while new, more realisitic opportunities may be uncovered. This process takes time. Money and resources committed to the new acquisition before this process is completed have been wasted.

Rapid changes instituted immediately after the acquisition have an additional negative effect. Either the acquired company's managers become demoralized because their input has been disregarded, or they become so distracted by the demands of the purchaser that they literally stop managing the company. In each case, the acquired company stops running effectively and new problems begin. The executives of the purchaser spend less time on their previous responsibilities and more time managing the acquired property.

Sameness Is Divine ...

The second popular operating philosophy which leads to disaster is that sameness is next to godliness. This concept is applied across industry lines, for companies of all sizes, in all corporate atmospheres. It is a rare occasion for a company not to utilize the same incentive compensation system for all managers or the same information system for all businesses.

A primary motivation for "sameness" is ease of administration of one program or one system company-wide. Such sameness eventually eliminates the unique aspects of companies which made them successful originally. The most obvious examples involve those companies whose success was dependent on quick responses to market changes. After acquisition, these companies become bogged down by paperwork and bureaucratic decision-making procedures. Many times sameness reduces the bonds of employee loyalty that exist in smaller organizations. Many companies immediately standardize labor contracts without realizing that plant work rules and productivity differ significantly. No adjustments are made in the contracts for such underlying differences.

Some companies are beginning to understand the need to retain variety among their various divisions and functional units. One of the stated benefits of the recent spinoffs planned at W.R. Grace is that each newly created company could then have its own stock options and its managers could be compensated directly for their performance. An executive at another company recently implemented a new policy for his company: "We can't pay people equally, but we will always pay people fairly."

Stars Conquer ...

Mergers and acquisitions are discussed frequently in terms of marriages, and as a goal this term may be relevant. The reality of historical acquisition relationships is rarely similar to even the worst marriage. It generally comes closer to rape, or, in softer terms, "the conquering army syndrome." The purchaser's managers descend on the acquired company and in their eagerness to exercise their new responsibilities, they begin giving orders. "We own you, so you will do it our way," is frequently heard. Or, "We know best."

The conquered do not willingly continue partnerships with the victor. At the first opportunity, key personnel of the acquired firm often leave or seek to undermine the acquisition. The partnership required for a successful acquisition or merger rarely results after a conquest. Instead, the "stars" must move to develop trust and a future working relationship.

"The Deal" and Integration Don't Mix ...

The last operating philosophy which leads to failure is the separation of the integration phase from pre-merger negotiation. The executive responsible for the integration frequently becomes involved only after the closing, although critical parts of the integration process have already occurred.

Covenants of the acquisition agreement which impact the integration process have been cast in stone prior to the integration phase. For example, earnout agreements are a popular vehicle for providing the acquired management an incentive to stay and maintain their prior performance levels. Earnouts however, may hamper integration. It is difficult to track capital added by the purchaser to insure that its benefits are not included for the earnout calculation; needed capital additions are delayed as a result. Improved profits from the elimination of redundancies may also be postponed until the earnout period ends.

Another technique is for management to hold a portion of the purchase price "in escrow" until the acquired company achieves the profits which it has forecast. In this situation, there is no incentive for the purchaser to assist the acquisition in attaining the forecast profit. As a result the purchaser might not make available to the acquired firm its less costly control systems and sources of supply.

The second critical aspect of an integration which begins before the deal is closed is the genesis of integration atmosphere. The anxiety and tension related to acquisition begins with the first rumor that something may be in the works. Even with tight security, announcements generally must be made before the contracts are signed. While a company may wait for the contract to be signed, the competitors will not. Raiding the acquired company of its best people can be expected to begin shortly after the first announcement. Without some attention and assurance from the purchaser, the key managers may not wait for the closing. In situations where the people are significant assets of a company, such as Wall Street brokerage and investment firms, waiting until the closing can result in buying the shell of the company, not the desired assets.

The third critical part of the integration process which starts before the contract is signed is the preliminary determination of profit impact and strategic direction. In most situations these are the primary reasons for the acquisition. When it is not recognized that these steps are part of the integration process, many problems occur. Preliminary profit impact and strategic benefit analysis tend to become unrealistic because those responsible for these preliminary determinations frequently are ...

1. Selling the "deal", but
2. *Not* responsible for its integration, and
3. Have limited experience with operations of a company.

Their reward comes from the signed contract and there is no direct penalty to them for unrealistic forecasts. The forecasts are generally overly optimistic and the operating risks are played down or ignored. Preliminary determinations tend to take on a life of their own. During integration, these forecasts are rarely refined or adjusted once the details of the acquired are known. The executives responsible for the integration may feel "stuck" with what they perceive to be impossible and incorrect expectations that can't be changed.

What can be done to significantly improve the probabilities of success? Avoid the "myths of integration", or ...

1. Move slowly and carefully.
2. Maintain critical uniqueness.
3. Develop a partnership.
4. Begin integration before the contract is signed.

These simple rules by themselves are not sufficient. They must be combined with a framework which allows the purchaser to think through and then develop a plan for the integration process in its entirety. Such a framework is described in detail in the following section.

The Integration Framework

This framework is based on the understanding that integration is a process which occurs over time. Four distinct phases exist ...

Phase I: Preparation Before Purchase
Phase II: Actions for Immediate Ownership
Phase III: Intermediate Profit Improvement Programs
Phase IV: Strategic Positioning and Development.

During each phase, several critical steps must be completed before the next phase is begun.

Phase I

Phase I of the integration process should begin once an acquisition candidate is seriously considered, that is, shortly after one clearly sees an opportunity and proceeds to promote the candidate. For some companies, this phase occurs when an evaluation team is officially formed, while at other companies, serious consideration does not begin before top management approval is obtained.

Six critical steps need to be completed during Phase I. These steps are:

1. *Selection of the integration executive.*

A formal team is not required but finding the executive who is willing and able to accept the task is critical. This executive then becomes a member of the evaluation and acquisition team.

2. *Preliminary assessment and statement of the opportunity.*

This assessment and statement will be refined once the integration begins, but it must be developed beforehand. It becomes the unifying goal for the many activities of acquiring. Also, it provides the basis for initial communications with the acquired company after the agreements are signed. It shows why the acquisition is valuable and what it brings to the partnership.

3. *Determination of what is critical for the acquired company's continued success during the next few years.*

This includes the identification of key managers, technologies, and customers. These will be the critical assets that must be maintained during the immediate post merger phase.

4. *Identification of industry norms for key details that must be considered in Phase II.*

In some cases, only sources of such information will be identified prior to the announcement. These industry norms should be obtained for executive compensation, labor contracts, billing procedures, etc.

5. *Development of the detailed plan for Phase II.*

Such a plan should include preliminary versions of announcements for employees of both companies and timing. It can also show the steps needed to assure continued employment of key managers. It may include designing the executive committee, with management from the purchaser and the acquired, which will implement the many parts of the integration once the contract is signed.

6. *Establishment of the people to visit the company between the letter of intent and the contract.*

At a minimum the auditors visit the potential acquisition. It is critical that not only the financial aspects of a company are examined. The integration executive should have a team which will examine those critical assets identified in Step 3 and begin to finalize the plans for maintaining such assets.

Of course, the preparation cannot answer all questions. The need for confidential evaluation and time limits restrict preparation efforts. One approach used successfully by several companies to maximize the results of this preparation is to hire industry experts. Generally, such experts can be hired on a per diem basis to advise the potential purchaser on:

1. What it takes to compete in the acquired's markets.
2. How competitive the acquisition is and where its weaknesses are.
3. What changes are occurring that will seriously impact the future of the acquired.

Some companies hire retired executives of either the acquired or its competitors. I have found that industry specialized consultants are more up-to-date and have a broader view of the market.

The preparation phase ends with the announcement of a letter of intent.

Phase II

Phase II includes the actions associated with immediate ownership. It begins when the letter of intent is signed, continues through the closing, and ends when the two companies are operating comfortably together. As such, it does *not* include the programs for profit improvement or strategic positioning.

The number of steps that have to be completed during this phase are few in number. But they are critical for the future outcome. The first step begins when the purchaser starts to examine the acquisition in detail. Many companies restrict this examination prior to contract to financial assets only. Extensive examination should be made of those assets believed to be critical for the successful functioning of the company. From an operational point of view, questions which should be answered during this stage include the following:

1. What are key sources of profits?
2. Who are the critical executives? Are they considering leaving?
3. Why do the acquired's customers prefer them over competitors?
4. Are there imminent cash or capital needs not previously anticipated?
5. Do critical assets exist and are they of expected quality?

The second major step, and the most important, is to *keep* whatever is critical for the continuing success of the acquired alive and functioning. One asset which is always critical is personnel. Management needs to feel that it is part of the acquisition process and that the purchasing company will be open and honest with them. It may only require dinners and individual meetings with key personnel. Other activities which support feelings of trust and confidence include circulating memoranda and documents about the acquisitions to top and middle managers.

Maintaining the continuing functioning of the acquired company is critical. Once the company is functioning effectively, the purchaser can begin to move into Phase III, where decisions will be made to achieve desired profit impact.

Phase III

This is the phase where extensive evaluations are made of each detail so that realistic profit improvement programs can be developed. This phase requires two preliminary steps. First, the integration executive must determine if the management of the acquired company knows how to manage its profitability. What is the impact of substantially increased volume? Can quality requirements be maintained? Do bottlenecks exist? Can effective cash management make a difference? Do the internal controls and management information system reflect an accurate picture of cost and revenue changes? These assessments become the basis of the decision about how much freedom the acquired management will have.

The second preliminary step is to establish the priority for profit-improvement programs. A list of possible programs can be generated either by the acquired's management, or the purchaser. The purchaser may want to identify these first, based upon the greater resources they bring to the acquired company.

With the assessment of the acquired's management team, indepth evaluations of the alternatives and priorities, a realistic implementation program can be designed and executed.

Phase IV

The last stage of the integration process involves the determination of strategic positioning and direction. It begins with a sharing by the purchaser of its preliminary assessment with the key executives of the acquired company. It then becomes the joint effort and responsibility of the integration team. From this review, the long term needs of the business are identified so that these resources can be built. It may include the training of middle management, or a program to locate and hire key managers might be implemented. The critical step is to determine what is needed for the acquired in the longer term and to begin developing those resources.

SUMMARY

This proposed framework for integration will not prevent all the disasters. It will assist companies in understanding the complexity of the process and that it is a process over time. By following some basic rules of integration the chances of success should be increased greatly. Although the task is demanding, in the future, hopefully, it will be more rewarding.

HAROLD BIERMAN, JR.

The Nicholas H. Noyes Professor of Business Administration
Graduate School of Business and Public Administration
Cornell University

A Cornell faculty member since 1956, Mr. Bierman formerly taught at Louisiana State University, The University of Michigan, and the University of Chicago. From 1964 to 1979 he helped the University of the West Indies establish a management program, and he held the Shell Chair of Management there in 1965 and 1966.

His industrial experience includes work with Arthur Young and Company, Shell Oil Company, Ford Motor Company, National Can Corporation, and Boeing. He has been a consultant to a wide variety of entities including Owens Corning Fiberglas and AT&T as well as the U.S. Government.

His teaching interests are in financial policy, investments, and accounting. He is the author or co-author of ten books, including *The Capital Budgeting Decision, Financial Accounting, Managerial Accounting,* and *Strategic Financial Planning,* and 100 journal articles.

19

Stock Market Impact*

HAROLD BIERMAN, JR.

There are two sets of stockholders affected by a merger or acquisition, those of the firm being acquired and those of the firm doing the acquiring. In this chapter we will primarily evaluate the effect of the acquisition on the well-being of the stockholders of the firm doing the acquiring. What is the perception of a common stockholder when a large premium over market price is offered? Consider a stockholder of a company which offers $30 a share for a company which is currently selling at $25 per share. This is a 20 percent premium over market price and well within reasonable bounds. Now assume the offer is rejected because of competition and the price offered shoots up to $50 per share. This is a 100 percent premium over market and the average stockholder has to start wondering whether the acquisition is being made in the interests of the stockholders or for the interests of management.

Let us consider the situation where a corporation has excess cash and the acquisition will be accomplished by the use of cash. If the firm's stockholders are in the 70 percent tax bracket and if the choice to the corporation is an acquisition worth $30 per share or to give the funds to the shareholders in the form of a cash dividend then the company can afford to pay as much as $100 per share for the firm which is only worth $30 per share and which is selling on the market for $25. Of course, a better alternative may be to find another firm where the gap between value and price per share is smaller. To keep the analysis simple we will assume there is only one firm to be considered for acquisition.

Why can the firm pay $100 for a stock that is worth only $30? If the $100 is distributed as a dividend the stockholders being taxed at a 70 percent rate would pay $70 of tax and would net out $30 and be able to buy only $30 of the stock. We assume reinvestment by the stockholders and the stock being acquired by the individual investor to have value exactly equal to its cost. If the firm bought the stock worth $30 at a price of $100 the stockholders would again have $30 of value. If the stock could be purchased for less than $100 the stockholders would actually be better off with the acquisition than with a cash dividend.

It could be argued that the company should pay only $83 for the stock because the individual shareholder receiving $83 could pay the 70 percent tax and still have $25. This $25 is enough to buy one share on the market of the firm being acquired. This is also the maximum price if the stock is only worth $25. The $100 maximum price is correct if the firm acquiring the shares can enhance the value of the acquired firm to a level of $30 per share. The $83 is correct if there is no value enhancement.

The amount that the firm could afford to pay would be somewhat reduced by the fact that the tax basis is increased with the cash dividend and then reinvestment. It is convenient to assume the tax basis change is worthless (and thus we obtain an offer price of $100). However, we can also compute an indifference price if there is assumed to be value to the tax base change. If we assume that capital gains are taxed at .25 at a time period 20 years from now and if a time value factor of .06 is used, we obtain a maximum value of $92.† Changing the time horizon or the rate of discount would change the maximum price the firm can offer.

---

*©1981 by Harold Bierman, Jr.

†Let X be the cash dividend or the stock price bid, t_p be the personal tax rate and t_g the capital gains rate.

$$(1 - t_p) X + t_g (30) (1+r)^{-20} = 30$$
$$.3X + .25 (30) .3118 = 30$$
$$.3X = 27.6615$$
$$X = 92.$$

There are tax incentives (at the personal level) for a company to engage in acquisitions rather than pay large cash dividends. The above example illustrates one reason why a company such as Kennecott Copper was willing to pay a premium of well over 100 percent of the market price of Carborundum Company's common stock to acquire the common stock of that company. If we add to tax considerations the synergy effect (the sum of the two firms as a joint operation is worth more than the sum of the individual firms) it is not difficult to justify offering prices that are more than 100 percent of the current market price of the stock of the firm being acquired.

In justifying the offering price we have assumed that the choice is between the acquisition of the firm and a cash dividend to be taxed at ordinary rates. Consideration of other alternatives will modify the maximum price that can logically be offered for the common stock. Also stockholders with different tax rates will have different perceptions as to the reasonableness of the price that is offered. If the stockholders have a zero tax rate, they will not be in favor of a premium over value. They would prefer a cash dividend to paying an amount in excess of the expected value of the common stock.

DEALING WITH ANALYSTS: THE EARNINGS PER SHARE

Analysts can be expected to be concerned with both the cosmetics of the transaction and the intrinsic values that are implicit in the transaction.

We will only consider the effect of the acquisition on the earnings per share. It is necessary to distinguish between the short and long-run effects. The short-run effects are easy to predict. Assume that the next period's earning will be the same as this period's earnings. The earnings per share will be increased if the price earnings multiplier of the acquiring firm is larger than the price earnings multiplier of the firm being acquired, and if market price is paid for the firm. This conclusion assumes common stock is used to accomplish the acquisition.

Assume that firm A is acquiring firm S for 125,000 shares and the facts apply as in Table 19-1

TABLE 19-1

	Firm A	Firm S	Combined A+S
Total Earnings	$10,000,000	$2,000,000	$12,000,000
Number of Shares	1,000,000	500,000	1,125,000
EPS	$10	$4	$10.67
Market Price	$80	$20	$80
P/E Ratio	8	5	7.5

Table 19-1 shows the price earnings multiplier is larger for Firm A than for Firm S and we can predict that the acquisition of S by A will increase the earnings per share of the joint firm compared to the earning per share of A ($10.67 compared to $10). To increase a firm's earnings per share it is only necessary to acquire another firm with a lower price earnings ratio, using common stock in the acquisition. The price to be used in this calculation is the price that has to be paid to accomplish the acquisition.

Now assume the earnings per share of S was $2 and total earnings of S were $1,000,000. Table 19-2 shows that the price earnings multiplier of A is smaller than for S. The acquisition will now reduce the earnings per share of the joint firm compared to the earnings per share of A (it will be $9.78 down from $10) (Table 19-2).

TABLE 19-2

	Firm A	Firm S	Combined A+S
Total Earnings	$10,000,000	$1,000,000	$11,000,000
Number of Shares	1,000,000	500,000	1,125,000
EPS	$10	$2	$9.78
Market Price	$80	$20	$80
P/E Ratio	8	10	8.18

In a situation where an acquisition or a merger affects the earnings per share, analysts will frequently try to compute a pro-forma earnings per share without the acquisition. A statement that the "acquisition contributed $.67 per share of the $10.67 total earnings per share" is then made. The analyst wants to distinguish the change in earnings caused by improved operations and the change caused by financial types of transactions, including mergers and acquisitions. Management likes to have an acquisition increase immediate earnings per share. On the other hand, a merger that reduces the immediate earnings per share from $10 to $9.78 would be very hard to justify in the board room of firm A. A decrease in earnings per share is a tough pill for a firm to swallow.

DEALING WITH ANALYSTS: THE PRICE EARNINGS RATIO

In Table 19-1 we start with a P/E ratio of 8 for Firm A and 5 for Firm S. What will be the price earnings ratio of the firm after the acquisition? It can be shown that if there are no special synergy effects the post acquisition P/E ratio is a weighted average of the P/E ratios of the component firms where the weights are the total earnings of the separate firms. For the situation described in Table 19-1 if we define E_A to be the earnings of firms A and Es to be the earnings of firm S, we have (all numbers in millions):*

$$\text{New P/E} = \frac{E_A}{E_A + E_S}(\text{P/E of A}) + \frac{E_S}{E_A + E_S}(\text{P/E of S})$$

$$= \frac{10}{10+2}(8) + \frac{2}{10+2}(5) = 7.5$$

This would imply a market price of the common stock of $80 after the acquisition (equal to 7.5 times $10.67). This is unchanged from the $80 market price of A before the acquisition.

For the situation of Table 19-2 we have

$$\text{New P/E} = \frac{10}{10+1}(8) + \frac{1}{10+1}(10) = 8.18.$$

This P/E would again imply a market price of the common stock of $80 after the acquisition (equal to 8.18 times $9.78) which again is equal to the before acquisition market price of A.

This model assumes that the market recognizes no gain or loss as a result of the acquisition transaction. Thus the stock price of A is the same before and after the acquisition. The P/E after acquisition is a weighted average of the P/E's before acquisition.

Returning to the situation of Table 19-1, why does A have a P/E of 8 and firm S has a P/E of 5? We will explain the level of the price earnings ratios with the aid of a popular valuation formula:

$$P = \frac{D}{k_e\text{-}g}$$

where

  D = current dividend
  k_e = cost of equity
  g = growth rate of dividends and earnings
  P = stock price.

For example, assume firm A is paying $6 per share dividends so that the retention rate is .4. The stockholders want a return of .15 and expect a growth rate of .075. We then have:

$$P = \frac{D}{k_e\text{-}g} = \frac{6.00}{.15\text{-}.075} = \$80$$

Note that Firm A has a .075 growth rate and a P/E ratio of only 8.

Firm S of Table 19-1 has a dividend of $2.80 per year and a growth rate of .01. We then have a price per share of

$$P = \frac{D}{k_e\text{-}g} = \frac{2.80}{.15\text{-}.01} = \$20.$$

S's growth rate is only .01 and the firm has a P/E of 5 (see Table 19-1).

Another way of explaining the low P/E ratios of A and S of Table 19-1 is to determine the implied growth rates and the implied expected returns on investment of retained funds.

If we define D = (1-b)E where (1-b) is the dividend payout percentage and E is the earnings per share then we have

$$P = \frac{(1\text{-}b)\,E}{k_e\text{-}g}$$

or dividing both sides of the equation by E:

$$\frac{P}{E} = \frac{1\text{-}b}{k_e\text{-}g}$$

This equation says that the price divided by earnings for a firm is equal to the dividend payout percentage divided by the difference between the cost of equity and the growth rate. Solving for the implied growth rate, we have:

$$g = k_e - \frac{E}{P}(1\text{-}b).$$

Assume that the stockholders for both firms of Table 19-1 want a return of .15. The retention rate for S is .3 and P/E ratio is 5. The implied growth rate for Firm S of Table 19-1 is:

$$g = .15 - \frac{1}{5}(1\text{-}.3) = .01$$

It can be shown that with zero debt that

$$g = rb$$

where r is the return on new investment.

With S having a retention rate of .3, this implies a return (r) on new investment of .033:

$$g = rb$$
$$.01 = r\,(.3)$$
$$r = .033.$$

---

*For a proof see Reference (1), p. 283.

The low returns expected on new investment and the resulting low growth rate help explain the low price earnings ratio being applied by the market to the stock of S. Assume Firm A has a retention rate of .4. It has a P/E of 8. The implied growth rate is:

$$g \;=\; .15 \;-\; \frac{1}{8} \; (1\text{-}.4) \;=\; .075.$$

This implies a return on new investment of .1875.

$$g = rb$$
$$.075 = .4r$$
$$r = .1875$$

Firm A has more desirable investment opportunities than Firm S and this leads to a price earnings multiplier of 8 for A compared to 5 for S. The P/E ratio of a firm reflects the market's perceptions of the earnings opportunities (growth) of the firm. When one firm has a P/E of 8 and a second firm has a P/E of 5 we can expect the new P/E of the joint firm to be between 8 and 5. The growth potential of the high P/E firm will be diluted by the addition of the firm with less growth opportunities.

Analysts are aware of the above models. Thus when an electronics firm with a P/E of 20 merges with a steel company with a P/E of 6 the earnings of the steel company after acquisition will not be capitalized with a P/E of 20. We can expect the new P/E of the merged firms to be between 20 and 6.

In Table 19-2 the earnings of S were only $1,000,000 (down from $2,000,000 of Table 19-1) but the stock price remained at $20. Assume the retention rate is .30 and the dividends are $1.40 per share and the growth rate is .08. We then have:

$$P = \frac{D}{k_e\text{-}g} = \frac{1.40}{.15\text{-}.08} = \$20.$$

A growth rate of .08 with a retention rate of .30 implies a return on investment of .267.

$$.30\,r = .08$$
$$r = .267$$

The P/E ratio of 10 for Firm S of Table 19-2 is justified because the firm is expected to earn .267 on new investment.

Let us consider why the merger summarized in Table 19-2 may be desirable even though the new earnings per share is reduced to $9.78. Table 19-3 shows the earnings of A without the acquisition and with the acquisition of Firm S. Not until a passing of 44.3 years does Firm A+S have higher earnings per share than Firm A. It is very unlikely that the board

of directors of Firm A would find Table 19-3 to be a persuasive argument in favor of the merger. There is too long a passage of time before the earnings per share of A+S catches up to A. If the switch had taken place in year two or three, there could be room for persuasion. A period of 44.3 years is too long a period to wait. The stockholders of A cannot be expected to be enthusiastic about such an acquisition.

TABLE 19-3

Year	EPS of A g=.075	EPS of A+S g=.07554
0	10.00	9.78
1	10.75	10.52
2	11.56	11.31
3	12.42	12.17
4	13.35	13.09
5	14.36	14.08
15	29.59	29.14
25	60.98	60.40
44.3	246.25	246.26
50	371.88	372.97

DEALING WITH ANALYSTS: THE DEBT LEVEL

Frequently an acquisition is accompanied by a significant change in the debt level of the firm after acquisition. Thus two changes are taking place, one in the basic nature of the firm, and a second in the capital structure of the firm.

As illustrated above, the acquisition of a firm is likely to cause a change in the P/E ratio being applied to the earnings. A change in the capital structure is also likely to cause a change in the return required by the stockholders. The addition of the debt increases the risk to the common stockholders which, in turn, results in the stockholders requiring a higher return.

The use of debt in connection with acquisitions follows naturally from the application of the following model:

Value of Levered Firm = Value of Unlevered Firm +

Tax Rate (Amount of Debt)

Assume the market value of firm A is $80,000,000 with a corporate tax rate of .46. If $50,000,000 of debt is substituted for common stock the value of the firm increases to $103,000,000.

$$80,000,000 + .46\,(50,000,000) = \$103,000,000.$$

If the firm can be acquired for $80,000,000 the acquiring firm could theoretically increase the value to

$148,000,000 by the use of a maximum amount of debt.*

Continuing the above example, assume that stockholders want a .10 return from investing in the firm, and the firm is expected to earn a constant $14,815,000 before tax. The $14,815,000 would be taxed $6,815,000 at a corporate tax rate of .46. The after tax income to investors if the firm is financed only with common stock is $8,000,000 and the value to investors of this perpetuity if the .10 is used as a discount rate is $80,000,000. More concisely, we have:

$$\frac{14,815,000 \ (1-.46)}{.10} = \$80,000,000.$$

Now assume $50,000,000 of debt can be issued to yield .10. The tax is now $4,515,000:

Earnings Before Interest	14,815,000
Interest	5,000,000
	9,815,000
	x .46
Tax	$4,515,000

The net after tax is:

$$14,815,000 - 4,515,000 = \$10,300,000$$

and the present value of this flow using a discount rate .10 is again $103,000,000.

While the above relationships are not supported by all, there is no question that the tax deductibility of interest combined with the contractual nature of interest (setting a maximum cost) does make debt seem to be an attractive means of financing acquisitions. If the acquisition is financed entirely with debt and if the amount of interest to be paid is less than the earnings before interest and taxes, the earnings per share will increase. This does not mean that the acquisition is desirable, but an increase in earnings per share is a number that is likely to shove management in the direction of the acquisition.

We can expect financial analysts to take careful note of the new level of debt and to attempt to identify the portion of the increase in earnings per share that is caused by the increase in debt.

Let us refer again to Table 19-2 where the acquisition of S, using common stock results in a decrease in earnings per share. Assume now that $10,000,000 of debt paying .09 is used to finance the acquisition. The tax rate is .46 and the earnings of S before taxes was

$1,852,000. With the $900,000 of interest tax shield the new tax is $438,000 and the new earnings of A are:

Basic earnings of A		$10,000,000
Earnings of S:	$1,852,000	
Interest	− 900,000	
Taxes	− 438,000	514,000
		$10,514,000

The new earnings per share are $10.51, an increase of $.51 compared to the $10.00 before the acquisition.

An intelligent analyst will look at the $10.51 and realize that there is now more risk. A not so careful analyst might conclude that firm A is merely more profitable.

DEALING WITH ANALYSTS: DIVERSIFICATION

An oil company (Mobil) acquires a retail firm (Montgomery Ward) and a packaging firm (Container Corporation). What is the reaction of the financial analysts? There are several possible reactions. If previously, Mobil was looked at as a rapidly growing energy company with a large number of profitable investments in the energy area, this evaluation would now be revised. Is there any set of assumptions that would lead to great excitement about Mobil and eagerness to buy Mobil stock? If previously it was felt that energy was a bottomless pit for investment funds with certain losses with "dry holes" and government regulation if oil was found, then the switch in investment direction might well be received with a sigh of relief, and more enthusiasm for Mobil stock. There is no advantage investing in the common stock of a company engaged in a series of gambles when the firm cannot win whatever the outcomes (this does not have to be an accurate description of the world, but merely an accurate description of the analysts' perceptions).

For most conglomerate acquisitions the analysts would not expect a drastic improvement in the common stock price of the acquiring firm. The selling firm has at least as much information as the buyer and there is no reason to think that the buyer rather than the seller will reap the surplus.

Market Share

One of the easiest bits of advice for a consultant to offer a corporation is "be a monopoly." Preferably

---

*That is, $\dfrac{80,000,000}{1-.46} = \$148,000,000.$

one wants to have a monopoly of a product where the demand is inelastic (that is, people cannot do without the product, if price is increased there will be a very small decrease in the amount demanded). The organization of OPEC is an example of the formation of such a monopoly. The world has not learned how to do without oil in the short run, thus the price of oil can be increased at a rapid rate to relatively large amounts without greatly decreasing the amount of oil consumed. The owners of the oil reap large profits. The corporate management which can find a product similar to oil, where the supply side can be legally organized in a manner similar to OPEC, has tremendous profit opportunities. Unfortunately for corporate managers, but fortunately for consumers, these "star" products are difficult to find since legislation makes it illegal to form monopolies by combining the operations of competing firms or by colluding on price. Thus mergers that tend to reduce competition are likely to attract governmental attention and are apt to be declared not in the common interest and to be disallowed. It may be possible to merge in an attempt to round out a product line where it can be argued that there is an increase in competition.

The merger that is least likely to attract attention is the merger that crosses over industry lines, and where the operations of the entities are highly independent. In 1976 Mobil Oil Corporation completed its acquisition of Marcor (Montgomery Ward and Container Corporation). This was obviously an attempt by a company in a beleaguered industry (officials of the United States Government including several presidents have indicated a distrust of "big oil") to move from an industry rapidly heading for controls, to an industry not yet so fettered. If the federal government reduces the profitability of one industry, they can expect funds to flow from that industry to other more profitable activities. Mobil executives were betting that stockholders would welcome a shift from funds invested in a controlled industry. The talk of taxing excessive profits and breaking up vertically indicated companies is likely to have a multiplier effect in terms of discouraging investment in the industry being reviewed for such taxation and dismemberment.

Another industry that considers itself under siege is the steel industry. Steel industry common stock (in 1980) is selling at one half of book value and a much smaller percentage of replacement cost. Management considers this situation to be the result of bad governmental policies concerning foreign trade (allowing the dumping of foreign steel) and the implementation of excessive pollution control legislation. Thus in 1979 National Steel Corporation acquired the United Financial Corporation of California. While the stated objective of the acquisition was to provide a source of earnings that would counter-balance the swings in earnings of a steel company, the facts that a finance company does not have environmental controls and there is no "dumping" problem probably were considerations. A common stockholder in a steel company in 1979 is likely to have trouble being enthusiastic about further investment in the steel industry. A shift to a financial corporation at least opens up the possibility of normal profits that have been missing for 20 years in steel.

Diversification and the Shareholders

For simplicity we generally assume the goal of a firm is profit maximization (in present value terms) in order to maximize the well-being of the common stockholders. Periodically we should question this assumption since corporations are also in existence to serve other groups, for example, management.

When a firm diversifies by merging or acquiring a firm in another industry, who benefits? Let us consider the position of the shareholder and for purposes of focusing on diversification let us assume zero personal tax rates.

The individual shareholder can diversify easily by buying stocks in different firms in different industries. When Marcor is selling at a price of $25 the holder of Mobil common stock does not need Mobil to bid $35 per share for Marcor stock to achieve diversification. The stockholder can easily achieve diversification by investing in mutual funds or buying stock in a variety of firms. The stockholder does not need the company to incur costs to achieve diversification.

The objective of diversification is risk reduction. The advice not to put all one's eggs in one basket is good advice if the objective is to avoid a feast or famine situation.

If diversification can generally be achieved efficiently by investors, then why do firms diversify? In the first place there are many investors who are not well diversified and would like to have the corporation diversify on their behalf. But even more importantly there is a group which has its major asset invested in the firm, and this asset is difficult to diversify. The major assets of managers are their careers. If a company goes bankrupt or enters a period of financial difficulty the middle-aged manager pays a heavy economic price. It is reasonable for such a manager to seek a higher level of security by trying to stabilize the income of the corporation.

Since the diversified stockholder does not benefit significantly from the diversification, why are there not more complaints from such shareholders? The shareholders may not seek diversification, but given an income tax schedule that reaches 70 percent for ordinary income there are sufficient other reasons for the shareholders to accept diversification.

DEALING WITH ANALYSTS: REAL CHANGES

The justification for many mergers and acquisitions is that they will lead to real changes in income. This is the synergy effect where one plus one equals three (or more). Bradley and Korn (2) think that the belief that synergy exists is one of the three most important factors leading to the current merger - acquisition boom. But Haugen and Langetieg (4) were able to find little evidence of synergy in their sample of 59 major industrial mergers taking place between 1951 through 1968.

Schick and Jen (5) present empirical evidence that mergers benefit the stockholders of acquiring firms.

Lorie and Halpern (3, p. 160) studied 117 mergers between 1955 and 1967 where the acquired firms were acquired for complex securities valued over $10 million. They found that if one measured the rate of return for the period six months prior to the merger to the date of merger (as well as one year after merger and two years after merger) the investors earned a return greatly in excess of the return earned on the Standard and Poor's Composite Index. They also measured the rate of return from the date of merger to one and two years after merger. While they found a return in excess of the return earned on the index, the difference was much smaller than the differential return earned during the period immediately preceding the merger.

The evidence would seem to be that the stockholders of the acquired firm tend to reap immediate (prior to operations of the merged firm) profits, but there still remain enough real gains as a result of the merger to benefit the stockholders of the acquiring firm (see Shick and Jen(5)).

Why does the joining together of two firms lead to increased rates of return?

There may be true synergy. In May 1979 Exxon bid $72 per share for Reliance Electric Company common stock which was selling for $36. The stated justification for offering over $1.17 billion for Reliance was that Exxon had developed an energy-saving electronic device for controlling the speed of electronic motors. The acquisition of Reliance would accelerate the entry of Exxon into the electric motor market and thus there would be synergy.

The situation may be one where one firm is doing something wrong and the other firm's management thinks it can correct the situation. It might be a cigarette company (Philip Morris) acquiring a beer company (Millers) and thinking it can supply marketing know how. Or it could be a company that thinks it can supply production and engineering improvements (Emerson

Electric has done this very successfully).

In situations such as this both the stockholders of the selling firm and the stockholders of the buying firm may benefit. The sellers may think it is worth $30 per share and be pleased to sell at $35 at the same time that the buyers see an intrinsic value of $45 once they institute the planned changes.

For the stock of the acquiring firm to reflect immediately the above judgements, they would have to be publicized. This publicity would not always be consistent with the best implementation of the corporate strategy. Philip Morris did not want to tell the world its plans for Millers when it acquired the beer maker.

If a firm feels it is not desirable to reveal all its plans either because of strategy considerations or because of the risk of claiming too much and then being embarrassed, all is not lost. If the predictions turn out to be valid, the financial statements will reflect the fact that the acquisition was a wise one, and the stock price will now go up. If the belated nature of the increase is troublesome, then some of the plans should be revealed to gain some of the stock price increase earlier.

CONCLUSIONS

The shareholders of a corporation should recognize that there are many motivations that lead to mergers and acquisitions. The payment of a large premium over market price does not necessarily indicate an unwise decision. Unfortunately, sometimes management might not be able to reveal all its reasons for offering the large premium. Thus stockholder unrest can arise where there would not be unrest if all the facts were known. But even worse, there can also be situations where management's analysis is faulty and the purchase price is excessive. Time will reveal which is the true situation. Looking back any one of us can be wiser than the wisest manager.

References

1. H. Bierman, Jr., *Strategic Financial Planning*, The Free Press, Macmillan, 1980.
2. J. W. Bradley and D. H. Korn, "Acquisition and Merger Trends Affecting the Portfolio Manager," *Financial Analysts Journal*, November/December, 1977.
3. J. H. Lorie and P. Halpern, "Conglomerates: The Rhetoric and the Evidence," *Journal of Law and Economics*, April 1970, pp. 149-166.
4. R. A. Haugen and T. C. Langetieg, "An Empirical Test for Synergism in Merger," *The Journal of Finance*, September, 1975, pp. 1003-1014.
5. R. A. Shick and F. C. Jen "Merger Benefits to Shareholders of Acquiring Firms," *Financial Management*, Winter 1974, pp. 45-53.

FINANCING THE ACQUISITION OR BUYOUT

THE FINANCING PACKAGE OF A MERGER, ACQUISITION OR BUYOUT is a primary part of the transaction. The terms and conditions under which a lender, or group of lenders, is willing to extend credit may actually shape the post-acquisition complexion of the business. This topical area considers the basic elements which determine capital structure and the amount of debt which can be supported. Also a unique device of corporate finance, the Employee Stock Ownership Plan, is examined as a financing vehicle which can increase cash flow. The discussion of credit will be somewhat technical although some elements such as the track record of management will obviously be important in analyzing the ability to obtain financing. For a more complete picture of the human resource impact the reader should turn to that section in this handbook.

Albert F. Reisman explores the concept and advent of the leveraged acquisition. He points out that finance companies are the specialists in short and medium-term financing against collateral while banks and insurance companies tend to be more comfortable with the longer term and more conservative end of the spectrum. This chapter is filled with cases and background material on asset-related lending. There is also a discussion of the alternatives to leverage such as venture capital and government guaranteed loans. One case study of a leveraged acquisition details the spinoff of the apparel division from a Fortune 500 company. Included are initial financial statements, pro-forma financials, and a discussion of deal structure. The footnotes to this chapter furnish an excellent compendium for the professional as well as the student.

An examination of the credit resources of the buyer focuses on the critical elements of credit worthiness. Donald Glickman addresses these elements by discussing internal cash generation, existing assets, utilization of assets, and the construction of a borrowing plan. He points out caveats in dealing with cash flow analysis and the reading of financial projections. Mr. Glickman discusses credit resources in a dynamic sense to meet the interest-carrying capacity required by a proposed transaction. There is also inclusion of information on sale/lease-back of property, suggestions on what to do when the buyer is short of cash, and an example of the purchase of a division of a major industrial corporation.

The widespread use of the Employee Stock Ownership Plan (ESOP) is a relatively new development. An ESOP is a type of employee benefit which has a financial side effect of improving the cash flow of a profitable company purchased in a leveraged transaction. Paul D. Ardleigh applies ESOP's to the transfer of ownership in closely held corporations and divestitures by larger corporations. He also points out the inherent risks and costs associated with this approach. This chapter has clear definitions, important historical material, and a series of examples which thoroughly explore the subject. Mr. Ardleigh has diagrammed and constructed the financials for the leveraged ESOP financing, the non-leveraged financing, conventional debt, and the equity financing. In addition there is a case study showing the use of an ESOP as an alternative to a more conventional merger.

ALBERT F. REISMAN

ALBERT F. REISMAN was admitted to the New York Bar in 1956. Mr. Reisman is a member of Otterbourg, Steindler, Houston and Rosen, PC, and was with Walter E. Heller & Company, Inc. for 12 years, initially as counsel to the New York office and then as a Vice President with both lending and legal responsibilities. He is a former president of the Association of Commercial Finance Attorneys and has been involved in the financing of numerous leveraged acquisitions.

20

Leveraged Business Acquisitions*

ALBERT F. REISMAN

I. INTRODUCTION

Archimedes had such confidence in the theory of leverage that he thought he could move the world with a long enough lever and a firm place to stand.[1] His theory would seem to be proven today, although in a fiscal rather than physical sense, by the increasing application in recent years of asset-based leveraged financing techniques to the acquisition and divestiture of business enterprises.[2] The structuring of leveraged buyouts, however, is still Greek to many in the financial community.[3]

The basic concept of the leveraged acquisition is that the buyer minimizes his equity investment in making the purchase by utilizing the value of the assets of the entity being acquired as a borrowing base against which to raise most or all of the purchase price.[4] In effect, the lender is willing to look initially to the future cash flow and earnings of the acquired enterprise as the source of funds from which its loans will be repaid and to the assets of the acquired entity as collateral for such loans. The seller receives most or all of the purchase price in cash and the acquisition loans become direct liabilities of the new enterprise.

In a typical leveraged acquisition (if indeed any leveraged acquisition can be called typical) a purchaser desiring to acquire a business with annual sales in excess of $50 million, assets of $20 million and an equity of $15 million might invest less than $500 thousand of its own money, borrowing the rest of the purchase price from one or more lenders against the collateral values of the acquired assets. The new debt-to-equity ratio may be more than 10 to 1 and, with the inclusion of subordinated debt from venture capital sources or taken back by the seller, may reach dizzying heights.

Although the concept of leveraged acquisitions is relatively simple to define, it is in practice one of the most complex forms of financing. Nevertheless, the potential benefits of a successful leveraged acquisition for all parties concerned more than outweigh the technical difficulties in structuring a viable project. The minimal capital investment, high reward to risk ratio, beneficial tax treatment of capital gains, immediate cash payment to the seller, limited new issue market and stock market discounts from book or asset values of established companies provide strong incentives for

---

*Copyright © 1980, Albert F. Reisman.

[1]This analogy has previously been pointed out in a similar context in Fritch, *Leveraged Leasing* in Fritch and Reisman, *Equipment Leasing-Leveraged Leasing* (PLI, 1977) at 97.

[2]See *It's All Done With Leverage*, Forbes, Aug. 20, 1979, p. 42; *How to Buy Your Own Company*, Dun's *Review*, Nov. 1977, p. 74; Little, *How I'm Deconglomerating the Conglomerates*, Fortune, July 16, 1979, p. 120; Wallner, *Leveraged Buyouts: A Review of the State of the Art, Mergers & Acquisitions Mag.*, Fall-Winter 4, 16 (1979).

[3]Frequently, the business press incorrectly categorizes a particular acquisition as a leveraged buyout. For purposes of this discussion, the term "leveraged acquisition" is not intended to mean asset or stock purchases financed by the buyer from either or both its own cash and borrowings based upon the buyer's (rather than the target company's) credit worthiness and asset values. Nor will it generally include contested tender offers or exchanges of securities. In the absence of a merger these types of transactions do not generally affect the post-closing debt structure of the target company or reduce its net worth by the borrowed portion of the purchase price, although post-closing dividends or loans upstreamed to the parent by the target company may fund the debt service on its acquisition loans.

[4]See Ruben, *Secured Financing: Creative Tool for Acquisitions*, Stock Market Magazine, October, 1978, p. 31. Grosse, *How to Finance Management Buyouts*, The Bankers Magazine, January, 1979, p. 76. The structure, problems and examples of leveraged buyouts are discussed in *Seminar on Leveraged Acquisition Financing*, Special Bull. No. 79 (National Commercial Finance Conference, 1978). Discussions of various legal, business, tax and accounting aspects, together with sample forms, are contained in Reisman et al., *Leveraged Business Acquisitions*, (Practicing Law Institute, 1979). See Also Wallner, *The Leveraged Buyout Manual* (1980).

both sellers and buyers to examine this financing technique as an alternative to traditional methods of acquisitions and divestitures.

II. THE ADVENT OF LEVERAGED ACQUISITIONS

The origins of leveraged acquisition financing go back to the war-born prosperity of many small to medium sized businesses during and in the aftermath of World War II. Burgeoning profits had led to the enactment of an excess profits tax which encouraged the sale of some enterprises to companies having higher earnings for the base years on which the excess profits were computed in order to mitigate the heavy tax impact. After the war years and through the early 1960's, aging entrepreneurs, concerned that continuity of the family business was not assured, or worried about the effect of potential estate taxes, were frequently willing to sell their businesses for less than book value to relatively younger men who were anxious to expand their own enterprises or to take advantage of an attractive purchase. The purchase price was often little more than the working capital of the acquired enterprise and frequently involved a substantial discount from the asset values of machinery, equipment and plant. Most of these leveraged acquisitions were of privately held, moderate sized enterprises and, generally, the purchaser made only a modest contribution of capital toward the amount required to fund the purchase price. The bulk of such funding was obtained through the secured lending facilities of commercial finance companies.

Commercial finance companies were, and still are, specialists in short- and medium-term lending against accounts receivable, inventory, equipment and real estate.[5] They had the special expertise necessary to analyze and evaluate the market or realizable value of these assets, verify and monitor their status, obtain a legally enforceable security interest in them and, if necessary, obtain their maximum "quick sale" value. Banks and insurance companies, which provide most of the private financing in this country, tend to shy away from highly leveraged balance sheets with little equity investment. They frequently refer these leveraged acquisitions to commercial finance companies who are more knowledgeable about assets values, comfortable with collateral and receptive to highly leveraged balance sheets. Literally hundreds of such acquisitions were handled by finance companies during this period in which the basic techniques of financing leveraged acquisitions began to evolve.

Leveraged acquisitions, however, became less common beginning in the late 1950's and through the 1960's. A go-go bull market led to a new issue craze in which thousands of family businesses from coast to coast, goaded by stock underwriters eager for commissions or a piece of the action, went public and saw their stock rise to astounding price-earnings multiples.[6] The original stockholders often grew rich on their paper values and, at times, in actual cash when they were astute enough to sell their own shares through a concomitant or subsequent secondary offering. By the early 1970's the party was over as reality replaced euphoria and new public issues could hardly be given away.[7]

Another mania of this period was the conglomerate and acquisition frenzy in which the magic concept of synergism combined with "creative" accounting techniques, such as pooling of the interests, and the arithmetic of stock multiples seemingly made $2 + 2 = 5$.[8] Thousands of privately and publicly held companies were acquired for seemingly fantastic prices in tax free exchanges of securities of over-valued conglomerates selling at extraordinary price-earnings ratios. Cash sales of companies became decidedly less attractive as the maximum federal tax rate on capital gains increased from 25 percent to nearly 50 percent between 1968 and 1978. When this bubble burst and the investing public finally came out of the ether in the late 1960's, the result was a stock market value in the 1970's for many conglomerates and recent new issues at less than book value so that the whole was frequently worth less than the sum of its parts or $2 + 2$ often equaled 3.

As a result, beginning in the 1970's, conglomerates began to divest many of their acquisitions as they realized that diversification for its own sake was not an end unto itself; that many types of business enterprises were not amenable to control from a distant executive suite or suitable for the constant ratio of profit increase or return on capital demanded by long range budget

---

[5]The most thorough discussion of secured financing techniques and criteria is contained in Lazare et al., *Commercial Financing* (1968). See also Reisman, *What the Commercial Lawyer Should Know About Commercial Finance and Factoring*, 79 Com.L.J. 146 (1974).

[6]See Brook, *The Go-Go Years*, 278-85 (1973).

[7]There were 1,026 new stock issues in 1969 and the total dropped to less than 30 by 1973. Last year, shares of only 81 companies traded publicly for the first time; a minor boomlet, considering that it was more than double the 1978 total and more than triple the 1977 figure. Most of 1979's new issues were in the high technology or energy related areas. New York Times, Business Section, Feb. 28, 1980, p. 2.

[8]See, Brook, note 6 supra at 150-81.

forecasts.[9] The solution in many cases was a spinoff of the previously acquired subsidiary or division for an immediate cash purchase price funded through a leveraged acquisition financing.[10] The resulting additional cash flow could be used by the seller to fund the development of more profitable operations or to acquire new operations more compatible with its corporate mix since the original acquisition.

The size of these divested units, ranged in annual sales from $5 million to more than $250 million; considerably greater than was the case of the typical leveraged acquisition of the 1940's or 1950's. Commercial finance companies are able to structure the increasingly complex framework of leveraged acquisitions and fund the significantly greater loans required for today's typical buyout because of the transformation that has taken place in this industry in the last 15 years.

In 1960, the commercial finance industry consisted of a few large, independent companies and many small regional firms or finance departments of factoring concerns. This form of lending was unacceptable to most banks, which viewed the administration of secured credits as arcane and better left to specialized finance companies. Structuring and monitoring loans secured by accounts receivable, inventories and other collateral was felt to be too costly administratively, legally complex and downright risky. Indeed any company that needed this sort of financing was almost considered suspect.

The general adoption of the Uniform Commercial Code in the 1960's simplified and made uniform techniques for obtaining and administering legally enforceable security interests in accounts receivable, inventory and other personal property collateral.[11] In this more permissive atmosphere, banks and other large financial institutions began to recognize that asset-based financing techniques could be a vehicle to support the needs of emerging companies growing at a faster pace than their capital base and which could not measure up to unsecured lending criteria. By the early 1970's many banks had begun to engage in commercial financing as an adjunct to other types of traditional bank services either by acquiring commercial finance firms, setting up their own commercial finance departments or participating in loans managed by established commercial finance companies.[12] At the same time, the largest independent commercial financing companies had become full service financial institutions; a few even acquiring commercial banks to expand their capabilities and range of services.

In 1960 the total annual volume of commercial finance loans was slightly over $10 billion. By 1979, as a result of the industry's increased resources and acceptance in the business community, the annual volume was in excess of $65 billion. Much of the recent increase in such volume is the result of the relatively larger outstandings resulting from leveraged acquisitions structured or funded by commercial finance companies.

The annual number of reported acquisitions peaked at about 6,100 in 1969 and dropped to 4,000 by 1973.[13] Most acquisitions in the 60's and early 70's involved mergers with public companies, the majority in exchange for the issuance of securities. By 1979, the number of reported acquisitions had further diminished to slightly more than 2,100 and all-cash purchases represented 53 percent of the total, with a combination package of cash and securities representing another 20 percent.

Even more significantly, divestitures of subsidiaries and divisions by public companies increased from 25 percent of the total number of acquisitions in 1970 to 55 percent in 1976. The percentage of divestitures leveled off to approximately 40 percent of total reported acquisitions in 1978 and 1979. This indicates that sales of many incompatible corporate units acquired during the conglomerate merger era had already taken place but that a substantial market continues to exist for divestitures resulting from nonfulfillment of corporate profit goals, incompatibility with the objectives of the parent firm, anti-trust considerations, the need to raise cash or other reasons.

As to size, in 1979 28 percent of all acquired companies had sales of $5 million or less, 16 percent had sales between $5 million and $10 million and 17 percent had annual sales between $10 million and $25 million. In the same year, 94 percent of all acquisitions were for a price in excess of $1 million, with 64 percent of all acquisitions being for a price of $15 million or less. The annual sales and borrowing availability of the typical commercial finance borrower would fall in the same general range; although some recent leveraged

---

[9]See, Davlin, *Dismantling the Corporate Dinosaur,* 79 Com.L.J. 196 (1974).

[10]See *New Credit Packages for the Smaller Borrower,* Business Week, Sept. 5, 1977, p. 74.

[11]See Reisman, *The Challenge of the Proposed Bankruptcy Act to Accounts Receivable and Inventory Financing of Small-to-Medium-Sized Business,* 83 Com.L.J. 169, 177-80 (1978).

[12]See Shay and Greer, *Banks Move Into High-Risk Commercial Financing,* 46 Harv. Bus. Rev. 149 (1968). A bank participation will generally reduce the effective interest cost of the over-all loan.

[13]The primary source for the following statistics is W.T. Grimm & Co., Chicago, Illinois.

acquisitions have involved substantially larger sums.

The figures on reported acquisitions are generally limited to transactions in which either or both the buyer and seller are public companies. They do not include the many acquisitions each year in which privately held companies are sold to management or outside investors, frequently with the assistance of leveraged acquisition financing.

The above statistics, coupled with recent growth in commericial finance volume, seem to indicate that at least 30 to 40 percent of all acquisitions today are funded through leveraged financing.

Asset-based lending techniques in recent years have provided most of the financing of the initial purchase price and assured a continual flow of working cash of divested subsidiaries or divisions of companies such as Ashland Oil, Squibb, Monsanto, Philip Morris, Whittaker Corporation, W.R. Grace & Co., Emhart Corp., Tenneco, FMC Corp., Clark Equipment, Elgin National Industries, Champion International, Thiokol, Celanese Corp., El Paso Gas, Kennecott Copper and other large corporations. The financing of such divestitures of businesses that might otherwise have been liquidated has, in effect, increased the number of independent small to medium sized business and preserved the jobs of thousands of employees.

The undervaluation in the stock market of shares of many publicly held corporations at substantially less than book value has also led to the growing use of leveraged acquisition financing to fund the cash sale of all operating assets of public companies, followed by their conversion to private companies. The purchaser, generally a newly organized private company, buys all of the assets and assumes the liabilities of the publicly held corporation for a cash purchase price at a premium above the market value of the stock. Shareholder consent and disclosure in proxy material is required for this type of transaction as the seller will terminate or change its business purpose. Existing management, which frequently owns a large block of stock, is hired to run the new company under a long-term employment contract.

The public company may then either pass through the cash from the sale to its shareholders through a liquidating dividend or offer to buy the shares of minority holders with the funds obtained from the sale of its assets. In the latter case, the public company is turned into an investment company that buys tax-exempt securities with the money left after the smaller shareholders are bought out. When the number of holders drops below 300, the seller now becomes exempt from the reporting and proxy provisions of the federal securities law as a closed-end investment company.

These types of leveraged acquisitions of publicly held companies have led to several recent SEC actions. In *Matter of Woods Corporation,*[14] the principal shareholders owned 37 percent of the company's stock and members of the acquiring group owned an additional 20 percent. The Commission held that full and fair disclosure was not made to minority shareholders concerning the tax benefits and purposes of the transaction, prior acquisition offers, negotiations leading to the offering price, the value of assets to be sold, the leverage financing of the purchase price and an investment banking opinion obtained by the companies as to the fairness of the transaction. The investment banker based its evaluation on public information, market price and trading volume of the stock rather than on an independent evaluation or inspection of the company's assets or prospects. The Commission required the retention of a "Special Review Person" to represent and negotiate on behalf of public stockholders for the sale, obtain such professional assistance as necessary and file SEC reports and proxy material.

In the Matter of Spartek, Inc.,[15] the principal stockholders owned 45 percent of the outstanding shares. Again, the Commission held that proxy material relating to the reasons for the transaction, including tax benefits and other information, was not sufficient for a shareholder to "fully understand and evaluate the terms, purposes and benefits to be derived from the transaction." A "Special Review Person" was required to be retained to represent the company's public shareholders in any sale of its assets.

On February 15, 1979, the Commission issued a release on "Disclosure in Proxy Statements Containing Certain Sale of Asset Transactions."[16] After summarizing the motivation and purposes of principal shareholders or management in transactions in which publicly held companies become private corporations through the cash sale of their assets, the release sets forth the standards of disclosure requirements to public shareholders before the sale may be consummated. These include: benefits and employment contracts received by management, difficulties in selling stock in the now-limited open market after the sale of assets and redemption of stock, conflicts of interest between management and shareholders, reasons for the sale,

[14]SEC Release No. 15337, Nov. 16, 1978, Adm. Proc. 3-5583.
[15]SEC Release No. 15567, Feb. 14, 1979, Adm. Proc. 3-5655.
[16]SEC Release No. 15572, Feb. 15, 1979. See also SEC "going private" and "self tender" releases, SEC Release Nos. 34-16075. Aug. 2, 1979, and 34-16112, Aug. 16, 1979.

effect on shareholders' tax liability, terms of financing, appraisal or other rights under state law and the underlying facts from which an evaluation of the fairness of the selling price may be determined.

The result of these SEC actions has not been to preclude leveraged acquisitions of the type described but to increase the degree of disclosure of the purpose and structuring of the sale of assets. Indirectly, however, such disclosure may limit the degree of self-serving benefits negotiated by principal shareholders and management in order to avoid shareholder litigation which might impede the sale.

Another area in which leveraged acquisition techniques have been utilized is in the funding of plans of reorganization of companies in bankruptcy proceedings which have "turnaround" possibilities or the purchase of their viable divisions or subsidiaries.[17] Generally, under the old Bankruptcy Act, consent of controlling shareholders was required to consummate a buyout by management or outside investors as only the debtor could propose a plan of arrangement. Thus, a potential acquiror had to deal with both creditors and shareholders. An attractive feature was that the reorganized company retained its tax loss carryforward despite forgiveness of debt by creditors under the plan of arrangement. The new Bankruptcy Code, effective as of October 1, 1979, provides that any party in interest may offer a plan for reorganization of an insolvent debtor if existing shareholders have not submitted their own plan within four months after another for relief.[18] The Bankruptcy Code also provides for the continuance of the federal tax loss carry-forward to the reorganized company,[19] but legislation is now pending in Congress at the request of Internal Revenue Service which may modify this tax shelter.[19a]

The limited new issue market for shares of privately held companies and the lowering of the federal capital gains tax rate have recently made leveraged buyouts more attractive to aging entrepreneurs who desire to "cash out" their investment in privately-held companies. Asset-based lending techniques are also being increasingly used to finance acquisitions by employees under Employee Stock Ownership Trusts or "Kelso plans."[20]

For the near term at least, it appears that the growth of leveraged acquisitions will continue due to stagnation in the public securities markets for smaller companies, continuing divestitures of prior acquisitions by larger corporations and the state of the economy. A recession may result in reduced earnings for many enterprises, leading to even lower stock market prices or a lower return on capital for the corporate parent. On the other hand, higher interest rates and a recessive economy may be drawbacks to financing this type of acquisition in which the acquired company's cash flow must repay the principal and interest of the acquisition loans.

III. THE ALTERNATIVES TO A LEVERAGED ACQUISITION

Once the buyers decide that a prospective acquisition is desirable, they may consider a number of alternative financing methods or a combination of such methods. Each of these techniques, however, may be utilized to some degree in the structuring of a leveraged acquisition.

Obviously, financing the purchase out of the buyer's excess cash is the easiest method. But, generally, even public or established privately held companies will not have sufficient "idle cash" to fund the full purchase price without eroding operating flexibility or balances necessary to support a bank relationship. Particularly in the case of managers, who have an opportunity to acquire their company, the excess cash alternative is simply not feasible. Maximizing the purchaser's cash investment, however, in the form of capital or subordinated debt will reduce interest costs and encourage more flexible terms by the lending group.

Venture capital sources may also be available to fund all or part of the purchase price in exchange for a substantial or controlling interest in the acquired company in the form of convertible debt, stock or warrants. Their investment may be as long term subordinated debt or equity which can facilitate obtaining bank and trade credit for the new company. In the long run, giving up 70 percent or more of authorized stock to venture capital sources may be the most expensive form of financing if the acquisition is successful. In addition to diluting management's equity, restrictions may also be placed on the permissible scope of its operations. Based upon an early payout of subordinated debt or redemption of preferred stock, the purchaser may be able to negotiate a reduction of the venture capital equity. For example: the stock interest

---

[17]See *The Miller Myers Formula for a Turnaround,* Business Week, Sept. 11, 1978, p.108.

[18]Bankruptcy Code Sec. 1121. See Rosenberg, *The New Chapter 11: The Creditors' Side of the Equation,* Credit and Financial Management, Feb. 1980, p. 26.

[19]Bankruptcy Code Sec. 346. See, generally, Sinrich, *Operating Losses: Tax Problems of the Going Concern and Failing Business* (PLI, 1979).

[19a]Bankruptcy Tax Bill of 1980, H.R. 5043, 96th Cong. 2d Sess. (1980).

[20]See Business Week, Aug. 11, 1975, p. 10; Nassberg, *Employee Stock Ownership Plans,* in Reisman, op. cit. note 4 supra at 275.

may be reduced to 80 percent if the payout or redemption occurs in 5 years, to 70 percent in 4 years and to 60 percent in 3 years.

Acceptance by the seller of the stock of a buyer which is a public company may seem attractive because there is no cash outlay, interest expense or impact on working capital. However, this financing alternative is not usually available in a buyout by management or by privately held companies. Furthermore, the experience of many sellers with the ''Chinese paper'' of the conglomerate merger era has made this an increasingly infrequent method of payment. At times, however, the seller in a leveraged acquisition may receive a preferred stock interest, subject to redemption within a designated period, if available cash funding is insufficient to cover the purchase price.

Issuing notes to the seller may be used when the desire for immediate cash payment is not paramount or to cover the balance of the purchase when other cash sources are not sufficient. The disadvantage is that the seller may seek purchase money security interests in the acquired assets or stock and impose restrictive covenants on the new operation. A limited amount of purchase money debt, however, is often utilized in connection with leveraged acquisitions.

Buyers that are publicly or privately held businesses may supplement a cash deficiency by borrowing under their own existing bank lines. This will usually involve a minimal lead time, minimize financing charges and improve the balance sheet ratios of the acquired enterprise. However, they must be concerned about the risk of jeopardizing their own borrowing or trade credit relationships by reducing working capital and depleting future financial flexibility. Funding a potentially long term asset, such as an acquisition, with short term debt may well have this effect.

Using long-term funding to obtain all or part of the purchase price may also be a viable alternative. The maturity dates of interest and debt amortization may be matched up to anticipated cash flow of the acquired enterprise, working capital flexibility is not diminished and interest rates may be lower than other alternatives. Bank and institutional lenders, however, will generally require a relatively low leverage ratio before they commit funds, thus requiring a substantial cash investment by the buyer or parent guarantees. Specialized intermediate term lenders secured by fixed assets, however, may fill this gap.

Publicly subsidized or government guaranteed loans, such as under programs of various federal and state agencies or industrial revenue bonds, may also be available to facilitate long term-financing. The relative inflexibility of documentation and amortization requirements, long lead time and bureaucratic delay inherent in such programs may make closing difficult to achieve by the tight deadlines which are typical in acquisition transactions. Bridge loans at the closing to be subsequently repaid from the proceeds of the government loan or guaranteed-loan commitment may cover the gap in the required cash purchase price.

Asset-based financing techniques have become an increasingly utilized alternative when the above approaches are not sufficient to fund an acquisition. Such techniques enable the buyer to make the acquisition with a minimal investment of its own cash and to leverage the new enterprise well beyond the level with which banks or institutional lenders would normally be comfortable. Of particular importance is the facility for advances against receivables and inventories which can be rolled over on an ''evergreen'' or non-amortizing basis and provide a borrowing base for the funding of the company's future cash needs after applying to the initial purchase price. Used in conjunction with the formation of an Employee Stock Ownership Trust, debt amortization on fixed assets can be paid out of pre-tax income. The asset-based lender does not ordinarily receive or retain an equity interest and, in the case of a successful acquisition, in the long run in a leveraged acquisition it may be the cheapest form of financing.[21]

IV. ASSET-BASED FINANCING TECHNIQUES

Banks and institutional lenders generally assess credit-worthiness for unsecured loan accommodations upon the borrower's liquidity, leverage, cash flow and management. The maximum amount of the loan is tied to a multiple of the cash flow of the borrower, generally 3 to 5 times its proven annual cash flow history. As an added measure of precaution, these lenders traditionally limit the borrower's availabilities to a low leverage ratio; the rule of thumb generally being not more than a 2-to-1 ratio of total liabilities to capital.

Asset-based lenders, on the other hand, place a greater reliance on collateral than on liquidity or leverage. Therefore, rather than tying the amount of its loan solely to the borrower's cash flow or leverage, the asset-based lender bases its loans upon the underlying values of the borrower's assets which serve as collateral. From a practical standpoint, the less one looks to leverage and liquidity the greater must be the reliance upon the collateral, the greater is the need for adminis-

[21]See Anderson, *In Financing Think High-Yield Debt-Not Equity,* Inc. Magazine, April, 1979, p. 74.

tration of collateral and the lower is the margin of error. Collateral becomes a hedge against inability to pay, but it is not a substitute for the viability of the newly acquired enterprise to meet its obligations.

To maximize this hedge, the asset-based lender takes three steps: perfection of a security interest in the assets of the borrower which are part of its collateral;[22] establishing a lending formula on the basis of the liquidating value of these assets, for instance 85 percent of amounts outstanding on accounts receivable and 30 percent of cost of inventory; and obtaining information on a daily or weekly basis as to the qualitative levels of all the collateral and the borrower's cash flow needs. Under this system, because the loan is protected by collateral, the commercial finance company need not restrict its loan to a conservative multiple of cash flow, require seasonal cleanups or limit borrowing leverage of the newly acquired enterprise.

Credit lines on accounts receivable are extended on a revolving basis in proportion to outstanding amounts due on eligible accounts receivable[23]. Thus, if the borrower had $1 million of accounts receivable and a 20 percent reserve to be held back for possible attrition of the receivables, through credit losses or disputes with customers, the borrower would have a loan availability or line of $800,000. Ineligible or restricted advance accounts would include consignment arrangements, progress billings, significant past dues, inter-company receivables, etc. The flexibility of this kind of arrangement is that the borrower has available on request the funds it needs to pay current expenses prior to maturity of its receivables. These loans do not have a fixed repayment date and are repaid as collections are effected in the ordinary course of business. It also means a saving in interest costs because there is no need for compensating balances as in an unsecured bank loan and there is no requirement for drawing down unneeded funds as in a loan for a fixed amount.

Some borrowers may also require inventory loans to bridge the gap between purchase, processing and conversion; first into receivables and then ultimately into cash. In addition to the initial acquisition financing, these loans may be made to accommodate a seasonal buildup, in connection with letter of credit financing for the importation of merchandise or floor planning for distributors and retailers.[24] In certain trades secured inventory financing may have a detrimental effect upon the borrower's ability to obtain trade credit. Today, however, most trade creditors are more concerned with the continued viability of their customers and their ability to pay on a timely basis. Inventory loan availabilities are based upon a fixed minimum percentage of the cost of acceptable inventory and are on a revolving basis. Therefore, the maximum loan availability will change directly in proportion to the value of acceptable inventory on hand and repayment is from the creation of customer receivables.

Some, but far from all, commercial finance companies also engage in factoring. While it serves some of the purposes of accounts receivable financing, factoring is not simply another way of lending money.[25] Factoring is essentially a service in which the factor purchases accounts receivable at the time of shipment of the goods, without recourse to the assignor for any credit losses. In leveraged acquisitions factoring has been used for the purchase of the acquired entity's receivables from the seller, thus reducing the total purchase price directly paid by the buyer and the allocation of any discount from book values to assets that might be subject to payment of a current tax liability. As an adjunct to purchasing the new entity's receivables without recourse, the factor assumes the responsibilities of credit investigation of customers, collection of accounts, ledgering of receivables and assumption of bad debt losses. The factor also makes advances prior to maturity on the receivables which it purchases, generally at a higher percentage of book value than in receivable financing because it has assumed the bad debt risk and has greater monitoring capability of their qualitative value.

Factoring services are particularly important to the newly acquired business in providing credit protection to avoid impairment of cash flow through bad debt losses and slow paying customers. It allows increased sales to marginal accounts and customer concentrations without jeopardizing the new enterprise's limited capital, eliminates the expense of establishing or expanding a credit and collection department, avoids the cost of ledgering and computer services for accounts receivable and places a lid on variable credit or collection costs in an inflationary era.

Part of the purchase price may also be obtained

---

[22]See, generally, *Carlin, Perfection and Enforcement of Security Interests* (PLI, 1979). See also *Kripke, The "Last Event" Test for Perfection of Security Interests Under Article 9 of the Uniform Commercial Code,* 50 N.Y.U.L. Rev. 47 (1975).

[23]See also Scults, *Accounts Receivable Financing Under the U.C.C.,* 3 U.C.C.L.J. 142 (1970).

[24]See Clontz, *Financing the Small Manufacturer and the Appliance Dealer Under the U.C.C.* 2 U.C.C.L.J. 152 (1969).

[25]See Naitove, *Modern Factoring* (American Management Assn., 1970); Moore, *Factoring, A Unique and Important Form of Financing, 14 Bus. Lawy. 703 (1959).*

through term loans or sale-leasebacks on fixed assets; machinery, plant and real estate.[26] Maturities may range from three to ten years with an amortization schedule providing for no principal repayments for six to twelve months, level payments, varying payments geared to the borrower's seasonal income, a balloon installment at the final maturity or other schedule to accommodate the new enterprise's cash flow needs. Institutional lenders, at times, may be willing to grant even longer terms on highly marketable real estate. Accommodations may also be granted for the financing or leasing of new or replacement equipment after the acquisition is closed.

To summarize, asset-based financing leveraged on the assets of the entity being acquired can generally minimize the initial cash investment by providing greater borrowing availability, result in a higher return on the buyer's equity than conventional financing, comfortably provide for growing working capital needs and generation of increased sales volume, maintain future operating flexibility and reduce interest costs by limiting borrowings to funds actually required on a day-to-day basis without any compensating balances.

PRELIMINARY CONSIDERATIONS

Any acquisition is a potentially risky undertaking, particularly leveraged acquisitions where the smaller equity investment magnifies the risk factor. In a corporate divestiture, the only initial certainty is that the division or subsidiary to be spun off generally has not met the parent's expectations as to profits or return on capital. A comprehensive review and analysis is required to minimize the unknowns that inevitably accompany an acquisition transaction.

Compounding the problem are the legal consequences of a business failure if the financing transaction is held to be *ultra vires* or the acquired entity is found to have insufficient capital or lack of viability after the closing to meet its obligations to existing and future creditors under fraudulent conveyance provisions of state law or the new federal Bankruptcy Code.[27] The very process of financing the acquisition results in the substantial substitution of debt for equity. The new company must be strong enough to meet its obligations and retain sufficient working capital to operate properly. An adverse judicial decision could strip the lender of its secured position or even result in equitable subordination of its claim to general creditors.[28] Moreover, control by the lender over its collateral might be construed as control of its borrower's business activities with concomitant liability for its obligations or Securities Act liability as an "aider or abettor" or "control" person.[29] Expertise in analyzing the potential viability and structuring of a leveraged acquisition can avoid or at least minimize these risks.

The new entity should have a balance sheet which clearly indicates solvency and cash flow projections, prepared on a reasonable basis and in good faith, which show the generation of sufficient cash by the new entity to repay its obligations in the ordinary course of business for a period of at least one year after the acquisition. Otherwise, the lender's security interest may be voided or its claim subordinated by a bankruptcy court if the acquisition loan is found to have caused the new enterprise to become insolvent or unable to pay its debts to existing and future creditors.[30]

The parties in a leveraged acquisition, particularly the lender, must also be concerned with the potential effect of a violation of margin regulations if the loan is secured directly or indirectly by (a) margin stock (b), even with respect to an unsecured loan or a loan secured by non-margin stock, if the acquisition loan is "arranged" by a broker in violation of Regulation T. The borrower or a trustee in bankruptcy standing in its stead may have a private right of action for losses or a defense based on the illegality of a margin transaction. The trend of recent cases is that there is no implied private right of action since the main purpose of controlling securities credit through margin regulations is the protection of the public securities markets rather than any private interests.[31]

Credit executives and personnel reviewing the

---

[26]*See Fritch and Reisman, Equipment Leasing - Leveraged Leasing* (PLI, 1980); Zweibel, *Equipment Financing*, 2 C.C.L.J. 215 (1970).

[27]See Rosenberg, *Fraudulent Conveyance and Preference Implications of Leveraged Acquisitions*, in Reisman op. cit. note 4 supra at 147; *In re Desert View Building Supplies*, 5 BCD 171 (D. Nev. 1977) affd __ F. Supp. __ (D. Nev. 1978); *In re Process-Manz Press, Inc.*, 236 F. Supp. 333 (N.D. Ill., 1964), revd on other grounds, 369 F. 2d 513 (7th Cir., 1966); *In re Terminal Moving & Storage Co., Inc.*, 6 BCD 332 (8th) Cir. 1980), *rev'd en banc*, 8th Cir. July 28, 1980.

[28]See Clark, *The Duties of the Corporate Debtor to Its Creditors*, 90 Harv. L. Rev. 505 (1977); Bankruptcy Code Sec. 510 (c).

[29]See *Monsen v. Consolidated Dressed Beef Company, Inc.*, 579 F.2d 793 (3rd Cir. 1978); *In re Falstaff Brewing Corp.*, 441 F.Supp. 62 (E.D. Mo., 1977). See also generally, Fortgang and Novikoff, *Creditors' "Control" of Debtors - Elements and Consequences of Lender Control*, in Reisman, op. cit. note 4, supra at 329; Herzel and Rosenberg, *Loans to Finance Tender Offers: Borrower's Problems That May Affect the Bank*, 96 Banking L.J. 581 (1979).

[30]See Herzog and Zwiebel, *Equitable Subordination of Claims in Bankruptcy.* 15 Vand. L. Rev. 83 (1961); Clark, note 26 supra; Bankruptcy Code Sec. 548. See also Douglas-Hamilton note 33 *infra*.

[31]See Herzel and Rosenberg, *Loans to Finance Tender Offers: The Bank's Legal Problems*, 96 Banking L.J. 676, 684-704 (1979). See, generally, *Symposium, The Impact of the Federal Reserve Margin Regulations or Acquisition Financing* 35 Bus. Lawy 517 (1980)

proposed acquisition should be aware of the importance of the written credit file in possible future legal proceedings as evidence of the new enterprise's solvency and ability to meet its obligations after the acquisition.[32] All memoranda on the basis for credit approval, discussions with management and investors, inspections of facilities, financial statements, projections, appraisals, credit committee minutes and the like should be placed in the credit file as a permanent record.

Obviously, the commercial finance company will look into the target company's past financial statements, its current products and markets, production facilities and labor force. Projected future cash flow, profit and loss and balance sheets will also be prepared on a realistic basis to include the effect of additional incremental costs resulting from the acquisition financing, such as additional interest expense arising from the heavy debt burden and the cost of services previously provided directly or indirectly by the corporate parent. Off balance sheet liabilities to be assumed by the new entity such as pending litigation or governmental regulatory requirements will be carefully reviewed. Future relations with trade creditors as to the amount and terms of credit and the impact of the acquisition on customers will be considered. The operating capabilities of new and retained management are at least as important as the financial statistics. Does such management have the necessary expertise, experience and depth to run the company effectively and establish adequate control systems?

Since the commercial finance company will be making its advances against specific collateral, it will also examine the quality of the assets to be purchased. Receivable agings will be analyzed for collection turnover (reflecting the general quality of customers) and probed for consignments, bill and hold sales, allowances, potential bad debts, unapplied credits or chargebacks, potential contras or offsets, concentrations to poor credit risks, etc. A physical inspection of the inventory and inventory records will be made to establish both quantitative and qualitative values, writing down obsolete and unmarketable goods. Fixed assets are appraised at realistic ''quick sale'' values by professional appraisers. At times, the liquidation value of equipment and real estate in an inflationary economy, such as we are experiencing today, may substantially exceed net book values. The sale of surplus fixed assets or even the mortgaging of operating

plant and equipment may result in increases to working capital greater than such book values. Values should also be placed on off balance sheet assets such as patents, trademarks, licenses, franchises, copyrights, molds, blueprints and the like. Under a fair market value test, which is the applicable standard for purposes of fraudulent conveyance and bankruptcy laws, the new entity's solvency may substantially exceed that reflected in its book value.

STRUCTURING THE LEVERAGED ACQUISITION

The acquisition may be effected by the purchase of all the capital stock of the acquired company or a purchase of assets, subject to liabilities. In either event, the acquiring entity may be either an active operating company or a new corporation especially organized for the purpose of the acquisition. On some occasions, for tax or other reasons, the buyers will form a holding company to own the stock of the acquiring company.

Divestitures of corporate divisions or where the seller desires to retain its corporate shell necessitate a sale of assets subject to liabilities. The asset-based lender makes a purchase money loan to the buyer and all or a substantial portion of the loan proceeds are paid to the seller. The asset sale may be subject to bulk sale and mortgage requirements of state law, although indemnities are frequently accepted from sellers who remain viable after the closing as they are primarily obligated on pre-closing debts of the acquired enterprise. Prohibitions on assignment of unexpired leases, licenses and executory contracts may present a problem in the asset sale and should be dealt with prior to the closing. To the extent possible, equity contributions and subordinated debt proceeds should be applied toward the purchase price with the balance drawn down from the asset-based lender's availability so that the new enterprise's remaining loan availability can be used for working capital purposes. Obviously, the buyer in an asset sale cannot take advantage of any tax loss carryforward available to the seller and the tax basis of the acquired assets will generally be based on the fair allocation of the purchase price to the various types of assets.

In many instances the buyer will change its corporate name to that of the seller after the transaction and the lender should insist that notice be given to creditors of the acquisition and change of name to avoid future

---

[32]Compare the SEC ''safe harbor'' rule for projections that have a reasonable basis and which are made in good faith. See SEC Release Nos. 34-15944, June 25, 1979 and 34-16076, Aug. 2, 1979.

allegations of bad faith or intent to deceive.[33] The consent of the seller's stockholders to the sale may be required if it will thereafter cease doing business or radically change the nature of its business. Disclosure requirements to shareholders of a public corporation and independent review by third parties in connection with cash sales of all assets of public companies have been the subject of recent Securities and Exchange Commission rulings.[34]

In the stock purchase acquisition, the lender makes the acquisition loan to the buyer with appropriate security agreements and a pledge of the acquired entity's stock. Immediately after the purchase, the target company is merged into the buyer with the buyer as the surviving entity. Frequently, the surviving company then changes its name to that of the target company. Again, the lender should insist that notice of the purchase and change of name be given to creditors in view of the substantial change in equity following the acquisition.

Payment of the acquisition loan proceeds is usually made directly to the seller pursuant to a letter of direction from the buyer. In some instances, in closely held corporations, the lender makes its loan directly to the target company which either dividends the proceeds upstream to its shareholders or to the buyer after the acquisition for the purpose of paying for the stock. A review of applicable state law is required to determine that the dividend or other distribution to shareholders does not violate legal restrictions on depletion of capital or surplus.[35] Normally, the closing of the acquisition, the asset-based loan closing, the pay-out and the merger all take place simultaneously.

Leveraged acquisitions by operating companies are generally accomplished through newly formed corporations, rather than by direct purchase or merger with the acquired entity, in order to avoid any possible detrimental impact that the merged structure would have on existing business and creditor relationships. If the parent's assets are to be used to partially support the acquisition by the subsidiary, joint and several security interests or secured cross-corporate guaranties should be avoided because of possible fraudulent conveyance problems.[36] Separate loans should be made to each entity based on the value of its assets and the proceeds of the parent loan may then be contributed to the

subsidiary as a capital contribution or subordinated debt by the parent for purposes of partial-payment of the acquisition purchase price.[37]

CASE STUDY OF A LEVERAGED ACQUISITION

As often happens in spinoffs or divestitures, the managers of the apparel division of a Fortune 500 conglomerate were offered the first opportunity to buy the business. The parent company preferred selling to insiders to avoid market repercussions and divulging internal finance data that might result if prospective outside buyers were invited to bid. It was an attractive acquisition and a once-in-a-lifetime opportunity for management. The division's quality clothing enjoyed an excellent market position and sales had grown to $50 million annually, but pre-tax profits had remained relatively flat at $1 million due to recurring design and promotional expenses inherent in the fashion industry. Expenses included $500,000 for parent interest charges and $250,000 for corporate EDP and management services.

Despite its potential, the parent had made a decision to sell off the division because of apprehension about the cyclical nature of the fashion industry and its incompatibility with long-range financial planning objectives. The net book value of the division was $13 million, but the asking price was $10 million on an all cash at closing basis, plus assumption of $5 million of current liabilities. A substantial capital gain on an earlier divestiture would more than offset the after-tax loss on the $3 million discount from net book value of the apparel division but the transaction had to close by December 31 of the current tax year. The simplified financial statements of the division were as follows:

Sales	$50,000,000
Pre-Tax Profit	1,000,000
Cash	$ 25,000
Accounts Receivable (net)	6,500,000
Inventories	7,500,000
Other Current Assets	375,000
Total Current Assets	$14,400,000
Machinery and Equipment (net)	1,600,000
Land and Buildings (net)	2,000,000
Total Assets	$18,000,000

[33]See, generally, Douglas-Hamilton, *Creditor Liabilities Resulting from Improper Interference with Management of a Financially Troubled Debtor,* 31 Bus. Lawy. 343 (1975).

[34]See notes 14-16 infra.

[35]See Model Business Corporation Act, Sections 6, 45, 46, 66; Note, *Bootstrap Acquisitions: The Risk of Subordination in Bankruptcy* ___B.U.L. Rev. 441 (19___). See also *Changes in the Model Business Corporation Act - Amendments to Financial Provisions,* 34 Bus. Lawy. 1867 (1979).

[36]See Rosenberg, *Intercorporate Guaranties and the Law of Fraudulent Conveyances: Lender Beware,* 125 U. Pa. L. Rev. 235 (1976).

[37]See Diamond, *Structuring a Secured Loan to a Multi-Corporate Organization,* J. Comm. Bank Lending, Feb. 1979; Seligson and Morris, *Multi-Debtor Petitions-Consolidation of Debtors and Due Process,* 73 Com.L.J. 341 (1968).

Accounts Payable	$ 4,750,000
Other Current Liabilities	250,000
Total Liabilities	$ 5,000,000
Equity of Parent	$13,000,000
Total Liabilities and Equity	$18,000,000

In early November, the managers obtained a purchase commitment for the sale of division from the parent which expired on December 31 of that year. The managers were only able to raise $250,000 from virtually all of their own personal resouces and therefore it was necessary that they borrow the bulk of the purchase price, but they could not obtain adequate credit from any banks due to the high borrowing leverage required for the acquisition. In mid-November they contacted an investment banker who brought the deal to a commercial finance company. Based upon a "quick sale" appraisal of the fixed assets, an insurance company had previously issued a written commitment to lend $2 million against all of the fixed assets on a long term basis at an interest rate only slightly above prime, but technical title problems (including ecological compliance certificates) precluded a closing of these mortgages before February of the following year at the earliest. A local bank, anxious to obtain deposits and additional service business of the new company, indicated a willingness to fund a bridge loan for the $2 million against the insurance company's commitment. Thus, the commercial finance company was asked to fund the additional $7.75 million required for the acquisition.

The initial question was whether the new company would have a sufficient cash flow to fund its operations, including debt service on almost $9.75 million of new acquisition debt, while it was establishing itself. This required preparation of cash flow, balance sheet and profit and loss projections; including verification of the factual assumptions on which such flow sheets were grounded. A realistic analysis of future expenses indicated that, freed of prior parental interest and service charges, the new entity could reduce fixed overhead items, eliminate certain overstaffing dictated by parental policy and close down one or two unprofitable product lines that would more than cover the additional interest and debt amortization charges. Revolving loans against receivables and inventory would be self-liquidating and not require a fixed amortization schedule. A review of the division's existing order position indicated that sales for the coming year would probably be higher and in accordance with historic profit margins.

The new company, on the other hand, would have to incur substantial start-up costs for credit, collections and EDP functions which were previously handled by the parent. An analysis of the division's customer list, however, indicated that its sales were suitable for factoring. The factoring division of the commercial finance company would purchase receivables without recourse to the new company for a fixed commission of 1 percent of sales and assume the functions previously performed by the parent. The new entity could then concentrate on increasing sales without concern for absorbing credit losses that might deplete its thin capital or incurring inflationary increases in expenses which might adversely affect its cash flow projections. Since virtually all customer credits would be approved by the factor, it felt comfortable in advancing 90 percent of the value of new receivables on the date of shipment. The commercial finance company also agreed to lend the new company, on a revolving basis, 50 percent of the cost of finished apparel inventory of $2.5 million but to exclude from its security interest the remaining inventory of raw material and work in process (having a cost of $5 million) in order not to jeopardize trade credit. All financing would be with a new corporation formed by the managers to acquire the assets and assume the liabilities of the division.

The seller was not willing to guaranty collectibility of the division's existing accounts receivable of $6.5 million, as is sometimes the case, and as to which the agings indicated there were some serious delinquency problems. Even though it had not checked the credit of these outstanding accounts, as would be the case under the factoring arrangement with the new company, the commercial finance company was prepared to loan the buyer 80 percent of the value of these receivables.

However, concern was expressed by management and their new accountants about the effect of allocation of the $3 million purchase discount on the new tax basis of the acquired receivables and the payment of the resulting tax liability on collection. Total book value of assets to be acquired was $18 million, of which receivables were $6.5 million, and at least $1 million of the discount would have to be allocated to reduce the tax basis of the receivables purchased by the new company. This would create an immediate ordinary income tax liability for the new company based upon collections in excess of $5.5 million, which was anticipated to occur within 90 days of the closing, materially affecting its cash flow in the crucial early months after the acquisition. The solution was for the factoring division of the commercial finance company to purchase the receivables outright from the division, without recourse to either the seller or the new company, immediately before the divestiture. The consideration for the purchase of the $6.5 million of outstanding receivables was (a) $5.2 million cash to be paid to the seller at the closing and (b) all collections on the $6.5 million of receivables in excess of $5.2 million (in effect, the excess was the factor's bad debt reserve as it did not have recourse to any of the parties), less a 1 percent factoring commission of $65,000 (which had the effect of reducing the book value of the divested assets and the discount by $65,000) and which would be due within 90 days. The seller would then assign the unliquidated amount due from the factor to the new company as part of the over-all acquisition. The result was to reduce the amount of receivables acquired by the new company by over 80 percent; with the appropriate allocation of the purchase discount and tax liability upon collection of such receivables.

Immediate tax liability for the increased portion of the purchase discount allocated to the tax basis of the acquired inventory would be avoided by a LIFO (last in, first out) valuation election. The increased allocation of such discount to fixed assets would substantially reduce their tax basis and lower allowable depreciation on building and equipment, but the effect on taxable income would be spread over the taxable life of such assets. Since the new company would now be acquiring approximately $12.7 million of total assets and $9.1 million of current assets at book value, a fair allocation of the discount in the purchase agreement and for tax purposes was determined to be $2.2 million on the quick assets and $735 thousand on the fixed assets.

At this point, early in December, the prospective buyer had been able to come up with the following financing to meet the cash purchase price of $10 million:

Management Equity	$ 250,000
Cash of Division	25,000
Term Loan on Fixed Assets	2,000,000
Receivable Advance	5,200,000
Inventory Loan	1,250,000
	$ 8,725,000

Thus, management was still $1.275 million short of the required purchase price. To close the gap and leave open some future borrowing availability for post-closing working capital, the parent was induced to take back a subordinated $1.5 million note secured by a second mortgage on the fixed assets, payable over six years with interest only during the first year and equal quarterly installments over the next five years. Prepayment was required to the extent of 20 percent of profits after the first year. However, the parent still

received an attractive price for the division since the $8.5 million cash paid at closing represented 90 percent of the division's working capital and the total purchase price was ten times the division's *pre-tax* earnings.

As a consequence, the new company's pro forma opening balance sheet after the closing would be summarized as follows, giving effect to its full borrowing availabilities:

PRO FORMA BALANCE SHEET I

Cash	$ 225,000
Due from Factor	1,235,000
Inventories	7,500,000
Other Current Assets	375,000
Total Current Assets (before allocation of purchase discount)	$ 9,335,000
Machinery and Equipment	1,600,000
Land and Buildings	2,000,000
Total Assets Before Discount	$12,935,000
Less: Purchase Discount	(2,935,000)
New Book Value of Assets	$10,000,000
Accounts Payable	$ 4,750,000
Inventory Loan	1,250,000
Other Current Liabilities	250,000
Current Portion Long Term Debt	200,000
Total Current Liabilities	$6,450,000
First Mortgage	1,800,000
Due to Seller	1,500,000
Total Liabilities	$9,750,000
Net Worth	250,000
Total Liabilities and Net Worth	$10,000,000

Allocating $2.2 million of the purchase discount to current assets would result in the new book value of current assets being reduced to slightly over $7.1 million, with current liabilities of $6.45 million, and working capital of $685 thousand. However, some of the larger trade creditors were reluctant to continue existing levels of credit lines for the new company, which would no longer have the backing of the parent, unless both working capital and net worth of $250,000 were increased. The commercial finance company was also concerned about potential legal problems that might result from the new enterprise's thin capital.[38]

A solution was finally achieved by the finance company's loan officers and the accountants for the new company. A holding company was organized which took title to the fixed assets and received

---

[38]See notes 28 and 30 supra.

management's equity contribution. The real estate and equipment were then to be leased to a newly formed subsidiary which would take title to all other assets of the division, assume its liabilities and operate the apparel division. The lease rentals were sufficient to fund the debt service on the mortgages to the insurance company and the seller. The fixed assets would be purchased by the parent for the seller's book value of $3.6 million less the allocated discount of $735 thousand or a net amount of $2.865 million. The seller was willing to take back a purchase money mortgage of $1.5 million so that only $1.365 million cash was required at closing. The holding company's equity of $250 thousand and excess cash of $635 thousand, from the $2 million insurance company mortgage, would then be down-streamed to the operating company as a capital contribution. The holding company's balance sheet would then be summarized as follows:

Machinery and Equipment	$ 1,600,000
Land and Buildings	2,000,000
Fixed Assets Before Discount	$ 3,600,000
Less: Allocated Purchase Discount	735,000
New Book Value	$ 2,865,000
Investment in Subsidiary	885,000
Total Assets	$ 3,750,000
First Mortgage	$ 2,000,000
Purchase Money Second Mortgage	1,500,000
Total Liabilities	$ 3,500,000
Net Worth	250,000
Total Liabilities and Net Worth	$ 3,750,000

After receipt of the cash portion of the $5.2 million from the factor for the division's receivables and $1.35 million from the holding company for the fixed assets, the seller would receive $1.95 million from the operating subsidiary for its acquired assets to complete payment of the $8.5 million cash portion of the total selling price.

The operating subsidiary's summarized balance sheet after the closing would then look like this:

PRO FORMA BALANCE SHEET II

Cash	$ 225,000
Due from factor	1,235,000
Inventories	7,500,000
Other Current Assets	375,000
Total Current Assets	$ 9,335,000

Less: Allocated Purchase Discount	(2,200,000)
New Book Value of Current Assets	$ 7,135,000
Accounts Payable	$ 4,750,000
Inventory Loan	1,250,000
Other Current Liabilities	250,000
Total Current Liabilities	$ 6,250,000
Net Worth	885,000
Total Liabilities and Net Worth	$ 7,135,000

Consequently, *Pro Forma Balance Sheet II* would result in a $200 thousand increase in working capital and a $635 thousand increase in net worth for the operating company over *Pro Forma Balance Sheet I*. Under the restructuring, the insurance company lender was satisfied to look to its first mortgage and an assignment of the lease rentals as security for its loan. The seller obtained its second mortgage (backed, in effect, by the parent's only other asset — the stock of the operating company) which would also be serviced by the lease rentals. Creditors of the operating company felt more comfortable with the new financial figures and ratios. Everything seemed on track to meet the December 31 closing deadline as legal documents were prepared and approved by the various parties.

Two days before the scheduled closing on December 30, however, word was received that the local bank, which was expected to make the bridge loan of $2 million against the insurance company's loan commitment, had backed out because of concern about the new company's ability to obtain environmental and anti-pollution certificates which were prerequisites to the permanent funding. After reviewing the circumstances and the fixed asset "quick sale" values, the commercial finance company agreed to make the bridge loan.[39] The closing began on the morning of December 31 and was finally completed six hours before the midnight deadline.

Confidence in the new company's profit potential and capabilities of its management-owners proved to be justified. In the first year of operations after the acquisition, sales increased by 20 percent to $62 million with an after-tax profit of $1.1 million. In the second year, sales were $64.5 million but profit declined by 15 percent. By the third year, sales had increased to $75 million and profit to $2.5 million. Last year, sales increased to over $85 million and after-tax profits were in excess of $3 million.

---

[39]The permanent mortgage was ultimately funded by the insurance company in April of the following year and the bridge loan was satisfied from the proceds.

DOCUMENTATION

The drafting of documents reflecting a leveraged buyout should not be undertaken without a careful analysis and appraisal of applicable law.[40] Future tax and accounting treatment, as well as achievement of the financial objectives sought by all parties, will depend to a large extent upon the form and structure of the transaction as reflected in the legal instruments.[41] Since virtually all the cash portion of the purchase price is funded by borrowings, with substantial credit and legal risks arising from the highly leveraged debt structure of the target company after the acquisition, the lenders and their counsel will play a much more active role in the negotiation and structuring of the acquisition than is usually the case. Care must be taken, however, that the lenders do not in fact or in appearance "control" the acquiror or the target company prior to or after the acquisition as adverse legal consequences may result from a determination to that effect.

In most cases, the transaction commences with a letter of intent between the seller and buyer or its principals briefly setting forth the basic terms; such as price, terms of sale, assumption of liabilities and closing deadlines. Frequently, the purchaser will be required to furnish the buyer, within a specified period, with a commitment letter from a recognized financial institution for the loans required to fund the acquisition. The letter of intent generally is conditioned upon the execution of formal agreements and often provides that it is not binding except for confidentiality provisions, certain out-of-pocket expenses, disclosure requirements if either party is a public corporation and an exclusive purchase option for a specified period, Usually, many material points are unsettled and left for future negotiation.

The lender's commitment letter demonstrates the buyer's financial capability to the seller and allows the lender to have access to the target company's records for credit evaluation purposes and to inspect operating facilities for appraisals. It will set forth the maximum loan availabilities, interest charges, ratio of advances against acquired assets and repayment schedule. The commitment letter is generally conditioned upon the lender's favorable approval of the new enterprise's economic viability and necessary levels of collateral values of acquired assets, as well as the execution of formal documentation acceptable to lender's counsel and the ubiquitous "no material adverse change" clause. A commitment or examination fee will be re-

quired, subject in some cases to being refunded or credited against future charges after consummation of the acquisition financing, and reimbursement of the lender's out of pocket expenses for legal fees, transportation, independent appraisers, etc. The lender is given the exclusive right to finance the acquisition by the buyer or any affiliated entity for the commitment period and liquidated damages may be provided for breach of this covenant, in view of the relative difficulty in ascertaining actual damages.[42]

The lender and its counsel will review title reports, lien searches, title insurance policies, litigation and contingent obligations assumed by the purchaser, bills of sale, deeds, significant contracts, important patents and trademarks, purchase obligations, leases, regulatory requirements and other aspects of assets to be acquired or assumed obligations which may affect the economic future of the acquiring company. This is done irrespective of whether the acquisition is in the form of a sale of assets, with assumption of certain liabilities, or of stock followed by a merger into the acquiring entity. Legal or business risks, which the buyer and its counsel may be willing to assume or waive in view of the limited capital investment, may be of much more significance to a lender which funds the bulk of the purchase price. Warranties or indemnities of a financially responsible seller, which are assigned to the lender, may tend to cure or alleviate many such risks.

Notice to existing creditors of the sale of assets must be given pursuant to the bulk sales law, particularly if all liabilities of the seller are not assumed, unless there is an indemnity from a financially sound seller. The buyer and the lender should seek to have all debt of the seller which is not assumed paid out of the purchase proceeds if the seller is not clearly solvent and financially responsible or will cease business operations following the divestiture.

The lender ordinarily assumes that the probabilities are that the acquisition debt will be paid at maturity without default based upon its credit evaluation of the new entity's pro forma and anticipated financial statements, cash flow projections, expertise, market conditions and other attributes. Collateral is taken as a "hedge" against the possibility of business failure, and not as a substitute for the probability of business success. At times, however, these judgments turn out to be incorrect as to the new enterprise's ability to repay its obligations or the realizable value of collateral. A single credit loss may be greater than the

---

[40]See, for example, notes 14-16, 18, 27-37 supra.

[41]See Stoney, *The Impact of Tax and Accounting Considerations,* in Reisman, op. cit note 4 supra at 35.

[42]See *Heller v. American Flyers Corp.,* 459 F.2d 896 (2d Cir., 1972).

lender's relatively small net profit on many transactions. Thus, the optimism of the lender's initial credit approval is tempered by the "acid test of bankruptcy."

The lender's secured loan under the "acid test of bankruptcy" of the new Federal Bankruptcy Code may be voided *in toto* if it can be successfully attacked by even one creditor,[43] subordinated on "equitable" principles if overreaching is found to exist,[44] attacked as a fraudulent conveyance under federal or state law if the new enterprise is unable to pay existing or future creditors,[45] subjected to judicially-created alteration of its rights and remedies if repayment or repossession of its collateral would adversely affect reorganization[46] and enjoined for an indefinite period from repayment of its loans through a foreclosure of its security interests.[47]

Shifting to a solvent and responsible seller, by appropriate undertakings or indemnities, the risk of existing and contingent liabilities to the extent possible may not only enhance the economic viability of the new enterprise but reduce the possible legal risks inherent in a leveraged acquisition financing.

Accordingly, the lender will encourage the buyer and its attorney to negotiate provisions of the following type in the formal acquisition agreement:

(i) Warranty of Balance Sheet, and of its preparation in accordance with generally accepted accounting principles ("GAAP";) consistently applied, and of its reflection of all liabilities. Warranty also that, except as disclosed, there have been no changes in the accounting principles applied in preparing financial statements for the past periods provided by the seller to the buyer, and that all such statements were prepared in accordance with GAAP. (ii) Warranty of, or indemnity against, all liabilities, known or unknown, accruing or arising from occurrences preceding closing. Specifically such warranties may be essential where the business, for example, entails substantial product liability risks. (iii) Warranty of net worth. (iv) Warranty of the collectibility (as well as validity and enforceability) of accounts receivable. (v) Warranty of no material adverse change since previous audited financial statements. (vi) Warranties of title to the assets sold (or of the transferred entity's title to its assets). (vii) Warranties that the transferred assets, or those of the transferred entity, are of such a nature and condition as will not prevent the transferred business from continuing the conduct of its business in the manner previously conducted. (viii) Warranties of the non-existence of any undisclosed labor disputes with, or concerted action by, employees. (ix) Warranties of compliance with OSHA, pollution control, environmental protection, and all other applicable law, and of the non-existence, except as disclosed, of any laws, future compliance with which will require a material adverse change in the transferred entity's conduct of its business or will cause the transferred business to incur material liabilities. (x) Warranties against undisclosed escalator clauses in lease and like agreements. (xi) Warranties that the transferred entity is not in material violation of any contracts, agreements or undertakings. (xii) Undertakings not to terminate any transferor guaranties of transferred entity obligations without the prior consent of the party guaranteed and its agreement to continue the obligation without change. (xiii) Warranties of no undisclosed employment or consulting contracts, or special loans, prerequisites or arrangements, between the transferred entity and any employees, directors or third parties. (xiv) Warranties that the manner in which the transferred business conducts its affairs, or markets it products, is not in violation of any laws, including trade regulation laws. (xv) Standard tax warranties and warranties as to compliance with ERISA in respect of any employee plan, including no unfunded pension obligations. (xvi) Warranty of the merchantability and salability (non-obsolescence) of inventory. (xvii) Warranties of the rights to, or to the use of, any trademarks, patents, copyrights, trade-names, etc.; and warranties as to the exclusivity of rights therein. (xviii) General indemnity agreement for breach of any warranty, preferably (together with the warranties) expressly running not only to the transferee but also the lender. All of the buyer's rights and claims under the acquisition agreement should be assignable to the lender in any event.

At times there is a fine line between the monitoring by a lender of its loan or collateral status and control of the borrower's business affairs. From a legal viewpoint, particularly in leveraged acquisitions, overreaching or overkill in documentation may result in litigation on the theory that the lender is the alter ego of the borrower or secondarily liable on its obligations under securities, tax, bankruptcy or other laws.

---

[43] Bankruptcy Code Sec. 544 (b); *Moore v. Bay,* 284 U.S.4 (1931).
[44] See note 30 supra.
[45] See note 27 supra.
[46] Bankruptcy Code Sec. 361, 363, 364. See Orr and Klee, *Secured Creditors Under the New Bankruptcy Code,* 11 U.C.C.L.J. 312 (1979).
[47] Bankruptcy Code Sec. 362.

The following are some guidelines as to what a lender might or might not do to avoid legal liability or appearances of control of the new entity in a leveraged acquisition:

1. Officers of the lender should not be directors or officers of the borrower or any of its affiliates.

2. If possible, some of the debtor's assets should be left free and clear to meet obligations to general creditors in the event of a liquidation, e.g., raw material and work-in-process. This may also enhance the new company's ability to obtain trade credit.

3. A stock pledge to the lender of the borrower's stock, particularly with voting powers, should be generally avoided. In any event, the lender has security interests in the borrower's other assets and the stock equity is subordinate to the claims of the borrower's creditors.

4. Equity "kickers", warrants or options on the borrower's stock generally should be avoided. Lenders should be lenders primarily and not co-entrepreneurs or partners.

5. Elimination of abnormally extensive or unusually restrictive loan covenants which suggest that the lender, and not the borrower's management, runs the company, such as:

  a. Right to select or veto management personnel and their compensation.
  b. Prohibition of *any* other financing sources.
  c. Selection of borrower's auditors by lender.
  d. Use of lender's counsel as attorneys for borrower.
  e. Absolute prohibitions on capital purchases, leases and improvements without lender's approval.
  f. Obtaining resignations in blank of borrower's officers.
  g. Required lender approvals on a discretionary rather than reasonable basis.

6. The obtaining of "clean" legal opinion letters as to corporate authority, enforceability of loans and security interests, non-violation of securities laws, etc.; which tend to establish good faith defenses. The opinion letter also serves the purpose of disclosing potential legal or business problems as to which counsel in unwilling to issue its opinion and the potential risks of which can then be considered in the context of the overall business decision.[48]

CONCLUSION

Managers, operating companies and outside investors having an opportunity for an acquisition should carefully consider the leveraged financing alternative. As early as possible, they should consult with a commercial finance company which specializes in arranging and has experience in this type of financing. The concept should be discussed with the prospective acquiror's financial advisors, investment banker, public accountant or attorney. The purchaser should also seek to obtain the maximum financial data and other pertinent information relating to the target company as is necessary for a sound business decision.

Asset-based lending techniques have come to occupy an important position in the leveraged financing of acquisitions and divestitures. These transactions are seldom routine because they always reflect the specific needs of the parties and the economics of the target company. By nature, the structuring of leveraged acquisitions must be open to new approaches in response to new situations and a changing business environment. This, more than anything else has been responsible for the growth and increasing use of leveraged acquisition financing for all types and all sizes of businesses.

---

[48]See *Legal Opinions to Third Parties; An Easier Path,* 34 Bus. Lawy. 1891 (1979).

DONALD GLICKMAN

DONALD GLICKMAN is currently Vice President—Region Head for the First National Bank of Chicago. Before joining FNBC in February 1974, he was Executive Vice President of Suez American Corp., a wholly owned investment banking subsidiary of Suez Financial Corp. In 1955 he received a Bachelor of Mechanical Engineering Degree from Cornell University and in 1960 a Master of Business Administration Degree from the Harvard Business School.

21

Examining the Credit Resources of the Buyer

DONALD GLICKMAN

The most critical element in any acquisition plan is the credit-worthiness of the buyer. Regardless of the merits of the deal, almost every potential lender will be addressing the issue of "Can the buyer repay the debt?" Buyers whose own financial stability is in question are, by definition, poor candidates for acquisition financing. In this chapter we will examine the various strategies by which a buyer can wring the most advantageous financing terms from potential lenders.

Before beginning to develop a borrowing strategy to meet the cash needs of the acquisition, the buyer should examine all of the potential sources of cash which exist within his own company. The conversion of under-utilized assets to cash provides a double bonus. First, it reduces the need for outside borrowings and second, it facilitates borrowing by increasing proforma earnings coverages. Often, asset conversion to cash also enhances the balance sheet, thus improving coverage ratios.

The most obvious place to look for internal cash generation is the current asset section of the buyer's balance sheet. In all too many companies, the ability to generate cash from existing assets is overlooked in the excitement of a "deal" and in the highly interesting dynamics of negotiating with sellers, lenders and lawyers. The cash lying under the noses of the participants is overlooked. For the aggressively thinking manager, an acquisition can often be the starting point for a searching review of asset utilization. If the manager addresses his attention to each element of his current assets he often discovers that:

Receivables can offer substantial opportunities for cash generation. As an example, for a company with $25 million of annual sales, shortening its average receivable period by only two days will produce almost $150,000 of additional cash. Changing sales terms, or tightening credit procedures/follow-up often can improve the average collection period by as much as a week. For our example company, these precedings could add $500,000 of interest-free cash to the company coffers.

Inventory is another resource often overlooked. In addition to the obvious tactic of reducing gross inventory levels, there are often more subtle elements which can be explored. The following questions should be posed concerning inventory:

1. Are there product lines which contribute nominal amounts of sales, but which absorb significant inventory resources?
2. Are there inventory items which can be provided by intermediate-level suppliers, e.g. steel supply warehouses for users of steel shapes?
3. Are there suppliers who can be induced to assume some inventory functions, even though it may require entering into annual supply contracts or similar arrangements?

The searching analysis of inventory levels and usage can often have a salutary effect on improving the balance sheet, as well as generating cash.

The second place to develop cash without borrowing is in fixed asset accounts. In addition to the obvious tactic of outright disposition of assets (excess land; unused machinery and similar items), there is the opportunity to sell and then rent or lease back such items as vehicles; computers, even furniture, and while these arrangements are frequently more costly than owning them, they can serve as another source of cash, without entering into leasing arrangements which would require balance sheet presentations in accordance with GAAP.

After the buyer has squeezed the last nickel of cash out of the various balance sheet items discussed above, it is time to develop a borrowing plan. The best place to start such a plan is a look at the buyer's own cash flow. The historical cash flow of the acquiring company is the surest prediction of how much money can be raised on the strength of the buyer's own resources. While we will discuss asset-based cash raising techniques later on in this chapter, the use of a cash flow analysis provides the quickest and surest method of obtaining the interest of banks and insurance companies in providing the acquisition financing.

Earnings before interest and taxes (EBIT) but after deduction for depreciation, amortization and similar non-cash charges, are the source from which the buyer will: (a) pay the interest on the debt that he is about to borrow; and (b) rely on most heavily to repay that debt. A good rule of thumb is to divide the EBIT by 2.5 to result in the annual interest charge which can be comfortably paid by the borrower. At interest rates prevailing in early 1980, each million dollars of EBIT can adequately support about $2.5 million of bank debt.

Now that the acquiring company has determined how much interest it can support with its own historical cash flow, the next step is to develop the "pro-forma" cash flow analysis. The two key elements are:

a) The on-going earnings stream of the acquired property.
b) The adjustments to the cash flow which will develop from the circumstances of the particular transaction.

In dealing with the on-going cash flow analysis several caveats are necessary. For those who have both created and read financial projections nothing is more surprising than projections which develop as predicted. For smaller and medium sized borrowers (below the Fortune 500 level) projections are often more useful as signposts to the future than as predicters of actualities. Nonetheless, lenders require the prospective borrower to look into the future, and to quantify the amount of cash which will be available to service the debt.

In preparing the projection, the borrower should be careful not to make radical departures from historical trend lines. If the acquired company has had a gross profit margin of 35 percent, projections of 40 percent to 45 percent will raise immediate questions. Unless there is a specific, quantifiable operating savings which will result from the merger (plant closings, cheaper raw material supply, etc.) it is best to stick closely to the historical ratios.

Since the combined cash flow will reflect the operations of both companies, many adjustments to historical data have to be made. Mergers often result in the elimination of many Selling, General & Administrative (SG & A) expenses. Typical categories for achieving savings are legal and accounting expenses, data processing facilities, reduction of staff services, duplication of office facilities and similar contributions to overhead expense. In making assumptions as to the magnitude and timing of these projected savings, the tendency to err on the side of optimism should be ruthlessly resisted. Savings come hard; hidden expenses, delays, operational and personal difficulties often interpose barriers in the realization of actual cash savings. No borrowing plan should be dependent on developing cash flow reserves not actually in hand at the time of closing.

Once the historical cash flow has been adjusted to meet the dynamics of the proposed transaction, the interest carrying capacity can be established. Now the borrower must answer the question "How is the debt to be repaid?" The most conservative point of view is that the debt should be capable of being repaid in the normal period of time from the after-tax earnings of the buyer alone. Obviously in many cases, the cash flow of the acquired company will be necessary to help amortize the debt in a reasonable period of time.

To determine the period over which the debt can be amortized, the pro-forma net income of the combined companies is added to the pro-forma depreciation and amortization. From this are deducted: estimates of anticipated capital expenditures; increases in working capital required to support the projected sales plan; dividends on equity and any expected extraordinary non-operating expenses. Fifty to 65 percent of the balance of the available cash flow can then be safely committed toward debt amortization. In preparing this analysis, very careful attention must be paid to estimates of future working capital needs. While it is often possible to delay or defer capital equipment purchases, working capital levels will have to be maintained to prevent a liquidity squeeze. This point is often overlooked when preparing the debt service analysis, and is often a root cause of credit crisis.

But what if the cash flow is inadequate to repay the debt in a normal time frame? The obvious answer is to extend the repayment period. Whereas most banks require full amortization in five to seven years, insurance company loans often have effective lives of seven to ten years or longer. Obviously, the longer life generally requires superior coverage tests, both in terms of assets (a minimum of 175-200 percent asset coverage) and in terms of interest and debt service coverage (a minimum of 2.5 to one). Many buyers will be unable to meet these rather stringent tests. What then?

The first solution is to borrow on a basis which does

not require repayment on a fixed schedule, because the borrower has taken a security interest on various assets in lieu of the fixed repayment schedule. Accounts receivable and inventory financing are the most common forms of borrowings which have no fixed repayment schedule. The level of borrowings is determined by the asset level, within an overall credit limit. As long as volume remains at predicted levels, these arrangements are often the best solution to the problem of how to schedule debt repayment. They are frequently used as an interim solution, pending a refinancing with longer term debt or with equity. Generally speaking, most banks (with some noted exceptions) are reluctant to provide "de novo" receivable/inventory secured financing, and the most likely lenders are commercial finance companies such as CIT, Heller, GECC, Aetna, etc. These companies have the experience to enable them to monitor asset levels, and quite frequently they will share deals with commercial banks where the commercial finance company will manage the collateral and the lending rate will reflect a blend of the commercial finance rate (400 to 500 basis points over prime) and bank rates. As long as the cash flow from operations can support the heavy interest charges (i.e., the ROA is good) asset-based financings are a good method of utilizing the available assets to raise money for the acquisition. A significant negative element in financings secured by current assets is that such financings generally preclude any other senior borrowings (except for real estate, discussed below) and that in some industries trade credit will also be adversely affected. The buyer must carefully weigh these factors when considering pledging current assets to raise the cash to effect a transaction.

Another common method of borrowing on assets is the mortgaging or sale-leaseback of real property. Mortgaging property is often a convenient way to obtain extended repayment terms by providing the lender with a first lien on the property. Similarly, sale-leaseback of real property often permits stretching the lease terms to the maximum degree possible, by providing the lessor with title to the property. Plants, warehouses, office buildings, etc. which have been on the property account for a many of years are carried at values which are often far below today's inflated replacement costs. These assets offer an opportunity for converting them to cash, while retaining the use of the property, and not drawing too heavily on the existing cash flow. Another virtue of real estate financing is that the detailed loan agreements and their accompanying restrictions which are characteristic of typical unsecured long-term debt agreements are generally not present in real estate-secured financings. Particularly in cases where the property is of general purpose use, the lender is often looking to the property itself, rather than the operating ratios of the borrower. Furthermore, such secured real estate borrowings generally have little impact on trade credit or the ability to borrow unsecured from senior lenders. The major drawback to such borrowings is that in periods of historically high interest rates, there is often some reluctance to "lock-in" interest rates for a period of 10 to 20 years.

What steps are open to a prospective buyer who has carefully followed the suggestions previously discussed and still finds himself short of the cash to complete his deal? If borrowings on a senior basis, secured or unsecured, are not feasible or adequate in amounts, then it will become necessary to examine the possibility of borrowing on a junior basis and/or expanding the equity base.

Because of the disclosure requirements, and the time element involved, it generally is not feasible to raise debt or equity from the public market prior to the conclusion of the proposed acquisition. Offerings of debt or equity subsequent to the consummation of the deal are quite common. Our analysis in this section will be limited to discussing private transactions with institutional lenders.

Subordinated borrowings have historically been an important part in the financing of acquisitions. Lenders such as Massachusetts Mutual and Allstate, have traditionally played active roles in the provision of junior debt to growing, acquisition minded companies. Venture capital firms; SBIC's, firms such as a Mass Capital Resources Corporation (formed by Massachusetts insurance companies) are experienced and sophisticated lenders. Quite frequently, they are willing to accept projections of cash flow as the basis to commence discussions while being fully aware of the risks inherent in such acceptance. Frequently, subordinated debt will not require amortization for three to five years, thus reducing the demands on cash flow, and permitting substantial paydown of senior debt prior to the commencement of the amortization of the subordinated debt. Subordinated lenders are reasonably lenient with regard to debt ratios … it is not uncommon to be able to borrow 75 percent to 125 percent of shareholders' equity on a subordinated basis. Obviously, each dollar of subordinated debt will also support $0.50 to $1.00 of additional senior debt. Consequently, the leverage inherent in these arrangements is excellent. The major inhibiting factor when one considers borrowing on a subordinated basis is that there is a price attached. Not only is the interest rate 100 to 250 basis points higher than the equivalent senior debt, but in almost all cases the lender will want an equity "kicker." Whether this is in the form of cheap stock, warrants, convertibility, contingent interest or some more esoteric concept, the fact remains that the subordinated lender will want to be paid for this increased risk. The buyer must make the calculation as to whether the increased dilution of the shareholders' equity will be adequately covered by the increase in earnings, after deducting all expenses attributable to the acquisition. Subordinated lenders often act in a dual role; as lenders, they are concerned with the safety of their loans; as potential equity holders, they are interested in the growth in value of their stake in the company. In particular, venture firms often seek representation on the Board of Directors, and their impact on overall corporate strategy and direction must be taken into account when considering the issue of subordinated debt.

In a similar fashion there are institutional investors who buy equity issues, either common or preferred. Generally these are "packaged" together with a debt instrument, and the entire package is calculated to produce a satisfactory yield on the overall investment. The comments made previously with regard to equity dilution and control aspects in relationship to the issue of subordinated debt apply equally well with regard to the issue of equity securities.

The hardest question to answer when discussing raising subordinated debt and/or equity securities is "What is a fair price for the equity portion?" Readers will be disappointed to learn that there is no rule, or even a guideline, as to what constitutes reasonable compensation for the risk of capital.

All one can say is that it is this area which calls for the utmost nicety of judgment. The services of a skilled professional are often required to guide the borrower in his negotiations with the lenders. Each deal is unique and represents a particular opportunity. The elements of risk and reward must be compared to those prevailing in the market place at that time, and the deal priced accordingly.

Discussed below is an acquisition which utilized almost all of the techniques outlined above, in an imaginative and creative fashion. The successful accomplishment of this transaction enabled the acquiring company to double its size from $50 million to $100 million in annual sales.

The acquisition involved the purchase of a division of a major industrial corporation. The division had been marginally profitable, but in the last several years earnings had declined to break-even. Consequently,

the buyer could only look to his own historical cash flow of approximately $2.0 million to service the additional debt, even though he anticipated making substantial operating savings and returning the acquired division to profitable operations. The acquisition price was a net of $13 million, equal to almost 65 percent of the acquiring company's assets. Shown in Table 21-1 are summary balance sheets prior to the acquisition.

TABLE 21-1
Balance Sheets
As of January 1, 1978
(000 omitted)

	ABC Corporation	To Be Acquired
Current Assets		
Cash	$ 500	
Accounts Receivable, Net	6,750	5,000
Inventories	6,200	7,500
Other	450	1,000
	$13,900	$13,500
Fixed Assets, Net	4,250	1,500
Other Assets	1,600	
Intangibles	1,000	
Total	$20,750	$15,000
Liabilities & Net Worth		
Notes Payable	1,200	
Other Payables	4,500	2,000
	$5,700	
Long-Term Debt	5,400	13,000*
Sub. Converted Debt	3,000	
Net Worth	6,650	
Total	$20,750	$15,000

*Net Price

As one can see, the ABC Corporation had already incurred a fairly significant amount of long-term debt and net tangible assets divided by senior long-term debt was 265 percent. Total asset/debt coverage (including subordinated debt) was a relatively thin 168 percent. The existing senior lenders were reluctant to permit ABC to add significant amounts of new debt either senior or junior. In addition, the available cash flow of $2 million was too thin to allow any significant amortization of new debt. What borrowing strategy should ABC Corporation employ?

The plan which was divised consisted of the following elements:

1. A revolving credit line of $9.0 million, secured only by the acquired accounts receivable and inventory. This line was provided by a group of finance

companies and banks. Under the formula which allowed borrowings equal to 80 percent of receivables and 40 percent of inventory, ABC Corporation could borrow $7.0 million in the acquired division (organized as a wholly owned subsidiary).

2. Sale to an institutional investor of $1.5 million of new senior preferred stock, with an annual dividend of 8 percent and with warrants to buy about 5 percent of the ABC Corporation common stock.

3. The seller purchased $3.5 million of new junior preferred stock, with a $6.00 dividend and a repayment schedule calling for redemption of the preferred over a five-year period.

4. $1.0 million of ABC cash which came from ABC short-term borrowings, subsequently repaid from liquidating ABC current assets.

The strategy accomplished its objectives very well. The receivables/inventory loan permitted loan levels to fluctuate in accordance with sales, and at the same time, did not burden ABC with a fixed schedule of repayments. ABC was subsequently able to tighten receivable terms and reduce inventory levels, thus reducing loan levels and cutting interest costs.

The sale of the preferred to the institution not only raised funds, but improved the overall ABC asset coverage by increasing ABC net worth.

The seller was induced to take back some preferred stock by a redemption schedule which assured him of a cashout within a reasonable period of time, and a modest yield while waiting. Because none of ABC Corporation's own assets were pledged to support the new borrowings, the ABC lenders were not disturbed by the secured financings and were appreciative of the increase in net worth.

The above example is only one of many which typify how an imaginative and flexible response can secure for an alert borrower the ability to acquire properties, which a routine approach would never permit.

PAUL D. ARDLEIGH

PAUL D. ARDLEIGH is a Vice President in the Corporate Financial Services Department of Bankers Trust Company. Mr. Ardleigh began his career as a professional Naval Officer in the Submarine Service. He subsequently joined Bankers Trust and was head of the bank's financial consulting division from 1973 to 1978, where he directed Bankers Trust's mergers and acquisitions, private placement and general corporate finance activities. For the past several years he has concentrated on counseling corporations on Employee Stock Ownership Plans, government financing programs and specialized financial structures. He has also spoken and written widely on strategic planning, mergers and acquisitions, and ESOPs. Mr. Ardleigh earned degrees at the U.S. Naval Academy and Harvard University Graduate School of Business, where he graduated With Distinction.

22

Use of Employee Stock Ownership Plans in Acquisitions, Divestitures and Buyouts

PAUL D. ARDLEIGH

One of the newest, and most widely misunderstood, acronyms in use today is—ESOP. The ESOP or Employee Stock Ownership Plan has been credited by some to be magical—the eighth wonder of the world; capable of leaping tall buildings in a single bound; able to solve a myriad of corporate problems. Others deride the ESOP pointing to its inherent risks and claiming that the ESOP does not achieve the objectives set for it. These extreme points of view tend to promote and perpetuate the misunderstanding surrounding ESOPs and inhibit the use of ESOPs in many legitimate and useful circumstances.

Since the attributes of an ESOP are so often misconstrued, this chapter has a dual purpose. First it will seek to lift the mysterious veil from ESOPs by defining the ESOP, tracing its historical origins, identifying its most important characteristics, and comparing its financing capabilities to those of other techniques of corporate finance. After the reader is familiar with the basic fundamentals of an ESOP, the chapter will endeavor to illustrate the ESOP's unique capacity to function as an instrument of corporate finance in the acquisition, divestiture and buyout area. To accomplish this objective it will present two case histories so the reader can study the structure and dynamics of an ESOP in a lifelike environment. These cases are fictional but have been studiously fashioned from the events of a number of ESOP transactions in which I was involved.

The scope of this chapter is primarily economic and financial. It is not my intention to cover all circumstances where ESOPs may be applied. Nor do I intend to deal with associated topics such as employee motivation and productivity or the legal issues associated with employee benefit plans and the securities laws. The reader should refer to more detailed texts or seek professional advice for assistance in these areas.

DEFINITION OF ESOP

Much of the confusion surrounding ESOPs can be attributed to conflicting and constantly changing definitions of an ESOP. Prior to the Revenue Act of 1978 and ESOP was defined in Section 407(d)(6) of the Employee Retirement Income Security Act of 1974 ("ERISA") and Section 4975(e)(7) of the Internal Revenue Code ("IRC" or "the Code") as a stock bonus or stock bonus and money purchase plan, qualified under IRC Section 401, that was designed to invest primarily in qualifying employer securities. The Revenue Act revised the definition of ESOP in the Code to limit its applicability to "leveraged" ESOPs, or plans that are using or have used borrowings to purchase employer securities. In addition, the Revenue Act added Section 409A to the Code which, among other things, includes what were commonly known as Tax Reduction ESOPs in the general definition of ESOPs. The definition of ESOP in ERISA remained unchanged.

The impact of the Revenue Act is that the various ESOP terms now have a new and different meaning under the law. However, for the sake of clarity, this chapter will continue to designate Tax Reduction ESOPs as TRASOPs. The term ESOP will refer to a "leveraged ESOP" which is a qualified stock bonus or a stock bonus and money purchase plan which is designed to invest primarily in the stock of the employer, but which is not eligible for an additional investment

337

tax credit. Non-leveraged ESOPs will be designated as such. Additionally the term Employee Stock Ownership Trust ("ESOT") may be interchangably used with ESOP. The reader should be aware that ESOP relates to the overall plan while ESOT refers specifically to the trust created under such a plan in which the employer's securities are held.

HISTORICAL BACKGROUND OF ESOP

ERISA marks the dawn of the modern ESOP age. Prior to ESISA's enactment in 1974 very few ESOPs as we know them today were in existence. Since that time there has been a steadily growing interest in ESOPs. One recent estimate suggests that between 1,000 and 3,000 firms have installed ESOPs since 1974. This strong surge of ESOP formation has been paralleled by the rapid rise in Congressional recognition of ESOPs as a viable capital formation device. With legislative support the ESOP has grown from a relatively obscure economic theory to a nationally recognized technique of corporate financing. A brief history of the evolution of the ESOP will help in placing it in proper perspective today.

The stock bonus plan, from which the ESOP takes its basic form, has been in existence for almost 60 years. The Revenue Act of 1921 established the legality of exempting from income taxes corporate contributions made to qualified stock bonus plans. In 1953, the Internal Revenue Service issued Revenue Ruling 46 which recognized the ability of qualified plans to borrow for the purpose of investing in employer securities. Thus the two most significant elements of the ESOP, the ability to deduct contributions and the ability to borrow, had regulatory authority almost 30 years ago.

Peninsula Newspapers, Inc. is generally credited with establishing the first modern ESOP in 1956. The company was able to maintain its independent character by becoming predominantly employee-owned. The architect of this transaction was San Francisco attorney, Louis O. Kelso. Kelso had developed an economic philosophy known as the "two-factor theory." Simplistically, the theory postulates that the real wealth of the nation is produced by capital, not by labor. Kelso argued that broadening the ownership of U.S. industry should be an objective of public policy. He concluded that should ownership of newly developed capital be widely spread among worker-owners, the benefits would be rapid economic growth accompanied by full employment, modest inflation, and a hard currency. Even those suffering from acute political naivete cannot fail to appreciate the attractiveness of "two-factor theory" claims to politicians and economists alike. Nonetheless, another 15 years was to pass before Kelso's theories, and the ESOP, were to gain any acceptance from classical economists or appeal to the Congress.

By the early 1970's Kelso found a powerful ally in Senator Russell B. Long, Chairman of the Senate Finance Committee. Senator Long has been an important influence in developing legislation that has brought the ESOP to its current form. In the Regional Rail Organization Act of 1973 Congress first gave recognition to the ESOP as a technique of corporate finance and a solution to the public policy questions of capital formation and full employment. The Foreign Trade Act of 1974 provided that companies establishing ESOPs would receive preference in certain loan programs established to assist firms hurt by foreign competition. ERISA was landmark legislation for the ESOP. In addition to formally defining the ESOP, ERISA established specific guidelines that differentiated ESOPs from other stock bonus plans. Some of the more significant features of ERISA were that it established statutory approval for borrowing by an ESOP trust, exempted ESOPs from the requirement to invest in a diversified portfolio, excluded ESOPs from new rules regarding minimum funding, and clarified the ESOP's exemption from certain prohibited transaction rules.

The Tax Reduction Act of 1975 created the TRASOP or tax reduction ESOP and also created a great deal of confusion between the TRASOP and the ESOP. The Tax Reform Act of 1976 attempted to resolve many of these ambiguities but for the greater part failed to achieve its purpose. It generated the feeling that ESOP regulations were too restrictive and that the regulations would inhibit the use of ESOPs contrary to the intent of Congress. As previously stated, passage of the Revenue Act of 1978 alleviated this situation and "final" regulations were issued in late 1978 bringing ESOP legislation up to the current "state of the art" with the exception of some relatively minor technical corrections. The Congress continues to support ESOP formation. ESOP appears to have an assured future as an instrument of public policy and as a financing vehicle.

CHARACTERISTICS AND REQUIREMENTS OF ESOPS

The basic requirement of an ESOP is that its provisions must satisfy Section 401(a) of the Code. As a qualified plan, the ESOP acts as a tax sheltering and a cash generating device that enhances its value as an instrument of corporate finance. Under ERISA the ESOP has been granted statutory authority to borrow.

Thus, the fundamental characteristics of the ESOP are its ability to generate cash and provide leverage. In order to obtain qualification the ESOP must meet numerous requirements set forth in ERISA, the Code, and in other Treasury regulations. These requirements are lengthy and subject to legislative and regulatory change. Nonetheless, a brief review of some of the more notable characteristics and requirements of an ESOP will help the reader to judge whether the ESOP is compatible with a transaction he may be contemplating.

Exclusive Benefit Rule

ERISA requires that a fiduciary exercise his duties in such a manner that benefits will accrue exclusively to the participants or beneficiaries of a plan. IRC 401(a)(1) modifies this requirement to the extent that benefits may accrue to other parties (i.e., the employer) as long as the benefit to the participants is not diminished. For example, if an ESOP buys stock on the open market the concept of exclusive benefit would not be violated, even if the sellers realize a substantial profit, because the purchase price would be fair and equitable to the ESOP.

Non-Discrimination

The ESOP must be for the benefit of all employees and discrimination by class of employee is not permitted. However, under IRC 410(b)(1) an ESOP may exclude union employees who are covered by their own plan or with whom employee benefits have been subject to collective bargaining. Furthermore, ESOPs may not be integrated with Social Security. These provisions are designed to prevent plans with a bias towards higher paid employees and/or management.

Vesting and Allocation

Vesting and allocation to participants' accounts must be predetermined and be in accordance with the provisions of Sections 411 and 415 of the Code, respectively. In addition, ERISA limits the amount of annual allocations to any participant's account. This provision has the effect of prohibiting a controlling shareholder from benefiting inordinately from the tax exempt features of the plan.

Investment Criteria

An ESOP must invest primarily in qualifying employer securities. In public companies an ESOP may invest in any marketable debt or equity security. Where there is no readily tradable common stock, an ESOP may invest only in stock having voting and dividend rights not less favorable than those of the sponsoring company's common stock, or in preferred stock that is convertible at a reasonable ratio into an equivalent common stock.

Diversification

There is no requirement that an ESOP must diversify. By qualifying as an eligible individual account plan an ESOP need not meet the requirement that limits investment to 10 percent or less of its assets in employer securities. ERISA Section 404(a)(1)(B) exempts ESOPs from the ''prudent man rule'' so far as the requirements to diversify and to receive a fair rate of return are concerned.

Adequate Consideration

Purchases of employer securities by the ESOP must be for adequate consideration. Adequate consideration is generally accepted to be ''fair market'' value which must be determined by independent valuation at least on an annual basis. Revenue Ruling 59-60 establishes the basic criteria for determining adequate consideration.

Contribution Limitations

Contributions to the ESOP must be made exclusively by the employer. They may be made in either cash or stock. The amount of the contribution is at the discretion of the employer's Board of Directors. However, the maximum contribution that the employer may deduct in any taxable year is established in the Code as 15 percent of covered compensation of the participants. Provisions have been made for carry-forward or carry-back. If the ESOP is combined with a money purchase plan, where the contribution is not variable, the total contribution may be as great as 25 percent.

Prohibited Transactions

An ESOP may engage in certain transactions prohibited by ERISA for other qualified plans. Two of the more important exemptions are the ability to purchase shares from a party-in-interest such as a controlling shareholder and the allowance of credit extension between disqualified persons. In general, an ESOP may borrow from the corporate sponsor or controlling shareholder, including purchase of shares on an installment basis, but other parties may not be indebted to the ESOP unless the indebtness is liquid and readily marketable.

Distribution of Shares

Distributions from an ESOP are made at the time of termination, retirement or death and are made in employer securities. The beneficiary or his estate has the right under IRC 4975(e)(7)(b) to exercise a ''put'' option to the sponsoring company over a reasonable period of time. The Code also provides that the company may have the "right of first refusal" on shares where the "put" is not exercised. This allows the company some latitude in limiting share distribution and, in the case of a private company, inadvertently "going public." It should be noted that distributed shares are subject to the securities laws and in many cases may be restricted securities.

Voting Rights

Publicly held companies must pass through to participants the right to vote their shares when the shares are allocated to the individual accounts. In the case of privately held companies voting rights may be exercised by a committee appointed by the sponsoring company's Board of Directors or may be passed through to participants. The Code currently provides that voting rights must be passed through to participants on issues that require a majority vote such as merger or consolidation.

CORPORATE FINANCING THROUGH ESOP

In order to better appreciate the applications of ESOP to the merger, acquisition, divestiture, and buyout discipline, an analysis of how ESOP compares to other techniques of corporate finance is necessary. The financial analysis of an ESOP may be performed from the point of view of numerous constituencies. Included among these constituencies are: the company, the employees, management, control shareholders, minority shareholders, public shareholders, the government, and the tax paying public. The attractiveness of ESOP in general or of any specific plan can vary widely among the constituencies. Because this is a financial rather than socio-economic analysis, we will approach our discussion of the ESOP as a financing vehicle on an aggregate or company basis and on an individual per share basis.

The Base Case

The following develops a case study of a corporate financing for a sample company. For the greater part, most other financial uses for an ESOP are modifications of the basic transaction. In constructing the case I have made a number of underlying assumptions about our sample company, which we shall call EXAMCO. Some of these assumptions are admittedly constructed to produce results that more clearly reflect the difference between ESOP and alternative methods of financing.

First let's assume that EXAMCO is a privately held manufacturing company. The company is capitalized with $20 million in common equity and has no long-term debt. Historically, EXAMCO has generated operating income at a rate equal to a 20 percent return on invested capital. In normal times capital expenditures have equalled depreciation. Its tax rate, including all federal, state and local taxes, is 50 percent. Although it provides normal retirement benefits to its employees, it does not have a profit sharing plan. The company has followed a policy of retaining earnings and does not pay dividends.

EXAMCO is faced with a perplexing problem. Its plant and facilities are becoming obsolete and therefore less competitive. A capital expenditure of $5 million will modernize its facilities and enable EXAMCO to continue to earn its historic return on capital. Debt financing is available from EXAMCO's bank. The bank has agreed to provide funds at an interest rate of 10 percent per annum with principal to be repaid in equal installments over a five year period. If equity is sold it will be priced at prevailing book value. Issuance costs are negligible. Table 22-1 summarizes our assumptions for EXAMCO.

Table 22-1
EXAMCO ASSUMPTIONS

Type Company:	Manufacturing; Privately Owned
Capitalization:	$20 million Common Equity; No Term Debt
Return on Invested Capital:	20 percent
Capital Expenditures:	Equal to Depreciation
Tax Rate:	50 percent
Required Financing:	$5 million
Interest Rate:	10 percent
Repayment Schedule:	5 years; equal installments
Equity Sales:	Prevailing Book Value
Dividends:	None

To further paint the scenario, covered payroll for the next five years is estimated to increase at a rate of 6 percent per year from a base of $11 million to $13.9 million. ESOP contributions may be made up to a maximum of 15 percent of covered payroll. (Table 22-2).

Table 22-2
COVERED PAYROLL & ESOP CONTRIBUTIONS
($000)

Year	ESOP Covered Payroll	Maximum ESOP Contribution (15%)
1	11,000	1,650
2	11,600	1,749
3	12,360	1,854
4	13,100	1,965
5	13,890	2,083

Since management is determined to finance the proposed capital expansion, the analysis will center around the various methods that might be employed. ESOP financing will be an alternative.

Conventional Debt and Equity Financing

The first alternative form of raising the required $5 million is a conventional debt financing (Figure 22-1). Typically this alternative would involve issuance of a note to the lender in return for a $5 million loan. The company would then invest the proceeds of the loan in earning assets. The loan would be serviced by the

Looking at the Conventional Debt Financing Schedule illustrated by Table 22-3, the reader will note that operating income is generated at 20 percent of the prior year's invested capital. Interest expense is reduced as principal payments are made. Annual additions to capital equal net income less principal payments on the outstanding debt. Over the five year financing period $11,502,000 of new capital is generated. No shares are issued so the original owners suffer no ownership dilution (page 342).

Table 22-4 indicates the financial results that could be expected if the company floats a common stock issue. Operating income grows more rapidly with an

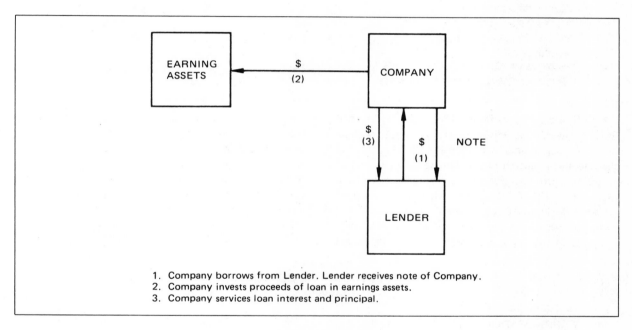

1. Company borrows from Lender. Lender receives note of Company.
2. Company invests proceeds of loan in earnings assets.
3. Company services loan interest and principal.

Figure 22-1
Conventional Debt Financing

return on invested assets and other general revenues as necessary. Interest, of course, is a tax deductible expense while principal would be repaid out of after tax cash flow.

As an alternative the company could have chosen to raise the required capital by an equity offering. This assumes that our relatively small company would in fact find the equity markets receptive to a common stock issue, a rather hazardous assumption at best considering the market for new issues in recent years. In the event that equity were issued the lender would be replaced by minority shareholders who would receive shares of common stock in lieu of notes.

equity offering than under the debt scenario because interest expense is eliminated and total capital increases faster. Since the new shares are issued at a book value of $10.00 (a reasonably conservative 10 times the previous year's net income per share) no per share dilution is immediately evident, but the original owners' position is reduced to 80 percent of the common equity (page 342).

Leveraged ESOP Financing

The leveraged ESOP is the next financing alternative. Tracing through the steps of this transaction, which is illustrated by Figure 22-2 we see that EX-

Table 22-3
CONVENTIONAL DEBT FINANCING SCHEDULE
($000)

End of Year	0	1	2	3	4	5	6
CAPITALIZATION DATA							
Long-Term Debt	5,000	4,000	3,000	2,000	1,000	0	0
Shareholders Equity	20,000	22,250	24,675	27,293	30,122	33,184	36,502
Total Capital	25,000	26,250	27,675	29,293	31,122	33,184	36,502
INCOME STATEMENT							
Operating Income		5,000	5,250	5,536	5,858	6,224	6,636
Interest Expense		(500)	(400)	(300)	(200)	(100)	0
Income Taxes		(2,250)	(2,425)	(2,618)	(2,829)	(3,062)	(3,318)
Net Income		2,250	2,425	2,618	2,829	3,062	3,318
CAPITAL ADDITIONS							
Net Income		2,250	2,425	2,618	2,829	3,062	3,318
Debt Service		(1,000)	(1,000)	(1,000)	(1,000)	(1,000)	0
Annual Increase		1,250	1,425	1,618	1,829	2,062	3,318
Cumulative Increase		1,250	2,675	4,293	6,122	8,184	11,502
PER SHARE DATA							
Shares Outstanding (000)	2,000	2,000	2,000	2,000	2,000	2,000	2,000
Earnings ($)	—	1.13	1.21	1.31	1.41	1.53	1.66
Book Value ($)	10.00	11.13	12.34	13.65	15.06	16.59	18.25
ORIGINAL OWNERSHIP RETAINED		100%	100%	100%	100%	100%	100%

AMCO first establishes its ESOP and the ESOP trust (ESOT). The company then opens negotiations with its bank to enter into an ESOP loan. EXAMCO agrees to make annual contributions to the ESOP sufficient to service both principal and interest on the loan. As in the case of most ESOP loans, EXAMCO also agrees to guarantee the loan. After the loan is executed the ESOP purchases stock from the company with its proceeds. The price of the stock is established by independent valuation and is at fair market value. To further secure the loan the ESOP pledges the stock purchased. EX-AMCO now invests the loan proceeds in earning assets. Finally, over the life of the loan the company makes an annual tax exempt cash contribution to the ESOP sufficient to meet the ESOP's full debt service, which the ESOP passes to the lender to satisfy its obligations (page 343).

The financial aspects of the ESOP transaction are

Table 22-4
EQUITY FINANCING SCHEDULE
($000)

End of Year	0	1	2	3	4	5	6
CAPITALIZATION DATA							
Long-Term Debt	—	—	—	—	—	—	—
Shareholders Equity	25,000	27,500	30,250	33,275	36,603	40,263	44,289
Total Capital	25,000	27,500	30,250	33,275	36,603	40,263	44,289
INCOME STATEMENT							
Operating Income		5,000	5,500	6,050	6,656	7,320	8,052
Interest Expense		—	—	—	—	—	—
Income Taxes		(2,500)	(2,750)	(3,025)	(3,328)	(3,660)	(4,026)
Net Income		2,500	2,750	3,025	3,328	3,660	4,026
CAPITAL ADDITIONS							
Net Income		2,500	2,750	3,025	3,328	3,660	4,026
Debt Service		—	—	—	—	—	—
Annual Increase		2,500	2,750	3,025	3,328	3,660	4,026
Cumulative Increase		2,500	5,250	8,275	11,603	15,263	19,289
PER SHARE DATA							
Shares Outstanding (000)	2,500	2,500	2,500	2,500	2,500	2,500	2,500
Earnings ($)	—	1.00	1.10	1.21	1.33	1.46	1.61
Book Value ($)	10.00	11.00	12.10	13.31	14.64	16.11	17.72
ORIGINAL OWNERSHIP RETAINED		80%	80%	80%	80%	80%	80%

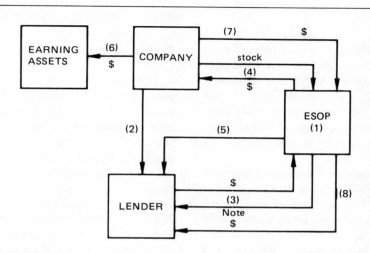

1. Company establishes ESOP.
2. Company agrees to make contributions sufficient to service the ESOPs debt and to guarantee the ESOP loan.
3. ESOP borrows from Lender. Lender receives note of ESOP.
4. Company sells new stock to ESOP for cash.
5. ESOP pledges stock to secure note.
6. Company invests proceeds of stock sale on earnings assets.
7. Company makes annual tax exempt contribution (in cash) to ESOP sufficient to service interest and principal of loan.
8. ESOP services debt.

Figure 22-2
Leveraged ESOP Financing

Table 22-5
LEVERAGED ESOP FINANCING
($000)

End of Year	0	1	2	3	4	5	6
CAPITALIZATION DATA							
Long-Term Debt	5,000	4,000	3,000	2,000	1,000	—	—
Shareholders Equity	25,000	26,750	28,725	30,948	33,433	36,237	39,961
ESOP Obligation	(5,000)	(4,000)	(3,000)	(2,000)	(1,000)	—	—
Net Equity	20,000	22,750	25,725	28,948	32,433	36,237	39,861
Total Capital	25,000	26,750	28,725	30,948	33,433	36,237	39,861
INCOME STATEMENT							
Operating Income		5,000	5,350	5,746	6,190	6,688	7,248
ESOP Contribution		1,500	1,400	1,300	1,200	1,100	—
Income Taxes		1,750	1,975	2,223	2,495	2,794	3,624
Net Income		1,750	1,975	2,223	2,495	2,794	3,624
CAPITAL ADDITIONS							
Net Income		1,750	1,975	2,223	2,495	2,794	3,624
Debt Service		—	—	—	—	—	—
Annual Increase		1,750	1,975	2,223	2,495	2,794	3,624
Cumulative Increase		1,750	3,725	5,948	8,443	11,237	14,861
PER SHARE DATA							
Fully Outstanding Method							
Shares Outstanding (000)	2,500	2,500	2,500	2,500	2,500	2,500	2,500
Earnings ($)	—	.70	.79	.89	1.00	1.12	1.45
Treasury Method							
Shares Outstanding (000)	2,000	2,100	2,200	2,300	2,400	2,500	2,500
Earnings ($)	—	.83	.90	.97	1.04	1.12	1.45
Book Value	10.00	10.83	11.69	12.59	13.51	14.49	15.94
ORIGINAL OWNERSHIP RETAINED		95%	91%	87%	83%	80%	80%

343

shown in Table 22-5. The income statement indicates that the ESOP contribution, equal to interest and principal on the ESOP loan and within the parameters established by Table 22-2, reduces net income below the levels exhibited in more conventional financings. As compared to the debt financing, cash flow is increased by the savings of the principal payment tax shelter (page 343).

Table 22-5 also illustrates the accounting treatment utilized for leveraged ESOPs. Since the Company has guaranteed the ESOP loan and agreed to fund the ESOP's obligations, the company is required to record the outstanding principal of the ESOP obligation as a deferred liability. The contra balance sheet entry is a reduction of shareholders' equity. As the ESOP loan is repaid the deferred liability is correspondingly reduced and equity shares are proportionately allocated. Earnings per share may be calculated in either of two ways: the fully outstanding method or the treasury method. The fully outstanding method utilizes the total number of shares issued to the ESOP in calculating earnings per share (EPS), while the treasury method permits a reduction of shares outstanding by an amount that could be purchased with the proceeds of the ESOP loan not yet allocated.

Non-Leveraged ESOP Financing

The primary advantage of leveraged ESOP financing over debt financing is the increased cash flow produced by tax sheltering the debt service. The principal disadvantage is dilution caused by share issuance. The leveraged ESOP requires contributions equal to principal and interest whereas the company only gains a tax advantage in the sheltering of principal payments. Since interest payments are tax deductible in any case, tax sheltering interest payments through an ESOP is redundant and yields no financial advantage. Furthermore, it increases the implicit cost of financing by requiring issuance of a greater number of shares.

In many cases where leverage in the trust is not essential a variation of the ESOP theme can provide an effective alternative financing method. As illustrated in Figure 22-3, the company borrows directly from the lender, makes the appropriate investment in earning assets, and services the debt in a conventional manner. However, it also establishes a non-leveraged ESOP (or another type of eligible individual account stock bonus plan). As principal of the ESOP loan is repaid, the company makes stock contributions of a like value, thus fully tax sheltering the principal payments.

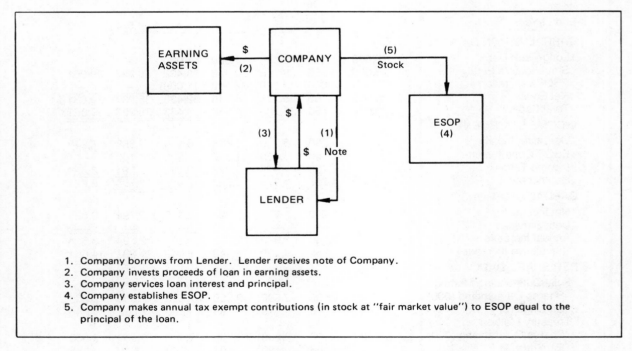

1. Company borrows from Lender. Lender receives note of Company.
2. Company invests proceeds of loan in earning assets.
3. Company services loan interest and principal.
4. Company establishes ESOP.
5. Company makes annual tax exempt contributions (in stock at "fair market value") to ESOP equal to the principal of the loan.

Figure 22-3
Non-Leveraged ESOP Financing

Comparing the results of this plan, shown in Table 22-6, to a leveraged ESOP we see that net income, cash flow and capital generation are identical. The principal difference is that equity is contributed at a fair market value annually rather than in a single transaction at the outset. In our example this proves favorable for the company and its shareholders since share value is increasing. Fewer shares are issued for the same tax sheltering effects. Less dilution results. However, we should quickly realize that the apparent advantages of this alternative, relative to the leveraged ESOP, would be reversed should EXAMCO falter and its shares diminish in value.

Advantages and Disadvantages of ESOP financing

The EXAMCO case has shown us the fundamental workings of an ESOP. As the data in Table 22-7 illustrates, the ESOP as a pure corporate financing vehicle lives up to its reputation as a cash flow and capital generator when compared to debt financing. However, the effects of dilution on earnings per share and ownership are significant and severely limit the practical applications of an ESOP as a capital raising technique.

For the greater part, ESOP makes the most sense to a closely held private company such as EXAMCO. In a

Table 22-6
DEBT FINANCING WITH NON-LEVERAGED ESOP
($000)

End of Year	0	1	2	3	4	5	6
CAPITALIZATION DATA							
Long-Term Debt	5,000	4,000	3,000	2,000	1,000	—	—
Shareholders Equity	20,000	22,750	25,725	28,948	32,433	36,237	39,861
Total Capital	25,000	26,750	28,725	30,948	33,433	36,237	39,861
INCOME STATEMENT							
Operating Income		5,000	5,350	5,746	6,190	6,688	7,248
ESOP Contribution		(1,000)	(1,000)	(1,000)	(1,000)	(1,000)	—
Interest Expense		(500)	(400)	(300)	(200)	(100)	—
Income Taxes		(1,750)	(1,975)	(2,223)	(2,495)	(2,794)	(3,624)
Net Income		1,750	1,975	2,223	2,495	2,794	3,624
CAPITAL ADDITIONS							
Net Income		1,750	1,975	2,223	2,495	2,794	3,624
Debt Service		—	—	—	—	—	—
Annual Increase		1,750	1,975	2,223	2,495	2,794	3,624
Cumulative Increase		1,750	3,725	5,948	8,443	11,237	14,861
PER SHARE DATA							
Shares Outstanding (000)	2,000	2,092	2,176	2,254	2,326	2,392	2,392
Earnings ($)	—	.84	.91	.99	1.07	1.17	1.52
Book Value ($)	10.00	10.88	11.82	12.84	13.95	15.15	16.66
ORIGINAL OWNERSHIP RETAINED		96%	92%	89%	86%	84%	84%

Table 22-7
COMPARISON OF ALTERNATIVES
($000)
End of Sixth Year

COMPANY VIEWPOINT	CONVENTIONAL DEBT	EQUITY	LEVERAGED ESOP	NON-LEVERAGED ESOP
Total Capital	$36,502	$44,289	$39,861	$39,861
Operating Income	6,636	8,052	7,248	7,248
Net Income	3,318	4,026	3,624	3,624
Cumulative Cash Generated	11,502	19,289	14,861	14,861
SHAREHOLDERS' VIEWPOINT				
Earnings Per Share	$ 1.66	$ 1.61	$ 1.45	$ 1.52
Book Value Per Share	$ 18.25	$ 17.72	$ 15.94	$ 16.66
% Ownership Retained	100%	80%	80%	84%

public company, where per share data is rightly a matter of serious concern for management, the reduction of earnings per share argues against the ESOP's use as a pure financial instrument. However, many private concerns consider minimization of taxes and maximization of cash flow to be significantly more important than EPS. Equity offerings are usually not a viable alternative because they can result in "going public" or potentially troublesome minority interests. Since management can control the minority block of stock in an ESOP in most instances, private owners may find circumstances where the increased cash flow is attractive enough to offset the dilution in their ownership.

ESOP financing can also be most useful to the highly leveraged company. Debt capacity is not infinite. Companies must maintain a proper capital structure. For rapidly growing companies, internal generation of capital is often insufficient to build a base for leveraging. The ESOP provides private companies with a vehicle for equity financing. The total effect of ESOP debt financing, supporting rapid growth in sales and earnings, may increase shareholder wealth more rapidly than if growth is slowed by financing limitations.

ESOP financing can also be cumbersome and expensive to administer, particularly when compared to debt. The plan must be formalized, trustees employed, accounts administered, and valuations performed. Unless the financing is substantial, the costs and management attention required may render ESOP financing infeasible.

In summation, the ESOP is not a financing panacea. It is a hybrid of equity and debt financing techniques. Whenever new shares are issued the positive attributes of improved cash and capital generation must be weighed against the negative features of earnings per share and ownership dilution. Careful and detailed analysis of all relevant factors is a prerequisite to implementing an ESOP for corporate financing purposes. Nonetheless, the ESOP does have a number of very valuable financial uses. We shall look at several of these unique applications in the case studies that follow.

ESOP AS AN ALTERNATIVE TO MERGER

Irving M. Swinger was the Chairman, President and 100 percent owner of Red Hot Stove Works ("Red Hot"). Red Hot was a small but rapidly growing manufacturer of home appliances with sales approaching $10 million. As a young man Irving had perfected several inventions that led to the development of a new improved cooking range which he had called the Red Hot Range. Quick market acceptance of his new range induced Irving to start Red Hot as a business and the business prospered as Irving added new appliances to the line. Belying his name, Irving was dedicated to Red Hot and as he approached the age of 50 found that his dedication was rewarded by the fact that he was a wealthy man. Nonetheless, Irving and his attorney, Sam Goodman, were very concerned. Because of Irving's single minded dedication to making Red Hot prosper, virtually his entire estate was represented by the value of Red Hot. Irving's children were grown and like many in their generation disdained continuing on in the family business. On the other hand Irving had developed a sound group of young managers capable of running the business in the future. Sam Goodman said to Irving, "Irving this is crazy. You're low on cash. If you die the estate can't pay the taxes. Red Hot will go in a fire sale. Your kids don't want it anyway. Sell!"

In fact, Irving had previously discussed the sale of Red Hot. Because Red Hot enjoyed the reputation of being a top-of-the line producer, a number of merger brokers and large companies had approached Irving with the thought of merger. Irving had rejected virtually all these approaches but had entered into serious negotiations with the National Appliance Co. ("National") because of National's reputation and the apparent "fit" of Red Hot into National's family of companies. Irving liked the National people but several things bothered him about the proposed transaction.

Irving had engaged my firm to appraise the true value of Red Hot. After having analyzed Red Hot fully, compared it to other similar companies, and used other tests of value outlined in Revenue Ruling 59-60, we informed Irving that in our opinion Red Hot should sell for about $50.00 per share. National was offering a maximum of $42.00 per share, a substantial discount from presumed value. National's offer contemplated a tax-free exchange of stock so Irving was not only bothered by the inadequacy of the offer but by the possibility that value received in exchange for Red Hot might further deteriorate in a volatile stock market. National told Irving that earnings dilution and other internal acquisition criteria precluded any improvement in their offer. National also said that if Irving did not accept the offer reasonably soon it would be withdrawn so National could pursue other acquisition candidates.

Irving was also concerned about the change in life

style a merger with National would bring. He had labored for 20 years at Red Hot and while, admittedly, he wanted to begin to enjoy the fruits of his labor more fully, he was uncertain that he was ready to cede ownership and direction of Red Hot to outsiders. Like many entrepreneurs Irving felt that Red Hot was more than an inanimate object; it was a living being of his creation. True, National had offered him a contract to manage Red Hot for the next three years, but what then? Irving had no taste for starting over at 50; neither did he aspire to counting coupons and watching the ticker. Furthermore, he was concerned for the welfare of the young managers he had trained. He rationalized that they might have broader opportunities in a larger company but again he was uncertain.

When push came to shove, Irving admitted that he really didn't want to sell Red Hot but felt compelled to do so. He was concerned that an offer like National's might not come along again until it was too late. He asked us if there was a viable alternative to sale. We advised Irving that he could consider sale of a minority block of stock. We cautioned him, however, that the likelihood of this method succeeding was small since insiders in the company didn't appear to have the money and independent parties were unlikely to take a minority position in a private company. We suggested that a buy-sell plan with his managment, to be funded

with the proceeds of life insurance, could be used to ease the estate problem, but would not resolve his desire for greater liquidity. We also told him that a stock redemption could provide liquidity but that the cash received would be taxed at ordinary income rates so he might as well just pay a larger dividend. Then we told him that given the circumstances, an Employee Stock Ownership Plan (ESOP) could be the answer to his problems. ''Tell me more!'', he said.

In order to develop the ESOP alternative we decided to first review the current position of Red Hot and forecast its performance for the next few years (Table 22-8). Red Hot's capital base had grown to $3,260,000 in common equity. It had no long-term debt. Operating earnings consistently equaled 11 percent of net sales which had been growing at a compounded rate of 20 percent for the last five years. For conservatism's sake we decided to project operating income in the future at a 15 percent compounded rate. Capital Expenditures generally equalled depreciation. All federal, state and local taxes cumulated to a 55 percent tax rate. Based on its performance and capital structure, Robert Moneypenny of Bingobancshares had agreed to lend up to $1,500,000 to the company, as required, at a rate of 10 percent. As a condition of borrowing, Irving agreed that he would suspend all dividend payments. (See Table 22-8 on page 348).

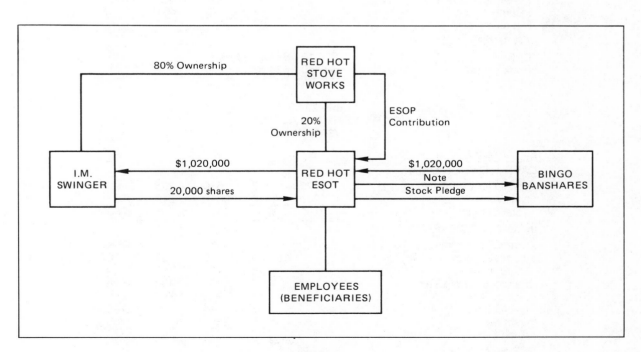

Figure 22-4
Red Hot ESOP Financing

Table 22-8
"RED HOT" ASSUMPTIONS

Type Company:	Manufacturer of Home Appliances
Operating Earnings:	Growing at 15 percent compounded
Capital Base:	$3.26 million equity; No term debt
Capital Expenditures:	Equal to depreciation
Tax Rate:	55 percent
Dividends:	None
Ownership:	100 percent owned by I.M. Swinger
Outstanding Shares:	100,000
Number Shares Sold:	20,000
Sales Price per Share:	$51.00 (10x an EPS of $5.10)
Interest Rate:	10 percent
Loan Repayment:	4 years; equal installments

Having completed our homework we then proceeded to describe to Irving how the ESOP would work. We drew a diagram, Figure 22-4 on page 347, to assist in our description. First Red Hot would establish an ESOP for the benefit of all its employees. Then Irving would sell to the ESOP trust 20,000 shares of Red Hot. To finance the purchase, Moneypenny would approve the loan of $1,020,000 to the ESOP. The loan would be evidenced by a note guaranteed by Red Hot and secured by the 20,000 shares held in trust. Red Hot agreed to make ESOP contributions of sufficient size to

Table 22-9
ESOP ALTERNATIVE
($000)

End of Year	0	1	2	3	4
CAPITALIZATION DATA					
Long-Term Debt	1020	765	510	255	—
Shareholder equity	3260	3647	4114	4655	5271
ESOP Obligation	(1020)	(765)	(510)	(255)	—
Net Worth	2240	2882	3604	4400	5271
Total Capital	3260	3647	4114	465	5271
INCOME STATEMENT					
Operating Income		1191	1338	1468	1604
ESOP Contribution		(357)	(331)	(301)	(276)
Other Income		25	30	35	40
Earnings Before Tax		859	1037	1202	1368
Income Taxes		(472)	(570)	(661)	(752)
Net Income		387	467	541	616
PER SHARE DATA					
EPS	$ 5.10	$ 3.87	$ 4.67	$ 5.41	$ 6.16
Book Value	$22.40	$28.82	$36.04	$44.00	$52.71

Table 22-10
STOCK REDEMPTION ALTERNATIVE
($000)

End of Year	0	1	2	3	4
CAPITALIZATION DATA					
Long-Term Debt	1020	765	510	255	—
Net Worth	2240	2486	2812	3210	3683
Total Capital	3260	3251	3322	3465	3683
INCOME STATEMENT					
Operating Income		1191	1338	1468	1604
Interest Expense		(102)	(76)	(51)	(26)
Other Income		25	30	35	40
Earnings Before Tax		1114	1292	1452	1618
Income Taxes		(613)	(711)	(799)	(890)
Net Income		501	581	653	728
Debt Service		(255)	(255)	(255)	(255)
Cash Flow		246	326	398	473
PER SHARE DATA					
Earnings	$ 6.38	$ 6.26	$ 7.26	$ 7.16	$ 9.10
Book Value	$28.00	$31.08	$35.15	$40.13	$46.04

fully service the ESOP loan which was to be repaid in equal annual installments over the next four years. As the loan was repaid, stock would be allocated to each employee's individual account so that at the end of four years the ESOP would own, free and clear, 20 percent of Red Hot for the beneficial interest of the employees. We pointed out that Irving would participate in the ESOP and as a beneficiary would ultimately give up less than the full 20 percent of Red Hot's equity sold. Red Hot's Board of Directors would appoint a committee to direct the ESOP trustee as to how to vote shares held by the ESOP. This power would be exercised in all cases except where a majority vote was required. Then the vote would be passed through to the employees in proportion to their beneficial ownership.

As financial advisors to Irving, we then proceeded to show Irving the financial impact that the ESOP alternative would have on Red Hot. We reasoned that Irving's major asset was still Red Hot and to paraphrase an old saying, ''What was good for Red Hot was good for Irving.'' Since a stock redemption was the only other alternative that would materially effect Red Hot short of a merger with National, we decided to compare the ESOP with redemption. The capitaliza-

tion data, abbreviated income and cash flow statements, and per share data for the ESOP and stock redemption alternatives that were generated are shown in Table 22-9 and Table 22-10, respectively.

We used Table 22-11 to summarize some of the key financial differences between the two alternatives. Net income of the ESOP was always less than an equivalent stock redemption by an amount equal to the after tax effect of principal payments. Conversely, cash flow and the incremental increase in net worth were greater by an amount equal to the tax savings. Earnings per share calculations were dramatically different because under the stock redemption alternative net income was higher and the number of shares outstanding were lower. Interestingly, other than in the first year there was no dilution in book value per share in the case of the ESOP. The reason for this was that although net worth was reduced equally by either alternative at the outset, accounting for ESOP permitted a gradual recapture of the ''lost'' net worth while redemption resulted in a permanent reduction. This factor coupled with the superior capital generative features of ESOP, resulted in substantially greater retention of capital under the ESOP alternative.

Table 22-11
COMPARISON OF ESOP TO STOCK REDEMPTION
($000)

End of Year	0	1	2	3	4
NET INCOME					
ESOP	510	387	467	541	616
Redemption	510	501	581	653	728
Difference	—	(114)	(114)	(112)	(112)
CASH FLOW					
ESOP	—	387	467	541	616
Redemption	—	246	326	398	473
Difference	—	141	141	143	143
Cumulative	—	141	282	425	568
NET WORTH					
ESOP	2240	2882	3604	4400	5271
Redemption	2240	2486	2812	3210	3683
Difference	—	396	792	1190	1588
EARNINGS PER SHARE					
ESOP	$ 5.10	$ 3.87	$ 4.67	$ 5.41	$ 6.16
Redemption	6.38	6.26	7.26	8.16	9.10
Difference	$(1.28)	$(2.39)	$(2.59)	$(2.75)	$(2.94)
BOOK VALUE PER SHARE					
ESOP	$22.40	$28.82	$36.04	$44.00	$52.71
Redemption	28.00	31.08	35.15	40.13	46.04
Difference	$(5.60)	$(2.26)	$ .89	$ 3.87	$ 6.67

The final phase of our work was to summarize for Irving what we felt were the most significant advantages and disadvantages of our ESOP proposal.

Irving would receive $8 per share more from the ESOP than under the proposed National merger. On 20,000 shares this meant a $160,000 advantage for the ESOP. Granted, an up front sale via the merger could prove superior under certain circumstances. However, Irving would have the opportunity to continue to sell shares to the ESOP in the future at a similar premium. Should Red Hot continue to prosper, Irving's profit would stand to be significantly greater by selling in installments.

The proceeds of a sale to the ESOP would be eligible for capital gains tax treatment while proceeds of a redemption would be taxed at ordinary income rates. Since Irving's beneficial interest in the ESOP would be less than 20 percent, no additional restrictions were going to be placed on the ESOP stock. Neither Irving nor Red Hot intended to redeem any stock purchased by the ESOP, so that Irving would be able to get an advanced ruling on this favorable tax treatment under the provisions of Revenue Procedure 77-30. With an ordinary income rate of 50 percent and a capital gains rate of approximately 35 percent, Irving would save $153,000 in income taxes, assuming a zero basis for his shares.

Irving would be able to achieve positive personal financial benefits without any effective loss of control of Red Hot. As a practical matter, only if he sold over 50 percent of his holdings and the employees voted as a block on a matter requiring a majority vote could his control be challenged.

Red Hot would generate almost $600,000 more cash using the ESOP alternative. This cash flow would in turn strengthen the credit-worthiness of Red Hot and increase the operating flexibility of the company.

Net worth would be $1.5 million greater than with a redemption. The larger capital base coupled with the increased cash flow would improve the leverage potential of Red Hot. This improved capital retention and leveraging capability could be used in numerous ways including investment for more rapid growth or purchase of larger amounts of Irving's stock.

The employees and management of Red Hot would have tangible evidence that ultimately the stewardship of the company would be theirs. Increased loyalty and productivity often are the by-products of such an arrangement. Even if Red Hot were ultimately sold to a third party, the employees would have been able to materially benefit from their stake in Red Hot.

The most obvious disadvantage of the ESOP was that Irving would suffer a dilution in ownership relative to a redemption. Since it was Irving's original intention to sell all or part of Red Hot, and since he would receive fair value for his shares without loss of control, it seemed that this factor would not be detrimental to Irving's interests.

Perhaps a more compelling argument against the use of ESOP emerged when it was compared to a direct sale to National. Irving would forego the opportunity for a tax-free exchange by choosing the ESOP alternative. This disadvantage would be mitigated by the fact that to gain liquidity Irving would have to sell National shares and pay taxes at that time. Therefore the merger's tax advantage was one of timing differential and in order to enjoy this timing advantage, Irving would have had to risk the possibility of National's stock price deteriorating. Additionally, Irving's flexibility in selling National shares most probably would have been restricted by the securities laws.

A side effect of the ESOP would be that in establishing a favorable value for share sales to the ESOP, precedent would be set in valuing the shares that Irving would continue to hold. Should Irving meet an untimely end, the value of his estate and the taxes due could be higher than if no ESOP had been formed. Conversely, the creation of an ESOP would provide a market for shares held by the estate. Taxes could be paid from the proceeds of additional share sales to the ESOP, negating the need to sell the entire company for tax purposes. Avoidance of a "fire sale" could be of significant advantage to the estate.

Irving carefully considered the alternatives and opted to go the ESOP route. He declined the National offer and established the ESOP on essentially the same basis that has been previously outlined. Nearly four years have passed. Red Hot has continued to prosper, growing more rapidly than we had projected. All parties concerned are extremely pleased with the results of the plan and it is Irving's intention to sell another 20 percent of his holdings to the ESOP.

ESOP SUBSIDIARY DIVESTITURES

Most large corporations have subsidiaries or plants which they wish to divest. The reasons are usually that product lines are incompatible with overall corporate policy, the parent cannot run them profitably, or they require too much attention for the small profit which is generated. There are many methods of accomplishing a divestiture after a decision has been reached to redeploy assets. The most widely used method is, of course, sale of the subsidiary to another corporation or third party with whom the subsidiary has operating or financial synergy. Unfortunately, many divestiture candidates are not attractive enough to develop interest in the market place at a return the seller can accept. In many cases the only viable method to free up corporate assets is through liquidation, and corporations look at liquidation as a last resort because of the adverse human effects that usually accompany a shut-down. The ESOP subsidiary divestiture offers an effective alternative to liquidation and often can be extremely competitive with a conventional sale.

PDQ Corporation ("PDQ") was a major manufacturing and natural resources company. Publicly listed on the New York Stock Exchange PDQ had recently reported sales of over $500 million and profits in excess of $50 million. The company was enjoying a period of rapid growth and investor popularity. PDQ's success was generally attributed to the leadership of its Chairman, Peter Quick. After assuming control five years earlier, Peter had adopted a corporate strategy of divesting some of PDQ's old line, staid manufacturing businesses and redeploying the assets into the natural resources area. His strategic plan was almost completed as most of the businesses targeted for divestiture had been sold to other corporations. Only a few small properties remained to be sold. One of these was the Northern Division ("Northern").

Northern's profits were cyclical and were now reaching what Peter reasoned would be their high point. Peter was determined to sell Northern at its peak but had no takers primarily because of Northern's poor performance in prior years and the fact that Northern's markets were limited with only modest growth potential. Northern's profits were not, on average, sufficient to provide an adequate return on invested capital. Failing to sell Northern, Peter decided to liquidate.

At this point my firm entered the scene and suggested that PDQ might maximize its return by selling Northern to its employees through an ESOP rather than by liquidating it. When asked for the basis of our rationale we cited three factors that should work in an ESOP's favor. First, an ESOP would be a willing buyer because of the employees' emotional and financial ties to the company. The employees would be willing to forego a high return on investment in order to continue their employment. Second, the ESOP would provide improved cash flow to service debt, increasing the probability of arranging loans. Third, saving jobs through the ESOP was encouraged by the government. This factor might improve the chance of obtaining favorable government sponsored loans or loan guarantees. Peter commissioned us to determine the structure that a ESOP purchase might take and to determine the feasibility of financing the transaction.

Before proceeding we decided to determine whether Northern's existing management had the enthusiasm and ability to run Northern as an independent entity, since a demonstrated capability to direct its affairs was a prerequisite to gaining the confidence of potential financing sources and maintaining Northern's market position. Peter introduced us to Mike Goodguy, Vice President and General Manager of the division. Mike was a bright aggressive manager, aged 37, who immediately impressed us with his ability to lead Northern. Reference checks in the trade and local community confirmed our initial impression. We were not as confident of the second tier of management, however, and concluded that Goodguy was the key to putting together the ESOP purchase. Any plan we divised would have to be structured to insure his continued involvement with Northern or its successor. Goodguy and his associates were enthusiastic about the prospects of purchasing the company. With this first major hurdle crossed we plunged into our feasibility analysis.

The initial step of our analysis was to determine a purchase price that would be acceptable to PDQ and which at the same time could be justified as "fair and equitable" to an ESOT in a formal valuation. Because of Northern's divisional status and because we wished to reduce the net purchase price to a minimum, an asset purchase was chosen as the favored vehicle for ownership transfer. PDQ would sell the fixed assets and inventories of Northern and would retain the remaining current assets and liabilities. Based on recent appraisals, the plant and equipment were valued at $1,800,000 and inventories at $1,900,000. PDQ had a policy of liquidating all unfunded vested pension liabilities of divested properties. Since the beneficiaries of this funding would be the new owners, PDQ felt the employees should share the burden of eliminating the pension liability. An amount of $200,000 was agreed upon. In addition, we estimated that the new company would require a minimum of $300,000 of working capital in excess of available trade credit to fund its receivables and incremental inventory increases during the first year of operation. Thus a purchase price of $3,900,000 and a total financing requirement of $4,200,000 were established.

To fund Northern's sale we considered a diversified group of financing sources. Among the sources considered were: commercial banks, finance companies, insurance companies, venture capital firms, state and federal agencies, private development corporations and PDQ itself. Having identified the most probable sources of funds a period of detailed investigation and negotiation followed. During the same period the fundamental structure of the ESOP divestiture plan also evolved.

The key element of the financing plan was issuance of an industrial revenue bond ("IRB"). Northern was located in a state that had created a state-wide industrial financing agency ("IFA"). The IFA was not only amenable to issuing an IRB on Northern's behalf but it also could underwrite insurance on a substantial portion of the principal amount of this issue. This had the effect of dramatically reducing a potential lender's risk since it protected against first dollars of loss. The IRB became more marketable. Several area savings banks agreed to subscribe to the issue which had a principal amount of $1,800,000 at an interest rate of 7 percent for a period of 15 years.

The ability to utilize an IRB issue to fund the purchase of the illiquid fixed assets materially enhanced the chances of assembling the rest of the financing package. The IRB's low interest rate and long maturity improved Northern's pro forma cash flow and ability to service other debt instruments.

The second feature of the financing plan was secured inventory financing. Inventories had a book value of $2,150,000, an estimated market value of approximately $1,900,000 and included raw materials and work-in-process as well as finished goods. Goodguy had developed sound working relationships with several local banks. One of them, the All Heart Bank, quickly committed to a $1,100,000 five year term loan at a rate of Prime plus 2 percent subject to the remainder of the financing package being assembled.

Armed with $2,900,000 of the required $4,200,000 we then approached several federal, state and private development agencies. We concentrated on private corporations because of the long lead times generally needed to complete the complex application procedures of the government agencies. The Capital Resource Company ("CRC"), funded by a consortium of banks and insurance companies headquartered in Northern's state, agreed to participate in the financing under certain conditions. CRC agreed to subordinate its loan to the IRB and the Bank financing but insisted that PDQ participate on a *pari passu* basis with them. Looking at the alternatives, PDQ acquiesced to this request and CRC committed to a $650,000 five year term loan with interest fixed at 9 percent per annum.

As suggested previously, a critical factor in arranging the financing package was assuring the lenders of Goodguy's continued involvement with Northern. Recognizing there are many methods of accomplishing this we concluded that giving Goodguy a "piece of the action" up front would provide him with the incentive, above and beyond a reasonable salary, to aggressively manage the facility. A 10 percent ownership was agreed upon. Because of the ESOP's participation, a straight "gift" of stock was precluded. Therefore a management incentive plan whereby Northern financed Goodguy's participation was created. Northern would lend Goodguy the funds to purchase 10 percent of the stock over a 10 year period at a reasonable interest rate. For Northern's, and the lender's, protection the loan would be tied to an employment contract. For Goodguy's protection, his shares would have an anti-dilution feature. Each year that Goodguy remained with the company, Northern would "forgive" interest and principal on his loan due that year.

Since the ESOP was to be the principal owner of Northern it was necessary to determine the ESOP's loan capacity. Based on the historical payroll for prior years and the assumption that covered compensation would grow at a rate of roughly 5 percent, we estimated the payroll of Northern over the next five years. Using the maximum allowable ESOP contribution rate of 15 percent we calculated the estimated ESOP contributions shown by Table 22-12.

Table 22-12
ESTIMATED ESOP CONTRIBUTION

Year	Contribution
1	$400,000
2	$420,000
3	$400,000
4	$470,000
5	$500,000

While the size of loan that this contribution could service would necessarily depend on terms and maturity, we estimated the ESOP's loan capacity to be between $1,000,000 and $1,250,000. It was decided to limit the ESOP obligation between these reasonably conservative parameters. If the ability of Northern to contribute to the ESOP grew more rapidly than we forecasted, we would use the "surplus" contributions to tax shelter the principal payments of loans made directly to the company.

To help illustrate the complex interactions among interested parties that the transaction structure and financing plan created, we drew the diagram shown as Figure 22-5. We then went through a step-by-step review of the various facets of the divestiture. (Figure 22-5 on page 353).

The first step would be to create a shell corporation to continue the operations of Northern. Goodguy had pooled the employees and the name NORCO, Inc. ("NORCO") had been selected. NORCO in turn would establish an ESOP. NORCO, the ESOP and

PDQ would then enter into a definitive agreement to purchase the plant, equipment, and inventories of Northern and to settle the unfunded pension liability. Subsequently, the following actions would be executed simultaneously.

NORCO would conclude a sale-leaseback agreement with the IFA. The IFA would purchase the fixed assets acquired from PDQ for $1,800,000. The IFA would then issue the Industrial Revenue Bonds, with insurance, to fund the purchase. The Bonds would be serviced by lease payments from NORCO and the fixed assets would serve as the underlying security.

The ESOP would borrow $1,100,000 from the All Heart Bank and use the proceeds to purchase 90 percent of NORCO's stock. This loan would be secured by a pledge of NORCO stock held by the ESOP as well as by NORCO's inventories. The loan would be serviced by cash contributions of NORCO to the ESOP.

Goodguy, the owner-manager, would purchase 10 percent of NORCO's stock. NORCO would finance this purchase by accepting Goodguy's personal note. The new management incentive plan would service this obligation.

Capital Resource Company ("CRC") would lend NORCO $650,000. This borrowing would be evidenced by a subordinated note and would be contingent upon NORCO receiving an equivalent financing from PDQ.

To complete the transaction, NORCO would pay PDQ $3,250,000 in cash and $650,000 in subordinated notes in consideration for the $3,700,000 in assets purchased and the $200,000 settlement of the unfunded pension liability. NORCO would retain $300,000 for working capital purposes. Table 22-13 summarizes the Sources and Uses of Funds of this transaction.

Table 22-13
NORTHERN DIVESTITURE
SOURCES AND USES OF FUNDS

SOURCES:

Industrial Revenue Bond	$1,800,000
ESOP/Inventory Loan	1,100,000
CRC Subordinated Loan	650,000
PDQ Subordinated Loan	650,000
	$4,200,000

USES:

Plant & Equipment	$1,800,000
Inventories	1,900,000
Unfunded Pension Liability	200,000
Incremental Working Capital	300,000
	$4,200,000

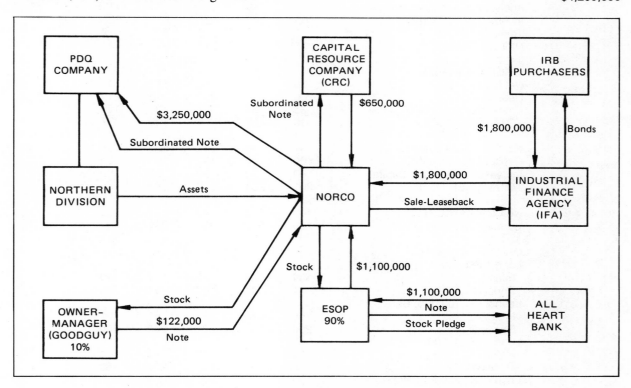

Figure 22-5
Northern Divestiture Financing

With the transaction structure finalized and the financing plan in place we then proceeded to determine the financial impact of the proposed divestiture so as to insure, as far as practically possible, that NORCO would succeed and be able to meet the heavy debt service demands inherent in an ESOP subsidiary divestiture.

We began this analysis by developing with Goodguy and his management team a conservative forecast or NORCO's operating income on a stand alone basis. We then impacted the structure of the transaction upon this operating plan to develop a detailed financial fore-cast for NORCO. The results of this effort are shown in Table 22-14.

A number of interesting observations became apparent when we reviewed the financial forecast. First and foremost, the forecast revealed that NORCO could enjoy a significant improvement in operating performance as an independent company. A good portion of the improvement was a result of cost cutting and elimination of corporate overhead while the remainder was caused by less tangible productivity improvements. Even when taken with a grain of salt, it was abundantly clear that a small, independent, entrepreneurially run

Table 22-14
NORTHERN DIVESTITURE
PRO FORMA CASH FLOWS
($000)

End of Year	0	1	2	3	4
NORCO INCOME STATEMENT					
Operating Income	809	963	1,142	1,336	1,513
Interest Expense	(251)	(248)	(241)	(210)	(165)
ESOP Contribution	(400)	(408)	(434)	(463)	(492)
Stock Bonus (10% of ESOP Stock) Contribution)	(4)	(9)	(15)	(20)	(16)
Additional Cash Compensation	(4)	(9)	(15)	(20)	(16)
Income Before Taxes	150	289	437	623	824
Taxes at 50%	75	145	219	312	412
NET INCOME	75	144	218	311	412
NORCO CASH FLOW					
Net Income	75	144	218	311	412
Depreciation	200	210	210	210	210
Proceeds from Sale of Stock	35	94	147	201	155
TOTAL SOURCES	310	457	575	722	777
Less: Principal Payments	41	94	347	501	555
Capital Expenditures	100	100	100	100	100
Increases in Working Capital	60	70	80	90	100
TOTAL USES	201	264	527	691	755
NET CASH FLOW	109	193	48	31	22
Cumulative Excess Cash	109	302	350	381	403
LOAN REPAYMENTS					
Loan 1 ($1,800,000) IRB					
Interest	134	131	128	124	120
Principal	41	44	47	51	55
Loan 2 ($1,100,000) Bank					
Interest	165	114	87	62	37
Principal	200	200	200	200	300
Loan 3 ($650,000) CRC Note					
Interest	59	58	57	43	22
Principal	0	25	150	225	250
Loan 4 ($650,000) PDQ Note					
Interest	58	59	56	43	23
Principal	0	25	150	225	250
Manager-Owner's Note ($122,000)					
Interest	10	10	9	8	7
Principal	0	10	10	10	15

NORCO would improve on Northern's historical performance. The second observation was that NORCO's projected payroll was large enough so that the maximum ESOP contribution would not only be sufficient to service the ESOP loan but also would fully shelter the principal payments of the other loans as they amortized. This would permit NORCO to maximize the cash flow effects of the ESOP. Since ESOP contributions to shelter principal payments of direct company loans would be made in stock rather than cash, the anti-dilutive provisions of Goodguy's contract would be evoked. Finally, we were pleased to see that the forecast generated a reasonable cushion of "excess" cash to protect against contingencies. We also knew that as the ESOP loan was repaid additional borrowing capacity would become available as the inventory collateral was released. All parties concerned were confident that NORCO would have the financial muscle to support the divestiture plan.

The transfer of ownership of Northern to NORCO was consummated as planned. We were truly amazed that the transaction, with all its complexities and the number of parties at interest, proceeded with "nary a hitch" until we rationalized that the deal had more than its share of that basic element of all successful transactions—significant benefits to all parties! PDQ was more than pleased. Peter had achieved his objective of freeing up needed growth capital and had done so by selling Northern at a price superior to that available in the market place. True, the $650,000 note would appear as a liability on PDQ's balance sheet but even that element was mitigated by fact that $200,000 of the amount was for the pension settlement. Even if NORCO should default on its note, the $3,250,000 cash received was greater than could have been reasonably expected in liquidation. Furthermore, the public image of PDQ was enhanced. Rather than being viewed as a ruthless and unfeeling liquidator, PDQ was seen as a company seeking enlightened and imaginative solutions to its problems.

For NORCO, which was faced with the burden of financing the transaction, the benefits were also apparent. First NORCO remained in existence. This permitted the company to improve its financial performance as an independent entity. The transaction helped to create a better identity between labor and management. Certainly, the lure of ownership helped in retaining critical and knowledgable employees. Lastly the ESOP provided additional cash flow from tax savings. Over the first five years the ESOP increased cash flow by over $1 million. It is unlikely that the lenders would have financed the divestiture had this additional cash flow not been available.

The employees saw the ESOP purchase as the vehicle that would preserve their jobs. The area in which NORCO was located had a relatively high unemployment rate and could not absorb almost 200 additional workers, particularly workers with specific job skills unique to NORCO. Thus for many, the ESOP provided the only practical alternative to unemployment or uprooting their families. In addition, the employees saw the opportunity to share in the growth of NORCO at no reduction in their take home pay. This caused them to more closely identify with NORCO because they had a stake in its future success.

The owner-manager, Goodguy, was also pleased with his prospects. The transaction provided him with investment capital without adversely effecting his current life style. His 10 percent stake plus his participation in the ESOP gave him effective control of NORCO at no direct cost to himself. True, if he had been able to structure a more conventional leveraged buyout his ownership position could have been much improved, but he considered the risk-reward ratio of the ESOP purchase to be very much in his favor.

Finally the lenders, agencies, and local government that made the transaction possible were fully satisfied that substantial economic and human benefits would result. The continuance of NORCO as an operating entity sustained the economic development of the area. On one side the high cost of providing public assistance to the unemployed was avoided. More positively, the combined payroll of almost 200 workers was retained in the local economy. This amounted to more than $15 million over a five year period. Loss of income of this size would have had a ripple effect throughout the community.

CONCLUSION

The ESOP is a valuable and flexible financing tool that can facilitate acquisitions, divestitures and buyouts. Nonetheless, it must be used selectively and only after careful and detailed analysis. The negative impact of earnings per share and ownership dilution limits the ESOP's applicability and inhibits its use as a vehicle for raising new capital. On the other hand, the ESOP exhibits great versatility when it is used to transfer ownership between parties. In ownership transfer situations the adverse dilutive factors are avoided since new shares are not issued. Furthermore, leverage capabilities are enhanced, relative to conventional debt financing, because cash flow is improved in direct proportion to the tax savings generated. While this chapter has discussed only two specific applications of ESOPs to acquisitions, divestitures and buyouts, the imaginative reader will be able to visualize many other instances where the ESOP can be used to transfer ownership immediately or in an orderly fashion over time.

TAX CONSIDERATIONS

Tax CONSIDERATIONS HAVE COME TO BE THE FOCUS OF ATTENTION in almost every area of corporate finance. The impact of taxes can virtually dictate the form and substance of a particular transaction. Unsophisticated planning may mean the loss of significant monies while creative use of Internal Revenue Code (IRC) provisions may make possible a merger or acquisition which appeared not doable on first impression. The tax law, as it relates to mergers, acquisitions and buyouts, is quite technical and complex. Our authors in this topical area are experts who have done an excellent job of translating the legal language of the IRC into concepts which will be meaningful to the layperson.

The subject of tax treatment of shareholders in mergers, acquisitions and buyouts is a broad one. Gerald Rokoff discusses the important factors in a tax-free exchange, reviews five types of acquisitive reorganizations and focuses on the treatment of a shareholder of the acquired company. Mr. Rokoff also explains the related problem of giving a small minority of stockholders of the acquired corporation tax-free treatment when the majority of the other stockholders receive cash. The chapter is divided and numbered so that the reader can easily cross-reference important points where it is appropriate. Ample footnotes with further comments, cases and rulings allow special research by the reader.

James Stevralia is the author of the chapter on taxable sales and liquidations. His example-oriented discussion begins with a simple sale of stock, works through installment sales and contingent payments, details a sale of assets, and simplifies the complex area of IRC Section 337 liquidations. Mr. Stevralia also discusses the boot-strap acquisition of stock, subsidiary liquidations, special business considerations, and determinations of basis in stock. Where desirable, the content of relevant Revenue Rulings and case law is supplied.

GERALD ROKOFF

GERALD ROKOFF is an associate in the tax department of Kramer, Levin, Nessen, Kamin & Soll. He graduated in 1974 from Yale Law School, where he was an Editor of the Yale Law Journal, and was selected by the Yale Law School faculty as an Assistant in Instruction. Following law school, Mr. Rokoff was the law clerk to Hon. Irving R. Kaufman, Chief Judge of the United States Court of Appeals for the Second Circuit. Mr. Rokoff received his B.A. from the State University of New York at Stony Brook in 1971, where he graduated *summa cum laude* and was the University valedictorian. He was an author of the "Report on the Internal Revenue Service 'Slush Fund Investigation'" issued by the Special Subcommittee of the Committee on Practice and Procedure of the New York State Bar Association, Tax Section.

23

Tax Consequences to Shareholders in an Acquisitive Reorganization*

GERALD ROKOFF

This chapter discusses the tax treatment to the shareholders of a corporation acquired in a reorganization. Section 1 considers briefly the factors that bear on the decision to employ a tax-free exchange. Section 2 reviews the five types of acquisitive reorganizations. Section 3 focuses on the treatment of a shareholder of the acquired corporation depending upon whether he receives solely stock (Section 3.1), stock and cash (Section 3.2), solely cash (Section 3.3), debt securities (Section 3.4), preferred stock (Section 3.5), installment notes (Section 3.6) and additional combinations of the above. Although Section 4 does not concern an acquisitive reorganization, it considers a related problem: giving only a small minority of stockholders of the acquired corporation tax-free treatment, where the overwhelming majority of the remaining stockholders receive cash.

Several steps have been taken in the hope of simplifying an otherwise complex mass of rules.[1]

First, to render the discussion less abstract (and less wordy), the following definitions are utilized:

"¶"   ¶ is the symbol for Section.
"P"   P refers to the acquiring corporation.
"T"   T refers to the acquired corporation.
"S"   S refers to a wholly owned subsidiary of P that may be a party to the reorganization (as described in ¶2 below).

"Mr. X"   Mr. X refers (where the context is appropriate) to a specific shareholder of T.

Second, examples are frequently utilized to illustrate the application and interplay of the rules discussed.

Finally, the chapter is divided into numbered and titled subheads to facilitate cross-references where appropriate.

One final introductory comment. Because the tax stakes in a reorganization are often very high and most public shareholders do not wish to bear either the expense of contacting a personal tax adviser or the tax risks of the transaction, almost every reorganization involving the shareholders of publicly held corporations, and most private transactions as well, are conditioned on a favorable ruling by the Internal Revenue Service (the "IRS") or are structured in such a way that counsel has no doubt that the transaction clearly qualifies under statutory and administrative guidelines. Thus, in the reorganization area, the administrative interpretations of the IRS enjoy a special status. Accordingly, the discussion in this chapter emphasizes the current policies and interpretations of the IRS (including those reflected in private as well as published ruling letters),[2] although the existence of more liberal or contrary authority is indicated, whenever appropriate.

---

*Grateful acknowledgment to Kevin J. O'Brien, a member of Paul, Weiss, Rifkind, Wharton & Garrison, who edited this chapter and made several insightful substantive contributions based on his experience in this area.

[1]Boris Bittker and James Eustice, in their seminal treatise, comment that: "[t]he reorganization provisions are extraordinarily complex, even for the Internal Revenue Code." Bittker and Eustice, *Federal Income Taxation of Corporations and Shareholders*, 1979, at 14-6.

[2]The Internal Revenue Code admonishes that a private letter ruling (in contrast to a published ruling) "may *not* be used or cited as precedent." Section 6110(j) (3). (All section references are to the Internal Revenue Code, unless otherwise indicated.) Notwithstanding this de jure lack of "precedential value", private letter rulings have become a major reference tool. They reveal the alternative types of tax planning done by other taxpayers that have previously engaged in similar transactions, but more importantly, they afford the tax practitioner a sense of what the IRS will and will not bless.

1. THE DECISION TO EMPLOY A TAX-FREE REORGANIZATION

There are a number of tax and non-tax reasons that so many P's acquire T's in tax-free reorganizations. Perhaps the most important is that offering T shareholders P shares tax-free (or the option to receive either P shares tax-free or cash) makes the proposed exchange more attractive to T shareholders and thus enhances the probability of P's making a successful acquisition. Alternatively, P may seek certain tax attributes of T (such as net operating loss carryovers or assets with a basis in excess of their fair market value) which a reorganization will generally preserve for P's enjoyment. Or, for financial reporting or business reasons, P may prefer to use its stock rather than cash or notes.

Where T's basis in its depreciable assets is substantially less than their fair market value , however, P may prefer a taxable acquisition. As noted above, where T is acquired in a reorganization, P generally inherits T's tax attributes including its basis in its assets.[3] If, however, T were acquired in a taxable transaction, P could "step-up" the basis of T's assets (by buying assets or by buying stock and then liquidating T)[4] and thus enjoy future tax benefits attributable to greater depreciation deductions. Thus, when the fair market value of T's assets exceeds their basis in T's hands, P should consider a taxable transaction.

In some cases, P could share a portion of the future tax benefits (attributable to a taxable acquisition) with T shareholders by in effect compensating them in whole or in part for the difference to them between a tax-free and a taxable deal.

> *Example 1*. T has an aggregate basis in its assets of $5,000,000 with a fair market value of $10,000,000. The T shareholders have an approximate basis in their stock of $9,000,000. The shareholders of T would accept $10,000,000 of stock in P in a tax-free deal. Instead, P pays $10,000,000 cash plus an additional $388,888.88 cash so that (assuming a 70 percent rate of tax and a 60 percent capital gains deduction) the T shareholders, after taxes, receive $10,000,000 (i.e., gain of $1,388,888 less 28 percent tax).

The T shareholders in Example 1 are clearly better off; their gain has not been deferred, but paid for. Moreover, the additional cost of $388,888.88 to P will certainly be worth the additional $5,000,000 of basis in T's assets.

The determination whether a taxable purchase transaction (assuming P pays more than it would if it offered P stock in a tax-free exchange to mitigate the T shareholders' tax burden on the transaction) is more favorable than a tax-free reorganization is, of course, generally somewhat more complex than the case presented in the example and depends upon a number of factors, including (i) the basis of the assets of T, (ii) the basis of the T stock in the hands of the T shareholders, (iii) the extent to which there will be investment tax credit, depreciation or other recapture on the purchase of T's assets or on the subsequent liquidation of T by P[5] and (iv) the respective fair market value and useful life of each of T's assets.[6] Where T is a public company, it may be difficult, if not impossible, to ascertain the amount of gain each stockholder of T would recognize on a taxable transaction or, in any event, P could not feasibly offer different amounts to different stockholders depending upon their gain on the transaction. Nevertheless, P and T should consider whether a price can be ascertained at which each would prefer a straight cash transaction to a tax-free reorganization.

If a cash transaction is selected, a number of techniques are available (as discussed elsewhere in this book), but P and T should have little difficulty in structuring the transaction so that shareholders of T enjoy capital gain treatment and a corporate level tax to T is avoided.

If a reorganization transaction is selected, an array of tax issues concerning the tax treatment of T shareholders emerge. These are considered in ¶3. First, however, it will be useful to briefly review the various forms of acquisitive reorganizations available to P with emphasis on the maximum amount of cash that may be used in each (in recognition of the increasing popularity of reorganizations in which T shareholders are offered a choice of cash or P stock).

2. THE FORM OF THE REORGANIZATION AND THE MAXIMUM AMOUNT OF CASH

Section 368 of the Code defines, effectively, eight types of reorganizations. Transfers between certain

---

[3] Section 362(b); Section 381. In a B reorganization, T remains a surviving entity so that its attributes are unaffected by the reorganization. *See* ¶2.2 below.

[4] P may liquidate T following a purchase of T's stock and secure a basis in the assets received in liquidation equal to the amount paid for the T stock if it adopts a plan of liquidation within 2 years after it acquires 80 percent of the stock of T and completes the liquidation within a specified time period. Section 334 (b) (2).

[5] Where P buys stock and then liquidates T, P, in effect, will be responsible for any recapture tax, since T will be a subsidiary of P at the time of liquidation. Where T sells its assets to P and then liquidates, the recapture tax paid by T will, in effect, be borne by the T shareholders as such tax reduces the amounts available for distribution to such shareholders. In any event, however, the ultimate price paid by P for stock or assets generally reflects whether it or the T shareholders will bear any recapture tax.

[6] A step-up in basis will be preferable to the extent that the present value of the additional depreciation deductions exceeds the immediate recapture cost, if any, triggered by the taxable transaction. Thus, the future depreciation deductions with respect to each asset must be ascertained for this computation.

related corporations (a type ''D'' reorganization), recapitalizations (a type ''E'' reorganization)[7] and a mere change of form, identity, or place of reorganization (a type ''F'' reorganization) are not normally of significance in a commercially motivated tax-free acquisition by P of the stock or assets of T. Thus, we are left with five statutorily recognized forms of acquisitive reorganizations.

2.1 The Type A Merger

In order to qualify as an A reorganization, the transaction must be a merger or consolidation of T into P effected pursuant to the laws of the United States, or a state or territory or the District of Columbia:

$$[T] \longrightarrow [P]$$

(T shares exchanged for P shares or cash. P acquires T assets which may be put into S.)

The A reorganization stands clearly as the most flexible reorganization technique. First, there is no requirement that P use solely voting stock and thus P may use voting or non-voting stock. Second, there is no requirement that P acquire substantially all of T's assets so that T can effectuate, for example, redemptions of stockholders or a spinoff of assets before merging into P. Third, and perhaps most important, the statute states no maximum amount of cash that may be used and the limitations articulated by the IRS and the courts allow substantially more cash to be used than in any other reorganization (except the subsidiary merger, discussed in ¶2.4 below).

The underlying rationale of the non-recognition provisions that attend qualifying reorganizations is that the surviving or acquiring corporation, after the reorganization, represents only a readjustment of a continuing interest in property under a modified corporate form.[8] Thus, the treasury regulations adopt the rule that requisite to a reorganization are a ''continuity of interest therein on the part of those persons who, directly or indirectly, were the owners of the enterprise prior to the reorganization.''[9]

The IRS takes the position for advance ruling purposes that this ''continuity of interest'' requirement is satisfied if at least 50 percent of the consideration received by the T shareholders consists of stock of P.[10] Stated conversely, P may acquire up to 50 percent of the stock of T for cash or notes and still qualify as an A reorganization. The IRS ruling guidelines also state that sales, redemptions, or other dispositions of stock occurring prior or subsequent to[11] the plan of reorganization will be considered in determining whether the 50 percent test is met. Thus, where P makes open market purchases in contemplation of a proposed reorganization and/or where dissenters will, under applicable state law, receive cash for their shares, the shares purchased in the market and the shares held by dissenters of T will count towards the 50 percent cash maximum[12]

Because cash option mergers often involve public corporations widely held by ''small'' investors, the business and securities law consideration for seeking an advance tax ruling generally outweigh any tax reason. Partly because an advance ruling has been a standard feature of cash option reorganizations, the 50 percent maximum cash test has taken on the status of a ''commandment.'' But P can use more than 50 percent cash—the IRS itself states in its ruling guidelines that its ''operating rules do not define, as a matter of law, the lower limits of continuity of interest.''[13] Indeed,

---

[7] A recapitalization may be useful where a minority of T shareholders want to have tax-free treatment with the remainder selling to P for cash. This is discussed in ¶4.1 below.

[8] Treas. Reg. §1.368-1(b).

[9] *Id.* This regulation also requires a ''continuity of business enterprise''—a requirement which has not generally posed any problem in connection with acquisitive reorganizations. Recently, however, the Treasury Department proposed regulations under section 368 which would require P either to (i) continue T's historic business or (ii) use a significant portion of T's business assets in its business. *See generally,* Prop. Treas. Reg. § 1.368-1(d). These regulations will apply only prospectively 30 days after they are adopted. First, however, hearings will be held and the Treasury has announced that no ''references are intended regarding the law prior to the effective date of this proposed regulation.'' *See,* proposed amendment of Regulations, published in the Federal Register on December 28, 1979.

[10] Rev. Proc. 77-37, 1977-2 C.B. 568, sec. 3.02. The Revenue Procedure states that it is not necessary that each shareholder of T receive in the exchange stock equal in value to 50 percent of his stock interest in T, so long as one or more shareholders of T have a continuing interest in P which is, in the aggregate, equal in value to at least 50 percent of the value of all former outstanding stock of T.

[11] The IRS takes the position that the continuity test will generally be satisfied if there is no ''preconceived plan or arrangement'' for disposing of the stock received. That individual shareholders may decide (after the reorganization) to sell some or all of the shares they received pursuant to the reorganization should not adversely affect the tax-free nature of the reorganization, nor should the fact that certain preferred stock received is redeemable by its terms. (See discussion of redeemable preferred in ¶3.5 below). The IRS has issued hundreds of private letter rulings finding a reorganization where specified percentages of the preferred stock issued is redeemable by its terms after a period of time, typically five years. Even where shareholders are required by court decree to dispose of their shares, the IRS treats five years of unrestricted rights of ownership as a sufficient period to satisfy the continuity test. Rev. Rul. 66-23, 1966-1 C.B. 67.

[12] In most reorganizations involving an advance ruling, P will generally take the conservative position that all shares previously purchased by it constitute ''cash'' shares and, therefore, reduce the maximum amount of additional shares that may be acquired for cash. However, shares purchased before the idea of a proposed reorganization first flickered should not count toward the 50 percent continuity test. The IRS has in at least one private letter ruling included ''old and cold'' T shares held by P in computing whether at least 50 percent of the T shareholders (as a result of owning T shares) hold P stock after the merger.

[13] Rev. Proc. 77-37 *supra,* section 2.03.

the Supreme Court has upheld reorganization treatment where 62 percent cash was used[14] and the Sixth Circuit Court of Appeals has found a reorganization where as much as 75 percent cash was used.[15] Thus, if P otherwise meets the requirements for an A reorganization, but wishes to acquire somewhat more than 50 percent of the T shares for cash, it should certainly be able to do so (at least to the extent of 60 percent cash) and qualify as an A reorganization—albeit at the cost of not being told so in advance by the IRS. An opinion of counsel should be considered where the cash exceeds 50 percent but is well within the judicial limits.

2.2 The Type B Stock Exchange

A type B reorganization involves the acquisition by P or S in exchange solely for P voting stock or solely for S voting stock of at least 80 percent (but typically 100 percent) of the stock of T.

(T shareholders receive P stock. P receives T stock and T becomes a subsidiary of P.)

The IRS and the court decisions interpret the "solely" for voting stock requirement to mean that absolutely no cash may be utilized (except for fractional shares[16] and the valid reorganization expenses of T and its shareholders).[17] Last year, however, a plurality of six judges of the Tax Court held that cash paid in a reorganization does not per se violate the statute if the requisite 80 percent of T's stock is acquired in one transaction for voting stock.[18] However, the Third Circuit recently reversed the Tax Court.[19] Accordingly, it remains advisable to dismiss a B if any cash is to be utilized.

2.3 The Type C Asset Acquisition

A type C reorganization involves the acquisition by P or S in exchange solely for P voting stock or solely for S voting stock of "substantially all" of the properties of T.[20] P may use cash

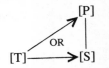

(T shareholders receive P stock or cash; S acquires T's assets.)

if property having a fair market value of 80 per cent of the fair market value of all property of T is acquired for stock.[21] *But,* if one penny of cash is used, the amount of any liabilities of T assumed or taken subject to by P or S is treated as money paid by P for the property of T. In other words, in a C reorganization, P may only use cash if T's liabilities are less than 20 percent of the fair market value of the T assets. If so, cash may be used, but the 20 percent maximum amount of cash is reduced, dollar-for-dollar, by the T liabilities assumed or taken subject to by P or S. Thus, because of the limitation on the amount of cash that may be used, a C reorganization is generally not an attractive alternative for a cash-option reorganization.

2.4 The Subsidiary Merger (type "(a)(2)(D)")

A subsidiary merger involves the merger or consolidation of T into S where shareholders of T receive stock of P.

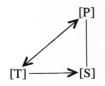

(T shareholders receive P stock or cash; S acquires T's assets.)

[14]*John A. Nelson Co. v. Helvering,* 296 U.S. 374 (1935).

[15]*Miller v. Comm'r,* 84 F.2d 415 (6th Cir. 1936). *See also, Helvering v. Watts,* 296 U.S. 387 (1935) (55 percent cash O.K.). In the following cases, the courts held the continuity of interest requirement was not met: *Banner Machine Co. v. Routzahn,* 107 F.2d 147 (6th Cir. 1939), *cert. denied,* 309 U.S. 676 (1940) (16.5 percent stock). *Yoc Heating Corp.,* 61 T.C. 168 (1973) (15 percent stock), Ltr. Ruling 7905011 (34 percent stock) and *May B. Kass,* 60 T.C. 218 (1973) (16 percent stock).

[16]Rev. Rul. 66-365, 1966-2 C.B. 116.

[17]Rev. Rul. 73-54, 1973-1 C.B. 187.

[18]*C.E. Graham Reeves,* 71 T.C. 727 (1979). The majority in *Reeves* decided that whether or not *prior* cash purchases of 8 percent of the target were pursuant to an integrated transaction, so long as 80 percent of the target's voting stock is acquired in one transaction the "solely" test is met. Two concurring judges would go further and allow payment up to 20 percent cash in the same transaction, a view subsequently adopted by a Delaware district court decision in the same case. *Pierson v. United States,* 472 F. Supp. 957 (D.C. Del. 1979). Five judges vigorously dissented in *Reeves* indicating that the majority view created uncertainty in an area which had long been considered settled.

[19]*Pierson v. U.S.,* No. 75-218 (3/25/80), *Daily Tax Reporter,* No. 65-1. The Third Circuit also reversed the district court decision. The First Circuit has recently agreed with the Third Circuit. See *Chapman v. U.S.,* 80-1 USTC ¶ 9322 (1st Cir. 1980).

[20]The IRS takes the position for advance ruling purposes that "substantially all" means at least 70 percent of the gross assets (i.e., the fair market value of the assets without regard to any liens or mortgages or indebtednesses) and 90 percent of the net assets (i.e., the fair market value of the assets reduced by any liens or mortgages).

[21]Section 368(a)(2)(B).

The great advantage to the subsidiary merger is that it is subject to the same continuity of interest requirements as an A reorganization. Thus, P can safely use 50 percent cash consideration in the merger.

The only stock that may be used in a subsidiary merger is the stock of P, but it need not be voting stock. However, unlike in an A merger, S must acquire "substantially all" of T's assets.[22] S must also be a first tier subsidiary of P.[23] Both S and P may each assume T's liabilities in a subsidiary merger and such assumption (unlike in a C reorganization) has no bearing on the tax-free nature of the reorganization. However, S must stay alive after the merger, although it can change its name to T's name at the effective time of the merger. If S is liquidated into P as part of the overall transaction, the transaction will be viewed as a C reorganization with all its attendant problems.[24] P's basis in S's stock after the merger will include an amount equal to T's net-basis in its assets.[25]

Under the merger laws of certain states, a subsidiary merger is preferable to an A since the subsidiary merger does not require approval of P's stockholders but only the approval of P's board of directors.

2.5 The Reverse Subsidiary Merger (Type "(a)(2)(E)")

The reverse subsidiary merger involves the merger of S into T where at least 80 percent of the stockholders of T receive voting stock of P:

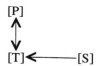

(T shares are exchanged for P shares or cash, T stays alive, but becomes a subsidiary of P)

The reverse subsidiary merger is akin to a B reorganization in that, in essence, P acquires T stock in exchange for P stock. Although the reverse subsidiary merger has a requirement that T hold "substantially all" of its assets and substantially all of the assets of S[26] (in each case defined as in a C reorganization)—a requirement that does not apply to a B—it permits P to use up to 20 percent cash (which it could not do in a B). Furthermore, unlike in a C, T's liabilities have no bearing on the maximum amount of cash that may be used. When the IRS tested "reverse mergers" under the B reorganization definition, it required that S be a transitory dummy corporation. However, under the statutory reverse subsidiary merger, S need not be a transitory dummy corporation.

The reverse subsidiary merger may offer tax advantages to the minority stockholders (i.e. less than 20 percent) who receive solely cash from P. These are noted briefly here but discussed more fully in ¶3.3 below. In an A, C, or subsidiary merger, stockholders who receive solely cash from P are treated as if they had their stock redeemed by T just prior to the merger. Redemption treatment may result in the cash received (not just the gain) being taxed at ordinary rates. However, in a reverse subsidiary merger, a stockholder of T who receive solely cash from P are treated as if they simply sold his T stock to P and, thus, the possible adverse consequences of redemption treatment should be avoided.

The reverse subsidiary merger is an especially attractive alternative where a transfer of T's properties, even though by operation of law only, will be burdensome, expensive or impossible. For example, T may be a party to agreements which require consent from other parties (and such other parties may demand something substantial for such consent) to transfer such agreement (whether by operation of law or otherwise) but which do not limit T's ability to acquire assets by merger.

A reverse subsidiary merger is often employed where T has several large shareholders who own over 80 percent of the T stock and have a very low basis in their T shares and thus desire stock. As a result, P knows that at least 80 percent will elect stock (or P can condition the reverse subsidiary merger on at least 80 percent of the T shareholders electing stock) and, thus, the remaining stockholders who hold only a minority of the stock can be offered cash or an election to receive stock or cash.

---

[22] As in a C reorganization "substantially all" means 90 percent of the fair market value of T's net assets and 70 percent of the fair market value of T's gross assets. Thus, unlike in an A or a B merger, there are limits on dispositions of T's cash or other assets (e.g., redemption, spin-off) prior to the reorganization.

[23] Rev. Rul. 74-564, 1974-2 C.B. 124; Rev. Rul. 74-565, 1974-2 C.B. 125.

[24] Rev. Rul. 72-405, 1972-2 C.B. 217. Only the basic requirements of the C reorganization have been discussed here. The tax practitioner, however, should be alert to the *Bausch & Lomb* [*Optical Co. v. Commissioner*, 267 F.2d 75 (2d Cir. 1959), *cert. denied*, 361 U.S. 835 (1959)] problem and possible solutions. *See* Rev. Rul. 57-278, 1957-1 C.B. 124, Rev. Rul. 58-93, 1958-1, C.B. 188, and Rev. Rul. 72-405, 1972-2 C.B. 217.

[25] At least the IRS will rule as much. Such basis will equal the basis P would include for S's stock if P acquired T in an A reorganization and contributed T's assets to S. Section 368(a)(2)(c) permits P to contribute the assets acquired in a reorganization to a "controlled" subsidiary.

[26] In computing whether T (after the merger of S into T) holds at least 90 percent of the net assets of S, the amount of any cash contributed to S by P for the payment of T dissenting shareholders, fractional share interests and S's expenses and the amount of P stock contributed to S to be used in the merger are not taken into account.

2.6 Summary

The maximum amount of cash that may be used and certain related considerations with respect to the various acquisitive reorganizations are summarized in Table 23-1:

Table 23-1

Type of Re-organization	Maximum Cash	Substantially all the Properties Requirement	Type of Stock
A	50% for advance ruling; higher under court cases	No	Voting or nonvoting, Survivor only
B	0% for advance ruling; 0% under weight of judicial opinion	No	Voting only, P or S
C	20% reduced by any liabilities of T assumed or taken subject to by S or P	Yes	Voting only, P or S
Subsidiary Merger (a)(2)(D)	Same as A	Yes	Voting or nonvoting, P only
Reverse Subsidiary Merger (a)(2)(E)	20%	Yes (T and S)	Voting only, P only

3. TAX CONSEQUENCES TO SHAREHOLDERS OF T

The tax consequences to a shareholder or security holder of T depend upon what he receives from P (or T) on the exchange.

3.1 T Shareholder Receiving Solely P Stock

A T shareholder who receives solely P stock in exchange for his T stock will recognize no gain or loss on the exchange.[27] The basis of the P shares received will be the same as the T shares surrendered.[28] The T shareholder's holding period for his P stock will include his holding period for his T stock.[29]

3.2 T Shareholder Receiving P Stock and Cash

3.2.1. *Amount of Gain; Basis.* A T shareholder receiving both stock and cash (which, for this purpose,

includes the fair market value of other property) recognizes gain, if any, but not in excess of the amount of cash received.[30]

Example 2. Mr. X owns 1,000 shares of T with an aggregate basis of $7,000. In the merger, he receives 600 shares of P stock with an aggregate value of $6,000 and $4,000 cash.

Total fair market value of consideration received	$10,000
Basis of shares surrendered	7,000
Total gain	3,000
Cash received	4,000
Gain to be recognized	$3,000

In Example 2, had Mr. X received 800 shares of P stock with a value of $8,000 and $2,000 of cash, his total gain would remain $3,000, but he would recognize only $2,000—the gain recognized is limited to the amount of cash received. If Mr. X had a basis of $12,000, he would have realized a loss of $2,000 on the exchange, which loss would not be recognized.[31]

The basis of the shares received by Mr. X is the same as the basis of the shares surrendered by him decreased by the amount of any cash received and increased by the amount of gain recognized on the exchange.[32]

Thus, in example 2, Mr. X's basis in his P shares would be determined as follows:

Basis of T shares surrendered	$7,000
Less: cash received	4,000
	3,000
Plus: gain recognized	3,000
Basis of P shares after the exchange	$6,000

Thus, Mr. X has lost $1,000 of basis attributable to the cash received without the recognition of any gain. Had Mr. X received shares of P stock worth $8,000 and $2,000 of cash (resulting in $2,000 of gain, as illustrated above), his basis for his P shares would be as follows:

Basis of T shares surrendered	$7,000
Less: cash received	2,000
	5,000
Plus: gain recognized	2,000
	$7,000

---

[27] Section 354(a).

[28] Section 358(a) (1). Where T stockholders own more than one class of stock and/or receive more than one class of stock an allocation of basis is made under the treasury regulations. *See* Treas. Reg. § 1.358-2.

[29] Section 1223(1).

[30] Section 356 (a).

[31] *See* ¶3.3.4 below.

[32] Section 358 (a) (1).

Thus, Mr. X would have a $7,000 basis in his P stock (with a fair market value of $8,000). Thus, the $1,000 of gain which was not recognized in the exchange would be recognized when and if Mr. X sells his stock for $8,000 or more. A portion or all of this gain will not be recognized if Mr. X sells his stock for less than $8,000 or if he holds this stock until his death.

Finally, in the case where Mr. X suffered a $2,000 loss, his P shares will have the same $12,000 basis as his T shares. This loss would be recognized when Mr. X sells his stock for $10,000 or less. Mr. X will not recognize such loss to the extent he sells the stock for $10,000 or more if he holds the stock until his death.

3.2.2 *Capital Gain or Dividend.* Once the amount of gain to be recognized is determined, the next issue is whether such gain will be treated as having "the effect of the distribution of a dividend" or whether it will be treated as gain from the sale or exchange of stock.[33]

If, under the rules discussed below, any cash received is treated as having the effect of a distribution of a dividend, then it is taxable at ordinary rates to the extent that it is not in excess of the T shareholder's ratable share of T's undistributed earnings and profits accumulated after February 28, 1913. The remainder, if any, of the gain is treated as gain from the sale or exchange of property.

Where T has substantial undistributed earnings and profits (which is more often the case than not), an individual shareholder of T will wish to avoid the adverse tax consequences of dividend treatment. If a shareholder has held his T stock for one year or more and enjoys sale or exchange treatment, he will be able to exclude 60 percent of the recognized gain from his taxable income.[34] If he suffers dividend treatment, 100 percent of such gain will be taxed at ordinary rates.

3.2.2.1. *Substantially Disproportionate Redemption.* In determining dividend equivalency, the current view of the IRS[35] is that the dividend equivalency tests of Section 302[36] (concerning redemptions of stock) should be applied as if T had redeemed its stock (to the extent its shareholders receive cash) just prior to the merger. However, the IRS has indicated that for this purpose the attribution rules (which apply in the case of section 302 redemptions and, in general, treat stockholders as constructively owning stock held by certain related persons or entities) will *not* apply.[37] Under this approach, a shareholder of T will enjoy capital gain treatment if his interest in T after the hypothetical redemption is 80 percent or less than his interest prior to the hypothetical redemption.[38]

Example 3. T has 1,000,000 shares outstanding. In the merger, T shareholders exchange 700,000 shares for P stock and 300,000 shares for cash. Mr. X owns prior to the exchange 40,000 shares of T. He exchanges 17,900 shares for cash and 22,100 shares for stock. Mr. X's percent diminution (or increase) in interest is determined as follows:

Mr. X's % of T before exchange:

$$\frac{40,000 \text{ (shares owned by Mr. X)}}{1,000,000 \text{ (total outstanding)}} = 4\%$$

Mr. X's % of T after exchange:

$$\frac{22,100 \text{ (shares exchange for P shares)}}{700,000 \text{ (treated as total outstanding, i.e., T shares not redeemed for cash)}} = 3.16\%$$

Mr. X's percentage decrease: $\dfrac{3.16}{4.00} = 79\%$

Thus, since Mr. X's interest in T after the exchange is less than 80 percent of his percentage interest before the exchange, the "substantially disproportionate

---

[33] Section 356 (a)(2).

[34] The discussion throughout this chapter assumes that the redeemed stock is a "capital asset" in the hands of the shareholder (which will be the case unless the shareholder is a dealer in securities). The statement that a "redemption" is to be treated as a dividend is posited on the assumption that the shareholder's proportionate share of T's earnings and profits are sufficient to cover the amount of the dividend.

[35] Initially the IRS took the position that any cash distribution in a reorganization would constitute a dividend to the extent of the lesser of the gain recognized or the distributing corporation's earnings and profits. Rev. Rul. 56-220, 1956-1 C.B. 191. However, this "automatic dividend" rule was rejected by most courts. *See Hawkinson v. Commissioner*, 235 F.2d 747 (2d Cir. 1956); *Ross v. United States*, 173 F. Supp. 793 (Ct. Cl. 1959), *cert. denied,* 361 U.S. 875 (1959); *Idaho Power Co. v. United States,* 161 F. Supp. 807 (Ct. Cl. 1958), *cert. denied* 358 U.S. 832 (1958). However, in *Wright v. United States*,482 F.2d 600 (8th Cir. 1973), the IRS agreed that the "automatic dividend" rule should no longer be applied.

[36] Rev. Rul. 75-83, 1975-1 C.B. 112; *See also* Rev. Rul. 74-515, 1974-2 C.B. 118; Rev. Rul. 74-516, 1974-2 C.B. 121.

[37] Rev. Rul. 74-515, 1974-2 C.B. 118. The attribution rules are relevant where a T stockholder receives solely cash and are considered in ¶3.3.3 below.

[38] The discussion in this ¶3.2.2.1 assumes that the exchanging T shareholder owns less than 50 percent of the total combined voting power of all classes of T stock exchanged for P stock in the merger. If a T shareholder owns before the exchange more than 50 percent of the stock of T exchanged for P stock, he cannot rely on the exception discussed herein. *See* section 302(b)(2)(B).

test'' is met and Mr. X is afforded non-dividend treatment.[39]

If, in Example 3, Mr. X exchanges the same number of shares for cash and stock (17,900 and 22,100, respectively) but in the merger P exchanged only 600,000 of its shares for T shares and acquired the rest for cash, Mr. X's interest after the merger would then be

$$\frac{22,100}{600,000} \text{ (shares exchange for P shares)} = 3.68\%$$
(treated as total outstanding, i.e., T shares exchange for P stock)

and his percentage interest after the merger would then be 92 percent of his interest before the merger and thus he would fail to pass the substantially disproportionate test.

$$\frac{3.68}{4.00} = 92\%$$

In such a case, the cash received (to the extent of the gain) would probably be treated by the IRS as a dividend.[40]

Thus, the probability of an exchanging stockholder passing the substantially disproportionate test will increase (i) the *more* shares he exchanges for cash and (ii) the *less* shares the other shareholders of T exchange for cash. Furthermore, since each shareholder will generally have to make its election at the same time, it is often very difficult for a T shareholder to assess his chances for passing such test. Nevertheless, by carefully structuring the type of elections that could be made by shareholders of T and by doing some simple algebraic computations based on the facts of a particular exchange, it is generally possible for a shareholder of T to elect cash and receive all cash, or to receive a mix of stock and cash (or even elect such a mix) and still be assured that his gain will not be treated as a dividend.

First, under an assumption that a certain maximum percentage of shares will be exchanged for cash (i.e., anywhere from 0 percent to 50 percent) it is possible to advise a shareholder of the exact percentage of his shares that he must exchange for cash in order to be assured the cash proceeds will be taxed at capital gain rates.

Example 4. T has 1,000,000 shares outstanding before the exchange. Mr. X owns 80,000 shares. It is known that no more than 45 percent of the shareholders will receive cash in the exchange.

Mr. X knows his percent ownership in T prior to the transactions.

$$\frac{80,000}{1,000,000} = 8\%$$

To meet the substantially disproportionate test, Mr. X knows that his interest in T after the reorganization will have to be less than 80 percent of 8 percent or less than 6.4 percent.

Mr. X also knows that for this purpose the minimum total of shares outstanding after the merger will be the shares not tendered for cash, or the shares tendered for stock. Thus, Mr. X knows that the number of shares held by him after the exchange (''y'') divided by 550,000 (the minimum number of T shares that will be exchanged for P stock) must be less than .064 or 6.4 percent.

$$\frac{y}{550,000} = .064$$
or
$$y = .064 \times 550,000 = 35,200$$

Thus, Mr. X knows that he must own less than 35,200 shares of T after the exchange to be assured he meets the substantial diminution test. Accordingly, he must receive for cash more than 44,800 shares or more than

$$\frac{44,800}{80,000}$$

or 56 percent of his shares for cash.

Second, the percentage of shares in excess of which Mr. X must exchange for cash where no more than 45 percent of the shares will be acquired for cash, i.e. 56 percent, *will apply to every shareholder no matter how many shares he holds and no matter what his proportionate interest in T is before the exchange.* By collapsing the various computations described above, the following formula states the percentage in excess of which each shareholder must exchange for cash (depending upon the maximum percent of T shares that P

---

[39] It should be noted that the Ninth Circuit has not adopted the IRS approach. Instead, it has held that dividend equivalence should be measured after the reorganization as if P had redeemed a portion of its (i.e. P) shares to the extent T shareholders receive cash. *Wright v. United States, supra* note 34. *See also Sellers v. United States*, 79-1 USTC ¶9202 (N.D.Ala. 1977). Of course, meeting the substantially disproportionate test under the IRS guidelines affords one comfort that reliance on the *Wright* approach does not.

[40] There is also the more general ''not essentially equivalent to a dividend test'' (*see* ¶3.2.2.2) which (unlike the substantially disproportionate test) cannot be passed with mathematical precision.

will acquire for cash) to be certain that he will meet the substantially disproportionate test.

$$\frac{\text{Minimum percent of T shares acquired for P stock}}{\text{Total T shares outstanding before exchange}} \times .8$$

In the above example, the formula would operate as follows:

$$1 - \left(\frac{550,000}{1,000,000}\right) \times .8$$

$$1 - (.55) \times (.8)$$

$$1 - .44 = .56$$

Thus, where the maximum number of shares to be acquired for cash is 45 percent of T's total outstanding stock, each shareholder of T would have to exchange more than 56 percent of his shares for cash to be assured non-dividend treatment. If in fact, Mr. X exchanges more than 56 percent of his shares for cash, but P uses less than 45 percent cash, Mr. X will still pass the substantially disproportionate test — albeit by a wider margin.

Therefore, since in every reorganization there is a statutory, administrative or judicial maximum on the amount of cash that may be used and in certain transactions P will state a maximum number of shares it will acquire for cash, a "safe-haven percent," i.e., the percent that must be tendered for cash by a T shareholder to assure capital gain treatment can be determined as follows:

Table 23-2

Maximum Percent of Shares to be Exchanged for Cash	Shareholder Must Exchange More Than the Following Percent of His Shares for Cash to be Certain of Capital Gain
5%	24%
10%	28%
20%	36%
30%	44%
40%	52%
50%	60%

The formula can be used to insure capital gain treatment to T shareholders whenever P cannot give every exchanging T shareholder his preference for stock or cash. This will occur in two situations.

1. More shares are tendered for cash than the maximum cash that P is permitted (to qualify as a reorganization) or is willing to use in the merger.
2. More shares are tendered for stock than the maximum amount P is willing to exchange in the merger.

The first is the more common problem. Typically, P will afford T shareholders in this situation two elections. A T shareholder could elect cash *unconditionally*, which means he will receive cash even if more shares are tendered for cash than the maximum cash available. In such cases, each shareholder electing cash unconditionally will receive his pro rata portion of the total available cash and risk dividend treatment. If a T shareholder wishes to avoid dividend treatment, he can elect cash *conditionally*, which typically means that he will receive cash only if he receives cash for all his shares. (As explained in ¶3.3 below, this is based on a faulty premise, as, under IRS guidelines, a stockholder may enjoy capital gain treatment if he receives a mixture of stock and cash where the same stockholder will suffer dividend treatment if he receives all cash). Under these traditional elections, cash is first allocated to those shareholders electing cash no matter what (i.e., unconditionally) and if there is any remaining cash, it is allocated to those stockholders electing cash conditionally. If there is insufficient cash to acquire all the shares for which a conditional election is made, the cash is allocated under a lottery system sometimes geared to give a preference to small stockholders.

By utilizing the simple mathematical concepts discussed above, more sophisticated conditional elections are possible that may be preferable than the "all or none" approach generally employed.

For example, where P will acquire only 30 percent of the shares for cash, we know that every shareholder will enjoy capital gain treatment if he exchanges more than 44 percent of his shares for cash.

Thus, the formula to determine the maximum number of shares that may be tendered for cash where each shareholder electing cash will receive an amount of cash for slightly more than 44 percent of his shares is:

$$\frac{\text{Cash maximum}}{\substack{\text{\% required to assure} \\ \text{capital gain treatment}}}$$

$$\frac{30\%}{44.01\%} = 68.16\%$$

Thus, in this case, P could allocate the total cash available among those electing cash as follows:

(i) if the total shares for which a cash election is made are less than 30 percent of the total shares outstanding, cash will be paid for all such shares;

(ii) if the total shares for which a cash election is made are more than 30 percent but less than 68.16

percent, the shareholders electing cash will receive cash on a pro rata basis (and each such shareholder will enjoy capital gain treatment with respect to the cash);

(iii) if the total of shares for which a cash election equals or exceeds 68.16 percent, a lottery will determine which shareholders will not share in the cash-stock mix described in (ii).

Under this allocation system, a much larger number of T shareholders may receive cash and still be assured capital gain treatment than under the typical all-or-none approach. In short, where P wishes to afford shareholders tax-sensitive elections, rather than allocate the cash available, after unconditional elections to shareholders under an all-or-none approach, it could afford more shareholders the safe-haven percentage of cash. If there is not enough cash to give all shareholders the safe-haven percentage, then the shareholders who receive such percentage could be determined by a lottery.

Typically, P will exchange as many of its shares as T shareholders elect. Nonetheless, there are situations in which P will place a cap on the number of shares it is willing to exchange in the transaction (because, for example, P does not wish to dilute its earnings per share or P is concerned about becoming a T).

In such a case P could offer ''stock'' as follows:

(i) T stockholders electing stock unconditionally would receive stock. To the extent the unconditional stock elections exceeded the total stock available, each such stockholder would receive cash on a pro rata basis and would risk dividend treatment.

(ii) T stockholders electing stock unconditional would all receive stock, if available. If conditional stock elections exceed the remaining stock available after satisfying unconditional elections, then T shareholders would receive cash, but each T shareholder receiving cash making a conditional stock election would receive the safe-haven percentage (thus assuring capital gain treatment). The shareholders receiving such stock-cash mix would be selected by lottery.

Example 5. T has 1,000,000 shares outstanding. P will accept a maximum of 600,000 shares for stock (60 percent). 100,000 shares are tendered with unconditional stock elections. 800,000 shares are tendered with conditional stock elections. 100,000 shares are tendered for cash. The safe-haven percentage where 40 percent is maximum number of shares to be exchanged for cash is 52 percent.

Thus, each T shareholder electing cash will receive cash and each T shareholder electing stock *unconditionally* will receive stock. The 80 percent who elected stock conditionally will have to receive the 30 percent of total cash remaining. A portion of such stockholders will receive more than 52 percent cash to insure capital gain treatment. The stockholders receiving the stock and cash mix can be selected by lottery.

3.2.2.2 *Not Essentially Equivalent to a Dividend.* The substantially disproportionate test affords mathematical certainty and its attendant comfort. Nevertheless, a stockholder may avoid having his cash treated as a dividend if he can meet the test contained in section 302(b)(1) which provides that a redemption will not be treated as a dividend if it is ''not essentially equivalent to a dividend.''

In Rev. Rul. 76-385,[41] the IRS gave some content to this conclusory test. There, a stockholder of Corporation Z owned, prior to the redemption, a .0001118 percent interest. Z had outstanding 28,000,000 shares, which means that such shareholder owned 31.30 shares prior to the redemption and .0001681 percent (or 30.27) shares after the redemption. The minority stockholder did not meet the substantial diminution test because his interest after the redemption was 96.6 percent of his interest before the redemption.

Nevertheless, the IRS ruled that the redemption qualified for capital gain treatment because (i) the redemption involved a minority stockholder whose relative stock interest in Z was minimal and who exercised no control over the affairs of Z and, in addition, (ii) as a result of the redemption, he experienced a reduction of his voting rights, his right to participate in current and accumulated surplus, and his right to share in net assets on liquidation. Then, citing the treasury regulation that provides that the ''not essentially equivalent to a dividend test'' depends upon the facts and circumstances of each case, the IRS concluded that in this case, under all the facts and circumstances, the redemption qualified for capital gain treatment.[42]

Since issuing the above ruling, the IRS has offered no further guidance in this area. Thus, there remains substantial uncertainty as to how small an interest in T a stockholder must have before he can be assured capital gain treatment on his boot without regard to the substantially disproportionate test. Parties to a merger of a widely-held target corporation have often sought to secure a ruling that T shareholders owning less than a specified percent (e.g., 1 percent or 5 percent) of T

---

[41]1976-2 C.B. 92.
[42]Treas. Reg. § 1.302-2(b).

stock who receive boot will have their gain taxed on the merger as if such stockholders had sold or exchanged their stock, notwithstanding that they fail to satisfy the substantially disproportionate test. However, as far as I know, the IRS has never issued such a ruling.

Finally, it should be noted that, as a practical matter, most minority stockholders receiving cash in exchange for all or a part of their shares probably report the transaction as a sale of stock on their tax returns. Thus, most stockholders, if not consciously, at least subconsciously rely on this exception if the substantially disproportionate test is not met. In this connection, almost every registration statement in a merger or acquisition alerts stockholders to the possibility that they might meet the ''not essentially equivalent to a dividend'' test, but because of its factual nature (and the scarcity of authority) combine this notice with a caution that each such stockholder should consult his or her own tax adviser as to the availability of this exception to dividend treatment.

3.3 Shareholders Receiving Solely Cash

Intuitively, one would think that if a T shareholder would enjoy capital gain treatment if he received a mix of stock and cash (because he passed the substantially disproportionate test) that he would be entitled to capital gain if he received all cash. Under the IRS guidelines, however, this may not be so.

3.3.1 *Redemption or Sale.* The IRS treats a shareholder who receives solely cash in an acquisitive reorganization (including shareholders who dissent from the merger) as if he received the cash in redemption of his T stock. The IRS treats the merger as if P transferred stock and cash to T in exchange for its assets and immediately prior to the merger T redeemed its shareholders who elected cash (presumably on the theory that this is the treatment generally afforded a taxable merger).[43]

It would appear that this logic should not apply to a reverse subsidiary merger where T is the surviving corporation, since such a reorganization is more akin to an acquisition by P of the T stock for P's stock and cash. The IRS itself recognizes in other contexts that the transitory existence of a subsidiary created solely for the merger should be disregarded and the transaction viewed as a direct acquisition of stock by P.[44] Indeed, I understand that the IRS is considering issuing a ruling in a reverse subsidiary merger that stockhold-

ers of T receiving cash from P will be treated as if they simply sold their stock to P without regard to the provisions and limitations that exist where such exchange is treated as a redemption.

3.3.2. *Redemption Treatment; Introduction.* In every acquisitive reorganization (other than a reverse subsidiary merger) a stockholder receiving cash will be treated as if his T stock were redeemed. Such redemption will be treated as if the T shareholder receiving solely cash had sold his stock (and thus be eligible for capital gain treatment) if, after the exchange, one of the following 4 conditions is satisfied: (1) he is not treated as ''constructively'' owning any stock of T as described in ¶3.3.3, (2) if he is considered to constructively own any stock, his percentage ownership of T after the exchange (taking into account shares considered as constructively owned by him after the exchange) is 20 percent less than his percentage ownership of T before the exchange (taking into account both the shares actually and constructively owned by him before the exchange), (3) he executes a special waiver described below, or (4) the exchange is not essentially equivalent to a dividend. If none of these conditions is satisfied, the *entire proceeds* received by the shareholder (not just the gain) are taxable at ordinary rates.

3.3.3. *Constructive Ownership of T Stock and the Non-Dividend Tests.* A shareholder of T who receives all cash will nevertheless be considered as constructively owning stock if certain persons or entities to whom he is related or in which he has an interest receive P stock in the merger. The constructive ownership rules are very complex, but the most common relationships which result in attribution of stock ownership to a shareholder of T are (1) stock owned by his spouse, grandparents, parents, children and grandchildren (but not brothers or sisters or in-laws), (2) a proportionate share of any stock owned by any estate, trust or partnership in which he has a beneficial interest, (3) a proportionate share of any stock owned by any corporation in which he owns either actually or constructively (under these constructive ownership rules) 50 percent or more in value of the outstanding stock, and (4) stock which he has an option to acquire.

If Mr. X receives solely cash and owns no T stock constructively after the merger, that is, if no person the ownership of whose stock would be attributed to Mr. X receives P stock in the merger, the cash received will

---

[43]*See, e.g., Raybestos-Manhattan, Inc. v. U.S.,* 296 U.S. 60 (1935), and *Texas Canadian Oil Corporation Ltd. v. Commissioner,* 44 B.T.A. 913 (1941).

[44]Rev. Rul. 67-448, 1967-2 C.B. 144 and its progeny. (The merger of newly created subsidiary into T in which holders of T received stock of P treated as a direct stock acquisition by P).

be taxed as if Mr. X sold his stock. If he has held his stock for more than one year, the gain will be taxed at capital gain rates.

Even if a T stockholder is considered to own stock constructively, he will enjoy sale or exchange treatment if he meets the substantially disproportionate redemption test described in ¶3.2 with respect to stockholders who receive cash and stock, but here both actual *and constructive* ownership is taken into account.

> *Example 6.* T has 1,000,000 shares outstanding. P acquires 450,000 T shares for cash and 550,000 T shares for P stock. Mr. X owns 5,000 shares and receives cash for all of them. His grandmother owns 10,000 shares, she exchanges 7,000 shares for cash and 3,000 shares for P stock. His son owns 8,000 shares, he receives P stock for all his shares.
>
> Mr. X's ownership before the exchange (actual plus constructive):

Mr. X's shares	5,000
His grandmother	10,000
His son	8,000
	23,000

Total outstanding before the exchange	1,000,000
Mr. X percent ownership (actual and constructive)	2.3%

Mr. X's ownership after the exchange

His grandmother	3,000
His son	8,000
	11,000

Total outstanding after the exchange (i.e. total T shares acquired for P stock)	550,000
Mr. X % ownership (constructive only)	2.0%

Thus, in this example, Mr. X fails to pass the substantially disproportionate test because his interest in T after the exchange is only 13.04 percent less than his interest before the merger. (He would pass the test if, after the exchange, he constructively owned less than 10,120 shares.) Note that, had Mr. X received one share of P stock in the reorganization, he would have enjoyed capital gain treatment because the cash received would be "additional consideration" under Section 356 and the IRS has indicated that attribution rules do not apply to that section.[45] Thus, in certain cases, a shareholder may insure capital gain treatment by exchanging a minimum number of shares for stock.[46]

Once again, as a practical matter, one can only wonder if minority shareholders have any idea whether their parents, grandparents, children or grandchildren own any stock of T, and probably report cash received as proceeds of a sale of exchange whether or not under IRS principles it should be reported as a dividend. Furthermore, at least one respected commentator has suggested that it is very unlikely a court would uphold dividend treatment in a case where the receipt of one share of P stock by the same stockholder would have insured capital gain treatment.[47]

If Mr. X's proceeds are treated as a dividend taxable at ordinary rates, then the family members whose ownership of T stock resulted in the adverse treatment to Mr. X should be able to increase the basis of their P shares by an amount equal to Mr. X's basis in his T shares (reduced by any proceeds received not treated as a dividend). Thus, in the above example, assuming all the cash received by Mr. X were treated as a dividend, Mr. X's grandmother and son's basis in their P shares (which after the exchange would initially equal the basis of their T shares surrendered reduced by cash received and increased by any gain recognized) should be increased proportionately by Mr. X's basis in his T shares before the exchange.[48]

Dividend treatment may be avoided, even if Mr. X fails to pass the substantially disproportionate test through waiver of the family attribution rules. If Mr. X signs an agreement which recites that he has not acquired, other than by bequest or inheritance, any interest (other than any interest as a creditor) in P since the exchange and that he agrees to notify the district director for the internal revenue district where he resides of any such acquisition (other than by bequest or inheritance) within 30 days after the acquisition (if the acquisition occurs within 10 years from the date of the exchange) the family attribution rules will not apply.[49] The agreement must be filed in duplicate as a separate

---

[45]The IRS position could be considered generous. Although the statute does not make Section 318 expressly applicable to section 356, the IRS could have taken the position that since in determining dividend equivalency under section 356 it looks to the principles under Section 302 (concerning redemptions) in so looking it would incorporate the principles of attribution that apply to such section.

[46]This might be accomplished by Mr. X buying a small number of shares from the family member electing shares and having such member elect P shares (as the nominee for Mr. X) for such T shares.

[47]Martin P. Ginsberg, outline entitled "Cash-option Mergers and Other Current Corporate Acquisition Techniques: Tax Aspects," 1979.

[48]Cf. Treas. Reg. §1.302-2(c).

[49]Treas. Reg. § 1.302-3(a) (1).

statement attached to the first return filed by the shareholder after the exchange.[50]

In short, a shareholder can avoid dividend treatment even where he fails to meet the substantially disproportionate test because of the family attribution rules if he agrees, in essence, not to purchase any P stock for 10 years.

Finally, Mr. X can rely on the more ambiguous, factually specific test, i.e., that the redemption is "not essentially equivalent to a dividend" as discussed above in ¶3.2.2.2. Here again, however, constructive ownership of P stock after the exchange will be taken into account.

3.3.4. *T Shareholders Who Realize Loss in the Merger.* If a T shareholder receives solely cash for his T stock and that shareholder realizes a loss on the exchange, the entire amount of such loss will be recognized. However, if cash is received for less than his entire interest in the T stock actually owned by a T shareholder, with the balance of such stock being exchanged for P stock, then any loss realized by the stockholder on the exchange will not be recognized. For the purpose of determining whether realized losses will be recognized by a T shareholder on the exchange, only actual and not constructive ownership is taken into account.

3.4 T Security Holder or Shareholder Receiving P Securities.

A T shareholder who exchanges his T debt securities[51] for (i) P stock, and/or for (ii) P debt securities of the *same or lower* principal amount, will recognize no gain or loss and will be governed generally by the rules discussed in ¶3.1.[52]

Gain will be recognized in two circumstances where P debt securities are received by a T shareholder or security holder.

First, if a T shareholder receives P securities for his T stock, the fair market value of the securities is simply treated as if cash were received. Gain or loss will be recognized in accordance with the rules discussed in ¶3.2 if P stock is also received and in accordance with

the rules discussed in ¶3.3 if no P stock is received by such stockholder.

> *Example 7.* Mr. X owns 1,000 shares of T stock with a fair market value of $1,600. He receives 500 shares of P stock worth $1,200 and securities of P worth $400. The $400 of securities received is treated as cash received. He is taxed under the rules described in ¶3.2 above.

> *Example 8.* Mr. X owns T stock worth $1,600. He receives securities of P worth $1,600. The $1,600 of securities received is treated as cash received. He is taxed under the rules described in ¶3.3.

Second, if a T shareholder exchanges securities with a principal amount of $80 and receives securities with a principal amount of $100, the fair market value of the $20 excess in principal amount is treated as cash received.

> *Example 9.* Mr. X owns T securities with a principal amount of $1,000 and an adjusted basis of $1,000. He receives from P a security with a principal amount of $1,500 which trades at 1,300. The fair market value of the excess principal amount (i.e. 1300/1500 × 300 = 260) is treated as cash received. He is taxed under the rules described in ¶3.2 above.

3.5 T Shareholder Receiving P Preferred Stock.

3.5.1. *Some Advantages.* The use of preferred stock by P is very popular in acquisitive reorganizations. First, preferred stock can be received tax-free by T shareholders in the same manner as common stock. Second, the preferred stock may be a more attractive instrument to T's shareholders because of provisions designed to maintain its value in the market place, such as a dividend preference, liquidation preference and an obligation by P to redeem stated percentages of the preferred at stated times. Typically, P will issue the preferred at a par value (e.g., $100) where the dividend preference is stated as a percentage (e.g., 9 percent) or as a dollar amount (e.g. $9.00) per share. The preferred will generally have a liquidation preference

---

[50]This agreement avoids the application of the family attribution rules and thus the shareholder will meet the complete termination test of Section 302 (b) (2). However, this special provision does not apply to an exchange if within 10 years prior to the exchange (i) the shareholder acquired the exchanged T stock from a person whose ownership of such stock would be attributed to him (at the time of the redemption), or (ii) if any such other person acquired stock from the exchanging shareholder (and such stock was not exchanged for cash in the same merger), unless the shareholder can show that such transaction did not have as one of its principal purposes the avoidance of Federal income taxes. Section 302(c) (2).

[51]There is always the issue whether a particular debt instrument is of sufficient dignity to qualify as a "security" as distinguished from "other property," the latter always being treated like cash. This classification problem appears throughout the tax laws and there is much case law on this issue. Suffice it to state that the longer the term of the instrument and the better the security, the more likely the debt instrument will enjoy the status of being treated as a "security"

[52]The aggregate basis of the various instruments received will be equal to the aggregate basis of the T stock or securities surrendered. The basis among the various P instruments received is allocated under rules contained in the treasury regulations. Treas. Reg. 1.358-2.

equal to or greater than its par value and may be subject to mandatory redemption by P after a stated period (e.g. 5 years) at a stated price (e.g. 100 percent to 110 percent of its par value).

Furthermore, to make the preferred even more attractive to T shareholders, its terms could permit conversion into common stock of P. Thus, a T shareholder could enjoy "upside benefits" at the same time as his "downside" risks are less than those of P's common stockholders.

Preferred stock may have additional advantages from P's perspective beyond offering T shareholders an attractive instrument. The P preferred stock may be issued with limited or no voting rights. Thus, P can acquire T by using stock and yet not increase (or appreciably increase) the amount of its voting stock held by the public. (Note, however, as explained in ¶2.2 and ¶2.3 above, nonvoting stock may not be used in a B or a C reorganization.) Furthermore, P may favor preferred stock where the acquisition of T common stock for P common stock would adversely affect P's earnings per common share for reporting purposes (a circumstance which may influence the price of P stock in the market place).

3.5.2 Tax Treatment. The tax treatment of preferred stock to a T shareholder is the same as the treatment discussed above with respect to the receipt of solely common stock (¶3.1) or a mix of stock and cash (¶3.3) in connection with the nonrecognition or partial recognition of gain and the treatment of such gain as a dividend or as gain from the sale or exchange of stock. Preferred stock, however, does add a few tax complexities of its own:

3.5.3 Section 306 Stock

3.5.3.1 *Defined*. Section 306 of the Code is designed to prevent a stockholder from receiving a nontaxable stock dividend and thereafter selling it under a plan, the purpose of which is to avoid the reporting of dividend income. Thus, Section 306 stock includes stock (other than common stock) received as a stock dividend.

Example 10. T has only one class of stock with 1,000 shares outstanding. Rather than declare a $10 dividend per share, T issues to each shareholder as a nontaxable stock dividend one share of $10 par preferred stock which may be sold or redeemed for $10 by a shareholder. The preferred stock received is Section 306 stock. A sale of the preferred stock will afford a T shareholder cash, at the same time he continues to participate in the ownership of the business by reason of his ownership of common stock.

Section 306 stock also includes stock (other than common stock) received in a tax-free reorganization, if the effect of the transaction is substantially the same as the receipt of a stock dividend.

Example 11. Corporation T (in Example 10) is merged into S, a subsidiary of P, in a tax-free statutory merger. Each shareholder of T receives one share of S common and one share of $10 par S preferred stock for his T common stock.

The S preferred stock received is Section 306 stock.[53]

3.5.3.2. *Tax Treatment*. The tax treatment of the disposition of Section 306 stock depends upon whether it is redeemed or sold.

If Section 306 stock is redeemed, the entire amount realized is treated as a distribution under Section 301, i.e., it will be taxed at the time of redemption first as a dividend (up to the shareholder's proportionate share of earnings and profits, if any) next as a return of capital (up to his basis) and then as capital gain (in excess of his basis).[54]

If the stock is sold, the amount realized is treated as ordinary income up to that amount that would have been a dividend *at the time of the distribution* (or exchange), if, instead of the stock, the corporation had distributed cash in an amount equal to the fair market value of the stock.[55] If the amount realized exceeds the amount treated as a dividend, the remainder is capital gain to the extent that it exceeds the adjusted basis of the stock.[56] Thus, if in Example 11, (i) the fair market

---

[53]Because the underlying purpose of Section 306 is to prevent dividend avoidance, if no part of a distribution to a stockholder of money in lieu of stock by the distributing corporation would have been a dividend, the stock distributed does not constitute Section 306 stock. Treas. Reg. §1.306-3(d). Section 306 stock also includes any stock (other than common) received for Section 306 stock by a stockholder where the stock received has a transferred or substituted basis, determined by reference to the basis of Section 306 in the hands of any person. Section 306 (c) (1) (C).

[54]Section 306 (a) (2). *See* Section 301 for treatment of amount distributed with respect to stock.

[55]Section 306 (a) (1) (A).

[56]Section 306 (a) (1) (B). Where Section 306 stock is received as a dividend, the basis of the stock with respect to which the distribution was made (e.g., the T common stock in the above example) is allocated between the old common and the new preferred stock in proportion to the fair market value of each on the date of distribution, Treas. Reg. §1.307-2. Where the Section 306 stock is received in a reorganization, its basis will be equal to the basis of the stock surrendered in exchange therefor.

value of preferred at the time of distribution was $10, (ii) the entire amount of a cash distribution of $10 would have been taxable as a dividend and (iii) the preferred stock would have been allocated $2 of basis, then a subsequent sale of a share of preferred for $15 would result in $10 being treated as ordinary income and $3 ($15 minus $10 plus $2) being treated as gain from the sale of stock.[57]

In no event is any loss allowed on sale or other disposition of Section 306 stock.[58]

3.5.3.3 *Exceptions.* The above rules as to the tax treatment of the amount realized on a disposition of Section 306 stock are subject to several important exceptions. Such treatment does not apply to any of the following dispositions:

(1) A complete redemption (within the meaning of Section 302 (b) (3)) of *all* of the stock (Section 306 and other stock) of the corporation held by the shareholder or a redemption in a partial or complete liquidation of the corporation. Thus, if in Example 11, a T shareholder had both his common and preferred redeemed by T and after such redemption he owns no stock of T either actively or constructively, Section 306 treatment would not apply.

(2) A sale of all of the stock (Section 306 stock and other stock) held in the corporation by the shareholder, where the sale is not to a related person under the constructive ownership rules, and such sale terminates his entire stock interest in the corporation (including stock constructively owned).

(3) If the stockholder can demonstrate to the IRS that (i) the distribution of the Section 306 stock, and its disposition or redemption, or (ii) in the case of a prior or simultaneous disposition of the stock with respect to which the Section 306 stock disposed of was issued, that the disposition of the Section 306 stock was, in each case, not in pursuance of a plan having as one of its principal purposes the avoidance of federal income tax.

Thus, if in Example 11, a shareholder of T first sold *his voting common stock* and then sold his Section 306 stock, the subsequent disposition of his Section 306 stock would not ordinarily be considered a tax avoid-

ance dispositon because the shareholder had previously parted with the stock which allows him to participate in the ownership of the business. (The "conditions" under which the IRS will issue advance rulings (i) in connection with this exception, or, (ii) that the stock received is simply not Section 306 stock are considered below.

(4) A nontaxable dispositon of Section 306 stock pursuant to a reorganization or other exchange where gain or loss is not recognized to the exchanging shareholder.[59]

3.5.3.4. Advance Rulings. The nonapplicability of the foregoing rules (concerning the tax treatment of Section 306 stock) can often be the subject of an advance ruling from the URS. Such a ruling makes life simpler to a T shareholder and to counsel for P and T because there is no need to disclose and explain these rather complex rules that in the particular merger may have no application. Thus, if T shareholders will receive preferred stock from P in the reorganization, an advance ruling is generally secured with respect to Section 306 treatment.

3.5.3.4.1 *Not "Section 306" Stock Rulings.*
Nonconvertible Preferred Stock. The IRS will usually rule that the preferred stock received by T shareholders (which is not convertible into common) is not "Section 306 stock" if the shareholders receive no common stock of P. Where T shareholders receive only preferred stock and no common, the transaction is not substantially the same as the receipt of a stock dividend (compare Example 11 above) and, thus, the stock received is not Section 306 stock.[60]

Convertible Preferred Stock. The IRS will usually issue a ruling that convertible preferred stock received by T shareholders is not Section 306 stock if (i) the T stockholders receive no common stock from P, (ii) the T shareholders, after the reorganization will own in the aggregate less than one percent of the common stock of P[61], (iii) the convertible preferred stock will be widely held[62] or it is represented that there will not be any conversion of the convertible preferred pursuant to a concerted plan which will result in both preferred and

---

[57]If the stock is sold for $10 (or less), what happens to the $2 of basis allocated to the preferred stock? This is popularly referred to by tax practitioners as the "disappearing basis" issue on which there is no useful authority.

[58]Section 306 (a) (1)(C).

[59]Treas. Reg. §1.306-2 (b) (2).

[60]Section 306 (c) (1) (B).

[61]The IRS will generally accept a representation to the effect that "the managements of P and T have no knowledge of any stockholders who will own, after the reorganization, in the aggregate one percent or more of the common stock of P."

[62]Where P preferred stock is traded on a national securities exchange, the widely-held standard should be easily met.

common stock being held by an exchanging stockholder.[63]

3.5.3.4.2 *Exception Rulings*. Even where the IRS will not issue a "clean" Section 306 ruling, i.e., that the preferred stock received by T shareholders will not constitute Section 306 stock, an alternative ruling (which, in essence, avoids Section 306 treatment, notwithstanding that the preferred stock issued may be Section 306 stock) may be received. The IRS will usually rule that the distribution of the preferred stock, and its disposition or redemption is not pursuant to a plan of tax avoidance if (i) P's stock is widely held, (ii) the P preferred stock is not redeemable for at least five years from the date of issuance, and (iii) P represents that it will not redeem, by tender or otherwise, the P preferred stock issued in the merger, within the five-year period.[64] The effect of such ruling is that the adverse tax treatment of Section 306 stock is avoided.

If the P stock is redeemable within five years from the date of issue, or if the P stock is not redeemable for five years, but P will not represent that there will be no tender within the five-year period, then the IRS will issue a ruling that a subsequent *sale* of the P preferred stock by a T shareholder (other than in anticipation of a redemption) will avoid Section 306 treatment.[65] However, it will not issue a ruling with respect to any redemption in such case. Thus, a subsequent redemption of such stock might result in ordinary income treatment if the stockholder fails to meet the complete termination test of Section 302 (b)(3), notwithstanding that he meets the substantial diminution test of Section 302(b)(2). To avoid this possible adverse tax treatment and the concomitant disclosure, P will generally structure the terms of its preferred to fall within the IRS advance ruling guidelines.

3.5.4. *Section 305 Problems*.

3.5.4.1. *General*. Section 305 is a very complex section which defines which distributions of stock (or of rights to acquire stock) are tax-free and which are taxable. Fortunately, Section 305 will generally not pose a problem in an acquisitive reorganization (except with respect to the unreasonable redemption premium issue, discussed below), because such a transaction will generally not have the effect of a taxable stock dividend.[66]

Where T shareholders exchange common stock for convertible preferred stock, there may be a Section 305 problem, but the IRS will generally rule that Section 305 does not apply to such exchange if the managements of P and T make the following representation:

> The managements of P and T have no knowledge of any concerted plan of conversion which will have the effect of the receipt of property by some stockholders and an increase of the proportionate interest of other shareholders in the assets or earnings of P.

3.5.4.2. *Redemption Premium*. Where P issues preferred stock which may be redeemed after a specified period of time at a premium higher than a "reasonable redemption premium", the difference is treated as a taxable distribution (of additional stock on preferred stock) which is constructively received by the shareholder pro rata over the period during which the stock cannot be called for redemption.

> *Example 12*. P issued its $100 par preferred stock to Mr. X for his T common stock worth $100. The P preferred stock is not redeemable for 5 years. Thereafter, it is redeemable at $150. Assuming that a reasonable redemption premium is $10, the $40 unreasonable redemption premium is taxable as an $8 stock dividend constructively received by Mr. X over the five-year period during which the stock is not redeemable.

The treasury regulations provide a safe-haven test that a redemption premium will be considered reasonable if (i) it is not in excess of 10 percent of the "issue price" and (ii) the stock is not redeemable by its terms for five years.[67] The treasury regulations provide also that a redemption premium not falling within the safe-haven test may still be considered as a reasonable redemption premium if it can be demonstrated that such premium does not exceed the amount that would be required to pay for the right to make such premature redemption in light of market conditions existing at the time of issuance of the preferred.[68]

---

[63]Rev. Proc. 77-37, 1977-2 C.B. 568, sec. 4. The IRS will generally accept a representation to the effect that "the managements of P and T have no knowledge of any stockholders who will convert P preferred into P common pursuant to a concerted plan whereby a T shareholder holds both P preferred and P common after the reorganization."

[64]Rev. Proc 77-37, *supra*, Sec. 5.01.

[65]*Id*. Sec. 5.02.

[66]Taxable stock dividends include stock dividends (i) where the stockholder can elect to receive stock or cash, (ii) where some stockholders receive property and others receive stock, (iii) where some stockholders receive preferred stock and others receive common stock, (iv) on preferred stock, (v) of convertible preferred stock (unless it established to the IRS that such distribution will not have the result described in (iii) above). Section 305 (b). Furthermore, transactions not involving in form the distribution of a stock dividend will be treated as such if the transaction has a similar effect on any shareholder. Section 305 (c).

[67]Treas. Reg. §1.305-5 (b) (2).

[68]*Id*.

Fortunately, for purposes of determining whether the redemption premium is reasonable, the IRS has taken the position that the "issue price" of preferred stock in a merger for shares of T is the greater of the market value of the T shares surrendered in the exchange on either the date the merger is approved by T's shareholders or on the date of the exchange, rather than the fair market value of the preferred stock issued in exchange therefor.[69]

Example 13. Each T shareholder exchanges his T stock for a share of $100 P preferred stock which is not redeemable for 5 years. The P shares are redeemable, thereafter, at $108.80 per share. On the date the merger was approved and on the date of the exchange, the T stock traded at $98 per share. Thus, the issue price for each P share is $98 and a reasonable redemption premium is $9.80 (i.e., the P preferred could be redeemable at $107.80).Thus, the redemption premium exceeds a reasonable redemption premium by $1. Unless a T shareholder can show that the redemption premium is otherwise reasonable, he will be required to include 20 cents per share each of the five years during which the stock is not redeemable (assuming sufficient earnings and profits at all relevant times). His basis in the P shares will increase in the amount that is includable as a dividend.

As a practical matter, P and T will avoid any constructive dividends to T shareholders by having the stock not redeemable for at least five years after the exchange (which may be the case generally, in any event, because of the Section 306 ruling discussed above) and creating a redemption premium that will almost certainly fall within the 10 percent safe-haven test. The IRS has issued private letter rulings to the effect that no part of a redemption premium will be considered as a distribution of additional stock under Treas. Reg. § 1.305-5 (b), if the stock is not redeemable for five years and the redemption premium is not in excess of 110 percent of the fair market value of the T stock on the date the merger is approved. Furthermore, where a "clean" Section 306 ruling can be secured (as discussed above in ¶3.5.3.4.1) unreasonable redemption treatment may be avoided by having the stock redeemable immediately.

3.5.5. *Conversion Privilege.* The subsequent surrender by the former stockholders of T of their P preferred stock pursuant to a conversion feature contained in the terms of the preferred should constitute a recapitalization and, therefore, a reorganization under the provisions of Section 368 (a)(1)(E). No gain or loss should be recognized on such exchange and the P common stock will have the same basis as the P preferred stock surrendered. The IRS has issued rulings to this effect.

3.5.5.1. *Sinking Fund.* Occasionally, the P preferred stock will be subject to a sinking fund which is an obligation on P's part to redeem a stated portion of the P stock at stated intervals. Such fund generally maintains the value of the P preferred since its fair market value will reflect the probability that it will be redeemed at the stated price.

The tax treatment accorded a sinking fund purchase is simply that of a redemption subject to all the principles and limitations on capital gain treatment discussed above in ¶3.3. P could consider building in protections, where possible, to avoid dividend treatment to a former T shareholder whose stock is called pursuant to the sinking fund or other mandatory redemption provisions.

A sample disclosure to T shareholders in connection with a sinking fund is as follows:[70]

> The tax treatment to be accorded to any sinking fund or other redemption by P (as distinguished from a sale or other disposition) of the P preferred stock to be issued in the merger can only be determined on the basis of particular facts as to each shareholder at the time of the redemption. For this reason, a ruling by the IRS of general applicability to such matters has not been requested. Under the Code, if shares of P preferred stock are held as capital assets, a holder of such shares would recognize capital gain or loss on redemption if (a) as a result of such redemption, his stock interest is completely terminated, (b) his percentage ownership of the voting shares of P immediately after the redemption is less than 80 percent of such percentage ownership immediately before the redemption or (c) the redemption is not essentially equivalent to a dividend. (In determining whether any of these con-

---

[69]Initially, tax practitioners were concerned that if principles similar to those that apply where debt is issued at a discount applied to section 305 in a case where the P preferred stock would be publicly traded, there would be no way of knowing whether a redemption premium was reasonable, because the "issue price" would be the price at which the preferred stock traded after the merger. *See* Treas. Reg. 1.1232-3 (b)(2)(iii)(c). However, the IRS has refused to determine the "issue price" as the fair market value of T stock on the date the managements of P and T reach agreement or on the date the merger is announced to the public. As a result, intervening market events that depress the value of the T stock between the date of announcement and the date of approval by T shareholders or the date of the exchange may create an unreasonable redemption premium problem where, at the date managements of P and T reached agreement in principle, no such premium existed.

[70]Adapted from the disclosure contained in the Joint Proxy Statement for Special Meetings of Shareholders of Georgia Pacific Corporation and Hudson Pulp & Paper Corp.

ditions has been met with respect to any shareholder, there must be taken into account shares actually owned by him and any shares considered owned by him by reason of certain constructive ownership rules contained in Section 318(a) of the Code. However, under Section 302(c) of the Code, a former T shareholder may under certain circumstances be able to avoid being treated as constructively owning shares owned by his family members for purposes of determining whether his stock ownership has completely terminated.) If none of these conditions is satisfied, the total amount of cash received in redemption will be treated as a dividend to the extent of the shareholder's ratable share of P's current and accumulated earnings and profits. There is support for the conclusion, based upon current law, which may or may not be in effect at the time of a future redemption, that the receipt of cash by a former T shareholder, as a result of the redemption of his shares of P preferred stock acquired in the merger, will not be considered essentially equivalent to a dividend, and therefore will not be taxed as a dividend, provided that: (a) on the date of the redemption there is no proportional relationship between the ownership of the P common stock and P preferred stock; (b) the shareholder being redeemed exercises no control over the corporate affairs of P; and (c) the redemption results in a meaningful reduction of the shareholder's proportionate interest in P after application of the constructive ownership rules of Section 318(a) of the Code. The IRS has indicated that a small percentage reduction in proportionate interest will satisfy the "meaningful reduction" requirement in the case of a small minority shareholder in a publicly held corporation; thus, for example, it has ruled that a redemption of all of the shares actually owned by such a shareholder satisfied that requirement even though, after application of the constructive ownership rules, the shareholder's proportionate interest was reduced by only 3.3 percent of such interest. However, there can be no assurance that any particular redemption transaction will qualify as "not essentially equivalent to a dividend."

3.6 Shareholders Receiving Installment Notes

3.6.1 *Qualification.* In addition to common stock, cash, securities and preferred stock, P could offer a T

shareholder the election to receive an installment note. The installment note affords a T shareholder the advantage of reporting his gain as he receives payment over two or more years.[71]

To qualify for installment treatment, (i) the sales price must exceed $1,000, (ii) there are no payments in the year of the sale, or the payments do not exceed 30 percent of the selling price,[72] and (iii) there are two or more payments under the sales contract.[73] [*Caution:* At press time, the President had signed H.R. 6883, the Installment Sales Revision Act of 1980, which is pending before the Senate. The bill eliminates the requirements described in clauses (i), (ii) and (iii) above and makes other important changes that generally liberalize the reporting of gain on the installment method. The provisions of this bill should be scrutinized prior to issuing installment notes in connection with an acquisitive reorganization.]

Example 14. On July 1, 1976, Mr. X sold his T stock to P for $100,000, payable $25,000 on December 31, 1970 and $25,000 a year on each of the three succeeding December 31's with interest at 10 percent per annum. At the time of the sale, Mr. X's basis in his T stock is $30,000.

The payment received in the taxable year equals 25 percent of the selling price determined as follows:

$$\frac{\$25,000 \text{ (payment of Dec. 31, 1976)}}{\$100,000 \text{ (total selling price)}} = 25\%$$

The gross profit to be realized after P pays in full is 70 percent of the total selling price, computed as follows:

$$\frac{\$70,000 \text{ gross profit (i.e., } \$100,000}{\$100,000 \text{ total selling price}} = 70\%$$
selling price less 30,000 basis)

Thus, Mr. X will report 70 percent of each payment under the contract as capital gain from the sale as it is received. If Mr. X did not qualify for installment treatment (or does not elect to report the gain on the installment basis)[74] the entire $70,000 gain would be taxable in the year of sale. The interest portion will be taxable as interest.[75]

Where a T shareholder receives both an installment note and P stock (permitted to be received tax-free) he should be able to report the boot (i.e. the note) under the installment method. However, the value of the P

---

[71]Sales of stock qualify as an installment sale of personal property under Section 453. See Rev. Rul. 56-153, 1956-1 C.B. 166; *50 E. 75th Street Corp. v. Commissioner,* 35-2 USTA ¶9549 (2d Cir. 1935).

[72]Section 453(b).

[73]See Rev. Rul. 69-462, 1969-2 C.B. 107; *Baltimore Baseball Club, Inc.,* 73-2 USTA ¶9549 (Ct. Cl. 1973).

[74]The installment method is elected by T shareholder in his return by reporting the sale on such basis in Part II of Schedule A, Form 1040.

[75]So long as there is stated interest of at least 6 percent, no interest will be imputed under section 483.

stock received tax-free in the year of the exchange is taken into account in determining the selling price and the payments received in the year of sale for purposes of the 30 percent test.[76] Under H.R. 6883, P stock received tax-free will not be treated as payments. Thus, under the bill, gain will be recognized only as cash is received.

3.6.2. *Readily Tradable Exception.* Where P's notes or bonds are (i) payable on demand, (ii) have interest coupons attached, or (iii) are in any form designed to render such obligation tradable on a national securities exchange or over-the-counter market, then such note will be treated simply as a cash payment.[77]

Example 15. On July 1, 1976, Mr. X sold his T stock (with a fair market value of $300,000 and a basis of $150,000) to P in exchange for 100 of P's 10-year registered bonds (which P is taking the steps necessary to create a market for on a securities exchange), each with a principal amount and fair market value of $1,000 and a promissory note (which is not readily tradable) for $200,000 payable $20,000 per year for 10 years commencing on the July 1, 1976. (Both the bond and notes provide for 10 percent interest per year.)

Since the bonds to be marketed are treated as payments of cash, the payments in the year of sale equal 33⅓ percent of the selling price (i.e., $100,000 worth of marketable bonds divided by $300,000 total selling price), and Mr. X does not qualify for installment treatment. His entire gain is reported in the year of sale. Had P issued only 80 bonds (and increased the note to $220,000 commencing on the same date), the sale would qualify for installment treatment. Mr. X would report as gain in the year of sale 50 percent of the payments received in that year (i.e., the readily tradable bonds or $80,000).[78]

3.6.3. *Convertible Note Exceptions.* Even if P's bonds or notes are not readily tradable, if they contain a right whereby a T holder may convert into P stock or securities which would be readily tradable, then the face amount of such note or bond is also treated as a cash payment in the year received; unless it is convertible at a substantial discount. Under the treasury regulations, whether a substantial discount is considered to exist depends upon all the facts and circumstances. However, two safe-haven tests are provided. First, if

the conversion privilege may not be exercised within a period of 1 year from the date the note is issued, then the note is considered convertible at a substantial discount. Second, if at the time the convertible note is issued, the fair market value of the stock or securities into which the note is convertible is less than 80 percent of the fair market value of the note, the note will be considered convertible at a substantial discount.

Example 16. T shareholders sell their T notes to P for P notes, each with a principal amount and fair market value of $1,000. The P notes are not tradable on any exchange and P is not taking any steps to make them tradable. The P notes, however, are immediately convertible into 10 shares of P stock at $10 per share. P stock is traded on the New York Stock Exchange. At the time P issues the convertible notes, the fair market value of the P stock is $88 per share.

The notes will not be treated as readily tradable because they are convertible at a discount of greater than 80 percent (i.e., 78 percent) determined as follows:

Fair market value of stock into which note is convertible (10 shares @ $88 per share)	880
Less amount that note-holder must pay to convert (10 shares @ $10 per share)	100
	780

$$\frac{\$780 \text{ (value of conversion)}}{\$1,000 \text{ (fair market value of notes)}} = 78\%$$

To avoid problems of valuation, however, P will generally provide that the notes are not convertible for one year from the date of issue.

Note that the P notes (although not readily tradable) may nevertheless, depending upon their terms, qualify as securities of P. If so, the subsequent conversion should be treated as a tax-free recapitalization to converting stockholders.

3.6.4. *No Original Issue Discount.* Where a T shareholder receives the P note pursuant to a tax-free reorganization (whether or not the transaction is taxable in part or in full to him as an individual shareholder), *no* original issue discount is created. Thus, original issue discount is present only where P acquires the T shares where the overall transaction is taxable.[79]

---

[76]*Cf.* Rev. Rul. 65-155, 1965-1 C.B. 356.

[77]Treas. Reg. §1.453-3.

[78]*See* ¶3.4

[79]Treas. Reg. §1232-3(d).

4. TAX-FREE TREATMENT TO THE MINORITY WHERE THE MAJORITY RECEIVES CASH

T may have a minority of shareholders (for example, less than 40 percent) (typically insiders with a very low basis in their shares) who desire a tax-free exchange, perhaps because such shareholders wish to afford their legatees a step-up in basis that will result upon their death. Where a stockholder holds appreciated stock until death, the gain inherent in such stock escapes free from income tax because his beneficiaries get a basis equal to the stock's fair market value at the time of death or at the applicable alternate valuation date.[80]

Although a tax-free reorganization would not be possible in such a case because the statutory, judicial or administrative rules concerning the minimum amount of P stock that must be used could not be met, see ¶2 above, there are alternatives available to provide tax-free treatment to the minority shareholders.

4.1 Recapitalization.

First, the common stockholders desiring to avoid recognition of gain could receive in exchange for their T common stock, a new preferred stock of T. Such exchange would be tax-free to exchanging stockholders since it constitutes a recapitalization of T.[81] Such stock could be redeemable at some future date, but (if so desired by a T stockholder) not before his death. (In a related context, the IRS has issued a favorable ruling where the redemption date was geared in part to the stockholder's death, see ¶4.2 below). P could purchase the remaining T common shares for cash or could merge a shell subsidiary into T where the remaining T shares are converted into cash.

In Rev. Rul. 77-479,[82] the IRS confirmed several cases which concluded that continuity of interest is not required for a recapitalization to qualify as a reorganization described in 368(a)(1)(E). Thus, the recapitalization will be tax-free, notwithstanding that a substantial portion of the stock held by stockholders not exchanging in the recapitalization is immediately thereafter sold (or even that the stock received by stockholders in the recapitalization is sold).

Where the fair market value of T's assets exceeds their basis, however, this approach will not afford P a step-up in basis to reflect the price paid for the stock, because a subsequent liquidation of T would result in a distribution to the preferred stockholders and thereby defeat their tax-free treatment.

4.2 Section 351 Exchange

A second approach is illustrated by the Unilever U.S. acquisition of National Starch and Chemical Company ("NS"). The form of acquisition was designed to allow a tax-free exchange to the holders of 15-20% of the NS stock, with the remaining stock being bought for cash.

1. Each NS shareholder was offered the choice of $73.50 or one share of the preferred stock described below for each of his shares of NS common. Based on the number of NS shares outstanding, the total cost to Unilever would be $484,000,000 in cash either currently or in the future when the preferred stock would be redeemed.

2. Those shareholders electing preferred stock received their preferred as part of a single Section 351 incorporation of a new corporation ("Holding").[83] Pursuant to the Section 351 exchange, the NS shareholders electing preferred received preferred stock of Holding in exchange for their NS common and Unilever received all of the common stock of Holding in exchange for $484,000,000 cash. At this point, assuming 15 percent of NS shareholders elected preferred stock, Holding owned 15 percent of the stock of NS and former stockholders of NS owned preferred stock of Holding.

3. Those NS shareholders who elected cash received their cash as follows. A shell subsidiary of Holding was merged into NS in a cash merger; all the shares of NS (other than those owned by Holding) were redeemed for cash. This cash was available from the $484,000,000 originally transferred to Holding. The result is that after the merger Holding owns (i) 100 percent of the stock of NS and (ii) exactly enough cash to ultimately redeem the new outstanding preferred of Holding. Unilever holds 100 percent of the common stock of Holding, with the 15 percent former NS shareholders holding the preferred stock of Holding with no vote.

---

[80]Section 1014.

[81]Section 368(a)(1)(E). Section 354.

[82]1977-2, C.B. 119.

[83]Section 351 provides that no gain or loss is recognized if property (which includes stock or cash) is transferred to a corporation by one or more persons solely in exchange for stock or securities in such corporation, and immediately after the exchange such persons are in "control" of the transferee corporation (i.e. own at least 80 percent of the then outstanding voting stock and at least 80 percent of the total number of shares of all other classes of the then outstanding stock of such corporation).

In some respects, the Unilever transaction goes further than the recapitalization followed by a purchase of the remaining T stock by P. In the latter case, the new preferred stockholders continue to have an interest in the target itself. In the Unilever transaction, the shareholders electing preferred have no gain on the exchange even though they now have stock in a totally new holding company which basically holds cash for an inevitable redemption. Presumably, the IRS blessed the Unilever transaction on the notion that its result could have been achieved within the framework of Rev. Rul. 77-479, if, following a recapitalization and a stock sale, T dropped its operating assets into a new operating subsidiary, and retained only cash to redeem its preferred stockholders.

To secure the ruling, Unilever represented that it had no plan to liquidate NS during the two-year period following the acquisition of more than 80 percent of the NS stock. (Such a liquidation would presumably enable Unilever to step up the basis of its assets to the extent it paid cash to NS shareholders electing cash.) However, Unilever represented to the IRS that it would not liquidate NS unless it received a ruling from the IRS to the effect that such liquidation would not affect the rulings requested in the exchange offer. Thus, it remains an open issue whether one could achieve the favorable (but doubtful) result of offering some shareholders of T tax-free treatment and at the same time have P get a step-up in basis to the extent it paid cash. [*Caution:* At press time, the IRS issued Rev. Rul. 80-284 in which the IRS reversed its position with respect to transactions similar to the NS transaction. Rev. Rul. 80-284 must be carefully considered prior to employing the NS approach.]

Finally, an interesting aspect of the Unilever-NS transaction is the nature of the preferred stock issue on the Section 351 exchange.

The Holding preferred stock issued has a liquidation preference of $73.50 and dividend preference at the rate of $3.31 per annum. Such stock is nonvoting, except upon certain defaults. The preferred stock contains covenants precluding Holding, in essence, from doing anything to jeopardize the cash it holds to be used to redeem the preferred shares. The preferred stock is subject to mandatory and optional redemption. If the owner is an individual (or is to be held under other arrangements which may result in the stock being included in the gross estate of any individual for Federal income tax purposes), the individual in whose estate the stock may be included may be designated as a "measuring life" for purposes of the redemption provisions. In that case (the IRS private letter provides) the stock *will be redeemed* at the latest of (i) the fifth anniversary of the date of issue, (ii) 180 days after the date of death of the individual who is designated as a measuring life, or (iii) 30 days after notice to Holding of the death of the individual who is designated as the measuring life. The terms of preferred also preclude Holding from any optional redemption prior to the death of any individual who is designated as a measuring life.

Thus, the preferred stock enables a holder, in essence, to ultimately receive cash for his NS shares, but to postpone the realization event until after his death, thus affording his estate the benefit of the step-up in basis. This ingenious approach bears one main caution: one must be very careful not to have the "preferred" stock instrument treated as debt for tax purposes (a risk that appears whenever a stock instrument is certain to be redeemed), since a note received in connection with the sale of stock will not, among other adverse tax consequences, enjoy a step-up in basis at death.[84]

---

[84] Section 1014(c); section 691(a)(2).

JAMES STEVRALIA

JAMES STEVRALIA is currently employed in New York in the law firm of Squadron, Ellenoff, Plesent & Lehrer. Previously, he was employed with major accounting firms as a specialist in valuation of assets acquired in taxable transactions.

Mr. Stevralia has a Bachelor of Engineering degree from Villanova University, a J.D. from the Fordham University School of Law, and an L.L.M. in Taxation from the New York University School of Law.

24

Taxable Sales and Liquidations

JAMES STEVRALIA

INTRODUCTION

When two individuals[1] begin discussions concerning the purchase and sale of a business, their foremost objective is to reach a meeting of the minds over the purchase price. The seller most likely has determined what he feels is the true value of his business and accordingly the amount which he desires and expects to receive. The purchaser also has arrived at what, to his mind, is a fair price for the business, perhaps limited to some extent by the financial resources he has available. In most instances a deal will be made at an actual selling price somewhere between the bid and asked prices.

Let us look at the dealings of Victor and George. Victor has interests in the processing of uranium as a fuel for atomic power plants. Fearing a surplus of petroleum products and its impact on his company's revenue, he decides to diversify. George, on the other hand, has grown tired of running his thriving, profitable "Big Car" dealership and wants to devote more time to recreational pursuits. He has determined that his business is worth $1.5 million and offers it to Victor. In addition, George, not wanting to get involved in managing a business, insists that the payment be made in anything except stock or securities in a corporation. Victor feels the price is a bit high and having lost a major utility customer as a result of a melt-down, cannot afford to pay that much anyway. He does, however, offer George $1 million, cash. After some discussions, Victor and George agree on a price of $1.25 million and they shake hands. It would seem that this is the end of the negotiations and all that is left to be done is for Victor to draw a check for $1.25 million and hand it to George in exchange for the keys.

What at first glance appears to be a simple,

straightforward, business transaction is, in good part because of the tax consequences, a sophisticated merger presenting many alternatives to the parties. The form of the acquisition will have a bearing on the character of the gain realized by the seller, the amount of the gain recognized in each year in the event installment payments are made, the tax bases of the assets being acquired and hence the future tax depreciation deductions, and whether or not the tax attributes existing at the time of transfer will remain with the company under its new ownership. Each of these results has an influence on the amount of money actually spent by the buyer and received by the seller.

The different methods for carrying out the acquisition will result in various combinations of benefits and disadvantages to each of the parties. There are several basic alternatives for the transaction.

1. Stockholder sells his stock to the purchaser.
2. Corporation sells its assets and does not liquidate.
3. Corporation adopts plan of complete liquidation, sells assets and completely liquidates within 12 months, distributing cash to shareholder.
4. Purchase of stock followed by a complete liquidation.

The word "liquidation," as used throughout this chapter, is to be given its tax definition. This is different from the meaning ordinarily associated with the term. A tax liquidation does not necessarily require the cessation of business together with a distress sale of the assets. Instead, it may be merely the dissolution of one corporate entity and a distribution of assets and liabilities to another corporation without an interruption of operations or change in ownership and management.

---

[1]For purposes of the following discussion, the word "individual" refers to any entity involved in acquiring or selling a business. It may be a person, partnership or corporation.

1. SALE OF STOCK

The cleanest, quickest and easiest method for transferring ownership in a corporation is the sale of its stock. The selling shareholder will be assured that the only gain realized by him is the capital gain resulting from the stock. He will not remain responsible for contingent liabilities, nor will he incur expenses of liquidation. The seller will also be relieved of any liability resulting from recapture of depreciation or investment tax credit.

The buyer, on the other hand, will have the option of liquidating the acquired corporation or continuing it. Hence he has the opportunity of determining, for himself, whether the basis of the assets can be stepped up and, if they can, whether he desires to do so.

Consequences to Seller

Ordinarily the difference between the amount realized by the seller and his basis in the stock will represent capital gain or loss to him. This gain or loss will be long-term if he has owned the stock for at least one year,[2] otherwise it is short-term. In some instances the gain or loss will not be capital. This is due to certain provisions of the Internal Revenue Code resulting from past actions by the seller. For instance, the sale of "Section 306 stock"[3] will result in ordinary income, as would the gain from the sale of stock in a "collapsible" corporation.[4] When the stock in a small business corporation (Section 1244 stock) is sold, any loss which may result is treated as an ordinary loss to the extent of $50,000 ($100,000 in the case of a husband and wife filing a joint return).[5]

As the seller will be paying taxes on the total amount of his gain (whether capital or ordinary), the resulting income tax may be substantial. This is especially so in a situation in which the seller has built the business through his own efforts and has a very low basis in the stock.

Deferral of Gain

Installment Payments.[5a] An alternative means of receiving payment which should be considered is in installment payments. If the amount of the installments conforms to the requirements as set forth in the Code, the seller will be able to defer his recognition and taxation until the payments are received and he has the cash to pay the tax. Care must be exercised in following the Code.[6] Section 453 requires that no more than 30 percent of the total consideration be received in the year of sale and that the remainder be paid in at least one other installment in a different taxable year. The amount being paid in installments must carry with it an interest charge for the right to defer payment. It is important to consider that, should the parties fail to specify payment of interest at a rate of at least 6 percent per annum simple interest, then it will be imputed at 7 percent.[7] This interest is treated as a business expense (ordinary deduction) to the buyer and as income to the seller. It is not a part of the purchase price of the stock, but is consideration for the time delay in making payment.

For example, let us assume George has an adjusted tax basis in the stock of his corporation of $250,000. Upon selling it to Victor for $1,250,000 he will realize $1,000,000 of long-term capital gain. If we assume this will be his sole income for the year 1979, his tax on this $1,000,000 of long-term capital gain will be $246,724.[8] Therefore George actually receives $1,003,276.

---

[2] I.R.C. Section 1222(3).

[3] "Section 306 stock" is defined in I.R.C. Section 306(c) as stock which was distributed to the selling shareholder and was not included in his gross income and which was not common stock distributed with respect to common stock already held by him. It is stock, other than common stock, which was received under a plan of reorganization under Section 368 or a distribution or exchange under Section 355 and with respect to which the Shareholder did not recognize any gain upon his receipt of such stock. Finally, it also includes stock received by the transfer of "Section 306 stock" with a carryover basis.

[4] I.R.C. Section 341 defines a "collapsible corporation" as a corporation used principally for the purpose of manufacturing, producing, constructing or acquiring property with a view to a sale or exchange of the stock of the corporation prior to the time the corporation realizes a substantial amount of taxable income from the property. The property held by the corporation includes inventory, property held for sale in the ordinary course of business, unrealized receivables or Section 1231(b) assets. This prevents capital gain on the sale of stock when the primary asset is not a capital asset.

[5] I.R.C. Section 1244.

[5a] A bill has been passed by the House and Senate modifying the installment rules. It will apply to all transactions occurring within a tax year ending after the date of enactment (including all transactions for calendar year taxpayers during 1980). Basically, the law eliminates the requirement for a 30% payment in initial year and the two-payment rule permits installment reporting of contingent sales, allows distribution of installment obligation in a Sec. 337 liquidation without recognition of gain by the receiving shareholder, and requires recognition of deferred gain where property sold to a related person (trust) on the installment basis is disposed of by such person.

[6] I.R.C. Section 453

[7] I.R.C. Section 483 and Regulations 1.483-1(c)(2)(ii)(B) and 1.483-1(d)(1)(ii)(B).

[8] This tax is computed as follows: Assuming 2 exemptions, no other income and 1979 rate tables:

Long-term Capital Gain	$1,000,000
§1202 Capital gain exclusion (60%)	600,000
Gross income	400,000
Exemption (2x$1,000)	2,000
Taxable income	398,000
Income tax	$ 246,724

In the event George and Victor agree to payment of the purchase price in installments, the resulting tax can be reduced. For example, suppose the payment in the year of sale is 30 percent of the total with the remainder in equal payments over the following five years.

The following chart illustrates the resulting payments and tax liability which George will incur:

Year	Payment	% of total payment	Gain[9]	Tax[10]	Net amount realized
1981	$ 375,000	30%	$ 300,000	$ 53,048	$ 321,952
1982	175,000	14%	140,000	16,738	158,252
1983	175,000	14%	140,000	16,738	158,252
1984	175,000	14%	140,000	16,738	158,252
1985	175,000	14%	140,000	16,738	158,252
1986	175,000	14%	140,000	16,738	158,252
Total	$1,250,000	100%	$1,000,000	$136,738	$1,113,262

By receiving installment payments, George reduces his overall tax liability and hence increases his net amount realized by $109,986.[11]

But there is one problem! The above example does not provide for interest payments by Victor on the amount of the price which is deferred. As such, the unstated interest provisions of Section 483 will come into play. Section 483 provides that when payment is to be made more than 6 months after the transaction, interest must be paid. The regulations stipulate that unless interest at a minimum annual rate of 6 percent simple interest is specified, an amount of 7 percent per annum, compounded semiannually, will be imputed.[11a] The effect of Section 483 on the installment payments in the example above is the following:

Year	Payment	Interest[12]	Principal	% of total Principal Payment	Gain
1981	$375,000	0	$375,000	35%	$294,065
1982	175,000	11,636	163,364	15%	126,028
1983	175,000	22,498	152,502	14%	117,626
1984	175,000	32,637	142,363	13%	109,224
1985	175,000	42,103	132,887	12%	100,823
1986	175,000	50,939	124,001	11%	92,421
Total	$1,250,000	$159,813	$1,090,187	100%	$840,187

A close look at the above transaction reveals another problem. By allocating a portion of each payment to interest, the total amount of principal is reduced, as well as the amount of each subsequent payment allocated to principal. However, the first payment, being all principal, is now more than 30 percent of the total amount to be paid. As a result the requirements for installment reporting are not satisfied, and all the gain is recognized in the year of the sale. To make matters worse, the seller will only receive the contract payment in this year and may end up owing more in taxes than he even receives.

In the event an individual desires to take advantage of the installment reporting of his gain, it is very important that the requirements be carefully followed and attention paid to the interaction with the remainder of the tax code, particularly the imputed interest of Section 483.

A further pitfall which can develop from installment payments is when the payments are contingent or uncertain. In this case, it is necessary to ascertain a fair market value of the total contingent payments primarily for the purpose of the 30 percent test. Should the IRS be able to prove a value different from what the seller determined it to be, the requirements for installment accounting again could fail.

Contingent Payment.[12a] If the contingency is such that it is not subject to valuation then, much to George's good fortune, the entire payment will be allocated to basis until it is fully recouped, after which gain will be realized.[13] However, the IRS will usually claim that a contingency is subject to valuation and the courts have, in most instances, agreed. The resulting effect of placing a value on a contingent payment is that such amount will influence the gain, usually capital, which the seller recognizes. Any payments which the seller receives in the future from the contingency in excess of its determined value will be ordinary income.

---

[9]I.R.C. Section 453(a) provides that when installment sale treatment is elected, the gain to be reported in each year is determined as follows:

Gain for year = Payment for year x $\frac{\text{Total Gain}}{\text{Total Payments}}$

[10]The tax payable in each year based on the 1979 tax rate schedules, assuming no other income and 2 exemptions is computed as follows:

	1979	1980 thru 1984
Long-term capital gain	$300,000	$140,000
§ 1202 capital gain exclusion (60%)	180,000	84,000
	120,000	56,000
Exemptions (2x$1000)	2,000	2,000
Taxable income	118,000	54,000
Tax (Schedule Y)	$ 53,048	$ 16,738

[11]This reduced tax liability should be considered in light of the present value of the opportunity cost resulting from deferring receipt of payment over the five year period.

[11a]Effective for contracts entered into on or after September 29, 1980, these rates have been increased to 9% and 10% respectively.

[12]Reg. 1.483-1(g)(2) provides a table to be used in computing the imputed interest of each payment. In this example Table V, column(b) was used.

[12a]See footnote 5a

[13]*Burnet v. Logan,* 283 U.S. 404 (1931).

Any amount below the value when the claim is finally settled will likewise be an ordinary loss.

When a contingent payment is included in an installment sale, the seller will have a choice of methods for deferring his gain. However, it is important to remember that the installment method of reporting must be elected at the time the return is filed. Once elected, the Code[14] specifically permits a revocation of the election. Unfortunately the reverse is not as easy. Failure to make the election at the time the return is filed will preclude reporting the transaction under the installment method[15]. This restriction could prove disastrous to a taxpayer who attempts to link his recognition of gain to his receipt of payments by reporting as an open transaction and it is subsequently declared to have an ascertainable value. At this time, the installment method is unavailable. If the taxpayer, on the other hand, elected the installment method and it was later determined that the contingency cannot be valued, the installment reporting should be disallowed. However, in such a situation the taxpayer can fall back on the open transaction method of reporting the contingent payments.

2. SALE OF ASSETS

In some cases it may be impossible or undesirable for the shareholders to sell stock. For example, the purchaser may have a stronger bargaining position than the seller and not want to expose itself to potential liabilities of the corporation.

On the other hand, George, the seller will prefer to dispose of the assets rather than stock when the assets are being sold at a loss. In this way, the loss can be used to offset his current taxes or carried back against prior year's taxes. It would be beneficial to allocate as much of the loss as possible to inventory and Section 1231 assets rather than the capital assets in order to maximize the ordinary loss. This would be undesirable to the buyer since the basis in the assets will now be less than it was to the selling corporation with the result that depreciation deductions will be reduced and gain on sale of inventory increased.

If the sale of assets would be at a gain, the treatment preferred by the seller would depend upon his plans after the sale. If the proceeds are to be kept in the corporation, George will desire to allocate as much as

possible to assets which will produce capital gains. He should attempt to lessen depreciation recapture and gain attributable to the inventory since these produce ordinary income, and try to maximize the value of capital and Section 1231 assets. If he intends to distribute the proceeds out of the corporation, then George may reduce the tax to the corporation by means of a twelve-month or Section 337[16] liquidation.

There are circumstances, however, when, even though the assets are sold at a gain and the proceeds are to be distributed, it may be desirable to have the corporation recognize gain and avoid Section 337. One such situation is where the gain determined from the shareholders' basis in their stock is substantially greater than that realized by the corporation with respect to the asset basis.

When the assets are sold it is necessary to allocate the proceeds among all the assets. The seller will desire as much as possible to be allocated to nondepreciable assets, i.e., goodwill, since this will produce capital gains and is not subject to recapture. The purchaser, on the other hand, will find this to be unfavorable since such an allocation will produce no amortization deductions. He also will desire a higher allocation to inventory, thereby lowering his ordinary income upon its sale. Often these tax benefits and detriments can be considered during the bargaining and reflected in the purchase price. When this happens, the parties should include their agreed-upon allocations in the purchase contract. Since the interests of each party are usually adverse, any allocation which they agree upon will be given significant weight in establishing the basis of the assets. As a matter of fact, the courts have upheld an allocation to a covenant not to compete absent "strong proof" showing the value to be different.[17] In another case the Third Circuit found an agreed-upon allocation to be binding unless fraud, undue influence, duress or mistake could be established.[18] In spite of the great weight which will be given to an allocation incorporated in the purchase agreement, there are certain situations where the element of adversity may be lacking, with the result that the allocation may successfully be challenged. Two primary examples are as follows. First, the seller may have sufficient net operating loss carryovers available to offset the effects of an allocation to ordinary income items and therefore will not object to an inflated allocation to inventory or depreci-

[14]I.R.C. Section 453(c)(4).

[15]Rev. Rul. 65-297, 1965-2 CB 152.

[16]I.R.C. Section 337 allows a corporation to sell the property without recognizing gain provided all the assets of the corporation are distributed within a twelve month period beginning upon adoption of a plan of complete liquidation. The sale must be within this 12 month period.

[17]*J. Leonard Schmitz*, 51 T.C. 306 (1968); *Harvey Radio Laboratories Inc. v. Commissioner*, 73-1 USTC ¶9121, 470 F.2d 118.

[18]*Commissioner v. Danielson*, 67-1 USTC ¶9423, 378 F.2d 771.

able assets. The second example occurs when there is a low allocation to inventory, thereby reducing ordinary income to the seller. When the purchaser acquires the inventory he can elect the last-in, first-out (LIFO) method of reporting. In so doing he revalues the inventory at a higher amount than that allocated in the contract on the FIFO basis. This reduces the buyer's ordinary income upon sale of the inventory in his course of business, while causing the seller to recognize a lesser amount of gain.

In these situations and others where the interests of the parties are not completely at odds, it is advisable that the allocation set forth in the contract be based on an independent valuation of all the assets. This valuation should include the amortizable and nonamortizable intangibles (i.e., goodwill, going concern, contracts, patents, etc.) as well as the fixed assets. It will not prevent the IRS from challenging the allocation; however, it can provide substantial support for a reasonable determination of basis.

At times, the seller may be in such a strong bargaining position that the purchaser's interests are best served by not including an allocation in the agreement. In this way, the buyer is free to determine the basis of the assets in the manner in which he feels is reasonable. The recommended method again is through independent valuation of all the assets. It should be recognized that the sum of the values of all the assets acquired will probably not correspond exactly with the amount actually paid for them. When this happens, the tax basis should be allocated among all the assets in proportion to their net fair market values.[19] The allocation to certain assets will be restricted. For example, cash and cash equivalents should be valued at their face amounts[20] and accounts receivable should not have a basis in excess of face value[21]. The IRS has expressed the opinion that inventory should not be assigned a basis which exceeds its selling price.[22]

Following are two examples of an allocation of basis; the first illustrates a step-up, the second a step-down in basis.

An examination of these two balance sheet illustrations will show various advantages and disadvantages to Victor as buyer. The most obvious benefit in the first is that the allocation step-up increases the basis in depreciable and amortizable assets as well as the inventory. This contrasts with the result in the second illustration wherein the taxpayer receives a basis lower than the fair market value in the assets, clearly a detriment.

EXAMPLE 1

	Fair market value	Allocated tax basis
Cash	$1,000	$1,000
Prepaid taxes	100	100
Accounts receivable	800	1,000
Inventory	3,000	4,183
Fixed assets	2,500	3,486
Contract rights	700	976
Goodwill	500	697
Going concern value	400	558
	$9,000	$12,000

EXAMPLE 2

Cash	$1,000	$1,000
Prepaid taxes	100	100
Accounts receivable	800	597
Inventory	3,000	2,241
Fixed assets	2,500	1,867
Contract rights	700	553
Goodwill	500	373
Going concern value	400	299
	$9,000	$7,000

A less obvious benefit of valuing all the assets is that, should the IRS challenge any part of the valuation, it is likely that the adjustment will be spread over all the assets and not just the amortizable ones. A closer look will show an unexpected advantage to the earnings-conscious corporation in the first example. While, for tax purposes, the excess cost over the fair market value of the assets is apportioned among all the assets and will result in reduced taxable income, the same treatment is not appropriate for financial reporting purposes. The proper accounting procedure[23] requires that the entire excess be included in goodwill and amortized over a period of up to 40 years. The effect on earnings will be less than that on taxable income. Therefore, the corporation will show lower taxable income and increased earnings. The cost of this benefit is a permanent accounting difference to be shown as a Schedule M adjustment on the buyer's tax return. It is advisable that the balance sheet for reporting purposes include the amortizable intangibles with the same fair market value as reported for taxes. Amortization should also be taken over the same period for both purposes.

---

[19]Reg. 1.167(a)-5.

[20]Allocation to cash in a subsidiary liquidation under Section 332 requires that the cash receive a basis allocation equal to its face amount under Reg. 1.334-1(c) (4) (viii). This principal should also apply in the case of an acquisition of assets.

[21]Rev. Rul. 77-456, 1977-2 C.B. 102.

[22]Letter Ruling 7750009.

[23]Accounting Principles Board Opinion 16.

3. DISTRIBUTION OF PROCEEDS FROM SALE OF ASSETS THROUGH A TWELVE-MONTH LIQUIDATION

Section 337

Where the corporation will distribute the proceeds of the sale of assets to the shareholders, the sellers should determine whether they desire to have Section 337 of the Internal Revenue Code apply to the sale and distribution. The benefit of Section 337 is that it enables the corporation to avoid recognizing gain or loss upon the sale of its assets.

Section 337 was included as part of the Internal Revenue Code of 1954. Prior to 1954, a corporation would be taxed on a sale of its assets even though the proceeds were immediately distributed to the shareholders. However, if the assets were distributed to the shareholders first and then sold, the corporation would not be taxed. In the *Court Holding Company*[24] case, the Supreme Court held a corporation liable for taxes where property was sold after distributed in liquidation to the shareholders because the corporation had, in fact, negotiated the sale. In a later case, *Cumberland Public Service Co.,*[25] the Supreme Court held no tax due from the corporation in a similar situation. This variance in opinion, based on distinctions in form where no economic difference resulted, led to much discussion over the effect to be given to the form of a transaction. In order to provide for the same treatment whether the assets are sold by the corporation or distributed to and sold by the shareholders, Congress enacted Section 337.

To obtain the benefits of Section 337, the specific statutory requirements must be satisfied. The primary advantage of 337 is that the corporation will not recognize any gain or loss resulting from the sale of assets within a twelve-month period beginning at the adoption of a plan of liquidation and ending with the final distribution. Exceptions to this nonrecognition include depreciation recapture and gain from the sale of inventory in the ordinary course of business.

Requirements for Section 337

Section 337 applies to prevent the recognition of gain or loss in every transaction satisfying the statutory requirements. Its application is not elective and it applies to any sale of assets during the twelve-month period between the adoption of a plan of liquidation and a final distribution. Since it applies to losses as well as gains it should be avoided in a loss sale. An attempt to recognize loss by selling a loss asset just prior to the adoption of the plan may be successful[26]; however, the IRS may claim that an informal plan was adopted at the time of the sale.[27]

Accordingly, in order to ensure avoidance of Section 337, the corporation should retain operating assets beyond the twelve-month period.

The Code and Regulations do not indicate what is to be included in the liquidation plan. However, it appears that very general terms are sufficient.[28] It is recommended that the resolution provide sufficient authority for the officers and directors to wind up the affairs of the corporation, formally dissolve it, and distribute the assets in redemption of the stock.

The time of adoption of the plan should be carefully planned. Not only is it essential to qualifying under Section 337, but it also allows for planning the time of recognition of gain by the shareholders. This is done by ensuring that the twelve-month period covers two tax years. The actual date on which the 12-month nonrecognition period usually begins is the date of the shareholder resolution authorizing the liquidation.[29] The timing of the sales of the assets is also extremely important since failure to dispose of all the assets during the statutory period will entirely prohibit the application of Section 337. However, Regulation 1.337-2(a) states that a contract to sell entered into before the adoption of the plan will not prevent Section 337 from applying if the actual sale takes place after the shareholder resolution. A "facts and circumstances" approach may, in certain situations, be applied to determine when the plan of liquidation has been adopted. Cases applying "fact and circumstances" to find an informal plan have been both beneficial and detrimental to the taxpayer.[30] The informal plan may provide relief to a careless taxpayer, but it should never be relied upon by one desiring Section 337 to apply. On the other side, the facts and circumstances may be used to indicate a plan prior to any sales of the assets where

---

[24]45-1 USTC ¶9215, 324 U.S. 331.

[25]50-1 USTC ¶ 9129, 338 U.S. 451.

[26]*Virginia Ice and Freezing Corp.*, 30TC 1251 and *City Bank of Washington*, 38TC 713.

[27]An informal plan of liquidation was found at the urging of the taxpayer in *Alameda Realty Corp.*, 42TC 273 and *Mountain Water Co. of La Crescenta*, 35 TC 418. The I.R.S. has asserted this position in Rev. Rul. 65-235, 1965-2 CB88.

[28]Rev. Rul. 65-257, 1965-2 CB89.

[29]Reg. 1.337-2(b).

[30]The Tax Court allowed non-recognition of gain resulting from the sale of assets prior to adoption of a formal plan where the taxpayer was able to show an informal plan had previously been adopted in *Mountain Water Co. of La Crescenta*, 35TC 418. In Rev. Rul. 65-235, 1965-2CB 88, the I.R.S. acknowledged that an informal plan may be adopted prior to a formal one. However, it is presumed that the government will assert this position to force non-recognition of losses.

the corporation attempts to straddle the adoption of a plan by selling the loss assets before the resolution (thereby recognizing a loss) and the appreciated assets after, to avoid recognition of gain. A corporation which will see a potential benefit in a straddle sale has little to lose and much to gain in attempting one. In this respect, a little planning should be done before any sales are made. It should be determined whether the overall result after selling the assets will be a gain or a loss. If it is a gain, then the corporation should time the sales of all the assets within the same twelve-month period. In that way, even if an informal plan is found, all the sales will be within the time limit prescribed for Section 337. On the other hand, if the overall result will be a loss, it is best to allow more than 12 months between the initial loss sales and the final ones at a gain. The effect of finding an informal plan will render Section 337 inapplicable and the loss will be recognized.

In other situations, the benefit or detriment of Section 337 may be uncertain. Therefore, for planning purposes, a liquidation plan should be adopted. Then, if it is subsequently apparent that the assets will be sold at a loss, the corporation can fail to dispose of all the assets during the twelve-month period. In Revenue Ruling 77-150[31] the IRS acknowledges that a corporation can avoid nonrecognition by retaining assets beyond the twelve-month period in excess of those needed to meet claims.

Complete Distribution of Assets

Section 337 requires that all the assets of the liquidating corporation be distributed within the twelve-month period commencing at the adoption of the plan. The corporation may, however, retain assets necessary to meet any claims against it, including the liquidating expenses. These include contingent as well as known claims, provided the amount being retained is a reasonable and good-faith estimate. The courts have been liberal in determining the extent to which assets may properly be held to meet future claims. The assets should be sufficient to ensure that a subsequent claim will not render the corporation bankrupt.[32] Regulation 1.337-2(b) indicates that the asset to be retained must be cash. Whether this standard will be accepted

by the courts is questionable; however, it is advisable that income-producing business assets be entirely disposed of.

The regulations[33] do not allow assets to be retained for the purpose of meeting claims of shareholders with respect to their stock. They also indicate that any distribution owing to shareholders which cannot be located should be made to a trustee, state official or other person authorized to receive a distribution for the benefit of a shareholder and not retained by the corporation. Again it is uncertain whether the courts will enforce this requirement.[34] Where the liabilities to be satisified include other debts to shareholders, problems concerning debt/equity questions may result. In the case of *John Town, Inc.*,[35] assets were retained to satisfy promissory notes held by shareholders. The Tax Court disqualified the liquidation from Section 337 treatment holding that the note was an equity interest and not a debt, hence, an excessive amount of assets were retained.

Quite often it will be difficult or even impossible to either sell or distribute all the assets within the required time limit. Situations in which this may occur include those in which a major asset is real estate or some other asset which cannot be readily divided among the shareholders and which may prove difficult to sell. When the number of shareholders is large, it will be difficult to distribute property to them as joint owners; the same is true where it may be difficult to identify or locate major shareholders. In order for Section 337 to apply, the corporation must somehow dispose of the property. An accepted technique is to transfer the non-cash assets to a trust which, in due course, can convert them to cash and then distribute the cash among the shareholders. The IRS will not accept the use of a trust for property which is readily convertible into cash. Various rulings have allowed the transfer to trust of a tax claim[36] and real estate.[37] The trust may also assume the contingent liability claims rather than having the corporation retain assets to meet potential claims.

Where the corporation is insolvent a problem in qualifying under Section 337 can result. Since Section 337 applies upon a distribution of assets to shareholders, the IRS is of the opinion that a corporation using all its assets to meet claims and making no distributions to

[31]Rev. Rul. 77-150, 1977-1 CB 88.
[32]*O.B.M., Inc.* 70-1 USTC ¶ 9437; 427 F2d 661.
[33]Reg. 1.337-2(b).
[34]See Bittker and Eustice, *Federal Income Taxation of Corporations and Shareholders,* paragraph 11.64, page 11-63.
[35]46 TC 107 (1966).
[36]Rev. Rul. 63-245, 1963-2 C.B. 144.
[37]Rev. Rul. 72-137, 1972-1 C.B. 101.

shareholders will not qualify for nonrecognition.[38] However, all the Service requires is a distribution to the shareholders; it is not necessary that any tax result.

Property to Which Section 337 Applies

There are certain categories of property which may or may not qualify for the Section 337 nonrecognition treatment when disposed of. Section 337 will not prevent recognition of gain upon a disposition of property subject to recapture under Sections 47, 1245, 1250 and 1251. Other items of property include:

Inventory. Since Section 337 is for the purpose of allowing nonrecognition of gain realized in winding up the corporation, it does not apply to sales of assets in the regular course of business even though such sales occur at the end of the corporation's life.[39] The Internal Revenue Code, however, provides for nonrecognition of gain upon a bulk sale of "substantially all" of the inventory.[40] The bulk sale must be to one person in a single transaction. The "substantially all" test is to be made at the time of the bulk sale; therefore, sales of the inventory in the course of business are permitted between the adoption of the plan and the bulk sale.[41] No such sales can be made after the bulk sale. Regulation 1.337-3(c) extends Section 337 treatment to more than one bulk sale where each sale relates to a different business.

If a bulk sale is not desired, it may be possible to avoid recognition of gain at the corporation level by distributing the inventory, in kind, to the shareholders. Doing so will result in a *Court Holding Co.-Cumberland Public Service Co.* type situation. It can be expected that the IRS will strongly assert that such sales should be attributed to the corporation. The argument will claim that the sales are to the same customers and in the same manner as if made by the corporation and that, even though in form made by the shareholders, should be regarded as producing corporate profits.[42] Where the inventory is accounted for, using the LIFO method, it is not necessary that the LIFO reserve be included in ordinary income upon a bulk sale.[43]

Installment Obligations.[43a] Section 337 will generally not apply to the sale of installment obligations. In addition, Section 453(d)(1) provides that a disposition of an installment obligation will require immediate recognition of the deferred gain. There are three types of installment obligations which a corporation being liquidated may hold. These are:

1. Installment obligations arising in the general course of business. These obligations are not considered to be "property" under Section 337(b); therefore, the deferred gain from sale would be recognized immediately.

2. Installment obligations resulting from a sale of noninventory property but which result in a recapture tax under Sections 1245, 1250 or 1251. Again this sale will result in immediate recognition of all the gain by the corporation.

3. The final type of installment obligation is one acquired from the sale of noninventory property which is not subject to recapture. Included in this category of property is inventory which is disposed of through a bulk sale after a plan of liquidation has been adopted. The sale of these obligations will not result in recognition of gain or loss to the corporation.[44]

Instead of selling these obligations, it may be decided to distribute them to the shareholders. The resulting effect to the corporation will be the same as if they had been sold. The first two types will cause recognition by the corporation while the third will not.[45] The result to the shareholder will be the same whether or not the corporation must recognize gain or loss. The shareholder will have to include the entire fair market value of the obligation in his amount received in the liquidation of his stock. This can be very detrimental to the shareholder since it will affect the tax he will have to pay, but not produce any cash with which to pay it. Recognizing this, it may be desirable to sell the installment obligations and distribute cash especially since the resulting tax effect will be the same either way.

One final feature of Section 337 as it relates to installment obligations is that, for nonrecognition purposes, it will apply to items which are not included as installment obligations under Section 453. The Tax

---

[38]Rev. Rul. 56-387, 1956-2 C.B. 189.

[39]Rev. Rul. 73-264, 1973-1 C.B. 178.

[40]I.R.C. Section 337(b)(2).

[41]*Winer v. Commissioner,* 371 F. 2d. 684.

[42]*U.S. v. Lynch,* 192 F.2d. 718.

[43]Rev. Rul. 74-431, 1974-2 C.B. 107. However, the Windfall Profits Act adopted April 2, 1980 included a provision requiring recognition of income resulting from including the LIFO reserve in income upon a corporate liquidation under Section 337 or 334(b)(2).

[43a]See footnote 5[a].

[44]Section 453(d)(4)(B) excludes recognition of gain upon a sale of installment obligations under Sec. 337. Section 337(b) provides that installment obligations are not "property" unless they result from a sale of non-inventory property without recapture or from a bulk sale of inventory after adoption of a plan.

[45]I.R.C. Section 453(d)(4).

Court has determined[46] that the accounts receivable of a cash basis taxpayer were installment obligations and upon their sale, gain had to be recognized.

Gain or Loss From a Sale or Exchange. Section 337 provides for nonrecognition resulting from a sale or exchange of property pursuant to a plan of liquidation. Just what constitutes a sale or exchange is not clearly indicated in the regulations under Section 337, nor have the courts provided much guidance. The term "sale or exchange" is also found in Section 1222 which deals with the definition of a capital gain or loss. As such, transactions which qualify as a sale or exchange under Section 1222 should also be a sale or exchange for Section 337. The Service at one time refused to treat a casualty as a sale or exchange for Section 337 purposes[47] even though it would have been under Section 1231. In a number of cases, the courts ruled against the IRS and finally the Service agreed that all involuntary conversions from a casualty should result in nonrecognition of gain or loss under Section 337.[48]

Even though a transaction may be considered to be a sale, it still must occur after adoption of the liquidation plan in order to come within Section 337. A particular problem in the past resulted in cases of an involuntary conversion or condemnation because the casualty or the public authority would take title without warning and not give the corporation time to adopt a plan. This changed for dispositions after November 10, 1978 as a result of enactment of Section 337(e). In effect, Section 337(e) allows the taxpayer to elect to have Section 337 apply to the disposition, provided the plan of liquidation is adopted within 60 days after the property is disposed of.

Transactions Not Qualifying for Nonrecognition

The purpose of Section 337 is to prevent a double tax on the sale of corporate assets followed by a liquidation. It is not to permit ordinary income to escape taxation by the corporation.

Assignment of Income. It has been widely accepted by the courts upon a disposition in complete liquidation that any accrued or potential income in an asset being distributed must be recognized by the distributing corporation. This principle applies as well to a Section 337 liquidation, at least insofar as the assets are distributed in kind. Since the underlying purpose of Section 337 is to ensure the same treatment whether assets are distributed in kind or sold and the cash distributed, it would seem that the same standards should apply in both situations.

Thus, the courts have denied Section 337 treatment to construction contracts,[49] antitrust claims,[50] and player contracts,[51] holding that the income resulting therefrom should properly be taxed to the corporation which earned it as ordinary income and not only as capital gain to the shareholders. Other items outside Section 337 include the sale of accounts receivable by a cash basis taxpayer[52] and accrued interest on notes.[53]

Tax Benefit Doctrine. Cases have developed a rationale that a sale of an asset which had previously yielded a tax benefit should not be permitted without recognition of gain determined by the amount of the past benefit. Such assets have included a sale of accounts receivable at an amount which included the reserve for doubtful accounts.[54] The amount to be reported as ordinary income is the excess value over the net amount of the receivables. The courts have, for the most part, agreed with the Service that the sale of items previously deducted as a business expense should not be permitted nonrecognition treatment under Section 337. Cases have held such sales to be excluded from Section 337[55], at least to the extent of the amount previously deducted. It can be expected that the tax benefit approach will be extended to the recovery of amortization deductions due to intangibles such as trademarks and trade names under Section 177 and research and development expenditures under Section 174. Payments made on a separately bargained-for covenant not to compete between the buyer and seller have been held to be outside Section 337.[56] Finally, expenses incurred in selling the assets should not be

---

[46]*Family Record Plan, Inc. v. Commissioner,* 36 T.C. 305, aff'd on other grounds, 309 F. 2d 208.

[47]Rev. Rul. 56-372, 1956-2 C.B. 187.

[48]Rev. Rul. 64-100, 1964-1 C.B. 130.

[49]*Pridemark, Inc. v. Commissioner,* 65-1 USTC ¶9388; 345 F. 2d 35; *Commission v. Kuckenberg,* 62-2 USTC ¶9768, 309 F. 2d 202; *Midland Ross Corp. v. U.S.,* 73-2 USTC ¶9678, 485 F. 2d 110.

[50]*S. Messer,* 71-1 USTC ¶ 9214.

[51]*Hollywood Baseball Association,* 70-1 USTC ¶ 9251, 423 F. 2d 494.

[52]*Family Record Plan, Inc.,* Supra. fn. 46.

[53]*Citizens Acceptance Corp. v. U.S.,* 72-2 USTC ¶ 9510, 462 F. 2d 751.

[54]Rev. Rul. 78-279, 1978-2 CB 135.

[55]*Commissioner v. Anders,* 48 T.C. 815, reversed by 69-2 USTC ¶ 9573, 414 F. 2d 1283 relating to the cost of rental uniforms recovered upon a sale. *Spitalny v. U.S.,* 70-2 USTC ¶9545, 430 F. 2d 195, which treated previously deducted cost of cattle feed which was recovered in the same year as ordinary income. *Connery v. U.S.,* 72-1 USTC ¶9441, 462 F. 2d 1130 involving prepaid advertising expenses subsequently recovered.

[56]*Harvey Radio Laboratories,* supra, fn. 17. and Rev. Rul. 74-29, 1974-1 C.B. 80.

deducted by the corporation, but rather are to offset the nonrecognized gain.[57]

Recapture: Finally, Section 337 will not prevent recognition of ordinary income resulting from the recapture of depreciation[58] and investment tax credit.[59] At the very least, the amount recaptured as ordinary income will be outside Section 337 and recognized to the distributing corporation.[60] It is possible that the *Corn Products*[61] doctrine could be applied to require the entire gain resulting from the sale of recapture property be excluded from Section 337. At present, this extreme approach has not been taken.

Effect of Section 337 on Deductions

In 1960, the Service ruled that Section 265(a) prohibited a taxpayer from deducting state income taxes and expenses attributed to unrecognized gain under Section 337.[62] This ruling was revoked in 1963[63] after the IRS lost several cases on the issue. The Tax Court has even allowed a corporation to deduct state excise taxes which were paid by the shareholders where the corporation was primarily liable and did not retain sufficient assets to meet the claims.[64] If the shareholders had computed their capital gain or loss from the liquidation without considering this liability, then they should be entitled to a capital loss deduction.[65]

In general, expenses incurred upon liquidation are not deductible but are considered to offset the proceeds of a sale reducing the gain or loss realized.[66] Under Section 337, however, the gain or loss is unrecognized and no benefit will result from an offset of the amount realized. The cases initially split in allowing deductions for these expenses.[67] However, they have become more consistent[68] in not allowing the deductions, reasoning, first, that the nonrecognition property is usually a capital asset and the consistent treatment is to apply selling expenses to reduce the amount realized and, second, since the gain is not recognized, the expenses incurred to realize the gain should likewise not be recognized.

Liquidations Not Qualifying for Nonrecognition

Section 337 does not apply to liquidation of three types of corporations. These include collapsible corporations, corporations electing to liquidate under Section 333, and liquidations of subsidiaries under Section 332.

(1) **Collapsible Corporations.** Section 337 cannot apply to collapsible corporations. If it did, the corporation could sell its assets without recognizing gain under Section 337 and the shareholders would avoid Section 341(a) because the corporation has *realized,* although not recognized, gain and would no longer be collapsible under Section 341(b). Although the statute does not clearly prohibit Section 337 from applying to collapsible corporations, the regulations and rulings do.[69]

Putting the transaction outside Section 337 does not always result in recognition by the corporation. For the corporation can distribute the assets to the shareholders who then sell them. The shareholders will be taxed on their gain under Section 341(a), but, if the requirements for *Cumberland Public Service* are met, no gain will be recognized by the corporation. If the sale were made by the corporation instead, gain would be recognized since Section 337 would not apply. However, the punitive provisions of Section 341 would no longer apply to the shareholders since the corporation would no longer be collapsible.

(2) **Liquidations Under Section 333.** Section 333 permits shareholders to receive property from a corporation without recognizing gain in certain situations. If Section 337 also applied, then gain would not be recognized by either the corporation or the shareholder. In order to ensure that the gain will not go totally unrecognized, Code Section 337(c)(1)(B) excludes Section 337 from applying in a Section 333 liquidation. If any shareholder elects Section 333, the corporation is barred from Section 337 even though there may be an advantage to other shareholders. When a corporation being liquidated under Section 333 sells its assets, a tax

---

[57]*Of Course Inc. v. Commissioner,* 74-2 USTC ¶ 9546; 499 F.2d 754.

[58]I.R.C. Sections 1245(a) and 1250(a).

[59]I.R.C. Section 47.

[60]*F. Clayton,* 52 T.C. 911.

[61]*Corn Products Refining Co. v. Commissioner,* 350 U.S. 46.

[62]Rev. Rul. 60-236, 1960-2 C.B. 109.

[63]Rev. Rul. 63-233, 1963-2 C.B. 113.

[64]*Royal Oak Apartments, Inc.,* 43 T.C. 243.

[65]*Arrowsmith v. Commissioner,* 344 U.S. 6.

[66]*Woodward v. Commissioner,* 397 U.S. 572.

[67]Selling expenses were deductible under Sec. 337 in *Pridemark, Inc.,* supra. fn. 49. and *U.S. v. Mountain States Mixed Feed Co.,* 365 F. 2d 244. They were not deductible in *Alphaco Inc. v. Nelson,* 385 F. 2d. 244; *U.S. v. Morton,* 387 F. 2d. 441; and *Lanrao, Inc.* v. U.S. 422 F. 2d 481.

[68]*J.T. Stewart III Trust,* 63 T.C. 682: *Of Course, Inc.,* supra fn 57 reversing *Pridemark, Inc.,* supra fn 49 and *Benedict Oil Co.* 78-2 USTC ¶ 9652, reversing *Mountain States Mixed Feed Co.,* supra fn. 67.

[69]Reg. 1.337-1; Rev. Rul. 58-141, 1958-1 C.B. 179; Rev. Rul. 63-125, 1965-2 C.B. 146.

may result which reduces the amount being distributed. The sale will also increase the corporation's earnings and profits, thereby increasing the amount of gain to be recognized under Sections 333(e) and 333(f). An alternative would be for the corporation to distribute the assets to the shareholders who, in turn, will attempt to sell them under *Cumberland Public Service Co.* In the event the transaction falls under *Court Holding Co.* instead, the gain will be taxable to the corporation and also increase the earnings and profits with a resulting increase in the gain to the shareholders.

(3) **Subsidiary Liquidations Under Section 332.** Once again, in order to prevent a complete nonrecognition of gain, Section 337(c)(2) excludes sales of assets from Section 337 treatment where the proceeds will be distributed to the shareholders tax free under Section 332. Where the liquidation is of a subsidiary with a carryover basis under Section 334(b)(1), the minority shareholders receive a tax credit which would, in effect, put them into the Section 337 situation. Section 337(d) provides the minority shareholder with a credit equal to the amount of his proportionate increase in distribution had the corporation been liquidated under Section 337.

If the subsidiary liquidation will have a stepped-up basis under Section 334(b)(2) then Section 337 will provide for nonrecognition to a limited extent. Gain from a sale, after adoption of a plan, will not be recognized to the extent the allocated tax basis (total tax basis allocated in proportion to net fair market values) exceeds the original tax basis. The Tax Court has held that this nonrecognition will not apply to exclude losses.[70]

The general prohibition of Section 337 under Section 332 will not apply where both the parent and subsidiary are liquidated. It does not matter whether the parent sells the subsidiary's assets after the subsidiary is liquidated or the subsidiary sells its assets after the parent is liquidated. Prior to the Tax Reform Act of 1976, gain or loss was recognized by a subsidiary which sold its assets prior to liquidating into its parent. The Tax Reform Act amended Code Section 337(c)(2) to provide that no gain or loss will be recognized to the subsidiary or the parent where both the subsidiary and parent adopt plans and distribute substantially all their assets within the same twelve-month period.

Recent cases have split on whether Section 337 will impose nonrecognition treatment in a transaction which is both a liquidation and a reorganization. In *FEC Liquidating*[71] the Court of Claims ruled that a transaction would be either a liquidation or a reorganization but not both. Since the reorganization provisions preempted the liquidation, Section 337 was held not to apply.

A contrary result was found by the District Court in *General Housewares Corp.*[72] Here the court held that a transaction could be both a liquidation and a reorganization. So long as the transaction was a valid liquidation, the liquidation provisions should apply.

Planning to Defer Capital Gains[72a]

A taxpayer planning to sell a closely-held corporation can defer reporting the capital gains from the sale through a Section 337 liquidation together with an installment sale of the stock. It is likely that a buyer, desiring the assets, will refuse to purchase the stock on an installment basis. In order to use the installment method of reporting, the shareholder would, after negotiating the asset sale and adopting the liquidation plan, sell his stock to a family trust under an installment payment plan. The trust can then sell the assets and the trustee will carry out the liquidation by distributing the proceeds of the sale to the trust. This technique is valuable for one who has a low basis, but high value, in the stock of his corporation. It also avoids the risk of having the buyer purchase on the installment basis since the trust can receive payment in full for the assets. The use of this technique was initially presented in *W.B. Rushing v. Commissioner*[73] which held the key to permissibility to be the independence of the trustee. The trustee must be free to decide not to liquidate. The corporation should be careful not to constructively sell the assets prior to adoption of the plan. There has been legislation introduced which prohibits installment sales between related parties. Enactment of this legislation would prevent the above deferral technique.

Steps in a Section 337 Liquidation

A liquidation under Section 337 requires that all the steps for any liquidation be taken as well as certain additional ones.

As in any liquidation, the directors and shareholders must adopt a liquidation resolution. Within 30 days after adoption of the liquidation plan, Form 966 must

---

[70]*United States Holding Company,* 44T.C. 323.
[71]77-1 USTC ¶ 9160, 548 F. 2d 924.
[72]78-2 USTC ¶ 9693.
[72a]See footnote 5[a].
[73]71-1 USTC ¶ 9339; 441 F.2d 593.

be filed with the Internal Revenue Service. Corporate business should be wound up and all assets should either be sold or distributed to the shareholders within 12 months after the plan is adopted. Forms 1099L and 1096 (information returns indicating value of property distributed) must be filed with the Internal Revenue Service by February 28 of the year after a distribution. The corporation is formally dissolved under state law and a final return filed by the fifteenth day of the third month after final distribution. The return should include a copy of the plan and shareholder resolution approving it, should indicate all assets sold under the plan and those being retained to meet claims and the date of the final distribution to shareholders.

Finally, minority shareholders wishing to claim the Section 337(d) credit should file Form 843 and indicate the name and address of the corporation together with information supporting its claim for credit.

Boot-strap Acquisition of Stock

In some situations the corporation which is being acquired may own assets in addition to the ones desired by the purchaser.[74] These unwanted assets may be disposed of through a "boot-strap" redemption. The ideal result would be for the distribution to be taxable as a redemption and not a dividend since a redemption generates capital gain while a dividend is ordinary income. In a redemption in which assets are distributed to a shareholder in complete redemption of his stock in the corporation the gain realized in canceling the stock is capital.[75] It is necessary that the redemption be complete and none of the remaining stock attributed to the selling shareholder[76] or that the attribution be waived.[77] A boot-strap redemption usually involves a redemption of only part of the stock while the remainder is sold to the new acquiring shareholder. This technique can be used to give the new shareholder complete control of the corporation while only acquiring the assets he desires or can afford. However, to

ensure the capital gain benefit of the boot-strap redemption it is essential that the redemption and sale be part of the same transaction.[78] In order to ensure that this requirement is met, it is best to have the sale precede or be simultaneous with the redemption. In the event that redemption occurs before the sale, the seller will still have a capital gain so long as the two steps were part of the same plan.

Another problem in the boot-strap redemption involves the tax treatment to the buyer. The problem here is that, in essence, the corporation is paying an obligation which properly belongs to the buyer. Accordingly it can be argued that he has received a distribution. Dividend treatment will result where the buyer pays for all the stock and later causes the corporation to redeem part of his stock. Such a redemption fails to satisfy any of the Section 302(b) exceptions to dividend treatment.[79] Similarly, a dividend will result if the corporation assumes or pays the buyer's obligations resulting from the acquisition.[80] However, if the boot-strap redemption is structured so that the corporation is redeeming stock of the seller which the buyer is not obligated to purchase, no dividend will result to the buyer.[81] This is so even when the buyer has an option to purchase the stock which is subsequently redeemed[82] if the buyer pledges his shares to guarantee the corporation's performance.[83] As this is an area in which the form of a transaction dictates the treatment which will result, it is important to abide by the formal requirements, not only when actually structuring the deal, but also as negotiations reach the final stages.[84]

Options Available to the Purchaser of Stock

The payment of $1,250,000 to George for his stock becomes Victor's tax basis in the stock. Victor has received a going business, organized as a corporation, which has a past tax history and a current tax status. The tax law presents Victor with several alternatives for continuing this business. His decision must be

---

[74]The corporation may possess assets unrelated to the business being acquired, there may be accumulated cash which the buyer does not need or want or the buyer may not have the financial means to purchase all the assets.

[75]I.R.C. Sec. 302(b)(3).

[76]I.R.C. Sec. 318.

[77]I.R.C. Sec. 302(c)(2).

[78]*Zenz v. Quinlivan,* 213 F. 2d 914 (6th Circuit, 1954) Acquiesed in Rev. Rul. 54-458, 1954-2 C.B. 167 and Rev. Rul. 55-745, 1955-2 C.B. 223.

[79]Section 302(b) provides that a redemption will not be considered a dividend if:

    1. It is not essentially equivalent to a dividend.

    2. It is a substantially disproportionate redemption or

    3. It is a complete termination of interest.

[80]An early case, *Wall v. U.S.,* 164 F. 2d 462, determined a dividend was paid to the purchaser where, after the acquisition, the corporation redeemed stock which the purchaser was obligated to purchase under an installment sale contract.

[81]Rev. Rul. 69-608, 1969-2 C.B. 43.

[82]*Commissioner v. Holsey,* 58-2 USTC ¶ 9816, 258 F. 2d 865 and Rev. Rul. 58-614, 1958-2 C.B. 920.

[83]*Ray Edenfield,* 19 T.C. 13.

[84]Bittker and Eustice, *Federal Income Taxation of Corporations and Shareholders,* warn that an initial binding agreement calling for a purchase of all the stock may prohibit a later attempt to restructure the acquisition as a combination sale/redemption.

made in light of the past, current and future tax attributes of the acquired corporation and his own requirements.

Victor, in purchasing the corporation, will not recognize any gain in this transaction since he is paying cash. However, if part of the consideration paid to George consisted of appreciated property, Victor would have a gain to the extent the fair market value of such property exceeded his adjusted basis in it. For example, suppose Victor gave George $1,000,000 in cash and 1,000 shares of stock in A Public Co., Inc. having a market value of $250,000 at the time of exchange. Victor would realize gain to the extent the $250,000 exceeded his basis in the stock, with the character of the gain being determined by his holding period in the stock. If Victor were acquiring this business through his company, use of the stock of this corporation would not result in recognized gain.

Continuing Existing Corporation

If Victor does nothing more once he acquires the stock, the corporation will continue generating tax history as if it had never changed ownership. For example, annual depreciation deductions will continue to be determined from the original cost of the assets and will not reflect the adjusted basis in the stock; net operating losses and unused capital losses generated in past years will continue to be available to offset post-acquisition operating income; the earnings and profits account will continue unadjusted; and the method of accounting will remain unchanged.

The purchaser of stock is not entitled to an investment tax credit or first year bonus depreciation as a result of his expenditure. This is not a significant detriment as both are restricted to limited amounts.[85] Recent additions to the Internal Revenue Code also limit the amount of beneficial carryforwards which will be available after a change in ownership of stock in a corporation. Section 382 limits the use of net operating loss carryforwards[86] while Section 383 imposes a limit on the amount of investment tax credit, work incentive program credit, new employee credit, foreign tax credit and capital loss carryovers which will survive the change of ownership.[87]

The addition of Sections 382 and 383 has reduced two of the primary tax reasons for continuing the existing corporation. An income tax benefit still remaining is that there is no restriction on the carryovers belonging to the purchasing corporation which may be used to offset income or reduce taxes resulting from the acquired business.

A final tax benefit which will result from not liquidating is in the situation where the fair market value of the assets is lower than their book value. In this case, larger depreciation deductions will be available when based on the higher existing book value rather than the allocated tax basis.

When purchasing stock there are no special filing requirements other than a filing of Schedule C by the seller to report his capital gain or loss. Mechanically, the transaction involves a simple transfer of the stock to the buyer.

4. LIQUIDATION OF ACQUIRED CORPORATION

Once Victor analyzes the tax impact and business objectives resulting from a liquidation of the newly acquired business and decides that the benefits from liquidation outweigh the detriments, he must follow the formal procedures required by the Internal Revenue Service and the state having jurisdiction over the corporation. The IRS, in certain situations, imposes time requirements on when a plan of liquidation must be adopted and over which the final distribution of assets must be accomplished. It also requires evidence of intent and adoption of a plan as well as the filing of the necessary forms at the proper times.

The simplest and most basic form for liquidation is where Victor liquidates the corporation distributing the assets directly to himself as an individual. The Internal Revenue Code, in Section 331, classifies a liquidation as a sale or exchange of the stock owned by the shareholders. Since, to Victor, the stock is a capital asset the liquidation could possibly result in the recognition of a capital gain or loss measured by the difference between the fair market value of the assets he receives and his basis in the stock.

For example, if we assume that he immediately liquidated the corporation, he would have to recognize a short-term capital gain or loss. However, most likely the fair market value of the assets would be approximately equal to the amount he paid for the stock and no gain or loss would result. In the event he chose to liquidate the corporation at a later time, a gain or loss would result.

Assuming Victor paid George the $1,250,000 for

---

[85]Investment Tax Credit on used property is limited to $100,000 of qualified investment; while the bonus depreciation is a maximum of 20% of $10,000 of investment.

[86]The Tax Reform Act of 1976 amended Code Section 382 to limit the net operating loss carryforwards available to a purchaser of the corporation. The new act originally was to be effective for taxable years beginning after June 30, 1980. However, the effective date was delayed by the House of Representatives (HR 5505) and the Senate (HR 5224) until 1982.

[87]I.R.C. Section 383.

the corporation on January 1, 1980, and liquidated the corporation some time later when the assets had appreciated and were worth $1,500,000, then Victor would realize $250,000 of capital gain. The character of the gain as short-term or long-term is conditioned on how long Victor waited before liquidating.[88] Now, you may be wondering that if the liquidation is treated as a sale or exchange and the fair market value of the assets has appreciated to $1,500,000, what happens, then, to the corporation when it distributes this property. If we assume the corporation had a basis in its assets of only $500,000, then it would seem that, somehow, a gain of $1,000,000 resulted. (That is receipt of stock worth $1,500,000 for property with a basis of $500,000.) Recognition of this gain at the liquidating corporation level is, however, expressly prohibited by statute in Code Section 336. This nonrecognition of gain results in a permanent forgiveness of taxation to the corporation.

In exchange for the recognition of the capital gain, Victor will receive a basis in the assets which he receives equal to their fair market value[89] of $1,500,000. In addition, the earnings and profits account of the corporation disappears without ever being taxed as ordinary income.

Liquidation of Subsidiary

In certain situations it is possible to avoid the recognition of gain upon liquidation of a corporation. This nonrecognition of gain results upon the liquidation of a subsidiary into its parent corporation.[90]

In order for Victor to take advantage of this nonrecognition it is necessary that he acquire the "Big Car" stock through an existing corporation.

The advantage of liquidating tax-free under Section 332 is that the gain or loss realized to the parent/stockholder will not be recognized. It must be remembered, however, that this gain or loss is measured by the difference between the corporation's basis in the stock and the fair market value of the assets being distributed. Accordingly,the tax benefit may not be that great when the subsidiary is newly acquired and, in fact, a detriment may result. This can be seen by comparing two situations.

In the first example, the basis in the stock is $1,250,000, while the fair market value of the assets is only $1,000,000. Hence a loss at liquidation $250,000 is not recognized. Also, since Victor Corp. takes a basis in the assets equal to that which the subsidiary had, a subsequent disposition of the assets may result in a gain. Assuming the basis is $750,000, then a sale of the assets at their current value would result in a recognized gain of $250,000. This is clearly an unfavorable result.

A definite benefit can be seen in a second situation. In this example, we assume Victor Corp. has a basis in the stock again of $1,250,000. However, this time the fair market value of the assets is $1,500,000 while their basis is even higher at $1,750,000. The result this time is an unrecognized gain at liquidation of $250,000. Upon sale of the assets at $1,500,000, Victor Corp. would have a loss of $250,000 which would not be recognized!

It is obvious that Victor must look carefully at the overall result of a liquidation of his new subsidiary. Care is especially important because the application of Sections 332 and 334(b)(1) is not elective. If all the requirements are satisfied, then the liquidation is within the nonrecognition provisions.

Requirements to Subsidiary Liquidation with a Carryover Basis

When all the requirements for a tax-free liquidation are satisfied Sections 332 and 334(b)(1) apply. These requirements are as follows:

(1) Control Is Required. The parent corporation must control the subsidiary. To have control, Victor Corp. must own 80 percent of the combined voting power of all voting classes of the subsidiary's stock and it must have 80 percent of the total shares of all other classes of stock. This test excluded non-voting stock which is limited and preferred in its dividends. The control requirement must be satisfied at all times from the adoption of the plan until the liquidation distributions have been completed.

The IRS has defined voting stock[91] as stock which participates in the election of the board of directors. Special stock which can vote only on certain matters or upon certain conditions is not voting stock for Section 332 purposes until the conditions are satisfied.

As for the non-voting stock it appears that the IRS requires that the parent own 80 percent of the shares of each class of nonvoting stock.[92] This requirement has not been clearly mandated and should not be relied upon to avoid Section 332.

[88]I.R.C. Section 1222 defines long-term as a period of at least 12 months.
[89]I.R.C. Sec. 334(a).
[90]I.R.C. Sec. 332(a).
[91]Rev. Rul. 69-126, 1969-1 C.B. 218.
[92]Rev. Rul. 59-259, 1959-2 C.B. 115.

These control requirements are met where an affiliated group of corporations, as defined in Section 1504 of the Code, in the aggregate satisfy the above 80 percent tests even though no one member does in itself.[93]

The control requirement is a principal means by which the taxpayer can take advantage of or avoid Section 332. However, the IRS has attacked attempts by taxpayers to manipulate control. In an attempt to keep the taxpayer outside Section 332, the Service has claimed that the actual plan of liquidation was adopted before the formal plan at a time when the parent did not hold control.[94] On other occasions, taxpayers have attempted to avoid Section 332 by disposing of stock just prior to adoption of a liquidation plan. Here, again, the IRS attempted to look for a plan before adoption of a formal one and this time keep the liquidation within Section 332. In several cases[95] the IRS has been unsuccessful in asserting this approach.

(2) Liquidation Completed within Required Time Period. A subsidiary liquidation must be accomplished within one of two time limitations specified in Section 332. The Code requires that the liquidation be completed within the taxable year or by the end of the third taxable year after the first taxable year in which a liquidation distribution is made. While the plan of liquidation must specify whether the liquidation will be accomplished within one year, a selection of the first time limit with a failure to satisfy cannot be relied upon to get the liquidation outside Section 332 since the Service may claim the second time frame was actually inferred. Failure to satisfy the second time requirement will put the transaction outside Section 332 unless the IRS can successfully show a constructive distribution.[96]

(3) Requirement of Plan of Liquidation for Complete Cancellation or Redemption of Stock. For the liquidation of a subsidiary to be within Section 332, Regulation 1.332-2(c) requires that there be a plan of liquidation. The plan must provide for the complete cancellation or redemption of stock in exchange for all the assets of the corporation. The plan must be adopted by the liquidating subsidiary as well as the parent and it must appear in the official records of each corporation.[97]

While the statute requires that all property, including cash, must be distributed,[98] the regulations permit the retention of some assets[99] for the purpose of winding up the corporation's affairs. Under no circumstances should the subsidiary retain assets to be used in carrying on either the old business or a new one.[100]

(4) Reporting Requirements for Liquidation under Section 332. In order for a liquidation to qualify under Section 332, certain requirements in addition to the general liquidation reports must be prepared. As in any liquidation, a Form 966 must be filed within 30 days after the adoption of the plan. The subsidiary must also file Forms 1096 and 1099L no later than February 28 of the year following each taxable year in which a distribution was made. A separate 1099L is required for each shareholder who receives a distribution of at least $600.

The regulations[101] require those who receive a distribution in liquidation, whether the parent or a minority shareholder, to provide certain information with respect to their interest in the liquidated corporation. This includes a copy of the plan and details of how it was carried out; a listing of the properties together with their basis and fair market values; details of any indebtedness of subsidiary to the parent and finally a summation of each class of stock owned together with its voting rights, basis and date purchased.

Special Business Consideration

Whenever acquisition of a new subsidiary is anticipated, Victor Corp., the acquiring corporation must decide first if a liquidation would be beneficial. This requires a comparison of the present value of future benefits of liquidation (step-up in basis of inventory and depreciable assets) with the costs of liquidating (primarily recapture of depreciation and investment tax credit). A second consideration, once a liquidation is desired, is to determine how the new business will fit into the organizational structure. That is, whether it is

---

[93]Rev. Rul. 74-441, 1974-2 C.B. 105.

[94]Rev. Rul. 70-106, 1970-1 C.B. 70.

[95]*Day and Zimmerman, Inc.*, 45-1 USTC ¶ 9403, 151 F. 2d 517; *Rhode Island Hospital Trust Co.*, 7 T.C. 211; *Granite Trust Co.*, 57-1 USTC ¶ 9201, 283 F 2d 670.

[96]Eustice and Bittker, "Complete Liquidations and Related Problems", 26 Tax Law Rev. 191, 224 assert that the IRS may have a very real threat where the sole purpose of the delay is the tax effect.

[97]Reg. 1.332-6(a).

[98]I.R.C. Sec. 332(b)(2).

[99]Reg. 1.332-2(c).

[100]Rev. Rul. 76-525, 1976-2 C.B. 98.

[101]Reg. 1.332-6(b).

to be part of the parent or an existing subsidiary or it is to be a newly formed subsidiary. Most often the latter is desired. It is important that this decision be made before the stock is acquired. The proper order of events is for the parent to organize NewCo. contributing cash in exchange for stock under Section 351. This cash is subsequently used by NewCo. to acquire the stock of the target after which the liquidation can take place. The reason this order is so important is illustrated by rearranging the sequence. Suppose that Victor Corp. acquire the stock of the target and then contributes this stock to NewCo. for its stock. NewCo. then liquidates the target and the same result is achieved.

However, NewCo. has received the target stock in a tax-free Section 351 contribution. Thus the "purchase" requirement, discussed below, will not be satisfied. Now suppose the parent acquires the target stock by purchase and liquidates it into the parent but then contributes all the target's assets to NewCo. The problem which results is the so-called "liquidation-reincorporation" concept. The IRS has argued and the courts have agreed that, in effect, no actual liquidation has taken place and again neither Section 332 nor 334(b)(2) will apply.

When determing the organizational structure many things should be considered. Of course, the primary one is how the target's business relates to the parent and its existing subsidiaries. Another important consideration is whether the business can be absorbed into the parent. For example, in certain businesses (i.e., insurance) some states prohibit non-resident corporations from engaging in business within their borders. Therefore, in order for the target to be liquidated it must be acquired by a resident corporation making NewCo. and the state of its incorporation extremely important to achieving the desired result.

Subsidiary Liquidation with a Stepped-up Basis— Kimbell-Diamond and Section 334(b)(2)

Prior to adoption of the 1954 Tax Code, the principle that a purchase of stock in a corporation to obtain assets which were distributed in a prompt liquidation should be viewed as a purchase of assets was adopted by the courts. The leading case, *Kimbell-Diamond Milling Co. v. Commissioner,* [102] involved the purchase,

in 1942, of a corporation to obtain its sole asset, a manufacturing mill. After the asset was distributed in liquidation, Kimbell-Diamond Milling Co. computed its depreciation deductions using the original basis in the hands of the liquidated corporation. The Service argued, and the courts agreed, that the "single transaction" doctrine required treating the transaction as a purchase of assets.

With the 1954 Code came Section 334(b)(2) for the purpose of codifying the principles of Kimbell-Diamond. Basically, Section 334(b)(2) provides that the basis in assets acquired in liquidation of a subsidiary should equal the parent's basis in the subsidiary's stock. The Code further requires, for Section 334(b)(2) to apply, that the parent acquire at least 80 percent of the subsidiary's stock by "purchase" during a period not exceeding 12 months. The assets must be distributed under a plan of liquidation adopted within two years of the purchase.

The *Kimbell-Diamond* rule was heavily conditioned on the intent of the acquiring parent while Section 334(b)(2) applies without regard to intent. For a non-statutory *Kimbell-Diamond* liquidation it is necessary that the intent of the purchaser be to acquire assets and not the corporate structure of the seller and that the acquiring entity intend to liquidate the corporation as soon as possible. The purchaser can acquire the seller's business and receive the benefit of its goodwill under *Kimbell-Diamond.* [103] A question remains whether Section 334(b)(2) preempts the *Kimbell-Diamond* opinion. This is important to one desiring to receive carryover basis treatment by attempting to avoid Section 334(b)(2) by not complying with the statutory requirements. The first case [104] on the preemption issue held that, because Section 334(b)(2) applied only to corporations, Congress did not attempt to prohibit *Kimbell-Diamond* from applying to individuals. Since *Kimbell-Diamond* was intended to remain alive for individuals, the court reasoned it should continue to apply to corporations as well. Current thought [105] indicates the acceptance that Congress did intend to preempt *Kimbell-Diamond* by enacting Section 334(b)(2).

Of the requirements for a Section 334(b)(2) liquidation, the one most likely to cause problems is that requiring acquisition of stock by "purchase." Section

---

[102] 14 T.C. 74, aff'd. per curiam, 187 F. 2d 718 (5th Circ.).

[103] Rev. Rul. 60-246, 1960-2 C.B. 462 and *M.O.J. Corp.,* 60-1 USTC ¶ 9209, 274 F 2d 713.

[104] *American Potash and Chemical Corp. v. U.S.,* 399 F. 2d 194.

[105] The Court of Appeals for the 7th Circuit in *Broadview Lumber Co.* Inc., 77-2 USTC ¶ 9615, 561 F. 2d 698; the 5th Circuit in *Supreme Investment Corp.,* 72-2 USTC ¶ 9689, 468F.2d 370 and *Chrome Plate, Inc.,* 78-1 USTC ¶ 9104; the 9th Circuit in *Pacific Transport Co.,* 73-2 USTC ¶ 9615, 483F. 2d 209 and the Tax Court in *International State Bank,* 70T.C. 173 have held Kimbell-Diamond to be preempted by Sec. 334(b)(2). However, in *Yoc Heating Corp.,* 61T.C. 168, the Tax Court allowed a cost basis in assets acquired in a transaction not qualifying under Sec. 334(b)(2).

334(b)(2) excludes carryover basis transactions (i.e., gift, inheritance, contribution to capital or tax-free reorganization), Section 351 exchanges and acquisitions from related persons from being considered a purchase. Section 334(b)(3) permits a parent corporation to liquidate a first tier subsidiary and then a second tier subsidiary with Section 334(b)(2) applying to the latter. As discussed above, this is another reason for the acquiring corporation to decide whether or not a separate operating subsidiary will be desired for the new business before the stock is acquired since, once acquired it cannot be transferred and continue to satisfy the purchase requirement.

Section 334(b)(2) imposes a time requirement during which a parent must acquire control of the subsidiary. Control is defined as it is for Section 332 as 80 percent of the combined voting power of all classes of stock entitled to vote and 80 percent of the total number of shares of all other classes of stock. This requirement can be met by decreasing the total number of shares outstanding by means of a redemption of the minority shareholders. For example, if P Corp. purchased 80 of the 120 shares of S Corp. outstanding and within the twelve-month period S Corp. redeemed 20 shares from minority shareholders, the control requirement would be satisfied. The redemption should be prior to the liquidation plan.[106]

Control must be acquired within the twelve-month period beginning on the first acquisition of the subsidiary stock by purchase. However, the twelve-month period will begin running upon purchase of an option to acquire stock even though the stock itself must be acquired during the twelve-month period for the purpose of satisfying the control requirement.[107] Where stock is purchased from another corporation whose shares are also owned by the parent, the date of purchase shall be deemed to be the date when ownership is first attributed under Section 318.[108]

The parent is required, under Section 334(b)(2), to adopt a plan of liquidation during the two-year period commencing on the day following the day of the last transaction required for control during the twelve-month period which began with the first purchase of stock.[109]

Once again, the Code calls for adoption of a plan of liquidation without indicating what should be included in the plan. Furthermore, it would appear that the IRS could argue that an informal plan was actually adopted prior to the date set out in the formal one. This may place the transaction outside Section 332 and hence Section 334(b)(2) as well in a situation such as one where control is to be acquired by redemption of the minority shareholders.

While it is easy to avoid the statutory requirements for Section 334(b)(2), and thereby obtain a carryover basis, the courts may look to the parent corporation's intent and apply the Kimbell-Diamond rule.

Mechanics of a Section 334(b)(2) Liquidation

There are two major steps to be taken in carrying out a Section 334(b)(2) liquidation. These are necessary because the purpose of Section 334(b)(2) is to assign the parent's basis in the stock of the subsidiary to the assets received in the liquidation. Accordingly, the first requirement is to determine the total cost of or basis in the subsidiary's stock. Since this basis is usually allocated to the assets received upon liquidation in proportion to their net fair market values,[110] the second step is to identify and value these assets. Prior to acquiring the stock and liquidating the target it is important that these steps be done on a preliminary basis, that is, using approximate but conservative amounts. This is extremely important so that the intitial costs of a liquidation (i.e., depreciation and ITC recapture) can be compared to the present value of the anticipated future benefit of a liquidation (i.e., depreciation and cost of goods sold based on a higher value). Most important, this is not the time to take favorable or aggressive positions.

Determining Basis in the Subsidiary's Stock

The basis of the stock is not simply the amount paid for it. It includes the basis in all of the stock held by the parent and not simply that acquired by purchase or during the twelve-month period.[111] It will also include various other costs such as liabilities assumed and liabilities inherent in the business which become due as a result of the liquidation. Furthermore, since the liquidation may not take place at the same time as the acquisition of stock, certain adjustments may be required to determine the actual basis to be allocated.

The objective of Section 334(b)(2) is to put a taxpayer who purchases stock and liquidates the acquired corporation in the same position as one who acquires only assets. As such, the basis must be determined with

[106]*Madison Square Garden v. Commissioner*, 74-2 USTC ¶ 9618.

[107]Reg. 1.334-1(c)(6)(iii).

[108]Reg. 1.334-1(c)(7)(ii)(b).

[109]I.R.C. Sec. 334(b)(2)(A); Reg: 1.334-1(c)(3)(i).

[110]Reg. 1.334-1(c)(4)(ciii).

[111]Reg. 1.334-1(c)(1).

respect to the date of acquisition and adjustment must be made for any transactions between that date and the liquidation. The regulations provide that the basis be reduced in the amount of all distributions from the subsidiary to the parent from the time the stock is first acquired through the adoption of the plan of liquidation (the "interim period").[112] It is irrelevant whether or not these distributions were considered as dividends.[113] The basis will not be reduced if the distribution is out of earnings and profits from that same period[114] or is required to reduce basis under Section 301(c)(2).[115]

The regulations require that the basis be increased by the unsecured liabilities assumed by the parent[116] and by the earnings and profits resulting during the period beginning on the date of purchase of the stock and ending with the final distribution in liquidation.[117] The liabilities assumed include liabilities owing from the corporation to its minority shareholders[118] as well as the tax liabilities from the liquidation. These tax liabilities may result from recapture of depreciation and investment tax credit and restoration of the reserve for doubtful accounts relating to the accounts receivable. The earnings and profits of the period between the acquisition of the stock and the liquidation include those produced by the corporation in its ordinary course of business. Cases have held that the increase in the earnings and profits account as a result of the income (net of the tax liability) produced by restoring a bad debt reserve to income[119] and by the recapture of depreciation,[120] both as a result of the liquidation, must be added to increase the basis being allocated to the assets. These courts held that, even though the acquisition of all the stock and the liquidation were on the same day, the adjustment to the earnings and profits account was due to a transaction in the interim period. Earnings and profits of lower tier subsidiaries are not considered to be earnings and profits of the subsidiary being liquidated for purposes of the interim period adjustment.[121]

The basis to be allocated to the assets is decreased by cash and cash equivalents received[122] and by the parent's share of any deficit in earnings and profits during the interim period.[123]

To determine the earnings and profits for purposes of increasing or decreasing basis, a subsidiary using the cash receipts and disbursements method of accounting will be considered to have used the accrual method prior to the interim period. That is, the earnings and profits account will not be affected by income or expense properly accruable to the period before acquisition of stock by the parent.[124]

In order to carry out the letter of the regulations it may be necessary to perform an extremmly complicated computation.[125] Where a delay takes place between the acquisition of stock and the liquidation, it will be necessary to prepare a hypothetical financial statement. This is required to determine the earnings and profits during the interim period. Income may be produced during this period from sales of inventory in the ordinary course of business or from sales of assets. Expenses and distributions to the parent during the interim period will reduce the earnings and profits. Expenses complicating the earnings and profits adjustment are depreciation and income taxes paid. This complexity occurs because, in computing the interim-period earnings and profits, the computation is to be made as though the corporation had liquidated at the date of purchase. To do this, the basis must be allocated to the assets as of the time of purchase and the deductions computed using this basis.

Allocation of Basis

The regulations require that the adjusted basis in the stock be allocated among the various assets received, including tangible and intangible assets whether or not they are depreciable or amortizable. This allocation is ordinarily made in proportion to the net fair market values of such assets. The net fair market value is

---

[112]Reg. 1.334-1(c)(4)(i).

[113]Reg. 1.334-1(c)(4)(iii).

[114]Reg. 1.334-1(c)(4)(iv)(b).

[115]Reg. 1.334-1(c)(4)(iv)(a).

[116]Reg. 1.334-1(c)(4)(v)(a)(1).

[117]Reg. 1.334-1(c)(4)(v)(a)(2).

[118]Rev. Rul. 59-412, 1959-2 CB. 108.

[119]*First National State Bank of New Jersey*, 51 T.C. 419.

[120]*R.M. Smith, Inc. v. Commissioner*, 79-1 USTC ¶591 F.2d 298 9179.

[121]*Pacific Transport Co.*, 29TCM 133, T.C. Memo 1970-41; rev'd on another issue, 73-2 USTC ¶ 9615, 483, F.2d. 209.

[122]Reg. 1.334-1(c)(4)(v)(b)(1).

[123]Reg. 1.334-1(c)(4)(v)(b)(2).

[124]Reg. 1.334-1(c)(4)(vi)(d).

[125]See June, 1978 issue of *Journal of Taxation* for a viewpoint of the computation of interim period earning and profits adjustment.

defined as the fair market value of the asset less any specific mortgage or lien against it.[126]

There are certain assets to which basis is not allocated or to which an allocation is limited. These assets include:

1. *Cash and cash equivalents.* The regulations provide that the basis to be allocated be reduced by the cash and its equivalent. Accordingly, they are to be assigned a basis equal to their face amounts. The IRS has defined cash equivalents to include only currency, bank deposits, checks, money orders, drafts, savings and loan accounts and like items readily convertible into cash. It does not include other current assets such as inventory, marketable securities or accounts receivable.[127]

2. *Property contributed to subsidiary.* Where the property distributed in liquidation is property which was contributed by the parent to the capital of the subsidiary the regulations provide that such property will retain the basis it had prior to the contribution.[128] To allow otherwise would enable the parent to change the basis of an asset without recognition of any gain or loss.

3. *Property not received for stock.* Here again the regulations deny an allocation of the stock basis to any assets which are distributed in satisfaction of indebtedness rather than in exchange for stock.[129]

4. *Accounts receivable.* Although accounts receivable are an allocable asset, the IRS has ruled that such an allocation is to be limited. In a Revenue Ruling[130] the service stated that, since a receivable will never result in payment greater than its face amount, the allocated basis cannot exceed this amount. When the fair market value of the receivables exceeds the amount net of a reserve, the excess results in ordinary income. However, if it is determined that fair market value is the net amount (or the net amount plus part of the reserve), no ordinary income should be recognized as a result of the subsequent increase in allocated tax basis.

Since there is no limitation on a step-down of the accounts receivable, a basis lower than fair market value can result where the total value of all the assets exceeds the total tax basis.

5. *Inventory.* Inventory, like accounts receivable, is an allocable asset which is limited in the amount of basis that may be allocated to it. The IRS has expressed an opinion indicating the proper technique for valuing inventory.[131] The Rev. Proc. indicates how inventory is to be valued in a lump sum purchase of assets and a Sec. 334(b)(2) liquidation. The best means of valuing readily replaceable inventory in a wholesale or retail business is the reproduction method. The second method, comparative sales, values the inventory at the actual or expected selling price giving consideration to the time of disposition, the expenses expected to be incurred (discounts, commissions, freight, and shipping charges) and a reasonable profit.

The final technique for valuing inventory is the income method. This considers the revenue to be produced by the inventory in its ordinary course of business. Consideration should be given to the historical financial results in determining the revenue due to finished goods together with the selling costs and a fair rate of return.

Work in process should be valued using the above techniques, with the result being reduced by the costs to complete and a fair rate of return. Raw materials are to be valued at their current replacement cost.

In Rev. Rul. 74-431[132] the IRS stated that the "tax benefit rule" would not require recognition of income as a result of a LIFO reserve to the selling corporation where the seller does not recognize gain because of a bulk sale of inventory under Sec. 337. The courts[133] have interpreted this ruling to prohibit recognition of gain from recapture of the LIFO reserve in other situations as well, including a Sec. 334(b)(2) liquidation. In effect, the result of Rev. Rul. 74-431 is that LIFO inventory can be disposed of and revalued without recovery by any party of the reserve set up by the seller. The IRS has recently condemned the application of Rev. Rul. 74-431 to liquidation situations other than those under Sec. 337 although it has agreed that, as currently structured, the ruling will apply to these situations. However, in order to officially do so it would have to revoke the ruling, a procedure which the IRS acknowledged would not have retroactive application.[134]

---

[126]Reg. 1.334-1(c)(4)(viii).

[127]Rev. Rul. 66-290, 1966-2 C.B. 112.

[128]Reg. 1.334-1(c)(4)(viii).

[129]Reg. 1.334-1(c)(1).

[130]Rev. Rul. 77-456, 1977-2 C.B. 102.

[131]Rev. Proc. 77-12, 1977-1 C.B. 569.

[132]Rev. Rul. 74-431, 1974-2 C.B. 337.

[133]*South Lake Farms, Inc.*, 324, F. 2d. 837.

[134]T.I.S. 79-195 (May 4, 1979) and T.I.S. 79-232 (July 31, 1979).

In order to require the recapture of the LIFO reserve the Treasury proposed, as part of the ''Windfall Profits Tax'' bill, a provision calling for the recognition of the LIFO reserve upon a liquidation resulting in a cost basis.[135]

The IRS has taken the position that, in the event the basis to be allocated to inventory exceeds the fair market value, the basis is limited to the selling price.[136]

The remaining assets of the acquired corporation are to receive their pro rata share of the remaining tax basis. In order to allocate the basis, the fair market values of all the assets at the time of liquidation must be determined. The primary classes of remaining assets are:

1. *Fixed assets.* The fixed assets are comprised of such tangible assets as land, buildings and improvements, machinery and equipment, furniture and fixtures and automobiles and trucks. All of these assets, with the exception of the land, give rise to a deduction for depreciation. As such, it is usually to the taxpayer's advantage to ascribe as much basis as possible to them. It is here that the most significant advantage of a Sec. 334(b)(2) liquidation manifests itself. The fair market value of the fixed assets is usually determined by an independent appraisal.

2. *Intangibles.* There are two categories of intangibles which are inherent in a business. These are the amortizable and the nonamortizable intangibles.

(a). *Amortizable intangibles.* In order for an intangible to be amortizable it must have a separately determinable value and a limited, ascertainable useful life. Examples of these assets include patents, copyrights and trade marks, customer lists, franchises, covenants not to compete, license agreements, beneficial contracts, leases and purchase agreements and other assets limited by the imagination of the valuation expert.[137] The basis allocated to these assets will be amortized over a reasonably estimated useful life. If the separately identified and valued intangible is disposed of or abandoned, the value will be expensed.

Where certain classes of intangibles are comprised of a number of assets, as in the case of customer lists,

the IRS will challenge amortization (or expensing as individual components are abandoned) claiming the list is a non-severable mass asset. Such a list, it may be claimed, does not deteriorate over time, but rather is self-regenerating. In a number of cases the taxpayers have successfully overcome this challenge.[138]

(b.) *Nonamortization intangibles.* The second category of intangibles are the nonamortizable ones. These include primarily goodwill and going concern value; although no intangible will be amortizable if a value and a reasonable estimated useful life cannot be determined.

Goodwill is generally considered to be that element which gives an enterprise an advantage over other concerns in the same business. Going concern value on the other hand is considered to represent the expenditures which the buyer avoids by purchasing an enterprise rather than building it entirely by himself. As such, cases have determined that businesses lacking in goodwill do, in fact, possess going concern value.[139] The courts have stated that going concern value is the ''... additional element of value which attaches to property because of its existence as an integral part of a going concern.'' and ''... any assemblage of assets into a functioning, on-going business is capable of giving rise to going concern value.''[140] Although the Tax Court has valued the going concern element by the residual method[141], it would seem that the definition would support an approach which reasonably estimates the expenses which the buyer saved.

The techniques for valuing goodwill have been primarily one of two methods. Both of these procedures have been asserted by the IRS in various situations, depending on which produces the most favorable result for the government. The first approach is that applied in situations where the purchase price exceeds the fair market value of the assets. It has been the IRS position that the excess or ''residual'' amount represents the goodwill value of the enterprise. In a number of cases the courts have accepted this approach although not always to the government's benefit.[142] When the residual method is applied it is done so

---

[135]This proposal was adopted as part of the Windfall Profits Tax on April 2, 1980.

[136]L.R. 790 7006 (Sept. 8, 1978).

[137]A number of cases have determined useful lives of different intangibles using various industry and statistical data. *Latendresse v. Commissioner*, 57-1 USTC ¶ 9623, 243 F.2d 577; *Seaboard Finance Co. v. Commissioner*, 66-2 USTC ¶ 9707, 367 F.2d 646; *Houston Chronicle Publishing Co. V. U.S.* 73-2 USTC ¶ 9537, 481 F.2d 1240.

[138]*Seaboard Finance Co. v. Commissioner*, supra fn. (137); *Sunset Fuel Co. v. U.S.*, 74-1USTC ¶ 9422; *Credit Bureau of Erie, Inc.* 54 T.C. 726.

[139]*VGS Corporation v. Commissioner*, 68 T.C. 563.

[140]*Black Industries, Inc.*, T.C. Memo 1969-61.

[141]*V.G.S. Corporation*, supra f.n. (139).

[142]The IRS was successful in asserting the residual method in *Plantation Patterns, Inc. v. Commissioner*, 29 T.C.M. 817, aff'd. 72-2 USTC ¶ 9494 and *Philadelphia Steel and Iron corp. v. Commissioner*, 23 T.C.M. 558, Aff'd. 65-1 USTC ¶ 9308. The taxpayer asserted the residual method successfully in *Jack Daniels Distillery v. U.S.*, 67-2 USTC ¶ 9499 and *Moss American Inc. v. Commissioner*, 33 T.C.M. 1121 in refuting the IRS attempt to establish a bargain purchase.

because of lack of substantiation to support any other technique and gives the most realistic indication of value.[143] The effect of the residual method goodwill on the taxpayer can be readily observed by comparing two simple situations. Assume the total tax basis in all the assets is $1,000,000. If the fair market value of all the assets (excluding goodwill) is $750,000, the residual value for goodwill is $250,000. On the other hand, if the fair market value of the assets is $1,000,000 or larger, the resulting value of goodwill is $-0-.

The second method of valuing goodwill is that outlined by the Service in Rev. Rul. 68-609[144] known as the formula approach. This ruling defines goodwill as a capitalization of the rate of return on net tangible assets in excess of a fair rate of return. The ruling indicates that the "formula" approach is one technique to be considered and should be used only where no better method is available. Looking at the example above it is readily apparent why the IRS has argued for the "formula" value of goodwill in the second situation.[145] In the Service's view, any amount of goodwill is better than none at all. The effect on the taxpayer in a bargain purchase situation of the formula approach can be very detrimental since it takes basis away from depreciable assets. It may be wise for a corporation in this situation to take the offensive by putting forth an independently determined value for goodwill (which may, in a given case actually be $-0-) and allocating the basis among the assets.

An interesting result can be seen by applying the "formula" method in the reverse of what is the IRS approach. Suppose in the above example where the fair market of the assets is $750,000, that the "formula" value for goodwill is only $150,000 and there are no other unidentified intangibles. The total fair market value of all the assets is only $900,000 while the tax basis is $1,000,000. The regulations require that the tax basis be allocated to the assets in proportion to their net fair market values.[146] The result is that the tax basis of the assets will exceed their fair market value yielding a larger amount of depreciation.

At first it may appear unlikely that a buyer would pay more for a business than the sum of the value of its assets. However, comparing the public tender offers being made in recent years with the respective trading prices on the stock exchanges immediately prior to the offer[147], it is obvious that acquisitions are being made at prices significantly in excess of freely traded value. The Third Circuit Court of Appeals criticizing the residual method, clearly indicated that, in economic reality, either the buyer or the seller will receive the benefit of the bargain in any given transaction. The Court stated:

"... the theoretical underpinning of the residual value method is that the total price paid for the stock equals the sum of the fair market values of all of the underlying assets. Although this is a sound principle in economic theory, in reality it has its shortcomings. Specifically, it fails to take into account the common situation when one party to the transaction achieves a bargain. If the purchaser of the stock obtains a "good deal" then the residual value method would undervalue goodwill. If, on the other hand, the price is too high, then the computation will result in a correspondingly inflated goodwill figure ..."[148]

The effect on a taxpayer of independently valuing all the assets acquired upon a Sec. 334(b)(2) liquidation and allocating the basis to these assets can be seen from the following example. We will assume the liquidation takes place immediately after acquisition of control.

Determination of purchase price:

Cash paid	$ 5,000,000
Notes	1,000,000
Liabilities assumed	10,000,000
Tax liability from depreciation and ITC recapture	400,000
Earnings and profits adjustments (recapture of depreciation and allowance for doubtful accounts less tax liability)	600,000
Total tax basis	$17,000,000

This tax basis was determined in accordance with *R.M. Smith* and *First National State Bank of New Jersey*[149] by including as an interim period earnings and profit adjustment the depreciation recapture net of tax liability (Table 24-1 on page 402).

It can be seen that the result of this allocation is to increase the tax basis in depreciable assets. If the residual method of valuing goodwill were used, then the basis of the fixed assets would remain at fair market

[143]*R.M. Smith Inc. v. Commissiner*, 69T.C. 317, aff'd. 79-1 USTC ¶ 9179.

[144]Rev. Rul. 68-609, 1968-2 C.B. 327.

[145]*Jack Daniels Distillery* and *Moss American Inc.*, supra f.n. (142).

[146]Reg. 1.334-1(c)(4)(viii).

[147]Various examples include the acquisition of Carborundum Corp. by Kennecott Corp. and Eltra Corp. by Allied Chemical.

[148]*R.M. Smith Inc.* supra fn. (143).

[149]Supra fn. (119) and (120).

value of $9,000,000 rather than the allocated amount of $9,840,000. In addition, in the event the value of the assets is subsequently challenged and changed, the change will be spread over all the assets. The result is that some of the reduced value will be allocated back to depreciable assets.

With respect to the amortizable intangibles, the useful life for tax and book purposes will be the same since both look for reasonableness. However, while depreciation deductions for tax purposes will be determined from the allocated basis, the deductions for financial reporting purposes will be based on fair market values. Hence, the taxpayer receives an increased tax deduction without a corresponding charge against earnings. There will, however, be a permanent schedule M adjustment on subsequent tax returns.

Table 24-1
ALLOCATION OF TAX BASIS

	Fair market value	Cash and cash equivalents	Allocable assets Fair market value	Basis	Total tax basis
Cash	$ 500,000	$ 500,000	$ —	$ —	$ 500,000
Accounts receivable (face net of reserve of $50,000)	500,000	—	500,000	546,700	546,700
Prepaid expenses	100,000	100,000	—	—	100,000
Inventory	3,000,000	—	3,000,000	3,280,000	3,280,000
Fixed assets	9,000,000	—	9,000,000	9,840,000	9,840,000
Amortizable intangibles (i.e. contracts)	1,000,000	—	1,000,000	1,093,300	1,093,300
Goodwill	1,000,000	—	1,000,000	1,093,300	1,093,300
Going concern value	500,000	—	500,000	546,700	546,700
	$15,600,000	$ 600,000	$15,000,000	$16,400,000	$17,000,000

CONCLUSION

The most important point to be gained from the foregoing discussion is that the cost of a business is not the amount being exchanged between the buyer and seller. Any transaction will have a tax cost which may be substantial and borne by either the buyer or seller. The tax implications should be considered early in the negotiations and should form a part of the final agreement. The objective of the tax advisor will be to determine what the total tax implications will be for each of the purchase alternatives available. In addition to the Federal tax issues, others must be considered. For example, what is the sales tax liability resulting from a sale of assets. Or, if a liquidation is decided upon, can the new corporation step into the old corporation's shoes or will state law prohibit the transfer of a license to do business. The tax cost of an acquistion can be substantial and should be addressed throughout the transaction from the earliest planning to the tax policies adopted by the new owners.

ANTITRUST, SECURITIES AND STATE LAW GUIDELINES

In MANY LARGER BUSINESS COMBINATIONS the ultimate success of the transaction may well depend on whether it can withstand antitrust and securities law scrutiny. On September 5, 1978, the Federal Trade Commission issued final rules implementing Section 7A of the Clayton Act which imposed notice and waiting period requirements on certain acquisitions. This gave further import and enforcement standards to the substantive antitrust regulation of the Commission and Antitrust Division of the Department of Justice. Practitioners in the field of mergers, acquisitions and buyouts are well advised to determine the antitrust implications inherent in a transaction to be certain there is a likelihood the merger would survive a future legal challenge.

William C. Pelster covers the antitrust topical area by first identifying the basic federal antimerger statutes. He then goes on to explain in detail some of the considerations which go into performing antitrust merger analysis. This is particularly useful because of Mr. Pelster's personal experience in the field. The chapter contains a framework of various forms of analysis, discusses horizontal and vertical mergers, relevant market, perceived potential competition, and entrenchment. Finally, various methods of resolving or curing antitrust problems are given to the reader. Even though the subject matter of antitrust is complex and often unpredictable, the method and material contained in this chapter will furnish the reader with a relevant overview of the area.

Continuing the discussion of federal antimerger statutes, Robert D. Raven examines the procedural framework. He details all the independent obligations that Section 7A imposes on the parties to an acquisition over and above the normal antitrust standards. The legal and practical significance of supplying enforcement agencies with information about corporate operations and the planned transaction are clearly laid out for the reader. The penalties, such as treble damages for private plaintiffs under Section 4 of the Clayton Act, are also included in the subject of anticompetitive consequences. Other information on premerger notification, entities of control, exemptions, agency approval and foreign investment are technical subjects included for a broader understanding of this involuted topical material.

Securities law is no less important to the longevity and ultimate success of a transaction than antitrust law. The scope of authority and enforcement capabilities of the Securities and Exchange Commission (SEC) has grown enormously in recent years. There have been numerous new interpretations of the Securities Acts of 1933 and the SEC has displayed an appetite for legal confrontations where they believe proper disclosure has been lacking. Samuel Feder explains Rule 133, Rule 145 and Rule 146 provisions. He details the responsibilities and burdens of preparing and filing the appropriate registration materials. In addition, Mr. Feder discusses financial statements, notice period, and Blue Sky laws.

Rounding out this topical area is the article by Robert Jay Haber which analyzes the state laws affecting sales. It is not within the scope of this handbook to detail the requirements of each state. Therefore, Mr. Haber points out the important issues which are common to many acquisitions and subject to state regulation. Included are bulk sale statutes, state merger and consolidation statutes, Blue Sky laws, and product liability of successor corporations.

WILLIAM C. PELSTER

William C. Pelster is a partner in the law firm of Skadden, Arps, Slate, Meagher & Flom. He received a B.A. in Economics from Oberlin College in 1964 and a J.D. from the University of Michigan in 1967. He was law clerk to Hon. Leonard P. Moore, Judge of the United States Court of Appeals for the Second Circuit during 1967 and 1968. He has practiced in the areas of antitrust and litigation, with primary emphasis on mergers and acquisitions.

25

Basic Antitrust Guidelines In
Federal and State Law

WILLIAM C. PELSTER

I. INTRODUCTION

When planning a merger, acquisition, or other business combination, familiarity with the antitrust laws is not just helpful; it is essential. Ultimate success of the transaction may well depend on whether it can withstand antitrust scrutiny. A thorough merger analysis ought to be undertaken during the early planning stages of the transaction to determine its antitrust implications and whether the merger can survive legal challenge at some future date.

This chapter identifies the basic federal antimerger statutes, explains some of the considerations which go into performing an antitrust merger analysis, and sets forth the antitrust framework in which various forms of mergers are analyzed. Finally, various methods of resolving or curing antitrust problems are discussed.

A thorough merger analysis will be useful not only to prepare for an antitrust challenge that may arise when a merger is announced, but also to determine whether or not a merger will be secure against potential antitrust challenges in the future. As there is no statute of limitations for violations of the basic antimerger statute, a merger is not immune from challenge once the deal is completed. For example, in 1957, the Supreme Court held that the purchase made 40 years earlier by E.I. duPont de Nemours & Co. of an interest in General Motors violated the law. The Court decided that an action could be brought at any time an incipient threat to competition is revealed, whether it is at the time of the transaction or several decades later.[1]

The severe remedies that courts can order provide a further incentive for focusing on antitrust considerations early in the transaction. Compliance with an order requiring the disposal of all or part of a business, for example, may be difficult and expensive. The adverse business effects of dismembering a newly created corporation, such as those effects on customer relations, employee morale, and investor confidence, may be quite detrimental, and the financial costs of a divestiture may be ruinous.

One further reason to keep antitrust considerations in mind is that it is not uncommon for a company found to have committed an antitrust violation to be enjoined for a period of years from making certain, otherwise legal acquisitions.[2] Such a restriction can be a serious impediment to business growth.

Performing an antitrust merger analysis during the planning stage of a proposed transaction will enable the parties to predict and possibly to avoid any antitrust litigation. Irrespective of outcome, antitrust litigation is extremely time-consuming and expensive. Horror stories of protracted merger antitrust cases abound. For example, the Department of Justice's legal challenge to the 1957 acquisition of Pacific Northwest Pipeline Corporation by the El Paso Natural Gas Company lasted 17 years.[3] The case went to the Supreme Court on eight different occasions and divestiture was finally achieved ten years after the Supreme Court had ordered that remedy without delay.

This is not to say that even the most careful antitrust

---

[1]*United States v. E.I. du Pont de Nemours & Co.*, 353 U.S. 586, 597-98 (1957).
[2]*See, e.g., United States v. Swift & Co.*, 286 U.S. 106 (1932).
[3]*United States v. El Paso Natural Gas Co.*, 376 U.S. 651 (1964).

review will reveal all possible problems or predict with accuracy the outcome of an antitrust challenge. As will be obvious from the discussion which follows, the various antimerger laws are deliberately vague and their interpretation by the antitrust enforcement agencies and the courts has not always been a model of consistency. It would be foolhardy for anyone, even the most seasoned antitrust practitioner, to attempt to predict with certainty the result of an antitrust challenge to a merger or acquisition.

II. THE LEGISLATIVE BACKGROUND

To appreciate the antitrust considerations involved in a merger, it is essential to understand the major provisions of the basic federal antitrust laws.[4]

A. Sections 1 and 2 of the Sherman Act

The Sherman Antitrust Act was the first Congressional enactment to embody the goal that the American economy be preserved as a fully competitive system. Passed in 1890, the Sherman Act was a legislative response to social pressures that grew in part out of America's rapid shift from an agrarian economy to an urbanized industrial economy. The late 19th century pressures for reform were generated both by the farmers' discontent over falling crop prices and rising prices of manufactured goods and railroad services and by a public outcry against the predatory practices of large national and international cartels which restricted output, boosted prices skyward, and drove small competitors out of business.

Section 1 of the Sherman Act makes it a civil and criminal violation to engage in "any contract, combination ... or conspiracy, in restraint of trade"[5] in interstate or international commerce. This section sought to condemn those business practices sufficiently restrictive of competition to constitute a "restraint of trade." Normal business activities which restrained trade solely in a reasonable and ancillary fashion were not reached by this section.[6]

For example, a contract by a merchant to sell a particular item to a customer restrains trade because the rest of the world is foreclosed from buying that particular item from that merchant at that time. However, such a reasonable restraint arising from normal business activity would not be sufficiently restrictive to constitute a violation of the antitrust laws. Contrast this with an agreement among merchants to sell the same goods only at one predetermined price. Such an agreement would seriously restrict competition and thereby violate the Sherman Act.

Just as an agreement among competitors with respect to the price at which they will sell their goods restricts competition, so may a merger or other business combination of competitors. Thus, Section 1 of the Sherman Act can be used to challenge mergers and other business combinations where, for example, the companies are major competitors and the combination results in a significant elimination of competition.[7]

Section 2 of the Sherman Act outlaws the ultimate consequences of unreasonable restraints of trade; monopolization and attempts to achieve a monopoly. The prohibition of monopolization in Section 2 makes it a civil and criminal violation to possess the power to control prices or exclude competition and engage in some deliberate act to acquire or maintain that power, to foreclose competition, to gain a competitive advantage, or to destroy a competitor. Thus, an acquisition or a series of acquisitions that creates a monopoly may violate Section 2 of the Sherman Act[8] if the resulting firm's power to exclude competition is coupled with the intent to do so.[9]

A firm that does not possess monopoly power, i.e., the power to control prices or exclude competitors, may nevertheless violate Section 2 by attempting to monopolize. Actions taken with an intent to monopolize the market, including acquisitions, constitute the offense of attempted monopolization if there is a dangerous probability of success.

Soon after its passage, the Sherman Act was used to combat several of the giant business trusts whose economic abuses had inspired the earlier public outcry. The United States attacked the Oil Trust[10] and the

---

[4]In addition to federal statutes, the field of antitrust also includes state enacted legislation concerning restraint of trade, monopolization, acquisitions of competitors and other practices. Many such state laws include prohibitions against anticompetitive acquisitions. State law antimerger actions, brought by either public authorities or private plaintiffs, are extremely rare.

[5]15 U.S.C. §1.

[6]*United States v. Addyston Pipe & Steel Co.*, 85 F. 271 (6th Cir. 1898), *aff'd*, 175 U.S. 211 (1899); *United States v. American Tobacco Co.*, 221 U.S. 106, 180 (1911).

[7]*United States v. First Nat'l Bank & Trust Co.*, 376 U.S. 665, 671-72 (1964).

[8]*United States v. Grinnell Corp.*, 384 U.S. 563, 576 (1966).

[9]*United States v. Paramount Pictures, Inc.*, 334 U.S. 131, 174 (1948)

[10]The leading case in the attack on the Oil Trusts was *Standard Oil Co. v. United States*, 221 U.S. 1 (1911). The United States sued Standard Oil, seventy other corporate defendants, and seven individual defendants including John D. and William Rockefeller alleging that they conspired to monopolize and restrain trade in the petroleum industry. The remedy awarded consisted of both injunctive relief to prevent the activities from continuing into the future and divestiture to dissolve the combination.

Tobacco Trust[11] and forced them to split up into a number of smaller firms.

The chief problem with using the Sherman Act to attack mergers is the severe standard which must be met to prove a violation. Under Section 1, the party challenging a merger must prove not only an actual restraint on commerce, but one that unduly restricts the course of trade.[12] An attack under Section 2 requires proof of power to control prices or exclude competition, together with proof of acts to acquire or maintain that power. As a result of these strict standards, the Sherman Act proved to be unsuitable for challenging smaller aggregations of economic power which did not result in a provable restraint upon competition, but were believed, nonetheless, to lessen competition.

B. Section 7 of the Clayton Act

Soon after it was enacted, it became apparent that although the Sherman Act was useful in combating flagrant competitive abuses, it failed to stem what was perceived as a rising tide of concentration in the American economy. Once again, public pressure mounted and once again Congress searched for ways to preserve an economic system which allowed and encouraged many small competitors to thrive. Congress passed the Clayton Act which contained a number of provisions to achieve these goals in 1914.

Section 7 of the Clayton Act was aimed at the merger movement. It was designed to prevent threats to competition before they became unreasonable restraints of trade or monopolies. To accomplish this, it prohibited acquisitions by one company of stock of another company where the effect "may be substantially to lessen competition, or to tend to create a monopoly."[13]

Because Section 7 was drafted in such terms as "may be" and "tend to," it is violated where only the *probability* of harm can be shown. This standard, less onerous than that of the Sherman Act, makes Section 7 a far more useful tool in challenging mergers.

However, the standard is not so lax as to bar all mergers. The mere "ephemeral possibility" of a lessening of competition will not constitute a violation.[14] To violate Section 7, the impact on competition need not be a certainty, but must be more than a mere possibility. It is upon this fine semantic difference that most of the substantial body of antimerger law rests.

Originally, Section 7 applied only to acquisitions of stock. This proved to be a significant loophole as corporations were able to combine with impunity by purchasing one another's assets rather than stock. Section 7 was amended in 1950 by the Celler-Kefauver Act, which brought acquisitions of assets within the scope of the Act's provisions.[15] In 1980 the Act was amended to apply to acquisitions by or from individuals as well as corporations. With these amendments, Section 7 became a far more useful weapon in combating the increase in economic concentration. Today, Section 7 of the Clayton Act is the major statutory provision used to test the legality of a merger from an antitrust viewpoint.

C. Section 5 of the Federal Trade Commission Act

The Federal Trade Commission Act ("FTC Act"), which was also enacted in 1914, created the Federal Trade Commission and gave it authority under Section 5 to act against "unfair methods of competition in commerce, and unfair or deceptive acts or practices in commerce."[16]

By virtue of its sweeping language, there is considerable overlap between Section 5 and the antitrust laws. For example, courts have held that an acquisition which violates Section 7 of the Clayton Act may also violate Section 5 of the FTC Act if the acquisition itself constitutes an unfair method of competition.[17] As a result, Section 5 of the FTC Act can also be used to attack mergers where the jurisdictional requirements of other antitrust laws are not met. For example, prior to 1980 Section 7 of the Clayton Act did not apply to acquisitions by entities other than corporations, to an

---

[11]The leading Tobacco Trust case, *United States v. American Tobacco Co.*, 221 U.S. 106 (1911), was decided by the Supreme Court just two weeks after the case against the Oil Trust. The Court held that the government had proven that five large Tobacco concerns had merged and subsequently used their combined power to drive competitors out of business or force them to join the combination; the Supreme Court ordered injunctive relief to prohibit similar activity in the future and divestiture to break up the combination which had violated the Sherman Act. Other trusts which dominated the 19th century American economy included the Whiskey Trust, the Lead Trust, the Sugar Trust, and the Cotton Oil Trust.

[12]*Chicago Bd. of Trade v. United States*, 246 U.S. 231, 238 (1918).

[13]15 U.S.C. §18. Until 1980 Section 7 applied only to corporations which were engaged in the flow of interstate commerce, and did not apply to firms engaged only in local activities, even though those activities may affect interstate commerce. *See United States v. American Bldg. Maintenance Indus.*, 422 U.S. 271 (1975). A recent amendment broadened the Act's coverage to include firms engaged "in any activity affecting commerce." Public Law 96-349 (1980).

[14]*United States v. Marine Bancorporation, Inc.*, 418 U.S. 602, 622-23 (1974).

[15]For a discussion of the full legislative history of the Clayton Act and its amendments, *see Brown Shoe Co. v. United States*, 370 U.S. 294, 311-23 (1962).

[16]15 U.S.C. § 45.

[17]*Stanley Works v. FTC*, 469 F.2d 498, 499 n.2 (2d Cir. 1972), *cert. denied*, 412 U.S. 928 (1973).

acquisition from individuals,[18] or to the formation of a corporation as a joint venture by two individuals.[19] Section 5 was used to challenge these transactions.[20]

D. Other Merger Statutory Authority

In addition to the basic antitrust laws, there are many federal statutes which have an impact on mergers in certain highly regulated industries. The statutes often contain provisions concerning mergers in the regulated line of commerce. Examples of this type of legislation include the Federal Reserve Act, the Interstate Commerce Act, the Federal Aviation Act, and the Webb-Pomerene Export Trade Associations Act.

Bank mergers were given special treatment under the antimerger laws by virtue of legislation enacted in 1966.[21] Merging banks must comply with other statutes which require that the banks obtain approval by either the Federal Reserve Board or the Comptroller of the Currency prior to merger. If the Attorney General is to challenge the merger at all, he must do so within 30 days of approval by the government authority. Moreover, in such an attack, the merger will be upheld if any anticompetitive impact is "clearly outweighed" by the convenience and needs of the community.[22]

The Interstate Commerce Act[23] exempts acquisitions or mergers involving motor, rail, and ship common carriers from antitrust laws provided the transaction is approved by the Interstate Commerce Commission (ICC).[24] The ICC examines the proposed transaction in light of the public interest benefit from the transaction as well as the effect on competition.[25] If the public interest outweighs the anticompetitive impact, the ICC must approve the transaction even if it would otherwise violate the antitrust laws.[26]

III. MERGER ANALYSIS

A. The Mechanics of a Merger Analysis

The three major resources used to analyze the antitrust implications of a merger are the antitrust statutes, the merger guidelines promulgated by the antitrust enforcement agencies, and the decisions of the courts interpreting the meaning of the statutes.

The Clayton Act, Sherman Act, and FTC Act, as previously noted, provide the broad fundamental rules governing the legality of business combinations. A major problem, however, is presented by the ambiguous language of the statutes. When is a merger a "restraint of trade," an event which "tends to create a monopoly," or a transaction which constitutes an "unfair method of competition"? The statutes themselves, therefore, are not particularly useful when attempting to analyze the legality of a specific transaction.

A more helpful tool for analyzing mergers consists of guidelines promulgated by the Antitrust Division of the Department of Justice and by the Federal Trade Commission. In 1968, the Department of Justice published a set of standards which, it said, the Antitrust Division would use in deciding whether a merger or acquisition might violate the antitrust laws and, therefore, be challenged.[27] The stated purpose in issuing these Merger Guidelines was to acquaint the business community and the legal profession with the standards used by the Department of Justice in determining whether to challenge a merger. Although the Merger Guidelines do not have the force of law and courts are not bound to accept them, a number of courts have relied upon them when judging the legality of mergers.[28] The Merger Guidelines certainly provide a good starting point for a merger analysis.

The FTC has also promulgated a set of merger policy statements. Like the Department of Justice Merger Guidelines, these policy statements indicate the types of mergers the FTC is likely to challenge in particular industries. Specific FTC merger policy statements have been issued for the cement industry, the dairy industry, and the grocery products distribution industry.[29] They are based, in part, upon that federal agency's experience in analyzing and prosecuting

---

[18]Honeywell Inc. v. Sperry Rand Corp., 1974 Trade Cas. ¶74, 874 at 95, 944 (D. Minn. 1973): Bender v. Hearst Corp., 152 F. Supp. 569, 578 (D. Conn. 1957), aff'd, 263 F.2d 360 (2d Cir. 1959).

[19]Hudson Valley Asbestos Corp. v. Tougher Heating & Plumbing Co., 510 F.2d 1140, 1145 (2d Cir.), cert. denied, 421 U.S. 1011 (1975).

[20]See Beatrice Foods Co., 67 F.T.C. 473 (1965), modified by consent, 1967 Trade Cas. ¶72, 124 (9th Cir. 1967).

[21]12 U.S.C. §1828(c).

[22]12 U.S.C. §1828(c)(5)(B). See United States v. Phillipsburg Nat'l Bank & Trust Co., 399 U.S. 350, 370-72 (1970). However, the banks must show that there are no alternatives to the merger. United States v. Third Nat'l Bank, 390 U.S. 171, 189-90 (1968).

[23]49 U.S.C. § 5.

[24]Id. at § 5b(9).

[25]Minneapolis & St. Louis R.R. v. United States, 361 U.S. 173 (1959).

[26]See Federal Maritime Comm'n v. Aktiebolaget Svenska Amerika Linien, 390 U.S. 238, 245 (1968).

[27]1 CCH Trade Reg. Rep. ¶4510.

[28]See, e.g., F. & M. Schaefer Corp. v. C. Schmidt & Sons, Inc., 597 F.2d 814, 817 n.5 (2d Cir. 1979); Allis-Chalmers Mfg. Co. v. White Consol. Indus., Inc. 414 F.2d 506, 524 (3d Cir. 1969), cert. denied, 396 U.S. 1009 (1970). Unfortunately, in an area of the law that is constantly evolving, the 1968 guidelines may be viewed as being somewhat out of date today.

[29]1 CCH Trade Reg. Rep. ¶¶4520, 4532, 4525. Policy statements regarding mergers of firms in the textile mill products industry and in the grocery products manufacturing industry were withdrawn in 1975 and 1976. 40 Fed. Reg. 21,078 (May 15, 1975); 41 Fed. Reg. 51,076 (Nov. 19, 1976).

mergers in those particular industries.

Both the Department of Justice Merger Guidelines and FTC policy statements can be helpful to the lawyer or business person in predicting whether or not a proposed transaction will be challenged by the antitrust enforcement agencies.

The primary analytical resource is the large body of decisions of the courts and of the Federal Trade Commission under the antitrust statutes. These decisions attempt to explain and clarify the broad language of the statutes. The logic of court decisions in the merger area is sometimes difficult to follow and often contradictory. As in other areas of the law, shifting sociological and philosophical viewpoints have resulted in shifting, and sometimes conflicting, analyses. Nonetheless, by studying how the courts have interpreted the meaning of the statutes and applied them to particular fact situations, it is possible to make certain predictions with respect to the situation at hand.

B. The Types of Mergers

From an antitrust viewpoint, there are three basic types of mergers: horizontal, vertical, and conglomerate. It will be obvious that many mergers are not "pure," that is, they do not fit squarely within one of these classifications, but rather contain elements of two or more types.

Horizontal mergers are those between firms which manufacture or sell similar products in the same geographical area.[30] *Vertical* mergers are those between firms which presently or potentially stand in a supplier-customer relationship with each other.[31] All the rest are conglomerate mergers.

Pure conglomerate mergers are those between firms with no discernible relationships in the nature of their business.[32] Geographic extension conglomerate mergers are those between firms engaged in selling the same products, but in different geographic areas.[33] Product extension mergers are those by which the acquiring firm expands its present product offering into a complementary product line.[34]

IV. THE CONCEPT OF THE "RELEVANT MARKET"

Because Section 7 of the Clayton Act is violated only if there may be a substantial lessening of competi-

tion "in any line of commerce in any section of the country," the concept of the "relevant market" is critical to any analysis of the antitrust ramifications of a merger. The definition of a "market" is important because it is only within the context of markets that economists and the courts can assess the competitive impact of a merger. Anticompetitive impact (the lessening of competition) cannot be measured until the nature and the extent of that competition are first defined.

Relevant markets have both product and geographic dimensions, both of which must be proven. Determination of the relevant market depends largely upon the facts of each case and it is often the crucial question upon which success or failure of a challenge to a merger depends.[35]

A. The Relevant Product Market

The product market, which is largely determined by consumer preference, is often defined in broad economic terms. A product's interchangeability of use with other products or the cross-elasticity in consumer demand between the product and substitutes for it mark the boundaries of a product market. Commodities which are "reasonably interchangeable by consumers for the same purposes" make up the product market.[36]

However, the inquiry does not stop at this point. The product market must be "relevant." That is to say, it must have some bearing on the merger or acquisition being analyzed.

In a certain sense, all products have some degree of cross-elasticity of demand. Elementary economics teaches that if consumers buy more guns, they will have less money to spend on butter. Therefore, an increase in the price of guns will have some form of impact on the demand for butter. In order to exclude such tangentially connected relationships, the examination must focus on the firms involved in the particular merger under consideration and on the products produced or sold by these firms.

The "relevant" product market has at times been found to include goods produced by different industries. For example, in analyzing the acquisition by the second-largest metal can manufacturer of the third-largest glass jar manufacturer, the Sup-

[30]*See, e.g., United States v. Pabst Brewing Co.,* 384 U.S. 546 (1966); *United States v. Aluminum Co. of America,* 377 U.S. 271, (1964).
[31]*See, e.g., Brown Shoe Co. v. United States,* 370 U.S. 294 (1962).
[32]*FTC v. Procter & Gamble Co.,* 386 U.S. 568, 577 n.2 (1967).
[33]*See, e.g., United States v. Falstaff Brewing Corp.,* 410 U.S. 526 (1973); *United States v. El Paso Natural Gas Co.,* 376 U.S. 651 (1964).
[34]*See, e.g., Kennecott Copper Corp. v. FTC,* 467 F.2d 67 (10th Cir. 1972), *cert. denied,* 416 U.S. 909 (1974).
[35]*See, e.g., United States v. Household Finance Corp.,* 602 F.2d 1255 (2d Cir. 1979), *cert. denied,* 444 U.S. 1044 (1980).
[36]*United States v. E.I. du Pont de Nemours & Co.,* 351 U.S. 377, 395 (1956).

reme Court, using industry recognition and the historical competition between of the products in its analysis, lumped both metal and glass containers into one market, even though the interchangeability of the products was far from complete.[37] Thus, what might have been viewed as a conglomerate merger of noncompeting firms was, in fact, analyzed as a horizontal merger of competitors within the same "relevant" market.

By contrast, the relevant market has also been narrowed to the point that a combination of two competitors could not help but have a significant impact on competition. For example, it has been held that aluminum foil used for decorating flower pots was in a product market different from the aluminum foil used for other purposes even though it was physically identical to the other aluminum foils. The result of this finding was that a firm which would have had a very small share of the aluminum foil market was suddenly viewed as having a very large share of the much smaller florist foil market.[38]

The determination of the relevant market in both of the above cases was made by identifying the products produced by the merging firms and then observing the commercial realities of the market in which the buyers and sellers of those products operate. In the case involving the metal and glass containers it was observed that the products were interchangeable for many uses and that glass manufacturers vigorously competed with can manufacturers for a number of applications, such as containers for beer or baby food. Likewise, the segregation of florist foil from all other aluminum foil was considered appropriate because both firms sold this product and the realities of the marketplace were such that only a few firms specialized in selling aluminum foil to florists.

Some important considerations in an analysis of the realities of the marketplace when determining the relevant market include: distinct customers (as in the florist foil example); functional interchangability (as in the metal and glass container example); industry recognition (how trade associations or trade publications view the market); and unique production or selling facilities.[39]

In challenging acquisitions, the antitrust enforcement agencies typically take the position that the market is large enought to establish the presence of competition between the merging parties; yet narrow enough that the merger's impact will be viewed as substantial. Defenders of an acquisition typically take the view that markets should be defined narrowly so that the parties to the acquisition are not viewed as competitors or, failing that, that the markets are so broad that the combination cannot be viewed as a substantial lessening of competition.

B. The Relevant Geographic Market

The geographic market, used to analyze whether there is a lessening of competition in "any section of the country," is generally defined by the area in which the acquiring firm, the target firm and competing firms sell their product or the area in which the firms' purchasers can reasonably turn to obtain the same goods.[40] This determination often can not, and need not, be made with precision. If most firms in that line of commerce sell nationwide, then the geographic market will probably be considered the nation.[41] But, the relevant geographic market can be as small as a single state or even a single small town.[42]

Transportation costs are probably the most significant factor in limiting the area where sellers can sell and where purchasers can practically turn to buy goods at the same price, and so transportation costs are a chief factor limiting the size of the relevant geographic area.

It can readily be understood that one can ship paper products farther than one can ship ready-mix concrete products. Not surprisingly, the relevant market for analyzing a merger involving firms engaged in selling ready-mix concrete has been held to be a single metropolitan area.[43] By contrast, the relevant market for analyzing a merger involving firms engaged in selling paper products has been held to be several states or the country as a whole.[44] Other factors which may have great significance in making a geographic market determination include natural boundaries and state regulation of particular industries.

---

[37]*United States v. Continental Can Co.*, 378 U.S. 441, 447-58 (1964).

[38]*Reynolds Metal Co. v. FTC*, 309 F.2d 223 (D.C. Cir. 1962).

[39]*Brown Shoe Co. v. United States*, 370 U.S. 294, 335 (1962).

[40]*United States v. Philadelphia Nat'l Bank*, 374 U.S. 321, 357-62 (1963); *Tampa Electric Co. v. Nashville Coal Co.*, 365 U.S. 320, 330-33 (1961). *But see United States v. Connecticut Nat'l Bank*, 418 U.S. 656, 666-71 (1974); *United States v. Marine Bancorporation, Inc.*, 418 U.S. 602, 618-23 (1974).

[41]*United States v. Grinnell Corp.*, 384 U.S. 563, 575-76 (1966).

[42]*Brown Shoe Co. v. United States*, 370 U.S. 294, 336-39 (1962); *FTC v. Food Town Stores, Inc.*, 539 F.2d 1339, 1344 (4th Cir. 1976).

[43]*United States v. M.P.M., Inc.*, 397 F. Supp. 78, 88-89 (D. Colo. 1975).

[44]*United States v. Kimberly-Clark Corp.*, 264 F. Supp. 439, 455-58 (N.D. Cal. 1967).

Products such as lead or coal, with more complex distribution economics, require considerably more detailed analysis in determining the relevant geographic market.

There may be regional submarkets where a number of local sellers compete with a number of nation-wide firms. As the statute prohibits a lessening of competition in "any section of the country," a court may find several geographic markets and designate any market as the relevant geographic market for purposes of its analysis.[45]

V. ANALYSIS OF VARIOUS TYPES OF MERGERS

A. Horizontal Mergers

In analyzing the antitrust implications of a horizontal merger (a merger of firms in the same relevant geographic and product market), the two factors which are considered most significant are (1) the respective market shares of the parties to the merger and (2) the existing level of concentration in the relevant market.

It is, of course, mergers of competitors which most clearly result in the lessening of competition to some degree. Therefore, horizontal mergers will receive the closest scrutiny by the antitrust enforcement agencies. The greater the market shares of the merging firms or the resultant firm, the greater the likelihood that the acquisition will be challenged and the greater the likelihood that it will be found to violate the antitrust laws.

In horizontal mergers, the increase in market share resulting from the combination of competitors has become the primary indicator of a lessening of competition. Where the increase in market share is small (de minimis) the probability of a substantial lessening of competition is remote. The larger the increase in market share, the more likely the combination will be found to be illegal. In one case, the Supreme Court went so far as to suggest that when the combined market share of the merging firms would be too large, the merger would be found to be illegal without a further showing of lessening of competition.

> [A] merger which produces a firm controlling an undue percentage share of the relevant market, and results in a significant increase in the concentration of firms in that market, is so inherently likely to lessen competition substantially that it must be enjoined in the absence of evidence clearly showing that the merger is not likely to have such anticompetitive effects.[46]

What precisely constitutes an "undue percentage share of the market" or a "significant increase" in concentration is not easy to define. In this case, involving the merger of two commercial banks, the Supreme Court found that a 30 percent market share constituted an "undue percentage" and hinted that lesser market shares could also suffice.[47]

Where there has been a trend over a period of years toward fewer and fewer firms holding increasingly larger shares of the relevant market, a merger precipitating even an extremely small increase in market share has been found illegal.[48] Similarly, where there is already a high level of concentration in an industry, typically measured by the combined market share of the top four or the top eight competitors, the courts will be hostile to proposed mergers. This is especially true if the acquired firm, even though small, is aggressive and innovative and exerts a strong competitive presence in the market.[49]

The Department of Justice Merger Guidelines state that mergers of firms in highly concentrated markets (markets in which the shares of the four largest firms amount to approximately 75 percent or more) will ordinarily be challenged if they involve firms accounting for the following percentages of the relevant market:[50]

Acquiring Firm	Acquired Firm
4%	4% or more
10%	2% or more
15%	1% or more

Mergers of firms in less highly concentrated markets will ordinarily be challenged if they involve firms accounting for the following percentages of the relevant market:[51]

Acquiring Firm	Acquired Firm
5%	5% or more
10%	4% or more
15%	3% or more
20%	2% or more
25% or more	1% or more

---

[45]*United States v. Pabst Brewing Co.*, 384 U.S. 546, 549 (1966).

[46]*United States v. Philadelphia Nat'l Bank,* 374 U.S. 321, 363 (1963).

[47]*Id* at 364.

[48]*United States v. Von's Grocery Co.*, 384 U.S. 270 (1966). *See also United States v. Pabst Brewing Co.*, 384 U.S. 546 (1966).

[49]*United States v. Aluminum Co. of America*, 377 U.S. 271, 278-81, (1964).

[50]Guidelines, ¶5.

[51]*Id.* at ¶6.

The presumption of illegality arising from high market shares can sometimes be overcome, however, by showing other countervailing economic factors. For example, where it was found that a coal company would not be able to maintain its historically high market share because of its depleted reserves, the probability of a future lessening of competition as a result of its acquisition by another coal company was held to be remote.[52] In that unusual case, market share was demonstrated to be an unreliable indicator of competitive significance.

Another circumstance in which a merger involving firms with large market shares may pass the scrutiny of an antitrust analysis is where the acquired firm is in a failing financial condition. The rationale of the "failing company defense" is that if a company is destined to cease acting as a competitive factor in any event, a merger with a competitor cannot be perceived as a transaction lessening competition.[53] However, this is not a defense that is viewed favorably by either the antitrust enforcement agencies or the courts. Recent Supreme Court decisions have insisted that there be no other alternatives open for the failing firm to remain a competitive factor and that no other purchaser could be interested.[54]

B. Vertical Mergers

Vertical mergers (those between a customer and a supplier) pose two related anticompetitive threats; they may foreclose supply or raise barriers to entry. To illustrate, consider a merger where a firm acquires its supplier (a backward vertical merger) which also supplies some of the acquiring firm's competitors. To the extent that the acquiring firm's competitors are cut off or foreclosed from a source of supply, they will be disadvantaged and competition will be restrained. If the acquired supplier were one of only a few sources, the foreclosure may be substantial enough so that the merger violates the antitrust laws.

Such vertical mergers also may make it difficult for new firms to enter into competition. Where there are many independent suppliers, a new entrant need simply contact one or more of them to satisfy its requirements. However, if most potential suppliers are already owned by existing competitors, the new entrant may face substantial difficulties in obtaining a source of supply.[55]

Because competitors are presumed to have a natural reluctance to deal with one another, some courts take the position that foreclosure of the supplier's competitors can be presumed in a vertical merger.[56] Other courts, however, require proof that the acquiring firm has post-merger plans to force the acquired company to purchase from or sell to it.[57] Proof of a mere chance of foreclosure is not enough to establish a violation.

Vertical mergers allow one company to enjoy the advantages of being supplier, manufacturer, and possibly even retailer. Such an integration of commercial tasks may well improve efficiency through combined management and coordinated performance and, thereby, enhance competition. However, the Department of Justice has taken the position in its Merger Guidelines that improved efficiencies will not necessarily protect the merger from challenge. While not disapproving of vertical integration, the Department of Justice would prefer that it be undertaken through internal firm expansion.

C. Conglomerate Mergers

A great deal of recent merger activity has involved conglomerate mergers, *i.e.,* those which are neither horizontal nor vertical. Because conglomerate mergers do not pose any immediate threat of market foreclosure or increased concentration, they are more difficult to challenge under antitrust laws. Four legal theories have been offered to answer the reasonable contention that mergers between non-competitors cannot lessen competition: the theories of perceived potential competition, actual potential competition, entrenchment, and reciprocity. Each of the four theories requires that the acquired company be a substantial competitor in an oligopolistic or noncompetitive market.[58]

1. *Perceived Potential Competition*

The perceived potential competition theory focuses on the competitive threat posed by a firm poised on the edge or "in the wings" of the relevant market, waiting for an opportunity to enter. When that firm's presence is perceived by those already in the market, it presumably exerts a procompetitive force in the market. That

---

[52]*United States v. General Dynamics Corp.,* 341 F. Supp 534, 538-39 (N.D. Ill. 1972), *aff'd,* 415 U.S. 486 (1974).

[53]*International Shoe Co. v. FTC,* 280 U.S. 291, 301-03 (1930).

[54]*Citizen Publishing Co. v. United States,* 394 U.S. 131 (1969).

[55]*United States Steel Corp. v. FTC,* 426 F.2d 592, 604-05 (6th Cir. 1970).

[56]*See United States v. E.I. du Pont de Nemours & Co.,* 353 U.S. 586 (1957). Proof of foreclosure was provided by evidence that 68% of finishes and 39% of fabrics purchased by General Motors were purchased from Du Pont. "The inference is overwhelming that Du Pont's commanding position was promoted by its stock interest and was not gained solely on competitive merit." Evidence of intent to use this power "to overreach ... competitors" was not necessary according to the Court. 353 U.S. at 607.

[57]*Fruehauf Corp. v. FTC,* 603 F. 2d 345, 354-55 (2d Cir. 1979); *Copperweld Corp. v. Imetal,* 403 F. Supp. 579, 593 (W.D. Pa. 1975).

[58]*United States v. Falstaff Brewing Corp.,* 410 U.S. 526, 531 (1973).

is, companies already in the market realize that if they raise prices too high or keep output far below demand, the firm "in the wings" will enter the market as a competitor. Because they know this, the theory postulates, they tend to keep prices down and output up. The Supreme Court once said:[59]

> The existence of an aggressive, well equipped and well financed corporation ... waiting anxiously to enter an oligopolistic market would be a substantial incentive to competition which cannot be underestimated.

Thus, the acquisition of a company already in the market by the perceived potential entrant violates the antimerger laws by eliminating that procompetitive effect.

An example of this theory is provided by the Supreme Court's decision that El Paso Natural Gas Co. had violated Section 7 when it acquired the Pacific Northwest Pipeline Corp.[60] The Court found that Pacific Northwest, a large western natural gas supplier, was a potential entrant into the California natural gas market. Pacific Northwest was clearly perceived as a potential entrant as it had attempted to enter the market, albeit unsuccessfully, on numerous occasions. By acquiring Pacific Northwest, El Paso, a substantial firm in the California market, had destroyed whatever procompetitive effect Pacific Northwest's presence "in the wings" had on those who were already in the California natural gas market.

It should be noted that, under the perceived potential competition theory, the acquiring firm's internal decision making process (whether the firm had actually decided to enter the market) is irrelevant. Rather, the important question is whether the firm *reasonably appeared* to those firms already in the market to be a potential competitor. Even if a firm had decided that it would never enter the market or never enter other than through an acquisition, it may still, in the minds of existing competitiors, be exerting an influence on competition in the market.[61]

2. *Actual Potential Competition*

The actual potential competition theory focuses, not on perceptions, but on the *means* of entry. Where a firm with the capability and incentive to enter an oligopolistic market has feasible alternatives available to it, such as *de novo* entry or a toehold acquisition, the theory holds that it should enter by those alternative means rather than by acquiring a substantial competitor in the market. *De novo* entry is entry by a firm into the market through its own internal expansion. A company simply builds a plant and begins competing with those already in the industry. A toehold acquisition describes a situation in which a firm enters the market by acquiring a very small company in the industry it seeks to enter.[62] Both *de novo* entry and *toehold* entry could, presumably, increase competition in the market either by creating new competition or by making a small competitor more vigorous. The actual potential competition theory posits that the acquisition of a large company in the relevant market by a firm willing and able to enter by other means violates the antitrust laws by eliminating the possible future procompetitive effects which could have been brought about by a *de novo* or toehold entry.[63]

The actual potential competition theory does not contemplate a possible lessening of competition, as does the perceived potential competition theory. Rather, it contemplates only a diminution of the possibility of an increase in competition. The lost opportunity for future deconcentration is sometimes referred to as the "entry effect." As one court stated:[64]

> The crux of the entry effect is that if the company which enters the market by acquisition had entered unilaterally, it would have supplied an additional competitive force without eliminating one already present in the market. An acquisition of a company in the market by a company which is likely to enter on its own thus has an anticompetitive effect on the market.

As noted above, Section 7 of the Clayton Act requires a showing that the effect of the acquisition under review "may be substantially to lessen competition, or tend to create a monopoly." Since the theory of actual potential competition does not contemplate the lessening of competition, there is debate as to whether it is even covered by Section 7. The Supreme Court has twice declined to approve this theory of potential competition.[65]

---

[59]*United States v. Penn-Olin Chem. Co.*, 378 U.S. 158, 174 (1964).

[60]*United States v. El Paso Natural Gas Co.*, 376 U.S. 651 (1964).

[61]*United States v. Falstaff Brewing Corp.*, 410 U.S. 526, 533-37 (1973).

[62]The Federal Trade Commission has defined a toehold acquisition generally as an acquisition of a company with a market share of less than 10 percent. *See The Budd Co.*, 86 F.T.C. 518, 582 (1975).

[63]Courts which have considered the actual potential competition theory have required clear proof that the acquiring firm actually considered entering the market by either a *de novo* or toehold acquisition and that it was reasonable to do so in the near future. *BOC Int'l Ltd. v. FTC*, 557 F.2d 24 (2d Cir. 1977).

[64]*United States v. Phillips Petroleum Co.*, 367 F. Supp. 1226, 1232 (C.D. Cal. 1973), *aff'd*, 418 U.S. 906 (1974).

[65]*United States v. Marine Bancorporation, Inc.*, 418 U.S. 602, 639 (1974); *United States v. Falstaff Brewing Corp.*, 410 U.S. 526, 537 (1973).

3. *Entrenchment*

The theory of entrenchment postulates that the acquisition of a dominant competitor in a concentrated market by a much larger firm provides the acquired firm with a substantial competitive advantage (name, finances, or expertise) which further "entrenches" its dominant position, raises barriers to entry, or discourages smaller competitors from aggressively competing.

The entrenchment theory was the basis for the Supreme Court's finding that the 1957 acquisition of Clorox by Procter & Gamble Co. violated the antitrust laws.[66] Clorox was by far the largest seller of household liquid bleach, having more than 48 percent of national sales and much larger percentages in various local geographic markets. Since all bleach is chemically identical, advertising and sales promotion was found to be vital to Clorox's dominant position. Procter & Gamble was not only the nation's largest seller of related household cleaning products, it was the nation's largest advertiser and enjoyed substantial advantages in terms of discounts and preferred space from the advertising media. The Supreme Court concluded that smaller liquid bleach competitors would be "more cautious" in competing and that new entrants would be "much more reluctant" to compete with P&G than with the smaller Clorox. This lessening of competition was found sufficient to violate Section 7 of the Clayton Act.

Situations similar to the facts of the Procter & Gamble—Clorox merger are rare.[67] The entrenchment theory has not been applied with much success in recent years to challenges of acquisitions.[68]

4. *Reciprocity and Reciprocity Effect*

Reciprocity or reciprocal dealing refers to a firm's practice of utilizing the volume of its purchases to induce others to buy its goods or services. Reciprocity effect refers to the tendency of a firm selling to a particular company to purchase goods or services from that company.[69] A merger which results in either reciprocity or reciprocity effect may eliminate price competition. Therefore, such a merger may substantially lessen competition and thereby violate Section 7 of the Clayton Act.

For example, the Supreme Court found that the 1951 acquisition of Gentry, Inc. by Consolidated Foods Corporation violated the antitrust laws because it created the opportunity for reciprocal dealing.[70] Gentry, was a manufacturer of dehydrated onion and garlic and a substantial supplier of these products to food processors. Consolidated owned a network of wholesale and retail grocery operations and was a substantial purchaser from food processors. The merger, therefore, created the possibility that food processors would favor Gentry as a supplier in the hope of encouraging sales to Consolidated.

Recent cases have held that to establish a Section 7 violation based upon the theory of reciprocity, the plaintiff must prove that the merger "significantly increased opportunities for reciprocal dealing by creating a market structure which is conducive to reciprocity or reciprocity effect;" that there is a "reasonable probability that those opportunities will be exploited;" and lastly, that the resultant reciprocal dealings have a tendency to substantially lessen competition.[71]

VI. CURING THE ANTITRUST PROBLEM

When the merger analysis discloses a serious antitrust problem, the parties to the proposed transaction are faced with three choices: (1) abandon the merger plan; (2) push forward with the hope of prevailing in any legal challenge that might be forthcoming; or (3) attempt to resolve the antitrust problem. The decision must, of necessity, be based upon a mixture of business and legal considerations.

When the antitrust obstacles are obvious and substantial (as where the parties to the proposed transaction are major competitors in the same relevant market), serious consideration must be given to abandoning the acquisition. If the cause is hopeless or the risk of loss is great, a reasonable business judgment may be that the money for the acquisition can better be invested in internal expansion or in a different acquisition.

In most cases, the legality or illegality of a proposed merger will not be clear. As noted above, the antimerger laws are vague and their application has not

---

[66]*FTC v. Procter & Gamble Co.*, 386 U.S. 568, 577-79 (1967).

[67]*General Foods Corp. v. FTC*, 386 F.2d 936 (3d Cir. 1967), *cert. denied*, 392 U.S. 919 (1968).

[68]*See Missouri Portland Cement Co. v. Cargill, Inc.*, 498 F.2d 851, 865-66 (2d Cir. 1974), *cert. denied*, 419 U.S. 883 (1974); *United States v. Black & Decker Mfg. Co.*, 430 F. Supp. 729, 773-76 (D. Md. 1976); *Carrier Corp. v. United Technologies Corp.*, 1978-2 Trade Cas. ¶62,393 (N.D.N.Y.), *aff'd*, 1978-2 Trade Cas. ¶62,405 (2d Cir. 1978).

[69]*United States v. Int'l Tel. & Tel.*, 324 F. Supp. 19, 41-42 (D. Conn. 1970), *appeal dismissed*, 404 U.S. 801 (1971).

[70]*See FTC v. Consolidated Foods Corp.*, 380 U.S. 592, 594-95 (1965).

[71]*Carrier Corp. v. United Technologies Corp.*, 1978-2 Trade Cas. ¶62,393 at 76,371 (N.D.N.Y.), *aff'd*, 1978-2 Trade Cas. ¶62,405 (2d Cir. 1978).

been entirely consistent. Therefore, where the outcome of a legal challenge is in some doubt, it may be reasonable to decide that the legality of the transaction be determined by the courts. Assuming that the acquisition is not enjoined before it is consummated, the expense of protracted litigation may be more than offset by the return on the investment in the acquired firm during the period of the litigation. Divestiture, should it be ordered at the conclusion of the litigation, is often accomplished at a profit.

In many instances, the antitrust problem discovered in the merger analysis will involve only a small portion of either the acquired or the acquiring firm's business. It may be that the parties are competitors in only one of many lines of business or in only a few localities. In such cases, it is often possible to resolve the antitrust issues by divesting the offending assets.

There are a number of methods by which a potential antitrust problem can be resolved by eliminating the competitive overlap between the two companies. For example, a part of a business, particularly if it has been operated as a separate subsidiary, can be sold or be placed under a trust for divestiture at some future time. It is common, in settling litigation brought or threatened by the antitrust enforcement agencies, to agree to the entry of an order requiring divestiture of certain assets within a specified period of time.[72]

Indeed, even if the antitrust enforcement agencies are unwilling to settle, an agreement to divest or actual divestiture during trial may defeat a government challenge.[73]

In order to be successful in curing an antitrust problem, all of the details of the proposed divestiture ought to be clearly worked out. Vague promises are not likely to satisfy either the antitrust enforcement agencies or the courts.[74] Following the divestiture, the divested business must be independent of the merged companies and must be a viable company, occupying a competitive position at least equal to its predivestiture position.[75]

VII. CONCLUSION

This chapter has introduced the reader to the antitrust laws as they relate to mergers and acquisitions and explained the theories that have been used to determine the legality of horizontal, vertical and conglomerate mergers. It has been emphasized that antitrust is a complex and often times unpredictable area of the law. The business planner must be cognizant of the antitrust considerations inherent in any merger or acquisition. However, unless the planner desires the excitement of being caught in a quagmire of complex and protracted litigation, expert antitrust counsel should be consulted at the earliest possible opportunity.

---

[72]*See, e.g., Cooper Industries, Inc.,* [1976-1979 Transfer Binder FTC Complaints and Orders] Trade Reg. Rep. (CCH) ¶21,551; *Crane Co.,* [1976-1979 Transfer Binder FTC Complaints and Orders] Trade Reg. Rep. (CCH) ¶21,557.

[73]*FTC v. Atlantic Richfield Co.,* 549 F.2d 289 (4th Cir. 1977); *United States v. Atlantic Richfield Co.,* 297 F. Supp. 1061 (S.D.N.Y. 1969), *aff'd,* 401 U.S. 986 (1971); *United States v. Connecticut Nat'l Bank,* 362 F. Supp. 240 (D. Conn. 1973), *vacated on other grounds,* 418 U.S. 656 (1974).

[74]*See FTC v. Food Town Stores, Inc.,* 539 F.2d 1339, 1345 (4th Cir. 1976).

[75]*See United States v. Jos. Schlitz Brewing Co.,* 253 F. Supp. 129, 183-84 (N.D. Cal.), *aff'd,* 385 U.S. 37 (1966).

ROBERT D. RAVEN

ROBERT D. RAVEN is a partner in the San Francisco law firm of Morrison & Foerster. He has an A.B. degree with honors from Michigan State University, and an LL.B. (Order of the Coif) from the University of California Law School. He has written and lectured widely on antitrust law for the American Management Association, Practicing Law Institute, American Law Institute, and American Bar Association.

Mr. Raven has been an active member of the American Bar Association and the State Bar of California, and President of the Bar Association of San Francisco. He is a Fellow of the American Bar Foundation and the American College of Trial Lawyers.

RONALD G. CARR

RONALD G. CARR is a partner in the San Francisco law firm of Morrison & Foerster. He holds an A.B. degree (with great distinction) from Stanford University, an M.A. from the University of California, Berkeley, and a J.D. cum laude, Order of the Coif, from the University of Chicago Law School.

Mr. Carr was Editor-in-Chief of the University of Chicago Law Review. He served as Law Clerk to Chief Judge David L. Bazelon in the U.S. Court of Appeals and as Law Clerk to Associate Justice Lewis F. Powell, Jr. in the U.S. Supreme Court. He was Special Assistant to United States Attorney General Edward H. Levi and has been a lecturer at the School of Law of the University of California, Berkeley.

26

Antitrust: The Procedural Framework

ROBERT D. RAVEN

RONALD G. CARR

On September 5, 1978, the Federal Trade Commission's final rules implementing Section 7A of the Clayton Act, 15 U.S.C. §18a,[1] became effective, subjecting certain acquisitions thereafter made to Section 7A's notice and waiting period requirements. Neither Section 7A, enacted by Congress as Title II of the Hart-Scott-Rodino Antitrust Improvements Act of 1976,[2] nor the Commission's implementing regulations in any way alters the substantive antitrust standards applicable to acquisitions. Section 7A was designed, instead, to eliminate practical difficulties in the standards' enforcement. In brief, its purpose was to assure that the Federal Government's antitrust enforcement agencies—the Commission and the Antitrust Division of the Department of Justice—have, in advance of a planned acquisition, information sufficient to judge whether the acquisition violates antitrust standards and sufficient time to launch preventive legal action if they conclude that it does.

While Section 7A does not alter antitrust standards, it does impose independent obligations that can have great legal and practical significance to parties to an acquisition. Section 7A requires parties to relatively large acquisitions to supply the enforcement agencies with prescribed information about their operations and about the transaction in which they plan to engage.[3] After having supplied information, the parties must await the expiration of a waiting period—15 days for

cash tender offers, 30 days for other acquisitions—before consummating the transaction.[4] During this initial waiting period, either of the agencies (but not both) may, in its discretion, request additional information about the acquisition. Such a request automatically imposes an additional waiting period of 10 days for cash tender offers, 20 days for all other acquisitions, after the requested information is supplied.[5]

Failure to comply with these requirements carries potentially severe legal sanctions. Under Section 7A(g) (1), the United States may recover from "[a]ny person, or any officer, director or partner thereof," who fails to comply with the Act a civil penalty of up to ten thousand dollars per day, *i.e.*, for each day from the point when, given the date the acquisition was consummated, the required information should have been filed. Moreover, if a party to an acquisition fails "substantially to comply" either with the initial notification requirement or a subsequent request for additional information, a district court, on application of the Government, "*may* order compliance," "*shall* extend the waiting period," and "*may* grant ... other equitable relief ..."[6]

It is therefore critical, from the point of legal obligation, to determine at the earliest possible moment in planning an acquisition whether Section 7A's requirements will attach. It is equally critical from a practical standpoint. Antitrust analysis of a planned acquisition

---

[1]Pub. L. No. 94-435, 90 Stat. 1383 (1976).

[2]16 C.F.R. §§801 *et seq.* (1978).

[3]Clayton Act §7A(a) (1)-(3); 15 U.S.C. §18a(a) (1)-(3).

[4]Clayton Act §7A(b)(1); 15 U.S.C. §18a(b)(1).

[5]Clayton Act §7A(e); 15 U.S.C. §18a(e); 16 C.F.R. §803.20(c).

[6]Clayton Act §7A(g)(2); 15 U.S.C. §18a(g)(2) (emphasis added). The Court may not, however, extend the waiting period because of the failure of the target of a tender offer to meet the filing requirements.

necessarily takes into account the likelihood that an acquisition will receive advance scrutiny from the enforcement agencies. Before Section 7A's enactment, the likelihood of antitrust challenge to an acquisition depended in some measure on the likelihood that the agencies would get news of the acquisition—from S.E.C. filings or other available sources—and on the kinds of information the agencies could gather in the often brief time available to them before the acquisition was consummated.[7] Section 7A, however, assures that all acquisitions subject to its requirements will be scrutinized, at least to the extent possible from the information filed. Moreover, although the initial 30 (or 15) day waiting period probably will not adversely affect the great majority of transactions, a request for additional information and the additional waiting period it entails may seriously, perhaps fatally, disrupt the acquisition schedule. Therefore, when the timing of the acquisition's consummation is critical, it is essential to take appropriate steps to avoid a second request's potentially adverse impact. Finally, although the enforcement agencies' failure to make a second request or to file suit to prevent the acquisition does not preclude a future action for divestiture, the agencies' failure to take advantage of the information and time available to them may make the courts somewhat more reluctant to regard divestiture as an appropriate remedy, at least where it would involve clear loss.

In short, Section 7A has become the procedural fulcrum for enforcement of antitrust acquisition standards. This chapter first describes the procedures and remedies available to the enforcement agencies and private parties when they believe that an acquisition, whether subject to Section 7A or not, violates the antitrust laws. It then describes in detail Section 7A's requirements and the preparation necessary to assure compliance and to minimize potential interference with the acquisition schedule. Finally, it describes the steps that can be taken, through the use of both antitrust clearance procedures and Section 7A's notification itself, to help avoid antitrust attack.

I. ANTITRUST PROCEDURES AND REMEDIES

The Antitrust Division, the Commission, or private parties may seek, on antitrust grounds, to prevent an acquisition from taking place by filing suit for injunctive relief in federal district court. Failure of the enforcement agencies or private parties to seek or to succeed in getting injunctive relief does not, however, immunize an acquisition from antitrust attack once it is consummated. The enforcement agencies may still seek divestiture, whole or partial, of the acquired assets or stock. The Division proceeds in federal court under Section 15 of the Clayton Act, 15 U.S.C. § 25, the Commission through institution of administrative proceedings. There is, moreover, no statute of limitations on government suits seeking divestiture or other equitable relief;[8] the agencies have challenged acquisitions long after they were consummated, and sometimes have coupled challenges to recent acquisitions with attacks on earlier acquisitions. The federal courts are divided as to whether divestiture is available to private plaintiffs. Private plaintiffs may, however, seek treble damages under Section 4 of the Clayton Act, 15 U.S.C. §15, if they can show that an acquisition has anti-competitive consequences and that those consequences have caused them injury.[9]

The potential that one or more of the antitrust remedies will be invoked must, of course, enter into an intelligent assessment of an acquisition's costs and risks. Antitrust challenge can augment an acquisition's costs significantly, not only because of the loss if the challenge succeeds, but because of the substantial expense in litigating frequently very complex antitrust issues. Moreover, the uncertainty generated by injunctive and divestiture suits can seriously impede the acquired firm's operations. It can, for example, make it difficult to get or to keep competent management and possibly force delay of important business decisions. In addition, business operations can be hampered simply by the diversion of time and energy to litigation. All of these factors, not only the ultimate probability of success on the merits of the antitrust challenge, must be considered in evaluating the antitrust costs of an acquisition and in identifying possible steps to mitigate them.

A. Injunctions

Actions for an injunction against undertaking an acquisition often end, as a practical matter, at the preliminary injunction stage. If a preliminary injunction is granted and upheld on appeal, acquisition parties often will abandon the project rather than undertake the protracted expense and delay of a full-scale trial on the merits, where the eventual result is, in light

---

[7]See, e.g., C. Hills, ed., Antitrust Adviser §3.52 (2d ed. 1978).

[8]*United States* v. *E.I. duPont de Nemours & Co.,* 353 U.S. 586, 597, 607 (1957). The Court held in *duPont* that "the Government may proceed at any time that an acquisition may be said with reasonable probability to contain a threat that it may lead to a restraint of commerce...." Moreover, the Court held, and has reaffirmed in subsequent decisions, that the potential anticompetitive consequences of an acquisition are to be gauged as of the time of suit, not as of the date the acquisition took place. See *United States* v. *General Dynamics Corp.,* 415 U.S. 486, 505 (1974); *FTC* v. *Consolidated Foods Corp.,* 380 U.S. 592, 598 (1965).

[9]*Brunswick Corp.* v. *Pueblo Bowl-O-Mat, Inc.,* 429 U.S. 477 (1977).

of the court's preliminary judgment, unlikely to be favorable. If the preliminary injunction is denied, the acquisition is likely to have been consummated long before a final judgment can be had. The enforcement agencies can, of course, convert the suits into actions for divestiture. Private injunctive suits, however, which are often brought by the acquisition candidate's management against unfriendly takeover attempts, normally will be dropped.

Under Section 15 of the Clayton Act, the Antitrust Division can obtain a preliminary injunction against an acquisition if it can establish a reasonable probability that it will be able to prove, in a full-scale trial on the merits, that the acquisition violates antitrust standards. Apart from probability of success, however, courts take into account the likelihood of serious business harm to the acquisition parties if the acquisition is delayed, weighed against the efficacy of divestiture if an antitrust violation eventually is proved.[10] As discussed more fully below, the great problem with the divestiture remedy is that the acquiring and acquired firms may have become so thoroughly integrated in operations and personnel after the acquisition that it is difficult to separate them into viable independent firms. Accordingly, the district court may condition denial of the preliminary injunction on the defendant agreeing to "hold separate," *i.e.*, to operate the acquired firm as if it were an independent entity. So long as this is an acceptable short-term business course and the acquiring company is reasonably confident either of ultimate success or that divestiture can be accomplished without significant loss, it may propose this sort of compromise to the court or negotiate it with the Division.[11] Indeed, a negotiated hold separate order also makes a good deal of sense in cases in which an acquisition promises substantial rewards if consummated but in which there are serious antitrust questions, and divestiture after integration would be difficult and expensive. In such cases, holding separate at once preserves the promise, by avoiding a preliminary injunction, and reduces possible divestiture costs.

Under Section 13(b) of the Federal Trade Commission Act, 15 U.S.C. § 13(b), enacted in 1973, the Commission may bring suit in district court for an order restraining an acquisition pending issuance of a Commission complaint and eventual termination of Commission administrative proceedings against the acquisition. Although termed a "preliminary injunction," the order does not contemplate further proceedings on the matter in the district court; instead, the order is simply a mechanism to allow exercise of the Commission's cease and desist power, subject to direct review in a Circuit Court of Appeals.[12] Under Section 13(b), the injunction is to issue "[u]pon a proper showing that, weighing the equities, and considering the Commission's likelihood of ultimate success, such action would be in the public interest."[13] Most courts have read this standard as substantively equivalent to that applicable to a Division preliminary injunction request under Section 15.[14]

The results of the cases under Section 13(b) as well as Section 15, however, turn less on the verbal formulations than on the antitrust theory on which the challenge to the acquisition is based. Injunctions are far more likely to be granted in horizontal than in vertical or, certainly, potential competition or entrenchment cases. In horizontal cases, the substantive standards are straightforward; indeed, the cases often are won or lost on the market definition issues. In contrast, preliminary injunctions very rarely have been granted on potential competition grounds, even in market extension cases, in part because of the great complexity of the standards and the corresponding difficulties of proof. Moreover, in potential competition cases, the likelihood of rapid or irreversible integration of the enterprises is relatively small, and divestiture is more likely to remain an efficacious remedy even after protracted antitrust proceedings.

This point applies in even greater measure to private actions to enjoin acquisitions under Section 16 of the Clayton Act, 15 U.S.C. § 26. Such suits theoretically can be brought by competitors of the acquiring or acquired firms, or by others, including customers, who can show that the acquisition may cause them some palpable injury. In practice, the suits usually are brought, often joined to securities actions, by management of a target firm against an unfriendly takeover bid made either through private or open market purchases, tender offers, or both. The courts generally have held that a target firm has standing under Section 16 to maintain an action for injunctive relief based on such injuries as adverse impact on employee morale, revelation of trade secrets, and, indeed, the probability that the government agencies eventually will bring suit, to

---

[10]See *United States* v. *International Telephone & Telegraph Corp.*, 306 F. Supp. 766, 769 (D. Conn.), appeal dismissed 404 U.S. 801 (1969).

[11]See *United States* v. *Ling-Temco-Vought, Inc.*, 1969 CCH Trade Cases ¶45,069, at 52712.

[12]If an injunction is granted, the Commission must thereafter, within twenty days or a lesser period specified by the court, institute an administrative proceeding; failing this the injunction dissolves.

[13]*E.g.*, *FTC* v. *Atlantic Richfield Co.*, 549 F.2d 249 (4th Cir. 1977).

[14]One court, however, has said that Section 13(b) requires not a, "reasonable likelihood of success," but merely a "fair and tenable chance of success.. *FTC* v. *Lancaster Colony Corp.*, 434 F. Supp. 1088, 1090-91 (S.D.N.Y.1977).

the target's loss.[15] To obtain a Section 16 preliminary injunction a private plaintiff must show both that it may suffer irreparable harm and, under what is now the standard formulation, either that it is likely to succeed on the merits or that the "balance of hardships tips sharply in [its] favor" and its antitrust claims raise "serious questions."[16] Again, however, the verbal formulas are less important than the courts' practice. In assessing irreparable injury, the courts have looked, to some degree, to whether the acquisition would be likely to injure the acquired firm's competitive potential—i.c., whether divestiture would not be an efficacious remedy if the Government eventually filed suit. Again, this is most likely—and preliminary injunctions will therefore most often be granted—in horizontal cases; it is somewhat less likely in vertical cases, and least in conglomerate cases.[17] Indeed, to the authors' knowledge, in no case has a private plaintiff succeeded in getting a preliminary injunction based on potential competition theories alone.

There is some reason to believe, moreover, that Hart-Scott-Rodino's pre-merger notice requirements will reduce the courts' willingness to credit private plaintiffs' irreparable injury claims. In the early cases recognizing that target companies are threatened with injury sufficient for Section 16 standing, courts often stated that targets' actions to enjoin acquisitions serve as critical adjuncts to government enforcement efforts; targets have sufficient information and notice to bring timely injunctive actions, advantages that, before Hart-Scott-Rodino, the Government often lacked. In short, private injunctions served the public interest by giving the Government agencies time in which to act. But other courts—notably the Second Circuit in the *Cargill* case—cast a skeptical eye on these notions and on targets' assertions of injury even before Hart-Scott-Rodino.[18] With Hart-Scott-Rodino, the skepticism can be expected to increase. As to acquisitions to which it applies, the pre-acquisition notification requirements give reasonable assurance that the enforcement agencies will have had both the time and information necessary to take action themselves if they believe it appropriate. If the agencies have allowed the waiting period (or periods) to elapse without themselves filing suit, their inaction may be taken to indicate at least a tentative judgment that the acquisition does not seriously threaten to transgress antitrust stand-

ards. At a minimum, it means that eventual Government suit is, although theoretically possible, unlikely; in any event, the private injunction is unnecessary to preserve an opportunity that the agencies themselves have decided to forego.

The options available to avoid or to settle private injunctive actions may, of course, differ radically from appropriate responses to Government suits. In the usual private action brought by incumbent management, the plaintiff's interest in the antitrust merits usually is tactical. Suit is brought to prevent a takeover that incumbent management believes contrary to the interests of the target, often for reasons having nothing to do with the purposes of the antitrust laws. Ways of avoiding or settling a private suit may accordingly have little to do with underlying antitrust difficulties and more with, for example, the price offered and, perhaps, assurances to incumbent management. In contrast, if Government determinations to sue are to be avoided, it is only by eliminating or at least reducing what the enforcement agency believes to be the acquisition's anti-competitive potential. So, for example, if the acquiring firm and the acquisition candidate compete in only one segment of manifold operations, the acquiring firm might, in advance of the acquisition, agree to sell its competing operation to an unaffiliated third party. Or the merger or acquisition agreement might provide for "spinning off" the acquired firm's overlapping assets in the form of a new corporation, with shares going *pro rata* to the shareholders. There are, of course, other possible options. The critical task is to identify as early as possible the genuine antitrust objections to an acquisition and to consider the business sense of the options available to cure them. This effort is easiest in the course of a negotiated acquisition. Indeed, it may be possible to use the Division's and the Commission's business review procedures, described below, and also the consultations that can accompany or follow the Hart-Scott-Rodino notification process to isolate the enforcement agency's concerns and to formulate reasonable business steps to mitigate them.

Once suit is filed, these possibilities may narrow. A partial divestiture accomplished during the course of suit may moot the antitrust issues and either avoid or justify vacating a preliminary injunction.[19] But such post-complaint divestiture may be difficult to arrange.

---

[15]*E.g., Allis-Chalmers Mfg. Co.v.White Consolidated Industries, Inc.*, 414 F.2d 506,510 (3d Cir. 1969), *cert. denied* 396 U.S.1009 (1970).

[16]*E.g., Charlie's Girls, Inc.* v. *Revlon, Inc.*, 483 F.2d 953 (2d Cir. 1973).

[17]Compare *Missouri Portland Cement Co.v.Cargill, Inc.*, 498 F.2d 851 (2d Cir.), *cert. denied*, 419 U.S. 883 (1974) with *The F. & M. Schaeffer Corp.* v. *C. Schmidt & Sons, Inc.*, 1979 CCH Trade Cases ¶62,573 (2d Cir. 1979).

[18]*Missouri Portland Cement Co.* v. *Cargill, Inc., supra*, 498 F.2d at 866-67.

[19]See *FTC* v. *Atlantic Richfield Co.*, 549 F.2d 289, 299 (4th Cir. 1977); *United States* v.*Atlantic Richfield Co.*, 297 F. Supp. 1075 (S.D.N.Y. 1969).

Moreover, courts may decline to regard an offer of partial divestiture made to avoid a preliminary injunction as sufficient, absent a convincing showing that the divested business will be a strong competitor.[20]

The possibility of injunctive actions presents significant risks of loss for both the acquiring and acquired companies (and their shareholders). The greatest difficulty can come if, in response to a Government challenge, the parties cannot agree on the appropriate course of action. It has therefore become customary to provide in the acquisition agreement that either party may withdraw if the Government enforcement agencies challenge the acquisition before it is completed.

B. Divestiture

Once an acquisition has taken place the usual remedy sought in Government actions is divestiture, often accompanied by a ban on future acquisitions in specified lines of commerce for a five- or ten-year period unless the enforcement agency approves. Although some courts have held that divestiture can take the form of rescission, *i.e.,* return of the acquired assets or stock to the company from which acquired,[21] rescission has never, to the authors' knowledge, been ordered. Accordingly, the primary risk of divestiture is on the acquiring company.

As noted above, the courts are divided as to whether divestiture is a proper remedy in suits brought by private plaintiffs under Section 16 of the Clayton Act. The Ninth Circuit has held that Congress did not intend the injunctive relief available under Section 16 to include divestiture and that private plaintiffs can obtain only an injunction directed at specific anti-competitive practices that result from an acquisition.[22] Courts in other circuits have disagreed.[23] But although divestiture is theoretically available to private plaintiffs outside the Ninth Circuit, to the authors' knowledge it has never been ordered in a private action.

In the *duPont* case the Supreme Court stated that, although the court may consider the potential for loss in choosing among equally efficacious remedies, divestiture "is simple, relatively easy to administer, and sure. It should always be in the forefront of a court's mind when a violation of §7 has been found." Accordingly, the Court held that where "complete divestiture is a necessary element of effective relief the Government cannot be denied (the divestiture) remedy because economic hardship, however severe, may result."[24] Therefore, in cases in which an acquisition presents potentially serious antitrust problems, the acquiring firm must take into account the possibility that complete or partial divestiture eventually may be ordered, and that the price obtainable in divestiture may be something less—perhaps substantially less—than the price paid, whether because of a declining market or because the assets have less value to possible potential purchasers than they had to the acquiring firm. A divestiture order, moreover, may significantly restrict the class of permissible buyers. If the acquiring firm is unable to locate a buyer at what it regards as a reasonable price within a reasonable time, the court may appoint a trustee to accomplish the sale subject to its approval. In order to assure the economic viability of the divested firm or assets, the court may also impose collateral responsibilities on the acquiring firm—for example, provision of adequate working capital, sharing trade secrets and customer lists, and, in vertical cases, agreements to purchase a certain percentage of production. Indeed, in some cases the Commission and the courts have refused to allow only partial divestiture of the particular operations which present antitrust difficulties, insisting instead on full divestiture to assure the economic health of the divested enterprise.[25]

The enforcement agencies have long believed that, despite these sorts of measures, divestiture is most often not an effective remedy. It may often be that the only available purchasers are large firms which themselves could be considered potential, independent entrants into the market. More frequently, the problem has been that, by the time an antitrust suit has come to final judgment, the acquired and acquiring firms have become completely intermeshed, and it is impossible to reconstitute the acquired firm as a viable independent entity.[26] There has, moreover, been a great deal of skepticism about the economic wisdom and efficiency of attempting divestiture, especially where it is a remedy, not for present anti-competitive effects, but for the kinds of probable future anti-competitive effects on which Section 7 claims are based.[27] These doubts have special weight where the economic viability of the

---

[20]*E.g., Chemetron Corp.* v. *Crane Co.,* 1977-2 Trade Cases §61,717 (N.D.Ill. 1977).

[21]*E.g., United States* v. *Phillips Petroleum Co.,* 1972 Trade Cases ¶73,900 (C.D. Cal. 1971).

[22]*International Telephone & Telegraph Corp.* v. *General Telephone & Electronics Corp.* 518 F. 2d 913 (9th Cir. 1975); *Calnetics Corp.* v. *Volkswagen of America, Inc.,* 532 F.2d 674 (9th Cir.) *cert. denied* 429 U.S. 940 (1976).

[23]*E.g., Fuchs Sugar & Syrups, Inc.* v. *Amstar Corp.,* 402 F. Supp. 636, 640 (S.D.N.Y. 1975).

[24]*United States* v. *E.I. duPont de Nemours & Co.,* 366 U.S. 316, 327-28, 330-31 (1962).

[25]*E.g., OKC Corp.* v. *FTC,* 455 F.2d 1159 (10th Cir. 1972).

[26]See Elzinga, The Antimerger Law: Pyrrhic Victories? 12 J.L. & Econ. 43 (1969).

[27]R. Posner, Antitrust Law: An Economic Perspective, 78-95, 223 (1976).

divested enterprise, and hence its future significance as an independent market factor, is uncertain.

Such concerns about the efficacy of the divestiture remedy were the major impetus to passage of Hart-Scott-Rodino's pre-merger notice requirements.[28] Section 7A can be taken, at least in some measure, not only as greatly facilitating the Government's ability to obtain preliminary relief, but also as encouraging its use, in preference to possibly costly post-acquisition remedies that have uncertain economic effects. In some cases, of course, the anti-competitive consequences of an acquisition may not be discernible until after the fact. This may be the case, in particular, where the acquisition is only the most recent of a series, each relatively small (and perhaps not subject to the notification requirements at all), but having a cumulative anti-competitive impact. More frequently, however, given pre-acquisition notice, predictions of anti-competitive effects for Section 7 purposes will be as readily made before an acquisition as after. In short, Hart-Scott-Rodino may to some degree deflate the kind of enthusiasm for divestiture that the Supreme Court expressed in *duPont*, since, in the usual case, advance notification will have provided the enforcement agencies with ample opportunity to take preventive action and so avoid both the private and public loss that divestiture after the fact can cause.

C. Treble Damages

In *Brunswick* v. *Pueblo Bowl-O-Mat* the Supreme Court held that to obtain treble damages for a violation of Section 7, a plaintiff must "prove more than injury casually linked to an illegal presence in the market." Instead, the plaintiff must show what the Court termed "antitrust injury," *i.e.,* that anti-competitive effects or acts, the probability of which rendered the acquisition unlawful under Section 7, had in fact occurred, and that those effects or acts damaged the plaintiff.[29] Subsequent cases, especially the Ninth Circuit's *Purex* decision,[30] suggest that the *Brunswick* formulation may have wide range. Purex, a competitor of Clorox, brought a treble damage action claiming that Procter & Gamble's acquisition of Clorox had in fact had the anti-competitive effects which had previously led the Supreme Court to hold the acquisition unlawful. The acquisition's illegality had been predicated on such matters as Procter's "deep pocket" and the possible increases in efficiency, advertising discounts, and

other competitive advantages that Clorox's access to Procter's "deep pocket" supposedly would allow. In the Ninth Circuit's judgement, if Purex could prove that these effects occurred and that, in consequence, Clorox's market position improved at Purex's expense, Purex could recover treble damages.

The *Purex* result may be theoretically sound, but its practical significance is difficult to discern. In practice, the critical point may be whether the courts will insist on reasonably persuasive proof of the extent to which improvement in competitive position *in fact* resulted from the acquisition rather than from a course of conduct in which the acquired firm might equally have engaged had it remained independent. Such proof would be difficult to come by. Indeed, in major part Section 7 was enacted because it is so difficult to discern, with any precision at all, the degree to which changes in market behavior or position result from acquisitions rather than market forces. If Section 7 treble damage actions require such proof, they may be as rare in the future as they have been in the past. Perhaps the only alternative, however, is to assume that *any* improvement in the acquired firm's position (and any harm to its competitors) was the result of the acquisition's anti-competitive potential. But this alternative would often greatly and unfairly exaggerate the extent of antitrust injury.[31]

In the short run, at least, *Purex* promises to make treble damages actions premised on Section 7 violations more common, especially where a divestiture judgment obtained by the Government can be invoked to estop litigation of the antitrust merits. In vertical and conglomerate cases the most likely plaintiffs will be competitors of the acquiring or acquired firms; in horizontal cases plaintiffs are likely to be purchasers or, perhaps, suppliers. In any event, the litigation inevitably would be complex and could add significantly to an acquisition's costs.

II. PREMERGER NOTIFICATION

Section 7A of the Clayton Act, in its initial section, provides that:

> [N]o person shall acquire, directly or indirectly, any voting securities or assets of any other person, unless both persons (or in the case of a tender offer, the acquiring person) file notification ... and the waiting period ... has expired ...

---

[28]See Smith & Lipstein, Premerger Notification: Coverage, Corporate Planning and Compliance, 47 Antitrust Law Journal 1181, 1182-83 (1979).

[29]*Brunswick Corp.* v. *Pueblo Bowl-O-Mat, Inc.*, 492 U.S. 477, 488-89 (1977).

[30]*Purex Corp.* v. *Proctor & Gamble Co.*, ___ F.2d ___ (1979).

[31]See Berkey Photo, Inc. v. Eastman Kodak Co. 603 F.2d 263, 296-98 (1979), *cert. denied* 48 U.S. L.W. 3517 (Feb. 19, 1980)

The requirement applies if the acquisition meets three basic tests—the "commerce" test, the "size of parties" test, and the "size of transaction" test—and if, under Section 7A(c) and the implementing regulations, the transaction is not exempt.

The statute generally does not define the terminology it employs. Instead, in Subsection (d), it empowers the Commission, with the concurrence of the Antitrust Division, to define its terms, as well as to exempt transactions "not likely to violate the antitrust laws" and to prescribe the form and content of the required notification. In carrying out this mandate, the Commission has constructed an extraordinarily complex framework of rules to govern both the applicability of the Act and proper completion of the notification form. It is possible here to describe only the basic elements of this framework and to provide an explanation sufficient, for the general run of acquisitions, to determine whether Section 7A's requirements apply, to guide proper completion and filing of the necessary notification, and to understand the mechanics of the waiting periods.

The regulations, however, interpret Section 7A broadly to reach transactions apart from the ordinary stock or asset acquisition primarily dealt with here. For example, the regulations apply the Act's requirements to the formation of certain corporate (but not partnership) joint ventures. Moreover, many apparently straightforward transactions will raise questions, particularly in completion of the form, to which the regulations seem to supply no very certain answer. On these points, first resort should be made to the Premerger Notification and Compliance Guide, prepared by the Commission's Premerger Notification Office and available from the Commission's Public Reference Branch, which contains detailed explanations both of the regulations themselves and of the various items on the form, and to the extensive Background Information that accompanied publication of the regulations in their final form.[32] But, on some points, the Compliance Guide, Background Information and the regulations themselves are equally obscure. If such points are encountered, counsel should feel free to consult the Commission's Premerger Notification Office to request either a formal[33] or informal interpretation. In the authors' experience, the Office has been unfailingly willing to provide, on a hypothetical case basis, its view of what the statute and regulations require. Informal advice that no notification is required may not legally estop the agencies from subsequently insisting on notification, but it should substantially reduce the possibility that either agency will seek civil penalties. Equally important, informal advice as to the notification's proper content will increase the probability that the Office will find the notification, as filed, in "substantial compliance" with the regulations' requirements and so sufficient to begin the running of the waiting period.[34]

A. Applicability

Persons: The critical first step in determining the applicability of the Act and in fulfilling the Act's notice obligation is to identify the "persons" to which the Act's requirements attach. The regulations define the term "person" as "an *ultimate parent entity* and all *entities* which it *controls* directly or indirectly."[35] The regulations then define each of these terms of the Act:

1. "Entity" means "any natural person, corporation, partnership, joint venture, association, joint stock company, trust, foundation, fund, institution, society, union, club or other group organized for any purpose, whether incorporated or not, wherever located and of whatever citizenship; or any receiver, trustee in bankruptcy or similar official or any liquidating agent for any of the foregoing ..."[36]

2. "Ultimate parent entity" means "an entity which is not controlled by any other entity."[37]

3. The pivotal term is thus "control." It means "(1) holding 50 percent or more of the outstanding voting securities of an issuer; *or* (2) having the contractual power presently to designate a majority of the directors of a corporation, or in the case of unincorporated entities, of individuals exercising similar functions."[38].

---

[32]43 Fed. Reg. 33450-33534 (July 31, 1978). On many points of the statute and regulations, an invaluable compilation of the relevant legislative and regulatory histories, as well as the authors' assessments of the regulations' probable interpretations, can be found in S. Axinn, B. Fogg & R. Stoll, Acquisitions Under the Hart-Scott-Rodino Antitrust Improvements Act (1978).

[33]See 16 C.F.R. §803.30.

[34]15 U.S.C. §18a(b) (1) (A), (g) (2).

[35]16C.R.F. §801.1(a)(1).

[36]16 C.F.R. §801.1(a)(2). The term also includes a joint venture which is to be formed and the voting securities of which are to be acquired. It does not include U.S. or foreign governmental units except "corporations engaged in commerce."

[37]16 C.F.R. §801.1(a)(3).

[38]16 C.F.R. §801.1(b).

4. Finally, the term "hold" means "having beneficial ownership, whether direct, or indirect through fiduciaries, agents, controlled entities or other means."[39]

These definitions allow identification of the "acquiring person"—the person that, as a result of the acquisition, will hold assets or voting securities directly or indirectly—and the "acquired person"—the person that includes the issuer of the voting securities or the entity whose assets are being acquired.[40] Assume, for example, that Corporation A has a wholly owned subsidiary X and a 50 percent stock interest in a joint venture Y. X is to acquire assets from Corporation Z, 70 percent of whose securities are owned by Corporation B. In this example, Corporation A is the ultimate parent entity; A, together with entities X and Y which it controls, are the "acquiring person." The "acquired person" is Corporation B, together with Z, an entity it controls. Assume, however, that A is to acquire voting securities of Z from N, a natural person, for cash. B, together with all the entities it controls, is again the acquired person, because Z, the issuer of the securities, is included within person B. Since Z is not controlled by N and therefore is not included within person N, N is not an acquired person and need not file notification.[41]

In some situations there may be more than one acquiring or acquired person. Thus if, in the example above, the acquisition was to be made by joint venture Y, the other 50 percent of whose stock was owned by Corporation C, Corporation C (together with all entities it controls) would also be an "acquiring person." In some transactions—for example, mergers and consolidations, and stock-asset exchanges—each person will be both an acquired and acquiring person.[42] Moreover, if, as a result of a merger, shareholders of the acquired firm will receive shares in the acquiring firm, the shareholders will themselves be acquiring persons and separately subject to the Act.[43] Finally, the

regulations apply the Act's requirements to what are termed "secondary acquisitions." A secondary acquisition occurs when the acquiring person— "A" —acquires control of an issuer— "B"—which in turn holds a less than controlling interest in a third corporation—"C." A's acquisition of shares in C is subject separately to the Act's requirements, with A as the acquiring person and the person including C as the acquired person.[44]

The task of identifying the acquiring and acquired persons and all entities they include is complicated by the extremely broad definition of "entity." Assume, for example, that acquiring person A has the right to designate the trustee of its employee pension trust. Under the regulations, A "controls" the trust because of its power of appointment and accordingly the trust is an entity included within Person A.[45]

Acquisitions: The Act applies to "acquisitions" of "assets" or "voting securities." The regulations nowhere expressly define the terms "acquisition" or "assets." In practical operation, however, "acquisition" means a change in the person that holds assets or voting securities unless accomplished by gift, intestate succession, devise, or creation of an irrevocable trust.[46] Thus, a transaction between two entities within the same person is exempt; it involves no change in the "person" holding the assets or voting securities.[47] "Assets" presumably has the broad meaning given it in cases under Section 7 of the Clayton Act.[48] Section 7A itself defines "voting securities" as:

"any securities which at present or upon conversion entitle the owner or holder thereof to vote for the election of directors of the issuer or, with respect to unincorporated entities, persons exercising similar functions."[49]

Thus, by the terms of the Act, the acquisition of convertible debentures would be subject to the reporting requirement. The regulations, however, provide that

---

[39] 16 C.F.R. §801.1(c)(1). The regulations require consolidation of the "holdings" of natural persons with those of their spouses and minor children; they also contain special rules to determine which entity "holds" the assets of a trust, and for collective investment funds and insurance companies. 16 C.F.R. § 801(c)(2-7).

[40] 16 C.F.R. §801.2(a), (b).

[41] See 16 C.F.R. §801.21(b).

[42] 16 C.F.R. §801.2(c), (d).

[43] 16 C.F.R. §801.2(e).

[44] 16 C.F.R. §801.4.

[45] See 43 Fed. Reg. at 33459.

[46] See 16 C.F.R. §802.71.

[47] 16 C.F.R. §802.30.

[48] See S. Axinn, B. Fogg, & R. Stoll, supra note 30, at 85-87.

[49] 15 U.S.C. §18a(b)(3).

the Act applies, not when such securities are purchased, but instead when they are converted into voting securities.[50]

As noted above, an acquisition is subject to the Act's reporting requirements only if it meets three tests:

1. *Commerce:* Either the acquiring person or the acquired person must, under Section 7(A)(1), be "engaged in commerce or in any activity affecting commerce." Under the regulations, the test is satisfied if any entity within either the acquiring or acquired persons is engaged in activities affecting commerce.[51] As a practical matter, almost any transaction involving United States firms and, indeed, many foreign firms will satisfy the test.

2. *Size of Persons:* Section 7A(2) sets out three alternative formulas for determining whether the persons involved in an acquisition are sufficiently large, in terms of annual net sales or total assets, to require notification. In brief, the test is satisfied if the acquiring person has "total assets or annual net sales" of $100 million or more and the acquired person has total assets of $10 million or more or, if "engaged in manufacturing," either annual net sales or total assets of $10 million or more.[52] The test is also satisfied if the acquiring person has annual net sales or total assets of $10 million or more, and the acquired person annual net sales or total assets of $100 million or more. Annual net sales and total assets are to be determined from, respectively, the person's "last regularly prepared annual statement of income and expense" and the "last regularly prepared balance sheet," adjusted as necessary to consolidate the net sales and assets of all entities included within the person.[53]

3. *Size of Transaction:* Under Section 7A(3), an acquisition is reportable only if, as a result of the acquisition, the acquiring person will hold *either* 15 percent or more of the voting securities or assets of the acquired person *or* an aggregate total amount of the voting securities and assets of the acquired person in excess of $15 million.

With respect to assets, the regulations require the following calculations to determine whether the 15 percent test is met:[54]

1. Calculate the value of the total assets of the acquired person, using its last regularly prepared financial statement, dated, in all events, within 15 months prior to the acquisition's consummation.[55]
2. Determine the value of the assets to be acquired, as shown on the acquired person's books.
3. Divide the value of the assets to be acquired, as determined in Step 2, by the total assets, as determined in Step 1.

If the resulting percentage is less than 15, the percentage standard is not met.

With respect to voting securities, the percentage standard requires the following calculation:[56]

1. Determine the total number of votes for directors of the issuer that the acquiring person will be able to cast after the acquisition is consummated. (The figure includes, in addition to voting securities to be acquired, those already held unless their acquisition was covered by certain exemptions).[57]
2. Determine, from the issuer's most recent SEC filing, the total number of votes that may presently be cast by all outstanding voting securities, or that will be entitled to be cast after the acquisition, whichever is greater.
3. Divide the acquiring person's votes (Step 1) by the total number (Step 2).

Again, if the resulting percentage is less than 15, the percentage standard is not met.

To determine whether the alternative $15 million test is met, it is necessary to calculate the value of the voting securities, assets, or both that the acquiring person will hold as a result of the acquisition. For this purpose, the acquiring person must add the value of all voting securities to be acquired, determined by the valuation methods set out in Regulations Section 801.10(a), to the value of voting securities already held, determined by the methods set out in Regulations Section 801.13(a)(2).[58] With respect to assets, it is necessary to value the assets to be acquired, plus all assets acquired from the acquired person within the

---

[50] 16 C.F.R. §§801.32, 802.31.

[51] 16 C.F.R. §801.3.

[52] A person is "engaged in manufacturing" if "it produces and derives annual sales or revenues from products," within the 1972 Standard Industrial Classification Manual's manufacturing codes - 2000-3999. 16 C.F.R. §801.1(j).

[53] 16 C.F.R. §801.11.

[54] 16 C.F.R. §801.12(c), (d).

[55] See 16 C.F.R. §801.11(b), (c).

[56] 16 C.F.R. §801.12(a), (b).

[57] 16 C.F.R. §801.15.

[58] Again, voting securities already held may be disregarded if their acquisition was subject to certain exemptions. 16 C.F.R. §801.15.

180 days previous to the acquisition agreement.[59] The valuations are to be made by the methods set out in Regulations Section 801.10 (b), (c).[60] If the total of all these figures is more than $15 million, the size of transaction test is satisfied.

If, however, the transaction satisfies the percentage test but does not satisfy the dollar value test, the "minimum dollar value" exemption comes into play. Under this exemption as it was amended,[61] an assets acquisition is exempt whenever the $15 million test is not met. A voting securities acquisition is exempt if the $15 million test is not met and either (1) the acquisition will not give the acquiring person control of the issuer *or* (2) the issuer has neither annual net sales nor total assets of $25 million or more. Assume, for example, that Corporation A will acquire voting securities of Corporation B valued at $14 million. So long as the securities amount to less than 50 percent of the total outstanding, the transaction is exempt because it does not confer control. Even if the securities confer control, the transaction is exempt if C has annual net sales and total assets of less than $25 million.

Notification Thresholds: If an acquiring person makes a series of acquisitions of the voting securities of an issuer, notification must be filed each time an acquisition results in crossing what the regulations term a "notification threshold."[62] The acquiring person must file, first, when, as a result of the acquisition, it will hold securities (and assets) valued at more than $15 million; second, when it will hold 15 percent or more of the outstanding voting securities if valued in excess of $15 million (the minimum dollar value exemption would otherwise apply); third, when it will hold 25 percent or more of the outstanding voting securities (again assuming the value exceeds $15 million); and finally, when, as a result of an acquisition, the acquiring person will hold 50 percent or more of the issuer's voting securities. As to the 50 percent threshold, the acquiring person will be obtaining "control" of the issuer; hence, the minimum dollar value exemption will apply only if the issuer's annual net sales and total assets are less than $25 million.

The purpose of the notification thresholds is to assure that the enforcement agencies are informed when, but only when, an acquiring person significantly increases its interest in the issuer. Accordingly, each acquisition that results in meeting or crossing one of the thresholds must be reported notwithstanding that an earlier acquisition was reported, or that the acquiring person's holdings crossed a threshold prior to the effective date of the rules, or that increases in market value or events other than an acquisition caused the acquiring person's holdings to cross a threshold.[63] Moreover, the acquiring person's notification with respect to an acquisition expires one year after expiration of the waiting period. If, within the year, the acquiring person does not meet or exceed the notification threshold as to which notification was filed, it must file a new notification if it wants to make additional purchases which would cross that threshold.[64] But if the threshold for which notification was given was timely crossed, the first filing will allow the acquiring person, at any time within five years after expiration of the waiting period, to increase its holdings up to the next highest notification threshold.[65] Thus, assume that A files notice that it intends to acquire 25 percent of B's voting securities. A observes the waiting period, but then succeeds in purchasing only a 20 percent interest during the next year. A must then file a new notification if it intends to make additional purchases which would cross the 25 percent threshold. On the other hand, if A succeeded in purchasing 25 percent of B's voting securities within a year of its notification, A may, at any time within five years after expiration of the waiting period, purchase up to 50 percent of B's voting securities. A may even sell its voting securities, and subsequently buy more without filing. But it may not increase its holdings to 50 percent or more without notification. Once, however, an acquiring person obtains "control," *i.e.,* an interest of 50 percent or more, any further acquisition is exempt from the Act.[66]

Exemptions: Many of the exemptions to the Act's requirements, especially the minimum dollar value exemption, have already been discussed. The most important of the other transactions exempted by the Act itself and the regulations are:

1. Acquisition *"of goods or realty in the ordinary course of business."*[67] This exemption and the regula-

[59] 16 C.F.R. §801.13(b). Previous asset acquisitions that were subject to the exemptions identified in 16 C.F.R. §801.15 need not be included.
[60] Assets previously acquired are to be valued as of the date of their acquisition. 16 C.F.R. §801.13)b)(2(ii).
[61] 16 C.F.R. §802.20 (January, 1980).
[62] 16 C.F.R. §801.1(h), 801.20.
[63] 16 C.F.R. §801.20.
[64] 16 C.F.R. §803.7.
[65] 16 C.F.R. §802.21.
[66] 15 U.S.C. §18a(c)(3).
[67] 15 U.S.C. §18a(c)(1).

tion expounding it are clear in concept but often obscure in application. The regulation expands the statutory exemption to cover acquisitions of voting securities of issuers whose sole assets consist of real property or assets incidental to the ownership of real property.[68] The regulation goes on to say, however, that an acquisition will not be deemed "in the ordinary course of business" if, as a result, the acquiring person will hold "all or substantially all of the assets of [an] entity or an operating division thereof," unless the entity's assets consist solely of real property and its incidents. This seems almost perfectly circular. It implies, however, that when an entity's assets are solely real property, an acquisition of either the assets or the entity's voting shares can be "in the ordinary course of business" even though, from the selling entity's standpoint, the sale may be quite extraordinary. In fact, of course, a broad interpretation of the exemption makes a great deal of antitrust sense. It will be rare that transfer of realty in itself will raise any conceivable antitrust objection.

2. *Agency approved or supervised acquisitions:* Certain acquisitions subject to advance approval by federal regulatory agencies are exempt, so long as the enforcement agencies are supplied copies of approval application materials.[69]

3. *Acquisition Solely for the Purpose of Investment:* Acquisition of voting securities is exempt if two conditions are met: (1) as a result of the acquisition, the acquiring person will hold 10 percent or less of the issuer's outstanding voting securities; *and* (2) will do so "solely for the purpose of investment"[70] *i.e.,* the acquiring person "has no intention of participating in the formulation, determination, or direction of the basic business decisions of the issuer." If the acquiring person takes advantage of this exemption and thereafter decides to participate actively in the issuer's affairs, notice must be filed.[71] Institutional investors, as defined in the regulations, are allowed a more generous investment exemption.[72]

4. *Foreign Investments:* The regulations contain elaborate rules exempting certain acquisition by "United States persons"[73] of foreign assets or voting securities,[74] and certain acquisitions by "foreign persons"[75] of foreign or U.S. assets or voting securities.[76] The exemptions contain various tests generally directed to determining whether the acquisition will have a significant effect on U.S. commerce. Acquisitions by or from "foreign govermental corporations"—corporations controlled by a foreign government or agency—are exempt if the acquisition relates only to assets located in the foreign government's territory or to voting securities of an issuer organized under the foreign government's laws.[77]

Summary: The complexity of the regulations reflects an effort by the enforcement agencies to apply the Act's requirements to almost all transactions that arguably could generate serious antitrust enforcement interest. Yet the regulations' elaborate structure inevitably leaves loopholes—possibilities for arrangements that technically would avoid the Act's reporting and waiting obligations.[78] The Commission has addressed these possibilities in Section 801.90 of the regulations:

> Any transaction(s) or other device(s) entered into or employed for the purpose of avoiding the obligation to comply with the requirements of the act shall be disregarded, and the obligation to comply shall be determined by applying the act and these rules to the substance of the transaction.

In short, it will ordinarily profit little to attempt to locate loopholes. Indeed, in ordinary circumstances, the only onerous aspect of complying with the Act may be the labyrinthine process of trying to determine whether, under the regulations, the Act applies in the first place. The mechanics of reporting and waiting are, at least by comparison, simple.

---

[68] 16 C.F.R. §802.1.

[69] 15 U.S.C. §18a(c)(6), (8); 16 C.F.R. §§802.6, 802.8.

[70] 16 C.F.R. §802.9.

[71] 16 C.F.R. §801.1(i)(1). The FTC has indicated that having a representative on the board, proposing corporate action, nominating a director, or simply being a competitor of the issuer may negate investment purpose. 43 Fed. Reg. at 33465.

[72] 16 C.F.R. §802.64.

[73] The term is defined in 16 C.F.R. §801.1(e)(1).

[74] 16 C.F.R. §802.50.

[75] The term is defined in 16 C.F.R. §801.1(e)(2).

[76] 16 C.F.R. §802.51.

[77] 16 C.F.R. §802.52.

[78] Assume, for example, that A acquires 49 percent of the voting securities of B for $14.5 million, and that this figure is the maximum valuation under the regulations (which do not necessarily reflect any premium for practical control). The transaction falls within the minimum dollar value exemption. B then redeems 5 percent of its outstanding shares from shareholders other than A, a transaction exempt under 16 C.F.R. §802.30, because both the acquiring person and the issuer are the same person. A now "controls" B, but not as a result of its acquisition.

B. The Mechanics

Timing: An acquisition may not be consummated until the applicable waiting period and the additional waiting period, if any, have expired. The assets or stock may, however, be held in escrow pending expiration. Moreover, as noted above, the acquisition must be consummated within one year after the end of the waiting period; if it is not, the notification is no longer effective.

In all instances, both the acquiring and acquired persons must file notifications. But the commencement of the waiting period—and hence the date when the acquisition may be consummated—turns on the nature of the transaction. In asset acquisitions, the waiting period always commences on the day the enforcement agencies have in hand the notifications, in acceptable form, of *both* the acquiring and acquired persons, and end 30 calendar days thereafter.[79] For securities acquisitions the situation is more complex. In mergers or consolidations, the waiting period begins only when both persons have filed and ends after 30 days. In almost all other securities transactions however—including tender offers, open market purchases, negotiated purchases from persons other than the issuer, conversion, exercise of options or warrants, and secondary acquisitions—all defined in Regulations Section 801.30,[80] the waiting period begins when the *acquiring* person files. It ends 15 days thereafter if the acquisition is a cash tender offer, 30 days thereafter in all other cases.[81] Where the waiting period begins when the acquiring person files, the acquiring person's notification must be accompanied by an affidavit attesting that the acquired person has *received* a prescribed notice of the acquiring person's intention to file.[82] The acquired person must then file on the fifteenth (or, in cash tender offers, the tenth) day after the acquiring person filed.[83] The acquired person's failure to meet this obligation does not, however, affect the running of the waiting period. If a tender offer is amended or renewed during or after the waiting period, special rules apply to limit additional filing requirements.[84]

Any person who is required to file can request the agencies to grant early termination of the waiting period. Under the regulations as interpreted by the agencies,[85] the agencies will exercise their discretion to grant early termination only when (1) both have concluded that they will take no further action during the waiting period and (2) the requesting party demonstrates serious business reasons for its request, such as financing contingencies. Moreover, the FTC has advised that early terminations will not be granted unless notification has been received from both parties.

When timing is critical to consummation of a transaction, these rules can present difficulties. In some circumstances, it may be possible to submit the necessary notifications well in advance of the critical consummation date, although, as discussed above, not more than one year. In other cases, early filing will not be possible. In Rule 801.30 transactions, the regulations require the acquiring person to attest that it has a good faith intention to make the acquisition and, in tender offers, that public announcement has been made. In non-801.30 transactions, the acquiring person must attest that "a contract, agreement in principle or letter of intent to merger or acquire has been executed."[86] In some situations, the acquiring person may find itself unable to so attest until shortly before the planned consummation date. In these situations, it may be possible to employ the enforcement agencies' business review procedures, described below, in combination with a request for early termination. In brief, the acquiring firm may be able to submit the equivalent of notification under the business review procedures, together with any additional information available to persuade the agencies that the contemplated acquisition presents no antitrust difficulty. If clearance can be obtained by this method, the agencies should be ready to grant early termination once notification is filed.

The Report Form and "Substantial Compliance": The required notifications are to be made on the Notification and Report Form prescribed by the regulations.[87] The acquiring person's form must be accompanied by the affidavit prescribed in Section

---

[79] 16 C.F.R. §803.10.

[80] 16 C.F.R. §801.30.

[81] 16 C.F.R. §803.10(b).

[82] 16 C.F.R. §803.5(a).

[83] 16 C.F.R. §801.30(b)(2).

[84] 16 C.F.R. §802.23.

[85] 16 C.F.R. §803.11(c) and the Formal Interpretation, Apr. 10, 1979.

[86] 16 C.F.R. §803.5.

[87] A copy of the Form, together with explanation of its various inquiries, is contained in the Premerger Notification Compliance Guide.

803.5 of the Regulations. Two notarized copies of the form are to be submitted to the Commission's Premerger Notification Office and three notarized copies to the Antitrust Division's Director of Operations, accompanied by one set of documentary attachments for each of the agencies.[88]

By the terms of Section 7A, the waiting period begins to run on the date that both agencies have received *either* the completed notification form *or* "if such notification is not completed, the notification to the extent completed and a statement of the reasons for noncompliance."[89]

As the legislative history explains:

[Section 7A] does not require absolute and complete compliance with either the required premerger notification form or any subsequent request for additional information before the waiting period or the extension period begins to run ... [Section 7A] provides that the waiting and extension periods will commence running upon receipt by the FTC and the Justice Department of the completed notification, together with a specific statement of the reasons for the partial non-compliance ... If the omitted data [are] withheld by the parties for frivolous, unjustifiable, or improper reasons, the Justice Department or the FTC may seek a court order, subsection (g) (2), extending the premerger waiting period until there has been "substantial compliance"—that is, until the notification form has been substantially completed ...[90]

The obligation, in short, is "substantial compliance." What this means in practice is that the Form must be formally complete, with all necessary affidavits and certifications. Moreover, there must be a response to each applicable question, with appropriate notations to those that are inapplicable. Most important, if a response cannot be made, or if the information available is incomplete, the filing person must state: (1) why it is unable to respond completely, (2) what further information would be necessary to respond completely, and (3) who has the necessary information and what efforts have been made to obtain it.[91] Unless these steps are taken and taken with care, the agencies

may give notice that the filing is deficient, and thus delay the beginning of the waiting period until a "substantially complete" form has been filed.[92]

In general, the information required by the form should present little real difficulty, although it may take some effort to extract it from corporate files and convert it to the required form. Briefly, the form calls for the following general items:

1. Certain basic information about the acquiring and acquired persons;

2. Basic information and documents describing the transaction;

3. Identification of entities within the person filing notification, their principal shareholders, and the entities' shareholdings, if any, in unaffiliated issuers;

4. Information about dollar revenues in various Standard Industrial Classification categories, restricted to revenues from U.S. operations, and, for acquired persons, to revenues from the assets being acquired or of the issuer, included within the acquired person, whose voting securities are being acquired;[93]

5. If two parties to the acquisition derived dollar revenues from the same SIC categories, or maintained a vendor-vendee relationship, additional information may be required as to the areas of overlap; and

6. Certain basic, recent financial documents, plus "all studies, surveys, analyses and reports which were prepared by or for any officer(s) or director(s) ... for the purpose of evaluating or analyzing the acquisiton with respect to market shares, competition, competitors, markets, potential for sales growth or expansion into produce or geographic markets ..."

The Form thus calls for what may be highly sensitive business information, but it is critical to note that Section 7A expressly exempts the submitted information from the Freedom of Information Act. The material may be disclosed to committees of Congress or, as relevant, in judicial or administrative proceedings. Apart from these possibilities, however, the Act prescribes that "no ... information or documentary material may be made public ..."[94]

---

[88]The addresses of the agencies are provided on the first page of the form.

[89]15 U.S.C. §18a(b)(1)(A).

[90]122 Cong. Rec. H 10293 (daily ed., Sept. 16, 1976) (remarks of Cong. Rodino).

[91]16 C.F.R. §803.3.

[92]16 C.F.R. §803.10(c)(2).

[93]16 C.F.R. §803.2(b), (c).

[94]15 U.S.C. §18a(h).

In completing the Form, two kinds of problems are most likely to arise. First, difficulties may be encountered in extracting the SIC data from corporate records. In such instances, the Form allows estimates, if necessary, identified as such and indicating their basis. Second, the "studies, surveys and analyses" called for in the Form's Item 4(c) may include items that are protected by privilege. Although the legislative history plainly does not contemplate that privileged material must be supplied,[95] the Commission has taken the position that failure to provide documents, within the scope of the request, on the ground of privilege constitutes non-compliance unless the bases for the asserted privilege are fully explained.[96]

Relying simply on explanations of non-compliance under the "substantial compliance" rule is, however, unwise on both this and other points. An explanation that the agencies believe inadequate may lead either to a deficiency notice or to a second request and a second waiting period, either of which can potentially disrupt the acquisition schedule. To avoid this, the wise course is to seek, at the earliest opportunity, express advice from the Notification Office as to the exact form of information or explanation it would find in "substantial compliance," and then to note on the form that the advice was sought and obtained and the information submitted in the manner advised.

Second Requests: At any time during the initial waiting period, either of the enforcement agencies may require additional information from any person that filed notification, or any of its constituent entities, their officers, directors, partners, agents or employees.[97] Such a request can substantially disrupt the acquisition schedule. In general, a second request made to any party automatically requires delay in the consummation of the acquisition until 20 days (or, for cash tender offers, 10 days) after the agency has received the required information. In tender offer situations there is an exception: no waiting period applies to second requests directed to the target.[98] In all other situations, the waiting period requirement applies, whether the request is made to the acquiring or acquired person. This can pose difficulties. A second request need only be complied with within "a reasonable time." Thus, in

Rule 801.30 transaction (apart from tender offers), an acquired person is able, intentionally or not, to impose a significant delay in completing the acquisition. Indeed, in some instances, an acquired person unfriendly to the acquisition could suggest to the enforcement agencies in its initial filing the kinds of additional information they might find useful and then take substantial time to provide it. Thus, despite Congress's intent, the rules are open to possibilities of abuse that may give targets of unfriendly acquisitions powerful tactical advantages.[99]

The Act places no limit on the scope of a second request. In some instances to date, second requests have been in the classic antitrust discovery tradition—asking for all information or documents "referring or relating to" whole series of transactions or events stretching over many years.[100] Compliance with such a request can take months of effort. Moreover, the substantial compliance rules apply. If the enforcement agency regards the response as incomplete, it presumably can give a notice of deficiency and thus delay the waiting period until what it believes a sufficient response has been filed. The legislative and regulatory history, however, strongly supports the view that deficiencies result only from failure to provide a response that is formally sufficient and either gives the information requested or explains why it cannot be supplied in whole or in part. If the agency regards such a response as not in substantial compliance, its proper remedy under the Act is to seek an injunction ordering substantial compliance not to assert a deficiency and then seek monetary penalties if the acquisition is consummated before the "deficiency" is cured. If the rule were otherwise, the enforcement agencies would have an almost limitless opportunity to delay an acquisition.[101]

In some cases, it may be possible to anticipate a second request and to take steps to avoid it or at least reduce its scope. This may be so, for example, when the data presented on the Notification and Report Form suggest areas of competitive overlap or supplier-customer relationships that in reality are insignificant. In this kind of situation, it may be wise—if timing is critical—to take advantage of the Rules' invitation to submit additional information helpful to the agencies

---

[95] 122 Cong. Rec. H 10293 (daily ed., Sept. 16, 1976) (remarks of Cong. Rodino).
[96] 43 Fed. Reg. 33526 (1978).
[97] 16 C.F.R. §803.20.
[98] 16 C.F.R. §803.20(c).
[99] See Axinn, Fogg & Stoll, Contests for Corporate Control under the New Law of Preacquisition Notification, 24 N.Y.U. L. Rev. 857 (1979).
[100] See, e.g., the request described in Smith & Lipstein, *supra* note 27, at 1198 n. 71.
[101] See the excellent discussion of this point, obviously based on unhappy experience, in Smith & Lipstein, *supra* note 27, at 1197-1203.

"in assessing the impact of the acquisition upon competition."[102] In appropriate instances, the submission might be accompanied by a request that, because of urgent business considerations, the agencies immediately inform the parties of any additional information they need so that it can be supplied on an informal basis.

If, however, the antitrust problems are potentially serious, this course could merely attract notice and, indeed, invite a second request. The fact is that, in cases that present apparently significant antitrust questions, the agencies may very well regard the second request power as a valuable way of gaining not only information but also time. While the parties are attempting to comply and so begin the second waiting period, the agencies may be putting together the witnesses and papers for a preliminary injunction. In such instances, a second request probably cannot be avoided, although it should be possible, from careful antitrust analysis, to anticipate what its subjects are likely to be and to prepare to respond as rapidly as possible. Moreover, the second request should itself go far in identifying the agency's sources of concern. Counsel are, of course, free at any time in the process not only to negotiate the scope and terms of the second request with the agency, but also to discuss the agency's antitrust concerns and, perhaps, possible means of resolving them short of suit.

There is, however, no absolutely certain way of avoiding a second request and its attendant delay through the notification process itself. Of course, where a second request is likely, notification should be filed as early as possible. Where early filing is impossible, however, but delay after filing would have serious adverse affects, it may be possible to use the Division's and the Commission's business review procedures to obtain advance clearance.

Business Review Procedures: The Commission's and the Division's business review procedures are set out. respectively, at §§1.1 to 1.4 of the Commission's rules of practice[103] and 28 C.F.R. §50.6.[104] The procedures have seldom been employed with respect to acquisitions. In the world before Hart-Scott-Rodino, requests for business review would simply give the agencies what they otherwise would not have had—advance notice and hence an enforcement headstart as to acquisitions that presented potentially serious antitrust questions. But, given the premerger notice requirements, advance clearance may be helpful whenever a second request could seriously disrupt the acquisition. In brief, the procedures could be used in advance of the notification process to reduce the likelihood of a second request or at least to limit its scope, and thus to reduce the attendant delay. They can also be used, much like the notification process itself, but with far greater certainty, as a means of assessing antitrust concerns and possible methods of avoidance.

The procedures present, however, one difficulty that may outweigh their advantages. Applications to both the Commission and the Division for clearance are presumptively matters of public record, open for inspection. Applicants may ask the agencies to retain certain information in confidence, or at least delay its disclosure, if they have sufficient justification. But the agencies have discretion to grant or deny the request. Moreover, the Commission's and the Division's response to the application for advice or clearance will be made public. The risk of public access may often make use of the procedures inadvisable. Where delay in the notification process will have serious consequences, however, and business review is the only reasonably sure means of avoiding or minimizing delay, it may be possible to negotiate with the agencies for confidential treatment before submission. Section 7A's Freedom of Information exemption reflects express Congressional acknowledgement of the business and competitive sensitivity of the information relevant to antitrust analysis of acquisitions. This, as well as recognition that the business review procedures often provide the only means of avoiding the difficulties in timing that Section 7A can cause, may induce the agencies to reasonable liberality in affording advance submissions confidential treatment.

---

[102]16 C.F.R. §803.1(b).

[103]3 CCH Tr. Reg. Rep. §§9801.01-04.

[104]3 CCH Tr. Reg. Rep. §8559.10.

SAMUEL M. FEDER

SAMUEL M. FEDER is a member of the New York law firm of Wender, Murase & White. He served as an attorney for the Securities and Exchange Commission from 1968 to 1972.

Mr. Feder has lectured widely on the subject of mergers and acquisitions for the Practicing Law Institute, the American Management Association, AMR International, and the NYU International Institute on Tax and Business Planning. He holds an A.B. from Yeshiva University and an LL.B. from George Washington University. He is a member of the District of Columbia Bar.

ROBERT G. ROBISON

ROBERT G. ROBISON graduated from the University of Chicago Law School in 1977. He took his undergraduate degree at Stanford University (A.B. 1970) and is currently an associate attorney with the law firm of Wender, Murase & White in New York City. He is admitted to practice in the State of New York and is a member of the American Bar Association.

27

Securities Law and Federal Registration Requirements

SAMUEL M. FEDER

ROBERT G. ROBISON

INTRODUCTION

Prior to January 1, 1973, a company which desired to acquire the stock or the assets of another company through a business combination was only subject to the registration requirements of the Securities Act of 1933, as amended[1] ("33 Act") under certain circumstances. An exchange of securities whereby the acquiring corporation (assumed throughout this chapter to be the surviving entity) issued shares in a voluntary exchange with the securities of the acquired company was subject to registration (unless an appropriate exemption could be found), while an acquisition by statutory merger or by an exchange of stock for assets was not. This distinction arose due to the fact that Rule 133 of the 33 Act[2] determined whether or not the issuance and exchange of securities by an acquiring corporation constituted a "sale", "offer of sale", or "offer" for the purposes of Section 5 of the 33 Act on the basis of how a combination transaction was structured.

Rule 133 provided that in the case of a stock for assets or merger acquisition submitted to the vote of the acquired company's stockholders, under circumstances where the vote of a required majority would either authorize or deny the transaction and would bind all stockholders (except to the extent that they exercised statutory dissenters' rights), the transaction would not be considered an offer or sale requiring registration under the 33 Act.

The rationale underlying this "no-sale" approach was that the transaction was accomplished by virtue of "corporate action," as opposed to the individual action of any stockholders affected by the transaction. Accordingly, Rule 133 did not exempt from registration acquisition transactions where each separate stockholder of the acquired company was required to make an individual decision whether to accept the exchange or tender offer. Therefore such transactions were treated as "sales" of the acquiring corporation's securities for the consideration of the acquired company's securities which were surrendered in exchange.

Rule 133(c) further provided that affiliates (usually a corporate "insider") of the acquired company would be deemed to be statutory underwriters with respect to public resales of the new securities received in the acquisition and therefore prohibited sales of their securities without registration. However, the Rule also exempted from registration routine brokerage sales which conformed to the "leakage" provisions of Rule 133(d) and (e) which, in effect, allowed large amounts of unregistered securities to reach the public without registration and concomitant disclosure protections of the 33 Act. The non-affiliate stockholders of the acquired company who received securities of the acquiring company in a Rule 133 transaction were free of any further restrictions on resale (assuming that such persons did not become affiliates of the acquiring company following the transaction).

On October 6, 1972, the Securities Exchange Commission ("SEC") issued Securities Act Release No. 5316 ("Release 5316"). In Release 5316 the SEC

---

[1] 15 U.S.C. §et. seq. (1977(a).
[2] 17 C.F.R. §230.133 (1980).

reversed its prior "no-sale" approach and rescinded Rule 133, adopting in its place Rule 145.[3]

Basic Provisions

Rule 145 requires compliance with the registration and prospectus delivery requirements of the 33 Act in connection with the issuance of securities in certain transactions, unless an exemption from registration is available. The transactions to which the rule applies, (*i.e.*, where an "offer", "offer to sell", "offer for sale", or "sale" is deemed involved insofar as security holders of a corporation are concerned) are those where there is submitted to such security holders for a vote or consent a plan or agreement for:

(1) A reclassification of securities which involves the substitution of one security for another (other than a stock split, reverse stock split, or change in par value); or

(2) A statutory merger or consolidation or similar plan of acquisition involving the conversion into or exchange of securities by security holders of one corporation for those of any other person (except where the sole purpose of the transaction is to change an issuer's domicile); or

(3) A transfer of assets to another person in consideration of the issuance of securities of such other person or any of its affiliates if:

    (a) the plan or agreement provides for dissolution of other person whose security holders are voting or consenting; or

    (b) the plan or agreement provides for a pro rata or similar distribution of such securities to the security holders voting or consenting; or

    (c) the board of directors (or similar representative) or such corporation or other person, adopts resolutions relative to (a) or (b) within one year after the taking of such vote or consent; or

    (d) the transfer of assets is a part of a pre-existing plan for distribution of such securities.

The theory behind the Rule is that the act of submitting these matters to security holders pursuant to which they may choose to accept a new or different security from the one they own, involves a new investment decision on the part of such security holders; and that since a new investment decision is being made, security holders should have available to them, through the processes of registration and delivery of a prospectus, all relevant information necessary for them to make such a decision.

Transactions Covered

Strictly interpreted, Rule 145 relates only to transactions ratified pursuant to a stockholder vote or consent. However, under certain state laws (such as the General Corporation Law of Delaware), a merger may take place between a parent corporation and its 85 percent or 90 percent (or more) owned subsidiary without stockholder approval (a "short-form" merger). In such a transaction, the minority stockholders are compelled to participate in the combination and make no investment decision except that they may choose to exercise dissenters' rights in lieu of accepting shares. However, Release No. 5316 states: "[T]he Commission is of the opinion that the [short-form merger] transaction involves an 'offer', 'offer to sell', 'offer for sale', or 'sale', within the meaning of Section 2(3) of the Act, and accordingly such transactions are subject to the registration provisions of the Act unless an exemption is available."

The three types of transactions specifically covered by Rule 145 are:

Reclassifications of Securities—This category covers internal reorganizations involving the substitution of one security for another security of the same issuer, as contrasted with a business combination or acquisition transactions. Reclassifications which effect a change in par value or which accomplish a stock split or similar numerical change in pro rata ownership are not subject to the Rule.

The introductory statement of the SEC preceding the Rule indicates that if a reclassification meets the requirements for an exempt transaction under Section 3(a)(9) (which exempts exchanges of securities by an issuer with its existing shareholders) or 3(a)(10) (exempting transactions involving a reorganization or receivership which has been approved by state or federal courts or agencies) of the 33 Act, those exemptions remain applicable, and there is no need to comply with the registration requirements of the Rule.

Statutory Mergers or Consolidations— Acquisitions, in which the securities of the acquired company will become or be exchanged for securities of the acquiring company, are covered by Rule 145(a)(2) except for transactions "where the sole purpose of the transaction is to change an issuer's domicile." The words "sole purpose" have not been read literally to deny the exception to a merger that, in addition to changing the state of domicile, also includes other

---

[3] 17 C.F.R. §230.145 (1980).

minor changes (for example, a change in a company's articles of incorporation not permitting the issuance of preferred shares).[4] Nonetheless, other SEC staff interpretations have required registration in cases where a change of domicile has also entailed changes which, in the SEC's view, amount to an "extensive reorganization."[5]

Assets for Stock

Acquisitions which call for the transfer of the acquired company's assets for the stock of the acquiring company on some pro rata distribution basis (including a distribution or dissolution occurring up to one year after the shareholder consent for the acquisition is given) is also subject to Rule 145.[6] Therefore, if assets are sold under a transaction resembling any of the enumerated types under paragraph (a)(3), then the shares must be registered when the transaction has been approved by the shareholders or when the acquiring company decides to distribute its shares. If the dissolution of the acquired company, or a pro rata distribution of the acquiring company's stock, is not part of the original plan submitted to the acquired company's stockholders (and the transaction is not registered at the time it is made), but some form of plan of distribution or dissolution is adopted within one year after the vote, Release No. 5316 provides that the acquiring company "should file a registration statement covering the dissolution and distribution of the securities on the appropriate form other than Form S-14, unless an exemption is available."[7]

Statutory Exemptions

It should be noted that Rule 145 specifically provides that covered acquisition transactions otherwise subject to registration may be exempt from the provisions of Rule 145 through the 33 Act Statutory exemptions. The exemptions specifically mentioned as being available and not affected by the Rule are those set forth in 3(a)(9)[8], 3(a)(10)[9], 3(a)(11)[10], and 4(2)[11]. Ac-

cordingly, if a transaction fits within one of these exemptions, registration will not be required at the time of the transaction.

Under Section 3(a)(9), any transaction (except for securities exchanged under Title 11 of the U.S. Code) whereby securities are exchanged by an issuer with its own shareholders exclusively, and where no payment or commission (either direct or indirect) is paid for soliciting such an exchange; is exempt from the 33 Act registration requirements. Any reclassification made under this exemption may (by SEC Rule 149)[12] include cash payments for dividend or interest adjustments. Rule 150[13] also permits payments made by an issuer to its shareholders in connection with the exchange of securities for outstanding securities when such payments are part of the terms of the offer of exchange. However, the SEC has been careful to also inject as a requirement that a company engage in a "bona fide" exchange offer (*i.e.*, one that is not designed for the sole purpose of circumventing registration).[14] Under section 3(a)(10) of the 33 Act, exchange transactions approved by federal or state courts or administrative agencies with the power to pass on the fairness of the terms of the exchange are exempt from registration. For instance, the exemption applies to bankruptcy reorganizations, receiverships, issuances and reorganizations approved by the SEC under the Public Utility Holding Company Act.[15] There is no prohibition of payment for solicitation, or of cash being included as part of the consideration by security holders. Accordingly, a creditor may exchange his claim plus cash for securities. A party receiving a large block of securities may, however, be subject to 33 Act restrictions on the resale of non-registered securities although the SEC has promulgated Rule 148 (17 C.F.R. 230.148) as a guide to effecting such resales.

Section 3(a)(11) exempts offerings of securities offered and sold only to residents of the state in which the corporation is incorporated and doing the principal part

---

[4]See Canadian Merrill, Ltd., SEC No-Action Letter dated January 1, 1978.

[5]See Beeline Fashions, Inc. (SEC 1976), '76-'77 CCH Dec. ¶80,923.

[6]17 C.F.R. §230.145(a)(3) (1980).

[7]There is still some ambiguity surrounding what the SEC deems to be an acceptable procedure to be followed if the acquired company adopts a plan of disolution or pro rata distribution more than one year after the ratification of the assets purchase. Most authorities have assumed that the acquiring company's securities that the acquired company would then hold would be "restricted securities" under Rule 144.

[8]15 U.S.C. §77c(a)(9) (Supp. 1972-1979).

[9]15 U.S.C. §77c(a)(10) (Supp. 1972-1979).

[10]15 U.S.C. §77c(11) (Supp. 1972-1979).

[11]15 U.S.C. §77(c)(2)(1971).

[12]17 C.F.R. §230.149 (1980).

[13]17 C.F.R. §230.150 (1980).

[14]17 C.F.R. §231.646 (1980)

[15]15 U.S.C. §79g, k(e) (1980)

of its business ("intra-state offerings"). For a Rule 145(a)(1) reclassification to be exempt, the issuer must do the principal part of its business in the state of incorporation, and all of the exchanging security holders must be residents of this state. In a Rule 145(a)(2) merger, all of the security holders of the disappearing corporation would have to be residents of the state of incorporation of the surviving corporation. In a consolidation, the security holders of both corporations would have to be residents of the state in which the new corporation would be incorporated. Also, in order for that corporation's principal business to be in that state, it would as a practical matter have to be the location of the primary businesses of both constituent corporations. In a Rule 145(a)(3) transfer of assets, the security holders of the transfer or corporation would have to be domiciliaries of the purchaser's state of incorporation. Furthermore, in any of these transactions, the issuer should not make any attempt to bring a combination within the exemption by freezing out out-of-state shareholders or giving them a different class of security as this will probably be challenged by the Commission.

In addition to the above requirements, a condition of the intrastate exemption is that the securities issued "come to rest" in the hands of residents of the state. Rule 147 (17 C.F.R. §230.147) has attempted to clarify and provide objective guidelines for compliance with this exemption. Rule 147 provides that an issuer, in order to qualify for this exemption, should be a resident and be doing business within the state in which offers or sales are made. To be a resident, an issuer should have approximately 80 percent of its assets (including those of its consolidated subsidiaries) located within the state. In addition, 80 percent of the net proceeds of the offering should be applied to operations in the issuer's state of residence. No part of the offering should be offered or sold to nonresidents within a period of 9 months from the date of the last sale by the issuer and no subsequent resales should be made to nonresidents during such period. Finally, appropriate legends and stop transfer orders should be used to implement these restrictions.

In addition to the above exemptions, a transaction covered by an exemption under Section 3(b)[16] (the most significant Section 3(b) exemption being Regulation A[17]) would also not be subject to the requirements of Rule 145. The Commission is empowered by Section 3(b) to exempt by rule, issuer offerings of up to $2,000,000. Under the general exemption of Regulation A, primary offerings of up to $1,500,000 in any twelve-month period are exempted from registration if certain conditions are met. These conditions include the filing of an offering statement, the contents of which are less extensive than a registration statement. In addition, Regulation A does not require audited financial statements to accompany the offering statement.

Section 4(2), the non-public offering exemption, allows an issuer to offer, exchange or sell its securities, without registration, to a limited number of "sophisticated investors" in a non-public manner, and not for resale through a distribution. The SEC has determined through its interpretive releases and no-action letters that sophistication is primarily a function of the potential investor's access to information about the issuer as well as his financial means. Generally, an issuer should only offer its securities in a private placement to those individuals and institutions who do not require the comprehensive disclosure and protections which would otherwise be available to them via the registration process.

The SEC, in an attempt to dispel widespread confusion over the terms of the availability of Section 4(2) issued the interpretive, safe-harbor Rule 146.[18] Rule 146 sets forth certain SEC criteria for investor sophistication. The Rule requires that potential investors be provided with an offering statement describing the issuer and the terms of the offering, which statement is not required to be as comprehensive as a registration statement, nor is it required to be reviewed and approved by the staff of the SEC. Moreover, investors who, because of their lack of financial wealth and knowledge of the company, may not rise to the level of a sophisticated investor, may be represented by an "offeree representative" under certain circumstances. The offeree representative, by his knowledge and acquaintance with the business of the issuer, may remedy any shortcomings of a potential investor whom he represents. Rule 146 is not the exclusive means by which a non-public offering may be made. Nonetheless, it is one of the few guiding lights out of the confusing 4(2) labyrinth of issues such as number and sophistication of offerees, extent of disclosure, and integration.

With regard to certain acquisitions and mergers. Rule 146 specifically provides that the requirements of "suitability" and "sophistication", otherwise essential to the availability of the Rule, are not required to be

---

[16]15 U.S.C. §77c(b) (1971).

[17]17 C.F.R. §§230.251-230.263 (1980).

[18]17 C.F.R. §230.146 (1980).

shown for each purchaser of a security in a transaction subject to the requirements of Rule 145.[19] It should be noted, however, that in the accompanying release[20], the SEC pointed out that exchange offers permit an acquiring company to choose prospective offerees and would, therefore, not be exempt from the suitability requirements of the Rule.

Securities acquired in exempt private placement transactions must be acquired with appropriate "investment intent." This means that an investor may not resell such securities for a period of two years from their acquisition, subject to certain exceptions contained in Rule 144.[21] While a discussion of the various aspects of Rule 144 is beyond the scope of this chapter, for the purposes of Rule 145 it should be noted that those shareholders of the company who are not "affiliates" of the issuer may avail themselves of the provisions of Rule 144 and sell the restricted securities acquired in the amounts provided in Rule 144. Those investors who, because of the extent of their ownership of the company or their relationship to management, may be deemed "affiliates" of the issuer, will be subject to continuous limitations on resale as well as the insider trading provisions of Section 16(b) of the 34 Act.

Responsibilities

Rule 145 places the burden of preparing and filing a registration statement on the corporation whose shares will be distributed (usually the acquiring company). In a transaction where the approval of the shareholders of both companies is required, each company must be careful to include such information about the other as will be material to the shareholder for the purpose of casting his or her vote. Moreover, the acquiring corporation must also include in its registration statement information relating to its management and financial condition as will be material to the acquired company's shareholders for the purposes of making an investment decision.

Rule 153A

Section 5(b)(2) of the 33 Act requires, in essence, that the jurisdictional means may not be used for the purpose of delivering a security for sale unless accompanied or preceded by a registered prospectus. In order to clarify the difficult issue of when to deliver a prospectus and to which shareholders an acquiring com-

pany should deliver a prospectus, the SEC adopted Rule 153A under the 33 Act. Rule 153A provides that for Rule 145(a) transactions the requirement that sales and offers of subject securities be "preceded by a prospectus" as used in Section 5(b)(2), will be satisfied if the prospectus is delivered prior to the vote (or regarding actions taken by consent, prior to the earliest date on which corporate action may be taken) to the shareholders of record of the acquired corporation entitled to vote on (or consent to) the transaction.

Rule 153A relates only to the delivery of prospectuses in connection with the initial transaction involving the sale of the acquiring company's securities to the acquired company's shareholders. It does not relate to subsequent resales of the new securities acquired by such shareholders. Section 4(3) of the 33 Act[22], which requires dealers in the newly issued securities to deliver prospectuses in transactions within 40 or 90 days (depending upon whether it is a first offering of the particular security being exchanged) is still applicable to dealers. If the acquiring company was subject to the 34 Act reporting requirements by virtue of Section 13 or 15(d) immediately prior to the filing of the registration statement, then 33 Act Rule 174 would exempt dealers from the prospectus delivery requirements of Section 4(3) on resale of the newly issued acquiring company's securities by the acquired company's shareholders.

Amendments to Form S-14

When the SEC adopted Rule 145 in Release No. 5316, it also amended the 33 Act registration Form S-14 to facilitate registration in connection with Rule 145 transactions.[23] The Amended Form S-14 is to be used for the initial issuance of the acquiring company's stock in the transaction itself. It may also be used for resale of such stock by underwriters (as defined by Rule 145(c)) following the transaction.

The prospectus in a S-14 registration statement may consist of a proxy statement or information statement relating to the transaction. Such a combination must, however, meet all of the SEC's requirements of proxy statement rules and regulations, which is to say that it must contain all of the information pertinent to the transaction that would be required by a proxy statement subject to the proxy (or information statement) rules

---

[19]17 C.F.R. §230.146(f)(2) (1980).

[20]SEC Release No. 33-5487 (1974).

[21]17 C.F.R. §230.144 (1980).

[22]15 U.S.C. §77d(3)(1970).

[23]The SEC also permits the use of Form S-1 which may prove useful in the case of "shelf-registrations".

under Sections 14(a) and 14(c) of the 34 Act.[24] Accordingly, the prospectus would typically include a description of voting rights and procedures, a brief synopsis of the proposed transaction, comparative and pro forma combined capitalization tables, audited financials of both companies, pro forma financial statements based on the assumed combination. In addition, such documents have also included the typical prospectus disclosures such as a description of the securities to be distributed, information as to which persons may be deemed underwriters under Section 2(11) as well as such persons' relationships to the parties to the transaction. The actual agreement between the companies involved is usually included in the document as an appendix.

Although this combination document will be distributed to the respective shareholders of both companies in situations where state corporate law requires the approval of both sets of shareholders, or only to the acquired company's shareholders in situations where only their approval is required, the acquiring company will shoulder the major burden of compliance with all applicable requirements and will be the primary subject to potential SEC liability.

Form S-15

The SEC has recently announced the adoption of new Form S-15[25], an optional experimental form which may be used in connection with securities issued either in a short-form merger or an exchange offer in which the amount of securities already held and the amount of securities to be sought in the exchange offer aggregate (at the time of filing) more than 50 percent of the subject securities of the offeree.

Form S-15 generally provides for a short prospectus which is to be delivered along with the issuer's latest annual report to offerees. This will allow the issuer's business description, financial statements, and other required information to be incorporated by reference from the annual report, rather than being presented in the prospectus itself.

Numerous other preconditions are set forth in the promulgating release which will determine the availability of this optional form to an issuer. Generally speaking, an issuer will be able to use Form S-15 if it meets the financial requirements for the use of Form S-7[26] and has furnished shareholders with its annual report as provided in the 34 Act.

Resales of Registered Securities

With regard to resales by individuals receiving registered securities, those individuals who are not affiliates of a party to a Rule 145 transaction and who are not deemed to be underwriters may immediately, publicly, resell the issuer's securities received in the transaction. Those individuals who are affiliates may utilize the provisions of Rule 144. Prior to May 15, 1978, underwriter status attached to certain persons involved in a Rule 145 transaction, which status was deemed to continue indefinitely. This resulted in substantial restrictions on resales by certain individuals who no longer effectively participated in the business affairs of the new combined entity. Accordingly, the SEC amended Rule 145 to permit an underwriter of Rule 145 securities to resell, without limitations, after the person has held them for two years, and provided further that he is no longer affiliated with the resulting issues and that the issuer is current in its 34 Act reports.[27]

Financial Statements

Item 15 of Schedule 14A requires that transactions fitting the description contained in Item 14 of Schedule 14A (*i.e.,* mergers, consolidations, sales of assets, etc.) must contain the same financial data required in an original 34 Act registration statement on Form 10 for each party to the transaction, with certain minor omissions. In addition, these statements must be prepared in accordance with the SEC's accounting regulation S-X and must be certified. However, Item 15(c) of Schedule 14A permits the Commission to allow the omission of any of the required statements, to permit the substitution of other statements for those required, and to require the filing of other statements in addition to, or in substitution for, the required statements. In the case of an acquired company not subject to the proxy rules which may presumably have difficulty meeting the Form 10 financial statement requirements, the financial statements to be included in Form S-14 need be certified only "to the extent practicable." Moreover, where such a company cannot comply with the Form 10 requirements even on an uncertified basis, then the SEC "generally" will use the lesser requirements of Regulation A[28] as a standard. The full S-14 registration statement will often consist of a facing sheet, a cross-reference sheet, the prospectus/proxy statement, and a brief Part II, which consists only of a requirement that

---

[24] 15 U.S.C. §§78n(a) and (c) (1971).

[25] 17 C.F.R. 239.29, promulgated in SEC Release No. 33-6232 (1980).

[26] 17 C.F.R. 239.26 (1972).

[27] Securities Act Release No. 5932 (1978).

[28] 17 C.F.R. §239.11 (1980) and 17 C.F.R. §239.11 (1980).

the interests of experts named in the registration statement be disclosed and a brief summary of provisions in both companies' charter documents concerning indemnification as well as the usual list of exhibits, undertakings, and the signature page (sometimes consolidated for both companies).

Notice Period

General Instruction A to Form S-14 provides that Form S-14 shall not be used unless the prospectus is delivered to the security holders whose vote or consent is solicited at least 20 days prior to the date of the meeting, or the date on which the transaction is to be effectuated if no meeting is held. However, if applicable law permits the furnishing of notice within less than the 20-day period, then compliance with such provision shall be deemed to satisfy the Form S-14 requirement. Note that this proviso relates solely to "the furnishing of a notice," and not to furnishing the full proxy statement. Thus, if state law requires 10 days notice for a merger, the literal requirements of General Instruction A would be met if a simple notice of the meeting were sent 10 days in advance of the meeting (which could be done under Rule 145(b)), even though the full prospectus/proxy statement were not sent until a later date, closer to the meeting). However, as a practical matter, most companies have chosen to comply with the SEC's notice requirements by having the full prospectus/proxy statement sent within the period specified by state law, not simply a notice of the meeting.

Blue Sky Laws

Compliance with Rule 145 will not obviate the necessity of complying with the various state securities statutes currently in effect. Many states have exemptions identical or similar to the federal exemptions discussed herein, and a majority of states have extremely simplified registration procedures for offerings which are to be registered under the 33 Act. This subject is dealt with at great length in Chapter 28 by Robert Jay Haber.

SUMMARY

Although Rule 145 has been in effect now for seven years, there remains a number of unanswered questions concerning its application and the mechanics of compliance. Fortunately, the staff continues to respond to no-action requests which relate to some of the exemptions discussed herein, although, with the promulgation of Rule 146, the staff has effectively decreased the issuance of letters relating to the private placement exemption. Once a decision has been made to effect a business combination through the registration process, the issuer can expect to receive direct guidance from the SEC staff as to compliance with the provisions of the Rule.

ROBERT JAY HABER

ROBERT JAY HABER received his undergraduate education at the University of Pennsylvania, graduating in 1963 with an A.B. He graduated from New York University School of Law with an LL.B in 1966 and an LL.M. (in Corporate and Commercial Law) in the following year. In 1969 he joined the Manhattan law firm of Bondy & Schloss and became a partner in the Summer of 1974. He specializes in the practice of corporate law.

28

Certain State Laws Affecting Acquisitions

ROBERT JAY HABER

INTRODUCTION

The discussions of law contained in other chapters in this book, for the most part, concern either Federal tax, antitrust, or securities law. But, of course, considerations of state as well as Federal law affect sales, and this chapter deals with certain aspects of the former.

To detail the special requirements of each state with respect to acquisitions is not within the scope of this book. Nevertheless, there are certain important requirements, common to many acquisitions, which are governed by state law, and which the buyer must consider when structuring the transaction. These requirements can have such a significant economic impact upon the buyer that, although frequently not capable of being reduced to prescriptions of broad application, they should be brought to the buyer's attention. They are: bulk sales law; state merger and consolidation statutes; Blue Sky regulation; and potential products liability of the buyer as a successor corporation.

Because of the peculiarities and diversity of the laws of the states, a preliminary caveat is in order: local counsel in those states whose internal law applies to the transaction should be consulted to assure compliance.

BULK SALES LAW

By March 31, 1968, the Uniform Commercial Code, a comprehensive statute governing commercial transactions, was effective in 49 of the states as well as in the District of Columbia and the Virgin Islands. By June 29, 1978, it became effective in substantial part in Louisiana, the last state to adopt it. Although the Code is a uniform law and there are uniform variations proposed by the drafters, various states have made individualized amendments to the Code. The specific law of each state must, therefore, be examined. The discussion that follows necessarily contains generalizations, but for certain key points there are listed in this chapter specific states which have adopted amendments, either uniform or individualized.

Most of the 10 Articles which comprise the Code cover topics with which the businessman is familiar such as sales of goods (''Article 2''); drafts, checks, certificates of deposits and notes (''Article 3'' entitled ''Commercial Paper''); letters of credit (''Article 5''); and warehouse receipts and bills of lading (''Article 7'' entitled ''Documents of Title''). But what is the purpose of ''Article 6'' captioned ''Bulk Transfers'' and frequently referred to as the ''bulk sales law''?

The main purpose of the bulk sales law is to afford protection to the creditors of a merchant who, owing debts, sells his inventory in a quick sale and disappears with the sale proceeds without paying his creditors.

To what type of transactions is the bulk sales law inapplicable? In those transactions where protection of the creditors—the goal of the statute—is accomplished, there is no need for the statute, and it does not apply. Thus, a transfer made in the ordinary course of business does not carry any bulk sales risk because the transferor is not engaging in any conduct which its creditors did not expect when credit was extended. If there is a statutory merger or consolidation, the assets remain intact and the state statutes require the surviving or consolidated corporation to assume the liabilities of the constituent corporations, so that the application of the bulk sales law would be unnecessary. (See the section below in this chapter entitled ''State Merger and Consolidation Statutes.'') In an asset purchase transaction the bulk sales law is applicable except in the following very limited circumstances where it is superfluous: the assumption of all of the seller's liabilities by a solvent buyer, with a known place of business in the same state where the goods are located, if the buyer gives public notice (as defined in the Code) of its assumption of liabilities. Of course, in a stock-purchase transaction, the balance sheet of the corporation remains intact, only the stockholdings changing hands, so that the bulk sales law would serve no purpose. Indeed, one of the advantages of the stock purchase is that in such a transaction it is not necessary to give the notice to the seller's creditors that the bulk sales law requires in an asset purchase. Thus, attention is not called to the change in management.

Whether the bulk sales law applies depends not only upon the type of transaction, but also upon the quantity and identity of the items being transferred and the nature of the transferor's business. In order for the sale to be considered a bulk sale, it must be a transfer in bulk not in the ordinary course of the transferor's business and that transfer must consist of a *major part* of the *materials*, *supplies*, *merchandise or other inventory* of an enterprise subject to the bulk sales law.

What is a ''major part''? Does it mean more than one-half of the transferor's total stock? Is this phrase used in the quantitative or qualitative sense, or both? Local variations must be consulted. California has substituted the phrase ''Substantial part,'' and a California case has held 25 percent of merchandise inventory to be within the meaning of the term. Is the transfer by a jeweler of one out of his entire inventory of ten diamonds within the statute when the transferred stone is valued at $90,000 and the remaining nine stones are valued at $10,000 in the aggregate? Idaho and Wisconsin have amended the phrase to read ''major part in value.''

The types of enterprise subject to the statute consist of those whose principal business is the sale of merchandise or stock, including those who manufacture what they sell. Thus, any business which is essentially a service business would not be subject to the bulk sales law, although eight states (California, Florida, Idaho, Maryland, Nevada, New York, Oregon and Washington) by modification of the Code include within their statute's scope some service businesses, the common addition being restaurants and, except for Maryland which limits its statutory expansion to restaurants, some of the following: cafe, food dispensing establishment, coctail lounge, beer parlor, tavern, bakery, garage, cleaner, dryer, hotel, club, barber shop, beauty salon, and gasoline service station. Furthermore, except in California and Washington, a transfer of a substantial part of equipment of an otherwise covered enterprise without a bulk transfer of inventory would not be a transfer subject to the bulk sales law.

Once it is determined that the transaction in question is within the province of the bulk sales law, there are two alternate courses of action which the buyer and seller can pursue: (1) compliance with the statute; or (2) waiver of the statute by buyer and seller and an indemnification of buyer by seller.

If the seller does not have audited financial statements and, as a result of the buyer's due diligence, the buyer learns that the seller has kept incomplete and shoddy records, and if the purchase price is to be paid either all at once without any escrow fund to protect the buyer, or on a deferred basis with installments represented by negotiable promissory notes against which the buyer may not assert an offset once the notes are in the hands of a holder in due course, the buyer should comply with the bulk sales law in order to be protected against undisclosed liabilities. In the event the seller liquidates quickly after the sale and before the buyer discovers the seller's undisclosed liabilities, and in the further event the buyer must pay the seller's creditors as a result of noncompliance with the bulk sales law, it may be difficult for the buyer to recover damages from the distributees of the liquidated seller.

In order to comply with the bulk sales law, the buyer must require the seller to furnish a list of existing creditors; both buyer and seller must prepare a schedule of the property to be transferred; and the buyer must preserve both the list and the schedule for six months subsequent to the transfer and permit inspection of the list and schedule and copying therefrom by any of the seller's creditors. Instead of preserving the list and schedule and permitting inspection, the buyer can file the list and schedule in a public place specified in the statute. The seller must sign and swear to or affirm the list of creditors which must contain names and business addresses, with known amounts owed, as well as the names of persons who are asserting claims against the seller which the seller disputes. The seller is responsible for the completeness and accuracy of the list of creditors, and, unless the buyer is shown to have had knowledge of an error or omission on that list, the transfer is not ineffective for errors or omissions made by the seller. As a further requirement of bulk transfers (other than those made by auction sale), at least 10 days before the buyer takes possession of the goods or pays for them, whichever first occurs, the buyer must give to the seller's creditors notice of the transfer as required by the statute. The statute sets forth the specific information which the notice must contain and requires that the notice be delivered personally or sent by registered or certified mail to all persons on the list of creditors furnished by the seller as well as to all persons who, to the buyer's knowledge, have or assert claims against the seller. Thus, if the list of creditors is extensive, this notice requirement can be quite costly.

In 19 jurisdictions (Alaska, Florida, Idaho, Kansas, Kentucky, Maryland, Mississippi, Montana, New Jersey, North Dakota, Oklahoma, Pennsylvania, South Dakota, Tennessee, Texas, Utah, Virgin Islands, Washington and West Virginia) of the 51 jurisdictions which have adopted Article 6 ("Bulk Transfers") of the Code (Louisiana not having adopted Article 6), a further burden is placed upon the buyer: it has the obligation (other than with respect to bulk sales at auction) to pay out of the purchase price those debts of seller which are either on the list of creditors furnished by the seller or filed in writing by a creditor, pursuant to the above-mentioned 10-day notice, within 30 days after the mailing of that notice. If any of the debts are in dispute, an adequate sum should be withheld from distribution until that dispute is settled or adjudicated. If the amount of the purchase price is insufficient to pay all of the debts in full, distribution must be made *pro rata*. This duty of the buyer runs to all of the seller's creditors, and may be enforced by any one creditor in a class action benefitting all such creditors. All but 8 (Alaska, Idaho, Kentucky, Mississippi, North Dakota, Oklahoma, South Dakota and Texas) of the 19 jurisdictions which have enacted this provision have adopted a further provision to the Code permitting the buyer, within 10 days after it takes possession of the assets, to pay the purchase price into an appropriate court and thereafter to discharge its duty to make distribution to seller's creditors who are on the list or who filed the written claim, by giving notice by registered or certified mail to those creditors that the purchase price has been paid into the court and that they should file their claims with the court. If this option to pay into court is elected by the buyer, the buyer has the additional expense of making a second mailing by registered or certified mail, the initial mailing having been for the 10-day notice discussed above. Even in those 8 states which have not adopted this Code provision, a similar procedure may be available under non-Code general interpleader statutes authorizing the buyer-stakeholder to deposit money into court.

If the buyer does not elect this option to pay all or part of the purchase price into court, it could save postage by mailing the distribution by ordinary mail, but such savings must be weighed against the administrative costs of preparing the checks, of withholding distribution with respect to disputed claims, and of calculating *pro rata* distributions if the purchase price is insufficient to pay the claims in full.

Strict compliance by the buyer with its duty to make arrangements to pay the seller's creditors out of the purchase price is compulsory in order for the buyer to reap the statute's benefits in those jurisdictions where this additional obligation is imposed. Thus, in the Pennsylvania case of *Atlas Merchandising Co.* v. *Johnny's Cal. Market, Inc.*, 25 U.C.C. Rep. 1427 (Pa. Court of Common Pleas September 27, 1977), the buyer had complied with all of the bulk sales rules except that, in order to fulfill his duty to have the seller's creditors paid out of the purchase price, the only measure taken was an express provision in the agreement by which the seller agreed to pay all of his existing liabilities. In holding that the buyer failed to comply with the Pennsylvania bulk sales law, the court reasoned:

> It will be noted that the comment to 6-106 [of the Code] expressly states that the purpose of the section is to give the transferor's creditors direct protection against improper dissipation by the transferor of the consideration received for the transfer. The comment goes on to suggest the methods by which the buyer may perform this duty, e.g., by holding the consideration in his own hands until the debts are ascertained and paid, or by depositing it in an account subject to withdrawal only by his countersignature, or by depositing it in escrow with an independent agency. If we were to hold that the procedure used here constituted compliance with the Act, then every purchaser of a business could escape responsibility by inserting a provision in the sales agreement to the effect that the seller would pay all existing debts. This is exactly what the bulk transfer provisions of the Code were designed to prevent.

Although the Code has a general provision in Section 1-105 granting to the parties to the transaction some leeway in selecting by agreement the law of which particular state is to apply, choice of law with respect to the bulk sales law is excepted from that Section, so that the parties cannot engage in forum shopping and thereby select the law of a state which does not impose upon the buyer the duty to pay the seller's creditors out of the purchase price. The Code, ignoring the location of the execution of the acquisition agreement, the location of the principal places of business of the seller and buyer, and the choice of law provision in the acquisition agreement, unequivocally requires that the controlling law be that of the state in which the goods to be sold in bulk are physically located.

Frequently a buyer intends to carry on the seller's business in the same manner as the seller had done, and to deal without interruption with the same suppliers. Often the buyer wants as smooth a transition as possible and is reluctant to give creditors the notice prescribed by the bulk sales law. The requirements of the bulk sales notice are quite technical, and the notice is usually couched in legalistic terms which the creditor cannot always understand. The notice may give to the creditor the erroneous impression that his receivable will not be paid. The buyer, paying substantial consideration for a business as a going concern, would like nothing better than to avoid this confusion and the necessity of repeating to each of the various inquiring creditors an explanation for the notice. If the buyer is reasonably confident that the amount of undisclosed liabilities will be minimal and that it will have some type of recourse against the seller to cover whatever undisclosed liabilities do exist, the seller and buyer can opt for an alternative to bulk sales law compliance, namely, waiver by buyer and seller of the requirements of the bulk sales law and an indemnification running from seller to buyer for such noncompliance. An example of such a provision for inclusion in the acquisition agreement is the following:

> Buyer herby waives compliance by seller with the terms and conditions of any applicable bulk sales law, and seller agrees to indemnify buyer and hold it harmless against any loss or damage arising from claims and demands of whatever nature, including counsel fees incurred in contesting the same, asserted by any creditor of seller against buyer or the assets and properties sold and transferred hereunder for noncompliance by seller or buyer with bulk sales laws or similar laws which may be applicable to the sale or transfer of the assets and properties hereunder.

Typically, the acquisition agreement will contain other indemnification clauses for other matters as to which the seller indemnifies the buyer, and such indemnification clauses will contain boiler-plate provisions such as those requiring buyer to give the seller timely notice of a claim which is subject to indemnification as well as those permitting the seller in good faith at its own expense to contest the claim. These kinds of boiler-plate provisions are equally applicable to the above sample of a bulk sales law indemnification provision, and can be added to it.

In this way, the buyer can, under the proper circumstances, ignore the requirements of the bulk sales law and thus avoid expense and possible delay in the consummation of the closing, yet still protect itself.

If the buyer complies with the bulk sales law, a creditor who already has a judgment against the seller could, during the 10-day period during which the buyer must wait to take possession of the goods or to pay for them, levy on the purchase price (usually cash) in the hands of the buyer. During this 10-day period a creditor without a judgment could, upon a *prima facie* showing that he would suffer irreparable harm unless the requested equitable relief were granted, obtain an injunction prohibiting or delaying the consummation of the sale, thereby gaining time to enforce his rights against the seller, or he might have a receiver appointed to take possession of the goods or the purchase price. In appropriate circumstances, the creditor without a judgment could put the seller into bankruptcy and thereby transfer the goods to be sold to the trustee in bankruptcy.

If the buyer fails to comply with the bulk sales law, the transfer of the property from the seller to the buyer is ineffective against any of seller's creditors who held claims based on transactions or events occurring prior to the transfer. (Of course, if the buyer in turn sells the transferred property to a purchaser for value who does not know about the noncompliance with the bulk sales laws, that purchaser takes the property free of any claims asserted by seller's creditors.) Such creditor may levy on the transferred property in the hands of the buyer, whether by execution, attachment, garnishment, trustee process, receivership or whatever proceeding is customary under local law. Such levy or action must be brought within six months (one year in California, Florida and Georgia) after the date on which the buyer took possession of the goods, unless the transfer has been concealed, in which event the levy or action must be brought within six months (or one year in those three states) after discovery of the transfer. In those jurisdictions which impose upon the buyer the duty to pay seller's creditors, the bulk sales law may impose upon the noncomplying buyer a trusteeship subjecting such buyer to personal liability for the value of the goods purchased. This is a further reason to induce the judicious buyer either to comply with the bulk sales statute or to obtain an indemnification from a responsible seller.

STATE MERGER AND CONSOLIDATION STATUTES

In the usual situation, the objective of the buyer is to purchase the entire business of the seller as a going concern. To accomplish this end, it is typically necessary to acquire all or substantially all of the assets of the seller.

Under the corporate asset-purchase approach, the goal of purchasing all or substantially all of the assets is accomplished by purchasing each asset or each type of asset individually. One of the most important documents executed and delivered by the seller to the buyer at the closing is the bill of sale and perhaps a separate assignment of intangibles. These documents frequently list the various assets being sold and then, to avoid neglecting any assets, contain a catch-all covering all other assets and properties of every kind and description, whether personal, real or mixed, whether tangible or intangible, and wherever located.

Futhermore, under the corporate asset-purchase method, agreements, contracts, franchises, licenses and leases — assets which are among the most vital being purchased — more often than not require the prior written consent of a third party in order to effect a transfer to the buyer, yet there is always the possbility that some third parties will refuse to grant such consents. To protect the buyer from such contingency, a customary provision in a corporate asset-purchase agreement imposes upon the seller, as a condition to closing by the buyer, the obligation to obtain such written consents before or at the closing.

Thus, although substantially all of the assets are being transferred, under the asset-purchase agreement the method of transfer is fragmented, and may entail many separate documents embodying the consents by third parties.

When a corporation purchases the assets of another corporation, it is purchasing assets in essentially the same way that a person purchases such assets. However, by virtue of being an artificial creature in the sense that it is created under and exists by virtue of a state statute, the corporation can use another acquisition method which is authorized by the same statute which created the corporation and which is not available to the individual buyer—the statutory merger or consolidation. Merger and consolidation were not permitted at common law; they are now permitted only by express legislative authorization.

A merger is the combining of two or more corporations into one corporation in such manner that one of those corporations survives and absorbs the other corporation which terminates its corporate existence. The disappearing corporation is frequently termed the "merged corporation." Consolidation is similar to merger except that two or more corporations combine into a new corporation, the original two or more corporations being dissolved and a "new" or "consolidated" corporation coming into existence upon consummation of the transaction. Although for convenience the discussion in this section sometimes refers only to a merger, it is equally applicable to a consolidation unless specially noted otherwise. Furthermore, for stylistic considerations this discussion re-

fers to the merged corporation in the singular, although there may be more than one merged corporation in a given transaction.

The corporation laws of each of the states empower the corporations organized thereunder to merge and, except for California, to consolidate, but in a few states this power is restricted in some way as, for example, under the Vermont statute which requires the foreign corporation in a domestic-foreign merger or consolidation to have qualified to do business in Vermont. Generally, the state statute dictates all aspects (other than Federal taxation and Federal securities, antitrust and other regulatory laws) of any merger in which its corporation participates. Therefore, if the specific procedural and substantive requirements of the statutes of the particular state governing each of the participating corporations are followed, the results decreed by the statutes take effect by operation of law.

By effecting a merger, various legal steps which would otherwise be taken separately occur simultaneously by operation of law, with the result that the multiple documents required to obtain these same results under the corporate asset-purchase are unnecessary. The assets of the merged corporation are transferred to the surviving corporation as a whole by operation of law. The documents of transfer discussed, such as the bill of sale and the assignment of intangibles, are superfluous because all the assets of the merged corporation are transferred to the surviving corporation by, virtue of the state's statute. (Still, to prevent any gaps in the chain of title, it is wise to file or record certain documents reciting the effect of the merger upon special kinds of assets being transferred, such as assignments of patents to be recorded with the Federal Patent Office and either certificates of merger (which are sometimes statutorily required) or confirmatory real estate deeds to be filed or recorded with the local land office official.) Similarly, all of the liabilities of the merged corporation are assumed by the surviving corporation without the latter executing any separate instrument of assumption. Upon the filing of appropriate documents with the state official, the following also occur simultaneously: (a) the merged corporation is dissolved without the filing of a separate certificate of dissolution; (b) the certificate of incorporation of the merged corporation is no longer effective; (c) the certificate of incorporation of the surviving corporation is amended; (d) the creditors of the merged corporation must look to the surviving corporation for satisfaction; and (e) the shares of stock of the merged corporation are cancelled and its shareholders become shareholders of the surviving corporation or, in a "triangular merger," become shareholders of the parent of the surviving corporation. All of these legal consequences are brought about by the merger which, as is detailed below, is accomplished with minimal paper work in contrast to the corporate asset-purchase.

The benefits of the merger which have been extolled above also can be its disadvantages: all the assets of the merged corporation are transferred to the surviving corporation and all of the liabilities of the merged corporation are assumed by the surviving corporation. At times there are specific assets which the buyer does not wish to purchase, and the corporate asset-purchase agreement will, unlike the merger, permit their exclusion, although if the asset-purchase is to be a tax-free reorganization under §368 (a) (1) (C) of the Internal Revenue Code (I.R.C.) (stock for assets), the net value of the assets permitted to be excluded from the acquisition is limited by the requirement that "substantially all of the properties" be acquired. Of course, the situations being discussed are those not in defraud of creditors, but rather those with legitimate business purposes, such as the exclusion from the acquisition of a division conducting a business unrelated to the seller's principal business. To accomplish this result with a merger, the assets must be transferred out of the corporation to be merged before the merger takes place. The same drawback is present in the merger with respect to liabilities. In contrast, under a corporate asset-purchase transaction, the acquisition agreement is usually very specific in detailing the liabilities which the buyer is assuming. Under that kind of acquisition agreement, it can be provided that the buyer assumes those liabilities of the seller revealed by a certified balance sheet as at a given date, and thereafter those liabilities arising only in the ordinary course of business, and can be further provided that no other liabilities or obligations are being assumed, including, without limitation, various kinds of liabilities or obligations which do not arise in the ordinary course and with which the buyer does not want to be saddled. To accomplish this result, there can be included in the acquisition agreement clauses such as the following, specifying those liabilities and obligations the buyer is not assuming:

> liabilities of the seller for Federal, state and local income or franchise taxes, property taxes, and use and sales taxes incurred by the seller for any periods ending prior to the closing date; liabilities and obligations of the seller to its shareholders respecting dividends and distributions to its shareholders in liquidation or redemption of stock; liabilities and obligations of the seller under or with respect to transactions occurring after the closing date, unless specifically assumed by the buyer; liabilities and obligations

of the seller incurred in connection with or related to this acquisition agreement or the transactions contemplated hereby or in connection with the liquidation or dissolution by the seller; and liabilities and obligations of the seller arising out of its violations of, or failure to comply with (a) any provision of the Federal securities act or any rule or regulation thereunder; and (b) the "Blue Sky" or securities laws of any state or rules and regulations of the authorities administering such laws, whether or not such violation or failure to comply under (a) or (b) is or was in connection with the transactions contemplated by this acquisition agreement or any other transaction entered into by the seller prior to the date of this acquisition agreement.

In this way, the buyer will not be assuming any undisclosed liabilities, liabilities which are unusual, or liabilities unrelated to the acquired business, so that the agreed upon purchase price will reflect the value of what the buyer expects to acquire. (But see the section below in this chapter entitled "Potential Products Liability of the Buyer as a Successor Corporation.")

Although the various state statutes necessarily differ markedly in detail, it is surprising how uniform they are in result. The best standard against which to compare some of the divergent state statutory provisions is the Model Business Corporation Act (the "Act"). Developed in 1946 by the Committee on Corporate Laws (Section of Corporation, Banking and Business Law) of the American Bar Association, it was first published as a complete act in 1950, and from time to time has been revised. It was used as the general basis for the corporation statutes of at least 26 jurisdictions: Alaska, Arizona, Arkansas, Colorado, District of Columbia, Florida, Georgia, Iowa, Kentucky, Mississippi, Montana, Nebraska, New Mexico, North Dakota, Oregon, Rhode Island, South Dakota, Tennessee, Texas, Utah, Vermont, Virginia, Washington, West Virginia, Wisconsin and Wyoming. The Act was used to a great extent in drafting the corporation statutes of at least 11 additional jurisdictions: Alabama, Connecticut, Louisiana, Maine, Maryland, Massachusetts, Michigan, New Jersey, New York, North Carolina and South Carolina. The Act has, therefore, directly influenced the legislatures of 70 percent of the states plus the District of Columbia.

The merger and consolidation provisions are contained in the Act at Sections 71 through 77 (exclusive of Sections 72A and 75) and Sections 80 and 81 and are respectively entitled: "Procedure for Merger;" "Procedure for Consolidation;" "Approval by Shareholders;" "Articles of Merger, [or] Consolidation ...;" "Effect of Merger [or] Consolidation...; "Merger [or]

Consolidation ... between Domestic and Foreign Corporations;'' ''Right of Shareholders to Dissent;'' and ''Rights of Dissenting Shareholders.'' The progression of the discussion which follows coincides with the subject matter covered by these Section headings.

Procedurally, the state merger and consolidation statutes fall into two categories: the ''agreement'' method and the ''plan'' method. Under the former, each of the participating corporations is a party to a contract which the shareholders of each corporation approve. Under the latter method, a plan rather than an agreement is generally first approved by the board of directors of each participating corporation and then by its shareholders. Substantively, the results of these two methods are the same, and the references in the following discussion to only ''plan'' are intended to also encompass ''agreement.''

Under the Act, which follows the ''plan'' approach, the board of directors of each participating corporation adopts resolutions approving a plan of merger or consolidation. The minimum information the Act requires the plan of merger to contain is generally also required under the state statutes: (1) the corporate names involved, that is, the name of each of the corporations proposing to merge and the name of the surviving corporation; (2) the terms and conditions of the proposed merger; (3) the ''manner and basis of converting the shares of each corporation into shares, obligations or other securities of the surviving corporation or of any other corporation or, in whole or in part, into cash or other property''; (4) the changes in the articles of incorporation of the surviving corporation to be effected by the merger; and (5) such other provisions with respect to the proposed merger as are deemed necessary or desirable. In addition, most statutes require other information itemized at a later point in this chapter. The contents of the plan are the same for both the merger and the consolidation except that, because a new corporation will come into existence at the time the appropriate document is filed with the appropriate state officer, the plan for the consolidation must also contain all of the information required to be set forth in the certificate of incorporation of a newly formed corporation.

The latitude afforded by item numbered (3) above to tailor the merger to the particular circumstances is indeed remarkable. Most states have comparable statutory provisions. The comment to this provision of the Act deserves to be quoted:

> This express reference to cash and to the securities of any other corporation is an important addition to flexibility. Thus it permits the shareholders of a merged corporation to receive securities of some third corporation, for example, the parent corporation of the surviving corporation, which may, by virtue of a broader market, be much more desirable. Or alternatively, it would be possible to maintain the separate corporate identity of the acquired corporation by merging into it a newly created subsidiary of the acquiring corporation and having the subsidiary issue to the shareholders of the acquired corporation shares of the acquiring corporation or of some parent of the acquiring corporation.
>
> . . . .
>
> Section 71 was amended in 1969 by adding to paragraph (c) a clause permitting the conversion of shares of each merging corporation in whole or in part into cash, property or shares, obligations or other securities of the surviving or any other corporation. Previously, the paragraph was limited to conversion into shares, obligations or other securities of the surviving corporation, which seemed to be needlessly restrictive and out of harmony with modern practices.

The statutory merger can qualify as a tax-free exchange under I.R.C. §368(a)(1)(A), although nonvoting stock and securities constitute the consideration. In contrast, the consideration for the assets under a tax-free exchange under I.R.C. §368(a)(1)(C) (stock for assets) must primarily be voting stock. Furthermore, note that although a merger, wherein substantial nonproprietary consideration is exchanged for stock of the shareholders of the merged corporation, can comply with state law, the transaction may not qualify as a tax-free reorganization under I.R.C. §368(a)(1)(A) due to the violation of the continuity-of-proprietary-interest doctrine. In addition, the money and other property exchanged in the merger constitutes ''boot'' and is taxed under I.R.C. §356. Yes, it is true that to qualify as not only a merger under state law but also as a tax-free reorganization under I.R.C. §368(a)(1)(A), there cannot be an inordinate amount of cash and other nonproprietary property exchanged. Nevertheless, the merger is relatively unrestricted in comparison to the reorganization under I.R.C. §368(a)(1)(C), which must comply with the stringent rules of I.R.C. §368(a)(2)(B) restricting the assets to be acquired for money or other property to no more than 20 percent of all of the assets of the transferor corporation. This restriction is particularly severe because liabilities assumed and liabilities to which any property acquired is subject are treated as money in determining whether 80 percent of all property of the transferor is acquired for voting stock.

Under the Act, the board of directors of each corporation, upon approving the plan of merger, by resolution directs that the plan be submitted to a vote at a meeting of shareholders. As in the Act, some statutes specify that the shareholders' meeting can be either annual or special; others, special; and still others do not specify. The period of notice for the shareholders' meeting under the Act is from "not less than ten nor more than 50 days" and, depending upon the state statute, varies from a minimum of ten days to a maximum of 60 days. Most statutes, like the Act, require that notice of such meeting must be given only to those shareholders of record entitled to vote, but a large minority of states require notice to shareholders whether or not they are entitled to vote. Under the Act and the statutes of some states, the notice must include a summary of the plan or be accompanied by a copy of the plan; other statutes require, in addition, a statement of the rights of dissenting shareholders and, sometimes, certain financial information. Of those state statutes requiring that the notice be sent to all shareholders, whether or not entitled to vote, some permit all voting and non-voting stock to vote on the merger, but others allow only voting stock to vote. The number of shares required to approve the agreement or plan varies from state to state from a majority vote, as under the Act, to a three-fourths vote, with almost all states falling into either the majority or two-thirds camp. The Act and many state statutes require any class of shares to vote as a class if the plan of merger contains any provision which, if contained in a proposed amendment to the articles of incorporation, would entitle such class of shares to vote as a class. The Act and some state statutes authorize the merger to be abandoned, pursuant to any provisions for abandonment set forth in the plan, at anytime prior to the filing of the articles of merger described below.

When compared with the corporate asset-purchase transaction, one of the disadvantages of the merger often cited is the extra expense and time expended in obtaining the approval of the shareholders of both the merged and surviving corporations. Only the approval of the shareholders of the acquired corporation is necessary in the corporate asset-purchase. This disadvantage is not present under the statutes of almost one-third of the states which permit shareholder approval by the surviving corporation to be dispensed with if certain conditions are met by the surviving corporation, the most usual being the absence of amendment to the articles of incorporation of the surviving corporation and the satisfaction of varying mathematical tests as to dilution of the shares of the surviving corporation resulting from the merger.

The Act advocates the minority position which distinguishes between the plan of merger and the articles of merger. After the plan of merger is approved by the directors and usually thereafter by the shareholders, it is executed by the corporate officers and filed with the appropriate public state official designated in the statute and, in some states, also with one or more local officials such as, depending upon the state, the county official where real property of a merged corporation is located, or the county official where the principal or registered office of the surviving corporation is located, or the county officials where the principal or registered offices of all participating corporations are located. The articles of merger set forth the plan of merger (the contents of which have been listed earlier in this chapter), plus recitals, as to each corporation, about the number of shares outstanding; if shares of any class are entitled to vote as a class, the designation and number of outstanding shares of each class; the number of shares voting for and against the plan; and, if shares of any class are entitled to vote as a class, the number of shares of each class voting for and against the plan. The majority of states do not differentiate between the plan and articles, but combine all of the information into the plan and require the plan to be filed. The state official will not file the articles or plan unless the state tax commission (or its equivalent) certifies that all franchise taxes have been paid. A certificate of merger or some other document evidencing the filing of the articles or plan is issued to the surviving corporation by the state official after he determines that the articles or plan conform to law and that the fees and taxes have been paid.

In Section 76, the Act contains the following comprehensive and clear statement of the effect of the merger or consolidation:

> A merger [or] consolidation ... shall become effective upon the issuance of a certificate of merger [or] consolidation ... by the Secretary of State, or on such later date, not more than thirty days subsequent to the filing thereof with the Secretary of State, as shall be provided for in the plan.
>
> When a merger or consolidation has become effective:
>
> (a) The several corporations parties to the plan of merger or consolidation shall be a single corporation, which, in the case of a merger, shall be that corporation designated

in the plan of merger as the surviving corporation, and, in the case of a consolidation, shall be the new corporation provided for in the plan of consolidation.

(b) The separate existence of all corporations parties to the plan of merger or consolidation, except the surviving or new corporation, shall cease.

(c) Such surviving or new corporation shall have all the rights, privileges, immunities and powers and shall be subject to all the duties and liabilities of a corporation organized under this Act.

(d) Such surviving or new corporation shall thereupon and thereafter possess all the rights, privileges, immunities, and franchises, of a public as well as of a private nature, of each of the merging or consolidating corporations; and all property, real, personal and mixed, and all debts due on whatever account, including subscriptions to shares, and all other choses in action, and all and every other interest of or belonging to or due to each of the corporations so merged or consolidated, shall be taken and deemed to be transferred to and vested in such single corporation without further act or deed; and the title to any real estate, or any interest therein, vested in any of such corporations shall not revert or be in any way impaired by reason of such merger or consolidation.

(e) Such surviving or new corporation shall thenceforth be responsible and liable for all the liabilities and obligations of each of the corporations so merged or consolidated; and any claim existing or action or proceeding pending by or against any of such corporations may be prosecuted as if such merger or consolidation had not taken place, or such surviving or new corporation may be substituted in its place. Neither the rights of creditors nor any liens upon the property of any such corporation shall be impaired by such merger or consolidation.

(f) In the case of a merger, the articles of incorporation of the surviving corporation shall be deemed to be amended to the extent, if any, that changes in its articles of incorporation are stated in the plan of merger; and, in the case of a consolidation, the statements set forth in the articles of consolidation and which are required or permitted to be set forth in the articles of incorporation of corporations organized under this Act shall be deemed to be

the original articles of incorporation of the new corporation.

When a merger [or] consolidation ... has become effective, the shares of the corporation or corporations party to the plan that are under the terms of the plan, to be converted ..., shall cease to exist, ... and the holders of such shares shall thereafter be entitled only to the shares, obligations, other securities, cash or other property into which they shall have been converted, ... in accordance with the plan, subject to any rights under Section 80 of this Act [*i.e.,* "Right of Shareholders to Dissent"].

The above-quoted section reflects revisions approved by the Committee on Corporate Laws of the Section of Corporation, Banking and Business Law of the American Bar Association at its meeting on January 30, 1976. One of these amendments permits the merger or consolidation to become effective on such date (not later than 30 days subsequent to the filing thereof with the state official) as shall be provided in the plan. The Comment made about this amendment states that "the procedure may validly be used not only by specifying a certain date or time, but by draftsmanship which would permit the date to be determined by a formula or by reference to other events, so long as the 30 day limitation is met." Over one-half of the states have a similar provision, the maximum period of time to which the effective date can be postponed ranging from 20 days to 90 days with at least one jurisdiction (Arizona) placing no limitation on the future date. Obviously the Act was amended to conform it to a beneficial trend in the statutes authorizing the effectiveness to be delayed either to a date certain or to the occurrence of an event. To be able to achieve certain tax objectives it is particularly important that the effective date of the merger not be dependent upon the vagaries of the state filing system, but rather be fixed with assurance. To illustrate, if a short taxable year is avoided by effecting the merger on the last day of the taxable year of the surviving corporation, in the year of the merger the loss carryover of the merged corporation will only be aged by one year rather than the two years which would otherwise be the case under I.R.C. §381. If there is no date certain or other referent specified, either because the particular state statute makes no provision for the concept or because the plan omits to state one, the merger usually becomes effective upon the date of filing, upon the date some official action is taken such as the issuance of a certificate, upon the certification of papers, or upon official approval in some other manner.

Prior to 1966 the Act contained a subdivision (g) in the equivalent of the above-quoted Section 76 which provided that the net surplus of the participating corporations available for the payment of dividends immediately prior to the merger would continue to be available for the payment of dividends by the surviving corporation to the extent that such surplus was not transferred to stated capital or capital surplus by the issuance of shares or otherwise. Due to the amendments of the sections of the Act defining earned surplus (§2(1)) and determining the amount of stated capital and earned surplus in connection with certain issues of shares (§21), the Comment states that subsection (g) became "surplusage," but "without any intent to restrict the carry-forward of earned surplus of the participating corporations." These accounting provisions pertaining to net surplus appear in approximately one-third of the statutes, and their most common formulation parallels the earlier version of the Act provision.

Mergers and consolidations between domestic and foreign corporations, like mergers between domestic corporations, must be authorized by grants of legislative power; naturally, in a domestic-foreign merger, the legislatures of both states must confer this authority, and, indeed, mergers and consolidations between domestic and foreign corporations are authorized under all of the state statutes except under the California statute which does not permit consolidation.

Under Delaware General Corporation law §252(a), foreign corporations which are parties to a domestic-foreign merger are defined as "corporations of any other state or states of the United States, or of the District of Columbia," and under the Florida statute, the definition is a bit more expansive in that, substantially in conformity with Treas. Reg. §1.368-2(b)(1) (1955, prior version; 1976, current version) it also includes corporations organized under the laws of any territory, possession or jurisdiction of the United States. On the other hand, the Act contains in §2(b) the following broad definition of "foreign corporation" which would include a corporation created under the law of a foreign country:

> a corporation for profit organized under laws other than laws of this State for a purpose or purposes for which a corporation may be organized under this Act.

However, under the above-cited Treasury Regulation and Rev. Rul. 57-465, 1957-2 C.B. 250, an exchange of stock under a merger statute of a foreign country is not a tax-free reorganization under I.R.C.

§368(a)(1)(A), but, with a favorable ruling from the Internal Revenue Service, may qualify as a reorganization under I.R.C. §368(a)(1)(C) (stock for assets).

Generally, the differing treatment afforded by the statutes to the domestic merger and the domestic-foreign merger result from specific considerations arising from the fact that one of the participating corporations is foreign. Almost all statutes require that the merger be permitted under the laws of the state in which the foreign corporation is organized. The Act and most state statutes specify that the domestic and foreign corporations must comply, in effecting the domestic-foreign merger, with the applicable provisions of the laws of the respective states under which each is organized. In the usual domestic merger, the surviving corporation will be conducting business in the state of the merged corporation, and must qualify to do business in that state, thereby protecting the creditors of the merged corporation. The Act and some of the state statutes specifically set forth this requirement. To protect the creditors and shareholders of the merged domestic corporation in a domestic-foreign merger, the Act requires that the surviving foreign corporation file with an official of the state of the merged corporation (1) an agreement that it may be served with process in any proceeding for the enforcement of any obligation of any domestic corporation which is a party to the merger and in any proceeding for the enforcement of rights of a dissenting shareholder of any such domestic corporation against the surviving corporation; (2) an irrevocable appointment of the domestic state official as its agent to accept service of process in any such proceeding; and (3) an agreement that it will promptly pay to the dissenting shareholders of any such domestic corporation the amount to which they are entitled under the provisions of the domestic law with respect to dissenting shareholders (discussed below). The Act and more than half of the state statutes provide that if in a domestic-foreign merger the surviving corporation is domestic, the effect of such merger shall be the same as in the case of the merger of domestic corporations, and if the surviving corporation is foreign, the effect of the merger shall be the same except insofar as the foreign laws provide otherwise. The Act contains a provision for abandonment of the plan in a domestic-foreign merger paralleling the provision for abandonment of the plan in a domestic merger.

It has been seen that, while some state statutes specify a shareholder vote for approval of a plan of merger greater than that necessary to approve most other action, no state statute requires a unanimous vote of shareholders for such approval. Hawaii comes closest to mandating unanimity by requiring a shareholder vote of three-fourths of all issued and outstanding shares of stock having voting power. As is the case with shareholder voting in general (other than in a situation involving the close corporation with a shareholders' agreement imposing voting unanimity), no one shareholder should have an absolute veto to thwart the will of the other shareholders with respect to the approval of merger. Yet, a merger is such a fundamental change that, to offset the inability of minority shareholders to prevent the merger so that they become shareholders of a different corporation or remain shareholders of the same corporation with substantially different or additional assets and business, all of the state statutes (except the West Virginia statute) grant to some if not all such shareholders what is variously called a "right to dissent" or "a right of appraisal" in the event the merger is consummated. Under the Act and the majority of state statutes, in order to exercise this right to dissent, the shareholder need only refrain from voting in favor of the merger; under a minority of statutes, the shareholder must vote against the merger. The Act and the statutes of some jurisdictions explicitly make this right to dissent or right of appraisal the exclusive remedy, and most decisions have held similarly when the statutory procedure was followed and neither fraud nor bad faith was involved. About a quarter of the states deny this right under certain circumstances, the most common being: the shares of stock are registered on a national security exchange; the outstanding shares are held by not less than 2,000 shareholders; or no shareholder vote is necessary to authorize the merger, such as when a wholly owned or virtually wholly owned subsidiary is merged into a parent. (For other instances where the requirement of shareholder approval is omitted and, therefore, the right to dissent or of appraisal is denied under the statutes of almost one-third of the states, see the discussion above.)

The state statutes governing the procedure for exercising the right to dissent or of appraisal are involved and detailed, and no useful purpose would be served herein by making an exhaustive comparison of the various provisions. A survey of the highlights of the Act as well as some of the more important deviations under state statutes should suffice.

These statutes set forth a mechanism by which the dissenting shareholders make a demand on the surviving corporation for payment of the "fair value" of their stock, or other statutory formulae, for example, "value", "fair cash value", "market value" and "full and fair value", such value being determined in most jurisdictions as of the date prior to the date on which the vote was taken approving the proposed cor-

porate action, or, under statutory variants, as at the time of the meeting, or the date of recording the merger agreement, or the close of business day on which voting occurs, or the date for determination of the shares entitled to vote at the meeting in which the vote occurs.

The Act requires that any shareholder electing to exercise his right to dissent file with the corporation, prior to or at the meeting of shareholders at which such proposed corporate action is submitted to a vote, a written objection. Most jurisdictions follow this provision of the Act by also requiring that the objection be made prior to or at the meeting, but a few jurisdictions permit the objection to be made only prior to the meeting; Delaware has eliminated the requirement that a written objection be filed with the corporation and has substituted therefor a written demand for appraisal to be delivered to the corporation before the taking of the vote on the merger. The surviving corporation is to make an offer to each such shareholder, and, if the shareholder accepts the offer, he ceases to have any interest in his shares upon payment of the agreed value. If the dissenting shareholder and the corporation disagree on the value offered by the corporation, or if the corporation makes no such offer, the corporation or the dissenting shareholder can petition the court to fix the value, either without the aid of appraisers under some statutes, or with the aid of appraisers which, under other statutes are discretionary with the court, and under still other statutes are mandatory. The Act requires that this petition be filed in any court of competent jurisdiction of the state where the registered office of the corporation is located. If the new corporation is foreign and without a registered office in the state, the petition is filed in a county where the registered office of the domestic corporation was last located. All dissenting shareholders, wherever residing, shall be made parties to the proceeding, a copy of the petition being served on each dissenting shareholder who is a resident of the state and being served on each non-resident dissenting shareholder by publication as well as by service of the petition by registered or certified mail. Some jurisdictions follow this approach by requiring that the value of all dissenting shares be determined in one suit, while other jurisdictions provide for permissive joinder or intervention.

The Act permits the judgment to include an allowance for interest at such rate as the court finds "fair and equitable in all the circumstances." Some states have similar provisions; a few states specify the rate of interest. Under the Act the costs and expenses (including reasonable compensation for, and reasonable expenses of, the appraisers, but excluding fees and expenses of counsel for, and experts employed by, any party) of the appraisal proceeding are to be determined by the court and are to be borne by the corporation except to the extent that all or any part of these costs and expenses are apportioned and assessed against the dissenting shareholders as the court deems equitable if it finds that their failure to accept the offer by the corporation was "arbitrary or vexatious or not in good faith." Even a sum which the court in its discretion determines to be reasonable compensation to an expert employed by a dissenting shareholder may be awarded in the court's discretion to the shareholder if the value of the shares as determined by the court "materially exceeds" the amount the corporation offered or if the corporation made no offer. Particularly in those states requiring only a simple majority of shareholders for approval of the plan of merger, there could be a substantial number of dissenting shareholders, thereby preventing the merger from being economically viable. In anticipation of such an eventuality, it would be wise to include in the merger plan a provision to abandon the plan (discussed above) if the jurisdiction involved permits abandonment after shareholder approval.

BLUE SKY REGULATION

Each of the states, including the District of Columbia, has a so-called Blue Sky statute which attempts to protect the public against being defrauded by schemes involving securities. These statutes are in addition to the Federal statutes regulating securities; the Federal securities laws have been considered elsewhere in this book and are outside the scope of this chapter.

Although there are as many versions of the previously discussed Uniform Commercial Code and the statutory merger and consolidation provisions as there are adopting jurisdictions, in the case of the Code, the variations from the statute are mostly the uniform ones proposed by the draftsmen of the Code and, in the case of the merger and consolidation statutes, the fundamentals underlying many of them are similar; consequently, significant variances from jurisdiction to jurisdiction are limited. However, the Blue Sky statutes of the various states are so greatly diversified that only very broad generalizations can be made to point up the issues and problems which are involved, and the caveat appearing at the beginning of this chapter deserves to be repeated, particularly in connection with Blue Sky matters: the Blue Sky statute, regulations and case law of each jurisdiction whose law applies to the transaction in question must be carefully examined. In this regard it is instructive to note that, while verifying the statutory citations appearing later in this section, the author discovered that, subsequent to his initial draft thereof, Tennessee had adopted a

new Blue Sky statute, effective July 2, 1980, whereby that State substituted an exclusion (as explained below) for the transactional exemption it had granted to statutory mergers, consolidations and corporate asset-sales in exchange for stock.

To the extent that any one statute can serve as a basis for creating some uniformity out of the statutory chaos, it is the Uniform Securities Act approved in 1956 by the National Conference of Commissioners on Uniform State Laws and by the American Bar Association. Substantial revisions of the Uniform Securities Act were approved by these two bodies in 1958. In order to permit the various states to retain their divergent philosophies toward securities regulation and still encourage them to adopt a uniform law, the Uniform Securities Act has been divided into the following four parts: Part I: anti-fraud provisions; Part II: dealer/broker/agent and investment advisor registration; Part III: securities registration; and Part IV: general provisions including definitions, exemptions, judicial review, and investigatory, injuctive and criminal provisions. A state can, therefore, adopt one or more parts of the Uniform Securities Act without the others and can amend or change the general provisions to suit its requirements. In their Prefatory Note to the statute, the Commissioners demonstrate its flexibility as follows: "The first three parts are designed to stand alone or in any combination. Appendix A specifies the changes required to be made in the Act if Part III is deleted. Appendix B specifies those portions of Part IV which are required for only a 'fraud' type of statute (Part I). The Act lends itself to four alternative treatments of investment advisers. These are specified in Appendix C." Thirty-three states (Alabama, Alaska, Arkansas, Colorado, Connecticut, Delaware, Hawaii, Idaho, Indiana, Iowa, Kansas, Kentucky, Maryland, Massachusetts, Michigan, Minnesota, Missouri, Montana, Nebraska, Nevada, New Jersey, New Mexico, North Carolina, Oklahoma, Oregon, Pennsylvania, South Carolina, Utah, Virginia, Washington, West Virginia, Wisconsin and Wyoming) and the District of Columbia, Puerto Rico and Guam have adopted Blue Sky laws which are based substantially on all or some part of the Uniform Securities Act.

Thus, when reading this discussion as to how the Blue Sky statutes must be satisfied in connection with a merger, consolidation or acquisition, the reader should bear in mind this general lack of uniformity in the statutory patterns and, to the extent that the following material is based upon the Uniform Securitites Act, should also remember that there are many states which have not adopted it or have adopted it only in part. The extent of this variety is evidenced by the following General Statutory Note for Alabama, a similar version of which forms a part of the General Statutory Notes for 22 of the 34 adopting jurisdictions: "Enacted a Securities Act which is a substantial adoption of the major provisions of the Uniform [Securities] Act, but it contains numerous variations, omissions and additional matter which cannot be clearly indicated by statutory notes."

The definition of "sale" appearing in Section 401 (j)(1) of the Uniform Securities Act is as follows:

"Sale" or "sell" includes every contract of sale of, contract to sell, or disposition of, a security or interest in a security for value.

Its wide breadth of coverage is representative of all Blue Sky statutes. Accordingly, unless there is some way for a merger, consolidation or acquisition to be excluded from the Blue Sky statutes, these transactions would be included because of the all encompassing definition of "sale".

What methods are there for removing mergers, consolidations and reorganizations from Blue Sky coverage?

In order to answer this question, the following concepts must be discussed: exclusion; exempt security; and exempt transaction.

An exclusion eliminates the dealing in question entirely from coverage of the Blue Sky statute. On the other hand, an exemption (whether of a security or of a transaction), while exempting the security or the transaction from registration, does not exempt that security or transaction from the anti-fraud provisions of the Blue Sky law. The distinction between an exempt security and an exempt transaction is as follows: the exempt security is exempt from registration no matter how frequently it is sold or offered for sale, and the exempt transaction is exempt from registration only with respect to that specific transaction, and, if the security involved in that exempt transaction is subsequently involved in another transaction, the initial exemption does not cover the second transaction and the security is subject to registration.

Section 401 (j)(6)(C) provides for an exclusion from the Blue Sky requirements by defining "sale", "sell", "offer" and "offer to sell" as excluding:

any act incident to a class vote by stockholders, pursuant to the certificate of incorporation or the applicable corporation statute, on a merger, consolidation, reclassification of securities, or sale of corporate assets in consideration of the issuance of securities of another corporation.

The draftsmen's commentary to this section sets forth several reasons for this exclusion, including the following:

[T]his area sufficiently impinges upon the corporation law and other general law of the states so that it seems better not to disturb whatever jurisprudence now applies by subjecting these corporate events to the special statutory sanctions and remedies afforded by the blue sky law... At the state level... there are the traditional civil and criminal remedies, both common law and statutory, of recission, deceit and obtaining property by false pretenses.

Except for New Hampshire, New York and (if the pre-transactional exemption discussed below is excluded) Arkanas, Blue Sky statutes of all jurisdictions contain either a specific exclusion or a specific transactional exemption for statutory mergers, consolidations and, usually, corporate asset-sales in exchange for stock.

The jurisdictions which have adopted the former approach are Colorado, §11-51-102 (8)(f)(III); Connecticut, §36-471 (k)(3)(C); Delaware, §7302(k)(5); District of Columbia, §2-2401 (k)(6)(C); Guam, §45401 (j)(6)(C); Hawaii, §485-1(10)(F)(iii); Indiana, §23-2-1-1 (i)(8)(iii); Maryland, §11-102(a)(3); Massachusetts, §401 (i)(6)(C); Missouri, §409.401 (j)(6)(C); Nevada, §90.080 (6)(c); New Jersey, §49:3-49(j)(6)(c); North Carolina, §78A-2 (8)f. 3.; Oklahoma, §2(18)(c); South Carolina, §35-1-20 (10)(f)(iii); Tennessee, §2(k)(vi)(g); Utah, §61-1-13 (10)(f)(iii); Virginia, §13.1-514 (c)(2); West Virginia, §32-4-401 (j)(6)(C); and Wyoming, §17-4-113 (a)(ix)(F)(III).

Those states which have enacted transactional exemptions are: Alabama, §8-6-11(a)(14); Alaska, §45.55.140(b)(15); Arizona, §44-1844 (6); California, §25103(c); Florida, §517.061 (9); Georgia, §97-109 (1); Illinois, §137.4.I.; Iowa, §502.203.13.; Kentucky, §292.410(1)(n); Michigan, §451.802(b)(19); Mississippi, §75-71-53.5.; Montana, §30-10-105(14); Nebraska, §8-1111 (14); New Mexico, §58-13-30.N.; North Dakota, §10-04-06.6.; Oregon, §59.035 (13); Rhode Island, §7-11-9 (d); South Dakota, §47-31-91; Texas, §581-5.G.; Washington, §21-20.320(14); and Wisconsin, §551.23 (13). A transactional exemption for mergers and consolidations, but not for corporate asset-sales in exchange for stock, is granted in Louisiana, §51:705 (6); Maine, §874-A.13.A.; and Vermont, §9-4204 (6).

In addition to the transactional exemption referred to above, California (§25103(a)) has a transactional exemption for negotiations or agreements prior to general solicitation of shareholder approval of a merger, consolidation or corporate asset-sale in exchange for stock. By Securities Rule 13, Arkansas in its definition of "OFFER OR OFFER TO SELL" has a transactional exemption, similar to California's, covering negotiations, agreements and similar communications with respect to a "proposed reorganization" which presumably includes a merger, consolidation and corporate asset-sale in exchange for stock, although Arkansas does not have a transactional exemption for the merger, consolidation or corporate asset-sale itself.

Some states place one or more conditions upon the transactional exemption. Alaska (§45.55.140(b)(13)) furnishes a transactional exemption for statutory mergers, consolidations and corporate asset-sales in exchange for stock if no commission or other remuneration (other than a standby commission) is paid for soliciting a security holder in Alaska and the issuer files a notice in the specified form not less than 30 days before making the offer. Consequently, it appears that even if the issuer neither is incorporated in Alaska nor conducts or transacts any business in Alaska, the issuer must file for a transactional exemption under the Alaska Blue Sky statutes if an Alaska security holder is solicited. Idaho (§30-1435 (13)) imposes virtually the same two conditions as Alaska, except the two conditions are in the disjunctive rather than the conjunctive. Thus, if no such commission or other remuneration is paid, the transactional exemption is effective without any filing. A commission or other remuneration can be paid for soliciting a security holder in Idaho, but if such is paid, the issuer must file the proper notice. In such case the filing is, as under Alaska's statute, required on the basis of a security holder being in the state irrespective of the fact that all other aspects of the transaction have no nexus to that state.

In Minnesota (§80A.15 Subd. 2 (1)) the only condition to the transactional exemption covering statutory mergers, consolidations and corporate asset-sales in exchange for stock is the furnishing to the state commissioner of securities of the department of commerce a general description of the transaction and such other information as he prescribes not less than 10 days prior to the issuance and delivery of the securities. Kansas (§17.1262(1)) imposes a condition similar to that of Minnesota except that the filing does not automatically guaranty the transactional exemption in that the state securities commissioner has 30 days in which to issue an order disallowing the exemption. Thus, any timetable for closing a merger, consolidation or corporate asset-sale where compliance with the Minnesota or Kansas Blue Sky statute is necessary must include an entry for a filing at least 10 or 30 days, respectively, in advance of the act to be exempted.

Perhaps the most involved statutory pattern is that of Ohio. Section 1707.03(U)(2) and (3) contains a transactional exemption for the merger, consolidation and corporate asset-purchase in exchange for stock if either (a) the securities to be issued are registered under sections 6 to 8 of the Securities Act of 1933 and offered and sold in compliance with section 5 of that Act or (b) at least 20 days prior to the date on which a meeting of security holders is to be held or the earliest date on which corporate action can be taken when no meeting is held, there is submitted to the security holders information substantially equivalent to the information that would be included in a proxy statement or information statement prepared by the management of an issuer subject to section 14(a) or 14(c) of the Securities Act of 1934. The issuer benefiting from this section would most likely be a public company offering registered securities. To register securities specifically for a merger, consolidation or corporate asset-sale in exchange for stock would in many cases be too costly, and to prepare proxy material would in many cases be too burdensome. Ohio Administrative Ruling 2 may provide some relief in that it answers in the affirmative the query whether an exemption can be claimed under §1707.03 (K) to cover the merger or consolidation of two Ohio corporations or of an Ohio and a foreign corporation. But see the discussion below that makes the availability of this interpretation doubtful.

A third alternative can be found in §1707.04 (A) permitting the Ohio division of securities to "consider and conduct hearings" upon any merger, consolidation or corporate asset-purchase in exchange for stock involving a corporation organized under the laws of Ohio or having its principal place of business in Ohio. The Ohio division of securities can after a hearing also approve the terms of the issuance and exchange and the "fairness of such terms." This hearing is initiated by application made by such corporation or by the holders of a majority in amount of any outstanding class of securities issued by such corporation. All persons to whom it is proposed to issue securities in such exchange have a right to appear at the hearing, and the statute specifies how notice of the hearing is to be made. If the merger, consolidation or corporate asset-sale in exchange for stock is approved by the division, the securities issued in connection therewith are excluded from coverage of the registration and anti-fraud provisions of the Ohio Blue Sky statute. An added advantage is that the securities which pass the "fairness hearing" are further protected by §3(a)(10) of the Securities Act of 1933 which, under the current interpretations of the SEC staff, exempts from the Federal registration requirement of that Act certain transactions approved by a state agency expressly authorized by law to grant such approval. Although both California (§25142) and Oregon (§59.095) also have enacted legislation to conform to §3(a)(10) of the Securities Act of 1933 and thereby furnish to the issuer this alternative by which to obtain a Federal registration exemption, those statutes require registration in addition to a "fairness hearing" and not, as in Ohio, in substitution therefor. The Ohio statute, therefore, is exceptional by offering, upon Federal registration or filing essentially proxy information, a transactional exemption, and, upon approval after a fairness hearing, an exclusion.

Pennsylvania takes a unique approach in that it includes within the scope of its Blue Sky statute the merger, consolidation and corporate asset-sale by specifically covering those transactions within its definitions of "sale" and "sell" (§1-102 (r)(i)), but thereafter granting a conditional transactional exemption. Like Alaska and Idaho, the connection between the transaction and the Pennsylvania Blue Sky statute is the location or residence of the security holder, but, unlike Alaska and Idaho, Pennsylvania reduces the burden of compliance by establishing a quantitative test of twenty-five percent: the Pennsylvania statutory scheme (§1-203 (o)) grants a transactional exemption to any party to a transaction where not more than 25 percent of the security holders of such party are residents of Pennsylvania. If more than 25 percent of such security holders are Pennsylvania residents, the transactional exemption requires either that: (a) one party to the transaction, who is required or permitted to file proxy materials under the Securities Exchange Act of 1934 or the Investment Company Act of 1940, files such materials with the Pennsylvania Securities Commission at least ten days prior to the meeting of security holders called for the purpose of approving such transaction, and the proxy materials be distributed to the security holders of each party to the transaction, or (b) such materials as the Pennsylvania Securities Commission specifies by regulation be prepared in connection with the proposed transaction and, after review by that Commission, be distributed to the security holders of each party to the transaction.

California, like Pennsylvania, also enacted a 25 percent test, but the consequences of passing the test differ. Under Pennsylvania law, if the Pennsylvania security holders constitute 25 percent or less, the transactional exemption is available without any filing; however, if the Pennsylvania security holders constitute more than 25 percent, the transactional exemption remains available, but a filing is required. Under California law, a transactional exemption is granted only if less than 25 percent of the outstanding shares of any class, any holders of which have received securities in the exchange, are held by persons who have addresses in California according to the records of the corporation of which they are shareholders (§25103(c)). In other words, the California Blue Sky statute requires registration for a merger, consolidation or corporate asset-sale in exchange for stock if 25 percent or more of such shares are held by residents of California. The 25 percent test being so crucial in that it determines whether the transactional exemption is available, the next section of the California statute (§25103 (d)) furnishes guidelines as to how that test is to be calculated: for the purposes of the 25 percent test, there are excluded: (a) securities held to the knowledge of the issuer in the names of broker-dealers or nominees of broker-dealers; and (b) any securities controlled by any one person who controls directly or indirectly 50 percent or more of the outstanding securities of that class. Presumably, as to the former group, the issuer should not have the burden of finding out the residences of security holders whose securities are in "street names," and, as to the latter group, the protection of the statute is not required. The California statute further details the method of calculation by providing that the determination of the 25 percent is to be made as of the record date for the determination of the security holders entitled to vote on the action or, if such approval is not required, as of the date of the directors' approval of such action.

The complexities in understanding the Blue Sky statutes are further compounded by the interpretations made by the state agencies administering these statutes — interpretations which may change as the agency's personnel changes. For example, Ohio Administrative Ruling 2 has been omitted from the official compilation of that State's Administrative Rulings because the chief of the Ohio division of securities takes the position that the Ruling is no longer in effect. The administrative interpretation of the Virginia statute can serve as another illustration: Section 13.1-514 (a) contains security exemptions; §13.1-514 (b), transactional exemptions; and §13.1-514 (c), exclusions, cited above as covering the merger, consolidation and corporate asset-sale; yet the Virginia State Corporation Commission considers the transactions listed in subdivision (c) as if they were listed in subdivision (b) and, therefore, transactional exemptions rather than exclusions. Obviously, it is imperative that after the Blue Sky statute in question is analyzed, the state agency administering it be consulted to assure compliance.

POTENTIAL PRODUCTS LIABILITY OF THE BUYER AS A SUCCESSOR CORPORATION

As discussed above, in the statutory merger or consolidation, the surviving or consolidated corporation by operation of law assumes the liabilities of the other constituent corporation to the merger or consolidation. However, in the case of an acquisition by a corporation of substantially all of the assets of another corporation, counsel for the buyer is usually scrupulous in drafting the acquisition agreement to provide for the assumption of only disclosed and certain other narrowly defined liabilities of the seller. In this way, the buyer expects that it knows what liabilities it will be assuming and paying. This knowledge is an important consideration in determining the purchase price. The typical acquisition agreement also provides for indemnification provisions and perhaps also escrow provisions or (if the purchase price is payable in installments) setoff provisions to protect the buyer in the event the assets purchased are subject to liabilities which the buyer has not assumed and did not expect to pay.

Until recently, it was a universally recognized principal of corporate law that a corporation which purchases the assets of another corporation is not liable for the obligations of the selling corporation in the absence of one of the following five exceptions: (1) the buyer expressly or by implication agrees to assume such obligations; (2) the transaction amounts to a consolidation or merger; (3) the buyer is a mere continuation or reincarnation of the seller; (4) the transaction is fraudulently entered into; or (5) the transaction is lacking some of the elements of a purchase in good faith, or the transaction is without consideration and the creditors of the seller have not been provided for.

Of course, exceptions numbered (4) and (5) cannot pertain to an acquisition entered into in good faith and at arm's length between unrelated parties. Furthermore, exception numbered (1) cannot be a problem if the buyer agrees to assume only specific liabilities. However, exceptions numbered (2) and (3) can impose upon the good faith buyer liabilities it did not know it was assuming. To determine whether either the de facto merger/consolidation exception or the continuation of the buyer exception is applicable to a given factual situation, the courts look to such factors as whether the corporate existence of the seller was terminated shortly after the transaction, whether the seller was contractually bound to dissolve as soon as possible

after the transaction, whether the seller is prohibited from engaging in normal business transactions after the transaction, whether the seller retains assets only sufficient for the expenses of the transfer, whether there is substantial continuity of ownership between the selling and the buying corporations, and whether the nature of the consideration paid by the purchaser for the assets of the seller is insubstantial. Other than the distinction between whether stock, an element of the de facto merger/consolidation exception, or cash, an element of the continuity exception, comprises the purchase price, "[a]pparently, there is considerable overlap of the traditional exceptions to the general rule. Indeed for most factual situations the de facto merger exception and the continuity exception are alternative rationales for achieving the same result." *Products Liability — Liability of Transferee for Defective Products Manufactured by Transferor,* 30 Vand. L. Rev. 238, 247 (1977) (footnotes omitted).

At least counsel for the buyer may be able to structure the acquisition in such a way as to increase the likelihood that the transaction will fail the de facto merger/consolidation and the continuation tests and thereby improve the chances that a court will not hold his client liable for the seller's liabilities his clients intended not to assume. If buyer's counsel is successful, the acquisition agreement will in fact control the terms of the deal between seller and buyer.

However, in 1976 and 1977 the highest courts of Michigan and California, respectively, handed down decisions which supplanted the traditional de facto merger/consolidation and the continuation exceptions with new products liability rules imposing liability on the buying corporation for injury to persons or property caused by products manufactured or otherwise dealt in by the selling corporation. This result was accomplished in the Michigan case by a fusion of the de facto merger/consolidation and the continuation exceptions, and, in the California case, by the creation of a new concept, continuity of the products line. The alarming aspect of these developments is that, in spite of an agreement to the contrary between seller and buyer, liability is imposed by operation of law upon the buyer for certain of the seller's liabilities which the buyer did not assume and did not expect to pay.

In the Michigan case, *Turner v. Bituminous Casualty Co.,* 397 Mich. 406, 244 N.W.2d 873 (1976) corporation A, a New York corporation, was organized in 1903. On April 13, 1964, corporation A and corporation B executed an agreement by which the latter was to purchase the entire business, good will, name and assets of corporation A as a going concern, only corporation A's corporate minute and stock record books, corporate seals and franchise to be a corporation being excluded from the books, records, documents and files sold. Although the acquisition agreement and the assumption of liabilities agreement were somewhat confusing, they were clear enough to be interpreted as excluding from the liabilities assumed by the buyer those which were future, contingent and unknown. (At any rate, the Court did not hold corporation B liable on the basis of an express or implied assumption of liability — certainly a less radical alternative for the Court if it had been available on the basis of the facts). The president of corporation A was to be employed by corporation B or its subsidiary, and corporation A agreed to use its best efforts to cause its employees to remain with corporation B. On April 27, 1964, corporation A changed its name, and on that same date corporation B formed under corporation A's former name a wholly owned New York subsidiary, corporation C, to accept the assets of corporation A. After the acquisition was consummated, on May 5, 1964, corporation A dissolved and distributed the cash purchase price of $6.38 million to its shareholders. Corporation C was merged into corporation B on July 24, 1968, when it became a division of corporation B. In 1968 the plaintiff's employer purchased a second-hand press which had been manufactured by corporation A prior to the acquisition by corporation B, and on July 26, 1969, the plaintiff during his employment was injured by the press, and, as a result, his hands were amputated. The plaintiff sued corporation B in tort on the basis of products liability.

After emphasizing that the case is one of products liability and not corporate law, the Court commented:

> Products liability law is a fast-developing area. All the rules have not yet been formulated and products liability law, as it matures, has to shake off various impediments associated with traditional concepts, which, while relevant to other problems, are inappropriate for this new area.

Then the Court discussed the competing interests of the party injured by the defective product, on the one hand, and the corporate acquirer, on the other hand:

> In order to develop a reasonable rule for products liability cases which arise subsequent to corporation transfers, it is necessary to go back to basics. In so doing we must review the problem from the standpoint of both the plaintiff injured person and the defendant acquiring corporation.
> To the injured person the problem of recovery is substantially the same no matter what corporate process led to transfer of the first corporation

and/or its assets. Whether the corporate transaction was (1) a traditional merger accompanied by change of stock of the two corporations, or (2) a de facto merger brought about by the purchase of one corporation's assets by part of the stock of the second, or (3) a purchase of corporate assets for cash, the injured person has the same problem, so long as the first corporation in each case legally and/or practically becomes defunct. He has no place to turn for relief except to the second corporation. Therefore, as to the injured person, distinctions between types of corporate transfers are wholly unmeaningful.

> From the corporate point of view likewise, the implications of a possible products liability suit after transfer do not depend on the form of corporate transfer. Regardless of the mode selected, both transferor [*i.e.*, the seller] and transferee [*i.e.*, the buyer] wish to know as exactly as possible what they are buying and selling in order to establish an appropriate price.

> Further, the transferee would be equally handicapped by products liability suits developing after the transfer has occurred, regardless of what that transfer is called. Once the deal is made and the transferor corporation is extinguished, the transferee has nowhere to go for relief.

> Despite this reality, the traditional corporate law approach in non-products-liability cases has been to largely condition successor responsibility on whether the transaction is labeled a merger, a de facto merger, or a purchase of assets for cash.

The Michigan Supreme Court concluded that, irrespective of whether the transaction is couched as a de facto merger or consolidation or a corporate asset-purchase, liability attaches to the buyer for products liability torts arising from products manufactured and sold by the seller pre-acquisition, but causing injury post-acquisition, if (1) there is a continuation of the enterprise of the seller with respect to management, personnel, physical location, assets and general business operations; (2) the seller corporation ceases its ordinary business operations, liquidates and dissolves as soon as legally and practically possible; and (3) the buyer assumes those liabilities and obligations of the seller ordinarily necessary for the uninterrupted continuation of normal business operations of the seller.

The defendant advanced several arguments concerning the economic impact of successor liability on corporate transfers. The Court's rebuttal has such a significant bearing upon the prospective corporate buyer that it deserves to be quoted in full except for the omission of footnotes:

> It is clear that the assumption of liability for

defective products by a successor corporation is not unknown, even under the "general rule" [that where one corporation sells or otherwise transfers all its assets to another corporation, the latter is not liable for the debts and liabilities of the former] ... Defendant acknowledges that if the transaction had been in the nature of a merger, there would have been no question that Harris-Intertype [*i.e.*, corporation B] would be liable. The same is true of a de facto merger. Yet corporate mergers continue to occur, even in the face of such contingent obligations. It has not been demonstrated that the possibility of liability would have a different effect on other forms of corporation acquisition.

Defendant contends that it is necessary to insulate transactions involving the purchase of assets for cash from the possibility of successor liability for defective products in order to avoid crippling the market for such purchases. This kind of objection was made and ultimately rejected, for example, when courts debated when the statute of limitations should start running in products liability cases. It is even less persuasive in the present context of an existing, thriving market in corporate mergers, where the possibility of such liability is already established.

Even the argument of surprise is likewise without merit.

While the first such successor to be faced with such a liability may claim surprise, the claim lacks legal force. For this kind of surprise is endemic in a system where legal principles are applied case by case and is no more an injustice than was the retroactive application of the strict liability doctrine in *Stephan* v. *Sears, Roebuck & Co.*, 110 N.H. 248, 266 A.2d 855 (1970)." [*Cyr* v. *B. Offen & Co.*,] 501 F.2d 1145, 1154 [1st Cir. 1974].

It is clear that once corporations considering such transactions become aware of the possibility of successor products liability, they can make suitable preparations. Whether this takes the form of products liability insurance, indemnification agreements or of escrow accounts, or even a deduction from the purchase price is a matter to be considered between the parties. Negotiations may be complex, but, with familiarity, they should become a normal part of business transactions.

Defendant argues that rather than go through this, corporations will opt for piecemeal divestiture. For some, this may be the solution. However, such sales usually realize less than the sale of the entire company. Therfore it may be more profitable for a selling corporation to sacrifice part of the ideal selling price rather than for it to take the more substantial loss resulting from piece-by-piece sales. In any event, these "cassandrian arguments", Juenger & Schulman, *Assets Sales and Products Liability,* 22 Wayne L.Rev. 39, 57 (1975), are far too speculative to cause us to reject the realities which direct our conclusion.

In the California case, *Ray* v. *Alad Corp.,* 19 Cal. 3d 22, 560 P.2d 3, 136 Cal. Rptr. 574 (1977), corporation A manufactured a ladder from which plaintiff fell on March 24, 1969, while working for the contracting company by which he was employed. On July 1, 1968,—after the ladder in question was manufactured, but before the injury occurred—corporation A sold to corporation B its stock in trade, fixtures, equipment, trade name, inventory, good will, and its interest in its real property used for its manufacturing activities. The sale excluded corporation A's cash, receivables, unexpired insurance and prepaid expenses. Corporation A had agreed to dissolve its corporate existence as soon as practical and to assist and cooperate with corporation B in the organization of a wholly owned subsidiary, corporation C. The principal shareholders of corporation A entered into an agreement not to compete with the purchased business for 42 months and to provide non-exclusive consulting services over that period of time. One of the principal shareholders of corporation A was employed as a salaried consultant by the acquired business for the first five months of its existence. Corporation A and its principal shareholders were paid in the aggregate more than $207,000 plus interest for the assets and good will of corporation A. On July 2, 1968, the day after the acquisition, corporation B filed and published a certificate of transacting business under a fictitious name, viz., corporation A's name. On August 30, 1968, corporation A filed a certificate of dissolution and corporation C filed a certificate of amendment changing its name to corporation A's. Thereafter corporation B transferred to corporation C all of the assets it had acquired from corporation A in exchange for all of the outstanding stock of corporation C.

With respect to the provisions contained in the agreement between corporations A and B by which the latter assumed the former's liabilities, the Court noted:

The only provisions in the sale agreement for any assumption of Alad I's [*i.e.*, corporation A's] liabilities by Lighting [*i.e.*, corporation B] were that Lighting would (1) accept and pay for materials previously ordered by Alad I in the regular course of its business and (2) fill uncompleted orders taken by Alad I in the regular from of its business and hold Alad I harmless from any damages or liability resulting from failure to do so. The possibility of Lighting's or Alad II's [*i.e.*, corporation C's] being held liable for defects in products manufactured or sold by Alad I was not specifically discussed nor was any provision expressly made therefor.

The plaintiff, claiming damages for injury from a defective ladder, asserted strict tort liability against corporation B which had neither manufactured nor sold the ladder, but which had continued to manufacture the same line of ladders under the same name, to use the same equipment and personnel, and to solicit its predecessor's customers through the same sales representatives with no apparent indication that the ownership of the business had changed.

The California Supreme Court agreed that none of the traditional exceptions to the general rule that a successor corporation (corporation B) is not liable for the liabilities of the selling corporation (corporation A) applied to this case. Nevertheless, the Court held that corporation B, which continued the product line of corporation A, was liable in strict tort for defective units of the same line which before the acquisition had been manufactured and distributed by the selling corporation (corporation A). The Court reasoned:

> Justification for imposing strict liability upon a *successor* to a manufacturer under the circumstances here presented rests upon (1) the virtual destruction of the plaintiff's remedies against the original manufacturer caused by the successor's [*i.e.*, the buyer's] acquisition of the business, (2) the successor's ability to assume the original manufacturer's risk-spreading rule, and (3) the fairness of requiring the successor to assume a responsibility for defective products that was a burden necessarily attached to the original manufacturer's good will being enjoyed by the successor in the continued operation of the business.

The Court concluded:

> [A] party which acquires a manufacturing business and continues the output of its line of products under the circumstances here presented assumes strict tort liability for defects in units of the same product line previously manufactured and distributed by the entity from which the business was acquired.

What can be done by the buyer to prevent the imposition of this products liability?

In the traditional purchase, the buyer will be continuing the enterprise and the product line, will be purchasing good will, and will be assuming seller's ordinary liabilities. Consequently, the only factor the buyer could manipulate to escape the reach of the *Turner* and *Ray* cases would be prohibiting the seller from liquidating for several years and requiring seller to maintain sufficient assets (at least the proceeds from the sale) to be responsive to a products liability suit. Of course, in the typical situation the seller will oppose this approach: if the seller's entire business has been sold, its shareholders will probably want to liquidate the seller under Internal Revenue Code §337 within 12 months from the date it adopts its plan of complete liquidation in order to substitute a single tax at the shareholder level, frequently at favorable capital gains rates, for the double tax which would otherwise be imposed first at the corporate level upon the profits from the sale and secondly at the shareholder level upon the distribution of the sale proceeds to the shareholders.

That an express provision in an acquisition agreement between corporations A and B to the effect that corporation B will not be liable for the products liability claims of corporation A is of no avail was suggested by the *Turner* and *Ray* cases in that they were based on tort rather than corporate law, but any doubt as to that conclusion is dispelled by the case of *Andrews v. John E. Smith's Sons Co.*, 369 So. 2d 781, Prod. Liab. Rep. (CCH) ¶8467 (Ala. S. Ct. 1979). A meat grinder was manufactured and sold by corporation A around 1949. This grinder had neither a guard over the opening to prevent feeding meat with the hand nor a stomper or mallet with which to feed and stuff the grinder, although other grinders marketed at the same time by corporation A had these safety features. In 1962 corporation A sold to corporation B for cash substantially all of its assets, including good will, orders, repair contracts, services, and all patents, including one on the grinder in question, and the safety devices used on similar models, and corporation B used corporation A's name together with the phrase "a division of corporation B, since 1868." Although two shareholders of corporation A retired at the sale, in other respects the business operation of corporation A remained with the same fiscal plan and employees. The sale included a non-competition agreement, and after 1962 corporation A participated in neither management decisions nor profits of corporation B. In the last several years corporation B had sold replacement parts for the particular meat grinder in question. In May, 1976, the plaintiff, an employee of a corporation which owned the meat grinder, had his right arm amputated below the elbow as a result of an accident at his place of employment. He had been stuffing ground meat into the meat grinder with his hand when it was caught and pulled into the grinding mechanism. Corporation A continued in existence under a new name until it was liquidated in 1977. Under the terms of the acquisition agreement corporation A specifically retained liability for all products liability claims on machines sold prior to June 20, 1962, and it continued to maintain product liability insurance until June, 1977, to cover claims arising from use of this machinery. Such insurance coverage was in effect at the time of plaintiff's accident. However, the plaintiff, being unable to sue corporation A, brought suit against corporation B.

Because only on appeal did the plaintiff raise for the first time the concept of products liability based upon continuity of the enterprise in reliance on the *Turner* case in Michigan, the defendant's motion for summary judgment was affirmed.

However, having cited approvingly the statement in the *Turner* case that "Justice would be offended if a corporation which holds itself out as a particular company for the purposes of sales, would not be *estopped* from denying that it is that company for the purpose of determining products liability," the Court stated in dictum that the reasoning of the *Turner* case is persuasive and compatible with Alabama law and that, if the complaint had properly pleaded this basis for recovery, corporation B would be "a prime candidate for application of an estoppel theory." The Court continued "justice requires that Hobam [*i.e.*, corporation B] be estopped from denying liability to innocent third parties, *even though it may have agreed with its predecessor that Hobam would not be liable for products liability claims*" (emphasis added). Thus, under the reasoning of the Alabama Supreme Court, the provision in the acquisition agreement between the selling and buying parties to the effect that the buying party would not assume products liability claims and that the selling party would retain them, would be ineffective against an injured party bringing a products liability action against the buying corporation although the injury arose out of a product manufactured by the selling corporation.

Because only a minority of the jurisdictions have adopted the approaches of the Michigan and California Courts, it is possible that one way to avoid imposition of products liability on the buying corporation would be to have the acquisition agreement contain a choice of law provision which would refer to the law of a state which follows neither the Michigan nor California approaches. The recent New Jersey case of *Litarowich v. Wiederkehr*, 170 N.J. Super. 144, 405 A.2d 874 Prod. Liab. Rep. (CCH) ¶8534 (N.J. Super. Ct., Law Div., Middlesex County, August 17, 1979), although involving the traditional de facto merger/consolidation exception, would seem to be equally applicable to the

Turner and *Ray* rationale and demonstrates that the attempted selection of a favorable forum may not be successful.

Corporation A, an Iowa corporation, manufactured a snow blower in 1966. In 1969 corporation B, a publicly traded Delaware corporation, purchased the assets of corporation A through its subsidiary, corporation C, a Delaware corporation formed in 1969 to receive the assets of corporation A. In 1976 the infant plaintiff was injured by the allegedly defective snow blower.

The defendants argued that under the law of Delaware, the buyer has no liability for this product liability claim. However, under the law of New Jersey, there could be a cause of action against the defendants on the basis of a de facto merger/consolidation because corporation B through its subsidiary not only bought corporation A's assets, but also bought its name, good will, plant, and facilities and then continued its business.

The following geographical facts were listed by the Court: Corporation A was an Iowa corporation with its manufacturing facilities in Dubuque; Arizona is the base for the headquarters of corporation B, and its connection with Delaware results only from the fact that it is incorporated in that state; the stock of corporation B is traded on the New York Exchange; corporation C, which was the vehicle for the purchase, is physically located in Dubuque, Iowa, from where it sells its products in many states just as corporation A had done before it; and the acquisition agreement executed between corporations A and B refers to their counsel in Washington, D.C. and New York, respectively, and contains a provision that the agreement be interpreted according to Delaware law.

In its discussion of two cases wherein other courts permitted the contract between the parties to control the choice of law to be applied to the products liability issue, the Court observed that "the corporations which made the contract were free to shape the consequences of their transaction and to choose a body of law and impose it on contingent tort claimants." The New Jersey Superior Court rejected this approach. It explained that the "case is about a New Jersey injury to a New Jersey resident caused by a snowblower manufactured for interstate sale and sold to a New Jersey retailer." The Court concluded that the contacts and interest of New Jersey were stronger than those of Delaware, Iowa or Arizona: "The corporate parties chose a body of local law to govern themselves, but they cannot thereby shut out a tort claimant whose concerns were unrepresented in the acquisition arrangements."

The Court recognized that the real interest opposing

application of the law of New Jersey, that is, the law of the state of residence and injury, was not the interest of either Delaware, Iowa or Arizona in applying its respective law, but rather was "the interest of the involved corporations in having an identifiable and reliable body of law by which to order their affairs. Corporate planners want to know when an acquisition will include contingent product liabilities and when it will not. Plans for escrows and indemnities can be made. The acquisition price may be affected."

The Court held that although predictability in corporate transactions may be desirable, "it does not weigh heavy against the need for a meaningful remedy for an injured person with a valid cause of action for product fault" and "it is more important that a worker's or consumer's cause of action for product fault not disappear in the shuffling of corporate papers and the invocation of protective foreign law."

Thus, it appears that the buying corporation, in spite of express provisions in the acquisition agreement for nonassumption of products liability by the buyer for products manufactured or sold by the selling corporation and for interpretation by the law of a favorable jurisdiction, cannot feel secure that it knows the extent of its liabilities arising out of an acquisition of a business with a product which can cause serious damage to persons or property.

At first blush it seems that the insulation of the buying corporation from such products liability and the simultaneous shifting of the burden of loss to the seller could be accomplished by escrowing part of the purchase price. But it may be difficult for the seller and buyer to agree on the duration of the escrow. Ideally, the buyer wishes to be protected from all possible claims. In this regard, if the products liability litigation is predicated upon an implied warranty of merchantability theory, it is generally subject to a statute of limitations of four years from the time of sale under Uniform Commercial Code §§2-725(1) and (2). If the products liability suit sounds in negligence or strict liability, it is generally subject to a statute of limitations running—depending upon the state—for one to five years from the date of injury, or from the date the defect in the product was or should have been discovered. Of course, again depending upon local law, the statute of limitations can be tolled by such factors as the infancy, insanity or imprisonment of the plaintiff. The interest of the buyer in prolonging the escrow must be weighed against the interest of the seller in terminating the escrow as quickly as possible to permit use of the sale proceeds. Another problem with this approach is to determine how much of the purchase price would be sufficient to cover unknown future claims. The claims could even exceed the purchase price.

If an insurance company will issue at affordable premiums products liability insurance covering the seller's pre-acquisition products, such insurance would be a better solution. The availability of such insurance, and the cost thereof, will be determined by a myriad of factors, including the nature and use of the product; the number and disposition of product liability claims made over the years; the manufacturer's quality control program; the extent of other, more profitable, insurance business placed by the assured with the insurance company; and the amount of the deductible or "retainage." No doubt, which party will bear the cost of this insurance will be a matter of negotiation and may affect the purchase price.

There are basically three kinds of policies offering this risk coverage. The Comprehensive General Liability Policies (and some Completed Operations-Products Liability policies discussed below) are of the "occurrence" type, that is, coverage is provided for all product related damages which occur during the policy period, the occurrence being neither the time of manufacture nor the time a claim is made, but rather the time when the product injures someone or something. The earlier the pre-acquisition inception date of the buyer's policy the greater the buyer's coverage insofar as the policy period is extended to a time to include any early, but unknown, pre-acquisition injuries. By its very nature, this kind of policy affords broad coverage (other than, of course, those risks specifically excluded under the terms of the policy), including coverage of liabilities newly created by operation of law such as those which are the subject matter of this discussion.

The coverage of Completed Operations-Products Liability Policy is limited to the two risks contained in its name. This kind of policy would cover, for example, damages arising not only from a defect in a product the firm manufactured (products liability), but also from a defect in installing that product by that firm (completed operations).

The coverage of the Products Liability Only Policies is the most restrictive of the three kinds of policies. They, as well as some Completed Operations-Products Liability Policies, are of the "claims-made" type, that is, coverage is provided only for claims made during *the policy period* with respect to a product which injures someone or something during that policy period. Some Products Liability Only Policies even limit coverage further by also requiring the sale to be made during the policy period. It is imperative, therefore, that the language of each policy be scrutinized to ascertain the perimeters of that policy's coverage.

For the same reasons as discussed with respect to the "occurrence" type of policies, the buyer's insurance protection under the "claims-made" type would be more comprehensive if it were continuing a policy which had become effective pre-acquisition. If the buyer is first obtaining this type of coverage as at the closing of the acquisition, the policy's "Retroactive Date," the date on which the policy period commences, should be made as early as is needed to cover pre-acquisition injuries with respect to which claims, not barred by the statute of limitations, have as yet not been asserted. Furthermore, the coverage of Completed-Operations Products Liability and Products Liability Only Policies is typically limited to scheduled products which have been manufactured, sold or distributed by the assured; consequently, the schedule should list the products manufactured, sold or distributed by the seller, and the seller itself should be named as an additional assured.

TENDER OFFERS

THE TENDER OFFER IS PROBABLY THE DOMINANT TECHNIQUE used to accomplish a corporate takeover where the management of the acquired company is likely to oppose the offer. In most cases the tender is one of cash for shares, but combinations of securities with or without cash are sometimes employed. The company to be acquired is referred to as the "target" and the offer itself as the "target tender." Over the years there has evolved a complex body of federal and state law, along with its attendant forms and documentation, which is part of making or defending against the tender offer process. A proliferation of new state laws has brought about decisions by state courts which tend to aid the target to the detriment of the acquiror. Until, and unless, federal action preempts such state regulations, these laws will be of substantial importance.

John C. Wilcox gives a detailed rundown on the advantages and disadvantages of conducting a cash tender offer. Topics include the costs of a tender, taxability, publicity, certainty outcome, and tactical advantages. There is also a discussion on analyzing the target, sources of information, shareholder profiles and the basics of organizing a team for execution of the transaction. When it comes to pricing the offer, Mr. Wilcox points out that setting the premium over the public market price is a relatively unscientific process of judgment as to ranges in which a variety of holders would be willing to give up their stock.

The position of the target company and its management is explored by Donald C. Carter. He explains the adoption of precautionary defensive techniques as a standard aspect of corporate planning and advocates an overall master plan to ensure that shareholders cannot be coerced into selling their stock at a price which does not reflect the true value of the company. Mr. Carter gives the characteristic profile of a target, defense techniques, composition of an ideal defense team and a list of defensive maneuvers.

Of course, the ultimate defense to a public tender offer and the lackluster public markets is to take the company out of public hands and make it a privately held entity. In the last five years many issuers have attempted this transition. Arthur Borden writes about this emotional issue which has provoked intense legal and corporate interest in recent years. On the one hand there is a school of thought which feels that when a corporation chooses to tap public sources of money it makes a commitment that it will remain a public investment. The opposition camp believes that the promised advantages of public participation have vanished in low price earnings multiples with thinly traded markets. Mr. Borden addresses techniques of going private, legal background requirements for the transaction, rules by the Securities and Exchange Commission, and actual cases of corporations who made the transition from public to private ownership.

JOHN C. WILCOX

JOHN C. WILCOX is a Principal of Georgeson & Co. Inc., New York, specialists in proxy and consent solicitations, proxy contests, tender and exchange offers, and shareholder and investor relations consulting. Mr. Wilcox received a B.A. from Harvard College, where he was a member of Phi Beta Kappa, an M.A. from the University of California, Berkeley, where he studied as a Woodrow Wilson Fellow, and a J.D. from Harvard Law School. He is a candidate for the LL.M. degree at New York University Graduate School of Law. During his seven years with Georgeson & Co. Inc., he has been involved in more than 200 tender offers.

29

The Practicalities of Planning a Cash Tender Offer

JOHN C. WILCOX

The decision to make a cash tender offer frequently comes at a relatively late stage in the process of planning an acquisition. Only after the prospective bidder has identified the type of acquisition that fits into its diversification or growth plan and then narrowed its selection to the target company that best meets its criteria, does it turn its attention to the techniques of acquisition that should be employed. In most cases a merger, exchange of securities or purchase of assets will be the favored mode of acquisition. But in cases where the traditional methods are inappropriate, the cash tender offer is the most popular alternative.

THE DISADVANTAGES OF A CASH TENDER OFFER

Despite its high visibility, dramatic impact and speed, a cash tender offer has certain disadvantages. The bidder should consider these matters carefully before embarking on a cash tender offer, whether friendly or hostile.

1. *Expense:* A cash tender offer is in the short run the most expensive form of acquisition. The initial cash outlay to purchase a majority or all the outstanding shares of the target company at a premium over current market price will usually involve borrowed funds. The cost of borrowing or a standby fee, in addition to the premium, the cost of advertising, a soliciting dealer's commission, the dealer-manager's override, legal fees, mechanical costs and various consultants' fees, must be factored into the overall expense of the tender offer. In a contested situation, litigation and other delays may force the offeror to maintain lending commitments over an extended period of time at substantial additional cost. The cost of litigation should be measured not only in attorneys' fees, but in executive time. On the other hand, a cash tender offer may be cheaper, dollar for dollar, than an exchange of securities. Some authorities maintain that the price to the acquiring corporation will be 15 percent higher where paper is used instead of cash.

2. *Uncertainty of Outcome:* As a practical matter it is impossible to acquire 100 percent of the outstanding shares of a company through a cash tender offer. There are always shareholders who cannot be located, who have lost their certificates, who are confused or who simply refuse to tender their shares (even in a friendly tender offer recommended by target management) through obstinacy or misunderstanding of the circumstances. If the bidder is unable to acquire the 90 percent-95 percent of outstanding shares necessary to effect a short-form merger, it may be left with a troublesome minority interest that cannot be easily disposed of.

Another factor leading to uncertainty, even in a friendly offer to which target management has given its approval, is the possibility of a competing bid. As sharks are drawn to bleeding prey, other acquisition-minded companies quickly assess the terms of a tender offer, and if a bargain is still possible at a higher price, competing bids will almost certainly develop. Although there is no way to prevent competing bids, the original bidder may attempt to discourage them by making its initial offer at a ''preemptive'' premium or by contracting for the purchase of substantial blocks of stock from insiders before commencing the public offer. In any case, ''white knights'' (competing bidders invited by target management) and ''black knights'' (uninvited competing bidders) are always a threat.

465

A third element of uncertainty results from the possibility that a federal regulatory agency (usually the Antitrust Division of the Justice Department or the Federal Trade Commission) may decide that the acquisition violates federal law. The Hart-Scott-Rodino Antitrust Improvements Act of 1976 lessens but does not eliminate the possibility of a post-acquisition divestment order.

In an unfriendly offer, the outcome of the struggle between the bidder and target management may be extremely unpredictable, depending on the vagaries of litigation, the attractiveness of the target to competing bidders, the stubbornness of target management, the persistence of the original bidder, the interest of various governmental regulatory agencies in interfering with the transaction, and other factors, none of which can be controlled by the acquiring company. No acquisition plan can provide fool-proof answers to the many questions that arise in the course of a takeover battle; the outcome is always uncertain.

3. *Lack of Warranties:* A cash tender offer, particularly when made without the cooperation of target management, is a unilateral act. It does not involve the exchange of information and the due diligence examinations that precede a negotiated merger. Although the acquiring company will examine all public information about the target, it does not have access to earnings projections and other undisclosed data about the target's operations. A tender offer is also nonselective; it cannot be used to acquire particular assets or operations. The bidder must therefore take the entire target company with all its blemishes (known and unknown) as well as its assets.

4. *Taxability:* A cash tender offer is a taxable transaction to the target company's shareholders. This may reduce its attractiveness to holders of large blocks with a low tax basis. The requirement of the Williams Act that all shareholders be treated equally disallows the possibility of a separate stock deal with selected shareholders. However, a first-step cash tender offer followed by a second-step tax-free merger is a frequently used alternative.

For accounting purposes a cash tender offer does not allow pooling of interest.

5. *Publicity:* A cash tender offer is a high-visibility transaction. Publication of the text of an unnegotiated offer or the appearance of a summary tombstone advertisement in a national newspaper will have the effect of a declaration of war. The interest of the investment community will immediately be drawn to the battle and the combatants. Litigation in a contest for control may lead to disclosures about the bidder that might not

otherwise have been made public. More than one tender offer has been defeated by litigation and discovery proceedings that led to embarrassing disclosures. Most acquiring companies will therefore examine their own vulnerability to publicity before undertaking the risks of a public confrontation and litigation. Some bidding companies, sensitive to the label "raider", simply refuse to make a hostile bid.

THE ADVANTAGES

Against these disadvantages the prospective bidder must weigh the advantages that have made the cash offer one of the most popular acquisition techniques.

1. *Speed:* Under the original Williams Act a cash tender offer could be completed in as little as seven or ten days, and the "blitzkrieg" tender offer became a highly publicized takeover device. Recent amendments to the Williams Act now require that a tender offer remain open for no less than 20 business days. State takeover laws may require even longer duration and may add a pre-offer waiting period or hearing provisions. The Hart-Scott-Rodino Act, while not affecting the duration of a tender offer, may delay the purchase of tendered shares. Despite these developments, a cash tender offer is still the fastest method to make an acquisition, and speed is always an important consideration. After announcing the terms of an acquisition, the bidder is always anxious to consummate the transaction before a move in the stock market disrupts the bargain, or changing financial conditions affect the cost of financing. Speed also reduces the possibility of competing bids by white or black knights.

2. *Certainty of Outcome:* Given enough information about the target company and its shareholders, the acquiring company can, with proper analysis and planning, determine with relative certainty the outcome of a negotiated cash tender offer endorsed by target management. This is very different from a statutory merger where almost anything can happen up to the closing. The shareholder vote on a merger is often uncertain, and factors affecting the stock market can seriously disrupt the terms of a merger involving an exchange of securities. The value of cash, however, is not subject to these disruptions.

3. *Tactical Advantages:* In both friendly and hostile tender offers, disclosure may not be required until the effective date of the offer. Assuming that there are no "leaks," that the market remains stable, that no purchases or agreements to purchase target stock are made in advance of the public offer, and that no other events

occur that might trigger a need for disclosure, companies can conduct their negotiations without publicity and keep the terms of the acquisition flexible until the tender offer becomes effective. Such confidentiality is impossible with a proxy statement (the fact of filing is not confidential even though the contents of preliminary proxy material are given confidential treatment) or with a registration statement for an exchange of securities.

Secrecy is particularly important for a company planning an unnegotiated tender offer and relying on the surprise and fear generated by a sudden unannounced takeover bid. The ability to work in secret, to plan unilateral action, to select the most advantageous timing, to retain the option of deciding not to make a bid right up to the date of effectiveness, gives an enormous amount of flexibility to the acquiring company.

If the bidder is itself concerned about an unnegotiated takeover, an acquisition made by a cash tender offer may provide a quick method to dispose of excess cash, thus serving as an effective "defensive" maneuver.

4. *Cost Savings:* The mechanics of a cash tender offer involve less direct cost than any other method of acquisition. The exhaustive financial reviews (of both companies in a statutory merger), due diligence meetings and disclosures are not required in a cash tender offer, nor are the expenses of preparing a registration statement under the '33 Act nor of qualification under state Blue Sky laws (with possible exceptions). There may also be long-range advantages to a company that pays cash for an acquisition instead of diluting its equity by the issuance of additional stock or increasing its interest burden by the issuance of debt.

Obviously, the transaction costs of a tender offer are substantially increased when the offer is unnegotiated and litigation ensues. Nevertheless, the costs of printing a relatively brief document, mailing it to target shareholders, processing the tenders and preparing payment are substantially below the costs of preparing a merger proxy statement, soliciting votes and holding a shareholders' meeting before the exchange of securities can occur.

Pre-Offer Strategy: Once the bidder has selected the cash tender offer as its method of acquisition, several preliminary questions must be addressed: Should negotiations with target management or directors be undertaken so that the offer can be made on a friendly basis? Even if negotiations are undertaken, is the bidder willing and prepared to proceed unilaterally if target management is opposed to the bid? In either case, should the bidder purchase target company shares on the market, from insiders, or from large block holders before the offer is made to the public?

Friendly or Hostile? Wherever possible, a tender offer should be made on a friendly basis with the support of the target company's management. A friendly transaction can be effected with greater speed and efficiency and with lower transaction costs. Management support generally assures the availability of the shareholders list and a favorable recommendation, both of which will substantially increase the number of shares tendered, particularly from individual shareholders who might not tender against management's wishes. Mutual disclosures and negotiations over terms and price will provide more complete information about the target company before the bidder makes a commitment to acquire it.

A friendly transaction also encourages continuity of key management personnel and better relations between parent and subsidiary after the acquisition. Agreements to acquire the stock of management and other insiders may also lock in a substantial percentage of the outstanding shares and thereby strengthen the offeror's hand against competing bidders. Overall transaction costs are greatly reduced in a friendly tender offer: there will usually be no need for a soliciting dealer's commission; a dealer-manager may not be necessary; and litigation costs are eliminated (except for possible shareholder actions). The offeror will also avoid the publicity that inevitably results from a hostile takeover. There is some question as to whether the premium will be lower or higher when the offer results from negotiations with target management rather than being set unilaterally by the bidder. This will vary with the facts of each case and the skill of the negotiators. However, to the degree that a friendly deal is successful in forestalling competing bids, the premium will be lower. Many state takeover statutes exempt tender offers that have been approved by the directors of the target company.

A friendly approach does not eliminate the bidder's option to make a hostile tender offer. A well-prepared bidder should be ready to proceed unilaterally before opening negotiations with target management for a friendly deal. The response will determine whether the offeror must proceed without management's blessing, but it must beware of "friendly" negotiations used by the target as a stall for time to find another merger partner or to develop strategies to block the proposed offer.

The basic strategic question for the bidder is whether or not it is willing to undertake a "hostile" tender offer, which will involve delay, litigation and publicity, and will probably produce one or more competing bids that must be met or exceeded. A realistic and thorough analysis of all these possibilities and their expense should precede any decision to make an unnegotiated bid.

If the bidder has concluded that it is willing to proceed hostilely if necessary, it may make an approach which is ostensibly friendly but which carries the threat of unilateral action should target management not acquiesce immediately or within a specified time. Such an approach is known as a "bear hug." There is an infinite variety in gradations of hug. The pressure to be applied to the target will depend on an evaluation of the degree of preparedness of the target, the strengths and weaknesses of its management, the attractiveness of the target to competing bidders, the position of each company with regard to possible litigation and other tactical considerations.

A bidder that decides to proceed hostilely must recognize that this course of action will almost certainly be long and difficult and the results uncertain, the chances of successfully acquiring the target company will be much lower than in a friendly transaction, and the costs will be higher than the bidder expects.

Pre-Offer Purchases: The bidder must consider whether it should purchase shares of the target company prior to making a tender offer. The purchase of target shares on the market will give the bidder a feel for availability of shares or "looseness" of the public float and the price at which substantial blocks may be available. In a thin market, however, even small purchases of target stock may produce an increase in the market price, leading to the necessity for a higher premium and ultimately a higher overall cost for the tender offer. A run-up in the market price may also generate rumors which can have the effect of bringing speculators into the market, further driving up the price, or giving warning signals to target management that a takeover may be imminent.

If substantial quantities of target stock can be purchased without affecting the market or generating rumors, the acquiring company can incur several advantages. Stock purchased on the market will not involve the payment of a premium and will thus lower the overall cost of the acquisition. In addition, the bidder who commences a tender offer already owning a substantial block of target stock has a stronger bargaining position in negotiations with management and a strategic advantage over competing bidders. These are extremely important tactical considerations.

The disadvantages of pre-offer market purchases are primarily legal. Although market purchases, even in volume, have never been held by a court to constitute a tender offer, a plan of coordinated off-market purchases at a premium from selected shareholders has been held to constitute a tender offer. The acquisition of certain percentages of stock will trigger various regulatory filings. The acquisition of 5 percent of a company's shares will require the purchaser (including members of its "group") to file a Schedule 13D, which includes a disclosure of the purpose of the investment. The acquisition of 15 percent or $15 million worth of stock will require a filing under the Hart-Scott-Rodino Act. There are various legal questions introduced by each of these filing requirements, and the advice of experienced legal counsel is essential. There is also the practical consideration that any public filing immediately eliminates the confidentiality of the acquiror's actions and requires a statement as to the purpose of the purchases and possible intentions as to a takeover.

Aside from these legal and tactical considerations, pre-offer market purchases rarely damage the acquiror and may result in a profit if the target is ultimately acquired by another company at a premium. In the jargon of market professionals, pre-offer purchases can lower the bidder's down-side risk.

Once a tender offer becomes effective the bidder is prohibited by Rule 10b-13 from acquiring shares of the target company otherwise than pursuant to the offer. Other companies, however, are not bound by this restriction. White knights or black knights are free to buy target shares that have been attracted into the market at the higher prices generated by the bidder's tender offer. There have been bids that were defeated, not by a competing offer, but by a competitor's purchase on the market of enough target shares to constitute control. This development is most likely to occur when consummation of the bidder's offer has been delayed, usually by litigation. During the period of delay sophisticated shareholders will retain their shares rather than tender them in order to preserve their option to sell or tender to the highest bidder. If the original bidder is unduly delayed and competing bids do not develop, these holders may decide to sell their shares into the market (where they may be purchased by a potential competing bidder), take a quick profit (even though the market price might be slightly or even substantially below the premium offered by the original bidder), eliminate the risk that the offer will fail, and move on with their cash to other investments. There is no way for a bidder to prevent a competitor from making this type of end run through the market, except by making the offer at a sufficiently high price to preempt all competing bids.

Analyzing the Target: Even though the bidder conducts an exhaustive business and financial analysis of the target company in determining its suitability as an acquisition and its "fit" with the bidder's own operations, additional analysis is necessary once the decision has been made to proceed with a cash tender offer. This analysis is primarily concerned with tactics. How much of a bargain is the target? Who are its shareholders and how loyal or dissatisfied are they? What kind of record does incumbent management have? Is the company prepared for a takeover bid? Is management likely to fight an unnegotiated bid, and if so, how effectively?

With these and many other questions in mind, the bidder must undertake a thorough examination of the target company, using all possible sources of information, in order to determine whether and to what degree a cash tender offer can succeed and to structure an offer that will have the best chance of success.

Sources of Information: In planning an unnegotiated offer, the bidder does not have access to earnings projections and other non-public information about the target company and must rely on public sources of information. These include reporting services such as Standard & Poor's, Moody's, Value Line, Vickers, Spectrum 13F reports of institutional ownership, brokerage and analyst reports, and various SEC filings. The company's own shareholder material — the annual report, interim reports, post-meeting report, shareholder relations materials — should be analyzed not only for the information they contain but for their effectiveness as shareholder communications. The target's most recent registration statement may contain dated financial information, but will prove useful in determining who has been the company's investment banker and which brokers were members of the underwriting syndicate. (These brokers should be contacted immediately when the tender offer becomes effective.) SEC filings, other federal and state regulatory filings, the company's own advertisements and promotional material will also provide valuable information and insights about the company. A clipping service can provide articles from newspapers and periodicals that may disclose unexpected and useful information about the company and its executives.

The Bargain: The analysis of the target company's business and financial background must answer the basic question of whether the offer will provide a bargain for the bidder and a profit for the shareholders (at least enough of them to pass a controlling interest to the bidder). The bidder will look at the target's price/earnings multiple: is it low by market or industry standards? The market price: is it below book value, liquidation value or going concern value? Dividends: are there any, and if so have they been paid regularly, increased or decreased recently? Earnings: have they been rising, declining, flat, erratic? Acquisitions: have there been many and have they been productive or disappointing? The stock: is it heavily or thinly traded; is its price at a low, a high, or at a stable average? These and many other questions about the health of the target company, its place within its industry, the way it is viewed by its shareholders, its competitors and the financial and investment community, must be analyzed to determine on what terms a tender offer should be made.

Target Shareholders: The cash tender offer, whether friendly or hostile, must be designed to appeal to a particular audience—the target company's shareholders. This is likely to be a diverse group of market professionals and non-professionals with widely different interests, and a marketing analysis should be made to determine how the offer can be structured to satisfy these interests. The individual shareholders of record are often large in number but small in their percentage ownership of shares. Insiders and others owning stock friendly to management may or may not have a significant ownership position, which will determine whether they have to be dealt with separately before a public tender offer is made. Street name holders and market professionals may have a large or small position in the target stock, but the terms of the offer can be designed to dramatically increase their participation.

(1) *Individual shareholders of record.* Individual shareholders who register their stock in their own names are generally characterized as conservative investors who purchase stock for long-term appreciation or income. As a group they are usually the most "loyal" to management, often to the point where they may refuse to tender their stock if an offer is opposed by management. The loyalty of these shareholders to management is subject to some qualifications, however. A long decline in earnings or in the market price for their stock, lack of a dividend or an interruption or reduction in dividend payments, scandal affecting management or a dispute involving executive "perks" are all matters that can undermine the traditional allegiance of individual shareholders to management.

The conventional wisdom is that an unhappy group of shareholders is far more likely to tender shares in a hostile bid, whereas a group of shareholders that has been treated well by management will often provide valuable support in resisting an unnegotiated offer. The bidder should therefore pay attention to the target's shareholder relations program in assessing the mood of the shareholders.

The bidder should also attempt to make a geographical analysis of the target shareholders. Concentrations of shareholders near the location of the target company's headquarters or operating facilities often represent shareholders who have strong feelings of loyalty to a "local" company. They may also represent employees of the target who would be concerned about their jobs in the event of a hostile offer leading to a change in management. On the other hand, an examination of the target's record of employee relations may lead to the conclusion that employees would be happy to "dump" incumbent management.

Without access to the target company's internal records, the bidder may be able to do only a limited analysis of the target's shareholders of record. Nevertheless, this analysis should not be neglected. Although the number of shares held by individuals is usually not a controlling interest, their support may make the difference between success or failure of a tender offer. In addition, federal and state takeover laws are ostensibly designed to protect the interests of individual shareholders more than any other group, and a tender offer that neglects these interests may be subject to regulatory pressure and private litigation.

(2) *Insiders.* The proxy statement for the target company will contain information as to the number of shares held by officers, directors and their families and by holders of 5 percent and 10 percent or more of the outstanding shares. The completeness of the disclosure in the proxy statement will vary from company to company. Those who have been well advised in tender offer defense tactics will often include extensive disclosures of the holdings of insiders' family members or other "related" persons (with appropriate disclaimers of beneficial rights) as a method of drawing attention to the substantial number of shares "controlled" by management. This disclosure is, in effect, a warning to potential raiders that an impressive amount of stock is held by family and friends who will presumably be loyal to management in the event of a hostile tender offer. Many companies, however, are less thorough in their disclosures. The bidder should beware of relying on the completeness of proxy statement disclosures in determining how many shares are held by insiders and others loyal to management.

Attention should also be paid to shares held by Employee Stock Ownership Plans (ESOPs and TRASOPs) and an attempt should be made to determine how these shares would be handled in the event of a tender offer. If the trustee for the ESOP is a member of the board of directors, the chances of shares being tendered in a hostile offer may be less than if the trustee is an independent agent.

Thrift plan and option shares should also be examined closely. Convertible securities, often issued in past acquisitions, may have special provisions triggering their conversion or may have unusual voting privileges. Shares issued in connection with acquisitions by the target company may constitute a significant percentage of the outstanding equity. An effort should be made to determine when such shares were issued and to whom, what is their tax basis, whether they are still restricted, and what relationship currently exists between the target company and the recipients of such stock. If the value of shares issued in an acquisition has fallen in an unfavorable subsequent market, the recipients may be disillusioned with target management and the shares may be accessible in a private transaction prior to the tender offer. On the other hand, if the value of such shares has been sustained or increased in the market and the management of the acquired company has maintained good relations with the target, these shares may share an identity of interest with management.

Large blocks of stock may be held by former target employees, and the availability of these shares may vary with the circumstances of the individual holder. For example, a former chairman of the target company who was forced into retirement against his will may be delighted at the prospect of seeing target management subjected to a takeover, and may even prove a valuable ally to the offeror.

(3) *"Street Name" holders.* Individuals may maintain their shares in street name either because they have been purchased on margin or because the holder wishes to maintain confidentiality and the convenience of having a broker or bank retain custody of the certificates. As a general rule, individuals who keep stock in street name take a more speculative view of their investments, are active traders interested in short-term gain, and may be more inclined to tender their shares in the event of an offer. They will generally be unconcerned whether an offer is friendly or hostile except in assessing the risk that the transaction may not succeed.

Street name share positions may also represent institutional investors — investment companies, insurance companies, pension funds, endowment funds and other professionally managed accounts. Almost without exception such accounts will look on a tender offer as presenting an investment decision, without regard to loyalties to management or other considerations of policy, and will tender their shares if it makes economic sense and is prudent to do so.

Arbitrageurs and other professional speculators will not usually have a position in target stock until the tender offer is announced. They will immediately assess the risks implicit in the terms of the offer (including the full range of legal and regulatory obstacles that will have to be overcome in order for the offer to be consummated), factor in their costs of borrowing money and will then buy target stock on the market. The price that these professionals are willing to pay is the most impartial measure of the likelihood of the offer's success. On occasion their price will actually be higher than offer price — usually an indication that a higher bid is expected. An offer endorsed by management for any and all shares will usually see the stock trading at a fraction below the offer price, or possibly a fraction above if there is a soliciting dealer's commission which the arbitrageurs can collect.

Target Management: Keeping in mind the basic tactical question of whether control can be acquired through an unnegotiated tender offer, the bidder must give careful attention to the strength and weaknesses of target company management.

How many shares does management control? If officers, directors and other reputedly friendly shareholders control an absolute majority of the target company's outstanding shares, an unnegotiated tender offer is practically out of the question. On the other hand, the insiders may not be as cohesive as they appear from the proxy statement. There may be dissatisfaction among members of the board and management; descendants of founding families may be interested in liquidating their investment; shareholders who received their stock by selling their companies to the target may be dissatisfied with the subsequent performance of target stock or may be unhappy after giving up control of their companies. These are just some of the issues that must be examined in determining the cohesiveness of a group of "controlling" shareholders.

The personality of key corporate officers is an important factor in determining how effectively the target will resist an unnegotiated tender offer. Hostile offers often develop into contests of wills. A strong or stubborn chief executive officer who is offended by an unnegotiated bid may attempt to save face by finding a white knight (*any* white knight) of his own choice rather than allow his company to be taken over by the original bidder.

Some CEOs have threatened to liquidate their companies rather than accede to an unnegotiated takeover (and in some cases the economics of liquidation have in fact been favorable to the target's shareholders). Obviously, the evaluation of corporate officers is subjective. Although it is impossible to know in advance how an individual will respond to a takeover proposal, the bidder should attempt to learn the reputation of the target's officers and directors, determine their experience in tender offers and examine how they have conducted their own acquisitions. A target company that has made its own hostile tender offer is likely to respond very differently from a target company that has always made acquisitions on a friendly basis.

The bidder should decide to what degree incumbent management is responsible for the success (or failure) of the target company and whether it is important to retain management to operate the company after it has been acquired. If the target company has been badly run and management has made poor use of its assets, one of the first post-acquisition moves contemplated by the bidder will be to replace key officers. At the other extreme, the target may be a service business whose major asset is its personnel. In the latter case a hostile takeover could drive out management, leaving the bidder with a worthless shell.

The existence of defensive provisions in the target's charter and bylaws may indicate the level of management's anti-takeover preparation and the degree of resistance that can be expected. Such provisions as a classified board of directors, supermajority votes for certain mergers, pricing formulas for minority freezeouts, removal to a state of incorporation with a protective takeover statute, long-term contracts and options for key employees, acquisition of a government-regulated business are usually intended by the target as a warning to prospective acquirors. These provisions indicate that the target has probably done its homework, that it may have retained professional assistance to prepare for a takeover and that the level of resistance is likely to be high.

ORGANIZING A TEAM

The planning and execution of a tender offer should be handled by a group of key management personnel and outside consultants. The group should be kept small in number so that its members can be assembled quickly and to ensure secrecy. Team members should be selected for their skill, experience and personal compatibility.

The most important member of the team is its leader, usually the chief executive officer of the acquiring corporation. (In large corporations which have an internal merger and acquisition group this role may be assigned to an executive other than the CEO, but the CEO will nevertheless retain a supervisory role.) The CEO's authority derives directly from the board of directors and he is responsible for making day-to-day tactical decisions as well as for implementing the general policies established by the board. In a tender offer, strategic moves must be made with speed and decisiveness, and the CEO's skill and leadership ability will be a determining factor in the offer's success.

During the tender offer the involvement of the acquiror's board of directors is usually limited to members of its executive committee, which will be empowered to act with the full authority of the board. This arrangement is essential to the proper execution of the offer because it eliminates the cumbersome and time-consuming requirement of convening all directors for each decision. If the full board is involved in strategic decisions, provision should be made for meetings of the board by telephone conference, and notice requirements should be waived.

Other corporate officers who should participate in the tender offer planning team are the vice-president for finance, the general counsel, corporate secretary, shareholder/investor relations manager and other officers normally involved with acquisitions. The selection of these participants depends on the management structure of the acquiring corporation and the involvement of outside consultants.

Legal Counsel

The legal framework governing tender offers involves five different areas of law: (1) direct federal regulation of tender offers under sections 13 and 14 of the Securities Exchange Act of 1934, the Williams Act; (2) direct state regulation of tender offers through the 36 state takeover statutes; (3) other federal regulation, giving general jurisdiction over corporate combinations (e.g., the Hart-Scott-Rodino Antitrust Improvements Act of 1976) or specific jurisdiction over regulated industries (e.g., administrative agencies such as the I.C.C., C.A.B., etc.); (4) other state regulation, including Blue Sky laws and special regulations covering certain industries such as banking and insurance; (5) foreign regulation.

Since every tender offer will involve one or more of the above categories of regulation, the role of legal counsel is central to the planning and execution of the offer. Lead counsel must include specialists in federal securities regulation who will be responsible for drafting the Offer to Purchase as well as reviewing news releases, advertisements and any other public documents relating to the offer. Lead counsel will also

decide whether it is necessary to have special counsel brought in for any unusual problems. For example, state takeover laws may establish jurisdiction not only in the state where the target company is incorporated, but in states where the target company has shareholders, does business, or has a certain portion of its assets located. Each of these jurisdictional questions must be reviewed, and if necessary, special counsel may be retained in states where jurisdiction might be claimed. (In several recent hostile offers, the constitutionality of state takeover laws has been directly challenged by the bidder.) If jurisdiction of a foreign agency or government is established, special counsel may also be required (e.g., the Canadian Foreign Investment Review Act may be involved if the target company has Canadian operations).

Lead counsel also takes responsibility for the conduct of litigation in connection with the offer. Litigation is generally regarded as the major weapon for both bidders and target companies in the battle for control. The speed with which a lawsuit is brought, the choice of forum and the skill with which the legal issues are presented can determine the outcome of a contest for control. Litigation can prevent the tender offer from ever reaching the shareholders of the target company, can move the battleground out of the marketplace and into the courts, and can substitute the decision of a judge for the will of the shareholders. The importance of legal counsel should never be underestimated, nor should the cost.

The Investment Banker

The investment banker is usually the first outside consultant to become involved in the planning of a tender offer. Most bidders will retain an investment banker to examine their own operations, to develop a business plan, to propose and evaluate various suitable targets for acquisition and to fix the price for the target that is finally selected. If the tender offer is made on a friendly basis, the investment banker plays a central role in negotiating the terms, often with another investment banker representing the target company. If the offer is unnegotiated, the investment banker serves as tactical adviser and will also conduct negotiations for a settlement while the tender offer and litigation are in progress. Whether the tender offer is friendly or hostile, the investment banker customarily serves as "dealer-manager," a term borrowed from underwriting that is not strictly appropriate when applied to a tender offer. In acting as dealer-manager for a tender offer, the investment banker organizes the mechanics of the offer and supervises the various participants —the information agent, depositary, forwarding agent, printer and public relations firm. He does not, however, establish a "syndicate" of broker-dealers to distribute the offer and solicit acceptances. He may distribute copies of the offering documents to broker-dealers who are members of his usual syndicate group, but he does not exercise the control over them that exists in an underwriting. The investment banker usually contacts large institutional holders of target company stock and may also arrange for customers' men or the syndicate department to contact shareholders. In this respect his function will overlap with that of the information agent.

Whether or not the investment banker takes an active role in the mechanics of the tender offer, his major role is as the bidder's financial advisor and specialist in mergers and acquisitions.

The Information Agent

The information agent will be selected by the bidder from among a handful of proxy solicitation firms, all located in New York City. The services provided by the information agent will vary with the type of firm selected and the experience of its personnel, the requirements of the tender offer and the presence or absence of an investment banker.

In every case the information agent is responsible for dissemination of the offering documents to Street name holders and to arbitrageurs and for answering questions from target company shareholders. When the list of target shareholders is available, the information agent will also organize a telephone campaign to contact target shareholders, alert them to the offer and determine how they are responding. The purpose of such a campaign is to make sure that the documents are not ignored by shareholders and to deal with any questions about the offer. In an unfriendly offer, where a shareholders list may not be readily available, distribution of the offer is limited to Street name holders, institutions whose portfolios are publicly reported and shareholders who request material.

When the offer is made on a friendly basis with the endorsement of target management, the bidder may decide that it is not necessary to use a dealer-manager. The information agent will then assume complete responsibility for coordinating the mechanics of the offer, the conduct of the telephone campaign and contacts with institutional holders.

If the information agent is experienced in tender offers and has shareholder and investor relations capabilities, he will play a key role in analyzing the target company, reviewing the offering documents, coordinating news releases and advertisements and planning strategy with the other members of the tender offer team. The information agent provides expertise in matters relating to shareholders and should be relied on to assess the reception that a tender offer will receive from target company shareholders and the investment community.

The Depositary and the Forwarding Agent

The bank which is selected as depositary for a tender offer should be experienced in tabulation and reporting procedures and should have had previous experience with tender offers. Most shares will be tendered during the few hours just before the offer expires, and the depositary must be equipped to handle the expected volume of tenders, process and tabulate them, select out defective tenders, eliminate duplicate tenders and guarantees of delivery, and provide preliminary statistics for a news release prior to the opening of the market on the next business day. Coordination between the depositary and forwarding agent is essential to avoid double counting of tendered shares. Brokers and banks have been known to send a guarantee of delivery by mail or Telex to the depositary and then deliver shares to the forwarding agent (which is usually located in New York City for the convenience of the major brokers and banks) to cover the guarantees. Care must be taken not to count guarantees and deliveries as a double tender which could inflate the preliminary statistics. In many cases the depositary is located outside New York simply to avoid transfer taxes.

Public Relations Firm

Public relations counsel is usually not necessary for a friendly tender offer. Drafting and issuance of news releases, placement of advertisements and other public relations matters are usually handled by legal counsel, the information agent or the investment banker. In a hostile offer, however, where a media campaign may be an important adjunct of the offer, a public relations firm is often retained. It is the target company, however, that derives most benefit from a public relations campaign to publicize its reasons for rejecting an offer.

Printer

The bidder should always engage an experienced financial printer with a reputation for speed, accuracy and dependability. The printer will be required to distribute proofs of the offering documents to members of the tender offer team, and to print final copy in bulk quantities sufficient for mailing and distribution to target shareholders. This must usually be accomplished overnight, to coordinate with a morning filing of the offer documents with the SEC and announcement of effectiveness prior to the opening of the stock market. The printer should also have the capacity to handle the mailing of the offer documents to target company shareholders.

SETTING THE TERMS OF THE OFFER

In drafting the Offer to Purchase, the bidder and the members of the tender offer team finally apply the results of their analysis of the target company, its management and shareholders. The Offer to Purchase, setting forth the terms on which target shares will be purchased and providing the mechanical means to tender, should be carefully tailored to fit the target company and the market for its shares. The basic terms of the offer—price, number of shares, duration and conditions—should be established, within the legal requirements for full and complete disclosure, to appeal to the audience of target shareholders and to satisfy the objectives of the bidder. Variations in the terms of an offer can give very different results, and the bidder should take care to balance the offer's terms to achieve the desired result.

Price

The offer price is generally viewed in terms of its premium above the current market price for the target company's shares, although it is also set in terms of the value of the company's assets or its value as a going concern. If the target's current market price is substantially below its book value, then the premium over market may have to be substantially higher than in a case where market and book are about equal or where market exceeds book. If the past market value of the target stock has been higher than current market, then a proportionately higher premium over current market may be required; but if current market is an all-time high, then the premium may be relatively low. Suppose, for example, that target stock is now trading at 25. A price of 35 may seem generous (depending, of course, on book value, price/earnings ratios and other considerations), but if the stock traded at 50 a year ago, the $10 premium will certainly not be sufficient to draw shares from holders who purchased at the previous year's high. The reason for the high and low trading prices must be examined. The volume of trading and the duration of the high are also important considerations, as are the same statistics for the stock at other price ranges. Such studies are always inexact because volume figures may represent the same shares of stock traded repeatedly while the bulk of the shares have continued to be held by holders who have not participated in the volatile market. The target company's transfer sheets and depositary position listings can provide useful information to evaluate the "float" of actively traded shares and to do an aging study of the stock.

It is important to remember that every tender offer is unique and every target company is unique. The reasons that dictate a certain premium in one offer may be inappropriate when applied to another. For this reason comparative statistics in setting a premium are of little use. It may, however, be of historical interest to review the percentage premiums paid in tender offers from year to year, but this information is of limited value in estimating the premium that should be paid in a particular offer. Nor will narrow changes in premium have much impact on the results of a tender offer. The nature of the investment decision made by a shareholder in a tender offer is quite different from the type of decision made in purchasing or selling stock on the market or purchasing shares of a new issue. In both of the latter cases, fine adjustments of price will have an impact on the decision to purchase shares. But in a tender offer the decision is to sell, and the existence of a premium over cost provides the shareholders' main incentive. Slight adjustments in the premium have no appreciable impact on the number of shares tendered. Setting the premium is an art based on relatively unscientific methods of assessing the range of prices at which a variety of holders will be willing to give up their stock. But even though the decision to sell stock is for most shareholders a much less refined decision than the decision to buy, the bidder can with experience achieve some accuracy in estimating how shareholders will respond to a given premium.

Although the main purpose of the offer premium is to encourage shareholders to tender, it should also be designed to block competing bids. Tender offers have become so competitive that every bidder is now aware that a low bid, even though perhaps sufficient to induce tenders from enough shareholders to give control, may immediately attract competing bids from rivals. Consequently, in setting the price the initial bidder will attempt to establish a premium sufficiently generous to discourage competing bids. This may also be accomplished by agreements to purchase stock from insiders or other arrangements reached before commencement of the offer.

Most tender offers used to provide for payment of a soliciting dealer's fee—an extra cash payment on shares of stock tendered through the efforts of a soliciting broker-dealer whose name appeared on the letter of transmittal. It was thought that with a soliciting dealer's fee an army of registered representatives would be enlisted to work on behalf of the bidder in soliciting tenders from target shareholders. The use of the soliciting dealer's fee has fallen out of fashion for friendly offers. Most experts believe that the premium over market supplies sufficient incentive and advise bidders to put their funds into the premium rather than reserving a separate payment for broker-dealers. In hostile offers, however, where the list of target shareholders may not be available and the bidder must rely on the marketplace for tenders, the soliciting dealer's commission is still considered an effective method to promote interest in the offer.

Number of Shares

If the bidder has no reason for limiting the number of shares it will accept, the offer should be made for any and all shares of target stock. An any-and-all offer provides certainty that tendered shares will be accepted and eliminates a troublesome element of risk. An offer for fewer than all shares raises the risk of proration. An offer conditioned on the tender of a minimum number of shares (usually 51 percent) raises the risk that no shares will be accepted if the minimum is not met. Both conditions raise questions for individual shareholders and for professionals. Individuals who hold round lots of target stock may be reluctant to tender if they run the risk of proration that could leave them with an odd lot. They may also be discouraged by the complex tax issues that must be disclosed when an offer is subject to proration. In the two-step cash election merger, in which a cash tender offer precedes an exchange of securities, the problem of proration is largely eliminated because unpurchased shares will subsequently be exchanged for securities. The market may value the second-stage securities below the first-stage cash, however, leading to a discount in the market value for target stock during the tender offer.

Arbitrageurs and other speculators who purchase target stock solely for the purpose of tendering always assess the risk of a proration which could leave them holding target stock to be sold in the after-market. Such subsequent sales must usually be made at a price substantially below the offer price, and this possibility is factored into the price that arbitrageurs are willing to pay for target stock during the offer. Where there is the risk of proration or a minimum share condition, the market price during the tender offer may be well below the offer price. This discount reflects the risk that the offer will be over- or under-subscribed as well as a variety of other risks that are of concern to professional traders.

If the bidder wishes to acquire the maximum number of shares, it will attempt to eliminate uncertainty and risk from the terms of the offer, with the obvious proviso that it must not sacrifice its own objectives in making the offer.

Duration and Payment

From the point of view of the bidder and the professional speculators, the best offer is the shortest offer with the earliest payment provisions. But the days of 7- and 10-day tender offers are now over. Amendments to the Williams Act, effective January 6, 1980, require that a tender offer remain open for no less than 20 business days (plus 10 days following an increase in compensation) and lengthen the withdrawal period to 15 days (and 10 additional days if a competing bid is made). The time frame of a tender offer may also be affected by operation of the Hart-Scott-Rodino law which can delay "consummation" of a tender offer (i.e., payment for tendered shares) for 15 days measured from the filing of certain documents with the Federal Trade Commission, and for an additional 10 days if further disclosures are requested. State takeover laws also contain a variety of waiting periods, hearing provisions and minimum time periods that are designed to prevent "blitzkrieg" tender offers. Within this array of regulations, the bidder should attempt to eliminate uncertainty and provide for speedy and certain expiration and payment dates.

Conditions

The fewer the conditions, the more attractive the tender offer will be to shareholders and other members of the "audience." However, conditions are designed to protect the bidder and to allow for termination of the offer in the event that adverse events occur. Most offers contain an array of conditions that have become little more than boilerplate. Nevertheless, a bidder should never make the mistake of being compelled to consummate an offer simply because it failed to provide the requisite conditions for termination. The bidder should stipulate every situation under which it might wish to abort the tender offer and make sure that these possibilities are covered in the stated conditions.

CONCLUSION

The planning of a cash tender offer should follow a logical sequence of analysis and preparation:

1. Select the target company that best fulfills the bidder's business purpose and growth plan.
2. Review all other methods of acquisition before determining that a cash tender offer is the best method for the proposed transaction.

3. Decide whether or not the bidder is willing to make the tender offer without the support of target management.

4. Assemble a team of experts to give advice at each step of the analysis and preparation.

5. Analyze the target company with care, paying attention to the shareholder mix, the characteristics of management and the history of the company's earnings and stock movements.

6. Set the terms of the offer to appeal to target shareholders and market professionals and to block competing bids.

7. Be strategically prepared for a prolonged contest against recalcitrant management and rich competing bidders.

DONALD C. CARTER

DONALD C. CARTER is the founder and President of The Carter Organization, a professional proxy solicitation firm based in New York City's financial district. A graduate of New York University's School of Commerce, Mr. Carter began his Wall Street career in arbitrage research specializing in securities valuations during mergers and takeover bids. He is well known for his successful war-games tactics employed during proxy fights and tender offers. Mr. Carter's other interests include the legitimate theater, where he was the producer of the Broadway hit revival, *Oklahoma!* He also serves as President of Top Cat Oil, a family owned energy exploration company. Mr. Carter lectures frequently on the subject of struggles for corporate control.

Resistance to Takeover Attempts

DONALD C. CARTER

The best executive talent in the American free enterprise system has been running scared for over two decades. Despite salaries that keep pace with inflation, recognition by their peers and the personal satisfaction inherent in a job well done, many successful senior officers of public companies cannot get a good night's sleep. Their collective corporate discomfort is due to the nightmarish presence of a possible takeover artist.

This growing demise in job security at high corporate levels is not due to widespread career failings. On the contrary, it is the combination of corporate financial success and an undervalued stock price that has led to an increase in "Situations Wanted" ads in the newspapers for more than a few successful independent management teams. The reason for these Fortune 500 fritters is the two-decade old sustained rise in the use of non-negotiated tender offers as an acquisition technique.

On Wall Street, where necessity is known to be the entire ancestry of invention, corporate scene onlookers were not surprised to see the victims fight back. Managements who thought the definition of a "target company" might soon apply to them have called upon their attorneys, investment bankers and proxy advisors to institute protective devices matching the strength of the early Dutch-built walled buildings that insulated the settlers on the southern tip of Manhattan from the Indians.

The adoption of precautionary defensive techniques as a method of combating the rise in tender offers has become an essential and standard aspect of corporate planning. In addition, companies have prepared response programs and strategies to be used once an unfriendly offer has been made. These tactics can be used separately or combined into one overall master plan. The amount of effort devoted to such planning will depend on the perception of danger held by management and the Board of Directors. Obviously, defensive planning should be undertaken only by those managements who make a good faith determination that a non-negotiated offer may not recognize the true value of the company and that their shareholders may not be fairly treated.

Advance defensive planning is deemed necessary by many companies because without it the raider[1] has a most crucial advantage with the ability to select the timing and initial terms of an offer. With time on his side, the raider can study the target company leisurely, arrange financing sources, assemble an attack team, and wait for the most opportune market conditions. On the other hand, the target company's response must be decisive, efficient and rapidly executed. Under the S.E.C. tender offer rules, an offeror need only keep its offer open for 20 business days. For targets with over a hundred years' existence, four weeks is indeed a short time to determine the course of the future. Once the offer is announced, there is obviously little time for a relaxed decision-making process.

There is little doubt that a carefully plotted defensive strategy has often spelled the difference between independence and corporate servitude.

CHARACTERISTICS OF A TARGET COMPANY

When framing a defensive strategy, the first step a potential target company must take is a complete analysis of its desirability as a takeover candidate. The corporate raider often searches for a company whose stock price in the public market is lower than what the assets and earnings power of the company would normally warrant. If, for example, the raider wants to go into a particular business line, he may discover that

---

[1]Or "potential buyer", or "offeror" — depending on which side of the equation one stands.

buying the stock of a public company already established in the field is less expensive than starting from scratch. This is especially true of companies engaged in capital intensive industries where the replacement cost of the company's assets can exceed the market price of its stock by huge margins. A company on the brink of a recovery from a period of depressed earnings or losses is apt to be significantly undervalued by the marketplace, and thus will interest raiders who might be interested in utilizing tax-loss carry forwards.

The "ideal" target company is one which can fund a significant portion of the transaction[2] from its own assets. In this regard a high cash position, large securities portfolio or substantial cash flow can have enormous appeal.

Less liquid assets such as subsidiaries, divisions or other properties which can be sold to third parties without affecting the earnings performance of the acquired company may also attract potential suitors. Raiders are particularly fond of undervalued assets such as real estate or equipment which can be used as collateral for institutional lenders who might finance the purchase. In addition, a company with a significant unused debt capacity may make it possible for the acquiror, after a successful bid, to increase borrowings and thus fund part of the purchase price. For those companies with significant debt positions, it has proven helpful to have loan agreements which contain covenants that enable the lender to accelerate a loan if large amounts of stock trade hands in a merger or acquisition or when new funded debt is added.

The most significant trait of a target company is the relatively small stockholdings owned or controlled by management. The Ivan Boesky's[3] of the world love nothing more than a scattered group of shareholders concerned only with the price performance of their shares. A substantial premium, or for that matter, any premium could entice them to sell. Even large institutional holders (traditionally pro-management in giving support to the election of directors each year) now analyze the terms of an offer carefully and are often the first ones to either tender or sell to the arbitrageurs.

D-E-F-E-N-S-E

Once a company has determined itself to be an attractive takeover candidate, there are a number of courses of possible defensive action that can reduce both its vulnerability and attractiveness without affect-

ing the ongoing responsibilities of growth and greater return in its shareholders' investment. These options range in scope and complexity from the ten-cent phone call (which, when coupled with a $50,000 extension cord, will ensure the availability of a specialized law firm) to changes in the basic structure or business of the company itself.

Well in advance of any unsolicited offer, a potential target company can assemble a defense team. Just like the gridiron eleven, a good defense will contain specialists in every area of the playing field. In addition to company personnel, the members of the defense team should include the company's investment banker, outside general or special counsel experienced in non-negotiated tender offers, a proxy solicitation firm and an outside public relations consultant. In most cases, all of these takeover defense specialists can be retained on standby basis to ensure their availability. Each can provide valuable input to the decision-making process as well as the expertise and manpower necessary for the proper execution of the defensive effort.

Investment Bankers

The opposition to a potential cash tender offer raid on the basis of price inadequacy requires a working knowledge of the asset value or stock market worth of comparable companies. The investment banker can offer various approaches to this evaluation including the development of a stock price performance study of the target company and its competition over the last few years. This review can be helpful in determining whether the raider's price is, in fact, a premium price. By itself, however, such a market analysis can be misleading. Not all stocks enjoy true liquidity and thus do not have prices reflective of what a willing buyer and willing seller would exchange for shares if informed of all facts. A small public float, control blocks, lack of trading volume and an overhang of unsold shares often distort public market prices.

An investment banker may also prepare a study of non-negotiated tender offers and their premiums which could assist the company's Board of Directors in their fairness determination. Of course, direct comparisons to other offers in the same industry would be helpful.

Attorneys

Careful consideration should be given to the retention of a special outside counsel with experience in both defensive tactics and litigation during non-negotiated offers. In addition to a handful of New York

---

[2]Most often in the form of a cash tender offer to all public shareholders.

[3]Ivan Boesky of Ivan F. Boesky & Co. is one of Wall St's leading risk arbitrageurs — a small band of moneyed professionals who are not afraid to put their blood pressure on the line when the first news of an unfriendly offer hits the Dow Jones Broad Tape.

law firms whose reputations in this area are well-known (including Skadden Arps and Shea & Gould), there are literally dozens of firms throughout the country whose competence and expertise in this field are equal to their New York counterparts.

Proxy Solicitation Firms

The retention of a proxy solicitation firm on an ongoing basis plays a vital role in potential target's defensive program. Proxy firms supply services which are designed to enhance and strengthen the target's ability to respond to a hostile offeror. Among these services are: (1) the maintenance of a current, accurate list of shareholders to be contacted if an offer is made; (2) the maintenance and review of transfer sheets and depository listings in order to provide an early warning of any unusual accumulation of the target's stock; and (3) improving relations with the "street-name" holders by establishing a communications network with brokers, banks and other nominees. Although most potential targets today perform their own review of transfer sheets and depository listings, a proxy solicitor will often read the same data and reach different conclusions (based on the solicitor's depth of experience). With the enormous rise in street-name ownership of securities — especially those of target companies — the transfer sheets alone cannot provide accurate data. At The Carter Organization, the author's company recently had certain available shareholder data that had been overlooked by our client's in-house counsel, which was subsequently analyzed by Carter professionals, turned over to special counsel and was the deciding factor in the resulting litigation in favor of the target. Unlike attorneys and investment bankers, there are only a few major proxy firms with top-level management expertise in takeover strategies. In choosing a proxy firm to assist in long-term planning and in defending against the actual offer itself, management should carefully consider the availability of the senior executives at these firms. It would be helpful to make certain that the firm to be retained is not too busy, especially during "proxy season" (April-June) to devote the proper amount of time and attention to a contested takeover attempt.

Public Relations

A target company should seek a firm with experience, and the name of Manning, Selvage & Lee of New York City is synonymous with tender offer defenses. A public relations consultant can aid management by formulating management's investor relations program in the interest of increasing the level of shareholder loyalty. These specialists maintain excellent relations with the financial press — a fact that is often critical in insuring the proper coverage of management's response to an offer.

BUILDING THE ANTI-TAKEOVER WALL

In an effort to reduce their attractiveness to raiders, many potential target companies have solicited stockholder approval for changes in the corporate charter or bylaws. The substantial increase in this defensive maneuver has prompted the concern of the S.E.C. In response to a request by the Advisory Committee on Corporate Disclosure, the staff of the Division of Corporate Finance published its position on disclosure of anti-takeover proposals in release #34-15320 (October, 1978). The staff focused on the two most general areas of defensive techniques: charter/bylaw amendments and defensive moves designed to delay the raider.

Charter/Bylaw Amendments

The Division of Corporate Finance has taken the position that when management sponsors anti-takeover proposals and other devices to insulate management from removal, the issuer's proxy material or information statement should disclose in a prominent place that the overall effect of the proposal is to render more difficult the removal of management. The Division's review of proxy and information statements containing anti-takeover measures continues to focus on three areas: the placement of the disclosure in the statement, the disclosure of anti-takeover proposals generally; and the disclosure of specific types of provisions being proposed.

With respect to charter/bylaw amendments, the S.E.C. requires certain basic information to be disclosed, including: (1) the reasons for the proposals and an explanation of the factors supporting the reasoning; (2) whether the issuer's charter or bylaws already include other provisions having an anti-takeover effect; (3) whether the current proposals are part of a broader plan by management to adopt anti-takeover amendments; (4) and whether management intends to propose other anti-takeover measures in the future. Management must disclose its knowledge of any efforts to accumulate the company's securities or to otherwise obtain control. The S.E.C. has identified the following anti-takeover measures that are commonly instituted through bylaw or corporate charter changes. Of course, the Commission is careful to note that the following list (as reported in Release #34-15230) may not be complete:

(1) Classification of directors or staggering of boards.
(2) Provisions to abolish cumulative voting.

(3) Provisions establishing supermajority approval requirements (for example, requiring an 80 percent favorable vote) for certain corporate transactions including, but not limited to, any proposed merger or sale of assets.

(4) Provisions requiring a supermajority vote to cancel a supermajority provision as described in category (3) above, but not to adopt one.

(5) Provisions requiring a supermajority vote to amend the corporate charter in any relevant respect.

(6) Provisions which reduce the supermajority required for a merger to a lesser majority unless the other party to the transaction is a "related corporation" (such as one owning more than 5 percent of any class of voting securities of the issuer) in which case a merger would require supermajority approval of the common stock as a class in addition to approval by the holders of the voting power to all securities of the issuer entitled to vote.

(7) The creation of a class of equity securities either common or preferred to be placed privately; the favorable vote of which is necessary to approve any tender offer, merger, sale or exchange of assets or other extraordinary corporate transaction.

(8) Provisions which prevent the removal of directors without cause or by a supermajority vote.

(9) Provisions prohibiting the removal from office for any reason of a director elected for a term longer than one year, notwithstanding any change in control due to tender offers, mergers or other transactions.

(10) Provisions prohibiting the calling of special shareholder meetings altogether or allowing them to be called only upon the request of a holder or holders of a supermajority of the shares outstanding.

(11) Provisions establishing the maximum permissible number of directors.

(12) Provisions providing for the election of stand-by successor directors at the same time as the regular directors, who will fill a position upon the death or resignation of a regular director.

(13) Reincorporation of the issuer in a state with an anti-takeover statute.

(14) Creation of an Employee Stock Ownership Plan, which because of its size, percentage of total outstanding securities of the issuer which it may own, voting or other provisions, may be used in defense in a contested takeover attempt.

(15) Provisions requiring the consideration for any merger following a tender offer to be no less than the highest consideration offered pursuant to the tender offer.

(16) Shareholder approval of long term "sweetheart" employment contracts with executive officers of the issuer which cannot be abrogated or rescinded.

Washington Service Bureau, Inc., a research firm that scrutinizes all filings with the S.E.C., has compiled a list of companies which have implemented anti-takeover proposals. A sample table is shown in Figure 30-1.

It is not unusual to find a number of anti-takeover proposals on one single proxy form. For example, IPCO Hospital Supply in 1979, sought shareholder approval of amendments to its Certificate of Incorporation and Bylaws which would provide: (1) for the division of company's board into three classes and the staggered election of directors thereof; (2) for an increase in the number of directors from the present three to eleven directors to nine to twelve directors the exact number to be determined by a resolution of a majority of the board; (3) that directors may be removed only for "cause" by the vote of a majority of shares entitled to vote (directors, at that time, could be removed for any reason by a majority of votes cast); (4) that vacancies and newly created directorships may be filled by the board and that the appointed director may then serve until the next meeting at which election of directors is in the regular course of business; (5) that special meetings may be called only by the chief executive officer or by the board; (6) that 80 percent of the shares entitled to vote must approve any merger or other consolidation of any disposition of company assets with or to an entity owning 10 percent of company shares entitled to vote unless the board approves the transaction prior to the time that the entity acquires the 10 percent, and (7) that 80 percent of the shares entitled to vote must approve any alterations inconsistent with these amendments.

STAGGERING THE BOARD TO AVOID A ONE-PUNCH KNOCKOUT

The most popular technique to prevent an immediate change in the board of directors at an annual meeting is to provide for a classified or staggered board usually consisting of three substantially equal classes of directors, each serving for a three-year term, with their terms ending in successive years. Even a substantial majority shareholder would have to wait for at least two successive annual meetings in order to elect a majority to the Board.

In presenting to shareholders a proposal for establishment of a classified board (as well as other defensive proposals) it is important to emphasize the positive aspects of the proposal. For example, the 1979 proxy

... a publication of the Washington Service Bureau, Inc.

TOPICAL INDEX   PROXY STATEMENTS

MONTH: _____ PAGE: _____

TOPIC ISSUER	WSB ABSTRACT # AND MICROFICHE CARD LOCATOR	MARKET OR EXCHANGE	STATE OF INCORPORATION	MEETING DATE
ANTI-TAKEOVER TECHNIQUES				
Creation of class of voting preferred stock				
Keene Corp.	6	NYSE	DE	04-04-79
IPCO Hospital Supply Corp.	96	NYSE	NY	11-16-79
Directors, appointment by board				
IPCO Hospital Supply Corp.	96	NYSE	NY	11-16-79
Directors, ''cause'' for removal of				
Topps & Trowsers	41	NYSE	CA	09-14-79
Bache Group Inc.	95	NYSE	DE	11-16-79
IPCO Hospital Supply Corp.	96	NYSE	NY	11-16-79
Calumet Industries, Inc.	169	—	DE	01-22-80
Reynolds and Reynolds Co.	180	OTC	OH	02-19-80
Directors, no enlargement of board of				
Topps & Trowsers	41	NYSE	CA	09-14-79
Bache Group Inc.	95	NYSE	DE	11-16-79
IPCO Hospital Supply Corp.	96	NYSE	NY	11-16-79
Directors, staggered election of				
Alba-Waldensian, Inc.	8	ASE	DE	04-18-79
Topps & Trowsers	41	NYSE	CA	09-14-79
Bache Group Inc.	95	NYSE	DE	11-16-79
IPCO Hospital Supply Corp.	96	NYSE	NY	11-16-79
Calumet Industries, Inc.	169	—	DE	01-22-80
Reynolds and Reynolds Co.	180	OTC	OH	02-19-80
Foreign concerns, discouragement of				
Great Lakes Dredge & Dock Co.	73	NYSE	NJ	06-12-79
Friendly offers				
UARCO, Inc.	2	NYSE	DE	02-01-79
UV Industries, Inc.	5	NYSE	ME	03-26-79
Reincorporations				
Keene Corp.	6	NYSE	DE	04-04-79
Topps & Trowers	41	NYSE	CA	09-14-79
Information Magnetics Corp.	91	OTC	CA	11-01-79
Shareholder action, limitation of				
Bache Group Inc.	95	NYSE	DE	11-16-79
Calumet Industries, Inc.	169	—	DE	01-22-80
Social factors, consideration of				
Alaska Airlines, Inc.	16	ASE	AK	06-08-79
CPT Corp.	47	OTC	MN	10-16-79
Special meetings, calling by board				
IPCO Hospital Supply Corp.	96	NYSE	NY	11-16-79
Supermajority vote for mergers, consolidations, liquidations or asset sales				
Alba-Waldensian, Inc.	8	ASE	DE	04-18-79
Alaska Airlines, Inc.	16	ASE	AK	06-08-79
Bache Group Inc.	95	NYSE	DE	11-16-79
IPCO Hospital Supply Corp.	96	NYSE	NY	11-16-79
American General Convertible Securities, Inc.	129	NYSE	MD	12-11-79
Calumet Industries, Inc.	169	—	DE	01-22-80
Reynolds and Reynolds Co.	180	OTC	OH	02-19-80
Supermajority vote to amend charter or by-laws				
Bache Group Inc.	95	NYSE	DE	11-16-79
IPCO Hospital Supply Corp.	96	NYSE	NY	11-16-79
Calumet Industries, Inc.	169	—	DE	01-22-80
Reynolds and Reynolds Co.	180	OTC	OH	02-19-80
Value of company, consideration of				
CPT Corp.	47	OTC	MN	10-16-79

Figure 30-1 All rights reserved   **Washington Service Bureau, Inc.**   **Washington, D.C. 20036**

statement of Treco, Inc. contained the following comments in addition to SEC-required statements:

> A classified and staggered Board facilitates continuity and stability of leadership and policy; assures that experienced personnel familiar with the Company will be represented on the Board at all times; and permits management to plan for a reasonable period of time into the future. The provision for a classified and staggered Board will also serve to moderate the pace of any change in control of the Board of Directors of the Company by extending the time required to elect a majority of the Board.

> Once the classified Board becomes fully operative, two-thirds of the Board following each annual meeting will consist of directors who have served during the previous year, thus making their experience available to the Board. However, such division into classes would, at the same time make it more difficult for shareholders to replace the entire Board of Directors (otherwise than for cause) in one annual meeting, even when this may be considered desirable by the holders of a majority of the Company's shares of common stock.

> Moreover, if the Company were to have a classified Board of Directors a corporation or group desiring to acquire or takeover the Company by merger, acquisition of its assets, or other means, would find it more difficult to obtain control of the Company's Board of Directors. If a takeover group were able to control the Board of Directors, the Company's management would be forced to negotiate the terms of any takeover bid with a corporation or group which had its own representatives on the Company's Board of Directors, thereby inhibiting management's independence to negotiate at arms-length for the interest of all shareholders. The provisions of Article Fifth, however, will be applicable to every election of directors and not only elections of directors occurring after a change in control of the Company.

> The Board of Directors believes that, with six of the present eight members of the Board being persons who are not officers or employees of the Company, it is unlikely that the proposed Article Fifth could result in perpetuation of the Company's present officers under circumstances detrimental to the shareholders, although shareholders should consider that the Board's determination with respect to takeover bids might be influenced by directors' self-interest in remaining directors of the Company.

Cumulative voting, when coupled with a classified board, can have the effect of extending the time it might otherwise take for a majority of dissident stockholders to obtain control of the Board. For example, with a board of nine, consisting of three classes of three directors each, it would take a majority of the votes cast to elect two of the three directors standing for election in any one year. Even a dissident stockholder who controls 70 percent of the votes cast, after two successive annual meetings, finds that he had been able to elect only four of the nine directors.

PREVENTING AUTOMATIC REMOVAL OF DIRECTORS

A substantial stockholder may be able to use the charter or bylaws to frustrate the incumbent board and force an early settlement even where, by reason of a classified board and other defensive provisions, management is in a position to maintain control of the board for a few more years. By amendment of the charter or bylaws, a substantial stockholder might (a) elect and determine the duties of corporate officers, (b) pack the board by filling vacancies, (c) call special meetings, remove directors without cause and destroy any protective provisions previously adopted, (d) abolish provisions indemnifying officers and directors, (e) require unanimous votes for all board actions, (f) require the board to act only at annual meetings in the state of incorporation.

For maximum protection, the charter or bylaws should provide that the stockholders shall have the right to remove directors only for cause. Furthermore, such provision and any provision requiring a higher than majority shareholder vote for removal can be "locked in" by a charter provision requiring the same higher percentage shareholder vote in order to amend or repeal any of the charter or bylaw provisions imposing these defensive measures. In order to prevent a majority shareholder from circumventing the effect of a classified board (whether or not coupled with cumulative voting), it is necessary to provide that the power to determine the number of directors, and the power to fill vacancies, be vested solely in the board. Otherwise, a majority stockholder could, by enlarging the size of the board and filling vacancies, obtain immediate control.

Several techniques are also available to defend against assaults upon the board prior to the annual meeting. The charter or bylaws provide that, to the extent permitted by law, only the board and not the stockholders can call special meetings or else allow for the calling of a special meeting by a supermajority of the shareholders. A charter amendment may eliminate the right of stockholders to act by written consent in jursidictions such as Delaware, where stockholders are permitted to act by less than unanimous consent in lieu of a meeting. Naturally, however, amending the charter requires a shareholder vote. The prevailing state law may play an important role in the stockholders' ability to remove directors. In Delaware, for example, stockholders owning a majority of the outstanding stock can remove any and all directors of a non-classified board, with or without cause, at any time, but can remove directors of a classified board only for cause. In New York, on the other hand, stockholders have the right to remove directors without cause only if so provided in the charter or bylaws.

On occasion management may be caught off-guard at an otherwise routine annual meeting by a surprising nomination for directors made by dissident shareholders from the floor. The management-supported nominees may be vulnerable if the opposition group making the nominations includes substantial holders. This situation will generally arise where dissidents did not solicit proxies and the dissidents' intentions were not disclosed early enough by Schedule 13-D filings. The risk of surprise can be avoided by providing in the charter or bylaws that nominations must be given to the secretary of the corporation not less than a specified number of days prior to the meeting. An additional limitation on the right to nominate directors is a bylaw provision requiring that directors meet certain qualifications, including residency in the country in which the corporation has its principal place of business.

DEFENSIVE MANEUVERS

Amending the corporate charter and bylaws are actions usually taken by a concerned Board well in advance of a substantial takeover threat. If the target waits too long, an unfriendly party may accumulate enough shares to block the approval of anti-takeover proposals. There are additional maneuvers that are management-action oriented that can be as effective as defensive charter provisions. The Securities and Exchange Commission, in release #34-15230 recognizes that these management actions might produce, what the Commission terms "the single most effective weapon in the arsenal of the subject company—delay." Although many of the following actions, as enumerated by the Commission's Division of Corporate Finance, are designed to lessen the attractiveness of a target, they can usually be implemented without any serious impediment to the ongoing business of the company:

   (a)   Repurchase of its own securities, to make it less likely for the tender offeror to obtain control of the company;

   (b)   Induce friendly third parties to make open market purchases of the target company's securities.

   (c)   Announce dividend increases, or a stock split;

   (d)   Issue additional shares or classes of stock.

   (e)   Take steps to create an incompatibility between the target company and the tender offeror, including possible anti-trust violations should the tender offer be successful.

   (f)   Arrange a defensive merger.

   (g)   Enter into restrictive loan agreements, with default to occur should the tender offer suceed.

   (h)   Institute litigation, challenging either directly or collaterally the conduct or effect of the tender.

   (i)   Arrange for cross or circular ownership of voting stock by parent and subsidiary corporations;

   (j)   Make the dismissal of directors expensive, by entering into costly employment contracts;

   (k)   Negotiate contracts—for example, labor, rent, loans or leases—which provide for acceleration, increase or renegotiation of payment in the event of a change of management;

   (l)   Acquire other companies or accelerate the payment of outstanding debt for the purpose of spending excess cash, thereby making the balance sheet of the target company less attractive to a potential offeror;

   (m)   Judicial action seeking a temporary or permanent injunction against the bidder alleging antitrust violations, inadequate disclosure and other securities laws violations; and

   (n)   Triggering the application of state anti-takeover statutes.

CONCLUSION

The unimpeded rise in the use of non-negotiated tender offers was halted in late 1979. It is interesting to note that this reversal of a trend that seemed to some observers as a permanent function of the marketplace, came about not because a genius finally devised the anti-takeover corporate charter amendment of all time. The slowdown in friendly tender offers resulted from the practical elimination of acquisition loans by banks; from the high interest rates on new loans of any type; from the inability to guarantee that an acquisition could generate the high rate of return needed to exceed the raider's cost of capital. In short, the United States economy was the only force capable of reducing the rise in takeover bids.

Wall Street, true to form, in early 1980, began to adapt to the lack of acquisition money. We have witnessed a revival of proxy contests as a replacement for the takeover bid. Proxy fights will remain in the forefront of corporate struggles until the economic pendulum swings back once more.

ARTHUR M. BORDEN

Arthur M. Borden received his B.A. at Yale University, 1940 and his LL.B. at Columbia University, 1948. He has been an adjunct Professor of Law, New York Law School.

He is the author of numerous articles, including a number on the subject of going private, and a frequent speaker at various securities law panels.

Mr. Borden is a partner of the firm of Sage Gray Todd & Sims.

31

Going Private

ARTHUR M. BORDEN

INTRODUCTION: A SHORT HISTORY

Beginning in the late 1950's, the securities markets underwent a series of boomlets. Small companies, particularly in high technology industries, but also many others, were able to sell their securities to the public at highly advantageous prices. For a while, those securities enjoyed amazingly high price/earnings multiples, only to be followed by periods of deep depression in the over-the-counter market, on which such securities generally traded, when almost no interest could be generated on their behalf.

By 1974, many issuers were convinced that there were no advantages, or at least no further advantages, in remaining a public company, and that there were a number of significant disadvantages associated with being public. Among them were the necessity of contending with a sullen and dissatisfied shareholder population, the generally increasing scope of liability under the federal securities laws, the sharply increasing costs of compliance with those laws, the competitive disadvantage of having to disclose the terms of material contracts and other sensitive information, and generally the *angst* of remaining a public company.

A short time before, in 1972, the United States District Court for the Northern District of Georgia, in *Bryan v. Brock & Blevins Co.*, 343 F. Supp. 1062 (N.D.Ga. 1972), *aff'd*, 490 F.2d 563 (5th Cir.) *cert. denied*, 419 U.S. 844 (1974), a case involving a close corporation, had considered the use of the cash-out merger technique to eliminate a minority shareholder from the corporation. In particular, the transaction involved a deposit by the controlling shareholders of their shares in a new corporation and a proposal of a merger between that new corporation and the old corporation under terms such that the minority shareholder to be eliminated would receive cash for his shares

and the majority shareholders would end up as the sole owners of the surviving corporation. In *Bryan*, the district court sustained the plaintiff-minority shareholder on the ground that the squeeze-out was a fraud under the federal securities laws. On appeal, the Court of Appeals for the Fifth Circuit affirmed, but on the ground that the majority violated its fiduciary duty to the minority under state law and avoided passing on the federal questions. 490 F.2d at 571.

No doubt because the entire subject was then of such intense interest to the huddling mass of little companies which were just itching to return to a more private corporate way of life, the Fifth Circuit's decision generated widespread comment, just as if it had involved a brand new tactic and opened a way to release the pent-up desire for a return to private status. This was amazing for a number of reasons. First, the decision involved a close corporation and not a public corporation, and as we shall see really had nothing to do with what we term going private. Second, the decision had gone against the insiders and in favor of the minority shareholder sought to be eliminated. Third, although the technique of a cash-out merger was relatively new, the technique of using an acquisition by a new company to force out minority shareholders was indeed a very old one. Perhaps the earliest reported case was that of *Ervin v. Oregon Ry. & Nav. Co.*, 27 F. 625 (C.C.S.D.N.Y. 1886), *appeal dismissed per stipulation*, 136 U.S. 645 (1890), where the technique used was a takeout by dissolution. In that case, the majority shareholders set up a new corporation to acquire the business and assets of the old company and subsequently dissolved the old company. Indeed, ever since then there have been a substantial number of cases involving what we today call going private techniques.

In any event, as if triggered by the Court of Appeals'

decision in *Bryan,* a number of companies shortly thereafter announced going private proposals of one kind or another. This trend was spotlighted and lines began to be drawn when Commissioner A.A. Sommer, Jr., in an address in November of 1974 at Notre Dame University, condemned these transactions in ringing words, saying that they were "serious, unfair, and sometimes disgraceful, a perversion of the whole process of public financing ...." [1974-1975 Transfer Binder], Fed. Sec. L. Rep. (CCH) ¶80,010 at 84,695 (1974).

Commissioner Sommer went on to say:

"Specifically, I would suggest that when a corporation chooses to tap public sources of money, it makes a commitment that, absent the most compelling business justification, management and those in control will do nothing to interfere with the liquidity of the public investment or the protection afforded the public by the federal securities laws. That liquidity is a benefit that the shareholder pays for and he should not be deprived of it by those who have fiduciary responsibilities to him. Further, absent such considerations, they must do nothing to deprive him of the value of his investment if he chooses to retain it.

"In my estimation, it is no longer possible for this overreaching to enjoy the protection of the mechanical provisions of state law. Increasingly the courts are correcting the deficiencies of state law by imaginative applications of federal securities law, particularly Rule 10b-5 which makes it unlawful to employ any device, scheme or artifice to defraud or to engage in any act, practice or course of business which operates or would operate as a fraud or deceit upon any person in connection with the purchase or sale of securities." *Id.* at 84,698.

If anything, the Commissioner's speech served to heighten the interest of small public companies in the possibility that they could go private, and transactions in the marketplace proceeded at about the same furious pace as did the Securities and Exchange Commission ("SEC") in an attempt to generate a governing rule. The result of all that activity was a proposal by the SEC in 1975 in which two alternative forms of a proposed rule under Section 13(e) of the Securities Exchange Act of 1934, as amended ("Exchange Act"), were published for comment—one of which required substantive fairness, while the other required both substantive fairness and the presence of what was termed "a valid business purpose." Exchange Act Release No. 34-11231 [1974-1975 Transfer Binder] Fed. Sec. L.

Rep. (CCH) ¶ 80,104 (Feb. 6, 1975). This proposal ran into a storm of criticism. As a result, the Commission in 1977 issued a second proposal in which it sought again to prescribe both substantive and procedural fairness. Exchange Act Release No. 34-14185, [1977-1978 Transfer Binder] Fed. Sec. L. Rep. (CCH) ¶ 81,366 (Nov. 17, 1977). All of this activity generated a further storm of comment and controversy, accompanied by still more actual transactions. Finally, in August of 1979, the Commission adopted its present Rule 13e-3, which purports to address the problem by application of the prophylactic effects of disclosure and to prescribe procedural fairness, but which, in fact, has a great deal to do with substantive fairness.

While all of this was going on, the going private phenomenon began to surface in the courts. Perhaps the most widely reported early case was *People v. Concord Fabrics, Inc.,* 83 Misc. 2d 120, 371 N.Y.S. 2d 550 (Sup. Ct. N.Y. Co.), *aff'd,* 50 A.D. 2d 787, 377 N.Y.S. 2d 84 (1975), in which the New York Attorney General, acting under the authority of that state's Blue Sky law (called the Martin Act), obtained an injunction against a "true going private" transaction as defined below. The transaction itself was characterized by some unfortunate idiosyncratic features, such as a tainting of the independence of the financial advisor In another early case in New Jersey, *Berkowitz v. Power/Mate Corp.,* 135 N.J. Super. 36, 342 A.2d 566 (Super. Ct. Ch. Div. 1975), the court expressed concern with the propriety of these transactions, and granted a preliminary injunction without expressing any conclusion as to their ultimate legality.

Most of the early cases were brought in the federal courts, and their clear trend was to adopt the view, following *Popkin v. Bishop,* 464 F.2d 714 (2d Cir. 1972), that unless there was a disclosure defect, the ultimate fairness of the transaction was of no federal concern. All of this, however, suddenly changed when the Second Circuit, in *Marshel v. A.F.W. Fabric Corp.,* 533 F.2d 1277 (2d Cir. 1976), on appeal from a district court determination in the *Concord Fabrics* matter, and in *Green v. Santa Fe Industries, Inc.,* 533 F.2d 1283 (2d Cir. 1976), emphatically and unequivocally adopted the view that these transactions constituted a substantive fraud within the range of Rule 10b-5. The *Green* case ultimately made its way to the Supreme Court where it was reversed, 8-1, with the Supreme Court taking the view that Section 10(b) and Rule 10b-5 could not be invoked absent manipulation in the narrow sense in which Congress intended that term, or actual deception, that is to say, a material disclosure defect. As we shall see, while that should have put an end to the federal interest in the substantive aspect of going private transactions, it has not quite succeeded in doing that. As a result of its decision in *Green*, the Supreme Court subsequently vacated the Second Circuit's ruling in *Marshel*, 429 U.S. 881 (1976).

In 1977 the focus of going private practitioners shifted to the state courts where the case of *Singer v. Magnavox Co.*, 380 A.2d 969 (Del. 1977) initiated a new and intensified review of going private transactions by the state courts and, in particular, Delaware courts.

Since the issue first came to prominence in 1974, there have been four major developments, all of which will be reviewed in this chapter:

1. A decision by the Supreme Court of the United States that going private is itself not a fraud within the scope of the federal securities laws;
2. A developing body of state law with respect to these transactions, particularly in Delaware:
3. The development of a series of conventions and techniques in order to conduct these transactions in a fair and equitable way; and
4. The adoption of Rule 13e-3 by the SEC on August 2, 1979.

True Going Private Transactions

To define the subject matter of this chapter, we must distinguish among three somewhat similar forms of transactions. First, there is what is commonly called a "squeeze-out." This term we shall use to describe a corporate transaction undertaken to eliminate the minority interest in a close corporation. Second, there is what this author has termed the "true going private" transaction, which is the subject of this chapter and which will simply be referred to as "going private." This is the transaction where the controlling stockholders of a public company seek to return it to private status by eliminating the minority interest through one or another form of corporate transaction. The paradigm of a going private transaction would be one where the very same controlling shareholders of a company who took it public not many years before now seek to reverse themselves and elect to return it to their own private ownership. Simply because the SEC has cho-

sen to include the transaction in its concept of "going private," we shall also include within that term a tender offer or other transaction which is a first step in such a program. The third form of transaction to be identified is where a third party, normally a corporation which has already acquired an interest in another corporation (commonly called the "target" corporation), as by way of a tender offer, a block purchase or open market purchases, thereafter desires to complete its acquisition of the target by effecting one or another form of so-called "takeout" transaction. This transaction will be referred to in this chapter as a "second stage takeout," meaning that it is the second stage of an acquisition program.[1]

It is apparent that the policy considerations underlying these several transaction forms differ vastly. There is little, if any, justification for a squeeze-out, that is, for eliminating minority shareholders in a close corporation. Persons investing as minority holders in a close corporation do so for the sole purpose of wagering that after a sufficient period their investment will ripen into significantly greater value either by way of the sale of the company or by its becoming public, or, occasionally, by way of substantial dividend payments. In any event, such investments are typically not made for the short haul and absent any unusual circumstances there is no excuse for depriving such investors of whatever opportunity of future success they originally envisaged when they plunked down their hard dollars. On the other hand, there is every reason, in an efficient capitalist society, to encourage the acquisition of one company by another, and accordingly to favor second stage takeouts. Certainly public policy favors second stage takeouts by which acquisitions are completed even if the Williams Act adopts a neutral posture with respect to tender offers themselves. On the spectrum of public policy considerations, this author, contrary to the view expressed by Mr. Sommer in his 1974 speech at Notre Dame, believes true going private transactions lie somewhere in between the squeeze-out and the second stage takeout. They have the social advantage of eliminating from the public roster companies which should never have been public and affording outside shareholders the opportunity to realize cash proceeds significantly in excess of what might otherwise be available to them in the open market. On the other hand, they present the insiders with an oppor-

---

[1] Of course, it may be in fact a third stage transaction, where the first step was a block purchase or open market purchase, the second step was a tender offer and the third and final step was the takeout transaction. Further, the definition may be deemed to include the transaction where the ownership interest in the target was acquired a substantial amount of time prior to the takeout. *See* Borden, *'Going Private' Fad: Infatuation Unlikely to Disappear Soon,* 174 N.Y.L.J. 114, Dec. 15, 1975, at 39, *reprinted in* Law Journal Press, ed; *IV SEC '76,* at 115 (1976).

tunity for abuse by attempting to acquire the public equity at what may be an unfairly low price.

The Structure of Going Private Transactions

A going private transaction may be structured in a variety of ways. The most common structure is a cash-out merger. In this format, shareholders (whom we shall call the "insiders") of a company (the "issuer") desiring to effect the transaction deposit their shares of the issuer in a new corporation ("New Corp") and cause a merger between New Corp and the issuer on terms such that the outside shareholders of the issuer receive cash for their shares and the insiders, now owners of New Corp, receive 100 percent of the equity of the surviving corporation, which may be either New Corp or the issuer. In a variation of this technique, the merger is effected between the issuer and a subsidiary of New Corp., again with either party surviving.[2]

The transaction may also be effected not for cash but by issuing debentures of a non-voting preferred stock, especially if the issuer cannot, or probably should not, effect a cash transaction. The debentures issued to outside shareholders in a going private transaction may be either short or long term and may or may not contain sinking fund provisions. Their common feature is that they are not convertible into common stock since the object of the transaction is the elimination of the equity interest of outside shareholders. The advantage of utilizing debentures is, of course, that the interest on them is deductible. On the other hand, interest payments constitute an obligation while preferred stock dividends do not, and accordingly, although such dividends are not deductible, the insiders may opt for the issuance of preferred stock as a more prudent security. In order to enhance the value of such a preferred stock, which again, of course, will not be convertible, and in particular to assure the outside shareholders that they will ultimately receive their cash-out payment in order to induce them to vote for the transaction, it is common to include in such preferred stock a sinking fund provision pursuant to which the issuer covenants to redeem the preferred stock over a fairly short period of years. Of course, preferred stock issues vary widely as to the penalty to which the issuer may be subject if the sinking fund payment is not made. Except for the form of consideration to be issued, a debenture or preferred stock going private transaction will normally be structured identically with a cash-out merger. Obviously, if debentures or preferred stock are issued to a sufficient number of persons, the issuer would have to continue to comply with the reporting requirements of the Exchange Act until such time as such securities are paid or redeemed.

Another format is the reverse stock split. In this technique, the issuer, with required shareholder approval, amends its charter to reverse split its shares so that each outside holder ends up with a fractional share of the issuer, which under applicable corporate law the issuer then redeems for cash in lieu of issuance of a fractional share. For example, if a single insider has 100,000 shares representing the largest outstanding block, then a reverse split by which any holding of less than 100,000 shares becomes a fraction of a share will achieve the desired objective.

It is also possible, although much more complicated, to go private by a sale of assets followed by a dissolution or by a dissolution followed by a sale of assets. In both of these formats, the insiders anticipate buying the assets on the sale and paying cash to outside shareholders.

LEGAL BACKGROUND OF GOING PRIVATE TRANSACTIONS

State and federal law are both applicable to these transactions. The state corporation statutes govern the form of the transaction, whether it be a merger, reverse split, asset sale or dissolution. In addition, directors and controlling shareholders effecting going private transactions are subject to fiduciary obligations imposed by state law.

As to federal law, although it was initially believed, at least in some quarters, that these transactions were subject to Section 10(b) and Rule 10b-5 under the Exchange Act, on the ground that they were *per se* fraudulent, that theory was laid to rest by the Supreme Court in *Santa Fe Industries, Inc. v. Green,* 430 U.S. 462 (1977).

In *Green*, a Delaware short-form merger was used to eliminate the minority interest of Kirby Lumber Company ("Kirby") in which Santa Fe Industries had acquired approximately 95 percent of the equity stock. Santa Fe had first acquired control of Kirby in 1936 and had in the succeeding years increased its equity interest to in excess of 95 percent. Santa Fe Industries offered to pay $150 per share, which was in excess of the "fair" price as determined by the investment banking firm retained by Santa Fe. The appraised value of the physical assets of Kirby exceeded $640 per share. Minority shareholders, claiming that the price was inadequate, sued Santa Fe Industries for violations of

---

[2]A second stage takeout may be similarly structured by merger between the acquiring company and the target, or by the acquiring company depositing its stock of the target in a subsidiary which then effects the cash-out merger.

GOING PRIVATE

Rule 10b-5. The District Court dismissed the complaint on the ground that if full and fair disclosure is made, transactions eliminating minority interests are beyond the reach of Rule 10b-5. 391 F.Supp. 849, 854-55 (S.D.N.Y. 1975). The Court of Appeals, reversing the district court below, concluded that Rule 10b-5 encompasses ''breaches of fiduciary duties by a majority against minority shareholders without any charge of misrepresentation or lack of disclosure,'' and that, therefore, the complaint taken as a whole stated a cause of action under the Rule. 533 F.2d 1283, 1287 (2d Cir. 1976).

The Supreme Court, while noting the gross discrepancy between the appraised value of the property of Kirby and the offered merger price, repeated its well-established principle that the fundamental purpose of the Exchange Act is implementing a philosophy of full disclosure. 430 U.S. at 477-478. Finding that breaches of fiduciary duty and mismanagement by directors and insiders traditionally have been within the purview of state law, and finding no Congressional intent to expand the federal regulatory scope into such areas through Rule 10b-5, the Supreme Court, reversing the Court of Appeals decision, went on to say ''once full and fair disclosure has occurred, the fairness of the terms of the transaction is at most a tangential concern of the statute.'' Id. at 478.

As we shall see, going private transactions are subject to Rule 13e-3 and, on occasion, Rule 13e-4 promulgated by the Commission under Section 13(e) of the Exchange Act. In addition, since Rule 13e-3 and Rule 13e-4 are not exclusive in the sense of replacing other applicable rules, the transactions remain subject to other pertinent provisions of the federal securities laws such as the proxy rules, registration requirements, tender offer regulation and the like.

State Statutes

The state statutes govern the form of the transaction. Most, but not all, permit a cash consideration to be offered in a merger. In addition to the general merger statutes, often called ''long form'' merger laws, most states also have so-called ''short form'' merger laws, pursuant to which a parent owning 90 percent or 95 percent, as the case may be, may merge with its subsidiary by the vote of the board of directors of the parent corporation. Most merger statutes provide for appraisal rights to dissenting shareholders.

In addition, it is to be noted that Wisconsin and California have adopted substantive going private statutes and/or regulations. See CAL. CORP. CODE §407 and §1101 (West); and Wisc. Admin. Code section SEC 6.05.

State Fiduciary Law Standards

The case law has been notably derelict in failing to distinguish among squeeze-outs, true going private transactions and second stage takeouts.

The seminal case in the modern era, *Bryan v. Brock & Blevins Co., supra,* a federal court decision applying Georgia law, was in fact a squeeze-out and thus was really not relevant to the issues raised by the going private phenomenon. Nevertheless, it became the bellwether of early discussion. In particular, the emphasis placed in that decision on the absence of a business purpose for the squeeze-out of the minority has continued to resound through the cases. The business purpose feature was specifically emphasized in *People v. Concord Fabrics, Inc., supra,* as already noted, a well-publicized proceeding in which the Attorney General of the State of New York sought successfully to enjoin a going private transaction as violative of the state Blue Sky law, called the Martin Act. In granting the injunction, the court emphasized the absence of a business purpose (83 Misc. 2d at 125, 371 N.Y.S.2d at 554), and the impropriety of the insiders taking the company public at as high a price as $20 per share, and proposing to take it private with corporate funds at a $3 per share price.

As of the moment of writing, there is really very little substantive law which can be authoritatively cited in a going private environment. At the state court level, clearly the leading authority is *Singer v. Magnavox Co., supra,* a case whose implications are still being explored.

Singer involved a 1974 tender offer made by a subsidiary of North American Phillips Corporation for the purchase of any and all shares of Magnavox Company. The offer disclosed the intention of North American Phillips to acquire all the equity interest of Magnavox and that in the event the tender offer did not accomplish that purpose, a subsequent merger to eliminate the minority shareholders was possible. A total of 84.1 percent of the common stock of Magnavox was acquired pursuant to the tender offer and subsequently a merger was proposed and consummated between Magnavox and another subsidiary of North American Phillips. Minority shareholders of Magnavox brought the subject action and contended that the merger was fraudulent because it was made without any ascertainable corporate business purpose and was designed solely to freeze out the minority stockholders. The trial court, after a review of the cases, concluded that to the extent that the complaint charged that the merger was fraudulent because of a lack of such purpose, it failed to state a claim upon which relief might be granted. On appeal, the Supreme Court of Delaware, reversing the court below, stated that it "recognized as established law in this State that the dominant corporation, as a majority stockholder standing on both sides of a merger transaction, has 'the burden of establishing its entire fairness' to the minority stockholders, sufficiently to 'pass the test of careful scrutiny by the courts.'" *Id*. at 976. The Court went on to state:

> "We hold, therefore, that a Section 251 merger, made for the sole purpose of freezing out minority stockholders, is an abuse of the corporate process; and the complaint, which so alleges in this suit, states a cause of action for violation of a fiduciary duty for which the court may grant such relief which it deems appropriate under the circumstances." *Id*. at 980

Singer stands for two propositions. The first is that a going private transaction must meet the standard of "entire fairness," which means that on an allegation of unfairness the proponents of the transaction have the burden of proving its fairness. The second is that the transaction must have what that case denominated as "a business purpose." When it comes to the implication, either in Delaware law or elsewhere, of what constitutes a business purpose, there is not a great deal of clarity. The so-called *Tanzer (I) case, Tanzer v. International General Industries, Inc.*, 379 A.2d 1121 (Del. Ct. 1977), stands for the proposition that in the context of a going private transaction, the valid business purpose of the parent corporation which seeks to eliminate the minority of the subsidiary will suffice to meet the Delaware standard. The Court in *Tanzer I*, while noting that the focus of *Singer* had been on the rights of minority shareholders, found that the *Singer* test should not be applied without taking into consideration majority as well as minority interests, and concluded that a majority shareholder would not be in violation of its fiduciary duty to the minority if it caused a takeout merger for a valid business purpose of its own. In that case the need to combine the business in order to obtain necessary financing was held to be a valid business purpose. A number of cases stand for the proposition that the elimination of conflict and the effect of economies in the combination of two operating companies will meet the standards. *See, e.g., Grimes v. Donaldson, Lufkin & Jenrette, Inc.*, 392 F.Supp. 1393 (N.D. Fla. 1974), *aff'd without opinion*, 521 F.2d 812 (5th Cir. 1975); *Schulwolf v. Cerro*

Corp., 86 Misc. 2d 292, 380 N.Y.S. 2d 957 (Sup. Ct. N.Y. Co. 1976). However, the relevancy of these cases is diminished by the fact that they are all what we have termed second stage takeouts and not true going private transactions. In *Teschner v. Chicago Title & Trust Co.*, 59 Ill.2d 452, 322 N.E.2d 54 (1974), the minority shareholders of Chicago Title & Trust Co. were eliminated by a reverse split of shares and the payment of cash in lieu of fractional shares. The court in considering the presence of a valid business purpose found that the reduction of corporate expenses and the simplification and facilitation of corporate procedures were acceptable reasons for eliminating the minority interest. In another case, patently spurious claims of elimination of conflict of interest and tax savings were rejected. *Young v. Valhi, Inc.*, 382 A2d 1372 (Del. Ch. 1978).

One significant proposition which seems to be on the way to establishing itself in the state courts is the proposition that if the inside vote is neutralized,[3] the insiders no longer have the burden of proving the fairness of the transaction, but the burden now shifts to the complaining outside shareholders to establish the unfairness of the transaction. This appears to be the view in *Weinberger v. U.O.P., Inc.*, 409 A.2d 1262 (Del. Ch. 1979). During 1975 the Signal Companies, Inc. ("Signal") became the owner of 50.5 percent of the outstanding shares of UOP, Inc. ("UOP"). During 1978, a merger of UOP with a wholly owned subsidiary of Signal was proposed and approved by the boards of directors of both companies whereby the 49.5 percent minority shareholders of UOP would receive $21 cash per share for their stock interest and UOP would consequently end up a wholly owned subsidiary of Signal. The plan of merger was submitted to the shareholders of UOP, with the Signal vote being neutralized, and overwhelmingly approved by outside shareholders. The complaint alleges that UOP's officers and directors, together with Signal and the investment banking firm which rendered the opinion that the consideration for the merger was fair and equitable, had violated their fiduciary duties to the minority by not (1) affirmatively taking steps to prevent a merger without a bona fide purpose, (2) opposing a merger whose purpose was to eliminate the outside shareholders, (3) opposing a merger in which the outside stockholders could be cashed out at an unfair price, and (4) refusing to enter into a plan, counter-conspiracy or scheme with others to accomplish any of the above. The court, finding that the plaintiff had indeed stated a cause of action under the *Singer* test, went on to point

---

[3]*See* the discussion of neutralized voting as a basic requirement of a going private transaction *infra*.

out that, unlike *Singer*, the majority here had neutralized their vote and had thus placed the fate of the minority shareholders in their own hands. The minority shareholders voted 12 to 1 in favor of the merger. The UOP decision was supported by the New York State Supreme Court in *Bromberg v. Stern*, N.Y. Sup. Ct. No. 19153/78 (N.Y. Co., February 16, 1979). In *Bromberg*, the challenged going private merger required the approval of a majority of the disinterested public shareholders. According to the court, that amounted to a 'situation in which shareholders are freely exercising their independent judgment with respect to this proposal, rather than one in which a majority shareholder, with the capacity to achieve his goal, is imposing his will on the minority.'' Furthermore, the court in *Bromberg* stated that where "the vast majority of shareholders favor" a corporate transaction, "the balance of equities is clearly struck against" those seeking to enjoin such a transaction. Consequently, the court refused to enjoin the going private merger.

Although the case law is obviously just beginning to develop, it seems fair to say that the posture of most practitioners in the field, at least as of the moment of this writing, is that business purpose is highly desirable and should be cited where it applies, but that on the other hand it is not of great moment, and particularly that there is no point in attempting to contrive one where one does not exist, since it is the fairness of the transaction that will ultimately govern.

The best judicial treatment of the fairness issue to date was by a Delaware Chancery Court in the so-called *Tanzer* II case, *Tanzer* v. *International General Industries, Inc.*, 402 A.2d 382 (Del. Ch. 1979). The Court, confronted with the scanty authority available to it in scrutinizing the transaction for "entire fairness," concluded that all elements of the transaction had to be considered. Starting with the issue of business purpose, the Court enumerated eight factors it considered relevant to its inquiry. Including such criteria as the possibility of alternative transactions, recommendations from investment bankers, and the existence of appraisal rights, the list was comprehensive and provided the Court with a solid footing for its judgment that the transaction was intrinsically fair.

A number of courts have commented on the propriety of the issuer's funds or credit being itself used to finance the transaction. No doubt the transaction will be better accepted if the funding is derived from the insider's own financial sources rather than from the issuer's treasury. *See Berkowitz v. Power/Mate Corp., supra.* Although the court in *Concord Fabrics, Inc., supra*, commented adversely on the use of corporate funds in that transaction, New York courts in two other cases, both involving second stage takeouts, have favorably commented on the fact that the corporate treasury was utilized to fund the transaction. *Tanzer Economic Associates, Inc. v. Universal Food Specialties, Inc.*, 87 Misc. 2d 167, 383 N.Y.S. 2d 472 (Sup. Ct. N.Y. Co. 1976); *Schulwolf v. Cerro Corp., supra.* Indeed, from a logical point of view, it should not make a great deal of difference to the outside shareholders whence the funds are derived.

As previously stated, in the federal courts, *Green* stands for the proposition that absent a disclosure defect, the federal courts have no interest in the substantive aspects of these transactions.

On the other hand, there is a concerted effort within the federal court system, led by the Second Circuit in *Goldberg v. Meridor*, 567 F.2d 209 (2d Cir.), *cert. denied*, 434 U.S. 1069 (1978), to avoid the strictures of *Green* on the ground that the failure to disclose to minority shareholders facts which, if they had been disclosed, presumably would have entitled the minority stockholders, and would probably have induced them, to go into state court and claim a violation of state fiduciary standards, creates a cause of action under federal law.[4] The complexity of this subject is beyond the scope of this chapter, but certainly this development constitutes one of the more intriguing aberrations in the long and tortuous history of Rule 10b-5.

THE BASIC REQUIREMENTS OF A GOING PRIVATE TRANSACTION

No transaction is more fraught with conflict of interest than a true going private transaction. Its essence is that insiders who propose to acquire the entire equity of the issuer, and who normally have the power to effectuate it both by their domination of the board and of the vote at a shareholders' meeting, are the very same persons who are fiduciaries for, and obligated to protect, those outside shareholders whose interests they are seeking to acquire. The basic requirement of a going private transaction is to structure it so as to overcome its inherent conflict of interest.

To do this, three basic requirements must be met:

1. The vote of the insiders should be neutralized so that the decision to effect the transaction will rest

---

[4]*See also Wright v. Heizer*, 560 F.2d 236 (7th Cir. 1977); *Kidwell v. Meikle*, 597 F. 2d 1273 (9th Cir. 1979); *Alabama Farm Bureau Mut. Cas. Co. v. American Fidelity Life Ins. Co.*, 606 F.2d 1602 (5th Cir. 1979); and *Spectrum Financial Companies v. Marconsult, Inc.*, 608 F.2d 377 (9th Cir. 1979).

entirely in the hands of the outside shareholders who cast their votes at the meeting;

2. The price must be fair; and

3. In all other respects, the transaction must be so structured and conducted as to promote and to demonstrate its fairness.

Each of these considerations is discussed in turn.

1. Neutralized Voting

Neutralizing the vote of the insiders bestows upon outsider shareholders the power to decide their own fate in a going private transaction. Two techniques are available to neutralize the insider vote. By one technique the insiders agree to vote their shares in favor of the transaction if, and only if, a majority of the shares voted by outside shareholders at the meeting are voted in favor of the transaction. By the other technique, the insiders vote their shares for the transaction in the same proportion as outside shareholders voting at the meeting vote their shares for or against the transaction. Clearly, if state law requires a superplurality, as, for example, the two-thirds requirement in New York, the first formulation is more likely to produce a successful transaction than is the second formulation. Indeed, the first formulation is most commonly used. On the other hand, if the insiders are confident of gaining a plurality even above the statutory plurality, they may condition the transaction on obtaining such a superplurality of outside shareholders. Clearly, the larger the voting obstacle they create for themselves, the more favorable and untainted the transaction will appear to be.

Very few, if any, transactions have been structured so as to require a majority of the votes of all outside shareholders, including those who do not cast their votes. The result of this procedure would be to cast as a negative vote the vote of all those who abstain from voting, or who are never reached by the solicitation. There is no reason to suppose that the class of non-voting shareholders would vote any differently than the class of those who are interested enough to vote, and accordingly, it is almost invariably concluded that there is no merit in this procedure.

2. Fairness of the Price

The fairness of the price is obviously the key element in the transaction .From a theoretical point of view, two different price levels may be deemed fair. On the one hand, it may be said that the price should be that price which would or could have been obtained, per share, if the business were to be sold as a whole. Such a sale would, of course, include the controlling majority interest in the company held by the insiders as well as the non-controlling minority interest held by outside shareholders. This measure of value we refer to as "acquisition value," "sale value" or "going concern" value. The other theoretical test is the price which would have been agreed upon by willing insiders, normally holders of a majority interest, and willing outside shareholders, normally a minority, if they had bargained at arm's length for the sale of the outside shareholders' interest to the insiders. This value will be referred to as "economic" or "arm's length" value. Both these standards may be contrasted with "fundamental value" which is an economic term meaning value as a function of book value, earnings record, dividend history, cash flow, and also of value based on a comparison with the market price of comparable securities.

The sophistication of judicial analysis of these issues has not yet reached the point of distinguishing among any of these measures, and particularly between sale value and economic value. As we shall see, Rule 13e-3, by focusing its principal attention in Item 8(b) of Schedule 13E-3 on elements of fundamental value, namely earnings, assets and market price, may be taken to suggest that fair price is equivalent to fundamental value. In general, sale value will be greater than economic value and economic value greater than fundamental value. This is because sale value includes the value of control while economic value normally will not, since the insiders will normally, but not always, already possess control. Since fundamental value is so much tied to earnings record and to the market value of comparable securities, it will normally be lower than either of the other measures of value.

If a transaction is to be effected on the theory that economic value is the proper measure, and if economic value should be significantly less than sale value, there may well be concern that the insiders, after consummation of the going private transaction, will simply turn around and reap for themselves the difference between economic and sale value. For this reason, under such circumstances, insiders should consider representing that they have no intention of selling the business and an appropriate covenant should be negotiated to secure for the former outside shareholders the economic benefit of any early sale of the business after the going private transaction.

Even if fundamental value is not deemed determinative, it is of course of considerable significance. It is the base from which both sale and economic value are computed, and from which certain conventions have developed as to the pricing of going private transactions. Typically, fair values fall within certain conventional ranges, reflecting a requirement to be at a substantial premium above current market, and to be quite clearly in excess of prevailing market levels in the recent past. Often these would seem to reflect an additional premium if book value is unusually high and an incentive to be at least at some respectable price/earnings ratio. Quite clearly no simple formula is available to dictate what should be a fair price in the context of any given transaction.

3. Conducting the Transaction Fairly

A number of additional techniques have been developed in order to insure an honest effort to determine a fair price and generally to promote, and to demonstrate, fairness.

First, it is essential that independent board members be involved in the process of price determination. It is preferable, although uncommon, to assign them the responsibility of recommending the price at which the transaction is to be effected; they should at least have the responsibility of assuring themselves that the price proposed by the insiders is fair. Obviously, the former is a more effective way of demonstrating a forthright approach though it is, in fact, seldom attempted.

As a second essential feature, the outside board members should engage independent financial consultants to assist them in assessing the fairness of the price. Although the SEC may be of the view that even where a price has been proposed by the insiders, the independent directors should engage financial consultants to recommend a price, it is easier, and again much more common, to ask them simply for their opinion as to the fairness of the price proposed by the insiders.

A word or two about hiring an investment banker or other financial consultant. It is important that the independent directors do the hiring. Further, in hiring their consultant, the independent directors must concern themselves solely with his qualification, the cost of the proposed study and the time which would be required to produce it. More particularly, the independent directors must conscientiously and assiduously avoid any discussion of the price, including such remarks as whether the prospective candidates believe that the proposed price is "in the ball park." Indeed, candidates for the assignment should be advised at the outset of their interviews that the independent directors have been specifically instructed to avoid any price discussions so that the candidate himself does not unfortunately introduce the subject. Obviously, the reason for this is that if the fairness of the price is pre-cleared with the consultant, his opinion is of no worth whatsoever. Further, failure to disclose this pre-clearance itself would be a material disclosure deficiency.

Normally, it is desirable to consider a number of candidates, all of whom should be interviewed by the independent directors. If the independent directors are not acquainted with qualified firms, counsel for the issuer may, at least in the opinion of this author, suggest a list of qualified firms, but should in no way discuss the matter with them.

Another matter often raised is whether the independent directors should have separate counsel. If warranted by the size of the transaction, it is clearly desirable. On the other hand, it is quite easy to proliferate experts in these transactions, including counsel for the insiders, counsel for the issuer and counsel for the independent directors. Wherever possible, engaging at least two counsel is desirable.

Another question which often arises is that of the source of funds. No doubt the transaction will have a better appearance if the funding is derived from the insider's own financial sources rather than from the issuer's treasury. See discussion of State Fiduciary Law Standards, *supra*.

Rule 13e-3

Rule 13e-3 was adopted by Exchange Act Release No. 34-16075 on August 2, 1979 and was effective September 7, 1979, [1979 Transfer Binder] Fed. Sec. L. Rep. (CCH) ¶82,166. It may generally be described as a fairness disclosure rule, and is expressly designed to make clear to the reader those elements upon which a judgment should be based as to the fairness of a going private transaction.

It is to be emphasized at the outset that the Rule is not in substitution of, but supplementary to, any other requirement of the federal securities laws. For example, if the going private transaction is to be effected by way of a proxy statement, than all of the rules relevant to proxy statements apply and Rule 13e-3 represents merely an additional requirement. Similarly, with a registration statement or a tender offer, Rule 13e-3 supplements the generally applicable provisions of the securities laws.

The first thing to understand about the Rule is when it applies. Three tests must be met for a transaction to be subject to the Rule. For purposes of the Rule, a transaction subject to the Rule is called a "Rule 13e-3 transaction" (Rule 13e-3 (a)(4)). The three tests for a Rule 13e-3 transaction are as follows:

1. The issuer of the securities sought to be acquired must have a class of securities registered under Section 12 of the Exchange Act or must be subject to the reporting requirements of Section 15(d) of that Act, or must be a closed end investment company registered under the Investment Company Act of 1940 (Rule 13e-3(b)(1)).

2. The transaction must be in one of three prescribed forms: either (A) a purchase of any equity

security by the issuer or an affiliate of such issuer, (B) a tender offer by an issuer or an affiliate, or (C) a solicitation subject to Regulations 14A, or a distribution subject to Regulation 14C, in connection with a "merger, consolidation, reclassification, recapitalization, reorganization or similar corporate transaction of an issuer or between an issuer (or its subsidiaries) and its affiliate, or a sale of substantially all of the assets of an issuer to its affiliate or a group of affiliates; or a reverse stock split of any class of equity securities of the issuer involving the purchase of fractional interest (Rule 13e-3(a)(4)(i)).

A purchase is defined very broadly to include almost any way in which shares or an equity interest may be acquired, including an acquisition pursuant to a reverse stock split or a merger (Rule 13e-3(a)(3)). The term "purchase" presumably, however, does not include a "contract to buy." In understanding these terms for purposes of this Rule, it is important to understand that they do not overlap and that, in fact, if a transaction is a tender offer or a proxy solicitation it is not a "purchase" for purposes of the dissemination requirements of the Rule. Any other reading would not make sense of the Rule.

3. The third test that must be met is that the transaction must either itself, or as one of a series of transactions, have either a reasonable likelihood or a purpose of causing an equity security registered under Section 12(g) or subject to Section 15(d) to be held of record by less than 300 persons or causing a class of equity securities which is quoted on a national exchange or quoted on NASDAQ no longer to be either so listed or so quoted. (Rule 13e-3(a)(4)).

Thus, in order to determine whether or not the Rule is applicable in the first place, it is necessary to determine the status of the issuer under Section 12 or Section 15(d) and whether its equity securities are traded on a national exchange or quoted on NASDAQ. Second, it must be determined whether the security is an equity security within the Rule. As there is no definition of an equity security within Rule 13e-3, the general definition of Section 3(a)(11) of the Exchange Act and Rule 3 (a)11-1 applies, and any security which is an equity security under that Rule, such as a convertible debenture or a warrant, is an equity security for purposes of Rule 13e-3. Third, it must be determined whether the transaction is to be effected by either the issuer or an affiliate of the issuer. Fourth, it must be determined whether in format it falls within the Rule, as almost all transactions will. And fifth, it must be determined whether it is by itself or is one of a series of steps having a reasonable likelihood or purpose of

terminating the active trading market of the subject security in the designated fashion. If all of those tests are met, one is then dealing with a Rule 13e-3 transaction and the Rule is applicable, absent an exception.

The Rule provides for two principal exceptions from its coverage. They are set forth in paragraph (g) of Rule 13e-3. The first exemption occurs if a tender offer is made by a non-affiliate, as a result of which he became an affiliate, and within one year after the tender offer the affiliate seeks to effect what would otherwise be a Rule 13e-3 transaction (Rule 13e-3(g)(1)). To qualify for the exception, the tender offer, if an any and all offer, must have firmly stated that the going private transaction would occur. If the tender offer was not an any and all offer, then it must have disclosed that there was a binding obligation to effect the going private transaction and the going private transaction must occur pursuant to that binding obligation. In either event, the transaction must occur within a one-year period of the expiration of the tender offer at a price at least as high as the consideration paid in the tender offer. Obviously, when you start the transaction in the belief that it is exempt under subsection (g)(1) of Rule 13e-3, you cannot be sure that the transaction will be completed within the prescribed one-year period. Shareholders suits, SEC investigation or other delays may prevent the timely closing. The Rule is unclear as to what the effect would be on the exemption if a person who reasonably believed that he would close the Rule 13e-3 transaction within one year of the tender offer failed to do so. It is the opinion of this author, however, that such a failure should not cause the transaction to be subject to Rule 13e-3, so long as the required dissemination was within the one-year period.

The other important exception is available if the going private transaction is effected by the issuance of common stock or, if not common stock, then of a security having substantially the same rights as the equity security which is going to be eliminated (or severely restricted in its trading) by virtue of the Rule 13e-3 transaction including, but not limited to, voting, dividends, redemption and liquidation rights (Rule 13e-3(g)(2)).

The justification for the first exception is that at the time of the tender offer, the party making the tender offer was not an affiliate and, therefore, not subject to the Rule and that the second transaction was in the words of Release No. 34-16075 merely a "second stage cleanup" transaction and, further, was one which was clearly disclosed at the time the original transaction was undertaken by a non-affiliate. The second exception was vociferously urged in letters of comment on the SEC's 1977 proposed rule. It is clear, of course, that equity transactions which would otherwise be subject to the Rule, but for this exception, are in some respects similar and in some respects dissimilar to a cash-out merger. They are similar in that the price at which the minority interest is exchanged is in effect set by the controlling majority. They are dissimilar in that the minority is not eliminated, but is allowed to maintain an interest in the entity and presumably will continue to receive reports which will display with hindsight whether or not the terms were or were not fair.

If a transaction should be deemed subject to the Rule, counsel must carefully study the Rule with respect to its filing requirements, its dissemination requirements and its disclosure requirements. In all cases, the filing is made on what is called Schedule 13E-3 (Rule 13e-3(e)). Normally the filing is made at the time you file the preliminary proxy statement, the tender offer or the registration statement which is the subject of the transaction. If the filing is in the form of a proxy statement, then the Schedule 13E-3 along with the proxy statement can be marked "premininary copy" and will not become public until the definitive proxy material is filed. If the transaction takes some other form such as, for example, an open market purchase, a block purchase or a short-form merger, which would not otherwise require any filing, then the filing must be made 30 days before the purchase. However, as a "contract to buy" is presumably not a "purchase" within Rule 13e-3, you can enter into a contract, although you cannot close until the expiration of the 30-day period.

The dissemination must be made at least 20 days before the meeting, vote or consent (Rule 13e-3(f)). It must be made to each shareholder who was a shareholder of record as of a date not more than 20 days prior to the dissemination date. *Id.* If a transaction is in the form which does not otherwise require a disclosure document, again, for example, as an open market purchase program, dissemination must be made to all shareholders of record as of a date not more than 20 days prior to the dissemination date and must be made at least 20 days prior to the purchase.

The disclosure requirements set forth in paragraph (e) and in Schedule 13E-3 are the heart of the Rule and should be studied closely by counsel before determining to undertake any transaction within the Rule, and then should be carefully reviewed after the required documentation is prepared in order to make certain that all of the required disclosures have in fact been included. There is a specific legend requirement which is found in paragraph (e) of the Rule (Rule 13e-3 (e)(3)(ii)(A)), and a requirement that the disclosure document contain in the forepart a section entitled "Special Factors" containing the information required by Items 7, 8 and 9 of the Schedule (Rule 13e-3(e)(3)(i)). The disclosure document provided to shareholders can either repeat or fairly summarize the other information required to be included in the Schedule. In most cases, issuers have been completing the Schedule 13E-3 by merely cross-referencing to the appropriate pages of the disclosure document.

Essentially, the disclosures required by Items 7, 8 and 9 are disclosures of how the transaction came about and why it is fair. Accordingly, Item 7 requires disclosure of the purpose of the transaction, of its anticipated results, of the benefits and detriments of the transaction to the interested parties which include, of course, the issuer, the inside shareholders and the outside shareholders, and a statement of the reasons for structuring the transaction as it was and for undertaking it at the time it is being undertaken, as well as an answer to the question whether or not alternative means were considered and, if they were, the reasons for their rejection.

A number of purposes have been claimed in the Schedule 13E-3's which have been filed to date. A principal purpose cited has been to allow a greater operating flexibility in the management of the business. Almost all of the filings have cited the cost savings to be effected by resuming private status. A number have emphasized the business advantage of not being obliged to make presently required public disclosures. In particular, it has been said that the requirement that a small company disclose details of its operations puts it at a disadvantage with larger companies against which it competes and which are not required to disclose similar details, especially when the larger companies are themselves divisions of significantly more substantial enterprises. In justification of a going private proposal, a number of filings have maintained that being public did not serve the original purpose for which the issuer had undertaken the responsibility of being a public company, and particularly that the company had been unable to raise capital or effect acquisitions by issuing its securities and further that its stock option plans had not been a useful incentive in attracting or retaining management personel because of the poor market performance of its common stock. It has also been said that the inability of all shareholders to realize their personal financial objectives in the public market because of lack of interest in the security was itself a justification for the transaction. From the issuer's perspective, it may be claimed that the best interest of the shareholders was deemed to be served by accepting the proposal.

The question of alternatives to the proposed transaction is usually of little significance, except that the SEC will be concerned if a particular structure was chosen to avoid appraisal rights, and is also interested in the reason for the structuring of a leveraged buyout situation when the transaction requires the payment of a tax at the corporate level which would not have been incurred if the transaction were otherwise structured.

Item 8 requires a statement whether the issuer or affiliate filing the Schedule reasonably believes that the transaction is fair or unfair. It would, of course, be amazing if anyone were to avow that he believed the transaction to be unfair, except, one should add, that in the case of an issuer tender offer the issuer may very well say that the offer is being made for the purpose of facilitating sale by shareholders in light of their own financial objectives or to increase the interest of the insiders but with no representation that the price is a fair price and, indeed, a representation that it would not be a fair price if the transaction were a true cash-out merger type of transaction. Although the Item speaks in terms of a statement on behalf of the filing party, it seems fairly clear that what it intended was a statement on behalf of both the affiliate and the issuer. Rule 13e-3 requires a discussion of material factors on which the filing party has based that belief and itemizes the factors which are normally taken into account in evaluating fairness of price including current market price, historical market prices, net book value, going concern value, liquidation value and the price paid in prior transactions. A statement is also required as to whether an independent evaluation of the price was made, whether there were other offers, whether the insiders' vote is to be neutralized, how the directors approved the transaction and whether these factors entered into a consideration of the fairness of the price.

Item 8(b) is the principal source of difficulty in complying with the Rule. The staff in at least some early letters of comment appears to desire a discussion of each of the enumerated factors.

Item 9 requires detailed information with respect to any fairness opinion from an investment banker or other financial advisor, including how the advisor was selected and, in particular, whether the advisor was asked to determine the consideration to be paid or to recommend what consideration would be paid.

Two techniques have developed to respond to the fairness discussions required by the Rule. One is what may be termed a question and answer format in which each of the Items is separately considered and responded to. On the basis of some early letters of comment, it would seem that a number of examiners appear to favor this format. On the other hand, a considerable number of disclosure documents have not used this mode of presentation but instead have used a more or less narrative format in which the genesis and reasons for the transaction are disclosed as events in time. It is the view of this author that the narrative format is more interpretative. In any event, it would appear particularly appropriate where bargaining ensued between the insider shareholders who proposed the transaction and the independent directors or the investment advisor hired by them for purposes of considering its fairness.

In addition, a number of conventions have developed in connection with a going private proxy statement which should be followed. Principal among these, of course, has been the development of a summary section in the forepart of the proxy statement which sets forth a summary of the terms of the transaction, the vote required, the availability of appraisal rights, summary financial information and the like. Counsel would be well advised to study recent examples of the form of transaction he is undertaking before preparing the required documentation.

Rule 13e-4

Shortly after the adoption of Rule 13e-3, the Commission issued Exchange Act Release No. 34-16112 adopting Rule 13e-4 which specifically provides dissemination and filing requirements for an "issuer tender offer." The Rule applies to tender offers by an issuer or an affiliate for any class of equity security of the issuer, if the issuer has a class of equity securities registered pursuant to Section 12 of the Exchange Act, or is required to file periodic reports pursuant to Section 15(d) of the Exchange Act, or is a closed-end investment company registered under the Investment Company Act of 1940. However, as tender offers by an affiliate for an equity security registered under Section 12 are subject to Section 14(d) of the Exchange Act and thereby exempt from Rule 13e-4, the Rule will typically only apply to issuer offers and to an "affiliate" of a Section 15(d) Company. Both Schedule 13E-3 and Schedule 13E-4 must be filed when both are required, although response by cross-reference is permitted.

The Rule requires that "prior to or as soon as practicable on the date of the commencement of the issuer tender offer," the issuer or affiliate must file the required "Issuer Tender Offer Statement" on Schedule 13E-4. The information to be provided in the Schedule 13E-4 and disseminated to the offerees is similar to that required by Rule 13e-3 for a going private transaction.

The heart of the information to be disclosed is found in Item 3 of Schedule 13E-4. Specifically required is a discussion of the purpose of the tender offer and any plans or proposals of the issuer or affiliate for such future transactions as purchases or dispositions of additional securities of the issuer, mergers, reorganizations, liquidations, sale or transfer of assets, change in the board of directors or management of the issuer or changes in the dividend rate or debt or capitalization structure of the issuer, or any change in the issuer's charter or bylaws which would impede the acquisition of control of the issuer by any other person. The offeror is also required to discuss any plans or proposals which may result in a class of equity securities of the issuer being delisted from a national securities exchange or to cease to be authorized to be quoted on NASDAQ, or for such class of such equity security to become eligible for termination of registration pursuant to Section 12(g) of the Act or for suspension of the issuer's obligation to file reports pursuant to Section 15(d) of the Act.

In addition summary financial information of the issuer for the two most recent years and any interim periods, ratio of earnings to fixed changes for the same periods, and pro-forma financial material should be included. It should be noted, however, that if only summary financial information is included in the offering circular, appropriate instructions stating how more complete financial information can be obtained should also be included.

Depending upon the type of tender offer, three methods of dissemination to security holders may be available. First, a cash tender offer may be disseminated by long-form publication, whereby all required information is printed in a newspaper of general circulation. Second, any tender offer may be disseminated by distribution to each security holder whose name appears on the most recent shareholder list of the issuer and by making available to nominee shareholders an appropriate number of offering circulars for the beneficial interest which they represent. The issuer in such case must agree to reimburse the nominee holder for reasonable expenses incurred in forwarding the offering circular to the beneficial owners. Third, if the tender is for cash and is not subject to Rule 13e-3, the offer may be disseminated by summary publication. This requires the publication in a newspaper of general circulation of certain information about the issuer and tender offer and the transmitting promptly of the offering circular and transmittal letter to any security holder who so requests.

Rule 13e-4 also contains procedural requirements. The tender offer must remain open for fifteen business days from its commencement, and securities tendered may be withdrawn for the first ten business days of the offer, and if not theretofore accepted for payment for the first seven business days from the date another tender offer is made for securities of the same class, and any time after the expiration of 40 business days from the commencement of the offer. If the offer is for less than all the securities of the class, and the amount tendered is greater than the amount to be purchased, securities tendered within the first ten business days must be purchased on a pro rata basis. Similarly if the consideration for the purchase of the securities is increased, the pro rata purchase provisions apply to securities purchased within ten business days of the date of notice of such increase. Exceptions to the pro rata purchase requirements are provided for shareholders owning and tendering less than 100 shares, and in certain cases shareholders tendering shares conditioned on the purchase of a specified amount.

BUYOUTS

THE NUMBER AND FORM OF FINANCING STRUCTURES and business combinations are limited only by the imagination. There are innumerable techniques which have been used successfully in the past and are likely to continue being used in future transactions. In addition, each year innovations tend to appear because of economic pressures or legislature initiatives which encourage the business community to adopt them.

One of these relatively new financial phenomena is the "leveraged buyout." Here a word on terminology is in order. When speaking of a merger or acquisition the authors have generally treated combinations of two ongoing concerns. On the other hand, a *buyout* involves the purchase of an ongoing business by a newly formed non-operating company explicitly formed for that purpose. This newly formed entity is essentially a shell which raises the capital needed to effect the transaction. Thus, a buyout is really a special category of merger. The term buyout indicates nothing about the sources or relative amounts of debt and equity used to fund the purchase. A "leveraged buyout" is simply a buyout which is highly leveraged. There is no clear consensus within the financial community as to what is or is not highly leveraged. This will turn on the type of business, the nature of the industry, and even the overall state of the economy.

Each of the three chapters in this section approaches the subject of leveraged buyouts from a slightly different perspective. Robert L. Frome and Alan M. Getzhoff have a legal emphasis and pay particular attention to public companies and going private techniques. They compare the sale of assets and cash merger formats. Two landmark cases, *Woods* and *Spartek*, are discussed at length. Emphasis is given to employee relations, employment contracts, and the use of partnership incentive profit funds.

Paul F. Balser analyzes the investment potential of leveraged buyouts as affected by growth and inflation. He shows certain analogies to real estate financing techniques. A detailed analysis of the Congoleum transaction is presented, as well as a recent transaction in which the author participated. Certain pitfalls of leveraged buyouts are pointed out—including unfunded pension liabilities, labor relations and accounting problems. These are germane to the larger area of mergers and acquisitions as well.

The overview chapter by Robert D. Colman places the subject in an historical context, and shows the evolution and likely future of this type of transaction. Several detailed case studies are presented as well as a comparison of six of the major public leveraged buyouts. The sources of leveraged buyout financing are considered with particular emphasis on the equity investors and "deal makers" (investment bankers) who initiate and structure the transaction.

PAUL F. BALSER

PAUL F. BALSER is Associate Director of the Corporate Finance Department at Thomson McKinnon Securities, Inc.

Previously he was Vice President in Corporate Finance with Wertheim & Co., Inc. He began his career at Empire Trust Company.

Mr. Balser is a graduate of Yale University and Lawrenceville School. He also attended NYU Graduate Business School. He is presently Trustee of The Hudson Guild and Secretary of the Class of 1960 for Lawrenceville School.

DEAN D. PORTER

DEAN D. PORTER is an Assistant Vice President in the Corporate Finance Department of Thomson McKinnon Securities, Inc. in New York City. He was previously a Vice President in the Cleveland investment banking firm of Golenberg & Co., and its affiliated SBIC, Intercapco, Inc. Prior to that time he was also associated with Prescott, Ball & Turbin.

Mr. Porter has a B.A. degree and an M.B.A. from Columbia University, and a J.D. from Case Western Reserve University. He is a member of the Ohio Bar.

32

Leveraged Buyout Financing

(or, the Kiss which turns the Frog into a Handsome Prince)

PAUL F. BALSER

DEAN D. PORTER

Every investment cycle creates different financing strategies. In the 1960's it was early public offerings of potentially explosive growth companies; conglomerate acquisitions to build earnings per share growth by using a higher price/earnings multiple stock to buy lower price/earnings multiple sellers; and a more liberal pooling of interests treatment for accounting purposes. In the 1970's it was leveraged buyout financing. Due to a dramatically undervalued stock market, effectively no new issue market, increasing reluctance on the part of professional investors to back start-up companies, and the availability of spin off operations from conglomerates no longer interested in managing them, this new financing technique evolved quickly.

The low growth, high asset value, stable companies which became the targets of leveraged buyouts were indeed ''Frogs'' to classical buyers because the return on investment and compound growth rates were unattractive given historic concepts of debt and equity ratios. When the real estate financing concept of 3-5x debt to equity ratios was applied to these ''Frogs'', buyers viewed them as ''Handsome Princes'' able to generate above average returns to all the financing participants within very acceptable overall risk parameters. Because of their attractiveness to buyers, the sellers could realize prices which more closely approximated perceived value and the number of transactions effected rose markedly.

WHAT IS A LEVERAGED BUYOUT?

Put simply, a leveraged buyout (''LBO'') is the layering of debt and other securities which are senior to a relatively small amount of common equity, to finance the acquisition of a company. Generally the acquired entity will be an established company with a visible and dependable record of cash flow as well as good prospects for continued profitability. This cash flow is pledged to repay the debt. Also, the acquired company often has a high ratio of fixed assets (older and largely depreciated) to total assets to provide the collateral security necessary for the debt financing.

An investor in an established business is aware that two types of risk are always present: business risk—failure of the company due to losses from fundamental causes, and financial risk—failure caused by inability of the company's cash flow to cover its fixed charges. If a company is facing substantial fundamental risks, such as investing heavily in unproven ideas, then it cannot also support substantial financial risks. But, if a company has a fairly stable earnings and cash flow growth rate, it can undertake increased financial risk. Unlike historic start-up venture capital investments, financed largely with equity, LBO's are akin to real estate investments—whose stable, predictable cash flows serve to repay a very high degree of secured leverage.

In the classic leveraged buyout candidate, several key criteria are important that significantly minimize business risk:

(a) An established, long standing, predictable cash flow from operations which provides adequate debt service coverages for potential lenders.

(b) A heavy preponderance of total assets represented by older, fully depreciated fixed assets—plants, property and equipment—

which are worth significantly in excess of their carrying "book" value.

(c) Operations in a relatively mature marketplace with moderate anticipated growth in revenues—this minimizes future capital expenditure requirements, freeing up cash flow for debt service. It also avoids dislocations from changes in technology.

(d) An in-place product line and management team—this should allow a continuation of earnings in the future without surprises and changes when the company is sold.

(e) Low existing current debt and long term debt to allow significant new acquisiton debt to be put on the books for the buyout. Such "leveragable" balance sheets take on great importance given collateral tests for lending limits generally used:

(1) 80-90 percent of Accounts Receivables under 90 days old;

(2) 50-60 percent of finished goods and raw materials inventories;

(3) 80-90 percent of the "under the hammer" or liquidating value of machinery and equipment;

(4) 70-80 percent of the fair market value of plant; and

(5) pre-tax, pre-interest, pre-depreciation cash flow coverage of pro forma fixed charges in the range of 2.0x.

ANALYZING THE INVESTMENT POTENTIAL

Given that a target investment meets these criteria, the mathematics of a LBO are illustrated by Tables 32-1, 32-2 and 32-3. As Table 32-1 indicates, with no growth in Sales or Pre-Tax, Pre-Interest Earnings, an equity investor could still enjoy a 17.4 percent compounded return on his initial equity over ten years with a relatively low risk. The similarity of LBO's to real estate transactions is clearly illustrated by comparing the results of Table 32-2 with Table 32-1. Given 8 percent inflation, the result of a fixed debt obligation (denominated in historic dollars and not inflation adjusted) and growing sales and earnings increased for this inflation is to greatly expand the growth rates for the equity investment. As with real estate investments, lenders are more than fully collateralized by fixed assets and look to a cash flow with an ample cushion for error to repay the LBO's obligations. As Table 32-2 indicates, returns from this simplistic example greatly exceed many other investment alternatives.

LOCATING INVESTORS

Finding equity investors for leveraged buyouts is generally not difficult because of widespread awareness that they are attractive, and because many venture investors have become disenchanted with traditional new business start-ups.

Such investors have found that start-ups commit and consume capital for substantial time periods. They cannot count on public underwritings to provide liquidity and financing either. For example, during the late 1960's, public offerings provided liquidity, secondary financing sources and frequently, increased market values. In 1969, there were 1026 new issues sold for a total value of $2.6 billion, according to "Going Public" (a Philadelphia publication). In 1979, 81 companies raised $506 million from the sale of equity. Thus, in a questionable securities market, going public is often not a realistic option for many companies.

Additionally, second stage financing, professional investors have learned, is frequently more expensive and harder to get. As a result, they're obligated to keep reinvesting their own funds, often before the company has grown enough to prove that their initial investment was sound.

In addition to being less risky than start-ups, leveraged buyouts are usually structured to provide a relatively high current return (i.e., subordinated debt with warrants). They often have a mechanism permitting the investor to liquidate his position while providing for a higher return on equity through the exercise of warrants.

FINANCIAL INTERMEDIARIES

Like the venture capitalists, financial intermediaries—banks, insurance companies and secured lenders—are interested in financing the senior debt layer of the transaction because of the attractive rates which such financing generates (prime plus 2 to 6 percentage points), the strength of the underlying collateral, and the historic earnings record. But, the key factors affecting lenders' decisions are most often cash flow coverages and the perceived competence levels of management.

Table 32-4 indicates the target rates of return and the layer of security preferred by the various equity sources and lenders. Table 32-5 lists some of the more well-known participants by type of preferred investment position as well as some of the more active packagers or arrangers of leveraged buyout financing.

Table 32-1—No Growth, No Inflation
($000 omitted)

Year	1	2	3	4	5	6	7	8	9	10
Sales	10,000	10,000	10,000	10,000	10,000	10,000	10,000	10,000	10,000	10,000
Pretax, Pre-interest Income	1,000	1,000	1,000	1,000	1,000	1,000	1,000	1,000	1,000	1,000
Interest Costs	540	504	464	419	368	314	253	186	113	34
Taxes (@ 50%)	230	248	268	291	316	343	374	407	444	483
Net After Taxes Income	230	248	268	291	316	343	374	407	444	483
Cash Flow Available for Debt Service	230	248	268	291	316	343	374	407	444	483
Principal Repayment	200	225	250	280	300	340	370	405	440	190
Discretionary Cash Flow/Year	30	23	18	11	16	3	4	2	4	293
Cumulative Net Cash Flow	30	53	71	82	98	101	105	107	111	404
Debt Outstanding at Year End	2,800	2,575	2,325	2,045	1,745	1,405	1,035	630	190	-0-

Assumptions:

(1) Company purchased at 8 times net income of $500,000. Acquisition price of $4.0 million financed with $1.0MM of equity and $3.0 million of debt at 18% interest.

(2) Depreciation equals capital expenditures in each year.

(3) No growth in sales, increase in prices or change in the margins of profitability.

(4) Working capital financing not reflected for this illustration.

(5) Debt repayment schedule assumes maximum use of excess cash flow to reduce outstanding debt.

Table 32-1 assumes no adjustment for inflation in revenues, thus with an 8 percent inflation rate the revenues show negative growth in real terms. Even with such a conservative assumption the debt is repaid in year 10.

Table 32-2—8% Increased Prices to Cover Inflation
($000 omitted)

Year	1	2	3	4	5	6	7	8	9	10
Sales	10,000	10,800	11,664	12,597	13,605	14,693	15,869	17,138	18,509	19,990
Pretax, Pre-interest Income	1,000	1,080	1,166	1,260	1,361	1,469	1,587	1,714	1,851	1,999
Interest Costs	540	504	457	399	327	237	129	-0-	-0-	-0-
Taxes (@ 50%)	230	288	355	431	517	616	729	857	925	1,000
Net After Taxes Income	230	288	355	431	517	616	729	857	925	1,000
Cash Flow Available for Debt Service	230	288	355	431	517	616	729	857	925	1,000
Principal Repayment	200	260	325	400	500	600	715	-0-	-0-	-0-
Discretionary Cash Flow/Year	30	28	30	31	17	16	14	857	925	1,000
Cumulative Net Cash Flow	30	58	88	119	136	152	166	1,023	1,948	2,948
Debt Outstanding at Year End	2,800	2,540	2,215	1,815	1,315	715	-0-	-0-	-0-	-0-

Assumptions:

(1) Company purchased at 8 times net income of $500,000 for a total of $4.0 million. Acquisition financed with $1.0 million of equity and $3.0 million of debt at 18%.

(2) Depreciation equals capital expenditures in each year.

(3) No growth in units sold; prices increased 8% per year to offset inflation. Pretax profit margins remain constant at 10%.

(4) Working capital financing not reflected for this illustration.

(5) Debt repayment schedule assumes maximum use of excess cash flow to reduce outstanding debt.

Table 32-2 reflects an inflation-adjusted 8 percent growth rate. The similarities between real estate financing and leveraged buyout financing are best demonstrated in this table. The repayment of debt in cheaper dollars and the inflation-increased earnings stream create a much higher market value for the company even given the same price/earnings multiple as was paid on the purchase price.

505

Table 32-3—Comparison of Examples I & II

	At Date of Purchase	At Year 10	Compound Rate of Growth
Table I Assumptions (with no growth)			
Value at 8X Net After Tax Income	$4.0MM	$3.9MM	—
Plus: Excess Cash	-0-	.3M	
Total Value	$4.0MM	$4.2MM	
Equity Investment	$1.0MM	$4.2MM	17.4%
Table II Assumptions (with 8%)			
Value at 8X Net After Tax Income	$4.0MM	$8.0MM	
Plus: Excess Cash	-0-	2.9MM	
Total Value	$4.0MM	$10.9MM	
Equity Investment	$1.0MM	$10.9MM	30.0%

Table 32-4—Financing Sources

Financing Sources	Investment Form	Term	Equity Position	Rate of Return Target
Banks	Senior Debt Secured by: Accounts Receivable Inventory Machinery and Equipment Plant (sometimes)	"Evergreen" (no repayment) on receivables and inventory; 5 to 7 years on plant property and equipment.	None	Prime plus 3-5%
Secured Lenders/Finance Companies	Same	5 to 10 years with a balloon at maturity.	None	Prime plus 4-6%
Insurance Companies	Longer term debt plus some equity.	10 to 20 years.	Cheap stock or warrants.	20-25% compound
Small Business Investment Companies	Longer term debt- usually subordinated.	7 to 10 years.	Warrants or debt with convertible features.	20-30% compound
Venture Capitalists, Private Groups	Preferred stock and/or common stock.	Often has buy back provisions after 5 years - "put" on part of investor and "call" on part of company.	All Equity	25-40% compound

SOURCES OF LEVERAGED BUYOUTS

There are generally three sources of leveraged buyouts; closely held private companies, divisional spinoffs and large public companies.

Such companies can be unearthed through approaching:

(1) Accounting firms, commercial banks, investment bankers, business brokers and lawyers;

(2) Bank trust departments - an estate may have a control position in a private/public company in which the bank trustee is unwilling and/or unable to manage the company long term;

(3) Managements of public or private companies which own a controlling interest in the company and which average over 60 years of age. Such individuals or groups are frequently concerned with:

(a) estate liquidity
(b) management succession
(c) continuance of the company as a viable competitive entity;

(4) Companies where the stock price has been static for a protracted period of time. Managements of these companies may have problems keeping and attracting younger management talent. Also, selling may offer the only alternative for realizing profits on stock options or stock positions.

(5) Companies selling for less than book value where the fair market value of the fixed assets may well exceed the original cost of such assets.

Table 32-5

The following lists are by no means all inclusive but reflect some of the participants involved in leveraged buyout financing.

Banks	—American Security (Washington, C.D.)
	Ameritrust (Cleveland)
	Bankers Trust Company (New York)
	Citicorp (New York)
	Continental Illinois (Chicago)
	First National Bank of Chicago (Chicago)
	Industrial National (Providence)
	Manufacturers Hanover (New York)
	National City (Cleveland)
	New England Merchants (Boston)
Insurance Companies	—Allstate
	Connecticut General
	Prudential
	Teachers
	Northwestern Mutual
Secured Lenders	—Aetna Business Credit
	Commercial Credit
	GE Credit Corp.
	FNB Financial (First National Bank of Boston)
	Walter Heller
SBIC's	—Allied Capital (Washington, D.C.)
	Citicorp Ventures
	Continental Illinois Venture Capital
	European American Bank (NYC)
	First Chicago Investment Corporation
	MorAmerica Corporation
	Narragansett Capital
	Virginia Capital (Richmond)
Equity Sources	—Adler & Co. (New York)
	Fidelity Ventures (Boston)
	Sprout Capital - Donaldson Lufkin & Jenrette (New York)
	Most Other Venture Capital Funds
Deal Makers	—First Boston
	Kohlberg Kravis & Roberts
	Gibbons, Green, van Amerorgen Ltd.
	Golenberg & Co.
	Hampshire Capital (Morristown, N.J.)
	Carl Marx
	Oppenheimer & Co.
	Rosenkranz & Company

TYPES OF LEVERAGED BUYOUTS

(I) Closely Held Companies (Public and Private)

Companies with a block of stock controlled by a close group of insiders or families. This type of company readily lends itself to the "Oppenheimer" financial structure, which, because of its tax advantages to the sellers has become popular:

Steps in Oppenheimer Financing:

The former XYZ Corporation sells all its assets to a new Corporation, ABC, in exchange for cash.

No taxes are paid if the purchase price is at book value or less. Any premium above book value is subject to capital gains taxes at the corporate, not individual shareholder, level.

The former XYZ Corporation becomes a closed end investment company under the Investment Company Act of 1940.[1]

The new regulated investment company invests the cash flow proceeds from sale of its assets into tax exempt bonds. Then, since it is a registered investment company, all income received on its investments is not taxed at the corporate level, as long as 90 percent of income is paid out to the shareholders. Since the dividends are a result of tax free income, shareholders are not taxed on their receipt of dividends either.

The stockholders of XYZ Corporation only pay capital gains taxes if they redeem their shares in this closed investment company. Their basis in the stock remains the same as before the sale of the company.

The "Oppenheimer" approach lets the controlling shareholders defer the tax impact of the sales of the company's assets on their net after-tax income, liquefy their assets and diversify their estates. Although there probably is only a limited public market for such closed end investment companies, the quality of the municipal bonds in the portfolio can remove most of the risk from the investment.

Thus, selling assets instead of stock creates a form of tax shelter. Future liquidity can come from redemption by the investment company or its ultimate liquidation.

To illustrate how appealing the "Oppenheimer" method can be, let's suppose a controlling stockholder decides to sell his company's stock for $20 million, or book value. Assuming he has a zero tax basis in his stock and also assuming he's in a 70 percent income tax bracket, he will pay a capital gains tax of 28 percent on the $20 million of proceeds, or $5.6 million. After taxes, he will have $14.4 million to invest in 7½ percent long term A-rated municipal bonds, and he'll wind up with annual income of almost $1.1 million after taxes.[2]

But, on the other hand, if the company decides to sell only its assets (also at book value), the $20 million proceeds can go into a closed end investment company, and the controlling shareholder won't have to pay a capital gains tax until he either redeems his stock or liquidates the investment company. $20 million invested in 7½ percent tax free bonds yields about $1.5

million in after tax income—39 percent more than if the stock were sold as described in the previous example.

Besides these attractive tax considerations, selling shareholders find the "Oppenheimer" method attractive because in many cases they can also receive lucrative management contracts to manage the company's assets after they have changed hands ...[3]

(II) Divisional Spinoffs

There are several reasons why a public or private company would sell off a division that it owned:

(a) Anti-trust problems: the Federal Government mandates sale of the business for competitive reasons.

(b) Such a company does not meet the return on assets or cash flow criteria mandated by the parent company's Board of Directors.

(c) The sale could raise cash for the reduction of the parent company's outstanding debt.

(d) The subsidiary's product line might be obsolete, unprofitable, or incompatible with the parent company's goals.

(e) Many conglomerates have moved from the broadly based diversification of the 60's to a "back to basics" approach. This frequently gives rise to the sale of smaller unrelated operations.

Such a seller normally will consider all of the alternatives before selling to a leveraged buyout purchaser. The obvious first alternative is sale to another large corporation. Some of the difficulties that are encountered here include anti-trust problems, possible time delay, and, most important, the possibility of a write-off on the seller's books. Since the seller is usually unwilling to take anything other than cash or cash and a small amount of notes, the purchaser's stock cannot be used. Therefore, a purchase (not pooling transaction) must result. Since the return on assets and growth rate in earnings of divisions that are being divested frequently are below the seller's minimum acceptance level, it is also often below those of the buyer as well. Corporate buyers focusing on returns on capital and growth are not likely to price an acquisition primarily on its undervalued lower returning assets. Additionally, the pooling of interests treatment and tax laws

---

[1]Generally, in order to qualify to be taxed as a regulated investment company under Section 851 of the Internal Revenue Code, a corporation must fulfill all of the following criteria:
—It must be registered under the Investment Company Act of 1940 at all times during the taxable year.
—It must not be a personal holding company, as defined in Section 542 of the code.
—At least 90% of its gross income must be derived from "dividends, interest and gains from the sale or other disposition of stock or securities."
—It must have at least 100 shareholders.
[2]Calculation does not take into account alternative minimum tax consequences.
[3]This aspect of the buyout has drawn criticism from the S.E.C., which is now in the process of deciding whether such management contracts constitute "additional consideration" paid to controlling shareholders who were insiders.

have changed which further impacts the difficulty of a transaction with a corporation buyer.

The second alternative, liquidation, is infrequently used because of the time delays, bad publicity, legal complications associated with customer accounts, stockholder suits, union problems, and ongoing pension obligations. Also, it is not clear that in many cases a liquidation can be implemented without still having the possibility of some future write-down of book value on the seller's books.

All of these factors tend to mitigate the apprehension of selling to the leveraged buyout financed purchaser. The slow growth rates and the high proportion of older depreciated assets are attractive to the leveraged buyout purchaser who needs the collateral assets more than he needs growth in cash flow to finance the acquisition. The LBO buyer will, therefore, pay a higher price as a multiple of cash flow. Secondly, where the buyers are the operating management of the corporate division, they may represent the most informed possible purchasers for the business. Since the risk of change in management does not become part of the risks in changing the company's ownership, financing may be more easily arranged for them. The seller certainly may believe that only the insider management could have a high enough level of confidence in the company to pay a full price for it. Finally, the seller may be comfortable in assuming some seller's paper since it is familiar with the existing management.

For these reasons, divisional spinoffs are frequently excellent candidates for leveraged buyout financing.

(III) Widely Held Public Companies

This is the latest—and perhaps most significant new source—of leveraged buyouts. The main reason for its growing popularity is the dramatic undervaluation of common stocks in today's market. Many equities are selling at substantial discounts from historic book values and way below true fair market value per share.

The inflation rate of the last 15 years has caused replacement values of assets to increase more than double historic costs. Therefore, companies may well be selling at less than half of fair market book value per share, a figure that is less than what banks and secured lenders would lend a purchaser on the same assets. With price/earnings ratios at 5-7x, the actual after tax cash flow as a percent of the market price of a company's common shares could easily be in the 15-25 percent range. Allowing for an acquisition premium of 100 percent would still leave substantial after tax cash flow to service the acquisition debt.

The recently completed Congoleum acquisition, which has drawn a lot of interest on Wall Street, illustrates the advantages of the leveraged buyout as applied to the widely held undervalued public corporation. Congoleum is a manufacturing, marketing and distribution company with principal operations in resilient flooring, shipbuilding and automotive and industrial products. The company manufactures resilient flooring for installation in residences, commercial buildings and institutions of various types. A large share of the resilient flooring business is directed to the home remodeling market. Congoleum also manufactures upholstered furniture, bedding, convertible cushions and dinette sets designed mainly for sale to the mobile home industry. Congoleum, through its Bath Iron Works subsidiary, builds, converts and modernizes naval vessels and merchant ships. The Automotive and Industrial Distribution segment distributes a wide range of automotive and industrial maintenance parts. In the automotive aftermarket, the products include battery and booster cables, ignition sets, spark plugs, carburetors, fuel pumps, mufflers, tailpipes and brake parts, as well as keys and key duplicating machines. Industrial maintenance parts include fasteners, terminals and chemicals.

Contributions from revenues and operating income, by product area were as follows:

| | At September 30, 1979 | |
	Revenues	Operating Income
Home Furnishings	40%	55%
Shipbuilding	40%	34%
Automotive and Industrial Distribution	20%	11%

The Congoleum transaction is best understood by examining three layers of the purchasing corporation's capitalization: bank debt, institutional debt and preferred stock, and common stock.

Set forth is the capitalization of Congoleum as of September 30, 1979, and the pro forma capitalization of the new entity as of September 30, 1979 giving effect to the Transactions and the Financing.

Bank Debt

Bank debt here is the most senior and as a result is the best security position. The rate is based on a formula which ranges from a minimum of 10 percent to a maximum of 14 percent. Based upon estimates of the value of Congloeum's receivables, inventory and fixed assets, the banks would most likely receive 100 cents on the dollar in the event of a liquidation. In addition, historical fixed charges coverage of 2 times would give the bank comfort that the new debt can be adequately serviced. The real issue is whether the company can

	Capitalization as at 9/30/79	Pro Forma for this transaction as at 9/30/79
	(In Millions)	
Long-Term Debt		
7-1/2%Subordinated Debentures due 1983	$ 12.2	$ 12.2
Other Long-Term Debt	4.7	4.7
Bank Term Notes	—	125.0
11¼% Senior Notes due 1995	$ —	$113.6
12¼% Subordinated Notes due 2000	—	89.8
Total	$ 16.9	$345.3
Less Current Portion	0.5	0.5
Total Long-Term Debt	$ 16.4	$344.8
Redeemable Preferred Stock		
$11.00 Cumulative Preferred Stock, $5.00 par value, authorized and issued 322,000 shares	$ —	$ 26.2
Common Stockholders Investment		
Common Stock, $.50 par value, authorized 20,000,000 shares, issued 11,783,210 shares	$ 5.9	$ —
Common Stock, $.01 par value, authorized 1,775,000 shares, issued 1,000,000 shares	$ —	$ .1
Capital in Excess of Par Value	11.2	24.9
Retained Earnings	200.3	—
Total Common Stockholders Investment	$217.4	$ 25.0
Total Capitalization	$233.8	$396.0

repay the principal during years three through eight. Unless growth projections are met, the company may very well have difficulty meeting its debt amortization schedule.

Stock Ownership

The common stock ownership of the new entity is divided up as indicated below:

Holder	Number of Shares	Percent of Total
First Boston, Inc.	90,000	9%
Century S. III	90,000	9
Byron C. Radaker Chairman, Congoleum Corp. Chairman, New Entity	70,000	7
Eddy G. Nicholson Vice Chairman, Congoleum Corp. President, New Entity	50,000	5
Other Congoleum Management	40,000	4
The Prudential Life Insurance Company of America	286,956	29
The Aetna Casualty and Surety Company	93,261	9
The Travelers Insurance Company	93,261	9
The Northwestern Mutual Life Insurance Company	66,717	7

Holder	Number of Shares	Percent of Total
Connecticut General Life Insurance Company	57,391	6
Teachers Insurance and Annuity Association of America	43,761	4
The Mutual Benefit Life Insurance Company	18,653	2
Total	1,000,000	100%

Institutional Debt and Equity

Institutional investors, which include such sophisticated institutions as Prudential, Aetna, Travelers, Northwestern Mutual, Connecticut General, Teachers, and Mutual Benefit Life, generally expect a compounded rate of return between 22-30 percent in leveraged buyouts. These returns are less than are usually anticipated in technologically oriented venture capital transactions due to the lower degree of business risk found in hard asset, historically proven cash flow companies. However, due to the leverage and investment risks involved, the returns are higher than those required in a conventional private placement. Thus the desired return represents a debt/equity hybrid, a layer of financing between bank debt and venture capital.

510

The structure combines both current yield and equity appreciation. The institutional investors receive a current yield of 12.6 percent after reducing their investment by the difference between the $25 per share which the other investors paid and the $10.40 per share which the institutions paid.

The institutional investors also receive 66 percent of the corporation's common stock. To fully appreciate how an institutional investor would analyze his potential equity appreciation, it is necessary to make some estimates of growth to create the following pro forma projections.

	From The Proxy Statement		Assumed 10% Revenue Growth Rate			
	($ Millions omitted)					
	1980	1981	1982	1983	1984	1985
Operating Income	97	112	123	135	149	164
Interest	41	41	41	41	41	41
Pre Tax	56	71	82	94	108	123
Taxes (50%)	28	35	41	47	54	61
Net Income	28	36	41	47	54	62
Less Preferred Dividend	4	4	4	4	4	4
Less Principal Repayment	0	8	24	24	24	24
Retained Earnings	24	24	13	19	26	34

Assuming the same price/earnings ratio in 1985 of 9x earnings as was the case in the buyout, the projected net earnings of $62 million for 1985 would provide a market capitalization of $558 million. The 66 percent owned by the institutional investors would represent a common stock value of $368 million. Over a period of six years these investors would have also received $172 million in interest and preferred dividends on an investment of $229 million.

Thus, the institutional investor received a high current yield, plus equity appreciation, and the eventual amortization of its capital generating an annual compounded rate of return of approximately 27 percent.

The question is usually raised in this and other examples as to the ability of the company to buy out the equity investment in year six. In those cases of inadequate cash, there are two alternatives:

(a) Releverage assets which have been amortizing its debt over this period of time, or by issuing a

(b) Participating Preferred—Banks such as Citibank have established a risk capital fund for ongoing businesses which do not qualify for institutional debt, but which do not wish to issue equity. In these cases the company issues a participating preferred dividend to the bank, which is 85 percent excluded from corporate taxable income. The instrument usually consists of a base yield with a participation in the company's earnings.

Management Compensation

Byron C. Radaker, Congoleum's Chairman and President, and Eddy G. Nicholson, Congoleum's Vice Chairman, will assume executive positions with the new entity as Chairman and President, respectively. Proceeds received from the sale of their Congoleum stock and compensation for the value of their unexercised stock options of approximately $2,900,000 provided the funds necessary for them to purchase 12 percent of the new common stock. As a result, management has every incentive to help all selling shareholders to receive an attractive price. The higher the price, the more dollars management has to reinvest. Other Congoleum management was permitted to purchase 4 percent of the common stock.

Radaker and Nicholson were also given nearly perpetual management contracts to run the new company at a pay level up to one-third higher than they were currently earning. Radaker can earn between $375,000 and 500,000 a year compared to his 1979 compensation of $370,000. Nicholson can earn between $290,000 and $380,000 a year, compared to $295,000 last year. Radaker's and Nicholson's generous compensation underscores the importance of existing key management in arranging a leveraged buyout.

Financial Advisors

First Boston Corporation, the investment banking firm that structured the leveraged buyout plan and arranged the financing, received fees of $3.3 million, a $350,000 annual advisory fee for three years and the right to purchase 9 percent of the new corporation's equity.

Century is an investment advisor which brought the idea of a leveraged buyout of Congoleum to First Boston. For its efforts it received the opportunity of purchasing 9 percent of the new entity's common stock.

Historic Congoleum Results
($ Millions omitted)

	Gross Revenues	Net Profit	Net Margin
1979 (1)	$602	$51	8.5%
1978	576	42	7.3
1977	389	25	6.4
1976	295	16	5.4
1975	279	10	3.6

	(3) Return on Assets	(3) Return on Equity	Dividend Pay Out Ratio
1979(1)	N.A.	N.A.	21.0%
1978	19.0%	22.3	18.7
1977	15.2	16.2	18.8
1976	11.0	11.9	24.3
1975	7.8	7.7	32.5

	Earnings Per Share	Book value Per Share	Dividend Yield (2)
1979(1)	$4.38	NA	3.3%
1978	3.58	$16.06	3.5
1977	2.13	13.17	3.4
1976	1.36	11.46	3.2
1975	.83	10.45	4.4

	P/E Ratio (2)	Price/Book (2)
1979(1)	5.9X	NA
1978	5.3	1.2X
1977	5.5	.9
1976	8.8	.9
1975	7.3	.6

	Cash Flow/Per Share	Price/Cash Flow (2)
1979		3.3X
1978		2.5
1977		2.9
1976		3.6
1975		2.8

(1) Trailing 12 months as of 9-30-79
(2) Based on average of high and low prices for year
(3) Net after tax

WHAT ARE THE PITFALLS OF THE LEVERAGED BUYOUT?

Despite the obvious advantages of the leveraged buyout, there are several key problem areas to watch out for when negotiating a transaction:

(1) Unfunded Pension Liabilities

Under ERISA, the future cost of pension liabilities for today's employees (as well as already retired employees) must be calculated each year. Independent actuaries are employed by a company to calculate the total future obligations as well as the present obligation, assuming all of today's employees remain until retirement at either today's or future compensation levels. This later figure is the vested unfunded past service liability of the business for those employees who have been employed long enough to have vested part or all of their future pension benefits. While this entire subject is complicated, the sheer magnitude of these liabilities, often two or three times the assets available in the pension plan, and sometimes a large part of the net worth of the target company, make it an area to analyze carefully. The selling company will probably not have booked the vested unfunded obligation as a liability since it is not required to do so. The target, however, if acquired in an asset purchase, will have to book the vested unfunded past service liability under present accounting requirements. The actual amount booked depends on the compound rate of return assumption for future investment returns which is applied to the starting pension asset base. Such assumed rates tend to range from 5-3/4 percent to over 9 percent. Secondly, a discount rate is applied to these hypothetical future assets, which usually ranges between 5-1/4 percent and 8-1/4 percent, to bring the future stream of earnings back to a present value figure. This number is then compared to the starting pension asset base to determine the pretax unfunded liability figure. Accountants seem to agree that the balance sheet figure to be booked is the after tax equivalent of this pretax number, generally using a discount rate of 6-1/2 percent - 7-1/2 percent. In a recent transaction, the book value of the target company was $10.6 million and the vested unfunded past service liability to the acquiror was $2.6 million pre-tax using an 8-3/4 percent discount rate. However, the discount rate on the parent companies books was 5-1/4 percent. Applying this rate to the subsidiary's future obligations would have almost doubled the pre-tax liability. Clearly, the assumptions chosen as well as the average age of the work force being carved out of the pension plan, the date of the last actuarial analysis and assumptions in that analysis as to salaries to be paid at termination, future inflationary increases in salaries and turnover rates all significantly affect the purchaser's financing. Once the variables are understood and agreed upon between buyer and seller, the appropriate discount from book value to reflect the new liability, on an after tax basis, can be taken. Interestingly, since this liability can be amortized (and funded) over as much as 40 years, it can represent excellent "in place" financing at the time of acquisition provided the liability is reflected in the purchase price negotiations.

(2) Labor Relations

Many companies that at one time gave labor unions exceedingly rich pension plans and health, welfare and insurance benefits later try to free themselves from these obligations by selling the company or its divisions. Although each union contract must be examined individually, a trend has been to tie these benefits to cost of living escalators. Therefore, each one must be carefully examined with respect to the impact on future projected cash flows and, as a result, on the purchase price.

(3) Accounting

Accounting practices differ a great deal. For example, many private companies have unaudited figures, and divisions of large public companies are audited infrequently. There are also choices between conservative and liberal methodologies used which may confuse the buyer as to the real receivables and inventory numbers.

Inventory methods in a small division of a large corporation may be much more liberal in treating obsolescence than a small privately held tax-conscious company and, therefore, careful investigation of the target company's inventory policies is critical. Certainly, the secured lenders will independently examine such policies and verify the actual inventory before closing so the sooner problems are discovered, the better.

(4) Cash Flow Projections

New owners always tend to overestimate cost cutting improvements and growth potential. It is best for both bank financing and internal budgeting to conser- ͏ sent these figures. Special attention should ͏ the company's cash flow performance in ͏ ars. Sellers are of little help in this since it ͏ est interests to have potential buyers use ͏ rates and smooth curves.

ss Cycles

͏ ies serving industries with constant cyclical ͏ as housing, automotive, chemicals, and ͏ ͏ment often have earnings cycles related to ͏ industry they serve. Purchases negotiated ͏ ͏om of the cycle and in a psychological ͏ ͏oor earnings can often be quite favorable if ͏ ing business is well positioned to partici- ͏sequent recoveries.

͏perational Problems

Positive results can be gained from checking for details at the target company which might otherwise be overlooked: caretaker top management, a lackluster or improperly compensated marketing effort, poor controls, manufacturing inefficiencies, price skittishness instead of leadership, and a host of other problems that can be used to improve future operations without an infusion of capital.

THE FUTURE OF LEVERAGED BUYOUTS

We believe that leveraged buyout financing for acquisitions will continue to be attractive and viable in the 80's because:

(a) politically mandated inflation will continue to reward the flight from cash into assets and further enhance the return potential from real estate type financing leverage.

(b) deconglomeratization will continue as return on capital grows in importance to inflation-sensitive professional managements.

(c) lenders will continue to finance such transactions as the ability to obtain high interest rates, good collateral security and cash flow coverage is attractive.

However, we believe that there will be some credit-based failures in recessionary times, with the attendent negative publicity, because increased competition for deals is driving prices up, quality standards down, and debt levels (as a percent of the total transaction) to new high levels.

A CASE STUDY: ABC CORP.

An interesting example of leveraged buyout financing is a company my firm worked on in the summer of 1979. As a study, it contains many of the key ingredients of a successful transaction and one fateful pitfall.

The target company, ABC Corp., was brought in by an entrepreneur who had met the principal shareholder in a prior acquisition situation. The company was publicly held and located on the edge of an older urban area. Its chief executive officer was in his sixties, owned over 50 percent of the outstanding common stock and had no family members interested in the business. He had done a good job of managing the company's business over the prior six years, but had no strong successor management in place. The company's Balance Sheet at 6/30/79, Summary Income Statements for the prior five years, stock price and P/E ranges, appropriately disguised, appear as Tables 32-6 and 32-7. At the time of our earliest conversations, the stock was 9 bid, up from $2.50 from the prior year, while earnings per share were $4.40 for the year ended 12/31/78. With a book value per share of $16.92 at the end of the same year, the company looked very attractive. The entrepreneur was young, well educated, aggressive and able to get along well with the owner/president. To the seller, the entrepreneur represented a potential way to:

(1) Assure liquidity in the seller's estate;

(2) Assure the continuity of the company's operations due to this new "equity-committed" management;

(3) Sell his company at an attractive price and increase his own after tax income from his investment. At a selling price of $22 per share with deferred income tax consequences due to the proposed "Oppenheimer" asset buyout, his after tax dividend income (assuming a 50 percent tax bracket) would have risen from $5,600 per year to $292,000 on his 55 percent of the stock. This presumes that the proceeds from the sale of the company's assets would have been reinvested at 7½ percent in tax-free municipal bonds and all of this income paid out to shareholders of the old ABC Corp.;

(4) A three year management contract to stay on and run the company at a 50 percent higher salary level;

(5) A method to personally gain access to the company's excess cash of over $2.0 million which was building rapidly. Dividends would have had to be taxed twice—once at the corporation level and once personally when received.

To the entrepreneur, the attraction of this deal focused on its highly financeable assets, worth significantly more than book value per share. At 6/30/79, the company's assets permitted the following borrowing:

Source (000's)	Book Value	Potential Financing	Funds Available
Cash	$2,600	100%	$2,600
Accounts Receivable	1,400	80%	1,120
Inventories			
Finished Goods	1,306	60%	784
Work in Process	924	10%	92
Raw Materials	370	50%	185
	2,600		1,061
Plant and Land	2,000 (1)	75%	1,500
Machinery and Equipment	2,000 (2)	50%	1,000
Equity			1,069
			$8,350

Uses (000's)	
Proceeds to selling corporation	7,100
Payment of Long Term Debt	390
Working Capital, Costs of closing, professional fees	$8,350

(1) Estimated fair market value
(2) Estimated liquidity value; "under the hammer" value would be somewhat less.

The assumptions here include an accounts receivable and inventory line of credit from a bank; a five-year maturity, 20 year amortization real estate mortgage and a seven year machinery and equipment term loan.

In addition, the entrepreneur was able to convince potential financing sources that a combination of his entrepreneurial talents and the president/seller's ongoing management expertise could successfully manage the company. $951,000 of equity was raised from a private venture capital group in the form of $869,000 of 10 year subordinated debentures plus $82,000 of equity for 41 percent of the common stock. The entrepreneur invested $118,000 personally for 59 percent of the common stock to be outstanding.

As is often the case, the entrepreneur was required to invest a sum of money which, if lost, would "hurt" his overall financial position. This is not intended to be cruel, but rather reflects a desire on the part of the other equity holders to assure themselves that the entrepreneur will stick with the company and help work out any

problems through good and bad times. Also, the venture group's $800,000 of Subordinated Debentures allowed them to get control of the new company, via the right to elect additional directors under various negative scenarios:

(a) if the company's earnings dropped 35 percent below budget for a year without correcting the trend in the subsequent two quarters, or;
(b) losses were recorded for two successive quarters; in both cases, the control situation could be reversed after two quarters of on-track results.

The entrepreneur was also required to guarantee the first $500,000 of bank secured financing. Again, the bank's intent here was to assure itself that the entrepreneur would stay involved in the company to help collect the outstanding receivables and liquidate the other collateral if the company ever got into trouble.

At this point, the transaction should have been closeable—all financing and agreements were in place. However, it did not close and shortly afterward the deal broke. The factors which led to this illustrate some of the key problems in such transactions. As the deal progressed, the seller began to experience "seller's remorse"—an epidemic of fears and concerns which really revolved around the fact that he had been his own boss for 17 years, taken the company from debt-ridden problems to cash-rich prosperity and was not sure that he now wanted to give up control of it all. His verbalized concerns included selling price, the economic risk to the company of preparing and circulating a proxy to secure shareholders approval and then having the deal not go through, and, finally, a fear that, at the last minute, the banks would pull their financing commitments and the deal would collapse. The buyer and his advisors did not fully realize the depths of these fears. The symptoms of the problem—requests for a higher selling price and an escrowed cash deposit to cover proxy and legal costs in the event the buyer did not close—were not difficult to overcome. However, these did not directly address the "seller's remorse" problem and therefore did not work. In retrospect, this problem would have been best handled by earlier sensitivity to the seller's fears and an escrowed deposit of significant proportions, on the seller's part, which would have gone to the buyer if the seller pulled out for any reason. This would have more completely committed the seller. The buyer's team, mindful of the need to avoid misleading publicity concerning this publicly held company, were persuaded not to require such a deposit.

In conclusion, the buyer and his advisors spent

significant amounts of time and money only to fail. The seller is now older, continuing to manage his company well and has not found the solutions to his original problems of liquidity and corporate succession. In spite of the attractiveness of this transaction to all parties, its positive conclusion came down to personalities and their interaction. Attractive numbers still could not guarantee the deal.

Table 32-6—ABC Corp.

Balance Sheet—6/30/79—(000-s)

Current Assets		Current Liabilities	
Cash	$2,600	Current Long-Term Debt	$ 150
Accounts Receivable	1,400	Accounts Payable	330
Inventory	2,600	Accrued Expenses	700
Total Current Assets	$6,600	Total Current Liabilities	$1,180
Gross Property & Equipment	3,000	Deferred Items	280
Net Property & Equipment	1,500	Long-Term Debt	390
Total Assets	$8,100	Equity	6,250
		Total Debt & Equity	$8,100

Table 32-7

Table — ABC Corporation
(000's)

	1974	1975	1976	1977	1978
Sales	$6,442	$5,100	$8,920	$11,738	$10,890
Pre-Tax, Pre-Interest Income	912	702	1,034	2,372	2,568
Net Income	392	328	440	1,122	1,328
Earnings Per Share	$1.20	$1.00	$1.34	$3.38	$3.94
Book Value/Share	$7.56	$8.52	$9.86	$13.24	$16.92
P/E Range	3.9-1.1X	5.7-1.3X	2.8-1.3X	1.9-.74X	4.7-2X
Price/Book Value	.63-.17	.68-.15	.38-.18	.49-.19	1.1-.47

ROBERT L. FROME

ROBERT L. FROME, a New York City attorney, is a member of the firm of Olshan, Grundman & Frome. He holds a Bachelor of Laws degree from the Harvard Law School, a Master of Laws degree and a Bachelor of Science degree from New York University. He writes a regular monthly column called "Buying and Selling Securities" in the New York Law Journal and is the author of "Private Placements: Forms and Techniques (Law & Business, Inc. 1980) and "Sales of Securities by Corporate Insiders" (Practising Law Institute 1977). He was also an associate professor of law at Brooklyn Law School, where he lectured on federal regulation of securities and taxes.

ALAN M. GETZOFF

ALAN M. GETZOFF, a New York City attorney, is an associate of the firm of Olshan, Grundman & Frome. He holds a Juris Doctor degree and Master of Business Administration degree from Syracuse University and a Bachelor of Arts degree from the State University of New York at Binghamton. He has on numerous occasions collaborated with Robert L. Frome in the preparation of Mr. Frome's regular monthly column called "Buying and Selling Securities" in the New York Law Journal.

33

Structuring the Buyout

ROBERT L. FROME
ALAN M. GETZOFF

A leveraged buyout ("LBO") is a transaction in which borrowings are used to fund all or a large portion of the price paid to buy a business. Generally, the borrowings are arranged with the expectation that the earnings of the business will repay the borrowings. The LBO potentially has great rewards for the buyers who, although they frequently make little or no investment, own the business free and clear after the acquisition loans are repaid by the earnings of the business. LBO's are often arranged to enable the managers of subsidiaries or divisions of large corporations to purchase a subsidiary or division which the corporation wants to divest. In addition, LBO's are used by groups of managers and investors to purchase private companies.

TECHNIQUES FOR THE LEVERAGED BUYOUT OF PUBLICLY HELD COMPANIES

The LBO is also a going private technique being employed by controlling shareholder/managers and/or acquisition minded investors, to acquire publicly owned companies. In these transactions, the LBO is accomplished by the sale of substantially all the assets of a company for cash to, or alternatively a cash merger into, a privately held corporation often owned by shareholder/managers of the public firm. The private company finances the acquisition largely with borrowed funds, the payment of which is secured by, or satisfied with, the newly acquired assets or the proceeds from the partial sale thereof. Typically, the private company employs the managers of the liquidating public firm under long-term employment contracts.

The Securities and Exchange Commission ("SEC") began to concern itself with going private

transactions during the mid-1970's, when it became attractive for majority shareholders of public companies to buy out the minority at depressed stock prices and in many instances, relieve the company from costly and burdensome SEC reporting and disclosure requirements.[1] Since conflicts of interest are inherent in such transactions, particularly in light of substantial benefits which accrue to participating shareholder/managers in the LBO, serious questions were raised with respect to proper disclosure and adequate protection of minority shareholders' interests.

In structuring the LBO, the practitioner should carefully consider the transaction from the perspective of the four main participants—the acquiring company, the majority shareholder/managers of the acquired company, the minority shareholders of the acquired company and the Securities and Exchange Commission.

SALE OF ASSETS FORMAT

The LBO transaction will generally take one of two basic formats: the sale of assets or the cash merger. Under the cash merger format to be discussed later, the acquired company disappears upon merger into the acquiring company and its shareholders receive cash for their shares. Under the sale of assets format, on the other hand, the operating assets become part of the buying company but the selling company will generally be given the option of either receiving cash or continuing to hold their shares in the selling company whose cash will then be used to make other investments.

---

[1]Proposed Rule 13e-3, Exchange Act Release No. 14185 (November 17, 1977) (1977-1978 Transfer Binder) FED. SEC. L. REP. (CCH) ¶81,366

General Description

In the typical LBO structured as a sale of assets, a public company (the "Seller"), agrees to sell substantially all of its assets to an unaffiliated, newly organized and non-operating company (the "Buyer"). As part of the agreement, the Buyer will assume substantially all the liabilities of the Seller.

The Buyer, which intends to continue the operations of the Seller's business, enters into long-term employment agreements with the management of the Seller. In addition, it amends its certificate of incorporation in order to assume the corporate name of the Seller and proceeds without interruption to conduct operations of the business thereunder.

The Buyer finances the acquisition primarily with debt, the substantial portion of which is secured by the assets purchased. Although the Buyer assumes the Seller's liabilities, the Seller usually remains secondarily liable on certain liabilities, such as long term leases.

Upon consummation of the sale, the Seller amends its certificate of incorporation to change its name and thereby make way for the Buyer to assume the business name of longstanding. The Seller has a number of alternatives at this point—having no liabilities and its only asset being the cash proceeds from the sale. Frequently, the Seller will offer to repurchase its shares for cash and use the proceeds from the sale remaining after the repurchase or redemption of its shares, to invest in tax-exempt securities or dividend paying stocks. The exact investment strategy is dependent on the Seller's objectives and status for federal income tax purposes. However, to obtain the best tax treatment, the Seller will generally seek to qualify as a registered, closed-end investment company under the Investment Company Act of 1940 provided more than 100 shareholders remain after the purchase or redemption is completed.

Financing

At the heart of the LBO transaction is the concept of financing an acquisition by employing the assets of the acquired company as a basis for raising capital. Large unused borrowing capacity is the characteristic which enables a Buyer to use the Seller's assets to borrow the purchase price. Specific factors which may exist to enhance borrowing capacity are: (i) large amounts of excess cash and cash equivalents such as certificates of deposit and other short term paper, (ii) limited debt outstanding, (iii) demonstrated ability over a number of years to achieve substantial earnings, (iv) substantial undervalued assets, which, when taken individually have a market value in excess of the depreciated value at which they are carried on the Seller's balance sheets, sometimes called "hidden equity," (v) subsidiaries with operations in unrelated industries which possess large amounts of excess properties that can be readily liquidated for cash without detriment to ongoing operations and (vi) the potential for "hidden cash flow" for the Buyer arising from income sheltered by depreciable property the basis of which is readjusted upward as a consequence of the sale.

Typically, the Buyer will consist of a parent corporation and a wholly owned subsidiary, the latter of which serves as the acquiring company. The purchase price for Seller's assets is raised in part by equity contributions by the Buyer's group in consideration for common shares received by them in the parent corporation. These funds are sometimes funneled to the subsidiary acquiring company. The remaining and principal portion of funds for the purchase, however, are raised from proceeds of loans obtained through a pledge of the newly acquired assets. The loan agreements may grant the lenders, as further protection, personal recourse against the members of the Buyer's group for all or part of the debt. For example, *In the Matter of Woods Corporation,*[2] the consideration to be paid was $30 million plus the assumption of federal and state income taxes of the Seller payable as a result of the sale of its assets and assumption of all other liabilities of the Seller. The purchase was to be financed primarily by two bank loans totaling $40 million. The terms of those loan agreements restricted the lenders to personal recourse against the individual members of the Buyer's group to the extent of $8 million and, in addition, enabled the lenders to force a particular member of the Buyer's group to purchase a subsidiary of the acquired company for $6.5 million, which obligation was secured by his personal stockholdings in an unrelated public company. In the event of default, the lenders would first proceed against the Buyer's group and, for the remainder of the $40 million loan package, against the assets of the acquired company. In other words, in the event the lenders received only 35 million on the loan, the guarantors would bear the 5 million loss and make the lenders whole.

Because of the complexities and uncertainties associated with arranging financing of this nature, the purchase agreement should provide that the obtaining of the financing by the Buyer is a condition precedent to the Buyer's obligations under the agreement. In addition, where there are several different types of

---

[2]*In the Matter of Woods Corporation,* Exchange Act Release No. 15334 (November 16, 1978)

debt and stock, often with significantly different and competing interests with respect to the extent of security and priority in the event of default, consideration should be given to allowing enough leeway to resolve these problems between the time the purchase agreement is signed and the final closing.

The amount of financing sought in the LBO transaction depends primarily on the purchase price negotiated between the Buyer and Seller. In general, this price is greater than the market value of Seller's shares outstanding but is often less than the book value. In addition, the Buyer assumes all Seller's liabilities including income tax up to and through the closing as well as all liabilities arising in connection with the claims of dissenting shareholders. With respect to Buyer's assumption of the latter liability, the Buyer's obligations, and those of its lenders, may be conditioned on there being no more than a specified percentage of the outstanding shares of the acquired company dissenting. This built in protection provides an escape valve for the Buyer in the event dissenting shareholders cause the LBO to vary too far from the terms agreed upon.

Typically, in a sale of assets transaction, the Buyer will pay all expenses of the Seller incurred in connection with the asset sale and in some instances, will even pay all taxes chargeable to Seller resulting from the sale of its assets. This may take the form of a loan from the Buyer to the Seller for Seller's tax liability from the sale of its assets, the repayment of which is subject to, and only to the extent of, any tax refund Seller receives from the sale. The purchase agreement may also provide for cross-indemnification by the parties for liabilities and expenses incurred as a result of material misrepresentations or omissions in the Seller's proxy statement furnished to its shareholders which is based on information given by the indemnifying party.

The Buyer must be careful in arranging financing to balance the following two key factors: first, to sufficiently leverage its debt to maximize return on its equity investment and second, to do so without unduly burdening the company with a debt structure that will drain it of funds needed for continued operations and future growth.

Although it appears that raising the necessary financing to pay the purchase price, providing for the various liabilities and contingencies, and continuing operations of the acquired business are the concerns of the Buyer, the Seller too has a vested interest in the Buyer's success in structuring the financial package. First, the Seller will have expended considerable time and money in legal, accounting, investment counseling and other related fees incurred in connection with

negotiating the transaction, preparing the proxy materials and communicating with its shareholders. These expenses will not be refunded if the Buyer is unable to complete its financial package by the closing date. The Seller may seek to protect itself by requiring a deposit to cover such a contingency, although this is not generally done. Second, if the transaction fails due to insufficient financing, the Seller might have sacrificed in the interim other buyout opportunities from competing bidders on favorable terms. Finally, even if the sale is consummated, the Seller usually will remain secondarily liable on certain obligations from which it is unable to obtain releases such as equipment leases and long term real estate rental obligations. Buyer's financing, albeit sufficient to consummate the sale, may soon cast the Buyer in default of its secondary liability if the financing package is over-leveraged.

Employment Arrangements

Essential to the LBO transaction is the structuring of employment arrangements with present management of the Seller. A well-conceived management plan with built-in incentives at all levels of management will assure the Buyer of continued operational success and will make the entire transaction more appealing to senior management personnel seeking continued employment and financial security. Simultaneously with the closing, and as a condition precedent to the Buyer's obligation to consummate the sale of assets pursuant to the purchase agreement, the Buyer and the senior management group of the Seller will enter into long-term employment agreements. Typically, this will take the form of a partnership and management agreement, individual employment agreements or a combination of the two. This format is best illustrated by the employment arrangements in the November, 1978 sale of assets transaction involving Donkenny, Inc. ("Donkenny") as discussed below.

The management group, comprised of the senior management personnel of the Seller, was organized as a general partnership and charged with the general management of the continued operations of the Seller's business subject to certain powers retained by the board of directors of the Buyer. The senior officer of the Seller was named managing partner, responsible for the business affairs of the partnership. Among the powers reserved by the board under the management agreement were the authority to act with respect to major capital expenditures and commitments; mergers, consolidations, major acquisitions and sales of all or substantially all of the company's assets; major debt financing; budget approval; and direction, oversight and control of operations in general. The management agreement and partnership agreement provided for a term of 15 years commencing with the closing of the sale transaction.

The management agreement further provided for the election of the partners as officers of the Buyer at prearranged salaries in excess of then current levels. Obtaining partner status in the future was conditioned upon being an officer or management employee of the Buyer. Separate employment agreements ranging in duration from five (5) to seven (7) years were entered into with the highest salaried partners. Fringe benefits were maintained in the management agreement, including deferred compensation arrangements with each of the officers in an annual amount equal to 20 percent of their annual salaries, which were previously available to the officers.

As a substitute for increases in regular salaries to the partners and other highly paid employees and as an inducement to maintain the high quality of management, the management agreement also provided for the creation of an incentive profit fund by the Buyer. Payments from the fund, if earned, were in addition to salaries and other fringe benefits, and were paid to the partners and other employees of the Buyer selected by the partnership. Increases in the salaries of partners and other employees who benefit from the profit fund however, required the specific approval of the board of directors of the Buyer.

The incentive profit fund was divided into three components:

1. *The Partners' Share.* This share amounts to 50 percent of the total fund and is payable to the partners only at fixed percentages as set forth in the management agreement. The fixed percentages are based on the partners' current compensation and range from 5 percent to 20 percent of the total profit fund for each partner. These percentages are subject to modification by the managing partner.

2. *The Discretionary Share.* This share amounts to 20 percent of the total profit fund and is payable at the discretion of the managing partner to partners or other employees, other than the managing partner.

3. *The Non-Partners' Share.* This share amounts to 30 percent of the fund and is payable at the discretion of the managing partner to employees of the Buyer who are not partners.

In allocating payments from the Discretionary Share and the Non Partners' Share, the managing partner takes into account with respect to each partner or other employee, as the case may be, the length of service, the current level of compensation and the performance during the year for which such profit fund is payable.

After the close of each fiscal year in which payments from the Buyer are due the profit fund, the Buyer is required to make payments from the Discretionary Share and Non-Partners' Shares to such employees and/or partners as the general partner directs. However, with respect to the Partners' Share, there is deducted pro rata from each such share any expenses of operation of the partnership.

Donkenny earned $8,044,276 in calendar 1977. In calculating the profit fund for the first fiscal year following the sale in 1978, $7,000,000 was agreed as the base earnings figure, and $8,000,000 for any fiscal year thereafter. The profit fund is computed to equal the sum of (i) net earnings for the fiscal year to the extent such net earnings exceed the base earnings figure in such fiscal year and do not exceed an amount equal to 100/90ths of the base earnings, plus (ii) 10 percent of the excess of net earnings over 100/90ths of base earnings. For example, if the Buyer has net earnings of $8,200,000 in its first fiscal year, the profit fund will be computed as follows:

(i) Net earnings ($8,200,000) to
     extent it does not exceed 100/90ths
     times base earnings ($7,000,000) ...$7,777,777.78
     less base earnings 7,000,000.00
          First Component of Profit Fund 777,777.78

(ii) Net earnings 8,200,000.00
     less base earnings ($7,000,000)
     times 100/90ths 7,777,777.78
     Subtotal   422,222.22

     Excess of net earnings over 100/90ths
     of base earnings times 10% .... × 10%
          Second Component of Profit Fund.   42,222.22
     Total Profit Fund $820,000.00

Net earnings for purposes of computing the profit fund are determined in accordance with generally accepted accounting principles before the deduction of federal and state income taxes. In addition, net earnings are determined as if the acquisition did not take place. This is done in order that valuation of pre- and post-acquisition earnings figures will not be materially altered as a consequence of changes in accounting which result from the sale. Accordingly, assets, including inventory, are valued and depreciated at historical cost basis in the hands of the Seller and no deductions are allowed for interest on Buyer's indebtedness incurred in connection with financing the acquisition or for interest expenses incurred on debt borrowed from the Buyer's parent company to the extent they exceed the cost of such funds if they were borrowed from an unaffiliated party.

Provision was also made in the management agreement to establish a minimum fund of $250,000 to be used as incentive compensation for all employees except the most highly salaried partners in the event earnings as computed above are not sufficient to result in a profit fund.

Finally, the agreement contained a termination provision which may be exercised at the sole option of the Buyer in the event the net earnings from operations are less than $4 million in each of two consecutive full fiscal years of the Buyer.

Repurchase or Redemption of Seller's Shares

Promptly after the closing of the sale of its assets pursuant to the terms of the agreement, the Seller will usually offer to purchase from its stockholders, all or any portion of their holdings for cash at a price equal to the net asset value per share. Shareholders who do not accept the offer will continue as shareholders of the Seller which will be operated as an investment company.

This aspect of the LBO transaction is typically structured to result in favorable tax consequences to controlling shareholder/managers who remain as stockholders after the sale. (See the discussion of *In the Matter of Spartek,*[3] *infra).* However, the minority shareholders may face numerous disadvantages if they do not sell. In structuring this aspect of the LBO transaction, the practitioner must consider the impact of the offer to purchase on both controlling shareholders and minority shareholders alike.

First, the repurchase of shares will result in a substantial reduction in the number of shareholders and the number of shares outstanding. Consequently, if the shares of the Seller public company were traded on a national exchange prior to the repurchase offer, it is possible that the reduction in shareholders and shares outstanding will cause limited trading of the Seller's stock or even de-listing from the exchange. Such limited trading or de-listing could adversely effect the liquidity and valuation of the Seller's stock.

Second, should the number of shareholders remaining after the repurchase amount to 100 or less, the Seller would, subject to the favorable vote of its remaining shareholders and the granting of an order by the SEC, terminate its registration under the Securities and Exchange Act of 1934 ("1934 Act") and the Investment Company Act of 1940 ("Investment Company Act"), if it was so registered at the time. In that event, the shareholders of the Seller would lose the protections afforded by these acts including the filing of periodic and other financial reports with the SEC, e.g., annual reports, current reports concerning specific events, reports on insider trading and proxy statements.

Third, as a consequence of the repurchase, the voting interests of the remaining shareholders will be proportionately increased. Since the controlling shareholders will commonly retain their shareholdings, their effective voting control over the future affairs of the Seller as an investment company will be even greater than before.

Fourth, the purchase offer by the Seller will allow each shareholder, after consideration of his own tax position and other factors, to either (i) retain his investment remaining a shareholder in the Seller constituted as an investment company and not paying any tax, or (ii) elect to sell his shares for the cash price and recognize taxable gain or loss. This transaction is structured to benefit substantial shareholders in high tax brackets who have a low basis in their shares since it permits these shareholders to convert their equity interests on a tax-free basis into an interest in the investment company paying regular income.

Fifth, in those LBO transactions where the Buyer agrees to pay the Seller's corporate taxes incurred on the sale of its assets, this payment may not be reflected in the tender price per share made to the Seller's stockholders. If this be the case, the remaining shareholders who do not tender their stock effectively obtain an added benefit. In the case of *Woods*[4], *supra,* where the tender price was $10.95 per share, payment by the Buyer of the Seller's corporate tax liability on the sale of its assets of approximately $2.8 million amounted to an added benefit of at least $1 per share to the remaining shareholders.

Sixth, if the Seller qualifies under the Investment Company Act to operate as a closed-end, diversified investment company after the purchase offer is completed, the stock of the Seller will not be redeemable at the holder's option. Furthermore, since the shares of a closed-end investment company customarily trade at a discount from net asset value, there is a likelihood of an immediate decline after the purchase offer expires in the market value of the Seller's shares relative to the tender price.

Finally, the investment policy of the Seller after it has become an investment company is usually designed to suit the particular tax requirements of the controlling shareholder/managers in higher tax brack-

---

[3] *In the Matter of Spartek Inc., et al.,* Exchange Act Release No. 15567 (February 14, 1979), (1979) FED. SEC. L. REP. (CCH) ¶81,961
[4] *Woods, supra* note 2

ets by gearing the Seller's portfolio to primarily tax exempt securities, the interest on which is distributed to the shareholders tax free if the Seller qualifies as a regulated investment company for Federal tax purposes. This investment policy will in all likelihood be less favorable for minority shareholders in lower tax brackets.

Registration of Seller as an Investment Company

As discussed above, the final stage of the LBO transaction may involve the change of the Seller's business following the sale of assets to that of a registered closed-end, diversified-investment company. The newly constituted investment company invests the proceeds from the sale in tax-exempt securities or preferred or other dividend paying stocks, the exact composition of which depends to a large extent on Seller's status for federal income tax purposes. The ultimate objective of this last step of the LBO transaction is to afford Seller's shareholder/managers in high tax brackets the benefit of receiving maximum tax-free distributions of income from their equity investment.

An investment company is defined under the Investment Company Act as a company engaged primarily in the business of investing, reinvesting, and trading in securities of other issuers.[5] The Seller will be required to register under the Act unless it qualifies for the exemptions for issuers whose securities are beneficially owned by 100 persons or less and which is not making, or proposing, a public offering of its securities.[6] As a practical matter, it is rare that in broadly held public companies 100 or fewer stockholders remain after the Seller's repurchase of shares. As a company registered under the Act, the operations and management of the Seller will be subject to SEC regulation as well as the reporting requirements of the Investment Company Act.

Furthermore, the Seller's investment policies will be limited to those investments set forth in its registration documents under the Act. Changes in investment policy after registration can be made only with majority shareholder approval, although the controlling shareholder/managers of the Seller will typically own sufficient shares to assure any such approval.

The Seller's holdings as a diversified company must be represented, to the extent of 75 percent of the value of its total assets, by cash and cash equivalents, government securities, securities of other investment companies and other securities limited in respect of any one issuer to an amount not greater in value than 5 percent of the value of its total assets and not more than 10 percent of the outstanding voting securities of such other issuer.[7] Since the primary investment purpose of the Seller will probably be to receive current income for its controlling shareholder/managers in higher income brackets, the Seller may seek to invest exclusively in tax exempt securities. As a regulated investment company, the Seller would then be permitted to distribute its income to shareholders without paying federal income taxes at the corporate level and to make tax-free distributions to shareholders of income received from the tax-exempt obligations.[8]

Typically, the Seller's assets will be managed by an investment advisor engaged by the Seller's board of directors and subject to shareholder approval. Furthermore, composition of the Seller's board of directors will have to be changed once it operates as a closed-end, diversified investment company in order to accommodate the requirement under the Investment Company Act, that "interested persons" may not constitute more than 60 percent of the Board.[9] "Interested persons" in this context refers to officers or employees of the Seller as well as its investment advisors or affiliated persons of the investment advisors.[10]

CASH MERGER FORMAT

Much of the discussion of the LBO transaction structured as a sale of assets is equally applicable to the cash merger format, particularly with respect to financing and employment arrangements. The following is a general description of the structure of the cash merger LBO.

General Description

The first step in structuring the cash merger format begins with the formation of parent and subsidiary shell corporations by the acquiring group. The subsidiary corporation is then merged into the acquired company on the effective date of the transaction with the acquired company surviving the merger as the

---

[5]Investment Company Act of 1940, §3(a)(1), 15 USC §80a (1970)
[6]Investment Company Act of 1940, §3(c)(1), 15 USC §80a (1970)
[7]Investment Company Act of 1940, §5(b)(1), 15 USC §80a (1970)
[8]Internal Revenue Code §852(b)(5), 26 USC §1 et seq. (1970)
[9]Investment Company Act of 1940, §10(a), 15 USC §80a (1970)
[10]Investment Company Act of 1940, §2(a)(19), 15 USC §80a (1970)

wholly owned subsidiary of the acquiring parent corporation. Also on the effective date, the shareholders of the acquired company will be entitled to receive cash for each share held by them, or in the alternative, elect to exercise their appraisal rights as dissenting shareholders pursuant to the provisions of the state law in which the acquired company is incorporated.

The primary purpose of the two-tiered corporate structure to the acquiring group is to provide maximum flexibility for future tax planning. For example, a preliminary review by the acquiring parent company may suggest that, following the merger of the acquired company and the subsidiary, a further merger of the surviving company into the parent would result in a substantial increase in the tax basis of the surviving company's assets for federal income tax purposes. This would result in higher costs of goods sold, increased depreciation deductions, reduced income or gain on the sale of other assets and, if the resulting company is sufficiently profitable, substantial reduction in future income taxes over a period of years. However, the advantages from this so-called "step-up" in tax basis could be offset by substantial current tax liability incurred as a result of recapture of previously deducted depreciation and other prior income tax benefits. If this is the case, additional funds might have to be borrowed to meet the current income tax liability. This decision of whether to merge the surviving company into the parent is best reserved until after the initial merger is complete for the following reasons: (i) it requires an in-depth study of the assets of the acquired company and the tax consequences to the parent of effecting the "step up" in basis which is time-consuming, is best accomplished when the assets are in the hands of the acquiring company, and may otherwise unduly delay the closing of the principal LBO transaction, (ii) it may upset the acquiring group's delicate financial package if it is determined that additional financing will be required to satisfy current income tax liabilities, and (iii) the "step up" treatment is a tax planning decision exclusive to the purchaser and does not directly affect the transaction, rights or interests of the acquired company and its shareholders.

As with the sale of assets transaction, the management of the acquired company are given long term employment contracts to continue operations, which is a condition precedent to consummation of the merger.

Financing for the cash merger is raised through borrowings, the sale of equity securities of the parent company and debt securities of the subsidiary. As part of the merger agreement the liabities of the subsidiary, evidenced largely by the borrowings and debt sec-

urities issued by the subsidiary, are then assumed by and become the obligations of the resulting company. However, the former shareholders of the acquired company who are "cashed out" have no secondary liability as a result of the merger.

Financing the cash merger, like the asset sale format, is to a large extent dependent upon the financial condition of the acquired company, particularly with respect to its existing cash reserves, potential earning power and debt capacity. The debt instruments issued by the subsidiary and assumed by the acquired company upon merger, will invariably contain numerous covenants restricting the sale of assets. In addition, it is generally anticipated in structuring financing arrangements, that promptly after the merger is consummated, a portion of the financing will be repaid with a substantial portion of the resulting company's excess cash as well as with the proceeds realized from the sale of certain excess properties not required in the areas of the resulting company's principal business. The first proceeds so realized are typically applied first to reduce bank and other indebtedness and the remainder to partially redeem preferred stock issued in connection with the financing.

Illustration of Financing

The LBO structured as a cash merger in May, 1979, involving Houdaille Industries, Inc. ("Houdaille") illustrates the complex capital structure often employed in financing transactions of this nature. In Houdaille, the merger was conditioned upon receipt of approximately $355 million in total financing of which $60 million (16.9 percent) was raised from bank borrowing under a revolving credit loan, $246.5 million (69.4 percent) from the issuance of debt securities including senior notes, senior subordinated notes and junior subordinated notes, and $48.5 million (13.7 percent) from the sale of two classes of preferred stock (senior and junior) and two classes of common stock (voting and non voting) of the parent company. This created a high debt to equity ratio of six which, in the judgment of the lenders participating in the transaction, could be supported by Houdaille's substantial earning power and large debt capacity — features which made the company a prime candidate for leveraged financing.

Participants in the financing were composed of more than twenty financial institutions including large banks, insurance companies, institutional pension and retirement plans and other financial institutions. Additional participants included the private investment firm which structured the transaction, two limited partnerships formed by members of the investment firm and certain officers and other key personnel of Houdaille.

Of the voting common stock issued by the parent company in connection with the transaction, the financial institutions were issued approximately one-half, certain key management employees received slightly more than 10 percent of the stock, and the investment firms and the limited partnerships formed by its members received one third of the voting stock. All the outstanding shares of the subsidiary company were owned by the parent company.

DISSENTERS' RIGHTS

In the LBO effected as a cash merger dissenting shareholders will generally have the right to seek the fair value of their shares in statutory appraisal proceedings. However, statutory appraisal rights are not universally available to dissenters in sale of assets transactions and therefore the law of the state of incorporation of the Seller should be consulted.[11] In order to illustrate the general procedures for exercising appraisal rights, it shall be assumed that such rights are available under the governing state law in both asset sale and cash merger transactions.

Where shareholders elect not to accept the cash price per share under the terms of the transaction, the shareholders are entitled to dissent therefrom and have the fair value of their shares judicially determined and paid to them by complying with the requirements of state law. In order to perfect their statutory rights to appraisal, however, shareholders who elect to dissent must deliver a written demand to the company for appraisal prior to the taking of the vote of shareholders on the proposed transaction and, in addition must not vote in favor of the transaction.

Statutes usually require that after the approval by a vote of the stockholders, or after the effective date of the transaction, the company must give written notice of same to the dissenting shareholders. Usually within a specified time set forth in the statute, the dissenting shareholder has the right to withdraw his demand for an appraisal and to accept the cash payment for his shares as orginally offered by the company. Assuming the shareholder's demand is not withdrawn, and that the dissenting shareholder and the company cannot agree upon a fair price to be paid for the shares, the matter will ultimately come before the state court to fix the value of shares upon the filing of a proceeding by the shareholder. The company also has the option to insti-

tute the proceedings, but it is unlikely that it will ever do so. The state court will then appraise the shares or appoint an appraiser to do so. In determining the fair value of the shares, any element of value arising from the accomplishment of the transaction is usually excluded. The costs incurred in the appraisal proceeding, including reasonable attorney's fees and the fees and expenses of experts, may be assessed against such parties as the court deems proper.

The procedures described above are intended to be very general in nature. However, the particular requirements with respect to appraisal rights may vary between jurisdictions and within jurisdictions between asset sale and cash merger formats. Therefore, in structuring the LBO, careful attention should be paid to the local law.

Occasionally, the agreement of sale of assets or the merger agreement will provide that the buyer or acquiring company will assume the liability for satisfying the claims of dissenting shareholders. However, in some instances, the obligations of the lenders and investors to extend financing may be conditioned on there not being written demands for appraisal by holders of more than a specified percentage of the outstanding stock of the Company. For example, in Houdaille, the entire transaction was conditioned on there being no more than 10 percent of the outstanding shares dissenting.

As a general rule, appraisal rights are more of a theoretical than a practical problem to the principals in a LBO. Insofar as small shareholders are concerned, they would generally prefer to take cash for shares immediately than to suffer the long delay, expense and uncertainty of an appraisal proceeding even if they comply with the technical prerequisites to enforcement of appraisal rights.

DISCLOSURE REQUIREMENTS UNDER THE FEDERAL SECURITIES LAWS

The increasing use and popularity of LBO's as an acquisition technique has heightened the concern of the SEC with respect to adequate disclosure to shareholders and adequate protection of shareholders' interests. In light of the conflicts of interest, the substantial benefits which accrue to participating shareholder/ managers and the absence of arms-length negotiations which are characteristic of LBO transactions, the SEC has taken the position that unaffiliated shareholders should be furnished with detailed infor-

---

[11]In an asset sale transaction, appraisal rights are available in New York and Illinois; New York Business Corporation Law §623, 910 (McKinney's); Illinois Ann. Stat. Ch 32 §73 (Smith-Hurd); but not available in Delaware and California; Delaware General Corporation Law §262; California General Corporation Law §1300(a)

mation so that they can determine whether their rights have been adequately protected and make an informed choice as to their alternatives.

One of the fundamental disclosure requirements under the securities laws, as discussed below, is that the Seller or acquired company state whether it reasonably believes that the transaction is fair or unfair to its unaffiliated shareholders. It is therefore essential in structuring the LBO transaction, to consider throughout, the interplay between the elements of fairness and disclosure.

In the Matter of Spartek, Inc.

In a well-publicized administrative proceeding instituted by the SEC, *In the Matter of Spartek, Inc., et al.*[12], the Commission addressed itself to disclosure requirements in a LBO transaction structured as a sale of assets. *Spartek* involved a proposed sale of assets to an unaffiliated investing group, followed by a tender offer to shareholders and thereafter conversion of the corporation to an investment company. The SEC charged Spartek, Inc. (''Spartek'') and its shareholder/managers with failure to file a current report on Form 8-K with respect to the proposed LBO transaction and conducted an investigation regarding Spartek's failure to disclose material information in its preliminary proxy statement. An offer of settlement consenting to the Commission's findings and agreeing to certain undertakings was submitted by Spartek and accepted by the Commission. The final order of the Commission reflects the views of the SEC Division of Corporation Finance which calls for full and adequate disclosure of the ''reasons for'' and ''effects of'' a proposed LBO and suggests special mechanisms to protect shareholders' interests.[13]

Spartek is a public company listed on the American Stock Exchange and engaged in the manufacture and sale of ceramic products for building and industrial use. The principal shareholders of Spartek were its chairman of the board and a director/vice president, who together owned approximately 39.6 percent of Spartek's outstanding common stock. Although approached on a number of occasions to sell its assets, it was not until the spring of 1977 that Spartek entered into serious discussions regarding a sale. This eventually led to an announcement on December 6, 1977 that an agreement in principle for the sale of assets had been reached. Spartek was represented in the negotiations by its two principal shareholders/managers. The proposed purchasers acted through a variety of entities and

consisted of a group of investors, none of whom were in any way affiliated with Spartek.

There were four main facets to the proposed transaction: the sale agreement, the long-term management agreement, the tender offer to shareholders, and the transformation of Spartek into an investment company.

The agreement provided for the sale of assets to Sparco Operating, Inc. (''Operating'') a corporation formed by the purchasing group for the purpose of making the acquisition and continuing Spartek's business. The agreed-upon purchase price was an amount equal to the number of common shares of Spartek outstanding at the closing date times $17.50. Virtually the entire purchase price of the assets was to be financed through a bank loan to Operating secured by all of the acquired assets and the personal guaranty of one of the investors. Upon consummation of the sale, Operating was to assume the name of Spartek, resume without interruption Spartek's business operations, and employ the senior members of Spartek's management under a fifteen-year management agreement providing in part for certain compensation increases over present salary levels along with a profit-sharing arrangement. Following the sale, a tender offer was to be made to Spartek's shareholders that would give them the option to sell their shares to Spartek at a price of $17.50 per share or continue as shareholders in Spartek, with the understanding that the company would amend its charter in order to become an investment company. In addition, the resulting investment company would seek to qualify as a regulated investment company for federal tax purposes which would permit tax-free income to pass through to its shareholders without taxation on the corporate level.

The findings of the Commission concern the failure of Spartek to file a current report on Form 8-K regarding the proposed sale of assets transaction which might result in a change in control at some future date. The Commission did not elucidate on this omission but its finding seems to imply that a report on Form 8-K is required to be filed when an agreement in principle to effect a LBO transaction is reached.

In July 1978, Spartek filed a preliminary proxy statement with the Commission in connection with the proposed special meeting of shareholders at which a vote was to be taken on the proposed transaction. With respect to the preliminary proxy statement, the Commission concluded that it ''failed to disclose certain principal reasons for the transaction, including the fact

---

[12]*Spartek, supra* note 3
[13]SEC Release No. 34-15572 (February 15, 1979), (1979) FED. SEC. L. REP. (CCH) ‡24,115, at 17,621-4, 17,621-5

that the transaction was structured to give management certain advantages not necessarily available to other shareholders."[14] Thus, the proposed transaction placed management in a significant conflict of interest in relation to Spartek's other shareholders and this was not disclosed.

The Commission based its conclusions on the findings contained in its Report of Investigation. First, the Commission addressed that portion of the preliminary proxy statement which set forth reasons for the proposed transaction. Although it stated that the cash price of $17.50 per share exceeded the market price prior to the public announcement of the transaction, the preliminary proxy statement failed to disclose the special and material benefits to be gained by the shareholder/managers including: "(1) the opportunity to earn tax-free income from Spartek operating as a regulated investment company, in excess of the potential after-tax income from their equity interest in the Corporation operating its current business; (2) the assurance that the [two principal shareholder/managers] and the other members of Spartek's management will be able to retain managing control of the day to day operations of the successor to Spartek; (3) the transfer on a tax-free basis, of their equity investment in Spartek into a more diversified and liquid investment in Spartek operating as a regulated investment company; and (4) the [two principal shareholder/managers'] personal estate liquidity."[15] The Commission's position is that these items are of material importance to shareholders in order for them to understand the potential conflicts of interest and thereby determine for themselves whether the proposed transaction is in their best interests.

Second, the preliminary proxy statement did not disclose representations by Spartek's management to the purchasing group that Spartek's land contained substantial deposits of natural gas with a potential market value in excess of its book value. The Commission concluded that such information is essential in order for shareholders to evaluate the fairness of the price offered. These representations also were of critical importance to the bank which eventually financed Operating's purchase of the assets.

Third, the Commission found in its Report that the preliminary proxy statement was defective in failing to accurately identify the principals behind Operating and its parent, Sparco Holding, Inc., and their respective percentage interests in the purchasing group. Also omitted was a description of the financing arrangements made by the purchasing group which were fundamental to the proposed transaction.

Finally, as to a matter not directly related to leveraged buyouts per se, the Commission concluded that certain misrepresentations were made by the chairman of the board of Spartek to officials of the American Stock Exchange in response to an inquiry regarding unusual trading in Spartek's stock prior to the public announcement of the proposed transaction.

The Commission accepted Spartek's Offer of Settlement in which Spartek agreed, among other things, to (1) retain a "special review person," disinterested in the transaction and with no material affiliations to the parties, who is empowered to represent its public shareholders, negotiate on their behalf the framework and details of the proposed transaction, obtain professional assistance if required, determine whether the transaction is fair in light of available alternatives, and report his findings, (2) file the report of the "special review person" on Form 8-K, (3) file proxy solicitation material with the Commission and hold a shareholders' meeting in the event management decides to proceed with the proposed transaction, and (4) comply with the reporting requirements of the Exchange Act. The two principal shareholder/managers also agreed that in the event a shareholders' meeting is held, they will "neutralize" their votes. That is, they will vote in favor of the transaction only the percentage of their shares equal to the percentage of all other shares voted for approval.[16]

By so ordering, the Commission has all but adopted the view of the Division of Corporation Finance (issued the day after the issuance of the orders, findings and settlement of *Spartek),* implemented its suggestions for such things as "special review persons" and "neutralization" of interested votes, and established a standard for full disclosure of conflicts of interests in LBO transactions.[17] In addition, the various mechanisms utilized in this case to insure that the best interests of the public shareholders are protected from the point of inception of the proposed transaction should be taken into consideration in structuring a LBO transaction.

Division of Corporation Finance

In its widely publicized views appearing in a Securities Exchange Act release[18] regarding disclosure in proxy statements involving "novel, multi-step, sale of

---

[14]*Spartek, supra* note 3 at 81,407
[15]*id.* at 81,405
[16]*id.* at 81,407-8
[17]SEC Release No. 34-15572, *supra* note 13
[18]*id.*

assets transactions," the Division of Corporation Finance of the SEC provided the first set of guidelines and recommended practices in LBO transactions. Although the release does not address itself to cash merger LBO's per se, the staff of the SEC suggested that the release is equally applicable to those transactions. The recommendations of the Division are summarized below.

A. *Actual and Potential Conflicts of Interest.* The release states that the LBO transaction is structured in part to accommodate the tax, investment and management needs of controlling shareholder/managers and the Buyer or acquiring company. Concerned that disclosure in the past has not adequately highlighted these conflicts of interest, the Division recommended, in appropriate cases, a "Special Factors" section be included in the forepart of the proxy statement containing the following disclosure items:[19]

> "1) Disclosure that the principal shareholders or management may have actual or potential conflicts of interest, and description of such conflicts.
>
> "2) Disclosure of the sale price per share compared to the net tangible book value per share.
>
> "3) Disclosure that the Public Seller may remain secondarily liable with respect to liabilities assumed.
>
> "4) Disclosure that certain officers and directors have entered into long term employment contracts with the Purchaser, and if applicable, that they will receive increased salaries and/or the opportunity to share in future profits of the business; and
>
> "5) Disclosure of such other factors with respect to the transaction which management believes require the particular attention by shareholders in making their vote decisions."

B. *Reasons for and Effect of the Transaction.* The Division stated that disclosure in the proxy statement with respect to the "effect of" the transaction should focus on the consequences to the company and its shareholders if the proposed transaction is approved, including legal effects, tax consequences and effects on market liquidity. Disclosure of the "reasons for" the transaction should highlight the reasons management is proposing the transaction. This disclosure should indicate: (i) a brief description of other offers or alternatives considered by the company in lieu of the proposed transaction, made within a reasonable time prior to concluding an agreement in principle and the reasons for rejecting them; (ii) whether management considered during negotiations their own particular

financial circumstances, personal goals and benefits to be derived from the transaction (such as investment diversification and tax advantages); and (iii) the opportunity to continue in management under favorable employment arrangements.

C. *Material Features of the Plan or Transaction.* In light of the fact that management, compromised by conflicts of interest cited above, may negotiate the structure of the transaction, selling price and employment agreements, the Division emphasized the importance of adequate disclosure of the material features of the plan.

The consideration paid to management under employment agreements may ultimately affect the fairness of the consideration received by the shareholders. Therefore, with respect to employment arrangements, disclosure should include a comparison of management compensation under the new arrangement with compensation under existing arrangements. If the compensation formula is, in part, based on future earnings, disclosure should indicate what management would have earned under such a formula based upon present earnings and for a reasonable time in the future based upon stated hypothetical assumptions of future earnings. In addition, any agreement by the acquiring company to make significant capital investments should be disclosed.

The terms of financing of the acquiring company should be described in detail and should provide pro forma financial statements of the acquiring company as well as the identity of the control persons of the acquiring company, particularly if they have guaranteed payment of the liability assumed. The purpose of this disclosure is to enable shareholders to assess, first, the risk that the Seller will be secondarily liable on the debts assumed if these liabilities are not discharged by the acquiring company due to inadequate financing, and second, the possibility that financing problems will forestall consummation of the transaction.

Disclosure is required of the facts which bear upon the fairness of the price offered. The Division has outlined such factors which may include: (i) alternatives to the proposed transaction such as a merger, reorganization or tender offer or terms of any recent or prior offers or negotiations; (ii) where appropriate, information about assets bearing on fair market value, such as real estate, mineral rights or marketable securities which are not necessary to Seller's business, which could subsequently be sold by the acquiring purchaser or its lender or otherwise be used as collateral and which are material to the lender's financing decision; and (iii) the material terms of the financing

---

[19]*id.* at 17,621-4

package of the acquiring company.

Finally, the Division recommended that discussion of the complex tax consequences inherent in LBO transactions should be in a manner easily comprehensible to the shareholder. Such discussion should emphasize the risk in asset-sale transactions that the Seller may be ineligible to realize favorable tax treatment afforded a regulated investment company subsequent to the sale should it fail to qualify as one.

D. *Rights of Shareholders under State Law*. Such discussion should outline the statutory appraisal rights or such other rights available under state law to shareholders who object to the transaction.

E. *General*. In this final category of the release, the Division offered a number of recommended procedures which had been employed in various transactions reviewed by the Commission and which in the Division's opinion assure careful consideration of the interests of shareholders. The first two provisions, neutralization of votes of persons having conflicts and engaging a ''special review person'' to represent and negotiate for the stockholders were contained in the order issued in *Spartek* and discussed above. The third recommendation calls for an independent appraisal of the assets and fairness of the consideration and should include disclosure of fee arrangements, material relationships, if any, between the appraiser and the parties to the transaction and the factors on which the appraisal is based.

It should be noted that the views of the Division in the release are not rules of the SEC. However, these views were, to a large extent adopted in Rules 13e-(3) and (4) subsequently adopted by the SEC.

Rule 13e-3 and Rule 13e-4

On August 2, 1979, the SEC announced the adoption of new Rule 13e-3 and related Schedule 13E-3 which require extensive disclosure of going private transactions by public companies or their affiliates and new Rule 13e-4 and related Schedule 13E-4 which impose substantive regulation and disclosure requirements with respect to tender offers by issuers for their own securities.[20]

Under the general antifraud provisions of the securities laws, prior to the adoption of new Rule 13e-3 and related Schedule 13E-3, there was no explicit requirement that the controlling shareholder/managers make statements respecting the fairness of the transaction. The going private rules are intended to augment and implement the antifraud provisions previously applied in going private transactions by requiring detailed disclosure of the terms of the transaction including the element of fairness. While these rules are not directed at the LBO transaction, the SEC has expressly stated that LBO transactions in the nature of going private transactions are intended to fall within the scope of Rule 13e-3.

A Rule 13e-3 transaction is defined as any of certain enumerated transactions or series of transactions which has a reasonable likelihood or purpose of producing the effect of reducing the number of shareholders of a public company to less than 300 persons or, alternatively, result in the delisting of shares of the company from a national securities exchange and the cessation of authorization for inter-dealer quotation of such shares. It should be noted that the transaction need not produce either effect stated above. All that is required to be subject to the going private rules is that there is a reasonable likelihood that either effect result from the proposed transaction. The reason given by the SEC for regulating those particular effects is because they provide objective criteria for identifying going private transactions.

The enumerated transactions or series of transactions referred to include the purchase or tender offer by an issuer or its affiliates of its own securities, the sale of its assets to an affiliate, or a merger. Although the asset sale LBO transaction typically involves a sale to an unaffiliated third party, the going private rules would still apply because in the second stage of the LBO transaction, the Seller makes a tender offer or purchases its own securities. A conceivable situation where Rule 13e-3 may not apply to such transactions is where a sale is made to an unaffiliated third party followed by a sale of the Seller's assets to a tax-exempt bond fund, distribution to its shareholders of shares of the tax-exempt fund and finally dissolution of the Seller. The SEC staff may justifiably feel that such transactions are within the purposes of and subject to the rule since the end result of the transaction is to eliminate the stockholders' interest in the business in which they had invested.

The end result of a going private transaction is the termination of a publicly held company and elimination of regulatory protections after the company becomes privately held. The main reason given by the SEC for acting in the going private area was to afford protection to shareholders where controlling shareholders, seeking to take advantage of depressed stock prices, offer a premium for minority stockholders' shares that exceeds the current market value but does not reflect the intrinsic value of the shares in the company as a going concern. In addition, the Commission was concerned that state law remedies such as

---

[20]Rule 13e-3, (1979) FED. SEC. L. REP. (CCH), ¶23,703A; Rule 13e-4; (1979) FED. SEC. L. REP. (CCH) ¶23,703B;

statutory appraisal rights of dissenting shareholders were inadequate to safeguard the interests of minority shareholders. The required disclosures under Rule 13e-3, in the Commission's view, may establish a basis for shareholder challenge of the going private transaction in state court.

Rule 13e-3 requires a statement by the company going private as to whether it reasonably believes the transaction is fair or unfair to unaffiliated shareholders and a detailed discussion of the factors upon which such belief is based. Among the factors which the rule requires to be discussed are (i) whether the consideration offered to unaffiliated shareholders constitutes fair value, (ii) whether there is provision for neutralization of votes, (iii) whether a majority of non-employee directors has retained an unaffiliated representative in the nature of a "special review person" to negotiate on behalf of unaffiliated shareholders and/or an appraiser to opine on the fairness of the transaction, and (iv) whether the transaction was approved by a majority of non-employee directors.

It should be noted that Rule 13e-3, as originally proposed, contained an antifraud provision that would have prohibited transactions that were unfair to unaffiliated shareholders. The Commission decided to eliminate the proposed fairness standard, and defer the question until it has had the opportunity to determine the efficacy of Rule 13e-3 as presently constituted and to monitor development of remedies in state law for unfairness in going private transactions. The proposed fairness standard was strongly objected to, however, by commentators of the proposed 13e-3 on the grounds that regulation of fairness amounts to substantive regulation of corporate affairs, which exceeds the authority that the Congress conferred on the SEC.

New Rule 13e-4 and related Schedule 13E-4 provide substantive regulation and disclosure requirements with respect to issuer tender offers. This includes the tender offer portion of a LBO structured as a sale of assets. In such transactions, therefore, compliance and disclosure under both Rules 13e-3 and 13e-4 and their related schedules is required.

Rule 13e-4 applies to issuers whose shares are registered pursuant of §12 of the Securities Exchange Act of 1934, which are required to file periodic reports pursuant to §15 of the 1934 Act, or which are closed-end investment companies registered under the Investment Company Act. Among the requirements under Rule 13e-4, which apply to the second step of the sale of assets transaction, are that (i) the tender offer remains open for a minimum of 15 days, (ii) shareholders have a right to withdraw their tendered securities during a specified time, and (iii) the tender offer must be made to all shareholders and on a pro rata basis. In addition, the rule requires detailed disclosure about the issuer and the purpose and term of the tender offer.

34

Overview of Leveraged Buyouts

ROBERT DOUGLAS COLMAN*

I. ELEMENTS OF A LEVERAGED BUYOUT

Definition

A leveraged buyout is a transfer of ownership of a going concern in which there is a financing involving highly leveraged loans plus venture capital. There is a wide divergence within the financial community as to what constitutes "highly leveraged," and the designation "leveraged buyout" is far from a term of art. For the purposes of this discussion, a leveraged buyout shall be designated as a transaction where the buyers of an ongoing business leverage their own equity money with at least twice as much borrowed funds in order to accomplish the purchase. That is, the leverage factor will be defined as the ratio of long-term debt to equity, of at least 2 to 1. Every example considered in this chapter meets this minimum criterion.

Many manufacturers have a leverage factor of 1 to 3 or less. Thus, even a ratio of 1 to 1 appears highly leveraged in terms of what is standard in most industries. However, the most frequent usage of the term "leveraged buyout" among lenders, investment bankers, lawyers and accountants occurs in situations where there is a leverage factor of at least 2 to 1. If the leverage factor is 1 to 1 or 1.5 to 1, it might be considered "highly leveraged" or "very highly leveraged," but it is not generally referred to as a "leveraged buyout."

There does, however, appear to be an uneasy consensus among those who use the term "leveraged buyout." One transaction which was clearly considered a "leveraged buyout" was the divestiture by a "Fortune 100" of its XYZ Division in 1979. The financing involved $7.8 million in equity and $18 million in

debt, resulting in a leverage factor of 2.3x. After the equity portion had been raised, this transaction was shown to over ten lenders in order to obtain the debt portion of the financing. In every case, the lenders demanded an equity kicker[1] as partial consideration for this loan because the transaction fell into the category of "leveraged buyout."

A distinction must also be made between a leveraged buyout and the more traditional acquisition of one corporation by another. The leveraged buyout is a species of acquisition where the financing medium consists primarily of borrowed funds. Such funds are borrowed against the physical assets and cash flow of the acquired business. This type of financing is not at all unusual in the traditional acquisition. However, the basic difference derives from the fact that there is no long-standing corporation which makes the acquisition in a leveraged buyout. Rather, the buyers in a leveraged buyout are a newly organized and non-operating company capitalized by their equity investment and borrowed funds. The entire resources of the new corporation are then used to pay the purchase price. Because the acquiring entity has limited resources, the acquired business in a leveraged buyout must stand completely on its own. This compounds the problems of obtaining the financing for the transaction. With no "deep pocket" to stand behind the acquisition, a sudden recessionary turn could seriously jeopardize the heavy debt repayments.

Financial Risk, Business Risk, and Cash Flow

There are, from an investment standpoint, two discrete elements of risk: business risk — the chance of a business failure as a result of operating losses caused

*The author gratefully acknowledges the editorial assistance of Jules Backman.
[1] Equity kickers are discussed at pages 531, 537 and 542. Bankers Trust Company; Corporate Financial Services acted as financial advisor in this transaction.

by fundamental factors, and financial risk — the chance of failure caused by the inability of a business to meet the fixed charges imposed on it by its capitalization. Unlike a venture capital investment in equity securities, where there is a low ratio of institutional debt to equity, the investor in a leveraged buyout situation seeks a high ratio. He looks to acquire an established business with a favorable earnings record of long standing and a slow upward trend; good prospects (hence low business risk); and to create a new capitalization structure that contains substantial financial risk.

One approach in identifying potential leveraged buyouts with low business risk is to stick to old-line, mundane companies that are historically profitable and well-managed. The investment banking firm of Carl Marks & Co. follows this approach. The firm stays away from high technology companies whose fortunes can be tenuous from one technological innovation to the next. The buyers are willing to bear the financial risk of leverage, but not the business risk. With some notable exceptions, the leveraged buyout candidate basically would be a manufacturing firm with a low technology, non-fad product line. Its products are proprietary or have an identifiable niche without significant head-to-head competition from heavily capitalized firms. The target firm also must possess sustainable earning power without any significant change in its mode of operation.

Generally, to create the desired amount of financial risk, the "investor" will attempt to finance the majority of the purchase price of the acquired business with borrowings. For example, in Houdaille Industries, Inc. (discussed in detail later in this chapter), the amount of debt securities issued in the financing ($306 million) was more than six times as great as the amount of equity securities issued ($23.5 million of preferred stock and $25 million of common stock).

Aside from the stable earnings history, only an existing company with a small amount of debt is able to support the high debt-to-equity ratios which make leveraged buyouts attractive to investors. Not coincidentally, a public leveraged buyout candidate is often an attractive takeover or acquisition candidate and the use of a leveraged buyout represents an alternative by which a company can remain independent while enabling its shareholders to sell at the full value of their investment.

The total risk involved in the buyout is clearly a function of both the business and financial risks. However, the investor can have a wide latitude in determin-

ing the total risk simply by varying the amount of borrowing employed. Recent transactions have had debt-to-equity ratios as high as 10 to 1, with the typical level between 3 and 5 to 1. The investor, in order to control the risk, does not always incur the maximum available debt load.

Another frequent characteristic of the leveraged buyout company is that the firm has a high proportion of its total assets in tangible property, much of which may have fair market value in excess of its net book value. In the case of a public company the market price is low — rarely a substantial premium over tangible book value — and generally a multiple of net earnings that is seven or less.

Leveraged buyouts are typically conceived and structured by an investment firm. In the last few years several firms have gained considerable recognition for their expertise in effecting these transactions, and these innovators are discussed in the following section. The investment firm searches for and finds acquisition candidates, and then arranges the financing of the acquisition with a group of investors. The investing group may include the investment firm itself, institutional investors, private individuals, investment partnerships and key management personnel of the acquired company.

Because of the high level of risk, the rate of return to the investor is a significant factor. Jerome Kohlberg, of Kohlberg, Kravis, Roberts and Co. has said that he looks for a return of six to seven times his investment over a five-to ten-year period because the successful transactions have to make up for the bad ones.[2]

The moneylenders, too, insist on a substantial return. Walter Heller & Co., for example, charges six percentage points above prime on a floating basis on loans secured by the assets of the acquired company. Bank rates are somewhat lower, but still usually several percentage points over prime. Insurance companies are almost always given the additional incentive of an equity kicker — the option to buy stock (usually through warrants) at a nominal cost — in return for debt financing. Though Teachers Insurance in the Syracuse China deal (discussed in detail in Section II) charged a fixed rate of only 9.5 percent on its $5 million loan, the astronomical return on its $5,000 equity investment substantially increased its effective yield.

The high rates charged by the lending institutions add to the overall financial risk of the leveraged buyout. High interest costs may make the transaction impractical. A leveraged buyout candidate should have a

---

[2]N. Galluccio, "Do You Sincerely Want To Be Rich?", *Forbes*, (July 24, 1978), p. 42

return on equity substantial enough to service the debt and still allow for a good return to the equity investors. Typically, the equity investors are looking for an after-tax return of at least 25 percent.

These high rates of return are justified on the basis of risk, which is evidenced by the number of deals that are failures. My estimates, based on discussions with a number of the leading investment firms, indicate that roughly one quarter of the leveraged buyouts have resulted in failure.[3] These include situations where there has been a default in debt payments, the company has been liquidated or subsequently sold at a loss.

Leveraged buyout dealers can not always count on public offerings to take them out at a profit. (Syracuse China used its public offering to obtain working capital). "In the mid and late Sixties you could go out and leverage a company with $10 million in debt and $2 million equity and after a six-month period have a public offering raise $5 million and reduce the debt by half," says Edward Gibbons of Gibbons, Green, van Anerorgen, Ltd. "But now with tight stock market conditions the initial financing is for a long period. It has to support the company both in the present and future. This has created greater risk for the lender."[4]

Few leveraged buyouts possess all the desirable attributes. Deals with many of them are bid for quickly. The absence of one or more of the core characteristics does not preclude the possibility of completing a transaction. For example, the controlling investor group can modify the deal (increasing its rewards and riskiness) by making post-acquisition changes in such areas as management, product line, assets and operating procedures.

The risks should not be underestimated. A bad recession can destroy carefully prepared cash-flow projections, or the new chief executive, on whom so much rides, dies suddenly. The backers of a leveraged buyout probably can not get out whole until the heavy debt has been at least partially paid down, and that depends on a relatively stable business and economic environment.

The Importance of Management

The investor group views the leveraged buyout as a financial transaction, and does not get directly involved in running the business. It is usually a requirement of the investment firm, which is arranging the leveraged buyout, that the acquired company's management team agrees to remain with the acquired company after the acquisition. As a management incentive, certain officers and other key management personnel of the acquired company may be given the opportunity to be participants in the investor group which purchases the equity portion of the financing for the transaction. Also, certain officers and key employees may be given employment contracts.

In the most common form of asset purchase leveraged buy-outs, the management of the acquired company is given long-term employment arrangements. These have taken the form of a partnership and management agreements pursuant to which officers and key employees form a partnership which enters into a management agreement with the acquiring company to provide general management for the acquired business. The partners, who are all officers or management employees, are paid salaries by the acquired company (with certain of the key people often entering into employment agreements) and also participate in a partnership profit fund. When this type of management incentive program is adopted, the officers and key management personnel usually are not given the opportunity to invest in the equity of the acquiring company.

The management needs of a business purchased through a leveraged buyout can not be filled by the young genius, fresh out of business school. Because of the high financial risk involved, hard-nosed money lenders and seasoned venture capitalists won't buy glib talk about concepts. "We look for those companies that have managers with the experience, wisdom and judgment that comes from being in business many years. Young managers don't know how difficult it is to run a business and how much perspiration goes into it," says Kohlberg.[5] Backers want a track record of performance. Thus, leveraged buyouts are the ideal platform for the person who is blocked in his job, though still energetic and ambitious, or for the top executive who, from his board's shortsightedness or greed, has not been given a chance to become anything more than a highly paid hireling.

The Deal Makers

There are two ways in which investment banking firms engage in the leveraged buyout business: (1) as participants and (2) as agents. The participating firms not only structure the transaction, but also invest a portion of their own funds as equity in the acquired business. The agent firms identify leveraged buyout candidates and/or structure transaction. However, the

---

[3]This figure is probably low because of hesitancy of the firms interviewed in admitting to the failures.
[4]Quoted in N. Galluccio, p. 43.
[5]Quoted in N. Galluccio, p. 43.

agents do not invest in the transaction. This group obtains equity money from unrelated venture capital sources.

Five companies illustrate the first approach of taking equity positions in the transactions which they structure. They are; Oppenheimer & Co.; Carl Marks & Company; Kohlberg, Kravis, Roberts & Co.; Gibbons, Greene, and van Anerorgen, Ltd. (formerly Gibbons, Green & Rice); and Donaldson, Lufkin & Jenrette, Inc.

Oppenheimer & Co. is a partnership that owns the long established Wall Street securities firm of the same name. Between 1976 and 1979 Oppenheimer either by itself or with partners had acquired the assets of six public companies having yearly combined sales of nearly $1 billion. The aggregate purchase price for these companies came to an estimated $138 million in cash. Included are the operating assets of Havatampa Corp., Tampa, Florida, the nation's largest wholesale distributor of tobacco products, and of Reliable Stores Corp., a Baltimore-based retail furniture and jewelry concern, whose shares were traded on the New York Stock Exchange. The Oppenheimer group bought the operating assets of Donnkenny, Inc., a New York-based maker of women's apparel, for a purchase price of $22 million. And Oppenheimer is a minority investor in the private group which purchased Spartek Inc., Canton, Ohio, a producer of ceramic floor and wall tile, for $13 million.

Previously, purchases by Oppenheimer included Automatic Service Co., an Atlanta Supplier for industrial vending machine operators; Shirley of Atlanta, Inc., an apparel maker; Wall Industries Inc., a manufacturer of insulated sports clothing, and Big Bear Stores Inc., a retail chain. Companies attracted by Oppenheimer often have the common feature of control by a top management owning large blocks of stock. The backing of these insiders at directors' and shareholders' meetings generally assures that the agreement to sell the companies' operating assets to Oppenheimer will proceed without undue problems. Oppenheimer has been one of the leaders in developing this method of avoiding conflict-of-interest problems created when corporate insiders purchase the holdings of public shareholders.

Management is almost always offered 15-year employment contracts to continue to run the business under the Oppenheimer name. These contracts virtually guarantee that the officials can stay in their high-salaried jobs until retirement. By contrast, the maximum term for such contracts at many public companies is five years, to avoid shareholder criticism that top management is enriching itself at shareholder expense.

Another common feature of Oppenheimer's leveraged buyouts is that the market price of these companies is static, giving the insiders an inducement to sell out. John Cable of Spartek, Inc. said unhappily, "We've been on the American Stock Exchange for 20 years, and there has been very little trading in the stock and very little appreciation in the stock's value"[6] Spartek's shares were trading for about $13 per share in December 1977 when the Oppenheimer/buyout group offered to purchase the operating assets for $17.50 in cash.

In addition, some of the top officials whom Oppenheimer has courted are nearing retirement age and facing the difficult question of how to dispose of some, or all, of their holdings in the companies they head. Frequently there is a second tier of management which is highly capable, but lacks sufficient funds to purchase the company independently. The owners realize that their heirs may be forced to unload large blocks of shares, and/or pay burdensome estate taxes. This, in turn, could depress the market price of the shares and reduce any capital gains profits from the sale of the shares.

Oppenheimer offers the owners and the management/purchasers a way out of the dilemma by structuring the purchase of the operating assets at a substantial premium over the shares' market price. Shareholders then have an alternative. They may elect to redeem their shares for cash and take an immediate profit. Or, as is usually the case with the insiders, they may retain their shares in the original company, which is only a shell. The survivor company takes the cash proceeds remaining from the sale of the assets and uses them to purchase state and local tax-exempt obligations. The interest from these municipal bonds then flows through the company in the form of dividends on which taxes do not have to be paid.[7]

Such an arrangement lifted a heavy burden from S.V. Bowen, president of Automatic Service Co., after the Oppenheimer investment group bought operating assets of his company for $8.7 million in 1976. Mr. Bowen was 60 years old and owned 34 percent of the stock, which was thinly traded over the counter. Upon his death, the underpriced stock would have been received by his wife, who would have had to sell it, driving the price down even further. Mr. Bowen, who remained as Automatic's president after Oppenheimer took over, retained his shares of Au-

[6]S. Penn, "Oppenheimer Group Fashions A Formula", *Wall Street Journal*, (September 14, 1978).

[7]On December 27, 1979 amendments to IRS Regulations and new Revenue Rulings severely restricted the sale of assets transaction immediately followed by a merger into an investment fund. This is particularly true where less than 100 shareholders remain in the newly formed fund.

tomatic instead of redeeming them for $10 a share. At the same time, the old automatic company, stripped of its business operations, became an investment firm and bought nearly $3 million of tax-free municipals.

Some of the corporate insiders end up collecting larger dividends from the new investment firms than they received from the predecessor companies. For example, Havatampa sold its assets to the Oppenheimer group and converted to Eli Securities, an investment firm. Eli Securities has purchased, on behalf of insiders who didn't redeem their shares, roughly $20 million of tax-exempt securities. Havatampa, prior to the takeover by Oppenheimer, had paid 44 cents a year per share in dividends. Shareholders in the upper 50 percent bracket were left with 22 cents a share after taxes. "Once Eli's portfolio is fully invested, it will pay in excess of 60 cents a year tax-free," says Thomas Power, who remained as Havatampa's executive vice president after Oppenheimer bought the business operations.[8]

It is interesting that the trend in leveraged buyouts has not been led entirely by the established firms. Two of the most active concerns in the business are relatively new, started by people who sensed early what was happening and moved while the big investment houses had their attention engaged elsewhere. The two firms are Kohlberg, Kravis, Roberts & Co. and Gibbons, Green & Rice, both New York-based.

Kohlberg, Kravis, Roberts & Co. has in the last five years, and prior to the huge Houdaille deal, negotiated and acted as principals in leveraged buyouts totaling $350 million. The Houdaille transaction, Sargent Industries, Inc., and U.S. Natural Resources, all structured by Kohlberg, are discussed in detail in Section IV. In the buyout of L.B. Foster Co., Kohlberg invested $2.5 million to purchase 40 percent of the equity. In addition to the $1 million put up by the company's management, $7.5 million was provided by insurance companies in the form of preferred stock. The remaining $85 million in debt was financed by bank and insurance companies.

Another investment bank which specializes in leveraged buyouts is the New York-based Carl Marks & Co. The 54-year-old firm is the nation's leading market maker in foreign securities, and is the principal owner in nearly 90 companies. Carl Marks has acted as principal in more than 25 leveraged buyouts deals in the last 15 years, five of them since 1975. Among recent transactions were Roberts Consolidated Industries, Inc., a consumer package-goods outfit spun off by Champion International Corp. in a $30 million deal, and Stern & Stern Textiles, Inc., an industrial textile manufacturer bought for $12 million.

The Marks firm has been doing leveraged buyouts longer than anyone else in the field, but its rival, Oppenheimer, has done the most public deals — eight for its own account and a dozen more for clients. Kohlberg has accomplished the largest single transaction, Houdaille Industries, for a price of $355 million and was about to snag Flintkote Corporation for $380 million before it was outbid in July of 1979.

In the Wall Street establishment, the leading "major" in leveraged buyouts is Donaldson, Lufkin & Jenrette, Inc. DLJ and its affiliated Sprout Capital Groups both execute and invest their own capital in buyouts. Since 1972, Sprout has negotiated 17 leveraged buyouts, 11 of them in the last three years alone.

Unlike the firms which act as principals in almost every deal, a number of investment bankers execute their transactions strictly as agents. That is, they put up none of their firm's capital and are paid a flat fee for arranging a transaction. A case in point is the firm of Paine, Webber, Jackson & Curtis, Inc. which has negotiated buyouts totaling $126 million. Another is Smith Barney, Harris Upham & Co. The Corporate Finance Departments in several of the larger banks, including Citibank and Bankers Trust Company, also act as agents in leveraged buyouts.

When a firm acts as an agent in a leveraged buyout it obtains equity funds from unrelated sources such as venture capital firms or wealthy families. The agent is entitled to a finder's fee or a financial advisory fee for structuring the transaction and arranging the financing. The agent, however, does not contribute its own funds in the equity portion of the financing. The firm would not be at risk after the transaction is consummated. Unlike the equity participants, the agent would not share in the future upside potential of the business through appreciation of the equity.

The fact that the managing firm is a principal or an agent will only impact the source of equity financing. It will not affect the debt financing, which will be supplied by banks, insurance, and finance companies. These sources of funds are discussed in Section III.

II. THE THREE TYPES OF LEVERAGED BUYOUT

The following types of businesses have lent themselves particularly well to the leveraged buyout format.

Divestitures of Divisions of Public Companies

The greatest number of leveraged buyouts, and the fastest growing area, involves the shedding of unwanted divisions or subsidiaries by big corporations. Although there is still a strong takeover movement,

---

[8]Quoted in Penn, p. 2.

there is a counterwave which may be viewed as a limited reversal of the conglomeration trend of the Sixties. Many large corporations are divesting divisions they either acquired or developed and, for one reason or another, no longer want. This type of leveraged buyout breaks down into two subcategories: (1) strategic divestitures—divisions which no longer fit into the company's strategic plan for marketing, geographic, regulatory or financial reporting reasons; and (2) financial divestitures—those which do not meet required corporate return-on-assets measures.

The strategic divestiture is often used by a large corporation to avoid a particular SEC or anti-trust constraint. A small, newly constituted buyout group not subject to the constraint in question can use the leveraged buyout technique, consummating the deal quickly with a minimum of regulatory difficulty.

The division or subsidiary which fits into the second category (financial divestiture) typically has a high book value relative to its after-tax earnings (greater than 9:1). In such cases, where the growth is not extraordinary, the parent company finds that it has assets invested at a yield significantly below its own weighted average cost of capital and that the division is not readily salable to another public company except at a loss (discount from carrying value). This is because the publicly owned buyer will generally pay a price based on the growth rate of the business rather than its book value. The small, private buyout group is less demanding of sustained high growth than is the large corporate buyer.

Often the selling public company may find a buyer who is willing to pay the asking price (i.e., the division's book value) if the seller provides a portion of the buyer's financing. This means that the seller will take back a subordinated note from the buyer for a portion of the purchase price. The buyer, who believes that he can improve the earning power of the business, reduce the assets employed in it, or both, is willing to bear the extra risk of higher leverage in the expectation of a significantly greater return. Such a deal requires less equity. For example, the seller may sell at book value and accept 70 percent of the purchase price in cash and 30 percent in eight-year, low interest notes of the buyer. The buyer regards these notes as "soft" (that is, less expensive and from a more benevolent source than his institutional debt) and is able to raise perhaps twice as much institutional debt as his obligation to the seller. The seller books no gain or loss on the sale of the division and is pleased to receive the bulk of the purchase price in cash with an orderly program for the payment of the balance. In such cases, it is quite common for the operating management of the division to be part of the entrepreneurial group.

Vapor Corp., a control systems producer was divested by Singer Co. in a $37 million leveraged buyout deal in 1972 as part of its slimming-down operation. Vapor clearly illustrates the balance sheet risk in a leveraged buyout. After the transaction, Vapor's debt-to-equity ratio was 7.8 to 1:

Long-Term Debt	$33.5 million
Stockholders' Equity	$ 4.4 million
Total Capitalization	$37.9 million

In the five years since the buyout, management has repaid the bulk of the debt and reversed the balance-sheet ratio.

Its debt-to-equity now stands at 0.35 to 1:

Long-Term Debt	$10.6 million
Stockholders' Equity	$29.9 million
Total Capitalization	$40.5 million

Below is the company's debt principal repayment schedule since the buyout (in millions of dollars).

	1973	1974	1975	1976	1977
Cash Flow	3.1	3.6	6.1	16.3[9]	7.9
Debt Repayment	1.1	1.4	2.6	15.0	1.6
Unrestricted Cash	2.0	2.2	3.5	1.3	6.3

Another example of a highly successful leveraged buyout was the divestiture by Amfac, Inc. of a $90 million-a-year high fashion retailer of women's apparel in San Francisco. Gibbons, Green, & Rice pieced together a group which included Edward Gorman, 61 years old and marketing assistant to the president at J.C. Penney Co. for 11 years. Gorman and other investors raised $6.3 million in equity, with Gorman's share at only $80,000. For Gorman's sweat equity he received 8 percent of the stock. This meant that Gorman's shares were tied directly to his efforts and the future performance of the company. A stock bonus plan would provide Gorman with shares if a certain performance level was met. Out of the total purchase price of $33 million, roughly $6 million involved a note to Amfac, with the remainder consisting of bank and insurance company loans.

Carl Marks has been quite active in buying divisions, in conjunction with their own management, from giant corporations and conglomerates that want to get out of unrelated businesses or are forced by anti-trust decisions to divest themselves of enterprises. Tyler Refrigeration, a Michigan company with $70

---

[9]The $16.3 million cash flow in 1976 includes $10 million raised in a public offering.

million in sales, is one example. It was purchased from Clark Equipment Company.

The case of Tyler Refrigeration is typical of how most of Marks' transactions are arranged. A Niles, Michigan, company with sales of $22 million a year, Tyler was a division of the Clark Equipment Company. Clark needed cash and decided to sell. However, Tyler's P. Linnen, with some of his key executives, hoped to buy Tyler. When he met John W. Jordan II of Carl Marks, they agreed to form a company and do the deal together. The price was $20 million.

On the equity side, Mr. Linnen and five of his management team members put up $400,000. Carl Marks put up $800,000 and Mr. Jordan invited in half a dozen venture capital funds, most of them owned by bankers, to ante $2.8 million, making the total equity investment $4 million.

Mr. Jordan and Mr. Linnen also arranged to sell an unprofitable segment of Tyler to Alcoa Standard Corporation for $3 million. The remaining $13 million was borrowed by selling notes to financial institutions. The leverage factor was 3-1/2 to 1. In three years since the buyout, three quarters of the debt has been paid off from the company's cash flow, and profits are running $3 million or better a year: a 75 percent return on the buyers' $4 million investment.

Other divestiture/leveraged buyouts in which Carl Marks has participated include Roberts Consolidated Industries, a $100-million maker of equipment for installing floor covering, that came out of Champion International Corporation; the Atlantic Research Corporation, a $40-million company in Virginia that makes solid propellant systems for rockets and was a division of the Susquehanna Corporation; P.C.I., a $22-million maker of shoe eyelets and fasteners in Massachusetts divested by Emhart Corporation; and Smith Pipe and Steel, a $25-million Arizona company sold by the Transway International Corporation. Because divestitures do not require public disclosure through a proxy statement, it is difficult to obtain the details of these transactions. However, it is believed that Marks' transactions involve a debt-to-equity ratio between 3 and 12 to 1, with 5 to 1 as the most typical.

In the era of corporate giants, the idea of taking pieces of corporations and making them independent appeals to the entrepreneurial instincts of many managers. "Every division we've acquired in partnership with management has operated substantially more efficiently and more profitably than under the parent corporation," says John W. Jordan II of Carl Marks. [10]

Mr. Jordan, who has handled a dozen deals, claims that the firm's return on its investment in these transactions averages better than 50 percent per year, as compared to a 20-25 percent range for the typical venture capital transaction.

Only on one occasion has Carl Marks sold one of its buyout companies. The firm bought Milwaukee's Pressed Steel Tank Company from Norris Industries near the end of 1975 for some $8.5 million. Only $2 million of that was equity, of which $356,000 was cash; the rest was in the form of convertible subordinated notes. Eighteen months later the company was sold to Giddings & Lewis, which covered the notes and offered $5.5 million of its stock, trading around $11 a share at the time, for the remaining equity. Adjusted for a stock split, those shares are now worth $22 each, and the original $356,000 investment is worth $11 million.

Privately Owned Businesses That Are Closely Held

Because the buyer in a leveraged buyout has broad flexibility in structuring his deal to suit the objectives of the seller, this type of transaction may be appropriate for some sellers of private businesses. Many such private businesses lack sufficient growth to be attractive corporate acquisition candidates. The leveraged buyout depends more on stability of earnings than growth and may solve the problems of selling these businesses.

Furthermore, the personal financial circumstances of the selling shareholders may be such that these shareholders are reluctant to sell for cash—the only acquisition medium offered by the buyer—because they are not anxious to recognize a substantial taxable gain or establish a value for estate purposes. In such cases, the shareholders of the target company may be able to achieve their objectives by causing the corporation (rather than the shareholders) to sell its assets to the buyer for cash. The ownership of their stock does not change, and if the sale is at book value, no gain or loss is recognized. The remaining cash-rich shell can then be operated as a personal holding company and can invest its cash in preferred stocks (dividend income from which is 85 percent excluded for tax purposes), tax-exempt securities and tax-shelter situations. The company can pay out substantial income to its shareholders, and upon the death of a shareholder, his shares pass into the hands of his distributees at a stepped-up tax basis (their December 31, 1976 value). [11]

---

[10]Quoted in W.G. Shepherd, "Carl Marks, Investor", *New York Times*, (June, 1979).

[11]The stepped-up basis rule was recently eliminated by Congress. The carryover basis rule was reinstated.

Milton Porter, 67, for ten years had been chief executive officer of the Pittsburgh-based L.B. Foster Co., a highly profitable family-owned manufacturer and distributor of industrial piping and rail, with sales in 1977 of $250 million. His equity in the company was negligible. Foster's owners agreed to sell last year to Porter and his eight-man management team, utilizing a leveraged buyout. The management group had to raise only $1 million in the $100 million transaction, for which they received 12 percent of the stock. Porter has the major portion of this 12 percent block. The remainder of the equity is held by a venture capital group and one of the long-term lenders.

Foster is one of numerous examples which underscore the fact that you do not have to be rich to participate. The leveraged buyout can give management a chance to use sweat equity as part or even all of its down payment. Because the management team gambles its future, and because it has a proven track record, other investors and moneylenders will take a chance along with them.

Public Companies Selling at Low Earnings Multiples and at a Substantial Discount From Book Value

Companies selling at low earnings multiples and at a substantial discount from book value are prevalent in low-growth or no-growth basic businesses. This phenomenon is heightened when the overall market is depressed, as it has been in recent years. It may serve the best interests of the shareholders for the company to sell its business and net assets for a price exceeding the current aggregate stock market value but still at a discount from book value. The difference between the book value and the sales price may, under the proper circumstances, represent an ordinary loss by the seller for federal income tax purposes. The loss can be used to offset other income, or it can be carried back as a net operating loss for a refund of previously paid taxes.

Syracuse China, cited earlier in Section I, was a public company whose stock and business were languishing in 1971. Its revenues were $16 million with negligible profits. The leveraged buyout involved a purchase price of $7.7 million. Of this amount, Teachers Insurance & Annuity Association provided $5 million in long-term debt. The equity capital, leveraged two-for-one by the Teacher's loan, came from the Allstate Insurance Co. and the Henry L. Hillman family of Pittsburgh, Pa.[12]

Robert J. Theis, an accomplished former sales and marketing manager for Philco-Ford Corp. and GTE-Sylvania, Inc. and ITT Corp. put up 8 percent of the equity capital but received 25 percent of the equity. He was, in effect, being paid in equity for his management skill and risk in becoming the chief executive and a major shareholder.

Syracuse is an example of a special type of leveraged buyout candidate—the turnaround situation. Gibbons, Green & Rice, the investment banking firm which packaged the deal, knew that Syracuse China, a restaurant chinaware maker that was operating unprofitably, was for sale. After months of investigating and making endless cash-flow projections, they concluded that new management and fresh capital could turn Syracuse around. What they needed was a top man to run it. Edward W. Gibbons, partner of the investment firm, approached Robert J. Theis through a mutual business associate.

It ended up as a rewarding deal for everyone concerned. However, Theis had to turn the company around. First he bought the Syracuse-based Will & Baumer Co. for $2 million in cash, borrowed against that company's receivables and real estate. This added candles as a natural complement to Syracuse's product line. By 1973 Syracuse China had enough of a record to make a public offering of common stock that raised an additional $2.6 million—in effect, almost doubling equity capital but giving away only 25 percent of the equity.

By 1977 Syracuse China was earning $2.3 million and looked good enough for Canadian Pacific to offer $21 million for the company—nine times what had initially been invested in it. Teachers, the moneylender, got an ordinary interest rate (9.5 percent) for its risk but it also demanded 20 percent of the company, for which it paid only $5,000—an "equity kicker." It resulted in Theis coming out with $5 million (his 25 percent interest) for his initial investment of $350,000 plus his salary of $147,000 per year. Teachers received $4 million plus its loan; Gibbons, Green & Rice $2 million (from an initial cash investment of $35,000); the Hillman family, $3 million for its original $350,000. Even the public stockholders came out more than whole. For shares that they purchased at offering for $10 each in 1973, they received $27 per share.

III. FINANCING

This section is broken down into five parts: (1) capital structure; (2) equity sources of financing for leveraged buyouts; (3) debt sources, (4) the signifi-

---

[12]This leverage factor is the minimum at which the transaction will fit into my definition. It was clearly considered a leveraged buyout by all parties involved.

cance of asset-based lending; and (5) the special financing techniques of Employee Stock Ownership Plans.

Capital Structure

Structuring the financing of a leveraged buyout will often involve the resolution of a number of complex and competing considerations. The objective will be the creation of a capital structure which is sufficiently leveraged to maximize the return to the equity capital. At the same time, the capital structure *can not* impose debt service requirements which drain the acquired company of the funds needed to sustain its growth. The ultimate capital structure results from a balancing between the objectives of the equity investors and the constraints of the lenders.

The equity holder seeks to increase his return through leverage. As leverage increases, risk increases, and the return required by the investor goes up. There is a spectrum of equity investors, each with different preferences regarding return and risk. The more conservative equity investors are more interested in smaller, safer returns (based on worst-case projections) than in larger potential returns with substantial risks. Some equity investors, as a matter of course, will not consider a leveraged buyout with a debt-to-equity ratio greater than 5 to 1. In any leveraged buyout which conforms to the definition of at least 2 to 1 leverage, few investors are interested in a minimum return of less than 25 percent.

Excessive leverage, however, reaches the point of diminishing returns. It is rare to see a buyout leveraged as high as 10 to 1, and the more common debt-to-equity ratio is in a range between 3 and 5 to 1. This is because large leverage factors result in debt service payments becoming so high that these use up profits, and reduce the cash flow, undermining the company's ability to service the debt.

For example, let us assume that a company is purchased for $48 million, consisting of $10 million in equity and $38 million in debt. Its earnings before interest and taxes are $8.8 million. If interest costs average 12 percent on $38 million, pretax earnings would be $4.24 million. With a combined local plus federal tax rate of 50 percent, the company would earn $2.12 million, or a return on equity of 21 percent. If, however, the capital structure consisted of $6 million in equity and $42 million in debt, there would be a greater return on equity (31 percent). Net earnings would decrease by 11 percent to $1.88 million. Although in the second case the return on equity would be more attractive, the lower earnings and cash flow increase the risks to both the lender and investor. A point is reached where the debt servicing ability of the cash

flow is threatened. This example is drawn from an actual situation at Bankers Trust Company. It shows how return on equity improves with leverage, but the higher leverage factor was not acceptable from a cash flow standpoint. The two alternatives appear as follows:

	Case 1 (Debt $38MM, Equity $10MM)	Case 2 (Debt $42MM, Equity $6MM)
EBIT	$8.8MM	$8.8MM
Interest	4.56	5.04
Pretax income	4.24	3.76
Taxes	2.12	1.88
Net Income	$2.12MM	$1.88M
Return on Equity	21.2%	31.3%
Leverage	3.8x	7.0x

Finally, a compromise was reached at a leverage factor of 5.0 to 1. This gave the equity investors a return of 25 percent, and the lenders felt comfortable with the cash flows.

From the lenders' standpoint, cash flow is the primary determinant of the point of maximum leverage. Conservative pro forma cash flow projections are constructed by the management/buyout group based upon historical performance and moderate expected rates of growth. The projections are usually scaled down by the lenders anywhere from 10 percent to 20 percent to provide a cash cushion for exigencies. What remains is a fairly "tight" cash flow projection, which is used as the basis for the lending decision.

Another important consideration in the lending decision is collateral. As a general rule in leveraged buyouts, cash flow is a more important factor for the banks and insurance companies. That is, collateral without cash flow will not carry the deal. Banks and insurance companies have even been known to lend entirely on cash flow. This is never the case with a finance company loan, for which collateral is the primary consideration. Except in the most attractive credits from a cash flow standpoint, the bank or insurance company will also look to be fully secured. Finance companies have loaned to situations in which they were fully secured, but had little expectation of being repaid out of cash flow. The importance of collateral is discussed in detail in the section on asset-based lending, starting on page 541.

Equity Sources of Financing

Earlier it was pointed out that some firms, such as Kohlberg and Carl Marks, provide equity financing. The agent firms, on the other hand, locate outside equity. Frequently, the participating firms will also have to tap these same sources of outside equity to supplement their investments.

These outside equity sources, also referred to as venture capital groups, range from private investors with domestic dollars to large, professionally managed pools of offshore funds. Certain leveraged buyouts are ideal for capital investments by federally licensed Small Business Investment Companies (SBIC).

Two fairly active equity sources in leveraged buyouts are First Chicago Corp. and Continental Illinois Venture Corp. First Chicago Corp. is the venture capital affiliate of First National Bank of Chicago. In 1978 it had half its assets of $20 million tied up in leveraged buyouts. In the brief two years that Continental Illinois Venture Corp. has been investing in leveraged buyouts, it has already committed more than 25 percent of its total assets there.

An equity investment may take the form of convertible subordinated debentures, warrants, preferred stock, common equity, or a combination of all of these. The structure of the equity portion of the capitalization depends largely upon the preference of the investor for income or appreciation.

Because management is such an important consideration in an investor's decision to proceed with a leveraged buyout, it is customary, and a condition required by some equity investors, that the members of the firm's management team have an investment of their own capital at stake. The advantages of such an investment are two-fold. First, it gives the management an incentive to make things work out in favor of the other shareholders. Second, it assures devotion to duty should the going get rough. Management is often restricted contractually to modest current compensation and must look to equity appreciation for the bulk of its reward. In order for such a reward to be attractive, the management group may receive a "carried interest," a share of the equity ownership that is disproportionate to their cash investment. Ideally, such interest is structured so that it will receive capital gains treatment.

Debt Sources

There are three major sources of debt financing: banks, insurance companies, and the commercial finance companies. Participation by the major banks and insurance companies has been critical to the success of the larger transactions. These institutions have provided intermediate and long-term financing in the purchase of highly capitalized companies such as Houdaille. Long payout periods are required and these can not be funded on a short-term basis by a finance company. The finance company is usually limited to

receivables and inventory financing although on occasion it will go out on an intermediate-term basis (3-7 years) in financing hard assets. Often the finance company will provide working capital, with a bank or insurance company financing the equipment or real estate.

Among the major New York banks, Citibank has been one of the most active lenders in leveraged buyouts. It has set up a separate lending division specializing in buyouts and has financed nearly $200 million worth of transactions. The majority of these are "leveraged" buyouts. Large banks such as Citibank usually participate with a syndicate of banks and insurance companies in the larger transactions. In Houdaille, for example, Continental Illinois was the lead bank. It was joined by Bankers Trust Company and Manufacturer's Hanover in furnishing a seven-year revolving credit for $60 million. The long-term debt of $245 million was provided by 13 insurance companies, of which the largest portion ($115 million) was provided by Prudential.

The debt portion of the company's capitalization varies in the proportion that is short-term, long-term, secured, or unsecured. Generally, as the deal becomes more highly leveraged, the more likely that debt is secured and at a high interest rate. Commercial finance companies, the most aggressive lenders, may be willing to lend up to 85 percent of the liquidation value (that is, auctioneer's "knock-down" value) of the assets acquired. Some of these institutions may lend the maximum because they are fully prepared in the event of financial difficulty to exercise their rights as secured creditors and to liquidate promptly at their expertly estimated liquidation values. Less aggressive lenders, such as the banks and insurance companies, are either less prepared to liquidate or lack confidence in their estimates and will make lower advances. The more aggressive commercial finance lenders even take on clients that from the beginning have only modest chances of long-term survival. The high interest costs and service fees, along with the estimated liquidation values, justify the risks for such lenders.

A bank is not likely to extend itself as fully as the finance company in the area of short-term credit (inventory or receivables financing due in less than one year) because it lacks the facilities to closely police the collateral. Thus, one or several commercial banks might participate by lending in step with the finance company that is managing the credit. The banks reap above-average returns on their loans while simultaneously lowering the borrower's net interest costs. In a typical case, the finance company, which lends the majority of the funds at a high rate (for example, 5 to 6 percent over prime), participates with a bank that is lending the balance of the funds at a lower rate. The net cost to the borrower is a lower, "blended" rate. The bank's portion of the loan on this basis is generally considered a bankable commercial credit. The higher rate charged by the finance company is due to the fact that the bank's claim to the assets would stand ahead of the finance company in the event of default.

XYZ Company's sale of its Plastic Parts division to its management is an example of a small leveraged buyout with bank financing.[13] The purchase price was $2,500,000 which approximated the fair market value of the net assets. The financing package consisted of a $1,250,000 collateralized long-term note from a bank, a $750,000 subordinated note from ABC Capital (a venture capital firm which also received 40 percent of the equity), and $500,000 in equity from ABC Capital and the division's executives. The division's assets and liabilities were transferred to a new corporation, Plas-

tic Parts Company. The balance sheets immediately before and after the purchase were as follows:

Balance Sheet of Plastic Parts Company ($000)

	Before	After
Assets		
Current Assets	$1,200	$1,200
Property, Plant and Equipment	700	1,800
	$1,900	$3,000
Liabilities and Equity		
Current Liabilities	$ 500	$ 500
Long-term Note	—	1,250
Subordinated Note	—	750
Equity		
XYZ Division Equity	1,400	—
Management	—	300
ABC Capital	—	200
	1,400	500
	$1,900	$3,000

Plastic Parts Company
Pro Forma Statement of Income
(In Thousands)

	Historical As Division	Pro Forma					
	19X0	19X1	19X2	19X3	19X4	19X5
				(In Thousands)			
Net sales	$4,000	$4,100	$4,700	$5,400	$6,200	$7,200
Costs and Expenses:						
Costs and expenses, excluding depreciation and interest	3,200	3,280	3,760	4,320	4,960	5,760
Depreciation	100	300	270	240	210	180
Interest	—	220	195	170	145	120
Income Before Income Taxes	700	300	475	670	885	1,140
Income Taxes (50%)	350	150	237	335	442	570
Net Income	$ 350	$ 150	$ 238	$ 335	$ 443	$ 570
Return on Equity		30%	37%	38%	36%	34%

Plastic Parts Company
Pro Forma Statements of Cash Flow

	Historical As Division	Pro Forma					
	19X0	19X1	19X2	19X3	19X4	19X5
				(In Thousands)			
Cash provided by:						
Net income	$ 350	$ 150	$ 238	$ 335	$1443	$ 570
Add back depreciation	100	300	270	240	210	180
New bank loan	—	—	—	—	—	2,000
Total Sources	450	450	508	575	653	2,750
Cash applied to:						
Additions to fixed assets	—	100	100	100	100	100
Debt principal payments:						
Bank loan	—	250	250	250	250	250
Subordinated note prepayment	—	—	—	—	—	750
Repurchase ABC equity interest	—	—	—	—	—	1,500
Total Uses	—	350	350	350	350	2,600
Cash Available For Growth And Dividends	$ 450	$ 100	$ 158	$ 225	$ 303	$ 150

---

[13]This case was developed by Ernst & Whinney in their brochure, *Leveraged Buyouts,* New York (1979), pp. 15-17.

The change in the property, plant and equipment account resulted from the recording of assets at appraised value. This resulted in an additional depreciation expense. The long-term note from the bank has the fixed assets as collateral, at an interest rate of 2 percent over prime, with annual principal payments of $250,000. The subordinated note from ABC Capital bears interest at 5 percent over prime, with a cap of 15 percent. Principal payments of $150,000 per year begin six years after the purchase.

Management invested $300,000 or 12 percent of the purchase price, and owns 60 percent of the voting common stock. ABC Capital obtained 40 percent of the stock for $200,000. Management will have the option to acquire this stock after five years at its then existing market value.

The pro forma statements of income and cash flow for the Plastic Parts Company are shown on the bottom of page 540.

In the pro formas, there are no significant adjustments for organizational changes. Amounts incurred for salaries, legal, accounting, data processing, and other services will be approximately the same after purchase. Interest expense assumes an 8 percent prime rate. The pro formas show that in 1985 the subordinated note will be prepaid, and the 40 percent equity interest will be repurchased at a negotiated price of $1,500,000. The company finances this principally through a new bank loan.

At the end of five years the original bank note of $1,250,000 has been repaid, the $750,000 subordinated note retired, and ABC Capital's stock repurchased so that the company is now 100 percent owned by the executives. Its balance sheet would appear as:

Plastic Parts Company
Pro Forma Balance Sheet in 1985
($000)

Current Assets	$2,436	Current Liabilities	$ 800
Property, plant and equipment:			
		Long-term note	2,000
Original purchase	1,800	Subordinated note	—
Subsequent additions	500	Equity:	
Less depreciation	(1,200)	Stock outstanding	500
	1,110	Retained earnings	1,736
		Less treasury stock	(1,500)
			736
	$3,536		$3,536

In the financing of a leveraged buyout by a finance company, such as Walter E. Heller & Company,[14] it is generally required that there be accounts receivable, inventory, or fixed assets which the lender can appraise at a reasonably predictable value. The value of the collateral must be sufficient to support a loan large enough to cover both the purchase price and, after the acquisition, adequate working capital for the new corporate entity. However, the lender can be less conservative in applying collateral ratios to a company with a history of profitability or strong projected profitability.

A comprehensive discussion of Heller financing is provided in the chapter by Albert Reisman (Chapter 20).

In recent years the federal government has been involved in financing specialized leveraged buyouts through the Economic Development Administration, the Small Business Administration and the Farmer's Home Administration. It is the primary purpose of these agencies to make or guarantee loans to keep plants open, preserve existing jobs and create new positions. Sometimes a bank, finance, or insurance company will fund a loan of this type with a 90 percent government guarantee, whereas without the guarantee it would not fund the transaction. In other cases, the federal agency might make a direct long-term loan to finance the acquisition, secured by a mortgage on fixed assets while a non-government lender finances or factors the receivables generated by the new company.

Certain insurance companies, such as Prudential and Teachers, have become increasingly active in providing term financing for leveraged buyouts. However, the institutional lenders as a group are rather conservative. It is estimated that less than 5 percent of the industry will consider a leveraged buyout. The large northeastern institutions have been the primary participants. Typically, these loans are repayable over the useful life of the assets that secure them. The rates charged are substantially higher than those of a BAA credit. While the interest cost of insurance company debt is considerably lower than that of finance company debt, the insurance company will frequently require an equity "kicker," while the finance company will generally refuse a "kicker" in order to purify its stand as a secured creditor under the Bankruptcy Act. The finance company is generally compensated by straight interest rate. Examples of insurance company participations are set forth in detail in Section IV.

Asset Based Lending

As pointed out earlier, the buyers in a leveraged buyout are not a large company with substantial resources. Rather, the buyers are small companies, managers of the spun-off companies and private investors,

---

[14]Discussions of Walter E. Heller are based largely on an article by H.E. Ruben, "Secured Financing: Creative Tool For Acquisitions," *Stock Market Magazine* (October, 1978).

alone or in groups. Because they have limited resources, maximizing leverage is a critical ingredient in the buyout decision. Asset-based financing is a means by which leverage may be increased beyond conventional bank financing.

In the conventional approach, the lender wanted protection primarily via cash flow of the borrowing entity. This required a stable cash flow history and the lender advanced an amount representing a conservative multiple of that proven flow. Furthermore, the lender stipulated that the loan had to be amortized over a specified period of time. The lender usually preferred situations where the leverage ratio was less than that of our minimum requirement for leveraged buyouts (i.e., 2 to 1).

In the asset-based approach, however, the lender ties all or at least part of his loan to the liquid value of the borrower's assets. The lender is thus not restricted to a multiple of cash flow. Indeed, frequently lenders can extend significantly greater amounts because they are basing protection on the assets, not solely the cash flow, of the borrowing entity.

The lender maximizes the liquid value in three ways: by taking a security interest in the assets of the borrowing entity, the lender establishes a lending formula on the basis of its liquid value, and the lender obtains periodic information on the nature and size of those assets and the borrower's needs.

The loan package often consists of an "evergreen" portion tied to current assets—that is, it has no fixed amortization schedule. Comprising the evergreen loan is a revolver which maintains the credit as long as the liquid assets are replenished. Sometimes there is an amortizing portion based on the value of the fixed assets. The formula may be 80 percent of accounts receivable, 50 percent of inventory at current cost, and 80 percent of the "quick sale" appraised value of the fixed assets.

Thus, with respect to cash flow, the revolving part of the loan can serve as a substitute for capital and give the borrower substantial flexibility. Because the revolver can actually grow as the borrower's asset values increase, an asset-based financing is particularly appropriate in highly leveraged situations. Buyers have used the asset-based approach in leveraged buyout financing for one or more of the following reasons:

(1) The buyer can maximize the leverage upon his initial cash investment. While lenders usually frown on no-equity, "boot-strap" acquisitions, deals have been done with 10 and 12 to 1 leverage (depending, of course, on the valuation of the assets).

(2) While the lending rates for an asset-based package generally run one to two percentage points higher than conventional rates, the higher leverage permitted can provide an investor with a greater return on his investment.

For example, if a company has sales of $25 million on assets of $10 million, with $2.5 million of trade credit and accruals, this leaves $7.5 million to be funded externally. Earnings before interest and taxes (EBIT) are 10 percent of sales.

Assuming that a conventional lender would require a leverage factor of no more than one-to-one and that an asset-based lender might readily permit a three-to-one leverage factor, the following table demonstrates a significant difference in the two approaches in the return on equity, even if the stipulated interest cost for the asset-based loan is two percentage points higher (that is, 10 percent vs. 8 percent per annum).

Financial Results with Conventional vs. Asset-Based Lending
Balance Sheet ($000,000)

	Conventional Approach	Asset-based Approach
Total Assets	$ 10.0	$ 10.0
Trade Credit & Accruals	2.5	2.5
Bank Borrowings	2.5	5.0
Total Liabilities	5.0	7.5
Equity	5.0	2.5
Equity plus Liabilities	10.0	10.0

Income Statement ($000)

	Conventional	Asset-based
Sales	$25,000	$25,000
EBIT at 10% of Sales	2,500	2,500
Interest	200(@8%)	500(@10%)
Pretax Income	2,300	2,000
Net Income (@50%)	1,150	1,000
Return on Equity	23%	40%

The capital structure under the conventional approach does not fall within our definition of leveraged buyouts (ie., 2 to 1 leverage). A substantial amount of equity is required and this results in the return of only 23 percent. However, the asset-based approach allows for a "leveraged" buyout. The return on equity increases to 40 percent by virtue of the greater leverage factor of 3 to 1.

(3) The formula approach of an asset-based loan permits future working capital flexibility. If sales suddenly pick up and/or additional inventory is needed, the resulting receivables and inventory are largely self-funding.

The non-amortizing nature of the current asset portion of the package helps create this situation. If sales growth were limited by insufficient working capital, as is often the case in highly leveraged situations, such working capital flexibility would have significant benefits to the bottom line of the growing enterprise in spite of the 2 percent higher borrowing cost.

In the situation shown in the preceding table a higher interest cost on $5 million in borrowings would represent an annual $100,000 incremental interest cost. At a pretax return on sales in the neighborhood of 10 percent, the company needs only $1 million ($1 million x 10% = $100,000) in incremental sales, or 4 percent higher volume to pay the greater interest cost. Even less than a 4 percent sales increase probably would cover the higher interest rate because margins normally improve on incremental sales. Thus, the opportunity for greater profits and/or market share can outweigh the higher cost of borrowed capital.

The asset-based approach is a potent tool for maximizing leverage where the assets of the proposed acquisition are strong enough to provide a significant portion of the cash price and have the strength to support the medium- or the long-term nature of the funding.

Employee Stock Ownership Plans (ESOPs)

An Employee Stock Ownership Plan (ESOP) has been used as the purchaser of a division or subsidiary of a company. It has also been employed in the transfer of ownership of a family owned business. The result of a transaction utilizing an ESOP is that part or all of the ownership of the new entity is broadly dispersed among management and employees.

The ESOP can be used in place of, or in combination with, the straight management buyout where management purchases ownership directly. Because it is a method of increasing cash flow, an ESOP can facilitate a transaction when a management group does not have sufficient cash to purchase the entire company. ESOP's are qualified under Internal Revenue Code Section 401(a) as an employee benefit plan, a form of stock bonus plan designed to invest primarily in qualifying employer securities (defined as employer's common stock and other marketable securities). Thus they can own up to 100 percent of the divested subsidiary or plant.

The major advantage of an ESOP is that the companies with such plans may deduct their yearly contributions to the plan up to 15 percent of total compensation. The contributions are not taken out of employee pay checks but are additional compensation. However, it is possible to contribute nothing at all, depending on the objective of the company in a particular year.

A second major advantage of an ESOP is its unique ability to borrow and leverage itself. This means that at the onset it may purchase a large block of stock of the employer. The tax deductible contributions by the employer to the ESOP are then used to repay the borrowings.

Because the ESOP is a tax-deductible device, it is applicable only within a profitable or potentially profitable company. It cannot, in and of itself, convert an unprofitable company or subsidiary into a profitable one. An ESOP divestiture, however, may relieve enough corporate overhead to produce taxable earnings in an otherwise unprofitable operation. The minimum ESOP candidate should have a pre-tax income equal to at least 15 percent of its payroll.

An ESOP was involved in the sale of "ABC" Division by XYZ Company for $4 million.[15] The management and employees of ABC Division strongly desired to purchase ABC but lacked the capital to do so. ABC, Inc. had sales of $12 million, payroll of $4 million, and pre-tax income of $1 million. ABC had a 52 percent combined tax bracket for federal and state taxes.

After ABC, Inc. was created, it established an ESOP. The ESOP borrowed $2.5 million from two banks. It paid the cash and issued $1.5 million in notes to XYZ for 100 percent of the stock of ABC. The stock and assets of ABC served as collateral for the loans.

Without an ESOP, the company with pre-tax income of $1 million would pay taxes of $520,000 and end up with $480,000 in after-tax income. With the same $1 million in pre-tax income, and a $600,000 (15 percent of $4 million) contribution to an ESOP, adjusted pre-tax income would be $400,000, federal and state taxes $208,000, and after-tax income $192,000.

Although the $600,000 contribution is a cash movement from the company to the ESOP, this cash is not lost since there is a commonality of interest between the ESOP and the parent company. The cash contribution is used to service the ESOP loan and builds the corporate equity base.

Comparing the ESOP contribution with after-tax income available to outside purchasers in a conventional transaction, there would be no contribution and after-tax income of $480,000. This is the amount that accrues to the shareholders. With a $600,000 contribution to an ESOP and after-tax income of $192,000, the total to shareholders is $792,000. The difference of $312,000 between these figures (which is really the tax savings produced by the ESOP contribution) is in effect a tax subsidy to the employee shareholders. A purchase price of $4 million for this company would represent 8.3 times earnings to an unrelated purchaser, but only 5.1 times earnings to the ESOP.

---

[15]This was an actual transaction completed by Bankers Trust Company.

IV. SOME NOTEWORTHY PUBLIC TRANSACTIONS

This section analyzes six examples of leveraged buyouts of public companies which have occurred over the past four years. There are two basic transactional formats which have emerged for effecting these transactions. One is the cash merger format (examples are Houdaille Industries, Inc.; Sargent Industries, Inc.; U.S. Natural Resources, Inc.) and the other is the asset purchase format (examples of which are the buyout of Spartek Inc.; Woods Corporation; Big Bear Stores Company.)

A leveraged buyout which is structured as a cash merger is in many respects no different from any other transaction effected in the form of a cash merger. Generally, in the cash merger format the acquiring group forms parent and subsidiary shell corporations. The subsidiary will merge into the acquired corporation with the acquired company surviving the merger. The acquired corporation's shareholders will receive cash for their shares and the acquired company will become a wholly owned subsidiary of the parent company. The two tiered structure is employed in order to provide tax planning flexibility in the event a step-up in the tax basis of the acquired company's assets proves advantageous. The parent corporation will issue the equity and the subsidiary will issue the debt securities which will provide the financing for the acquisition. The lenders in the leveraged buyout typically prefer that the debt securities be issued at the subsidiary level so that they will avoid the possibility that their loans will be subordinated to trade creditors of the acquired company into which the shell subsidiary will be merged.

The asset purchase format involves the formation of a shell corporation which will purchase substantially all the assets of the acquired company for cash. The asset purchase format is typically employed in situations where the purchase price is less than or approximately equal to the tax basis in the shares. Because the assets are purchased at a price less than, or approximately equal to, their tax basis, the selling corporation should realize little or no tax on the sale.

After the purchase of its assets, the selling corporation (which, as a result of the purchase, holds only cash) offers to repurchase or redeem its outstanding shares of stock. When the repurchase or redemption is completed, the selling corporation usually amends its certificate of incorporation to change its business to that of an investment company and invests its remaining cash in tax-exempt securities or other income-producing securities, depending on its tax status. If the selling company has more than 100 shareholders, it will have to register as an investment company under the Investment Company Act of 1940. A variation of this pattern involves a second sale by the selling company of its assets (which consist solely of cash after its first sale of assets transaction) to a tax-exempt bond fund. Therafter the selling company is dissolved and its shareholders receive shares of the tax-exempt fund.[16]

The repurchase or redemption of the selling company's outstanding shares is usually implemented through a tender offer at a price equal to the per share purchase price paid by the acquiring company for the assets. Although there are certain apparent disadvantages for shareholders with small holdings to continue as shareholders, such as lack of liquidity (as a result of delisting, no trading market, etc.) making disposition of the shares difficult, the price of the shares will probably be at a discount from net asset value (since the shares of most publicly traded closed-end investment companies sell at a discount from their net asset value), and the investment policy may be beneficial for high-bracket shareholders—more than 100 shareholders can be expected to remain after the completion of the offer to repurchase or redeem shares. Since the selling company's activities thereafter will be to invest in securities and since it will have more than 100 shareholders, it will be an "investment company" as defined in section 3(a)(1) of the Investment Company Act of 1940 (which section defines an "investment company" as a company which is or holds itself out as being engaged primarily, or proposes to engage primarily, in the business of investing, reinvesting, or trading in securities") and will be required to register under such Act.

Where the "sale-of-assets" feature is most advantageous is in purchasing public or private companies whose controlling shareholder wants to make his assets liquid and diversify his estate. Selling assets instead of the company (i.e., stock) offers the seller a tax shelter. For example, if the owner of a company with a $28 million net worth and a selling price of $32 million sells his company, he will very likely have to pay personal capital gains taxes at the 42.5 percent rate, or $14 million. That leaves him $18 million, which, if invested at 8 percent, would yield about $1.4 million per year.

If he sells only the assets, however, the proceeds go into the remaining shell corporation, which can be converted into a personal holding company, and he

---

[16]See Note 7 on page 533.

will not have to pay personal capital gains taxes until he liquidates the company. Meanwhile, the proceeds are subject only to a 35 percent capital gains tax on the amount that the selling price exceeds book value, which is $4 million. So the seller pays only $1.4 million tax; the 30.6 million residue, invested at 8 percent, yields about $2.4 million a year.

Standards for Analysis

The tables on the following pages compare three cash mergers and three asset-purchase transactions.

The value of these transactions (measured as the total cash raised by the purchaser) varies from $15 million in the case of Spartek to over $389 million for Houdaille. With the exception of Big Bear Stores, which was a retail operation, five of the six companies were engaged in manufacturing as a primary line of business. Woods Corporation was also involved in transportation. The majority of these companies produce proprietary products and occupy a unique position in their respective industries. Every one of these situations had impressive earnings and consistent cash flow in recent years.

COMPARISON OF SIX LEVERAGED BUYOUTS—1

	Houdaille Industries Inc.	Sargent Industries Inc.	Spartek Inc.	Big Bear Stores Company	U.S. Natural Resources	Woods Corporation
Date of Transaction	May 1979	January 1979	March 1979	August 1976	November 1977	December 1978
Type of Transaction	Cash Merger (KKR)	Cash Merger (KKR)	Asset Purchase (Oppenheimer)	Asset Purchase (Oppenheimer)	Cash Merger (KKR)	Asset Purchase (Insiders/DLJ)
Type of Business	Manufactures pumps, industrial products, machine tools.	Manufactures' highly engineered, proprietary energy control devices using mechanical, hydraulic and pneumatic power.	Manufacture and sale of engineered building and industrial products (ceramic floor and tile) and industrial plastics and metals.	Retail food supermarkets and discount department stores, drugstores and a central bakery.	Designs and manufactures large scale capital equipment for forest products industry. Also coal mining and highway products.	Transportation of new motor vehicles by motor carrier and manufacture of pre-engineered metal building systems.
Historical Earnings	Impressive earnings growth over past twelve years (current management's tenure)	Proven history of profitable operations, good cash generator, and record-high order backlog.	Consistent earnings over past five years and positive cash flow.	Steady earnings growth for past five years.	Consistent earnings growth over prior four years.	Consistent earnings and cash flow over past five years.
Value of Transaction	$389,783,000 - of which $338,200,000 used to repurchase outstanding common.	$39,125,000 - of which $33,135,000 used to repurchase outstanding common.	$15,000,000 of which $13,275,903 to shareholders.	$41,602,362 to shareholders.	$23,000,000 of which $22,300,000 to shareholders.	$32,570,000 of which $30,120,000 to shareholders, partly in stock of subsidiary.
Price Paid Per Share	$40.00 for common stock.	$9.50 for common stock. $53.00 for preferred stock.	$17.50 for common stock.	$33.00 for common; $105.00 for preferred.	$8.25 for common stock.	$11.45 for common stock.

COMPARISON OF SIX LEVERAGED BUYOUTS—2

	Houdaille Industries Inc.	Sargent Industries Inc.	Spartek Inc.	Big Bear Stores Company	U.S. Natural Resources	Woods Corporation
Book Value Per Share	$20.18 (12/31/78)	$6.12 (9/30/78) $50.00 stated value of preferred.	$22.14 (9/30/78)	$35.17 (2/28/76)	$9.27 (12/31/76)	$10.23 (6/30/78)
Pre-Announcement Market Price	$20.75 (10/78) $32.00 (3/79) ($37-31 in 1979)	$6.63 ($8.63 - 3.50 in 1978)	$13.88 (1/79) ($15.25 - 14.88)	$26.50 ($32.0 - 22 in 1976)	4.88 (7/6/77) ($3.88 - 7.13 in 1977)	$7.00 ($7.0 - 8.63 in 1978)
Pre-Announcement Market Price/Book	1.03x	1.08x	.63x	.75x	.53x	.69
Last Twelve Months EPS	$3.32 (12/31/78)	$.66 (12/77)	$1.12 (10/31/78)	$5.63 (2/28/76)	$1.04 (1976)	$1.45
P/E = Lowest Market Price (12 Mo.)/12 Mo. EPS	6.25x	5.30x	13.28x	4.71x	3.7x	4.8x
P/E = Price Paid/12 Mo. EPS	12.05x	14.39x	15.63x	5.86x	7.9x	7.9x
Leverage Before Deal = LTD/Equity	.12x (12/78)	.27x (9/78)	.09x(10/78)	.18x	.05x	.31x
Leverage Factor After Deal	305.5/48.5 = 6.3x	35.8/3.9 = 9.1X	5.3x	Not disclosed in proxy.	3.8x	3.1x (Treats subordinated debt and guaranteed loans as equity).
Sources of Funds	Funds from Financing 354.0; Cash Balances 34.8; $388.8	Funds from Financing 39.1; Tax refunds plus Cash Balances 3.9; $43.0	Funds from Financing 12.5; Tax Refund 2.5; 15.0	Funds from Financing 39.9; Cash on Hand 12.9; Tax refund 1.6; 56.1	Cash from Financing 18.0; From cash balance 5.0; Sale of division .08; 23.8	Cash from Financing Plus Petroleum Stock 33.1; 33.1

COMPARISON OF SIX LEVERAGED BUYOUTS—3

	Houdaille Industries Inc.		Sargent Industries Inc.		Spartek Inc.		Big Bear Stores Company		U.S. Natural Resources		Woods Corporation	
Uses of Funds	For common	343.0	For common	30.5	For common & Investment Fund	13.2	For Common & Preferred Investment Fund	41.6	Cash to Shareholders	22.3	Cash and Stock to Shareholders	30.1
	Prepay Long Term Debt	22.2	For ppd	2.5								
			Reduce debt	7.0								
	Redemption of Preferred	9.5			Repay Long Term Debt	1.5	Prepay Debentures				Payment of Tax Liability	2.4
	Fees & Expenses	6.0	Fees & Expenses	1.0	Fees Expenses	.2	Loan for Tax Refund	5.0	Fees and Expenses	.7		
		$381.0		$41.0		$14.9				23.0		
							Fees and Expenses	1.6			Fees and Expenses	.6
	Remaining Cash Balance	$ 8.3	Remaining Cash Balance	$ 2.0	Excess Cash Balance	.1	Excess Cash Balance	1.0	Remaining Cash Balance	.8		33.1
Capital Structure After Deal	7 Year Bank R/C	60.0	5 Year Bank Term Loans	9.5	8 Year R/C	2.5	Excess Cash Balance	6.9	Bank debt (existing)	1.9	Bank debt (existing)	9.5
	20 Year 10¾ Senior Notes	140.0	15 Year Senior Notes	9.5	8 Year Bank Term Loan	8.0	Not disclosed in Proxy.		Bank R/C	1.5	Bank debt (New)	21.0
			pfd (ORICO)	16.75					Bank Term Debt	12.5	Bank debt (New Guaranteed by s/h)	8.0
	17 Year 12% Sen. Sub. Notes (with 10% equity at no additional cost)	75.0	pfd (Sargent)	2.5	Common Stock	2.0			Common & Preferred	4.0		
			common (ORICO)	.45		12.5				$19.9	Subordinated Debentures to Common s/h	1.0
	17 Year 12% Junior Sub. Notes (with 25.6% equity)	31.5	common	1.0							Common	1.0
	17 Year 9% red. pfd (with 24.4% equity)			$39.125								40.5
	Common @ 2.52/sh	25.5									(No detailed disclosure in proxy).	
		$355.0										

548

COMPARISON OF SIX LEVERAGED BUYOUTS—4

	Houdaille Industries Inc.	Sargent Industries Inc.	Spartek Inc.	Big Bear Stores Company	U.S. Natural Resources	Woods Corporation
Ownership of Equity	– Senior Subordinated Lenders — 10%	– Former Preferred Shareholder — 28.5%	– Outside Investor Group — 100%	– Outside Investor Group — 100%	– Management — 34.8%	– Outside Investor Group (Primarily owned by president and two directors). — 100%
	– Junior Subordinated Lenders — 24%	– All other Public Shareholders — 37.6%	– Profit Fund for Management	– Profit Fund for Management (Not detailed disclosure in proxy).	– KKR — 65.2%	
	– Preferred Shareholders — 32%	– KKR — 12.8%			100.0%	
	– Management — 8%	100.0%				
	– KKR — 25%					
	100%					

549

In all the buyouts considered, the price paid per share reflected a substantial premium above the pre-announcement market price. Houdaille showed the largest premium of 92.7 percent with an average of 55.2 percent. This is not surprising because a substantial premium would be required to induce current shareholders to tender their shares. Furthermore, buyout groups would only be attracted to those situations where the company was undervalued by the market. If the market were truly reflective of the company's value, then there would be no justification in paying a higher price for the company.

Another significant ratio shows the relationship between market price and book value. In every case book value was at or above the pre-announcement market price. This again would tend to support the fact that these were undervalued situations. At first glance, it is difficult to reconcile the relationship between price paid per share and book value. Only three of the companies were purchased above book value, and two of these—Houdaille and Sargent—were purchased at 98.2 percent and 55.2 percent above book value respectively. The apparent discrepancy in the price paid/book value ratio can be attributed to lack of accuracy in using book value as a measure of value. With the exception of Houdaille and Sargent, the price paid tends to cluster around book value, averaging a mere 7 percent below book for the remaining four companies.

With Houdaille and Sargent, book value was not a good indication of inherent value. In these two companies, book value failed to reflect the high replacement cost of plant and equipment. The value of plant and equipment for Houdaille and Sargent had been appreciating at a much greater pace than indicated by its depreciable book value. It was not a coincidence that Houdaille and Sargent had highly engineered industrial products used for pumps and hydraulic power. The tremendous appreciation was characteristic of their particular industry.

Thus, book value may be a useful way of screening potential leveraged buyout candidates. It may show that the market is undervaluing a particular company. However, this measure must be applied with extreme caution in determining a company's true value. Substantial appreciation of assets, as in Houdaille and Sargent, is not reflected by book value. Conversely, obsolescence of plants and valueless inventories are not revealed by book value.

A very important characteristic of the six transactions was the low leverage factor prior to the transaction. The ratio of long term debt/equity averaged .17x with a high of .31x for Woods. It is essential that the leveraged buyout candidate have a large debt capacity

since the majority of the purchase price will be paid with debt. The tremendous swing in the leverage factors goes to the essence of leveraged buyouts. The average leverage factor after the transaction was 5.5x with a high of 9.1x for Sargent and a low of 3.1x for Woods Corporation.

Each of the six companies obtained the bulk of their financing from outside sources, particularly banks and insurance companies. However, these sources were supplemented by excess cash balances in Houdaille, Sargent, Big Bear and U.S. Natural Resources. In Sargent, Spartek, and Big Bear Stores, additional cash was generated through tax refunds. These refunds resulted from the sale of assets below their tax basis. In U.S. Natural Resources, one of its divisions was sold simultaneously with the buyout, resulting in the generation of additional cash. In Woods, the Petroleum division was spun-off simultaneously with the transaction. The stock of this division was distributed to Woods shareholders in lieu of cash payment for these assets.

The Houdaille transaction provides an example of the complexity of the capital structure which may be created. In Houdaille, two classes of common stock (voting and non-voting), two classes of preferred stock (senior and junior), bank notes under a revolving credit agreement, senior notes, senior subordinated notes and junior subordinated notes were issued.

In Houdaille, Continental Illinois was the lead bank and was joined by Bankers Trust and Manufacturers Hanover to supply $60 million in the form of a seven-year revolving credit. Prior to the transaction Houdaille had a tangible net worth of approximately $170 million, long-term debt of $20 million, and a current ratio of nearly 3.8 to 1. For these reasons it was considered a first-rate banking credit.

However, Houdaille after the transaction was quite another matter from a banking point of view. It had equity of only $25 million in common stock, $23.5 million in preferred stock and $106.5 million of subordinated debt to support $200 million of senior debt. The current position decreased to 3 to 1. The asset base and earning power of the assets were subject to due diligence appraisal by the lenders and independent appraisal for valuation purposes. The ability of Houdaille after the transaction to carry its financial burden was supported by financial projections prepared by Kohlberg. Nevertheless, the bank loan was priced at 1 percent above prime. In addition, balances were required to be maintained on 10 percent of the outstanding loan and 5 percent of the committed but unused portion.

The long-term lenders supplied Houdaille with $215

million in senior and $31.5 million in subordinated debt. This group, consisting of 12 insurance companies and one pension fund, was led by Prudential which loaned $115 million. Other major lenders included Teachers, Massachusetts Mutual, Connecticut General, and Travelers Insurance. Because of the thin interest coverage for the subordinated loans, an equity kicker was required. The senior subordinated lenders received 10 percent of the equity and the junior subordinated lenders 24 percent.

The final criterion in the table is the ownership of the equity. Houdaille, Sargent, and U.S. Natural Resources were cash-merger transactions. In these situations, Kohlberg structured the transaction, raised the financing, invested its own funds, and obtained a substantial percentage of the common equity. In Houdaille and U.S. Natural Resources, management put up additional money for which they received substantial interests. Sargent differs from these transactions because management did not contribute any of its own funds. The management did however, receive 15,000 shares of phantom stock as an incentive to remain with the company.

Unlike the cash mergers, management did not receive ownership interests in ths asset-purchase transactions. Instead the management group, comprised in each case of the senior management of the Seller, was organized as a general partnership. This partnership was charged with the management of the continued operations of the Seller's business. As an inducement to maintain the high quality of management, an incentive profit fund was created by the Buyer. Payments from the fund, if earned, were paid to the partners and other employees of the Buyer selected by the partnership. The profit fund for each fiscal year was to be comprised of the excess earnings above an established base figure.

SEC Problems with Leveraged Buyouts[17]

One consequence of the increased use of leveraged buyouts as acquisition tools for public companies has been a heightening of the interest of the Securities and Exchange Commission ("SEC") in these transactions. Recent transactions involving Woods Corporation and Spartek, Inc. encountered severe problems with the SEC during the processing of their proxy statements. In fact, SEC investigations in both Woods and Spartek resulted in the institution by the SEC of administrative proceedings and settlement agreements with the companies.

In the case of asset-purchase transactions, the SEC was concerned about the purchase of the company's assets at a price equal to or less than their tax basis and the presence of shareholders with large blocks of low-basis stock. These factors seem to have fueled the SEC's belief that these transactions were actually being done to benefit specific shareholder groups as opposed to all the shareholders of the corporation. Furthermore, the incentive which management receives in these transactions also raised concerns within the SEC with respect to potential conflicts between management interests and the interests of the other shareholders.

Because of Woods and Spartek, the SEC issued Release No. 15572 on February 15, 1979, concerning disclosure in leveraged buyouts, with particular emphasis on actual and potential conflicts of interest, including (1) Disclosure that the principal shareholders or management may have actual or potential conflicts of interest; (2) Disclosure of the sale price per share compared to net tangible book value per share; (3) Disclosure that the public seller may remain secondarily liable with respect to liabilities assumed; (4) Disclosure that certain officers and directors have entered into long-term employment contracts with the purchaser, resulting in increased salaries or profit sharing; and (5) Disclosure of such other factors with respect to the transaction which management believes require shareholder cognizance in making their voting decisions.

A second major area of disclosure under the release involves the reasons for and effect of the transaction. This includes the consequences to the shareholders and to the issuer if the proposed transaction is approved, including the legal effects, tax consequences and effects on market liquidity. Reasons for the transaction should focus on the reasons management is proposing the transaction and any particular reasons for structuring the transaction in the manner proposed.

Material features of the plan must also be disclosed, including employment agreements, terms of financing, tax consequences and the fairness of the price. Rights of shareholders under state law, such as appraisal rights available to dissenting shareholders, must also be disclosed.

In addition, the SEC has recently held that leveraged buyouts are going private transactions for Rule 13e-3, which imposes further substantive and disclosure requirements. Thus, aside from the difficulties of structuring and financing the public leveraged buyout, there

---

[17]This section is based upon a series of recent articles in the *New York Law Journal,* including R.S. Aaron, "Two Formats Available For Leveraged Buyouts," New York (June 4, 1979), and R.L. Frome, "SEC Takes Position on Leveraged Buyouts", (April 5, 1979).

is an important legal dimension which must be considered as well.

THE FUTURE OF LEVERAGED BUYOUTS

The leveraged buyout has been likened to the so-called "bootstrap" deals, where an entrepreneur borrows all (or substantially all) of the purchase price of a company and then pays back his borrowings either from the proceeds of the sale of unwanted assets of the acquired company, from the proceeds of a public equity offering, out of the firm's operating earnings, or any combination of the three. The result of even a modest dollar return from the ultimate sale of the property is an extremely large return on equity. Such transactions were common in the early days of the conglomerate era and, in fact, formed the basis for a few well-known latter-day enterprises.

Some believe that the popularity of the bootstrap financing in general and leveraged buyouts in particular may be waning, in large measure as a result of more sophistication among sellers. Among other reasons offered for its possible decline are:

(1) Tightening of cash tender offer rules. One must now disclose the source of one's financing and be subject to more crippling and expensive litigation than before.

(2) More conservative lending policies among commercial banks, the traditional source of bootstrap financing. These institutions have incurred large loan losses in recent years and tend to shy away from acquisition loans during periods of credit restraint because they are economically unproductive.

(3) Increased awareness of leveraged buyouts, competition for leveraged buyouts, together with the availability of equity capital for leveraged buyout transactions.

Other doom-sayers believe that, like all investment trends, leveraged buyouts will eventually be carried to excess. In their greed, investors, lenders and brokers will start reaching for marginal deals. Other brokers will find a way to bring the public in at an early stage when the risk is still high. There will be failures and scandals and big loan losses, and the whole game will get a bad name.

Aside from the new SEC rules requiring greater disclosure, the recent Louisiana Pacific/Flintkote deal (where Louisiana Pacific outbid KKR's bid of $380 million for a leveraged buyout) may make managements in public companies more cautious in considering this type of transaction. The required disclosures

and publicity could well attract larger companies (particularly foreigners) to outbid the buyout group. Therefore, the management of the prospective company might be hesitant to consider it.

There is, however, another side to the story. While there are no exact figures, it is estimated that several hundred leveraged buyouts took place in 1978 and an even greater number occurred in 1979. The major firms alone—including Carl Marks, Kohlberg, Oppenheimer, Gibbons, DLJ—accounted for nearly 50 of these. Bankers Trust Company acted as lender or financial advisor in five leveraged buyouts in 1978 and seven in 1979. Banker's Trust's activity is indicative of that of another 12 to 15 major banks in the country. The remainder of the leveraged buyouts were conducted by the numerous, but less active, investment banks.

Jerome Kohlberg, Sr., says that "In the last two years we have had the greatest environment ever for management buyouts. There is plenty of money available. The institutions have generated a lot of cash that they have taken out of the stock market and out of venture capital deals. With very low stock prices, companies are increasingly disenchanted with being public, and you have private companies that can't go public. There is no favorable market. So, many instead are going the buyout route."[18]

Many of the large corporations that rushed feverishly to conglomerate during the acquisition binge of the Sixties are increasingly divesting those business that have become obsolete, unprofitable or incompatible with the technology and goals of the parent company. If the parent closes them down, it risks taking writeoffs. Sales to another big company might result in antitrust problems and the delay could be interminable. Thus, selling them as going concerns for cash to existing management is in most cases preferable to liquidation. Smaller public companies are finding the buyout route an alternative to being acquired by larger corporations. They are afforded a means of going private until more favorable stock market conditions warrant a public offering. Rather than go through the difficulties of takeover (witness Exxon/Reliance and CIT/RCA) many firms will retain the incentive of going private.

The advocates of leveraged buyouts argue that the financing of leveraged buyouts is becoming easier because, with the refinement of techniques, big lenders in the insurance companies and venture-capital affiliates of major commercial banks are becoming more involved. Big buyouts like Houdaille and the purchase of Congoleum Corp. for $430 million are a logical exten-

---

[18]Quoted in Galluccio, p. 42.

sion of the trend that has been building for several years. In a way, the trend is feeding on the same essentials as the takeover craze. Many companies are selling so far below replacement value in the stock market that they have become increasingly good buys.

One interesting formula was proposed by James McN. Stancill for finding companies that could finance a buyout by borrowing on the target company's assets and cash.[19] Inventory will have the potential for generating 50 percent of its costs, receivables 70 percent to 80 percent, fixed assets 90 percent to 100 ~~~~ of their "quick-sale" appraised value. There-~~~~ ~~~~kly eliminates companies whose assets ~~~~ ~~~~rily of inventory, such as distributor ~~~~ service-type companies. Manufactur-~~~~e most promising area. Owners of ~~~~ manufacturing companies would ~~~~o sell, and certainly at anything less ~~~~ompanies with unusual fixed assets, ~~~~lt machinery for a particular pur-~~~~ candidates because the assets' ~~~~ve to cost is usually quite low. ~~~~rrow to a manufacturer owning ~~~~ assets (machinery) in propor-~~~~l rather old fixed assets, with greatly deprecia~~~~ k value relative to quick-sale value. Machine tools ~~~~ ten have economic lives far in excess of their depreciable lives. Most important there should be sufficient cash flow to service debt and provide a reasonable salary for the entrepreneur as well. Although a proprietary product is desirable, a job shop should be considered as well.

Publicly traded leveraged buyout candidates are the easiest to spot because of the accessibility of public information. I have developed the following criteria for selection of potential target companies in the Compustat Data Base:

(1) The Market Price/Tangible Book Value on a per share basis must be equal to or less than .75. (This is near the average of .78 for the six cases examined in the preceding section.) A market price well below book value will allow for a purchase price at or near book value while at the same time offering an attractive premium to current shareholders.

(2) The Price/Earnings ratio must be equal to or less than 7x. The average of the six cases in the preceding section was 6.3x, but only one of the six had a multiple above 7.) This restriction will eliminate those situations where the market might have overvalued the stock. A high current multiple would reduce the likelihood of a purchaser offering a substantial premium above market to existing shareholders.

(3) Leverage defined as Long-Term Debt/Equity must be equal to or less than .25. (The highest leverage factor among the six cases was Woods' .31x, with an average of .17x). Large unused borrowing capacity, which may be indicated by this ratio, is the characteristic which allows for the use of the company's assets to borrow the purchase price. If a company is already highly leveraged, it is unlikely that the buyer can borrow the purchase price against the remaining unencumbered assets.

(4) The net income figures after taxes over the last three years must be positive and increasing. Stability in earnings and cash flow is essential to attract the lenders.

(5) The universe selected excludes most service industries (such as Banking, Insurance, Transportation, etc.), all regulated industries, agriculture, forestry, fishing, mining, construction and communications. Highly capitalized manufacturers in industries where regulatory approval (aside from SEC) would not be required are most desirable.

Thirty-one companies are found to meet these preliminary criteria (see table starting on page 554).

These companies might be further screened to determine which are in low risk industries, and which have large amounts of excess cash and marketable securities balances. One potential source of cash comes from subsidiaries or operations in unrelated industries which possess properties that can be readily liquidated without detriment to ongoing operations. Preference should also be given to companies with large blocks of shares held either by a group of individuals or a large institutional investor. The quality of management, undervalued assets, complexity of capital structure, and cash flow would also weigh heavily in the selection process. It is likely that a majority of the companies on the remaining list will be involved in this year's leveraged buyout or acquisition activity.

The end of the leveraged buyout game is still a good way off. Right now, leveraged buyouts are playing a constructive role in keeping opportunity alive for venturesome executives and venturesome investors.

---

[19] J.M. Stancill, "Search For A Leveraged Buyout", *Harvard Business Review*, Boston (1977).

LEVERAGED BUYOUT CANDIDATES
COMPANIES SCREENED FOR BOTH LEVERAGE AND DISCOUNT

COMPANY	SALES (mill.)	NET INCOME (mill.)	PRICE PER SHARE	SHARES OUT-STANDING (thous.)	MARKET VALUE (mill.)	P/E RATIO	LEVERAGE	TANG. BOOK VALUE (mill.)	TANG. BOOK PER SHARE	MARKET DISCOUNT FROM BOOK VALUE
AMERICAN MTRS CORP	3117.050	68.144	5.250	31883.	167.386	4.27	0.146	428.817	13.450	0.390
UNITED STATES GYPSUM	1525.380	123.547	28.000	15911.	445.508	3.69	0.206	625.365	39.304	0.712
HORMEL GEO A & CO	1414.020	30.612	14.750	9607.	141.703	4.00	0.151	190.373	19.816	0.744
TIMKIN CO	1282.070	102.131	45.875	11204.	513.873	5.20	0.041	705.859	63.001	0.728
U S INDS IMC	1273.850	51.158	7.125	24761.	176.422	4.14	0.221	438.807	17.722	0.402
SMITH A O CORP	836.433	29.612	14.375	4906.	70.524	2.99	0.180	220.092	44.862	0.320
SPRINGS MLS INC	827.861	35.063	14.000	8699.	121.786	3.44	0.248	335.827	38.605	0.363
CANNON MILS CO	608.718	38.145	22.375	9381.	209.900	5.23	0.000	316.896	33.781	0.662
V F CORP	544.310	38.822	19.500	8311.	162.064	5.04	0.120	220.022	26.474	0.737
NORTHWESTERN STL & WIRE	477.155	40.059	23.125	7506.	173.576	5.03	0.005	241.823	32.217	0.718
A P S INC	391.791	17.005	7.125	12085.	86.106	4.98	0.193	126.904	10.501	0.679
STEWART WARNER CORP	365.971	21.744	22.250	5188.	115.433	5.55	0.012	166.195	32.035	0.695
DIBRELL BROS INC	320.877	4.229	12.000	1314.	15.768	3.82	0.189	32.403	24.660	0.487
SEALED PWR CORP	279.390	20.899	14.750	4809.	70.933	4.09	0.165	116.736	24.275	0.608
BASSETT FURNITURE INDS	272.069	23.726	15.750	7289.	114.802	4.54	0.014	156.311	21.445	0.734
TI CARO INC	222.046	14.462	18.599	2704.	52.728	3.61	0.204	91.724	33.922	0.575
THOROFARE MKTS INC	218.348	0.767	3.250	1245.	4.046	5.33	0.195	13.906	11.170	0.291
OGLEBAY NORTON CO	193.690	17.112	36.000	2310.	83.160	4.79	0.113	112.660	48.771	0.738
CTS CORP	187.951	10.991	15.750	4583.	72.182	6.62	0.000	100.703	21.975	0.717
CUNNINGHAM DRUB STORES	182.890	11.682	8.50	1191.	10.124	6.85	0.021	28.677	24.078	0.353
RICHARDSON CO	159.808	4.604	14.625	2076.	30.362	6.90	0.110	59.336	28.582	0.512
LANE INC	158.931	11.422	20.000	2421.	48.420	4.09	0.000	87.093	35.974	0.556
BELKNAP INC	125.763	2.608	11.625	1504.	17.484	6.80	0.000	28.098	18.682	0.622
SCHOLASTIC MAGAZINES	125.125	4.545	8.500	1719.	14.612	4.36	0.183	29.789	17.328	0.481
MEANS SVC INC	113.359	5.005	16.000	1696.	27.136	5.42	0.000	42.765	25.215	0.635
FAB INDS INC	112.710	8.654	10.250	2350.	24.088	2.70	0.049	34.440	14.655	0.699
MOUNT VERNON MLS INC	111.404	5.005	16.000	823.	20.678	3.59	0.156	47.666	57.917	0.434
TORIN CORP	97.977	3.160	13.750	1052.	14.465	4.58	0.156	47.666	28.356	0.485
LOUISVILLE CEM CO	90.022	8.875	23.750	1580.	37.525	4.22	0.037	69.813	44.185	0.538
ALTAMIL CORP	88.198	4.317	11.250	1246.	14.018	4.15	0.158	24.568	19.718	0.571
CONROY INC	86.335	4.326	4.625	4089.	18.912	4.17	0.003	30.338	7.419	0.623
SIMKINS INDS INC	83.159	5.183	8.000	1407.	11.256	3.02	0.162	35.496	25.227	0.317
BUCKABEE MEARS CO	74.000	4.339	6.250	3077.	19.231	4.28	0.083	31.970	10.390	0.602
AMERICAN FURNITURE INC	71.403	2.920	3.938	2817.	11.092	3.90	0.156	25.170	8.935	0.441

554

LEVERAGED BUYOUT CANDIDATES
COMPANIES SCREENED FOR BOTH LEVERAGED AND DISCOUNT

COMPANY	SALES (mill.)	NET INCOME (mill.)	PRICE PER SHARE	SHARES OUT- STANDING (thous.)	MARKET VALUE (mill.)	P/E RATIO	LEVERAGE	TANG. BOOK VALUE (mill.)	TANG. BOOK PER SHARE	MARKET DISCOUNT FROM BOOK VALUE
TOOTSIE ROLL INDS INC	69.619	3.085	7.250	2444.	17.720	5.75	0.000	26.600	10.883	0.666
BRIGADIER INDS CORP	67.617	1.358	2.750	2007.	5.519	3.99	0.118	8.769	4.369	0.629
PAT FASHIONS INDS INC	65.785	2.316	5.875	969.	5.693	3.25	0.000	26.600	17.173	0.342
SHATTERPROOF GLASS CP	65.588	2.155	8.250	1272.	10.494	5.46	0.103	30.219	23.757	0.347
SELAS CORP AMER	64.284	1.256	6.000	1213.	7.278	3.77	0.073	11.745	9.683	0.620
BERKLINE CORP	63.181	1.973	5.375	1506.	8.095	4.07	0.117	18.935	12.573	0.428
MICHIGAN SUGAR CO	61.217	1.903	13.750	1210.	16.638	4.63	0.127	24.680	20.397	0.674
FEDERAL SCREW WKS	60.180	3.828	9.000	1036.	10.224	4.74	0.205	21.743	19.140	0.470
AINLEEN INC	60.080	0.315	2.125	5061.	10.755	4.62	0.208	34.946	6.905	0.308
MEM INC	59.428	3.467	9.625	1697.	16.334	4.72	0.027	31.951	18.828	0.511
BUELL INDS INC	59.187	2.179	7.000	1422.	9.954	6.19	0.224	24.706	17.374	0.403
FRITZI CALIF MFG CORP	56.244	2.128	9.750	841.	8.200	4.60	0.021	13.400	15.933	0.612
JACO ELECTRS INC	48.639	0.779	5.250	751.	3.943	4.43	0.153	6.429	8.561	0.613
NORTHWSTN STS PORT CEM	40.696	5.129	24.000	944.	23.856	4.72	0.141	43.889	44.154	0.544
PRATT-READ CORP	38.161	1.961	4.375	1556.	6.888	4.17	0.045	16.039	10.308	0.424
JACLYN INC	37.263	1.216	4.375	1450.	6.344	4.92	0.112	11.800	8.138	0.538
VERIT INDS	35.679	0.275	1.375	768.	1.056	4.04	0.000	2.405	3.132	0.439
VAN SCHAACK & CO	33.067	2.188	6.625	1382.	9.156	4.17	0.139	14.704	10.640	0.623
NOBILITY HOMES INC	30.130	0.978	2.750	1423.	3.913	3.24	0.061	6.282	4.415	0.623
RONCO TELEPRODUCTS INC	29.188	0.404	2.500	1256.	3.140	5.81	0.000	7.023	5.592	0.447
SCHRADER ABE CORP	28.754	0.063	2.250	1712.	3.852	6.82	0.000	10.185	5.949	0.378
REALEX CORP	25.818	1.259	6.250	699.	4.369	4.19	0.032	10.128	14.489	0.431
THREE D DEPTS INC	25.429	1.395	3.375	1514.	5.112	3.38	0.000	8.900	5.876	0.574
KEYSTONE PORTLAND CEM	22.436	0.813	7.250	542.	3.930	4.83	0.232	12.705	23.479	0.309
CREST FOAM CORP	21.851	0.677	3.375	1312.	4.428	6.25	0.164	6.641	5.062	0.667
KENWIN SHOPS INC	21.015	0.982	10.250	410.	0.722	4.74	0.000	7.289	17.778	0.577
NOEL INDS INC	20.734	0.123	1.625	1109.	1.802	5.42	0.154	5.465	4.928	0.330
PENOBSCOT SHOE CO	19.851	1.014	5.500	879.	4.835	4.07	0.007	9.056	10.303	0.534
CHADWICK MILLER INC	18.410	1.244	6.625	1008.	6.678	5.39	0.000	10.062	9.982	0.664
ALLES ORGAN CO	15.990	1.793	13.000	565.	7.345	3.93	0.000	12.995	23.000	0.565
DISCOUNT FABRICS INC	14.819	0.253	1.375	993.	1.365	6.88	0.171	3.593	3.618	0.380
UDS INC	13.407	0.243	1.875	965.	1.809	4.17	0.019	5.629	5.833	0.321
UNIVERSAL METALS & MACHY	11.511	0.335	2.750	469.	1.290	3.82	0.172	2.786	5.950	0.463

DISSOLUTION AND DIVESTITURE

Dissolution and divestiture can be viewed from very similar vantage points. Corporate dissolution occurs when it is determined by management and shareholders that a company is worth more dead than alive. By this we mean that the underlying value of assets sold in the marketplace to the highest bidder represents a return on investment which the operating entity employing those assets is not able to match. Divestiture, for a large corporation, is a method of partial dissolution. The sale of an unwanted subsidiary or plant enables a company to employ the capital tied up in this investment in a more productive purpose. Divestitures from such corporations are a primary source of merger, acquisition and buyout activity.

W. Peter Slusser employs an example-oriented approach to explain liquidation of companies to realize value. He suggests that finding undervalued companies is in some respects the same as searching for oil or gold. One must be systematic in his approach and utilize the best and most practical analytical tools available. This chapter details the cases of the Belridge Oil Company, UV Industries, Inc., Hammermill Paper Company and Western Pacific Industries, Inc. Material on the principal types of liquidation and quasi-liquidation is clearly and concisely formulated for the reader.

The troubled or non-essential subsidiary is the prime candidate for corporate divestiture. Milton L. Glass addresses a structure for a divestiture program in the corporate world as the phenomenon of the business conglomerate becomes increasingly less fashionable. There is a wide range of considerations for the divesting company, including establishing a proper price, using third parties to locate potential purchasers, antitrust problems, employee-relation problems, pension problems, and tax considerations.

W. PETER SLUSSER

W. PETER SLUSSER is a Managing Director, Blyth Eastman Paine Webber and heads its Merger & Acquisition/Corporate Development Department. Prior to his joining Paine Webber in December 1975, Mr. Slusser was a Senior Vice President, Director and a member of the Executive Committee of Shields Model Roland Inc., and Manager of its Corporate Finance Department. He was formerly the Vice Chairman of Pacific Holding Co., a Director of Armstrong Chemcon and Gemini Computer Systems, a privately owned European company. He was a founder, original stockholder and a Director of Associated Mortgage Companies, Inc., now a subsidiary of First Pennsylvania Corp. Mr. Slusser is an honors graduate of Stanford University and the Harvard Business School. He is a member of the Finance Advisory Board, Columbia Graduate School of Business.

35

Liquidating the Company to Realize Value

W. PETER SLUSSER

I. BACKGROUND—THE BELRIDGE OIL COMPANY

"Beauty is in the beholder's eye." So said a top official of the Shell Oil Company when his company recently won the competition to purchase the Belridge Oil Company.

The shareholders of Belridge had in substance waited since January 25, 1911, when the Company was founded, for this moment. As recently as 1974, the year after the Arab oil embargo, the stock of Belridge was selling for as little as $90 per share. The final Shell offer made on December 10, 1979, amounts to $3,665 per share in cash or $916 in cash and $2,749 principal amount of installment notes, for each Belridge share.

On the basis of the 996,800 outstanding Belridge shares, this price placed a value on the Company of $3,653,272,000 as contrasted with a 1974 market value of $89,712,000. The cash and installment notes and cash were paid to the shareholders in late January 1980. And on January 25, 1980, Belridge gave notice of commencement of voluntary proceedings to liquidate and to wind up and dissolve the business.

II. THE KEY QUESTIONS IN BELRIDGE /SHELL TRANSACTION

1. What accounted for the extraordinary increase in the value of Belridge?
2. How does one find these very undervalued situations?
3. How does one force, in effect, the liquidation or sale of the business?
4. What are the principal types of liquidations, dissolutions or quasi-liquidation/sales?

III. SOME OF THE ANSWERS FOR BELRIDGE /SHELL QUESTIONS

Belridge is used as the primary example in this chapter because of its outstanding and somewhat unique characteristics. It was a little known OTC stock in the Los Angeles market. There was a large concentrated ownership in four groups: Mobil Oil (17.9 percent), Texaco (17 percent), and the Whittier, Buck, and Green families (estimated at approximately 50 percent), and a few knowledgeable or lucky undervalued-situation seekers.

It had a very solid balance sheet. At December 31, 1974, about the time the writer first noticed the Company, Belridge had net working capital of $26,099,000 of which $24,630,000 was cash and cash equivalents. In addition, the Company had investments in state and municipal bonds and common stocks of $15,882,000. The Company had *no long-term debt,* and book value of $80,194,000, or $80.36 per share, and it was trading in a range of $90.00 to $120.00 per share.

Belridge was generating sizable amounts of cash, i.e., $33,794,000, or $33.90 per share.

The Company's net income was also strong, i.e., $21,416,000 on $69,337,000 of revenues, or an after tax margin of 30.9 percent. The earnings per share were $21.48.

In addition, the company owned an oil field in Kern County, California, and approximately 16,000 acres of farm land in the Belridge Water Storage District. The one major negative was that no one except the officers and directors knew the size and value of the oil reserves, and they made no effort to disclose the size or nature of the reserves.

The mystery of the reserves was unlocked because the Company grew to more than 500 shareholders and was, therefore, required under the SEC disclosure rules to provide its shareholders with reserve estimates. These reserve estimates were revealed to shareholders by means of a letter from Leland K. Whittier dated April 30, 1979. In that letter, Mr. Whittier pointed out that De Golyer and McNaughton, one of the country's most prestigious independent petroleum engineers, had provided the following estimates of proved reserves of crude oil and natural gas:

	Crude Oil (barrels)	Natural Gas (MCF)
Proved developed	134,740,000	60,488,000
Proved undeveloped	241,532,000	87,366,000
Total proved	376,272,000	147,854,000

Various analysts began assigning values to these reserves. The initial estimates were approximately $6.00 per barrel of oil and $1.00 per MCF for gas. Using these rough figures, this put a value of approximately $2,400,000,000 on the reserves or equal to about $2.400 per share of Belridge common stock.

This very interesting letter to shareholders also included a bombshell: "We also wish to inform you that the Company has received inquiries with respect to a possible sale to or merger with other corporations, and as a result and pursuant to the discretion of the Board of Directors, the Company has engaged the investment banking firm of Morgan Stanley & Co., Incorporated to act as a financial advisor and to explore the possibilities for a sale or merger of Belridge."

The Company had, in effect, put itself up for sale, with the bids due on September 17, 1979. The oil giants were obviously interested, including such names as Standard Oil of California, Getty Oil Co., Texaco, Mobil, Shell, Union Pacific Corporation and Veba AG (an energy group 43.75 percent owned by the West German government), among others.

One side effect of this announcement was a lawsuit brought by Texaco, Inc. and the Mobil Oil Company, which together owned about 35 percent of the Company's stock, to block the sale on the grounds that it would jeopardize their minority interests. Belridge counter-sued and asserted that Mobil and Texaco did not criticize the proposed September 17th auction until very late in the game and opposed the sale because "that method reduced their chances of acquiring control of Belridge."

Despite these legal skirmishes, the acquisition of Belridge by Shell Oil Company moved ahead. On October 15, 1979, Belridge and Shell jointly announced the signing of a definitive merger agreement providing for the merger of a wholly owned subsidiary of Shell with Belridge.

On November 26, 1979, the Company mailed its proxy statement to its shareholders setting forth in detail the form and substance of the proposed transaction with the Shell Oil Company and called for a special meeting of shareholders to be held on December 10, 1979. The special shareholders' meeting was held on December 10, and the merger of Belridge with a subsidiary of Shell Oil Company was approved and consummated.

Payment, as previously mentioned, was accomplished in January of 1980. An investment of $90 in 1974 turned out to be worth $3,665 in 1980!

IV. SOME THOUGHTS ON FINDING UNDERVALUED SITUATIONS

Finding undervalued companies is, in some respects, similar to searching for oil or gold. One must be systematic in his approach and use the best but most practical analytical tools available. Certain tests are useful:

1. The stock should be selling near or preferably below book value.
2. The stock must assuredly be selling at a substantial discount from adjusted book value—that is, book value adjusted for the present market value of its current and fixed assets including such items as oil and gas reserves, mineral reserves, timber reserves, real estate values, etc.
3. The Company should have a strong balance sheet—that is, a balance sheet that has a substantial cash position, little or no short or long-term debt, and the ability to generate annual sizable and positive cash flow.

Certainly, Belridge met the three tests outlined above, particularly, test No. 2.

Other recent, well-known examples of liquidation or sale in order to realize value are UV Industries, Inc., (successful), Hammermill Paper Company (not successful, to date), and Western Pacific Industries, Inc. (certain quasi-liquidating steps).

UV Industries, Inc:

The shareholders of UV Industries approved a Plan of Liquidation and Dissolution at a special meeting on March 26, 1979. The Company's subsidiary, Federal Pacific Electric Co., was sold for $345 million on March 26, 1979, and the first liquidating dividend of $18 per share was distributed on April 30. The plan provided that all assets would be sold, or distributed to shareholders within a twelve-month period, and the net proceeds distributed to shareholders.

On November 26, 1979, Sharon Steel Corp., which controlled about 23 percent of UV, purchased the remaining assets of UV for $518 million in cash and debentures. This was after the sale of substantially all of its oil and gas properties to Tennaco Corp. for $135 million in October, 1979. The Sharon action completed the liquidation program. The shareholders thus received or were to receive the following:

1. Initial cash payment,
   April 30, 1979   — $18
2. Final distribution,
   when legally permissible:
   a. debentures   —   27*
   b. cash   —   7
          Total Estimated Value   = $52*

*prior to any discount on value of debentures

The important aspect of these financial moves is that UV's directors felt that the Company's common stock was substantially undervalued. On December 15, 1978, the stock was selling for $19⅜ as contrasted with a book value estimated at approximately $25 per share.

It is interesting to review some of the Board's logic in recommending liquidation:

1. "Given ... the present status of the economy;
2. "The speculation among economists ... as to the possibilty of a recession in 1979;
3. "The uncertainties of an acquisition program;
4. "The relationship of the cash position after the sale of Federal Pacific Electric ... and the potential asset value of the remaining assets to the recent market value of UV; and
5. "The federal income tax to be paid upon the gain from the sale of Federal if the proposed Plan of Liquidation and Dissolution is *not* adopted; it has been concluded by the Board that it is in the best interest of all stockholders to adopt the Plan of Liquidation and Dissolution."

In its liquidation, UV stated that it intended to comply with Section 337 of the Internal Revenue Code, which requires distribution of cash and assets to or for the benefit of stockholders within a period of 12 months following stockholder approval. By complying with Section 337, UV sought to benefit from the non-recognition of gain provisions of the Internal Revenue Code which could result in a tax savings of approximately $42 million.

The end result of the UV liquidation is that its shareholders have received $18 in cash and were to receive a debenture with a face value of $27 and $7 more in cash when legally permissible or $52 in value for a stock that was selling for $19⅜ in December of 1978. In this case, it is difficult to argue that the shareholders were not well rewarded for the Board's recommending a Plan of Liquidation and Dissolution.

Hammermill Paper Company

In July, 1980, Hammermill's management won a proxy contest spearheaded by Carl C. Icahn who held about 10 percent of the stock and who sought to sell or liquidate the company. Mr. Icahn nominated himself to the board, committed to selling the business on the assumption that the sale would exceed the market value of the Company's common stock. (At the end of July, 1980, Hammermill common was quoted at $25½ versus a book value of $36.84 at December 31, 1979).

Two important elements in the contest were the vigorous opposition to the Icahn proposals waged by management, and management's strong 1978, 1979 and interim 1980 earnings results.

The problem for the "sale or liquidation protagonists" in Hammermill was that as contrasted with Belridge and UV Industries, they were outsiders. A vigorous contest was held in the spring of 1980, but with only 10 percent of the stock, and with the machinery to fight the dissidents in the hands of management and the board of Hammermill, the dissidents lost.

However, with little in the way of concentrated ownership, and the stock (on August 15, 1980) trading in the $30 area with a book value of over $38 and earnings in the range of $5 per share, the Company may well hear from the dissident group again. Hammermill has the characteristics of a candidate for liquidation, particularly with 420,000 acres of low cost timberland. It is obviously management's job to see to it that market values more adequately reflect the underlying values of the Company if they hope to avoid liquidation or sale proposals in the future.

Western Pacific Industries Inc.

Western Pacific Industries is not in liquidation in the classic sense, but it has in effect liquidated certain major assets in order to improve the overall return to its shareholders. In April, 1979, the Company completed the sale of the assets and business of its railroad subsidiary, Western Pacific Railroad Co., to the public. The sale price was $14 million cash plus the assumption of approximately $116 million in liabilities. The sale generated a substantial tax-loss carry forward credit (after-tax benefits of $44.8 million).

On November 7, 1979, the directors of Western Pacific Industries declared an extraordinary cash dividend to stockholders in the amount of $23 per share payable December 31, 1979. Based upon the applicable provisions of the Internal Revenue Code and Letter Rulings and other determinations, the distribution would not constitute a taxable dividend, but rather a return of capital to be applied as a reduction of the tax basis of the shareholder in his stock. To the extent that the amount of the distribution exceeded the shareholder's basis and, if the stock was held as a capital asset, the excess would be treated as a long-term or short-term capital gain.

It is interesting to note that in December, 1977, shortly before the February, 1978 announcement that the Company, through its transportation subsidiaries, agreed to sell their assets and business to corporations formed by the management of such subsidiaries, the stock of Western Pacific Industries was trading at $24¾. The stock was trading (August 15, 1980) in the $43 range, and the shareholders received a special cash dividend of $23 per share paid on December 31, 1979, or a total value of $66 through quasi-liquidation.

The Board's reasoning for the distribution of $60,000,000 to its shareholders is worth noting:

1. "The highly competitive corporate acquisition market of the past few years has created an exorbitant price level related to fundamental values, and we have been unwilling to purchase another large business on terms which do not meet our acquisition criteria."
2. "We believe our stockholders can invest the cash to be distributed on more attractive terms than we presently can if we were to pay overly inflated prices to stockholders or other companies for control or full ownership of another business."

Once again, the patient investor had been rewarded, and the undervalued company had been partially liquidated to the benefit of shareholders.

V. HOW TO FORCE THE LIQUIDATION OR SALE OF A BUSINESS

This is, of course, the most difficult action for any group or party to instigate and carry out. As previously discussed, recent examples of this type of activity are Belridge Oil, UV Industries, Inc., and Hammermill Paper Company. In the case of both Belridge and UV Industries, the companies are in the process of completing their liquidations. Hammermill Paper Company has recently defeated a movement by certain of its shareholders to force the sale or liquidation of the Company.

It would appear that the following forces must be present:

1. A strong commitment on the part of the Board and management to realize the maximum benefit to shareholders through the liquidation or the liquidating sale of the corporation.
2. Lacking a unanimous Board or management support for liquidation, or a liquidation-sale, then there must be a very strong group of shareholders who have the will-power and financial resources to force, through appropriate shareholder processes, the liquidation or liquidation-sale of the corporation.
3. Basically, there must be sound and rational reasons for a liquidation or liquidation-sale, and these reasons must be documented and made very clear to the shareholders and the Board of Directors.

VI. THE PRINCIPAL TYPES OF LIQUIDATIONS, DISSOLUTIONS OR QUASI-LIQUIDATION SALES

Liquidation means the conversion of assets into cash, the payment of all liabilities, and the distribution of the remaining assets to the shareholders, and the legal processes to carry out the dissolution of the corporation. The liquidation process is generally protracted in nature because of the time that it takes to sell non-liquid assets such as real estate, oil properties, etc.

Dissolution means the termination of corporate existence. The purpose of this chapter is not to discuss the negative aspects of liquidation to avoid insolvency, but rather voluntary dissolution to achieve maximum benefits for the shareholders.

In most states, laws have been enacted that allow the dissolution of a corporation by a vote of a specified majority of the outstanding stockholders.

Quasi-Liquidation-Sale can mean several things:

1. The sale or merger of 100 percent of a company with the final outcome of liquidation as was the case with Belridge Oil.
2. The sale of a major asset in order to partially achieve the shareholders' goals in terms of value realization. Western Pacific Industries' sale of its transportation subsidiary is an example.
3. A "going private" transaction which is not discussed in this chapter, but is dealt with in some detail in Arthur Borden's chapter of this handbook, (Chapter 31).

VII. CONCLUSION

This chapter has reviewed three examples of liquidation to realize value:

1. Belridge Oil Company, through the liquidation-sale to the Shell Oil Company.
2. UV Industries, through the complete liquidation process.
3. Western Pacific Industries, through a sale of a principal subsidiary which resulted in a partial liquidation.

In each of these cases, the shareholders benefited to varying degrees, the greatest, of course, in Belridge Oil. The example of Hammermill Paper Company had a different result in that the sale or liquidation plans by a minority shareholder group were recently defeated. The basic question is what are the majority of the shareholders' aims and objectives. Should a company be liquidated or sold at a given point in time to maximize shareholders' profits? This frequently is a difficult question to answer, and it must be studied carefully by Boards and their advisors. Obviously, there are many companies in today's stock market environment that are worth more to the shareholder in liquidation or sale than what he can fetch on the stock market.

MILTON L. GLASS

Vice President and Treasurer
The Gillette Company

MILTON L. GLASS, in 28 years with Gillette, has been responsible for the management of almost every Controller's and Treasury function, leading to his present position as Corporate Treasurer. He holds BBA and MBA degrees, from Northeastern University and graduated from the Program for Management Development at the Harvard Business School. He has lectured at universities and before business groups on a wide variety of financial subjects and has contributed to numerous published works. His outside interests cover a wide range of civic, charitable, governmental and health care activities, among which is service as Vice Chairman of the Board of Blue Shield of Massachusetts.

36

The Troubled or Non-Essential Subsidiary

MILTON L. GLASS

UNDERTAKING DIVESTITURE

Divestment can be defined as a process for ridding an enterprise of certain business assets, thereby putting an end to the business activities associated with those particular assets.

A troubled or non-essential subsidiary, by definition, constitutes a prime candidate for divestment. At the very least, the existence of such a division, subsidiary or product line acts as a stimulus to force a management decision as to whether retention or divestment is an appropriate plan of action.

If retention is decided, management is faced with a host of decisions that must be implemented to effect changes needed to correct the trouble. In some cases, divestment is the preferable plan of action or may be the only action possible in the case of court-ordered divestiture.

While the ''merger craze'' of the Sixties was responsible for an increase in corporate divestitures in the Seventies, divestitures of subsidiaries were certainly not uncommon before the Sixties and are quite frequent at this time, long after divestment associated with conglomerative mergers has ceased to be fashionable. Divestment most often results from management's decision that a subsidiary, division or product line no longer fits the enterprise's longer-range strategy and must therefore be excised from the corporate body. This process has been compared with weeding or pruning a garden so as to insure maximum health and productivity for the remaining part over the longer run. Rather than waiting for a subsidiary or division to become troubled, the strategy review should be a continuous process allied with a budgeting or scheduled business review procedure rather than a ''fire-fighting'' exercise.

ALTERNATIVES TO DIVESTMENT

At the point in time when management has identified a troubled or non-essential subsidiary or division as a divestment candidate and has decided that retention and rehabilitation are not indicated, other divestment alternatives should be considered.

It may, for example, be possible to partially divest with better after-tax results than full divestiture. On the other hand, abandoning assets or shutting down operations may be the best choice, given all of the accounting, tax and legal considerations. There may, similarly, be some advantage in delaying the divestment, during which time the business can be ''cleaned up'' to bring a better price when finally divested, or during which profits may be squeezed out of the operation while it is being contracted in scope and operated solely for profit maximization in the short term.

Since there is such a wide range of alternatives to full immediate divestment, management must first eliminate those choices that are obviously not desirable and concentrate on an analysis of a limited number of alternatives. This analysis should include consideration of the profit aspects, legal implications and possible additional risk to the total enterprise which has already experienced trouble with the subsidiary or division. Other considerations relating to corporate policies, governmental actions and alternative uses of the assets by the remainder of the enterprise must also be reviewed.

If the review is comprehensive and objective, it should be possible to identify alternative choices quickly rather than allow a potentially difficult problem to become more severe. Top management is then put in the position of making a firm decision to adopt an alternative or proceed with the divestiture forthwith. If an alternative is adopted, plans must be implemented to effect the new action plan. Again, this should be done quickly so that morale problems and resulting aggravation of existing business problems may be kept to a minimum.

ANALYZING AN INDIVIDUAL SUBSIDIARY OR DIVISION

The decision to consider divestment is usually a "top down" management action. Subordinate managers may not share with the same enthusiasm activities that could lead to the elimination of a portion of the business and the possibility of reduced personal opportunity which that might imply.

Yet, unless there is an automatic review process in place and in operation, divestment candidates are often discovered by lower echelon managers who must communicate that information to upper management levels where the review and decision responsibility resides. Having been alerted to the need for a review and analysis, management must undertake an intensive examination of the subsidiary or division to determine whether divestment is desirable.

The investigation must examine the reasons for unsatisfactory performance, lack of longer-range potential or the reasons for the poor fit with the long-term strategic aims of the enterprise. The analysis should proceed along purely logical lines. A check list of difficult questions must be prepared for the analysis and review to be conclusive and objective. Some typical questions which management must analyze would be:

- Why did we go into this business originally or why was this company or product line acquired?
- What business is the subsidiary really in?
- Would the remaining business be improved if this business were divested?
- Have our goals for the total business changed thereby making this operation unnecessary?

While every divestment situation will have a different set of difficult questions that must be analyzed, it is most important that the list of questions be drawn objectively and unemotionally, and that the resulting analysis be prepared professionally and without regard to personalities involved either in the original decision to go into the business or in the current management of the business operation.

USE OF CONSULTANTS

Since most companies do not have an on-going program for divestment appraisal, a divestment situation will require the use of consultants to achieve maximum success. It is not always necessary, however, to hire outside consultants as the development of a team of staff specialists is often possible and in many cases preferable. The team leader, however, should be someone with specific experience in the general area of acquisitions and divestitures. The balance of the team should incorporate broad business backgrounds in marketing, finance and technical fields. This team approach may be used to develop an on-going review process as well as the specific planning for a selected divestiture.

In some cases, an outside consultant should be employed to augment the work of the internal team. Outside consultants are particularly useful in assembling information necessary for a divestiture when the involvement of the company should be kept confidential. Even after the divestiture is announced, outside consultants may be helpful in finding new positions for personnel to be terminated.

ANTITRUST CONSIDERATIONS

Court-ordered divestitures are frequently based on antitrust considerations. Usually, the court will require management to submit a divestiture plan specifying detailed actions to be taken, along with a timetable for such actions.

Alternatively, management may decide to accept the findings of a governmental body in an antitrust matter and divest under the conditions specified in a consent decree. By accepting a consent decree, management avoids any admission of a violation of law. Additionally, it may be possible to reduce the often lengthy and always costly burden of litigation.

In preparing a divestiture plan or consent agreement, management should attempt to receive fair value for property divested. Perhaps equal in importance, management should plan the divestment so as to avoid any disruption to the balance of the enterprise while the process is underway and after it is completed.

In some cases, voluntary divestitures are undertaken for the specific purpose of avoiding governmental challenge and the potential damage this could cause to the enterprise. Often, the most promising acquisition parties for such a divestment will be companies presently engaged in the same or similar businesses. It is possible, therefore, that the proposed sale and acquisition could attract the attention of regulatory agencies thereby complicating or even terminating the transaction. Management should take every precaution to examine the antitrust implication in such a divestment decision and if the sale is to be made to a buyer with possible antitrust problems, reflect that possibility clearly in the terms of the contracts so as to protect the enterprise from undue loss or delay.

EMPLOYEE RELATIONS PROBLEMS

The activity involved during the planning or study period preceding a decision to divest or retain an operation may result in a particularly traumatic experience for employees as well as affected management people. Rumors will often race through the organization unsettling employees and causing apprehension among their families as well. Competitors may attempt to capitalize on rumors by contacting key employees with offers for employment before plans are finalized.

If handled poorly, the employee relations problems created could cause lasting damage to the reputation of the enterprise in the industry, the community and among employees unaffected by the divestment far beyond the monetary significance of the divestment project itself.

To keep this situation from developing or getting out of hand ought to be one of the primary goals of the planning and analysis. A management that is sensitive to employee relations in the first place will be better able to avoid problems than one which is not. In cases where a history of trouble with labor organizations exists or where a unionized work force is involved, problems may become particularly severe.

Initially, during the preliminary evaluation and analysis phase of the divestment study, extreme confidentiality should be observed. There is no point in creating problems prematurely, particularly since many early studies lead to decisions to retain operations or seek alternatives other than complete and immediate divestiture. If a rumor does leak out, management should seek to reassure employees that such evaluation of subsidiaries, divisions or product lines is a continuous and necessary process and does not mean that decisions have been made or plans formulated or that jobs are at risk at this particular time.

Of course, if planning has proceeded to a point where a decision is imminent, management may wish to withhold comment entirely, or may be forced to abstain from validating rumors due to legal considerations. It helps if the enterprise has had a standing policy not to comment on rumors publicly until a general release can be made. Sometime, the fact that rumors have broken out may accelerate the decision so that a publicity release may be made and employees thereby reassured or notified. On advice of counsel, it may be possible to speak to key employees in advance of a general release to acquaint them with the plans, reassure them about their future, or advise them of specific programs affecting their future.

If divestment is decided, part of the planning process will be devoted to personnel implications. There should be a clear understanding with the prospective acquiror as to the future of the employees involved. The best situation is one in which the buyer will agree to take the subsidiary or division as a package, retaining existing personnel and providing relatively the same salary and fringe benefits scale. In most cases, the buyer will want to change one or more management people and effect some personnel changes among key employees or in the number of lower-level employees. If a clear plan can be developed regarding the specific personnel moves, management can arrange to absorb, relocate or provide re-employment assistance where necessary. In most cases, severance pay will be available for terminated employees. The sooner these factors can be communicated to affected employees, the less likely employee relations problems will occur.

In the event that the acquiror intends to make wholesale personnel reductions, the severance pay program should be worked out and communicated before rumors seriously affect employee morale and harm the ability of the organization to function while divestment details are worked out.

In some cases, management may want to do something special to attempt to retain key employees who will be subsequently terminated upon divestiture. Special "staying" bonuses may be developed or employment contracts for specific time periods may be negotiated, increasing the remuneration as the termination date draws nearer.

PENSION PLANS

In negotiating the sale of a subsidiary or division, the effect of changes in employee benefits programs may become an important consideration both from a financial and an employee morale viewpoint. The pension plan can be a particularly sensitive area if the acquiring company has a substantially different plan. If the plan is more generous; the acquiring company may find that it will incur substantial new expenses for funding and might therefore reduce the price it is willing to pay for the assets to be divested. Alternatively, if the acquiring company has a less generous plan it may find that employee morale may suffer unless the benefits are improved for new employees. Employee relations in this case may be strained with existing employees of the acquiring company even if those employees may be working in a different legally constituted subsidiary or separate business area. Again, this could seriously affect the price the acquiring company is willing to pay for the divested assets, and could jeopardize the economic basis for an otherwise successful divestment.

The status of the pension plan, therefore must be negotiated with the prospective buyer of the assets before the divestment takes place. The divesting company has a limited number of alternatives available to it. It may terminate the plan prior to sale of the divested assets thereby permitting the acquiring company complete flexibility in structuring its pension benefits for the newly acquired employees. In this case, the employees who are terminated or transferred to the new employer will receive 100 percent vesting of their funded accrued pension credits. Alternatively, if agreement is negotiated with the acquiring company, a transfer of the plan to the new employer is possible, wherein the plan continues in effect exactly as before. This will entail the transfer of fund assets as well as the accrued benefit liability to a fiscal agent chosen by the acquiring company.

In some cases, the divesting company may have generous early retirement benefits which may be used to good advantage insofar as it may be necessary to reduce the number of people involved in the operation to be divested. A cost comparison between retaining and retiring the employee can be prepared with consideration given to retraining and relocation costs. Intangible benefits and risks should also be assessed when considering benefits of early retirement, such as hardships of transfer or demotion because of lack of equal positions available.

TAX CONSIDERATIONS

Tax considerations often dictate the form of divestiture and the timing of the transaction. In certain cases, a corporation may find that outright abandonment of assets or a donation to a charitable institution may result in a better after-tax situation than the sale of assets to a third party. In still other cases, the distribution to shareholders may provide the most effective tax treatment.

A careful review of the corporation's tax situation is imperative before any firm decisions are made on divestiture. Many divestitures which have appeared to be unfavorable financially have turned out to be financially beneficial after the tax planning had been completed.

The most frequent divestiture method is a sale of the assets or business to an independent third party. In some cases, the sale may be consummated through a nontaxable exchange of securities. The ultimate effect of a tax-deferred exchange must be studied carefully to be certain that the ''halo effect'' of a tax-free gain in the short term is measured objectively against the longer term tax ramifications. In cases where the sale of assets results in a taxable event, such factors as depreciation recapture, loss of investment tax credit, installment or deferred purchase arrangements, earnings ''buyout'' schemes and other methods of structuring the transactions should be weighed carefully. In some cases, distribution of divested business to shareholders may be advantageous, and the tax on such receipt may be deferred if structured properly.

Finally, donation to a qualified charitable institution or outright abandonment, with consequent tax write-off, may prove to be the most feasible method of divestiture after considering the after-tax effect.

USE OF AN ESOP TO FACILITATE A DIVESTITURE

Employee Stock Ownership Plans (ESOP's) have received increasing attention as vehicles for divestitures in recent years. Proponents had originally considered ESOP's as a novel, but effective way for employees of a corporation to become owners of newly issued stock. However, it has become apparent that in some specific situations the ESOP also works well as a financing scheme for divestitures, using tax incentives in the process.

In some cases, a corporation wishing to divest assets, or required legally to promptly begin divesting operations, cannot find a buyer at a fair market value. In other situations, some corporations find that the operation to be divested represents a complete entity, with employees who are anxious to remain with the entity and would otherwise want to acquire the unit had they financial means. In these cases an ESOP divestiture can be of great benefit both to the divesting corporation and the acquiring employees.

The organizational concept is quite straightforward. A corporation wishing to divest can create a shell corporation to acquire the assets to be divested. The new shell corporation creates an Employee Stock Ownership Trust (ESOT) which borrows part, or in some circumstances, all of the funds needed to purchase the stock of the new corporation from the corporation divesting the assets. The new company then proceeds to use this money to acquire the divested assets, which completes the divestiture.

The ESOT is managed by a trust committee composed of employees of the new corporation. The new corporation guarantees to the lender that it will make annual payments into the ESOT in sufficient amounts to amortize the debt. The tax incentive comes into play in that these payments are deductible by the new corporation as payments to a qualified employee deferred compensation trust.

As the ESOT receives annual payments, usually limited to 15 percent of the payroll of participating employees, principal and interest due are paid to the lender. The shares of stock which have been hypothecated during the loan period become free of lien as the loan is repaid and are allocated to each participating employee's individual account. This has the effect of passing ownership to the employees over a period of years at a price fixed at the time the stock was first purchased by the new corporation.

The use of ESOP's for divestiture will work best where there is a strong entrepreneurial leadership among the management employees of a subsidiary to be divested, and those management employees are willing to invest personal capital in the new entity. The concept may not be known by the management employees as ESOP's have not received a great deal of publicity. Additionally, the employees may never have considered an ownership role before. The possibility of such a program, therefore, could be presented to the top management group even before a discussion of possible divestiture is undertaken. In this way, the group could get used to the idea of a possible ownership role before the decision is thrust upon them as an alternative to the sale of the subsidiary to a third party.

SHUTDOWN AS A FINAL ALTERNATIVE

In some cases, after all searches for alternatives have proven to be unproductive, shutdown becomes the final alternative. Notice must be given to all concerned with the shutdown on a timely basis and in as complete and detailed form as is necessary to insure a minimum of confusion.

Management should develop a comprehensive checklist showing precisely who should be notified and the timing for such notification. If a union contract is in force, it will usually spell out the terms of a shutdown as to advance notice and employee rights and benefits. In a non-unionized situation, management should be sensitive to the public relations effect of a shutdown as well as the humanitarian aspects.

Notification to customers and suppliers is important as well. Supply and service contracts will usually specify terms of cancellation, but non-contracted goods and service suppliers are also entitled to advance notice so that the effects of the loss in their business may be minimized. Customers should be notified in time to secure alternative sources of supply, particularly if the product is sensitive or vital to their own business operations.

Finally, relations with the community should be considered and releases to the press and other media should be carefully drawn and timed so as to leave the most favorable image possible in an otherwise traumatic and sorrowful event.

SPECIAL TOPICS

As MENTIONED IN THE OVERVIEW OF THIS HANDBOOK, there are numerous subjects interwoven in the fabric of a successful transaction. The chapters in this final topical area discuss some important elements in the merger, acquisition and buyout litany which do not fit neatly elsewhere.

The psychological positions and differences of the buyer and seller are dramatized by Theodore Birnbaum. Mr. Birnbaum applies a highly original format to the same basic questions being asked by the buyer and seller on matching pages. The technique of matching pages affords a glimpse into the negotiation process that is probably not available in any other place. Hammering out an agreement is a technical process surrounded by disorder of individual emotions. The reader will obtain the advantage of understanding the opposition's thinking. Questions are sequenced as they would probably occur during actual negotiations.

James B. Young Jr. constructs a unique theory as to the causative elements which promote failure in acquisitions and mergers. He concludes that the root of the problem is the lack of a planned, coordinated methodology in the acquiring company. There are many case studies and suggestions which will aid the reader to prepare a proper strategy that is more likely to result in a successful transaction. The total research behind this chapter took Mr. Young three and a half years and we are fortunate to have secured the results for this handbook.

The end of the road in any business combination is not the verbal agreement of the buyer and seller. David I. Karabell points out that despite the belief of parties that they have negotiated a contract, documentation in a final form which all parties will sign, may prove to be as much a starting point as striking the deal. Mr. Karabell covers role playing, structuring, preliminary agreements, due diligence memoranda, the details of an acquisition agreement, and relevant mechanics of the closing itself.

THEODORE BIRNBAUM

Theodore "Ted" Birnbaum is founder and president of his own financial and management organization at 60 East 42nd Street, New York, N.Y. 10165.

He also personally invests in small operating businesses where his experience and directorial skills can help. Currently he is a stockholder/officer with Mechanical Music Center, Darien, Conn., a major dealer in antique musical instruments. Among others is an investment in an exciting, new publishing venture.

He is a graduate of the Wharton School of the University of Pennsylvania, lives in Westchester County and plays a lot of tennis.

Lengthy merger/acquisition equity and debt funding/underwriting and senior executive management experience has variously been gained in the data processing, printing, computerized typesetting, writing instruments, automotive parts, motion picture, cosmetic and other industries, both domestic and foreign.

37

The 15 Most Frequently Asked Questions In Buying and Selling Companies

THEODORE BIRNBAUM

Unless one has had hands-on experience as a corporate buyer or seller, it is difficult to fully understand how and why each situation is unique. It is paradoxical that although the questions asked of themselves by the sellers and buyers are similar or even identical, the answers are not. Inevitably each party values each asset higher or lower as a direct reflection of his ownership.

To dramatize this point, each basic question, as separately asked by buyer and seller, is shown on matching pages. Variations in the detailed wording reflect such opposite viewpoints.

The technique employed here is to provide questions only rather than answers. (For answers, read the rest of this handbook.)

It has been said that formulating and refining the right questions is more than 90 percent of the eventual solution to most problems. Therefore, the 15 basic questions here have each been supplemented by a number of complementary questions. Many times the solution to a perplexing problem is best approached by the asking of one or more secondary questions, (as arbitrarily titled here) rather than by use of the basic question alone.

The 15 most frequently asked questions which follow should be used as a checklist. Buyers or sellers who take the few minutes to ask themselves all the questions, both those for the opposite side as well as their own, will undoubtedly prevent the overlooking of one or more keypoints. Many negotiations become emotional and, hence, disorderly. The use of a checklist such as this can result in good discipline as well as simple insurance.

It is always good strategy to try to study your opponent's thinking. By asking yourself all those questions he is probably asking himself you might develop some fascinating tactics which can be used to improve your bargaining position. You might prevent a terrible error such as the one committed by the Persian Emperor Darius in 492 B.C. He demanded such tribute of Greece in the form of earth and water that the war continued for another 40 years before Persia lost.

The reader may obtain maximum benefit, and occasional enjoyment by reading across the pages rather than conventionally from top to bottom. Your good question should be seen in the light of the other fellow's equally good question.

In a most general way, the questions are sequenced as they probably occur during a transaction. Basic questions 1 through 5 or 6 reflect the initial stages of the deal. They encompass the emotional gyrations of the first few days before the parties settle into the details and into hard bargaining.

Questions 6 through 8 sometimes develop after the initial night's sleep and are the beginning of strategy. Questions 9 through 11 review strategy and directly concern themselves with financial and technical matters. Questions 12 and 13 reflect the inevitable worries and second thoughts that crop up. Question 14 is highly personal. Question 15, more than any of the others, dramatizes several almost universal human traits. When the hard-sought reward is assured, why share it with more people than absolutely necessary?

In your next transaction, whether you are on the offense or defense, try to ask yourself all of the following questions. Your batting average should improve.

Seller
Question #1:   Why is the bid price so low?

— How can they offer us a multiple of earnings lower than their own?

— Do they think we're going to let them steal our company?

— Can't they see that with their financial strength, they'll make greater profits with our company than we've achieved?

— Who knows the value of this company as well as we who built it do?

— Are they penalizing us because of one bad year? Our sales and profits are at record levels!

— Why are they ignoring our off-balance sheet items? Could we liquidate and get more? Could we divide ourselves into several companies and get more?

— Isn't it obvious to all that the replacement cost of our plant and equipment alone is greater than their bid price?

— How can they derogate the fact that our hard assets alone are equal to their bid price which doesn't reflect any value whatever for our accumulated goodwill, position in our marketplace, etc.?

— Do they know that a while back Company X, one of our competitors, actually received more than our current offer and they're not in our league? Also, don't they know that we turned down an offer of the same size as today's bid several years ago and our earnings were much less then?

— Isn't it completely apparent to everyone who has spent five minutes studying our industry that the real growth of our company hasn't commenced? Isn't it equally obvious that our future growth rate will exceed that of yesterday's heroes such as IBM and Xerox?

— Are we now being penalized because we expensed everything we possibly could to save on taxes? Wasn't that policy rather elementary good management?

— Who has to be taken care of first, the stockholders or the employees?

— How much of a loss will we take when we discount their notes and other paper in order to wind up with cash? Isn't the net price too low?

> — But once in a great while:
>> — Why is the bid price so high?
>> — What do they know that we don't?
>> — Have we underpriced ourselves?

Buyer
Question #1:   Why is the asking price so high?

— How can we have a built-in profit if we pay them a multiple of earnings even equal to our own? Don't they read the papers? Do they know that such Goliaths as Ford and GM sell for lower multiples?

— Did we bid too high? Should we have started a little lower?

— Why pay them for *our* contribution of capital, etc.?

— Is it possible that their self-evaluation is a mite prejudiced?

— Can we ignore their living proof that their business is not invulnerable? Since when did they take the eraser off their pencil? When might, or will, it happen again? What is the prudent safety margin for error we need to build into the numbers?

— How can we do anything but ignore their claimed off-balance sheet assets until we can audit them most carefully along with all off-balance sheet contingent liabilities? How much of their claims have substance and what is merely fluff? How does our bid compare to what they can realize via liquidation or split up?

— Isn't that the rub? Aren't much of their future profits needed to keep them modern and merely even-up competitively?

— If they didn't have an excellent reception in their field, would we or anyone else be interested at any price? Who pays for balance sheet goodwill anymore?

— Why mention that a while back all acquisition prices were higher than today's? Why didn't they sell back then? Don't both of us have to deal with today's reality and acquisition formulas and not with what-might-have-been?

— Can we let them have it both ways? It it so difficult for them to see that either they wait to sell until all those marvelous but theoretical future earnings are in hand or that they sell now at the most advantageous price letting the buyer take the risks, and winnings, of the uncertain future? Is "chutzpah" the word to use to describe their comparing themselves to IBM and Xerox?

— Is it necessary to point out that if they hadn't saved on taxes, they wouldn't have had enough capital to grow and profit as they did? Isn't it enough to give them credit for those partially non-recurrent earnings, but only once, not twice?

— How much of a reserve in the price should we hold back to permit large salary increases to their staff to cushion the blow and to buy loyalty?

— How much cheaper is it to overpay in the currency of long-term debt rather than cash? Is our debt discountable? At what rate?

> — But once in a great while:
> > — Why were they so eager to accept our offer?
> > — What do they know that we don't?
> > — Have we overpriced the deal?

Seller
Question #2:   Are they fishing, or are they serious?

— What are their real motives?

— Is this action merely a smoke screen or otherwise diversionary?

— Do they have anything to lose?

— How far will they go?

— Who in our industry would be their first choice?

— Are they badly in need of a deal to impress Wall Street, their bankers, stockholders, or discourage *their* prospective acquiror?

— Could we wind up looking foolish?

— Are we naive?

— Are the odds of eventual success at the onset good enough to chance losing the time and money to negotiate?

— Is it possible to negotiate in good faith? Are they basically moral or immoral?

— Should we play hard-to-get to test their seriousness?

— Can we risk giving them confidential information? And trade secrets?

— Would we be risking the support of our key men if we negotiate?

— Can we keep this whole affair confidential?

— Why do they want to buy?

— Are there any conflicts between us so basic that no deal will ever be completed? If so, why continue?

Buyer

Question #2: Are they serious, or merely fishing?

— What are they really thinking?

— Do they have a different objective and are merely using us? Is it an ego trip? Are they bored? Do they need to be flattered?

— What do they have to lose?

— How far will they go?

— Who in or out of our industry would be their first choice?

— Are they badly in need of a deal to impress Wall Street, their bankers, stockholders or to discourage an undesirable acquiror?

— Will we wind up looking foolish?

— Are we naive?

— Are the odds of eventual success at the onset good enough to justify the cost in time and money?

— Is it possible to negotiate in good faith? Do they understand the morality of acquisitions?

— Can we be both aggressive and diffident?

— Are they willing to trust us with their confidential information? And trade secrets?

— Will their key men stick around when they find out that we may acquire their company?

— Is it possible to keep this deal completely confidential?

— Why are they willing to consider selling?

— Are there any conflicts between us so basic that no deal will ever be completed? If so, why continue?

Seller
Question #3:   Should we shop around?

— Would shopping around be positive and good tactics? If we shop around, will the buyer back out or pay more?

— What have we got to lose? How risky is it?

— Do we have an obligation to our stockholders to shop around?

— Will our big cash position act as a lure to attract a higher price? Is there someone else out there who'd be better able to use our cash to leverage a higher price?

— Up to now we've been amateurs or dilettantes on the subject of marketing ourselves—isn't it time we developed some professionalism?

— If we shop around, who does the work? Should we hire an agent such as an investment banker?

— Can we afford an investment banker? Will they pay for themselves via a higher price? Would a competent or prestigious investment banker be interested in us?

— Who is the buyer's outside advisor or investment banker? Do we know them personally?

— Can one really trust an investment banker? Do they play both sides of the street?

— What can we learn via shopping around that we can't learn via serious and direct negotiations?

— Are they interested in our company, with its premier market position, simply in order to submerge it into one of their own operations? If so, what happens to each of our executives? Will they keep us on for a limited time merely long enough for *their* consciences to be assuaged?

— If they let us go after a minimum period, what will be the effect on our reputations? Will prospective employers think we were fired for incompetence? Will the buyers extend themselves to help us land on our feet? What is their track record in the area of executive terminations?

— Now that we're at this stage in the discussion, is there any better way to acquire an objective valuation of our company than by engendering a little friendly competition?

Buyer
Question #3:   Will they shop around?

— Would we continue to be interested in them if we found out that they were shopping around?

— Would we gain or lose if they shop around? How cold a cold world is it out there?

— How much of an obligation do they have to their stockholders to check around or are they permitted to negotiate only with us?

— Are they likely to try to use their big cash position to engender another offer?

— What do they know about how to sell themselves?

— If they do shop around, will we find out? Would they do it themselves or more discreetly via an investment banker?

— Can they afford outside help such as a prestigious investment banker? Are they attractive to a first rank investment banker? Would it drive the price up? Are we fixed as to price or is there any give in our numbers?

— Who are the seller's outside advisors or investment bankers? Do they have any real friends?

— Are their and our investment bankers completely honorable? In case of push and shove, who comes first in each instance?

— Can we ''lay it all out'' for them so there is no need for them to shop around?

— Are their executives afraid that we want the company and not them? How honest and open should we be? If we let it all hang out, will this drive them to someone else?

— What techniques should we employ to defuse opposition by their important personnel? For example, can we absorb them into our other divisions or guarantee that we'll help them to get jobs elsewhere?

— Would we prefer a little friendly competition or do we really prefer to have the field to ourselves? How can we prevent competition?

Seller

Question #4:   Who are these guys? What makes them tick? What homework do we have to do?

— What do we in fact know about them?

— Can we organize a fact-finding group to update and correct our information in time to be useful?

— How do we make sure we don't underrate them? Have they merely been lucky or are they competent?

— Do we or would we like them? Are they up to our level socially?

— Can we trust them?

— Do they negotiate strenuously but fairly?

— Are they too young? Do they have any respect for tradition?

— Is their track too fast for us? For example, will we be forced into slipshod controls of product and project developments solely to create the aura of progress?

— Will they constantly increase our sales and profit budgets regardless of reality? Do they cut costs to the bone as a basic policy? Can we do without any or all of our perquisites?

— Are they overreaching, not only for us, but overall? Are they steady enough? Are they merely noise and fluff and riding for an inexorable fall?

— Will we be able to talk to them, communicate? Do they listen?

— Do we respect and agree with their methods and tactics? Is their political power the result of questionable contributions to both parties? Is their reputation for strong-arm tactics justified?

— What will our friends, customers, suppliers and relatives think of them?

— Do they already have a "spy" in our group?

— Are they always pushing for volume regardless of risk? Can we adjust our thinking to a new philosophy and arithmetic?

— Are they capable of understanding that some of our losses were taken to save cash and were not objectives unto themselves?

— What Rosetta Stone can we utilize to decipher the spread between what they say to the press and what they appear to be saying to us?

— Will they ever learn to pronounce our names correctly? How can they fail to remember that our town is spelled "Cairo" and not "Caro"?

Buyer

Question #4: What do we really know about these guys? What makes them tick? Do we need to do further homework?

— How good and how complete is our information?

— Are we capable of perfecting our information and of constantly checking it against developments?

— How do we make sure we don't under-or overrate them? Were they lucky or are they capable of repeating their performance?

— Are they nice people? Are they too concerned or insufficiently concerned about social prestige and background?

— Are they trustworthy?

— What kind of negotiators are they?

— Are they too old? Are they mired in out-of-date traditions?

— Are they walkers or sprinters? Are they strategists or detail-oriented? Do they delegate? Do they "nickel and dime" every project and product development to death?

— Will we have to constantly flog them into better performance? Can they unemotionally cut costs when necessary to increase profits?

— Can they swing with us for bigger pieces of the pie or will they hold us back? Are they too "steady" to move quickly when an unexpected opportunity develops?

— Will we communicate? Do they listen?

— Can they adjust to our methods and tactics? Are they versatile enough to manage in tomorrow's climate as well as they were able to build in yesterday's world?

— Do we need their obsequious friends and suppliers and relatives? Will their customers care who we are? Will Wall Street like them?

— Should we or can we develop a "friend at court"?

— Do they understand that, regardless of taxes, income is better than no income? Do they see that even at a 70 percent tax rate, one keeps 30 percent which is much better than nothing?

— Do they understand that losses, regardless of deductibility, are never preferential objectives?

— What is the difference between their public pronouncements and what they really think and what they actually do?

— Dammit, why are they so sensitive to our innocent mispronunciation of their names?

Seller
Question #5:   What would we do with the money if we got it?

— First of all, do we need money more than we need owning our own company?

— If we sold for cash (taxable), Uncle Sam would be happy, but would we?

— Are there personal demands we *now* are unable to satisfy—tuition, wife, alimony, home improvements, hobbies, back taxes, other debts, retirement home?

— What *new* demands for funds will we be suddenly hit with if we sell—church, college or secondary school, wife, ex-wife, mistress, my children, her children, indigent relatives, vacation home, creditors, home town, grandchildren, other charities?

— Will we have time to manage the remaining proceeds? Or will we be twice as busy? Can we work for men who have less personal money than we do?

— Will the proceeds be enough to finance that secret project?

— Will we be personally more or less liquid as a result of the terms of the deal?

— If we agree to sell for stock, will they be willing to make us large repayable loans at low interest rates?

— Are our real personal motivations to sell transparent or will they accept the corporate objectives we've published?

— What we can afford to do with our money depends on their plans for us, so the basic question is, is this goodbye? If so, when?

— Do we really want to be rich? After the smoke settles, would we actually be rich? How many steaks can be eaten in one day?

Buyer

Question #5: What will they do with the proceeds? What will be their future roles?

— First of all, is money really important to them or do they prefer owning and managing their own company?

— Does the price have to be uneconomically inflated to provide for Uncle Sam's share?

— What private demands for funds are now bugging them?

— What new financial demands on them will further dissipate the proceeds? Are there mistresses or other bottomless (sic) pits into which the money will disappear? Are there existing personal debts that we are unaware of? What effect will these have on the deal?

— Will they spend too much time trying to manage their money? Dammit, will we be successful in managing men who are personally richer than we are?

— Are they likely to use the money to finance sideline businesses, also demanding time, emotion and energy?

— Should the deal be structured so that their money is tied up? Will they take letter stock?

— Are they going to ask us for large, low interest loans which could sharply reduce the advantages of our buying for stock?

— What are their personal motives and how are such hidden within their announced corporate objectives?

— Are they looking for "out"? Is this goodbye? When?

— Is becoming rich their major incentive? If not, what is?

Seller

Question #6:   Are we powerful enough to handle the negotiations and decisions our own way? Are we pros at this game?

— When "big money" appears on the horizon, who else is going to get into our act? Who might attempt an end run? Or go over our heads?

— Running down the list, who specifically do we have to worry about:

> big stockholders
> outside directors
> outside auditors
> outside attorneys
> investment bankers
> commercial bankers
> factors
> other lenders/relatives
> suppliers
> customers

— Do we have the health and energy to control the negotiations? How tired are we? Do we have competent backup for each task?

— Do we "control" our side because everyone else is a sycophant or yes man? Who can be helpful as a devil's advocate?

— Who of our enemies would like to undercut any deal?

— Who can be trusted to keep his/her mouth shut?

— Do we need professional outside help? Are we too naive to go it alone?

— Of what use will our "unlimited patience" technique be when it becomes apparent that we may not get what we want? Do we know any other negotiating ploys?

— In the final analysis, whose finger is on the "button"?

— In a complicated deal such as this one, who does what to whom?

Buyer

Question #6:   Are we negotiating with the right guys?

— When it looks like ''big money'' will change hands who else will try to get into the act, not only on their side, but also on ours?

— Running down the list, who specifically do we have to worry about on both sides:

    big stockholders
    outside directors
    outside auditors
    outside attorneys
    investment bankers
    commercial bankers
    factors
    other lenders/relatives
    suppliers
    customers

— Do the people we are initially talking with have the stamina to survive through a long negotiation? Or should *we* push for backup people on their side?

— Are they surrounded by/or managed by yes men? Will they use a devil's advocate? Who?

— Who are their enemies, or ours, who might undercut the negotiations?

— Who on their side/our side is a blabbermouth?

— Unless they have professional outside help from the start will any deal we attempt to negotiate with their senior executives survive to signing?

— Will we be able to out-wait them? Who will fumble first? Is the game of chicken applicable in this deal?

— In the final analysis, whose finger is on the ''button''?

— In this specific deal, who should do what to whom?

Seller

Question #7: **Now that this discussion looks like it might be for real, what do we truly want? If we had a magic wand?**

— First, it's a new day—so let's ask ourselves again, do we really want to sell?

— If the answer is yes, or at least maybe, do we in fact have a plan, a goal? Is it updated? What does it in fact say?

— If the answer is no, or at least doubtful, can we: continue to go it alone; obtain enough capital; manager proper R & D; hold or improve our market share; compete with the existing giants?

— Further, if the answer is unclear: will they buy our competitor and can we compete with still another giant; will our executives become encouraged or discouraged?

— Could we protect ourselves from an unfriendly takeover by these guys or anyone else? Can we: make acquisitions of our own; buy in our debt and/or outstanding shares; or even liquidate? Can we retire, happily? Could we go private? Should we get rid of our other stockholders by the ESOT or some other complicated technique?

— Do we prefer our present life of big fish in a small pond—the advantages of privacy? Can we deal with security analysts, SEC, etc.?

— Do we care whether our corporate name survives? Is immortality more important than money?

— Can we be happy taking orders from remote bosses whom we may not get close to? Are we capable of committing ourselves to someone else's management system?

— Will our employees and community continue to give us the deference and respect we've earned, and enjoy?

— Will we have to move? Could we enjoy commuting and the New York sophistication?

— Is it too far-fetched to consider buying them?

— Are we honestly interested in greater responsibility or do we want to gradually tread water until the time to get out?

Buyer
Question #7:   **Since this looks like it might be for real, what might they really want and we now want? If we had a magic wand?**

— First, in the clear light of a new day, do we really want to buy this company?

— If the answer is yes, or at least maybe, do we in fact have a plan, a goal,? Is it updated? What does it say?

— Do we have to worry about their ability to fight us off? In fact, could they: go it alone; raise necessary capital; develop new products; retain or gain market share; compete with giants like us?

— How anxious are we to get into their industry? Should we switch emphasis onto their competitors? Will the entire hassle result in a Pyrrhic victory if their executives leave?

— Would we attempt an unfriendly takeover? Could we win? Do we have the financial muscle, allies and intestinal fortitude to employ all the techniques needed to succeed? Would they try to go private to stop us? Have they heard of ESOT?

— Can we convince them that they will become bigger fish although in a tremendously bigger pond? Do they possess the latent abilities to move into the goldfish bowl, deal with the SEC and security analysts, etc.?

— How are they going to react to the elimination of their corporate name? Who is immortal anyway?

— Will they be happy taking orders from our distant world headquarters, especially when we're unlikely to develop close friendships? Will they learn our system of operations?

— Are they excessively dependent upon the respect and deference they receive locally?

— Would they relocate if *we* felt it beneficial for the future? Are they capable of surviving in New York?

— Are they dumb enough to try to buy us? Could they?

— Are they merely treading water until the right time to get out?

Seller
Question #8:   Do we realistically know how attractive we are? What is the real world?

— Has our insularity on the subject of our total value in this marketplace been so complete that we don't really know? It may have been a wonderful dream world, but can it last?

— What do other acquirors think?

— Will competition develop? Do we want competition?

— Do we care what our factual value is as long as we get top price? If we oversell, will there be personal problems later on? If the price is too high, will the business ever be offered back to us at a major price discount? Would we buy?

— What's the true value of our LCF?

— How much does our unfunded pension liability detract from the price?

— Are we synergistic or are we an oddball?

— Are there important duplications to be eliminated? Will the merger immediately result in higher profits? Can we get a higher price?

— Will standardizing fringe benefits materially reduce profits?

— Can our expensive buyout and key-man insurance be dropped? Can we personally buy those policies?

— How much is the business worth without our CEO, etc.?

— Are we currently in vogue? Are buyers suddenly hot-to-trot in our field? Are we the leading edge in a dynamic growth industry or merely a camp follower?

— Do we possess intangible values (i.e., a name like Rolls Royce) the acquisition of which will make the buyer look good?

— Is our dependence on a large group of young men for the future, good or bad? Will the buyer see that we saved a lot of money or think that we are afraid of management competition?

— Based on our cash flow, how long will it take the Buyer to recoup his investment?

— Are we a "sure thing" acquisition or are we a high risk?

Buyer
Question #8:   Do we, in fact, know how attractive they are?

— With the information in hand, are we safe enough with our bid? Or should we take additional steps to determine their true market price in today's arena?

— What would our competitors pay?

— Will anyone else compete with us or will we have the field to ourselves? Is competition to our benefit?

— Can we confine the price negotiation to the real world? Would "stealing" the company be to our benefit over the long haul? Will they continually resent the low price? Does anyone not ever afterwards feel that they could have gotten more? Could we become so hungover that we'd have to sell it back to them at a discount? Would they buy?

— Why discuss their LCF? Are they worth the price regardless?

— Can we rely on the accuracy of their unfunded pension liability calculations? Can we risk the assumption of this burden or is there a technique to finesse it? Are they guilty of racial or religious discrimination?

— Are they an oddball company or would a merger be synergistic?

— Can we eliminate enough duplications, in overhead, manufacturing, etc. to recoup a major portion of the purchase price in a short while? Have we already fully priced these eliminations?

— If we bring their people into our fringe benefit plans, will the added cost seriously diminish their profit contribution?

— Because no one man is indispensable in our overall picture, why not eliminate their key-man insurance? Further, can we make money by selling the policies to them?

— Can we figure out the worth of their business without the continued services of the CEO?

— Is the real reason we started looking at them that they are currently in vogue rather than truly exciting? Or is it that their industry is the only thing that's exciting?

— Why don't they have a name like Rolls Royce so we could afford to pay more?

— Are we accurate in judging that their organization has no real middle management? Is it figuratively made up of hundreds going through business puberty managed by a few who are experiencing menopause?

— How exciting is their cash flow? How long will it take to get our dough back?

— How risky is this deal? Can we miss badly?

Seller
Question #9:   Can we have our cake and eat it too?

— How can we improve the price without killing the deal?

— Can we tack on to the price long-term employment contracts followed by long-term consulting agreements payable to our estates if we die? Yet, can we resign midterm without penalty if we don't like the way things are going or we're bored?

— Can we tie in escalation clauses in case of increased inflation, only up?

— Can the price be set in today's dollars but paid in that value in shares at the closing? Or better still, six months later?

— What special fringe benefits to us personally wouldn't seriously affect the total price?

— Can we use up our cash surplus to pay a big dividend without reducing the bid price?

— Can we avoid non-compete clauses?

— Will they let us have such a large block of stock that we will wield a big stick in *their* company?

— Can we get the basic price plus a big contingent bonus if we perform as we now claim? Can the bonus be taxed at capital gains rates?

— Can we exercise our own company's options and still receive their options?

— How can we arrange enough personal time to manage our new estates?

— Can we use our loss-carryforward to improve our sales price by technically buying them? Who has to trust whom? Will Uncle Sam see through it? What's to lose?

— Since some people may feel that our management is receiving a particularly favorable deal, will the buyers take on the task of ''selling'' the terms to our other stockholders, etc.?

— How can we get certain contractual rights and privileges at no cost, just in case we may need them someday? Which, if any, are worth insisting upon? Which ones were suggested by our super-cautious lawyers and aren't important?

Buyer
Question #9:   Is there a way to let them believe they can have their cake and eat it too?

— What is our fall-back price? Is the increase above our initial bid enough to give them a sense of victory?

— In structuring our intitial bid do we hold back a reserve to provide for long-term employment contracts to be followed by non-compete consulting agreements? How important are these personal items? Can we give them ice-in-the-winter privileges such as unilateral freedom to resign after a minimum period? Since employment contracts generally favor the employee over the employer, why not let them win this latter one?

— How naive do they think we are? Doesn't everyone know that it cannot be all one way?

— First of all, who is smart enough to know what will happen in six months? Will they chance the downside risk?

— How much extra will their special fringe benefits cost? What are they willing to trade?

— Should we suggest they use their cash surplus to pay a big dividend before the sale? Will this make them more receptive to our bid? Since this dividend will not reduce their corporate earning power from operations will we appear to have acquired at a cheap price?

— If we do not insist on non-compete clauses, can we trade off for something more valuable?

— If we can succeed in getting them to sell only by paying with a large tax-free block of our stock, can we negotiate a mandatory, but partial, secondary to reduce their power in our group? Or will they take part in non-voting shares?

— Should we lower the fixed price, but up the contingent bonuses so we win either way? Can the bonuses be tax-deductible?

— As long as our price, as expressed in a lump sum, is for the full company, rather than on a per-share basis, do we care if their management manages to get a bigger slice of the pie?

— How can we insure their continued corporate efficiency while they are worrying about competent management of their newly enlarged personal estates?

— Can we "sell" to them for a sufficient number of future shares to give *us* full control of the resultant company and yet enable us to shelter our certain profits against their loss-carry-forward? Since the tax laws require that they continue to hold some of their shares, will they be happy with down-the-road profits? Do they have a better alternative?

— Can we or they get an investment banker to render an opinion, inexpensively, that the deal is "equitable" and thus convince all minority shareholders to go along?

— What extraneous clauses or terms should be eliminated before they become too expensive? Which of their useless garbage should be left in for trading purposes?

Seller
Question #10:   How can we do better?

— Can our sales or profits or assets be "re-engineered" to improve our attraction in their eyes and hence the price?

— Should we sell off, or liquidate our one losing division?

— Can we bring forth our "reserves" thus improving current profits and making us appear to be growing more rapidly? Can we afford the risk that the deal might collapse? Will the IRS cause trouble?

— Should we hire a financial PR firm to improve our image and drive up our price? Is this cricket?

— Is there a friendly mutual fund or institutional buyer who would take some of our stock off the market? Remember Robert Young and his N.Y. Central takeover?

— Is there another buyer not quite so large and impersonal? Can we find a niche only two levels from the throne rather than four or five?

— Can we secure long-term employment contracts for sons, daughters, brothers, in-laws, etc. so that we won't have to continue to support them?

— Will they let us personally buy the real estate at depreciated book value?

— Is there any way that we can corporately borrow large sums productively, especially from lenders, seeing that we might be sold soon to an even better credit risk? Will such borrowings make us more or less attractive? Can we "clean up" our balance sheet? Can we use such borrowings to pay off debt to individuals which otherwise would have to be subordinated at the request of the buyers?

Buyer

Question #10: **Of the techniques to improve a takeover price, which should we use and which of theirs should we watch out for?**

— Are their financial numbers consistently arrived at or are there sudden increases and decreases not fully explained or even logical which indicate manipulation?

— Can we get them to do the dirty work of liquidating their losers? If so, can we improve the price?

— How have they been handling the whole subject of reserves? Did they manipulate their reserves so as to appear to be a solid growth company when in fact the recent increase only reflects a non-recurrent gain? On the other hand, are all the reserves used up? If not, how can we make use of them?

— What effect did their new PR guy have on the price of their stock? Was the run-up merely fluff? How much did it cost?

— Can we pick up some large blocks from institutions or from friends at today's market prices so that the overall average, when we tender for the balance, won't be too high? Do we know how to do this without running afoul of the SEC?

— How can we convince them that we're not too big and impersonal and yet that our tremendous size and strength will make more money for them?

— Can we reduce the purchase price by an amount greater than the cost of employment contracts for their incompetent dependents? How could such top men produce such nitwit children?

— Can we capitalize on their deep-seated and emotional need to own something physical by letting them keep the building at depreciated book value thus lowering the total price by a greater amount?

— Have we properly analyzed their debt structure? Should we encourage them, and even help them, to re-do it before the acquisition? Yet if they re-do it after negotiations start without talking to us, is that a sign of bad faith? Can we trust them? Do we need continued subordination of their personal loans to their company as a vehicle of maintaining our control? How much more or less expensive will bank debt be than their own loans?

Seller

Question #11:   How can we reduce or eliminate taxes on the transaction? Will Uncle Sam get it all?

— What are the applicable taxes? Corporate, personal, national, international, state and city? Which are final and which permit future recapture?

— How much of our expenses of the deal can be written off personally and not treated as capital items? Can the buyer help out?

— Which of the basic formats does the best tax job: stock, cash, asset, statutory merger, etc?

— Do we need to hire special experts?

— Are we able to understand some of the recommended razzle-dazzle techniques? Are we certain that we'll do the correct things at steps 2, 3, etc. unless we are led by the hand?

— Are the chances to gain via use of that new and clever technique more than offset by the consequences of a possible tax audit reversal? Should we wait until we get an IRS ruling in advance, assuming they'll give one in time?

— Is it possible that *we* treat the transaction one way for tax purposes and the other side treats it differently so that we each get maximum mileage? Would this enable us to lower our price and yet keep more?

— How can we avoid ''recapture'' of accelerated depreciation and amortization?

— Is there enough time left in the year to ''shelter'' our personal profits? Or should the entire deal be held over until after January 1?

Buyer
Question #11:   What is the best way to structure the deal from a tax standpoint? Ours? Theirs?

— What are the applicable taxes? Corporate, personal, national, international, state and city?

— Can we help them write off some expenses without it costing us anything? Will a small gesture on our part buy us a lot of goodwill?

— Which of the basic formats does the best tax job: stock, cash, asset, statutory merger, etc.?

— Should we encourage them to hire special experts? Do we also need specialized outside professional help?

— Do we fully understand the razzle-dazzle techniques suggested by the various advisors? Will they produce near-term profits but long-term losses?

— What are the chances of obtaining favorable IRS rulings in sufficient time on all of the clever but tricky suggestions? Who pays for the IRS rulings? What to do if the deadline occurs first?

— Is it possible that *we* treat the transaction one way for tax purposes and the other side treats it differently so that we each get maximum mileage? Would this enable us to increase our price and yet net more?

— Are they miracle men or do they know something about tax law that we don't?

— Should we get involved in their personal tax problems? Can we risk telling about the tax shelter deals we're into without being held responsible if they don't work out?

Seller
Question #12:   How can we minimize or eliminate the various risks? What's the worst that can happen?

During Negotiations:

— Are they capable of accurately analyzing us? Will they be scared off by seeming weaknesses: patent expiration; reliance on certain customers and suppliers; end of favorable lease; foreign competition; unfunded pension liability?

— How can we assay their management, competitive position, financial strength and non-public information? How can we do this without appearing to be too anxious?

— How can we "control" their contacts with our customers/suppliers so that none become worried?

— How can we find out if they have failed in other acquisition tries, and why?

— Should we volunteer information or let them dig it out? Will we learn much from the nature of their questions? How can we find out what data they truly think is key, particularly that which we do not voluntarily supply?

— To preserve the amount of our sales price can we refuse to have the stock we receive restricted?

If Deal Is to Be Signed:

— What written guarantees do we need?

— What written guarantees can we get? How good are their guarantees?

— If new information regarding the past is subsequently discovered, such as foreign bribes, non-fraud tax liabilities, how can we make this the buyer's problem?

— How can all provisions covering future performance by the buyer be made airtight?

— How can we marshall full support in advance from our team? What added incentives can we obtain to make the deal sufficiently interesting?

— How can we put into the contract their oral promise that we will be permitted a great deal of autonomy?

If Negotiations Are Collapsing:

— What should we do to minimize injury to our reputation and to the morale of our staff?

— Can anything be done to control what the buyer will say to the press?

— How do we account for all the time and money we spent with no result?

— How can we keep them from using the trade secrets they've learned?

— Will our lawyers and accountants bill us at modest rates since there is no big winning to divvy up?

— Since the collapse of discussions is their fault, can we get them to pay our expenses?

Buyer
Question #12:   How can we minimize or eliminate the various risks? What's the worst that can happen?

During Negotiations:

— Are we capable of accurately analyzing them? How important to the future are their lapsing patents, reliance on a few customers and suppliers, expiration of their favorable lease, advent of strong foreign competition, unfunded pension liability?

— Without appearing too anxious, how can we assay the non-public information and intangibles? How good are the sons and daughters in the business? How can we get all this without coming on too strong?

— Can we talk to their leading customers/suppliers, bankers, etc. without weakening the company and creating a Pyrrhic victory for ourselves? Is their market position strengthening or eroding?

— How can we find out if they have been turned down by others, and why?

— What data do they seem to suppress? What's the problem? Are they hiding anything? Are we asking the correct "catch-all" questions?

— Who should receive restricted stock? Is there anyone who shouldn't?

If Deal is to be Signed:

— What written guarantees do we need?

— What written guarantees can we get? Can we hold anyone personally liable? How good are their guarantees?

— How can we tie them up so that they will be around and involved if new information is subsequently discovered, especially past liabilities?

— How can all provisions concerning future performance, especially personal services by the biggest stockholder/managers, be made airtight?

— Will all of their employees fully support the deal? What incentive can be offered to replace equity?

— What should we do to rapidly achieve *de facto* as well as *de jure* control?

If Negotiations Are Collapsing:

— What can we do to keep from looking foolish? Will this, our fourth failure in a row, prevent anyone else from taking us seriously?

— Can anything be done to control what they will say to the press?

— How will our accountants record all the monies wasted? Can these be buried?

— How should we utilize the trade secrets we picked up?

— Will our lawyers and accountants bill us at modest rates since there is no big winning?

— Since the collapse is their fault, can we get them to pay any or all of our expenses?

Seller
Question #13:   **What if unexpected or uncontrollable events occur just before the deal is signed? What happens? Are we vulnerable?**

— What are the chances of a Three-Mile Island happening to us?

— What if Ralph Nader or a Congressional Sub-Committee says our key product is dangerous to the health of unborn Eskimos?

— What if a dissident small shareholder or ambitious lawyer tries to get an injunction against the merger?

— Is there a religious or minority group that will choose this moment to complain about our one-tenth of 1 percent of sales to South Africa?

— What if a clerk in our accounts receivable department loses all at Las Vegas? And at craps, rather than Chemin de Fer?

— What if some headline seeker claims our commissions paid to that foreign air force general were really bribes?

— What if the long-lost nephew of our founder suddenly decides he wants to be CEO? Does a forty-year absence from the company come under the Statute of Limitations? How much stock does he own? Can we buy him off?

— What is our contingency plan if our CEO gets hit by that mythical streetcar?

— Since they are a big customer, what happens to us if Chrysler doesn't get the government's $1.5 billion support money?

— Do we have enough token minority members in the wings somewhere to be able to handle most emergencies?

Buyer
Question #13: **What if unexpected or uncontrollable events occur just before the deal is signed? What happens? Are we vulnerable?**

— Will we be Babcock & Wilcox or United Technologies?

— How can we find out what Ralph Nader or the pertinent Congressional sub-committee is working on without giving them any ideas?

— Do they have any bitter enemies? Do we? Are they particularly vulnerable to annoyance suits by unscrupulous lawyers, etc.? Are we?

— What is our policy or what will be our policy toward sales to South Africa? Will our combined figures be big enough to attract trouble?

— Are we properly protected in the purchase agreement and by insurance against fraud and defalcation?

— Have they been engaged in bribery? Was it intelligently kept at a low level? How can we find out? Do we want to find out?

— How much of the stock do we need? Is it less than 100 percent? Can we afford it and is it wise to sweat out the remainder? Good grief, can't they handle their own dissidents? Did some idiot on our side talk to that nephew?

— Is their CEO's health good? Is he indispensable? Could we back out of the deal or could the price be lowered? Do we or they have a qualified backup? Would we be better off if the old curmudgeon did retire or die?

— How dependent are they on sales to Chrysler? Can the purchase price be tied to the amount of government loans, if any?

— Do we have enough token minority members in the wings somewhere to be able to handle most emergencies?

Seller
Question #14:   Can we live happily with them? How long should we plan to stick around?

— How can we spend four days of each week attending meetings? What can be discussed at such length? How do they keep awake? Who runs the show back home? How many extra people are needed to make up for absence of top people in meetings? If our assistants are also tied up in meetings-of-assistants do they think our night watchman will. be able to make the key decisions?

— An hour or two once in a while with their tough CEO is more than enougth, but four days at a time? Will they completely revamp our management system and take away all the fun? Do they possess a sense of humor to help ameliorate the inevitable conflicts?

— Will our wives believe such a situation—or will they prefer it? Can we trust them to spend our money wisely when we are always in meetings?

— Who's responsible for finding, identifying and training our successors?

— Do they realize that our policy of buying for $1, selling for $2 and being "satisfied with a 1 percent profit" is all we know? Are B-school type five-hundred page budgets, forecasts, fast tracks, and alternative strategies beyond us? How about autonomy?

— Will they let us continue to use our friendly auditors?

— Can we forgive and forget that they never let us "win one"? Didn't every controversial point go their way? Isn't it important to be a good winner or do they believe that winning big is the sole criterion?

— What business atmosphere do they maintain? Will there be solid teamwork or will we always have to give in? Can we overlook their attitude that a punch in the nose plus a kind word is better than a kind word alone?

— Are they the types who will castigate us for our small errors and also blame us for losses caused by their insisting on policies over our objections?

— Are we correct in our visceral judgment that they are always planning and scheming to get an extra edge and would even be willing to commit the business equivalent of murder if necessary to win?

— Are we willing to be peremptorily assessed for *their* CEO's favorite political campaign?

Buyer

Question #14: Can we live happily with their top guys? How long should we demand that they stick around?

— Are they the old-fashioned types who figuratively "sweep the floors" constantly getting involved in minutiae? Do they really understand the need for group meetings to coordinate and communicate long-term plans and budgets? Do they understand and practice modern management techniques? For example, are they capable of developing a foreign operation? Who will run their show at home when they're with us?

— Can we split up the responsibility now held entirely by their CEO by creating the separate position of chief operating officer? Would they benefit from an "Office of the President"? Are they hedgers or gamblers? Do they make only visceral judgments or do they analyze as thoroughly as we do? What do they understand about advertising, franchising or discounting? How good is their sense of timing? Do they laugh too much?

— What influence do their wives wield? Will they help or hinder? Will our respective wives get along? Do they and their husbands understand the need for good community relations?

— Can and will they train their successors? Do we have to supply their replacements or will they?

— How much autonomy can we give them? Sure, they've made money *in the past,* but will they be willing to comply with our reporting and financial control requirements?

— Is there anything to worry about because they want to continue *their* auditors?

— Do they realize how often the deal almost collapsed because of their numerous "cockamamie" requests? Are they sore losers? Can we teach them that excuses, no matter how justified, are unacceptable?

— How quickly do we require that they do exactly as we request, at least on the important issues as determined by us? What independent decisions can we leave to them? Will we always have to pat them on the back regardless of their achievements?

— Are they the types who will constantly try to avoid responsibility by totally hedging their recommendations and then blaming us if anything goes awry?

— Are they afraid of being tough? Don't they know that the real MacBeth enjoyed the spoils for 14 long years after he murdered Duncan?

— Are they going to rock the boat when they're asked to make "voluntary" contributions to our political war chest?

Seller
Question #15:   Why do our outside advisors get paid so much?

— Who did all the negotiating anyway?

— How come they get paid a great deal more per hour than we do?

— We've paid them a retainer for years—why a giant fee now?

— Wasn't a great deal of the professional work done by the buyer's lawyers and accountants?

— Come to think of it, was there ever much room for maneuver considering the number of bank loans, employment contracts, state regulations, etc. that we were encumbered with? Did their work change the final price in any way?

— How come their fees are the same regardless of how tough the deal? Is it a case of what the traffic will bear?

— Are they trying to create an annuity from this one deal?

— Why all the gobbledegook that no one understands?

— Are they conspiring with the buyer's lawyers/accountants to stretch out their hours and complicate matters thus requiring their services to untangle?

— Would they settle for a bigger share of the glory (tombstone ads we'll pay for) and a smaller piece of the pie?

— If it's a lousy deal, who suffers? Can *we* find an occupation where one gets paid regardless of the risk?

— Will we ever need them again?

— Will they ever need us again?

Buyer
Question #15:   Why do our outside advisors get paid so much?

— Who did all the negotiating anyway?

— How come they get paid a great deal more per hour then we do?

— Is there a duplication or overlap between their annual retainer and their charge for this deal?

— Wasn't a great deal of the professional work done by the seller's lawyers and accountants?

— Wasn't much of the effort limited to hack work such as looking at bank loan documents, corporate charter, employment contracts, state regulations, etc.? What help did they actually give us on the price itself?

— Why don't their fees vary in direct relationship to the difficulty of the deal? Is there a conspiracy to constantly increase fees? How much are they charging us to finance the time they spend doing public service, conscience salving work?

— Are they trying to create an annuity from this one deal?

— Why all the gobbledegook that no one understands?

— Is there an unwritten conspiracy with the seller's lawyers/accountants to stretch out their hours and to complicate matters requiring their services to untangle?

— Can we save money now by letting them have a greater share of the glory or a promise of more business in the future?

— If it's a lousy deal, who suffers? Can *we* find an occupation where you get paid regardless of risk?

— Will we ever need them again?

— Will they ever need us again?

JAMES B. YOUNG, Ph.D.

Assistant Controller - Accounting Operations
Arrowhead Puritas Waters Division
Coca-Cola of Los Angeles

During the past ten years, James B. Young has concentrated on developing, implementing and managing various aspects of business operating systems. With a keen eye on effectiveness, logistics, systems and profitability, Jim has successfully participated in developing three new operating and accounting systems for Quaker Oats, Pet, Inc., and Standard Brands. In Jim's new position with CCLA at Arrowhead, he is responsible for developing Operating Systems; the functional direction of 15 branch accounting offices; managing Accounts Receivable, Data Control, and Equipment/Customer Records Control.

While developing a sound career path, Jim completed all formal requirements leading to a Ph.D. in Business Administration (Concentration, Corporate Finance) from California Western University in 1968. In completing the requirements for graduation, Jim spent four and a half years researching over 280 companies that had engaged in expanding their businesses via acquisitions or mergers. The concluding dissertation develops and explains the unique elements associated with acquisition and merger failure rates and assembles a step-by-step program for coordinating the acquisition/merger sequences. The 376 page dissertaton is entitled, *Business Acquisitions and Mergers: A Conclusive Investigation Into the Causative Elements of Failure*. Jim also has his M.B.A. (Corporate Finanace, C.W.U.), and B.A. (Lycoming College) and has completed the Industrial Management program at Penn State University.

38

A Conclusive Investigation into the Causative Elements of Failure in Acquisitions and Mergers

JAMES B. YOUNG Ph.D.

Business shortfalls, regardless of type and degree, are certainly a distasteful experience of all businesses. An assembled listing of all business shortcomings no doubt would be endless. However, after conducting a detailed survey, identifying only those problems that persist year after year and are not mutually exclusive to any particular type of business, it was discovered that one perennial dilemma, capable of producing more loss of capital, degradation to consumer confidence and distasteful legal entanglements, is clearly in a class by itself. Simply, this dilemma is business' inability to achieve, by means of a well-planned, coordinated methodology, a successful acquisition or merger. In this application, success must be measured in the ability to operate a business profitably for extended periods of time (measured in years). In reviewing the Standard & Poor's Industrials, an astounding 45.3 percent of all acquisitions/mergers fail. An additional 6.4 percent experience a very restricted degree of success and are very likely candidates for failure. Though these figures seem high, statistical surveys on this subject over the past 40 years indicate that there has been very little change.

A thorough investigation of the available body of knowledge demonstrates that there exists a very definite lack of subject attention by businessmen and educators alike. The underscored bottom line of this matter suggests that the undesirable consequences of acquisition/merger failure can only be reconciled by management. But management, in order to operate successfully, needs basic tools of the trade and the knowledge of how to operate them. Currently, the business community is at a great disadvantage simply because it does not have a proven format from which to work. The need for concise coordinating procedure for acquisition/merger development is virtually self-evident.

By observing actual field performance of hundreds of businesses, it can easily be seen that management does not properly coordinate and control the complicated mechanism of Acquisition/Merger Management. This observation was seen to intensify in smaller businesses or in businesses that attempt to diversify in interests outside the area of their expertise and/or experience. It must further be stated that an alarmingly high number of businessmen would not follow an acquisition/merger format in any event. This group not withstanding, the author hypothesizes that, provided management understands the basic elements of business, possesses a coordinated, sequential program controlling acquisitions/mergers, and has a desire to use these tools, a major reduction in the rate of acquisition/merger failures can, in fact, occur.

After completing my total research, a task which required three-and-a-half years, a thorough, well-coordinated program was developed that details the three basic business areas of concern: marketing, financial and legal aspects. By paying close attention to all phases of an acquisition/merger, management can better control the incremental variables, thus manipulating all associated events in reference to each application of business and demands of the situation. As a consequence, emphasis on timing and communicative coordination has been observed to be a most critical concern. Further, most successful acquisition/mergers are coordinated by one competent individual who centrally controls and directs the total effort.

The author's investigation considered a wide variety of control points which included the effectual motivation for selling/buying, the various degrees of emphasis on marketing, financial and legal matters, the desired short- and long-term goals of both the seller and purchaser, and the modes of conduct and professionalism observed during the actual acquisition/merger event. Probably the most striking observation made was that most businessmen easily become overwhelmed by the initial multiplicity of questions and uncertainty of acquisitions and mergers. The definite trend to over-react by over-simplification, which dilutes the effectiveness of the entire program, usually occurs. Over-simplification in most occurrences results in the over-development of one business aspect or another, which by doing, shifts attention away from the central focus, a successful transaction. It makes little sense trying to describe an entire forest by concentrating solely on one type of tree.

> "The combination of phenomena is beyond the grasp of human intellect. But the impulse to seek causes is innate in the soul of man. And the human intellect with no inkling of the immense variety and complexity of circumstances conditioning phenomena, any one of which may be separately conceived as the cause of it, snatches at the first and most easily understood approximation and says, 'Here is the cause.'"
>
> Count Leo Tolstoy

Complicating the matter further, management often attempts to incorporate data and/or use text materials which are in excess of ten years of age. Relative age is of utmost importance when considering the dynamic nature of tax laws and legal statutes.

In the final analysis, it is the business community that must deal with the consequences of poor acquisition/merger management. When control points go unidentified, thus causing the acquisition programs to proceed unguided, the relative effects of random chance defer achieving the greatest possible degree of success.

The acquisition/merger basically is split into two organizational phases, pre-closing controls and post-closing follow through. The areas of developmental investigations, negotiations, determining worth, determining price, contract development, changing con-

trol of the business, and assimilation and direction are all critical. A calculated, weighted moving effort similar to the one outlined by the author, will insure the greatest degree of success. By understanding what totally occurs during an acquisition/merger, management's confusion intimidation and trepidation will be virtually eliminated.

DEVELOPMENT OF THE SELECTED PROBLEM

Many American businesses consist of an organization of operating divisions and/or corporations. But even if there is only one profit center within the organization, the basic elements of business administration persist to interplay. From the quantifying elements of accounting to the more artful aspects of marketing, a complicated set of factors intermingle to determine the life or death of a business.

Business includes many inherent complexities, organizational variability and the interaction of administrative prerogatives. Many firms have found extreme difficulty in dealing with the more complex problems of business largely due to poor organization, according to Dun & Bradstreet. This lack of continuity becomes even more evident when companies are compared to each other. Virtually without exception, elemental business programs, like cost or inventory accounting, follow straightforward business principles that are more easily understood than the more complicated aspects of financial analysis or marketing's strategic planning. Those business aspects that are more complex relate to a set of business problems that require greater technical expertise and administrative aptitude. The degree of disturbance that follows a series of decisions made within a business addresses this very point. One specific example that clearly demonstrates a detailed and complex business sequence is that of acquisition management. The gravity of this is exemplified by a review of Table 38-1[1]

Table 38-1
Performance Schedule—Business Acquisitions

Category	Number of Companies*	Percentage
Failure	78	45.3
Limping Group	11	6.4
Rejuvenations	3	1.8
Success	80	46.5

*172 major public corporations.

The basis for presenting business failure statistics,

[1]*Standard & Poor's Index: Industrial, 1975.*

as defined within the meaning of this chapter, does not represent the sum total of all business discontinuances. Those acquired or merged businesses that discontinue because of court proceedings or voluntary actions involving loss to creditors are classified as failures. Those business discontinuances that occur for various other reasons, such as loss of operating capital, inadequate profits, ill health, retirement, etc., but which entail no residual debt, are not classified as business failures. The non-failure groupings, as presented in Table 38-1, are summarized in the Limping Group (representing depressed profit margins compared to industry averages), Rejuvenated (representing a business turn-around with improving profit margins), and Success (profits are equal to or better than the industry average), all of which conduct liquid and solvent businesses where creditors are being paid.

During the period 1973 through 1977 (according to Dun & Bradstreet, Inc. of New York), more than 7,000,000 businesses per year changed ownership or control on a national basis. In 1976 alone, cumulative business failures amounted to $3,011,171,000. Considering this large dollar amount, the businessman can more readily understand the gravity of the failures and the resulting undesirable economic impact.

As a result of a business' change in financial status (business failure or degree of business success), more than 5,000 changes are made daily in the Dun & Bradstreet Reference Book: new names are added and discontinued businesses are deleted, name styles are altered, and credit and financial ratings are revised up or down. This high activity level evidences a very dynamic condition in the business population. Further, acquisition/merger failure rate trends (based upon the relative status of the economic environment) are directly comparable to the overall failure rate trends of business at large. Thus, as the total business community failure rates increase, the tendency for failures of acquired/merged businesses also increases. This relationship fluctuates with the overall change in business activity, the changes observed in operating and profit margins.

Except for the Depression and World War II years, there has been an average of over 750 mergers and acquisitions of major firms per year since 1920. In the period 1965 to 1969, the pace of new business combinations accelerated, particularly in the area of conglomerate combinations. In 1968, the number of major conglomerate mergers was triple the number in either 1964 or 1971. The assets of the acquired forms in major conglomerate combinations for 1968 totaled nearly $12 billion, almost ten times the assets of firms acquired in horizontal or vertical mergers that year.[2]

In 1975, corporations bought more than $12 billion worth of publicly held companies, according to financial consultants W.T. Grimm & Co. of Chicago. A total of 2,300 mergers of major private and public businesses took place in 1975.[3] After a six-year lull (period 1970 inclusive of 1975), the acquisition/-merger[4] action is once again advancing. Figure 38-1[5] demonstrates the merger action levels from 1969 to 1978 (est.) of major public corporations (page 608).

The year 1975 provided a situation that changed the style of business acquisitions. Today's trend involves bigger cash transactions negotiated in the form of a statutory merger or a sale of assets. The motivation for this is threefold: (1) There is an abundance of money available; (2) Foreign capital is flowing into the United States; and (3) Both rising costs and environmental restrictions are convincing many an expansion-minded management that it is often easier, cheaper, and more efficient to buy a business or facility than to build one.[6] With building and equipment costs growing higher with each passing day, there exists even greater support for the position, "Why build when a facility, many times more fully equipped, is available at yesterday's cost?"[7] Purchasing an existing facility includes no demanding campaign to plan a new building, no initiative requiring the development of new process flows, usually no serious alteration in facility layout, no major entanglements with contractors and time schedules, and an overall reduction in the complicated ramifications associated with new facility construction. An older facility generally costs less, potential sales withstanding. The extent of required modifications on an older facility is easily determined by means of engineering inspection of the physical structure(s).

In 1976, thirty-seven mergers were announced involving more than $100 million each.[8] Companies have discovered that if they are planning to diversify, they must buy companies large enough to have a meaningful impact on their overall operations, including

---

[2] United States Department of Commerce, Bureau of the Census, *Statistical Abstract of the United States: 1973* (94th Ed..), Washington, D.C.. 1973.

[3] J. Madrick, "Merger Guide to Good Buys," *Business Week,* January 16, 1976, p. 72.

[4] The FASB (Financial Accounting Standards Board), created in 1973, refers to both of these kinds of transactions as business combinations and therefore uses the terms interchangeably; so shall it be in this text.

[5] J. Perham, "Mergers on the Rebound," *Dun's Review,* May, 1977 p. 62.

[6] Ibid.

[7] J. Costello, "Why It's Cheaper to Buy than to Build," *Nations Business,* November 1977, p. 70.

[8] The largest merger was Peabody Coal Co., acquired by Newmont Mining Corp. for $1.2 billion.

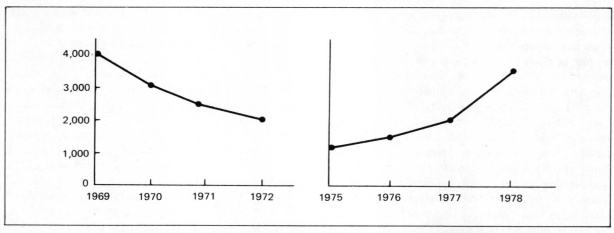

Figure 38-1   Number of Mergers by Year, Major Public Corporation

their net earnings. Where total 1975 mergers numbered 2,300, only 979 were of major publicly controlled corporations. The 1977 trend indicates that the business community will increase the merger rate in the group of major public companies by approximately twofold.[9]

With the increased occurrence of acquisitions, including the activities of other major acquirors such as Litton Industries, Ling-Temco-Vought, Gulf and Western Industries, I.T. & T., Textron, Esmark, Kraftco, Pepsico, Bendix Corp., Crown Zellerback Corp., Marshall Field and Co., Revlon, etc., it becomes even more important for business managers and negotiators to minimize or eliminate doubts, uncertainty, and hesitancy. To further explain the thinking of acquisition-minded companies, consider the current position of Standard Brands, Inc.

Chiefly, new leadership moves by SBI are toward a more frequent and ambitious new product introduction program ... by means of aggressive efforts in business acquisitions.[10] Chairman F. Ross Johnson and President Reuben Gutoff last year screened about 3,000 companies as potential acquisition targets.[11]

All this ambitious enterprise, however, too often falls victim to its own good intentions. "Jim Walter Broke Law By Acquiring Panacon, FTC Rules."[12]

This is but one example of many firms that have run into technical problems. Other examples of problems arising from acquisitions can be as diverse as circumstance itself. Pott Industries, sold to Houston Natural Gas Corp., has created operational problems that could require years to correct, thus delaying the expected rate of return on investment.[13] United Technology's attempt to purchase Babcock & Wilcox developed into a "tender offer that went sour."[14] As Bic discovered, it was better to terminate negotiations, taking preliminary losses of negotiation efforts, than lose capital on a potentially disastrous scale.[15] "Contran Corporation's Valhi Incorporated reports that bid to merge with unit has been enjoined."[16] In October, 1977, holders of a total of 10,000 to 12,000 Valhi shares filed a class-action suit against Valhi seeking to enjoin the merger between Contran Corp. and Valhi, Inc. on the grounds that it was designated solely to eliminate Valhi's minority stockholders at a grossly inadequate price. Because of this, Valhi said it expects the order to be entered, whereupon it intends to abandon the merger proposal.

Another complicating condition exists with a very large number of presidents of privately held companies having no idea of what their net worth is.[17] It is further observed that smaller companies desiring to sell are in

[9]"Great Takeover Binge," *Business Week,* November 14, 1977, p. 176.
[10]"Standard Brands: A Blueprint For a New Packaged-Goods Drive," *Business Week,* February 6, 1978, p. 90.
[11]Ibid., p. 91.
[12]*The Wall Street Journal* (New York), February 2, 1978, p. 7, Col. 2.
[13]"Bittersweet Deal: Pott Industries, Sold to Houston Natural Gas Corp.," *Forbes,* April 1, 1977, p. 76.
[14]"Not-so-Tender Offer United Technologies at Attempted Acquisition of Babcock & Wilcox," *Time,* March 14, 1977, p. 5.
[15]"Why Bid Dropped Its U.S. Razor Deal," *Business Week,* March 7, 1977, p. 23.
[16]*The Wall Street Journal* (New York), February 27, 1977, p. 8.
[17]"The Tough Time of the Finder," *Dun's Review,* January 1976, p. 45.

non-growth or profit-loss modes. Because of the complicated difficulties that can attend acquisitions, Corporate Marriage Brokers[18] have become a new major factor in locating and negotiating a successful transaction. The firm Niederhoffer, Cross and Zeckhauser finds sellers for buyers and receives 3 to 5 percent of the purchase price for their service. In the past six years, 38 mergers have occurred through this firm. Harlan J. Brown provides the same service working out of McLean, Virginia. One of Mr. Brown's larger successes is included in the series of mergers recently negotiated by the Kroger Company. Davis Associates of New York exemplifies yet another firm whose prime function is to act as financial consultant to acquisition-oriented companies of all types. There are others, and the list of Corporate Marriage Brokers continues to grow. Following a fundamental law of economics, the need for technical assistance is obvious; these professionals are supplying a need that is presently lacking in industry and business at large.

In spite of the 1973 recession and current economic uncertainty, there is no indication that the business advance is in jeopardy from any internal economic imbalance.[19] Supporting this position, the Acton Corp. and Bachman Foods, an acquired company of the Culbro Corporation, have extended their respective businesses by acquisition during fiscal 1977. Specifically, the Acton Corp., a once troubled enterprise, through careful financial assessment and the acquisition of 13 operations, has increased revenues for the nine month period (ending September 30, 1977) to $32.6 million from $10.6 million in the previous period of 1976. Net income for the period in 1977 was $3 million, compared with $1 million the previous year. That resulted in EPS of $1.13 compared with $.41 of the prior year. Income increased by $850,000 compared with $819,000 the prior year.[20]

The fiscal impact can be demonstrated positively, as with Acton's newly gained success, or it can become a disaster. Recall that 45.3 percent of all major business acquisitions fail; 6.4 percent just limp along. This entire unaddressed problem suggests that management has been remiss in controlling the events and circumstances of the acqusition process. The energy and driving forces behind Acton's success are Messrs. Sam and George Phillips, who have extensive financial backgrounds through both education and business ex-

perience. Why should the mechanics of the purchase-sell transaction be so mysterious and often times unattainable?

As Charles William Eliot suggests,[21] the business environment is a functional and interacting set of dynamic elements, ever changing. In the final analysis, it is the businessman's responsibility to perceive course and direction within the acquisition environment. The obvious measure of success is found in that degree of expertise management demonstrates in the technical use of the available information and an understanding of the mechanisms involved within the transaction sequence.

STATEMENT OF THE PROBLEM

Considering that a total of 51.7 percent of all acquisitions measure up unsatisfactorily, the business community is commissioned to give careful consideration to the multitude of thoughts that pass through the minds of buyers and sellers:

> Should this business be sold—What is it worth—Can an interested buyer be found—How much information should be permitted to the prospective buyer—Will the buyer lower his initial offer—Should this business really be sold—Could we have gotten more for this business—Will this business succeed under new management?

> Should this business be purchased—What is the real reason behind the sale of this business—Can our current operation afford this purchase—How can any remaining costs be financed—How reduced could the selling price become—After acquisition, how should the old management be converted to our management concepts and style—What hidden skeletons will surface after acquisition—Everything will work out well, won't it?

Considering the complex nature of an acquisition or merger, it can be easily observed that many questions arise and require, actually, demand attention. Remember, 45.3 percent of the major corporations, those who could afford greater proficiency, fail at acquiring businesses, and 6.4 percent barely survive; it is apparent that proper coordination and programming of the processes that comprise an acquisition do not occur.

---

[18] "The Tough Time of the Finder," *Dun's Review,* January 1976, p. 45.

[19] "Business Outlook," *Business Week,* January 16, 1978, p.23.

[20] Financial data obtained from "Acton Now Among Top Snack Firms," *Snack Food,* December 1977, p.20.

[21] All business proceeds on beliefs, on judgements of probabilities, not on certainties.

Obviously, the specific critical elements in the purchase-sell sequence have been overlooked or superficially handled. Obviously, there may be other more obscure situations that could cause acquisition failure. But whatever the circumstance, it makes a great deal more sense to eliminate uncertainty by reducing the undesirable and variable impact of the unknown.

When elements of random chance enter into a transaction, unfavorable results can be expected. Elements of random chance in an event guide the process out of control. For the newly acquired organization(s), or for the parent company itself, the financial burden of less-than-anticipated successful performance has resulted in limited fiscal success or absolute business failure. Current business trends further demonstrate that significant future changes in the acquisition failure rate are not expected.

With these considerations in mind, the author recognized an overriding need for inquiry into the reasons behind acquisition failure. By evaluating the impact of events that comprise a transaction, the author concluded that a thorough and organized procedure for expediting an acquisition is required. As a consequence, the alternative method of Acquisition Management became the primarily desired conclusion of this research. Identifying a problem and defining its elements would prove fruitless without a detailed method for correction. As a businessman, it is extremely frustrating to be subjected to the whims of random chance. Possessing the ability to control variable situations gives positive direction to any enterprise.

The interaction between a purchaser and a seller of a business, as well as the type of business being transacted, gives rise to conditions that enlarge and overwhelm most business managers. The successful transfer of ownership in the final analysis results from comprehensive, factually complete analysis. Rigorous negotiations follow, resulting in final terms of varying quality based upon the congruence and reliability of the development data and analysis of the transaction. The purchase-sell contract can contain numerous conditions, liabilities, and other modifying attachments. Generally, business managers fail to utilize proper investigative methods due to identifiable causes (capital limitations) and/or unidentifiable causes (lack of practical knowledge). Those managers whose operations fail are usually those who have been overwhelmed by the jointly shared professional frustration of other unresolved failures. Considering the potential gravity of the purchase-sell transaction, it seems unusual that better handling hasn't occurred.

Interstate Brands, Inc. (name concealed by request) in September, 1977, did not follow detailed research during an acquisition. As a consequence, it was legally required to expend $13 million beyond the negotiated business' purchase price because of inadequate negotiations and contractual research.

The Bradford Company failed to research potential marketing impact and the value-added leverage of a newly acquired business it had purchased. Three years later, the newly acquired business was divested because of irretrievable losses. The actual losses decreased the gross margin to the point that a negative cash flow and a large short-term debt were created.

Business failure is certainly an experience to be avoided. However, over half of all acquisitions fail or demonstrate very restrained, or a limping degree of success. What causes such situations; what can be done about them?

RESEARCH METHODOLOGY

Considering the interdependent aspects of a transaction, there exist ten decision factors. A business normally changes owners after management considers and acts upon a series of decision elements. The actual sale or purchase of a business is the final decision made, which reflects the efforts of earlier decisions in a unique process characteristic of an acquisition. The relative success of any buyer or seller can be measured by the degree in which the problem elements are realized, the depth in which they are studied, and the application of results obtained. Due to the singular nature of the individual decisions and how they relate to each transaction, it is better to identify decisions by a series of steps or elemental categories.

(1) Motivation—a decision to attempt the sale or purchase of a business.
(2) Contact—a decision as to the method of determining a buyer/seller of a business with specified characteristics.
(3) Information—a decision on the information needed to purchase/sell a business.
(4) Sources—a decision on the logistics and cost impact requirements governing the development of information.
(5) Analysis—a decision on the significance and reliability of obtained information.
(6) Value—a decision on what the actual worth of the business should be.
(7) Price—a decision on how much capital is to be expected for the business
(8) Financing—a decision on the method of transacting capital (or other asset equity).

(9) Contract—a decision on the form and content of the contractual relationship.

(10) Implementation—a decision on the mechanism to be utilized in effecting ownership transfer.

As a means of further expansion, these ten decisions were considered by the author due to their logically progressive nature in describing the events within the complex mechanism of the transaction. Obviously, management does not like to publish the full extent of their failure no matter what the degree. Because of this and the resulting lack of documented cases available to analyze, it was necessary to conduct further investigative research in an attempt to understand the actual procedures involved.

The basic information available to the businessman was demonstrated to be technically complicate or generalized beyond use. Thus, it can be concluded that there exists an improper balance of available information which, as a result, is improperly and/or incompletely organized for use. The business professional, consequently, falls victim to frustration, confusion, and disillusionment accompanied by a functional lack of understanding in the matters of acquisition analysis. It must be stated that analysis only occurs when the need for it is perceived and not necessarily when the need for it exists.

Because of the variable nature of the transaction environment, the author's research demanded that determination of the contributing events comprising the transaction needed to become a major issue. Since a continually high acquisition failure rate persists, as demonstrated by the poor results of newly acquired businesses, it became imperative that acquisitions be evaluated by means of first-person exposure. For all practicle purposes, it is impossible for each manager to indulge himself in learning the aspects of acquisitions and mergers when the actual event begins. Knowing what to do at the appointed time can make the difference between achieving success or failure.

RESULTS BASED UPON THE DECISION ELEMENTS OF ACQUISITION

In order to develop the real concerns of the purchaser and seller, a review of the basic questions used during the decision-making sequence is required. Decisions must be made sequentially, usually one answer leading to another question as the puzzle works its way together. The following is a description of the history of an actual situation reported as a result of the business interviews. In order to make this situation typical of other business transactions, specific considerations characteristic to the other cases researched have been included in the following exaxple of a low-value-added business, the grocery store.

Jim's Food-Villa. Frank Aaron has worked 13 years in various grocery stores in Youngstown, a city of 450,000 population. Beginning his career as a carry-out boy, Frank progressed through virtually all phases of store operations. During 1977, Frank decided to own his own store. Since he and his wife were 37 years old, he concluded that they should not delay any longer. A business purchased now could be turned over to their children when their education was completed. Toward achieving this goal, the Aaron's decided to invest their $8,000 savings. Frank was confident in his operations knowledge and his wife's capabilities in maintaining the accounting responsibilities.

The Aaron's pursued many leads secured from their newspaper's classified section. This process produced business possibilities either too large to finance or too run-down to salvage. Frank also allied himself with two real estate agents specializing in business properties; however, no leads were developed within the Aarons' guidelines.

In August, Frank discovered from a sales representative that Jim Adamley was in the market to sell his store. Jim's Food-Villa was a relatively small store which had operated for many years across town.

Jim had been trying to sell his business for over a year. However, he was reluctant to aggressively pursue selling because the store had been established by his father, which associated strong personal feelings. Yet he was approaching retirement age, and the responsibility and long hours required to operate the store presented a serious hardship. Further, the business had lost sales from a high of $200,000 in 1973 to $125,000 in 1976 with gross '77 sales amounting to $8,000 a month. Jim concluded that these sales declines were due to the increased competition from six new supermarkets in the local area. Finally, he was concerned about an unused area of approximately 1,100 square feet located at one end of the building contiguous to the store. Jim owned the entire building and had been unable to find a tenant for this area for five months. A discount paint company had offered Jim a local franchise, and he thought that the vacant area could easily handle that operation with much less effort. What remained was the sale of the grocery business so that he could lease the store space to the new owner. Jim concluded that, with all things considered, this would be a very equitable arrangement.

After discussing preliminary items with the sales representative, Frank called Jim and expressed an interest in the business. A meeting was arranged, followed by several more. Frank discovered that Jim wanted to sell in order to take advantage of the paint store opportunity. When Jim announced that he was asking $25,000 cash and $300 per month rent, the discussion proceeded as follows:

Frank: Because of my serious interest, I think it's only fair that I review your books.
Jim: You can't do that! Most of my personal affairs are in those books. Besides, I don't want to give away certain details about my business to a potential competitor.
Frank: But I must have some facts to base my decision on.
Jim: Well, you ask me what you need to know, and I'll tell you if and when I can.

During subsequent discussions, Frank discovered the following about the operation:

The modern fixtures and equipment had cost $30,000 in 1971 and had a depreciated value of $15,000. The inventory had a wholesale cost of $10,000. Gross sales were $8,000 during September with a gross profit of 15.5 percent; Frank discovered that sales in the past had been as high as $200,000. The 3,900 sq. ft. store space appeared well organized, clean, and in good repair.

From this information and general observations, Frank determined that sales could be increased to $20,000 a month within one year with aggressive sales promotion, using handbills, radio spot announcements, a specially designed illuminated sign, and more personal service. As a result, Frank concluded that the working inventory should be enlarged to $12,000. In order to improve net profit performance which had been averaging 2 2/3 percent of gross sales before Jim's salary was withdrawn, Frank considered raising the average markup from 18 percent to 20 percent. Further reductions in the costs of operations, according to Frank's analysis, could be realized by cutting the staff by one full-time and one-part time clerk.

Frank found it difficult to borrow the difference between his $8,000 savings and the initial $25,000 price. Five banks refused to grant a loan before one agreed to a loan with terms that provided $10,000 at 8½ percent interest with monthly payments over a five-year period.

Jim refused Frank's $18,000 offer, but stated that he would finance part of the purchase price. After a series of discussions, final purchase terms were agreed upon:

(1) $12,000 cash.
(2) $11,000 unsecured note, payable monthly over a five-year period at 8½ percent interest.
(3) $200 a month rent.

With the $6,000 borrowed capital remaining, Frank concluded that working capital and the ability to increase inventory would be available.

On October 1, store operations changed owners. Frank had initially only an $8,000 inventory at wholesale cost. Therefore, $4,000 was expended to increase his shelf stock. During November, sales increased to $15,000, and Frank was confident that $20,000 gross sales per month could be attained. This notwithstanding, net profit was only 1.96 percent of gross sales. Attempts to increase net margin and reduce operating costs were unsuccessful.

Five months later, the net profit deteriorated to .27 percent, whereupon the grocery store was closed. The remaining $6,000 inventory was sold to a wholesale outlet for $5,400. The fixtures were sold for $8,200. Frank was struggling to close out his payables and debts and to forget the complete loss of his savings ($8,000).

As a result, Jim was faced with an empty building, no prospective occupants, and no prospects of recovering the loan to Frank; he had lost in excess of $2,000 rental income and was confused about appropriate action, if any, that he should take to recover the loss.

To the Frank's and Jim's of the business world, one should ask: "How does one purchase or sell a business?" This is an obviously important and difficult question to answer. The acquisition of a business includes personal, economic, and management decisions which deny easy and superficial comment.

Therefore, the series of decision elements, as previously outlined, must be collectively addressed in proper perspective and sequence.

DECISION ELEMENTS OF AN ACQUISITION

The preceeding vignette described a business bought and sold. Frank, the purchaser, and Jim, the seller, thought that each had negotiated a deal of fair value. However, the final analysis clearly demonstrated that the decision to change business ownership was successful; the results were not. The losses included savings (capital funds), future income, and a source for gainful employment. This section will reduce the task of evaluating the aspects of business ownership transfers into its simplest elements. By representing this task in basic terms, the complicated and peripheral aspects will be placed in proper perspective, and a more effective decision-making course of action will be available for use.

The most difficult and most important step in the process focuses on the question, ''What is this business worth?'' Referring to Jim's Food-Villa in the example, most people conceive the worth of a business to be the total of the value of machinery and equipment, land and building(s), inventory, and applied receivables. These items, which are easily retrieved from the balance sheet, are important considerations; however, the sum of these values does not constitute the value of the business. Frank probably paid a reasonable price for the equipment, but did the selling price of $23,000 reflect the value of Jim's market? Obviously not—the business failed. How businesses deal with assets, liabilities, and potential sales is determined by the sequence of decisions that lead to the final ownership change.

Motivation. What causes an owner to sell his business (or a profit center) to another controlling group? An infinite number of reasons follow which could include change of a company's strategic direction and policy, business disagreements, an over-extension of an organization's working capital, a desire to retire from business, health problems, etc. An analysis of the cases provided in this text demonstrates this point.

In Jim's situation, the primary motivating factor was change. Jim found his sales decreasing, competition increasing, and an empty building space impossible to rent. Both internal and external factors had created conditions which adversely affected business.

From an owner's point of view, changed economic conditions should be analyzed carefully before they are accepted as reasons to sell the business. Guidelines from this analysis can be outlined by referring to these questions:

(1) Have changes actually occurred in my business?
(2) Are the causes for the changes beyond my control?
(3) Are the causes for the changes within my control?

It would be unfortunate for an owner to sell a business because of changes which he could control and, by such control, recapture a successful and satisfying operation. Every owner, therefore, should evaluate closely his motives for wanting to divest the business.

What causes an individual or organization to purchase a business? Once again, motivations will range the spectrum of desires (including business-oriented political circumstances and pressures) from simple economic gain to social-ladder climbing. Frank's prime motivating factor was to expand a special skill he had acquired into a desired application, a business of his own. However, in the final analysis, Frank did not, in fact, possess the required business skills. The particular factor of personal skill is a dominant motivation causing companies or individuals to purchase a business. It is an emotional motive, in numerous instances, based upon ego and wishful thinking and, therefore, must be recognized as a potentially dangerous motive to be handled accordingly.

Any business must be managed. Possessing the operating skill does not necessarily equate with possessing managing ability. Based upon an operator's orientation, a particular mode of operation will reflect those skills in which the operator is most proficient. Frequently, an orientation to a skill encourages a person, manager/or operator, to spend his time operating the said skill instead of managing. The management function includes planning for the future, organizing resources, staffing the business with competent people, directing the coordination of people, and operating and controlling business results.

Consequently, those who seek to purchase a business in which to apply operating skills should evaluate their motivation by means of asking the following pertinent questions:

(1) How important is management ability in this business? Occasionally, a business is sufficiently simple or unique to manage itself. However, where it is imperative to be competitive, and where integration is necessary, management ability is probably the most critical factor.

(2) Can the existing management team manage successfully? Effectiveness with people (customers and employees), eagerness to tackle difficult, complex problems and make decisions, and intelligence concerning routine business operations are key factors in management ability.

(3) Can management skills specific to this business be obtained? Most people can learn to manage if they recognize the need. This requires participation in educational programs, either professional, self-improvement programs, seminars, graduate school, etc. Room to make mistakes is also a consideration that must be addressed carefully. The intensity and result-

ing cost of error will be dramatically reduced with a competent staff.

After the actual motive for purchasing/selling has been evaluated and the impetus to continue with negotiations established, the next step is to develop the purchaser-seller contract.

Contact. Because there appears to be no best way of locating a purchaser or seller, a multitude of possibilities exists, which defies the cataloging of a specific procedure. Those successfully seeking contact virtually always include basic salesmanship and marketing techniques.

From the position of the seller, the task of locating prospective buyers is the more difficult. Since there are many avenues for the seller to exploit (other than using advertisements in newspapers), those most adept at making contact should attend the following questions:

(1) Have the business's employees and other associates been informed of the intentions to sell the business?

(2) Have the broadcasting abilities of salesmen, who call on similar businesses, of association meetings, and of other trade contacts been explored?

Obviously, those who know the business, or the type of business, generally are excellent prospects as buyers, providing they have the financial capacity. The seller is expected to realize that informal advertising requires the same kind of information output as does more formal advertising. Business associates, trade contacts, and friends generally are provided data dealing with asking price, terms, and anticipated return. Without this knowledge, a potential buyer probably will not respond authoritatively. He needs to know in advance how the possibility relates to his financial capacity.

From the purchaser's position, locating purchase opportunities is relatively uncomplicated. The real problem lies in locating a business that can be analyzed confidently. When dealing with unfamiliar businesses, a prospective buyer feels a desire for more information and a suspicion about the basic quality of information received. If the purchaser is competent in analyzing the type of business in question, the following considerations will be made:

(1) Have personal contacts included the use of credible persons, with whom the purchaser is familiar, concerning individuals who are considering the sale of business?

(2) Has the purchaser made personal contacts with prospective sellers?

It was through such informal means that Frank met Jim. Purchasers or sellers should not neglect the efficacy of this type of contact.

Information — Kinds and Sources. This is the point at which the purchaser and seller determine what information (about the business) must be secured or released. In the case of Jim's Food-Villa, three factors determined the type of communicated information:

(1) The nature of the business in the past.

(2) The present condition of the business.

(3) Relating the past and present to future expectancy.

Frank's approach was in order, but the information he received was meager support for decision making.

During the sequence of developing sources of information, the astute purchaser will face a difficult problem. Desired information will often be expensive to develop or will require considerable time to obtain. Therefore, a purchaser is expected to decide which sources should remain unused. Certainly, then, the types of information for decision-making and business analysis are not separable elements in actual transactions, but are closely integrated in the acquisition proceedings.

Considering the experience in Jim's Food-Villa, Frank might well have inquired about the general conditions of local economics. A full documentation would require an expensive economic analysis. However, there were readily available sources of information which included these facts:

(1) Sales in the market had declined in excess of 50 percent.

(2) Jim had been unable to rent commercial space in the same building in which the grocery store was located.

(3) Competition was increasing with new, larger supermarkets.

(4) Lending institutions (banks) were hesitant to gamble with Frank on the future of Jim's Food-Villa.

Frank might have developed information about the future business trends; this required time. He should have known, however, the following facts about his financial program. Table 38-2 presents a financial survey reviewing the known data secured from Jim.

Frank had sufficient information available to ascertain that his sales expectations were overly optimistic, and that even if his hope about sales materialized, he would never be able to satisfy the cash demand on the operations. The final result was predictable.

Table 38-2
Financial Summary — Jim's Food-Villa

Available Funds		$18,000
Use of Funds		
Payment to Jim	$12,000	
Inventory Increase	2,000	
Advertising	500	
Display Sign	500	15,000
Available Working Capital		$ 3,000
Anticipated Monthly Income		
($15,000 x 3%)		450
Probable Expense		
Payment to Bank	$ 170	
Payment to Jim	190	
General Administrative	?	

Evaluation of the word "predictable" suggests that there is a pattern that coordinates and organizes the information of acquisition. From this pattern, an analysis of the findings can be determined. A purchaser should be able to follow through the steps listed below and ascertain with confidence the future of the business:

(1) (a) What factors affect sales?
How will these market factors behave?
Therefore, what sales can I expect?
(b) What constitutes the costs of sales?
How will these cost factors apply to expected sales?
Therefore, what gross profit can I expect?
(c) What expenses are required to run this business?
How will expenses develop under my ownership?
Therefore, what net profit can be predicted?
(2) (a) What assets will the business need and possess?
What is the condition of these assets?
Therefore, what asset improvements can be anticipated?
(b) What credit does the business assume?
What is the condition of the credit position?
Therefore, what changes, if any, can occur in the debt structure?
(3) (a) How much cash is on hand?
How much cash will the business generate?
Therefore, what will be the available cash position after acquisition?
(b) What should be the purchaser's immediate cash outlay?
What will be the cash needs of the business?
Therefore, what cash outgo will be experienced?

(c) What will be the new owner's net cash position?
What additional cash resource, if any, will be required?
Therefore, what financing plan will be required?

This outline is a basic model from which are derived decisions on information needed, sources of information available, and techniques of analysis.

Value. The value of any business is only the conclusion of the purchaser's and seller's analysis. What remains is defining the precise meaning of value as it pertains to the business.

All businesses have a purpose. That purpose is to provide a satisfactory return on the owner's investment. Consequently, determining value involves measuring the future profit of the new business.

The seller frequently considers value as representing the money he has invested during his period of ownership. The purchaser often considers value as a fair price for the physical plant including building, land, equipment, and inventory. While these factors are important, they have value only to the extent they contribute to the attainment of future profits. An owner may have invested $20,000, the tangible assets may have a present value of $10,000, but there may exist a profit potential that must be considered when establishing the net value of the total business.

A carefully prepared marketing estimate of future sales used in the preparation of the financial estimate of future profit will provide the base for determining payment ($) for each dollar of profit potential. Summarizing the elements of value determination suggests these considerations:

(1) What is being bought (or sold)? A business as future sales or a facility full of equipment and inventory on some property, as fixed assets?
(2) What return could be realized on alternative investments such as stocks, bonds, diversified investments, or other business opportunities?

Frank considered the assets of the grocery, was strongly motivated to own his own business, and gave superficial treatment to projecting future sales. Further, these projected future sales were never considered in the final decision leading to determining actual value of the business.

Price. It might seem that price, the monies expended or received, would be synonymous with value. However, value refers to what a business is worth; price refers to the amount of money for which ownership is transferred. In the final analysis, there will usually be a difference between price and value because those purchasing and those selling have different opinions as to the worth of the business. Therefore, the price will represent negotiation and compromise.

The following offer suggestions for a fruitful negotiation:

(1) Discussion between purchaser and seller should focus upon future profit performance of the business. Since anticipated profit is fundamental to valuation determination, it can be a valuable negotiation leverage point.

(2) Specific assumptions and risk attend every profit projection. Generally, the more tenuous the assumption and the more apparent the risk, the less value an expected profit can support. Consequently, identifying and analyzing risks involved in future operations can make significant discussion between purchasers and sellers.

These two points assist in bringing the negotiation of different conclusions as to value toward a mutually acceptable price. It is obvious that Jim and Frank did not address price based upon value. Nevertheless, by whatever means price is determined, financing must follow.

Finance. As a result of the field research, the aspects of finance in acquisition management involve:

(1) The amount of required capital.
(2) The type of required capital.
(3) The intended uses of the capital.
(4) The required length of time for capital repayment based on generated capital from operations.
(5) The sources of available capital.

The conditions in Jim's Food-Villa characterize a universal problem: underestimating the amount of capital required to purchase a business. Capital must obviously be available to pay the purchase price. However, capital must also be available to meet the requirements of (a) funds to operate until the business is generating cash, (b) funds to meet unexpected expenses, and (c) funds as a reserve to provide for errors in expectations. The purchaser must think or project beyond the purchase price to determine the amount of required working capital, otherwise capital resources would be at least embarrassingly, or more probably, disastrously wanting:

(1) Is there enough capital to pay the purchase price?
(2) Is there enough capital to support one-to three-months' operations, including payroll and other cash expenses if the business is less than self-supporting (Payback Analysis)?

(3) Is there an extra amount of capital to cover unexpected needs, probably 10 percent to 15 percent of the purchase price?

There exist two basic types of capital: (1) Equity capital, investment capital invested in the business by the owner(s) or operating officers, and (2) Debt capital, borrowed capital which must be repaid.

Equity capital is frequently referred to as risk capital. Those who furnish the equity capital are expected to absorb the primary risk of failure and to receive the benefits of success. The equity capital provides a safety margin for a lender. The greater the amount of equity capital, if other items are equal, the less difficult it becomes to secure debt capital.

The primary source of equity capital is from cash on hand, sales of stock, capital surplus, retained earnings, or investment capital (including savings) of the purchaser of the business.

In the event that sufficient equity capital is not available, debt financing must be utilized. Borrowing money for the purchase of a business may be short or long in term. Sources of such debt financing can be secured from debentures, sinking funds, notes, etc. Small business proprietors usually borrow via personal loans, against insurance policies, or through refinancing the home mortgage. These methods are not direct business debts; however, the debts of a business and the personal debts of the owner cannot be distinctly separated.

In Jim's Food-Villa, the purchaser's savings plus a bank loan were insufficient to completely finance the purchase. Frank, requiring more financing, and Jim, desiring to sell the business, reacted in a manner quite common in the financing of the sale of a business. Jim agreed to accept payment of part of the purchase price over a specified period of time. Consequently, a rather unique source of capital to the purchaser of a proprietorship business is the seller himself. However, this type of capital is usually not available to those involved in purchasing partnership or incorporated businesses. If it is a possibility, the successful purchaser should usually consider the following:

(1) Determine and evaluate existing reasons why commercial lenders refuse the purchaser's loan request.
(2) Determine if the seller is so intent on selling the business that he is willing to take imprudent risks.
(3) Reascertain what the business' actual worth is. Re-evaluation of the reasons for purchasing the business should occur.
(4) Be certain that the business can support the acquired debt repayment obligation.

Recalling Jim's experience, the seller should consider the following before accepting an extended payment plan:

(1) How serious will it be if the purchaser defaults payment?

(2) What security is there that protects the seller's position?

(3) How capable is the buyer at operating this business successfully?

Contract and Implementation. Each step in this discussion has involved the problems of forecasting. From motivation to finance, the purchaser and seller have been encouraged to anticipate characteristics, developments, and problems before they develop. The resulting contract presents the details of the negotiated agreement and describes the present and future relationship between the purchaser and seller. However, a well-written contract will not function if previous decision elements in the process have been executed carelessly or not at all.

It was unnecessary for Frank and Jim to have sacrificed so much as a result of their acquisition. A review of the techniques of acquisition is available upon request from the author. For those who use these techniques, the measure of success will be dramatically increased.

DECISION-MAKING INFORMATION

As a result of the initial desire to purchase or sell a business, the businessman is confronted with two basic questions: "What kind of information is required?" and "Where and how can this information be obtained?" This section will analyze these questions which are classified under three general categories: (1) Marketing information, (2) Financial information, and (3) Legal information. The discussion at this point identifies the kinds and sources of information to which the purchaser and seller should seek answers, while the actual methodology for securing data must be considered relative to the circumstances at hand. Each situation must, of its own merits, dictate the actual procedure.

Beyond questions into the nature of the information, purchasers and sellers might ask, "How much information is required?" Obviously, the answer would be, "Enough to enable the involved people to reach an intelligent decision so that objectives could be successfully accomplished." This statement is not very quantified or qualified. However, it is important to keep this response in mind since all acquisition situations are unique.

In considering sources of information, the author concluded that it would be appropriate to ponder where information is most likely found. In effect, there are two basic source areas; Internal Sources include records of the business and personal observation; External Sources, information from sources separate from the business, include records and other documents as well as observation information.

Inadequate records, non-availability of certain information, lack or cooperation, etc., cause increased complication in the task of securing usable information. The seller has the advantage concerning internal data, since he has access to his own records where the purchaser does not. If the prospective purchaser has need for internal information in order to reach the final decision of acquisition, such information should be provided in a factual manner. The purchaser should insist that business records be made available for review. A purchaser must be wary of those sellers who refuse access to records.

External information research may require a relatively long expenditure of time due to inaccessability. The same would apply to circumstances in which specific observations of certain factors would be required to assist in progressing through the series of acquisition decisions. In many instances, the records of smaller businesses are inadequate, or at times, non-existent. This trend is inversely proportional to the overall size of the business. Further, it is virtually impossible to presume in advance the kinds of internal records that may be available. The investigator(s) will be required to use considerable ingenuity when information is provided in non-standardized fashion. Non-accurate sales information is a particularly good example of poor record keeping. As a result of the field research, the following sections present a general overview of the information sources that will assist a researcher in gathering the basic types of information and data necessary in the decision-making process.

Market Information

In the order of events occurring in an acquisition, the first and most logical step would be in conducting or analyzing information from a market analysis. This market analysis describes the position of the business within its operating market to establish present status and to reflect future patterns. The desired concerns of such an analysis would be with the nature of the business growth, the state of the market, the nature and extent of competition, and all other factors which would identify both the present position and future expectancy of the business.

An initial market analysis would indicate the status

of market conditions revealing the desirability of considering further the purchase or sale of the business. Such an analysis can be expected to be of value to the seller in determining the valuation to be placed on the business for sale purposes. The value to the purchaser would also be a matter of price determination, but further to assist him in gaining a clearer picture of just what it is he is buying. A market analysis has the added value of providing information leading to the development of sales forecasts and projections. The emphasis of conducting an investigation into marketing aspects stresses the importance of fact finding and de-emphasizes wishful thinking and guesswork.

For those businesses or individuals who cannot afford a full-time marketing department, the purchaser or seller should give himself the advantage of obtaining professional advice and counsel. While certain records and documents will serve as a basis upon which to make decisions, a substantial portion of the information required may not be obtainable through readily available sources. This would be especially true in studying external conditions, such as competition. Professional marketing counsel would assist in developing a systematic and orderly procedure in information gathering.

The specific nature of the business being bought or sold would determine much of the required market information. A manufacturing business with problems of marketing and distribution would need certain information sources as would more likely be true of financial statements and specific types of contracts.

Consider the following areas of marketing that provide desirable information for use in the acquisition sequence.

Internal Sources: Company Sales Records. A thorough investigation is recommended into the history of the business' sales. In order to realize significant trends, a minimum three-year sales period is required, but preferably a ten-year period, or to the point of origin if the seller is a relatively new company of less than ten years. Availability of sales information will largely depend upon the manner in which the records are kept. The size of a business is usually directly proportional to the way the sales records are maintained. With small businesses, the only records that are kept are those that satisfy the necessities of the I.R.S., state, and local tax agencies.

During the research, it was noted that many smaller businesses maintain bookkeeping systems designed by business machine manufacturers, i.e., NCR, Sweda, etc. Others utilize systems established by trade associa-

tions or professional accounting services, such as Mail-Me-Monday. In all cases, however, those businesses that employ standardized accounting procedures, as those described in the Official Opinions of the American Institue of Certified Public Accountants (AICPA), will provide more useful information for analysis purposes.

Since virtually all states have instituted sales taxes and many localities have an extra added tax of their own, proper sales records are required by law, except where the type of business grants immunity to taxation. Sale tax laws are non-uniform state to state. However, those businesses that conduct an interstate business generally follow official methods in accounting for sales.

If the majority of sales are done on a credit basis, accounts receivable will give useful sales information, even if work sheets or journals need to be audited. In this application, the secured data would be used to establish amount of sales on a credit basis and not necessarily inclusive of the effectiveness of collections.

In certain isolated situations, ingenuity and perception will lead to methods for accurately accounting sales. This can be exemplified in the review of sales for a self-service laundry where figuring water capacity per machine, price per load, and the amount of water consumption based on city water readings determined the business' sales.

No matter what source is available for determining sales information, the need to establish sales trends over time including projected future sales, remains constant in all businesses. Market share potential, then, must be determined so that a strategic plan can be developed. Consequently, the realized sales information should be related to volume changes of sales over the last three years minimum, ten years ideally.

It cannot be sufficiently stressed that the sales history investigation is the major element in determining the value of the business, over and above the value assigned to the assets.

Internal Sources: Records of the Cost of Goods Sold. In conjunction with sales determination of market position, the business costs associated to sales also must be determined. Cost of goods sold represents the cost associated with all phases from manufacture or merchandising through warehousing and distribution to the business' final customer(s). The difference between the cost of goods and the sales represents gross margin (or in some applications, gross profit). As cost of goods increase, the gross margin decreases and, consequently, the net profit.

Since the interaction of events affects the cost of goods sold based on business and market causes, an investigation including the following is expected:

(1) Average rate of inventory turnover as compared to the average rate as described for the type and size of business.

(2) Extent to which invoices are being discounted. Discounting of invoices, accounts payable, will result in increasing gross margin/net profit if shown as a reduction in the cost of goods sold, or as a direct increase in net profit if shown as other income.

(3) Determination that freight costs of incoming transportation charges are within reasonable expectations.

(4) Analysis of capital turnover or cash flow as an indicator of the relationship between the mean inventory at cost by period and the net sales during the same period.

While an analysis of the cost of goods sold only provides an indirect relationship to marketing activity, the investigator will be provided with additional information on the state of the business in question.

In review, those specific records that require examination are vendor invoices, accounts payable, shipping records (bills of lading), and the past three years' material inventories.

Internal Sources: Sales Effort Records. In this regard, the investigator evaluates the cost of sales to volume of sales ratio. This must not be confined to a minimum period, but rather considered on a quarterly basis over a minimum three-year period. Specifically, this analysis reviews advertising cost from invoices and statements of various forms of advertising and promotion, and for salaries and wages paid to support the selling effort. Salaries and wages are determined from payroll accounting records or from Social Security records.

Where the business maintains a sales force, as with manufacturers, information regarding reimbursed travel expenses must be reviewed since this affects resulting selling expenses.

The results of gathering selling cost information will provide information describing how efficiently these costs are being handled and a comparison between these costs and average figures for the particular business in question.

Internal Sources: General Observation. A personal inspection of the business and the personnel comprising the business' manpower will be helpful in developing the negotiations. While this will vary depending upon the business' nature, the following represents specific points which need to be investigated, thus subscribing to the purchaser's requirements:

(1) The general appearance of the premises, internally and externally. General cleanliness, housekeeping, and repair will be factors supporting negotiations, particularly in businesses that include direct customer contact therein or where regulatory agencies demand good conditions to prevail.

(2) The physical layout and apparent efficiency of operation. The manufacturer or retailer finds operational difficulty where ease of flow or the proper utilization of space has not been addressed.

(3) The employee morale and general attitude toward the business. This factor is highly important, especially if the current employees are scheduled to be retained after ownership has changed.

(4) The status of personnel records. This information will indicate the existence of wage payment plans, employee evaluation and merit rating programs, employee training programs, or any other employee benefit program that might modify the results of the negotiations.

External Sources. Sources of information available outside those related within a business are quite numerous and variable and are predicated upon the type of business being acquired. For classifying purposes, these sources can be grouped within two general categories: (1) Business competition, and (2) The total market in which the business competes, including the factors that are governing elements. Generally, the competent investigator will realize that market characteristics are dynamic so that the resulting analysis will only be acceptable if variable trends are identified and their impact acknowledged. As a counterpoint, the internal analysis largely considers the historical trends (and not the future estimates) of a business's performances to the point of transaction.

External Sources: Competition. Since monopolies are restrained legally, an investigation of the forces of competition are required as a definitive part of the market analysis. The competition's market geography, regarding market penetration/saturation and the percent of control of the market share, must be identified. Trade associations and other data-collecting agencies (including governmental and nongovernmental) are often helpful in determining competitive pressure.

A considerable amount of information on competition can be secured through direct investigation on a business-by-business basis. Such factors considered would be projected sales, type and amount of advertising and promotion, nature and degree of sevice offered, performance ratios of sales personnel based on sales potential, recent additions of new competitors, recent deletions of existing competitors, changes in the competitive structure through the product mix or services offered and pricing policies, as well as others that contribute to the competitive patterns for specific types of businesses. One extremely vital aspect of competition deals with the extent to which the total weight of competition has expanded the market for product types or business types, and the direction in which this aspect is moving.

Any investigation should begin with businesses that are established and equal to or smaller, rather than larger, than its type in the market area. This not only establishes a point of perspective, but provides the investigator with the ability to analyze actual market position. Larger businesses with greater market dominance and purchasing power usually are sufficiently entrenched so that limited inroads can be expected into their market position. Analysis of large competitors should be directed toward the share of the market held and the effectiveness of operation on which leverage might provide a lowered cost of goods.

External Sources: Location. In certain businesses, location may not contribute to operations effectiveness, provided that the physical aspects of the facility demonstrate that the business is structurally sound and otherwise suitable. However, other situations in varying degrees rely on location, which may be a vital factor in the business's success. An important consideration concerns the status of the location and proposed plans describing changes which may adversely affect the future success of the business. Urban renewal programs, changes in highways and streets, flood control programs, changes in zoning ordinances, property limitations on expansion, condition of the local area (junk yards, refuse disposal areas, public land, government land, leased land, etc.), and so forth, may seriously restrict business growth or future business success.

Of particular interest to the purchaser are considerations of future expansion. As alluded to, property and facility limitations, such as owned or leased property or buildings have been observed to restrict future expansion and must be considered a negative characteristic. It has been observed that using the skills of an engineer or architect may avert later difficulty.

The specific factors associated with location management should take the form of a checklist. The checklist concept can be applied to all forms of businesses where location is an issue.

External Sources: Population and Purchasing Power. Population represents the number of individuals comprising a specific market area, and purchasing power represents the amount of spendable income vested in the population. Population may also represent a limited effect upon a given type of business. For many kinds of businesses, the total population will be less important than certain segments of the population. For example, a business selling eyeglasses would be interested primarily in that section of the population having difficulties with seeing.

Demographic figures are available from Federal, state, and local governmental sources. The U.S. Census Bureau provides population figures that represent a multitude of subdivisions with the national population. A census packet providing a wide scope of information is available at no charge from the Data User Services Division, Census Bureau Department, Washington, D.C. 20233. In areas of the country where population density is high, census figures are further developed and refined into a system of classifying sections on the basis of certain population, economic, racial, income, age, sex, social class, religion, education, family size, and occupational aspects.

Business population figures are usually available from numerous sources. Of immediate use are the telephone directory and city directory. Chambers of Commerce, trade associations, or industrial advisors as A.C. Nealson, Fortune, Standard & Poor, or Dun & Bradstreet can often be of assistance.

Population income and sales by states and counties can be secured from Sales Management's "Survey on Buying Power."

Many trade associations report the actual results of research on consumer expenditures. Other income data sources would include planning commission offices, employment offices, research done by newspapers, building permits (especially in newly developed or growth areas), and mortgage or lending companies. As a factor observed by the author in review of the collected case studies, fact-gathering efforts to understand trends or environment of consumer income and expenditures for various classes of goods and services are, unfortunately, not usually evaluated by acquisition investigators.

External Sources: General Market Conditions. The general state of the market is a much broader, yet significantly vital aspect of market analysis. The majority of the above-noted factors have been equated against the business on the basis of immediate influence on the business being evaluated — company sales, location, competition, etc. In the final analysis, these are influenced by the overall economic conditions of the country or more specifically, the market's target area. These may be of a broad nature, such as national cycles in macro-economy of a business, or they may be confined to a specific market region. The two extremes do not necessarily complement, or correlate with, each other.

A clear understanding of economic factors that potentially affect a market must be examined in depth so adverse marketing trends, based on economic (macro and micro) shifts, can be anticipated and evaluated as an alternative which may shift the current status of the business being acquired. The significance of this detail becomes clear when forecasts and estimates are developed.

In the past, accurate measuring of marketing opportunities was confined to those who practiced making estimations based on intuition after reviewing, to some degree, the sales market. However, since the mid-1970's more objective and quantifying techniques for measuring and analysing marketing opportunities have become an increasingly more viable marketing tool. Consumer markets and buyer behavior; producer, reseller, and governmental markets; demand measurement and forecasting; planning market program; formulating product strategies; and assembling the market mix all demand the use of EDP evaluation systems with utilized programmed calculations based on historical, current, and future trends.[22]

Financial Information

The purchaser and seller are both interested in financial information relative to acquisition management. Inasmuch as this information is readily available to the seller, it becomes a major requirement for the purchaser to avail himself of as much financial data as is possible.

The purchaser, under normal conditions, can secure financial information in the following documents: (1) Financial Statements, (2) Income Tax Returns, (3) Other internal records, (4) Other external sources, and (5) Miscellaneous sources. The accounting of financial data must be consistent and conform to standard methods, i.e., standardized AICPA Opinions.

The details of finance have been presented in detail in other sections of this text. The impact of financial matters must not be minimized since the ability to measure profitability accurately is imperative.

Internal Records: Financial Statements. The results of the financial transactions of every company should be reflected in its periodic financial statements. These statements have been demonstrated as extremely

important elements in acquisition management. Inasmuch as these statements were prepared for the seller and the contents of such statements are available to the seller, the purchaser should be aware of the financial statement's contents early in the acquisition proceedings.

The financial statements discussed will include the balance sheet, income statement, and statement of change in financial position based on working capital. The balance sheet is described as a statement of stocks, thus providing an evaluation of financial position as of a stationary moment in time. The income statement and SCFP (statement of change in financial position-working capital) are statements that summarize capital flows of an accounting unit or group of such units for a specified period of time. Financial statements provide an historical review of any business' transactions and the results of the future operations may or may not parallel trends in the historical sense. Financial statements reveal information relative to capital utilization, flow, and return (or loss); however, maximum usefulness of these statements generally results from properly employed and detailed financial analysis. Any complete financial analysis includes a review of the methods in which the statements were prepared. This will probably include a thorough review of the accounting records and control features of the system. Usually, financial statements of smaller businesses are not prepared as professionally as the statements for larger companies. In reviews of smaller businesses, the investigator must determine who compiled and completed the available financial statements. In any event, it is evident that an accountant (CPA or company's financial accountant or controller) should be brought into the negotiations as early as possible. The intention is not to restrict these statements to the purchaser's accountant; the seller should also be advised of this required information's status by his accountant prior to the initial negotiations.

In many transactions the statements are supplied by the seller, where the purchaser reserves the right to conduct an audit of the seller's records. This type of analysis is usually a modification of the customary general audit. As noted from the case studies, the accounting investigation usually includes specified accuracy tests on a selected group of accounts rather than an analysis of all accounts. These special audits are usually referred to as "purchase audits."

Where the seller supplies the financial statements, the purchaser is well-advised to require the seller to warrant those statements. Warranty of financial state-

---

[22]Philip Kotler, *Marketing Management,* 3rd Ed. (Englewood Cliffs, New Jersey: Prentice-Hall, Incorporated, 1976), p. 67-402.

ments by the seller must be carefully detailed due to the non-uniformity that exists in the definition of the term.

If the financial statements were prepared by an independent accounting firm, the statements usually reflect one of two types of reports—statements prepared after a completed audit, or statements prepared from records supplied by the seller without audit verification. If the financial statements were prepared by an independent accountant without audit verification, there may be considerable similarity or even complete uniformity in the statements had they been prepared by the seller's own accountant. However, in this there is no assurance. If the financial statements were prepared by an independent accountant after an audit, the statements would include an attached summary by the accountant including the observed audit's scope with an appropriate opinion. Financial statements prepared without such an audit may or may not reflect the current financial status (balance sheet), the results of operations (income statement), or the financial trends (statement of change in financial position—working capital). Good business practice dictates that accounting audits verify accuracy of previous accounting practices; thus, these audits are required since this forms the basis of all determinations that follow. Larger firms conduct, as a rule, annual audits. However, it was observed that many smaller businesses do not conduct annual audits.

As a minimum request, the purchaser must secure at least the balance sheets and income statements for a minimum of three years and preferably ten years, or to the point of the business' origin if the company to be sold is less than ten years old. Most acquisitions are concerned with assets being sold. The purchaser usually continues the operation under very similar, if not exact, conditions to those established by the seller. This, however, usually changes during the first year in order to accommodate the new owner's management style. But the purchase of assets must be tempered by the consideration and analysis of future income, which financially is the actual item being exchanged. Marketing ramifications dictate potential future income which must be included in evaluating asset value, one of which is goodwill. As well, one must evaluate the technical aspects of measuring actual financial valuation of a business.

Other financial statements may be available to the buyer. These may include the Statement of Cost of Goods Manufactured, Statement of Application of Funds, Statement of Variances from the Buyer, Inventory Statement, and the Statement of Net Present Value. It is rather obvious that assessment of various financial statements will provide a better understanding of the actual state of the business.

Yet another purchaser consideration is in the cutoff period for the financial statements. It is a possibility that these statements were prepared at the end of a low or a high period during the business cycle. The cutoff date will enable the investigator to understand financial position by establishing the fiscal point of perspective.

The preceding describes the events surrounding the purchase method of gaining control of a business. The second method is referred to as pooling of interests. This accounting approach may be used only under the following circumstances:

(1) The businesses to be merged were autonomous and independent firms for at least two years prior to the acquisition.
(2) The acquisition is completed in a single transaction or within one year according to a fixed plan.
(3) The shares offered by the acquiring firm are identical to those already outstanding.
(4) The acquiring firm acquires at least 90 percent of the business or voting stock of the acquired firm.
(5) There have been no changes in the equity interest of the voting stock in contemplation of the merger.
(6) The acquired firm's shareholders will maintain a proportional equity interest in the combined firm.
(7) The former accounting basis is retained.
(8) No significant disposal of the acquired firm's assets is planned by the merged firm.

The balance sheet and income statement will reflect the addition of the acquired business' assets, liabilities, and stockholders' equity, net earnings after taxes, and number of shares. Further, this pooling of interests can only be applied to the joining of two firms. A situation similar to the sale of Jim's Food-Villa would not apply.

Internal Records: Income Tax Returns. It is possible, depending upon the type and relative size of the business, that the seller may or may not possess a complete set of statements. By law, however, the seller must maintain an annual income statement for tax purposes. If the seller is a partnership or corporation, the tax returns usually have a balance sheet attached. However, if the seller is a sole proprietorship, the tax return usually will exclude the balance sheet data.

Legal Information

A prospective buyer can provide the vehicle for discovering legal problems which could affect not only the business' value, but also the purchaser's decision whether or not to buy. Legal opinions usually are concluded by the business' attorney. However, a deficiency usually arises when the attorney's source of information is the purchaser. Therefore, it becomes important that the purchaser have some conception as to what the attorney will be expecting.

As in any sale, the basic legal problem in the purchase of a business involves the transfer of ownership or title to the property. The title-related problems are business specific and are predicated upon the nature of the assets being purchased. Since a title transfer includes more than a single piece of tangible and permanent real estate, the transaction usually includes varying degrees of complexity. The full impact of this fact is realized when an inventory of nonpermanent property is taken into account. The transaction usually involves a mixture of inventory, equipment, vehicles, office equipment, furnishings, assorted contract rights under leases, sales agreements, patent licenses, etc., which are tangible. Since the asset has its own ownership aspects, it is actually pertinent to inquire as to each asset: Is the purchaser receiving the ownership rights which he assumes he is to receive?

Where the buyer either assumes liabilities or purchases the corporation's stock, a most stringent legal investigation of the business is required. Obviously, the purchaser's fear of unassignable, thus uncontrollable, liabilities become less significant the more he is able to learn about the business. Even at the risk of potential liabilities, those liabilities which may accrue in the future based on past events, may be significantly reduced by proper investigation.

For examination, internal and external sources of legal information are usually available to the purchaser and his attorney. Among the more obvious internal sources are copies of contracts, evidences of ownership and organizational documents which may be obtained from the seller. Personal examination of the business premises and an inquiry of the seller and his employees may reveal partial information as to particular assets. However, the buyer should refrain from relying solely upon oral representations. The seller's statements which are relied upon should either be incorporated into the final contract as expressed warranties or substantiated by supportive information. The most available external sources of legal information are public records, governmental agencies and third parties with whom the seller has had dealings.

To what extent should a purchaser investigate a business so that an accurate analysis can lead to a commitment to a purchase? There exists no simple answer. The purchaser must realize that the unidentified and potential legal risk he assumes is proportional to the amount of information obtained about the business. A more detailed presentation on the subject of legal matters has been presented in other chapters of this handbook.

DETERMINING THE VALUE OF A BUSINESS

In many respects the most difficult aspect of acquisition management rests with the determination of the business's worth as a going concern. In the final analysis, value must be acceptable to both the purchaser and seller. Value must reflect the most logical and objective efforts of the parties involved.

Just as no two acquisitions are alike, neither will be the procedure for business value determination. The purchaser evaluates from one viewpoint, while the seller evaluates from another. Consequently, many judgement decisions must be made. Usually the seller is more intimately acquainted with the facts and, therefore, his problems are not as troublesome as the difficulties facing the purchaser.

Valuation Methods

Valuation, in effect, can be determined by two basic methods. The first and most desirable is based on future expectations of profits and return on investment. Such a method will include attention to specific factors as trends in sales and profits, capitalized value of the business, the expectancy of return on investment. At the outset, however, one must realize the inherent danger in this method of valuation. Any attempt to project into the future includes varying degrees of risk which increases when long-range estimates are established.

The second valuation method is based on the appraised value of the assets at the time of negotiation, usually with the presumed notion that these assets will be used in the continuation of the business. Little consideration is usually given to future business; rather, the purchaser's concerns are with the current value of assets. In practical application, this asset valuation method is more commonly used, not because of its superior reliability and business soundness, but rather because it is easier to determine where projections are not utilized.

Value Based on Future Anticipation

Sale Forecasting. Prior to any forecasting, an estimate of sales must be made where a pro forma statement of sales and profit can be constructed which addresses business value. In this regard, the forecast over several years differs little from forecasts made generally in business. One of the principal purposes of general business forecasts is to determine the financial requirements necessary for continued, or perhaps expanded, operations. In a general sense, the forecast generated for purchasing and selling purposes is finance-oriented and employed to place a value on the business as a viable entity. While valuation methods are designed to produce a negotiated price, such finance-oriented methods serve also as an initiation point for future negotiations.

In practice, past sales records will establish the foundation for projecting future sales. The relative success with which these records are used rests largely upon (1) the manner in which sales records have been maintained, and (2) the frequency with which they are recorded. The more accurate and systematic the records of sales, the greater will be the confidence with which it is possible to present these data in future sales estimates.

"Over how long a time period is it necessary or possible to forecast sales?" At best, a forecast of any length is subject to uncertainty, and the more the forecast is projected into the future, the greater the uncertainty. Even if reasonable control over internal operations is possible, the external economic and market factors make forecasting difficult due to unidentifiable variations in control.

Perhaps a more appropriate method to approach the length of a forecast would be in terms of the expected or anticipated return on investment. At this point, the purchaser would calculate net present value, evaluate the break-even point, and investigate capital-time ratios in terms of cash flow, payback, and unadjusted return on investment. If it is estimated that a 20 percent return on initial investment should occur, the investment should be returned in five years. For discounted cash flow/return on investment analysis, a 20 percent DCF/ROI could be at break-even at a nonlinear rate. DCF/ROI calculations are generally more sensitive to benefit/revenue and cost projections. At the point of break-even, the owner/investors have recovered their original investment. Therefore, it seems logical that sales and profits (supported by sufficient working capital) be projected over a span of time comparable to that estimated for return on investment. However, any such forecast should give careful consideration to expected or anticipated changes in the economy and/or changes in the market which may affect sales performance. It is mathematically possible to forecast sales with absolute precision. However, the precision is dulled in light of

the lack of controllability over the more vital market and economic factors. Because of this variability, the trends of historical performances as an element in projecting sales, may also become nonconsequential.

Of primary concern, the purchaser must address the trend of sales, whether they are increasing or decreasing. Without calculations, one can expect a trend to continue, economic and market factors or internal business influence notwithstanding.

Where forecast periods exceed one, or better, two years, a more detailed forecasting technique is most desirable. This technique should be designed to weigh out extreme variations regarding year-to-year inconsistencies and thus provide a more realistic pattern for future sales. However, there is no guarantee as to the quantitative or qualitative value of the forecast since variability in economic and market conditions will skew results in future estimations. Though not precisely measurable, the possible influence thereof can be realized and certainly be anticipated.

Risk and Return on Investment. Invested money should be expected to yield a fair rate of return on investment. While many new businesses can realize a profit in a reasonably short period of time, one to five years, very few smaller businesses increase appreciably over a long period (ten years and more) of time. The actual rate of return is usually predicated upon the risk factor. By comparison, U.S. Government Bonds, often considered the safest investment, yield 5½ percent to 6½ percent, where Blue Chip stock or major corporate bonds yield 5 percent to 10 percent. More speculative stock investments yield 10 percent and often a 16 percent to 21 percent return, but involve a much higher risk factor. Likewise, varying risk is associated with a new business based upon its type and historical performance. The purchaser, therefore, must realize the new business's risk factor and project future profits accordingly and as far into the future as reasonably possible.

Next, the purchaser must consider with care the minimum return on investment that is acceptable. The purchaser must determine maximum acceptable risk and identify those observable conditions, actual or potential, that could affect sales and the profit-making capacity of the business.

Pro Forma Statements. In preparing the statement of future operations, the seller should prepare a sales estimate, or forecast, for a twelve-month period accompanied with a matching estimate of the cost of goods sold and operating expenses. The pro forma will reflect the net profit estimated by the seller. Likewise, the purchaser would determine his own separate estimate of sales, cost of goods sold, operating expenses, and net profit for the last 24 months and project the trend into the future, preferably over the next two years. Preparation of a pro forma statement of income, costs, expenses, and profits requires the purchaser to analyze historical statements of profit and loss for at least the preceeding five years.

Almost without saying, the purchaser must be certain of the accuracy of the information provided. Inaccurate information will logically yield inaccurate results. Further, contemplated operational changes must be recognized before the projections are estimated. These estimates would include an understanding of economic alternations and a knowledge of competition. The most important pro forma numbers to be determined would be the sales figures. Figures expressing costs, expenses, and profit are relatively easy to secure. In the event the purchaser is not competent to complete a pro forma, he should secure the abilities of CPA, who would include in the opening statement of presentation, an attachment which specifies the CPA and seller liability for the pro forma's accuracy. The expense involved in developing the pro forma outweighs the potential risk if financial accord is out of phase or otherwise inaccurate or altered. Future negotiations must rest upon the outcome of this pro forma development and the resulting investigation.

ACQUISITIONS: MARKETING ANALYSIS

The author's experiences during the research and development of this study led to the following basic questions: "What elements of marketing analysis need attention? What must a purchaser of a business understand about the market he is entering or expanding?"

In order to establish continuity, it is necessary to investigate and understand the methods of marketing analysis used. This satisfies a prerequisite requirement that answers the question of whether the market is accepting the new business's current sales effort. Unfortunately, many businesses, regardless of size, do not invest the required time or possess the proclivity or ability to involve themselves in the required development of a detailed market study.

Subsequent to an acquisition, an investigator must expeditiously and accurately survey the market to determine both value and applied use of the specifically designed and targeted analysis. Further, the language or method of expression must reflect the project demands in order to serve the investigative purposes and management. This often becomes a critical element which in itself can manipulate and possibly alter desired results.

Considering the problem of market analysis from a fundamental approach, the procedure that yields the best information entails a series of questions and responses, constructed with specific regard to technique, sources of information, and desired benefit. This approach requires the investigator to use specific guidelines that are dependent upon the uniqueness of the application. By design, the language and technical phraseology should be as uncluttered as possible.

As a result of the field research, it was established that little if any attention has been given to market impact upon the business. As an adjunct to the acquisition, undesirable results following an acquisition have been identified and classified as internal problems with management, ultimate insolvency and/or illiquidity, poor purchase timing, apparent overpayment for the business, questionable financing methods, undisclosed litigation, etc. Unequivocally, one who enters into an acquisition sequence from a position of control will have a much improved probability for success than someone who does not. The investigator must content himself with the accuracy of results far and above the possible expenditure of time and perhaps some money.

This notwithstanding, most businessmen do not avail themselves of any sort of market analysis. The author observed that two very strong motivations in the negotiation, at least in the purchaser's mind, are (1) his immediate means and methods for financing, and (2) his rather alarming optimism that he can make the new business a success in spite of the relatively good or bad history of the business, in spite of the state of the market, and in spite of his own possible shortcomings.

The task of organizing and conducting a market analysis has been observed to be very difficult for businesses in general. Many new businesses that share the market are usually quite small and will have little practical effort on the market. Further, the nature and type of records maintained may leave much to be desired in organizing data for analysis.

In developing such an analysis, directions provided by the body of knowledge have not been extremely helpful. The search for information sources on market analysis has led to two conclusions: (1) the literature is invariably directed to a specific and isolated audience (usually the larger business enterprise); and (2) the literature is invariably limited to descriptive and definitive terminology of analytical techniques. The lack of useful data has resulted in the necessity of drawing from experience and conducting market analysis for a considerable number of businesses and using this experience as a basis for a major part of this recommendation.

By design, this research focused upon the controlling aspects associated with the processes of business acquisitions. Admittedly, some bias exists toward the prospective buyer of the business. Based on the position of future liability, this appears to be a logical position. The seller's immediate concern is in divesting himself directly of further obligations to the business, although the case studies have shown that this may be more desirable than factual, particularly with respect to methods of financing. The purchaser, if he becomes so, assumes all the risk and uncertainty of the continuance of the business. In approaching the issues of market analysis, both sides of the transactional relationship have been weighed with equal objectivity. At the negotiations table, the applicability of a market analysis is equally shared by both the purchaser and the seller.

MARKET ANALYSIS OVERVIEW

It is at this point that the responsibility of acquisition management addresses itself to the estimated future market opportunity of the firm. Every purchaser and indeed every seller should have some measurement of what the future will offer regarding not only the business's ability to attract sales as in the past, but also its opportunity to improve.

It is imperative that the purchaser develop a realistic idea of what he is acquiring aside from the physical assets of the business. The actual basic fact of the acquisition matter is that the purchaser is obligating himself to continue his new operation at a profit. The actual value, therefore, should be in the ability of the business to generate sales at least equal to his current position in the market. This calls for a careful investigation and analysis of two factors: (1) the historical pattern and growth of the company within its market; and (2) an estimate and forecast of the future sales pattern. Present value of the business, at least from the point of view of physical assets, is largely a monetary evaluation of what the company is worth, where balance sheet accountability is required. The real value, at least to the prospective purchaser, is the actual use of these assets to maximize the future opportunity of the business. Judgment and experience notwithstanding, the purchaser should be able to undertake, or have accomplished for him, a thorough analysis of the market as circumstances reasonably permit.

The seller, on the other hand, is not immune, for he also needs a market analysis of the business he proposes to sell. While the nature of his analysis would not differ significantly from the purchaser's, the importance would differ. The seller would be presumed to desire the best possible price for the company he is proposing to sell. The more economically favorable the business's future is, the greater the likelihood is that the asking price would not be adjusted downward, all other factors considered.

The question arises as to whether a single market analysis provides sufficient data to determine the future of the business. Recalling Count Leo Tolstoy's quotation, there is a combination of events that will interact and adjust the course of the current market which can only be realized by a series of market studies. Independent analysis by both purchaser and seller would logically offer a better means of understanding the current state of the market. The seller has access to historical data which could be available to the purchaser. Unless the purchaser has had reasonably wide and recent experience in the kind of business being considered, he may be handicapped by his lack of knowledge of market conditions and, correctly or incorrectly, tend to rely on the seller's estimation of the business's market position. It is also conceivable that no two studies of the same business will derive the same results. Further, it would be expected that the analysis conducted by the purchaser would tend to be more conservative, particularly when presented at the negotiating table. Negotiating the value of the business will usually be the result of a series of compromises based upon the market analysis. As a consequence, the determined value of the business will be legally agreeable to both parties.

Who should undertake the market studies? The purchaser or seller could conduct the studies on their own, or they could employ specialists to evaluate current state of the market and historical sales trends. As to which alternative should be used, there are no ready answers. Depending upon the situation, however, it is suggested that all market studies should be conducted by the parties involved in the transaction. The cost of having such studies conducted by a market analyst is not insignificant. If a market study is kept within the bounds of reason, a highly technical, statistically-oriented approach can be avoided. The reasonable market survey is more likely to provide at least preliminary information regarding the present and future market positions of the business. The degree of sophistication in the study depends on the competency of the analyst, the nature and extent of desired information, and the techniques employed during the analysis. As the foundation for this market research, the parties must not sacrifice the accuracy of the results in order to reach conclusions that may be too superficial to be considered. The market analyst must incorporate the appropriate amount of technical controls so that a concluding market estimation can be appraised as a credible work in which unsupported guessing has been avoided.

Though the circumstances of the acquisition will dictate the degree of complexity of the market analysis, the basic purpose of any analysis should be to obtain a clearer picture of the individual's business in the marketing scheme of things and to give some indication of the general direction of the business. Prerequisite to a market analysis, it is important that the degree of complexity be determined in addition to a consideration of the impact of time and cost.

The type of questions considered and the depth in which they are probed will be contingent upon the requirements as dictated by the business' nature. In all probability, the principal value lies in focusing the individual's attention on certain aspects of the market that might otherwise be overlooked, however unintentionally. It is imperative that the investigator not collect data for its own sake. The purpose of the market analysis must be remembered at all times (e.g., scope and direction).

Caution should also be taken that there will be no dilution of results of the market analysis. Unique or unusual situations will arise from business to business in which any composite list will be guilty of errors or omissions. In such instances, the purchaser or seller would have to exercise judgement in determining what other analysis or pertinent data should be investigated.

An especially difficult problem lies in determining how important a specific market characteristic is within itself and, further, its degree of importance. What may prove to be vital in one investigation, may be of little or no consequence in another. The suggested method in developing a specific program of investigation would be to list the specified order of importance, the major subject areas in the study, and the relative importance of each subject area. Afterward, the investigator can develop a system for cataloging each item within the analysis and thus arrive at a method of evaluation. This might be accomplished by means of a numerical rating scale, such as 1 through 5, or a verbalized form such as high, medium, low, and not significant. Obviously, judgment would have to be used in placing an evaluation on each subject investigated. This demonstrates in itself that the market

analyst needs to be familiar with the business he is evaluating. As an example of how this would work, let us consider Table 38-3. Since sales of the company compared with time is one characteristic most likely to be studied, the investigator should develop a method of evaluation along the lines described in the table.

Table 38-3
Significance of Sales Rating

1. Business' Sales

Year*	Dollar Sales	Percent Change by Year
1974	1975	1976
1977	1978	

Total Dollar increase 1978 over 1974 $ _____
Percent Sales increase 1978 over 1974 _____ %
Degree of Performance Rating Level: 1 2 3 4 5

2. Market Share

Year	Total Sales	Business Sales	Share % of Market
1974			
1975			
1976			
1977			
1978			

Change in share of market 1978 over 1974 _____%
Degree of Performance Rating Level: 1 2 3 4 5

*Years shown for illustrative purposes only. Appropriate years would be assigned by the investigator.

Obviously, it would not be practical to attempt to schedule an analysis for each type of business; the variations preclude such a possibility. A further suggestion, however, would be to consult trade associations and other specialists who engage in maintaining methods of market evaluation and of specific kinds of businesses. The U.S. Government and various marketing analysis journals have prepared numerous aids in establishing the future trends of retail and service businesses. Principal among these are: The U.S. Department of Commerce; Bureau of Foreign and Domestic Commerce; Dun & Bradstreet; *Journal of Marketing; Journal of Business; Harvard Business Review; Fortune; Business Week;* etc. Organizations like The National Cash Register Company have prepared numerous publications dealing with the operations of specific types of businesses. These are often quite helpful in determining what aspects of the market should be investigated.

MARKET ANALYSIS—SPECIFICS

At this point a specific market analysis guideline must be developed and used during the process of investigation. As alluded to earlier, any such cataloging in a finite sense will be incomplete. Some elements will apply to all businesses, some only to certain businesses. There will be questions not addressed in this listing; there will be questions that will have to be modified. It is obvious that the experience of the marketing analyst will be called upon to extract those necessary elements in order to yield acceptable and usable results.

There is the inevitable question as to whether or not the individual doing the investigation can obtain sufficient data regarding a given subject and whether the time and cost justify pursuing the subject further. This recommendation does not propose to rate the degree of difficulty in obtaining data, but rather to indicate what the investigator should consider.

One of the significant purposes of the analysis is to forecast the market opportunity. Generally, the data necessary for such projections must of necessity come from past performance and from present conditions. The data may be internal, relating to certain aspects of the growth of the business in terms of market demand and market share potential. Or the data may be external (with economic and specific erratic effects causing a random variation in sales performance) and involve the market of the business. The relationship of one to the other is obvious, particularly the effect of external market characteristics on the business. The analysis of the market addresses the internal and external conditions which construct a historically developed assessment of the business. Sales forecasts are a simplified technique of projecting and forecasting the position of the business into the future.

CONCLUSION

Why should we businessmen be bothered with these detailed controlling sequences comprised as Acquisition Management? After a reading of this chapter, the answer becomes self-evident; and yet, virtually half of all acquisitions enjoy a limited degree of success, many of which conclude as dismal failures.

After detailing the case studies and reviewing the available body of knowledge, one finds the lack of expertise and competence in coordinating the acquisition most obvious, actually glaring. When one considers that competence and incompetence are exquisitely strange bedfellows, one can appreciate, at least to some degree, the resultant incongruous progeny that results.

Management problems, as numerous and varied as they can become, cannot be surrendered to or ignored. These problems or opportunities, as it were, are most certainly solvable and controllable. As presented in this chapter, the task of Acquisition Management is not a task that can tolerate superficiality or ulterior motivation. There are too many critical aspects to consider. Management that recognizes the elements of risk will be in a position to understand and, thus, deal with, the various aspects that conclude in a change in business ownership.

Within the successful acquisitions, management has recognized that an organized, well-thought-out approach will yield very positive results. But what the entire business community does at this point must be reconciled within the hallowed walls of American business. There is no mystery to Acquisition Management; there is, however, a path that leads to successful acquisition if business, in fact, desires it.

DAVID I. KARABELL

DAVID I. KARABELL is a partner in the New York law firm of O'Sullivan, Wolff, Karabell & Graev, and is a member of the New York Bar. He has a B.A. degree from Temple University and an LL.B. from New York University Law School. He has been working on mergers, acquisitions, divestitures and other matters since 1967.

39

The Acquisition
Contract and Closing

DAVID I. KARABELL

The heading of this chapter may seem to indicate contents dealing with the end-of-the-road in the long walk together by a buyer and seller before finalizing their transaction. However, despite the belief of the parties that they have struck a business deal in final form, the documentation and the intense involvement of lawyers and accountants at this stage of the business transaction may prove to be as much a starting point as a completion of the job. If the professionals perform effectively and the parties have agreed to terms, and are willing to live with inevitable changes caused by detailing those terms in documentation, the transaction may, in fact, both start and finish at this stage.

The scope of this chapter includes not only a description of the acquisition contract and closing, but also of options, restrictive letters and letters of intent. It is not my intention to present an outline or a textbook discussion. I have attempted to provide the flavor of the kinds of issues which may arise in the context of the documentary underpinnings of a specific kind of transaction indicating, where relevant, an alternative focus which might arise in another type of transaction. To the extent the transaction concerning the reader differs from that described, other and more detailed textual discussions should be consulted.

ROLE PLAYING

Sellers and buyers have different and, frequently, opposing interests. They each should be aware of the interests and needs of their opposite numbers. The professionals representing the seller and the buyer must also understand fully not only their clients' desires and needs, but also the desires and needs of the parties on the other side of the table. That awareness will help smooth over difficulties which inevitably

arise and provide a basis for compromising issues. Every business negotiation requires some posturing by its participants. Variations in emphasis and the ability to clarify murky issues can sometimes overcome the frequent hurdles of deal-making. Screams and whispers each may have a place in the transaction if invoked in an intelligent and perceptive manner. The ability to creatively articulate solutions to conflicting interests is a basic asset of the successful deal-maker, and detailing and documenting those solutions is the stock in trade of his attorney.

The following, woven from the threads of many acquisitions, is a purely fictional account of one particular transaction. I call it the "100% Leveraged Buyout."

THE 100% LEVERAGED BUYOUT:
BACKGROUND OF A TRANSACTION

Myron Rushmore was President of a medium-size public company, Fabulous Consolidated, Inc. ("Fabulous"), with revenues of approximately $110,000,000. Fabulous was engaged in various business lines headed, in the corporate summaries, recreation, communications and electronics. Fabulous had been through a major acquisition campaign during the nine-year tenure of Myron's stewardship and had grown from a small, profitable electronics enterprise, grossing approximately $8,000,000, to its present size through Myron's acute ·efforts and marvelous sales ability. Many of the acquisitions had been made in exchange for preferred and common stock of Fabulous. Other acquisitions had been paid for in cash or a combination of cash and notes. Often, the cash was borrowed. In the early years of Myron's activities, the market price of Fabulous stock had increased. However, Fabulous had suffered continuing losses in several of its basic businesses and, during the past five years, a precipitous decline in the book value of Fabulous and the market value of its stock had occurred. Since bank debt incurred in connection with several transactions and the cash needs of the ongoing businesses had become unmanageable, Myron was forced to sell off some of the businesses owned by Fabulous in order to reduce bank debt and maintain the viability of Fabulous.

Igloo Chomp-Chomp, Inc. ("Chomp-Chomp"), a subsidiary of Fabulous, was engaged in the manufacture of frozen dog food and other pet products. Headquartered in the southwest United States, it had been at least nominally profitable for many years. Its revenues of approximately $8,000,000 had generated earnings of $250,000 after taxes in the preceding year. Its year-end tangible net worth was $1,400,000. Its assets included manufacturing equipment and vehicles. Chomp-Chomp also owned a parcel of realty on which its plant was located. Myron believed that the sale of Chomp-Chomp could raise sufficient money for Fabulous to satisfy its bank's immediate requirements. Chomp-Chomp's equipment had been depreciated and Myron believed that it was worth more than its book value indicated. In addition, Myron had obtained an appraisal for Chomp-Chomp's real estate in an amount substantially exceeding its book value.

Myron wanted to sell Chomp-Chomp for cash—as much as he could get. However, he recognized that Fabulous might be required to extend credit to a buyer in connection with the sale and that it might then accept cash and promissory notes or, conceivably, cash and securities such as a preferred stock of the buyer.

The Broker

Myron, while attending a luncheon of the Conglomerate Trade Association, had been impressed by a talk by Jonathan Worthington, an investment banker with a major brokerage house in a large midwestern city. Myron approached Worthington concerning the possibility of seeking a suitable candidate to buy Chomp-Chomp. Worthington, not only an effective lecturer, but also a sensible businessman, immediately placed under Myron's nose a fee agreement providing for the payment to Worthington's firm of a brokerage fee in the event a suitable candidate for the acquisition was found. The brokerage fee was equal to 5 percent of the first $1,000,000 of consideration, 4 percent of the next $1,000,000 of consideration, 3 percent of the next $1,000,000 of consideration and 2 percent of all consideration thereafter. The fee agreement set forth

methods of determining value if the consideration was not paid in dollars and provided for an exclusive brokerage arrangement with Mr. Worthington's firm for a period of one year. A non-returnable fee of $2,500 monthly (a total of $30,000) was to be paid to Worthington's firm during the one-year period of exclusivity. This fee was deductible from the brokerage fee and would cease in the event a transaction for Chomp-Chomp was consummated before the year was up.

The agreement presented by Worthington to Fabulous was not dissimilar from the fee agreements used by many investment bankers. Worthington required a written agreement covering his fee to insure that it was collectable. Business brokers or finders, unlike realtors and attorneys, are rarely protected under state laws unless their compensation arrangements are set out in writing.

Having been an acquiror, Myron recognized that a finder's fee could be an obstacle in negotiations. It affects the pricing of a transaction and has significance for both tax and accounting purposes. He also recognized that Worthington had substantially greater access to prospective buyers than Myron and could provide aid in structuring and negotiating the transaction by using not only the experience he and his firm could bring to the negotiating table, but also the prestige which they could lend to a transaction.

Myron had previously discussed the prospective sale of Chomp-Chomp with his accountants and attorneys, each of whom had had experience in connection with mergers and acquisitions. The brokerage arrangements were negotiated through counsel seeking to achieve Myron's two goals: (i) non-exclusivity so that the finder would get paid only if he found a transaction which closed; and (ii) less money for the finder. Within a week, an agreement was reached with Worthington's firm providing it with a non-exclusive brokerage arrangement at a fee, not to exceed $135,000, ranging from 4 percent to 1 percent of the amount of consideration received. No retainer was to be paid and the lack of exclusivity would enable Myron to use other brokers without concern about payment of two fees, or to seek a direct transaction without the necessity of paying a broker. Worthington then went to work. So did Myron.

The Buyer

Our law firm entered this transaction one bright morning when I received a phone call from Willington Lafayette, IV. Lafayette had successfully bought and sold several businesses as a principal and was comfortably enjoying the fruits of his business acumen. He also, occasionally, acted as a business finder. He was a close friend of the president of a corporate client of our office and had been referred to us by him. Lafayette arrived at my office at 10:00 A.M. with Finbar McQue, a voluble Irishman, whose Spanish ancestors had landed in County Cork two hundred years before and started a line of McQues, many of whom had engaged in unusual business activities over the years.

McQue was then employed by another large public company as chief executive officer of a wholesale food division and Vice President of Acquisitions. After making many successful acquisitions for his employer, he had decided to do it for himself. McQue's current status generated a series of questions not relevant to this story. Did he have an employment agreement? If so, what restrictions were imposed which were relevant to this negotiation? Was there a possibility that McQue would forfeit benefits such as pensions or profit shares from his current employer? How could he best time termination of his current employment?, etc. After my review of relevant documents, these questions were answered in a manner permitting the acquisition to proceed with risks and losses which McQue found tolerable.

Lafayette had ascertained at another cocktail party that Chomp-Chomp might be for sale. He had contacted McQue and obtained from McQue a written commitment to pay Lafayette a finder's fee if McQue purchased Chomp-Chomp. He and McQue had then met with Myron Rushmore to discuss McQue's acquisition of Chomp-Chomp.

McQue, an individual unaffiliated with any substantial entity had a credibility gap to overcome. Although Myron knew and respected Lafayette, he had no basis to believe McQue could arrange funding for the acquisition. McQue, however, had a relationship with a friendly banker, Winston Largess, Jr. Largess had participated with Lafayette and McQue in preliminary discussions and analysis of the acquisition of Chomp-Chomp. During the course of McQue's initial discussions with Myron, Largess had contacted Myron directly, and had overcome Myron's skepticism concerning the availability of financing for the transaction. Largess had even convinced Myron to refrain from requesting a deposit from McQue to assure Fabulous of his good faith and financial solidity. If, like McQue, you are not a well-known and well-heeled institution, a banker like Largess can be a critical asset—worth far in excess of the interest charges paid to his institution.

After obtaining from Lafayette and McQue personal information and the background of the transaction, I requested details concerning the purchase price for Chomp-Chomp. McQue indicated that a transaction at approximately $2,500,000 cash had been agreed upon. This price would be based on the book value of Chomp-Chomp at closing plus $1,000,000. I asked him where he would obtain the money. He indicated that all the money would come from Largess' Bank. I made a note to insure that I contacted Mr. Largess, to see if he could overcome *my* skepticism. I then asked McQue if any cash would be invested by him in the transaction. "No cash at all," he said. "None." This was, obviously, a leveraged buyout with unusually high leverage. It is *not* typical of most purchases which require at least *some* equity.

McQue then provided additional details concerning the transaction, peppered with spicy portions of his life story and frequent references to his interest in my secretary. Despite his many digressions, McQue managed to communicate to me his complete grasp of the transaction. By the end of his narrative, I was confident in his ability to carry it off.

The equipment and realty owned by Chomp-Chomp, carried on its books at only $500,000, had, according to McQue, a value exceeding $2,000,000. The equipment and realty, coupled with the inventory and accounts receivable of Chomp-Chomp, would provide more than sufficient collateral for Largess' bank. McQue assured me that an appraisal would be available for the equipment and real estate and that Winston Largess would accept the valuation. I returned to my earlier notes to underline three times, in red, *"Call banker."*

I asked McQue for a retainer in order for us to commence work on the transaction. "Retainer?" McQue said, blanching. He excused himself and left the room with Lafayette. I immediately surmised that when McQue indicated that no cash would be required, he really anticipated that *no* cash would be required. At the end of our meeting, McQue had not committed to provide the retainer and we had not committed to commence work. However, within three hours I received a call from McQue indicating that the retainer would be sent and requesting that I contact counsel for Fabulous to start work on the transaction. The retainer did, in fact, arrive within a week. McQue had induced Lafayette to put up the money in exchange for a piece of the deal. The finder's fee to Lafayette was eliminated in the process.

STRUCTURING THE TRANSACTION

Other chapters of this handbook deal with the various alternatives available in structuring transactions and the criteria applied to determine the structure to be used. Since I am dealing with a specific example, I will not attempt to duplicate here analysis of transactional structure. However, since McQue had available to him several alternative methods of making the acquisition, I will mention some of those alternatives.

I determined it would be best for McQue and Lafayette to form a corporation which would act as the buyer and acquire the assets of Chomp-Chomp. The acquisition of assets would enable the buying entity to increase the book value of assets acquired to the price being paid for those assets. Thus, for tax and accounting purposes the value of the assets acquired would be $1,000,000 higher than the book value reflected on the financial statements of Fabulous. The direct acquisition of assets by a buying entity would also enable the buyer's lender to acquire a better-secured position in the assets acquired by advancing funds directly to the acquiring entity. Loans in connection with purchase of capital stock require some gymnastics in order to provide a lender with a security interest in assets of the entity whose stock is acquired.

It should be noted that the transaction under discussion involved a subsidiary of a public company. If assets of a corporate division were to be acquired, an additional layer of problems would arise in defining the assets purchased since a division does not maintain a separate legal status. If all or a significant portion of the assets of a public company were to be acquired, it would have necessitated grappling with additional considerations, including shareholder approval and compliance with proxy rules under the Securities Exchange Act of 1934.

McQue had initially obtained an oral indication from Winston Largess that his bank would fund 100 percent of the acquisition cost of Chomp-Chomp, subject to the banker's satisfaction with certain conditions. However, we were confronted with a period of rising interest rates and decreasing availability of loans and it became increasingly clear to McQue that full bank funding of the acquisition by Largess was unlikely. Even if full bank funding were available, McQue wanted to reduce the high interest expense which would be required in the foreseeable future to service the loan. McQue did have available investors who could have provided in the form of equity and subordinated loans approximately 20 percent to 25 percent of the price for Chomp-Chomp. One partner, Mr. Lafayette, was enough for McQue. He detested the thought of further diluting his ownership interest for mere money and he placed outside investors on a shelf with the idea of taking them off the shelf and into the transaction only if absolutely necessary to close the deal.

Since McQue did not want to raise outside equity and Myron was not willing to defer a substantial portion of the purchase price, I therefore decided to seek McQue's leverage both from Largess and from the seller by deferring payment of approximately 25 percent of the purchase price, that portion which might otherwise have been provided by investors.

McQue's use of leverage has become a common device in acquisitions (as evidenced by the emphasis given to leveraged buyouts elsewhere in this handbook) and increasingly available in situations where the value of underlying assets equals or exceeds the price being paid for those assets. In a period of high interest rates and decreasing availability of bank credit, leverage is more difficult to obtain from third-party lenders and more readily available from sellers.

The corporation wholly-owned by McQue and Lafayette would purchase from Chomp-Chomp substantially all of the assets of Chomp-Chomp subject to assumption of certain specified liabilities. Concurrently, the lender would acquire as security for its loans security interests in those assets subject to the Uniform Commercial Code, principally inventory, accounts receivable and machinery and equipment. It would also acquire security interests in assets covered under the local Motor Vehicle Title Law and a mortgage on Chomp-Chomp's realty. The money advanced by the bank to the new corporation (called by McQue, "Ice Cold Doggie Bisquits Ltd." ("Ice Cold Doggie")) would, in turn, be paid over to Chomp-Chomp for the assets being transferred. To "belt and suspender" the transaction, some banks might require individual stockholder guarantees secured by a pledge of all capital stock of the borrowing entity and by other unrelated assets. Largess, however, was not so demanding.

McQue hoped that Myron's participation in financing would be via issuance of preferred stock. Preferred stock, even if subject to redemption, would not only defer payment of part of the purchase price, it could also help beef up the equity section of the balance sheet of Ice Cold Doggie. If a "purchase money" promissory note were to be taken by the seller as a part of the purchase price for the acquisition, McQue was willing to secure that promissory note by granting to the seller a "second" secured position in the assets being transferred. In addition, McQue was prepared to deliver to the seller, if required, a "non-recourse" guaranty by Lafayette and himself of a purchase money promissory note secured by a pledge of the capital stock of Ice Cold Doggie.

The banker was comfortable with the management changes proposed by McQue for Chomp-Chomp and Chomp-Chomp's ability to service from its cash flow the debt being incurred. Debt service would be facilitated not only by designated cost reductions, but also by income tax savings resulting from additional depreciation deductions available because of the high price being paid for the assets of Chomp-Chomp. We hoped Myron would be willing to allocate a substantial portion of the purchase price to equipment which could be depreciated at a relatively rapid rate. Although Fabulous would recapture and take into ordinary income the depreciation previously deducted, the losses available to Fabulous which had been carried forward from prior years and its current losses would eliminate any immediate tax consequence for Fabulous from the depreciation recaptured. Those losses also served to eliminate the tax payable upon 100 percent of the sale price of Chomp-Chomp even though less than 100 percent of the sale price was paid in cash. Installment sale treatment under the Internal Revenue Code (limiting the tax to that imposed on cash received) was not available to Fabulous since one basic test then required for an installment sale, that not more than 30 percent of the purchase price for the assets sold be paid in the year of sale, was not being met in this transaction. I anticipated that I would spend some time with the buyer fine-tuning the cash projections and that, in fact, before the transaction was completed, some equity might be required. However, the banker's willingness to make a loan with little or no equity cushion behind it, coupled with the deferral by Fabulous of part of the price, as we assumed, might permit consummation of the buy with no money other than our retainer.

Lafayette's presence as a principal in the transaction had an unforeseen benefit and added a few complications. As a benefit, Lafayette had torn up his finder's fee agreement with McQue thereby providing more room to McQue in negotiating price with Myron. The complications concerned the relationship between Lafayette and McQue which was negotiated by me with Lafayette's counsel and embodied in a pre-incorporation agreement which contemplated the execution of, and to which was attached as an exhibit, a stockholders' agreement among Lafayette, McQue and Ice Cold Doggie.

PRELIMINARY AGREEMENTS; OPTIONS, RESTRICTIVE LETTERS AND MEMORANDUMS OR LETTERS OF INTENT

When a buyer and seller reach agreement concerning the business to be sold and the price to paid therefor, they often want to memorialize that agreement in a preliminary memorandum or letter of intent. Although such a memorandum is not usually binding, it can provide moral suasion which will be taken seriously by businessmen and it may serve to reduce later misunderstandings by providing a written summary of the preliminary accords reached. However, negotiating a memorandum of intent is often difficult and may absorb substantial energy and time which might be better spent on drafting and negotiating final documents.

As counsel for Lafayette and McQue, I wanted to insure that this transaction became binding upon the seller as soon as possible. I did not, however, wish our clients to be bound until they had the opportunity to fully investigate the business and financial condition of Chomp-Chomp.

McQue was eager to get almost anything in writing from Fabulous. He believed that once Fabulous had signed a letter of intent and issued a public announcement of the sale of Chomp-Chomp, the pressure from its bank and the problems which would arise with the business of Chomp-Chomp if the sale did *not* occur, would facilitate negotiation of a better deal for McQue. Even though acquisitions may collapse for perfectly sound reasons unrelated to the condition of the business being sold, McQue knew that outsiders often conclude that a terminated transaction reflects negatively on that business.

I had available various documentary alternatives prior to the time we might execute definitive agreements. The preliminary agreement chosen would depend upon (a) the information to be released publicly concerning the transaction, (b) the degree that negotiations have been definitive and necessary information gathered, (c) the cost to the buyer and the seller of proceeding with the transaction prior to the making of binding commitments, (d) the rapidity with which the parties estimated a final agreement could be signed and (e) the degree of confidence in the good faith of each party and the absence (or presence) of other parties competing for the transaction.

Although our clients had negotiated the basic economic terms of their cash transaction with Myron, they had not attempted to detail in depth the terms of the acquisition. McQue had a salami theory of bargaining: "Don't try to bite off the whole thing; one slice at a time is enough!" He based the theory on a strong desire to avoid unpleasant issues in the early stages of deal-making and a sophisticated understanding of the momentum achieved when a deal keeps moving. Like a rolling snowball, an acquisition tends to pick up bulk and speed as it develops. I was delighted that McQue did not want to completely negotiate the transaction himself and that he provided us the opportunity to participate with him in basic decision-making involved in this transaction. It would simplify our task (and would help maintain his credibility and ours) if we were able to avoid renegotiating items which might have been agreed to without a full understanding of legal and tax implications. I also agreed with McQue's analysis of Myron's position, including the difficulty Myron would have unwinding the transaction after a public announcement had been made.

With McQue, I decided to use a preliminary document, but of minimal size. We wanted a meeting of the minds in written form which would require that Fabulous publicly announce Comp-Chomp's sale and which would restrict its ability to negotiate with others. This would maintain the momentum of the transaction and help protect the buyer's substantial expense of documenting and investigating the transaction.

We presented to Myron and his counsel a restrictive letter in which Ice Cold Doggie and Fabulous acknowledged their initial discussions and in which Fabulous agreed for a 60-day period not to negotiate concerning the sale of Chomp-Chomp with any other party. During this time, the agreement for the acquisition by Ice Cold Doggie of the assets of Chomp-Chomp would be negotiated in good faith by the parties and the investigation of the business of Chomp-Chomp completed (in confidence) by the buyer. A restrictive letter of the nature presented to Fabulous might not be enforceable against a public company since the legal duty of a publicly held enterprise to its stockholders may override the contractual duty to a proposed buyer arising from the restrictive letter. However, I did not anticipate that Fabulous would sign a binding preliminary agreement. An agreement triggering a public announcement of the transaction would be enough. A restrictive letter fulfilled that goal and might serve to proscribe any actions of the seller designed to violate its terms—even if the letter was not enforceable in court.

The contracting party on the restrictive letter was the purchasing corporation rather than our individual clients in order to reduce the potential legal exposure for the individuals if disputes arose at a later date. Formation of the buying entity required consideration of a series of elements ranging from those arising out of the stockholders' agreement between Lafayette, McQue and the entity, to the legal (including tax) implications of incorporation of the entity in any one of a number of jurisdictions. I decided to incorporate in the state in which Chomp-Chomp's business was located. This would be less expensive on an ongoing basis than incorporating elsewhere and qualifying to do business in that state. With a two-man private entity, there were no pressing considerations requiring a jurisdiction such as Delaware with a more liberal corporate

law. A local attorney was contacted at this point in the transaction for input concerning the local law. I also arranged for independent review by our firm of the legal elements involved and consulted with the buyer's accountants concerning state tax elements of the transaction.

I considered seeking an option for our buyer to purchase the business of Chomp-Chomp. However, an option satisfactory to us would have required either preparation and attachment of a complete purchase contract (which would then necessitate negotiating all terms of the contract prior to signing of the option) or an option exercisable over an agreed-upon time period so long as the buyer was satisfied, in its discretion, with the investigation of the business and financial condition of Chomp-Chomp. I believed that it was unrealistic to expect Myron to sign an option leaving so much discretion to the buyer without exacting an unacceptably high price. In addition, such an option might provide a basis for Myron to seek an "as is" transaction with few representations and warranties and limited indemnities. I wanted full protection provided by representations, warranties and indemnities from Chomp-Chomp and Fabulous since our clients were strangers to the business being acquired.

As an alternative to a restrictive letter, McQue was willing to accept a memorandum or letter of intent. We were willing to make the memorandum binding so long as it provided for the flexibility we needed to insure that the buyer was satisfied with the business investigation of Chomp-Chomp and that financing from Winston Largess would be available.

It was nearing the end of the fiscal year of Fabulous and Myron was under pressure to consummate a sale prior to the year's end in order to satisfy his bank. However, he had learned something from his prior mistakes and wished to insure that he did what was best for Fabulous (and himself). In addition, his counsel was sufficiently competent to stymie any unusual requests we might make at this time. Although Myron wanted to announce the transaction to increase his bargaining power with the bank and help his image in the public market, he did not want to publicly announce the transaction until he was confident a full agreement had been reached. He was therefore inclined to skip a preliminary agreement and to negotiate and sign a full acquisition agreement as soon as possible. If a preliminary agreement was to be executed, Myron wanted that agreement to contain as much detail as possible in order to reduce later problems.

After a long meeting at which the opposing views of the seller and the buyer were vigorously expressed, McQue eloquently pleaded, as a compromise from our restrictive letter, for execution by buyer and seller of a memorandum of intent which would outline in detail the essential terms of the transaction. Myron's counsel suggested that the memorandum be non-binding and subject to a definitive acquisition document, the approval of the Board of Directors of Fabulous and the approval of its bank. He also spoke of the good intentions of Fabulous and its desire to consummate the transaction with our clients but he did not feel that Fabulous should restrict itself in any way from speaking to other people.

Since a substantial amount of money and a large expenditure of time and energy was involved on the buyer's part in negotiating the transaction, I urged McQue to insist on restricting the seller's ability to negotiate with other parties. I also indicated that in our view, Board and bank approval of the transaction must precede execution of the memorandum. It was unreasonable, in our belief, for Fabulous to have the right, based on its Board's actions or the actions of its bank, to accept or reject our offer *after* signing a memorandum of intent.

McQue was convinced of his uniqueness—as a buyer and in every other way—and that Myron would, in fact, negotiate with him in good faith. Myron, according to McQue, not only needed the deal, but he had no idea of the real value of Chomp-Chomp's realty and equipment. After I explored the pros and cons of a non-binding memorandum of intent and the elements which we would seek to include in the memorandum, McQue agreed to a non-binding memorandum without Board or bank approval and including as much detail as Myron desired, subject to our satisfaction with the terms stated.

Following his salami theory, McQue had initially suggested to Myron an all-cash transaction. Subsequently, based on increases in interest rates and a decrease in bank loans nationwide, McQue had suggested that Fabulous accept redeemable preferred stock of Ice Cold Doggie for $600,000 of the purchase price. By the time the letter of intent was completed, McQue and Myron had agreed that $300,000 of the price was to be a promissory note, $300,000 preferred stock of the buyer and the balance, cash.

The memorandum we finally prepared covered the following points:

(1) the sale by Chomp-Chomp to Ice Cold Doggie of substantially all of the assets of Chomp-Chomp subject to assumption by Ice Cold Doggie of substantially all of its liabilities;

(2) the payment to Chomp-Chomp of book value plus $1,000,000 for the assets being sold, of which price $300,000 was to be evidenced by the buyer's 5-year promissory note, which was subordinated to the bank and any outstanding institutional financing and $300,000 was to be represented by issuance by the buyer of its redeemable preferred stock with a liquidation preference in that amount;

(3) the preparation by the parties of a definitive acquisition agreement as soon as practicable providing, among other things, that

(a) the buyer's obligations were to be subject to appraisals satisfactory to the buyer's bank indicating a fair market value of not less than $1,000,000 for Chomp-Chomp's equipment and realty and the assumption by Fabulous of pension liabilities under the pension plan maintained by Chomp-Chomp and termination of that plan; and

(b) representations and warranties involving the business of Chomp-Chomp reasonably satisfactory to the buyer to be made by both Chomp-Chomp and Fabulous and other terms to be mutually agreed upon; and

(4) the seller's provision to the buyer and its representatives of full access to Chomp-Chomp and information concerning its business and financial condition and, in the sole discretion of Fabulous, certain of its personnel, to enable the buyer to fully investigate the business and financial condition of Chomp-Chomp. The buyer, in turn, agreed to maintain in confidence the information acquired in the investigation.

Although additional discussion occurred concerning indemnities and the scope of the potential liability of Fabulous for breach of representations and warranties, these discussions were not embodied in written form in the memorandum of intent. The memorandum specifically recited that it was not to be deemed a binding contract. Upon execution of the memorandum of intent, Fabulous issued its press release after review thereof by McQue and our firm. Concurrently with issuance of the release, Myron contracted Jonathan Worthington to thank him and provide notice that Worthington's firm was off the case.

DUE DILIGENCE MEMORANDUM AND TIMETABLE

While negotiating with Myron's counsel with respect to the memorandum of intent for this transaction, we prepared a due diligence memorandum setting forth in detailed form the legal aspects of the investigation, which we believed the buyer should perform, of the business of Chomp-Chomp.

At my urging and the urging of Winston Largess, McQue and Lafayette had engaged accountants to review (and, after closing, audit) the books and records of Chomp-Chomp. Notwithstanding the relatively small size of this transaction, we believed that a review by accountants independent of the seller would provide an important security blanket for our clients, their bank and for our firm, as the attorneys in the transaction. The accountants, as early members of the acquisition team, can also perform preliminary work which will aid them in rendition of auditing services for the acquiring entity. The buyer's accountants also prepared a due diligence memorandum dealing with those financial and accounting items which they believed should be reviewed. Our firm and the accountants then coordinated memoranda in order to minimize duplication of effort, although some duplication and overlap occurred because of the need for both the accountants and the lawyers to review various aspects of Chomp-Chomp's business.

With the buyer's accountants, and after review by McQue, we also prepared a timetable setting forth an outline of what we believed was a reasonable estimate of the timing for completing various stages of the transaction.

The due diligence memorandum and the timetable were presented to Myron and his attorneys and accountants. The timetable went through some changes as each of the parties involved in the transaction attempted to estimate his needs to accommodate the transaction to other business activities and to the time required to comply with the various elements involved.

The due diligence memorandum was designed to investigate all relevant information concerning the business and financial condition of Chomp-Chomp. Myron and the professionals working with him were sufficiently sophisticated to agree to opening all aspects of the business being sold to full inspection by the buyer in order to insure that the buyer was satisfied. In general, approaching the mergers and acquisitions business with a buyer's bias, I believe it is unwise for buyers to limit their investigation of entities to be acquired. Particularly in a transaction such as the acquisition of Chomp-Chomp in which a substantial part of the purchase price is being paid in cash to the seller at closing, the buyer is entitled to full disclosure concerning the merchandise for which he is paying; and, the seller should bear the risk if the merchandise is not as represented.

If you are a seller without a strong need to sell and are capable of maintaining a "take it as is or leave it" attitude toward your prospective purchaser, it may be possible to narrow the scope of a buyer's investigation of your business—and reduce the related disruption that investigation may cause.

THE ACQUISITION CONTRACT
Who Prepares the Documents

McQue initially wanted Fabulous to do (and pay for) everything, leaving him (and us, as his counsel) mere spectators commenting on the documents. In my experience, however, he who prepares the documents controls the negotiating process and can better protect his client. Mere commentary is no substitute for the opportunities provided by drafting. Decisions are made in preparing documents which affect the substantive aspects of transactions and the pacing of transactions can be determined by the speed with which documents are delivered. As the buyer's counsel, we could use our documents to define the disclosure necessary to protect our clients, the representations and warranties relating to the material disclosed and the indemnities protecting the buyer against damage if the agreement was violated. I therefore believed, as is traditional, that it was appropriate for us, as buyer's counsel, to control preparation of the agreement. I convinced McQue of the validity of the approach, obtained the agreement of seller's counsel, and went to work.

Simultaneous or Delayed Closing

An early decision to be made in drafting an acquisition agreement is whether to have a simultaneous execution of the agreement and closing or a closing delayed to some point in the future.

In many transactions, particularly those involving public companies, a delayed closing is essential. Often, the acquisition agreement must be approved by stockholders. This approval requires filing proxy material with the Securities and Exchange Commission, and forwarding that material to stockholders after the Commission has reviewed it. Since the transaction cannot be closed until stockholder approval has been obtained, the closing must be delayed for some period of time after the acquisition agreement is signed.

Other situations requiring delayed closings include those requiring compliance with bulk sales laws and provision of written bulk sales notices to creditors of the seller and those in which government agencies must act prior to consummation. Such transactions may include those involving approvals or tax rulings required by one or both of the parties, approvals in connection with businesses regulated by governmental agencies such as the Interstate Commerce Commission or Civil Aeronautics Board, and approvals required by acquisitions of a scale triggering Federal Trade Commission review under the Hart-Scott-Rodino Antitrust Improvements Act, dealt with elsewhere in this handbook.

A transaction such as the one to be engaged in by Lafayette and McQue does not necessarily require a delay between signing and closing. However, the prospective transfer of assets in the Chomp-Chomp transaction would require substantial paper work and because of the real estate involved, the delay required to investigate title to realty. I also had to insure that bank documents were negotiated and completed prior to negotiation and completion of the acquisition agreement. Largess had indicated his desire for a signed acquisition agreement *before* loan documents would be completed to insure his satisfaction with the provisions of the agreement, including the provisions of the buyer's preferred stock, the purchase money note to be issued to the seller and the security agreements with the seller. These facts clinched the decision to prepare an agreement providing for a delayed closing.

Agreements involving delayed closings are more complex than those contemplating simultaneous closings and signings. With a simultaneous signing and closing, covenants established in the documents pending the closing and the conditions of closing can be eliminated since the closing takes place at the same time as the signing. There are no detailed provisions required for opinions and letters from lawyers and accountants since they are present at the time of closing and signing. Only representations and warranties intended to survive closing need be included in the agreement. The agreement we finally prepared contained substantially more detail.

GOALS OF BUYER AND SELLER

Frequently, a seller is unwilling to fully disclose all facts concerning the business and financial condition of the entity to be sold until a purchase agreement is signed. However, substantial time pressure existed for Fabulous because of its desire to complete the transaction by year-end. Winston Largess also wanted to lend his money before year-end and our buyers were eager to acquire Chomp-Chomp. I therefore decided with counsel for Fabulous and, after careful explanation to

McQue of the possibility of incurring substantial legal and accounting bills without completing the deal, to proceed on all fronts at once. Our clients determined to bear the risk of this expense, notwithstanding the absence of a binding contract, in order to facilitate rapid completion of the transaction.

For the buyer, the acquisition agreement is designed to do several things:

(a) provide as much detail as possible concerning the business to be acquired;

(b) insure that the seller focuses completely upon the business and financial condition of the assets or entity to be sold in order to discipline the seller's analysis and presentation of facts in a manner useful to the buyer;

(c) set up factual representations and warranties which shift to the seller risks of loss concerning the business and which provide (i) grounds for the buyer to terminate the transaction if the representations and warranties prove untrue, or (ii) a basis for renegotiation if facts develop indicating that the transaction, as structured, is not what the buyer had bargained for; and

(d) provide a basis subsequent to consummation of the transaction for the buyer to seek monetary damages from the seller under indemnity provisions should the representations, warranties and covenants of the agreement prove untrue.

For the seller, the acquisition agreement does not necessarily serve the same function as it does for the buyer. If the transaction is for cash and the seller is satisfied with the buyer's ability to pay, very little need be said about the buyer. The agreement merely need articulate various legal representations concerning the buyer and insure that the price is paid. Facts concerning the buyer's business are not significant. If the seller is receiving securities from the buyer, the seller may desire the same type of business information from the buyer as is provided by the seller. Full disclosure is required because of the seller's prospective ownership of the buying entity. If the buyer is publicly held, much of the disclosure may be available in public documents — but the seller should still require that the buyer stand behind the accuracy of that information by provision for representations and warranties.

Key Provisions: Representations, Conditions, Covenants and Indemnities

The seller's representations and warranties provide a statement by the seller at a particular point in time of facts concerning the business being sold. In an agreement providing for delayed closing, the seller will also represent that these facts will be substantially the same at the closing date as they were at the time the agreement was signed. Thus, the buyer is protected from unpleasant deviations which may occur in the business being sold between the time of signing and the time of closing. The seller, on the other hand, will want to insure that the factual representations are not so stringent as to prevent the business from operating in the normal course and that the agreement reflects changes anticipated in connection with the operation of the business being sold.

Rather than embodying all facts concerning the business to be sold in the acquisition agreement itself, most agreements will refer to a schedule or exhibits— which will be prepared by the seller and reviewed— very carefully—by the buyer. The schedule or the exhibits will contain the myriad facts concerning the entity to be sold and will relate to the representations made in the agreement.

In addition to representations and warranties, the acquisition agreement should contain conditions to the obligations of the parties to assure each of them that the facts upon which they rely in connection with the transaction will be true. In the case of Chomp-Chomp, conditions included the release by Fabulous's principal bank of its lien on the assets of Fabulous and, essential for Mr. Largess and his loan, appraisals of not less than $1,000,000 for the real estate and equipment of Chomp-Chomp.

The convenants which were to constitute part of the acquisition agreement included agreements related to the operation of the business of Chomp-Chomp prior to and after the closing and various other commitments to insure a smooth transfer of ownership.

The fourth major aspect of the acquisition agreement which would undergo substantial negotiation prior to closing involved indemnification provisions under which the parties would agree to make one another whole in the event of breach of any representations, warranties and agreements.

Preparing the Acquisition Agreement

Preparing the first draft of an acquisition agreement is an activity in which the attorney often engages alone. Sometimes he will prepare the agreement without having met or spoken in detail with counsel for his opposite number and without having participated in the ebb and flow of initial negotiations and the activity surrounding execution of a preliminary agreement such as a letter of intent. Under such circumstances, thorough discussions with the client, review of documented facts and a decent understanding of the business to be acquired are essential preconditions to setting pen to paper. With the acquisition of Chomp-Chomp, I had been fortunate. Not only had I obtained backgrond

from the preliminary negotiations, but McQue and Layfayette were sophisticated deal-oriented clients, having the capacity to provide insights and guidance concerning the decisions to be made as the agreement was drafted.

Our firm's form file provided relevant documentary precedent for this transaction. Also relevant was data concerning Chomp-Chomp's business — including publicly available documents from its competitors — and specific information, including financial statements, delivered to our clients by Fabulous and its counsel. I assembled prior first drafts of asset acquisition agreements. These provided the benefit of a buyer's document undiluted by negotiations and eliminated the time which would have been required to re-do a fully negotiated form agreement.

An Agreement Outline

The draft agreement prepared contained the provisions outlined below.

1. A preamble identifying the parties, stating their relative roles, and the assets being sold;
2. Provision for transfer of the assets being sold, the price to be paid and the manner in which the price will be paid (in the event securities are being issued in payment of the purchase price, methods of valuing those securities might be appropriate in this section) and, in connection with transfer of assets, provision for the buyer's assumption of liabilities;
3. Representations and warranties of the seller;
4. Representations and warranties of the buyer;
5. A statement of the manner in which the seller will conduct the business prior to the closing;
6. Those conditions which are to precede the obligations of the buyer to be performed at the closing;
7. Those conditions which are to precede the obligations of the seller to be performed at the closing;
8. A summary of the closing itself, the mechanics thereof and the documents to be delivered at the closing;
9. Agreements and commitments relating to the relationship of the parties and the activities of the business sold after the closing;
10. Agreements relating to the survival of the representations and warranties of the parties and, importantly, the indemnification provisions to be provided by the seller and buyer;
11. For an asset transfer, provisions relating to bulk sales laws;

12. For a stock transfer, provisions relating to the securities laws and rights to resell securities issued pursuant to registration statements or otherwise;
13. A provision relating to brokers;
14. Provisions related to employee benefits; and
15. Miscellaneous provisions including notices, the completeness of the agreement, the law governing the interpretation of the agreement, whether or not the provisions of the agreement will be severable and other general provisions desired by the parties.

THE ACQUISITION AGREEMENT IN DETAIL

The initial draft I prepared was a reasonable starting point for the agreement and had assembled in cohesive form the material from which it was derived. McQue had reviewed the document and had suggested changes which, in his belief, would present to our seller a reasonable document rather than a tough one-sided initial draft. The latter would require haggling and, possibly, engender rancor in the process. McQue was not, however, undermining what he believed were his basic needs. He wanted firm representations concerning Chomp-Chomp and its business in the agreement without qualification as to "materiality" or the "best knowledge" of his seller. He also wanted a firm indemnity with no floor and no ceiling on the amounts which could be claimed thereunder. Since materiality, knowledge and indemnities are three of the most common arguing points in acquisitions, he hadn't really conceded much at all.

Preamble

The parties to the agreement were Fabulous, Chomp-Chomp and Ice Cold Doggie. Although Chomp-Chomp was the party transferring the assets owned by it, I believed it critical to insure that Fabulous was included and fully liable for representations, agreements and indemnities. Once the transaction had closed, the seller would be an empty shell, a funnel distributing proceeds to its stockholder, Fabulous. To insure that the buyer had a real party to deal with in the event of problems or losses arising out of breaches of the agreement, the presence of Fabulous was important.

The Property Being Transferred; the Liabilities Assumed; Mechanics

In the acquisition of the assets of Chomp-Chomp, our initial paragraphs were straightforward. We detailed all of the items to be transferred which included the following:

(a) real estate, machinery, equipment and other items of personal property either described or located at facilities of Chomp-Chomp;
(b) work in process and inventories as well as containers and other material relating to the items being shipped either on hand or in transit;
(c) rights of Chomp-Chomp to contractual commitments set forth in an exhibit or made in the ordinary course of business;
(d) accounts and notes receivable;
(e) business records of Chomp-Chomp;
(f) sales data; and
(g) trademarks, tradenames, etc. and rights to use them and the good will connected therewith.

We also provided for the transfer of other assets which were eliminated in the course of negotiations including cash, specified pre-paid expenses in cases where the buyer would not obtain the benefit thereof, deferred credits and insurance policies and insurance reserves. Exclusion of these items did not affect price since the price was to be adjusted at closing based upon a closing pro forma balance sheet.

Chomp-Chomp's insurance was in large part covered by the blanket insurance of Fabulous. At closing, Fabulous would terminate that aspect of its blanket insurance coverage related to the business of Chomp-Chomp and the buyer would be obligated to obtain its own coverage. Fabulous was also terminating its pension plan to the extent it related to the employees of Chomp-Chomp and would cover those employees separately to the extent of vested service. The buyer was, in turn, commencing a new profit-sharing plan in connection with its operation of Chomp-Chomp's business which would be less expensive and, in the buyer's opinion, would provide a better incentive to the employees of Chomp-Chomp to perform in the future. In determining whether or not to continue the pension plan of Fabulous to the extent it was applicable to Chomp-Chomp's employees, the buyer had engaged its own actuary to independently review the data relating to the pension plan.

This section of the agreement also described in broad brush strokes the kind of instruments to be utilized in the transfer of the assets and further provided that anything which needed to be done, in the reasonable opinion of the buyer, would be done to insure that the buyer received the benefit of all the assets transferred in connection with the buyer's operation of Chomp-Chomp's business.

We set up in the acquisition agreement a separate section relating to the liabilities and obligations of Chomp-Chomp to be assumed by the buyer. These included current liabilities and obligations reflected on a pro forma balance sheet to be attached to the acquisition agreement to the extent remaining unpaid as of the closing date, current liabilities and obligations for trade accounts payable incurred by Chomp-Chomp in the ordinary course of its business subsequent to the date of the balance sheet through the closing date, and liabilities and obligations of Chomp-Chomp arising under agreements which were to be assigned to the buyer. The agreement specifically negated the buyer's assumption of other liabilities including tax liabilities, liabilities to customers for shortages and defects in goods and liabilities based on events occurring before the closing date or on products sold before the closing date.

The Purchase Price

If the purchase price for the acquisition of Chomp-Chomp's assets had been all cash, the purchase price section of the agreement would have merely provided for a cash payment to the seller at the closing equal to book value of Chomp-Chomp plus $1,000,000 against delivery of all the documents required. I also would have argued for an escrow with a third party of a portion of the purchase price in order to protect the buyer against obligations for which Fabulous had indemnified the buyer.

Since McQue had successfully negotiated for deferral of part of the purchase price, the purchase price section of the agreement provided for a method of determining price (book value as shown on the pro forma balance sheet at closing plus $1,000,000), the payment of $300,000 of the price by delivery of a 5 year promissory note in the form attached to the agreement as an exhibit, $300,000 of the price by issuance of preferred stock in the form attached to the agreement as an exhibit and the balance in cash.

Exhibits designated in the purchase price section of the agreement included the following documents:

1. a purchase money promissory note to the seller;
2. a "non-recourse" guaranty by McQue and Lafayette of the promissory note;
3. a pledge agreement securing the guaranty;
4. a security agreement granting to the seller a second security interest in the assets being sold;
5. a second mortgage on Chomp-Chomp's realty;
6. an amendment to the Certificate of Incorporation of Ice Cold Doggie defining the relative rights of the preferred stock to be issued to the seller; and
7. a pro forma balance sheet.

In a subsection relating to the purchase price, we provided for preparation of a pro forma balance sheet of Chomp-Chomp at the closing date upon which the final price would be based. An adjustment would be made if the pro forma book value on the closing date exceeded or was less than the book value shown on the pro forma balance sheet attached to the agreement. A schedule to the agreement set out an allocation of the purchase price to the assets being transferred, much of which had been previously discussed with Myron and his counsel. Accounts receivable and inventory were to be purchased at the face amount thereof and the real estate and equipment were allocated with reasonable relationship to the appraisals obtained therefor.

The purchase price section of the agreement contained or referred to many "toothy" items upon which all parties to the transaction spent much time chewing. The section had expanded from what I had originally believed would be a simple statement of a cash payment to its present state since Fabulous was to be given purchase money security interests in assets.

The Purchase Money Note and Security Therefor

Preparation of the exhibits to the purchase price section of the agreement opened a "Pandora's Box" of possible provisions which I examined. Although this chapter is not designed to deal with loan documents, loans are often a critical part of acquisitions and must be a standard number in the repertory of every acquisition attorney. The decisions reached in drafting the purchase money note and related documents involved many provisions, only a few of which are dealt with below.

The purchase money note was a two-edged sword. To protect the buyer, the note was to be subject to offset and non-negotiable, so that it could not be transferred to a good-faith purchaser, thereby cutting off defenses to payment which might be available to the buyer. The note was specifically subject to the provisions of the acquisition agreement including those provisions which might entitle the buyer to be paid by the seller.

The seller, of course, wanted the note to serve as an evidentiary basis for payment by the buyer of the amount of principal and interest agreed upon. However, the twists and turns of the transaction complicated that simple purpose. Not only was payment of the purchase money note subject to offset, but it was made subordinate to payment of the buyer's obligation to the bank. However, to benefit the seller the note was to be secured by a second security interest in the assets being sold and the course of negotiations had resulted in a commitment from Lafayette and McQue to further secure the note with all capital stock of the buyer. To make Lafayette and McQue parties to the arrangement, I provided for their guaranty to the seller of payment of the note with the guaranty secured by their pledge to the seller of the buyer's capital stock. The guaranty was without recourse personally against Lafayette and McQue. The remedy of the seller in the event the guaranty was drawn upon was solely against the capital stock securing the guaranty.

Since the seller would continue to be interested in the buyer and its performance until payment of the promissory note (and redemption of preferred stock to be issued to the seller), I had to consider the kind of negative and positive covenants of a continuing nature which would be provided by the buyer to Fabulous so long as the note remained outstanding. These covenants were built into the security agreement under which the buyer granted to the seller a second security interest in the buyer's assets. Ultimately, the covenants and agreements provided to Fabulous in the security agreement mirrored substantially those covenants and agreemeents provided by the buyer to Winston Largess's bank. In my initial draft of the security agreement, I specified in brackets under sections headed, respectively, "Affirmative Covenants" and "Negative Covenants" "[to be provided based, in part, on bank documents]."

Although the borrower under a security agreement will typically provide detailed representations and warranties to the secured party concerning its ownership rights and the condition of title to the assets serving as security, those were not present in my draft. In those transactions where the secured party is transferring the assets to the debtor and concurrently taking back a security interest, I believe that the secured party should not require the debtor's representations and warranties as to facts better known to the secured party than the debtor and it would be unwise for the debtor to assume those responsibilities. I was also reluctant to provide to Largess's bank representations and warranties from the buyer concerning title to the property. The solution to the bank's desire to be protected was an assignment to the bank of the buyer's rights against the seller and Fabulous in the event of breach of representations and warranties in the acquisition agreement. However, many banks will not accept such an assignment in lieu of a direct representation from the borrower. In that case, the borrower must weigh the business risks involved in providing full title representations and counsel must determine its ability to legally opine thereon.

The extent of subordination by the seller of its right to payment under the promissory note had to be determined as did the scope of the guaranty to be delivered. I focused upon issues such as these while I was drafting. Typically, it was the preparation and submission of documents which brought to the negotiating table these many issues not discussed by the parties.

Preferred Stock

In the prolonged negotiation of preferred stock provisions with Myron, McQue had agreed upon a $300,000 liquidation preference, a dividend of 10 percent and a mandatory redemption of the stock within five years. Preferred stock has five basic elements: dividends, preference on liquidation, voting rights, redemption and conversion. Within these elements are diverse variations limited only by the imagination of the draftsman. Accounting treatment of the preferred stock on the balance sheet of the issuer is also an important element to be considered in determining provisions of that stock.

McQue, a man with a strong aversion to paying taxes, had reconsidered a 10 percent dividend in light of its non-deductibility as a corporate expense and had determined, with Myron, to provide an average 10 percent return on the $600,000 of the purchase price for Chomp-Chomp which was being deferred—14 percent under the purchase money note and 6 percent as a dividend under the preferred stock. Myron acquiesced, notwithstanding better tax treatment available to a corporation upon receipt of a dividend than upon receipt of interest, since a large percentage of the dividend received is excluded from taxation. My initial draft provided for a cumulative 6 percent dividend payable semi-annually; a liquidation preference for $300,000 plus accrued and unpaid dividends; voting rights to elect one director (out of five) only in the event of failure to pay dividends for two years or failure to redeem; redemption—at the option of Ice Cold Doggie—in the fifth year for $300,000 plus accrued and unpaid dividends and no conversion.

The preferred stock finally agreed upon included sinking fund provisions and mandatory conversion of the stock to a demand promissory note if it had not been redeemed by the sixth year after issuance.

Stock (whether preferred or common) is *not* equivalent to a direct obligation to pay even after the stock may have been transmogrified into a promise to pay. The payment of dividends on stock and payment of a redemption price therefor are generally subject to the existence of a "surplus" (frequently defined as the excess of net assets over liabilities), as defined by the applicable corporation law. The payment may also require that a corporation be "solvent" at the time it is made. Thus, a corporation may have an absolute defense to payment under a contract requiring that it redeem stock or under a promissory note issued to redeem stock if the corporation does not meet the corporate law tests at the time payment is to be made. The jurisdiction in which Ice Cold Doggie was incorporated imposed such restrictions on payment of dividends and payment in connection with redemption.

The Closing

Deciding the time and place for a closing requires deliberation. To be considered are sales and other transfer taxes, the desires of any lender and the myriad number of considerations affecting the business needs and convenience of the parties. Winston Largess's bank maintained a small "promotional" office in New York which Winston was willing to utilize to close the transaction. He had indicated his desire to preclose and execute loan documents in the Midwest so that he could reasonably apply local law to the interpretation of those documents. He would then wire funds directly to Fabulous's bank in New York when all the additional elements of the transaction had been completed to his satisfaction.

Since we had the option to close in New York, my agreement recited that the closing was to be held at our offices, a convenience which I deem the prerogative of the party preparing the agreement if all other elements permit a local closing.

Representations and Warranties of the Seller

As we have stated before, the representations and warranties in the agreement are designed to disclose to the buyer all pertinent facts concerning the business of the seller, and to shift to the seller the risks from untrue statements concerning those facts. These provisions give the buyer basis for terminating the agreement or, possibly, renegotiating its terms. Subsequent to the closing, the representations and warranties provide a factual basis for utilization of indemnity provisions in the agreement.

In addition to general representations concerning Fabulous and Chomp-Chomp and their organization, corporate power and power to enter into the agreement and consummate the transactions provided for in the agreement, several business representations were necessary. In order to provide the buyer with an accurate snapshot of Chomp-Chomp's business at a given point in time, balance sheets and statements of income and changes in financial position as of the end of the fiscal year and as of the end of its most recent interim period were to be attached to the agreement. Often, financial statements of subsidiaries of public companies are not separately certified by accountants. However, Chomp-Chomp for many years had been separately certified by an accounting firm which did not audit the statements of Fabulous. If a separate certification is not available, the buyer might have to settle for non-audited financials (which should be carefully reviewed by buyer's accountants and accompanied by appropriate representations).

I requested that Chomp-Chomp represent with Fabulous that the certified financial statements, together with the notes, were complete and correct, presented fairly the financial condition and results of operation of the business of Chomp-Chomp at the dates and for the periods indicated, and were prepared in accordance with generally accepted accounting principles consistently applied. This reference to "GAAP" was a key to the financial protections which we desired. Accounting standards have been relatively solidified and to the extent generally accepted accounting principles are referred to, disputes can frequently be resolved by accounting firms. Even with application of generally accepted accounting principles, accountants (and lawyers and principals) can differ, but the utilization of this familiar terminology goes a long way toward solving potential problems. The pro forma balance sheet referred to in the purchase price section of the agreement consisted of the numbers on the "GAAP" balance sheet, adjusted based upon those assets and liabilities excluded from the transaction. That pro forma balance sheet would be used in the purchase price calculation at closing.

I provided that there were no liabilities not disclosed on the balance sheet and that all reserves established on the balance sheet were adequate. In addition, I provided that since the balance sheet date, the business of Chomp-Chomp had been operated in the ordinary course and that no material changes or damage or destruction had occurred. Provisions were added pursuant to which Chomp-Chomp and Fabulous represented that no labor trouble had occurred, no statutes had been adopted adversely affecting the business of Chomp-Chomp, no termination or waivers of rights had occurred and that no increase in compensation had occurred except as disclosed.

I also provided for representations concerning tax payments, notwithstanding the fact that in connection with this acquisition, the buyer was only assuming certain narrowly proscribed tax liabilities. The representations and warranties then refered to specific facets of the business of Chomp-Chomp and provided for the schedule to relate details concerning each of these.

The real estate of Chomp-Chomp was dealt with in detail including a legal description of the realty and representations concerning compliance with law, its title condition, zoning, etc. Leases and agreements were to be described in detail and the schedule was to completely itemize personal property, trademarks and tradenames, insurance, all contracts, including a list of specific contracts which were to be disclosed, and accounts receivable, including a firm representation as to collectability of those accounts which would later tie into the buyer's ability to ''put'' the accounts to the seller in the event they were not collected within a 90-day period. The schedule was to particularize information relating to litigation, laws and compliance with laws affecting the business of Chomp-Chomp and inventories including the usability and quantity thereof. The agreement also contemplated full information on the schedule concerning compensation of employees, pension plans, union arrangements and major customers and suppliers and arrangements, if any, between Chomp-Chomp and Fabulous.

Additional representations related to overall accuracy of the information supplied, the general business of Chomp-Chomp and the fact that the business would be operated in its normal course to the closing date and, importantly, that the assets being transferred to the buyer were sufficient for the buyer to operate the business of Chomp-Chomp in the ordinary course.

Representations and Warranties of the Buyer

If the deal had been all cash, the buyer would provide to the seller only limited representations as to incorporation, authority and compliance with law. The promissory note and preferred stock increased the complexity of the buyer's representations. However, I managed to convince the attorneys for Fabulous to permit many of the buyer's representations to appear, not in the acquisition agreement, but in the security agreement which would be executed at closing. This is not necessarily the best place for the seller to have the representations since the consequence of a breach is generally acceleration of the obligation secured rather than damages. Representations and warranties in the acquisition document, rather than the security agreement, might better protect a seller against losses for breach thereof.

Additional representations made by the buyer included those concerning the capitalization of the buyer, its commitment from a reputable financial institution for loans sufficient to finance the purchase price and, combined with other funds to be available, to operate the business of Chomp-Chomp after the closing, and honor its contracts and agreements. An assertion was made by the buyer that its ownership of the assets would be free and clear of liens and encumbrances (other than those of Largess's bank). Other items designed to make Fabulous comfortable with its legal claim to monies under the purchase note included maintenance by Ice Cold Doggie of its business in an agreed-upon financial state.

Substantial negotiation had occurred when the seller's counsel requested that McQue personally obligate himself for the representations and warranties in this agreement. McQue kicked and shrieked when the issue arose. His passion, and the logic with which it was presented, resulted in the issue being dropped. The compromise involved the nonrecourse guaranty secured by capital stock which McQue and Lafayette provided for the purchase note.

The Hiatus Between Signing and Closing

We had provided in the seller's representations and warranties that the business of Chomp-Chomp would be operated in the ordinary course to the closing date. In addition, I provided for the following:

— Full access by the buyer's representatives to books, records and other data pertaining to the business of Chomp-Chomp to enable a complete investigation to occur;

— no diminution of the representations, warranties and agreements by reason of the investigation;

— best efforts to preserve relationships with customers, suppliers, etc.; and

— delivery of monthly interim financial and other data.

If stock or substantially all assets of a public company are being sold, this section must also set out and require compliance with regulatory mechanics prior to closing. This includes preparation and submission of proxy material to stockholders to permit them to vote on the transaction.

Seller's counsel may request that the representations and warranties exclude adverse information known to the buyer—in effect, that those representations and warranties diminish based upon the buyer's investigation. The seller doesn't want the buyer to close the transaction and then sue for a breach of representations and warranties which was known at closing. However, whether the buyer had knowledge of a fact is a difficult question to answer, and a seller has the ability to protect itself by carefully disclosing in schedules or exhibits all facts concerning the business to be sold.

Conditions Precedent to the Obligations of the Parties

There are certain relatively standard conditions to closing contained in acquisition agreements. These conditions are designed to insure that the representations in the agreement remain accurate at closing and that the commitments in the agreement have been complied with by closing if compliance by closing is required. To nail down these conditions, most acquisition attorneys will provide for the delivery by the parties of certificates as to compliance with conditions and as to accuracy of representations and warranties.

As additional backup for the accuracy of representations and warranties, corporate proceedings reasonably satisfactory to counsel for each party were required to have been completed, and attorneys' opinions relating to matters of law contained in the representations and warranties were required to be delivered. I also requested a comfort letter from the accountants for Chomp-Chomp which would indicate to a date not later than five days prior to the closing that they had performed a review of the financial statements of Chomp-Chomp and would stand by the scheduled financial statements as disclosed in the comfort letter. An accountant's comfort letter would probably not have been available to the buyer if separately audited financial statements had not been prepared for Chomp-Chomp.

Letters from attorneys and accounts are very important to the preparers thereof. McQue scoffed at the concern of our firm and of counsel for Fabulous about the respective opinions we prepared. However, the opinions provided additional insurance to the recipient and placed at risk the providers of the opinions.

There were certain additional conditions which I believed were crucial to the buyer. These included confirmation from certain major customers of orders, appropriate title insurance on the real estate and appraisals for the real estate and equipment indicating a minimum value of $1,000,000. In fact, McQue was confident the appraisal would be made at $2,000,000 but we did not wish to include a number so large as to provide grounds for additional inquiry from Myron and his counsel. A five-year non-compete agreement from the seller and Fabulous was also provided for in this section and attached as an exhibit.

Because Fabulous wished to insure that the buyer obtained appropriate insurance relating to the business of Chomp-Chomp, including product liability insurance, I inserted a condition to the seller's obligations relating to the kind and nature of insurance to be obtained. I also provided for the consent of Chomp-Chomp's unions as a condition to the seller's obligations because of the seller's concern about its relationship with those unions in other businesses. Myron's request for the buyer to maintain such items as insurance and union relationships after closing was provided for in the security agreement.

Closing Adjustments

I had not discussed with counsel for Fabulous those items which were to be adjusted at the closing and, as the drafter of the document, was in a position to exactly determine the cards I would initially place on the table. I assumed that subsequent meetings would result in additions and deletions to the agreement which would be satisfactory to all the parties.

The agreement provided for termination of utilities service at the closing date, a request by the seller for final bills to that date and the commencement of new service in the name of the buyer. These utilities included telephone, gas and electric. In order to help maintain the continuity of the business, the buyer and seller were to request that the same telephone numbers be used subsequent to the transfer of the business to the buyer.

Salaries, including fringe benefits and vacation accruals, were to be adjusted to the last shift on the closing date. Since Chomp-Chomp paid its employees in arrears, this item would require a rebate from the seller to the buyer once the specific amount of the adjustment had been determined. Taxes accruing on real estate and personal property were prorated. Special assessments relating to real estate which dealt with work commenced prior to the closing date would be paid by the seller and assessments, if any, for work commenced after the closing date were to be paid by the buyer. Certain miscellaneous items such as water, fuel, sewer expenses, license and permit fees, rentals on equipment and obligations under service contracts were to be apportioned to the close of business on the closing date. I also provided for the payment by the seller to the buyer of trade accounts payable in excess of the maximum number agreed upon.

Proration adjustments were to be paid within 30 days after the closing date based upon an adjusted amount to be agreed upon by buyer and seller after examination of the books and records of Chomp-Chomp. In case of a problem, I set up a method to resolve disputes in a later section of the agreement which contemplated utilizing the services of an arbitration association.

At closing, the buyer would deliver to the seller the purchase money note, preferred stock and cash based upon the pro forma balance sheet attached to the agreement. I wanted closing adjustments to be made quickly based upon McQue's estimate that, due to a seasonal shift in business, the closing pro forma balance sheet would result in a purchase price adjustment in favor of the buyer.

I had advised McQue that we should seek to maintain the purchase money note at $300,000 and provide that other adjustments be paid in cash when incurred. Offsets under the purchase note were not as good as cash since the note was due five years from the closing and only semi-annual interest thereon (at 14 percent) could be used for offset prior to that time.

Counsel for Fabulous wanted the principal amount of the purchase note to be adjusted six months from closing if adjustments were required in buyer's favor. By adjusting the note, Fabulous would obtain the maximum cash possible. Ultimately, after much effort and several concessions to Fabulous, we agreed that adjustments would be made in cash.

After the Closing

In order to mechanically expedite adjustments, a closing pro forma balance sheet was to be prepared promptly after closing. A list of post-closing activity included insurance adjustments, purchase by the seller of accounts receivable unpaid within 90 days after the closing, adjustment of inventories which did not meet terms set forth in the representations and warranties provided by the seller, adjustments in connection with credits and adjustments for goods returned for credit or otherwise. I also provided for the seller's right of access to the business operated by the buyer after closing to deal with the items to be adjusted and for the seller's assumption of claims relating to product liability.

To help maintain continuity of the business of Chomp-Chomp, the agreement provided that Fabulous would continue to provide to the buyer computer servicing of certain accounting functions for up to 90 days after closing. Compensation for computer services was based upon the cost of those services to Fabulous.

A mechanism was provided to resolve disputes which might occur in connection with preparation of the closing pro forma balance sheet. Initially, that balance sheet was to be prepared by the accountants for the buyer and submitted to the accountants for the seller. The two accounting firms were to agree upon the pro forma balance sheet and if they did not agree, arbitration by a third accounting firm was provided for. The buyer and the seller were to split the costs relating to the preparation of the closing pro forma balance sheet.

The agreement also provided for the seller's payment of all its liabilities not assumed and for the change of the seller's name to something other than Chomp-Chomp. McQue wanted to continue using that trade name after closing for certain products. In acquiring all or substantially all assets of public companies, plans of liquidation should be required that will not only require payment of creditors, but also distribution of funds to stockholders and compliance with other conditions of proxy material relating to the transaction.

Further Agreements of the Parties

The acquisition agreement included a series of commitments from the parties which were not representations and warranties, but which related to activities in which the parties were to engage in connec-

tion with the acquisition.

A series of meetings had occurred with counsel for Largess's bank in connection with the loan documents. The bank's counsel had arranged, prior to closing, to pre-file Uniform Commercial Code Financing Statements in order to perfect, upon execution of security agreements, the bank's security interest in inventory, accounts receivable and machinery and equipment. The first mortgage to the bank (and the second mortgage to the seller) had been fully negotiated and the title company engaged had indicated that it would issue at closing to the bank a firm title insurance policy based upon delivery to its representative of the executed mortgage and the deed to the property. No substantial mortgage tax was imposed in the jurisdiction in which Chomp-Chomp was located. This eliminated the high cost of mortgage tax which is encountered in jurisdictions such as New York. At the 1-1/2 percent tax rate imposed in New York City, the tax on recording a $2,000,000 mortgage is substantial.

The seller's security interests did not require advance filing. However, the agreement did provide for the mechanics of preparing and filing the documents required to perfect the seller's security interests and impose its liens.

Survival of Representations; Indemnification

My initial draft of the agreement simply provided for the survival of representations, warranties and agreements subsequent to closing and the consummation of the transaction contemplated by the agreement. If that provision had stood, the buyer would have had a period of time equal to the appropriate statute of limitations within which to bring any actions under the acquisition agreement. In many states, that time period is six years.

To insure that the schedule and other attachments to the agreement would be included as part of the representations and warranties made in the agreement, I provided for their inclusion in this section of the document. I also provided that any material delivered by the seller to the buyer concerning the business and financial condition of Chomp-Chomp would be deemed a representation and warranty by Fabulous and the seller as to the contents thereof. Counsel for Fabulous said that was "cute" and we agreed to delete the line.

I assumed that Fabulous would request a limit upon survival of its representations and warranties. I hoped that our five-year promissory note might provide a reasonable basis for five (rather than six) years limitation within which claims could be asserted. However, a two-year limitation on enforcement of representations and warranties was, in the process of compromising issues, ultimately built into the agreement at the urging of the seller and its counsel.

My initial indemnity provision was broad. I sought a full indemnity of the buyer by Fabulous and Chomp-Chomp against any liabilities not assumed and any damages or loss (including costs and expenses) which were incurred due to inaccuracy of representations, warranties or agreements. A mechanism was established to implement the indemnity provisions requiring that a party claiming indemnity provide specified written notice of those claims to the other party and permit the other party to assert defenses for such claims under stipulated circumstances. The party indemnified was granted the right to be represented by its own advisory professional help at the expense of the other side. The agreement provided for mutual access to all material relevant to the claim and that no claim would be settled without the written consent of the indemnified party. The indemnity provisions were designed to make the injured party whole if damages occurred, including giving effect to the tax consequences of the damage.

Indemnity provisions, along with opinions of counsel, are usually among the most hotly negotiated items in an agreement. Fabulous, in addition to hewing to a two-year period within which the buyer could enforce the agreement, was unwilling to provide a complete indemnity. Counsel for Fabulous was ultimately successful in negotiating a $100,000 "basket" as part of the trade-off for cash adjustments and no personal liability for the buyer's stockholders. Thus, if the aggregate claims for which the buyer wished to be indemnified did not exceed $100,000, no indemnity could be sought and the buyer would only be entitled to indemnification for amounts in excess of $100,000. If a "trigger" rather than a "basket" had been built into the indemnity, the "trigger" would provide that the buyer would not seek indemnity unless the aggregate amount for which it was to be indemnified exceeded the triggering amount, in this case $100,000. However, once the amount for which indemnity was sought did exceed $100,000, the buyer would have the right under the indemnity to recover from the seller all monies from the first dollar involved. The indemnity section clearly stated that any remedies available to either party were cumulative, that they could be exercised one on top of another, and that they could be exercised at any time.

Since the indemnity provisions were reciprocal, the seller also had the right to recover against the buyer for damages caused by buyer's breach of representations and warranties. However, since the seller was not exposed to the exigencies arising from operation of a "new" business and since the buyer made far fewer representations than the seller, I did not anticipate that the indemnity provisions would be meaningful to the extent that the buyer was the indemnifying party. They were provisions principally designed for the buyer's benefit.

Employee Benefits

The complexities of employee benefits, particularly insofar as they are controlled by the Employee Retirement Security Act of 1974 ("ERISA") and its regulations, may often warrant separate provisions. The representations and warranties had referred to details pertaining to employee benefits in the schedule to the agreement, including actuarial reports. This particular section of the agreement was designed to insure that there were no violations of law in connection with any of the plans maintained by Fabulous for the employees of Chomp-Chomp and that all funding had occurred thereunder. Since the buyer would be employing the employees of Chomp-Chomp after the closing and would rely upon those employees in operating the business acquired, the agreement should insure that the benefits which had accrued to those employees during the period that the business was under the aegis of Fabulous were properly funded and available. Maintenance of good employee relations is critical in connection with any business acquisition and various sections of the acquisition agreement, including the representations and warranties, covenants, conditions to closing and special employee benefit sections, are relevant to those relations.

As facts developed, underfunding of the Fabulous pension and profit-sharing plan became a major problem in connection with this transaction and required not only a commitment for Fabulous to pay a portion of the cash proceeds from the sale of Chomp-Chomp to increase funding of the plan, but also an agreement from Fabulous to maintain contributions at specified levels over a period of time.

Brokers

The agreement included cross-representations by the parties that none of them had dealt with any brokers or finders in a manner requiring payment of a fee in connection with the transaction and that each party would, to the extent a fee was payable because of their actions, pay the fee and indemnify the other party with respect thereto. Although both Fabulous and McQue had dealt with finders, neither was obligated to pay them fees in connection with the acquisition.

Miscellaneous Provisions

Miscellaneous provisions are crucial. They may include an allocation of expenses, a reference to the parties in interest to the transaction, that the agreement is complete, provisions pertaining to the headings of the agreement and other items which may seem superficially to warrant the appellation of "boilerplate," but which are important enough to require careful preparation.

Notices under the agreement require attention not only as to address, but as to the method to be used to give notice and the time within which notices are to be received. Since I expected that many of the notices would issue from the buyer and involve the making of claims or a request for data from the seller, as buyer's counsel I wanted easy and "loose" notice provisions: "notice will be given by personal delivery or by first-class mail, postage pre-paid, and will be deemed given when delivered or mailed at a post office box." The seller wanted a tighter procedure which would require that notices be deemed given only when actually received. Registered or certified mail or personal delivery were finally chosen as the methods for notifying parties and, for greater evidentiary certainty, notices were deemed to be delivered based upon the receipts provided by the post office or facts concerning delivery.

Other miscellaneous provisions in the agreement included a reference to consultation on publicity, the designation of governing law and reference to the fact that waivers would not be deemed continuing and that any waiver of a provision would not operate as a waiver of any other provision. Detailed arbitration procedures, referred to earlier, were also set forth under this section of the agreement.

Bulk Sales Laws

The provisions of bulk sales laws are often waived in connection with the purchase of assets from a division or subsidiary of a large company. Buyers often believe that an indemnity will be sufficient to protect them if problems arise. In addition, since bulk sales laws are designed to protect buyers against claims of creditors of the seller affecting assets acquired, they may be less important in situations, like this one, which include the buyer's assumption of obligations to those creditors.

Largess's bank, notwithstanding what was typical, initially demanded full compliance by Chomp-Chomp with the Bulk Sales Law. Bank counsel believed that seller's creditors might, in this divisional acquisition case, have priority in a bankruptcy over the secured position of the bank. Compliance with bulk sales laws would have required that Fabulous notify all creditors of Chomp-Chomp in order to cut off claims which

might affect the assets being acquired. This procedure is cumbersome and would have delayed closing. It also has the effect of putting suppliers on notice of the sale, enabling them to reassess relationships with the business being sold. However, the bank's lawyers finally agreed with our conclusion that failure to comply with bulk sales laws could be made without undue risk and the transaction proceeded without compliance.

THE MECHANICAL CLOSING PROCESS

Finally, after four weeks of investigating the business of Chomp-Chomp, negotiating with Fabulous, Largess and their counsel and arranging for completion of all of the acts contemplated by the agreement, we set a closing date. The acquisition agreement had not yet been signed and, notwithstanding a contemplated delay between signing and closing, it was not, in fact, signed until the closing date. This is not a desirable state of facts for either buyer or seller, but is not an uncommon development in some mergers and acquisitions.

In the event that a transaction involves delay between signing and closing, a signing of the acquisition agreement would occur first. All exhibits and schedules to the agreement would be in final form and attached to the agreement. Subsequent to signing, documents related to the closing would be prepared, reviewed and negotiated by the parties, and delivered at the actual closing.

Prior to the concurrent signing and closing of the Chomp-Chomp transaction, I prepared closing memoranda for circulation, one for the acquisition of Chomp-Chomp and the second for the financing to be engaged in by the buyer. The memoranda contained detailed descriptions of the items to be delivered by each party at closing and a full list of all documents related to the transaction. The circulation list, which had expanded as negotiations proceeded, included three sets of lawyers (including bank counsel), two accountants, McQue, Lafayette, Myron and the Treasurer of Fabulous, the President and Treasurer of Chomp-Chomp, Largess and, with respect to limited documents, the title company—a total of 13 copies!

Once our final documents were circulated, I advised both McQue and Lafayette to warm their right arms in preparation for signing.

From the foregoing, it should be clear that the success of a merger or acquisition depends, in substantial part, upon the availability of talented support staff and the reliability of the automated office machinery which they operate. The mechanics of any transaction must be assiduously attended to in order to avoid a shift of focus from the substantive problems which often arise.

Some of the problems arising prior to closing have been mentioned in the description of the acquisition agreement itself. In addition to pension and profit-sharing plan difficulties, our title report indicated encroachments on the real estate of Chomp-Chomp which could potentially affect the salability thereof and which could not be removed without negotiating with an adjoining land owner. This real estate was, of course, critical to the buyer's financing requirements and the operation of the business. The negotiations with the adjoining land owner, in which Fabulous's counsel played the major role, resulted in an agreement which removed the encroachments, at a cost of approximately $75,000 to Fabulous. Thus, the encroachments, along with pension and profit-sharing requirements, decreased meaningfully the cash available to Fabulous from this transaction. By the time the additional dollars had to be expended, it was difficult to back out. Fabulous had agreed to firm representations in the agreement which were violated by the facts and, despite the failure of the parties to execute the agreement before closing, Fabulous adhered to its word.

The investigation of Chomp-Chomp's business preceding the closing process indicated that certain agreements should be reached with suppliers and three distributors to insure their continued relationship with the business after closing. In attempting to ferret out problems and facts, McQue also determined that two present employees of Chomp-Chomp were sufficiently important to warrent employment agreements. A condition for those agreements had been included in the acquisition agreement after negotiations with Fabulous and its counsel.

A Uniform Commercial Code search report was delivered prior to closing to reveal any security interests in the assets of Chomp-Chomp other than the interest of Fabulous's lender. That lender had provided to the buyer a written commitment to release its lien at closing, subject to payment of $1,000,000, and Largess had arranged to wire the payoff amount direct to that lender at closing.

Transfer documents relating to registered motor vehicles, along with documents creating liens on those vehicles, had been prepared prior to closing and reviewed by the bank.

In connection with the acquisition, I attempted to prepare all documents reflected in the closing memoranda as early as possible so that they could be fully reviewed by the various parties. Legal and accounting letters often undergo substantial negotiation and should be delivered sufficiently in advance of closing to permit study and negotiation and avoid the all-night sessions often required in order to finish transactions. Pre-closings prior to the time the principals are available for signing often help diminish the frequent problems which arise on a closing date and sometimes pre-signing of an agreement may be desirable.

The lawyers in our firm, along with counsel for Fabulous, had worked well into the night the day before a pre-closing was to occur in order to finalize all documents. At the pre-closing, additional changes were made as required and virtually a full day was spent correcting and organizing all documents in form for signing.

The buyer had pre-signed all of its documents with the lender at the request of Largess and those documents remained in escrow with the attorneys for the lender. At closing, the buyer would deliver to its lender the mortgage and title policy along with documents related to registered equipment. Based upon delivery of those documents (along with the deed for the real estate being transferred) and evidence of the closing of the asset acquisition, the lender was prepared to wire funds. Wires, however, often get lost. Notwithstanding my reluctance to wire funds, it was the only method seemingly available in this situation since Largess would not issue checks prior to the time all documents had been completed and delivered.

We planned to finish as early as possible on the day of closing in order to insure that wired funds might, with luck and constant attention, arrive prior to the close of business on that day. The principals of the buyer, the seller, Fabulous, the title closer and counsel for the parties arrived at our offices at 8:00 A.M. to commence signing the ten execution copies of documents. By 11:00 A.M. documents had been executed and instructions issued to wire funds. Acknowledgement of arrival of funds was not received until 2:45 P.M. when the transaction was finally completed.

WHAT HAPPENED AFTER CLOSING

McQue had resigned from his current job two weeks before the closing occurred and on the day of closing immediately flew to the facility of Chomp-Chomp to commence running its business. The pro forma closing balance sheet was not prepared without many threats and, eventually, preparation by us of a summons and complaint against Chomp-Chomp and Fabulous. We never got together on arbitration. Final resolution, however, did occur. When last I heard from McQue, he was happily engaged in the dog food business and looking for another deal.

Model Merger, Acquisition and Buyout Forms

CONTENTS

DRAFT

GENERAL BUYER'S FEE LETTER

I. Compensation for Services

In consideration for the submission of

_____

by _____ as an acquisition candidate for _____ (the "Company"), it is the Company's understanding that if the Company or any of its affiliates acquire, by means of a merger, consolidation, joint venture, exchange offer, purchase of stock or assets or other transaction, any entity as a result of any submissions or introductions made by _____ within two years of such submission or introduction, the Company shall pay _____ or cause _____ to be paid, at the closing of such transaction, a

fee equal to 5 percent of the aggregate consideration up to $2 million but not exceeding $4 million, plus 3 percent of such consideration in excess of $4 million but not exceeding $6 million, plus 2 percent of such consideration in excess of $6 million but not exceeding $8 million, plus 1 percent of such consideration in excess of $8 million but less than $20 million, plus one half of 1 percent of the amount in excess of $20 million. Aggregate consideration is defined as:

A) The total proceeds and other consideration being paid upon the consummation of the sale (including payments made in installments) inclusive of cash, securities, notes liabilities assumed, consulting agreements and agreements not to compete.

B) If a portion of such consideration includes contingent payments (whether or not related to future earnings or operations) aggregate consideration will include 50 percent of the maximum amount of such payments.

C) If the transaction involves the disposition of assets, the net value of any current assets not acquired by the Company will be included in aggregate consideration.

D) In the event that the aggregate consideration for a transaction by the Company consists in whole or in part of securities, for the purposes of calculating the amount of aggregate consideration, the value of such securities will be (in the case of the existence of a public trading market therefore) the average bid or closing prices for twenty days preceding the consummation of the sale, or (in the absence of a public trading market herefor) the fair market value thereof as the Company and _____ agree on the day preceding the consummation of the sale.

II. Indemnification

If during the effective period of this agreement _____ concludes that a situation develops for which _____ feels it requires indemnification, either a) the Company will provide _____ with customary indemnification or b) if the Company does not provide with customary indemnification then _____ will have the right to terminate this agreement without liability on the part of _____ .

III. Entire Agreement, Etc.

This Agreement sets forth the entire understanding of the parties relating to the subject matter hereof, and supersedes and cancels any prior communications, understandings, and agreements between the parties. This Agreement cannot be modified or changed nor can any of its provisions be waived, except by a writing signed by all parties.

IV. Confidentiality

The Company also agrees that each submission will be treated by it as confidential, and will not be discussed with any parties other than those involved in the decision-making process within its organization.

V. Governing Law

This Agreement shall be governed by the laws of the State of New York.

Please confirm that the foregoing is in accordance with your understanding by signing and returning to _____ the duplicate of this letter attached hereto.

Very truly yours,

BY _____

Accepted and Agreed to:

BY _____

DRAFT

EXCLUSIVE SELL ASSIGNMENT FEE LETTER

This letter will confirm that _____ _____ is hereby authorized to represent _____ (the "Company") as its exclusive agent for a period of one year from the date on which you acknowledge acceptance of this letter (the "exclusive period") in connection with the possible sale of the business of the (Company, the _____ Division, or the _____ Subsidiary) by means of merger, consolidation, joint venture, exchange offer, purchase or sale of stock or assets, or other transaction resulting in any change of control of the Company, the acquisition of any shares of its stock or the disposition outside the ordinary course of business of any of its assets or business.

I. Performance of Services

_____ agrees to use its best efforts in attempting to consummate a transaction which will be satisfactory to the (Company or shareholders). In completing this assignment _____ will:

A) Work together with the Company and its management in preparing a descriptive memorandum of the (Company the _____ Division, or the _____ Subsidiary) and its operations for use in discussions with prospective acquirers or merger partners. It is understood that it is the Company's responsibility to assure the accuracy and completeness of the information in the memorandum.

B) Prepare a list of potential acquirers and merger partners concurrently with the preparation of the memorandum, which will be submitted to you for the purpose of eliminating companies which are unacceptable to you and establishing the order in which the acceptable acquirers and merger partners will be contracted. The list of approved acquirers and merger partners ("the approved list'') may be supplemented and amended from time to time by mutual agreement.

C) Contact the companies on the approved list, establish and attend exploratory meetings, value the properties to be sold, analyze prospective buyers and structure and negotiate a transaction.

II. Referral of Prospects

In order to coordinate the efforts to complete a transaction satisfactory to the Company and its stockholders, during the period of _____ 's engagement hereunder, only _____ will have the authority to initiate discussions with companies on the approved list. In the event the Company, its management or its stockholders receive an inquiry concerning the availability of the Company for purchase, they will promptly refer the party to _____ in order that _____ can follow through on any discussions. In addition should the Company have been contacted by a prospective purchaser prior to _____ 's engagement they will be identified and included under this agreement.

III. Compensation for Services

The Company will pay _____ a retainer fee of $_____ at the time this agreement is signed. If a transaction is consummated (a) during the exclusive period to any Company on the approved list, the Company shall pay _____ or cause _____ to be paid, at the closing of such transaction, a transaction fee equal to 5 percent of the aggregate consideration up to $2 million but not exceeding $4 million, plus 3 percent of such consideration in excess of $4 million but not exceeding $6 million, plus 2 percent of such consideration in excess of $6 million but not exceeding $8 million, plus 1 percent of such consideration in excess of $8 million but less than $20 million. Also the Company will reimburse _____ for reasonable out-of-pocket expenses incurred in carrying out the terms of this Agreement. The retainer fees paid by the Company to _____ for the twelve month period prior to the closing of the transaction will be credited on a one time basis, against the transaction. Aggregate consideration is defined as:

A) The total sales proceeds and other consideration received by the company and its stockholders upon the consummation of the sale) including payments made in installments) inclusive of cash, securities, notes, liabilities assumed, consulting agreements and agreements not to compete.

B) If a portion of such consideration includes contingent payments whether or not related to future earnings or operations) aggre-

gate consideration will include 50 percent of the maximum amount of such payments.

C) If the transaction involves the disposition of assets, the net value of any current assets not sold by the Company will be included in aggregate consideration.

D) In the event that the aggregate consideration for the sale of the Company consists in whole or in part of securities, for the purposes of calculating the amount of aggregate consideration the value of such securities will be (in the case of the existence of a public trading market therefor) the average bid or closing prices for the twenty days preceding the consummation of the sale, or (in the absence of a public trading market therefor) the fair market value thereof as the Company and _____ agree on the day preceding the consummation of the sale.

IV. Indemnification

If during the exclusive period _____ concludes that a situation develops for which _____ feels it requires indemnification, either a) the Company will provide _____ with customary indemnification or b) if the Company does not provide _____ with customary indemnification then _____ will have the right to terminate his agreement without any liability on the part of

V. Entire Agreement, Etc.

This Agreement sets forth the entire understanding of the parties relating to the subject matter hereof, and supersedes and cancels any prior communications, understandings, and agreements between the parties. This Agreement cannot be modified or changed nor can any of its provisions be waived, except by a writing signed by all parties.

VI. Governing Law

This agreement shall be governed by the laws of the State of New York.

Please confirm that the foregoing is in accordance with your understanding by signing and returning to _____ the duplicate of this letter attached hereto.

Very truly yours,

BY _____

Accepted and Agreed to:

BY _____

Date: _____

CONFIDENTIALITY AGREEMENT

(to be signed before exchange of information and meeting in order to protect seller)

Dear Sirs:

You have requested information from _____ _____ in connection with our consideration of the possibility of a transaction between _____ (the "Company") and _____ or its shareowners. As a condition to our furnishing such information to you, we are requiring that you agree, as set forth below, to treat confidentially such information and any other information we or our agents furnish to you, whether furnished before or after the date of this letter (collectively, the "Evaluation Material").

You agree that the Evaluation Material will not be used by the Company in any way detrimental to _____ in the judgement of _____ management and that such information will be kept confidential by the Company and its agents; provided, however, that (1) any of such information may be disclosed to directors, officers, employees and representatives of the Company who need to know such information for the purpose of evaluating a possible transaction between the Company and _____ or its shareowners (it being understood that such directors, officers, employees and representatives shall be informed by the Company of the confidential nature of such information and shall be directed by the Company to treat such information confidentially), and (2) any disclosure of such information may be made to which _____ consents in writing.

Without the prior written consent of _____, the Company will not, and will direct its directors, officers, employees and representatives not to, disclose to any person either the fact that discussions or negotiations are taking place concerning a possible transaction between the Company and _____ or any of the terms, conditions or other facts with respect to any such possible transaction, including the status thereof. The term "person" as used in this letter shall be broadly interpreted to include without limitation any corporation, company, partnership and individual.

In the event that the Company is requested or required (by oral questions, interrogatories, requests for information or documents, subpoena, Civil Investigative Demand or similar process) to disclose any information supplied to the Company in the course of its dealings with _____ or its representatives, it is agreed that the Company will provide _____ with prompt notice of such request(s) so that they may seek an appropriate protective order and/or waive the Company's compliance with the provisions of this Agreement. It is further agreed that, if in the absence of a protective order or the receipt of a waiver hereunder the Company is nonetheless, in the opinion of its counsel, compelled to disclose information concerning _____ to any tribunal or else stand liable for contempt or suffer other censure or penalty, the Company may disclose such information to such tribunal without liability hereunder.

In addition, you hereby acknowledge that you are aware (and that your directors, officers, employees and representatives who are apprised of this matter have been advised) that the United States securities laws prohibit any person who has material non-public information about a company from purchasing or selling securities of such company.

In view of the fact that the Evaluation Material consists of confidential and non-public information, the Company agrees that it will not acquire in any manner, for a period of two years from the date of this Agreement, any securities of _____ , except pursuant to a transaction approved by _____ Board of Directors.

In the event that no transaction is effected between the Company and _____ or its shareowners after the Company has been furnished with Evaluation Material, the Company will promptly upon the request of _____ deliver to _____ the Evaluation Material, without retaining any copy thereof.

The term "Evaluation Material" does not include information which (i) becomes generally available to the public other than as a result of a disclosure by the Company or its representatives, (ii) was available to the Company by _____ or its representatives, or (iii) becomes available to the Company on a non-confidential basis from a source other than _____ or its representatives, provided that such source is not bound by a confidentiality agreement with _____ or its representatives.

Although you understand that we have endeavored to include in the Evaluation Material information known to us which we believe to be relevant for the purpose of your investigation, you further understand that we do not make any representation or warranty as to the accuracy or completeness of the Evaluation Material. You agree that neither _____ nor its representatives shall have any liability to you or any of your representatives resulting from the use of the Evaluation Material by you or such representatives.

It is further understood and agreed that no failure or delay by _____ in exercising any right, power or privilege hereunder shall operate as a waiver thereof, nor shall any single or partial exercise thereof preclude any other or further exercise thereof or the exercise of any right, power or privilege hereunder.

This letter agreement shall be governed and construed in accordance with the laws of the State of _____.

If you are in agreement with the foregoing, please sign and return one copy of this letter which will constitute our agreement with respect to the subject matter of this letter.

Very truly yours,

_____

BY _____

Name:

Confirmed and Agreed to:

BY _____

Name:
Title:
Date:

DRAFT

BUYER'S FEE LETTER—REQUEST FOR INFORMATION

This letter will confirm your request that _____ _____ obtain for you certain material which it has requested in respect of _____ the "Company").

I. Confidentiality

This will confirm that such material contains confidential information, and, consequently, will not be disclosed by you to any third party. You have further agreed to restrict the dissemination of such information with your organization to those executives involved in the decision-making process.

II. Compensation for Services

If you acquire, by means of merger, consolidation, joint venture, exchange offer, purchase of stock or assets or other transactions, all or a portion of the Company within a period of two years from the date hereof, you will pay _____ or cause _____ to be paid, at the closing of such transaction, a fee equal to 5 percent of the aggregate consideration up to $2 million, plus 4 percent of such consideration in excess of $2 million but not exceeding $4 million, plus 3 percent of such consideration in excess of $4 million but not exceeding $6 million, plus 2 percent of such consideration in excess of $6 million but not exceeding $8 million, plus 1% of such consideration in excess of $8 million but not exceeding $20 million, plus one half of 1 percent of the amount in excess of $20 million. Aggregate consideration is defined as:

A) The total proceeds and other consideration being paid upon the consummation of the transaction (including payments made in installments) inclusive of cash, securities, notes, liabilities assumed, consulting agreements and agreements not to compete.

B) If a portion of such consideration includes contingent payments (whether or not related to future earnings or operations) aggregate consideration will include 50 percent of the maximum amount of such payments.

C) If the transaction involves the disposition of assets, the net value of any current assets not sold by the Company will be included in aggregate consideration.

D) In the event that the aggregate consideration for the sale of the Company consists in whole or in part of securities, for the purposes of calculating the amount of aggregate consideration, the value of such securities will be (in the case of the existence of a public trading market therefor) the average bid or closing prices for the twenty days preceding to consummation of the sale, or (in the absence of a public trading market therefor) the fair market value thereof as the Company and _____ agree on the day preceding the consummation of the sale.

III. Indemnification

If during the effective period of this agreement (_____) concludes that a situation develops for which _____ feels it requires indemnification, either a) the Company will provide _____ with customary indemnification or b) if the Company does not provide _____ with customary indemnification then _____ will have the right to terminate this agreement without any liability on the part of _____ .

IV. Entire Agreement, Etc.

This Agreement sets forth the entire understanding of the parties relating to the subject matter hereof, and supersedes and cancels any prior communications, understandings and agreements between the parties. This Agreement cannot be modified or changed nor can any of its provisions be waived, except by a writing signed by all parties.

V. Governing Law

This Agreement shall be governed by the laws of the State of New York.

Please confirm that the foregoing is in accordance with your understanding by signing and returning to BTCo. the duplicate of this letter attached hereto.

Very truly yours,

BY _____

Accepted and Agreed to:

BY _____

Date _____

DRAFT

SPECIFIC BUYER'S FEE LETTER—REQUEST FOR MEETING

This letter will confirm your request that _____ arrange a meeting between yourselves and _____ (the "Company").

I. Confidentiality

This will confirm that the occurrence and subject of this meeting will be treated in confidence, and that all matters discussed at such meeting will be restricted within your organization only to those executives involved in the decision-making process.

II. Compensation for Services

If you should acquire, by means of merger, consolidation, joint venture, exchange offer, purchase of stock or assets or other transaction, all or a portion of the Company within a period of two years from the date hereof, you will pay _____ or cause _____ to be paid, at the closing of such transaction, a fee equal to 5 percent of the aggregate consideration up to $2 million, plus 4 percent of such consideration in excess of $2 million but not exceeding $4 million, plus 3 percent of such consideration in excess of $4 million but not exceeding $6 million, plus 2 percent of such consideration in excess of $6 million but not exceeding $8 million, plus 1 percent of such consideration in excess of $8 million but not exceeding $20 million, plus one half of 1 percent of any amount in excess of $20 million. Aggregate consideration is defined as:

A) The total proceeds and other consideration being paid upon the consummation of the sale (including payments made in installments) inclusive of cash, securities, notes, liabilities assumed, consulting agreements and agreements not to compete.

B) If a portion of such consideration includes contigent payments (whether or not related to future earnings or operations) aggregate consideration will include 50 percent of the maximum amount of such payments.

C) If the transaction involves the disposition of assets, the net value of any current assets not sold by the Company will be included in aggregate consideration.

D) In the event that the aggregate consideration for the sale of the Company consists in whole or in part of securities, for the purposes of calculating the amount of aggregate consideration, the value of such securities will be (in the case of the existence of a public trading market therefor) the average bid or closing prices for the twenty days preceding the consummation of the sale, or (in the absence of a public trading market therefor) the fair market value thereof as the Company and _____ agree on the day preceding the consummation of the sale.

III. Indemnification

If during the effective period of this agreement _____ concludes that a situation develops for which _____ feels it requires indemnification, either a) the Company will provide _____ with customary indemnification or b) if the Company does not provide _____ with customary indemnification then _____ will have the right to terminate this agreement without any liability on the part of _____ .

IV. Entire Agreements, Etc.

This Agreement sets forth the entire understanding of the parties relating to the subject matter hereof, and supersedes and cancels any prior communications, understandings and agreements between the _____ parties. This Agreement cannot be modified or changed nor can any of its provisions be waived, except by a writing signed by all parties.

V. Governing Law

This Agreement shall be governed by the laws of the State of New York.

Please confirm that the foregoing is in accordance with your understanding by signing and returning to _____ the duplicate of this letter attached hereto.

Very truly yours,

BY _____

Accepted and Agreed to:

BY _____

Date _____

DRAFT

RETAINER CLIENT FEE LETTER

This letter sets forth the basis on which _____ _____ is engaged by _____ (the "Company") to act as its financial advisor for its acquisition program for a one year period beginning the date this agreement is confirmed.

I. Performance of Services

_____ is prepared to provide the following services:

A)   _____ will work with the Company's staff in developing acquisition criteria both from the point of view of business compatibility and financial acceptability.

B)   _____ will assist the Company in identifying companies in the targeted industries, which may include public companies, divisions of public companies, and privately held companies, and after evaluating such companies assit in ranking them in terms of priority.

C)   _____ will develop financial information on target companies. In those cases where the company is private or a division of a public company, _____ will utilize its contacts and sources of information to develop as complete a financial profile as possible. In the event outside consulting studies are desirable, _____ will recommend such consultants and be prepared to retain them on behalf of the Company.

D)   _____ will evaluate the target companies from a financial viewpoint, providing an opinion as to value and the price level necessary to consummate a transaction.

E)   _____ will provide its judgment as to the receptivity of the target company's management or principal shareholders to be acquired, and will analyze tactical approaches to the target company and indicate the probabilities of success.

F)   _____ will contribute to the analysis of the target company's desirability from both a business and product viewpoint, combining these conclusions with the judgment as to the likelihood of success.

G)   _____ will assist the Company structuring and negotiating the transaction.

II. Compensation for Services

In consideration for the above described services, the Company agrees to pay to _____ a retainer fee of $_____ (per quarter per month), payable on the last day of each (quarter month) for the term of this Agreement. In addition if the Company or any of its affiliates acquire, by means of merger, consolidation, joint venture, exchange offer, purchase of stock or assets or other transactions, any entity as a result of submissions or introductions made by _____ within two years of the termination of the Agreement, or if the Company uses the services of _____ in conducting or assisting in negotiations or structuring a transaction with any party, the Company shall pay _____ or cause _____ to be paid, at the closing of such transaction, a transaction fee equal to 5 percent of the aggregate consideration up to $2 million, plus 4 percent of such consideration in excess of $2 million but not exceeding $4 million, plus 3 percent of such consideration in excess of $4 million but not exceeding $6 million, plus 2 percent of such consideration in excess of $6 million but not exceeding $8 million, plus 1 percent of such consideration in excess of $8 million but not exceeding $20 million. 1 percent of the amount in excess of $20 million less any retainer fee. Also the Company will reimburse _____ for reasonable out-of-pocket expenses incurred in carrying out the terms of this Agreement. The retainer fees paid by the Company to _____ for the twelve month period prior to the closing transaction will be credited, on a one time basis, against the transaction. Aggregate consideration is defined as:

A) The total proceeds and other consideration being paid upon the consummation of the transaction (including payments made in installments) inclusive of cash, securities, notes, liabilities assumed, consulting agreements and agreements not to compete.

B) If a portion of the consideration includes contingent payments (whether or not related to future earnings or operations) aggregate consideration will include 50 percent of the maximum amount of such payments.

C) If the transaction involves the disposition of assets, the net value of any current assets not acquired by the Company will be included in aggregate consideration.

D) In the event that the aggregate consideration for a transaction by the Company consists in whole or in part of securities, for the purposes of calculating the amount of aggregate consideration, the value of such securities will be (in the case of the existence of a public trading market therefor) the average bid or closing prices for the twenty days preceding the consummation of the sale, or (in the absence of a public trading market thereof) the fair market value thereof as the Company and _____ agree on the day preceding the consummation of the sale.

III. Entire Agreements, Etc.

This Agreement sets forth the entire understanding of the parties relating to the subject matter hereof, and supersedes and cancels any prior communications, understandings, and agreements between the parties. This Agreement cannot be modified or changed nor can any of its provisions be waived, except by a writing signed by all parties.

IV. Indemnification

If during the exclusive period _____ concludes that a situation develops for which _____ feels it requires indemnification, either a) the Company will provide _____ with customary indemnification or b) if the Company does not provide _____ with customary indemnification then _____ will have the right to terminate this agreement without any liability on the part of _____ .

V. Termination

This Agreement may be terminated by either party at the end of any calendar month, by the terminating party giving written notice to the other party at least 15 days prior to such termination.

VI. Governing Law

This Agreement shall be governed by the laws of the State of New York.

Please confirm that the foregoing is in accordance with your understanding by signing and returning to _____ the duplicate of this letter attached hereto.

Very truly yours,

BY _____

Accepted and Agreed to:

BY _____

Date _____

PURCHASE AGREEMENT

$1,100,000 Principal Amount
13% Subordinated Notes
Due September 30, 19

150 Shares of $1.00 par value
Common Stock

October 25, 19

To the Purchasers (the "Purchasers")
 Named in Exhibit A attached:

Dear Sirs:

The undersigned, _____,
a New York corporation, having its principal place of
business at _____ (the
"Company") proposes to issue and sell to the Purchasers for cash (1) its 13% Subordinated Notes (the
"Notes") in the aggregate principal amount of
$1,100,000 due September 30, 19 , to be sold at par,
and 150 shares of its $1.00 par value Common Stock
(the "Stock") to be sold at a purchase price of $200.00
per share. The Notes and Common Stock will be issued
pursuant to and subject to all of the terms and conditions of this Agreement (the terms "this Agreement"
or "Purchase Agreement" as used herein or in any
Exhibit hereto shall mean this Agreement and the Exhibits hereto individually and collectively as they shall
from time to time be modified or amended).

In connection with the foregoing, the Company
agrees with each of the Purchasers, and each of the
Purchasers severally agrees with the Company, as follows:

Section 1. Purchase and Sale of Notes; Payments

1.1 The Company agrees to sell, and each Purchaser severally agrees to purchase from the Company,
at par, on the date on which this Agreement is executed
and delivered (herein called the "closing date"),
Notes aggregating as to each Purchaser the amount set
forth opposite its name in Exhibit A. Each Note shall
(a) be dated the closing date, (b) be substantially in the
form of Exhibit B attached with the blanks appropriately filled in conformity herewith, (c) be payable
on September 30, 19__, and (d) bear interest on the
unpaid principal amount thereof until paid at the rate of
13% per annum, payable on the first full business day
of each calendar month commencing December, 19__,
and at maturity or at prior prepayment of the Notes in
full.

1.2 The Company agrees that, until payment in full
of the Notes, it will apply to the prepayment of the

Notes, without premium or penalty, and without duplication or overlap, on the date set forth below, if a full
business day, otherwise on the first full business day
thereafter, the amount (the "Mandatory Prepayments") set forth opposite such date:

Schedule

Dec. 31, 19__ - $10,000	Dec. 31, 19__ - $55,000
Mar. 31, 19__ - 10,000	Mar. 31, 19__ - 55,000
June 30, 19__ - 10,000	June 30, 19__ - 55,000
Sept. 30, 19__ - 10,000	Sept. 30, 19__ - 55,000
Dec. 31, 19__ - $25,000	Dec. 31, 19__ - $65,000
Mar. 31, 19__ - 25,000	Mar. 31, 19__ - 65,000
June 30, 19__ - 25,000	June 30, 19__ - 65,000
Sept 30, 19__ - 25,000	Sept. 30, 19__ - 65,000
Dec. 31, 19__ - $40,000	Dec. 31, 19__ - $80,000
Mar. 31, 19__ - 40,000	Mar. 31, 19__ - 80,000
June 30, 19__ - 40,000	June 30, 19__ - 80,000
Sept. 30, 19__ - 40,000	Sept. 30, 19__ - 80,000

TOTAL = $1,100,000

1.3 The Company shall have the right at any time
and from time to time to prepay the Notes in whole or in
part in multiples of $50,000 without premium or pen-
alty (the "Voluntary Prepayments"). Any Voluntary
Prepayment in excess of the amount due on account of
a Mandatory Prepayment in accordance with Section
1.2 above, shall be applied against the immediately
succeeding Mandatory Prepayment or Mandatory Prepayments to become due. Any Mandatory or Voluntary prepayment shall be applied (to the extent thereof)
to the Notes, *pro rata*.

1.4 Payments and prepayments of principal and
interest on the Notes shall be made to the Purchasers at
their addresses (as they appear on the register maintained by the Company) by mailing the Company's
good check in the proper amount to the Purchasers at
least three days prior to the due date of each payment or
prepayment or otherwise transferring funds so as to be
received by the Purchasers on the due date of each such
payment or prepayment.

Section 2. Purchase and Sale of Stock

2.1 The Company agrees to sell, and each Purchaser severally agrees to purchase from the Company, on the closing date, the number of shares of Common Stock set after such Purchaser's name on Exhibit A, at a price of $200.00 per share (such stock is hereinafter called the "Purchasers' Stock").

2.2 The Company has furnished to the Purchasers the written appraisal of _____ dated September 28, 19__, appraising the value of each such share of Common Stock at $783 per share. The Company represents that it accepts such appraisal as true and correct and as having been prepared in accordance with principles generally accepted by independent appraisers in determining the value of property such as the Common Stock. The Company has disclosed to _____ all facts believed by the Company to be relevant to the appraisal of the shares of Common Stock and has no knowledge of any facts which would affect the accuracy or independent nature of the appraisal of which would affect the Purchasers' reliance thereon. Notwithstanding any other term of this Agreement, the parties hereto accept such appraisal and agree that the fair market value of the shares of Common Stock sold hereunder is $117,500 in the aggregate, which amount (less the $30,000 paid by the Purchasers) will be treated by the Purchasers as additional interest and amortized over the term of the Notes.

Section 3. Conditions of the Closing

The Purchasers shall not be obligated to purchase the Notes or Common Stock described in Sections 1 or 2:

3.1 If any event has occurred and is continuing which is, or with the giving of notice or lapse of time, or both, would constitute, an event of default under this Agreement had this Agreement been in effect on, and immediately after, the closing; and unless prior to the closing hereunder the Company has furnished to each of the Purchasers a certificate (in form and substance satisfactory to them) of the Company's President or a Vice President to the effect that no such event has occurred and is continuing.

3.2 Unless all representations and warranties of the Company to the Purchasers are true in all material respects on the closing date; and the Company has delivered to each of the Purchasers a certificate signed by its President or a Vice President to that effect.

3.3 Unless there has been delivered to each of the Purchasers resolutions (in form and substance satisfactory to them) of the Company's Board of Directors authorizing this Agreement and the transactions herein contemplated, certified by its Secretary.

3.4 Unless each of the Purchasers has been fur-

nished with (a) the Certificate of Incorporation of the Company and all amendments thereto, certified of recent date by the Secretary of State of the State of New York, (b) the By-Laws of the Company certified by the Company's Secretary, (c) certificates of good standing and payment of taxes of recent date of the Secretary of State of New York and of all states in which the Company is qualified to do business as a foreign corporation, and (d) telegrams bringing down to the closing the items referred to in Section 3.4 (a) and (c).

3.5 Unless _____ and _____, and _____ has each sold to the Company for a consideration of $1,060,000, an aggregate of 530 shares of the Company owned by them, pursuant to an Agreement executed in October, 19__, heretofore entered into by them with the Company, and the Purchasers have received such corporate authorizations, documents and instruments, including opinions of counsel, as they shall require in respect of such sale.

3.6 Unless the Company has purchased or owns a life insurance policy or policies in the total amount of $700,000 on the life of _____ and a life insurance policy or policies in the total amount of $100,000 on the life of _____ , with the Company as the owner and beneficiary of each, and each is in form and substance satisfactory to the Purchasers.

3.7 Unless each of the Purchasers has been furnished with (a) the Articles of Incorporation of each Subsidiary of the Company (which shall mean each corporation of which the Company or another Subsidiary shall own at least 51 percent of the stock of any class having power under ordinary circumstances to vote for the election of directors) and of _____ , a New York corporation ("affiliate") of which the Company owns 50 percent of the stock having power to vote for the election of directors, and of all amendments thereto, certified by its Secretary, (b) the By-Laws of each Subsidiary and Affiliate, each certified by its Secretary or other appropriate officer, and (c) certificates of good standing and payment of taxes of recent date of the Secretary of State of the Subsidiary's and Affiliate's respective states of incorporation and of all states in which the Subsidiary and Affiliate are qualified to do business as a foreign corporation.

3.8 Unless the Purchasers have received the Basic Agreement dated August 31, 19__, between the Company and _____ , a Belgium corporation, owner of 50 percent of the stock having the power to vote for the election of directors of the Affiliate in respect of the ownership and operation by them or either of them of such Affiliate, and unless such

Agreement has been duly certified by an officer of the Company to be in all respects accurate and complete.

3.9 Unless the Purchasers have received the appraisal referred to in Section 2.2.

3.10 Unless there has been delivered to each of the Purchasers, an opinion of _____ in form and substance satisfactory to each of the Purchasers.

3.11 Unless the Company has substantially performed and complied with all agreements and conditions contained herein required to be performed or complied with by it prior to or at the closing, and the Company has delivered to Purchasers a certificate signed by its President or a Vice President to that effect.

3.12 Unless all corporate and other proceedings in connection with the transactions contemplated hereby and all documents incident thereto shall be satisfactory in form and substance to each of the Purchasers and their counsel and they shall have received all such counterpart originals or certified or other copies of such documents as they may reasonably request.

3.13 Unless a Shareholders' Agreement dated as of October 25, 19__ between Bankers Trust New York Corporation ("BTNY") and BT Capital Corporation ("BTCC"), the Purchasers, and _____ _____ and the Company, in respect of the control of the Company and its stock (the "Shareholders' Agreement"), in form and substance satisfactory to the Purchasers and their counsel, has been duly entered into and is valid and enforceable, and unless to the satisfaction of the Purchasers all prior shareholders agreements or other agreements between the Company and its shareholders have been cancelled.

3.14 Unless the proposed amendments to the Certificate of Incorporation and By-Laws of the Company have each been duly and properly adopted in the forms thereof attached hereto as Exhibits C and D respectively, it being understood that the amendment to the Certificate of Incorporation will be filed promptly after the closing date.

3.15 Unless the Shareholders of the Company immediately before and immediately after the Closing are as set forth in Exhibit F (as used elsewhere in this Agreement, the term "Shareholders" means the shareholders of the Company immediately after the Closing as set forth in Exhibit F).

Section 4. Affirmative Covenants

The Company covenants and agrees that, unless the Purchasers shall otherwise consent in writing, it will, so long as the Notes are outstanding:

4.1 Furnish or cause to be furnished to each of the Purchasers the following financial statements and information, which shall be prepared in accordance with generally accepted principles of accounting practice consistently applied:

4.1.1 As soon as available, but in any event within three months after the close of each fiscal year of the Company, audited consolidated and consolidating balance sheets of the Company and of each of its Subsidiaries and Affiliates as of the close of such year, and audited consolidate and consolidating statements of income, stockholders' equity, and changes in financial position of the Company and each of its Subsidiaries and Affiliates for such fiscal year, together with (a) copies of the reports and certificates relating thereto of _____ or other independent certified public accountants of recognized national standing, selected by the Company and satisfactory to the Purchasers, and (b) a certificate of such accountants to the effect that they are familiar with the terms and provisions of this Agreement and that in making their audit they have not discovered, insofar as they relate to accounting matters, any condition, act or omission to act which would constitute an event of default or which with notice or lapse of time, or both, would constitute such an event of default, under this Agreement, *provided however* that the Company shall not be in default under this clause (b) in the event that, after using its best efforts, (i) it is unable to obtain such a no-default certificate from such accountants because of a policy adopted by them, and applied on a consistent basis nationally, that they will no longer issue such certificates or any similar certificate and (ii) such accountants so represent to the Purchasers.

4.1.2 As soon as available, but in any event within two months after the close of each of the first three quarters of each fiscal year of the Company, consolidated and consolidating balance sheets of the Company and of each of its Subsidiaries and Affiliates as of the last day of such quarter and consolidated and consolidating statements of income, stockholders' equity, and changes in financial position of the Company and of each of its Subsidiaries and Affiliates for the period from the beginning of the then current fiscal year to the last day of such quarter, each such balance sheet and statement of income, and changes in financial position to be certified by the acting principal financial officer of the Company, such Subsidiary or Affiliate, as the case may be, provided that any such certificate may state that the accompanying balance sheet and statements are subject to adjustments based on year-end audit.

4.1.3 With each of the statements of the Company

and its Subsidiaries referred to in Section 4.1.1 and 4.1.2, a certificate (executed on behalf of the Company) of the acting principal financial officer of the Company to the effect that he is familiar with this Agreement, and that to the best of his knowledge there exists no condition, act or omission to act which would constitute an event of default under this Agreement, or if any such condition, act or omission exists, specifying the same and what action the Company is taking to remedy the same.

4.1.4 Such information as BTCC, one of the Purchasers, shall reasonably require in order to furnish reports to the Small Business Administration, including, without limitation, the report required on Form 684 of the Small Business Administration.

4.1.5 From time to time, with reasonable promptness, such additional financial statements and information with respect to the financial condition of the Company and of its Subsidiaries and Affiliates as any of the Purchasers may reasonably request, including without limitation and without further request, any financial statements or reports furnished to the Company, any Subsidiary or Affiliate by its independent certified public accountants which relate to the Company, any Subsidiary or Affiliate, all registration statements and periodic reports filed with the Securities and Exchange Commission pursuant to the Securities Act of 1933 or the Securities Exchange Act of 1934, and all press releases.

4.2 Maintain, and cause its Subsidiaries to maintain, insurance to such extent and covering such risks as shall be required by law and such additional insurance as is customary for companies engaged in the same or similar business.

4.3 Use the proceeds of the sale of the Notes hereunder solely (a) to purchase 530 shares of the Company's common stock at a price of $2,000 per share, (b) for working capital purposes, and (c) for the legal and other reasonable expenses of this financing.

4.4 Provide each of the Purchasers with such information concerning the operations of the Company and of its Subsidiaries and Affiliates as such Purchaser may from time to time reasonably request in writing, and at reasonable intervals permit representatives of the Purchasers and each of them full and free access during normal business hours to the properties, books and records of the Company and its Subsidiaries and Affiliates, and information obtained by the Purchasers in accordance with this Section 4.4 to be treated by them as confidential and, except as required by law and the rules and regulations governing them, not disclosed by Purchasers or used by Purchasers other than for

purposes of evaluating the condition of the Company; provided however that nothing in this Section 4.4 or in Section 4.1.5 of any governmental contract or regulation or any private agreement relating to proprietary information or trade secrets.

4.5 Maintain consolidated net worth plus the outstanding Notes (excluding intangible assets), determined in accordance with generally accepted principles of accounting practice consistently applied, of not less than $800,000.

4.6 Maintain an excess of consolidated current assets over consolidated current liabilities, both determined in accordance with generally accepted principles of accounting purposes of this Section, at any date as at which the amount thereof shall be determined, "consolidated current assets" means all assets which should, in accordance with generally accepted accounting principles, be classified as current assets of the Company and its Subsidiaries, and "consolidated current liabilities" means all indebtedness and other liabilities which should, in accordance with generally accepted accounting principles, be classified as current liabilities of the Company and its Subsidiaries.

4.7 Duly pay and discharge, and cause its Subsidiaries to duly pay and discharge, all taxes, assessments and governmental charges upon the Company and its Subsidiaries, or against their respective properties, prior to the date on which penalties attach thereto, unless and to the extent only that such taxes shall be contested in good faith and by appropriate proceedings.

4.8 Duly pay and discharge, and cause its Subsidiaries to duly pay and discharge, all lawful claims, whether for labor, materials, supplies, services or anything else which might or could, if unpaid, become a lien or charge upon the properties or assets of the Company or any Subsidiary unless and to the extent only that the validity or amount thereof shall be contested in good faith and by appropriate proceedings.

4.9 Maintain, and cause each Subsidiary and Affiliate to maintain, its corporate existence, keep its property, and cause each Subsidiary to keep its properties, in good repair and carry on itself or through its Subsidiaries the business described in Section 5.14; keep and maintain in full force and effect the insurance referred to in Section 3.6 and the beneficiary designation as referred to in such Section.

4.10 Promptly give written notice to the Purchasers of (a) any action, proceeding or claim, of which the Company, any Subsidiary or Affiliate have notice, which may be commenced or asserted against the Company, any Subsidiary or Affiliate, unless such action, proceeding or claim involves payment of a fixed sum of money of less than $50,000 or is fully covered by insurance, (b) the occurrence or claimed occurrence of an event specified in Section 5.19 or 6.8, or (c) the occurrence of any other event specified in Section 6 within ten days after it becomes known to the Company.

4.11 Furnish promptly to each of the Purchasers, any subsequent modifications or amendments to any of the agreements or instruments referred to in herein.

4.12 Execute and deliver or cause to be delivered such further instruments and to do or cause to be done such further acts as may be reasonably necessary or proper to carry out the purposes of this Agreement.

Section 5. Negative Covenants

The Company covenants and agrees that, without the prior written consent of the Purchasers, it will not, so long as the Notes are outstanding:

5.1 Contract, create, incur, assume or suffer to exist, or permit any of its Subsidiaries to contract, create, incur, assume or suffer to exist, any mortgage, pledge, security interest, lien or other charge or encumbrance of any kind (including the charge upon property purchased under conditional sale or other title retention agreement) upon or with respect to any of its or their property or assets, whether now owned or hereafter acquired, except mortgages, pledges, security interests, liens or other charges or encumbrances as follows:

5.1.1 Liens in connection with workmen's compensation, unemployment insurance or other social security obligations;

5.1.2 Deposits or pledges securing the performance of bids, tenders, contracts (other than contracts for the payment of money), leases, statutory obligations, surety and appeal bonds and other obligations of like nature made in the ordinary course of business;

5.1.3 Mechanics', carriers', warehousemen's, workmen's, materialmen's or other like liens arising in the ordinary course of business with respect to obligations which are not due or which are being contested in good faith;

5.1.4 Liens for taxes, assessments, levies or governmental charges imposed upon the Company or its Subsidiaries or their respective properties, operations, income, products or profits, which shall not at the time be due or payable or if the validity thereof is being contested in good faith by appropriate proceedings;

5.1.5 Security interests on inventory and receivables securing indebtedness not exceeding $1,400,000 to Bankers Trust Company, under a Security Agreement dated March 21, 19__, a copy of which, together with all notes, commitment letters and other agreements with Bankers Trust Company, have been delivered to each of the Purchasers. It is understood that at its discretion, the Company may change the $1,400,000 indebtedness, or any part thereof, secured as provided in this Section 5.1.5, to a lender other than Bankers Trust Company.

5.1.6 Obligations in the form of leases, incurred for the purchase of real or personal property, provided that the aggregate purchase price of all such property subject to such leases shall not exceed $200,000.

5.1.7 Mortgage on the real property of the Company located at _____ and securing indebtedness of $865,460.17 on October 25, 19__, maturing December 1, 19__, with installments of $8210.42 payable monthly to _____ , and bearing interest at 10% per annum, a copy of which, together with all notes, commitment letters and other agreements with (_____) have been delivered to each of the Purchasers.

5.1.8 Mortgage on the real property of the Company's wholly owned subsidiary, _____, a Massachusetts corporation (_____) located at _____, and securing indebtedness of $185,480.84 on October 25, 19__, maturing July 29, 19__, with installments of $2088.46 payable monthly to _____, and bearing interest at 9½% per annum, a copy of which, together with all notes, commitment letters and other agreements with _____ have been delivered to each of the Purchasers.

5.1.9 Pledge of U.S. Treasury Bills and Notes aggregating not more than $89,000 to secure 6% notes outstanding in the amount of $81,065.64 on October 25, 19__, maturing May 1, 19__, with installments of $27,021.88 payable quarterly, due to former stockholders of the Company and of _____ (a predecessor since merged into the Company), copies of which notes, together with all commitment letters and other agreements with such stockholders have been delivered to each of the Purchasers.

5.1.10 Liens on equipment, furniture, fixtures and inventory of _____ located at _____ securing notes payable to _____, in the amount of $18,000 on Octoxer 25, 19__, maturing September 16, 19__, with installments of $9,000 each payable semi-annually and bearing interest at 6% per annum. A copy of the instrument creating such liens, together with all commitment letters and other agreements with _____, have been delivered to each of the Purchasers.

5.1.11 Any mortgage, encumbrance, security interest or other lien hereafter granted upon any property hereafter acquired by the Company or a Subsidiary created contemporaneously with such acquisition to secure or provide for the payment or financing of any part of the purchase price thereof, or the assumption of any mortgage, encumbrance, security interest or lien upon any such property hereafter acquired existing at the time of such acquisition, or the acquisition of any such property subject to any mortgage, encumbrance, security interest, or other lien without the assumption thereof, *provided* that the indebtedness secured by any such mortgage, encumbrance, security interest or lien so created, assumed or existing shall not exceed 80 percent of the cost of the property covered thereby to the Company or a Subsidiary acquiring or owning the same or of the fair value thereof (as determined in good faith by the Board of Directors of the Company) at the time of such acquisition, whichever is less, and *provided further* that every such mortgage, encumbrance, security interest or lien shall attach only to the property so acquired and fixed improvements thereto or the proceeds therefrom and that the aggregate principal amount of indebtedness secured by all mortgages, encumbrances and liens permitted by this Section 5.1.11 shall not in the aggregate for the Company and its Subsidiaries exceed at any one time outstanding the sum of $1,400,000; and

5.1.12 Any mortgage, encumbrance, security interest, or other lien securing the renewal, extension or refunding of any indebtedness secured by any mortgage, encumbrance, security interest or other lien permitted by Section 5.1.7, 5.1.8, or 5.1.11, *provided,* that the principal amount secured is not increased and that the mortgage, encumbrance, security interest or lien is not extended to any property or assets of the Company or any Subsidiary other than property formerly securing the indebtedness so renewed, extended or refunded.

5.2 Create, incur, assume or suffer to exist, or otherwise be, become or remain liable, directly or indirectly, or permit any Subsidiary to create, incur, assume or suffer to exist, or otherwise be, become or remain liable, directly or indirectly, on any indebtedness for borrowed money or any other liability evidenced by bonds, debentures, notes or similar instruments, except (a) to the Purchasers, (b) indebtedness referred to in Sections 5.1.5 to and including 5.1.12, (c) other outstanding or future unsecured indebtedness in the amount not to exceed $500,000.

5.3 Lend money or credit, or make or permit to be outstanding loans or advances, to any person, firm or corporation or other enterprise, or permit any Sub-

sidiary to lend, make or permit any thereof, except:

5.3.1 Loans or advances in the nature of prepayments to sub-contractors, suppliers, and others in the ordinary course of business;

5.3.2 Loans or advances by the Company to its wholly owned Subsidiaries and by wholly owned Subsidiaries to the Company or other wholly owned Subsidiaries;

5.3.3. Loans or advances to its Affiliate, not exceeding $100,000.

5.3.4 Advances to salesmen not exceeding $5,000 in the aggregate at any one time outstanding to all salesmen, or more than $2,000 to any one salesman.

5.4 Purchase, acquire or own, or make any investment in, or permit any Subsidiary to purchase, acquire or own, or make any invesment in, the stock or obligations of any person, firm, corporation or other enterprise or any government or instrumentality thereof, except (a) direct obligations of the United States of America, (b) certificates of deposit of banks having total assets in excess of one billion dollars, (c) stock of newly formed Subsidiaries having an aggregate cost _____ to the Company of not more than $10,000 and (d) the stock of _____ and _____ presently owned.

5.5 Agree to purchase or repurchase the indebtedness of, or assume, guarantee (directly or indirectly or by instrument having the effect of assuring another's payment or performance or capability of so doing), endorse, or otherwise become obligated upon the indebtedness, stock, dividend or other obligation of, any person, firm, corporation or other enterprise, or suffer any thereof to exist, or permit any Subsidiary so to do, except (a) by endorsement of negotiable instruments for deposit or collection in the ordinary course of business, (b) guaranties by the Company or a wholly owned Subsidiary of indebtedness of the Company or a wholly owned Subsidiary, or up to $100,000 of indebtedness of the Affiliate, or (c) guaranties by a Subsidiary of indebtedness of the Company or a wholly owned Subsidiary.

5.6 Wind up, liquidate its affairs or dissolve, or permit any Subsidiary except wholly owned Subsidiaries so to do; enter into any transaction of merger or consolidation, or permit any Subsidiary so to do, except mergers and consolidations between the Company, wholly owned Subsidiaries and other wholly owned Subsidiaries; convey, sell, lease or otherwise dispose of all or any substantial part of its assets or properties, or permit any Subsidiary to purchase or lease, any assets or properties if (i) such assets or properties would constitute a substantial part of the assets or properties of the Company or any Subsidiary and (ii) such purchase or lease would not be in the ordinary course of the business of the Company or any Subsidiary.

5.7 Enter into or be a party to, or permit any Subsidiary to enter into or be a party to, any arrangement providing for the leasing to the Company or any Subsidiary of real or personal property, provided that the Company and its Subsidiaries may enter into or be a party to such arrangements if (a) the aggregate of the rental payments for all such real or personal property would not exceed $100,000 per annum, and (b) the term of any such arrangement entered into after the date of this Agreement for any such property shall not exceed five years, *provided* that the foregoing shall not be deemed to prohibit leasing arrangements permitted in Section 5.1.6.

5.8 Declare or pay dividends upon any stock of the Company now or hereafter outstanding or return any capital to any of its stockholders or make any other distribution, payment or delivery of property or cash to its stockholders in their capacities as such, or redeem, retire, purchase or acquire, directly or indirecly, any shares of its stock now or hereafter outstanding, except as expressly permitted in the Shareholders' Agreement referred to in Section 3.13.

5.9 Enter into, or permit any Subsidiary to enter into, any arrangement with any bank, insurance company or other lender or investor providing for the leasing to the Company or any Subsidiary of real property now owned or hereafter acquired by the Company or any Subsidiary which at the time has been or is to be sold or transferred by the Company or any Subsidiary to such lender or investor, or on which one or more buildings have been or are to be constructed by such lender or investor for the purpose of leasing such property to the Company or any Subsidiary.

5.10 Sell, assign, or dispose of, or permit any Subsidiary to sell, assign or dispose of, any of its accounts receivable or any instrument evidencing, or executed in connection with, any such accounts receivable, except (a) as permitted in Section 5.1.5, and (b) assignment of accounts for collection.

5.11 Make, or permit its Subsidiaries to make, capital expenditures for fixed assets exceeding either (a) $150,000 in the aggregage for the Company and all such Subsidiaries in any fiscal year, or (b) $50,000 for any particular expenditure.

5.12 Pay or permit any Subsidiary to pay, directly or indirectly, as salary, finge benefits, expenses, drawing accounts, or otherwise, compensation for personal services to any officer, employee or stockholder or to any relative of any officer, employee or stockholder, or to any corporation or enterprise directly or indirectly affiliated with any officer, employee or stockholder, or to any person, firm, corporation or other enterprise, except that the Company or any Subsidiary may pay compensation for personal services in an amount not greater than the value of the services rendered, (a) to any one person who is not a stockholder, officer or employee up to $20,000 per year in the aggregate for the Company and all Subsidiaries, (b) to any one officer or employee not named in clause (c) of this Section 5.12 up to $40,000 per year in the aggregate for amounts indicated (it being understood (i) that such amounts may, but need not be, increased in the future by way of cost of living adjustments which shall not exceed seven percent for any one person within any twelve months' period; and (ii) that this provision is not intended to amend or modify in anyway the Employment Agreement intended to amend or modify in any way the Employment Agreements with _____ dated April 15, 19__ and August 20, 19__).

Name	Amount Per Year
	$120,000
	50,000
	50,000
	50,000
	45,000
	50,000
	50,000
	20,000

and, in addition, the Company and its Subsidiaries may reimburse their respective officers and employees for reasonable out-of-pocket expenses incurred in performing services for the Company; and may maintain reasonable major medical, hsopitalization and disability plans, employee group or term life insurance in accordance with policies in effect at the time of closing; and may continue the Company's Pension Plan as amended Jan. 1, 19__; _____ and shall be entitled to any compensation expressly provided in the Employment Agreement dated April 15, 19__ and August 20, 19__ which is in excess of $120,000 per annum; and the Company may maintain, or extend on similar terms, its existing Administrative Incentive Plan, Manufacturing Incentive Plan, and Inside Sales Incentive Plan.

5.13 Engage in any business other than that now conducted, namely designing, servicing, manufacturing and selling metal and plastic materials, including, but not limited to, wire cloth, wedge wire screens and fabricated products, used for filtration, separation and other purposes, in industries processing paper, wood pulp, food, minerals and other materials.

5.14 Engage, or permit any Subsidiary to engage, directly or indirectly or through other entities, in transactions with any director, officer, employee or stockholder, or any entity directly or indirectly affiliated with any of them, including the Affiliate, or for or on behalf of any director, officer, employee or stockholder, or any entity directly or indirectly affiliated with any of them, including the Affiliate, or at the request of any director, officer, employee or stockholder, or any entity directly or indirectly affiliated with any of them, including the Affiliate, which will result in the income or profits of the Company or any Subsidiary being transferred to any director, officer, employee or stockholder, or any entity directly or indirectly affiliated with any of them, including the Affiliate, or the losses of any corporation or other entity, including the Affiliate, being transferred to the Company or a Subsidiary; *provided, however,* that a director, officer, employee or stockholder shall not be deemed affiliated with any entity if such entity is a corporation the stock of which is actively traded on a national securities exchange or over the counter market and the sole affiliation of such director, officer, or employee or stockholder is title to a nominal number of shares purchased solely for investment purposes and without regard to any transactions with the Company.

5.15 Enter into or be a party to, or permit any Subsidiary to enter into or be a party to, any contract for the purchase or use of materials, supplies, or other property if such contract requires that payment for such materials, supplies or other property, or the use thereof, shall be made by the Company or such Subsidiary regardless of whether or not delivery is ever made of such materials, supplies or other property.

5.16 Enter into or be a party to or permit any Subsidiary to enter into or be a party to, any contract for the sale or use of materials, supplies or other property if such contract provides that payment to the Company or any Subsidiary for such materials, supplies or other property or the use thereof, shall be subordinated to any indebtedness (or any instrument evidencing such indebtedness) owed or to be owed to any person, firm, corporation or other enterprise.

5.17 Change, or permit any Subsidiary to change, its fiscal year.

5.18 Issue, or permit any Subsidiary to issue, any additional shares of stock of any class, including without limitation treasury shares.

5.19 Terminate any plan defined in Section 4021(a)

of Employee Retirement Income Security Act of 1974 ("Erisa") in respect of which the Company or any Subsidiary is an "employer" or a "substantial employer" as defined in Sections 3(5) and 4001(a)(2) of Erisa, respectively, so as to result in any material liability to the Pension Benefit Guaranty Corporation ("PBGC") established pursuant to Subtitle A of Title IV of Erisa; engage in any "prohibited transaction" (as defined in Section 4975 of the Internal Revenue Code of 1954, as amended) involving any such plan which would result in a material liability for an excise tax or civil penalty in connection therewith; or incur or suffer to exist any material "accumulated funding deficiency" (as defined in Section 302 of Erisa), whether or not waived, involving any such plan.

5.20 Except as provided in Section 5.15 and 5.16, nothing in this Section 5 shall be construed as restricting the dollar amount or length of term of any purchase of raw materials, supplies or inventory, or the sale of any of its products, which the Company may make in the ordinary course of its business.

Section 6. Events of Default

In the event that:

6.1 The Company defaults for more than twelve days after demand in the payment of (a) any principal or interest due on the Notes or any payment required to be made thereon, or (b) any other obligation for the payment of money to purchasers; or

6.2 Any representation or warranty made to Purchasers in writing in this Agreement, or in any certificate, application, agreement, or other instrument executed and delivered to them by any person, firm or corporation as provided in this Agreement or in connection with the financing contemplated in this Agreement, is false, inaccurate or incomplete in any material respect on the date as of which made; or

6.3 The Company or any Subsidiary defaults in the performance of any term, covenant, agreement, condition, undertaking, or provision of Section 5; or the Company or any Subsidiary defaults in the performance of any other term, covenant, agreement, condition, undertaking or provision of this Agreement or of any other agreement or instrument executed and delivered by the Company or any Subsidiary to the Purchasers as provided in this Agreement or in connection with the financing contemplated in this Agreement, and such default is not cured or waived within 30 days after it becomes known to the Company or after written notice thereof is given to the Company by either of the Purchasers; provided, however, the Company shall have sixty (60) days to cure any default otherwise provided for in this Section which default involves a fixed sum of money of $5,000 or less; or

6.4 The Company and its Subsidiaries suffer (a) a cumulative consolidated operating loss exceeding $100,000 incurred from June 30, 19 to the end of any interim or annual accounting period as disclosed in any financial statement provided for in Section 4.1, or (b) a consolidated operating loss exceeding $100,000 during any fiscal year as disclosed in the annual audited financial statement for such year provided for in Section 4.1.1; or

6.5 Any person, firm or corporation, shall acquire or shall for the first time control or be able to vote (directly or through nominees or beneficial ownership) after the date of this Agreement (other than through either Purchaser or as permitted in Section 9 or in the Shareholders' Agreement) more than ten percent of any class of stock of the Company having at the time power to vote for directors of the Company, which acquisition, control or ability to vote is not satisfactory to each of the Purchasers; or

6.6 The Certificate of Incorporation or By-Laws of the Company are at any time amended or modified from the forms thereof in effect immediately after the Closing, except for amendments to the By-Laws made for corporate housekeeping reasons and which do not adversely affect rights of the Purchasers or the holders of the Purchasers' Stock; or the stockholders of the Company fail, after request by the Purchasers, to elect and keep in office at least one director designated by Purchasers, but this shall not obligate the Purchasers to name any director; or

6.7 Any default occurs for a period longer than the grace period, if any, specified therefor under the provisions of any instrument evidencing indebtedness (including without limitation, any indebtedness assumed or guaranteed) of the Company or any Subsidiary for the payment of borrowed money or of any agreement relating thereto; or of any guarantee or assumption agreement; or if any obligation of the Company or any Subsidiary for the payment of borrowed money becomes or is declared to be due and payable prior to its expressed maturity, or is not paid when due; or

6.8 Any warrant of attachment, execution or other writ is levied upon any property or assets of the Company or any Subsidiary and is not discharged or stayed (including stays resulting from the filing of an appeal) within 60 days thereafter; or all or any substantial part of the assets or properties of the Company or any Subsidiary are condemned, seized or appropriated by any government or governmental authority; or any order is entered in any proceeding directing winding up, dissolution or split-up of the Company or any Subsidiary; or

6.9 The Company or any Subsidiary makes an assignment, for the benefit of creditors, or files a petition in bankruptcy as to itself, is adjudicated insolvent or bankrupt, petitions or applies to any tribunal for the appointment of any receiver of or any trustee for the Company or any Subsidiary or any substantial part of the property of the Company or any Subsidiary under any bankruptcy, reorganization, arrangement, readjustment of debt, dissolution or liquidation law or statute of any jurisdiction, whether now or hereafter in effect; or if there is commenced against the Company or any Subsidiary any such proceeding and an order approving the petition is entered or such proceeding remains undismissed for a period of 60 days, or the Company or any Subsidiary by any act indicates its consent to or approval of or acquiescence in any such proceeding or the appointment of any receiver of, or trustee for, the Company or any Subsidairy or any substantial part of their respective properties, or suffers any such receivership or trusteeship to continue undischarged for a period of 60 days; or

6.10 The occurrence of any event set forth in Section 4043(b) of Erisa with respect to, or the institution of proceedings by PBGC to have a trustee appointed to administer or to terminate, any plan referred to in Section 5.19, which event or institution of proceedings is, in the reasonable opinion of either Purchaser, likely to result in the termination of such plan and such termination would have a material adverse effect upon the business operations, assets or financial adverse effect upon the business corporations, assets or financial condition of the Company and its Subsidiaries as a consolidated entity, and the continuance of the same unremedied for 10 business days after notice of such event pursuant to Section 4043(a), (c) or (d) of Erisa is given or such proceedings are instituted, as the case may be; or a trustee shall be appointed by a United States District Court to administer any such plan with vested unfunded liabilities that are material in relation to the business operations, assets or financial condition of the Company and its Subsidiaries as a consolidated entity, or such plan shall be terminated;

then, and in any such event, and at any time thereafter, if such event shall then be continuing, either of the Purchasers may, by written notice to the Company, declare due and payable the principal of, and interest on, the Notes, whereupon the same shall be due and payable without presentment, demand, protest or other notice of any kind, all of which are hereby expressly waived.

Section 7. Consents; Agent

7.1 Any provision in this Agreement to the contrary notwithstanding, with the written consents of Purchasers holding 67% or more in principal amount of the Notes then outstanding hereunder, the Company may be relieved to the extent provided therein from the effect of any event of default or from compliance with any covenant, agreement or undertaking contained herein or in any instrument executed and delivered as herein provided, except in any case the terms of the Notes. Each Purchaser agrees that it will reply to any request from the Company for a consent hereunder within fifteen business days after it actually receives such request.

7.2 Each purchaser hereby designates Bankers Trust New York Corporation ("BTNY") to act as its agent under this Agreement and BTNY agrees to act as such agent. BTNY shall as agent act in accordance with the written instructions of the holders of 67% or more of the unpaid principal amount of the Notes (including those held by BTNY) and upon payment of its reasonable charges and the expenses anticipated in carrying out such instructions. BTNY shall be under no obligation as agent to see to the performance or enforcement of the covenants or agreements of this Agreement, the Notes, or any other instrument executed in connection with the financing contemplated in this Agreement. BTNY may employ agents and attorneys and take such other action as in its sole discretion appears necessary and proper to carry out the written instructions of the holders of the Notes and shall not be held liable or responsible for any neglect or misconduct of any agent or attorney appointed by it or for any unwise exercise of any duty, power or discretion, except for its own willful misconduct or gross negligence. The expenses of carrying out such agency shall be paid by all holders of the Notes (whether or not joining in executing written instructions to BTNY) *pro rata,* according to the outstanding principal amount of Notes held by each, and shall be due upon demand by BTNY. Each holder of Notes hereby indemnifies BTNY from any loss or liability it may suffer by reason of its acting as agent hereunder. BTNY shall hold any proceeds collected by it as such agent for the *pro rata* benefit of the holders of the Notes. BTNY may resign as agent upon 30 days written notice and the holders of 67% or more of the Notes then outstanding may appoint a successor, and the successor so appointed must be acceptable to and approved in writing by the Company, which consent shall not be unreasonably withheld. In any case, BTNY's resignation shall not be effective until its successor has been appointed.

Section 8. Investment Representations; Registration Agreements

8.1 The Purchasers severally acknowledge that the Notes and Purchasers' Stock are not being registered under the Securities Act of 1933 on the ground that the issuance of the Notes and Purchasers' Stock is exempt from registration under Section 4(2) of the Securities Act of 1933 as not involving any public offering, and that the Company's reliance on such exemption is predicated in part on the following representations and agreements made to the Company by the Purchasers severally:

8.1.1 Each is acquiring the Notes and Purchasers' Stock for investment for its or his own account, with no present intention of dividing its or his participation with others or reselling or otherwise distributing the same; and neither of the Purchasers is aware of any particular occasion, event or circumstance upon the occurrence or happening of which it intends to dispose of any Notes or Purchasers' Stock; subject, however, to Section 9.

8.1.2 Each is aware that the Notes and Purchasers' Stock constitute "restricted", "letter" or "investment" securities.

8.1.3 The knowledge and experience of each in financial and business matters is sufficient to enable it to (a) understand and utilize the type of information concerning the Company that would be provided by a registration statement under the Securities Act of 1933, (b) evaluate the risks of its investment in the Notes and Purchasers' Stock and (c) make an informed investment decision with respect thereto; and its financial resources are such that it is able to bear the economic risks of its investment in the Notes and Purchasers' Stock.

8.1.4 Except as provided in Section 9.1, neither of the Purchasers will sell or transfer all or any part of the Purchasers' Stock acquired by it unless and until it shall first have complied with the Shareholder Agreement referred to in Section 3.12, and the Company will place a legend in the form of Exhibit E on the Purchasers' Stock concerning the restrictions set forth therein.

8.2 Nothing contained in this Section 8 shall limit the full force or effect of any representation agreement or warranty made herein or in connection herewith to the Purchasers.

8.3 The Company has agreed that if there is a registration or registrations of the Company's Common Stock under the Securities Act of 1933 at any time or times in the future, the Company will give to the holders of the Purchasers' stock the same rights as given to the other holders of its Common Stock as to participating on a pro rata basis in such a registration or registrations.

Section 9. Participations of Investors; Transfers

9.1 The Company and BTCC understand that BTNY is or may be acting on behalf of itself and various Investors (not exceeding 15 persons) who are presently stockholders or directors of BTCC (the "Investors") and may wish to grant participations in the Notes and Purchasers' Stock to such Investors or some of them. The Company agrees that without notice to or consent by it (a) BTNY may grant such participations and (b) BTNY and the Investors may from time to time among themselves purchase and sell participations in the Notes and Purchasers' Stock. BTNY agrees that upon granting such participations and at the time of any such purchase or sale of participations it will notify the Company with respect thereto setting forth the name and address of each Investor holding a participation and describing the amount of such participation.

9.2 The Purchasers shall be entitled to assign and transfer all or any part of the Notes (and their related rights under this Agreement) held by such Purchaser, or any interest or participation therein, to not more than 15 persons provided each such assignee or transferee represents to the Company that such assignee or transferee is acquiring for investment and not with a view to distribution, and upon the assignment or transfer by a Purchaser of all or any part of the Notes or any interest or participation therein, the term Purchaser or Purchasers as used herein shall thereafter mean, to the extent thereof, the purchaser or purchasers of that interest. Subject to the restrictions of the preceding sentence, the Company will at any time, at its expense, at the request of the holder of a Note, and upon surrender of such Note for such purpose, issue a new Note in exchange therefor, payable to the order of the holder or such person or persons as may be designated by such holder, dated either (a) the last date to which interest has been paid on the surrendered Note or (b) the Closing Date, if such exchange shall take place prior to the due date of the first interest payment, in such denominations, which shall not be less than $1,000, as may be requested, in an aggregate principal amount equal to the unpaid principal amount of such Note so surrendered.

9.3 In case any of the Shareholders' shares are transferred to any other person (not in violation of this Agreement or the Shareholders' Agreement dated October 25, 1979) such other persons shall be entitled to receive from the Company copies of all financial statements and reports that the Company is required to furnish to the Purchasers under this Purchase Agreement.

Section 10. Effectiveness of Agreement

The covenants contained in this Agreement shall continue in full force and effect until the Notes and all indebtedness outstanding under this Agreement are paid in full, except that the covenants contained in Section 8.3, 9 and this 10, shall continue in full force and effect, after the payment of the Notes. Until the Company has securities registered under Section 12 of the Securities Exchange Act of 1934 or under the Securities Act of 1933, the Company will furnish to each holder of its Purchaser's Stock financial statements as required by Sections 4.1.1 and 4.1.2 of this Agreement. So long as any Purchaser is the holder of any stock of the Company, the Company will also comply with Sections 4.1.5 and 4.4 of this Agreement. So long as BTCC is a holder of any stock of the Company, the Company will also comply with Section 4.1.4. Where covenants continue to be binding and effective, any supplemental covenants shall be binding and effective.

Section 11. Subordination of Notes

11.1 Anything in this Agreement or the Notes to contrary notwithstanding, the indebtedness evidenced by the Notes shall be subordinate and junior in right of payment, to the extent and in the manner hereinafter set forth, to all indebtedness of the Company for money borrowed from banks or other financial institutions whether outstanding at the date of any of the Notes or incurred after the date of any of the Notes (such indebtedness to which the Notes are subordinate and junior being herein called "Superior Indebtedness").

11.2 In the event of any insolvency or bankruptcy proceedings, and any receivership, liquidation, reorganization or other similar proceedings in connection therewith, relative to the Company or to its creditors, as such, or to its property, and in the event of any proceedings for voluntary liquidation, dissolution or other winding up of the Company, whether or not involving insolvency or bankruptcy, then the holders of Superior Indebtedness shall be entitled in any such proceedings to receive payment in full of all principal and interest on all Superior Indebtedness before the holders of the Notes are entitled in any such proceedings to receive out of the assets of the Company any payment on account of principal or interest upon the Notes, and to that end (but subject to the power of a court of competent jurisdiction to make other equitable provisions reflecting the rights herein conferred upon the Superior Indebtedness and the holders thereof with respect to the subordinate indebtedness represented by the Notes and the holders thereof by a lawful plan of reorganization under applicable bankruptcy law) the holders of Superior Indebtedness shall be entitled in any such proceeding to receive for application in payment thereof any payment or distribution of any kind or character, whether in cash or property or securities, which may be payable or deliverable in any such proceedings out of the assets of the Company in respect of the Notes, except securities which are subordinate and junior to the payment of all Superior Indebtedness then outstanding.

11.3 The provisions of this Section 11 are solely for the purpose of defining the relative rights of the holders of Superior Indebtedness on the one hand, and the holders of the Notes on the other hand, and nothing herein shall impair, as between the Company and the holder of any Note, the obligation of the Company, which is unconditional and absolute, to pay to the holder thereof, the principal and interest thereon in accordance with its terms, nor shall anything herein prevent the holder of a Note from exercising all remedies otherwise permitted by applicable law or otherwise, subject to the rights, if any, under this Section 11 of the holders of Superior Indebtedness to receive cash, property or securities otherwise payable or deliverable out of the assets of the Company to the holders of the Notes. No present or future holder of Superior Indebtedness shall be prejudiced in such holder's right to enforce a subordination of the Notes (to the extent and in the manner herein provided) by any act or failure to act on the part of the Company.

11.4 Anything in this Agreement or the Notes to the contrary notwithstanding, any payment or prepayment of principal of or interest on the Notes received out of the assets of the Company by the holders of the Notes shall become the sole and absolute property of the holders of the Notes and shall not, by virtue of the provisions of this Section 11 or otherwise, be subject to any payment over or any distribution to or claim by any holders of Superior Indebtedness or any other person, unless at the time of receipt of such payment or prepayment the holder so receiving such payment had actual notice from a holder of Superior Indebtedness of the occurrence of an event specified in Section 11.2

Section 12. Miscellaneous

12.1 All notices, requests, demands or other communications to or upon the respective parties hereto shall be deemed to have been given or made, and all financial statements information and the like required to be delivered hereunder shall be deemed to have been delivered, when deposited in the mails, postage pre-

paid, addressed to the Company at _____ and to the Purchasers at their respective addresses set forth on Exhibit A, or to such other address as any of them shall specify in writing to the others. The Company will maintain a register of the holders of the Notes, which shall contain the last address specified to the Company as provided in the preceding sentence. No other method of giving notice is hereby precluded. Upon request of any Purchaser, the Company will deliver to such Purchaser, at the Company's expense, up to six additional copies of all financial statements, information and the like required hereunder.

12.2 No failure or delay on the part of the Purchasers or any of them in exercising any right, power or privilege hereunder, and no course of dealing between the Company and the Purchasers or any of them shall operate as a waiver thereof nor shall any single or partial exercise of any right, power or privilege hereunder preclude the simultaneous or later exercise of any other right, power or privilege. The rights and remedies herein expressly provided are cumulative and not exclusive of any rights or remedies which the Purchasers or any of them would otherwise have. No notice to or demand on the Company in any case shall entitle the Company to any other or further notice or demand in similar or other circumstances or constitute a waiver of the rights of the Purchasers or any of them to take any other or further action in any circumstances without notice or demand.

12.3 This Agreement may not be changed or terminated orally and shall be binding upon the Company and the Purchasers and their successors and assigns. All agreements, representations and warranties made herein or in connection herewith shall survive the delivery of the Notes and Purchasers' Stock. This Agreement may be executed in any number of counterparts and all of such counterparts taken together shall be deemed to consitute one and the same one and the same instrument.

12.4 The Purchasers shall not be jointly obligated hereunder; their obligations are several. The sales of Notes and Purchasers' Stock to the Purchasers shall be deemed a separate sale to each Purchaser. Notwithstanding any provision of this Agreement, the Company shall not be obligated to sell less than all of the Notes and Purchasers' Stock hereunder.

12.5 The Company and the Purchasers represent and warrant to the other that each has employed no brokers, agents or finders in carrying on the negotiations relating to this Agreement or to the financing herein contemplated and the Company and the Purchasers, respectively, shall indemnify and hold the others and each of them harmless from any loss, liability or obligation incurred by them or any of them by reason of the breach of the aforesaid representaion and covenant.

12.6 Whether or not the transactions herein contemplated shall be consummated, the Company agrees to pay and save the Purchasers and the Investors and each of them harmless against liability for the payment of all out-of-pocket expenses arising in connection with the preparation, execution, delivery, administration and enforcement of this Agreement, the Notes, any security therefor, and the Purchasers' Stock, including the reasonable fees and expenses of _____ or other counsel selected by the Purchasers (which counsel fees shall not exceed $3,000 in the event the transaction herein contemplated shall not be consummated).

12.7 Upon receipt of evidence reasonably satisfactory to the Company of the loss, theft, destruction or mutilation of any Note or certificate evidencing any Purchasers' Stock and of a letter of indemnity reasonably satisfactory to the Company, and upon reimbursement to the Company and all reasonable expenses incident thereto, and upon surrender or cancellation of such Note or certificate, if mutilated, the Company will make and deliver a new Note or certificate of like tenor in lieu of such lost, stolen, destroyed or mutilated Note or certificate.

12.8 The Purchasers agree among themselves that, with respect to all sums received by the Purchasers applicable to the payment of principal of or interest on the Notes, equitable adjustment will be made among the Purchasers so that, in effect, all such sums shall be shared ratably by all of the Purchasers whether received by voluntary payment, by realization upon security, by the exercise of the right of setoff, by counter-claim or cross-action or by the enforcement of any or all of the Notes. If any Purchaser receives any payment on its Notes of a sum or sums in excess of its *pro rata* portion, then such Purchasers receiving such excess payment shall purchase for cash from the other Purchasers an interest in their Notes in such amounts as shall result in a ratable participation by all of the Purchasers in the aggregate unpaid amount of Notes then outstanding.

12.9 Calculations hereunder shall be made and financial data required hereby shall be prepared, both as to classification of items and as to amounts, in accordance with generally accepted accounting principles consistently applied.

12.10 This Agreement and the rights and obligations of the parties hereunder and under the Notes shall be construed in accordance with and be governed by the laws of the State of New York.

IN WITNESS WHEREOF, the parties hereto have executed and delivered this Agreement as of the day and year first above written.

BY _____
President

Accepted and Agreed to:

BANKERS TRUST NEW YORK CORPORATION

By _____
Vice President

BT CAPITAL CORPORATION

By _____
Treasurer

EXHIBIT A

Name and Address of Purchaser	Percentage of participation in Notes	Dollar participation in Notes	Number of Shares	Purchase Price of Shares
Bankers Trust New York Corporation 280 Park Avenue New York, New York	85.00%	$ 935,000	127.5	$ 25,500
BT Capital Corporation 39th Floor 600 Third Avenue New York, New York	15.00%	$ 165,000	22.5	$ 4,500
	100%	$1,100,000	150	$ 30,000

EXHIBIT B

New York, New York
October 25, 19__

FOR VALUE RECEIVED, the undersigned _____, a New York corporation (herein called the "Company"), hereby promises to pay to the order of _____ at the office of Bankers Trust New York Corporation, 280 Park Avenue, City, County and State of New York, the principal sum of _____ in lawful money of the United States of America, on or before September 30, 19__.

The unpaid principal balance of this Note shall bear interest from the date hereof until paid in like money at the rate of 13% per annum, payable on the first full business day of each calendar month commencing December, 19__, and at maturity of prior prepayment in full of the Notes.

This Note is one of a series of Subordinated Notes (the "Notes") identical in all respects except as to the principal amount and payee, issued by the Company in the aggregate principal amount of $1,100,000 pursuant to and subject to the terms of a certain Purchase Agreement dated October 25, 19___ (the "Purchase Agreement") between the Company and the original Purchasers listed on Exhibit A attached thereto. Reference is made to the Purchase Agreement for a description of the agreements of the parties, the extent to which the Notes are subordinated in right of payment to the Superior Indebtedness as defined in the Purchase Agreement, and the circumstances under which the maturity of the Notes may be accelerated. In the event that the Notes are declared due and payable prior to their expressed maturity, the same shall become due and payable without presentment, demand, protest or notice of any kind, all of which are hereby expressly waived.

The Company has the right to repay this Note in whole or under certain circumstances in part at any time or from time to time and, as provided in the Purchase Agreement, the Company is required to make certain mandatory prepayments on the Notes.

This Note is made and delivered in the City and State of New York.

By _____ _____

, President

EXHIBITS C and D

PURCHASE AGREEMENT

Amendments to the Certificate of Incorporation and By-Laws of _____ to be adopted by directors and shareholders.

JOINT ACTION BY UNANIMOUS WRITTEN CONSENT OF THE BOARD OF DIRECTORS AND SHAREHOLDERS OF

The undersigned, being all of the shareholders and all of the members of the Board of Directors of _____ a New York Corporation, in accordance with the authority contained in Sections 615 and 708, respectively, of the Business Corporation Law of the State of New York, hereby unanimously consent and agree to take and by the execution hereof do take the following actions:

RESOLVED: That the President be and he is hereby authorized and directed in the name and on behalf of the Corporation to execute and deliver two certain agreements dated October ___, 19___ to which Bank-

ers Trust New York Corporation, BT Capital Corporation and others are parties, hereinafter respectively referred to as the "Purchase Agreement" and the "Shareholder's Agreement"; and further

RESOLVED: That Article Fourth of the Certificate of Incorporation of the Corporation be amended to read in its entirety as follows: "The principal business office of the Corporation shall be located in the County of _____, State of New York."; and, further

RESOLVED: That Article Sixth of the Certificate of Incorporation of the Corporation be amended to read in its entirety as follows: "The number of directors of the Corporation shall be not less than three nor more than nine." and, further

RESOLVED: That Article Seventh (a) of the Certificate of Incorporation of the Corporation be amended to read in its entirety as follows: "(a) The votes of the holders of 76 percent or more of the outstanding voting shares shall be necessary to amend the By-Laws of the Corporation."; and, further

RESOLVED: That Article Seventh (b) of the Articles of Incorporation of the Corporation be amended to read in its entirety as follows: "(b) Amendments to the Articles of Incorporation shall be authorized only by (i) the Board of Directors pursuant to Subsection 803(b) of the New York Business Corporation Law with respect to the matters set forth in such Subsection; or (ii) the vote of the holders of 76 percent or more of the outstanding voting shares of stock of the Corporation."; and further

RESOLVED: That an Article Eighth be added to the Certificate of Incorporation of the Corporation to read in its entirety as follows: "Eighth. Any issued and outstanding stock of the Corporation, from time to time, held by any person who is a party to or subject to the Shareholder's Agreement dated October ___, 19___, on file with the Secretary of the Corporation transferred after the date of said Agreement, other than through Sale Priority pursuant to Paragraph 3 of said Agreement, shall, upon such transfer, become non-voting unless such transfer is to _____ Bankers Trust New York Corporation, or BT Capital Corporation."; and further

RESOLVED: That, at such time as the loans by Bankers Trust New York Corporation and BT Capital Corporation to the Corporation pursuant to the Purchase Agreement dated October ___, 19___ shall have been repaid, the Shareholders agree to vote in favor of an amendment of the Certificate of Incorporation of the Corporation to reduce the percentage of the outstanding voting shares required to amend the Certificate of Incorporation of the Corporation and the By-Laws of the Corporation from 76 percent to 60 percent, and, further

RESOLVED: That Article I, Section I of the

Corporation's By-Laws be amended to read in its entirety as follows: "The number of directors of the Corporation shall be not less than three nor more than nine, and shall be annually elected by ballot at the annual meeting of the shareholders. They shall serve for the term of one year and until such time as their successors are elected. Any vacancy in the Board of Directors, caused by death, resignation or otherwise, may be filled by the remaining directors of the balance of the year, and until the next annual election."; and further

RESOLVED: That Article I, Section V of the Corporation's By-Laws be amended to read in its entirety as follows: "The Corporation shall not enter into any contract, agreement, understanding or any other commitment or arrangement, except for routine purchases of materials used by the Corporation or routine sale of products of the Corporation, which extends for a period in excess of one year or which involves a commitment of a principal amount in excess of $150,000 in the aggregate or exceeding $50,000 for any particular expenditure in any fiscal year without the prior consent of the greater of (a) three (3) directors or, (b) a majority of directors then in office."; and further

RESOLVED: That Article II, Section III of the Corporation's By-Laws be amended to read in its entirety as follows: "At all meetings of shareholders, all motions and resolutions shall be passed only upon the affirmative vote of the holders of 76 percent or more of the outstanding voting shares of stock of the Corporation prior to the repayment in full of the loans plus interest thereon, by Bankers Trust New York Corporation pursuant to the Purchase Agreement dated October __, 19__ and 60 percent or more of such shares thereafter, to authorize the Corporation to:

(A) Issue any additional shares of its capital stock including treasury shares;

(B) Purchase on a pro-rata basis from all of its Shareholders as defined in the Shareholders Agreement dated October __, 19__ any shares of its own common stock at a price in excess of the Purchase Price as defined in said Agreement;

(C) Waive any provision of the Shareholders' Agreement of October __, 19__ on the part of the Corporation;

(D) Sell any of its assets of a value in excess of one hundred thousand dollars ($100,000) during any fiscal quarter, other than in the ordinary course of its business;

(E) Merge or consolidate into or with another corporation;

(F) Increase the number of directors to more than three."; and further,

RESOLVED: That _____ be and hereby is elected Vice President of this Corporation to serve at the pleasure of the Board; and further,

RESOLVED: That a certain Employment Agreement entered into between the Corporation and _____ dated August 20, 19__ be and the same hereby is ratified, confirmed and approved and the Vice-President __be and hereby is authorized to execute and deliver said Agreement in the name and on behalf of the Corporation; and further,

RESOLVED: That the appropriate officers of this Corporation be, and each of them hereby is, authorized and directed to execute and file in behalf of the Corporation any and all documents, certificates and other instruments and to take any and all action which may be necessary or desirable in order to effectuate the foregoing resolutions, including without limitation the provisions of the Purchase Agreement and the Shareholders' Agreement.

IN WITNESS WHEREOF, the parties to this action have affixed or caused to be affixed their hands this__ day of October 19__.

BOARD OF DIRECTORS:
SHAREHOLDERS:
Bankers Trust New York Corporation

_____ by _____
BT Capital Corporation
_____ by _____
_____ _____
_____
_____
_____

Filed with the undersigned on October__, 19

_____
Secretary of

EXHIBIT E

Legend on Common Stock

Each share of Common Stock shall bear the following legend on the face thereof:

"The shares represented hereby have not been registered under the Securities Act of 1933, as amended, and the transfer of such shares is subject to the restrictions set forth in a Shareholders' Agreement dated October 25, 19__ among _____ and the Shareholders named therein. Copies of said Shareholders' Agreement are available for inspection at the office of _____ and no transfer of said shares shall be valid or effective unless and until the terms and conditions of said Shareholders' Agreement in respect of transfer shall have been complied with.''

EXHIBIT F

Common Stock Outstanding
After Closing

Name	Shares
	240
	60
	100
	50
Bankers Trust New York Corp. 280 Park Avenue New York, N.Y. 10017	127.5
BT Capital Corporation 39th Floor 600 Third Avenue New York, N.Y. 10016	22.5
Treasury Shares	400
Total	1,000

EXHIBIT F (Continued)

Common Stock Outstanding
Immediately Prior to Closing

Name	Shares
	240
	60
	100
	50
	330
	75
	75
	50
Treasury Shares	20
Total	1,000

PURCHASE AGREEMENT

THIS AGREEMENT is made this ____ day of September, 19__ by and between _____ an Ohio corporation (the ''Seller''), and _____ an Ohio corporation (the ''Buyer'').

WHEREAS, Seller desires to sell and Buyer desires to purchase all of the assets of Seller's Tractor Division (the ''Division'') other than its cash, receivables and prepaid expenses upon the terms hereinafter set forth;

NOW, THEREFORE, in consideration of the premises and the mutual covenants herein contained, the parties hereto, intending to be legally bound hereby, agree as follows:

I. BASIC TERMS OF TRANSACTION

1.1 Sale of Assets. Seller hereby agrees to sell, transfer, assign and deliver to Buyer on the Closing Date (as hereinafter defined), and Buyer hereby agrees to purchase from Seller, free and clear of all liens, security interests, charges and encumbrances, all of the Division's assets and business as a going concern, of every kind, nature and description and wherever stiuated, tangible and intangible, owned by Seller at the close of business on the Closing Date, including, but not limited to: the Division's land, plant facility and office space located at a legal description of which is attached hereto as Exhibit A, machinery and equipment (including, but not limited to, those items set forth on Exhibit B), furniture, office equipment, business machines, vehicles, inventory (including, but not limited to, the raw materials, work in process, finished goods and supplies set forth on Exhibit C), trade secrets, know-how, trade names, trademarks, logos, rights under contracts, tooling, patterns, dies, jigs, fixtures, patents, product designs and claims, rights, choses in action, operating data and records (including customer lists, credit information and correspondence), and all rights to use, to the exclusion of Seller, the names _____ and _____ either alone or in conjunction with other words, EXCEPT, however, for the following assets of the Division which shall not be included in the purchase and sale transaction herein contemplated:

(a) the Division's accounts receivable existing on the Closing Date;

(b) the Division's prepaid expenses existing on the Closing Date; and

(c) the Division's cash and bank deposits existing on the Closing Date.

The assets of the Division being purchased and sold hereunder are hereinafter called the ''Acquired Assets.'' Coincident with such sale, assignment and transfer Seller shall place Buyer in effective possession and control of the Acquired Assets.

1.2 Purchase Price. Buyer agrees to pay Seller the following separately identifiable purchase price for the Acquired Assets:

(a) for the Division's inventory of finished goods, raw materials, supplies and work in process, a purchase price of _____ ($_____); which shall be allocated among the items of inventory in the manner set forth in Exhibit C;

(b) for the Division's land, plant facility, and office space located at _____, a purchase price of _____ which shall be allocated $_____ to the building comprising the office space and plant facility; and

(c) for all other Acquired Assets a purchase price of _____ ($_____) which shall be allocated among the Acquired Assets in the manner set forth in Exhibit B attached hereto.

Seller shall, prior to the Closing Date, conduct a physical count of all inventory of the Division in the presence of a representative of Buyer, which shall be adjusted to the Closing Date for activity subsequent to said count. Said physical count, as so adjusted, shall be used as the basis for determining pursuant to Section 2.1 the increase or reduction (if any) in the purchase price of said inventory as stated above.

1.3 Assumed Liabilities. Buyer agrees to assume, perform and/or discharge the following obligations and liabilities of the Division (the ''Assumed Liabilities''):

(a) all customers' orders relating to the purchase of the Division's products, accepted in the ordinary and usual course of business, which are on hand and unfilled or incomplete as of the Closing Date (all of which are set forth on Exhibit D) and all orders for the purchase by the Division of goods, materials and supplies, entered into in the ordinary and usual course of business, which are outstanding and unfilled or incomplete as of the Closing Date (all of which are set forth on Exhibit D);

2. PAYMENT OF PURCHASE PRICE

2.1 Inventory Purchase Price. The purchase price for the inventory of the Division, computed according to the provisions of Subsection 1.2(a) shall be paid by check at Closing in the amount of $_____ subject to the reconciliation provided for below.

It is the intention of the parties that Buyer shall purchase all of the Divison's inventory but that Buyer be obligated to pay for hereunder only such inventory of Seller relating to the Division which is not defective, substandard, obsolete or slow moving in every case where the same had remained in Seller's inventory of finished goods for and has not been sold during a period of one (1) year from the date it was manufactured. Subject to the foregoing standards, the purchase price for all the Division's inventory of raw material, work in process, finished goods and supplies shall be either reduced or increased dollar for dollar to the extent the Division's inventory on hand at Closing (valued at the lower of actual cost or net realizable value) is (a) either greater or less than _____ _____ and (b) not defective, substandard, obsolete or slow moving. Said inventory shall be certified by an officer of the Company based upon inventory taken by Price Waterhouse & Co.

2.2 Other Acquired Assets Purchase Price. The purchase price for all the other Acquired Assets shall be paid at the Closing by check in the amount of $_____ and by delivery of Buyer's Subordinated Promissory Note in the principal amount as set forth in Exhibit E.

3. ADDITIONAL COVENANTS AND UNDERTAKINGS

3.1 Bulk Sales Law. Buyer and Seller agree to waive compliance with any laws relating to the bulk sales and bulk transfers applicable to the transaction contemplated by this Agreement, and in consideration of such waiver Seller agrees to defend and indemnify Buyer against and hold it harmless from any and all loss, liability, damage or expense (including all reasonable costs and expenses, including attorneys' fees) arising out of or resulting from such noncompliance.

3.2 Change of Name. Promptly after the Closing, Seller shall cease to use the names _____ and _____ or any other trade name heretofore used in connection with the Division's business.

3.3 Pro-Ration of Labor Costs. Seller shall, as promptly as reasonably possible after the Closing or the date payable, if later, pay directly or reimburse Buyer for all compensation of employees of the Division (including FICA contributions) earned for services rendered prior to the Closing together with Seller's pro rata share of the cost of any and all fringe benefits of said employees for the period prior to the Closing including, but not limited to, life and disability insurance premiums, contributions to health and welfare or supplemental unemployment benefit plans and other fringe benefits set forth in the Labor Agreement. Seller's pro rata share of any such expense which is payable periodically for a period ending subsequent to the Closing shall be equal to such expense multiplied by the ratio that the number of days in such period occurring prior to Closing bears to the total number of days in the period. Notwithstanding anything herein to the contrary, Seller shall, within 10 days after the Closing, pay to Buyer in cash an amount equal to the full amount of all vacation pay and sick leave accrued or accruable as of the Closing for all employees of the Division.

3.4 Assignments. Seller agrees to obtain and deliver to Buyer at the Closing duly executed consents to the assignment and transfer by Seller to Buyer of all rights of the Division in and to all agreements, commitments, and other specific assets and properties to be assigned and transferred to Buyer hereunder in all instances in which the same may, in the opinion of Buyer's counsel, be necessary to vest in Buyer all of the Seller's right, title and interest therein and thereto.

Notwithstanding anything herein to the contrary, to the extent the assignment of any right to be assigned to Buyer pursuant to the provisions hereof shall require the consent of any other party, or shall be subject to any equity or option in any other person by virtue of a request for permission to assign or transfer, or by reason of or precedent to any transfer to Buyer, this Agreement shall not constitute a breach thereof or create rights in others not desired by Buyer. Seller shall use its best efforts to procure consent to any such assignment. If any such consent is not obtained, Seller shall cooperate with Buyer in any reasonable arrangement designed to provide for Buyer the benefit of any such right, including enforcement of any; and all rights of Seller against the other party to any contract arising out of the breach or cancellation thereof by such party or otherwise.

3.6 Purchase of Plant Facility. Simultaneous with the Closing Seller shall execute and deliver to Buyer a general warranty deal pursuant to which Seller will transfer and convey free and clear of all liens, encumbrances, charges and imperfections of title, all its right, title and interest in and to the real property comprising its plant and office facility located at a complete legal description of which is contained in Exhibit A.

3.7 Transfer and Sales Taxes. Seller shall pay directly, unless Buyer is required to tender payment in which case Seller shall promptly reimburse Buyer for, all sales or other transfer taxes, if any, applicable to the transaction contemplated by this Agreement.

3.8 Further Assurances and Assistance. Buyer and Seller agree that each will execute and deliver to the other any and all documents in addition to those expressly provided for herein that may be necessary or appropriate to effectuate the provisions of this Agreement, whether before, at or after the Closing. Seller

further agrees that at any time and from time to time after the Closing, it will execute and deliver to Buyer such further assignments or other written assurances as Buyer may reasonably request to perfect and protect Buyer's title to the Acquired Assets.

The parties agree to cooperate with each other to any extent reasonably required in order to fully accomplish the transaction herein contemplated and put Buyer in possession and control of the Acquired Assets. The parties acknowledge that the customers of Seller and other third parties may not fully and immediately appreciate the consequences of the transaction herein contemplated, and Seller and Buyer each agree to remit promptly to the other any payments received by such party which are properly for the account of the other.

3.9 Employee Pension Benefit Plans. Seller shall take all necessary measures including, where applicable, adopting or causing to be adopted appropriate amendments to its relevant employee pension benefit plan (as such term is defined in Section 3 (2) of The Employee Retirement Income Security Act of 1974), to fully vest every person employed by the Division as of the Closing Date, in his accrued benefits, determined as of the Closing Date, under the relevant employee pension benefit plans, and, for all purposes of said employee pension benefit plans, to treat such employees as participants who have terminated their employment with the Division.

4. THE CLOSING

4.1 Time and Place of Closing. The transfers and deliveries to be made pursuant to this Agreement shall take place at the Closing at the offices of _____ at 10:00 A.M., local time, on _____,1978, or such other place, time and/or date as Seller and Buyer agree upon in writing (the "Closing Date"), and shall be deemed to be effective as of the begining of business on the Closing Date.

4.2 Deliveries at the Closing. At the Closing, Buyer and Seller respectively shall deliver the following documents in substitution therefor as are satisfactory to the recipient:

(a) Seller shall deliver to Buyer:
   (i) an Incumbency Certificate with respect to the officers of Seller executing documents or instruments on behalf of Seller;
   (ii) good standing certificates for Seller from the Secretary of State of Ohio dated not more than 10 days prior to the Closing Date;
   (iii) certified copies of the proceedings of Seller's Board of Directors and Shareholders with respect to approval of this

Agreement and authorization of the consummation by Seller of the transaction herein contemplated;

(iv) the certificate specified in Subsection 9.1.1;

(v) such bills of sale, endorsements, assignments and other good and sufficient instruments of transfer as shall be deemed necessary or appropriate by counsel for Buyer to transfer and assign to Buyer good and marketable title to the Acquired Assets;

(vi) the general warranty deed described in Section 3.6;

(vii) an appropriate amendment to the Labor Agreement, in form and substance satisfactory to the parties and their respective counsel, substituting Buyer as the employer thereunder, properly executed by Seller and the union; and

(viii) an opinion of Seller's counsel in form and substance satisfactory to Buyer confirming Seller's representations and warranties set forth in Sections 5.1, 5.2, 5.9 (first sentence only), and 5.17.

(b) Buyer shall deliver to Seller:

(i) an Incumbency Certificate with respect to officers of Buyer executing documents or instruments on behalf of Buyer;

(ii) a good standing certificate for Buyer from the Secretary of State of Ohio dated not more than 10 days prior to the Closing Date;

(iii) certified copies of the proceedings of Buyer's Board of Directors with respect to approval of this Agreement and authorization of the consummation by Buyer of the transactions herein contemplated;

(iv) the certificate specified in Subsection 9.2.1;

(v) Buyer's check in the aggregate amount determined pursuant to Sections 2.1(a) and 2.2;

(vi) Buyer's Subordinated Promissory Note executed by Buyer in the form set forth in Exhibit E;

(vii) an instrument evidencing the assumption by Buyer of those obligations of Seller described in Section 1.3; and

(viii) the amendment referred to in Subsection 4.2(a) (vii), properly executed by Buyer.

5. REPRESENTATIONS AND WARRANTIES OF SELLER

As an inducement to Buyer to enter into this Agreement and consummate the transaction contemplated herein, Seller represents and warrants to Buyer as follows:

5.1 Organization; Corporate Power; Qualification. Seller (i) is a corporation duly organized, validly existing and in good standing under the laws of the State of Ohio; (ii) has all requisite corporate power and authority to own the Acquired Assets and to sell and transfer the Acquired Assets to Buyer; and (iii) has all requisite corporate power and authority to own, lease and operate the properties of the Division and carry on its business as and where such properties are now owned or leased and such business is presently being conducted. Seller is qualified to do business as a foreign corporation in the State of _____ _____ and, to the best of Seller's knowledge and belief, the business and properties of the Division do not require that Seller be qualified as a foreign corporation in any other jurisdiction.

5.2 Title to Property. Seller has, and at the Closing, Buyer will be vested with good and marketable title to all of the Acquired Assets free and clear of any liens, security interests, claims, charges, restrictions, easements or other encumbrances.

5.3 Use of Premises. Seller has all necessary permits and licenses with respect to its operation of the business of the Division, all of which are valid and continuing. Seller's use of the factory and office facilities of the Division, including all machinery and equipment, conforms to all applicable environmental, safety, health, building, zoning or other laws, ordinances and regulations. Seller has received no notice of any zoning, health, safety or other violations or of any assessments, either general or special, relating to the operations or properties of the Division.

5.4 Contracts. Seller is not a party to or bound by, nor has it any rights under, any contract or commitment relating to the Division except for (i) the customer orders and purchase orders listed on Exhibit D all of which were entered into in the ordinary course of business, (ii) the Labor Agreement, and (iii) the *(names of all employee pension benefit plans)* to which Seller contributes with respect to employees of the Division. Seller has not defaulted, nor is there a valid basis to claim any such default on the part of Seller, under any of the customer orders or purchase orders listed on Exhibit D or under the Labor Agreement. None of the customer orders listed on Exhibit D nor any outstanding binding quotation with respect to the products or services of the Division involves the future sale and/or delivery of products or services of the Division at prices other than the Division's regular prices as in effect at the time of delivery.

5.5 <u>Compensation and Benefits</u>. Exhibit F sets forth a complete listing and description of all current compensation and benefits for each employee of the Division.

5.6 <u>Proprietary Rights</u>. With respect to the conduct of the business of the Division, Seller does not own or use any patents, inventions (whether or not patentable) trademarks, copyrights or service marks other than those set forth on Exhibit G attached hereto, and with respect thereto Seller has not received any notice or claim of conflict with the asserted rights of others. Seller is not required to pay any royalty, license fee or similar type of compensation in connection with the current or prior conduct of the business of the Division.

5.7 <u>Employment of Labor</u>. Seller has complied in all material respects with all applicable Federal and state laws and local ordinances relating to the employment of labor of the Division, including the provisions thereof relating to wages, hours, employee benefit plans (as defined in Section 3(3) of the U.S. Employee Retirement Income Security Act of 1974) and the payment of social security taxes, and is not liable for any arrearages of wages or any tax or penalties for failure to comply with any of the foregoing. There are no controversies pending or, to the knowledge of Seller threatened, between the Seller and any employees of the Division, nor have there been any such controversies within the past three years. Seller has complied with all Federal and state labor laws, if any, applicable to the transaction contemplated by the Agreement. In the event of any labor dispute arising after the Closing based upon acts arising prior to the Closing or as a result of this transaction, Seller agrees to cooperate with Buyer in the resolution of any such disputes and agrees to hold Buyer harmless from any costs and expenses including reasonable attorney fees incurred in connection therewith.

5.8 <u>Books and Records</u>. The books and records of Seller relating to the Division are in all material respects correct and complete, and have been maintained in accordance with sound business practices.

5.9 <u>Litigation</u>. There is no litigation, proceeding or governmental investigation existing or pending, or any order, injunction or decree outstanding, against Seller with respect to the Division or its assets or business, nor does Seller know or have reasonable grounds to know of any basis for any such litigation, proceeding or governmental investigation. Seller is not, with respect to the Division, acting, or suffering to exist a condition which is, in material contravention or violation of any applicable law, regulation, ordinance, order, injunction or decree, or any other requirement of any governmental body or court, nor has Seller failed to remedy any such previously existing violation.

5.10 <u>Acquisition Balance Sheet</u>. The unaudited balance sheet for the Division for the period ending September 30 is set forth on Exhibit H (hereinafter the "Division Balance Sheet"). The Division Balance Sheet has been prepared in conformity with generally accepted accounting principles, consistently applied, and presents fairly the financial condition of the Division at the date stated.

5.11 <u>Real Property</u>. Exhibit A contains a description of the real property owned or used by the Division, the legal description thereof, and lists all the buildings and facilities pertaining to the operation of the Division as of the date hereof. Seller owns all such real property and has good and marketable title thereto, free and clear of all mortgages, hypothecs, liens, charges, pledges, security interests, encumbrances and other claims whatsoever except as disclosed in Exhibit I, none of which materially interfere with the operations of the business or the marketability of the premises. All buildings and other improvements to the real property are situated wholly within the limits of the real property and there are no encroachments on the real property of buildings or structures adjacent thereto. Seller's operations on and use of real property in connection with the operation of the Division conform to applicable zoning regulations, including use, set-back and area requirements, and other restrictions and covenants on the use of said real property. The real property and all improvements located thereon comply in all material respects with all other applicable municipal and other governmental law, by-laws, orders, regulations and restrictions including, without limitation, those with respect to building, safety, fire protection, access, parking, pollution, elevators and boilers. Seller has not received, nor does it have any knowledge of, any notice of violation or any zoning regulations, ordinance or other law, regulation or requirement applicable to the Division's real property nor has it received any notices of assessments, either general or special, relating to the Division's operations or its owned or leased properties for which an accrual has not been made on the Division Balance Sheet. There are not outstanding work orders relating to the real property described in Exhibit A from or required by any police or fire department, sanitation, health or factory authorities or from any other federal or municipal authority, or any matters under discussion with any such departments or authorities relating to work orders.

All licenses and permits required for the operation and use of the real property, buildings, fixtures and equipment have been obtained and are in full force and effect.

5.12 Products Liability. No claims based upon any theory of product liability have been made or threatened against Seller or the Division, which claims arose by reason of the manufacture, sale or use of any product of the Division. Neither Seller nor the Division has breached any product warranty or contract made by either of them to customers in connection with the business of the Division. No written or oral warranties or guarantees have been made or are being made by Seller and/or the Division in connection with the present or prior operations and products of the Division.

5.13 Accounts Receivable. The accounts receivable of the Division reflected in the Division Balance Sheet arose in the ordinary course of business of the Division and are good and enforceable in full, without any defenses, set-offs or other deductions. Seller has not received any notice or threat that merchandise previously shipped by the Division, or by Seller on behalf of the Division (payment for which has not yet been received) is to be returned to Seller for any reason other than returns made in the ordinary course of business and has no knowledge or reason to believe that unusual returns of merchandise will occur subsequent to the date hereof.

5.14 Taxes. Seller has filed all Federal, state, county and local tax returns presently required to be filed in connection with the operations of the Division, and all taxes owing by Seller in connection therewith have been paid when due, including all estimated corporate income tax payments due and payable through the date hereof.

5.15 Inventories. The Division's inventory of raw materials, work in process and finished goods reflected in the Division Balance Sheet is good and usable, and has been valued at the lower of actual cost or net realizable value consistent with prior practices and computation methods of the Division, and reasonably can be anticipated to be sold, use or consumed in the usual and ordinary course of business of the Division now conducted. The inventory of the Division has been maintained at levels consistent with past practice and prior periods and Seller has not caused the inventory of the Division to be increased or decreased except as was required in the ordinary course of its business. Items included in the Division's inventory have been paid for or the liability therefor recognized in the Division's Balance Sheet. Neither Seller nor the Division has received payment or downpayment from any vendor with respect to those items of inventory set forth in the Division Balance Sheet.

5.16 Supply of Raw Material. Seller is not aware of any shortage of raw materials from any source(s) which would materially adversely affect the operations of the Division as presently and heretofore conducted.

5.17 Customer Lists. Exhibit J contains a complete and accurate listing of all customers of the Division to which the Division has made sales and/or provided services in the ordinary course of its business operations.

5.18 Authorization of Agreement. This Agreement, the consummation of the transaction herein contemplated, and the performance, observance and fulfillment by Seller of all of the terms and conditions hereof on its parts to be performed, observed and fulfilled, have been approved and authorized by the Board of Directors and Sole Shareholder of Seller. This Agreement has been duly and validly executed and delivered by Seller and constitutes the valid, binding and enforceable obligation of Seller. Seller has the right, power, legal capacity and authority to enter into and perform its obligations under this Agreement, and no consent of any third party is necessary with respect thereto. The execution and delivery of this Agreement by Seller, the consummation of the transaction herein contemplated, and the performance of, fulfillment of and compliance with the terms and conditions hereof by Seller do not and will not (i) violate any provisions by any judicial or administrative order, award, judgment or decree applicable to Seller, (ii) conflict with any of the provisions of Seller's Articles of Incorporation or Code of Regulations, (iii) conflict with, or result in a breach of, or constitute a default under any agreement or instrument to which Seller is a party or by which it is bound, or (iv) result in the creation or imposition of any lien, charge or encumbrance against any of the Acquired Assets.

5.19 Continuing Accuracy. Each representation and warranty made by Seller in this Agreement or pursuant hereto shall continue to be true and correct at the time of the Closing as though such representation or warranty is being made again at and as of such time.

6. REPRESENTATIONS AND WARRANTIES OF BUYER

As an inducement to Seller to enter into this Agreement and consummate the transactions herein contemplated, Buyer hereby represents and warrants as follows:

6.1 Incorporation, Corporate Power. Buyer is a corporation duly organized, validly existing and in good standing under the laws of the State of Ohio and has all requisite corporate power and authority to enter into this Agreement and consummate the transactions herein contemplated.

6.2 <u>Authorization of Agreement</u>. This Agreement, the consummation of the transaction herein contemplated and the performance, observance and fulfillment by Buyer of all of the terms and conditions hereof on its part to be performed, observed and fulfilled, have all been approved and authorized by the Board of Directors of Buyer. This Agreement has been duly and validly executed and delivered by Buyer and constitutes the valid, binding and enforceable obligation of Buyer. The execution and delivery of this Agreement, the consummation of the transaction herein contemplated and the performance of, fulfillment of and compliance with the terms and conditions hereof by Buyer do not and will not (i) violate any provisions of any judicial or administrative order, award, judgment or decree applicable to Buyer, (ii) conflict with any of the provisions of the Articles of Incorporation or Code of Regulations of Buyer or (iii) conflict with, result in a breach of, or constitute a default under any agreement or instrument to which Buyer is a party or by which it is bound. Buyer has the right, power, legal capacity and authority to enter into and perform its obligations under this Agreement, and no consent of any third party is necessary with respect thereto.

6.3 <u>Continuing Accuracy</u>. Each representation and warranty made by Buyer in this Agreement or pursuant hereto shall continue to be true and correct at and as of the time of Closing as though such representation and warranty is being made again at and as of such time.

7. SURVIVAL OF REPRESENTATIONS AND WARRANTIES: INDEMNIFICATION

7.1 <u>Survival</u>. The parties hereto agree that the representations and warranties contained in this Agreement or in any document, certificate, instrument or Exhibit delivered in connection herewith shall survive the Closing and continue to be binding regardless of any investigation made at any time by the parties.

7.2 <u>Indemnification</u>. The seller shall indemnify Buyer against and hold it harmless from: (i) any and all taxes and other liabilities and obligations of Seller not expressly assumed by Buyer hereunder, including, without limitation, all liabilities of Seller and/or the Division arising from the Seller's or the Division's hiring, firing or employment of labor, all liabilities and obligations of Seller with respect to any product manufactured, sold or delivered prior to the Closing Date resulting from any and all claims (including the expense of defense and settlement thereof) for or relating to bodily injury, wrongful death or property damage allegedly caused by a defective or faulty product or based upon any theory of product liability (tort, absolute or otherwise), resulting from any and all claims based upon any theory of product warranty; (ii) any and all liabilities, obligations, losses, damages and deficiencies resulting from or arising out of any inaccuracy in or breach of any representation or warranty made by Seller in this Agreement or pursuant hereto, or from any nonfulfillment or breach or default in the performance by Seller of any of the covenants made by Seller herein, and (iii) any and all costs and expenses (including reasonable legal and accounting fees) relating to the foregoing.

7.3 <u>Notice of Claim; Defense of Action</u>. In the event that any legal proceedings shall be instituted or that any claim or demand shall be asserted by any third party in respect of which the obligation to indemnify may arise under the provisions of Section 7.2, Buyer shall give or cause to be given to Seller written notice thereof, and Seller shall have the right, at its option and expense, to be represented by counsel of its choice in connection with the defense of any claim or proceeding, but not to control the defense or settlement thereof. The parties agree to cooperate with each other in connection with the defense of any such legal proceeding, claim or demand, provided, however, that Buyer shall be reimbursed for all direct and indirect payroll expenses, and Seller shall pay all living and travel expenses related to out-of-town assistance, with respect to employees of Buyer who are called upon to provide assistance in connection with such defense.

8. ADDITIONAL COVENANTS OF THE SELLER

8.1 <u>Access to Information</u>. During the period between the date hereof and the Closing Date (the "Interim Period"), Buyer and its representatives may make such investigation of the properties, assets and business of the Division as Buyer may reasonably request, and Seller shall give to Buyer and to its counsel, accountants and other representatives, full access during normal business hours throughout the Interim Period to all of the properties, books, contracts, commitments, records and files of the Division, and shall furnish to Buyer during the Interim Period all such documents and copies of documents (certified as true and complete if requested) and information concerning the business and affairs of the Division as Buyer may reasonably request.

8.2 <u>Conduct of Business Pending the Closing</u>. During the Interim Period, except as Buyer may consent in writing:

8.2.1 The business of the Division shall be conducted only in the ordinary course (which, without limitation, shall include the maintenance in force of all existing insurance policies) and in such a manner as to avoid any breach of any of the representations and warranties made by Seller in this Agreement; and

8.2.2 Seller shall use its best efforts to preserve the business organization of the Division intact, to keep available the services of the present employees of the Division and to preserve the goodwill of all those having business relations with it.

Seller will give Buyer advance written notice of its desire to, and without the advance written consent of Buyer will not, enter into any transaction in which Seller:

8.2.3 Transfers, leases or otherwise disposes of any material assets or properties of the Division, or causes the Division to acquire or lease any material assets or properties;

8.2.4 Cancels or compromises any debt or claim relating to the Division;

8.2.5 Waives or releases any rights of material value relating to the Division; or

8.2.6 Transfers or grants any material rights under the lease, licenses, agreements, patents, inventions, trademarks, trade names, service marks, copyrights or with respect to any know-how relating to the Division.

9. CONDITIONS PRECEDENT TO OBLIGATIONS TO CONSUMMATE THE TRANSACTIONS

9.1 Conditions Precedent to Obligations of Buyer. The obligations of Buyer to consummate the Closing as provided in Section 4 of this Agreement is subject to the fulfillment, at or prior to the Closing Date, of each of the following conditions:

9.1.1 All representations and warranties of Seller contained herein shall be true at and as of the Closing Date with the same effect as though such representations and warranties are made at and as of such time, Seller shall have performed and complied with all obligations, covenants and conditions required by this Agreement to be performed or complied with by it prior to or at the Closing Date, and Buyer shall have been furnished with a certificate executed by the President of Seller, in form and substance satisfactory to Buyer, certifying that (a) each of the foregoing conditions has been fulfilled and (b) that the value of the Division's inventory computed at the lower of actual cost or net realized value is reflected in the Division Balance Sheet.

9.1.2 Buyer shall not have learned of any fact or condition with respect to the business, properties, assets or earnings of the Division which is materially at variance with one or more of the representations or warranties of Seller set forth in this Agreement or which in Buyer's reasonable opinion materially and adversely affects such business, properties, assets or earnings, or the ownership, value or continuance thereof.

9.1.3 Seller shall have obtained all consents, approvals and discharges of lenders which may be necessary to complete the transaction contemplated herein.

9.1.4 There shall not be any actual or threatened action, proceeding or investigation which, in the reasonable judgment of Buyer, is directed toward challenging, restraining, prohibiting or invalidating the transaction contemplated herein or which, in the reasonable judgment of Buyer, may affect the right of Buyer to own, operate or control after the consummation of the transaction contemplated herein any of the Acquired Assets or business of the Division.

9.2 Conditions Precedent to the Obligations of Seller. The obligations of Seller to consummate the Closing as provided in Section 4 of this Agreement is subject to the fulfillment, at or prior to the Closing Date, of each of the following conditions:

9.2.1 All representations and warranties of Buyer shall be true at and as of the Closing Date with the same effect as though such representation and warranties are made at and as of such time, Buyer shall have performed and complied with all obligations, covenants and conditions required by this Agreement to be performed or complied with by it prior to or at the Closing Date, and Seller shall have been furnished with a certificate of an executive officer of Buyer in form and substance satisfactory to Seller, certifying to the fulfillment of the foregoing conditions.

10. MISCELLANEOUS

10.1 Finder's Fees.

10.2 Ratings and Deposits. Promptly after the Closing Seller will use its best efforts to make available to Buyer the unemployment and workmen's compensation ratings held by Seller and relating to the Division and to assign to Buyer any unrefundable deposits made by Seller with respect to such programs, to the extent permitted by law.

10.3 Expenses. Buyer shall bear and pay all of its own expenses incident to the transaction contemplated by this Agreement, and Seller shall bear and pay all of its own expenses incident to the transaction contemplated by this Agreement. Such expenses include, without limiting the generality thereof, legal fees, accounting fees, and costs of public document certificates.

10.4 Best Efforts to Meet Conditions. Each of the parties agrees to use its best efforts to fulfill as soon as practicable after the date hereof the conditions precedent to the Closing which are dependent upon such party's action or forbearance.

10.5 Amendment. At any time prior to the Closing, Seller and Buyer, with the authorization or consent of their respective Boards of Directors, may amend or modify this Agreement in such manner as they may mutually agree upon provided such amendment or modification is set forth in a writing executed by both parties with the same formality as this Agreement has been executed.

10.6 Waiver. Buyer may waive compliance by Seller with any of the conditions set forth in Section 9.1 of this Agreement, and Seller may waive compliance by Buyer with any of the conditions set forth in Section 9.2 of this Agreement, provided in each case that any such waiver shall be set forth in a writing executed, with the same formality as this Agreement has been executed, by the party granting such waiver.

10.7 Termination. This Agreement may be terminated at any time prior to Closing:

10.7.1 By the mutual agreement of Seller and Buyer with the authorization or consent of their respective Boards of Directors, provided such termination is set forth in writing executed by both parties with the same formality as this Agreement has been executed;

10.7.2 By Buyer, with the authorization or consent of its Board of Directors, if any of the conditions specified in Section 9.1 shall not have been timely met and shall not have been waived by Buyer pursuant to section 10.6; or

10.7.3 By Seller, with the authorization or consent of its Board of Directors, if any of the conditions set forth in Section 9.2 shall not have been timely met and shall not have been waived by Seller pursuant to Section 10.6.

Any termination pursuant to Subsection 10.7.2 or 10.7.3 above shall be effective immediately upon the giving of notice by the terminating party to the other party.

10.8 Notices. All notices and other communications made pursuant to this Agreement shall be in writing and shall be deemed to have been given if delivered by hand or mailed by registered or certified mail to the parties at the following addresses (or such other address for a party as shall be specified by notice given pursuant hereto):

(i) If to Buyer, to it in care of:
(ii) If to Seller, to it in care of:

10.9 Headings. The headings in this Agreement are intended solely for convenience of reference and shall be given no effect in the construction or interpretation of this Agreement.

10.10 Exhibits. All Exhibits to this Agreement constitute an integral part of this Agreement as if fully rewritten herein.

10.11 Execution in Counterparts. This Agreement may be executed in two or more counterparts, each of which shall be deemed an original, but all of which together shall constitute one and the same document.

10.12 Entire Agreement. This Agreement and the documents to be delivered hereunder constitute the entire understanding and agreement between the parties hereto concerning the subject matter hereof. All negotiations between the parties hereto are merged into this Agreement, and there are no representations, warranties, covenants, understandings or agreements, oral or otherwise, in relation thereto between the parties other than those incorporated herein or to be delivered hereunder. Nothing expressed or implied in this Agreement is intended or shall be construed so as to grant or confer on any person, firm or corporation other than the parties hereto any rights or privileges hereunder.

10.13 Governing Law. This Agreement shall in all respects be interpreted and construed in accordance with and governed by the laws of the State of Ohio.

10.14 Binding Effect. This Agreement and all of the provisions hereof shall be binding upon and insure to the benefit of the parties hereto and their respective successors and assigns, provided, however, that neither party hereto may make any assignment of this Agreement or any interest herein without the prior written consent of the other party hereto.

IN WITNESS WHEREOF, the parties hereto have caused this Agreement to be executed by their duly authorized officers as of the date and year first above written.

Attest:

By _____

_____
Secretary

Attest:

_____   By _____
Secretary

CREDIT AGREEMENT

THIS CREDIT AGREEMENT, dated as of the day of _____, 1978, by and between _____ (the "Borrower"), and _____ an Ohio banking association

WITNESSETH:

The Borrower and _____ desire to contract for the establishment of a revolving credit in the amount of _____ pursuant to which the Borrower may obtain certain interim loans until one year from the date of this Credit Agreement, at which time the revolving credit shall be converted into a term loan, and for the establishment of a line of credit in the amount of _____ pursuant to which the Borrower may obtain certain interim loans until August 31, 1979 at which time said line of credit shall terminate, all upon the terms and conditions hereinafter set forth.

Certain terms used herein are defined in Section 11 hereof.

In consideration of the mutual covenants herein contained, the parties hereto agree as follows:

SECTION 1. REVOLVING CREDIT

_____ hereby establishes a Revolving Credit for the Borrower as follows:

(a) Amount of Revolving Credit Commitment. The Revolving Credit Commitment hereunder established by _____ for the Borrower shall be in the amount of _____

(b) Term. The Revolving Credit shall become effective as of the date of this Credit Agreement and shall remain in effect until the conversion of the Revolving Credit into a Term Loan pursuant to subsection (b) of Section 3 or the termination of the Revolving Credit pursuant to any provision hereof, whichever of the foregoing shall first elapse or occur, whereupon the Revolving Credit shall end and no longer be in effect.

(c) Compensating Balance. The Borrower agrees to establish a commercial bank account at _____ and, so long as either the Revolving Credit or Term Loan shall remain in effect, not to maintain therein a cash balance less than ten percent (10%) of the amount of the Revolving Credit Commitment as set forth in subsection (a) of this Section 1.

SECTION 2. LINE OF CREDIT

_____ hereby establishes a Line of Credit for the borrower as follows:

(a) Amount of Line of Credit Commitment. The Line of Credit Commitment hereunder established by for the Borrower shall be in the amount of _____

(b) Term. The Line of Credit shall become effective as of the date of this Credit Agreement and shall remain in effect until August 31, 1979, or the termination of the Line of Credit pursuant to any provision hereof, whichever of the foregoing shall first elapse or occur, whereupon the Line of Credit shall end and no longer be in effect.

(c) Compensating Balance. The Borrower agrees to establish a commercial bank account at _____ and, so long as interim loans made under the Line of Credit shall remain unpaid, to maintain therein a balance at least equal to ten percent (10%) of the amount of the Line of Credit Commitment as set forth in subsection (a) of this Section 2.

SECTION 3. LOANS.

_____ agrees to grant the Borrower Interim Loans and a Term Loan as follows:

(a) Interim Loans. Subject to the conditions of this Credit Agreement, _____ will grant the Borrower such Interim Loans (each in an amount not less than _____ or a multiple thereof) pursuant to the Revolving Credit as the Borrower may from time to time request in a writing received by _____ at least five full business days before the date of a requested Interim Loan; provided, that in no event shall the aggregate unpaid principal balance of all Interim Loans outstanding at any one time under both the Revolving Credit and the Line of Credit exceed the sum of the amount of the Revolving Credit and the amount of the Line of Credit. The obligation of the Borrower to repay the unpaid principal amount of each Interim Loan shall be evidenced by an appropriate Interim Note bearing a stated maturity date of one year from the date of this Credit Agreement in the case of the Revolving Credit, and August 31, 1979 in the case of the Line of Credit, bearing interest at a rate per annum equal to 1-½% higher than the prime commercial interest rate for unsecured short-term loans to substantial borrowers in effect at _____ from time to time and otherwise being in the form and substance of Exhibits A1 or A2, as the case may be, to this Credit Agreement, with the blanks therein appropriately filled. The interest rate provided above shall be adjusted on the effective date of any change in the Prime Rate. The principal amount actually due and owing to _____ at any time shall be the aggregate unpaid principal amount of all Interim Loans made pursuant to this Credit Agreement. _____ shall endorse on the reverse side of the Interim Notes an appropriate notation evidencing the date and amount of each advance for an Interim Loan made by _____ as well as the date and amount of each repayment by the Borrower with respect thereto.

(b) Term Loan. Subject to the conditions of this Credit Agreement, _____ will at a date one year from the date of this Credit Agreement, convert the Revolving Credit into, and thereby _____ shall grant the Borrower, a Term Loan which shall be in such principal sum not exceeding the amount of the Revolving Credit as the Borrower may request. The obligation of the Borrower to repay the Term Loan shall be evidenced by an appropriate Term Note payable to _____ in twenty consecutive quarter-annual installments of principal (each such installment to be in an amount determined as provided in Exhibit B to this Credit Agreement), bearing interest at a rate per annum equal to 2% higher than the _____ for the first two years of the term of such note, and 2½% higher than the _____ thereafter until maturity, and otherwise being in the form and substance of Exhibit B to this Credit Agreement, with the blanks therein appropriately filled. The interest rate provided above shall be adjusted on the effective date of any change in the Prime Rate. Concurrently with obtaining the Term Loan, even if that should occur before the maturity of an Interim Note, the Borrower shall pay in full to _____ the principal of and interest on all Interim Notes then outstanding.

(c) Possible Default. The Borrower shall not be entitled to obtain any Interim Loan or Term Loan if any Event of Default shall then exist or immediately thereafter would exist. Each execution and delivery of a request for a loan hereunder and an Interim Note or Term Note by the Borrower shall, in and of itself, constitute a continuing representation and warranty by the Borrower that the Borrower then is, and at the time the proceeds thereof are disbursed the Borrower will be, entitled under this Credit Agreement to obtain the loan.

(d) Optional Prepayments. The Borrower shall have the right at all times to prepay an Interim Note or the Term Note in whole or in part subject to the conditions of this subsection (d).

(i) Each prepayment of the Interim Note evidencing loans granted pursuant to the Revolving Credit or the Term Note evidencing the Term Loan shall be in the aggregate principal sum of $40,000 or any multiple thereof. Any prepayment of the Term Note shall be applied to the principal installments thereof in the inverse order of their maturities.

(ii) Each prepayment of the Interim Note evidencing loans granted pursuant to the Line of Credit may be in any principal sum in excess of _____

(iii) Each prepayment of the Interim Note evidencing loans granted pursuant to the Line of Credit may be made without the payment of any premium. Each prepayment of the Interim Note evidencing loans granted pursuant to the Revolving Credit or the Term Note evidencing the Term Loan may be made without the payment of any premium, if such payment is made solely with funds generated in the normal course of operation of the business of the Borrower. If any part of such prepayment is made with funds obtained in any manner from parties other than _____ then Borrower shall pay a premium of _____ to _____ at the same time as such prepayment.

(e) Loan Purposes. The proceeds of the Interim Loans granted pursuant to the Revolving Credit shall be used to purchase certain operating assets of The _____ pursuant to the Purchase Agreement, and the proceeds of the Interim Loans granted pursuant to the Line of Credit shall be used for general working capital purposes.

SECTION 4. SECURITY AGREEMENT, MORTGAGE DEED, PLEDGE AGREEMENT, ASSIGNMENT OF LEASES, AND PERSONAL GUARANTEE

Repayment of all loans hereunder, interest, premium, if any, and all costs and expenses incurred by _____ shall be secured as follows:

(a) Security Agreement. The Borrower shall, prior to the first loan hereunder, execute and deliver to _____ a Security Agreement (the "Security Agreement") in the form and substance of Exhibit C to this Credit Agreement, with the blanks therein appropriately pursuant to which the Borrower shall grant to _____ a security interest in all of the Collateral referred to therein.

(b) Mortgage Deed. The Borrower shall, prior to the first loan hereunder, execute and deliver to _____ a Mortgage Deed (the "Mortgage Deed") in the form and substance of Exhibit D) to this Credit Agreement, with the blanks therein appropriately filled, pursuant to which the Borrower shall grant to _____ a first lien upon the real property referred to therein.

(c) Pledge Agreement. All the shareholders of the Borrower shall, prior to the first loan hereunder, execute and deliver a Pledge Agreement (the ''Pledge Agreement'') in the form and substance of Exhibit E to this Credit Agreement, with the blanks therein appropriately filled, pursuant to which all the issued and outstanding stock of the Borrower shall be pledged to _____

(d) Personal Guarantee. shall, prior to the first loan hereunder, execute and deliver a Personal Guarantee (the ''Personal Guarantee'') in the form and substance of Exhibit F to this Credit Agreement, with the blanks therein appropriately filled, pursuant to which _____ will guarantee a portion of the indebtedness incurred hereunder.

(e) Assignment of Leases. The Borrower and the lessees whose consent is provided for therein shall, prior to the first loan hereunder, execute and deliver the Assignment of Leases in the form and substance of Exhibit H to this Credit Agreement.

SECTION 5. REPRESENTATIONS AND WARRANTIES OF THE BORROWER

The Borrower represents and warrants to _____ as follows:

(a) Organization of the Borrower: Business and Property. The borrower is a corporation duly organized, validly existing, and in good standing under the laws of the State of Ohio and has all requisite power and authority to execute, delivery, and carry out the provisions of this Credit Agreement and of the Interim Notes and the Term Note and to borrow money as contemplated hereby and to execute, deliver, and carry out the provisions of the Security Agreement, the Purchase Agreement, and the Mortgage Deed. The Borrower has, on the date of this Credit Agreement, no subsidiaries. The Borrower has full power, authority, and legal right to own and operate its properties and to carry on the business in which it engages and intends to engage. The Borrower is qualified or otherwise entitled to do business and is in good standing in all jursidictions in which such qualification is required by reason of its business, activities, or ownership of property.

(b) Authorization. All necessary actions on the part of the Borrower relating to the authorization of the execution and delivery of this Credit Agreement, the Interim Notes and the Term Note, the Security Agreement, the Assignment of Leases, the Purchase Agreement and the Mortgage Deed and of the performance of the obligations of the Borrower herein and therein contained have been taken. This Credit Agreement, the Assignment of Leases, the Security Agreement and the Mortgage Deed, when executed and delivered, and the Interim Notes and the Term Note, when executed and delivered pursuant to this Credit Agreement, will be valid and enforceable in accordance with their respective terms. No consent, approval, or authorization of, or registration or declaration with, any governmental authority is required in connection with the execution and delivery of this Credit Agreement, the Assignment of Leases, the Security Agreement, the Mortgage Deed, or the Interim Notes and the Term Note or the performance of the obligations of the Borrower herein and therein contained, and contained in the Purchase Agreement.

(c) Purchase Agreement. The Purchase Agreement has been duly and lawfully executed and delivered by the parties thereto for valid consideration, is a valid and existing agreement binding upon the parties thereto in accordance with its terms, is now in force and will not be amended without the prior written consent of _____. To best of the knowledge of the Borrower, the representations and warranties of the seller, therein, including references to the schedules attached as exhibits to the Purchase Agreement, are true and correct as of the date of the Purchase Agreement and, except as otherwise specified in writing by the Borrower to _____ as of the date hereof.

(d) Property acquired Pursuant to the Purchase Agreement. The list of equipment, real property, and inventory as set forth in the Purchase Agreement and documents related thereto is a complete and correct list of the equipment, real property, and inventory of the Borrower required to be listed thereon as of the date hereof. The inventory listed therein has a market value of not less than _____. The real property listed therein has an appraised value of not less than _____, as determined by an independent real estate appraiser satisfactory to _____.

(e) Projections. The Borrower has furnished to _____ the projections attached hereto as Exhibit G. Such projections represent the Borrower's best estimate of projected future operations as of the date of this Credit Agreement, based on the notes and assumptions stated therein (which the Borrower believes to be currently valid assumptions), and the Borrower does not presently anticipate any material deviations from such projections.

(f) Financial Condition at Date of Credit Agreement. The Borrower does not have on the date of this Credit Agreement any material amount of liabilities, contingent or otherwise and the Borrower does not have outstanding or existing on the date of this Credit Agreement any unusual commitments for the purchase of land, buildings, equipment, materials, or supplies, or any unusual contracts for services nor is it a party to any bonus or profit-sharing plan for any of its employees, except as otherwise disclosed in the Purchase Agreement or in a letter from the Borrower addressed to _____ dated the date of this Credit Agreement.

(g) Title to Properties: Patents, Trademarks, Etc. The Borrower has or will have good and marketable title to all of its properties and assets, including, without limitation, the properties and assets set forth in the Purchase Agreement. There are no mortgages, liens, charges, or encumbrances of any nature whatsoever on any of the properties or assets of the Borrower other than those permitted under this Credit Agreement. None of the properties or assets of the Borrower is held as lessee under any lease or as conditional vendee under any conditional sale contract. To the best knowledge of the Borrower, the Borrower owns or possesses or will own or possess at the time of consummation of the transactions contemplated by the Purchase Agreement all the patents, trademarks, service marks, trade names, copyrights, and licenses and rights with respect to the foregoing necessary for the conduct of its business, without any known conflict with the valid rights of others which would be inconsistent with the conduct of the business of the Borrower substantially as now conducted and as proposed to be conducted.

(h) Litigation. There are no actions, suits or proceedings pending or, to the knowledge of the Borrower, threatened against or affecting the Borrower, at law or in equity or before or by any Federal, state, municipal, or other governmental department, commission, board, bureau, agency, or instrumentality, which involve the possibility of any judgment or liability not fully covered by insurance or which may result in any material, adverse change in the business, operations, properties, or assets or in the condition, financial or otherwise, of the Borrower.

(i) Indebtedness. The Borrower has outstanding no indebtedness other than permitted under this Credit Agreement.

(j) Compliance with Other Instruments. The Borrower is not in default in the performance, observance, or fulfillment of any of the obligations, covenants, or conditions contained in any evidence of indebtedness of the Borrower, or in any lease to which the Borrower is a party. Neither the execution and delivery of this Credit Agreement and the Interim Notes and the Term Note, the Security Agreement, the Purchase Agreement, the Assignment of Leases, and the Mortgage Deed, nor the consummation of the transactions herein and therein contemplated, nor compliance with the terms and provisions hereof and thereof will violate the provisions of any applicable law, or of any applicable order or regulations of any governmental authority having jurisdiction of the Borrower and will not con-

flict with or result in a breach of any of the terms, conditions, or provisions of any restriction or of any agreement or instrument to which the Borrower is now a party, or constitute a default thereunder, or result in the creation or imposition of any lien, charge, or encumbrance of any nature whatsoever upon any of the properties or assets of the Borrower, except as provided therein.

(k) Material Restrictions. The Borrower is not a party to any agreement or other instrument or subject to any other restriction which materially and adversely affects its business, property, assets, operations, or condition, financial or otherwise.

(l) Correctness of Data Furnished. The projections attached hereto as Exhibit G, do not, nor does this Credit Agreement, the Purchase Agreement, the Assignment of Leases, the Security Agreement, or the Mortgage Deed, contain any untrue statement of a material fact or omit a material fact necessary to make the statements contained therein or herein not misleading; and there is no fact which materially affects, nor so far as the Borrower can now foresee, will materially affect adversely the business, prospects or condition (financial or otherwise) of the Borrower or its properties.

(m) Capital Contributions. _____ has made, or will have made at the time of consummation of the transactions contemplated by the Purchase Agreement, equity cash contributions to the Borrower in an aggregate amount not less than _____.

(n) Regulation U Compliance. None of the proceeds of any loans made or credit extended under the Credit Agreement have been, nor will any of the proceeds of any future loan be, used by the Borrower for the purpose of purchasing or carrying any margin stock, as that term is defined in the Code of Federal Regulations §221.3.

(o) Employee Benefit Plans. Based upon ERISA and the regulations and published interpretations thereunder, _____ and the Borrower are in compliance in all material respects with the applicable provisions of ERISA. No Reportable Event (as defined in Section 4043(b) of Title IV of ERISA) to the best of their knowledge has occurred with respect to any Plan. Neither _____ nor the Borrower has, and upon the closing under the Purchase Agreement, the Borrower will not have, any accrued liability of any kind to or in respect of any such Plan.

SECTION 6. CONDITIONS TO BORROWING

(a) Conditions Precedent to First Loan. The obligations of _____ to make the first loan hereunder shall be subject to the satisfaction of the following conditions prior to or concurrently with the making of such first loan hereunder:

(i) Representations and Warranties. The representations and warranties of the Borrower contained herein shall be true on and as of the time of the first loan, with same effect as if made on and as of such date.

(ii) No Defaults. There shall exist no condition or event constituting an Event of Default, as defined hereinafter, or which, after notice or lapse of time, or both, would constitute such an Event of Default.

(iii) Performance. The borrower shall have performed and complied with all agreements and conditions contained herein required to be performed or complied with by it prior to or at the time of the first loan.

(iv) Certificate. The Borrower shall have delivered to _____ a certificate dated the date of the first loan and signed by the chief financial officer of the Borrower, certifying to the matters covered by the conditions specified in subsections (a)(i), (a)(ii), and (a)(iii) of this Section 6.

(v) Insurance report. The Borrower shall have delivered to _____ the insurance report required by subsection (e) of Section 7.

(vi) Execution and Delivery of Credit Agreement and Notes. This Credit Agreement and Interim Notes shall have been duly executed and delivered and _____ shall have been furnished with an executed counterpart of this Credit Agreement.

(vii) Purchase Agreement. The transactions contemplated by the Purchase Agreement shall have been consummated without the waiver of any of the material terms, conditions or provisions thereof by the Borrower and all necessary documents with respect thereto shall have been delivered so that the Borrower shall have good and marketable title to the assets of _____ which are the subject of the Purchase Agreement.

(viii) Security Agreement. The Borrower shall have executed and delivered to the Security Agreement covering all of the Collateral referred to therein, together with all Financing Statements required in connection therewith and referred to therein, and all Financing Statements required in connection therewith shall have been filed in all places where necessary in order to perfect the priority of the liens and security interests of _____ upon the Collateral described therein against all third parties.

(ix) Mortgage Deed and Assignment of Leases. The Mortgage Deed and the Assignment of Leases shall have been duly executed, witnessed, notarized and delivered in escrow with a title company satisfactory to _____ that shall have issued a preliminary title report on the property described in the Mortgage Deed, containing no exceptions to title that are unacceptable to _____ ; the Mortgage Deed and the Assignment of Leases shall be accompanied by instructions to the title company to file the same upon the Borrower's telephone instructions: and the title company shall have indicated its willingness and ability to issue its ALTA Mortgagee's Policy of Title Insurance in an amount satisfactory to _____ insuring the priority of the Mortgage Deed as the first and best lien upon the property therein described, showing only those exceptions on Schedule B thereof as have been approved by _____ . The Borrower shall have delivered to _____ the appraisal of real property contemplated by Section 5(d) of this Credit Agreement, showing the appraised value of the real property to be acquired by Borrower pursuant to the Purchase Agreement to be not less than __.

(x) Personal Guarantee. The Personal Guarantee shall have been duly executed and delivered to _____ by_____

(xi) Pledge Agreement. All the shareholders of the Borrower shall have executed and delivered the Pledge Agreement with _____ and shall have delivered share certificates for all the issued and outstanding shares of Capital Stock, together with executed and completed assignments separate from certificates to _____, so that _____ shall have a valid lien on and pledge of the shares represented by the certificates so delivered.

(xii) Federal Reserve Form U-1. The Borrower, upon the request of _____ shall have executed and delivered a statement or Federal Reserve Form U-1.

(xiii) Opinion of Counsel for the Borrower. _____ shall have received the favorable opinion of counsel for the Borrower, in form and substance satisfactory to _____ substantially to the same effect as the Borrower's representations and warranties in subsections (a), (b), (c), (d), (h), (j) and (o), of Section 5. Such opinion shall also include the favorable opinion as to the priority of the security interests and the liens of _____ pursuant to the Security

Agreement, the Pledge Agreement, the Assignment of Leases, and the Mortgage Deed, and such other matters relative to the transactions contemplated by this Credit Agreement as _____ may reasonably request.

(xiv) Opinion of Special Counsel for _____ _____ shall have received from Messrs. _____ of _____ its special counsel, a favorable opinion, satisfactory in form and substance to it, covering such matters incident to the transactions contemplated hereby as _____ may reasonably request.

(xv) Proceedings. All proceedings to be taken in connection with the transactions contemplated by this Credit Agreement and all documents incident thereto are reasonably satisfactory in form and substance to _____ and their special counsel; and _____ shall have received copies of all documents or other evidence which they and their special counsel may reasonably request in connection with said transactions and copies of records and all proceedings in connection therewith, in form and substance reasonably satisfactory to _____ and its special counsel.

(b) Conditions Precedent to Subsequent Loans. The obligations of _____ to make any loan hereunder subsequent to the first loan hereunder (including, without limitation, the Term Loan to be evidenced by the Term Note) shall be subject to the satisfaction of the following conditions prior to or concurrently with the making of such loan:

(i) No Defaults. There shall exist no condition or event constituting an Event of Default, as defined hereinafter, or which, after notice or lapse of time, or both, would constitute such an Event of Default.

(ii) Performance. The Borrower shall have performed and complied with all agreements and conditions contained herein required to be performed or complied with by it prior to or at the time of such loan.

(iii) Certificate. The Borrower shall have delivered to _____ a certificate dated the date of such loan and signed by the chief financial officer of Borrower, certifying to the matters covered by the conditions specified in subsections (b)(i) and (b)(ii) of this Section 6.

SECTION 7. AFFIRMATIVE COVENANTS OF THE BORROWER

While any part of the principal of, or interest or premium, if any, on, the Interim Notes or the Term Note remains unpaid:

(a) Payment of Amounts Due. The Borrower will make all payments of the principal of, and interest and premium, if any, on the Interim Notes and the Term Note promptly as the same become due thereunder or under this Credit Agreement.

(b) Existence, Business, Etc. The Borrower will cause to be done all things necessary to preserve and to keep in full force and effect its corporate existence, rights, and franchises and will take all action which may be required to comply with all valid laws and regulations now in effect or hereafter promulgated by any properly constituted governmental authority having jurisdiction.

(c) Maintenance of Properties. The Borrower will at all times maintain, preserve, protect, and keep its property used or useful in conduct of its business in good repair, working order, and condition and, from time to time, make all needful and proper repairs, renewals, replacements, betterments, and improvements thereto, so that the business carried on in connection therewith may be properly and advantageously conducted at all times.

(d) Payment of Taxes, Etc. The Borrower will pay and discharge all lawful taxes, assessments, and governmental charges or levies imposed upon it, or upon its income or profits, or upon any of its property, before the same shall become in default, as well as all lawful claims for labor, materials, and supplies which, if unpaid, might become a lien or charge upon such property or any part thereof; provided, however, that the Borrower shall not be required to pay and discharge any such tax, assessment, charge, levy, or claim so long as the validity thereof shall be contested in good faith by appropriate proceedings, and the Borrower shall set aside on its books adequate reserves with respect thereto and shall pay such tax, assessment, charge, levy, or claim before the property subject thereto shall be sold to satisfy any lien which has attached as security therefor.

(e) Insurance. The Borrower will keep adequately insured, by financially sound and reputable insurers, all properties of a character usually insured by business entities engaged in the same or similar activities and business against loss or damage resulting from fire or other risks insured against by extended coverage and of the kind customarily insured against by such business entities and maintain in full force and effect public liability insurance against claims for personal injury, death, or property damage occurring upon, in, or about any properties occupied or controlled by the Borrower, or through the operation of any motor vehicles or aircraft by the agents or employees of the Borrower, or arising in any manner out of the businss carried on by ,the Borrower, all in such amounts as the Borrower may reasonably determine. The Borrower will deliver to _____ on or before the date of the first loan hereunder and at such other times as material changes may be effected in the insurance carried by the Borrower, certificates of the chief financial officer of the Borrower containing a statement of the policies of insurance covering the risks described herein in effect on the date of such certificate and a statement that such policies comply with the provisions of this subsection.

(f) Accounts and Reports of the Borrower. The Borrower will maintain a standard system of accounting in accordance with generally accepted accounting principles and furnish to _____ the following reports:

(i) As soon as available, and in any event within 90 days after the end of each fiscal year of the Borrower, a complete accountant's report with respect to the Borrower, together with all notes thereto, prepared in reasonable detail and certified by independent public accountants of recognized standing selected by the Borrower and satisfactory to _____ which report shall contain (w) a balance sheet of the Borrower, (x) an income and expense statement of the Borrower, (y) a statement of changes in financial position, and (z) a statement that the examination made in preparing and certifying such report has not disclosed the existence of any condition or event which constitutes an Event of Default, as hereinafter defined, or which, after notice or lapse of time, or both, would constitute such an Event of Default; and shall otherwise comply with the requirements of this clause:

(ii) As soon as available, and in any event within 30 days after the end of each month, a report certified by the chief financial officer of the Borrower, which report shall contain (w) a monthly aging of all accounts receivable of the Borrower, (x) a balance sheet of the Borrower as at the end of such month, (y) an income and expense statement of the Borrower for such month, and (z) a statement of changes in financial position of the Borrower for such month, setting forth in each case, in comparative form, corresponding figures for the corresponding month in the preceding fiscal year; and

(iii) Copies of all such financial statements, audits, and reports which the Borrower may have had made of its respective accounts, books, or records, or which it shall send to its shareholders generally or file with the Securities and Exchange Commission.

(g) Performance of Obligations Under the Purchase Agreement. The Borrower shall make all payments and perform all other terms and provisions required to be made and performing under the Purchase Agreement or documents related thereto.

(h) Information and Inspection. The Borrower will furnish to _____ from time to time, upon the request by _____ full information pertinent to any covenant, provision, or condition hereof or of the Security Agreement or Mortgage Deed, or to any matter in connection with its activities and business, and at all reasonable times and as often as _____ may reasonably request, permit any authorized representative designated by it to visit and inspect, at the expense of _____ any of the properties of the Borrower, including its books (and take extracts therefrom) and to discuss its affairs, finances, and accounts with its officers.

(i) Management. The Borrower will at all times maintain executive management satisfactory to _____ and will continue to employ Riley Miller as its chief executive officer. For purposes of this Credit Agreement, _____ agrees that the executive management of the Borrower as presently constituted is satisfactory.

(j) Other Borrowing. The Borrower will pay any and all installments of principal and interest due as a result of borrowing when the same become due and payable, and will keep and perform any and all obligations to be kept and performed by it pursuant to any instrument executed in connection with such borrowing.

(k) Adverse Change. The Borrower will promptly advise _____ of any material, adverse change in its business, operations, or condition, financial or otherwise.

(l) ERISA Reports. Regarding ERISA, the Borrower shall furnish to the Bank the following:

(i) As soon as possible, and in any event within thirty (30) days after any executive officer of the Borrower knows or has reason to know that any Reportable Event (defined in Section 4043(b) of Title IV of ERISA) with respect to any Plan has occurred, a statement of the chief financial officer of the Borrower setting forth details as to such Reportable Event and the action which is proposed be taken with respect thereto, together with a copy of the notice of such Reportable Event given to the Pension Benefit Guaranty Corporation:

(ii) Promptly after the filing thereof with the Internal Revenue Service, copies of each annual and other report with respect to each Plan; and

(iii) Promptly after receipt thereof, a copy of any notice it may receive from the Pension Benefit Guaranty Corporation relating to the intention of the Pension Benefit Guaranty Corporation or the Borrower to terminate any Plan or to appoint a trustee to administer any Plan.

(m) <u>Maintenance of Operating Cash Flow</u>. The Borrower will, during the fiscal years set forth below, maintain Operating Cash Flow at the respective levels indicated:

SECTION 8. <u>NEGATIVE COVENANTS OF THE BORROWER</u>.

While any part of the principal of, or interest or premium, if any, on, the Interim Notes or the Term Nota remains unpaid:

(a) <u>Limitation of Indebtedness</u>. The Borrower will not create, incur, assume, become or be liable in any manner in respect of, any indebtedness except:

(i) indebtedness in respect of the Interim Note or the Term Note:

(ii) unsecured current indebtedness (other than for borrowed money or represented by bonds, notes, or other securities) incurred in the ordinary course of business:

(iii) indebtedness secured by liens permitted hereby:

(iv) indebtedness for taxes, assessments, governmental charges, liens, or claims to the extent that payment thereof shall not be required to be made by the provisions hereof: and

(b) <u>Limitation on Liens</u>. The Borrower will not create, incur, assume, or suffer to be created, or incurred, or assumed, or to exist, any pledge of, or any mortgage, lien, charge, or encumbrance of any kind on any of its property or assets, or own or acquire, or agree to acquire any property of any character subject to or upon any mortgage, conditional sales agreement, or other title retention agreement; provided, however, that the foregoing restrictions shall not prohibit:

(i) liens and security interests pursuant to the Security Agreement, the Assignment of Leases, the Pledge Agreement, and the Mortgage Deed;

(ii) liens for taxes, assessments, governmental charges, levies, or claims, if payment thereof shall not at the time be required to be made by the provisions hereof;

(iii) liens of carriers, warehousemen, mechanics, laborers, and materialmen incurred in the ordinary course of business for sums not yet due or being contested in good faith; provided, how-

ever, that the Borrower shall have set aside on its books such reserve, if any, as shall be required by generally accepted accounting principles;

(iv) liens in the ordinary course of business in connection with workers' compensation or unemployment insurance;

(v) liens in respect of judgments or awards with respect to which the Borrower shall, in good faith, by prosecuting an appeal or proceeding for review and with respect to which a stay of execution upon such appeal or proceeding for review shall have been secured; and

(vi) minor title defects, or liens or encumbrances consisting of minor survey exceptions or encumbrances including easements or rights-of-way for sewers, water lines, utility lines, and other similar purposes, and zoning or other restrictions as to the use of real property, which title defects, liens, and encumbrances do not, in the aggregate, materially impair the use of such real property in the operation of the Borrower's activities and business.

(c) <u>Guarantees</u>. The Borrower will not guarantee, directly or indirectly, or otherwise become surety in respect of the obligations of, or lend its credit to, any other person, or enter into any working capital maintenance or similar agreements.

(d) <u>Leases</u>. The Borrower will not lease any Fixed or Capital Assets, except leases under which the Borrower pays not in excess of _____ in rent annually.

(e) <u>Management Agreements</u>. The Borrower will not make or enter into any so-called management agreement whereby management, supervision or control of its business shall be delegated to or placed in any persons other than its duly elected Board of Directors and officers, or any contract or agreement, whereby any principal functions are delegated to or placed in any agent or independent contractor.

(f) <u>Investments, Loans, and Advances</u>. The Borrower will not purchase or otherwise acquire, hold or invest in the securities (whether capital stock or instruments evidencing indebtedness) of, or make loans and advances to, or enter into any arrangement for the purpose of providing funds or credit to, any other person.

(g) <u>Assignment or Sale of Accounts or Notes Receivable</u>. The Borrower will not assign, sell, discount, or otherwise dispose of, any accounts or notes receivable or trade acceptances.

(h) <u>Liquidation, Merger, or Consolidation</u>. The Borrower will not liquidate or consolidate with or merge with or into any other business entity.

(i) <u>Amendment of Articles of Incorporation or</u>

Regulations. The Borrower will not amend, modify, or supplement its Articles of Incorporation or its Regulations; provided, however, that Borrower may change the name of the Borrower to _____.

(j) Dividends: Purchases or Redemption of Capital Stock; Issuance of Shares. The Borrower will not declare or pay any dividends, or make any distributions of cash or property, to holders of any shares of its capital stock, except dividends payable in shares of such stock of the Borrower, or, directly or indirectly, redeem, purchase or otherwise acquire for a consideration any shares of any class of its capital stock, except that the Borrower may pay cash dividends on its common stock in an aggregate amount not to exceed fifty percent (50%) of the Operating Cash Flow of the Borrower for each fiscal year commencing with the fiscal year ending September 30, 1982.

(k) Disposition of Assets. The Borrower will not sell, lease or otherwise dispose of any substantial part of its assets, except that Borrower may lease to third parties satisfactory to _____ no more than 20,000 square feet of warehouse space for terms no longer than two years, at a rate not less than comparable rental rates for such space generally prevailing in _____.

(l) Acquisition, for Cash, of Going Concern Business. The Borrower will not pay cash to acquire property or assets of any character, real or personal, tangible or intangible, constituting a going concern business, or the stock or partnership or other equity interests of a corporation or partnership or other business entity constituting a going concern business.

(m) Purchase of Fixed or Capital Assets. The Borrower will not purchase Fixed or Capital Assets in any fiscal year if, after giving effect to such purchase, the aggregate amount expended in such fiscal year exceeds the amount of depreciation on or obsolescence of fixed or Capital Assets and of amortization of intangibles and leasehold improvements for such fiscal year, computed on a straight-line basis in accordance with generally accepted accounting principles.

(n) Long-Term Debt: Shareholders Equity Plus Subordinated Indebtedness. The Borrower will not maintain at any time (a) a ratio of total liabilities to the sum of (i) Shareholders' Equity plus (ii) indebtedness of the Borrower expressly subordinated to the Interim Notes and the Term Note, or (b) a ratio of unsubordinated indebtedness to Shareholders' Equity, greater than the respective ratios set forth below:

Fiscal year ending September 30,	Ratio of total liabilities to Shareholders Equity plus subordinated indebtedness	Ratio of unsurbordinated indebtedness to Shareholders Equity
1979	1.5 to 1	3.0 to 1
1980	2.5 to 1	2.5 to 1
1981	1.5 to 1	1.5 to 1
1982	1.5 to 1	1.0 to 1
1983	1.5 to 1	1.0 to 1
1984	1.5 to 1	1.0 to 1

(o) Working Capital. The Borrower will not maintain at any time Working Capital less than the amounts set forth below:

Fiscal year ending September 30,	Amount of Working Capital
1979	
1980	
1981 and thereafter	500,000

(p) Receivables. The Borrower will not at any time permit more than 5% of the total amount of its accounts receivable to be overdue by more than 60 days. For purposes of this subparagraph, accounts receivable shall be overdue if they have not been paid in full within 30 days of the date invoices are sent to the account debtors.

SECTION 9. WAIVERS

Any of the acts which the Borrower is required or permitted to do or prohibited from doing by any of the provisions of Section 1 or Section 8 may, notwithstanding such provisions of said Sections or any other provisions of this Credit Agreement or of the Interim Notes or the Term Note, be omitted or done, as the case may be, if _____ by an instrument in writing, consents thereto.

SECTION 10. EVENTS OF DEFAULT: REMEDIES

If any one or more of the following events (herein termed ''Events of Default'') shall happen, that is to say:

(a) default shall be made in the payment of any principal of the Interim Notes or the Term Note, with premium thereon, if any, when and as the same shall become due and payable, whether at maturity or by acceleration, or otherwise; or

(b) default shall be made in the payment of any interest due on or with respect to the Interim Notes of the Term Note when the same shall become due and payable; or

(c) default shall be made in the due observance or performance of any covenant, agreement, or provision contained in Section 7 or Section 8 to be performed by the Borrower; or

(d) default shall be made in the due observance or performance of any other covenant, agreement, or provision of this Credit Agreement or of the Interim Notes or the Term Note to be performed by the Borrower, or any representation or warranty herein contained or in the Interim Notes or the Term Note or as provided in subsection (c) of Section 3 or in any report, financial or other statement, or instrument furnished pursuant hereto shall be false in any material respect, and such default shall remain unremedied, or such falsity shall not be corrected or cured within 30 days after written notice thereof has been given to the Borrower by _____ or

(e) default shall be made in the due observance of any covenant, agreement, or provision of the Security Agreement, the Assignment of Leases, or the Mortgage Deed to be performed by the Borrower, or any representation or warranty therein contained or in any instrument furnished pursuant thereto shall be false in any material respect, and such default shall remain unremedied, or such falsity shall not be corrected or cured within 30 days after written notice thereof has been given to the Borrower by _____ or

(f) default shall be made with respect to any evidence of indebtedness of the Borrower (other than the Interim Notes or the Term Note) or under any agreement under which such evidence of indebtedness may be issued, or upon any instrument of security for any such evidence of indebtedness and such default shall continue for more than the period of grace, if any, therein specified; or

(g) default shall be made by any of the shareholders of the Borrower in the due observance or performance of any covenant, agreement or provision of the Pledge Agreement, or by Riley Miller in the due observance or performance of any covenant, agreement or provision of the Personal Guarantee, and such default shall have continued for any applicable grace period; or

(h) The Borrower shall become involved in financial difficulties as evidenced by:

(i) any admission in writing of inability to pay its debts as they become due; or

(ii) filing a petition in bankruptcy, or for reorganization, or for the adoption of an arrangement under the Bankruptcy Act, as now or in the future amended, or filing any answer or admission asking such relief; or

(iii) making an assignment for the benefit of creditors; or

(iv) consenting to the appointment of a trustee or receiver for all or a major part of its property; or

(v) being adjudicated a bankrupt; or

(vi) the entry of a court order appointing a receiver or a trustee for all or a major part of its property, or approving a petition filed against it under the Bankruptcy Act, as now or in the future amended (in both cases without its consent), which order shall not be vacated, denied, set aside, or stayed within 60 days from the date of entry; or

(vii) the entry of a final judgment or judgments for the payment of money aggregating in excess of _____ against the Borrower, and the same shall not be satisfied and discharged within 60 days from the date of entry thereof, or an appeal or other proceeding for the review thereof shall not be taken within said period and a stay of execution pending such appeal shall not be obtained; or

(i) If any representation or warranty made in writing by or on behalf of the Borrower in connection with or in the Purchase Agreement, or by or on behalf of the Guarantor, as defined in the Personal Guarantee, or the Pledgors, as defined in the Pledge Agreement, shall prove to have been false or incorrect in any material respect on the date on or as of which made and shall not have been cured or corrected within 30 days after written notice thereof shall have been given to Borrower by _____.

(j) A Reportable Event (as defined in Section 4043(b) of Title IV of ERISA) shall have occurred with respect to any Plan of the Borrower and, within thirty (30) days after the reporting of such Reportable Event to the Bank, (a) the Bank shall have notified the Borrower in writing that (i) it has made a determination that, on the basis of such Reportable Event, there are reasonable grounds for the termination of such Plan by the Pension Guaranty Corporation or for the appointment by the appropriate United States District Court of a trustee to administer such Plan and (ii) as a result thereof an Event of Default exists hereunder; (b) a trustee shall be appointed by a United States District Court to administer any such Plan; or (c) the Pension Benefit Guaranty Corporation shall institute proceedings to terminate any such Plan.

Then, and in every such event, Lender may, at any time (unless all defaults shall theretofore have been remedied or waived in accordance with the terms of this Credit Agreement), by written notice to the Borrower, declare the unpaid principal of all Interim Notes or the Term Note then outstanding and all interest and premium, if any, then accrued thereon to be immediately due and payable, and such principal, interest and premium, if any, shall thereupon be immediately due and payable, without presentment, demand, protest, notice of protest, or other notice of any kind, all of which are hereby expressly waived by the Borrower. In such event, all commitments of Lender hereunder shall terminate forthwith.

Any principal of and interest on the Interim Notes or the Term Note not paid when due and payable shall bear interest thereafter as provided therein.

In case any one or more of the foregoing Events of Default shall happen and be continuing, the Lender shall be entitled to recover judgment against the Borrower for the amount due on the Interim Notes or the Term Note, either before, or after, or during the pendency of the proceedings for the enforcement of any security for the Interim Notes or the Term Note, and, in the event of realization of any funds from any security and application thereof to the payment of the amount due on the Interim Notes or the Term Note, Lender shall be entitled to enforce payment of and recover judgment for all amounts then remaining due and unpaid upon the Interim Notes or the Term Note, whether for principal, interest, or premium. Lender may proceed to protect and enforce its rights by suit in equity, action at law, and/or by any other appropriate proceeding, whether for the specific performance of any covenant or agreement contained in this Credit Agreement or in the Interim Notes or the Term Note, or in aid of the exercise of any power granted in this Credit Agreement or in the Interim Notes or the Term Note, or may proceed to enforce payment of the Interim Note or the Term Note or to enforce any other legal or equitable right.

The Lender may pursue any rights or remedies as the holder of the Interim Notes or the Term Note or under this Credit Agreement, independently or concurrently. All rights, remedies, or powers herein conferred upon Lender shall, to the extent not prohibited by law, be deemed cumulative and not exclusive of any others thereof, or of any other rights, remedies, or powers available to Lender. No delay or omission of Lender to exercise any right, remedy, or power shall impair the same or be construed to be a waiver of any Event of Default or an acquiescence therein. No waiver of any Event of Default shall extend to or affect any subsequent Event of Default or shall impair any rights, remedies, or powers available to Lender. No single or partial exercise of any right, remedy, or power shall preclude other or further exercise thereof by Lender.

To the extent permitted by law, the Borrower agrees to waive and does hereby absolutely and irrevocably waive and relinquish the benefit of any valuation, stay, appraisement, extension, or redemption laws now existing or which may hereafter exist, which, but for this provision might be applicable to any sale made under any judgment, order or decree of any court, or otherwise, based upon the Interim Note or the Term Note or any claim for interest due thereon.

To the extent permitted by law, the Borrower agrees

that if default shall be made in the payment of the principal of, or interest or premium, if any, on the Interim Notes or the Term Note, when the same shall become due and payable, it will pay to Lender such additional amount as shall be sufficient to cover the cost and expenses of collection, including reasonable compensation to its agents and attorneys and any expenses or liabilities incurred by Lender in the collection thereof.

The Lender shall not be required to make or renew any loans hereunder if an Event of Default specified in this Section 10, or if an event which, but for the lapse of time or the giving of notice and the lapse of time, would become an Event of Default under this Section 10, has occurred and is continuing.

SECTION 11. <u>DEFINITIONS</u>.

As used herein and in the Interim Note and the Term Note, the following terms shall have the following meanings:

(a) "Revolving Credit" means the commitment of Lender to grant the Borrower loans upon the terms and conditions of this Credit Agreement: and "Revolving Credit Commitment" means the commitment of Lender to grant the Borrower loans as set forth in subsection (a) of Section 1:

(b) "Line of Credit" means the commitment of Lender to grant the Borrower loans upon the terms and conditions of this Credit Agreement; and "Line of Credit Commitment" means the commitment of Lender to grant the Borrower loans as set forth in subsection (a) of Section 2;

(c) "Interim Loan" means a loan obtained by the Borrower pursuant to subsection (a) of Section 3 hereof: and "Interim Note" means a note which evidences such a loan and is in the form of Exhibit A1 or A2 to this Credit Agreement;

(d) "Term Loan" means a loan made pursuant to subsection (b) of Section 3 hereof; and "Term Note" means the note which evidences such a loan and is in the form of Exhibit B to this Credit Agreement;

(e) Lender's Prime Rate" means the prime commercial interest rate of Lender in effect from time to time, as defined in subsection (a) of Section 3;

(f) "Shareholders Equity" means the aggregate sum of the capital stock, capital surplus, and retained earnings (deficit) accounts of the Borrower.

(g) "Working Capital" means the excess of current assets over current liabilities of the Borrower, as determined by generally accepted accounting principles.

(h) "Operating Cash Flow" for any fiscal year means the net income of the Borrower during the fiscal year involved, in each case determined as provided in the definition of Net Earnings, plus, in each case, the amount of depreciation on or obsolescence of Fixed or Capital Assets and of amortization of intangibles and leasehold improvements for such fiscal year, computed in accordance with generally accepted accounting principles, over the sum of (i) the amount of the fixed quarter-annual payments of principal of the Term Note payable during such fiscal year in accordance with the terms of the Term Note, and (ii) the amount of the expenditures for Fixed or Capital Assets which the Borrower shall have made in such fiscal year in accordance with the terms of the Term Note, and (ii) the amount of the expenditures for Fixed or Capital Assets which the Borrower shall have made in such fiscal year in accordance with subsection (m) of Section 8.

(i) "Purchase Agreement" means the agreement for the sale and purchase of certain assets of The _____ by and between The _____ Inc. and the Borrower, dated _____, 1978, in the form heretofore delivered to _____ providing for the sale of certain of the assets of The _____ to the Borrower.

(j) "Net Earnings" for any period means the net income (or deficit) for such period, after taxes, of the Borrower, after all proper charges and reserves, excluding nonrecurring special charges and credits, all as determined in accordance with generally accepted accounting principles.

(k) "Fixed or Capital Assets" means and includes all assets which are defined or classified as fixed or capital assets in accordance with generally accepted accounting principles.

(l) "ERISA" means the Employee Retirement Income Security Act of 1974, as the same may be amended, and "Plan" means any employee benefit plan subject to the provisions of Title IV of ERISA which is maintained for employees of the Borrower.

SECTION 12. MISCELLANEOUS

(a) Payment of Expenses. If any taxes shall be payable, or ruled to be payable, to any state or Federal authority, with respect to the execution and delivery of this Credit Agreement or the Interim Notes or Term Note, by reason of any existing or hereafter enacted Federal or state statutes, the Borrower will pay all such taxes, including interest and penalties thereon, if any, and will indemnify and hold Lender harmless against any liability in connection therewith. The Borrower will also pay the fees and disbursements of Lender for their services to Borrower with reference to the subject matter of this Credit Agreement and any amendment hereof or modification hereto and the Interim Notes or the Term Note and will reimburse Lender for any out-of-pocket expenses in connection herewith. The obligations imposed upon the Borrower by this subsection (a) shall survive the payment of the Interim Notes and the Term Note.

(b) Notices. Any notice to or demand upon the Borrower shall be deemed to have been sufficiently given or served for all purposes hereof when mailed, first class, postage prepaid, addressed to the Borrower, care of _____ or to such other address as may be furnished in writing to Borrower for such purpose by the Borrower, as the case may be.

Any notice to or demand upon _____ shall be deemed to have been sufficiently given or served for all purposes hereof when mailed, first class, postage prepaid, addressed to Lender or to such other address as may be furnished in writing to the Borrower for such purpose by Lender.

(c) Survival of Representations and Warranties. All representations and warranties contained herein shall survive the execution and delivery of this Credit Agreement, any investigation at any time made by Lender and the execution and delivery of the Interim Notes and the Term Note and shall continue in full force and effect so long as the Interim Notes or the Term Note are outstanding and unpaid.

(d) Entire Agreement: Amendment. This Credit Agreement embodies the entire agreement and understanding between the Borrower and Lender and supersedes all prior agreements and understandings relating to the subject matter hereof. The Borrower and Lender may enter into further and additional written agreements to amend or supplement this Credit Agreement and the terms and provisions of such further and additional written agreements shall be deemed a part of this Credit Agreement as though incorporated herein.

(e) Parties in Interest. All the terms and provisions of this Credit Agreement shall inure to the benefit of and be binding upon and be enforceable by the respective successors and assigns of the parties hereto, whether so expressed or not and, in particular, shall inure to the benefit of and be enforceable by any holder of the Interim Notes or the Term Note.

(f) Governing Law. This Credit Agreement and the Interim Notes and the Term Note are and will be contracts made under the laws of the State of Ohio and together with the rights and obligations of the parties hereunder shall be construed and enforced in accordance with and governed by the laws of such State.

(g) <u>Interest Calculations</u>. The interest payable on the Notes shall be computed on a 360-day-per-year basis.

IN WITNESS WHEREOF, the parties have caused this Credit Agreement to be executed at the time first above written by their respective officers thereunto duly authorized.

By _____
President

By_____
Loan Officer

STOCK OPTION AGREEMENT

In consideration of the sum of Twenty-five Thousand Dollars ($25,000), the receipt whereof is hereby acknowledged, Seller Corp., a New York corporation having its principal office at New York, New York ("Seller") hereby grants to Buyer Enterprises, Inc., a New York corporation having its principal office at Albany, New York ("Buyer") an option to acquire all of the stock (the "Stock") of Subsidiary, Inc. ("Sub") on the terms set forth below:

1. <u>Exercise</u>. This option is exercisable by notice in writing sent to the Seller by certified or registered mail not later than 90 days after the date hereof. Said notice shall specify a closing date not later than 30 days after the expiration of said 90 day period. If this option is not so exercised, it will terminate and said sum of Twenty-Five Thousand Dollars ($25,000) shall not be refundable.

2. <u>Price</u>. The price and terms of payment shall be those set forth in Subsection 2.1 or Subsection 2.2 hereof, as selected by the Buyer at closing.

2.1 The sum of Six Million Dollars ($6,000,000), payable by certified or cashier's check at closing.

2.2 The sum of Six Million Five Hundred Thousand Dollars ($6,500,000), of which Four Million Dollars ($4,000,000) will be paid by certified or cashier's check at closing, and the balance of Two Million Five Hundred Thousand Dollars ($2,500,000) in the form of the Buyer's promissory note, delivered at closing, payable over a five (5) year period in monthly installments of Fifty-three Thousand One Hundred Eighteen Dollars ($53,118) each (applicable first to interest and the balance to reduction of principal), commencing 90 days after closing. The Buyer may prepay said note in whole or in part at anytime; prepayments shall be applicable to the installments due thereunder in inverse order of maturity.

3. <u>Representations and Warranties of Seller</u>. Seller represents and warrants to the Buyer as follows:

3.1 <u>Corporate Standing</u>. The Seller and Buyer are New York corporations duly organized, validly existing and in good standing under the laws of its State of incorporation. Each has the corporate power to own, lease and operate its powers and is duly qualified as a foreign corporation and is in good standing in every state in which its operations require such qualification.

3.2 <u>Capital Stock</u>. The issued and outstanding capital stock of Sub consists of Two Hundred (200) shares of common stock without par value, all of which are owned by Seller. The issued and outstanding capital stock of Trust consists of Two Hundred (200) shares of common stock without par value, all of which are owned by Seller. There are no outstanding options, warrants, contracts or agreements of any kind for the issue or sale of any additional shares of the capital stock of Sub or for the issue or sale of any other securities or obligation of either of them or for the purchase of either of them of any of their outstanding shares of capital stock.

3.3 <u>Title to Stock</u>. Seller has good title to and owns the Stock beneficially, free and clear of all liens, encumbrances and restrictions on transfer except such as will be discharged at closing, and has full right and authority to sell the same upon the terms and conditions set forth herein.

3.4 <u>Financial Statements of Sub.</u> The financial books, records and accounts of Sub have in the past been and are now kept in accordance with generally accepted accounting principles and practices applied on a consistent basis..The audited balance sheet as of December 31, 1978 and the related statements of operations and retained earnings and of changes in financial position for the year then ended, copies of all of which have heretofore been furnished to Buyer, have been prepared in accordance with generally accepted accounting principles and practices applied on a consistent basis and fairly present the financial condition of Sub as of such date and the result of its operations for the period then ended, subject to the opinion of Price Waterhouse & Co. dated March 10, 1979 attached thereto.

3.5 <u>Liabilities.</u> Except to the extent reflected or reserved against in Sub, said balance sheet or in the footnotes thereto, as of the date of said balance sheet Sub had no liabilities of any nature, whether accrued, absolute, contingent or otherwise, including, without limitation, tax liabilities due or to become due, and whether incurred in respect of or measured by Sub's income for any period prior to the date of said balance sheet, or arising out of transactions entered into, or any state of facts existing, prior thereto.

3.6 <u>Conduct of Business.</u> Since the date of its said December 31, 1978 balance sheet, the business and operations of Sub have been carried on in the usual course under business policies and otherwise in the manner theretofore conducted; and since said date there have not been (i) any changes in the financial or other condition, assets, liabilities or business of Sub which have been materially adverse, (ii) any change or alteration in the terms of the compensation payable to or to become payable to officers or other personnel of Sub, except for historic and usual annual increases and labor union contractual agreements, (iii) any material transaction of Sub not in the ordinary course of business (including but not limited to capital expenditures, purchases in excess of Sub's customary levels, and commitments for any such purpose), or (iv) any declaration or payment of any dividend or other distribution with respect to Sub's stock.

3.7 <u>Subsidiaries.</u> Sub does not own any stock or securities evidencing an ownership interest in any corporation, business trust, firm or business.

3.8 <u>Litigation.</u> Except as disclosed in the footnotes to the balance sheet referred to in Article 3, Section 3.4, there is no action, proceeding or investigation pending or (to the knowledge of Seller) threatened against Sub before any court or any governmental department, commission, board, agency or instrumentality, which involves the possibility of any judgement or liability not fully covered by insurance or which might result in any material adverse change in the business, operations, properties, assets or financial condition of Sub. Sub is not subject to any order, injunction or decree of any court, governmental department, commission, board, agency or instrumentality.

3.9 <u>Contracts.</u> Sub is not a party to any (i) labor agreement, (ii) contract of employment, (iii) contract for the purchase, sale or lease (as lessor or lessee) of real estate or personal property, (iv) contract for services to be rendered to it, (v) employee insurance, hospital or medical expense program or (vi) pension or profit-sharing plan, retirement plan, bonus or incentive

agreement or plan, stock purchase or stock option plan, whether formal or informal, except as disclosed in writing by Sub to Buyer within the 10 day period immediately preceding the date of this option.

3.10 <u>Other Agreements of Sub.</u> Sub is not a party to or bound by any contract or agreement, or subject to charter provision or other legal restriction (other than restrictions applicable to corporations or businesses generally) which adversely affects its business, operation, properties, assets or condition, financial or otherwise. Sub is not in default under any material contract, lease, agreement or other undertaking to which it is a party or by which it is bound.

3.11 <u>Other Agreements of Seller.</u> Neither the execution or delivery of this option nor the consummation of the transactions contemplated hereby, nor compliance with the terms and conditions hereof, will conflict with, or result in a breach of the unwaived terms and conditions of, or constitute a default under, the Certificate of Incorporation or by-laws of Seller or any contract, agreement, commitment or other undertaking to which it is a party or by which it is bound.

3.12 <u>Title to Assets.</u> Sub has good and marketable title to all the properties and assets reflected on the balance sheet referred to in Section 3.4 of this Article (except such as have been disposed of in the ordinary course of business) free and clear of all liens, charges and encumbrances of any nature, except as reflected in said balance sheet.

3.13 <u>Condition of Property and Equipment.</u> The properties and equipment of Sub which are necessary or useful in the conduct of its business are, with no material exceptions, in good operating condition and repair.

3.14 <u>Insurance.</u> Sub is adequately insured with respect to risks normally insured against by business similarly situated.

3.15 <u>Taxes.</u> All Federal, State and other tax returns and reports respecting Sub, required by law to be filed, have been duly and timely filed and set forth accurately the information called for thereby for tax purposes, and all taxes shown by said returns and reports to be due have been paid. Except as disclosed in the footnotes to the balance sheet referred to in Article 3, Section 3.4, no claim is being asserted by the Federal Government, State of New York, or any other municipality or political subdivision for any such taxes in respect of any such period.

3.16 <u>Accounts Receivable.</u> The accounts receivable and unbilled services included as assets in the said balance sheet of Sub, are good, valid and collectible.

3.17 <u>Authorization.</u> The execution and delivery by

Seller of this option have been duly and sufficiently authorized by appropriate proceedings of the Board of Directors of Seller.

3.18 <u>Broker</u>. The parties agree that Bankers Trust Company ("Bankers") assisted in this transaction and that Seller is responsible for the payment of the fees stated in Bankers' letter of April 19, 1979 to Sub. Any monies for fees paid by the Buyer or by Sub to Bankers for feasibility study, preliminary work, and financial aid in the consummation of this transaction shall be deducted from the monies payable at closing under Article 2 thereof.

3.19 <u>General</u>. No representation or warranty contained herein by or on behalf of Seller, nor any statement or certificate furnished hereunder or in connection herewith, contains or will contain any untrue statement of a material fact or omits or will omit to state a material fact necessary to make the statements contained therein not misleading.

4. Covenants of Seller. Seller covenants that from and after the date of this option and until the closing (or until expiration of this option) it will cause Sub to:

4.1 Continue to conduct its business diligently and in the ordinary course.

4.2 Use its best efforts to preserve its business organization intact, retain the services of its officers and key employees, and preserve its relationships with suppliers, customers, creditors and other business contacts.

4.3 Maintain in full force and effect insurance policies providing coverages and amount of coverage as now provided.

4.4 Not (without the prior consent of the Buyer) declare or pay any dividends or make any other distribution of assets; make any change in its Certificate of Incorporation of assets; make any change in its Certificate of Incorporation or By-laws; issue or sell, or issue rights to subscribe to, or grant options to purchase, any shares of its stock or make any changes in its capital structure; enter into any commitment not in the ordinary course of business; purchase any of the outstanding shares of Sub stock; or grant any unusual increases in salaries or benefits payable to any employee other than negotiated through collective bargaining.

5. Conditions Precedent to Obligations of Buyer. The obligations of the Buyer, after exercise of this option, to consummate the purchase provided for herein are, at the option of Buyer, subject to satisfaction of the following conditions on the closing:

5.1 All representations and warranties of Seller which are contained in this option or in any written statement which shall be delivered by Seller pursuant to this option, except as affected by transactions contemplated hereby, shall be true on and as of the closing as though such representations and warranties had been made on and as of the closing; and Buyer shall not have discovered any material error, misstatement or omission in any of such representations or warranties.

5.2 Seller shall have performed and complied with all covenants and agreements required by this option to be performed and complied with by it.

5.3 All inter-company debt between the Seller on the one hand, and Sub on the other hand, shall have been deleted by appropriate entries on their books.

5.4 Sub shall have received the resignations of such directors of Sub as Buyer may request by notice given at least five days prior to closing.

5.5 Buyer shall have received a certified copy of a resolution of the Board of Directors of Seller approving this transaction.

5.6 Sub shall have received a certificate, executed by Seller and dated the closing, in such detail as Sub shall reasonably request, as to the fulfillment of the conditions specified in Sections 5.1, 5.2 and 5.3 of this Article.

5.7 All proceedings of Seller in connection with the authorization, execution and delivery of this option and the authorization of all transactions contemplated hereby shall be reasonably satisfactory in form and substance to Sub and its counsel, and Sub shall have received all documents which it shall reasonably request in connection with the transactions contemplated hereby and copies of all corporate proceedings in connection therewith, in form and substance satisfactory to Sub and its counsel.

5.8 Sub shall have received an opinion or opinions of Seller's counsel, dated the closing date, in form and substance reasonably satisfactory to Sub and its counsel, to the effect that (i) the representations and warranties of Seller contained in Article 3, Sections 3.1, 3.2, 3.3, 3.7, 3.8, 3.9, 3.10, 3.11 and 3.17 hereof, are true and correct as of the closing date and that counsel has no reason to believe that any of the other representations and warranties in Article 3 are untrue and incorrect; (ii) this option has been duly and validly authorized, executed and delivered by Seller and is valid and binding upon Seller and its shareholders in accordance with its terms; and (iii) all proceedings and actions required by law or the provisions of this option to be taken by Seller on or prior to the closing in connection with the transactions contemplated by this option have been duly and validly taken.

6. Conditions Precedent to Obligations of Seller. The obligations of the Seller to consummate the sale

provided for herein are subject, at the option of Seller, to satisfaction of the following conditions on the closing:

6.1 This option shall have been exercised as provided in Section 1 hereof.

6.2 The option price shall have been paid as provided in Section 2 hereof.

7. Closing. This option shall be closed at the office of _____, New York, at 10:00 a.m. on the date specified in the notice of exercise of this option was provided in Section 2 hereof, or at such other time and place as may be mutually agreed upon. All references herein to the "closing" or "closing date" shall be deemed to refer to such time and place. At the closing, all transactions shall be deemed to be simultaneous, and none shall be effective until all have been completed.

8. Headings. The headings to the articles and sections herein are inserted for convenience of reference only and are not intended to be a part hereof or to affect the meaning or interpretation of this option.

9. Survival. All warranties and representations, covenants and agreements, made hereunder or in connection with the transactions contemplated hereby, shall survive the closing and remain effective in accordance with the terms hereof regardless of any investigation at any time made by or on behalf of Buyer.

10. Publicity. All publicity with regard to the transactions provided for in this option shall be released jointly by the parties hereto.

11. Benefit. This option shall bind and inure to the benefit of the successors of the parties hereto.

IN WITNESS WHEREOF, the Seller has executed this option this _____ day of May, 1979.

Seller Corp.

By:_____

JOINT VENTURE AGREEMENT

AGREEMENT, made as of _____, 1980, by and between _____ Corporation ("ABC"), a _____ corporation having its principal office at _____, O&H Corporation ("O&H"), a Delaware corporation having its principal office at New York, New York and B&B Corporation ("B&B"), a _____ corporation having its principal office at _____, (ABC, O&H and B&B being hereafter collectively referred to as the "Joint Venturers").

ARTICLE I
FORMATION OF JOINT VENTURE

1.1 Formation. The Joint Venturers hereby form a joint venture (the "Joint Venture") and constitute themselves as the only Joint Venturers of the Joint Venture to operate and conduct business in accordance with the provisions of this Agreement.

1.2 Name. The name of the Joint Venture is XYZ. The Joint Venturers agree that each of them shall execute and file all certificates and documents necessary or appropriate for the formation of the Joint Venture or the qualification of the Joint Venture to do business.

1.3 Principal Office. The principal office of the Joint Venture is located at _____ or such other place as the Joint Venturers shall determine.

1.4 Purpose. The purpose of the Joint Venture is (a) to acquire substantially all the business and assets, wherever located, of Banco, Inc. and its subsidiaries (all such corporations being hereafter collectively referred to as "Banco" and all such business and assets to be acquired being hereafter referred to as the Banco Operations); (b) to carry on the business of Banco; (c) to employ personnel to manage the Banco Operations; and (d) to take all actions necessary and appropriate in order to consummate such acquisition and thereafter to carry on such business. The Joint Venture shall conduct no other business.

1.5 Term. The term of the Joint Venture shall commence on the date of the execution of this Agreement and continue until September 30, 2020 unless earlier terminated by consent of all Joint Venturers, provided, however, if the acquisition of the Banco Operations has not been consummated on or before October, 1, 1980, the Joint Venture shall terminate at the written election of any Joint Venturer.

1.6 Representation. Each Joint Venturer represents and warrants that it is a corporation duly organized, validly existing and in good standing under the laws of the jurisdiction of its incorporation; that it has full corporate power and authority to enter into and perform this Agreement, and that all actions necessary to authorize the execution and delivery of this Agreement and to carry out its obligations hereunder have been duly taken.

ARTICLE II
CAPITAL

2.1 The intitial capital contribution to the Joint Venture shall be $1,500,000 of which ABC will contribute $1,000,000, O&H will contribute $250,000 and B&B will contribute $250,000. In addition, O&H will use its best efforts to secure personnel to be employed by the Joint Venture to manage the Banco Operations.

2.2 Capital Accounts. A capital account shall be established for each Joint Venturer on the books of the Joint Venture and there shall be credited to each Joint Venturer's capital account the amount of its initial capital contribution and its share of undistributed profits of the Joint Venture. There shall be charged against each Joint Venturer's capital account the amount of all distributions from the Joint Venture and the Joint Venturer's share of any losses of the Joint Venture. The Joint Venture will not pay any interest on the capital accounts except as provided in Section 7.2 hereof. Additional capital contributions may be made only with the consent of all Joint Venturers, and none of the Joint Venturers shall be required to make additional capital contributions to offset losses charged to its respective capital account except that on termination of any Joint Venturer's interest in the Joint Venture by way of retirement or withdrawal or by termination of the Joint Venture, such Joint Venturer shall pay to the Joint Venture in cash any deficit balance in its capital account.

ARTICLE III
PROFITS AND LOSSES

3.1 Allocation. All income and deductions, profits and losses of the Joint Venture for its first fiscal year and for the following (number) full fiscal years shall be allocated 90% to ABC, 5% to O&H and 5% to B&B. Thereafter, such income and deductions, profits and losses for each fiscal year shall be allocated 10% to ABC, 45% to O&H and 45% to B&B. All allocations to the Joint Venturers shall be credited or charged to their respective capital accounts.

ARTICLE IV
DISTRIBUTIONS

4.1 Distribution of Real Property. Simultaneously with the acquisition of the Laneco Operations, the Joint Venture will distribute certain real property to or for the account of each of the Joint Venturers. The book value of such real property shall be charged against the capital account of the Joint Venturers in proportion to the balance of such acccounts immediately before such distribution. If such real property is subsequently con-

tributed to the Joint Venture by or on behalf of the Joint Venturers, the capital accounts of the Joint Venturers shall be credited in an amount equal to the amount charged to such capital upon the initial distribution of such property.

4.2 Distributions to ABC. Within 90 days after the close of each fiscal year of the Joint Venture ending on or after _____ , the Joint Venture shall distribute to ABC an amount of cash equal to the greater of (a) an amount equal to 1 1/2% of the net profits of the Banco Operations (computed without regard to any taxes imposed with respect to income) or (b) $300,000, *provided, however,* that the amount of such distribution shall not exceed the then remaining balance of the capital account of ABC (in excess of original capital contributions).

4.3 Distributions on account of Income Taxes. Each of O&H and B&B may, at any time after the close of each fiscal year of the Joint Venture, and ABC may, at any time after the close of each fiscal year of the Joint Venture ending on or after _____ , deliver to the Joint Venture one or more verified certificates setting forth the amount or amounts of federal, state and local income or similar taxes payable by such Joint Venturer solely because of the inclusion in its taxable income of the amounts of income and deduction, profit and loss allocated to such Joint Venturer hereunder with respect to such fiscal year (without regard to any losses or credits which may be available to reduce such taxes). Within 30 days after the receipt of such certificate, the Joint Venture shall make a distribution to such Joint Venturer an amount of cash equal to the lesser of (a) the balance of its capital account (in excess of original contributions) or (b) the amount or amounts set forth on such certificates. Notwithstanding the foregoing, no distribution permitted by this Section 4.3 shall be made if, after giving effect to such distribution, the sum of all liabilities of the Joint Venture shown on the Joint Venture's most recent audited financial statement plus the aggregate amount of original capital contributions of all Joint Venturers exceeds the assets of the Joint Venture shown on such financial statement.

4.4 Interim Distributions of Profits. At any time after _____ , the Joint Venture may make interim distributions of the remaining balance of each Joint Venturer's capital account (in excess of original capital contributions) in such aggregate amounts and at such times as O&H, in its sole discretion, shall determine, provided, however, that (i) all distributions under this Section 4.4 shall be deemed to be made out of the profits of the Joint Venture for the immediately preceding fiscal year, (ii) such distribution shall be allocated among the Joint Venturers in the same proportion as the allocation of profit and loss for such year and (iii) the aggregate amount of the distributions made with respect to any fiscal year pursuant to this Section 4.4 and pursuant to Section 4.3 above shall not exceed 75% of the net profit of the Joint Venture for such year (computed without regard to taxes imposed with respect to income).

4.5 Final Distribution of Profits and Capital Accounts. Upon the termination of the Joint Venture and after providing for or paying all expenses of and claims against the Joint Venture, the balance of the capital account of each Joint Venturer (in excess of original capital contributions) shall be distributed to such Joint Venturer and the original capital contribution of each Joint Venturer shall be returned to it. Distributions pursuant to this Section 4.5 may be made in cash or property or both and any property distributed pursuant to this Section 4.5 shall be valued at its fair market value at the time of such distribution and charged against the Joint Venturers' capital accounts at that value.

ARTICLE V
MANAGEMENT

5.1 Management of Banco Operations. The conduct and management of the Banco Operations shall be carried out by the persons serving as employees of the Joint Venture under that certain Partnership and Management Agreement (the "Management Agreement") dated as ____ of (a copy of which is attached hereto as Exhibit A) subject to the control of the Joint Venture as set forth herein.

5.2 Management of the Joint Venture. Except as otherwise set forth herein, the management of the Joint Venture, including, without limitation, the exercise of all powers of the Joint Venture under the Management Agreement, shall be conducted by majority vote of the Joint Venturers, with each Joint Venturer having one vote.

5.3 Designation of Representative. Each Joint Venturer agrees that it will designate in writing to the other Joint Venturers the name of one of its officers who shall serve as that Joint Venturer's representative, agent and attorney in fact for all purposes of the Joint Venture. Each Joint Venturer agrees that such designated representative shall have the authority to take all actions required or permitted to be taken by such Joint Venturer hereunder and that the actions of such representative shall be binding upon such Joint Venturer.

ARTICLE VI
OPERATION OF
THE JOINT VENTURE

6.1 Books and Records. The Joint Venture shall maintain its books and records on a full accrual basis of accounting in accordance with generally accepted accounting principles. The Joint Venture shall also keep all other records necessary or convenient for the recording of the Joint Venture's business and affairs and for the accurate allocation of profits, losses and distributions as provided for herein.

6.2 Fiscal Year. The first fiscal year of the Joint Venture shall begin as the date of this Agreement and shall end on September 30, 1980 or as the Joint Venture may otherwise determine or as otherwise may be required by law.

6.3 Reports. Promptly after the end of each quarter of the fiscal year, there shall be prepared and delivered to each Joint Venturer a statement showing the results of operations during such quarter and for the portion of the fiscal year then ended. At the time any distribution is made by the Joint Venture, there shall be delivered to each Joint Venturer a balance sheet as of the end of the fiscal period in respect of which the distribution is made. The Joint Venture shall have an annual audit of the books made by the firm of certified public accountants in accordance with generally accepted auditing standards and shall prepare a balance sheet, a statement of the capital accounts of the Joint Venturers and a statement of income of the Joint Venture for the fiscal year. Each Joint Venturer shall be furnished a copy of such annual financial statements as certified by said accountants, as soon as reasonably practical after the close of the Joint Venture's fiscal year.

Upon termination of the Joint Venture or any interest of any Joint Venturer therein, an audit shall be conducted by said accountants and financial statements of the same type described above shall be provided to each Joint Venturer. In addition, within ninety (90) days after the end of each fiscal year, said accountants shall prepare and mail to each Joint Venturer a report setting forth in sufficient detail all such information and data with respect to the business transactions effected by or involving the Joint Venture during such fiscal year as shall enable such Joint Venturer to prepare all its tax returns in accordance with the laws, rules and regulations then prevailing. Said accountants shall also prepare all tax or information returns required of the Joint Venture. The Joint Venture shall also furnish to each Joint Venturer such other reports on the Joint Venture's operations and condition as may be reasonably requested by any Joint Venturer.

6.4 Bank Accounts. The operating accounts of the Joint Venture shall be maintained in such bank or banks as may be designated by the Joint Venture and withdrawals from said accounts shall be made as the Joint Venture may determine. There shall be no commingling of the moneys or funds of the Joint Venture with moneys or funds of any of the Joint Venturers or any other entity.

ARTICLE VII
WRONGFUL TERMINATION

7.1 <u>Intent of Joint Venturers.</u> Each Joint Venturer acknowledges that it intends that this Joint Venture Agreement shall continue until terminated by consent of all Joint Venturers. Each Joint Venturer understands that (i) the date of termination of this Joint Venture Agreement is indefinite, (ii) the other Joint Venturers are relying on the mutual expectation that this Joint Venture shall continue for a substantial period of time and (iii) if the Joint Venture is terminated without the consent of all Joint Venturers, one or more of the Joint Venturers will suffer irreparable harm and will not have an adequate legal remedy. Accordingly, each Joint Venturer agrees that any one or more of the Joint Venturers may bring a proceeding in any court of competent jurisdiction seeking (i) an injunction or other equitable relief to prohibit the termination of this Joint Venture Agreement other than by consent of all the Joint Venturers and (ii) damages and costs for the attempted wrongful termination of the Joint Venture.

7.2 <u>Continuance of Joint Venture.</u> In the event of withdrawal by any Joint Venturer or the termination of its participation in the Joint Venture (whether by operation of law or otherwise) without consent of all Joint Venturers, the Joint Venture shall not terminate and shall be carried on by the remaining Joint Venturers, *provided, however,* that the non-participating Joint Venturer shall have no liability for the continued actions of the Joint Venture. The capital account of such non-participating Joint Venturer shall be credited with the profits and losses of the Joint Venture up to the date of such withdrawal or termination in accordance with the allocation formula then in effect. The Joint Venture shall thereafter credit on the capital account of the non-participating Joint Venturer with interest at the rate of 3% per annum and, subject to any claims for damages, shall continue to make the annual payments described in Section 4.2 hereof. In no event shall the Joint Venture be required to make any other payment (or distribution) on account of such Joint Venturer's capital account except upon termination of the Joint Venturers or otherwise, all the remaining Joint Venturers, in their sole discretion, shall determine.

ARTICLE VIII
GENERAL

8.1 <u>Limits of Joint Venture.</u> The relationship between the Joint Venturers shall be limited as set forth in this Agreement. This Agreement shall be construed and deemed to create a joint venture for the sole purpose of carrying out the purposes described in Article I, and nothing in this Agreement shall be construed to create a general partnership among the Joint Venturers or to authorize any Joint Venturer to act as general agent for any other Joint Venturer except as set forth herein. No Joint Venturer may engage in any activities which are competitive in any way with the business of the Joint Venture.

8.2 <u>Assignment.</u> Neither this Agreement nor any interest of any Joint Venturer herein, including any interest in moneys belonging to, or which may accrue to, the Joint Venture may be assigned, pledged, transferred or hypothecated without the prior written consent of the other Joint Venturers.

8.3 <u>Disputes and Arbitration.</u> In the event that a dispute should arise among the Joint Venturers under or in connection with this Agreement, such dispute shall be submitted to arbitration. Such arbitration shall be conducted by a board of five arbitrators, one of whom shall be appointed by each Joint Venturer and the fourth and fifth to be appointed by the three arbitrators so selected and such arbitration shall be conducted at New York City under the rules of the American Arbitration Association then obtaining.

8.4 <u>Inspection.</u> Each Joint Venturer or his authorized representative may examine any of the books or records of the Joint Venture at any time upon reasonable notice during the business hours of the Joint Venture.

8.5 <u>Integration.</u> This Agreement is the entire agreement among the parties and, except as otherwise provided herein, no alteration, modification or interpretation thereof shall be binding unless in writing, signed by all Joint Venturers.

8.6 <u>Notices.</u> All notices required or permitted by this Agreement shall be in writing and shall be sent by registered or certified mail, addressed, in the case of the Joint Venturers, to their addresses as they appear in the records of the Joint Venture or to such other address as shall from time to time be supplied in writing by any Joint Venturer.

8.7 <u>Severability.</u> If any provision of this Agreement or the application of any such provision to any party or circumstances shall be determined by any court of competent jurisdiction to be invalid and unenforceable to any extent, the remainder of this Agreement or the application of such provision to such person or circumstance other than those to which it is so determined to be invalid and unenforceable, shall not be affected thereby, and each provision hereof shall be validated and shall be enforced to the fullest extent permitted by law.

8.8 <u>Governing Law</u>. This Agreement shall be interpreted in accordance with, and the relationship between the Joint Venturers shall be governed by, the law of the State of New York (including the Uniform Partnership Act as adopted by the State of New York).

8.9 <u>Counterparts</u>. This Agreement may be executed in counterparts, each of which shall be deemed to be an original and all of such counterparts together shall constitute one and the same instrument.

IN WITNESS WHEREOF, the undersigned have executed this Agreement as of the day and year first above written.

ABC Corporation   O&H Corporation

By _____   By _____

                         B&B Corporation

                         By _____

STOCK PURCHASE AGREEMENT

Relating to the Acquisition of

SELLER, INC.

by

BUYER, INC.

Dated:_____, 19__

STOCK PURCHASE AGREEMENT

THIS STOCK PURCHASE AGREEMENT is made and entered into as of this ___ day of _____, 19__ by and among those individuals listed on Schedule A attached hereto (individually "Stockholder" and collectively "Stockholders"), being the owners of all the issued and outstanding shares of capital stock of SELLER, INC. _____ , a New York corporation (the "Company") and BUYER, INC. ("Buyer"), a California corporation, with reference to the following RECITALS:

A. The number of shares of the Common Stock of the Company owned by each Stockholder is listed on Schedule A hereof, the aggregate amount of Stock being sometimes referred to herein as the "Company Stock".

B. Buyer is newly formed and wholly-owned subsidiary of XYZ Company.

C. The Stockholders desire to sell all of the Company Stock owned by them to Buyer for the aggregate amount of $3,781,200, upon and subject to the terms and conditions hereinafter set forth.

NOW, THEREFORE, in consideration of the recitals and of the respective covenants, representations and agreements herein contained, it is hereby covenanted and agreed by and among the parties that they shall carry out and consummate the following Stock Purchase Agreement (the "Agreement"):

1. <u>Purchase and Sale of Stock</u>. Each Stockholder, in reliance on the representations, warranties and covenants of Buyer contained herein and subject to the terms and conditions of this Agreement, shall sell all of the shares of the Company Stock which he owns for the purchase price of $15 per share of Company Stock. Buyer, in reliance on the representations, warranties and covenants of the Stockholders contained herein and subject to the terms and conditions of this Agreement, shall purchase the Company Stock for the aggregate purchase price of $3,781,200, which will be paid by the Buyer at the Closing as follows:

(i) $776,240 in cash (the "Cash Payment"), by delivery to the Stockholders of checks payable to the order of each Stockholder as set forth in Schedule A; and

(ii) $3,004,960 in principal amount of the Buyer's Promissory Notes guaranteed or secured by a letter of credit issued by The Bank of New York (the "Notes Payment"), by delivery to each Stockholder of the Buyer's Promissory Notes in the form of Exhibit 1 annexed hereto, dated the Closing Date and payable to the order of each Stockholder in the principal amount which is set forth beside his name in Schedule A hereto.

2. <u>Closing</u>. The Closing (herein the "Closing") of such purchase and sale of stock shall take place at the offices of _____ , at _____ A.M. on that date which is ten days after receipt by the Buyer of the

certified financial statements referred to below in Section 7, or at such other time and place as shall be mutually agreed upon by Buyer and the Stockholders (the date of Closing being herein referred to as the ''Closing Date'').

At the Closing, the Stockholders shall deliver, free and clear of all liens, encumbrances, claims and other charges thereon of every kind, the certificates for the shares of the Company Stock in negotiable form, duly endorsed in blank or with separate stock transfer powers attached, with signatures guaranteed by a bank or trust company or by a firm having membership in the New York Stock Exchange, Inc., to Buyer upon delivery by Buyer to the Stockholders of the Cash Payment and Notes Payment on the basis provided in Section 1 hereof.

3. Default at Closing. Notwithstanding the provisions of Subsection 3.1 hereof, if any of the Stockholders shall fail or refuse to deliver any of the Company Stock as provided in Section 2 hereof, or if any of the Stockholders shall fail or refuse to consummate the transactions described in this Agreement prior to the Closing Date, such failure or refusal shall not relieve the other Stockholders of any obligations under this Agreement, and Buyer at its option and without prejudice to its rights against any such defaulting Stockholder, may either (a) acquire the remaining Company Stock which it is entitled to acquire hereunder, or (b) refuse to make such acquisition and thereby terminate all of its obligations hereunder. The Stockholders acknowledge that the Company Stock is unique and otherwise not available and agree that in addition to any other remedies, Buyer may invoke any equitable remedies to enforce performance hereunder, including, without limitation, an action or suit for specific performance.

3.1. Damages. Each of the parties hereto shall be liable to each other party for a material breach of its representations, warranties and covenants which results in a failure to perform under Sections 1 and 2 hereof, but then only to the extent of the expenses incurred by the other parties in connection with transactions contemplated by this Agreement.

4. Representations and Warranties of the Stockholders. The Stockholders, jointly and severally, represent and warrant to Buyer as follows:

4.1. Organization, Standing, Qualification and Capitalization.

The Company is a corporation duly organized, validly existing and in good standing under the laws of New York, and has the corporate power to perform its business as presently conducted and to own and lease the properties used in connection therewith. A complete and correct copy of the Articles of Incorporation and all amendments thereto of the Company certified by the Secretary of State of New York and a complete and correct copy of its By-Laws and all amendments thereto, certified by its Secretary, will be delivered to Buyer within 10 days from the date hereof. The Company is duly qualified to do business and is in good standing in [_____] and the conduct of its business or the ownership of its property does not require such qualification in any other jurisdiction.

The total authorized capital stock of the Company consists of 1,100,000 shares of Common Stock, par value $.01 per share, of which 252,080 shares are validly issued and outstanding, fully paid and nonassessable. Neither the Company nor any of the Stockholders at the Closing will be a party to or bound by any written or oral contract or agreement which grants to any person an option or right of first refusal or other right of any character to acquire at any time, or upon the happening of any stated events, shares of Common Stock of the Company whether or not presently issued or outstanding.

4.2 Stock Ownership. Each Stockholder is the lawful owner of record and beneficially of the number of shares of Company Stock set forth on Schedule A hereto, free and clear of all liens, encumbrances, claims and other charges of every kind, and each Stockholder has full legal power and all authorization required by law to transfer and deliver said shares in accordance with this Agreement.

4.3 Subsidiaries of the Company. The Company owns no shares of any corporation and has no interest in any partnership, joint venture or other legal entity.

4.4 Financial Statements. The Stockholders have delivered to Buyer copies of the following financial statements, all of which have been prepared in accordance with generally accepted accounting principles except as otherwise disclosed therein applied on a basis consistent with that of the preceding fiscal year,

(i) Balance sheets of the Company as of December 31, 1979 and December 31, 1978, certified by Main Lafrantz Company, certified public accountants, and as of October 31, 1980, prepared by the Company, which balance sheets together with any notes to the respective balance sheets present fairly the financial condition and assets and liabilities of the Company as of their respective dates. The balance sheet as of October 31, 1980 will be hereinafter called the ''1980 Balance Sheet''.

(ii) Statements of operations for the Company for the fiscal years ended December 31, 1982 and December 31, 1980 certified by Main Lafrantz & Company, and for the ten months ended

October 31, 1982, prepared by the Company, which statements together with any notes to the respective statements of net income present fairly the results of operations of the Company for the said periods.

(a) Accounts Receivable. The Accounts Receivable of the Company as set forth on the 1979 Balance Sheet and all Accounts Receivable acquired by the Company or arising subsequent to October 31, 1979 are collectible in full in the ordinary course of business in the aggregate reported amounts less any reserves reflected on the 1978 Balance Sheet.

(b) Inventory. All inventory of the Company as set forth in the 1979 Balance Sheet consisted, and all such inventory as of the Closing Date will consist, of a quality and quantity usable or salable in ordinary course of business of the Company. The value at which inventories were reflected in the 1979 Balance Sheet was the lower of cost (defined as invoice cost) or replacement market value and with adequate provision for obsolete material, all in accordance with generally accepted accounting principles applied on a basis consistent with that of the prior fiscal year.

(c) Other Assets. The prepaid expenses and other assets of the Company as shown on the 1979 Balance Sheet or arising thereafter prior to Closing represent amounts which will benefit the Company in future periods. All material tangible assets owned and used by the Company in its operations were reflected in the 1979 Balance Sheet.

(d) Fixed Assets. The fixed assets of the Company are stated at cost in the 1979 Balance Sheet. The reserves for depreciation and amortization provided against these assets have been established in accordance with the notes to the financial statements and are adequate to reduce any idle fixed assets to net realizable value.

4.5. Title to Properties. The Company has good and marketable title to all its properties and assets reflected in the 1979 Balance Sheet (except properties and assets sold or otherwise disposed of since October 31, 1980, in the normal and ordinary course of business), free and clear of all mortgages, liens, pledges, charges or other encumbrances of any nature whatsoever, except (i) any mortgages, liens, pledges, charges or other encumbrances disclosed in the 1982 Balance Sheet; or (ii) liens for current taxes not yet due and payable. The Company has valid and enforceable title insurance coverage on all real property reflected on the 1979 Balance Sheet and will deliver a true and correct copy of any policy or policies of such insurance within 10 days from the date hereof. All plants, struc-

tures and equipment owned or used by the Company are, with minor exceptions, in good operating condition and repair.

4.6. Tax Matters. The amounts set up as provisions for taxes on the 1979 Balance Sheet are sufficient for the payment of all foreign, federal, state, county and local taxes, and all employment and payroll related taxes, including any penalties or interest thereon, whether disputed or not, of the Company accrued for or applicable to all periods ended on or prior to October 31, 1980. The Company did not and will not realize any gain or income of any kind with respect to activities subsequent to October 31, 1980 and through the Closing Date except gain and income incurred in the ordinary course of business subsequent to October 31, 1980. The Company has duly made all deposits required by law to be made with respect to employees' withholding taxes. The Company has duly filed all income, foreign, franchise, excise, employment and payroll related, real and personal property, sales and gross receipts tax returns and all other tax returns which were required to be filed by it, and has paid, or has set up adequate reserves for the payment of, all taxes shown on such returns. All federal income tax returns filed by the Company have been examined and accepted by the Internal Revenue Service through [_____], and no agreement for the extension of time for the assessment of any deficiency or adjustment with respect to any tax return filed by the Company has been assessed, and the Stockholders have no knowledge of any unassessed tax deficiency proposed or threatened against the Company.

The Company has made the following elections under Section 455 of the Internal Revenue Code of 1954, as amended; [_____]

4.7. Litigation and Labor Matters. Except as provided for or disclosed in the 1982 Balance Sheet or in Schedule B hereto:

(a) there is no litigation, proceeding or governmental investigation pending or to the knowledge of the Stockholders threatened, against or related to the Company, or its properties or business;

(b) the Company is not in default with respect to any order, writ, injunction or decree of any court or federal, state, municipal or governmental department, commission, board, bureau, agency or instrumentality; and

(c) The Company has not committed, and neither the Stockholders nor the Company has received any notice of or claim that the Company has commited any unfair labor practice under applicable federal or state law.

4.8 Insurance. The Company is insured under various policies of fire, liability and other forms of insurance, as set forth in Schedule C hereto, which policies are valid and enforceable in accordance with their terms and provide adequate insurance for the business of the Company and its assets and properties. The Company shall continue to carry all such policies or similar policies during the pendency of this Agreement, and all outstanding claims under such policies are described in Schedule C. There is no liability for retrospective insurance premium adjustments for any period prior to the date hereof.

4.9 Patents, Trademarks and Copyrights. Schedule D attached hereto sets forth all patents, patent applications, registered trademarks, registered service marks, trademark and service mark applications, unregistered trademarks and service marks, copyrights and copyright applications, owned or filed by the Company or in which the Company has an interest and the nature of such interest. No other patent, trademark or service mark, copyright or license under any thereof, is necessary to permit the business of the Company to be conducted as now conducted or as heretofore or proposed to be conducted. No person, firm or corporation has any proprietary, financial or other interest in any of such patents, patent applications, registered trademarks, registered service marks, trademark and service mark applications, unregistered trademarks and service marks, copyrights and copyright applications, and there are no violations by others of any of the rights of the Company thereunder. The Company is not infringing upon any patent trademark or service mark, or copyright or otherwise violating the rights, of any third party, and no proceedings have been instituted or are pending or, to the knowledge of the Stockholders or the Company, are threatened, and no claim has been received by the Company, alleging any such violation. The Company is not a party to or bound by any license agreement requiring the payment by the Company of any royalty payment, except as set forth in Schedule D.

4.10 Contracts and Commitments. Except as listed and identified in Schedule E hereto, the Company is not a party to any written or oral:

(a) contract or commitment with any present or former director or employee or consultant;

(b) contract or commitment with any labor union or employee group;

(c) contract or commitment for the future purchase of, or payment for, raw materials, supplies or products, involving in any case $10,000 or more;

(d) contract or commitment to sell or supply products or to perform services for a specific price involving $10,000 or more without the ability

on the part of the Company to increase such price or to cancel the contract or commitment without any liability to the Company;

(e) contract or commitment continuing over a period of more than six months from the date of this Agreement;

(f) representative or sales agency contract or commitment;

(g) lease under which it is either lessor or lessee;

(h) bonus, pension, profit sharing, retirement, stock purchase, stock option, hospitalization, insurance, vacation pay or any other similar plan or practice, including but not limited to any welfare benefit plan as defined in Section 3(1) of the Employee Retirement Income Security Act, formal or informal, in effect with respect to any of their employees or former employees;

(i) contract or commitment for the borrowing of money or other agreement or arrangement for a line of credit;

(j) contract or commitment for any charitable contribution;

(k) contract or commitment for capital expenditures in excess of $5,000;

(l) contract or commitment limiting or restraining it from engaging or competing in any lines of business with any person, firm, corporation or other entity; or

(m) contract not made in the ordinary course of business.

Except as stated in Schedule E and for delays, minor failures to meet specifications or other minor defaults which are normal in the conduct of business between the Company and other parties to the above contracts, all parties to the above contracts have complied with the provisions thereof, no party is in default thereunder, and no event has occurred which but for the passage of time or the giving of notice would constitute a default thereunder.

4.11 Absence of Undisclosed Liabilities. There are no liabilities or obligations of the Company either accrued, absolute, contingent or otherwise, including, but not limited to, any tax liabilities due or to become due, except:

(a) to the extent reflected in the 1982 Balance Sheet and not heretofore paid or discharged, and

(b) those incurred, consistently with past business practice, in or as a result of the normal and ordinary course of business since October 31, 1978.

4.12. Absence of Default. The Company is not in default in the performance, observance or fulfillment of any material obligation, covenant or condition contained in any debenture or note, or contained in any conditional sale or equipment trust agreement, or loan or other borrowing agreement to which the Company is a party.

4.13. Existing Condition. Except as disclosed in Schedule F, since October 31, 1979, there has not been (i) any material adverse change in the financial condition or in the combined operations, businesses or properties of the Company; (ii) any damage, destruction or loss, whether covered by insurance or not, materially and adversely affecting the operations, businesses or properties of the Company; (iii) any declaration, setting aside or payment of any dividend, or any distribution in respect of capital stock of the Company, or any redemption, purchase or other acquisition of any of such shares of the Company; (iv) any increase in the compensation payable or to become payable by the Company to any of its officers or directors; (v) any change in the terms of any bonus, insurance, pension or other benefit plan for or with any officers, directors or employees which increases amounts paid, payable or to become payable thereunder; or (vi) any complaints or other concerns which have been brought to the attention of the Stockholders and which relate to the Company's labor relations.

4.14. Validity of Contemplated Transactions. Neither the execution and delivery of this Agreement nor the consummation of the transactions provided for herein will violate any agreement to which the Company or any of the Stockholders is a party or by which it or any of them is bound or any law, order or decree or any provision of the Articles of Incorporation, Charter or By-Laws of the Company. The Stockholders have full legal authority to execute and deliver this Agreement and to consummate and perform the transactions contemplated hereby, and this Agreement constitutes the valid obligation of the Stockholders legally binding upon them and each of them in accordance with its terms.

4:15. Restrictions. The Company is not subject to any charter or other corporate restriction or any judgment, order, writ, injunction or decree, which materially and adversely affects or, so far as the Stockholders can now foresee, may in the future materially and adversely affect, the combined businesses, operations, prospects, properties, assets or condition, financial or otherwise, of the Company.

4.16. Pension Plans. Schedule G fairly sets forth the financial and actuarial condition of all plans described in Schedule E in response to Section 4.10(h) and fully discloses the current liabilities and any unfunded past service liabilities of the Company based

upon the assumptions that all such plans and arrangements will remain in force afd further contains those actuarial assumptions upon which such condition and projections are premised. All such plans and arrangements described in Schedule E to which the Employees Retirement Income Security Act ("ERISA") applies, in whole or in part, are in compliance with those existing provisions of ERISA which are presently applicable to such plans and arrangements and either (a) substantially comply with those provisions of ERISA which will in the future apply to such plans and arrangements or (b) can, without incurring an expense in excess of $2,500 and without decreasing any benefit or otherwise making such plans and arrangements less advantageous to participants and beneficiaries thereunder, be brought into compliance with those provisions of ERISA which will in the future apply to such plans and arrangements. The Company has not breached any of its fiduciary obligations under ERISA nor has any other fiduciary breached any of its obligations for which the Company would be liable as a fiduciary under ERISA.

4.17. Compliance with Laws. The Company has complied with and are not in default under, or in violation of, any laws, ordinances, rules, regulations or orders (including, without limitation, any safety, health or trade laws, ordinances, rules, regulations or orders) applicable to the operations, businesses or properties of the Company which materially and adversely affect or, so far as the Stockholders can now foresee, may in the future materially and adversely affect, the combined businesses, operations, prospects, properties, assets or condition, financial or otherwise, of the Company.

4.18. Disclosure. No representation or warranty by Stockholders in this Agreement contains any untrue statement of material facts or omits to state any material fact necessary to make any statement herein not misleading.

4.19. Transactions with Affiliates. No director, officer or Stockholder of the Company owns or during the last two years has owned, directly or indirectly, or has, or during the last two years has had, an ownership interest in any business, corporate or otherwise, which is a party to, or in any property which is the subject of, any business arrangement or relationship of any kind with the Company, except as described in Schedule H.

4.20. Bank Accounts and Officers. Schedule I contains a true and correct list of the name and location of each bank in which the Company has an account, each safety deposit box or custody agreement and the names of the persons authorized to draw thereon or to withdraw therefrom and also sets forth the names of all directors and officers of the Company.

5. Representations and Warranties of Buyer. Buyer represents and warrants to the Stockholders that:

5.1. Organization, Good Standing and Authority. Buyer is a corporation duly organized, validly existing and in good standing under the laws of the state of New York, and has full corporate power and authority to own its properties and assets and to carry on its business as it has been and is conducted. The execution and delivery of this Agreement and the consummation of the transactions contemplated hereby are within the corporate power of Buyer and have been duly authorized by all necessary corporate and other action. This Agreement constitutes and the Notes Payment will constitute when delivered in accordance with the terms hereof the valid obligation of the Buyer legally binding upon it in accordance with its or their respective terms. All of the Buyer's issued and outstanding capital stock is owned by Buttin Company.

5.2. Validity of Contemplated Transactions. Neither the execution and delivery of this Agreement nor the consummation of the transaction provided herein will violate any agreement to which Buyer is a party or by which it is bound or any law, order or decree or any provision of the Certificate of Incorporation or By-Laws of Buyer.

5.3. Investment Representations. The Company Stock being delivered pursuant to the provisions of this Agreement will be held by Buyer for its own account and not with a view to, or for resale in connection with, the distribution thereof.

5.4. Litigation.

(a) There is no litigation, proceeding or governmental investigation pending, or to the knowledge of the officers and directors of Buyer, against or relating to Buyer, or its properties or business, and

(b) Buyer is not knowingly in default with respect to any order, writ, injunction or decree of any court or federal, state, municipal or governmental department, commission, board, bureau, agency or instrumentality.

6. Conduct of Business Pending Closing. The Stockholders jointly and severally, represent, warrant and agree with respect to the Company that, pending the Closing and except as otherwise approved in writing by Buyer:

6.1. Business in the Ordinary Course. The Company shall refrain from engaging in transactions other than in the ordinary course of business. The Company shall also refrain from entering into any transaction involving a capital expenditure (including any borrowings in connection with such transaction) of more than $1,000 or the disposal of any property or asset (other than inventory in the ordinary course) with a value of more than $1,000. or the disposal of any property or asset (other than inventory in the ordinary course) with a value of more than $1,000.

6.2. Accounting and Credit Changes. The Company shall not make any change in its accounting procedures and practices or its credit criteria from those in existence at October 31, 1979.

6.3. Capitalization, Options and Dividends. No change shall be made in the Articles of Incorporation of the Company, it shall not issue or reclassify or alter any shares of its outstanding or unissued capital stock, it shall not grant options, warrants or other rights of any kind to purchase, or agree to issue any shares of its capital stock, it shall not purchase, redeem or otherwise acquire for a consideration any shares of its capital stock and they shall not declare, pay, set aside or make any dividends or other distribution or payment in respect of its capital stock.

6.4. Encumbrance of Assets. No mortgage, pledge or encumbrance of any of the properties or assets of the Company shall be made.

6.5. Employment Agreements, Etc. The Company shall refrain from entering into any employment agreements, and shall keep in effect its present salary administration program (including pension plans and other fringe benefits).

6.6. Real Property Acquisitions, Dispositions and Leases. The Company shall refrain from acquiring or agreeing to acquire, or disposing or agreeing to dispose of, real estate and from entering into or agreeing to enter into leases of real estate or equipment for a period in excess of one year.

6.7. Litigation During Interim Period. The Company will promptly advise Buyer in writing of the commencement or threat against the Company of any claim, litigation, proceeding or tax audit not covered by insurance when the amount claimed is in excess of $10,000.

6.8. Access. Buyer and its officers, attorney, accountants and representatives shall be permitted to examine the property, books and records of the Company, and its title to any real estate, and such officers, attorneys, accountants and representatives shall be afforded access to such property, books, records and titles, and the Stockholders will upon request furnish Buyer with any information reasonably required in respect to the Company's property, assets and business and will provide Buyer with copies of any contract, document or instrument listed in any Schedule hereto.

6.9. <u>Good Will</u>. The Company will use its best efforts to preserve the good will of its customers and suppliers and others having business relations with it.

7. <u>Audit and Termination</u>. Within 60 days following the date hereof, the Stockholders shall deliver to the Buyer a balance sheet of the Company and a statement of operations of the Company for the year ended December 31, 1979, prepared in accordance with generally accepted accounting principles applied on a basis consistent with that applied in the financial statements described in Section 4.4 and reported on without qualification by Dan Lafrentz & Company, whose report shall accompany the delivery of such statements (the "Audited Financial Statements"). If net income after provision for taxes of the Company for the twelve months ended December 31, 1979 as shown on the Audited Financial Statements is less than $750,000, then notwithstanding any other provision in this Agreement to the contrary, Buyer shall have the right to terminate all obligations hereunder and shall notify the Stockholders of any decision to so terminate within 10 days of the delivery to it of the Audited Financial Statements.

8. <u>Covenants of the Buyer and the Stockholders</u>.

8.1. <u>Pension Plan</u>. Buyer agrees that it will take no action after the closing which would result in an adverse change in the benefits to the employees covered by the Company's Pension Plan described in Schedule E.

8.2. <u>Employment Agreements</u>. Mr. Jones and Ms. Smith shall have entered into Employment Agreements with the Company in the form attached as Exhibit 2 with annual base compensation payable thereunder and a term thereof as follows: Mr. Jones $___,___ years; Ms. Smith - $___,___ years.

8.3. <u>Covenant Not to Compete</u>. Each of the Stockholders agrees that for a period of five years from and after the date of the Closing, he will not, unless acting as an employee of or consultant to the Company or with Buyer's prior written consent, directly or indirectly, own, manage, operate, join, control or participate in the ownership, management, operation or control of, or be connected as as officer, employee, partner or otherwise with, any business engaged in any of the businesses which are presently conducted by the Company within any State in which the Company presently maintains an office, other than by owning not more than 5% of a class of securities registered under Section 12 of the Securities Exchange Act of 1934. Each person agrees that the remedy at law for any breach of the foregoing will be inadequate and that the Company and

the Buyer shall be entitled, inter alia, to temporary and permanent injunctive relief without the necessity of proving actual damage to the Company or the Buyer.

9. <u>Liability and Responsibility of and Indemnification by Stockholders</u>.

9.1. Subject to other Subsections of this Section 9, the Stockholders shall indemnify and hold harmless Buyer and the Company against and in respect of any and all liability, damage, loss, deficiency, cost and expenses arising out of or otherwise in respect of:

(a) any misrepresentation, breach of warranty or non-fulfillment of any agreement or covenant or from any misrepresentation in or omission from any Schedule or list contained in this Agreement, certificate or other instrument furnished by the Stockholders, and

(b) any and all actions, suits, proceedings, audits, demands, assessments, judgements, costs and legal and other expenses incident to any of the foregoing or the enforcement of this Section 9; provided, however, that the Stockholders shall not be liable to Buyer under this Agreement for any matter, other than matters relating to taxes, which was not set forth in a claim presented in writing to the Stockholders pursuant to Section 22 within four years from the Closing Date. Notwithstanding anything to the contrary herein, the Stockholders shall be liable, responsible or obligated to indemnify Buyer for claims under this Section 9, only if the aggregate amount of such claims exceed $15,000. The total liability and responsibility of each Stockholder under this Section 9 shall be limited to the aggregate purchase price received under this Agreement.

9.2. Promptly after the receipt by any party hereto of notice of any claim or the commencement of any action or proceeding, such party will, if a claim with respect thereto is to be made against any party obligated to provide indemnification (the "Indemnifying Party") pursuant to this Section 9, give such Indemnifying Party written notice of such claim or the commencement of such action or proceeding. Such Indemnifying Party shall have the right, at its option and upon posting a bond or other security equal to such claims, to compromise or defend, at its own expense and by its counsel, any such matter involving the asserted liability of the party seeking such indemnification. Such notice, and opportunity to compromise or defend, shall be a condition precedent to any liability of the Indemnifying Party under the indemnification agreements contained in this Section 9. If any Indemnifying Party shall undertake to compromise or defend any such asserted liability, it shall promptly notify the party seeking indemnification of its intention to do so, and the party seeking indemnification agrees to cooperate fully with the Indemnifying Party and its counsel in the comprise of, or defense against, any such asserted liability. In any event, the indemnified party shall have the right at its own expense to participate in the defense of such asserted liability.

10. Conditions Precedent to Buyer's Obligations. All obligations of Buyer under this Agreement are subject to the fulfillment, prior to or at the Closing, of each of the following conditions:

10.1. Representations and Warranties. The Stockholders' representations and warranties contained in this Agreement or in any list, certificate or document delivered pursuant to the provisions hereof shall be true at and as of the time of Closing as though such representations and warranties were made at and as of such time (except to the extent that they are stated therein to be true as of some other date) and the Stockholders shall have delivered to Buyer a certificate dated the Closing Date and signed by them to such effect.

10.2. Compliance with Agreements. The Stockholders and the Company shall have perfomed or complied with all agreements and conditions required by this Agreement to be performed or complied with by them prior to or at the Closing, and the Stockholders shall have delivered to Buyer a certificate dated the Closing Date and signed by them to such effect.

10.3. Opinion of Counsel. The Stockholders shall have delivered to Buyer an opinion of their counsel, White and Williams, dated the Closing Date and in form and substance satisfactory to Buyer to the effect that:

(a) Each of the Stockholders is the lawful owner of record and beneficially of all the number of shares of the Company's Stock set forth beside his name in Schedule A, free and clear of any liens, encumbrances, equities and claims and has full legal power and all authorization required by law to transfer and deliver said shares in accordance with this Agreement, and by delivery of a certificate of certificates therefor will transfer to Buyer title to said shares, free and clear of any liens, encumbrances, equities and claims.

(b) This Agreement constitutes the valid obligations of the Stockholders legally binding upon them and each of them in accordance with its terms.

(c) The Company is not a party to, or bound by any written or oral contract or agreement which grants to any person an option or right of first refusal or other right to acquire at any time, or upon the happening of any stated events, shares of the capital stock of the Company.

(d) The Company's authorized capital stock consists of 1,100,000 shares of Common Stock, par value

$.01 per share, of which 252,080 shares have been validly issued, are presently outstanding, and are fully paid and non-assessable.

(e) The Company is a corporation duly organized, validly existing and in good standing under the laws of its state of incorporation and it has the corporate power to conduct its business as presently conducted and to own and hold the properties used in connection therewith.

(f) The Company is qualified to do business as a foreign corporation in [_____].

(g) The consummation of the transactions contemplated by this Agreement will not result in a breach of any term or provision of or constitute a default under the Articles of Incorporation or Charter or By-Laws of the Company, or any indenture, agreement, instrument or understanding known to such counsel to which the Company or any of the Stockholders is a party or by which it or any of them is bound.

(h) The Company has good and marketable title to the properties described in Subsection 4.5 hereof subject to no liens or other encumbrances except those listed in phrases (i) through (ii) of said Subsection 4.5. The opinion required by this Subsection shall be based solely upon matters which have come to such counsel's attention and which are contained in a title insurance policy and any judgment, federal tax lien or financing statement searches in respect of the Company referred to in such opinion.

10.4. Directors. The Stockholders shall have caused the By-Laws of the Company to be amended so that its Board of Directors will be increased by three members and the three nominees of the Buyer set forth in Schedule J shall have been elected directors of the Company.

10.5. Material Damage. The business and properties of the Company taken as a whole, shall not have been and shall not be threatened to be materially adversely affected in any way as a result of fire, explosion, earthquake, disaster, accident, labor dispute, flood, drought, embargo, riot, civil disturbance, uprising, activity of armed forces or act of God or public enemy.

10.6. Employment Agreements. The four employment agreements with those Stockholders referred to in Section 8.2 shall have been executed and delivered.

10.7. Approval of Counsel. All steps to be taken and all resolutions, papers and documents to be executed, and all other legal matters in connection with the purchase and sale of stock and related matters, including compliance with applicable State securities laws, shall be subject to the reasonable approval of ABC'S counsel.

11. Conditions Precedent to Stockholders' Obligations. All obligations of the Stockholders under this Agreement are subject to the fulfillment, prior to or at the Closing, of each of the following conditions:

11.1. Representations and Warranties. Buyer's representations and warranties contained in this Agreement or in any certificate or document delivered pursuant to the provisions hereof or in connection with the transactions contemplated hereby shall be true at and as of the time of Closing as though such representations and warranties were made at and as of such time, and Buyer shall each have delivered to the Stockholders a certificate dated the Closing Date and signed by its President or a Vice President to such effect.

11.2. Compliance with Agreements. Buyer shall have performed and complied with all agreements and conditions required by this Agreement to be performed or complied with by each corporation prior to or at the Closing, and shall have delivered to the Stockholders a certificate dated the Closing Date and signed by its President or a Vice President to such effect.

11.3. Opinion of Counsel. Buyer shall have delivered to the Stockholders an opinion of ABC'S counsel dated the Closing Date, and in form and substance satisfactory to the Stockholders, with respect to the matters referred to in Subsections 5.1 and 5.2 hereof.

11.4. Material Damage. The business or properties of Buyer shall not have been, and shall not be threatened to be, affected in any way materially adverse to the enterprise of Buyer as a result of fire, explosion, earthquake, disaster, accident, labor dispute, flood, drought embargo, riot, civil disturbance, uprising, or activity of armed forces or act of God or public enemy.

11.5. Employment Agreements. The four employment agreements with those Stockholders referred to in Section 8.2 shall have been executed and delivered.

11.6. Letter of Credit. The Bank of New York shall have guaranteed the Company's obligations under the Notes Payment, which may be in the form of a letter of credit.

12. Broker and Finder's Fees. The Stockholders represent and warrant to Buyer that they have not engaged or dealt with any broker fee or commission in respect of the execution of this Agreement or the consummation of the transactions contemplated hereby, except Mr. Jones whose fees shall be paid by the Stockholders. Buyer represents and warrants to the Stockholders that neither it nor any corporate affiliate has engaged or dealt with any broker or other person who may be entitled to any brokerage fee or commission in respect of the execution of this Agreement or the consummation of the transactions contemplated hereby.

Each of the parties hereto shall indemnify and hold the others harmless against any and all claims, losses, liabilities or expenses which may be asserted against such other parties as a result of such first mentioned party's dealings, arrangements or agreements with any such broker or person.

13. Survival of Representations and Warranties. All representation, warranties and agreements made by Buyer and the Stockholders in this Agreement or pursuant hereto shall survive the Closing for a period not to exceed four years, except for representations, warranties and agreements relating to taxes of all kinds which shall survive until claims based thereon shall have been barred by the relevant statutes of limitations. Notwithstanding any investigation or audit conducted before or after the Closing Date, the parties shall be entitled to rely upon the representations and warranties set forth in this Agreement.

14. Expenses. Except as otherwise provided in Section 3.1, the Stockholders shall bear their expenses, and Buyer shall bear its expense, in connection with the Agreement and the transactions contemplated thereby.

15. Announcements. Buyer and the Stockholders will, and the stockholders will cause the Company to, consult and cooperate with each other as to the timing and content of any announcements of the transactions contemplated hereby to the general public or to employees, customers or suppliers.

16. Further Actions and Assurances. Buyer and the Stockholders will execute and deliver any and all documents, and will cause any and all other action to be taken, either before or after Closing, which may be necessary or proper to effect or evidence the provisions of this Agreement and the transactions contemplated hereby.

17. Counterparts. This Agreement may be executed in several counterparts each of which is an original and any Stockholder may become a party hereto by executing a counterpart hereof. This Agreement and any counterpart so executed shall be deemed to be one and the same instrument. It shall not be necessary in making proof of this Agreement or any counterpart hereof to produce or account for any of the other counterparts.

18. Contents of Agreement; Parties in Interest, Etc. This Agreement sets forth the entire understanding of the parties. Any previous agreements or understand-

ings between the parties regarding the subject matter hereof are merged into and superseded by this Agreement. All representations, warranties, covenants, terms, conditions and provisions of this Agreement shall be binding upon and inure to the benefit of and be enforceable by the respective heirs, legal representatives, successors and assigns of the Stockholders and Buyer.

19. New York Law to Govern. This Agreement is being delivered and is intended to be performed in the State of New York and shall be construed and enforced in accordance with the laws thereof.

20. Section Headings and Gender. The section headings herein have been inserted for convenience of reference only and shall in no way modify or restrict any of the terms or provisions hereof. The use of the masculine pronoun herein when referring to any party has been for convenience only and shall be deemed to refer to the particular party intended regardless of the actual gender of such party.

21. Schedules. All Schedules referred to in this Agreement are intended to be and are hereby specifically made a part of this Agreement.

22. Notices. All notices, requests and other communications which are required or permitted hereunder shall be sufficient if given in writing and delivered personally or by registered or certified mail, postage prepaid, as follows (or to such other addressee as shall be set forth in a notice given in the same manner):

If to Buyer to: BUYER, INC.

If to Stockholders:

23. Confidential Information. Notwithstanding any termination of this Agreement, Buyer and its corporate affiliates and its representatives agree to hold in confidence any information not generally available to the public or the trade received by them from the Company or the Stockholders pursuant to the terms of this Agreement. If this Agreement is terminated for any reason, Buyer, its corporate affiliates and its representatives will continue to hold such information in confidence and will, to the extent requested by the Company, promptly return to the Company all written material furnished to Buyer, its corporate affiliates or its representatives pursuant hereto.

IN WITNESS WHEREOF, this Agreement has been executed as of the day and year first above written.

BUYER, INC.

Attest:

By _____

_____
Secretary

STOCKHOLDERS:

STOCK PURCHASE AGREEMENT

LIST OF SCHEDULES

Schedule A - List of the Stockholders and the number of sharees of the Common Stock of the Company owned by each Stockholder, and allocation of cash and notes - Recital A, ¶1, ¶5.2

Schedule B - Litigation - ¶5.7 [To be prepared by the Stockholders]

Schedule C - Insurance - ¶5.8 [To be prepared by the Stockholders]

Schedule D - Patents, Trademarks and Copyrights -¶5.9 [To be prepared by the Stockholders]

Schedule E - Contracts and Commitments - ¶5.10 [To prepared by the Stockholders]

Schedule F - Existing Condition - ¶5.13 [To be prepared by the Stockholders]

Schedule G - Pension Plan Information - ¶5.16 [To be prepared by the Stockholders]

Schedule H - Transactions with Affiliates - ¶5.19 [To be prepared by the Stockholders]

Schedule I - Bank Account Information - ¶5.20 [To be prepared by the Stockholders]

OPTION AGREEMENT FOR ASSET PURCHASE

THIS OPTION AGREEMENT, made and entered into this _____ day of June 1982, by and between Seller Company, a Delaware corporation (hereinafter referred to as "Seller"), and Buyer Company or his designee (hereinafter referred to as "Buyer").

WHEREAS, Seller owns certain land, buildings, machinery and equipment in Boston, Massachusetts, including Seller's ABC Division (hereinafter referred to as the "Plant Facilities"); and

WHEREAS, Seller and Buyer have entered into a Consulting Agreement as of the date hereof which grants to Buyer an option to purchase the Plant Facilities on the terms and conditions included herein.

NOW, THEREFORE, in consideration of said Consulting Agreement and of the premises herein Seller hereby grants to Buyer an option to purchase the Plant Facilities on the following terms and conditions:

1.0 DESCRIPTION OF ASSETS INCLUDED IN OPTION

1.1 Real Estate. All of the land, buildings, improvements and appurtenances thereto owned by Seller in the City of Boston, Massachusetts as more particularly described on Exhibit A, attached hereto and made a part hereof.

1.2 Machinery, Equipment and Fixtures.

(a) All of the machinery, equipment, tools, office furniture, fixtures and all of the physical assets, whether real or personal property, located at and constituting a part of the Plant Facilities, including those assets utilized by Seller's ABC Division, except as provided or limited by Subsections 1.2(b) and (c) below.

(b) Prior to the exercise of the option as provided herein, Seller shall, subject to the limitations of Subsection 1.2(c) below, have the right to sell or otherwise dispose of for its account all of the machinery, equipment, tools, furniture and fixtures presently constituting a part of Seller's Biney Mill (which is a part of the Plant Facilities), except that Seller shall not have the right as long as this Option Agreement is effective and outstanding to dispose of the equipment listed on Exhibit B, attached hereto and made a part hereof, which is presently included as a part of the Biney Mill assets.

(c) Up to and including November 1, 1982, Seller agrees not to dispose of machines No. 3 and No. 4 in the Greene Mill provided that if Buyer so requests, Seller will include such machines No. 3 and No. 4 in the machinery and equipment to be sold to Buyer upon

exercise of Buyer's option as provided herein.

1.3 Intangible Assets. All of Seller's manufacturing processes, trade secrets, know-how, trademarks and brand names used exclusively by Seller in the manufacture and sale of products at the ABC Division, including those trademarks listed on Exhibit C, attached hereto and made a part hereof.

1.4 Patents. Seller presently knows of no patent rights which are necessary to the manufacture and sale of products currently being manufactured at the ABC Division. However, to the extent that Seller has the right and can do so without violating the rights of third parties, Seller will at the Closing, grant to Buyer a nonexclusive license at no cost to Buyer covering any patent rights which Buyer may reasonably require in order to manufacture and sell the products being manufactured and sold by the ABC Division at the time of the exercise of this Option.

1.5 Inventories. All of the raw materials, supplies, work-in-process and finished goods inventories which are included as a part of Seller's ABC Division assets at the Closing Date or such other date as may be mutually agreed to by the parties.

1.6 Leased Assets. Seller will use its best efforts to obtain any necessary consents to assign or sublease to Buyer, as of the Closing Date, any assets which are used by the ABC Division at the closing and which are at that time being leased by Seller from third parties.

2.0 LEASES

2.1 Seller has presently leased certain space in the Biney and Kitter Mills constituting a part of the Plant Facilities and Seller may, prior to the exercise of the option provided herein, lease additional space in the Plant Facilities which does not constitute a part of and will not interefere with the ABC Division operations and assets. The parties agree that Seller's obligation to sell and transfer the assets described under Section 1.1 above will be subject to the rights of any lessees of any portion of the Plant Facilities as such rights may exist as of the Closing Date, and Seller agrees to assign to Buyer its interest in any of such leases as of the Closing Date.

3.0 PURCHASE PRICE

3.1 As the full consideration and purchase price for the assets described in Section 1.1, 1.2 and 1.3, Buyer agrees to pay to Seller the sum of One Million Eight Hundred Thousand Dollars ($1,800,000), except that if Buyer elects to include paper machines No. 3 and No. 4 in the Greene Mill in the machinery and equipment to be acquired as described in Section 1.2 hereof, Buyer shall pay to Seller an additional sum equal to Seller's net book value for such paper machines No. 3 and No. 4 as of the Closing Date.

3.2 As the full consideration and purchase price for the finished goods inventory described in Section 1.5, Buyer agrees to pay to Seller an amount equal to Seller's published list prices for such inventory less a discount of 15.3% which represents Seller's normal profit and an allowance for freight costs, cash discounts, returns and allowances and any special sales commissions.

3.3 As the full consideration and purchase price for the raw materials, supplies and work-in-process inventory described in Section 1.5 above, Buyer agrees to pay to Seller a sum, determined as of the Closing Date or such other date within fifteen (15) days thereof as may be agreed to by the parties, equal to the cost to Seller of each of such items as determined by Seller's accounting practices and procedures, consistently applied, and generally accepted accounting principles.

3.4 If at the date of exercise of the option granted by this Agreement there shall be any items in finished goods inventory for which Seller has not invoiced shipments within the twelve (12) months preceding, at Buyer's option any such item may be purchased at such price and upon such terms as shall be mutually agreed by the parties. Seller will retain the items described in this subparagraph on which the parties are unable to reach agreement. Buyer shall provide storage at no charge for the inventory retained by Seller for a reasonable time (not to exceed six (6) months) and during such period shall ship such inventory in accordance with Seller's directions at Seller's expense plus a reasonable handling charge.

4.0 METHOD OF PAYMENT

In payment of the purchase price of the assets to be sold and transferred to Buyer hereunder as called for under Section 3.0 above, Buyer shall pay or deliver to Seller at the Closing Date the following:

4.1 Buyer's Promissory Note in the principal amount of One Million Eight Hundred Thousand Dollars ($1,800,000) in the form as set forth on Exhibit D, attached hereto and made a part hereof.

4.2 A Mortgage, Security Agreement and Financing Statement securing the Promissory Note described above, in a form acceptable to counsel for Buyer and Seller, which will, in the opinion of both such counsel, effectively vest in Seller a security interest in the assets described in Sections 1.1 and 1.2 hereof.

4.3 A bank cashier's, certified check or other method of payment acceptable to Seller for the full purchase price of the assets described in Section 1.5 hereof.

5.0 PHYSICAL INVENTORY AND VALUATION

5.1 Not later than forty-five (45) days after the exercise by Buyer of the Option granted herein the parties agree to take a physical inventory of the assets described in Sections 1.2 and 1.5. Such inventory shall be conducted and supervised by personnel of the Seller, provided, however, that Buyer shall be entitled to have as many representatives and agents as it so desires observe and assist Seller in the taking of such inventory. The procedures for the taking of such physical inventory shall be negotiated and agreed to by Buyer and Seller in good faith prior to the taking of the inventory.

5.2 Inventory Valuation. The valuation of the inventory items included in the physical inventory taken pursuant to Section 5.1 shall be made as set forth under Sections 3.2 and 3.3 hereof and such valuations shall be conclusive evidence of the purchase price of all of such inventory items.

6.0 TRANSFER OF ASSETS

6.1 Transfer. At the Closing, Seller shall transfer, assign, deliver and set over to Buyer all of the assets described in Section 1 hereof.

6.2 Delivery of Documents. To effect such transfer at the Closing, or as may be required by the Buyer or its counsel subsequent to the Closing, Seller shall deliver to Buyer such deeds, bills of sale, assignments and other documents of transfer in a form satisfactory to Buyer hereunder. Upon the request of Buyer at any time subsequent to the Closing, Seller shall execute and deliver such further documents and perform such other acts as Buyer may reasonably deem necessary as advisable in order to transfer, protect title to or protect Buyer's rights to the ownership, use or enjoyment of any property, assets or rights intended to be transferred pursuant to this Agreement.

6.3 Books and Records. At the Closing or as may be requested by Buyer within a reasonable period of time thereafter, Seller shall deliver or cause to be delivered to Buyer all of the books, records, documents and other data in its possession pertaining to the assets to be sold and transferred to Buyer hereunder, including, but not limited to, accounting and sales records, purchase orders, customer lists, engineering and manufacturing drawings and production records pertaining to the ABC Division operations. Buyer agrees to retain all of such records for a period of time at least equal to the record retention times as specified in Seller's current record retention policy. Buyer further agrees that it will make available to Seller or its agents, representatives, counsel or accountants, at any reasonable time upon request of Seller, any of such books or records and agrees to provide Seller at no charge with office space at the Plant Facilities in order to permit Seller to fully enjoy the rights granted to it by this Section.

7.0 EMPLOYEE AND EMPLOYEE MATTERS

7.1 <u>Employees</u>. At least thirty (30) days prior to the Closing Seller will deliver to Buyer a list of all persons employed at the ABC Division showing their current job classification, and copies of all union and collective bargaining contracts and agreements, group life, hospital and medical insurance plans and pension and retirement plans which are then in effect with respect to employees working at the ABC Division. Seller agrees to use its best efforts to encourage all such employees, including hourly, salaried and management employees, to enter into employment with Buyer from and after the Closing Date.

7.2 <u>Employee Agreements and Benefits</u>. Buyer agrees to assume all of the obligations, duties and liabilities of Seller under the union contracts and employee benefit plans for the hourly employees of the ABC Division in effect at the Closing, subject to the express understanding and agreement by Seller that all liabilities and obligations incurred or accruing under any of such plans to the Closing Date shall be and remain the obligation of Seller, and Seller does hereby indemnify and hold Buyer harmless from any of such obligations.

8.0 PENSION PLANS

(a) Seller agrees to be responsible for the payment of any liabilities for pension or retirement benefits that have accrued at the Closing Date under Seller's Pension Plan No. 12 for all present or former hourly employees of the ABC Division and under the Seller Company Retirement Plan for all present or former salaried employees of the ABC Division. Seller agrees to be responsible for the administration, operation and funding of such pension plans and the investment of all pension fund assets applicable to such plans and to comply with all applicable statutory and actuarial funding requirements and reporting and disclosure requirements concerning such pension plans. Seller hereby indemnifies and holds Buyer harmless from and against any claims, demands or liabilities that may be hereafter asserted by any employee of the ABC Division for pension or retirement benefits earned or accrued by such employee up to and including the Closing Date.

(b) Seller agrees that by this Agreement Buyer is not assuming any liability for pension or retirement benefits with respect to salaried employees who may elect to continue their employment at the ABC Division with Buyer after the Closing. Buyer, however, does expressly agree to assume the contractual liability, if any, which Seller has or will have under its union and collective bargaining agreements in effect at the Closing covering employees at the ABC Division for pension and retirement benefits which may accrue to such employees subsequent to the Closing Date as a result of employment by Buyer at the ABC Division.

(c) Seller represents to Buyer that the liabilities for benefits under Pension Plan No. 12 are substantially fully funded and Seller shall be responsible for the full funding of any such liabilities and Buyer shall have no responsibility whatsoever for the funding of any pension liabilities accrued to the date of Closing under Seller's Pension Plan No. 12. Seller also represents that the liability for pension benefits to present and former salaried employees of the ABC Division who are covered under Seller's retirement plan for salaried employees is not fully funded and that the unfunded present value of of such benefits is presently estimated at One Hundred Eighty-Five Thousand Dollars ($185,000). In consideration of Seller's agreement to remain fully responsible for all pension benefits to present or former salaried employees of the ABC Division which have vested and accrued as of the Closing Date. Buyer agrees to deliver to Seller at the Closing its Promissory Note in the form as set forth on Exhibit E, attached hereto and made a part hereof, in the principal amount of One Hundred Thousand Dollars ($100,000), said Note to be secured by the Mortgage, Security Agreement and Financing Statement provided for under Section 4.2 above.

9.0 ACCOUNTS RECEIVABLE

At the Closing Date Seller shall retain for its account all accounts receivable for sales made by Seller prior to the date of the physical inventory taken pursuant to Section 5.0 above. Buyer agrees to use its best efforts to assist Seller in the collection of all such accounts receivable retained by Seller. Buyer's assistance shall include all reasonable collection efforts, including any legal proceedings that Seller may determine to be necessary in order to effect such collections provided that the cost of any such legal proceedings shall be borne by Seller. The parties agree that the procedures for the collection and payment to Seller of all of its retained accounts receivable shall be as set forth in Exhibit F to be prepared by Seller and attached hereto by August 1, 1978 and made a part hereof. Such procedures may include procedures with respect to Seller retained accounts receivable customers for check handling, invoicing and credits, records and analysis possession and control, interfacing and communication, disputed payments and claims settlement, payments by Buyer of customer amounts collected for Seller and other matters involved in the collection of accounts receivable. Buyer and Seller agree at the time of execution that this agreement is complete in all material respects despite the absence of Exhibit F and Buyer agrees that it will be bound by the procedures prepared by Seller despite the fact that it does not yet know what these procedures are and agrees that it hereby waives, and agrees not to raise, any claim or defense relating to the fact that Exhibit F is not in existence at the time of entering into this Agreement.

10.0 RESPONSIBILITY FOR LIABILITIES AND EXPENSES

Except as otherwise in this Agreement provided, seller shall be responsible for all liabilities and expenses arising out of its operation of the ABC Division up to the Closing Date, and Buyer shall be responsible for all liabilities and expenses arising out of its operation of the ABC Division business after the Closing Date.

11.0 ACCOUNTS PAYABLE AND PURCHASE COMMITMENTS

11.1 Seller agrees to be responsible for the timely payment to the suppliers of all equipment, materials and supplies included as a part of the ABC Division assets to be sold and transferred to Buyer hereunder. Buyer agrees to be responsible for and assume all payment obligations of Seller under any orders placed by Seller in the ordinary course of business for the purchase of raw materials, supplies or other goods intended for use in the manufacture of products in the ordinary course of business at the ABC Division provided that any of such items have not been received at the ABC Division and included as a part of the assets included in the physical inventory as provided under Section 5.0 above.

11.2 Buyer further agrees to assume the obligations of Seller for work performed and materials furnished on and after the date of the physical inventory provided under Section 5.0 above with respect to capital improvement projects for the ABC Division which are outstanding as of that date.

11.3 Seller agrees to assign to Buyer at the Closing all of its right, title and interest under all of the orders, the obligations, of which are to be assumed by Buyer

pursuant to Sections 11.1 and 11.2 above.

12.0 POLLUTION CONTROL MATTERS

Seller makes no representation or warranty with respect to any pollution control matters that might affect or involve the Plant Facilities or the ABC Division. Seller does, however, agree to assign to Buyer as of the Closing Date all of its right, title and interest under any agreements which it may then have with the City of Boston or any other Federal, state or local agency or any private firm or organization concerning any pollution control matters or facilities, or the use thereof, as such might apply to the Plant Facilities or the ABC Division. Seller further agrees to use its best efforts to assist Buyer in the transfer to Buyer of any such rights and interests, including any applicable pollution control permits.

13.0 CLOSING

The completion of the sale and purchase contemplated by this Agreement shall take place on or before sixty (60) days after Buyer's exercise of the option provided herein, but in no event later than August 31, 1983, at such time and place as the parties may agree to and such event and date is referred to herein as the "Closing" or "Closing Date." In the event that such sale and purchase is not completed by August 31, 1983 or by such later Closing Date agreed to in writing by the parties to this Agreement, the option and purchase rights granted to Buyer in this Agreement and the consulting Agreement referred to above shall expire (whether exercised or not) and shall be cancelled, null and void.

14.0 CLOSING ADJUSTMENTS

On and as of the Closing Date the parties shall equitably apportion the responsibility for payment of all charges and bill for all utility services, fuel oil, gasoline and diesel oil, salaries, wages, payroll taxes, lease payments and all real and personal property or other taxes applicable to the Plant Facilities or the ABC Division or any of the assets to be sold and transferred to Buyer hereunder.

15.0 TRANSFER AND SALES TAXES

Seller shall pay all real estate transfer taxes, deed taxes, recording fees and similar impositions respecting the conveyance of the Plant Facilities and all transfer taxes or other sales and use taxes respecting the sale and transfer of all other assets. Buyer will pay all title insurance costs.

16.0 BUYER'S FINANCIAL INFORMATION

Upon exercise of this Option, Buyer agrees to furnish to Seller such reasonable financial information as

Seller may reasonably request, including a statement of Buyer's net worth or a balance sheet of any corporation, partnership or organization which Buyer designates to receive title to the assets being sold and transferred to Buyer hereunder. Buyer agrees that Seller or its agents or representatives shall have an opportunity to make a reasonable audit of any such financial information prior to the Closing Date.

17.0 REPRESENTATIONS AND WARRANTIES OF SELLER

The Seller represents and warrants that:

17.1 Due Organization and Qualification of the Seller. The Seller is a corporation duly organized, validly existing and in good standing under the laws of the State of Delaware, with full power and authority (corporate and other) to own or lease its properties and conduct its businesses as now being conducted, and is qualified to do business as a foreign corporation in good standing in the State of Massachusetts. The Seller has taken all necessary and proper corporate action to authorize and approve this Agreement and to perform all of the covenants and conditions on the Seller's part to be performed contained in this Agreement.

17.2 Title to Assets. Seller has and on the Closing Date will have good and marketable title to all of the assets to be transferred to Buyer hereunder free and clear of all covenants, conditions, charges, liens, encumbrances and security interests of any kind or nature whatsoever, except as shown on record or as may be disclosed by a visual inspection of such assets.

17.3 Condition of Assets. Buyer has or will by the Closing Date have had an opportunity to fully examine and inspect all of the assets sold and transferred to Buyer hereunder, and Buyer has conducted such examination and inspection of such assets as it deems necessary. Seller makes no representation or warranty with respect to the condition of any of the assets to be sold and transferred to Buyer, except that all of such assets are usable and operable in the manner as being used and operated by Seller immediately prior to the Closing Date.

EXCEPT AS EXPRESSLY SET FORTH IN THIS AGREEMENT THERE ARE NO OTHER REPRESENTATIONS AND WARRANTIES EXPRESSED OR IMPLIED WITH RESPECT TO THE ASSETS TO BE SOLD OR TRANSFERRED TO BUYER AT THE CLOSING.

17.4 Taxes. Seller has filed or will file all tax returns required by law to be filed in connection with the operations of the ABC Division up to and including all of Seller's obligations to make payment or adequate provision for all social security, withholding, sales and use, unemployment insurance taxes, excise taxes or any other applicable taxes or duties which may become due with respect to the operations of the ABC Division prior to the Closing Date.

17.5 Litigation. Seller represents and warrants that as of the Closing Date there are no actions, proceedings or claims which have been filed or threatened with respect to the operations of the ABC Division or which might affect the Plant Facilities or if there are any such actions, proceedings or claims (except any actions, proceedings or claims involving environmental matters), Seller agrees to hold Buyer harmless from any liabilities which might be incurred by Buyer or Seller in connection with any such actions, proceedings or claims.

17.6 Insurance. Seller will provide for and pay the premiums on such insurance policies or renewals thereto as Seller presently maintains with respect to the Plant Facilities and the business and operations of the ABC Division and such insurance coverage will be kept in full force and effect through the Closing Date.

17.7 Approval of Transaction. This Agreement is binding, valid and enforceable against the Seller in accordance with its terms and conditions and the Seller has obtained all authorizations, consents and approvals necessary for the execution, delivery and performance by Seller of this Agreement. No order, rule, permit or approval of any Federal, state or local authority or administrative agency or body is required to authorize the execution or consummation of this Agreement by the Seller of the transactions contemplated hereby.

17.8 Validity of Transactions. The consummation of the transactions contemplated by this Agreement will not result in any breach, termination or violation of any term or provision of, or constitute any default under any indenture, security agreement or instrument, loan agreement, joint venture agreement, note, any mortgage, deed of trust, or any other agreement, instrument or understanding to which the Seller is a party or by which it is bound or the Articles of Incorporation or By-Laws or other similar instruments of the Seller.

17.9 Survival of Warranties. All of the representations and warranties of Seller will be true and complete on the Closing Date and shall survive the Closing; provided, however, except in the case of fraud, and except as to the representation and warranty contained in Section 17.2 hereof, Seller shall not be liable to the Buyer for breach of any such representation or warranty after three (3) years from the date of Closing, unless a claim is made with respect thereto prior to the expiration of such three (3) year period.

18.0 REPRESENTATIONS AND WARRANTIES OF BUYER

The Buyer hereby represents and warrants:

18.1 Due Organizaiton and Qualification of the Buyer. The Buyer is a corporation duly organized, validly existing and in good standing under the laws of the State of New York with full power and authority (corporate and other) to own or lease its properties and conduct its businesses as now being conducted and to enter into and perform all of the covenants and conditions of this Agreement required by it to be performed. Buyer has taken all necessary and proper corporate action to authorize and approve this Agreement, and to perform all of the covenants on the Buyer's part to be performed and contained in this Agreement.

18.2 Approval of Transaction. This Agreement is binding, valid and enforceable against the Buyer in accordance with its terms and conditions and Buyer has obtained all necessary authorizations, consents and approvals necessary for the execution, delivery and performance by Buyer of this Agreement. No order, rule, permit or approval of any Federal, state or local authority or administrative agency or body is required to authorize the execution of this Agreement by the Buyer, or the consummation of the transaction contemplated hereby.

18.3 Validity of Transaction. The consummation of the transactions contemplated by this Agreement will not result in any breach, termination , or violation of, any term or provision of, or constitute any default under any indenture, security interest or agreement, loan agreement, joint venture agreement, note, any mortgage, deed of trust, or any other agreement, instrument or understanding to which the Buyer is a party or by which it is bound, or the Articles of Incorporation or By-Laws, or other similar instrument of the Buyer.

18.4 Financial Information. Buyer has furnished to Seller a financial statement disclosing Buyer's financial position as of a date within a period of forty-five (45) days prior to the Closing Date showing Buyer's financial position as of that date and such financial statement has been prepared in accordance with generally accepted accounting principles and fairly presents the financial position of Buyer as of such date. If such financial statement is not audited, Seller or its agents shall be afforded a reasonable opportunity prior to the Closing Date to audit such financial statement.

18.5 Survival of Warranties. All of the representations and warranties of the Buyer will be true and complete on the Closing Date and shall survive the Closing; provided, however, except in the case of fraud, Buyer shall not be liable to the Seller for breach of any such representations and warranties after three (3) years from the Closing Date unless a claim is made with respect thereto prior to the expiration of such three (3) year period.

19.0 COVENANTS OF THE SELLER

Seller covenants for the benefit of Buyer not to make any capital commitments or enter into any orders for capital equipment or any leases or material contracts or agreements affecting the ABC Division prior to the Closing Date without first having obtained the written consent of Buyer.

20.0 COVENANTS OF THE BUYER

Buyer covenants for the benefit of Seller:

20.1 To make all reasonable efforts to maintain the ABC Division as a going concern so long as any of Buyer's obligations to Seller hereunder remain outstanding or are unfulfilled.

20.2 To maintain, keep and preserve all of the Plant Facilities free and clear of all liens, encumbrances and security interests, except as to those assets which may be disposed of as permitted by Section 20.3 below, provided however, that Buyer shall be free to impose or place a lien, encumbrance or security interest on any of the Plant Facilities which is junior and subject to the Mortgage, Security Agreement and Financing Statement in favor of Seller as provided under Section 4.2 hereof.

20.3 Not to remove from the Plant Facilities, except in the ordinary course of business, any of the assets being sold and transferred to Buyer hereunder, except that Buyer may dispose of for its account, and Seller agrees to release from the security agreements provided herein, any machinery, equipment, furniture or fixtures acquired as a part of the Plant Facilities which are not necessary for the operations of the ABC Division as conducted at the time of Closing.

20.4 To maintain all customary insurance coverages with respect to all of such assets so long as any of Buyer's obligations to Seller hereunder remain outstanding or are unfulfilled.

20.5 To furnish to Seller audited financial statements covering the operations of the ABC Division at the end of each fiscal year of such Division subsequent to the Closing Date until such time as all of the obligations of Buyer to Seller under this Agreement have been performed, and unaudited financial statements covering the operations of the ABC Division for each fiscal quarter subsequent to the Closing Date, such statements to be prepared in accordance with generally accepted accounting principles. Such audited financial statements shall be furnished by Buyer to Seller within ninety (90) days after the close of Buyer's fiscal year and such unaudited financial statements shall be furnished to Seller within forty-five (45) days after the end of each such quarterly period.

21.0 CONDITIONS PRECEDENT FOR THE BENEFIT OF THE BUYER

The obligations of the Buyer hereunder are subject to the satisfaction on or prior to the Clsoing Date of all of the following conditions, compliance with which or the occurrence of which may be waived in whole or in part by the Buyer in writing, and the delivery of all of the documents and authorizations required herein.

21.1 Performance of Covenants. All terms, covenants and conditions of this Agreement to be complied with and performed by the Seller prior to the Closing Date shall have been duly complied with and performed or satisfied.

21.2 Representations and Warranties. The representations and warranties made by the Seller shall be true and correct as of the Closing Date with the same force and effect as though said representations and warranties had been made at the Closing Date. The Exhibits attached to this Agreement and delivered hereunder shall also be true and correct as of the Closing Date.

21.3 Other Approvals and Consents. There shall have been secured such approvals, consents and waivers, if any, as may be required under the provisions of any contract, agreement or instrument to which the Seller is a party in order to consummate the transactions contemplated by this Agreement and the Board of Directors of the Seller shall have duly taken all action necessary to authorize the consummation of the transactions contemplated hereby.

21.4 Damage or Destruction of Purchased Assets. Between the date of this Agreement and the Closing, Plant Facilities being sold hereunder shall not have been materially and adversely affected by reason of any loss, destruction or physical damage, whether or not insured against.

21.5 Absence of Litigation and Proceedings. On the Closing Date there shall not be pending or threatened any investigations, litigation before any court, state, or other governmental commission, board or agency, or any arbitration pending or threatened against or affecting any of the assets of Seller to be sold hereby, or to which any of the assets of Seller to be sold hereby is or may be subject, which will result in any material adverse change in any of the assets to be conveyed hereunder or any such investigations, litigation, proceedings or arbitration pending or threatened

against any party to this Agreement in which it is or would be sought to restrain, to prohibit, or to obtain damages or other relief in connection with the consummation of the transactions contemplated hereunder.

21.6 Opinion of Counsel. Buyer shall have received from, Seller's General Counsel, an opinion, dated the Closing Date, in form and substance satisfactory to Buyer and its counsel, to the effect that:

21.6.1 The Seller has the full right, power and authority to consummate the transactions contemplated by this Agreement, the Board of Directors of the Seller have duly and validly taken all action necessary to authorize the sale of the assets as herein provided, and this Agreement is binding upon the Seller in accordance with its terms.

21.6.2 To the best of the knowledge of such counsel the conditions set forth in Subsections 21.3 and 21.5 hereof are satisfied.

21.6.3 The representation of Seller contained in Section 17.1 is true and correct as of the Closing Date.

21.6.4 After due inquiry, to the best of the knowledge of such counsel the consummation of the transactions contemplated by this Agreement will not result in any breach, termination or violation of any term or provision of, or constitute any default under any indenture, security agreement or instrument, loan agreement, joint venture agreement, note, any mortgage, deed of trust, or any other agreement, instrument or understanding to which the Seller is a party or by which it is bound or the Articles of Incorporation or By-Laws or other similar instruments of the Seller.

21.7 Instruments of Transfer. The instruments of transfer, conveyance and assignment, opinions and all other documents to be delivered hereunder, and the validity of all transactions herein contemplated shall be satisfactory in all respects to the Buyer and its counsel.

22.0 CONDITIONS PRECEDENT FOR THE BENEFIT OF SELLER

The obligations of the Seller hereunder are subject to the satisfaction on or prior to the Closing Date of all of the following conditions, compliance with which or the occurrence of which may be waived in whole or in part by the Seller in writing, and the delivery of all of the documents and authorizations required herein.

22.1 Performance of Covenants. All terms, covenants and conditions of this Agreement to be complied with and performed by the Buyer prior to the Closing Date shall have been duly complied with and performed or satisfied.

22.2 Representations and Warranties. The representations and warranties made by the Buyer shall be true and correct as of the Closing Date with the same force and effect as though said representations and warranties had been made at the Closing Date.

22.3 Other Approvals and Consents. There shall have been secured such approvals, consents and waivers, if any, as may be required under the provisions of any contract, agreement or instrument to which the Buyer is a party in order to consummate the transactions contemplated by this Agreement and the Board of Directors of the Buyer shall have duly taken all action necessary to authorize the consummation of the transactions contemplated hereby.

22.4 Litigation and Proceedings. On the Closing Date there shall not be pending or threatened any litigation before any court, state or other governmental commission, board or agency, or any arbitration pending or threatened against any party to this Agreement which, if adversely determined, would restrain or prohibit the consummation of the transactions contemplated hereunder.

22.5 Opinion of Counsel. Seller shall receive an opinion dated as of the Closing Date from counsel for the Buyer, in form and substance satisfactory to Seller and its counsel to the effect that:

22.5.1 The Buyer has the full right, power and authority to consummate the transaction contemplated by this Agreement, the Board of Directors of the Buyer have duly and validly taken all action necessary to authorize the sale of the assets as herein provided, and this Agreement is binding upon the Buyer in accordance with its terms, except to the extent that the same may be subject to modification under any applicable bankruptcy, reorganization, arrangement, insolvency, readjustment of debt, dissolution or liquidation law of any jurisdiction, whether now or hereafter in effect.

22.5.2 To the best of the knowledge of such counsel the conditions set forth in Subsections 22.3 and 22.4 hereof are satisfied.

22.5.3 The representation of Buyer contained in Section 18.1 is true and correct as of the Closing Date.

22.5.4 After due inquiry, to the best of the knowledge of such counsel the consummation of the transactions contemplated by this Agreement will not result in any breach, termination or violation of any term or provision of, or constitute any default under any indenture, security agreement or instrument, loan agreement, joint venture agreement, note, any mortgage, deed of trust, or any other agreement, instrument or understanding to which Buyer is a party or by which it is bound or the Articles of Incorporation or By-Laws or other similar instruments of the Buyer.

22.5.5 No consent, approval, authorization or order of any court or governmental or regulatory

agency, or body not obtained and in effect as of the Closing Date is required for the consummation by the Buyer of the transactions contemplated by this Agreement.

22.5.6 The Mortgage, Security Agreement and Financing Statement have been duly executed and delivered and appropriate recordings of such documents have been made so as to effectively create a mortgage and security interest in favor of Seller in the assets referred to in such documents, and Buyer is duly obligated under all of such documents in accordance with the terms thereof.

22.6 Damage or Destruction of Purchased Assets. Between the date of this Agreement and the Closing, the Plant Facilities being sold hereunder shall not have been materially and adversely affected by reason of any loss, destruction or physical damage, whether or not insured against.

23.0 BULK SALES LAW

Seller agrees to hold Buyer harmless from any cost liability or expense which may be incurred by Buyer, either directly or indirectly, as a result of Seller's non-compliance with any applicable "bulk sales" or similar law designed to protect the creditors of a business being sold.

24.0 EXPENSES

Each party shall bear its own costs and expenses in connection with the transactions contemplated by this Agreement.

25.0 BROKERS' AND FINDERS' FEES

The Seller and the Buyer each respectively represent to the other that they have not incurred any brokers', finders', or any similar fee in connection with the origin, negotiation, execution or performance of this Agreement or the transactions contemplated thereby, and each party agrees to indemnify and hold harmless the other against any loss, liability, damage, cost or expense incurred by reason of the breach of this representation.

26.0 MISCELLANEOUS

26.1 Entire Agreement. This Agreement and the Exhibits attached hereto or to be delivered herewith constitute the entire Agreement between the parties hereto pertaining to the subject matter hereof, and supersede all prior and contemporaneous agreements, understandings, negotiations and discussions, whether oral or written, of the parties, and there are no warranties, representations, or other agreements between the parties in connection with the subject matter hereof, excepting as specifically set forth herein. No supplement, modification or waiver or termination of this

Agreement shall be binding unless executed in writing by the party to be bound thereby. No waiver of any of the provisions of this Agreement shall be deemed or shall constitue a waiver of any other provision hereof (whether or not similar), nor shall such waiver constitute a continuing waiver unless otherwise expressly provided.

26.2 Rights of Others. Except as otherwise provided herein, nothing herein expressed or implied is intended, or shall be construed, to confer upon or to give any person, firm or corporation, other than Buyer and Seller and their respective legal representatives, heirs, successors and assigns, any rights or remedies under or by reason of any term, provision, condition, undertaking, warranty, representation or agreement contained in this Agreement.

26.3 Headings. Section and subsection headings are not to be considered part of this Agreement, and are included solely for convenience, and are not intended to be full or accurate descriptions of the contents thereof.

26.4 Counterparts. For the convenience of the parties, any number of counterparts of this Agreement may be executed and each such executed counterpart shall be, and shall be deemed to be, an original instrument, and to have the same force and effect of an original, but all of which shall constitute and shall be deemed to constitute, in the aggregate, but one and the same instrument.

27.0 SUCCESSORS AND ASSIGNS

This Agreement shall be binding upon and inure to the benefit of the lawful successors and assigns of Seller, but this Agreement shall not be assigned by Buyer, except, as provided in this Option Agreement, Buyer may upon exercise of such option acquire all or a part of the Plant Facilities in the name of a firm or organization owned or controlled by Buyer.

28.0 GOVERNING LAW

The parties hereby agree that this Agreement and any performance thereunder shall be construed and governed by the laws of the State of New York.

29.0 NOTICES

Any notice or other communication required or permitted hereunder shall be in writing, and shall be deemed to have been given if placed in the United States mail, registered or certified, postage prepaid, addressed as follows:

If to the Seller: Seller Company

If to the Buyer: Buyer Company

Each of the foregoing shall be entitled to specify a different address or person to whom notice should be given by giving notice as aforesaid to the other.

30.0 FURTHER ASSURANCES

Subsequent to the date hereof Seller and Buyer agree to execute and deliver from time to time any further instruments, documents, assignments and other assurances, and to obtain any approvals, authorizations, consents, licenses, orders or permits of any governmental agencies, whether Federal, state or local, as may be required in order to vest in and confirm in Buyer or any successor in interest of Buyer the full right, title and interest to and the right to use and enjoy the assets to be transferred hereunder.

31.0 EXERCISE OF OPTION

The option to purchase the assets as provided herein, may be exercised at any time from and after August 1, 1982 and prior to August 1, 1983 upon the delivery to Seller of Buyer's written notice to exercise such option and upon such exercise, the parties hereto agree to use their best efforts to complete the sale to Buyer of the Plant Facilities as contemplated by such option as soon as possible, but in any event not later than August 31, 1982.

IN WITNESS WHEREOF, the parties hereto have caused this Agreement to be duly entered into and executed as of the date and year hereinabove first set forth.

ATTEST: SELLER COMPANY

_____   By_____
                                 BUYER COMPANY

                                 _____

                                 BUYER COMPANY

The Lawyer's Checklist for Due Diligence Inquiries In Acquisitions*

ROBERT A. McTAMENY

Partner, Carter, Ledyard & Milburn

The following checklist is designed for due diligence investigation, evaluation and basic documents and procedures with respect to a proposed acquisition of a privately-held corporation by an office client. The due diligence checklist is keyed to the usual representations which would be set forth in a basic stock purchase or assets purchase agreement.

The checklist is intended only as a guide since every acquisition will be unique and more emphasis will be required with respect to specific problem areas that inevitably will arise. Where relevant, documents should be secured for the target company and each of its significant subsidiaries.

I. Due Diligence Investigation

1. Organization and Good Standing.

   1.01 Certificate of Incorporation, as amended.
   1.02 By-Laws.
   1.03 Good-Standing Certificates (long form) and Tax Status Certificates.
   1.04 List of states where the Company is (or should be) qualified as a foreign corporation, or has offices (then secure certificates of authority, good standing and tax status certificates).
   1.05 Minutes and stock books of the Company, including minutes of executive and other committees (board and non-board).

   1.06 Partnership or joint venture affiliations.

2. Capitalization and Shareholders.

   2.01 List of shareholders, cross-checked against stock certificate book.
   2.02 Preemptive rights confirmation.
   2.03 Shareholders' status - minors, trustees, etc.
   2.04 Trust agreements or other documents if shares are held in a fiduciary or entity capacity.
   2.05 ESOP, stock bonus or other agreements to issue shares.
   2.06 Letter from auditors regarding fully paid and non-assessable character of shares and correct accounting entries.
   2.07 Consider Power of Attorney and Stock Escrow Agreement.

3. Authorization.

   3.01 Review specific authorizing resolutions.
   3.02 Consider stockholder approval if partial asset transaction.
   3.03 Confirm fiduciary or entity powers to approve.
   3.04 Voting trusts, outstanding proxies or agreements as to voting.
   3.05 Restrictive share transfer agreements (if so, confirm prior compliance).

4. Financial Statements and Quality.

*Copyright © 1980. Prepared by Robert A. McTameny, Esq. for The National Law Journal.

4.01 Five years consolidated and consolidating statements, with access to auditors and work papers.

4.02 Most recent unaudited statements, with comparable statements for prior year.

4.03 All projections.

4.04 Auditors' letters to management for five years.

4.05 Auditors' inquiry letters and replies for five years.

4.06 Arrangements for businessman's review or other review by Client's auditors.

4.07 Accounts Receivable Review (Quality, Aging, Special Cases).

4.08 Inventory Valuation, Turnover and Obsolescence Review.

4.09 Secure credit reports.

4.10 SG&A and factory overhead.

4.11 Backlog.

4.12 Cost Accounting (Government Contracts); Small business and minority business subcontractors.

4.13 Pricing Policies and Compliance.

5. Tax Matters.

5.01 Copies of returns for latest closed and all open years (federal, state and local).

5.02 Audit and revenue agents' reports (federal, state and local).

5.03 Settlement documents and correspondence for three years.

5.04 Agreements waiving statute of limitations or extending time.

6. Employees, Benefit Plans and Salaries, Labor Disputes.

6.01 Union agreements.

6.02 Management and employment agreements; secrecy agreements.

6.03 Pension plans and actuarial reports; confirm current assumptions.

6.04 Profit-sharing plans and agreements.

6.05 ESOP and stock bonus plans and arrangements.

6.06 Calculations of liabilities and of fund assets using various assumptions of PBGC, Company and Client.

6.07 Fringe benefits, perquisites, holidays, vacation.

6.08 Labor disputes, requests for arbitration, grievance proceedings, etc.

6.09 History of recent union negotiations.

6.10 Employee size, turnover, absentee history, distribution.

7. Other Contracts and Commitments.

7.01 All loan agreements (bank loans, IDA, etc.).

7.02 Customer lists.

7.03 Supply and customer contracts.

7.04 Deeds.

7.05 Leases.

7.06 Compensation balance arrangements.

7.07 Contracts with insiders or other arrangements.

7.08 Samples of all forms of purchase orders, invoices, etc.

7.09 Installment sale agreements above designated dollar amount.

7.10 Secrecy or non-compete agreements.

7.11 Membership agreements or other relations with trade associations.

7.12 Terms review and possible renegotiation of contracts being assumed or continued.

7.13 Guarantees.

8. Licenses.

8.01 Material license agreements running to and from Company.

8.02 Material permits or governmental consents.

9. Insurance.

9.01 All insurance contracts.

9.02 Key-man insurance and present value calculation.

9.03 Contact Client's carrier regarding continuation of coverage.

9.04 Workers' Compensation.

10. Litigation.

10.01 Complete litigation list.

10.02 Contact local counsel.

10.03 Confirm acceptance of insurance coverage.

10.04 Consent decrees and applicable injunctions, etc.

10.05 Pending or threatened proceedings.

10.06 Regulatory Compliance (FTC, F&DA, OSHA, EPA, EEOC).

10.07 Questionable Payments.

11. Patents and Trademarks.

11.01 Patent list and arrange for patent analysis.

11.02 Trademarks list (confirm continuation notices).

11.03 Copyright list.

11.04 Examine common-law protections.

12. Properties.

12.01 Title reports and insurance policies.

12.02 UCC searches in relevant states.

12.03 Judgment searches in relevant states.

12.04 Condition of Plant, Machinery and Equipment.

12.05 Energy sources and cost.

12.06 Government-owned equipment.

12.07 Depreciation and Investment Credit Check (calculate recapture).

13. Inventory.

13.01 Inventory schedule and valuation assumptions.

13.02 Confirm carrying value at lower of cost or market.

13.03 Turnover and Obsolescence.

14. Access to Books and Records.

15. Broker or Finders' Agreements.

II. Organize Acquisition Vehicle

(a) Reserve name in relevant states.

(b) Draft charter, by-laws and initial organization action.

(c) Minute and stock books.

(d) Taxpayer identification number.

(e) Organize and qualify in relevant states.

(f) Authorizing resolutions.

III. Preparation of Purchase Agreement

1. Description of Purchase Transaction.

1.01 Stock or assets.

1.02 Purchase price (cash, property or stock; options, if any) and payment.

1.03 Escrow provisions.

1.04 Allocation agreements (consider excess good will).

1.05 Instruments of conveyance and transfer.

1.06 Further assurances.

2. Takeover of Business.

3. Closing.

4. Bulk Sales Law (if applicable).

5. Representations and Warranties of Company and Shareholders.

5.01 Representations in accordance with due diligence results.

5.02 No material misstatements or omissions.

6. No adverse change and designated pre-closing transaction prohibitions.

7. Indemnification provisions.

8. Client representations.

9. Client indemnification.

10. Conduct of business prior to closing.

11. Conditions of Client's Obligations.

11.01 Representations and warranties true; convenants performed.

11.02 Related agreements, if any, executed.

11.03 No litigation.

11.04 Opinions.

11.05 Auditors' letters.

11.06 Consents, Assignments, Approvals.

11.07 Other conditions.

12. Conditions of Company's Obligations.

12.01 Representations and Warranties true.

12.02 Other agreements executed.

12.03 No litigation.

12.04 Opinions.

12.05 Other conditions.

13. Other Agreements of Company and Shareholders, if any.

14. Guarantee of Parent of Acquisition Vehicle, if necessary.

15. Survival of Representations and Any Negotiated Limits on Scope of Indemnification.

16. Expenses.

17. Entire Agreement.

18. Arbitration (if agreed).

19. No Brokers.

20. Publicity Provisions.

21. Miscellaneous.

21.01 Binding effect.

21.02 No assignment (include voidance language).

21.03 Counterparts.

21.04 Governing law.

22. Notices.

IV. Draft Employment Agreements

1. Engagement and Term.

2. Duties.

3. Compensation. Vacation, Travel.

4. Termination (Cause, Death or Disability, etc.).

5. Covenant Not to Compete.

6. Trade Secrets and Confidential Information.

7. Injunctive Relief.

8. Survival.

9. Entire Agreement.

10. Arbitration (if agreed).

11. Miscellaneous.

11.01 Binding effect.

11.02 No assignment (include voidance language).

11.03 Counterparts.

11.04 Governing law.

12. Notices.

V. Consents

1. Antitrust Review (Hart Scott Rodino or Business Review Letter).

2. Loan Agreements.

3. Lease Agreements.

4. License Agreements.

5. Supply and distribution Arrangements.

6. Confirm Continuation of Non-Contractual Arrangements, if Material.

VI. Receipt of Required Audits, Appraisals and Interim Financials

VII. Closing Preparation

1. Closing Memorandum and Checklist.
2. Schedules to Agreement.
   2.01 Remuneration.
   2.02 Contracts and Commitment.
   2.03 Insurance in Force.
   2.04 Litigation.
   2.05 Title Exceptions.
   2.06 Trademarks.
   2.07 Certain Warranties.
   2.08 Insider Transactions.
   2.09 Pre-Closing Transactions.
3. Definitive Agreement.
4. Definitive Employment Agreements.
5. Escrow Agreement.
6. Powers of Attorney and Stock Escrow Agreements.
7. Certified Certificates of Incorporation.
8. By-Laws Certified by Secretaries.
9. Good-Standing Certificates.
10. Tax Status and Lien Docket Certificates.
11. Certified Resolutions.
12. Representation Certificates.
13. Consents.
14. Assignments, if Applicable.
15. Resignations of Certain Directors and Officers.
16. Assignments of Patents, Trademarks and Copyrights.
17. Assignments of Bank Accounts.
18. Legal Opinions.
19. Checks.
20. Promissory Notes.
21. Cross-Receipt.

VIII. Post-Closing Matters

1. Subsequent Audit and Price Adjustment.
2. Merger or Liquidation of Acquisition Vehicle.
3. Commerce Department Forms.
4. Bound Volumes and Closing Files.

INDEX

INDEX

Stock market impact *(cont.)*
earnings per share, 304
price earnings ratio, 304-306
real changes, 309
Stock options, 271
Stock watch, 39
Street name holders, 470-471
Structure, deals, 21
Structuring transaction, 633-635
Subsidiary:
pooled, 263
troubled or non-essential, 565-569 *(see also* Troubled subsidiary)
Subsidiary corporation:
capitalization, 68
organizing, 66-67
Subsidiary liquidation:
basis of stock, 397-402
accounts receivable, 399
allocation, 398-402
allocation limited, 399
amortizable intangibles, 400
cash and cash equivalents, 399
fixed assets, 400
inventory, 399
nonamortization intangibles, 400
not allocated, 399
property contributed, 399
property not received for stock, 399
carryover basis, 394-395
control required, 394-395
plan, 395
Section 332, 395
time period, 395
nonrecognition of gain, 394
Section 334 (b)(2). 396-397, 399
special business consideration, 395-396
stepped-up basis, 396
Subsidiary merger, 362-363
"Substantially all," 206, 267
Substantially disproportionate redemption, 365-368
Sunset Fuel Co. v. U.S., 74-1 USTC ¶9422, 400
Supplemental pension, 121
Supreme Investment Corp., 72-2 USTC ¶9689, 468 F.2d 370, 396
Swift & Co., U.S. v., 286 U.S. 106 (1932), 405
Syndicated service data, 146
Synergism, 150
Synergistic combinations, 21

T

"T," definition, 359
Takeout transaction, 489
Takeover attempts, defense, 479-485
Takeover fever, 14
Takeover premiums, 17

Tampa Electric Co. v. Nashville Coal Co., 365 U.S. 320, 330-333 (1961), 410
Tanzer Economic Associates, Inc. v. Universal Food Specialties, Inc., (Sup. Ct. N.Y. Co. 1976), 493
Tanzer II case, 493
Tanzer v. International General Industries, Inc., (Del. Ct. 1977), 492
Target company, characteristics, 479-480
Tax-accounting procedures, 21
Tax benefit doctrine, 389-390
Tax-deferred mergers, 192
Taxes:
advance rulings, 373
amount of gain, 364-365
"A" reorganization, 361-362
best way to structure deal, 595
"B" reorganization, 362
capital gain or dividend, 365
cash tender offer, 466
constructive ownership of T stock, 369
conversion privilege, 375-376
convertible preferred stock, 373
"C" reorganization, 362
divestiture, 568
form of reorganization, 360-364
installment notes, 376-377
convertible note exceptions, 377
no original issue discount, 377
qualification, 376-377
readily tradable exception, 377
maximum amount of cash, 360-364
minority where majority receives cash, 378-379
nonconvertible preferred stock, 373
non-dividend tests, 369
not essentially equivalent to dividend, 368-369
not "Section 306 stock," 373
P preferred stock, 371-376
P securities, 371
P stock, 364
P stock and cash, 364-369
recapitalization, 378
redemption or sale, 369
redemption premium, 374-375
redemption treatment, 369
reduce or eliminate, 594
reverse subsidiary merger (type "(a)(2) (E)"), 363
Section 305 problems, 374-375
Section 306 stock, 372
Section 351 exchange, 378-379
shareholders receiving solely cash, 369-371
sinking fund, 375-376
subsidiary merger (type "(a)(2)(D)"), 362-363
substantially disproportionate redemption, 365-368
taxable sales and liquidations, 381-402
tax-free reorganization, 360
T security holder or shareholder, 371